Allan Dwan and the
Rise and Decline of the
Hollywood Studios

ALLAN DWAN PROD.
MR. DWAN

Allan Dwan and the Rise and Decline of the Hollywood Studios

Frederic Lombardi

McFarland & Company, Inc., Publishers
Jefferson, North Carolina, and London

***Frontispiece:* Allan Dwan as The Thinker, ca. 1920 (courtesy Robin Allana Wallace).**

LIBRARY OF CONGRESS CATALOGUING-IN-PUBLICATION DATA

Lombardi, Frederic.
Allan Dwan and the rise and decline of the Hollywood studios / Frederic Lombardi.
p. cm.
Includes bibliographical references and index.

ISBN 978-0-7864-3485-5
softcover : acid free paper ♾

1. Dwan, Allan, 1885–1981. 2. Motion picture producers and directors — United States — Biography. I. Title.
PN1998.3.D95L55 2013 791.4302'33092 — dc23 [B] 2012030281

BRITISH LIBRARY CATALOGUING DATA ARE AVAILABLE

On the cover: Allan Dwan publicity shot for Republic Studios, which he joined in 1946 (Photofest); background image Dwan's gangster drama *Big Brother* was shot on the streets of New York (courtesy Kevin Brownlow)

Manufactured in the United States of America

McFarland & Company, Inc., Publishers
Box 611, Jefferson, North Carolina 28640
www.mcfarlandpub.com

To Lucy

Table of Contents

"Consequently, there may be much more to be said about Dwan."—Andrew Sarris, *The American Cinema*

Acknowledgments

I have spent more than seven years working on this book and had little idea when I started just how daunting a task it would be. Allan Dwan's staggeringly large body of work was just part of the challenge. There were such formidable obstacles as the fact that Dwan left a slim paper trail and had no children, and that the vast majority of his associates were dead by the time I embarked on this project. In addition, Dwan garnered relatively little press coverage in the second half of his career.

Various archives, libraries, and museums became the major part of my focus. But my climb was made less steep by the assistance and kindness of a remarkable group of individuals.

I must cite first the eminent biographer and film historian Joseph McBride. No one has so consistently and frequently been in contact with me regarding this book as Mr. McBride. Although we only had some brief contacts when both of us were working at *Variety* on opposite coasts, I on the East Coast and Joe in L.A., Joe has offered a helping hand to me since the inception of this project. Although he has a very busy schedule both lecturing and writing, he has periodically taken the time to advise me and to read several of my chapters which he then critiqued. He has also shared with me his own reminiscences of Allan Dwan. Joe and I have communicated only by e-mail and have never met, but he has made me feel I have found a true friend.

I have also been gratified and totally overwhelmed by the generosity of such formidable figures as Peter Bogdanovich and Kevin Brownlow. These two men, who introduced Allan Dwan to a new generation of film fans, have helped spread the notion that cinema's past and even its distant past should be just as loved and savored as the most current film release that catches our fancy.

Kevin Brownlow has, of course, done more than any other individual to revive interest in the silent film medium, trumpeting it as a source of great artistic expression despite all the technological changes that have followed. This is an essential element in appreciating the contributions of Dwan. Brownlow has been most kind in sharing with me his vast knowledge and collection of material. He also read portions of my manuscript and offered very helpful comments and corrections.

Peter Bogdanovich is one prominent film director who has never forgotten what he owes to the filmmakers of earlier generations. His book-length interview with Dwan is a landmark achievement as well as a gateway to a larger and more complex story that exists beyond it. In addition to granting me two interviews and providing numerous e-mail responses, he has done everything possible to give me access to material I needed, including his personal papers and the Dwan interview that appeared in his books *The Last Pioneer* and *Who the Devil Made It,* and permitted me to use it in this volume.

Marilyn Moss, who resides in Los Angeles, was introduced to me by Joe McBride, again by e-mail. Fortunately, I did get to meet Marilyn during her research trip to New York as she worked on her biography of Raoul Walsh. As Walsh and Dwan were friends and associates, we were able to swap information that was mutually beneficial. Our emerging friendship and exchange of e-mails were also most helpful in getting this book finished. As we both toiled on our books, it was a great morale-booster to be communicating with someone who was going through the same experience.

Tracey Goessel is, for my money, the greatest living specialist on all things relating to Douglas Fairbanks. She was kind enough to share information with me and even to provide me with a very rare photograph for this book. My chapter on Fairbanks is much the better for having been submitted to her scrutiny. She is presently working on the definitive biography of Fairbanks.

For information and insight on Dwan's first years as a director, I was most fortunate to make the acquaintance of Dana Driskel, who has been studying the pioneering Flying A Company since 2002. It was a great pleasure to compare notes with Dana and discuss different theories about what was going on behind the scenes in those years. Dana's great experience in this realm made his input invaluable. He also graciously permitted me to read the transcript of his interview with Allan Dwan and to quote from it in this book.

I am deeply indebted to Larry Suid for generously supplying me with his interviews with the major participants of *Sands of Iwo Jima*, both from the military and motion picture spheres, as well as sharing with me his letter from John Wayne. These were but a portion of the primary sources for his fascinating book *Guts & Glory: Great American War Movies*. This material should also prove invaluable to future historians.

I am also very grateful for the feedback provided me by my former *Variety* colleague John Dempsey after he read several of my chapters. It was good to get the perspective of a non–film historian as well as listen to his suggestions on improving the quality of the writing based on his meticulous standards. Another friend and former *Variety* reporter, Bob Marich, was very helpful in keeping me abreast of news and information relevant to my book.

I would also like to thank Bob King, the editor of *Classic Images*, who published my first article on Dwan and who was instrumental in helping me make some key contacts. I am especially grateful that he was able to put me in touch with one of *CI*'s most colorful contributors, Blackie Seymour, who passed away shortly before completion of this manuscript. I am also very grateful for Mr. Seymour's assistance.

Especially crucial to this book were contacts with people who knew and/or worked with Allan Dwan. The most critical of these was Dwan's goddaughter, Robin Allana Foster Wallace. It took a while to locate Ms. Wallace but it was well worth the effort. In addition to doing two long interviews, we have also communicated in numerous phone calls and she has provided me with an enormous storehouse of information as well as photographs from Dwan's personal life. Her deep affection for her godfather has always been evident and energizing but she has also not hesitated to be very frank as well. My work on this book has been enriched by the kindness of Robin and her family.

I am also very grateful for the correspondence of two of Dwan's former associates, Harry Carey, Jr., and the late Edward Alperson, Jr. I am also deeply appreciative of other Dwan collaborators and friends who kindly granted me interviews including Robert Blees, Wally Cassell, Arlene Dahl, Richard Erdman, Lisa Montell Janti, Joan Leslie, Marcy McGuire, Andrew V. McLaglen, Debra Paget, Gregg Palmer, Evelyn Rudie, Kevin Thomas, Audrey Totter, Stuart Whitman, and those who have since passed on, Teddy Infuhr, Lillian Kinkela Keil, Steve Mitchell, William Self, and Gloria Stuart. I would also like to thank Marvin Paige for helping to arrange some of these interviews.

I also deeply appreciate the time given to me by other Dwan interviewers including Joe Adamson, Gary Morris and Howard Mandelbaum. All three of these gentlemen were very forthcoming in going beyond the contents of their interviews to tell me what they recalled about Dwan — their impressions of the man and things he said outside the interviews. Mr. Mandelbaum was especially generous with his time and also helped me with illustrations in his capacity as head of Photofest. I am also grateful to Patricia Eliot Tobias for helping to arrange my contact with Mr. Adamson.

Richard Koszarski was kind enough to send me his transcript of his interview with Dwan and discussed other Dwan-related matters with me by e-mail. Another prominent film historian, Cari Beauchamp, kindly took the time to communicate with me both by phone and e-mail. Other distinguished film historians who shared with me their knowledge and views of items concerning Dwan were Jeanine Basinger, Michael F. Blake, Aljean Harmetz, David Kiehn, Anthony Slide and R.M. Hayes. John Gallagher, both a film historian and filmmaker, guided me to some of his interviews with Dwan's players and provided me with viewings of rare Dwan films. Two authors of separate biographies of Wallace Reid, E.J. Fleming and David Meneffee, took the time to supply me with information regarding Dwan's early directing years. Leonard Maltin, one of America's great treasures among cineastes, kindly sent me a copy of the shooting script of *Sands of Iwo Jima*.

The bulk of the research for this book was conducted at the Library for the Performing Arts in New York City. Among the individuals who assisted me there were Susan Shute, Christopher Frith, Daniele Rogers, Caleb Cadet and Margarita Canal. Also in New York, at the Museum of Modern Art, numerous screenings of Allan Dwan films were arranged for me with the kind help of Charles Silver. Through the assistance of Megan Forbes at the Museum of the Moving Image in Queens, I was able to obtain a complete recording of the lengthy Joe Adamson interview with Dwan as well as a rare photo for my book.

I also spent time researching at the Margaret Herrick Library in Los Angeles where I received the assistance of the ever-helpful Barbara Hall. I received help at the Motion Picture Academy Library from Mae Woods, who appropriately had compiled the Allan Dwan filmography for Peter Bogdanovich's book *The Last Pioneer*.

My research at the Library of Congress was facilitated by the courteous and very diligent assistance of Josie Walters-Johnson, Madeline Matz, and Zoran Sinobad. I have also benefited from the helpful advice of the Library's literary manuscript historian, Dr. Alice Lotvin Birney.

For information on Dwan's very early years, I am most grateful for the assistance of Sharon Sumpter at Notre Dame University. With the help of two student researchers, Nicholas Derda and Abigail Braun, she was able to provide me with material by and about Dwan during his college days from university periodicals.

Ned Comstock at the Cinematic Arts Library at USC was very helpful to me before, during and after my visit to California. His generous assistance of film historians must have enhanced the quality of numerous books. I know it has with mine.

I was also ably assisted at USC in researching the Warner Bros. Archives by Randi Hokett, Noelle Carter and Haden Guest.

At UCLA, my research was ably assisted by Lauren Boisson and Julie Graham. Screenings of Dwan films were arranged for me by Mark Gens of UCLA's Archives Collection Services Department. I wish to extend particular thanks to Lisa Fuguet who ran those screenings for me and valiantly stayed until I saw all four Dwan features and a short even though the L.A. streets were by then snarled by the festivities for Halloween.

I would also like to thank Rosa Gomez and Shirlette Smith for helping me overcome some of the transportation problems of my L.A. visit.

I would like to thank the curator James D'Arc for his assistance regarding the Republic files in the Jack Mathis Collection at Brigham Young University. I also appreciated the assistance of Karen Pederson, the library director at the Shavelson Webb Library of the Writers Guild Foundation, for information on screenwriting credits.

My thanks also go to Katrina Stokes of the British Film Institute and Ad Pollé of the Filmmuseum in Amsterdam for information regarding prints of Dwan films.

For arranging for me special screenings of Dwan films at Eastman House in Rochester, New York, I would like to thank Jared Case. Jared also has my gratitude for continuing to answer my questions about prints after my Rochester visit.

For a screening arranged for me at NYU, I would like to thank Ann Harris and Michael Belkewitch.

I was able to obtain copies of documents and photographs from the Allan Dwan Collection at the University of Wyoming through the kind efforts of Gregory John Kocken, John R. Waggener and Shaun Hayes. I would also like to thank Emil Hoelter and Dorinda Hoffmann at the Wisconsin Center for Film and Theater Research.

At the Harry Ransom Center at the University of Texas, I was given very considerate research assistance from Steve Wilson, Albert Palacios and Leslie DeLassus in locating and obtaining copies of documents from the Gloria Swanson Collection.

For permitting me to obtain copies of excerpts from Fox film scripts and, particularly, document copies from the Peter Bogdanovich Collection, I am very grateful to Cherry Dunham Williams and Mary Sue Presnell. Some of this material appears in my book courtesy of the Lilly Library, Indiana University, Bloomington, Indiana.

Daniel Tenkman of the DGA Special Projects gets my sincere thanks for arranging for me to see and quote from the transcript of the DGA interview with Dwan's former assistant director and future director H. Bruce Humberstone. For permitting me to obtain copies of relevant interviews from the Ronald L. Davis Oral History Collection at Southern Methodist University, I would like to thank Cynthia Franco, the librarian at the De Golyer Library. I would also like to convey my gratitude to Margaret Hrabe, reference coordinator at the University of Virginia, for permitting me to see Booton Herndon's notes from his interview with Dwan for his book *The Most Popular Couple the World Has Known: Mary Pickford and Douglas Fairbanks.*

I tried to handle personally as much of the research for this book as possible. However, because of the limitations of my personal budget for this project, it was necessary for me to hire researchers for some institutions I could not visit or could not spend more than a limited time. I would therefore like to express my thanks for the assistance of my researchers, who were not affiliated with any of the institutions at which they did their probing. They included Will Gartside (Wisconsin Center for Film and Theater Research), David Coon (University of Indiana), Walt Wilson (Chicago History Museum), Sadie Menchen (UCLA) and John Christensen (Brigham Young University).

For information on Dwan's Toronto roots I would like to express my thanks to Shirley Hughes of the Toronto Silent Film Society and Paul Sharkey of Toronto Archives.

Some individuals supplied me with just one item of information but those "bits" can be invaluable and I am very grateful for them. The film historian Robert Birchard brought to my attention one of his early interviews which contained a vital piece of information about Dwan's life. James Roots alerted me to a book containing a 1920 article by Dwan with revealing and crucial info. In that same spirit, I would also like to thank the noted author Patrick McGilligan, Eric Chadbourne, Walter Mirisch, Phillip Oliver, Marc Wanamaker and Tom Weaver. Bruce Goldstein of the Film Forum supplied me with some helpful info and contacts. My friend Stephen Breen also deserves my thanks for some helpful comments. I also appreciated the opportunity to discuss Dwan with Joe Franklin.

I would also like to thank the following individuals for helping to supply me with photographs: Donald Albrecht, Louis Azzollini, Robert Birchard, the late Richard Bojarski, Bruce Calvert, John Cocchi, Lisa Montell Janti, Jon Mirsalis, David Smith and Adrianne Whitmore. I would also like to thank Mirsalis for providing me with some helpful information regarding Lon Chaney. I also appreciate being able to speak to Ms. Whitmore about her mother, the late Lillian Kinkela Keil, the heroic Air Force nurse who was the role model for a Dwan heroine. For photos from the Motion Picture Academy, I would like to thank Faye Thompson and Janet Lorenz of the National Information Service. In addition to various institutions cited in the photo credits, I also purchased pictures from eBay, Kate Shackleton, Movie Goods and the Jerry Ohlinger Store in Manhattan. I would like to thank Dollie Banner at Ohlinger's for her kind help in finding the photos I needed. At Photofest, the always helpful Howard Mandelbaum helped me locate some rare pictures.

I also received help at the Elmwood Park Library in New Jersey including the kind assistance of Carole Skeen in locating whatever I was seeking that was in the Bergen County Library system.

I am very grateful to many critics and film authors not mentioned who have inspired me, particularly Andrew Sarris, who encouraged us all to think more of unsung directors. I thank the various essayists cited in this book who extended their insights about Allan Dwan.

I would also like to thank some of my friends at *Variety*, where I worked for thirteen years. These include my former boss, Syd Silverman, who phoned me regarding some information I was seeking for this book. I would also like to thank a very good friend from *Variety*, Morton Bryer, who first showed me how formidable it was to launch an important project. My thanks also go to Larry Cohn, from whom I learned much in observing him as *Variety*'s film editor and to Jeremy Gerard who kindly tracked down info for me for this volume. The late Roger Watkins and Peter Besas were the first to respond to print news of my book on the Simesite website. Many of my other *Variety* friends, both dead and living, were also in my thoughts as I wrote this book including Hank Werba, who did see something in my aspirations.

This book might not have been successfully completed without the generous assistance of my neighbor and good friend, Raymond Marrero, whose invaluable expertise with computers has spared me from numerous nervous breakdowns. He has truly been a godsend.

I am also grateful to family members who showed their support during the writing of this book including my cousin Sandra Cassinelli, who has always encouraged me. I would especially like to express my deep gratitude for the support of my brother Robert, my mother and lastly my father, who died as this book was being completed.

My deepest thanks to all who helped me on this book and my humble apologies to anyone who was inadvertently left out.

Preface

Why a book on Allan Dwan? His film output is staggeringly large and his directorial career began in 1911, just three years after D.W. Griffith completed his first film. But where Griffith's directorial career ended in 1931, Dwan's last release came 30 years later.

Yet, Dwan had to be re-discovered first by Kevin Brownlow, who interviewed him in 1964 for his celebrated history of the silent film in *The Parade's Gone By...*, and then be treated to a book-length interview by Peter Bogdanovich, which was published in 1971.

Although I had seen Allan Dwan movies long before I had any idea of who Allan Dwan was, the first time I recall seeing a reference to him was as an entry in Andrew Sarris' seminal book *The American Cinema: Directors and Directions: 1929–1968*. There, classified under the heading "Expressive Esoterica," was this description: "Dwan's career is still being mined for a possibly higher assay of gold to dross. Recent findings — *Silver Lode, The Restless Breed, The River's Edge*— represent a virtual bonanza of hitherto unexplored classics. It is too early to establish any coherent pattern to Dwan's career as a whole, but it may very well be that Dwan will turn out to be the last of the old masters."

But how was it that Dwan could have been working since the dawn of commercial cinema and it was only in the mid-1960s that he had begun to be appreciated as one of the old masters, as if he had somehow been misplaced for decades?

Bogdanovich titled his book *The Last Pioneer* but I wondered if Dwan hadn't been the *lost* pioneer. Through the filter of Dwan's reminiscences, Bogdanovich fleshed out a directorial career that was virtually unknown to the burgeoning number of English-language readers who wanted to learn about cinema's past. Dwan's wit and amiability were so ingratiating that few cinephiles questioned if there was a more complex narrative behind his breezy storytelling. Forty years later, there has still not been a book-length critical study of his work and life although a book of essays about Dwan was published in conjunction with a Dwan tribute at the 2002 Locarno Film Festival. Despite his astonishing productivity, he has remained elusive to critics.

During the winter 2003 retrospective of twenty Dwan films at New York's Walter Reade Theater, Elliott Stein wrote in *The Village Voice*, "Dwan is hardly a subject for auteur analysis. He loved making movies, and would often shoot whatever came along. But he did his job with such economy and narrative flair that the most banal material could be transformed into something personal." But how is it that Dwan is "hardly a subject for auteur analysis" while he could "transform the most banal material into something personal"? Isn't that part of a definition of what makes a director an auteur, particularly one working in an unfashionable genre? But both Dwan's themes and subject matter seemed too diffuse to be easily calibrated. With genres he seemed to operate like a whirling dervish, specializing, for example, in cinematic farce in the mid–1940s before switching to Republic and RKO with a hodgepodge of genres with Westerns dominating. Nor could the ambiance of his films be as easily summed up as, say, with Raoul Walsh and the love of adventure or Edgar G. Ulmer and his fatalism. Even more disconcerting, there was no cult masterpiece that could be used to "spin" his reputation, no *Rio Bravo*, no *White Heat* or *Detour*.

Dwan is something of an anomaly in how he allegedly entered the motion picture business both as an engineer and as a writer — a seemingly ideal combination for the technological requirements of the cinema. Dwan also developed a reputation as a problem-solver. He said he assisted D.W. Griffith in shooting one of his most famous sequences in *Intolerance* by putting an elevator on a railroad track so that it could go upwards and backwards at the same time. Dwan also had the same ability to evaluate scripts and decide how their weaknesses could be overcome, sometimes tilting a script previously considered "serious" more toward comedy.

There is indeed something of the scientist in Dwan's style. He knows the inner mechanics of each story and its visualization thoroughly. He can sometimes add meanings by extending the length of a shot beyond its ostensible function or by re-showing certain images. In this, he somewhat resembles the deist God who does not impose himself on his creations but lets their inner clockwork reveal himself. Some of his minor films seem to carry a spark that suggests something far greater.

In this approach may lay both Dwan's strengths and weaknesses. His careful intelligence usually prevents him from falling into the crudeness that characterizes some of the lesser films of say, Raoul Walsh. Yet, there is something of passionate outrageousness missing in Dwan's sensibility that made possible such Walsh masterpieces as *White Heat* and *High Sierra*.

Dwan is essentially a director without a masterpiece although arguably several of his films have come close to that status. There are certainly notable highlights throughout his career and in the silent era he was one of the highest regarded and most highly paid directors. (Some of his most impressive achievements of that era may be lost forever.) Yet one cannot chart his career as moving toward that one towering opus that guarantees immortality. He seemed to be too preoccupied with doing his best for many lesser assignments.

A still more transcendent view of Dwan comes from the Austrian film critic Christoph Huber. In 2002 he wrote, "Probably the most exhilarating experience all year was the Locarno Film Festival's extensive retrospective for Allan Dwan, who seemed incapable of directing a movie badly. If the script was no good, he'd make an interesting movie, if the script was so-so, the film was near-great, if the script was good, the film was brilliant."

Huber's comments may smack of hyperbole and Dwan often did his best to have his scripts improved before they were shot. But as Huber suggests, Dwan brought careful planning and intelligence into the making of his films. The joy of the creative process seems to have been a sustaining force that guided him through such an astonishingly large output of work.

Under the strain of limited budgets, he would also find more artistic means to make his points. There were also tensions in his own personality that would help ignite the art in his work.

Like Walsh and Howard Hawks, Dwan claimed to have sworn off making consciously artistic or prestigious films early in his career. Yet there appear to have been at least three periods in the silent era where Dwan strove to make arty or "important" movies. While he ultimately abandoned that approach, he continued to fight throughout his career to maintain his independence as a director. In exchange, he would provide his employers with films made both economically and with commercial appeal. In the sound era, the cost of such an arrangement sometimes left Dwan with meager material to make his films. But he did not lose his knack of doing much with little, even if it earned him scant recognition. He also grasped (or convinced himself) that the fame he had won in the silent period could be a hindrance to longevity. Some of Dwan's most expressive films came late in his career, when few seemed to notice.

Dwan remained attuned to the basic rules of filmmaking he had learned early and which he felt served him with infinite variety. Those principles may have been far from old-fashioned for those who scrutinized them carefully. The film director John Sayles has stated, "There is one thing I learned from a book about screenwriting. There was an interview that Peter Bogdanovich did with Allan Dwan.... He had this rule, which I also use in my fiction writing, that if you drew lines of emotional connection between the characters, you had to have at least two coming from every person."

Bogdanovich noted, "To follow Dwan's career is to watch the evolution of an art." It is certainly that but it is also to watch the evolution and history of the film industry in the United States. By necessity, histories of the film industry are full of generalities. In closely following Dwan's career, you can understand the history of the film industry as you never have before. That is because it is full of particulars and the drive of one man to find his way through the thickets of emerging and failing companies to the entities that offered the best opportunities for him to work and to develop as a filmmaker. In the silent era, Dwan looked for the most forward-looking corporations. But late in his career, he made his way through the backwaters of the industry to seize available opportunities to preserve his independence.

He learned that he could not remain at any firm too long and became always prepared to move on.

This book covers a great many factors that were involved in the dynamics of Dwan's career and the quality of his work. These included the tumultuous changes in the film industry in its early years, Dwan's alliance with some major stars and his collaborators behind the camera. There are also glimpses of his personal life in the midst of his workaholic dedication to his craft. Not all the chapters in this book move in the same direction but they are all intended to give a broad context and understanding of what propelled the man and his career.

There is also a shift in the second half of the book. The director of the second half is much less of a public man and tends to disappear into his films. Consequently, there is a greater emphasis on discussing his movies in the second part. A number of these lesser-known films indeed merit more attention.

I also make no pretenses of this book having the final word on Allan Dwan. I might have gone on for additional years finding other bits and pieces, while some information may already be lost forever. And after seven years' work, I have already obtained more material than I could comfortably squeeze into one volume. Bogdanovich's book was a great leap forward in uncovering Dwan's neglected career. (That Dwan was so overlooked probably confirmed the director's own suspicions about the nature and brevity of fame.) I hope that this book will be seen as another great leap that answers some vital questions, corrects some inaccuracies and provides a much fuller account of Dwan's marvelously prolific career than was heretofore available. But there may be a bit more; "missing" films that may yet be found and individuals, whom I was not able to locate, who will step forward. I hope my book will encourage such developments and further consideration of Allan Dwan's status in film history.

As always, historians of all kinds must continue to build on each other's work.

Part One

The Lusty Child

It has become a habit to say that the motion picture is still in its infancy. That is not true today. The motion picture has outgrown its swaddling clothes and has become a lusty child.— From a speech by Adolph Zukor on radio station WOR, as quoted in *Film Daily*, January 15, 1925

1. Prelude

The elderly film director, now in his nineties, entered the Sunset Strip restaurant and took his place at the table. It was a critics' award banquet and he was to be honored with a lifetime achievement award for his body of work.

He would enjoy the honors but the real trick was to see if his renewed status of celebrity could help sell his screenplay. It was a project he had first considered while he was still an active director, when he was "only" in his seventies. He was now in another period of exile, as he had been before and would be again. His current exile was a common one. It was the one shared by aged film directors who still had the physical and mental ability to work but who would never again be permitted behind the camera.

The director had a very mottled face, with many reddish spots and scars caused by his long exposure to the sun. He evidently had little skin cancers removed over the years. He seemed to have bad eyes, with one looking kind of skewed and dead and the other getting most of the use. His typical way of talking was sardonic with a wry smile.

He felt that his mind was still spry and resourceful and that he could be just as creative as he had been. But could he be wrong?

The director had turned to his friend, the film critic in his early forties, whom he had asked to read his scenario. But he had given his friend a stiff admonition: "Please, if you're going to do this, you've got to promise to give me a totally honest response."

The director's script was an adaptation of Thornton Wilder's novel *The Bridge of San Luis Rey*.

The film critic took his duty seriously but he wondered if he was the best person to perform this service. Critics weren't necessarily equipped to evaluate the potential of a script or indeed anything that was short of a finished film splashing on a screen. Still, over the course of the years, he had been given a number of screenplays to judge and done his best.

He found that he had never read a script that was so completely visualized as that of his director friend. He felt he could see every frame of the film. It befitted the work of someone who had been a great silent film director and a trained engineer. All the camera angles, camera movements and other technical specifications were there; so was a detailed description of how the bridge would come apart.

The power of the imagery, the pacing, all led the critic to believe this was a wonderful script.

The one drawback, the critic felt, was that the dialogue, much of it probably drawn from Wilder's novel of fifty years ago, needed updating. He suggested to the director a writer he thought could contribute the necessary refinement.[1]

The director thanked the critic for his suggestion but the elderly man had still larger concerns. He knew that he was now considered too old to be permitted to direct the film. He was back to where he had started, seventy years ago, when selling scripts had first brought him into the business. And a quarter of a century after that, it had been his writing talents that got him back when he had seemed to be forgotten and cast away by the movie industry.

He felt that he had a good name director for the project in Peter Bogdanovich, the man who had helped restore the director's fame in his interview book

He would also need a big name star to help get his project afloat. And the social contacts accessible at events like this dinner could be crucial.

The director's acceptance speech for his award was brief. He simply expressed his gratitude for being recognized and remembered.

When the ceremonies ended, Allan Dwan alighted to join the social whirl. Despite his age, the director was still sprightly and he approached Liza Minnelli, the Oscar winner of four years ago, who was among the guests.

"This part would be perfect for you," Dwan told the actress, who was seated next to Martin Scorsese. A little over a month earlier, Scorsese had written to Dwan to thank him for his supporting the protest against the way American International Pictures had handled the film *A Matter of Time*, directed by Liza's father Vincente Minnelli.[2] Producer Samuel Arkoff had taken over editing of the picture and discarded much of its flashback structure.

Minnelli probably did not know Dwan's work but she understood from her father the trials and tribulations of film directors. She treated Dwan with courtesy and respect. Scorsese, with his encyclopedic knowledge of film history, could appreciate all Dwan's efforts and hustle.

Dwan knew, of course, that he might have made no progress that night. In Hollywood, people could be kind and have the best of intentions but that did not mean that your project would see fruition. And at his age, all the odds were against him, no matter how good his ideas were.

Even Dwan's former boss, the once mighty but always realistic tycoon Adolph Zukor, in an interview shortly after his 100th birthday, conceded, "I cannot tell people how to make pictures any more."[3]

Dwan's good friend, the film critic Kevin Thomas of the *Los*

Angeles Times, along with Bogdanovich and Kevin Brownlow, had ushered Dwan into a world of honors and appreciation that had eluded him in the latter part of his career. But Dwan just wanted to continue as he had before, still working, no matter how far removed he was from the centers of power.

Like some of the noted film directors of his era (John Ford, Leo McCarey and Raoul Walsh), Dwan was of Irish ancestry. However, he was not born in the U.S. or Ireland but in Toronto, Canada, where he entered this world on April 3, 1885, with the moniker Joseph Aloysius Dwan. His mother was the former Mary Hunt and his father Joseph Michael Dwan was a clothing merchant. He was the second of their two children, having been preceded two years earlier by his brother Leo.

Dwan recalled that he was "a fairly normal kid" but that there was one aspect that branded him "odd." At a very young age, he was infatuated with the theater although even in 1920 Dwan could not recall when he had first seen a play.

At the age of about seven, Dwan was already "stage struck" and at that time he wrote and produced his own play for his friends. "I learned that my companions did not particularly care for the work of rehearsing in my shows, so I played all of the parts myself. I was my own publicity agent and incidentally, the ticket collector. The admission was, I think, two marbles.... When the table cloth curtain was lifted I began my show and I was playing all the parts. It went very well until one of the audience said that he did not think I talked like an actor, and the fight started. When my mother untangled us, the show was over."[4]

The infant Allan Dwan (1885) (courtesy Academy of Motion Picture Arts and Sciences).

Dwan recalled that his father's business interests necessitated a move to Chicago. According to a document at the Margaret Herrick Library, the eight-year-old Dwan and his family entered the U.S. on April 15, 1893, first arriving in Detroit, Michigan.[5] Dwan's family stayed briefly in Detroit, then moved on to Chicago in time for the 1893 Chicago World's Fair, known as the World's Columbian Exposition, as it was celebrating the 400th anniversary of Columbus' discovery of the New World. The Exposition, dedicated in late 1892, opened to the public on May 1, 1893, and closed on October 30.

There was much there that would have fascinated the young Allan Dwan. The Electricity Building was full of exhibits that may have proved inspirational to a boy who would later study electrical engineering. The eight-year-old might have also been taken to visit Buffalo Bill's Wild West show which was situated just outside the fair grounds.

One exhibition may have made little impression on the youngster. At least one of Thomas Edison's Kinetoscope machines, which showed moving pictures through the window of their cabinet housing, was demonstrated at the fair. But even into his adolescence, Dwan had little interest in motion pictures except for their mechanical value.

Dwan still retained his theatrical ambitions when he went to the University of Notre Dame to study electrical engineering. At Notre Dame, he exhibited interest in a broad range of activities and proved popular. He was unanimously elected president of the Illinois club. (Illinois was said to have a larger number of students at Notre Dame than any other state.) He was also president of the Electrical Society and one of the editors of the Dome, the university yearbook.

Dwan also tried his hand at football and in 1906 played quarterback in two games, appearing in one game for twelve minutes. The *Scholastic*, the university newspaper, reported, "Dwan, the man to whom the propeller of the team was to be given, had been forced to withdraw because of parental objections.... [F]rom his work in the two games he played in he gave every indication of making a great quarter-back. He possessed an abundance of speed and nerve, and was learning the game fast."[6]

But the stage remained Dwan's greatest interest outside his studies and this was recognized by his fellow students. An entry in the 1906 yearbook noted, "Undoubtedly Mr. Joseph A. Dwan was the leading spirit in dramatics about the University this year.... His ability to carry successfully such diverse roles as 'Shylock,' old 'Adam,' and a present day college-man, stamp him as an actor of no mean power" ("Dramatics" from the 1906 Dome, Notre Dame University). Years later, Dwan told Charles Foster of his college theatricals, "I wasn't really that good. It was simply that everyone else was so bad."[7]

The day after Easter in 1907, Dwan played the title role in the University's production of Bulwer Lytton's *Richelieu*. The

Scholastic cited his work as "masterful. Dwan has been in dramatic circles for some time but his appearance Easter Monday was the climax to a brilliant college career in this line. His interpretation of the Cardinal and his rendition of Lytton's famous lines were little short of perfect." The *Scholastic* believed he had a great professional future ahead of him, adding, "His part was heavy and required a good man to do it justice, and Aloysius J. Dwan filled the bill perfectly."[8]

Note how in the second of the two above stories, Dwan's first and middle names are transposed. Dwan did not care for the names Joseph or Aloysius and would soon be known as "Allan." Explaining the name change to Kevin Brownlow, Dwan said, "At school they used to say, 'Aloysius to be a girl.'"[9] The 1907 yearbook cited Dwan's nickname as "Allie." This yearbook went on to note of Dwan,

> His personality is all his own. This young man is singularly blessed with talents. As a singer, he would put the famous Mary McLane to shame. What may be the source of his wonderful strain, we hesitate to conjecture, except that it has been inherited from one of his ancestors, who was a bard in Ireland. The oratorical voice of this prodigy has moved many a callous soul to prayer, and won for him sumptuous dinners, of a Sunday, at the homes of the fair belles of the parish. As an actor, he is a luminary among the stars. Unfortunately he was one of "the troupe that was stranded in Peoria." Since that time, owing to parental objections, he has not appeared in the limelight.[10]

A family portrait from the early 1900s: From left to right, Leo Dwan, Joseph A. Dwan, Mary Dwan, Allan Dwan, Michael Dwan (paternal grandfather of Allan). Note that only Mary Dwan is not facing camera and is detached from the others. Had there been an argument before the picture-taking or was she basically aloof? (courtesy Academy of Motion Picture Arts and Sciences).

Exactly what happened when things did not play in Peoria is not clear but it is interesting that for a second time "parental objections" curtailed Dwan's extracurricular activities. It leaves open the question about how heavy a hand his parents applied.

Little information is available about Dwan's parents. According to the 1886 Toronto Directory, Joseph Dwan was listed as a "traveller" (traveling salesman) who lived at 265 Berkeley Street. Dwan's mother Mary Hunt also hailed from Toronto. Interestingly, when Dwan was making films in Santa Barbara in the teens, his mother was cited in the Santa Barbara Morning Press as entertaining visitors to his home. No mention was made of Dwan's father, who may have still been in Chicago (which is where he died in 1917).

Dwan would later tell his goddaughter that his parents were quite prosperous from their ownership of a lumber company in British Columbia.[11] But that leaves open the question of why the family would need to move to the U.S.

According to the U.S. Census report of 1910, when his father was only fifty-three, Dwan's twenty-seven-year-old brother Leo (a physician) was listed as head of the household. A newspaper clipping citing Dwan's activities at college noted that his family resided at 608 La Salle Avenue in Chicago.[12]

After his graduation from Notre Dame in 1907, Dwan stayed on to teach at the Notre Dame Preparatory School. In the 1907-08 season, he is recorded as having been an instructor in English and mathematics as well as serving as an assistant in physics and electricity. In the 1908-09 season he taught mathematics and physics. Dwan also said he worked as an assistant football coach, which is possible, but I have not found it officially recorded.

Dwan said that his family had sent him to the Massachusetts Institute of Technology for post-graduate work. Dwan remarked in 1920, "The family were [sic] certain that I had an engineering future. Poor family! If they had only known that my studies were always hurried, and my best thought dwelled constantly on the theatres in Boston...."[13] There is no record of Dwan having received a post-graduate degree from M.I.T. He may have just been auditing courses or perhaps abandoned them for his theater interests.

In the same narrative, Dwan said he left teaching at Notre Dame to go to New York to sell a play he had written. Dwan confidently felt that he would make a fortune for some theatrical manager. Instead he found that one firm after another "rejected the manuscript,

Mary Dwan appearing alone and this time looking directly at the camera (Allan Dwan papers. Collection number 3566. American Heritage Center, University of Wyoming).

and believe me when I solemnly say that they were right. It was a *very, very* bad play."[14]

Because youthful pride kept him from writing home for money to return to Chicago, Dwan had to make an important decision. "I had told the family when they asked me not to leave my college position, that they were hindering talent. I slept in Bryant Park — a sure sign of arriving fame, only I did not know it then — and decided that I would lower my ambitions. I would be an actor."[15]

Breaking Into Movies

In 1920, discussing his early pursuit of an acting career, Dwan recalled, "I started a round of managerial offices, but they had never heard of me.... And as I needed to eat, I went a further step down — I hunted a cheap vaudeville agency. Yes, they needed a man, a "heavy" in a dramatic act.... So I became a villain and made eyes at the leading lady."[16]

Dwan here apparently learned the importance of working not for art but for a paycheck. As he remembered it,

> The leading man and leading lady used to do an acrobatic act earlier on the bill, by way of earning a few more dollars, and many a night when I needed the money I used to stand in the wings and watch them at work, wondering if she should fall, whether we would get our salary.
>
> Finally, we reached Passaic. No, the lady did not fall, but the manager did. He looked us over and came down with a heavy hand.
>
> "It's rotten," he remarked poetically, "rotten. You're closed."
>
> "You mean that we are not going to act any more?" I questioned.
>
> "I mean you never did act, any of you. You're rotten," and that was all there was to it.
>
> By this time I was cured of pride. I went home on the family money.[17]

But in Dwan's case, pride vanished before his rise. Dwan said that the day after he returned to Chicago he got a job as an electrical engineer. One of his tasks was "to inspect the installation of an arc light system for the Essanay Motion Picture Studio in Chicago."[18]

Readers of Bogdanovich's long interview with Dwan are familiar with what happened next and how his electrical assignment brought him into the film industry.

Dwan explained how lights then being used for illumination for motion picture photography were very rough on the eyes of the actors. Dwan said he worked on the mercury vapor arc, "which was the great-grandfather of the neon light."[19] These lights did not create problems for the actors' eyes. Dwan said he was approached by George Spoor, one of the co-founders and owners of Essanay (the other was G.M. Anderson; "Essanay" was derived from the first letters of their last names), who asked if these tubes could be useful for motion picture photography. Dwan responded that he thought so and an experiment was arranged.

Dwan told Bogdanovich, "I designed some lights for this experiment ... and then stayed to see that they operated properly.... And so in the process of supervising the lights, I watched these movies being made ... and I finally said, 'Where do you get these stories you're doing?' And they told me they bought them from any source possible — paid as much as $25 for a story. Now that intrigued me. I had written a lot of short stories for the scholastic newspaper at Notre Dame, so I brought a load of them over. And they bought about thirteen or fourteen of them from me at $25 each, and were so impressed with me as a writer they asked me if I'd be their scenario editor."[20]

In his later years, Dwan also recited this story to Kevin Brownlow and others. In 1920, he wrote that it was only his job as electrical engineer to inspect the installed lights. But by the 1960s he was claiming to have actually developed these lights and was supervising their installation.[21]

But in his earlier years when he was riding high, Dwan gave other versions of his entry into the film business. Though many of the basic elements of the story usually remained the same, there were enough variations and departures to position Dwan somewhere between Scheherazade and Baron Munchausen.

In 1920 alone, Dwan gave three different versions of the Essanay story. He told the Canadian magazine *MacLean's* that while at Essanay he was approached by Tom Ricketts, the director of the studio,[22] who asked Dwan if he had ever acted. Dwan assured Ricketts that he was "the best actor in the world," adding, "I'm afraid that I believed that."[23] Ricketts then cast Dwan as the villain in a one-reel film.

That first picture demonstrated to Dwan that Essanay needed better stories. He then wrote a story which he sold to Essanay for ten dollars. Dwan then "went home, much elated, sat up all night writing the second film story, and sold it for twenty-five dollars. When they sent me the check for the second story, they offered me a staff position in the scenario department. All I had to do was to keep the directors busy by turning out sufficient stories."[24]

In the *Photoplay* interview that appeared in August 1920, Dwan also told Adela Rogers St. Johns that he was sent to Essanay to install some Cooper Hewitt lights. He explained, "They were new then and I took an expert to handle them." This again suggests that he was not involved in developing the lights.

He then told St. Johns, "Now comes the horrible part of my confession. I had written a story. Personally, I thought it was a durned fine story and the more I read other people's, the more I decided I'd have to send it out for the poor editors to see.... So the next time I was sent out, I took it along. They bought it. Then I wrote some more. They bought them, too."[25]

At an informal dinner given to the members of the trade and daily press in Chicago on October 19, 1920, Dwan recalled going to Essanay in "the capacity of electrical engineer. Suddenly, the director cast his professional eye on me and shouted, 'Say, we're looking for a man to play the hero's weaker brother, and you're just the type!'"

Dwan continued, "Well, I slipped into the part and then came a scene where big brother, who was played by [Warren] Kerrigan, gets rough with me. I was almost fed up on the weaker brother stuff by that time and instead of dealing him a stage blow, I came back at him with all my force and actually knocked him out."[26]

In 1923, Dwan told *Picture Play Magazine* that when he went to supervise the installing of lights at the Essanay Studio, "while he was hanging around, a director mistook him for an actor and put him in a scene.... For several weeks he worked pretty regularly at the studio." Dwan then began writing and selling stories to the studio.[27]

In a 1927 article, nobody at Essanay, mistakenly or not, approached Dwan for an acting job while he was installing lights. Instead, "I talked myself into a job as an actor — and I got away with it. Being on the inside then I was heeded when I submitted my first scenario."[28]

On occasion, Dwan departed completely from the basic Essanay narrative. In a 1921 article in the *Washington Post*, a youthful Dwan was still in New York, down to his last nickel. Using that nickel to buy some chewing gum and perhaps appear more confident, Dwan then approached the theatrical producer A.H. Woods for a job. Woods had no position for him but as he watched the disappointed young man turn toward the door, he asked him, "Up against it?"

When the youth could only stammer, "Well..." Woods handed him a $10 bill. "With Al Woods' $10 bill Dwan got himself a shave and a shine and a meal," the article continued. "His faith restored in others and in himself, he tucked his manuscript (the one he had come to New York to sell) under his arm and he radiated such enthusiasm and confidence when he reached the studios that he sold the darned thing and on the strength of it was later given the job as scenario editor of American Film Company."[29]

In this version, Dwan seems to have amalgamated his fruitless experience trying to sell his play in New York with his later successful selling of scenarios at Essanay. This story is also of interest because the fable of the invigorating effects of the $10 gift presages the Depression plot of Dwan's 1948 *The Inside Story* where the act of passing $1000 from one individual to another, resuscitates the fortunes of all involved.

"The Dynamic Allan Dwan," a 1919 article in *Motion Picture Magazine*, provides an even more dramatic incident. Here again, Dwan got his cinema start in New York: "It was at the old Bison studio in New York that he started his film career as an extra. During his first day's work he was a soldier, and in the excitement of the battle scene, the man next to him jabbed a sword into his leg as he lay on the ground, having been 'killed' in the first skirmish. He endured the pain until the camera stopped, fearing that the slightest move would destroy the illusion."[30]

While Dwan's act of valor on a cinematic battlefield may not have occurred, it is possible that he did take on work as an extra at Bison while he was running low on funds in New York. If there was any truth to this particular story, it certainly takes Dwan's reputed capacity for restraint to a new level as well as his obsessive dedication to a theatrical career.

True or not, the story also served to elevate Dwan's "stooping" to extra work to a more ethereal level. As the purple prose of this article puts it, "This incident was entirely indicative of the inherent demand for realism that was to mark his work and was like a finger pointing up the path he was to climb to fame."[31]

Neither the uplifted finger nor the rest of the wayward sword story appears to have been included in the accounts Dwan gave in his later years.

Like a presidential candidate, Dwan needed to provide his own mythology of his rise to prominence. Some of this was to fulfill the publicity requirements of the time but the myth-making may have been also satisfying Dwan's own inner needs.

Given that the stories of Dwan breaking into films as an actor were each told a different way, it is tempting to conclude that they were all fabricated. Most of them involve him being discovered on the spot and only in the version told in 1927 does he have to exert himself so much as to "talk" himself into getting a part. Also, in the later years of his life when his acting career must have meant much less to him, none of his narratives of how he got started in the film business make reference to acting.

However, there is some evidence to give credence to Dwan working as a screen actor. In 1912, when Dwan was directing films at the American Film Manufacturing Company, his star actor J. Warren Kerrigan was interviewed by the local paper at Santa Barbara. The article cites Kerrigan's previous association with the Essanay Company. The piece goes on to note that "Mr. Kerrigan has an interesting photograph of those days, a drawing room scene with the players finely groomed and gowned, in which Mr. Dwan, the director of the company, played the villain."[32]

Another piece of evidence, though less compelling, is a newspaper blurb about Dwan hiring his former boss Tom Ricketts for a small acting part in his 1936 B movie *Human Cargo*. The article notes, "Years ago, Ricketts, then a director for Essanay in Chicago, hired Dwan for a bit and then fired him when his too-enthusiastic punch knocked out the leading man." This story might appear to confirm Dwan's anecdote of having knocked out Kerrigan. However, the newspaper piece does not make clear if the story originated with Dwan or Ricketts. Also, if he was the source, Ricketts by this time was eighty-three years old and it's impossible to know how accurate his power of recall was or if he was prone to embellishment.[33]

The telling of different accounts of his acting career seemed to suit different purposes. Each variation in the breakthrough story could serve a specific need. In the version where Dwan played Kerrigan's younger brother, Dwan was able to express his satisfaction in telling how he pulverized an actor he strongly disliked. In the *MacLean's* story, Dwan was able to follow up on the pathetic tale of his dismal performance as a villain on stage with a depiction of a director seeing him as a convincing villain for the cinema.

While Dwan's stint as an actor disappeared from his career breakthrough stories in later years, his talents as an engineer magnified into that of a designer. In this narration, he was well on his way to making a moderate living in a very practical capacity when he was lured away by the glamour and riches of the film business. As if in some kind of a fantasy psychodrama, in these stories Dwan the Scientist and Dwan the Actor had to lead the way to Dwan's ultimate vocation as a writer and, later, director.

The one part of the story that remains consistent is that Dwan ultimately won a place in the Essanay Company by selling it stories but even here there is a crucial divergence in detail. The versions of the story given when he was younger have him writing his initial stories on the spot or having written them relatively recently. Even as late as 1950, Dwan told an interviewer, "They looked easy to do and I figured I could write the kind of stories they used. So I knocked out a couple and before I knew it I had sold ten of them to Essanay."[34] But late in life, as with the citation above from Bogdanovich, Dwan says he used stories he had written for the *Scholastic*, Notre Dame's college paper. For the Bogdanovich interview the number of stories sold is quantified as "thirteen or fourteen."[35] Dwan told Brownlow in his interview for *The Parade's Gone By...* that he sold Essanay fifteen of his *Scholastic* stories.[36] In a later interview with Brownlow, Dwan said that he sold twelve of his *Scholastic* stories.[37] For his contribution to Tay Garnett's book *Directing: Learn from the Masters*, the number is fixed at thirteen.[38]

Research on indices conducted at Notre Dame on old issues of the *Scholastic* turned up only one short story by Dwan, the not particularly cinematic "As Heard by Central." It is unlikely that a dozen or so stories could have been missed the indices for their respective years.

The effect of saying that the stories he sold were simply lifted from the *Scholastic* makes Dwan's entry into the film business seem almost effortless. Learning about this opportunity through an electrical engineering assignment makes it seem serendipitous.

Even in 1920, Dwan had regarded his decision to want to sell a story to the movies to be the "horrible part of my confession."[39] He had told Bogdanovich, "All of us great actors sneered at motion pictures...."[40] But Dwan had accepted the need to lower his sights.

There is one account of Dwan's entry into the film industry that not yet been examined. It comes from a 20th Century–Fox studio biography meant to be circulated when Dwan started work in late 1935 on the film *Song and Dance Man*. Dwan was then toiling on B movies and with much less need to promote himself. The release stated of Dwan, "His education thus completed in 1909, his first act was to write a scenario which he sold by mail to the Essanay Film Company. This brought him a job with Essanay as a scenario writer."[41]

Dwan may have felt no need to talk about his days struggling to sell a play. And at this low point in his career, Dwan may have felt little of the horror in confessing that, plain and simple, in 1909 he was out to sell a script to the movies. That was probably true, regardless of whether he ever installed or inspected mercury vapor lights at Essanay.

The Essanay Company, founded in 1907, was the major production firm in the Midwest. Grasping the commercial value of the Western, G.M. Anderson took his cast and crew on a location trip out West in 1908. They found suitable landscapes around Golden, Colorado, and the results were successful enough that they returned in September 1909. Anderson directed and starred in his films and later developed the character of "Broncho Billy" for which he is best remembered. Although Anderson wrote many of his scripts, it's possible that Dwan wrote some of the Westerns since that genre had become Essanay's "gold mine."[42]

Essanay, however, had to reckon with an entity known as the Motion Picture Patents Company (MPPC). The Patents Company had brought a strong measure of standardization and stability to the film industry but it also amounted to a royalty scheme for which by virtue of his patented camera, producers had to pay Thomas Edison a royalty for every film made. The MPPC was able to use its influence to control not only the production of films but their distribution and exhibition. Only film companies accepting their terms would be granted licenses by the Patent Companies. Essanay decided it had to comply.

But not everyone buckled under. Among the figures operating in the film exchanges who had incurred the wrath of the Patents Company were Harry Aitken, John Freuler, Samuel Hutchinson and Charles Hite, who all became locked in legal battles with the MPPC. To fight back, they started their own production company and offered the Patents Company some new competition.

Essanay's business manager Aubrey M. Kennedy and production supervisor Gilbert Hamilton joined in the plan but they would not be the only defectors moving to the new outfit to be called the American Film Manufacturing Company. In September 1910, the nascent company conducted a "raid" of Essanay's personnel. When it was over, Essanay had lost forty-seven of sixty employees to American. These included J. Warren Kerrigan, Essanay's newest star who had joined the company in January, actress Dot Farley, director Tom Ricketts, and scenarist Allan Dwan. Dwan recalled, "Their trick of getting everybody was to double salaries in those days because they weren't very high."[43]

The first public announcement of the new company was made in the first week of October. It proclaimed;

> American Film for the American People
> Manufactured by the
> American Film Manufacturing Company[44]

In the listing of company credits, Dwan (misspelled Dewan) was referred to as "scenario expert." Since his was the only name listed in the scenario department, he was almost certainly the scenario editor.

American was able to boast that although it was a new company, it had an experienced staff. An enraged George Spoor filed an injunction against American to prevent it from luring away any more of his employees. As a face-saving gesture, Spoor issued a publicity release explaining that Essanay was upgrading its personnel and therefore had to release numerous employees while they added an entire new stock company.

With its contingent of former Essanay staffers, American or Flying A (so-called because of its logo of the letter "A" bearing wings) could produce the same types of films that were most popular at Essanay: Westerns and comedies. Flying A would have three units, one led by director Ricketts to produce dramas, one under Sam Morris to make comedies and another under Frank Beal to do Westerns. The first two units remained in the Chicago area; Beal's troupe was sent to the Southwest.

Dwan recalled that his first assignment for American involved a location trip. He was sent

> to work with Frank Beal who was a very good stock company director they got from the theater and sent out to make pictures in Tucson, Arizona. I went as a sort of unit manager — handled the money, took care of the payroll — and did work with him on stories. If he saw something he wanted to get into a story, I'd write it in for him.... And then something happened, because the Chicago office sent word for us to stop operating, discharge everybody on the spot and come back to Chicago. Well, that didn't sit well with me because these people had been brought out from Chicago and how would they ever get back? So, against orders, I arranged for everyone to get back, and the company got sore about it because they thought they were going to save that fare money — a couple of hundred dollars or so.... Anyway, they got sore and I got fired.[45]

Dwan told much the same story in his 1920 Canadian article but here more clearly identified the reason for the disbanding of the company. "My first job was an errand to Tucson, Arizona, where I was to discover why one of the company's directors, located there, was not making pictures. I discovered the company was in a high state of incompatibility; nobody spoke to anybody else, and consequently, good work was an impossibility. I sent a wire to Chicago, telling them what I found. They told me to discharge the crowd, and not pay any car fares home."[46] And in this version, too, Dwan did not follow orders and was dismissed.

Dwan told Bogdanovich that after a management change, he was re-hired by A.M. Kennedy. Kennedy had been American's first general manager and remained in that post until 1912. However, Flying A's superintendent, Gilbert Hamilton, either left the company or was relieved of his duties around the time Dwan returned, so there may be something to Dwan's explanation.[47] Dwan's 1920 account noted, "I was not exactly worried over the situation, for I wrote and sold scenarios with fair regularity. Then one day, the American people wanted me back."[48]

Whether Dwan worked for any other company in the interim before he re-joined American is open to speculation. Tom Ricketts has told a story of how Dwan worked for him as an assistant after they had both left Flying A but his account is vague and even confusing on details.[49]

For the first few months of its existence, American's output was evenly divided among dramas, comedies and Westerns. Reviews for their films were mixed. By April 1911, Flying A decided that it would concentrate exclusively on Westerns with their ballyhooed quality of actually being made in the west. But a problem arose with the Western company. Dwan said he was told that the unit had no stories. Dwan was again asked to go out west to work with Beal, who had returned to the fold. What happened next was chronicled in what is surely Dwan's most memorable anecdote:

> And after a long search I finally found our company at San Juan Capistrano in a little hotel. There were about eight actors, a lot of cowboys, some horses, and everyone was sitting there, doing nothing. I said, "Why aren't you working?" They said, "Well, our director has been away on a binge for two weeks in Los Angeles, and we don't see him very often, so we haven't made any pictures." It looked like a pretty sad situation and I wired the Chicago office, "I suggest you disband the company. You have no director." They wired back, "You direct." So I got the actors together and said, "Now either I'm a director or you're out of work." And they said, "You're the best damn director we ever saw. You're great." I said, "What do I do? What does a director do?" So they took me out and showed me. And it worked.[50]

Dwan repeated this story throughout his life and (unlike the Essanay story) with few variations. In his later years, he did add a few more details and some dialogue to his account.

The one questionable part of the story is Dwan's suggestion that the company be disbanded. Dwan must have been aware that Flying A was depending on Westerns for its survival. Isn't it more likely that he would have asked the company to get another director out there as soon as possible?

In fact, Dwan himself once acknowledged this very point. In 1920 he wrote, "[T]he home office said they would send on another director. A week or ten days passed and the order came through that as no one else was available, I had to direct."[51]

Clearly, Dwan's emergence as a film director was accidental. Perhaps that was one reason why he continually tweaked his Essanay story so that his entry into the film business might appear just as accidental. It would be another symmetry that could explain Dwan's passage into the culturally disreputable habitat of the movies.

But accidental or not, Dwan was now a movie director.

2. Pioneering

I Am the Motion Picture ... I am the matinee idol of slatternly wives, the dime novel of detective boys. I am opium to ambition. I am the drama's illegitimate child. I am literature's idiot brother.

I am the profoundest possibility of modern times. I am one day old—and on my brow the sages have already found the seal of immortality...

My feet flounder in the clay, but my eyes are with the stars....—"I Am the Motion Picture" by Julian Johnson, *Photoplay*, March 1917

And I say it's the doggone most fascinating game there is—directing motion pictures. It's a sense of power and a sense of creation in one. It's a gamble. Even if you know something about it, you're not so sure you know anything about it at all.—Allan Dwan quoted in "Artistic Efficiency—That's Dwan," *Photoplay*, August 1920

A new westward movement was now in progress to make Western films. Earlier Westerns had been produced in the East, usually in New Jersey. But by 1910, film companies were increasingly using the more convincing landscapes of the West, primarily California. Essanay, which in 1910 established a permanent studio in Niles, California, had set a standard which the new Chicago-based Flying A now followed. Remnants of the actual Western frontier days sometimes converged on this new westward movement. In 1911, the Wild West was still in recent memory and many of its most notable participants were still accessible for the new medium.

Around the time that Dwan found the idle troupe of Flying A players and crew in San Juan Capistrano in mid–April 1911, Buffalo Bill Cody's "Wild West" began its 1911 farewell tour in Washington, D.C. (Cody preferred not to use the word "Show" in its title.) Cody, however, was forced to take his western show on another tour the following year when 1911's receipts failed to produce enough profits to pay his debts and support his various enterprises.

With his touring show gone and forced into bankruptcy by his creditors, Cody (who had already dabbled in films) became involved in a major project, a history of Indian Wars on the plains, played by many of the actual participants. The epic feature, known as *Buffalo Bill's Indian Wars*, as well as other alternate titles, premiered in early 1914. Less than a reel of this invaluable historical document is known to exist today.[1]

In June 1914, producer Thomas H. Ince said he had secured the services of legendary lawman "Bat" Masterson but apparently nothing came of it. Dwan said he met another famous lawman, Wyatt Earp, in 1916 and supposedly gave him a part as an extra in one of his films. Even the former outlaw Emmet Dalton appeared in a film based on his book on the exploits of the Dalton gang, *Beyond the Law*.

With numerous participants of the West still living, it was natural that film companies would want to show that they shared in that personal knowledge of what the frontier was like and would make use of it in their films. One press release, published in the trades, noted,

> Much of the success attained by the American Company, in their "Flying A" Cowboy releases, can be attributed to the interest taken ... by Mr. S.S. Hutchinson, the president of the American Film Manufacturing Company. Mr. Hutchinson is a Westerner. He was born in Cheyenne, Wyo., in the early Sixties. Cheyenne at that time was a frontier cowboy town and the center of the cattle industry in the United States. The Western Indians were, for the most part, as yet unfettered, and it was a comparatively uncommon occurrence for him to see the entire garrison manning Fort Laramie, which was located close to Cheyenne, called out to subdue some savage squad of blood-thirsty redmen, who were running amuck in close vicinity to his birthplace. The knowledge gained by Mr. Hutchinson of Western life generally of the habits, eccentricities, and peculiarities of the cowboy during his early years, was used by him to the great advantage of the company, upon its organization in the West. Through his relatives, some of whom are still residing on the fringe of civilization, were located the best riders, the best ropers, and the best all-around cowboys that the West can boast of.[2]

(While Hutchinson had become president of the company, John Freuler was its secretary-treasurer. Freuler and Harry Aitken headed the Mutual Company, which by 1912 would be distributing the Flying A films.)

Hutchinson had thus established his own "mythic" credentials for making Westerns. There was a different tone for another figure from Flying A being introduced in the trades:

> The producing force of the Western Company of the American Film Manufacturing Company has recently been augmented and its efficiency greatly improved by the addition of Mr. Allan Dwan. Mr. Dwan is well known in theatrical circles as one of the promising playwrights of the younger school. Two or three of his productions have already entertained Broadway under the management of Wm. A. Brady. The latest of his plays has been acquired by Liebler & Co. for Broadway production during the coming season with Walter Whiteside

> as the star. The production is entitled *Into the Light* and is confidently predicted by the various critics, who have seen the scenario, that it undoubtedly will be accepted favorably by the theatergoing public.
>
> Mr. Dwan's penchant, however, is moving pictures. He is not only a capable producer, but likewise inaugurates each and every picture made by him. He is versatile in that his pictures are extremely laughable and original and his dramas invariably enthrallingly interesting.[3]

There was probably nothing in Dwan's biography that American's publicity thought it could exploit for establishing him as an expert on the Old West or sharing in any way in its myths. If they had chosen to divulge it, they could have noted that he was a tenderfoot who went out west on a job and then, because of a derelict director, became the leader of a group of actors and cowboys, providing their "salvation."

As with many biographical announcements, film companies relished pointing out the achievements of their personnel on the legitimate stage. Dwan doubtlessly embellished his Broadway career, which was virtually non-existent. Exactly which "two or three of his productions have already entertained Broadway" is something Dwan does not share with us, nor has any record of such productions been retrieved. In 1913, when he joined Universal, Dwan again maintained that he was not working exclusively in films and that he was a "very successful writer of vaudeville sketches and playlets."[4] Perhaps his "Broadway productions" (if they existed at all) were in vaudeville where contributions were usually anonymous. Similarly, darkness surrounds the fate of his play *Into the Light*. If nothing else, these "credits" suggest that Dwan may not have yet given up his hopes of becoming a playwright.

But while Dwan was myth-deficient in this article, one part of the description adheres to what would become one of the most valued and consistent parts of his résumé, his "efficiency."

Dwan learned directing on a picture set with, as he recalls, the actors instructing him when to say, "Camera ... action ... cut." Dwan summarized what he learned this way:

> I found it was a good idea to let the actors have a lot of free play. I learned that in the beginning and I never got over it. I don't believe in telling an actor every move to make.... Your job is to sort of keep everything going together, as a coach does with a lot of fine athletes. Keep them coordinated, keep them doing their job, and not let them run away from the rest or be too slow so they can't catch up. And see that the story is getting its full value — that's the director's job. But a lot of directors make the mistake of trying to teach the actor every move or gesture he makes.[5]

A story in *Moving Picture World* about American's Western company referred to Dwan as "the producer in charge. Mr. Dwan is one of the most ambitious and hard-working playwrights of the younger school."[6] But the story added, "The second division of the Western stock company will be under the management and dramatic direction of Mr. Charles Earle, who has had many years' experience in moving picture work."[7]

But over the period of weeks that followed while American continued to be able to release two films per week, available records indicated they were all directed by Dwan, at least those made in California. Earle is not listed among directors used by American in Tim Lyons' book *The Silent Partner*, and Lyons had access to the fragmented surviving records of the company. Nor is there any record elsewhere of any Flying A film directed by Earle. And although it was claimed he had "many years' experience in moving picture work," this author has found no record of any films worked on by Charles Earle.

It also seems odd that, after American turned to Dwan in desperation, they suddenly had two working directors. Whether for reasons of management or finance or whatever else, American appeared to have trouble at this point procuring directors. Why else would they again have used Beal after his previous company was so troubled that it had to be disbanded?

Charles Earle may have proved inept or argumentative and was let go without completing any films out west for American. Or ... he may have never existed and was a "phantom" concocted by Flying A to disguise the fact that one director was grinding out all the company's films.[8] In replacing Beal, Dwan not only sped up production but got better notices for his movies.

The studio also saw to it that Dwan had his mythic moment in the papers. Two weeks after the first press story about Dwan as producer of Flying A's Westerns, a piece appeared in the same publication citing a visit by American's general manager, A.M. Kennedy, to their western locations.

In this story, on "one sunny Sunday afternoon" Kennedy suggested to Dwan that this would be a good opportunity to check out the scenic beauties of nearby Foster Canyon. Kennedy and Dwan obtained a "buggy" which was hitched to, yes, an "old gray mare." Kennedy was driving the buggy when the horse began to behave peculiarly. After going on a mad dash on this mountain trail, the horse stopped and acted as if it was going to kick the buggy to pieces. Dwan dismounted. The horse made a spurt for the end of the trail. "On one side of Mr. Dwan was a 200-foot drop into a rugged ravine, on the other side a balky old mare with an inexperienced driver. The position was a peculiar one for Mr. Dwan but his decision was made in a moment ... he decided that if he was going to perdition he would take the mare with him. Grasping the mare's bridle, he hung on for dear life. This so surprised the horse that she hesitated and the momentary hesitancy was all that Mr. Kennedy required to right affairs in a satisfactory manner. The horse was quieted, the harness straightened out, and Mr. Dwan encouraged in his broncho busting proclivities.... Mr. Dwan walked, in a precise and dignified manner, back to El Cajon Valley, quietly leading the mystified and humbled steed."[9] The decision by Dwan to act by surprising the horse sounds typical of his clever resourcefulness. If he did not actually experience the event, he may have at least helped to write it.

In his own account to Bogdanovich, Dwan remembers in

Allan Dwan roughing it out West with Flying A. Note that he wears a holster and pistol (courtesy Academy of Motion Picture Arts and Sciences).

his early greenhorn days being the butt of a cowboy joke. For his film *Rattlesnakes and Gunpowder*, Dwan asked the cowboys to get a rattlesnake for close-ups. Dwan said he was holding the snake by the back of its head when it suddenly stretched out and bit his nose. The cowboys had neglected to tell Dwan that they had already removed the rattler's poison sacs so Dwan thought he was really in peril. The cowboys told him that to keep him from dying they would have to apply a pint of whiskey. Dwan thought they meant to place it on the wound but they said he would have to drink it. Dwan claimed he had never had a drink in his life. (Dwan would have been twenty-six years old at the time.)

When Dwan began to feel the ill effects of the liquor, he thought the poison was taking its course and that he "was going fast." While under the influence, Dwan resolved to get as much shooting done as he could while "I can see my way." Dwan remembers, "I told them, 'Let's get some scenes.' So we started chasing. Well, I made so many chases that the horses dropped exhausted, and finally, so did I.... They took me in and pumped me out — and when I came out of it I realized I was stone drunk and not hurt by the rattlesnake."[10]

Regardless of whether this is exactly what happened or if the truth was as stretched as far as the attacking rattlesnake's head, Dwan demonstrated that he was on top of his game here. The plot of *Rattlesnakes and Gunpowder*, which Dwan also wrote, concerned a game of courage and wits between a Western sheriff and an eastern salesman both vying for the affection of a hotelkeeper's daughter. To help her make up her mind, the men submit to a test where each one of them must thrust his arm into a rattlesnake hole. The easterner became panic-stricken because he knew this meant doom. The sheriff, aware that rattlesnakes always avoid tobacco, sprinkled the hole with tobacco and then fearlessly inserted his arm in the hole. The sheriff thus won the woman's heart.

But the eastern drummer managed to figure out the trick played by the sheriff. He then returned to the hotel and appeared to hold a paper full of gunpowder as he sat close to it with a lit cigar. Actually, this was "fake" gunpowder but looked enough like the real thing for the sheriff to be called. When the sheriff arrived, the salesman struck a match and told him, "Drop that gun or I'll drop this match." The sheriff ran away in terror, leaving his fiancée with the "drummer." "The fate in store for her, however, is a complete revulsion of feeling and she decides that eastern wit is better than cheap heroics."[11] A reviewer observed, "This is a cowboy comedy that kept the audience laughing from beginning to end. The amusing stunts follow each other in such rapid succession that the laughs are without intermission."[12]

Moving, Moving, Moving

An essential element of Western mythology is the continuous sense of movement, whether it was settlers heading for their destination on a wagon train, a cattle drive bringing steers to market or the solitary cowboy hero just wandering.

The early filmmakers who came to California were pioneers in two senses. They were founding a new industry, an entertainment resource and, possibly, an art form. They were also seeking out a new land where that industry would flourish, promising abundant sunshine and good weather year-round.

But another reason has been given for the move to California. The filmmakers, it has been asserted, were trying to escape the menacing surveillance and armed attacks of the Patents Company. Dwan said that *Rattlesnakes and Gunpowder* was begun "in San Juan Capistrano, but moved out of there because of its proximity to the railroad — a convenience for the Patents Company men to get at us. I wanted to go some place a little more remote where we could protect ourselves. Someone steered me to Lakeside...."[13] San Juan Capistrano is roughly halfway between Los Angeles and San Diego. With the move to Lakeside, Dwan took his company further south, just 22 miles from San Diego.

The numerous stories told by early filmmakers of the violent attacks by Patent Company thugs and detectives have been met with some skepticism by many modern film historians. There are some basic reasons why these accounts have been contested. One recent volume, referring to the origins of the American Film Manufacturing Company, noted that Flying A avoided harassment by the Patent Company lawyers and their cohorts by following Anderson's example of moving west. But American also had two companies operating in the city of Chicago. If these companies were able to operate in the city without being shut down, there was no logical reason why another company would have to flee to the west.

One perspective on the situation by an eyewitness to this era comes from the distinguished cinematographer Arthur C. Miller. Having previously worked with the Bison Company, at the end of 1909, Miller began to work in New York City for the Defender Company, run by Joe Engel and film pioneer Edwin S. Porter:

> After being chased and hounded by the Patents Company while with Fred Balshofer and the Bison company, the lack of harassment came as a surprise when I worked for Porter and Engel at Defender and later when [William] Swanson joined them to form the Rex company. The reason for this might have been caused by the change in the independent field. One big factor was that the few independents who had skipped out of reach of the Patents Company had been more than replaced by the rapid growth of the new independent companies and this made the job of policing more difficult. This was the beginning of trying times for the Patents Company in their efforts to enforce their monopoly, and it began to look as if they were faced with an almost impossible task. Whatever the reason, the Rex continued to make their exteriors on Staten Island without the slightest interference.[14]

Miller's comments are but one bit of evidence that suggests that by 1910 the Patents Company could not depend on large-scale intimidation to work. This doesn't preclude that they may have still carried out isolated acts of harassment to keep up the pressure. These may have been reflected in the stories of some filmmakers about violent attacks.

Whatever the truth of the matter, trade paper stories indicate that feelings ran strongly about the battle between the independents and the Patents Company. In the account Dwan gave to film historian Dana Driskel, Dwan's defensive measures border on paranoia. Dwan had armed cowboys standing guard all around the hills, including the three Morrison brothers carrying Winchesters. He told them to stop anyone seen bearing a gun. As a result, Dwan said, "All the little farm boys around there going out to shoot ducks or something were getting pulled in by the cowboys wanting to know what the hell they were doing with that gun, taking their guns away from them and everything. So the gangsters got on to that."[15]

Dwan also recounted an incident that depicted him confronting a rough-looking character trying to drive his company out of town until Dwan bested him in a display of marksmanship. "We stopped at a bridge over an arroyo where people had thrown some tin cans. There was a bright one sitting out there, so to impress me he whipped a gun out of his shoulder holster and shot at the can and missed it by about five yards. I pulled out my gun and hit the can twice, and that afternoon he left town.... From that time on we were never molested."[16] Years later Dwan would use a scene involving the tin challenge in a film with Douglas Fairbanks. Did the true incident inspire the scene or did the movie scene inspire this story in Dwan's old age?

For Dwan's celluloid adventures, the man who provided the heroics at Flying A was usually J. Warren Kerrigan. Dwan and Kerrigan had both toiled at Essanay, and it was Essanay that had signed Kerrigan after some of its officials had spotted him performing on the Chicago stage. Kerrigan attracted enough admirers that eventually American had their publicity department promote him. Though often a cowboy hero, Kerrigan did not appear particularly rugged. He did have a "pigeon" chest which, thrust forward, projected stature to audiences of the time. Kerrigan also won over fans with his handsome,

A 1912 photograph of J. Warren Kerrigan, one of the world's first movie stars and Dwan's rival for power at Flying A (courtesy Dana Driskel).

boyish face, and his characters would be known to use brain more than brawn to triumph. Kerrigan has been called "the first true superstar of the movies."[17] He won the very first popularity poll for male star run by *Photoplay Magazine* in 1913. Kerrigan would win the second as well, in addition to polls by other organizations.

But Kerrigan also had a secret, or at least a secret from the public. He was homosexual and his effete, pampered manner evoked derision from the cowboys on the set. Kerrigan also did not get along well with Dwan.[18]

Flying A's western company also acquired a new leading lady as Dwan took over directing chores. Twenty-five-year-old Pauline Bush made her film debut in *Rattlesnakes and Gunpowder*. A native of Lincoln, Nebraska, she was already a veteran of the stage where she was said to have started her career in 1907. After performing with eastern stock companies, Bush came out west to join the Liberty stock company in Oakland. Bush later recalled that on a visit to Los Angeles, she was "talking to a friend at the Belasco Theater when a director from the American Film Manufacturing Company was there seeking a woman lead. I was introduced and joined the company...."[19] The Flying A publicity department described Bush as "an extremely versatile actress, young, winsome, graceful and an extremely good rider."[20]

Dwan would get along with her much better than with Kerrigan.

As Dwan knew from experience, no stock company would be complete without a heavy and the man who would fill that bill for American's western company was Jack Richardson. He made his first appearance for Flying A in *$5,000 Reward: Dead or Alive*, which was released on June 8, 1911, following *Rattlesnakes and Gunpowder* by less than two weeks. A year younger than Kerrigan, Richardson was born in 1883 in New York City but early in life he and his family moved to Cleveland, Ohio. Richardson started his film career with the Selig Company in 1909.

Dwan continued to make offbeat Western comedies like the half-reel *The Yiddisher Cowboy* where the peddler Ikey Rosenthal shows he can outsmart the roughnecks who treat him derisively. But Dwan also made Western melodramas like the still extant *The Ranchman's Nerve* where Kerrigan and Richardson enacted one of their many confrontations of good and evil.

In the latter film, ranchman Kerrigan accepts the challenge to lead a posse after a bandit (Richardson) known as the Terror of the Mountains. When they come under fire from the rocks, the ranchman decides to try to capture the outlaw single-handed. Kerrigan manages to outfox the thief but relents when he sees that Richardson lives with his mother and sister. Kerrigan gives Richardson a chance to escape.

But Richardson then tries to ambush Kerrigan while he is drinking from a spring. The outlaw's sister (Bush), who has been smitten by the posse leader, shoots her brother. Mortally wounded, he falls over the cliff to the table rock below.

Pauline Bush, Allan Dwan's first leading lady, on a postcard from 1914-15.

As the short description indicates, the landscape was often an integral part of these one-reel Westerns. Dwan gave Bogdanovich an example of how he would get the inspiration for his plots in those days, riding around in a buckboard. "Once we were looking around and I saw a flume. It carried water from one ranch to another in the air like a great bridge — came from a reservoir up the hills. It fascinated me, so I immediately said, 'We've got to use that for a picture.' And I wrote something called *The Poisoned Flume*. Jack Richardson was putting poison in the flume and the water was killing J. Warren Kerrigan's cattle so that's why he threw Richardson off the cliff. That was the typical way of making pictures in those days. All off the cuff."[21] Or as Dwan put it in another article, "When we saw a nice cliff that we had not used the week before, we used it to push the villain off."[22]

Richardson was the lucky recipient of these cliff discoveries. For the next two years, in a ceaseless tide of these Westerns, he would render his Sisyphean efforts to foil Kerrigan only to be done in again and again. One popular line about the actor was that "he has been killed so many times that he finds it hard to believe that he is really alive."[23]

Richardson would suffer injuries in some of his falls. On one occasion, the company was enacting a scene over a cliff with a wide slope extending downward. The slope was outside of camera range, making it look like a straight drop. Two cowboys were positioned to catch Richardson at the end of the fight. Kerrigan and Richardson became so involved in their struggle that they missed the mark where the cowboys were waiting. A newspaper article reported, "While the cowboys were standing off somewhere else waiting for this climax, Richardson struck with a bang and rolled about thirty feet down in the brush.... Mr. Richardson is very anxious that this scene comes out well as he has no desire for further rehearsal."[24]

But Richardson was not the one who would receive real-life punishment on the set of *The Poisoned Flume*. Dwan had begun to find Kerrigan insufferable and decided to play a cruel prank on the actor. During one scene, Dwan had Richardson hold Kerrigan's face down in the water for longer than was necessary for the scene. According to one description, "The villain held him by the back of the neck, keeping him facedown in the flume. Behind him, the crew slapped their knees in laughter, and the director, barely able to conceal his own mirth, ticked off the extra seconds in his mind. When finally he called 'cut' up from the flume staggered the Great God Kerrigan — cursing, spitting, gasping for air."[25]

How much of the reason for this treatment is attributable to the fact that Kerrigan was gay? That's open to debate. Dwan did make derisive references to gays, and late in his life told an interviewer that Kerrigan was "quite a lady himself." In this interview Dwan also "says there were many such 'pansies and poseurs' because 'Hollywood sucked them all in.'"[26] But in 1922, Dwan also worked well with Mitchell Leisen, the homosexual costume designer for *Robin Hood* with no reported problems. (Leisen later became a celebrated film director, most notably at Paramount.)

The greatest part of the conflict between Dwan and Kerrigan most likely arose because of personality differences and the rivalry of egos between a movie star and a star director. Though Dwan and Kerrigan continued to work together, that rivalry would not end and would have future consequences.

By the late summer of 1911, it was time for the Flying A Company to continue its western odyssey. Dwan told Bogdanovich, "We kind of outgrew Lakeside, and wanted to get a little different background and a little closer to people. We couldn't get enough extras there so we came down to La Mesa which was not too far from San Diego and stayed there awhile."[27]

On August 12, the American Company moved to its new Western headquarters, just seven miles away from San Diego. La Mesa was in the center of El Cajon Valley. Although the company was now closer to a large city, Flying A trumpeted the move by proclaiming, "Southern California is actually 'the last West.' Nowhere else on the American continent can one find the diversity of characteristic Western scenery that El Cajon Valley contains. In no other portion of the Western hemisphere can one find the magnificent range country, the untrammeled cowboy, and the actual ranch life which is here native to the land."[28] Flying A wanted its audience to believe that they were not just filming the Old West but living in it.

Dwan had first set up developing facilities for his films in Lakeside. In his interview with Bogdanovich, Dwan said that the method of post-production that Beal had espoused was to ship "the negative back to Chicago — until I decided that it

This 1911 photograph of Flying A's western team has been identified as being taken at the Morrison home, probably in Lakeside shortly before the move to La Mesa. In the front row from left to right are J. Warren Kerrigan, the cameraman Al Heimerl, Louise Lester, Anna Morrison, Jack Richardson (in straw hat), and Scott Beal. In the back row are Wallace Kerrigan, Peter Morrison, Chick Morrison (Anna's husband), George Periolat, Robert Coffee, unidentified (the woman in white), Allan Dwan and Pauline Bush (courtesy Dana Driskel).

would be better to develop the negative ourselves and know what we had — not leave it to them to send us word about our 'mistakes.'"[29] After the move, there were published reports of a $10,000 studio and developing plant built at La Mesa for American.[30]

Dwan explained his schedule. "We would work say, Monday, Tuesday and Wednesday and make two pictures. Then on Thursday and Friday I'd develop and cut them and take Saturday and Sunday off— go down to San Diego or Los Angeles for the weekend."[31] Apparently, the preparation for the next film took place somewhere between the weekend and early Monday morning.

The editing would be done by Dwan himself, even before he had a laboratory. At that time, "I cut the negative — never saw a print — and put it together the way I wanted the picture to run. They'd simply print it that way when it got to Chicago, and that's the way it stayed." Dwan said the intertitles were scratched on the negative with a pin and that once in Chicago they would be properly photographed and inserted in the film.[32]

The lessons learned from doing his own editing would stay with Dwan for his entire career. "I am of the opinion that, of all the director's many duties, there is — perhaps — no one single function that is more vital to the ultimate quality of the film than the editing."[33] Like many modern directors, Dwan believed that the director should have the final say on the cutting. He said, "There's no doubt that a good editor can enhance a director's work immeasurably. Nevertheless, I always stayed as close as possible to my film throughout the entire editing process. Because of my long and intimate knowledge of every facet of the story, I knew the values to be derived from the many little touches I had added during the shooting, and I knew how to jockey them around to take maximum advantage of them — perhaps to eliminate a dull spot, or to pick up the pace."[34] Dwan also understood the value of editing "in the camera." "In my opinion, to be a good director, one must have a pair of scissors in his brain at all times while shooting. He must know exactly why he makes every camera set-up."[35]

There was a business manager with the company, Kerrigan's twin brother Wallace, but it was Dwan who made the ultimate decisions. Not long after the move to La Mesa, Kennedy left his post of general manager. With the departure of Hamilton and Kennedy, Hutchinson gradually took a more hands-on approach that would eventually clash with Dwan's local control of operations.

At La Mesa, there was a new member of the company who would many years later attest to Dwan's increasing sense of cinematic sophistication. Jean Hathaway (nee Weil) took the kind of character parts being played at Flying A by veterans Louise Lester and George Periolat. A couple of months later, she also brought out her young son Henry to play juvenile roles and add to the family's bank account. In the sound era, Henry Hathaway would direct a vast array of films ranging from *The Lives of a Bengal Lancer* and *Peter Ibbetson* to *True Grit*. But now, as a small boy, he would have a chance to observe firsthand how films were made in cinema's early years.

He remembered vividly, "Every stage in those days was open because we had no lights and you needed the sunlight. They worked outside and just diffused the sun.... It was a stage with no background and no ceiling. They couldn't have a ceiling because they had to use the natural sunlight. They had this little wall and a desk in front of it. There was a discussion because a man had to come in and deliver a letter and there wasn't room to get back with the camera to hold the height of the guy without shooting off the set. Dwan said, 'Just have him put his hand in.' They said, 'Well, it'll look idiotic, a guy putting his hand in from the side.' Oh, there was a hell of an argument about it.... Everyone agreed it would look kind of funny just to see a hand coming in from the side without seeing who it was. Dwan said, 'Motion pictures are illusion anyway.'"[36] The scene was shot Dwan's way.

In 1911, scenes were almost always played out in a long shot (as if it was a scene onstage and viewed by a fixed onlooker) until there was a cut to another scene. Dwan comprehended, as perhaps no one else in the company did, that visual shorthand was possible; audience members did not always have to see an actor make an entrance to know that someone had entered a room. Insertions of a hand giving or receiving a message were among the small aesthetic breakthroughs in films at that time.

Dwan had a fateful encounter with another new face in La Mesa. He recalled, "And it was in La Mesa I decided to buy an automobile for transportation. It was brought to me by a young fellow from the auto company who had to stay to teach me how to drive it. And I got to like him. His name was Marshall Neilan. I said to him, 'Would you like to be an actor in the pictures?' He said, 'Sure. What's it pay?' I told him — pretty good pay. I needed a character to play Kerrigan's weak brother, so Neilan was elected and played that in the next fifty films we made."[37]

Dwan had an unfortunate tendency to embellish some of his stories of lending a helping hand to new (and sometimes to old) talent. While he did often play a significant mentoring role, as he did with Neilan, it was not enough that his pupil was a young, relatively inexperienced actor. He had to demonstrate that his subject was totally outside the film industry until Dwan discovered him.

Neilan had indeed been a salesman for an auto firm, the Simplex Motor Car Company, and performed well enough to be made manager of its Los Angeles branch. But the restless Neilan abandoned that job to become a chauffeur for theater director Oliver Morosco, who was presiding over a Burbank stock company. Neilan already had some stage experience (as a teenager) and he later chauffeured for film pioneer D.W. Griffith (a onetime member of the same stage company as Neilan). Griffith may have then helped him get a job with the Kalem Company in Santa Monica where Neilan quickly rose from bit parts to leading man.

According to Neilan's biographer Jack Spears, Neilan met Dwan at one of Griffith's lavish parties in early 1912.[38] Neilan then joined Dwan's Flying A company and his first film for them was *The Reward of Valor*, released on May 27.

Neilan was a native Californian who had roamed through much of the state. Dwan recalled asking Neilan, one day before his prodigy went to visit Los Angeles, "Why don't you go a little further and find me a place where I can have the ocean and the mountains and ranches and everything we need to make pictures?" Dwan told Driskel that he was looking for a new location because he "ran out of places up around La Mesa"[39]; it was also reported in a newspaper story that, after a year in La Mesa, "the scenery commenced to pall on the entire company as it became 'worn out.'"[40] In any case, Dwan said a few days later he received a phone call from Neilan who told him, "I've found exactly what you want down here."[41] Actually, the direction was not down. Neilan had found Santa Barbara, 78 miles north of Los Angeles.

According to a story published months later in the *Santa Barbara Morning Press*, after it was decided that a new location was needed, "Wallace Kerrigan then visited Santa Barbara and upon his report of conditions here Director Dwan very quickly decided to move and early in July the company was located with its studio at the old ostrich farm on upper State Street."[42] In a trade story, it was stated that Kerrigan's negotiations in Santa Barbara followed Dwan's own personal tour of the area. Thus, Kerrigan's trip may have followed visits by both Neilan and Dwan. Flying A now had another new beginning.[43]

Up and Out in Santa Barbara

Sounding like a veteran wagon master, Dwan described his last move with Flying A: "So I packed up the outfit, put them on their horses and their wagons and off we went from La Mesa to Santa Barbara. It took us about two or three days to get there."[44]

Actually, it took the cowboys a week to make the 250-mile journey to Santa Barbara.

The Flying A troupe came into Santa Barbara by different vehicles. Wallace Kerrigan arrived by train. The local paper noted, "The cowboys under the direction of C.P. Morrison, came clattering up State Street at 3 o'clock in the afternoon and they surely looked the real thing. They were travel stained and dusty but rode their horses with true western grace."[45] Dwan and his actors entered Santa Barbara in automobiles.

Santa Barbara offered a number of scenic advantages to the filmmakers. It had both mountain scenery and beaches that remained pristine and undeveloped. There were also islands scattered twenty miles off the coast. A trade story of the time noted, "Mr. Dwan has undoubtedly recognized the fact that in coming to Santa Barbara it will be possible to deviate from so-called Western pictures. The famous Santa Barbara mission, the best preserved in California, will suggest a vast material of stuff from early days in California, while for regal or medieval subjects, beautiful homes and estates in Montecito, a fashionable suburb, would serve."[46]

The company arrived in Santa Barbara on July 6, 1912. Four days later, the first Flying A film was shot in the community, *The Greaser and the Weakling* with Kerrigan and Richardson reprising another of their Manichean struggles. With a former ostrich farm as their new headquarters, American was once more without a laboratory to develop its films and again they had to be shipped to Chicago for developing. But within a few months, a new facility was established.

At Santa Barbara, a future cameraman and director joined the ranks of Flying A. When he was having trouble with his car, Dwan recollected meeting a young mechanical wiz who quickly identified the problem and began fixing it. As he worked on the car, Dwan said he noticed in the corner of the garage a lot of photographic equipment. Dwan then asked the man if he was interested in photography, and when the young man answered affirmatively, Dwan inquired if he'd be interested in doing photographic work in the motion picture industry. And with that, Dwan drew Victor Fleming, the future credited director of *Gone with the Wind* and *The Wizard of Oz*, into the picture business.[47]

There are several other versions of how Fleming joined Flying A and the reader can take his pick. Dwan's cameraman Roy Overbaugh has his own account in which Fleming comes to the Flying A studio "many times and wanted to know if I couldn't possibly engineer him in somehow because he did want to get in the picture business. So, eventually I was able to work it and Vic came on as my assistant cameraman."[48] There are other versions including one in which Fleming was dating Charlotte Burton, an actress at American, who here likely helped bring Fleming into the company.[49]

From his beginnings as a director, Dwan had brought his own wit and resourcefulness into Flying A but he still needed to learn and indeed help develop film technique which was still evolving at the time. As an example of Dwan's early primitive sense of *mise-en-scène*, Lyons cited one of Dwan's films at Lakeside, *Three Million Dollars*, released on September 7, 1911. The film consists of eighteen shots, each less than a minute long. "This one-reel film (approximately fourteen minutes) has no editing within scenes, but instead the progression of the narrative merely follows from one locale to another with each shot revealing a different camera setup."[50] Lyons considers the film below average "technically and dramatically" even for 1911 although outside of Griffith's work, comparisons are difficult. Lyons acknowledges that the "exterior locales eliminate any studio consideration such as light and shadow."[51] But Lyons also notes, "The reliance upon natural scenery, moreover, works as a credit to the film, matching well the naturalistic style of acting."[52]

Over the course of a year, Dwan's style had grown more

refined. The incident described by Hathaway at La Mesa suggests that Dwan was already advancing as a filmmaker. When asked by Bogdanovich what helped him develop so quickly, Dwan replied, "I'd probably been down to the theater and seen a few more of Griffith's pictures and was beginning to learn. I had to learn from the screen. I had no other model. We picked up and manufactured what technique we could, watched the other fellow. The only man I ever watched was Griffith, and I just did what he did." Dwan claimed he also sent Neilan "on an expedition once to work for Griffith for a while" and then report back to Dwan on everything he had observed.[53]

The surviving films Dwan made at Santa Barbara show a significant leap in cinematic sophistication. *Man's Calling* (released on November 11, 1912) again shows Dwan's sensitivity to the dramatic values of locale but with far greater command of his craft and more narrative complexity. It opens in the mountains. Here, "The religious old mountaineer desires his son to follow the calling of the Church."

There is a long shot of the mountaineer, and in the immediate background we can see a procession of friars moving left to right with their staffs. The friars appear to visualize the thoughts the mountaineer has about his son's future.

After parting from his father, we see the son (Kerrigan) stopping before the fence that stands before the Mission.[54] It is a sacred moment as he removes his hat and makes the sign of the cross. In the next shot, as Kerrigan moves to the right of the fence, he sees a young woman (Bush) carrying a canteen coming toward him. Later he follows her to her home and gets to meet her.

He returns to the fence before the mission. He stops, turns back to look, then looks ahead to the mission. He turns back again and then towards the mission again. A conflict in his mind is apparent as he walks to the left out of the frame.

After again seeing the young woman, he is once more in position before the mission. Kerrigan then puts his hand to his forehead and in front of his eyes as if blinded. He is being tortured by a decision he must make but he then turns and extends his arm forward, in the direction of the young woman. Kerrigan goes into the woods, crying on the ground. The next day he asks the young woman's mother (Louise Lester) for work and she hands him a rake. A title informs us, "After a time the call of love conquers the call of the Church." Walking hand in hand, Kerrigan and Bush go before her mother, who gives them her blessing. The next shot is the same one we've seen earlier before the Mission but this time we see the backs of Bush and Kerrigan who are going forward to the Mission.

Dwan shows the dramatic values he can endow with limited surroundings. He repeats images in changing dramatic contexts and in the course of the editing, the images change in meaning. The mission is first a source of solace and inspiration for Kerrigan. Then the Mission becomes the source of a dilemma and finally a horror from which he must avert his eyes. In the final shot in the sequence, the Mission again becomes sanctified as it will be the source of the protagonist's marriage and happiness.

A title then informs us, "A year later The Old Man yearns for his son he supposes has become a priest." The old man is again shown watching the friars going by. The friars again reflect the old man's thoughts about his son but in the repetition of images, they have also become a kind of silent Greek chorus heralding what is to come. The film cuts back to Kerrigan now with his mother-in-law, wife and ... a baby. The young family then goes to visit Kerrigan's father. Although initially disappointed, the father accepts his son's decision and puts his arms around the couple.

The father looks out and in the next shot we see the friars going off into the distance, as if a seeming constant in his thoughts and dreams has passed away forever.

A week before the appearance of *Man's Calling*, an apparent companion piece to that film was released: *Maiden and Men*. It highlights a father and daughter but this time it is the daughter who has aspirations she wants to follow. An old bearded man is seen sitting outside a building with a young woman (Bush) appearing in a doorway. A title notes, "Only these two in many miles." As with the young man of the mountains in *Man's Calling*, the young woman has grown up in an isolated environment, cut off from the outside world.

The daughter's one source of worldly ambition is, according to a title, "Her Secret Treasure a Romantic Novel." The young woman is seen pulling a book out of the bough of a tree. She begins reading it. A passage states, "Will I find my Lover o'er the Sea?" There is then a shot of her appearing before a body of water. When the next passage asks, "Or in the mountains?" it is followed by a shot of her looking over the mountains.

Both the protagonist's hiding place in the tree and the book's romantic images stress her closeness to nature. Implicit is her naiveté about how her quest for a lover must wind through the thicket of human society. These passages are also reminiscent of Griffith in expressing a character's psychological state and act of decision-making.

Not long after, "The Lonesome Maiden forsakes her devoted Father to Seek a Lover."

Bush takes a job on a ranch. She makes an error in ignoring other interested cowboys and accepting the attentions of "the Bully of the Ranch," portrayed by a black-hatted Richardson. After Richardson finishes with her, all of the other cowboys walk away from her. The woman who hired her (Lester), apparently deciding that Bush has loose morals, tells her to go back where she came from and shakes her violently. Snapped out of her reverie, the chastened young woman walks past the gate which looms as portentously as the fence in *Man's Calling*. It is as if she has been expelled from the paradise of her imagination.

The film returns to the images of the first part of the film. Bush goes back to the tree bough of what was once her romantic secret. She picks up the book which now, like an accursed object, seems to fly out of her hands. She rips it up. There is then a shot of her father who remains in the same position seen in the beginning of the film. His daughter enters the frame from the right; then falls down crying in his lap.

Like *Man's Calling*, this film utilizes a repetition of images that change in meaning. It is a device that Dwan will use in later films and carries the basic truth that many familiar places and situations change their value to us with the passage of time. This seems particularly true for youths entering on their rites of passage. By having these images at the beginning and end of the film, they suggest a cyclical scheme of things. Both the dreams that we cherish and the responsibilities that ensnare us, come back to haunt us.

The Reformation of Sierra Smith (released October 12, 1912) shows Dwan, like Hitchcock, being able to use an object as a visual correlative. Kerrigan plays a doctor on a stagecoach robbed by Richardson's highwayman. Richardson takes Kerrigan's watch and brings it to his home. When Richardson's young daughter is taken seriously ill, Kerrigan's doctor is summoned and finds his watch in the child's bed, which he will use to check her pulse. The watch, initially a gift of love from Kerrigan's parents, becomes an object of plunder, evidence of guilt, an instrument aiding the physical salvation of the girl and then the moral regeneration of the father. There is some Victorian sentimentality in how this gift of doting parents ultimately inspires a spiritual rebirth. This is the kind of economic and unpretentious use of symbolism that Dwan would continue to use in his career.

The Thief's Wife, released on November 18, shows Dwan impressively composing shots throughout the film. Using doorway and window framing, he creates a sense of foreboding and of the tense divide between husband and wife. It also presages his voyeuristic use of windows much later in his career. The woman has come to suspect that her husband may be a criminal. A posse (led, of course, by Kerrigan) comes to the thief's house. Richardson shoots at them through the doorway and closes the door. The camera has been placed just behind Richardson and helps establish immediacy to the action.

After the title "A Narrow Escape," there is a long shot from a very low angle from the bottom of the hill so that the viewer can feel he is just behind the posse as they move up toward the house. As they advance to the door, Richardson can be seen climbing out of the second floor window on the left side of the frame. The men take pursuit and head downhill, all in the same shot.

Kerrigan is later wounded and stays with Bush while the posse chases the thief. There is an overhead shot of the posse pursuing Richardson on horseback (with all the foliage around the winding road, it looks like a maze). Richardson is then wounded and taken alive.

The period of 1912–1913 was one of increasing violence and instability in Mexico that culminated in the execution of President Francisco Madero and was followed by insurrection against the new government and more violence that sometimes spilled across the American border. That was certainly one of the reasons that stereotyped Mexican villains (usually Richardson with a mustache) recurred in Dwan's Flying A films. On the other hand, Native Americans tended to be treated more sympathetically. For example, in *White Treachery*, Kerrigan is the Indian hero and Richardson plays the black-hearted white villain.

But the quality of Dwan's Flying A films was about more than stylistic innovation and ethnic conflicts. Not only were the films praised in their own time but film historian Scott Simmon has written admiringly of Flying A films made "under director Allan Dwan, near Los Angeles, where their Westerns show an off-the-cuff charm unmatched by any other company to judge again from surviving examples."[55]

Some of the charm of the Flying A Westerns was prominent in a series centering on a character called Calamity Anne. Most likely, Dwan was looking for a novelty to provide a new wrinkle to the seemingly eternal confrontations between Kerrigan and Richardson and possibly to spin off something new in a comic vein. The name of the character was most probably inspired by the two most legendary female figures of the West, "Calamity Jane" Canary, the frontierswoman and scout, and Annie Oakley of "Wild West" Show fame.

Calamity Anne was not a glamourous figure. She was played by Flying A's character actress Louise Lester, who was forty-five years old when the first Calamity Anne film was made. Lester, a veteran stage actress, had appeared in stock companies in Cleveland, Newark, Philadelphia and Chicago. She toured

An early example of Dwan framing characters before windows is this scene from *The Thief's Wife* (1912). Pauline Bush is the silhouetted figure in the foreground awaiting her husband Jack Richardson, seen approaching the house (courtesy Library of Congress).

in her own company before joining American. Lester had for a time been married to Frank Beal, the derelict director whose disappearance had caused Dwan to be pressed into service. They had a son, Scott Beal, who would later work as an actor for Flying A and then became an assistant director.

The first film featuring the character was *Calamity Anne's Ward,* released on September 30, 1912. The plot initially concerns a brother and sister who are the sole survivors of a wagon train. An outlaw (Richardson) spots them and when the boy challenges his attentions to the young woman, Richardson shoots him.

Richardson brings the girl (Jessalyn Van Trump, Flying A's ingénue) to his camp. He entrusts her to a member of his gang, Calamity Anne, who is distinguished by her long clay pipe, slouched hat with hair jutting out, wearing a jacket and bandana. The girl cries on Calamity Anne's shoulder, and Calamity is deeply moved and resolves to become the girl's guardian. When one of Richardson's men comes to get the girl, Calamity shoots him in the arm. Richardson tries to grab Calamity Anne, but she shoves him away.

In *Calamity Anne's Ward* (1912), Louise Lester's Calamity protects Jessalyn Van Trump from villainous Jack Richardson (courtesy Library of Congress).

A ranger (Kerrigan) who has found the boy's body pretends to be an outlaw and enters the camp. When the ranger and young woman escape, Calamity shoots the hapless Richardson, who had been drawing a bead on the ranger. With her rifle, Calamity keeps the rest of the gang at bay as the ranger and girl make their getaway.

More Calamity Anne films followed. While Dwan was making the films, it was said that he had originated the series.[56] After Dwan left American and Flying A was still trying to cash in on the series, it was reported, "Calamity Anne is a real character whom Miss Lester encountered some years ago, before her advent in motion pictures."[57] By this time, Lester was writing the Calamity Anne films. Available evidence indicates that Dwan wrote the scenario for the first Calamity Anne picture. Lester was still working for American in 1915 when it told the trades, "Miss Lester was the originator as well as the impersonator of the role."[58]

In the spring of 1916, there was a reunion of Lester, Richardson, Kerrigan, Bush, and Dwan and it was reported that "Director Dwan and Miss Lester mapped out the 'Calamity Anne' series for Miss Lester."[59] This is likely closest to the truth. Lester may have suggested the basic look and temperament of the character with Dwan figuring how to fit her into a story.

The sense of male insecurity fomented by an assertive female figure would recur in Dwan's work as it would for Howard Hawks, and often be used for comic effect.

And what effect would this have on Richardson, already resigned to being regularly beaten by Kerrigan, to be now pummeled by a woman? Apparently, the impact was not adverse. Lester and Richardson were married in June 1914. The bride was Richardson's senior by sixteen years.

By the fall of 1912, Dwan and Flying A were riding high and the move to Santa Barbara had proved satisfactory. Hutchinson was now conferring with local architects and planning the construction of permanent buildings and a real studio to replace the ostrich farm. Neilan bowed out of American, where he was playing juveniles, to return to Kalem as a leading man. But Flying A was expanding its labor force and a second company of actors and crew was being organized. It was reported that the cost of the second company would increase the payroll by approximately $100,000 per year.

It was noted in an article in the *Santa Barbara Morning Press* that it was the first time in a year that Hutchinson "has seen the western players in person."[60] To be precise, Hutchinson had last been with his western players during a two-week visit to La Mesa that had ended February 5.[61] The article stated that Hutchinson would be staying for at least a week but he wound up remaining in the area for three weeks. When he left for Chicago on November 21, it was announced that he would be returning to Santa Barbara in January and that he might then make a more extended stay.[62]

Dwan was not used to having the president of Flying A lingering with the western company for any considerable length of time. In the *Morning Press* piece in which Hutchinson announced plans for the permanent home and the second company, it was noted, "The plans which have been set afoot by Mr. Hutchinson were suggested some time ago by Allen [sic] Dwan...."[63] But increasingly, only Hutchinson's name would be mentioned in the local newspaper stories referring to Flying A's business decisions.

The same article cited only Hutchinson going to Los Angeles for the engagement of actors for the second company. Hutchinson returned from Los Angeles on November 9. It was mentioned that Dwan remained in Los Angeles, completing arrangements for the new company. It is not clear how long he was there or how much influence he had in selecting the actors. Knowing Dwan's character, it is likely that at the very least, he had significant input.

It was announced shortly thereafter that the new company would include the actors Wallace Reid, Ed Coxen and Lillian Christie. They arrived in Santa Barbara on November 17. Again, Dwan told both Bogdanovich and Brownlow that Reid was another star he had plucked from obscurity and that Reid had been his prop man. Actually, Reid, the son of the playwright Hal Reid, had been acting in films since 1910, before Dwan had started directing. In 1912, he had already starred in films for Bison/Universal and Vitagraph.

Flying A was still shooting films in Chicago but with the assemblage of the second company, Hutchinson stated that all of American's product would be filmed in Santa Barbara. With some fanfare it was announced that William J. Bauman would arrive from Chicago to assume the duties as director of the second company. Bauman was referred to as a California native who had written both plays and vaudeville sketches.

But on November 20, it was abruptly announced that Wallace Reid would be the director as well as star of the second company. It was cryptically reported, "Conditions have suddenly arisen which have necessitated William J. Bauman resigning as director and he will return to Chicago."[64] Was there some personal problem or had Bauman clashed with Reid and/or others in the company? There were other personnel changes to come and it was telling that if there had been a conflict between Reid and Bauman, it was the star, not the director, who triumphed. Further reinforcing the idea that Santa Barbara had been selected for having locations useful for films other than Westerns, Flying A asserted that Kerrigan would be given the opportunity to star in non–Western films.[65]

With Hutchinson having departed Santa Barbara on the twenty-first, negotiations were concluded by telegraph on November 23 for Flying A to purchase the north corner of Mission and Chapala Streets in Santa Barbara for constructing their new facilities. The *Morning Press* story that revealed that the deal also carried a reaffirmation that in addition to directing the first company, Dwan would have "general charge of the affairs of the concern."[66]

After the second western company was formed, it was announced that together they would make three films per week, with the premier company fulfilling its usual quota of two per week and the second company making one. But the end of the *Morning Press* piece concluded, "The two companies will start to produce four plays in a week in a short time. The American releases three each week, but by laying up a stock it will give the two companies an opportunity to work together occasionally on two-reel spectacular features."[67] The idea to increase production likely originated with Hutchinson, who would want to get his money's worth out of having a second company. Dwan, who prided himself on his efficiency, no doubt felt that he and his associates could rise to the occasion and the idea of the two-reeler may have even had some appeal for him. But he probably did not appreciate the pressure from above.

When Hutchinson returned to Santa Barbara in January, he was with his wife and it soon became clear that he intended to spend a good part of the year in Santa Barbara. Having shed his frontier image, Hutchinson appeared to be setting roots in Santa Barbara as he allied himself with the city. He told the press,

> But the American company is now just as much at home in Santa Barbara as anybody else, with nearly fifty employees and a good payroll.... The American Film company will do its share to boost Santa Barbara, and all we ask is the assistance of the community, and that I understand we already have. We are already advertising Santa Barbara through our pictures.... We intend to use the words "Santa Barbara" as frequently as possible and in all our advertising we state we are making our pictures here.[68]

This sense of advertising had also begun to affect Hutchinson's view of film production. "Mr. Hutchinson yesterday indicated an intention of deviating somewhat from the western stuff that has played such a spectacular part in literature as well as moving picture plays, by reproducing a few things that are actually of the west. He is acquainting himself with industrial conditions and what is being done along horticultural and agricultural lines."[69] Hutchinson was quoted as saying, "The people of the cities are anxious to know how things are done in the great free country and it will be the purpose of the American Film Company in the future to overlook no opportunity to let them know."[70] Flying A would be making films about the rice, poultry and walnut industries, among others. Hutchinson may have genuinely believed in the educational value of these films but as the precursors of modern industrial films, he also knew that the promotional values would secure him financing.

Flying A was now ensconced in Santa Barbara and with his hands-on approach, Hutchinson would mine all the commercial prospects. He had given business authority to Dwan when he needed a trail boss as well as a director. But now the Flying A western odyssey that had begun in Sante Fe was over and in the Biblical parlance of the early settlers, they had found the Promised Land. For Flying A personnel, the days of being strolling players and the lost children of Hutchinson were over. Civilization had ensnared them in the form of Santa Barbara.

In early 1913, Hutchinson's pride and joy was in the construction of the Mission Street Flying A headquarters, which was expected to be "the most artistic moving picture studio in the world."[71] Architect J.C. Poole had been chosen to design Flying A's new home, which would consist of twelve buildings including a concrete and glass studio, 25 feet high and 40 by 60 feet long. Like the film moguls who would aim even more ambitiously in the next decade, Hutchinson was seeking the perfect film factory. Given his interest in micro-management, he did not need a production supervisor. Dwan had been Flying A's pioneer leader in guiding the company's production to the West Coast, even though he would later be adamant in his dislike of California. In this new atmosphere, the business powers that had been granted Dwan now seemed oddly superfluous. With Hutchinson's looming presence, conflict was probably inevitable.

There may have been contention about any number of changes Hutchinson was making in construction, organization and personnel. But it was Dwan's rivalry with Kerrigan that appeared to finally bring matters to a head.

Dwan told Bogdanovich that Kerrigan was unhappy about having a second company, mainly out of resentment at having a rival star in Reid. According to Dwan, "Kerrigan was pretty fond of himself at the time so he put a knock into the company by letter saying *I* was getting out of hand and that unless I was replaced, he was going to leave the company."[72]

While it's quite possible that Kerrigan did resent the second company, there was no way that Hutchinson could be persuaded to drop it. He was intent on boosting the number of films produced by Flying A and had invested considerably in that effort. Hutchinson could, however, placate Kerrigan with Dwan's exit and provide him with additional benefits while also solving some of his own problems.

Dwan's sense of hubris probably contributed to his downfall. He had undoubtedly read all the material about Kerrigan's importance to the company but probably dismissed it as publicity pabulum. Dwan had modulated Kerrigan's performances from the more rough-and-tumble characters he had earlier portrayed to thoughtful figures more consistent with his actual personality, resembling Theseus rather than Hercules. So he may have thought his guiding hand was essential for Kerrigan's success.

Dwan was only twenty-eight years old at the time and may have felt both the arrogance and invulnerability of youth. In any case, he took an inflexible stance and claims he told Hutchinson, "Things are going to be just the way I want or else they're not going to be at all, as far as I'm concerned."[73]

One day Dwan came in to work and found a note that said he was no longer with the company. "It was quite a shock. It was terrifying — never having been with any other company — to suddenly find myself out of work."[74]

On April 13, 1913, the *Santa Barbara Morning Express* carried a story with the headline, "American Changes Presage Improvement in Photoplays." Both Kerrigan brothers are mentioned in the lengthy sub-heading. The first sentence reads tersely, "As a result of an arrangement mutually agreed upon, Allen [sic] Dwan severs his connection with the American Film Manufacturing Company (Flying A)."[75]

Having disposed of Dwan in the first sentence, the rest of the story sounds like a coup by the Kerrigan brothers, with the name "Kerrigan" mentioned nine times. While Albert W. Hale is cited as the new director of the premier company, it is made clear that there will be a separation of responsibilities and the director will no longer handle business matters.

In lieu of the old arrangement, "[a]ll business matters will be taken charge by Wallace Kerrigan as President S.S. Hutchinson's Pacific coast representative. Wallace Kerrigan has been attending to business matters in a general way during the last two years, but under the new arrangement his authority in that department becomes absolute."[76]

For brother Jack, there were also encouraging words. It was stated that the first company would center more on him: "The demand from the public has been so insistent that it has been decided to produce plays that will give him greater opportunities."[77]

With the new separation of responsibilities, a director was now just a director and much less of a potential drag on Hutchinson's aims. He had transferred power to the Kerrigans but the power was split between two men. With Jack, at least, there would always be much greater interest in his stardom than in running the company, and Hutchinson had acquiesced that J. Warren Kerrigan was the company's number one box-office draw. Hutchinson probably also saw Wallace Kerrigan as more pliable than the independent Dwan.

Less than three weeks before his sacking, Dwan had showed up in Santa Barbara with a new $6,000 Simplex 90-horsepower roadster which he intended to use for scouting locations.[78] He apparently had no idea of what was coming and his recollection of shock was probably accurate.

Dwan had been fired not because he had failed but succeeded too well. One western production unit had already failed and another was on the brink of collapse when with little (if any) experience, Dwan became both director and business overseer of the troupe. He may have ridden in an auto as often as in a buckboard but beyond the publicity hype, Dwan and the members of his company were true pioneers, roughing it under primitive circumstances. In making their films, they had lived off the land, their stories often inspired by the rugged landscapes on which they were shot. In two years, the company had achieved strong financial success and found stability and good business prospects in Santa Barbara. It was now much simpler for an executive like Hutchinson to take over.

Dwan's first stint as director had also involved him in running business affairs for the company. Dwan would never forget this and the importance of practical business knowledge for direct-

Dwan seated proudly in his roadster before Samuel Hutchinson lowered the boom on him (courtesy Kevin Brownlow).

ing. Later, he would often portray himself as a businessman as well as a director but implicit in this claim was his belief that he understood the mechanics and business of moviemaking as well, if not better, as any executive. Dwan would continue to savor the open range independence that he had enjoyed and then lost at Flying A and in future years would have little patience with studio supervisors.

Now he was a pioneer without a job. On April 12, Dwan sent a telegram to the Selig Company in Chicago: "AM OPEN FOR ENGAGEMENT. FOR TWO YEARS I HAVE WRITTEN AND PRODUCED ALL PREMIER COMPANY 'FLYING A' FILMS AS WELL AS MANAGED THE WESTERN STUDIO. HAVE YOU ANYTHING TO OFFER THERE OR IN CALIFORNIA WIRE COLLECT."[79] Given the above date of the telegram and that the *Morning Press* story of his departure from Flying A appeared in the April 13 issue, April 12 is the likely date on which Dwan was fired.

Dwan's importance to the staff of Flying A and their loyalty to him is indicated by the fact that it was thought necessary to place the following item in the *Morning Press*: "There were unfounded rumors in circulation yesterday that the retirement of Allen [sic] Dwan as director, has resulted in much dissatisfaction with the company. Mr. Hutchinson said last night that the loyalty of members vital to good production was unquestioned. This was demonstrated during the day by the willing response to Mr. Hale's exacting direction."[80] But it was announced on April 20 that both Pauline Bush and Jessalyn Van Trump were quitting Flying A. Bush may have had a personal reason for following Dwan in departing the company.

Dwan said he called his friend Neilan, who told him, "Don't make a move till you talk to me. Meet me at the Van Nuys Hotel as soon as you can and we'll do something."[81] At the hotel, Neilan introduced Dwan to two representatives from Universal Pictures. Dwan told Brownlow that their names were Kennedy and Engel. Kennedy must have been A.M. Kennedy, who had been general manager at American and was now in the same position at Universal.[82] Aside from his familiarity with Dwan at Flying A, both Kennedy and his associate had screened Dwan's films at their studio and were impressed.

Although Dwan was being offered far more than he had been paid at American, Neilan scolded the Universal executives by saying, "Look, I didn't bring you here to insult him."[83] (In the Brownlow interview, Dwan said he had been making $400 per week at Flying A.) At this point, they had already offered him at least $200 a week more than he was making with Flying A. Dwan told Bogdanovich they finally agreed to pay him approximately $1500 a week.[84]

It was reported in the *Santa Barbara Morning Press* on April 22 that both Pauline Bush and Jessalyn Von Trump were heading south to join Universal so Dwan may have been already in contact with the company by that time.[85] There were also reports that Dwan was in Los Angeles on April 14 so it's possible that's when he met with the Universal executives.[86]

In May, Wallace Reid also left American to follow the path to Universal. Reid's biographer E.J. Fleming states that it is unclear whether Reid left of his own accord.[87] It is possible that Kerrigan goaded Hutchinson to release his possible rival. But it is equally possible that Reid left, not only out of loyalty to Dwan, but because his own hopes of stardom might have seemed limited in a company that was so publicly committed to Kerrigan as its premier star.

It was announced in early May that Dwan was joining Universal accompanied by his former colleagues from Flying A, Reid, Bush, and Von Trump.[88] But this small exodus from the American Film Company was part of a larger Universal employee raid on Flying A, according to what Dwan told Brownlow and Dana Driskel. Dwan said that when he met Carl Laemmle in New York, the executive told him that "we want you to bring some of your company," referring to the premier company Dwan ran at Flying A. Dwan said he then showed Laemmle his whole payroll and was told all their salaries would be doubled if they came to Universal. Laemmle wanted the second company too.

Dwan recalled, "Well, I wired out to J. Warren Kerrigan's brother, Wallace Kerrigan, who had been my business manager, and I said I have a definite offer for all of you including everybody and er at double salary if you'll join me at Universal. Not later than next Monday. And I got back a wire, all will join you next Monday at Universal. And all including J. Warren Kerrigan who'd caused the break up he came too, and the only man left in Santa Barbara was Hutchinson, all alone, in his studio. And Hutchinson had to start to build from there, but while they tried hard, they never got back up again, they spent a lot of money, built a fine studio and went out of business."[89]

Dwan, however, was not speaking the whole truth. Jack Kerrigan, his business manager brother Wallace and ten other Flying A actors did join Dwan at Universal but that was not until months later. Also, Flying A did not go out of business in the short term but continued with new stars like Mary Miles Minter. The American Film Manufacturing Company continued to exist before succumbing in 1921.

Dwan may have confused the situation with American's raid on Essanay which nearly rendered George Spoor alone in his studio. These raids persisted in the early silent film era and Flying A had come full circle in being victimized, though not as badly as Essanay was in 1910. These events might have also become a kind of fantasy revenge in Dwan's memory, especially when he told Driskel, "I even offered Hutchinson a price. The poor guy nearly died. I think he went to the hospital."[90]

But if we overlook the details, Dwan was correct in the long view. A decade after his firing, the American Film Manufacturing Company no longer existed. But Dwan was still directing with a long future ahead of him.

The Universal Year

Carl Laemmle is alleged to have thought of the name "Universal" for his film company when he looked out the window and saw a dray wagon pass with the inscription, "Universal Piping Company" on its side.[91]

At that time, it was not actually "his" company. Laemmle's picture firm was then the Independent Motion Picture Company (more popularly known as IMP), which had been in existence since 1909. But the name "Universal" was brought up at a meeting in the spring of 1912 when various independent production outfits were looking for an effective way to combat the Patents Company. Their strategy was that by merging into one corporation, they would have the financial resources to challenge and defeat the Patents Company in court, having it declared a monopoly. The new corporation was to be a stronger version of the Motion Picture Distributing and Sales Company, the anti–Patents combine that had just floundered.

Aside from IMP, the companies involved in these negotiations included the New York Motion Picture Company, Powers Company, Nestor, Champion, Éclair and Rex. On June 2, 1912, all the parties signed an agreement to pool their assets in a corporation that, following Laemmle's suggestion, was to be called the Universal Film Manufacturing Company. Despite the title, this was supposed to be a distribution company that also held the capital for its production branches.

There was now to follow a battle for control that would determine which of the production heads would wind up running the company.

Adam Kessel and Charles Baumann, former bookies, owned the New Motion Picture Company that controlled the 101 Bison Company that made Westerns and Keystone where Mack Sennett produced his comedies. Kessel and Baumann thought they were in the strongest position. Baumann had been elected president of Universal and because he and Kessel brought the most assets into the company, they held the largest block of stock shares. Laemmle had been elected temporary treasurer.

Laemmle, however, anticipated a power move by Kessel and Baumann and outmaneuvered them. He was able to rally enough support to have Baumann voted out as president by the end of June. Pushed out of management, Baumann and Kessel vowed to take their assets out of Universal but Laemmle challenged them on contractual grounds. Because of a technicality, Baumann and Kessel were able to work out a settlement whereby they could take their companies with them but the name "101 Bison" remained the property of Universal.

One by one, Laemmle was able to nudge all of his remaining partners into selling their interests to him until he had total control of Universal.

This turmoil was already in play when Dwan joined Universal and that may have even contributed to the ease of his being hired. The same issue of *Moving Picture World* that carried news of Dwan and his colleagues joining Universal noted, "Resignations and dismissals have separated more than thirty persons from the payroll of the Universal Company this week. Several of the directors have left to join other companies and a number of well-known actors and actresses are among the missing."[92] So Universal had reasons for being eager to enlist Dwan and whomever he could bring with him.

Just three weeks later, *Moving Picture World* had another story about Universal, this time that David Horsley, former head of Nestor, had resigned from Universal's board of directors. It was at the Nestor studio at Sunset and Gower in Hollywood that Dwan would recall making films for Universal. By June 12, an announcement was issued from Universal's office that Laemmle was in full control of the company.[93] W.H. Swanson, the former head of Rex, had been removed as vice-president and sold his interests to Pat Powers of the Powers Company. Powers, the last of Laemmle's rival founders, would hang on to his holdings at Universal until 1920.

Dwan was assigned by Universal to work with the Bison Company. One of his fellow directors there was Francis Ford. At the time Dwan joined Universal, Ford was about to direct *The Stars and Stripes Forever*, featuring Ford in the lead with his popular co-star, Grace Cunard. In a year, Francis Ford would be joined at Universal by his younger brother Jack. The younger Ford would work both as an actor and crew member. Before he became the celebrated director John Ford, he would also be part of the crew for two Allan Dwan films.

Dwan made longer films at Universal, usually two reels instead of one. He had made one two-reel film at Flying A. Before making it, Dwan had directed *Ashes of Three* from a story by Stuart Edward White, a noted writer who lived in Santa Barbara. It was then said that White "with Owen Wister and Ralph Connor have done more to familiarize the world with stories of the West than any other set of authors...."[94] White was also known for writing travel books. In later years, he and his wife Betty would author books they claimed were received by channeling with spirits.

For his Flying A two-reeler, Dwan said he came up with an idea to use White's name for a story he had already written. "I had an idea for a story called *Oil on Troubled Waters*, using the oil wells in the ocean off Carpenteria. Now I wanted to make it sound important, so I arranged to pay Stuart Edward White for the use of his name on this story. I told it to him and he said, 'Let's do it better than that. Let me have that story.' So he took the idea, wrote it and sold it to the *Saturday Evening Post* who published it and then I made it."[95] This was probably the first case where a literary work was based on a film story.

In discussing Dwan's work at Universal, one must penetrate a great void. Although Dwan made over thirty films there in the course of a year, as of this writing, not a single one of them is known to exist. So this phase of Dwan's development must be put together by surviving descriptions and reviews.

When Dwan started working for Universal, Civil War films were in vogue and several of his early pictures for the company were in that vein. In *The Powder Flash of Death*, the Civil War begins and three devoted friends go their separate ways. One joins the Union army (Reid), another the Confederacy (Neilan, who also followed Dwan to Universal) and one becomes a guerrilla fighter (J.D. Kirkland). At the film's climax, the young men and their respective forces converge on the same area. The three friends meet in a home in which resides a beautiful Southern belle (Bush). All three men succumb to her charms and crave her love. "As their companies fight, the three captains agree, knowing that the girl can be had by only one of them, to stand backwardly to the points of a triangle, lay a fuse to the charge of powder in the center, and at the flash, turn and begin firing — the winner to claim the prize."[96] All three men are shot and die, but not before the Confederate and Union chums can grasp each other's hands. Aside from Dwan's usual adept use of geometry, this may rank as one of the most ludicrously melodramatic conclusions to any of his films. It's also indicative of a much darker tone that is apparent in many of Dwan's Universal pictures.

Dwan provided a different kind of Civil War film in *The Picket Guard*, released July 15, 1913, a week after *The Powder Flash of Death*. The film was based on a poem of the same title, also known as "All Quiet Along the Potomac." It was originally published in *Harper's Weekly* on November 30, 1861. Written by Ethel Lynn Beers, the poem drew from news reports of "all is quiet tonight" based on telegrams sent to the Secretary of War by Major-General McClellan following the First Battle of Bull Run. Beers had also noted that this report was followed by a small item about the killing of a picket guard.

The poem begins:

> "All quiet along the Potomac," they say
> "Except now and then a stray picket
> Is shot, as he walks on his beat, to and fro,
> By a rifleman hid in the thicket.
> 'T is nothing — a private or two, now and then,
> Will not count in the news of the battle;
> Not an officer lost — only one of the men,
> Moaning out, all alone, the death rattle."

There are six more stanzas in a poem that does not qualify as great literature. Some lines are quite plaintively sentimental.

But the poem does succeed in establishing an empathy with the average soldier whose thoughts are more with his family than with any grand strategy and whose death will be reduced to a statistic in battlefield reports. The poem was popular enough to have been adapted as a song in 1863, ironically by a Confederate composer. The first line of the poem, which is twice repeated, carries a resonance that finds a parallel in the title of Erich Maria Remarque's celebrated novel of World War I, *All Quiet on the Western Front*.

According to the studio-provided synopsis, Dwan's film, not wanting to give away too much plot too soon, begins with titles citing the beginning of the second stanza,

> "All quiet along the Potomac tonight,
> Where the soldiers lie peacefully dreaming,
> Their tents in the rays of the clear autumn moon,
> Or the light of the watchfires gleaming."

Reid is then seen portraying a Federal sentry on guard duty that night. Then a Confederate officer dispatches an advance picket. There is a cut to more lines from the poem and then the Confederate rifleman is seen advancing on the slumbering Union camp.

Reid is shown having reveries of his courtship of his wife and her consent to marry him. His thoughts of their early married bliss are interrupted when something attracts his attention and he raises his rifle for a moment. But he then resumes his reverie, thinking back to events that prompted him to enlist in the army. There are more quotes from the poem and then the sentry leaves his musings to focus on his guard duty. The action proceeds, with the poem providing the title descriptions, and continues to the fatal shooting of the picket guard.[97]

The description indicates a flashback structure that must have been complex for a film of 1913. Dwan appears to have deftly orchestrated audience attention and emotion so that no confusion was provoked by his editing. The reviewer in *Moving Picture World* wrote that the film "illustrates effectively a well known war poem. Wallace Reid appears as the sentry on guard along the Potomac. Homesick and lonesome, he reviews the scenes leading up to his enlistment. Later he is mortally wounded in a skirmish and scenes are shown back at his home when the news is brought to his wife, impersonated by Pauline Bush. The close is tenderly pathetic. This offering is notable for its artistic effects and appealing story. A fine production."[98]

In Dwan's next three films, *Mental Suicide*, *Man's Duty*, and *The Animal*, he used Reid and Bush in somber melodramas with disturbing elements. The reviewer for *Moving Picture World* described respectively each of the three as "not a very pleasant type of story," "unpleasant," and "not a pleasant one."[99] In *Man's Duty*, Reid eschews his usual stalwart image to play a rotter who abandons his pregnant sweetheart. Reid then takes up with a blind girl (Bush) who has just lost her father. But learning of his situation, the blind girl admonishes him to return to his lover and infant child, even though it means she will be left alone in the world.

Reid plays a similarly unsympathetic character in *The Animal*: a brutish father who becomes jealous when he sees the loving attention his wife gives to their newborn baby. He takes the baby away and gives it to a loving couple whose baby has died. His wife becomes frantic when she discovers the baby is missing. Her old beau, played by Neilan, pleads with Reid to find the child. Reid then forcibly takes the child back from the other couple and returns the infant to his wife. This time the joy and love of the mother awakens Reid's own paternal instincts. Over a year later, Reid cited *The Animal* as his best work.[100]

Part of the reason for the change in subject matter may have been that, beginning with *Mental Suicide*, Dwan had been shifted from 101 Bison to the Rex company. For Rex, he produced but did not direct *The Harvest of Flame*, which was helmed by Reid. (Neilan's biographer Jack Spears says that Neilan co-directed the film with Reid but did not receive credit.[101]) The film concerned a greedy factory owner who tries to bribe an inspector (Reid) to prevent him from reporting safety violations in the factory.

Dwan directed Reid in another factory saga, *The Wall of Money* (written by Neilan), and then the two went their separate ways.[102] Reid became a major star but, when making *The Valley of the Giants* (1919) on location in Oregon, he was injured in a train wreck. In order to continue work on the film, Reid was given large doses of morphine which resulted in addiction. Reid later tried to fight his addiction in sanitariums, but in his weakened state he was overtaken by the flu and died in 1923.

In late July 1913, Dwan made a three-day visit to Universal's offices in New York. Referring to his meeting with Laemmle the previous day, Dwan told the company's publicity organ, *The Universal Weekly*, "I met Mr. Laemmle for the first time yesterday...."[103] Most likely this was the meeting where, as Dwan described it, Laemmle asked Dwan to tell his former colleagues at Flying A that he could double their salaries if they jumped to Universal. Just a few weeks after this meeting, it was announced that J. Warren Kerrigan was joining Universal.[104] Kerrigan made his first Universal appearance in *The Restless Spirit*, reuniting him with Dwan.

Dwan told Bogdanovich that he once said he could make a motion picture out of anything. "So somebody wanting to stop me, said, 'You can't make one out of Gray's "Elegy," because that *would* be pretty difficult — in the first place it's a long poem.' So I studied it a little bit and began to dream about it, and more or less as a challenge, on a bet, I made it."[105] This was the project that became *The Restless Spirit*.

Dwan may have felt emboldened by his success with *The Picket Guard* to believe that he could translate poetry or anything else to the screen. But the poem "The Picket Guard" had a clear narrative thread and appealed to the emotions. As the description above emphasizes, Dwan was well aware that he was dealing with a far more complex and contemplative poem in Thomas Gray's "Elegy Written in a Country Church-Yard." He may have found comfort as the poem also dealt with universal themes and that since it had no "real story" he could provide his own allegorical plot.

Even more amazing is that Dwan was able to convince his employers that these universal themes could generate a Universal film where eighteenth century poetry could deliver at the box-office. The advertising for the picture suggests that Universal saw *The Restless Spirit* as a big prestige vehicle to depict Kerrigan's ascension into the Universal fold: "*The Restless Spirit*, a modern allegorical play, suggested by "Grey's [sic] Elegy" and written and directed by Allan Dwan, will be the first play the star, Warren Kerrigan, will appear in under the Universal Rex brand. Kerrigan will undertake a number of different characters in the one man. We are to see him both as a farmer, a musician and again as a king. It is a magnificent scope seldom allowed to any actor." This announcement also sought to calm exhibitors and audiences about its cemetery setting: "While the play is strongly psychological in its nature, it does not dwell so much upon the grave...."[106]

In the film, Kerrigan "is seen first as a restless disappointed dreamer with a wife and child. He gazes at his hands, the hands of a conqueror, and he feels that he is destined to become one. He is wrathful because chance fails to come to him, and yet he does nothing but dream. In the small town, he becomes the object of derision and his wife of pity."[107] Kerrigan leaves his wife and community to pursue his dreams. The wife goes to live with her father who urges her to marry "a man of polished manners."

The dreamer comes to a desert where he collapses from exhaustion. A woman finds him and takes him to her lonely hut. "She learns the dreamer's story and, in a series of wonderful vision scenes and double exposures, shows him the futility of trying to conquer unknown worlds when he has not even conquered the small world he has lived in."[108]

To visualize the ethereal aspects of the story and the above-mentioned double exposures, Dwan made twenty-four dissolves in the film. In later years, these could be constructed in a laboratory but in those days, all dissolves had to be made in the camera. This was a painstaking process that could easily go astray. Dwan recalled, "You'd reach the point you wanted to dissolve and you'd take eight counts to get out, and then you'd wind back the film and take the eight counts again on the next scene, which would be on another set with another crowd of people. But with twenty-four of these on one roll of film, it was quite a risk. If one shot was wrong and the cameraman made a mistake in the counts, the whole thing was gone."[109] Walter Prichard was the cinematographer who had to go through this ordeal and Universal publicity stated that he was "one of the company's oldest men."[110] Dwan claimed the cameraman wound up in a hospital.[111]

The story climaxed as Kerrigan returns home, "a dreamer no longer," banishes his rival to the desert and "becomes a power in the town, in the small world he has conquered and in the hearts of his wife and child."[112] Students of Gray's poem, if any did see the film, were no doubt appalled to see Gray's musings on the dead reduced to this kind of "stay in your own backyard" theme.

One can see in this outline how this story was shaped by Dwan. Throughout his career he always asserted the power of his practical side over the dreamer. This was apparently one of those periods in his career where he was interested in making more overtly artistic films, even (by his own admission) dreaming about it. But even then he would feel the need to keep the dreamer under control and make that the theme of his film.

The Restless Spirit was released as a three-reel film under the Victor brand on October 27, 1913. The reviewer for *Moving Picture World* opined, "The production is very elaborate, containing a number of very picturesque settings to illustrate the lines quoted from the Elegy. The drama was apparently written with an eye for these scenes, and they are the most meritorious part of the play. The story is none too strong."[113] Other responses may have been even more tepid and Dwan made no more Universal films of such an experimental nature. Pretentiousness was a quality that Dwan was usually careful to avoid.

In Dwan's next film with Kerrigan, the two-reeler *Back to Life*, he tried to give the star the kind of complex role he had permitted Reid to handle. A reviewer at *Motion Picture News* sounded a skeptical note. "The part played by him ... did not seem suitable. Kerrigan makes a wonderful hero, if he has the part exactly suited for him. He is best as a matinee idol, and where he performs wonders in bravery and skill. In this picture he has to become a man hated and despised by all for his alleged cowardice until one day he kills a man in self-defense and is forced to run away."[114] Dwan may have recognized the limitations of working with Kerrigan or they may simply have preferred to work with others. Whatever the reason, except for a promotional film (*The Great Universal Mystery*) and two other one-reelers (*The Barrier of Bars* and *The Field Foreman*), after *Back to Life*, Dwan and Kerrigan did not again collaborate.

In his interview with Bogdanovich, Dwan also complained about a supervisor at Universal. Unlike American, Universal had Dwan working in an open air studio in the same area with other production units, usually separated by only a makeshift partition. Dwan recalled a supervisor whom he described as "a vicious little guy." Dwan said while he was working on a scene the supervisor would come to complain about something he saw in the rushes. He would ignore Dwan's insistence on discussing it with him later. Dwan remembered, "He annoyed me so much one day coming in there that I picked him up and threw him over the separating wall into Bob Leonard's set. And Bob Leonard threw him back!"[115] (Leonard, Dwan's fellow director [and occasional actor] at Universal, would later become better known as Robert Z. Leonard working at MGM during the sound era.)

Laemmle may have employed supervisors, including some from his prodigiously large family, but according to I.G. Edmonds, who wrote a volume on Universal's silent days, directors at Universal then had relative freedom. "Once story and budget were passed, the 'producer'— actually the director and frequently the writer as well — was on his own. He was only required to make an entertaining film that made money."[116]

In mid–September 1913, Dwan left Universal to join Aubrey Kennedy of the Western Features Film Company. Dwan took with him Murdock MacQuarrie, who had played leads in a couple of Dwan films, Pauline Bush, and others. Dwan may have again been following his old associate Kennedy, who had recently left Universal.

Apparently, the venture did not work and by mid–November, Dwan and the other members of his company were back at Universal.[117] The only film Dwan is alleged to have made in this endeavor is a two-reel picture called *The Battle of Wills* but almost no information exists about it.

Dwan also had a new member in his acting company. While Dwan used him in supporting roles, Lon Chaney was destined to become one of the legendary stars of the silent era.

Dwan gave this account of how Chaney came to work for him. "I picked up a new property man at Universal who was quite a nice guy. He used to come around with funny teeth in his mouth and weird makeups. I guess he was hinting — nobody goes around with a putty nose on unless he wants to be noticed. But he loved makeup. Finally, I said to him, 'What the hell is this? Do you want to get in front of the lens?' He said, yes, he'd tried acting once in a stock company and had liked it. He was a property man because he had to make a living. So I put him to work as a couple of weird characters and he caught on — people began to notice him — and I took the tip right away and said, 'I'll feature him.' And that was the start of Lon Chaney."[118]

This sounds uncomfortably like the Neilan–Fleming–Reid "Cinderella syndrome," right down to Chaney, like Reid, having been Dwan's prop man. It is difficult to ascertain what if any of this is true. In fairness, it should be observed that Dwan did serve a mentoring role to the above named individuals even if he exaggerated the magnitude of his discoveries.

A large part of the problem here is that not only are all of Dwan's Universal films missing; so is most of Universal's total output for that period. Chaney's first known screen credit is *Poor Jake's Demise*, directed by Allen Curtis and released by Universal on August 16, 1913. But in his early career, Chaney did film bits without credit. Photo stills have helped identify some of those films but many have disappeared without leaving a trace so it is impossible to identify all of Chaney's early movies.

Chaney's unbilled appearance in Dwan's *The Restless Spirit* is a relatively recent discovery. According to Chaney expert Jon Mirsalis, a still from this film was found on the estate of George Chaney, Lon's youngest brother. An "X" was marked above Lon Chaney's head in the photo and on the back, Chaney had written, "This is me just below the X sign. Here I am a Russian prince." This may have been the last of Chaney's uncredited films.[119]

In Chaney's first year with Universal, he and Dwan made at least eighteen films together, more than Chaney is known to have made for any other director in that time. These were all melodramas with Chaney usually, but not always, playing the villain. In *Remember Mary Magdalen* (released February 1914), Chaney plays a halfwit who defends a fallen woman (Bush) but is hit with a brick and killed. This was probably one of the earliest of his pathetic screen characters. In *Discord and Harmony,* released three weeks later, Chaney actually plays a romantic hero. Perhaps Dwan was checking how far Chaney's talents could be stretched.

Chaney wrote his first screenplay for Dwan's lurid melodrama *The Menace to Carlotta* where Chaney tries to regain his gambling losses by selling his fiancée into white slavery. *Moving Picture World* credits Chaney with writing the screenplay for Dwan's two-reel *The Tragedy of Whispering Creek*.[120]

Dwan and Chaney also made a Gothic melodrama called *The Forbidden Room* that may have been a precursor to Chaney's later horror excursions. Universal's publicity organ stated that Dwan "recently employed two specialists with expert knowledge in mental telepathy and allied subjects, to review with him and criticize his latest production entitled *The Forbidden Room*, a three-reel story delving deep into the fascinating field of the occult. Mr. Dwan is exceedingly careful in handling stories, the development and subject matter of which implies a scientific knowledge of established facts."[121]

In the film, as part of a scientific experiment, Pauline Bush is put under hypnosis and ordered to murder another person in the room. She is given a paper knife so that when she stabs him, no harm is done. Unseen by the others, the young woman's demented mother (also played by Bush) recognizes the "victim" as the man who impregnated her and then abandoned her.

An early glimpse of Lon Chaney (left) in Dwan's *Red Margaret, Moonshiner* (1913). Murdock MacQuarrie is at right and the central figure is unidentified (courtesy Jon Mirsalis).

Chaney is the victim of the madwoman who kills him and then leaves bloodstains on her sleeping daughter, creating the impression that she is the murderer. Matters are finally rectified when the mother is found dead in her room clutching a watch she took from Chaney's body.

Moving Picture World commented, "This melodrama depends upon the powerful, thoroughly human situations involved rather than any sensational, hair-raising incidents. *The Forbidden Room* is ... distinctly original, with powerful situations and strong climaxes." The review praised Bush's dual performance as "wonderfully impressive, realistic and human." Chaney's contribution as victim went unmentioned.

On at least one occasion, Dwan was able to work with his company on location. In late 1913, for the films *Bloodhounds of the North* and *The Honor of the Mounted*, both dealing with the Canadian Northwest Mounted Police, Dwan brought his actors and crew to the summit of Mt. Lowe on the southern fold of the San Gabriel Mountains. There were two alleged mishaps during the shooting. According to the *Universal Weekly*, "During a heavy downpour of rain one morning Lon Chaney and Arthur Rosson became lost in a deep canyon. Hunting parties failed to locate them that afternoon and at night the situation became serious as neither of the men had any cartridges with which to signal. However, the two men were located at ten o'clock."[122]

Arthur Rosson had written the scripts for both of the films being shot on Mt. Lowe as well as having already written *The Picket Guard*. He had also acted in Dwan's 1913 Rex film *Criminals*, as did his brother Dick. (There was also a brother Hal who became a celebrated cinematographer.) The Rossons would be consistent collaborators with Dwan in different capacities during his films of the silent era.

Dwan told Bogdanovich that he knew the Rossons before they came into the film business. "In fact," he noted, "I rented a house from them when I moved into Universal at Gower and Sunset, and took their house over for my offices."[123]

Another accident at Mt. Lowe, as claimed by the *Weekly*, involved Pauline Bush, who slipped on a mountainside and fell to the very edge of a precipice. But ropes pulled her back to safety.

Bush was a very valuable member of Dwan's company but she had also become an important part of his personal life. She was a high-spirited, independent woman and at the time a supporter of the suffragette movement. She was said to have written a number of articles under a pen name on "deep" subjects and had also written several scenarios.[124] As she had followed Dwan to Universal, the relationship between them had intensified.

It is perhaps revealing that a number of Dwan's early films at Universal (*The Animal*, *The Restless Spirit* and *Back to Life*) deal with men who have difficulty adjusting to marital responsibilities. Dwan at this time was still struggling with his options.

So little is known about Dwan's personal life but thanks to the efforts of a noted film historian in recording an elderly actress' reminiscences, a sad and harrowing part of that story has been preserved. Bob Birchard has related this narrative in an e-mail which I repeat verbatim.

> At Universal in late 1913 or early 1914 Allan Dwan was dating a young actress who went by the name Beatrice Van. He was also seeing Pauline Bush at the same time.
>
> Well, as sometimes happens, Allan proposed to Pauline ... but Beatrice was pregnant with his child.
>
> With no place to turn for help, Beatrice Van attempted to perform her own abortion with a coat hanger. She collapsed and was found bleeding on the floor of her dressing room by Lon Chaney who took her to the hospital.
>
> After she recovered, Dwan learned what happened and arranged with his former employer the American Film Company of Santa Barbara, to get Beatrice a job and get her out of Los Angeles. She went on to a long and fairly distinguished career — not as an actress, but as a screenwriter — but she could just as easily have died on her dressing room floor in Universal City...
>
> Van became an alcoholic, but later recovered as one of the early members of Alcoholics Anonymous and [had] a relatively happy life ... but she felt somehow compelled to tell this story to a young fellow with his tape recorder who sat down to interview her in the early 1970s. That young fellow, of course, was me.[125]

Pauline Bush, in a dual role as Dr. James Gibson's sister and niece, is surrounded by stern men as she is implicated in a bizarre murder in *The Forbidden Room* (1914) (courtesy Jon Mirsalis).

Van died in 1983, a month before her ninety-third birthday. There is, of course, no way to confirm her story. Her first film script appears to have been for Dwan's *Small Town Girl*, which was not released until late 1914, after Dwan had left Universal.

In this film, Bush plays the niece of a hotel proprietor in a small rural town. A city slicker from the East gets her drunk and takes advantage of her. When Bush tries to follow him to the East, he throws her out. She gives birth to a child but neither the father nor his family will have anything to do with her.

The distraught and impoverished mother considers both prostitution and suicide as a way out of her dilemma. Fortunately, her previous boyfriend saves her and brings her back to the hotel which he has been running since the death of her uncle.

If Van's story is true, *Small Town Girl* takes on the quality of expressing some sense of guilt on the part of the director as well as an act of expiation in employing Van. In fact, the plot of the lost or missing father would recur in many of Dwan's films for the remainder of his career. Given the time frame mentioned above, *The Forbidden Room*, which was released on June 20, 1914, and scripted by Bess Meredyth, may have been made after Van's asserted brush with death. In that context, the film seems even more eerie with Dwan's future wife assuming the roles of both the abandoned mother and the heroine happily engaged at the end.

Dwan would never have children. Perhaps the thought that Van might have had his child and did not reveal it to him is what kept him coming back, time and again, to the lost father figure in his films.

There is still another reason to go back to Dwan and his cast and crew stationed on Mt. Lowe. During five consecutive days of heavy rain, the company was virtually imprisoned in their mountain retreat. The *Universal Weekly* noted, "However, the days were put to good account. All members of the company gathered before a blazing fire and studied and rehearsed Bulwer's *Richelieu*, which Mr. Dwan is about to produce."[126]

Dwan not only intended to bring to the screen the play that was his college triumph as an actor; he would do it as a feature-length film, the first in his career. In late 1913, feature-length films, even when defining them as being a minimum of four reels long or around forty minutes, were not the norm. Carl Laemmle was vehemently opposed to them. Nevertheless, in 1913 Laemmle was persuaded to produce and release the feature-length *Traffic in Souls*, directed by George Loane Tucker and dealing with the subject of white slavery, emanating from a celebrated police report. The film was a resounding box-office success and Laemmle relented a bit on longer films. Early in 1914, Universal released a four-reel adaptation of *The Merchant of Venice* with Philips Smalley and Lois Weber serving as both stars and co-directors.

Dwan's meticulous work on *Richelieu* was given ample coverage in the *Universal Weekly*. Noted were the film's adherence to historical accuracy and such details as employing six angora cats as Richelieu's pets to help establish his "cold, feline" character.[127]

In January 1914, a fire broke out at Universal, destroying the cutting rooms. Fortunately, the recently assembled positives of two Universal features, *Samson* and *Richelieu* were saved. Dwan would not always be so lucky in such cases.

Virtually, all of the advance publicity for *Richelieu* referred to it as a four-reel feature. But in March 1914, a six-reel version was released. (Perhaps Dwan had convinced Laemmle to give a chance to a longer edition.) But this version does not appear to have been well received. *Moving Picture World* observed, "A six-reel production of the celebrated story of Cardinal Richelieu, following the famous play by that name.... There are some good characterizations in this and some that seemed inadequate. The plot is a highly interesting one toward the close, but the action in the first three reels is rather slow and confusing. This would have been much stronger as either a three- or four-reel production. Not a thoroughly artistic production, but one on which much care and thought have been expended."[128]

Laemmle was not slow in taking the hint. *Richelieu* was withdrawn and slashed to four reels for release in late summer. Resistance to longer films was still much in evidence and even Griffith had difficulty making the four-reel *Judith of Bethulia*.

In June, in one of his "Straight-from-the-Shoulder Talks" in the *Universal Weekly*, under the apocalyptic heading "Long Features Doomed!" Laemmle railed against making any films longer than four reels.[129] Dwan surely grasped that at a time of change in the film industry, he would be working under constrictions at Universal.

Pauline Bush is the ostracized unwed mother in *The Small Town Girl* (1915). Note the writing credit given to Beatrice Van. Writing credits were then rare, especially on publicity stills (courtesy Jon Mirsalis).

Richelieu had been intended to be released as a "Universal Special," meaning that exhibitors would be charged an extra $5 for showing it. But shortly before the film's release on the week of August 31, Laemmle withdrew its "Special" status and sent it out as a regular 101 Bison release. Since Universal claimed to have no fewer than 10,000 exhibitors, it was foregoing $50,000. Universal's publicity apparatus reported, "The decision to put *Richelieu* on the regular program without extra charge, was brought about by a conference between President Laemmle and the exchanges, at which the present unsettled condition in the amusement field, owing to the present war in Europe, was discussed."[130] World War I had begun in Europe and Laemmle contended that with a period of instability ahead in the industry, Universal's generosity would encourage cooperation among the exchange men, manufacturers and exhibitors. It's more likely that some exhibitors were expressing doubts that this film was worth accepting the $5 per week charge. Laemmle's decision suggests a further loss of confidence in the film. By this time, Dwan had left Universal.

In *Richelieu*, set in 17th century France, machinations revolve around Julie (Bush), the ward of Cardinal Richelieu. The latter was played by Murdock MacQuarrie, then far more celebrated than Chaney as a character actor.

Dwan wrote the script with the unenviable task of compressing the play's Byzantine plot into six reels and later to a four-reel film. The four-reel version appears to have gotten a better reception than the earlier edition. *Moving Picture World* (which had been tepid about the first release) commented, "This finely photographed four-reel production of *Richelieu*, besides being good entertainment, has a pleasing historical interest." The review noted that there were quotes from the play in the final reel including, "Beneath the rule of men entirely, the pen is mightier than the sword."[131] *Motion Picture News* wrote of the film, "Allan Dwan is the director who undertook the task, and with the players and resources at his disposal, there was every prospect of his success. Therefore it is hardly necessary to say that he has succeeded in really reproducing a section from the most momentous and troublous times in the history of France...."[132]

Before his departure from Universal, Dwan had also completed a one-reel promotional film, *The Great Universal Mystery*, which featured many of the company's stars and other personnel including Laemmle, Bush, Kerrigan, Cunard, Weber, Smalley, King Baggot, Ford Sterling, Francis Ford, Florence Lawrence, Herbert Brenon, Al Christie and many others.

Dwan left Universal but this time Bush remained with the company and became the head of a new Rex unit where she was supported by Lon Chaney, Joseph King and others. Joseph De Grasse was the director of this group and he had a much greater opportunity than Dwan to develop Chaney's talents, as they made sixty-four films together.

Chaney had served a useful apprenticeship with Dwan and with *Richelieu* had made his first appearance in a feature film. Whether because of Bush or De Grasse or the Universal executives, Chaney was mentioned in generous terms in the release announcing the new company. "Lon Chaney has worked opposite Miss Bush continually since her engagement by the Universal. He is almost as well known as Miss Bush and is considered to be the most versatile makeup artist and the most capable 'heavy' in his own line in the business."[133]

Dwan had specialized in dark melodramas at Universal and one wonders if his career path might have been different if he had stayed with that studio. Despite its grandiosity, *Richelieu* appears to have fit the pattern of those films. But it would not be the last time Dwan would depict Cardinal Richelieu's exploits on the screen.

The Unwelcome Feature Film

Explaining to Peter Bogdanovich why he left Universal, Dwan said, "[A]long came an outfit I thought would make a mark called Famous Players. They were going to bring big theater stars to films. That intrigued me. Having always had a little inkling for the theater, having once been a great actor myself, I thought, 'Well, that's a step up — now *my* class of actor is coming in.' So when Famous Players made me an offer I was very happy to accept."[134]

It is easy to understand how the once-stage struck Dwan, with his dreams of first being an actor and then a great playwright, was attracted to the concept of Famous Players. The idea of a better "class" of actor must have appealed to his desire both for greater respectability for the film medium and for the medium's ability to advance. It is also likely that Dwan's own frustration with the treatment of his first feature *Richelieu* and the aesthetic conservatism of his boss Laemmle had something to do with his change of workplace

Adolph Zukor, who headed and founded Famous Players, was diametrically opposed to Laemmle's viewpoint on the feature-length film. Zukor was a Hungarian immigrant who had achieved success as a furrier. A $3,000 loan to a cousin in 1903 got him involved in a penny arcade in New York that, among other things, showed moving pictures. By 1906, Zukor had his own film theater, known as the Comedy Theater, on Fourteenth Street.

Zukor became convinced that the future of the film business rested with the feature-length film and that it would bring motion pictures beyond the status of a novelty. In 1910, while traveling through Europe, he met Laemmle and tried to persuade him to make features. Laemmle demurred but he later introduced Zukor to the pioneer film director Edwin S. Porter, who had made the landmark film *The Great Train Robbery* (1903).[135] Porter alerted Zukor that Joseph Engel of Rex Films (apparently the same Engel who would later be part of the duo that approached Dwan for Universal) had purchased the American rights to a four-reel French film, *Queen Elizabeth*, with the renowned stage star Sarah Bernhardt. Zukor then bought the rights from Engel. With a star of Bernhardt's stature and a notable historical subject, *Queen Elizabeth* was tailor-made for Zukor's purposes of lifting the value of motion pictures. And even more importantly, it was a success at the 1912 box office.

Queen Elizabeth became the pilot project for Zukor's new company, Famous Players. Porter was named technical director. The slogan for the company became "Famous Players in Famous Plays." It was therefore important for Zukor to have a prominent theater man involved, not only for prestige purposes but to help reassure stage actors that they were involved in a dignified enterprise. Daniel Frohman, along with his brother Charles and David Belasco, were considered the Big Three producers of the Broadway stage. Daniel Frohman had been plagued by a series of flops on stage in the last few seasons so he was eager to accept Zukor's offer. He became the managing director of the company. Frohman helped prod actor James K. Hackett to see Zukor. Hackett had played so often in the play *The Prisoner of Zenda* that he had become completely identified with the lead role. Zukor convinced him that at Famous Players his acting in *Zenda* would be preserved for posterity. He would also be well compensated. In 1913, *The Prisoner of Zenda* starring Hackett became the first release of Famous Players.

By the summer of 1913, five productions had been completed for Famous Players including *The Count of Monte Cristo* starring James O'Neill, the father of playwright Eugene O'Neill.

Dwan told Kevin Brownlow that he "shot a wire to Zukor asking him if he had a space for me in his company. I got an immediate reply that he had, if I could come at once. So I jumped away from Universal and went to Famous Players...."[136] Since Dwan had waited until the spring of 1914 to join Famous Players, it again suggests that the flap over *Richelieu* had something to do with his departure from Universal, after roughly one year of service. Dwan may have also waited to see if Famous Players could survive producing feature films exclusively.

It is not entirely clear which film was the first Dwan made for Famous Players. *The Unwelcome Mrs. Hatch* is listed in Dwan's filmography in Bogdanvoich's book but it has not been subsequently confirmed that Dwan did indeed direct this film. It was announced in *Variety* in its May 29 issue that Henrietta Crosman (now best known for her starring role in John Ford's 1933 *Pilgrimage*) would be working for Famous Players. Though it was not mentioned in the article, her first film was based on her old stage vehicle *The Unwelcome Mrs. Hatch*. The *New York Dramatic Mirror* carried this item in its June 3, 1914, issue: "Under the direction of Allan Dwan, formerly of the Universal, *The County Chairman* is being produced ... by the Famous Players Company, with Macklyn [*sic*] Arbuckle in the leading role which he played for four years on the legitimate stage."

Regardless of which film was shot first and of who directed *Mrs. Hatch*, it was *The Unwelcome Mrs. Hatch* which premiered first, opening on September 10. The film appears to have been well received.

The County Chairman (opening on October 26) was five reels long, surpassing the four-reel limit Laemmle had set for Dwan at Universal. Maclyn Arbuckle was a cousin of the celebrated comic actor Roscoe "Fatty" Arbuckle and a familiar figure on the stage. Arbuckle recreated his role as Jim Hackler, the irascible and wily political boss who is the title character. The story is set circa 1880 and it was observed that the film "should be preserved as a convincing record of a phase of American political life rich in comedy material."[137] Unfortunately, *The County Chairman* has apparently not survived on film.

Another Dwan film, made probably after *The County Chairman* but released eleven days earlier, was called *Wildflower*. It introduced a new star to the screen.

Marguerite Clark, who was raised on a farm in Ohio, made her Broadway debut in 1900 at the age of seventeen. By 1914, she had starred in over a dozen plays on Broadway including co-starring with John Barrymore in *The Affairs of Anatole*.

Zukor's interest in Clark was supposedly first aroused after he saw a photograph of her in *Prunella*.[138] Despite a generous offer, Clark hesitated to work in the flickers. Cora Clark, her sister and manager, later said that she persuaded Marguerite to sign the three-year contract by telling her that "pictures were a fad and in three years would be dead. So she might as well sign."[139]

Four foot ten and with a cherubic face, Clark had an elfin appearance that made her look distinctly younger than her thirty-one years. It was thought that she could play the same kind of juvenile roles as Mary Pickford, even though Pickford was already under contract to Famous Players. Dwan speculated, "I guess they wanted to cover their bet and keep anybody else from having this girl who might become Mary's rival."[140] Dwan was then assigned to direct Clark's first film *Wildflower*, based on a story by Mary Germaine. He also collaborated on the script with Eve Unsell. The company was here gambling on the personality and not on a popular play.

In a 1979 interview, Dwan recalled Pickford being resentful about Clark's signing and said that her resentment extended to Dwan. He remembered in particular one encounter with Pickford. "She wouldn't even say, 'How do you do' to me. I knew her. She walked right by as if I didn't exist. I got mad at her. I turned to stop her and said, 'You listen to me, bitch. This girl is going to outdo you and she's going to be so much better than you that you're not going to exist. You better change your attitude.'"[141]

Pickford's insecurity regarding Clark may have been fanned by the fact that whereas Pickford had entered the movies while she still had a promising theatrical career, Clark had already been a star on stage. Pickford might have also seen Clark's potential as diminishing her own value to the studio. Canadian writer Charles Foster, who says he first got to know Dwan and Pickford in the 1940s, has offered another possible reason for tension between the director and Pickford. Foster's writings about Dwan include some very unreliable accounts but his story here is quite plausible. According to Foster, Pickford used her influence to have her brother Jack, just short of his eighteenth birthday, cast as the male lead in *Wildflower*. Dwan found him all wrong for the role as well as arrogant and disruptive to the rest of the cast. Jack, whose brief life and career would be blighted by alcoholism, was already toting bottles of liquor on the set.

Dwan said his contract gave him total control over casting but Zukor claimed that Mary had an even better contract that gave her total control over all casting for Famous Players. While that much power for even a star of Pickford's stature sounds dubious, Zukor had good reason not to want to do anything to alienate his top box-office attraction. Dwan left his meeting with Zukor threatening to see a lawyer.

Later that afternoon, Dwan had a visitor at his apartment, a doleful looking Mary Pickford. Dwan invited her in and offered to have Pauline make her a cup of coffee. "I'd rather have a glass of whiskey," Pickford is said to have responded.

In this account, Pickford then related how concerned both she and her mother were about Jack being rejected for the role and the effect it might have on him, saying she was afraid that he'd "do something drastic." Dwan thought it over briefly and then offered a compromise solution. "I would write in a comedy role of the leading man's valet for Jack. Was I thinking fast! I told Mary it would give him the chance to use some of the comedy abilities I'd heard he had. It wouldn't be the lead, but people would, I promise, remember him."

A tearful Mary Pickford appeared to be placated.[142]

It is difficult to confirm if part or any of this story is true. But several factors suggest that Pickford may have exerted some power behind the scenes against the Dwan–Clark working relationship (including Dwan's deep-seated resentment against Pickford's attitude toward Clark surfacing in the Adamson interview over sixty years later). Despite the fact that Dwan had directed a smash hit debut for Clark in *Wildflower*, they worked together at Famous Players on only one other film and in both pictures, Jack Pickford had a key role. There was also, as we shall see, a sense of unease in the Dwan–Pickford working relationship, though each clearly respected the other.

Perhaps Dwan merely suspected that Pickford had played a conspirational role since he supposedly told Foster in 1943, "Perhaps Mary stepped in, I don't know, but only once more was I allowed to use [Clark] in any of my films."[143]

A May item in the *New York Dramatic Mirror* said that Dwan would be directing Clark in a film called *Wild Flowers*.[144] However, the film was probably not shot until some time later as the *Mirror* had a gossip item in mid–July saying that Dwan was "staging the production of *Wild Flowers*."[145] The film was shot in and around New York City.

The story concerned a young farm girl, Letty Roberts (Clark), who lives as a child of nature surrounded by her beloved animals. Wealthy stranger Arnold Boyd (Harold Lockwood), seeking the seclusion of the forest, meets Letty and sees her as more child than woman. However, Arnold's wastrel brother Gerald arrives and is more appreciative of Letty's womanly qualities. Gerald elopes with the unsophisticated girl. Arnold finds them after the wedding ceremony and takes Letty to New York where Letty struggles to fit into a world of which she is totally ignorant. She must then contend with a far more serious and devastating blow, learning that Gerald is already married and has betrayed her. But the fragile beauty known as "Wildflower" proves strong enough to withstand this shock and to grasp that it is the better man, Arnold, who really loves her.

Dwan said that when they saw the finished film, Zukor and his associates were deeply disappointed. He told Bogdanovich, "They were going to scrap it — thought it was a complete loss of money — but they couldn't afford that — they didn't have the money — so they *had* to get it out."[146]

However, when in August, Famous Players released its schedule of upcoming releases, *Wildflower* was dead last on the list, not scheduled to debut until November 30.[147] But something must have made the executives change their minds. *Wildflower* was moved up to be released on October 15. It then proved a huge success.[148]

Part of the appeal of *Wildflower* was that it was a fetching Cinderella story. Dwan continued to make such films into the 1920s with variations reflecting the changing mores. Letty was also a figure of pastoral innocence, who would have to struggle to learn the ways of urban civilization now on the rise in America.

Motion Picture News commented that the film "is simple in plot and situation, and flaws could be picked in its dramatic construction, but the great outstanding fact is that it tugs at the heart strings of the spectators, and makes them completely forget themselves in the charm of the story. In other words, it accomplishes its end perfectly."[149]

The *New York Dramatic Mirror* attributed half of the film's success to the combination of story and atmosphere but the other half to the power of a new screen personality. The publication, which was mindful of Clark's stage performances, noted, "Miss Clark really seems to jump back into her early teens for the purposes of this charming picture, and then with perfect naturalness she proceeds to reveal the fascinating nature of a girl 'who just growed up' without anybody bothering to tell her about the correct use of knives and forks and other equally trifling matters of etiquette."[150]

Naturalness was one of the attributes that Dwan prized most in his actors and Clark's presence had a great impact on the public. Clark's biographer Curtis Nunn recalled seeing the film as a child. "In the midsummer of 1914 at the Airdome Theater in Georgetown, Texas, I saw Marguerite Clark on the screen for the first time. The film was *Wildflower*, and stumbling barefoot out of that roofless, hard-benched so-called theater, I knew that the nickel I had spent for admission had been well expended, for — unknown to anyone else in the world — I had discovered the girl of my dreams. I was a pre-adolescent Edgar Allan Poe who had lost his heart to the shadow of Lenore on a flickering screen. Hereafter, I knew Mary Pickford and Blanche Sweet would have to stand aside for her."[151] In 1916, *Motion Picture Magazine* asked its readers what they considered the greatest screen performances to date. Clark's performance in *Wildflower* took second place, beating out Pickford, Lillian Gish, Norma Talmadge and others. Only Earle Williams' performance in *The Christian* finished ahead of Clark.[152] Clark recalled in 1917, "On the part of Mr. Zukor and Mr. Frohman it was a prodigious gamble as nobody had the faintest idea whether *Wildflower* would be a success or an utter failure. Fortunately, it was a success thanks to the directors who pushed me through. To this day *Wildflower* is the one of all my pictures I like best."[153]

Popularity polls showed that Clark was now a clear rival to Mary Pickford. *Wildflower* was so successful and highly regarded that it was re-released in 1918.

Dwan's next film *The Straight Road* was a decided change of pace from *Wildflower* with his heroine not a child of nature but a child of the gutter. Reared in the slums by a drunken mother, Moll O'Hara (Gladys Hanson) becomes an alcoholic but fights to improve her station.

Dwan followed this picture with *The Conspiracy*. John Emerson, who co-authored the stage play with Robert Baker, made his film debut starring as the author-detective role he created on stage. Like *Traffic in Souls*, the story concerned a white slavery ring. Peter Milne of *Motion Picture News* wrote of the film, "Credit for its success should go largely to Alan [sic] Dwan, the director. In practically every point he has shown us that as a director he has no large number of superiors, if any. In adapting the play for the screen[,] Mr. Dwan has plainly retained its attractive powers, besides changing it to suit the requirements of the motion picture."[154]

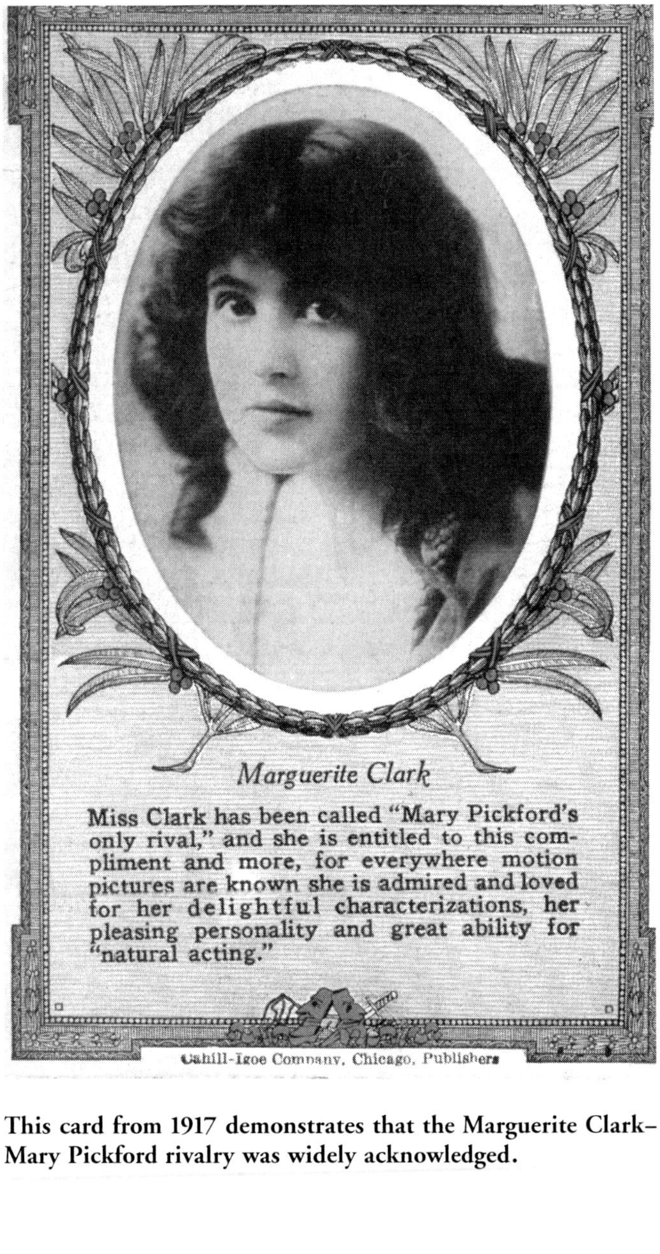

This card from 1917 demonstrates that the Marguerite Clark–Mary Pickford rivalry was widely acknowledged.

The reviews indicate that both *The Straight Road* and *The Conspiracy* consisted almost exclusively of interior scenes. Dwan's next project *The Dancing Girl* was, like the previous two, based on a stage play. But this film marked the debut of stage actress Florence Reed and it was reportedly stipulated in her contract that some of the scenes would be photographed at Sebago Lake in Maine where she and her husband, Malcolm Williams, spent their summers on Indian Island.[155]

Dwan had started making films by trying to find the stories in his locations as his gypsy caravan of actors and crew moved from one spot to another. Dwan also learned that he could extract the best sense of atmosphere from location shooting. A glimpse of Dwan at work here is provided in an article in *Moving Picture Weekly*.

> For the scene at the Quaker church a number of the villagers and summer visitors were impressed into service, and the staging of the scene drew a considerable crowd of their friends, who came by all manner of conveyance, automobile, surrey and wagon, as well as on foot — all to look on and see just how it was done.... Here as at the scene staged at the cottage in the afternoon, the onlookers ranged themselves at a safe distance to the rear, while Mr. Dwan and his assistant, A.H. Rosson, posed the players and made them rehearse, before the camera trained by Operator Buenning [sic] recorded the scenes.... Director Dwan, hatless, coatless and with sleeves rolled up, posed, suggested, ordered, criticized — in short directed ... until he had things going to his liking...[156]

The article stated that much of the rest of the film had been shot in England, which is highly unlikely. The studio publicity arm apparently felt that the production would be convincing enough for audiences not to notice the difference.

As in *Wildflower*, the use of location shooting helped enhance the stark differences between two locales. The synopsis for *The Dancing Girl* noted, "The colorful exteriors of the rocky coast of 'The Isle of Endillon' contrast with the rich interiors of the home of the profligate Duke of Guiseberry, under whose patronage the dancing girl lives for a time in this film, and there is the dramatic comparison of the sober life of the grave Quakers on the island with the gay life of London society and the bright Bohemia of the singers and artists, with whom the Quaker girl mingles, when she becomes the favorite of the duke."[157]

Drusilla Ives (Reed) leaves her community of solemn Quakers to become the London servant of the duke. With the duke's help, she is soon London's most popular dancer. Drusilla's father curses her and causes her to faint and fall down a staircase. When the duke is ruined financially, she leaves him and returns to Endillon. They later meet there when both are contemplating suicide. Instead they marry and begin a new life.

Dwan and his cinematographer Hal Rosson make playful use of depth of field in this shot from *David Harum* (1915). William H. Crane as Harum is in the foreground. Note the horse standing on its hind legs in the distant background (courtesy George Eastman House).

(The struggle between a Puritanical society or father and a young woman's free-spirited impulses was another plot that would recur with variations in Dwan's silent film output.)

The Dancing Girl, another five-reeler, was released in January 1915. The film received kudos, as did its star. The critics were also beguiled by the atmosphere and look of the production. George Blaisdell in *Moving Picture Weekly* commented, "In the telling of the story we feel the breezes of the ocean and hear the surf pounding on the cliffs as we also feel the atmosphere of the ballroom and the luxurious homes."[158] *Motion Picture News* noted, "Some of the scenes were taken over the water and are unusually beautiful. The photography is excellent."[159]

In October 1914, still another prominent stage star, William H. Crane, signed with Famous Players. Crane, who was sixty-nine years old and had been acting on the Broadway stage since the 1870s, had long resisted lavish offers to appear in films. This time it was Charles Frohman who helped persuade him to join Famous Players.

Crane was selected to repeat one of his great stage triumphs on the screen, *David Harum*, to be directed by Dwan. In 1900, Crane had appeared in the first Broadway production of *David Harum*, based on a popular novel by Edward Noyes Westcott, and had subsequently starred in two Broadway revivals. Dwan said that although he had worked out a script when he met Crane, the actor was adamant that he wouldn't do the film unless it was done exactly like the play. "He didn't want to change anything in this play, and so with that handicap I had to start out to make this famous play with William H. Crane and I had to use all the trickery in the world."[160]

David Harum turned out to be an important film both for its success and for Dwan's technical bravura in bringing the play to the screen. It also has the distinction, as of this writing, as being the only Dwan feature from his first tenure at Famous Players to survive. A print is stored at Eastman House in Rochester, New York.

The title character of *David Harum* is a country banker, horse trader and philosopher who lives with his sister Polly (known as Aunt Polly) in a small rural town in central New York. Because of his eccentric behavior and gruffness, he has the reputation of a grouchy miser but is in reality a philanthropist who does not want his charitable work known.

An opening title card proclaims, "The busiest man in Homeville." But Dwan does not show us a close-up of the character's face or even a portrait in long shot. Instead we get an insert of a dining table, centering on a cup, plate and hands. We see food being cut for eating and a cup being stirred and coffee or tea being poured into a saucer. An iris unfolds to show Crane as David Harum blowing on the saucer. The camera than pans across the table to reveal Aunt Polly. Some critics appreciated this as a novel way of introducing a beloved character. The *New York Dramatic Mirror* noted, "However, the face soon came to view and the sharp features of William H. Crane gazed upon a new and friendly audience for the first time. Whoever thinks of David Harum without at once recalling his whimsical, shrewd and kindly old man?"[161]

Dramatic necessity prompted Dwan to use a more significant innovation. Dwan recalled that one scene "required David Harum to walk down the street talking to people as he went, to show that he was well-acquainted with everybody.... He'd greet one person and stop to chat with another as he moved down the street."[162] There were two conventional ways Dwan thought he could shoot the scene. Dwan could position the camera so that Harum could be seen in the distant background and that as he continued walking, he would draw closer and closer until his face was clearly visible. Dwan felt that much of the shot would be wasted since you couldn't tell it was Harum until he moved close enough to the camera.

The other option was to break up the shot into a series of

tableaus so that each time Harum moved out of recognizable camera range, there would be a cut to another shot of Harum greeting the next individual or group of people.

This also seemed awkward so Dwan decided to try another solution. "Well, instead of setting the camera backwards each time, it occurred to me, wouldn't it be nice if we could just *move* it backward with him."[163] But just how would they move the camera (which was usually anchored in a tripod) so there would be no vibrations? Dwan ruled out the idea of carrying it and instead proposed moving it in a Model T Ford. The cameraman was still concerned that it would jiggle too much. Dwan said that they then got "a farm scraper and we scraped the street flat, got all the bumps out. And then we softened the tyres [sic] so they wouldn't joggle, we locked the springs and fastened on securely with a few two-by-fours, got it well wired down so it wasn't bobbley, and it worked great."[164] Dwan told Brownlow that they didn't use the engine of the car. "I just used muscular strength to push it...."[165]

The Guinness Book of Movie Facts and Feats cites *David Harum* as one of two 1915 films (the other being *The Second-in-Command*) using the tracking shot in the United States for the first time.[166] Traveling shots filmed from trains and ships actually go back to the very early days of silent cinema. But *David Harum* was an important milestone in developing the expressive possibilities of the tracking shot. And though (according to Dwan) it was shot from a car, it pioneered the kind of fluidity that would be achieved by camera dollies mounted on tracks.

Another sequence had to do with Harum's shrewdness as a horse trader. Harum's sagacity is reflected in his credo which goes back to the novel, stating, "Do unto your neighbor what he would do unto you — but do it fust." Harum plots to get back at Deacon Perkins (Guy Nichols) who once sold him a wretched horse. Harum in turn sells Perkns a horse at what Perkins thinks is a bargain price until he is confronted with the horse's odd behavior.

At one point, Harum watches and can see across a pond the difficulties the new horse is giving Perkins. The use of depth of field, especially for a comic shot, is impressive, as we see Harum in foreground on his carriage laughing uproariously while in the distant background across the pond we can see Perkins' horse on his hind legs. In fact, the act of Harum throwing back his head in laughter is almost in sync with Perkins' horse raising itself up.

Later the scene cuts back to Perkins and we see the Deacon forced to get out of his carriage and lead the horse as the camera follows the action with a reverse tracking shot until an iris closes in on the hapless Perkins.

These scenes of Harum's impishness give way to a straight (and conventional) plot involving John (Harold Lockwood, again the romantic interest), a young man who comes to clerk for Harum and falls in love with Mary Blake, the new "school marm" (May Allison). John is unfairly imprisoned for passing counterfeit bills. As vengeful citizens surround the jail, Harum stops the mob by having the real culprit confess to the crime. As with *The County Chairman*, Harum is the lovable curmudgeon at the center while the young couple provide the romance.

David Harum opened in February 1915. Although there were some complaints that the five-reel film developed a bit slowly, it was well received by the critics and, apparently, by the audiences of the day. *Variety* noted, "[T]his feature will undoubtedly pull money. The story of the life in a country village was exceedingly well depicted, the producer having gone out of his way to secure a few novelties that were most effective."[167]

In November 1914, shortly after Dwan completed *David Harum*, Famous Players decided to reopen its West Coast studios which hadn't been used since the spring. Despite her reluctance to go west, Marguerite Clark was dispatched to the California studio along with Dwan, who was to direct her in an opus called *The Pretty Sister of Jose*. Since *Wildflower*, Clark had already made another film in New York, *The Crucible*, which again paired her with Lockwood (under the direction of Edwin S. Porter). Dwan was to be stationed in the west for some time. One can speculate as to whether Dwan was again permitted to direct Clark because Jack Pickford was given a major role in the film. By early January, Mary Pickford would also be headed to work at the Famous Players West Coast studio. In early 1915, Marshall Neilan joined Famous Players and would soon be again working with Dwan.

After shooting had been completed, *The Pretty Sister of Jose* was not released for some time. Dwan then made two unremarkable-sounding melodramas, *The Love Route* and *The Commanding Officer*. Neilan played supporting roles in both features.

Dwan's next film, *May Blossom*, a Civil War romance based on a play by David Belasco, may have been more interesting. *Moving Picture World*, comparing the film to the play, noted, "[I]t so happens that the film version is fully strong enough to stand on its own merits, for there is a romantic Civil War story of marked appeal, ably directed by Allan Dwan and acted with sincere feeling by Gertrude Robinson, Donald Crisp and Marshall Neilan at the three points of the lovers' triangle.... Pictorially, the film is of exceptional quality, with a wealth of splendid locations photographed on the summit of a cliff bordering on the sea. *May Blossom* always pleases the eye...."[168]

Dwan, now enjoying his life in California, showed that he had not lost his knack for athletics. There was some intense competition going on for the handball championship of the Film Athletic Squad, according to one trade column. "Jack Pickford is still leading for the cup with Dwan and Crisp right behind him.... Mr. Dwan has lost weight but no money. He is a very cautious young man."[169]

The Pretty Sister of Jose was finally released on May 31, 1915. In this film, Marguerite Clark is not physically isolated as her character was in *Wildflower* but she experiences a childhood trauma that creates a psychological isolation. When Pepita

(Clark) and her brother Jose (Pickford) are just children, their mother commits suicide after being abandoned by their father. This horrific event imbues in Pepita a hatred of men and a determination never to marry. Clark, still bearing her ingénue looks, begins her portrayal as the child who undergoes this shocking experience.

As an adult, Pepita is pursued by the famous toreador Sebastiano, played by Rupert Julian (later the director of Lon Chaney in *The Phantom of the Opera*) but resists him until melodramatic events take their turn.

Overall, the reviews were excellent. As with *Wildflower*, the critics were torn about what aspect of the film deserved the most credit. *Moving Picture World* opined, "Whether the first appeal in *The Pretty Sister of Jose* be attributed to the sympathetic personality of Miss Clark, or to the artistic tone and superior quality of the production in its entirety, is of small consequence. Everything is made to harmonize in the creation of a completely artistic picture...."[170] The *New York Dramatic Mirror* noted, "The very valuable contribution of photography to a picture result was never more in evidence. Alan [sic] Dwan has gone boundlessly into big sweeps and winding roads. It is almost useless to try and describe the exotic effect that has been accomplished by a judicious placing of the lens. It succeeds in contributing novelty to every scene, and especially is this true in a picture supposed to take place in Spain."[171]

At this still very early period of film history, critics were noticing that Dwan was departing radically from the staid conventional ways of shooting films. He was also adding a measure of subtlety. Feature films were now achieving a level of sophistication.

In one interview, Dwan claimed that Clark's only films were the two she made with him. This is incorrect. But he was correct that her career was relatively brief. For years Clark ran neck and neck with Mary Pickford in the fan polls. In its poll of motion picture exhibitors for 1920, Quigley Publications ranked Clark as the top film actress.

Shortly after that, Clark decided to call it quits. In 1921, at the age of thirty-eight, she retired with her husband to their country estate in New Orleans. She had made all but the last of her forty films for Famous Players. Clark died in 1940 at the age of fifty-seven. Only a handful of her films survive.

A Flight for Mary Pickford and a Lost *Foundling*

In a sign of Famous Players' growing confidence in him, Dwan was next assigned to work with the company's reigning star and his fellow Canadian, Mary Pickford.

At that time, Pickford had just completed a string of nine films under the direction of some-time actor James Kirkwood. According to Pickford biographer Ellen Whitfield, Kirkwood "was just the sort of man Mary liked: flamboyant, irreverent and raffish," traits he shared with Dwan's friend Neilan who would later also become Pickford's favorite director. (Neilan also worked on a couple of the Pickford–Kirkwood features as an actor or writer.)

Kirkwood may have also provided a sympathetic ear to Pickford as she continued a rocky marriage with actor Owen Moore. In later years, Kirkwood told his son that he and Pickford had had an affair.[172]

But on March 24, Kirkwood left California to resume making films in the east. Dwan filled the void and directed the final two West Coast productions on Pickford's schedule.

The brief collaboration between Pickford and Dwan did not produce notable results. Aside from past tensions, one possible strain was that Dwan was replacing an intimate friend of Pickford's. For his part, Dwan had reason to be wary of working with a powerful star after his experiences with J. Warren Kerrigan.

Booton Herndon judged that Dwan and Pickford did not have a successful working relationship because "each was too strong."[173] Dwan told Herndon that when he once informed Pickford, "This is what we're gonna do today," Pickford shot back, "Who says that's what we're gonna do today?" Dwan then backpedaled and asked, "Don't you think it would be a good idea?" The now placated Pickford queried, "Why didn't you ask in the first place?"[174]

While there may have been a clash of chain of command between director and star, available evidence suggests their relationship on the set was cordial and respectful. Cari Beauchamp, biographer of Pickford's friend Frances Marion (who had a supporting role in Pickford's first film with Dwan), wrote that the "friendly atmosphere" generated by Dwan on the set extended to "his inviting everyone to his wedding" during a weekend break.[175] Discussing Pickford and other acting talents at Famous Players decades later with Peter Bogdanovich, Dwan observed, "Mary was terrific."[176]

In the "Along the Pacific Coast" column in the *New York Dramatic Mirror*'s issue of March 17, 1915, there appeared a curious item: "Allan Dwan is mournful. He says that no one ever writes him. His address is the Los Angeles Athletic Club."[177]

Was Dwan, the successful director and "popular toastmaster," reduced to making a public appeal for pen pals? Could this have been some kind of inside joke between Dwan and other pranksters? (Kirkwood had been given a sendoff in the blue room of the Athletic Club where diners filed in to a funeral dirge before Kirkwood was "roasted" in a manner popularized on TV by Dean Martin decades later.) Or was this some kind of publicity stunt?

Three weeks later, a follow-up entry appeared in the April 7 column: "Allan Dwan is no longer lonesome. Our invitation for writers to cheer him up increased the director's mail to such an extent that he cut us on the street. Thus is true friendship rewarded."[178]

On April 24, 1915, Dwan and his former leading lady Pauline

Bush were married. Dwan's demeanor certainly sounds strange to have been so described shortly before his wedding. Could these entries have been a part of some kind of private message conveyed from Dwan to Bush in the column? The *Motography* story about their nuptials said that on Dwan's return from the East Coast, which was in late 1914, "they quickly agreed upon a wedding date."[179] But the marriage may have been more recently decided for they were given a dispensation from the Catholic custom of having the banns (intention of marriage) read aloud in church three times, usually over a period of weeks before the ceremony. Had something given their relationship a pause before their final decision to wed? They had been seen in public together at least as late as February 13 when at the grand ball of the Photoplayers Club, they were part of the grand march led by Mary Pickford and the club president Del Henderson.[180]

In any case, Dwan moved toward his goal of being "no longer lonesome."

The wedding ceremony was performed at Mission San Juan Capistrano and presided over by Father O'Sullivan, at that time a very influential and well-known priest in California. It was at San Juan Capistrano on the same date four years earlier that Dwan had worked with Bush for the first time as a performer in his company.[181] Another dispensation was granted for one of the parties (Bush) who was not a Christian and not baptized.[182]

Mary Pickford, then working with Dwan, attended the wedding and chose to have a parallel ceremony with her husband Owen Moore. Pickford and Moore had been married years before by a justice of the peace so this gave them a chance to renew their vows while having a belated church wedding.

Pickford undoubtedly hoped that the renewal of her wedding vows might give a boost to her troubled marriage with Moore. This was not to be, nor was the Dwan–Bush union to be long-lived.

Dwan's wedding occurred after he had begun shooting his first film with Pickford, *A Girl of Yesterday*. For the first time in her career, the story was written by the star herself. Pickford's character Jane Stuart and her brother John have been brought up with strict, old-fashioned conservatism by their Aunt Angela. Jane has even adhered to wearing old, outmoded clothes. Then Jane inherits a fortune. Her brother John starts to live the life he craved but Jane clings to her traditional way of living. With their acquisition of wealth, the Stuarts gain the attention of the neighboring Monroe family who had previously shunned them. Jane reluctantly tries to smarten her wardrobe before going to the Monroes where a frequent guest is Stanley Hudson (Neilan), who has fallen in love with her.

The storyline permitted Pickford to continue with her persona of the naïve innocent who is then goaded into a more modern and fashionable lifestyle, like an Edwardian version of *Grease*. It was surely hoped that this would make her appeal and image more timely. A publicity release for the film asserted that it "is probably the first screen play to contrast all the phases of courtship in a generation gone by with the most modern of romantic auxiliaries — the aeroplane, the palatial steam yacht, the tennis court, the golf course and other adjuncts...."[183]

For the yachting scenes, Dwan was able to secure the use of a "five million dollar yacht" owned by John D. Spreckles.[184] Dwan and Bush also reportedly spent some of their short honeymoon on that yacht.[185]

The "aeroplane" flight was a more difficult matter. Local aviator Glenn Martin was hired to fly his own plane and play a small part in the movie. (Martin would later rise to prominence in his field and design the Martin bombers.) The flight was anticipated with a drumbeat of press announcements in the trade papers like *Variety*'s blurb "Pickford Taking Chances,"[186] and a piece in the *Motion Picture News* that stated, "If the weather permits, the big scene of the subject will be made at Griffith Park where Miss Pickford is scheduled to come to take a ride in the aeroplane of Glenn Martin."[187]

Adding a little drama, the story continued, "Manager Al Kaufman has made a trip and is using his utmost persuasive manner to convince the popular star that it is perfectly safe, including in all of his talks that he is going up and will be there turning the crank if anything should happen." *Moving Picture World* followed with another story noting, "The aeroplane scenes will be conducted and participated in by Glenn Martin and, already trial flights have been made by Miss Pickford in his new four-seated machine...."[188]

The anticipated flight had succeeded in garnering publicity. (Frances Marion claimed that the use of the airplane was suggested by Pickford's press agent.[189]) But did little Mary really fly?

Recounting the incident almost forty years later, Adolph Zukor proclaimed that this was "the first time a movie scene in a flying plane was photographed."[190] According to Zukor, it was his manager Al Kaufman who thought of substituting an airplane for a speeding automobile in the script as the vehicle abducting the heroine. (Zukor was not in California at the time and probably got his information from Kaufman.) Both Pickford and Dwan were pleased with the idea. Zukor noted that the one potential dissenter was the actor who played the heavy, Douglas Gerrard. Being older than the others, he dwelt on the risks involved.

Kaufman invited the press to cover the event but he had not reckoned on an authority almost as formidable as Zukor's. Mary's mother Charlotte had assumed that the scene was to be shot on the ground and when she learned otherwise, she became adamant: Mary would not fly.

In desperation, Kaufman concocted a scheme to follow Charlotte's dictates while deceiving the assemblage of reporters. A wig of blonde curls and a dress was fetched from the studio and transported to a house at the other end of the field. Kaufman donned the wig and dress and the plane taxied to pick up the Pickford imposter out of the range of vision of the journalists.

Mary Pickford appears about to embark on her famous flight in *A Girl of Yesterday* (1915). Glenn Martin is the pilot, and Douglas Gerrard appears as the villain on the left (courtesy Academy of Motion Picture Arts and Sciences).

Zukor's manager was now not only in drag but, in keeping with the requirements of the script, was "bound hand and foot ... struggling to get loose while Gerrard held him down, and he could keep his face turned away." According to Zukor, the scene was being photographed by a cameraman perched on a cliff.

But when the flight was over, Kaufman found that the angry newsmen had gotten no suitable pictures and were getting suspicious. At that point, Pickford agreed to make the flight herself. Charlotte was still able to secure a pledge that the plane would not fly above five hundred feet for whatever dubious safeguard that provided.

The mollified news photographers now got their pictures as Gerrard had to make still another flight. Kaufman later learned that the actor had taken the precaution of writing out a will the night before.

Dwan's account as told to Peter Bogdanovich complements Zukor's but also differs in some details. Dwan does not mention the need to substitute Kaufman for Pickford in the first flight but acknowledges that "we had a hard time getting Mary's mother to agree to let her go up." In Dwan's version, Charlotte's stipulation was not five hundred feet but that Mary must not go over *one* hundred feet high.[191] Characteristically, Dwan found Charlotte's edict to be a technical challenge to which he must engineer a solution:

> Now it's ten times more dangerous at one hundred feet than at ten thousand feet, but we said fine, she won't be over a hundred feet from ground at any time. I said "ground" not "the ground" because my scene was a peculiar one. She had to ride in the back with the heavy with Glenn Martin up front at the controls.... [W]e were driving right along beside them on a road along the top of the Griffith Park mountains; they flew parallel to us and that's how we were able to photograph them. Followed them right along the contour of the mountain for miles. We had to go like hell to keep up with it, really give it the gun, but we did. It was a great shot. They were within twenty feet of us at all times, very close.

Poor Gerrard was again made the butt of the story. At one point, pilot Martin teased Gerrard, showing him that he didn't even have to hold on to the controls. "And this fellow fainted dead-away. We could see him flop right over — with Mary trying to support him and shaking him...."

Dwan concluded, "But I had kept my word to Mary's mother. She was never over 100 feet from us on the mountain — so she was close to ground."

Still another account appeared in the *Los Angeles Times* on May 25, the day after the ballyhooed flight. None of the intrigues mentioned in the Zukor or Dwan versions are noted here. Mrs. Pickford again issues a decree to her daughter but this time her ceiling is down to a mere *fifteen* feet. However, to the satisfaction of the reporter, Mary did fly and in the *Times*' reckoning ascended to 8,000 feet. The headline flashed, "While Her Frantic Mother Waited on the Ground Below, the Moving Picture Star Soared."[192]

For all the hoopla the aviation story gathered, the plane flight was mentioned fleetingly, if at all, in the reviews. In his critique for *Moving Picture World*, George Blaisdell wrote, "There are following sessions on the golf links, there is a trip on a yacht, and an adventure in an aeroplane in which Glenn Martin is introduced. Jane is supposed to take a ride in an aeroplane, but you can't prove it by the film."[193]

This creates some question about Dwan's claim that his camera was never more than twenty feet away from the plane in flight. Unfortunately, no print of *A Girl of Yesterday* appears to be extant for study.

A Girl of Yesterday may have been a film more of gimmicks than substance. Aside from fashions and other modern accoutrements shown, the movie was played up as the first instance in which Pickford's brother Jack also played her brother on screen.

Reviews were quick to focus on this being lightweight material, even for Pickford. Probably the most enthusiastic trade review came from *Motion Picture News* which asserted, "It is one of the best vehicles that Little Mary has ever appeared in, for it offers her opportunities innumerable in which to utilize practically every pretty gesture and expression that she possesses."[194]

This was, of course, before Pickford had made her most memorable films. And the reviewer was quick to add, "The story or rather the substance of the story is almost negligible, the incidental touches being the mainstay of the picture."

Wid's more harshly bemoaned, "It seems a crime that they should wish such awful stories onto poor 'Little Mary.' Just because this little lady has such a wonderful personality and can do so much with little touches is no reason why she should be handicapped with stories that wouldn't hold together as half reel offerings on their own merits."

In 1915 Wid Gunning founded the important film trade publication *Wid's Films and Film Folks*. The name was later changed to *Wid's Daily*, but it was often referred to as *Wid's*.

Wid apparently was not informed that Pickford herself had written the story nor did he seem aware of the film's other behind-the-camera credits. "I didn't catch the name of the producer but it struck me as one of Jim Kirkwood's with a script that should have been completely forgotten, and I certainly will say that whoever the director was, he did his very best to forget that there was a 'drammer' to be thought of. But for the clever touches of character and comedy inserted by the director and the leading players this film would be awful."[195]

Photoplay put the matter even more succinctly: "Written by Miss Pickford the play ... proves that Miss Pickford had better stick to acting."[196]

The June 12, 1915, issue of *Motion Picture News* reported, "The Famous Players Company this week take up a new subject featuring Mary Pickford, supported by Frank Mills, Donald Crisp, Harry Ham and others.... The title of this subject has not been announced. The scenario has been prepared by Miss Frances Marian [sic]...."[197]

This film was *The Foundling*, the second of Dwan's Pickford films and the first written by Marion, who played a "vamp" in *A Girl of Yesterday*. Marion went on to become a frequent writer for Pickford and even directed one of her features. Since *Motion Picture News* actually appeared in print a week before the publication date, *The Foundling* probably went into production in very late May or in early June.

Dwan and his company were also about to receive an important visitor. On Saturday, May 29, 1915, Famous Players' president Adolph Zukor, accompanied by his wife, son and daughter, left New York City for the West Coast. But he was not coming just to observe his brightest star in action but to purchase more land for the erection of additional studios.

Famous Players had already purchased an almost completed plant from Fiction Pictures. In early May, Dwan and his filmmaking unit, now the last Famous Players company working on the West Coast, had moved to the new quarters at Santa Monica Boulevard and Gower Street. With the completion of *The Foundling*, Famous Players' shooting season in California was over and Dwan, Pickford and company returned east. But more ambitious plans for West Coast production were now being developed.

A number of future Pickford films to be directed by Dwan were now announced. Upon their arrival in New York, preparations were to be made for *Miss Jinny*, a tenement story by Edith Barnard Delano, who had also written a recently completed Pickford film, *Rags*. Still to come would be *The Heart of Sally Temple*, from a novel and play by Rupert Sargent Holland, and *Audrey*, adapted from a novel by Mary Johnson and the play by Harriet Ford. Sounding more typical of Dwan's inventiveness, Pickford and company would also enact a story en route to the East as the plot was constructed to start in California and end in New York where subsequent scenes would be filmed.[198]

Dwan may have been less than enthralled with these prospects for both the *New York Dramatic Mirror* and *Variety* now reported that he had signed to work for the Fox Film Corporation. The *Mirror* noted that Dwan had signed with Fox for "a very gaspy salary."[199]

Interestingly, even before the trade paper announcements of Dwan's signing with Fox there was an intriguing story that was a special to *Motion Picture News*. It said that Pauline Bush would leave Universal to become a member of the stock company of Fox. The story even stated that she would be joined there by her frequent Universal co-star and now director, Lon Chaney.[200] Had the engagements of either Dwan or Bush led to the other coming to an agreement with Fox?

But all this evaporated rather quickly. Within a week, *Motography* reported, "Pauline Bush will remain with the Universal despite the rumors to the contrary." She remained bound with Big U to appear in a movie called *Betty's Bondage*.[201] Chaney, too would remain with Universal. As for Dwan, he was the subject of a *Variety* story that said that both Famous Players and Fox were claiming he was under contract to them.[202]

The stories of Dwan signing with Fox petered out. But he did not make any of the films that had been announced by Famous Players. In fact, even Dwan's filming of *The Foundling* would never be seen by any audience.

At 6:55 on the evening of Saturday, September 11, 1915, smoke was spotted pouring out of the third floor of 213 West 26th Street, between Seventh and Eighth Avenues in New York City. The third and fourth floors housed the offices and studio of Famous Players. A fire had supposedly started in a braid works on the second floor but had quickly begun to spread throughout the building and there was fear that it would advance still farther. "The building was surrounded by tenements housing negroes, Greeks and Italians, and these persons, hundreds of them, fled in wild panic when the flames burst through the roof of the old armory building and from all the windows."[203]

Twenty-five fire engines responded to the blaze. The fire was brought under control by nine o'clock, before it could extend beyond the edifice, but sparks carried by a northwest wind were reported as far east as Second Avenue.

The three employees of Famous Players present in the building managed to escape. But there were devastating losses in the property department involving furniture, sets and costumes. More importantly, the office vault contained several negatives of soon-to-be-released features. The fate of these films remained unclear as company officials had to wait for three days to open the vault. Fortunately, the print of Dwan's *A Girl of Yesterday* was undamaged, as was the upcoming *The Prince and the Pauper.* The survival of the negative of *Zaza* starring Pauline Frederick was even used by Famous Players in their publicity campaign for the film.[204]

But *The Foundling,* which was slated for release before *A Girl of Yesterday,* was not among the survivors.

The Foundling had been scheduled for release on September 6, five days before the fire but, in a last-minute change, was yanked in favor of *Esmeralda*, an earlier Pickford film directed by Kirkwood.[205] That postponement proved fatal. Also, *The Foundling* had not been already reviewed by the trades, as has been stated by some sources. What had been published were descriptions of the movie appearing under headings like "Manufacturer's Advanced Notes" in *Moving Picture World.* Such notices usually were run shortly before films were actually reviewed. The notices that appeared in *Moving Picture World, Motion Picture News* and *Motography* were clearly differently edited versions of the same press release.[206]

But this was not the end of the *Foundling* saga. Pickford decided that *The Foundling* was worth remaking and, after completing her role in *Madame Butterfly*, she set out to do just that. Dwan had by this time left Famous Players so John B. O'Brien was brought in as director. A new supporting cast consisted of Edward Martindale, Maggie Weston, Mildred Morris, Marcia Harris and Tammany Young. This new edition was shot in New York, not California. This new version of *The Foundling* was released on January 3, 1916.

The story concerns an artist whose wife died in childbirth. Embittered against his baby girl for causing the death of his wife, the artist has the child deposited in an orphanage and goes to Italy to pursue his career. Years later, regretting his decision, the artist goes back to the orphanage to get back his daughter but is tricked into taking the orphanage director's illegitimate niece instead. By chance, he later meets his real daughter (Pickford) in the street and, thoroughly charmed by her, brings her to his home. Through a chain of events, the chicanery is discovered and the artist and his true daughter are happily reunited.

Again the critics regarded the plot as inconsequential. The *New York Dramatic Mirror* opined, "We doubt if any other actress now appearing on the screen could have taken *The Foundling* and made of it the highly interesting and attractive picture that Mary Pickford has.... The whole picture is a refutation of the asserted fact that a good story is necessary for a good picture."[207] It was already, as *Variety* acknowledged, an "old, old story."[208]

It was also one of what would be numerous cases of Pickford regressing into a waif role after playing an adult part.

A print of this version of *The Foundling* does survive and is available at the Library of Congress. The movie is not without its charms. The problem is that this is basically Mary Pickford 101, an amalgam of standard Pickford situations that could serve as a template for better developed Pickford "waif" movies like *Daddy Long Legs.*

Given the various changes in personnel and locale, it is very difficult to conjecture how close this came to the Dwan version. But it seems reasonable to say that the destruction of the earlier film, while regrettable, was not a major loss on the Dwan filmography.

Perhaps the most interesting aspect was the plot device of a "lost father," which Dwan would pursue still more obsessively in later films.

The Move to Triangle and Griffith

Why was Dwan so intent in the summer of 1915 on leaving Famous Players? He told Bogdanovich, "Well, one of the reasons was my disappointment in the legitimate players emphasized at Famous Players. Mary [Pickford] was terrific and one or two others came through pretty well, but most of them suffered and disappeared back to the theater."[209] But Famous Players had already announced that Dwan would do a string of projects with Pickford.

A more practical explanation was that, newly married and with more responsibilities, Dwan would have been receptive to a deal that would have boosted his salary. Shortly before the Fox deal was announced, a trade column noted, "Allan Dwan was observed counting his money just outside a contractor's office and then making a slow exit, shaking his head sadly."[210]

Dwan also stated on numerous occasions that he was not happy with supervisors imposed on him. During his California sojourn for Famous Players, Dwan's name repeatedly appeared in tandem with Al Kaufman in trade stories apparently culled from company press releases, as if Kaufman was always casting a watchful eye. Even an account of Dwan's bachelor party ended not with Ms. Bush being telephoned to hear a toast in her honor but that "Al Kaufman entertained the party at the theater and at Levy's after the dinner."[211]

A hint of Dwan's mindset may also be gleaned from the *Variety* story on the dispute between Famous Players and Fox for

Dwan's services where Dwan is referred to as "the former aid [sic] to D.W. Griffith on the coast."[212] There is no evidence that Dwan ever worked for Griffith up to that time nor did Dwan ever claim in his post-career interviews to such an early liaison with the great director.

However, as noted earlier in this chapter, Dwan did tell Bogdanovich he was studying Griffith's films while directing at Flying A and had sent Neilan on an expedition to work for Griffith. But appreciation of Griffith's artistry became universal in March 1915 when the master director's epic *The Birth of a Nation* was released.

While there was an outcry of protest against the film's racism, there was also widespread agreement that the motion picture had been taken to a new serious level it had not known before.

Dwan must have grasped the magic of Griffith's name at this time so he likely had something to do with *Variety*'s mistaken credit. But Dwan could not have known that the very making of *The Birth of a Nation* would set off a chain of events that would create an opportunity for him to work with Griffith.

After the friction created because of his feature-length *Judith of Bethulia*, Griffith left Biograph in October 1913 to join Harry Aitken and his Reliance–Majestic studios. Aitken, who worked with his brother Roy, was a Wisconsin native who had forged ahead in the film business with grandiose ambitions. Back in 1911, Aitken had hired Mary Pickford away from Carl Laemmle's Imp Pictures while Laemmle was in Europe. In March 1912, with the support of Wall Street investors, Aitken had helped found the Mutual Film Corporation, a distribution company which could handle any films "regardless of the seller's other affiliations."

Aitken was chief executive of Mutual but he had an uneasy rivalry with two of his partners from the American Film Manufacturing Company, John R. Freuler and Dwan's old nemesis, Samuel S. Hutchinson.

Mutual also handled the distribution of the New York Motion Picture Company run by Adam Kessel and Charles Baumann, who had broken from Universal. Making films for them was the producer-director Thomas H. Ince, the most notable American filmmaker of the time aside from Griffith. Also appearing through the New York Motion Picture Company–Mutual axis were Mack Sennett's Keystone comedies.

So Aitken already had a full plate when Griffith approached him about funding a 12-reel epic first known as *The Clansman* and then as *The Birth of a Nation*. The $40,000 budget Griffith proposed was four times the amount of each of his five-reel films but was far less than what the epic would ultimately cost. Even this amount caused consternation among Aitken's Mutual partners, most vociferously from Freuler. They refused to let Mutual assume the financing of *Birth* and Aitken had to raise the money on his own, taking a loan on his Majestic stock.[213]

The $40,000 was quickly used up and Griffith was badgering Aitken for more money. Aitken managed to raise another $20,000 but this was still not enough. Griffith then started taking small investments from his employees, his suppliers, from anyone he could find who would put money in the film. *Birth of a Nation* opened at the Clune's Auditorium in Los Angeles on February 8, 1915, because its manager, William Clune, had provided the final $15,000 to complete the picture. Since Mutual would not distribute *Birth*, the Epoch Producing Corporation was founded on that same date for the purpose of distributing that one film.[214]

The Birth of a Nation was probably the most successful film in motion picture history until *Gone with the Wind*. Aitken and all the small investors reaped huge profits. By rebuffing Aitken, Mutual had lost a chance to share in the bonanza.

Logically, this should have bolstered Aitken's standing at Mutual and hurt Freuler but just the opposite happened. Aitken's status at Mutual had declined since his financing of *Birth* had been rejected and he had created dissension with his independent ways. Freuler shrewdly sought out the 700 stockholders to gain the votes to replace Aitken. On June 23, 1915, Aitken was unseated and Freuler was elected president of Mutual.

But Aitken was already hatching a new and more ambitious idea for a film organization. He found partners in Kessel and Baumann, who had their own quarrel with Freuler for not permitting a renegotiation of their Keystone contract.

What Aitken had in mind was a film company that joined all three of the major creative forces of the time, Griffith, Ince and Sennett. He was sure that he could get Griffith's involvement after their triumphant partnership in *The Birth of a Nation* while Ince and Sennett had already been working through Kessel and Baumann's company. To gain capital for his venture, Aitken went to Wall Street and approached F.S. Smithers and Co., an investment banking firm. The enormous profits accrued by *The Birth of a Nation*, as well as Aitken's acquired skill in inflating the size and value of his assets, helped put his prospective backers into a receptive mood.

So Aitken would embark on his corporate plans with an impressive $5,000,000 worth of capital.[215] This would be a precursor to future Wall Street investments in the film business that would one day be prominently cited by Allan Dwan.

Because of the involvement of three major producer-directors, Griffith, Ince, and Sennett, the company would be known as the Triangle Film Corporation. Its creation was formally announced in La Junta, Colorado, on July 20, 1915.

Three production companies, Griffith's Fine Arts, Ince's Kay-Bee and Sennett's Keystone, would make the films which would be distributed by Triangle. Triangle would also furnish the operating capital to the companies. The films would be distributed only to theaters holding Triangle contracts, an arrangement which presaged the future ownership of theater chains by the major film companies. Thus, these theaters would become like Triangle franchises.

The intended benefit would be that these theaters would be receiving films of high quality and the Triangle name was meant to convey that. Kessel wrote in *Motion Picture News,* "The public wants better pictures. That is the kind we are going to make: the best pictures the world has ever seen, and we are ready to spend enormous sums of money to do that."[216]

Recalling the success he had in charging $2 admission for *Birth,* Aitken intended that Triangle films would be shown for the same premium prices. The admission price was to be seen as a further mark of quality.

In the pages of *Motography,* Adolph Zukor responded sneeringly, "I believe in the so-called $2 picture but I do not believe in charging $2 for the privilege of seeing them."[217]

As Aitken believed he was elevating movies to a new cultural level, he also thought higher quality stars had to be created. For this reason, he decided to hire a flock of performers from the Broadway stage. (Zukor had tried a similar gambit with Famous Players.) New York stage stars were not known in most parts of the country and their ability to adapt to the film medium would vary, with many prominent actors not making the grade. The gap between the hefty sums paid to lure these actors to the screen and their actual drawing power would come back to haunt Aitken. Ironically, Dwan had said that he had left Famous Players because of his disappointment with the stage actors employed there.

But in order to put its program into practice, Triangle also needed more talented directors. This would be especially true at Fine Arts where Griffith was preparing to make another lengthy epic and other filmmakers would be required to keep up the flow of product.

D.W. Griffith, the greatest of the film pioneers. As one of the three points in the Triangle, he offered some opportunities to Allan Dwan.

The July 10, 1915, issue of *Motion Picture News* announced that Dwan had joined the New York Motion Picture Company. It reported the signing as taking place on June 26, three days after the fateful Mutual meeting that ousted Aitken, so the company's executives Kessel and Baumann may have already known that they were soon to become part of a large new combine. The *Motion Picture News* article cited Dwan as being from "Famous Players, with which company he has been head director for some time."[218]

The following week, *Motion Picture News* had to print a retraction: "Although Mr. Dwan directed important productions, he was not head director. That position is held by Daniel Frohman and Edwin S. Porter who have immediate supervision of Famous Player productions."[219] So as with the earlier *Variety* article, Dwan may have been embellishing his credentials to the press.

In August 1915, the *New York Dramatic Mirror* reported that Dwan was one of a growing number of directors signed to work at Griffith's Fine Arts Company.[220] In their March 1916 issue, *Photoplay* had an article on the new crop of directorial "lieutenants" now working at Triangle. The article observed, "Allan Dwan came to the Griffith studios a journeyman director and is the only one of the 'Lieutenants' who was not brought up in the Griffith service. He is the one exception to the Griffith rule of not going abroad for directors and was engaged because of his excellent work for other concerns and his close sympathy with Griffith methods."[221]

So after years of admiring Griffith from afar, Dwan would now be working for the greatest of the film pioneers.

Griffith's Ghost

As Dwan headed out to California to begin his new stint as director, Griffith and his co-workers now saw a whirlwind of changes at their old studio. Karl Brown, who started working for Griffith as an assistant to cameraman Billy Bitzer, recalled "the fantastic expansion of activity within the studio itself. Directors, stars, cameramen, and crews for half-a-dozen companies were hired. The carpenter shop was working day and night, turning out sets for stages, while other crews of carpenters, plumbers, electricians, and maintenance men were swarming all over the place building more and more new structures to this influx of talent."[222]

Griffith himself now became immersed in a grandiose project that was to dwarf *Birth of a Nation.* He was still intent on answering the critics of *Birth of a Nation* and what he regarded as an encroachment of free speech. The film that started out as a relatively modest film called *The Mother and the Law* mushroomed into a story of four separate segments told with parallel editing. Some of his assistants were not let in on this and could only wonder in perplexity as one project after another was begun, all seemingly unrelated but with the same title of *The Mother and The Law*. Only later did they learn that he was attempting a new kind of film storytelling in an epic intended to show intolerance through the ages. It would ultimately bear the title of *Intolerance*.

To launch an undertaking the size of *Intolerance*, one that would take up almost a year, would seem the worst way to begin an enterprise where Griffith was, in effect, supervising production of an entire studio. Unlike his partners Ince and Sennett, Griffith would always remain more a director than producer, and *his* films came first. But it's possible that even had this project not consumed so much of his time, Griffith may not have believed in being heavy-handed. As the *Photoplay* article pointed out, most of the directors were of the Griffith school and already understood his methods. Griffith would sometimes write scripts for his directors under the pseudonym Granville Warwick, but he did not exercise an iron hand.

Frank Woods, the head of the Fine Arts scenario department, told the *New York Dramatic Mirror*, "To each of the Fine Arts five-reel pictures, Mr. Griffith gives a measure of supervision both before and after they are filmed. But it is the policy of the organization to give the individual directors the fullest possible freedom to work out their own artistic salvation."[223]

This does not mean that Griffith lacked a keen interest in ensuring that Fine Arts films maintained his standards. According to actress Bessie Love, he exercised his own form of quality control, commenting that he "had a great deal to do with the cutting" and that he screened and approved each film prior to release.[224] Some films received more of his attention than others; the official Triangle publicity journal listed five films that he "supervised" though none of these were made by Dwan.

When asked about how Griffith's supervision manifested itself, Dwan replied, "Only in a pleasant way. When we were going to make a picture, we'd all go into a room with two or three of the actors assigned and the script we were going to do — or a synopsis of it.... And he was just seeing that I wasn't going to do the same thing one of the other fellows was doing. Or seeing if maybe I should use Lillian Gish instead of Mae Marsh or someone else out of his stock company. After that we got whatever we wanted and were completely independent."[225]

It is likely that from his viewpoint, Griffith appreciated that talented filmmakers did better work with less interference. Another point that Dwan makes is that Griffith's stock company supplied his other directors with very disciplined and skilled actors. "They had learned economy of gesture which I love. They projected their personalities and didn't try to cram them down your throat. They let your mind work."[226]

The colossal Babylon set for *Intolerance* was actually on a separate lot but Brown remembered that the Fine Arts studio "was packed to its smallest crevice with people working at all sorts of unimaginable tasks."[227] These included everything from wardrobe people producing simulated armor to painters decorating chariots.

Griffith wanted a shot of this set where the camera would move to show its tremendous breadth and then bear down to its smallest detail. This would be one of the most famous shots in cinema history. But how could it be executed? There were no camera cranes at that time. Dwan told Bogdanovich and others that he was the one to come up with the solution and this story has been repeated in numerous books. "Put an elevator on a railroad track. Go backwards and upwards at the same time."[228] But is it true?

This is difficult to confirm since Griffith took pains to hide the tricks of his trade and may not have wished to divulge how the problem was solved. But we can at least look at the plausibility of Dwan's claim.

Lillian Gish's account suggests that Griffith did indeed have trouble figuring out how to handle the shot. According to Gish, "He wanted the camera to record every detail of the fantastic scene, so he installed [cameraman Billy Bitzer] in a balloon that could be raised or lowered. But the wind played havoc with Billy's attempts to keep within the limits of the set...."[229] When this strategy failed, Gish said Griffith came up with the elevator-on-rails idea. Leaving aside Gish's often criticized adulatory treatment of Griffith, she would have no way of knowing if he hadn't first heard this from someone else.

Gish also gives us a tantalizing detail. "As the sets grew in magnitude, Allan Dwan, one of the assistant directors on *Intolerance*, as well as director for many of the other films being made at the studio, said to Mr. Griffith, 'You've bitten one hell of a chunk. How are you going to get actors to dominate all this magnificence?'

"'If it's good,' Mr. Griffith answered with a wry smile, 'you'll be doing it yourself next year.'"[230]

Joseph Henabery, a Griffith assistant, disputes Gish. According to Henabery, "Dwan told me he never worked on it [*Intolerance*]."[231] This is probably true, given Dwan's busy filmmaking schedule, but does not preclude that Dwan, like any other director on the lot, might have discussed the massive project with Griffith.

Griffith was a man who planned things deliberately. He surely knew that Dwan had an engineering degree and had earned praise for his use of elaborate tracking shots in *David Harum*, so it would have been logical for Griffith to ask his advice.

Recalling the story as Dwan related it to him, film historian Kevin Brownlow observed, "When Dwan told me that he had given Griffith the idea for the siege tower, it made perfect sense because he had been an engineer, and this was hardly a filmmaker's solution. He said that it was his only contribution. I sensed sometimes that Dwan was helping a story along a little

Griffith couldn't figure out how to capture every part of his titanic Babylonian set in the elaborate tracking shot of *Intolerance* (1916). Dwan said he provided the solution.

bit, but in this case he was very terse. However, Hollywood seldom kept a record of where ideas came from!"[232]

So while we cannot confirm Dwan's claim, it does appear quite plausible.

Dwan was now a part of the corps of directors that would be churning out the Fine Arts films. His fellow directors included John B. O'Brien (who had remade Dwan's *The Foundling*), Lloyd Ingraham, William Christy Cabanne, and Paul Powell.

Dwan's first film at Triangle was *Jordan Is a Hard Road*, a carryover Mutual project. Mary H. O'Connor was first hired to write the scenario but the script used would be credited to Dwan in most accounts. The star was Frank Campeau, noted stage actor and Dwan's fellow Notre Dame alumnus. Dorothy Gish, Griffith's frequent star, was set for the female lead. The cast also included Pickford's husband Owen Moore.

Moving Picture World (September 11, 1915) reported how "D.W. Griffith's big plant" was humming with activity and that seven productions were underway. It noted, "One of the more pretentious of the coming Fine Arts productions is *Jordan Is a Hard Road*, a film adaptation from Sir Gilbert Parker's popular novel.... The scenes are laid in Canada, and in order to secure a true atmosphere, a complete Canadian village is being constructed."[233]

Dwan sought to enhance the atmosphere with location shooting and two weeks were spent filming exteriors at Bear Lake Valley. Pauline Bush, phasing out her own career, accompanied her husband to the site.

The story of *Jordan Is a Hard Road* features an outlaw and evangelist so Dwan got expert help from representatives of both professions. Al Jennings was a lawyer turned bank and train robber who, after being pardoned by President Theodore Roosevelt in 1907, resumed his law practice. He had made an early appearance in motion pictures in 1908 with his former nemesis, the famed lawman Bill Tilghman, ironically serving as director. Six years later, after his memoirs were published in *The Saturday Evening Post*, Jennings was hired to play himself and act as technical advisor by the Thanhouser Company in a film called *Beating Back*. Perhaps not illogically, Jennings' next move was into politics and he ran for governor in the 1914 Oklahoma Democratic Primary, finishing third.[234]

So Jennings was then again available for film work. He did not have an imposing appearance and actually looked somewhat frail. One young Hollywood acquaintance recalled that Jennings "had the palest blue eyes I had ever seen and his thick wavy hair was worn in the style of Rudy Vallee."[235] Dwan said, "I remember him as an ordinary little man who might have been cast as a grocery clerk."[236] But Jennings certainly knew his past "business" in supervising the film's bank robbery. One critic wrote appreciatively, "The robbing of the bank was handled in manner which registered ten times better than the ordinary 'bank robbery.'"[237]

Dwan also strove for verisimilitude for the portrayal of the preacher so he said he engaged the most famous evangelist of his day, Billy Sunday, as his technical advisor.

To give the scene maximum impact, Sunday brought his tent and assistant and Dwan had big signs put up, stating that Sunday would be there on the day specified and "that everybody was invited." Dwan explained that there was no ready source for extras at that time so by staging a genuine revival meeting featuring Sunday, "we made it legitimate for them to come."[238] The incoming crowd easily filled the tent. Dwan claimed that five or six thousand had to be turned away.

Dwan remembered, "Now, in the story Campeau is supposed to harangue them about religion and make them come to God, but I got Billy Sunday up there and he let them have one of his best hot lectures, and I had about three cameras filming only the audience. And pretty soon these people began to feel it, and the first thing you know they were crawling up the aisles on their knees, coming up to Billy Sunday to be saved, hollering 'Hallelujah' and going into hysteria. A terrific scene. No bunch of million-dollar actors could have done it. You could see the frenzy in their faces. And after we cut, he actually went on with a religious revival right there."[239]

Dwan could now film his actor giving his sermon and intercut shots of him with the scenes of the overcome faithful. Dwan considered the effect "astonishing."[240]

But he might have also felt astonished when he saw Al Jennings falling to his knees in front of Sunday like many others in the tent. Jennings was so impressed with the experience that for a time he too assumed the mantle of an evangelist. He later returned to the screen to make starkly realistic Westerns that de-glamorized the outlaw.

Dwan was now striving with greater resources to attain not just greater realism but the character that could be distilled from atmosphere. He would continue to pursue this atmosphere in locations he thought appropriate for each film, while always shooting with an economy that boosted commercial viability.

No prints are known to exist of *Jordan Is a Hard Road* but its plot can be thus synopsized: An armed robber named Bill Minden (Campeau) learns that his wife is dying. Before he is arrested, he gives his infant daughter Cora to the care of a religious woman, Mrs. Findlay. The story resumes years later after Bill is released from prison, a free man but still not reformed, avoiding riskier ventures for confidence games. He then learns that his now grown daughter is living in the border town of Askatoon. Settling in the town and seeing his daughter (Gish) singing at a religious revival meeting, Bill converts. He helps Mrs. Findlay and Cora get established. Cora is led to believe that Bill was a friend of her father.

When the funds lost in a bank robbery threaten the livelihood of his daughter and Mark (Moore), her lover, Bill robs a train to replace the stolen money. Mortally wounded, he turns the money over to Mark but pretends he has been shot in an accident and dies as Cora sings the hymn ("Jordan Is a Hard Road") that helped convert him.

As with *The Foundling,* the protagonist is another "lost father" though here one who cannot reveal himself. Even his final sacrifice must remain secret to avoid disillusioning his daughter. The narrative has inherent sentimental pitfalls and one can better understand the importance of creating a vivid and colorful background.

At the premiere theaters, the new Triangle productions were originally presented in triple bills consisting of one film each from the Keystone, Kay-Bee and Fine Arts companies. Although *Jordan Is a Hard Road* did not go into general release until December 19, it was shown on the Triangle bill at the Knickerbocker Theater in New York in November. It was the seventh Triangle program to be presented since the first one debuted on September 23.

For this latest Triangle program, the first entry exhibited was Ince's *The Winged Idol,* a drama of "an inebriate who falls under the spell of a Russian seeress." It was followed by the Keystone comedy *A Submarine Pirate* starring Syd Chaplin, Charlie's older half-brother. Both films were four reels long. After an intermission, the five-reel *Jordan Is a Hard Road* was shown.

The *New York Times* interestingly saw Dwan's film as a "Bret Harte sort of story of the Golden West" but did not comment further other than to acknowledge that Campeau and Gish did some "effective acting."[241]

Moving Picture World commended *The Winged Idol* and *A Submarine Pirate* but judged *Jordan Is a High Road* to be a "labored and loosely made adaptation from a novel, containing some bright spots and fair acting, but so badly put together that it drags along like a two-reel play stretched to five. The least interesting Triangle yet shown."[242]

But this turned out to be the minority view in the trade press. *Motography* noted, "After the intermission, Frank Campeau and Dorothy Gish make their Triangle debut in the production staged under the direction of Allen [sic] Dwan and a most successful one it proves, for many were overheard declaring as they left the theater that it was the single best offering yet seen on the Triangle program. The director has chosen some truly wonderful locations and these, combined with the unique and excellent allegories used in the telling of the story make *Jordan Is a Hard Road* a picture decidedly out of the ordinary."[243] *Variety* also believed that it "lived up to every prediction and promise made by the Triangular group of producers...."[244]

Wid Gunning may have been the most enthusiastic, opining,

"Director Dwan deserves much credit for the manner in which he handled the little touches, introducing and 'planting' these characters. This is truly a great film.... Where there were scenes which were 'quiet' as to definite 'action,' Mr. Dwan found spots of striking beauty or he lighted them most artistically." Gunning, the critic cited who praised the robbery scene, added, "The revival scenes were splendid and carried all the little effective touches that helped to make them 'real.'"[245] These were perhaps the best reviews Dwan had received since *Wildflower.*

The impact of *Jordan Is a Hard Road* resonated strongly enough that in 1965, seventy-four-year-old former cowboy star Tim McCoy wrote to Dwan about playing Bill Minden in a remake. "I've added a few ideas of my own to the original," McCoy wrote, "and the result should make a good strong Western picture. It certainly was good the way you made it."[246]

Campeau went on to a successful career as a character actor in the silent era. Dorothy Gish and Owen Moore resumed working with Dwan in another opus called *Betty of Graystone.* For this film, they would all be deployed to the East Coast.

The press sometimes saw all the Fine Arts directors as extensions of Griffith. In its October 29 issue, *Variety* ran a blurb erroneously stating that "D.W. Griffith is to begin work in the East on Nov. 2 at the Willat Studio, Fort Lee, N.J. He will have as one of his assistant directors Allan Divan [sic]."[247]

Actually, Dwan's was the second company Griffith had sent to work in the east. A short time earlier, Dwan's former leading man now converted to director, John Emerson, had also taken his crew and players east.

Dwan had been part of filmmaking's original westward movement. But now four and a half years after he began his career as a director, not only were there still studio facilities on the eastern seaboard but new ones were being opened. One explanation given was "that the long rainy spells of the last two years on the Coast ... caused the price of negative to jump skyward."[248]

In an article in *Motography*, Adolph Zukor provided a fuller explanation, emphasizing, among other things, that the "importance of obtaining the proper atmosphere for every production has never failed to impress me...." Zukor was convinced that the east provided a greater variety of surroundings.[249]

Dwan, who had probably already grasped all of Zukor's points, would become increasingly drawn to working in the east. But for the time being, Dwan was simply concerned with filming *Betty of Graystone* which, because of its setting in New England and New York, was deemed a subject for the eastern studios. Fine Arts had two facilities in the east, the Willat Studios in Fort Lee and the studios at 537 Riverdale Avenue in Yonkers, New York, often referred to as the Riverdale Studios.

Biograph had been churning out films in Fort Lee since 1908 and other film combines had also established facilities there. The Willat Studios were at the corner of Main Street and Linwood Avenue. Channing Pollock, a playwright and a visitor to Fort Lee in 1915, wrote, "Willat's, the Éclair and the Peerless occupy what would be the same block, if there were any blocks in Fort Lee. The former is composed of two big brick buildings, surrounded by a high cement wall.... They are all brick buildings, with plenty of glass, grouped together so that, when they don't suggest mushrooms, they do suggest the Crystal Palace, or a section of a World's Fair."[250] The walls and roofs of glass were constructed to maximize the effect of daylight needed for the proper exposure of film. After *Betty of Graystone,* Dwan would make another film in the east so that by March, *Photoplay* facetiously referred to him as Fine Arts' "oriental representative."[251] Dwan was reported to have shot some additional *Betty* scenes on location in upstate New York and Connecticut.

The story is set in a New England town where Betty (Gish) is strongly attached to her scholarly father who serves as a caretaker at Graystone Gables. When her father dies, the lonely girl seeks refuge in the Graystone mansion. Meanwhile, her mother marries a widower with two grown sons who treat Betty cruelly.

Betty's presence at Graystone Gables is discovered by David Chandler (Moore), a young New Yorker who owns the estate as a summer home. When Betty and David are seen together there, it is considered a scandal. Betty is driven from the village but is then permitted to live with David's friends, the Sherwoods in New York. There she wins the love of David. But when she suspects David of being unfaithful, she returns to her mother, who is dying. Her stepbrothers refuse to let Betty see her. In her despair, she goes back to the Gables, where one of her stepbrothers follows her and makes unwelcome advances. David arrives in time to rescue her. Reconciled, Betty and David marry.

The plot is, of course, a mixture of Cinderella story and a tale of "intolerance." The film was the first Fine Arts feature scripted by F.M. Pierson but its affinities to Griffith are apparent.

Variety noted that the plot was elemental but thought it "a good program feature with plenty of comedy and 'class.'"[252] Julian Johnson in *Photoplay* extolled, "No photoplay produced in the past month has been more a fragment of life, nor has more subtly stimulated imagination than *Betty of Graystone,* a Fine Arts Fort Lee product, shaped under the hands of Allan Dwan, all of whose previous work made not the slightest impression upon me." (Johnson was apparently unaware that Dwan was the director of *Jordan Is a Hard Road,* which he had praised as an "exquisite Fine Arts idyll.")[253]

Johnson further noted, "I cannot recount the full hundred touches of vivid pathos, humor, narrow suspicion and innate innocence or nobility which Mr. Dwan and his actors have bewitched this implement, so that it is not a play, but a window opening onto the path of life, through which any of us may look.... Dorothy Gish does the best work of her life as Betty...."[254]

Betty of Graystone was apparently popular enough that in 1919 Triangle re-released it along with two Ince films, and with

Dorothy Gish is caught up in an unpleasant family situation in *Betty of Graystone* (1916), with the title spelling apparently changed for the 1919 re-release. The actor next to her is Kid McCoy (born Norman Selby), a former champion boxer. In a precursor to the O.J. Simpson case, in 1924 the athlete turned actor was put on trial for the murder of his lover. Found guilty of manslaughter, he was in prison until 1932.

much fanfare. The full page *Betty of Graystone* ad consisted of a head shot of Gish against a black background with the caption "A classic of the motion picture art, re-created for the highest class audiences of to-day. Dorothy Gish and Owen Moore in a guaranteed success."[255]

Interestingly, Dwan's name was not mentioned in the ad but under the title were the words "Supervised by D.W. Griffith." At the time of its original release, Triangle publicity did not make any claim to Griffith's supervision of the film since he was 3,000 miles away from where *Betty of Graystone* was being shot. The press sheets for the film's re-release noted, "Two names which will serve as extra 'pullers' are those of the directors. Allan Dwan handled the megaphone for Dorothy Gish in this production which was supervised by D.W. Griffith."[256]

The linkage of Dwan's name with Griffith recurred in later years though for aesthetic rather than commercial reasons. Dwan was seen as the heir to Griffith, particularly decades later when he was working on less esteemed low-budget films; a few erudite critics professed admiration at his preservation of Griffith's sense of narrative and editing. Andrew Sarris has written, "Some of the French critics treat Dwan as Griffith's ghost," then added, "But in a very marginal conception of his career. The French always seem to be most fascinated by those directors engulfed in the damnation of necessity."[257]

As Dwan was being rediscovered by the French critics, the Griffith legacy must have seemed a useful rallying point to celebrate a director who was then toiling in cinema's lower depths. It also provided a helpful explanation for a filmmaker whose themes and style did not seem easily identifiable.

In his last years, Dwan was not keen on pushing the Griffith connection. One interviewer recalled that Dwan became defensive when asked about Griffith's influence on him and proceeded to do an impression of Griffith being terribly pompous.[258]

John Dorr, an American, was among the most insistent on linking Dwan to the Griffith tradition and its reliance on editing. Of the Griffith legacy he wrote, "In the montage tradition, each shot becomes a fact whose meaning is determined by its juxtaposition to another fact." Dorr contrasts this with the Murnau Tradition (from the German director F.W. Murnau) of the moving camera.[259]

Dorr wrote, "Of all the directors of the Griffith Tradition who maintained careers well into the sound period, Allan Dwan was the least affected by the Murnau Tradition.... Dwan's visual style was the purest expression of the Griffith tradition; and it is the purity of this style (and its thematic implications) that sustained Dwan's creative energy.... In Dwan's later work the mathematical perfection of his visual style best illustrates the primal power inherent in the Griffith Tradition."[260]

There are some simplifications as well as insights in Dorr's approach but it is of interest here as a basis to make some observations about Dwan and Griffith.

As we have seen, Dwan had developed dramatic values out of the principles of editing quite early in his career at Flying A. Dorr notes that "like classical Greek art, the artisans of the Griffith tradition valued order, balance, graceful proportions, symmetry — ideals of structure and geometry."[261] Educated in engineering, Dwan embraced these values, perhaps even more than Griffith himself. He would assert these values both within and outside of the Griffith tradition and in areas of sheer practicality, such as his method of working economically by eliminating what he regarded as "extraneous matter." He expounded on this to Bogdanovich and stated "that there's always a mathematical solution to everything." Asked how this manifested itself, Dwan responded, "In logic. In naturalness. The inevitable laws of mathematics. They apply to drama and life."[262]

There is, of course, no mathematical formula for art. But the editing principles of the Griffith Tradition provided Dwan with a structure to play with and to study different creative possibilities.

Interestingly, Dorr notes that unlike Dwan, Griffith himself seemed to depart from the Griffith Tradition in his later years of filmmaking. Dwan may have been more committed to this Tradition because to his scientific mind it provided a sound structure and remained most alive with possibilities. Through the teens and twenties, Dwan was open to other kinds of technological and stylistic experimentation but none altered his basic style of filmmaking so that by the end of his career, some of his colleagues found him ponderously old-fashioned. But Dorr also arguably overemphasizes Dwan's sense of formal purity.

Even greater than his adherence to the Griffith Tradition was Dwan's commitment to functionalism. Myron Meisel has written, "The profundity of Dwan's style lies in its functional beauty; the exquisite calibrations of its analysis of the dramatic moment."[263] Part of the essence of his style was to reject any device that called attention to itself or was unduly expressionistic. Dwan did not shun Murnau's moving camera or restrict its use if it served a narrative purpose. Donald Phelps has pointed out that Dwan's "single takes are often filled with some of the most elaborate sustained tracking shots done by an American director aside from Cukor."[264] In a sense, Dwan was totally unaffected by the Murnau tradition because Dwan was using elaborate tracking shots before Murnau started making films.

Meisel has perceptively acknowledged, "Dwan's impassive, contemplative style is perhaps inherent in the gaze of the camera itself; for him the camera not only sees with his eye but thinks with his sensibility."[265] The films of Dwan's last years fully reveal this contemplative aspect of looking but while never shedding the mask of functionalism, one can detect a burgeoning self-consciousness. Dwan was not, as Dorr believes, "oblivious"[266] to the limitations of his players and studios but we will see he could also figure out how to engage them as well as fit them into the context of his style. The remarkable sense of order one sees in Dwan's films comes not from a blind commitment to the Griffith Tradition but an all-embracing playfulness that has already examined every aesthetic option.

The *Variety* review of *Jordan Is a Hard Road* observed, "A pretentious prologue showed the 'mob' walking around the road to Jordan wherein all men are finally judged, etc., but this portion had an indirect bearing on the theme proper, which was of perfect dramatic construction." Dwan may have cut back to this or similar allegorical scenes since the *Motography* review refers to the "unique and excellent allegories used in telling the story."[267] These sound like similar visionary scenes Griffith would insert in *Birth of a Nation* and *Intolerance*. Dwan would abandon such apparently heavy-handed editorializing in his later films. But he would learn to internalize his spiritual values and in later years, his films would sometimes exhibit a capricious mysticism that would manifest itself in various ways.

If Dwan could be said to have stood steadfast with the Griffith Tradition, he would also embellish it and take it into realms that Griffith could not have anticipated. Perhaps another indicator of the difference between Dwan and Griffith is that Dwan told Stuart Oderman that while he admired and worked with both Gish sisters, he considered Dorothy the better and more versatile actress.[268] For Griffith, of course, Lillian, the primal Victorian heroine, figured much more crucially as his star and muse. (It should be added that Dwan had far more interest and empathy for the cinema's "bad girls.") Unfortunately, none of the three films that Dwan directed with the Gish sisters are available today so it is not possible to explore this realm of difference between the two directors.

But there is another performer who would also divide Griffith and Dwan as to his merits. Griffith would have little use for him but with the assistance of Dwan and others, this actor would emerge as one of the cinema's greatest and most influential stars. As with much else that was significant in the rest of Dwan's silent film career, this development would begin in the cast.

3. The Age of Fairbanks

The hero has died as a modern man; but as eternal man—perfected, unspecific, universal man—he has been reborn. His second solemn task and deed therefore ... is to return then to us, transfigured, and to teach the lesson he has learned of life renewed.—Joseph Campbell, *The Hero with a Thousand Faces*

Fairbanks is a faun who has been to Sunday-school. He has a pagan body which yields instantly to any heathen or gypsy impulse—such as an impulse to balance a chair on its nose while hanging from the club chandelier by one of its knees—but he has a mind reliably furnished with a full set of morals and proprieties: he would be a sympathetic companion for anyone's aunt. I don't know his age; I think he hasn't any. Certainly he never will be older—unless quicksilver can get old.—Booth Tarkington, "Send us this word about Douglas Fairbanks," *The American Magazine*, July 1917

If while he was at Essanay, Allan Dwan had been reading the theatrical section of the *Chicago Tribune*, he might have seen a piece that appeared on May 1, 1910. It consisted of an interview with an actor only two years older than Dwan but far more experienced. The *Tribune*'s Percy Hammond observed,

> Mr. Douglas Fairbanks is a very young actor as actors go; but he seems to be animated by a strain of reason which is uncommon as far as we have seen and heard in actors of any age. This, at least, so far as concerns the public attitude toward the stage.... Mr. Fairbanks believes that of all the cant that finds its way into circulation in matters of the theater, none is more absurd than that which has to do with the duty of the public toward the stage and its players. Authors' cant about lack of encouragement; producing manager cant because audiences do not flock to see unknown plays; actors cant because their "creations" are not regarded by the public as attractive enough to offset the qualities of a bad play. The public owes no more toward the theater than toward grocery stores, canning factories or livery stables. The theater with theatergoers is a matter of what Faulconbridge calls "commodity" and nothing else; it has never been anything else and never will be...
>
> "Some of us," says Mr. Fairbanks—"authors, managers and actors—may be 'creative artists,' even in the best meaning of the phrase; but if so we are self-elected artists.... We impose ourselves on the public—a public that would be just as happy if we had elected to remain clerks, or salesmen, or typesetters or yacht owners, or even butchers."[1]

Fairbanks was at this time just emerging as a stage star and this kind of salvo may have been calculated to boost his public image. We hear in his words a kind of swagger as he assaults established pieties about the theatergoer's duties. In identifying the theater with terms like "commodity" and "commerce," he emphasizes the stage's free market context as Dwan would with the cinema in interviews in which the director touted himself as a businessman.

There is also a glimmer of the satirist as he knocks the pre-

Competitive athletes Douglas Fairbanks and Allan Dwan fought hard to keep up with each other, as seen in this 1917 photograph (courtesy Academy of Motion Picture Arts and Sciences).

tensions of theater folk. The very last play in which he would appear, would poke fun at theater life.

With apparent reluctance, Fairbanks also acknowledges the potential status of the practitioners of the stage as "artists." But by emphasizing the innate arrogance of actors who do not and should not have a safety net from failure, he is also depicting acting as a romantic and adventurous profession.

At the time of the *Tribune* article, Fairbanks had been a professional actor for about a decade. In 1907, he married Beth Sully, the oldest daughter of Daniel Sully, a tycoon known as the Cotton King. Due to pressure from his father-in-law, Fairbanks quit the theater and worked for a time as a salesman in Sully's Buchan Soap Company. But by August of 1908, he was back on the Broadway stage as the star of *All for a Girl*. Now having both his girl and his old career back, Fairbanks zestfully flashed his teeth throughout the play. The audience apparently found this engaging and Doug's producer advertised the "Fairbanks Smile" in the papers the following day. After the play folded, this trait would remain a fixture of Fairbanks' theatrical persona. In his subsequent plays, flamboyant physical action would become an increasing hallmark of his stagecraft.

By the age of twenty-nine, Fairbanks was becoming a well-known theatrical star. It was around this time that Fairbanks met Roy and Harry Aitken at the Algonquin Hotel when they were still involved with the Mutual Company. Although this blossomed into a friendship, Fairbanks was then unimpressed with motion pictures. He did agree to appear as a guest interviewee in a Mutual film released in December 1914 but harbored no larger interest in the medium. That same month, Fairbanks opened in the play *The Show Shop*. It would prove to be his last.

While *The Show Shop* ran on Broadway, Griffith's *Birth of a Nation* was released and Fairbanks was said to have been at its premiere. He was apparently impressed enough to re-think his prejudices about the movies.

The Aitkens signed Fairbanks at $2,000 a week for a trial period of ten weeks. They also agreed to the stipulation that Fairbanks would be personally supervised by Griffith, which apparently assured him that he would be appearing in quality productions. With that, Fairbanks headed out to California in the summer of 1915.

Fairbanks and Griffith did not hit it off well at the Fine Arts studio. The reasons for this lack of rapport have been the subject of some speculation among film historians. Fairbanks' behavior at this time apparently rubbed Griffith the wrong way. Alistair Cooke noted that during routine tests, "Fairbanks buoyantly vaulted tables and discommoded the crew...."[2]

This factor, however, probably played a secondary part in Griffith's attitude towards Fairbanks. At this time, the great director was engaged in the burgeoning project that would become *Intolerance* and was latching onto it with Ahab-like tenacity. It is unlikely that any upstart would distract him from this pursuit and certainly not one as far removed from his methods as Fairbanks.

Under his usual pseudonym of Granville Warwick, Griffith did agree to write the scenario for Fairbanks' first film, which would suggest that he did not write off Fairbanks completely. He also supervised the production, probably along the detached means described in the last chapter. The film was loosely based on Fairbanks' theatrical success *The New Henrietta* and went out under the title of *The Lamb*. One of Griffith's lieutenant directors, William Christy Cabanne, helmed the production.

The plot concerned Gerald, the wealthy son of a deceased "old War Horse." Gerald is an effete idler though it's suggested he has more daring aspirations. When his fiancée breaks away from him to follow a visitor from the West, the virile "Cactus-Fed Goat from Arizona," the disheartened Gerald takes up boxing and jiu-jitsu lessons. He then follows her and they meet on the Mojave Desert where Gerald proves himself fighting against an enemy of overwhelming odds.

After the film was completed and screened for the Aitkens, they were impressed. They put *The Lamb* on the opening Triangle bill and began negotiations with Fairbanks for a long-term contract.

The first program of the Triangle Film Company was presented on September 23, 1915, at the Knickerbocker Theater in New York City. *The Lamb* outshone the other two films on the bill, Ince's *The Iron Strain* and the Keystone entry *The Valet*, in the eyes of both the audience and the critics. "Unquestionably the honors of the evening went to the Griffith production *The*

Douglas Fairbanks flashing his signature "Fairbanks smile."

Lamb," pronounced *Moving Picture World*. "There were moments when the audience fairly rose with excitement, which is saying something for a 'mere motion picture.'"[3]

Seen today, *The Lamb* looks cruder than the Fairbanks films that followed. But Fairbanks' winning personality is clearly in evidence and, except for one brief scene of stagy histrionics, he seems to have fully adapted to the motion picture in a manner that eluded most of the stage actors of the time.

Fairbanks next appeared in *Double Trouble*, again under Cabanne's direction. He plays a character with split personalities, with one replacing the other during bouts of amnesia.

Well before that film was released and roughly around the time *The Lamb* opened, it was announced that Fairbanks had been signed to a three-year contract by Triangle. For Fairbanks' third film, a new director was selected to work with him, John Emerson. This was the same Emerson who had been the author of the play *The Conspiracy* and starred in Dwan's film version for Famous Players. Emerson not only shared a theatrical background with Fairbanks; they were friends and fellow members of the Lambs' Club in New York.

Emerson supposedly found suitable material for Fairbanks by rummaging through the file of scripts in the Fine Arts scenario department. They were the witty scenarios written by 22-year-old Anita Loos. Loos had been selling screenplays since her teens but while numerous films had been produced from her work, Griffith had not used one since the 1912 *The New York Hat*. John C. Tibbetts commented, "Her fate at his hands parallels that of her future partner, Douglas Fairbanks. Both found their forte in comedy. For her, it was the snappy, wisecracking kind of satire that could never fit in with Griffith's pastoral lyrics like *True Heart Susie*."[4]

Both Fairbanks and his wife Beth wanted a chance to return to New York and it was determined that this was a good time to initiate use of the Triangle East Coast facilities. The resulting film was *His Picture in the Papers*, which premiered on February 13, 1916. The film opens with the title, "Publicity at any price has become the predominant passion of the American people." The film then introduces us to a modern disciple of this philosophy, one Proteus Prindle, who produces Prindle's 27 Vegetarian Varieties which includes items like "Predigested Prunes" and "Desiccated Doughnuts."

Fairbanks plays his son Pete who, as in *The Lamb,* is something of an idler. However, he resolves to win his father's favor by showing that he can bolster publicity for the family product by getting his name in the newspapers.

Loos' satiric depictions became a mainstay of Fairbanks' films and she proceeded to write at least nine of them. Emerson, who became Fairbanks' second most frequent director, married Loos in 1919.

His Picture in the Papers was a major critical and box-office success and solidified Fairbanks' standing as a major star. He would later be better known for his swashbuckler adventure films of the 1920s, but it was these comedies that first earned him the affection of filmgoers. And Fairbanks would set a standard for movie heroes yet to come.

He was also very much a product of his time. Fairbanks' passion for exercise and love of the outdoors was a reflection of the ideals of President Theodore Roosevelt, who had run his last (unsuccessful) presidential campaign just four years earlier and followed it with an expedition into treacherous territory down the Amazon River. Fairbanks was one of Roosevelt's admirers and said of him, "He is the living incarnation of kinetic energy — of active force."[5]

But there was a broader social context in which Fairbanks' career can be understood, perhaps most trenchantly articulated in a chapter on Fairbanks in Gaylyn Studlar's book *This Mad Masquerade*. The early twentieth century had its equivalent of what would be called in the early twenty-first century a "boys' crisis." America was becoming increasingly an urban country and in the process, men were abandoning more physical work for "softer" and more impersonal jobs. Studlar notes,

> There was a new system of "command and obedience" for the middle class in contrast to the pre–Civil War situation when 88 percent of American men were farmers or self-employed businessmen. Middle-class men were expected to take up salaried employment in hierarchy-structured corporations and in sedentary white-collar jobs increasingly shared with women. Not only were women perceived as invading white-collar domains of work, but new corporate structures were perceived as undermining autonomy and individuality, qualities that had been important in defining masculinity.[6]

These social changes produced anxieties about the rearing of male children and fears of boys being brought up as "sissies." There was even concern about the effeminizing effects of religion; a book was published to maintain the right perspective, *The Virility of Christ*. Cults of the body ideal of physical development sprang up as well as back-to-wilderness movements. It was against this backdrop and to uphold these ideals that the Boy Scouts of America was founded.[7]

The movies were also becoming a part of the culture. As the flickers progressed into features and into the fringe of respectability, how did they fit into the equation? Adolph Zukor's Famous Players was in the vanguard of developing a film product for the middle class. In an ad that appeared in the June 5, 1915, *Saturday Evening Post* (shortly before Fairbanks began acting in his first film), portraits of twelve of the leading stars of the Famous Players Film Company were displayed. Of the twelve, ten were women. These included Mary Pickford, Elsie Janis, Marguerite Clark, Pauline Frederick, and Blanche Sweet. John Barrymore and the character actor George Fawcett were the only males included. (The men had a slightly better percentage in the text of the ad which referred to 16 stars, twelve of them female.)

In July 1916, the noted director Herbert Brenon announced that he was founding his own independent film company. An "innovation in this new company will be the lack of masculine stars. Mr. Brenon from his long experience in the work has come to the conclusion that the public wants women stars and he is going to fill the desire."[8]

Griffith's films contained virile action scenes such as large scale battles and the Ku Klux Klan ride to the rescue but the heroines were still his major protagonists.

There had been celluloid masculine heroes such as Broncho Billy Anderson, J. Warren Kerrigan, Wallace Reid and Francis X. Bushman. But none proved as developed as the Fairbanks persona. Watching Fairbanks' early films in succession, one has the sense of the idea of the hero being reconstructed for film. A large part of this constructivist sense derives from the fact that we literally see the hero created in these films as the protagonist undergoes a transformation.

This became a basic formula in the Fairbanks comedies. In his book, Studlar divides it into two variants. The first is simple enough, as in *The Lamb,* where a character who appears weak but has aspirations of manliness, is given an opportunity to develop and release the hero inside him. Studlar sees the second category as when a "Fairbanks character often starts out with vigorous, manly qualities, but must prove their appropriateness."[9] *His Picture in the Papers* is a manifestation of that aspect although this second variation could get much more complicated.

Interestingly, Fairbanks' chief rival for masculine heroics on the screen at the time was William S. Hart, many of whose films also depended on a transformation of character. Hart had been making Westerns since 1914 but gained prominence as a star in 1916 at Triangle, working for Ince's Kay-Bee Studios. His characters were often bad men who because of a chance encounter, usually with a good, upright woman, underwent a conversion. Religious values often played an important part in his stories. Hart's characters were hardened men of experience so it was appropriate for him to be an older man. This worked well for Hart who was pushing fifty when he began his film career in earnest.

In contrast, Fairbanks' films were about youthful exuberance. They depicted the transition to manhood and were full of speed and movement. As Tibbetts noted, "Fairbanks was forever in motion, like a clock."[10] And there was the rub. Fairbanks was already thirty-two years old when he began his film career playing juveniles. It has been pointed out in comparison that Rudolph Valentino was only 31 when he died. Fairbanks exercised regularly and kept trim and in shape, looking years younger than his real age. But how long could Fairbanks maintain his boyish guise and physical agility and how would this affect the aesthetic choices of his films over the years?

There was another temporal tension to Fairbanks' career and that was the question of what time period he represented. Was the Fairbanks hero a throwback to an earlier, more romantic age that masculine reformers wanted to recapture? Or did he represent the new modern man, especially in his mania for speed? Studler sees the Fairbanks hero as a reconciler between past and present. He saw him combining an old-fashioned boyhood with "the notion of the body as a machine, turbo-charged and built for the heightened, physically centered play activity that was the work of the man-to-be."[11] However, there would soon be disillusionment with the "man as machine" philosophy. By the time of the Depression, its dehumanization was ripe for parody by Fairbanks' good friend Chaplin in *Modern Times.* The reconciliation enacted by Fairbanks was purely poetic, that is as Robert Frost defined poetry, "a momentary stay against confusion."[12] Fairbanks started making films in a period of anxious social change with a world war on the horizon. This temporal paradox may have had an inherent appeal because audiences sensed that an era was coming to an end.

Having completed *His Picture in the Papers*, Emerson was now selected to direct Herbert Beerbohm Tree in *Macbeth.* With Emerson departing for California, still another director would be called upon for the next Fairbanks film to be shot in the east.

Allan Dwan would now have his chance to direct the Fairbanks phenomenon.

A Collaboration Begins

In an interview with Richard Koszarski, Dwan says that he did some work on *His Picture in the Papers.*[13] Regardless of whether or not Dwan's memory was accurate on this count, when he arrived in the east in late October 1915 to make *Betty of Graystone,* his unit and Emerson's were the only Fine Arts personnel working there. So it is likely that Dwan and Fairbanks got to know each other during this time (if they hadn't already met in California) and they must have found mutual interests. Booton Herndon has written, "Like Doug's image of Doug, Dwan was a college man and an athlete, the only difference being that Dwan's background was real."[14] Herndon was referring to stories Fairbanks told of having been accepted by Harvard but found in his research no record of such acceptance nor was such conceivable since Fairbanks had only one credited year of high school. As a balance to this reality check, it should be noted that Fairbanks had the kind of stage career that Dwan had fantasized for himself.

Herndon has not inaptly called Dwan "the director with whom he [Fairbanks] was most in tune and who had the most to offer."[15] This is also demonstrated by the fact that Fairbanks worked more frequently with Dwan than any other director. Dwan helmed ten of his films and on at least one other (*Headin' South*) served in a supervisory capacity.

But how great a role would a director play in the films of an actor who had achieved the superstar status of Fairbanks? Richard Schickel, citing as his source Fairbanks Jr., says that Doug's first two films were the only ones in which he was not the *de facto* boss of the production.[16] Fairbanks' power would only increase in the coming years when he would start his own production company and assemble a formidable staff of collaborators. Dwan, who had worked with both Fairbanks and Pickford and appreciated the deft capabilities of both, believed that "Doug's grasp of production was deeper than Mary's."[17] Dwan's influence therefore may have been greater in the period when Fairbanks was still learning the technical ropes.

Dwan appeared adroit in his method of directing Fairbanks, possibly because he recognized aspects of his own personality in Doug. "I was a bit like that myself ... a restless, athletic type. So I'd move *with* Doug—work with him and surround him with athletes."[18] Dwan also learned to cope with the other particulars of Fairbanks' personality. Herndon, who interviewed Dwan and other Fairbanks associates for his book, wrote, "Even with a friend as close as Dwan, Doug would soften any question on Dwan's direction by asking, 'Vous avez raison?' Dwan, who liked him and put up with him, would quickly give a reason. [Dwan and Fairbanks apparently didn't know or care that the actual translation of the query was 'Are your right?'] With other directors Doug might suddenly start playing tricks, start clowning or just take off. He would never face up to confrontation but he'd get his way just the same."[19]

Fairbanks Jr. recalled of Dwan, "I was a little bit frightened of him as a boy. I don't know why because I learned later there was nothing to be frightened of. But I was."[20] While Doug's son couldn't identify the reason, this does suggest that Dwan conveyed some sense of authority.

Fairbanks Jr. was himself puzzled by their working arrangement. Regarding his father's attitude towards Dwan, he said, "I knew my father was fond of him and had great respect for him. And I know that Dwan was very fond of working with my father. I never knew quite why, because my father tended to be the absolutely complete boss of his films, and he really didn't need directors. He told directors what to do.... And Allan's direction was quite strong in its own right. Of course, I wasn't around much when he was working with my father, but I often wondered how they managed."[21]

Herndon not surprisingly maintains that Fairbanks was the true auteur of his films and certainly his dynamic personality was buoyant with creative ideas. But Dwan also had an opportunity to convince Doug about directions in which he wanted to go. Indications are that they were often on the same page and were congenial collaborators. Even Herndon notes somewhat romantically of their first pairings, "[L]ike Doug, he [Dwan] admired the films of D.W. Griffith but found the man himself pompous. Two rebels, Dwan and Fairbanks made several films together, in Triangle's New York studio or on location in the West—anywhere so long as it was away from Griffith."[22]

The first film which Dwan directed with Fairbanks, *The Habit of Happiness,* was actually shot in Fort Lee and at the Riverdale studios. An important element in the story involved a group of derelicts. Future film star Adolphe Menjou, then an extra, recalled how they were realistically cast: "Dwan decided that rather than hire actors to pretend that they were Bowery bums, it would be simpler to go to the Bowery and hire the real thing. One morning he drove down to the flophouse, rounded up every man in the place, and ordered them all into the bus. At first these Bowery characters thought they were being pinched and they set up a terrible yammer protesting their innocence. But when they learned that they were to get five dollars for acting in a movie, they went along peaceably. The whole crowd was ferried across the river and delivered to Fort Lee, where a duplicate of the Bowery flophouse had been built."[23]

The plot concerns a cheery Fairbanks optimist named Sunny Wiggins, the scion of a family rapidly rising in wealth. Unlike his sister, who uses their riches to build social contacts, Sunny prefers to help the downtrodden.

While in many ways the Fairbanks character was already established with *The Lamb*, Emerson and Loos had added in *His Picture in the Papers* a background of amusingly satiric targets to serve as foils for Doug. A continuance of such scenarios would keep the films appearing trendy while the witty use of intertitles added another layer of humor to Fairbanks' talent for physical comedy.

When one looks at the first four films he made with Dwan, Fairbanks seems to be looking for new and alternative paths without completely abandoning the successful road map. It also says something about his confidence in Dwan that he was willing to take some chances over this stretch of moviemaking.

Contrasting *The Habit of Happiness* with Fairbanks' previous film, Tibbetts wrote, "If in *Picture* we encountered a generally breezy attitude toward strength, health, and vigor, in *Habit* we find a much more consolidated and directed attitude toward defining the good life and the means to obtain it. *Picture* was satirical—*Habit* was a sermon. It is a bit of Teddy Roosevelt, Horatio Alger and Billy Sunday."[24]

It should be pointed out that when Tibbetts refers to *The Habit of Happiness* as a sermon, he is not using it in the critical sense of Fairbanks being heavy-handed. Rather he is saying the film bore a similarity to the style of sermons then popularized by Billy Sunday. Yes, the same Billy Sunday who electrified the faithful and mesmerized Al Jennings in the tent set of *Jordan Is a High Road,* who in the days before radio spoke to over a hundred million people[25] and who was critiqued in Sinclair Lewis' 1927 novel *Elmer Gantry.*

Known as the "Baseball Evangelist," Sunday adroitly packaged his past professional baseball experience into his revivals. During his sermons, his activities included "not merely walking, but sliding, jumping, falling, staggering, whirling and throwing himself about the platform."[26] It is not surprising that he seized on the Rooseveltian theme of linking vigorous health to morality.

Both Fairbanks and Sunday have been termed gymnastic

evangelists. In a 1913 magazine article, well before he had begun his film career, Fairbanks stated, "Farce and satire are potent stage preachers. I have come to the conclusion that they are much more potent preachers than is the drama."[27]

Alistair Cooke wrote of Fairbanks, "He was a muscular itinerant preacher sailing gaily into the social novelties and the occupational neuroses of a new era dizzy with growing pains."[28]

The Habit of Happiness begins with Loos-like titling describing the Wiggenses as a "family of climbers, who have spent years in mounting to the point where they can be snubbed by the best people in town." Actually, the screenplay was written by Dwan and Shannon Fife.

The first shot we see of Sunny-Doug is a close-up of him enclosed in an iris as he awakens in his bed. The iris opens to show that Sunny is flanked by two middle-aged men with long beards. For a second, Sunny seems puzzled but then he flashes the famous Fairbanks smile and we know that Sunny has an innocuous and good-spirited rationale for all this. A title explains that he is putting his brotherhood of man philosophy into action by plucking men off a bread line. The next shot shows Sunny struggling to put on his slippers while surrounded by men scattered all over his room, sleeping on the floor. After feeding them, he sends off each of his newfound friends with some extra cash. He also finds that his sister Clarice does have one guest worth talking to, the charming Elsie (Dorothy West).

Sunny is called into his father's study where his father berates him for "not dropping anchor." Sunny counters that the family has ten times the money they need and he is taking the responsibility for returning some of it to people who haven't any. Sunny is no radical but, as Dwan has described him in interviews, he is a "philanthropist"— a concept that was beginning to take hold in the country where it was felt that the wealthy needed to give back something of what they had accumulated. As Sunny makes his plea, it is illustrated with a series of contrasting images of rich and poor, such as a shot of Clarice's parasitic friends at the dinner table juxtaposed with a shot of a poor family short on food. This was the kind of editing that Griffith had developed and Soviet filmmakers would adopt.

Adding to the discomfort of Wiggins *pere* may be another quality of Sunny, who was described by one critic as a "masculine counterpart, rendered inoffensive of Pollyanna."[29] Sunny, unlike the go-getter of the previous *Picture*, seems to have a much more nurturing side. Also, at its most idealistic, the Fairbanks hero of this film may have been in the vein of the more virile Jesus that was being championed at the time.

The senior Wiggins challenges Sunny, "Go down there and live for a while, without money, and you'll find out for yourself what a worthless lot they are." Without funds, Sunny must construct another philosophy to help them.

Sunny proceeds to "A Sargasso Sea of humanity where the derelicts of life are drawn to await Potter's field." Dwan's decision to use actual "Bowery actors" demonstrates that his instincts for "neo-realist" casting serve him well. The denizens of the flophouse, in both group shots and a close-up, convey a documentary gallery of human beings with bitter memories and no future prospects. It establishes a base of reality to Fairbanks' fanciful theatrics and gives palpable weight to the plea of one of the downtrodden pals to Sunny: "They need cheering up."

There is undeniably something infectiously uplifting in watching Fairbanks rouse these men out of despair and into torrents of laughter with his gospel of humor. Dwan and Fairbanks are also abetted here by the nature of the silent medium. We do not have to know how good the jokes are or how effective Sunny's pep talk reads and there are no titles to translate them. (According to Dwan, the jokes were pretty raw.)[30] All we have, without distraction, are the joyous communal images of Sunny interacting with the men. This later includes laughter (and of course, smiling) exercises.

Sunny is then given a higher calling, that is in terms of social standing. Sunny's success in rousing the spirits of the depressed derelicts has come to the attention of a doctor who is treating a wealthy patient suffering from dyspepsia and chronic depression. He has rebuffed the doctor's recommendation of diet and laughter with the retort, "I can't eat and I won't laugh." For finding a cure, the doctor offers Sunny good money, which he can use to help the derelicts.

Dwan's dynamic editing is instrumental in propelling his social comedy. Intercut with the lively scenes of the "exercising" derelicts is the first glimpse of the home presided over by the millionaire Jonathan Pepper. Sarcastically introduced in a title as the "House of Laughter," Pepper's household is glimpsed in a long shot fade-in that shows practically everyone inert from Pepper (George Fawcett) at the center, propped up in his chair, to the elderly cellist in the far background, slowly grinding out a funeral march. There are then tighter shots of a dour-looking butler and an even more grim-faced maid. The one bright spot in the house is the elusive Elsie, the girl Sunny had met as one of his sister's guests. She is Pepper's daughter.

Sunny's entrance is depicted by cutting from a static shot of Pepper seated next to his cellist to the image of a suitcase hurtling into the frame past the ducking butler. Entering Pepper's home with playful confidence, Sunny has a letter from the doctor introducing him as "Dr. Smile." But the enthusiastic and strenuous efforts of Sunny and the Fairbanks smile are met with the cold catatonic stare of Fawcett's Jonathan Pepper; he looks like the brainwashed soldiers in *The Manchurian Candidate* but with less cheer. The view of the glum and repressive Pepper household presages the screwball comedies of the 1930s where the restrictive atmosphere of the rich is liberated by some frenetic and chaotic activity. Fairbanks' apostle of optimism in this film could be the prototype of the populist hero who would emerge in Frank Capra's films. And of course, it is the rich man in *Habit* who proves much gloomier and less vulnerable to Sunny's charms than the suffering poor.

Sunny does manage to get the cellist to "rag" the *Miserere* and the resultant rhythms induce the butler and maid to dance and shortly thereafter depart for a honeymoon. While the static compositions now give way to dancing and even brawling, Pepper remains recalcitrant and Sunny decides to lock him in his room and starve him to submission.

Meanwhile, the senior Wiggins' new business partner, Foster (as in foster son?), is hatching a Wall Street scheme. He tells Sunny's father that if Pepper can be restricted to his house, they can make a million.

But Wiggins, perhaps from his own sense of ethics and friendship, phones Pepper to alert him that Foster is trying to ruin him and that he had better telephone his broker the next morning. Foster, who is visiting Pepper's house to court Elsie and perhaps to eavesdrop, overhears this and sends a group of roughnecks to Pepper's house the next day. By locking Pepper in his room in an effort to starve him, Sunny is unintentionally abetting Foster.

However, the fastidious Pepper, suddenly left completely without food, develops a desperate craving where all thoughts of business are forgotten. The next day when Sunny finally brings Pepper a tray of food, he tears at it greedily.

Foster's gangsters enter the house and are soon engaged in a fierce struggle with Sunny. Dwan can still mine the scene for humor by crosscutting to Pepper remaining oblivious to the situation as he continues to gorge himself. While the Fairbanks hero has been here proving his mettle by a totally different means than in the previous three films, he must still satisfy the audience expectation of using his athleticism to save the day.

Sunny manages to triumph with help from local toughs he had befriended. Sunny, however, has been wounded.

Pepper now bursts out of hiding, full of the life and the pep he has been missing. And watching the mayhem before him, he has finally found something to make him laugh. He calls his friend Wiggins and tells him to wipe Foster's stocks out; then goes off to see Wiggins, who has suffered some kind of collapse. He tells the doctor to take good care of Sunny, whom he intends to make his partner. Wiggins, of course, does not know that the man at Pepper's home is his son nor does Sunny know that Pepper's colleague is his father.

In his resistance to accept Sunny's philosophy, Pepper has functioned like a surrogate father to Sunny. In fact, Sunny's own father was first identified by a title noting, "Father had so little sense of humor that he wasted a lifetime in accumulating a fortune." So Pepper seems like a more extreme version of Dad. When Pepper visits Wiggins, he also reflects Wiggins' view that his son is worthless, not knowing that this is the same man he wants to make his partner.

Billy Sunday may have delivered baseball sermons but Fairbanks' filmic sermon (co-written and directed by Dwan) has something of baseball's structure, if not all its bases. Sunny's mission takes him first to one place (the poor) and then to a second (the rich man) but it all leads him back to home. The reinvigorated Pepper tells Wiggins, "I'm going to send a wonderful young man to doctor you. He cured my dyspepsia and saved my life." It might be even more accurate to say that this structure is geometric and how apt it was for Dwan to be working at a company called Triangle.

We do not have to wait for this fortuitous meeting to right things because Elsie phones Wiggins. The wounded Sunny does not open his eyes until he hears Elsie on the phone speaking to his father. Both father and son need recovering as the shots alternate between parallel images of Wiggins in his sickbed and Sunny supine on the couch. A single title covers their phone talk: "Waiting for the laugh man to come back." But we see in a subsequent shot an exultant Wiggins sharing his discovery with Pepper. In the final shot, Elsie kisses the wounded Sunny, who just manages to keep his eyes open. The *New York Times* critic complained that the film "ends suddenly as if the director had reached the end of his reel before the end of the story."[31]

Indeed, the story ends with the audience involved with its characters and wanting to know more. Sunny has inadvertently shown that his qualities also might make for a good businessman and that he can be the success that his father wanted. But how will his reform for the poor proceed? Displaying another of Dwan's symmetries, the film ends with Sunny literally opening his eyes to new possibilities just as we saw this dreamer doing in the beginning. The lines of interlocking relationships Dwan has drawn between his characters also carry us into more primal drama. *His Picture in the Papers* ends more cheerily but *The Habit of Happiness* concludes with more emotional resonance.

Into the West: *The Good Bad Man*

Dwan worked briskly (reflecting Fairbanks' own tempo) and efficiently. The budget of *The Habit of Happiness* was lower than that of any of the previous three Fairbanks movies though admittedly none of them cost very much.

Fairbanks' next project was a Western that would eventually be titled *The Good Bad Man*. This was, in fact, the moniker often given to Fairbanks' chief rival as the movie hero of his era, William S. Hart. In February 1916, *Moving Picture World* was already complaining of Hart's repetitious plot of the "western badman reformed through the sweet and humanizing influence of a pure-minded girl."[32] Yet that same plot was appropriated by Fairbanks with his own peculiar nuances. The heroine of Fairbanks' picture was Bessie Love, who had also been the leading lady in the recently completed Hart film *The Aryan*.

Why would Fairbanks and Dwan choose to go in this direction? Early in his film career, Fairbanks acknowledged, "I prefer the screen to the stage because of the unlimited space which really makes possible my attempts at athletic stunts."[33] The Western, of course, thrived on "wide open spaces" and was an innately American genre that suited Fairbanks' image.

Hart, bolstered by the financial resources of Triangle and quality productions, had elevated the status of the Western to weighty action dramas. There was a chance for greater gravitas to Fairbanks' screen persona here if he wished to pursue it.

Of course, *The Lamb*, Fairbanks' first film, was a sort of Western. Gerald completed his transformation to hero in the West with a little help from the cavalry in vanquishing the savage foes. There would be other Fairbanks films playing on the East-West dialectic to follow.

Fairbanks' idol Theodore Roosevelt was then the living embodiment of the East-West paradigm. Born with a sickly body, he strove in his youth to overcome his weaknesses with strenuous physical exercise, and like Fairbanks' protagonist in *The Lamb,* took boxing lessons. On February 14, 1884, both Roosevelt's mother and first wife Alice died. That autumn, Roosevelt quit his post as a New York assemblyman and set out to put his grief behind him by heading out West to his ranch in the Badlands of Dakota. Spending two years there, he became skilled at roping and riding and for a time served as a lawman, on one occasion apprehending outlaws and taking them back on a long trek to justice.

In the new industrial America with its teeming cities and perceived threats to traditional values and masculine ideals, the West appeared as an antidote. The West was seen as a testing ground that would develop manhood and build character as the easterner would have to submit to its challenges. Roosevelt, of course, was among the advocates of this "wilderness cult" as was the artist Frederic Remington and the novelist Owen Wister, whose novel *The Virginian* was allegedly inspired by Roosevelt's experience.

Fairbanks himself was a Westerner, having been born in Denver, Colorado, in 1883. By the time of Fairbanks' boyhood in Denver, the Wild West era was fading. But there was another aspect to his origins that might not meet the Western ideal.

John Fairbanks, the first husband of Doug's mother Ella, is said to have died of tuberculosis in 1873, the same year that she gave birth to her first son, also named John. When a business partner absconded with the senior Fairbanks' considerable fortune, Ella was forced to leave her home in New Orleans and move in with her sister in Georgia. With a son to support, Ella there married one Edward Wilcox, who proved to be an abusive alcoholic. She sought the aid of a New York lawyer, Hezekiah Charles Ulman, who had tried unsuccessfully to recover the funds of her first husband. After Ulman helped get her a divorce, the married lawyer became romantically involved with Ella.

With young John in tow, Ulman and Ella went off to Denver in 1880. Two sons were born to Ella during this time, Robert and then Douglas a year later. Ulman ceased the practice of law in favor of several mining ventures, none of which proved to be successful. Ulman, like Ella's last husband, took to drinking heavily and in 1888 left his family, supposedly to work as a campaign speaker for Benjamin Harrison's presidential campaign. He had, in effect, abandoned them.

Ella took up the task of raising her three sons alone. Although Doug was christened Douglas Elton Ulman, Ella had both him and Robert take the name of her first husband, Fairbanks. While at first resistant, Ella also did what she could to help Doug's aspirations for the New York stage. Fairbanks' Western biography was closer to Edna Ferber than to Owen Wister.

There is certainly much that is admirable in the courage displayed by Roosevelt in his journey to the West. However, Roosevelt could return to other matters when his sojourn in the West was over. But a different kind of courage was required for the much larger numbers of men who tried to eke out a living in the West and support their families. The many opportunities promised were balanced by an even greater potential for failure. Charles Ulman could not cope with his and this would leave its mark on Douglas Fairbanks.

Fairbanks' Westerns, as with most others, did not deal with the everyday, mundane challenges of the West. But in *The Good Bad Man*, Fairbanks incorporated an unusual premise for a Western, a young man seeking the identity of his father. We know this was his contribution because for the first time Fairbanks is credited with the script to one of his films. Herndon observed, "It is a romantic fable, almost embarrassing when compared with the life of its author and star...."[34]

Actually, Fairbanks had already shown his character's concern with paternity in his very first film. Near the end of *The Lamb*, after Gerald has proved himself and is about to be married, there is a lingering scene of Gerald looking at the portrait of his father, the "old War Horse." He may be contemplating whether he has lived up to his father's expectations. In *His Picture in the Papers*, Pete Prindle is trying to impress his father by getting his name and the family product in the newspapers but their relationship seemed only a means to an end of Doug proving his mettle and getting his girl. With Dwan in *The Habit of Happiness* the relationship between father and son cuts more deeply. Dwan's first film for Triangle, *Jordan Is a Hard Road*, was the story of a young woman whose father cannot reveal his identity to her. The theme of the "lost father" would appear in Dwan films for many years. Fairbanks may have realized that he and Dwan both had an affinity for this subject and that may have encouraged him to develop it into a screenplay. Although Fairbanks would work on future scripts, he would use a pseudonym when it included him and his collaborators. This was one of the few he did solo.

Dwan had encouraged the creative contributions of his players and it should be remembered that Lon Chaney wrote his first screenplay when working for Dwan. Early in his career, Wallace Reid also wrote stories for the director. However, Fairbanks' effort was probably not in the form of a fully written screenplay. Nearly all of Fairbanks inspirational books and other writings appear to have been ghost written. When he did apply himself to writing, he rarely produced anything of any kind of length, usually less than one page.

As witnesses had seen Doug do with Dwan on other films,

he most likely pitched most of his ideas orally. Director and star probably discussed their mutual thematic interest without ever touching on their respective traumatic sources. As Herndon wrote of Fairbanks, he "obviously concealed his inner feelings well." But their chats around such sensitive areas may have helped establish a bond of trust between Fairbanks and Dwan.

According to one story in the papers, Fairbanks decided on casting Bessie Love as his *Good Bad Man* leading lady while watching the shooting of *The Aryan*. The Hart people at first refused to release her to Fairbanks but after he wrote a scenario in which only she could play the part written, the Hart people relented. This obvious bit of press gimmickry performs the double duty of romanticizing both the selection of the leading lady and the inspiration that moved Fairbanks to write.[35]

Love was given a less romantic explanation. "Very soon I was chosen as Douglas Fairbanks' leading lady in *The Good Bad Man*.... I wanted to jump over the moon and was rushing off to tell him so when my informant said, 'Thank Mrs. Fairbanks. She's the one who chose you.'"[36]

To make *The Good Bad Man,* Fairbanks and Dwan returned to California. According to trade paper accounts, at least part of the film was shot in the Mojave Desert.

Fairbanks still had much to learn about production and Dwan and his cameraman Victor Fleming provided him with a technical education in shooting *The Good Bad Man*. Using nothing but the camera and a piece of black paper, Dwan and Fleming gave Fairbanks a lesson in matte photography, a process that has grown much more complicated. By blocking out different parts of the frame and then combining the unhidden parts of each shot, Dwan was able to combine a shot of Fairbanks on his horse jumping over flat land with a shot of a ravine so that it appeared the horse was jumping over the ravine.[37]

Love also remembered lighter moments during the making of the film. "When Vic and Mr. Fairbanks were traveling on the Sante Fe Express one time, they had a bet to see which of them could go from their compartment and drawing-room to the dining-car without touching the floor. So they 'walked' through the coaches, hanging on to anything overhead and clinging to the seats which faced each other."[38] Practical jokes and offbeat games were habitual sports for Fairbanks. Dwan also recalled participating in such pranks.

The surviving print of *The Good Bad Man* (now in the Library of Congress) is from an edited re-release of the film. The observations below are based on a viewing of that print. It starts out wistfully with two old cowboys sitting by a campfire swapping stories about a mysterious figure. When one of them starts talking, we see an insert of a newspaper page with the headline "'Passin' Through' Heard from Again. Sticks Up Pacific Express — Takes No Loot." The newspaper story explains that the lone bandit known only as "Passin' Through" held up a train but the robber chose to take only the conductor's ticket puncher.

The other old cowboy tells how he was present when Passin' Through stuck up a saloon and forced its occupants to put all their watches on a table. There is then a cut to the actual scene with a shot of Fairbanks as Passin' Through telling the men, "Now grab for your watches! Any man who gets the wrong one pays me five dollars." Some do indeed have to pay him and then Passin' Through rides off amid gunfire. It is then explained by the storyteller that Passin' Through gave the money to a woman whose child had no father. Another story follows of a robber who gave his booty to an orphan. The storytelling exchange ends with the observation, "Yeah, he's an odd one — always helping kids born in shame."

This bit of narrative hijinks and distancing creates a playful tone for the film. It supplies a good deal of exposition while establishing the protagonist as a legendary figure. It also not only minimizes the extent of his outlaw deeds but it shows them as a kind of humorous, childlike behavior. As many sources including Love indicate, Fairbanks was known for his fondness for playing pranks and getting adults to engage in games. This is his boyish prankster mania with a slight sting to it as Passin' Through gives all his plunder to children born out of wedlock. These opening ramblings and flashbacks also contrast with the more somber flashbacks to follow in the film.

We get our first good look at Fairbanks as Passin' Through when he approaches a frontier settlement near Maverick City. Love plays Amy, the daughter of the sick man who takes him in. Amy is being menaced by a character known (appropriately) as the Wolf. Passin' Through puts a scare into the Wolf by throwing a playing card up in the air and shooting a hole in the middle of it. (This recalls the story Dwan told of discouraging the Patents gunman by scoring a direct hit on a tin can.)

Not surprisingly, Amy and Passin' Through develop a relationship and the bandit begins to confide to her the details of his strange outlaw life, e.g., how he stole firecrackers from a Chinese man. Passin' Through shows her some of the items he stole in a bit of childish play. But when Amy asks why he makes these curious thefts, Passin' Through becomes serious.

"I like to keep two jumps ahead of the law. It helps me to forget. To forget there's no decent way I can make a livin' 'cause I had no father." This Freudian assertion may have sounded questionable, especially in 1916, but Passin' Through's behavior shows how he has been affected by his lack of a father. When Amy asks about his mother, this prompts a flashback from Passin' Through. We see an iconic close-up of a woman in fear ... his mother. She is surrounded by a black background and slowly turns her head to look back in trepidation. She bites her lip, closes her eyes, and then we see something she has written. It tells her son to give her enclosed letter to a man named Bob Evans. The letter states,

> Dear Bob,
> I haven't told my son about his father. I'm afraid he might kill Frazer. But if Frazer would die, please tell my son the whole story.

Fairbanks shows his high spirits in front of his cast, holding his revolvers in the air during production of *The Good Bad Man* (1916). Dwan in helmet and holding megaphone is at his left. The leading lady, Bessie Love, stands between them (courtesy Kevin Brownlow).

Passin' Through rejoins that if he ever meets Frazer, "I'll kill him with my bare hands!"

Passin' Through's image of his fearful mother is no doubt as strongly emblazoned in his memory as the letter. The implication is clear that Passin' Through suspects that Frazer is his father in a combined quest for identity and vengeance. This is also a case where there is a clear thematic reason why the protagonist is known only by a sobriquet. It also follows that Passin' Through considers himself unworthy of his beloved.

The film's passage in tone from the comic to dark drama is effectively and convincingly made. While the opening flashbacks distance us from the narrative and frame it with a touch of whimsy, the later flashbacks carry us into deeply personal territory, shrouded in nightmarish black imagery. Even Griffith's pioneering applications of cinematic psychology may not have proceeded as far.

Passin' Through arrives in Maverick City where he encounters Bob Evans, who is a U.S. marshal. He gives Evans the letter and the marshal recounts to Passin' Through what appears on the screen in flashback. In a saloon, a man in a black suit approaches his mother and she protests, "I'm not that kind, Bud Frazer, and you know it." A man then enters to whisk his mother away from Frazer and propose marriage. They are married and Passin' Through is born. But shortly after Passin' Through's birth, his father is fatally shot in the back by Frazer. The process of creating an enigma with a flashback and then resolving it with a later one was a technique later used memorably in Sergio Leone Westerns but with greater elaboration and lyricism.

Passin' Through acknowledges that he had thought that Frazer was his father but still wants to help look for him. Then Evans, the former friend of his mother, assumes the responsibility of not arresting Passin' Through if he promises to reform. So Passin' Through has learned his real father's identity while gaining a surrogate father. He rides back to Amy and blithely announces, "I've come to tell you. I just found out I had a regular father! I'm all through being an outlaw." But then the Wolf's gang attacks and Passin' Through has to shoot his way out. Amy is kidnapped and held by the Wolf, who wants her to marry him.

Passin' Through goes to Wolf's cabin and, finding a picture of his mother and a letter from her, realizes that the Wolf is Fraser. In the actions that ensue, Fraser is killed by Evans and Passin' Through flees with Amy, pursued by the Wolf's gang. A posse follows them and in the chase and gunfights across the desert, all is righted. The wild melodramatic action across wide open spaces in scenic long shots seems liberating after Fairbanks' hero has been freed from the bondage of his identity nightmare. Passin' Through sets out to start a new life with Amy. A title in which she asks Passin' Through his name is mischievously followed by the last shot of them riding away from the camera.

The Good Bad Man deftly interweaves Fairbanks' frolicsome image with a more somber drama. Certainly, one cannot describe him as a comedian in this film. Passin' Through's childlike demeanor permits him to make uninhibited and direct remarks about the sources of his maladjustments without sounding pretentious. The humor notwithstanding, the film remains an early psychological Western.

The critics acknowledged the film as a leap forward for Fairbanks. The *New York Dramatic Mirror* noted, "*The Good Bad Man* has the charm of being unique; we cannot remember ever having seen a photoplay just exactly like it. Furthermore, it has the added charm of introducing Douglas Fairbanks in a brand new screen role, that of a typical Westerner of the old days.... We had supposed that Douglas Fairbanks would be satisfied with his well-earned laurels as a first class screen comedian, but lo and behold, he must now set out and endeavor to take those of William S. Hart and Frank Keenan."[39]

Motion Picture News said, "Allan Dwan's direction is first rate, and is nowhere more successful than in his capturing of wide sweeps of Western mountain and plain scenery as backgrounds for fights, furious riding, and other thrills."[40]

Moving Picture World also praised *The Good Bad Man* for its originality but couldn't resist citing the Roosevelt connection. Louis Reeves Harrison wrote, "Mr. Fairbanks is very intense, and he is almost as strenuous as Ex-President Teddy."[41] *Wid's* pronounced it as "absolutely sure-fire with any kind of an audience."[42]

The Good Bad Man was the opening attraction at the new Rialto Theater in New York City. At the Los Angeles premiere, Bessie Love appeared in person to sing "The Rosary." Her musical talents revived her flagging career during the sound revolution when she appeared in the 1929 *Broadway Melody*.

Fairbanks' own father had died in 1915, the year before *The Good Bad Man* was made. His widow had intended to apply publicly for a pension because of his Civil War service. Fairbanks provided her with a private pension so there would be no publicity.[43]

Fairbanks Without the Smile

Before they made their next film, Fairbanks and Dwan briefly worked separately at Triangle. Fairbanks returned to Christy Cabanne, who had directed his first two films. In *Reggie Mixes In*, Fairbanks plays a rich and spoiled college kid who falls in love with Agnes (Bessie Love again). When he learns that Agnes is forced by circumstances to work as a dancer in a cabaret, Reggie becomes the establishment's bouncer and runs afoul of the neighborhood gangsters. The film is engaging but also coarsens the impressions of *The Habit of Happiness* and could be titled *Doug Goes Slumming, Part II*.

Fairbanks and Dwan were now back with Griffith at the Fine Arts studio in Los Angeles. Both were surely riding high. Fairbanks had vanquished whatever doubts Griffith may have had about his potential as a star. As for Dwan, his status is reflected in Love's recollection that at Fine Arts, "[s]ome star directors, like Allan Dwan, were allotted their own units, with a stage used exclusively for their sets and their own studio carpenters, paper-hangers — the works."[44]

Dwan recalled an incident when he and Fairbanks were discussing a future film in front of their bungalow. Dwan was illustrating something by scratching in the sand when both men looked up and saw a large lion hovering over them. Not knowing what to do, both men froze. "And suddenly along came Griffith. He walked up, took the lion by the mane, and said, 'Come, little pussycat,' and he walked away with it. He had done that as a gag — but we never sat on those steps again!"[45] The ostensibly staid Griffith showed that he could hold his own against these two modern pranksters and "rebels."

The big cat was most likely appropriated from the *Intolerance* set. Dwan got an inkling of the theme of that film from a more businesslike encounter with Griffith. Dwan had made a film that he wanted to open with an inscription from a poem, something that was in vogue at the time and which Dwan confessed he loved to do. As Dwan recalled, the final line of the poem had to do with "tolerance of opinion and speech," which Dwan remembered as the basis of his story. Griffith asked Dwan not to use the poem because he was going to call his film *Intolerance*. Dwan complied, "And that's how I knew he was going to make a thing and it was going to be called *Intolerance*."[46]

The most interesting aspect of Dwan's account is that it suggests the extent to which Griffith and Dwan were on parallel tracks. This should not have been entirely surprising since Dwan's next film *An Innocent Magdalene* was based on a story by Griffith and starred Griffith's favorite actress, Lillian Gish.

The plot features a number of elements that sound Griffith-like. Gish plays Dorothy Raleigh, the daughter of an aristocratic and "unreconstructed" Southerner. Dorothy falls in love with a Northern gambler. Though her father dismisses him as "white trash," they marry and he promises to be an idler no longer. After Dorothy's father disowns her, her husband is arrested for his past gambling activities and sentenced to a year in prison.

Appearing to be abandoned, Dorothy discovers she is pregnant. Adding to her tribulations, a woman appears who claims to be the gambler's wife. Ostracized by small-town society, Dorothy goes to her old black mammy's cabin and bears her child. Dorothy, driven by a guilt urged on her by others, believes her child to be illegitimate and that she is a "Magdalene." Dorothy contemplates suicide by jumping over a cliff (like Mae Marsh in *Birth of a Nation*). But her husband returns in time to save her. He also reveals that the other woman claiming to be his wife is an imposter. All is made right and the father finally gives his blessings.

But there were also aspects of *An Innocent Magdalene* that related more directly to Dwan. The film bears some resemblance to *Betty of Graystone*. Gamblers would play a continuous role in Dwan movies, especially in his later films. In this one, the gambler was played by Sam De Grasse, who had played the Wolf in *The Good Bad Man*. He was Fairbanks' suspected father in that one and Dwan's "lost-father" figure here.

The church is of no help to Dorothy; the review in *Wid's* observes, "Gossiping neighbors and a well meaning minister make life unbearable for her...."[47]

Dwan's films often take the viewpoint of outcasts and the manner in which Dorothy (ostracized by "decent society") finds refuge and acceptance only with black people raises interesting dramatic possibilities. How well Dwan rose above the maudlin elements can only be speculated upon unless a print of this film suddenly turns up. Gish's biographer Charles Affron says the actress rarely spoke of the films she made at Fine Arts without Griffith's direction. The trade reviews were quite favorable for this film.[48] *An Innocent Magdalene*, like many of Fine Arts' dramatic offerings, did not fare well at the box office.

Beyond their use in *An Innocent Magdalene,* the strands of characterizations of the "lost father," gamblers, outcasts and the unhelpful minister against a background of bigotry and intolerance are all elements that Dwan called upon in his next film with Fairbanks, carrying them beyond (or at least in different directions than) anything Griffith had done.

In the meantime, Fairbanks was being kept busy in two projects, including, oddly enough for a star of his stature, a two-reel film. Fine Arts explained that to fill the demand for two-reel films to run with features, even big stars had to be used.[49] The Fairbanks short was called *The Mystery of the Leaping Fish*, a piece of slapstick surrealism crudely put together under the direction of Emerson. Fairbanks starred as Coke Ennyday, a parody of Sherlock Holmes who is seen constantly injecting himself and his adversaries with a syringe, producing instantaneous paroxysms of hopped-up pleasure. A cult movie for silent film fans today, its modest charms are bound with its artlessness with Fairbanks hamming it up as if he was in some kind of vanity production. Fairbanks continued to do comedy in Cabanne's feature *Flirting with Fate*, a dark farce where Fairbanks spends much of the film fleeing in terror from imagined assassins.

While Fairbanks was working on *The Mystery of the Leaping Fish*, Dwan was sent on an auto trip through central California to select locations for his next Fairbanks film. *The Half-Breed.* Based on Bret Harte's *In the Carquinez Woods*, it would be shot in the Sequoia National Park, Yosemite Valley near Santa Cruz and the surrounding area.

Race, of course, was an incendiary issue. It was a mere year after Griffith's *Birth of a Nation* and the controversies it aroused in the depiction of the Civil War and Reconstruction. Griffith had tried in his way to show that his racial portrait was balanced by depicting two black servants who remained loyal to their white masters. But there was not even an attempt to provide a balance on the presentation of mulattos; both mulatto characters in the story are ruthless and vilely ambitious.

The portrayal of those with mixed Indian and white blood was not much better. Film historian Kevin Brownlow noted that although there had been movies that treated Indians sympathetically at the time, the half-breed was "fair game as villain in anyone's picture. In Ben Wilson's *One-Eighth Apache* (1922), written by Peter Kyne, it was enough for the heroine to discover in her husband the merest hint of Indian blood to cause her nervous collapse. While prominent Americans boasted of their Indian blood, the half-breed was portrayed as a menace to society.... He did not appear in a sympathetic light until 1916 when Douglas Fairbanks played *The Half-Breed* under Allan Dwan's direction."[50]

For Dwan, this was an opportunity to do a film about outcasts based on the work of an author whom he would long admire. As for Fairbanks, a news blurb noted, "Douglas Fairbanks, who has always hankered after heavy-roles, and who made a success in the first feature of this class, *The Good Bad Man*, is rejoicing that he is to enact another role of this character in Bret Harte's *In the Carquinez Woods*."[51] It was another opportunity to boost his stature as an actor and to show he was not dependent on the Fairbanks smile.

Fairbanks' role in *The Half-Breed* would be his most dour. But if that was out of character for his screen persona, it was not alien to his character for all his protestations of boundless optimism. Dwan remembered, "Doug could be serious, moody, sensitive as any woman. Every now and then I'd see signs of depression coming on, something inside gnawing at him. All of a sudden he'd just disappear, take his anguish and hole up with it. He hid his black moods well. I doubt if a handful of people ever noticed it."[52]

This film, like Fairbanks' previous one with Dwan, dealt with a protagonist who does not know the identity of his father. But there may have been other aspects of his background that may have linked him to the character. Herndon notes that Fairbanks from infancy was unusually dark-skinned and that years later, he would joke about that. Fairbanks was once quoted as saying, "I was so dark even my mother was ashamed of me. When all the neighbors came around to look at the new baby, Mother would say, 'Oh, I don't want to disturb him now — he's asleep and I'd rather not.'"[53]

Fairbanks may have inherited his dark looks from his father Charles Ulman, who was Jewish. Douglas was raised in his mother's Catholic faith and did not think of himself as Jewish. In fact, he remained secretive about this part of his heritage all his life. The prejudices common in his era were surely a factor in that.

When his first wife Beth asked him a question that prompted him to reveal his father and his origins, she said that "from his tone of voice and the expression on his face she had thought he was going to confess that he had robbed a bank."[54] Aside from his own innate reticence, Fairbanks might have sensed that a woman of his wife's prominent background would gravitate to snobbery. This seemed to be confirmed by her aversion to the cowboys and Indians who became Doug's companions in California. "When Douglas Jr. came home from the lot with stories of being picked up by Eagle Eye, the studio Indian, she rushed him to the bathtub."[55]

This also parallels Dwan's story of encountering Beth's objection to her husband making *The Half-Breed.* Dwan says she told him, "Why, a half-breed's such a dirty, filthy character and so greasy — I just don't see Doug running around that way."[56] For his solution, Dwan said he inserted a scene early in *The Half-Breed* of Fairbanks' character diving into a river and then coming out almost completely naked and drying himself. That seemed to satisfy Mrs. Fairbanks but a bemused Dwan surely grasped that more was involved than an intense concern with hygiene. (Interestingly, after Fairbanks' character dresses himself he throws a rock at a man who has called him a "filthy half-breed.")

The Triangle Film Corporation had another hero demonstrating a strong point of view about half-breeds. The films of William S. Hart with their hero's moral turnabouts had developed a religious fervor. In Hart's *The Aryan*, a strongly racist ideology is also seen emerging. Andrew Brodie Smith has pointed out, "Racism was not new to the western but it had never been articulated in such a sophisticated fashion."[57] In the story, Hart's protagonist Steve Denton, betrayed by his lover and disillusioned, turns to a life of crime in a town called Devil's Hole. He leads a gang of vicious outlaws, the "Scum of hell" as one review cited, who are mostly half-breeds, Indians and Mexicans.[58] Sporting a sombrero, a serape, and an Indian belt, Denton even begins to dress like a mixed blood.

After an outdoor bath, Fairbanks' title character in *The Half-Breed* (1916), Lo Dorman, shows off his physique while paying tribute to his natural surroundings (courtesy Museum of the Moving Image, Photograph Number 1996.017.0476).

When a wagon train is lost in the desert, members of the party suffering from thirst come to Steve's town. Steve refuses to help. The presence of women in the party only inflames his misogynistic bitterness. He is ready to leave them at the mercy of his non-white cutthroats but one woman refuses to give up.

The film's centerpiece is the encounter between Steve and this woman, Mary Jane (Bessie Love). According to Triangle's original synopsis (appropriately described as "The Story of a White Human Heart Turned Black"), Mary Jane refuses to believe his indifference because "He is a white man, she can see that although he lives among half-breeds and Indians, and she knows he will run true to the creed of his race — to protect its women."[59] At the crucial moment, Steve realizes he must act and so he saves the white women from his followers and then guides the party out of the desert.

This was the period when Pancho Villa's raids across the border and his pursuit by American troops helped to entrench Mexicans in popular fiction as stereotyped villains. As Diane Koszarski points out, Hart was particularly emphatic about the use of Mexican bad men and women.[60] Smith notes the similarity of *The Aryan* to *Birth of a Nation*. Hart's Denton, like the Radical Republican leader in *Birth*, betrays his race by taking on a following of half-breeds and other non-whites with mixed blood, a clear sign of degeneracy.[61]

Fairbanks and Dwan were most likely familiar with *The Aryan*, especially as its leading lady was picked to star in *The Good Bad Man*. In that film, Fairbanks and Dwan had appropriated the Hart persona and reconstructed it in Doug's image. There is no direct evidence that *The Half-Breed* was intended as a reply to *The Aryan*. But given that in his first period Western, Fairbanks had vaguely emulated Hart, it is a distinct possibility that *The Half-Breed* was intended to mark a contrast between the two heroes.

Location shooting was an important element of *The Half-Breed*. Dwan and his company traveled over four hundred miles by automobiles from Los Angeles to Calveras County. For the last leg of the journey in the Sequoia Park district, they traveled by mountain burros since the roads were too narrow to accompany autos.

An important decision made in adapting Harte's book was that the film would not be as largely dominated by its location in the Carquinez woods, no matter how magisterial that site may be. There is much more of a view of the town life in the film version and it was likely important to Dwan to establish the contrast of the two locales.

The film establishes the political and social context of the story in its opening titles: "In the early pioneering days in California, a majority of the settlers considered the Indians uncivilized and inferior." After showing a squaw and her papoose, the titles continued, "However, this did not stop some of them from taking advantages of the natives as Silver Fawn discovered to her sorrow."

It is the early imagery of the film that establishes the power of Nature, its beauty and terror. There is a great scenic long shot of a river with no human in sight but then we see a figure who appears to be climbing a hill in the foreground.

This is Silver Fawn, the Indian mother. She is going to see John Bowers, a white man and "a self-made scholar who knows enough about Indians to respect them and make friends with them." Silver Fawn tells Bowers that she has seen the baby's white father, who rejected the child. She entrusts the crying infant to Bowers, then walks away as Bowers calls out to her. Silver Fawn is next seen in extreme long shot, raising her arms at the edge of a precipice. She disappears over the cliff.

It was at that time an established fictional convention that any interracial love affair must end tragically. It was usually the woman who bore the brunt of this and suicide was often her dramatic exit. One of the most famous vehicles for this theme of the day was the play *The Squaw Man*, which was translated into a film directed by Cecil B. DeMille in 1914. Realizing that she is only an impediment to her son being raised as a civilized "white" man, the film ends with her committing suicide, with her husband's white romantic interest conveniently standing in the wings. *The Half-Breed* begins at this usual departure point, delving into what happens to the child of mixed blood.

The movie flashes forward to the child having grown to manhood under Bowers' tutelage and known by the name Lo Dorman. When Bowers dies, Lo is told by white men that as an Indian he has no rights to Bowers' property and should be glad that they have no proof that he killed the old man.

There is a cut to the town of Excelsior and to its "center of social and political life."

We then see a saloon and gambling house. But there are some provocative images for a film of that era. We see a black man in a stovepipe hat dealing cards to white men at the table. In the next shot we see whites and Chinese playing cards together. The characters seem to get along without any problem. The minister, Pastor Winslow Wynn, enters the saloon. He seems convivial and takes a drink at the bar while urging the saloon patrons to come to his church. But when someone collecting money for Yuba Bill's widow comes to the minister explaining she's sick with lung trouble, the minister demurs. "My dear brother," Wynn explains, "she was not a member of my congregation."

From this and the minister's somewhat pompous manner, we are led to see him as a hypocrite. A minister is also seen to be a hypocrite in William S. Hart's *Hell's Hinges*, released just a few months earlier. But in the latter film the young minister's downfall to temptation was sealed when he started congregating with the unsavory elements of the saloon and dance hall. Won over by the minister's more dedicated and inspiring sister, Hart's "good bad man" defends the church against the miscreants who want to burn it down. Hart's reformed character ultimately traps the prostitutes, gamblers and dance hall girls in the saloon and, in a Sodom–Gomorrah like finale, shoots out the oil lamps and precipitates a conflagration that sweeps through the whole town. In *The Half-Breed*, the gamblers and "disreputable" ladies seem more generous and humane than the minister.

The other *dramatis personae* in the story are pointedly revealed. A title introduces us to Sheriff Dunne as the betrayer of Lo Dorman's mother and thus his father. Dunne is mustached and wears a black hat and his character is consistent with these symbols of Western storytelling. The audience is thus clued in very early to the identity of Lo's paternity, something that none of the other characters share and a free-floating irony that hovers over them. And yes, Dunne is played by Sam De Grasse, the "Wolf" of *The Good Bad Man.*

Pastor Wynn's daughter, Nellie the "unapproachable," is first seen piecemeal and gradually materializes as she descends a flight of stairs. The camera initially catches a glimpse of her feet encased in fine bowed shoes. When she steps down, we get to see her dress and finally her face as she smiles into the camera coquettishly. She is revealed as the sum of her parts and a creature of artifice. This is an interesting contrast to the earlier beefcake shot of Fairbanks' Lo Dorman emerging almost totally nude from the waters. As played by Jewel Carmen, her calculating and teasing nature also make Nellie a strong contrast to the vulnerable white women threatened by half-breeds in *The Aryan* and similar kinds of fiction. It is likely that Anita Loos with her pungent wit was called upon to do the adaptation from Bret Harte to focus on the film's satirical targets. As Scott Simmon observes, "Although the film runs through the standard white woman–Indian man plot points, it rewrites them with sharp satire. This time the woman's coy lust is played with awareness of the absurdities ('I hear you have a very nice wigwam') and with a casual sensuality so rare in the Western...."[62]

Lo turns up in Excelsior dressed in his usual buckskin outfit. Pastor Wynn seems to be boring his parishioners with his sermon on intolerance when he spies Lo waiting outside the church. He beckons him to come in, telling Lo that his appearance "gives me an opportunity to illustrate my sermon."

Wynn is using the half-breed as a prop but when he later learns that his daughter is consorting with him, the minister will be moved to remark, "No white woman will be safe with a savage like that being treated like an equal." One wonders if this view of hypocrisy, where someone preaches against intolerance until the possibility of miscegenation arises, might have made Griffith wince.

Simmon has pointed out that caricatures of ministers were not unusual in the silent era Western where they were sometimes depicted as "too physically weak and usually too hypocritical to confront the depth of evil found in the Western."[63]

Dwan's films are often suffused with a perplexing mysticism but they are just as often marked by a distrust of sanctimoniousness. *The Half-Breed* romantically favors the virtues of Nature over Civilization, and it is the authority figures like the sheriff and the minister who are the least sympathetic. Nellie toys with Lo but adheres to her father's plans to marry someone influential.

In a more restrained place of worship, Fairbanks' half-breed participates in the service with the minister's daughter Nellie (Jewel Carmen) (courtesy Photofest).

crisscross of desert and town in favor of the spectacularly scenic, even monumental locales of the Grand Canyon or the Hopi mesas. In a magazine article entitled "Why I Was Disappointed by the Grand Canyon," Fairbanks allegedly explained his disappointment in that he could not jump it. He said had been led to believe that he "could jump anything. Here, on the rim of the world I met defeat. And I went down gladly. Impressions? Unconveyable."[69] Regardless of whether he did say this, the Fairbanks persona did find transcendence pitting his speed and energy against what seemed unfathomable. In *The Mollycoddle*, the regenerated character ecstatically runs through the spectacular vistas, once trodden by his forbearers, shouting, "Hurray for God!"

Fairbanks' fascination with the use of these sites in his films certainly began with Dwan and *The Half-Breed*. Dwan carefully uses lighting and composition to further enhance the majesty of the Sequoia setting.

Lo Dorman is in his element in the Carquinez woods, living in the hollowed-out trunk of one of the giant Sequoia trees, quite literally merging with his environment. We do get a few glimpses of the Fairbanks smile in Lo's cavorting in the forest. The *New York Times* reviewer said that he looked "rather more like Peter Pan than not."[64] In his novella, Harte wrote of his protagonist, "But for the rifle he carried and some modern peculiarities of dress, he was of a grace so unusual and unconventional that he might have passed for a faun who was quitting his ancestral home."[65] The faun imagery appropriately coincides with Tarkington's description of Fairbanks.

The frontiersman of legend that had developed from the primitivist view of Daniel Boone had been celebrated in the works of James Fenimore Cooper and other writers as having developed a mystical bond with nature and through nature to God.[66] Noting the change in popular Western fiction as the way west reaches the plains, Henry Nash Smith in his book *Virgin Land: The American West as Symbol and Myth* wrote that now gone was "the power to commune with nature. The Wild Western hero has been secularized — if the term may be employed with this connection — and magnified. He no longer looks to God through nature, for nature is no longer benign.... The scene has been shifted from the deep fertile forest east of the Mississippi to the barren plains.... It throws the hero back upon himself and accentuates his terrible and sublime isolation."[67]

The forest of the giant redwoods is, of course, much more than benign, but a magnificent locale for Fairbanks' hero to inhabit, deeply evocative of the metaphor of trees for a natural church.[68] Fairbanks' Westerns would often avoid the usual

In *Photoplay*, Julian Johnson described the film by saying, "Allan Dwan staged this forest symphony and every scene manifests laconic grace combined with force."[70]

The mythology Smith describes about this man of the forest can also be seen to overlap with that of Hart's Westerns. The sylvan half-breed is the mystic figure while the far West hero like Hart is the "secularized" one. It follows that he is the one most in need of moral reform as exhibited in Hart's conversions in various films. Moving from Hart to Harte, the author had transplanted the Cooper frontiersman to California but the frontiersman and his Indian companion have been combined into one figure of mixed blood. He would have no need of an Aryan code for his moral purpose.

The racial and moral drama of *The Half-Breed* is displayed most conspicuously in the saloon confrontation between Lo and Sheriff Dunne. Dunne has encouraged the Indians of a touring medicine show to get drunk and dance for the pleasure of the crowd. It is the creation of a stereotype and Lo upbraids the Indians, asking them, "Haven't you any more pride than to make fools of yourselves for the amusement of these people?" He then berates Dunne, telling him, "I'd call your evening's sport a rather cheap type of fun."

But the scene is most strongly infused with the undercurrent tension of the relationship between the two men. Dunne is cruelly mocking the Indians before the man who is the product of his liaison with their race. The scene carries a resonance of the long legacy of racists in their secret attraction to sexual relations with the "inferior race." Adding to the tension is that both Lo and Dunne are pursuing Nellie Wynn.

Unlike Passin' Through in *The Good Bad Man*, Lo shows little interest in finding the identity of his father. He has accepted the fact that there is no way he can fit into this society. Far from feeling resignation, he has independence in his own domain in the forest. With the education he has received from a white man, he can also function in the white world as a botanist.

But there is another woman in the story, a Mexican named Teresa (played by the dark-haired beauty Alma Rubens), who works at the touring medicine show. Teresa is fiery and volatile, the kind of character who, like the half-breed, would normally register solely as a stereotype. But she asserts herself in the confrontation between Dunne and Lo, telling the older man, "That half-breed is worth a dozen of you, sheriff!"

Later, in a jealous rage she wounds her lover Curson with a knife after she finds him with another woman. Teresa also wounds Dunne as she makes her escape. Lo's stately forest now becomes a place of refuge for Teresa and he provides her with private quarters in his hollowed-out tree home.

Dunne, still in a weakened state and convinced that Nellie is with Lo, enters the forest to kill the half breed. Instead he finds Teresa alone in Lo's home and is so relieved that he offers to let her go while scolding her for not picking someone better than an Indian. But in that home, Dunne finds the proof that Lo is his son. After laughing at the irony, he collapses to the ground and will fall prey to a fire that is sweeping the forest. (The effect was achieved convincingly with a fire limited to a patch of trees about a hundred yards from the real forest.)

While Dunne perishes, Lo saves Teresa. This forest finale is what one might imagine from the final act of a very dark Shakespearean romance. This denouement spares Harte's final bleak irony. In the novella, Lo's sylvan paradise becomes a deathtrap as he and Teresa also die in the fire.

Still, *The Half-Breed* works on its own terms with the outcasts, who would be doomed in most films of the era, surviving together. In the final shot of the Library of Congress print, Lo is seen standing defiantly under a stark tree bough with Teresa sitting at his feet.

In gauging Dwan's contribution to the Fairbanks films, John Tibbetts uses quotes from interviews later in the director's career to emphasize Dwan's disavowal of artistic pretensions. But Dwan and Fairbanks clearly tried for something daring and different in *The Good Bad Man*, and the bolder *The Half-Breed* was definitely the most original and risky of Fairbanks' Triangle features. It was also a precursor of Fairbanks' big-budget adventure films of the 1920s such as *Robin Hood*.

The trade reviews were generally enthusiastic for *The Half-Breed* and for Fairbanks' turn to drama. Harrison in *Moving Picture World* noted, "At last we have a picture in which the intense personality of Fairbanks does not bulge out of the story, one in which the characterization is difficult and where it is not made dominant to story interest. The result is not only an artistic achievement, but a stronger proof of his ability...." In *Motography*, George Graves wrote, "The story has that vim, originality and power which exalts it as high above the numerous tedious five-reelers of the day as the sun above the clouds."[71] Most of the reviews also cited the film's visual splendors of the forest which the *New York Times* headline called "stunning."[72]

But while praising the film in the *Motion Picture News*, Oscar Cooper observed, "Those who look for stirring fights in every Fairbanks picture will find none of them in this."[73]

The Half-Breed was a disappointment at the box office. This may have been due less to its offbeat racial views than to this lack of action anticipated from Fairbanks. Also, while effective in this somber role, Fairbanks does not exude the same kind of charisma that he does in his comedy and adventure films.

After completing *The Half-Breed*, Fairbanks was interviewed in New York by *Moving Picture World*. Asked if he had met William S. Hart, he replied, "He's one of my best friends. The boys gave me a dinner at Los Angeles just before my departure. Bill Hart sat on my right. Alan [sic] Dwan in his speech said he would like Bill Hart and Doug Fairbanks to do a picture together. Hart remarked that he was agreed."[74]

Neither Dwan nor anyone else would make a feature starring Hart and Fairbanks (though they did both appear in a short promoting war bonds). But they would remain friendly rivals. A few months after *The Half-Breed* was released, there appeared *The Dawn Makers* in which Hart starred as a half-breed. But in this film, Hart's character realizes that he can never help the Indian people the way the whites can. "In the end he dies of hunger that the young white couple may live and propagate a people, giving this world the progress one of his native limitations could never rise to."[75]

If Dwan was doing his own riff on the theme of intolerance, Fairbanks served him as perhaps no other star of the period could have. Dwan would romantically continue to favor Nature over Civilization in a number of his later films.

Fairbanks and Hart projected different social and religious values, some of which reflected the difference in ages between the two men. Fairbanks espoused a more optimistic and expansive spirituality that could be more inclusive; Hart's was closer to the darker hellfire and damnation legacy of Jonathan Edwards which required his protagonists to purge all evil before they could reform. Hart's racism, while obviously appalling today, was also a product of his times and did not evoke the same kind of controversy that Griffith's did. It should be pointed out that even as Hart's popularity dwindled in the 1920s, black Americans remained among his most faithful fans. The depiction of traditional religious values and message of redemption apparently resonated deeply in the African American community. Hart's popularity with blacks was strong enough that in Washington, D.C., his epic *Tumbleweeds* was shown in a black theater before it was projected in a white theater.[76]

Fairbanks would make other Westerns and occasionally, Indians would take their turn as the bad guys. But in his *The*

Man from Painted Post, the villain was a white man who abused his Indian wife and child. After the criminal was brought to justice, Fairbanks' hero adopted the half-breed boy. However, Fairbanks would make no other pictures of such a serious nature as *The Half-Breed* until his very last silent film.

When in 1917 Dwan returned to work as Fairbanks' director after a one-year separation, he was greeted enthusiastically. Fairbanks declared to the *Los Angeles Times* that *Manhattan Madness, The Good Bad Man,* and *The Habit of Happiness* were the three best American photoplays he had ever done. Those films constituted nearly all the movies he had made with Dwan at Triangle.

The only title missing was *The Half-Breed.*[77]

Manhattan Madness

Manhattan Madness is perhaps the breeziest, most enjoyable and highly regarded of Fairbanks' early films. Journalist Heywood Broun opined, "People who think they don't like motion pictures should see Douglas Fairbanks in *Manhattan Madness....* If they derive no amusement from this merry farce-melodrama they are correct in supposing that they are film blind."[78]

Manhattan Madness was also the last of the unofficial trilogy of Westerns made by Fairbanks and Dwan in 1916 and incorporated elements of each of the last two films directed by Dwan. Like *The Half-Breed,* there is the Dwan contrast of locales; the forest and civilization of the latter converted to the rivalry between West and East in *Manhattan Madness,* with the distinction being less stark and more comic. But where in *The Half-Breed,* Fairbanks played an atypical dramatic role, in *Manhattan Madness* he was back to his old screen persona with a vengeance. The film harped not only on that image but on the public personality of Fairbanks himself and, as in *The Good Bad Man,* his obsession with pranks.

The plot deals with a former Easterner (played by Doug) returning to New York from Nevada with horses he's selling to someone in the East. Meeting up with his old buddies, he is adamant that everything about New York is wrong and inferior to the West.

Anita Loos said that she contrived the plot for *Manhattan Madness,* which required New York exteriors.[79] Loos is not credited with the script of *Manhattan Madness* and her track record for accuracy in her reminiscences is not a good one. But it is possible that she may have contributed the original idea.

Dwan told Bogdanovich, "Fairbanks and I wanted to work in New York and they wanted him to be a Western character, so we said, 'All right, we'll do a Western in New York.' How do you do that? Well, you bring a Westerner to New York and have him buck the New York racket."[80]

According to Herndon, after making his first two films, Fairbanks was eager to return to the east. Los Angeles lacked the good restaurants, theater and society that were available in New York. Fairbanks' mother also resided there. But Fairbanks' wife may have been a stronger proponent of returning to the east since there was little to preoccupy her while Doug was at the studio.

By early 1916, however, when Fairbanks was returning to the West Coast, stories appeared in the trade press that he was planning to make his permanent home in California. "He enjoys the active out-of-door life which California affords and is planning a trip to settle down to home-building as a welcome variation to hotel living."[81]

In that first visit back to New York, Fairbanks' enthusiasm for the West Coast was already palpable, as his good friend Frank Case, owner of the Algonquin Hotel recalled. "Hollywood has everything," Fairbanks gushed, "great climate, great people and a great new frontier."[82]

California also represented to Fairbanks the chance to make movies and do them in wide open spaces. In *Manhattan Madness,* there is a scene where Fairbanks talks to a weed and bemoans the fact that it's not out West where it would have sufficient space to grow. As he had told the magazine *Motion Picture,* space was what he needed to perform stunts he could not do on the stage in New York. Dwan, on the other hand, was much more disposed to the east, so this clash in geographic preference may have spilled over into the film.

The picture opens with the title, "The argument of this story contrasts the East with the West in respect to their joy yielding qualities."

East and West are then introduced as if they were individual characters in the film. An overhead shot of New York's Times Square is shown to signify what is meant by the East. The other side of the country is then introduced by a shot of an uninhabited Western desert. But this is then followed by energetic scenes from a corral where a cowboy is attempting to ride a bucking bronco while cheered on by his pals leaning on the railings.

These locales having been introduced, we are then presented with the first human character, a young man "out of the West." He is aptly named Steve O'Dare and we first see Fairbanks' hero in long shot scampering across the roofs of freight cars and then coming down, walking up to the camera and winking. We are back in the realm of the Fairbanks smile, promising all kinds of mischievousness.

Steve takes a cab to his old college club just as Fairbanks probably visited the Lambs Club on his earlier return to New York. With ultra Fairbanks pugnacity he takes on each of his old chums as if trying to tackle them until they all restrain him to tell him how glad they are to see him.

After a title informs us that they have been visiting various New York sites together, Steve and his buddies dine at a country club. O'Dare tells his friends, "New York is all wrong — superficial, un-American, overcrowded. I can't breathe — can't sleep — can't eat. I tell you I wouldn't give an acre of Nevada cactus for Manhattan Island." This sounds like an extreme rendering of the comments Fairbanks made to Case on his return from Hollywood. It also certainly reflects some of the heartland's distrust of big cities.

O'Dare also becomes increasingly overbearing to his friends as he belittles everything about the city in favor of Nevada. As they discuss each aspect of their respective regions, they are visualized on screen. Thus, if the New Yorkers talk about the ferocity of a brawl they saw in the city, it is seen onscreen and answered by a Western gunfight where the combatants still fire at each other as they lay on the ground. Words instantly beget images and the cutting between them becomes a comic interplay of dueling images.

At another point, when confronted with a New York newspaper headline about a theft of pearls, Steve regales his friends with tales of a Western bandit named Black Burke, who materializes on the screen committing nefarious deeds while dressed in black with the lower part of his face masked with a bandana.

The dynamic editing style that Dwan's earlier Fairbanks films had demonstrated is here brought to its zenith. Kevin Brownlow has written that the film's "editing style was as innovative as if Dick Lester had worked for Thomas Edison.... But *Manhattan Madness* did things that no one else dared do until years later.... Dwan cut back and forth between the West and East, bravura editing of the kind historians think only Griffith capable of."[83]

Steve finally does find something in New York that interests him when an attractive young woman (Jewel Carmen) walks into the country club with some companions. They both eye each other but no introductions are made.

In the next scene at the college club, Steve is still thinking about the girl and a close-up of her appears. Steve muses somewhat poetically whether he'd prefer to look for her smile or return to the "sting of the cactus and swing of my bronc." There follows two shots of Steve as a lone rider on the range. The dueling images of East and West take a different turn to suggest that for all his macho posturing, the West is a place where Steve can get away from women and hide his insecurities.

When Steve complains he hasn't had a thrill since he came to the city, his exasperated College Club chum Cupid Russell offers a $5,000 wager that Steve will have a thrill if he stays in New York for one more week. O'Dare accepts the bet but then receives a phone call for him to complete his horse deal.

Steve takes leave of his companions to meet his buyer "at one of those mysterious old mansions on the fringe of Manhattan." Not only does Steve meet the count but discovers that the girl from the country club is there as his ward. Steve learns from the maid that the girl is in great peril. When Steve goes upstairs to look for the girl, the sinister butler hits a button that opens a trap door and Steve falls into a closet where he is tied up and locked away by the butler's cohorts.

But through a grating, Steve is able to see and hear a meeting taking place between the count and his confederate. They have in their possession the stolen necklace Steve saw mentioned in the newspaper. They make clear that the count intends to do O'Dare in and is keeping his ward prisoner because she has overheard the plot.

This melodramatic twist in a Fairbanks film should by now sound familiar. But here an entirely new atmosphere is created in the film in something akin to a mystery story. As the criminal forces swell, it even takes on the ambience of the conspiracy serials of Louis Feuillade.

Low-key lighting is impressively used for a film of this early era. In the closet, Steve's barely visible face is surrounded by darkness. After being freed by the maid, Steve again climbs the stairs. The butler again follows him. In a rapid succession of shots we see the maid press the trap door button, the butler fall through the trap, Steve turning back to look, the maid stabbing the butler in the closet and finally the count and his confederate hearing the noise and remarking, "It's the end of that interfering American." All this flashes by in a few short seconds.

Commenting on *Manhattan Madness*, Dwan has said, "And we paced the film fast — which was done in the camera, not in the cutting room."[84] Of course, some of it had to be done in the cutting room, but this suggests that there was already an established shooting plan which made the editing easier.

After Steve reaches the top of the stairs, a beckoning arm brings him into the girl's room. She confesses that she has loved Steve since she first saw him in the country club. Then making the conspiracy appear even more alarming, she says she has heard state secrets. She argues against Steve calling the police but asks if he has friends they can depend on. Steve predictably calls his club friends but then, as a precautionary measure, also calls the stockyard for four of his cowboys to come to the rescue.

Traveling by auto, Steve's club chums get to the mansion well before the cowboys on their mounts. There is then plenty of scuffling and shooting, unfolding in a rapid series of shots. Steve is chased over the roof of the mansion and manages to escape in true Fairbanks fashion. Later re-entering the house, he finds it totally and mysteriously empty. After catching a glimpse of the apparently still living butler peering out from a secret panel, Steve punches his way through one of the panels and enters another room. There he finds a huge dinner table where both the count and the butler are seated, appearing alive and well though both seemed to have been killed, as well as his club buddies, the elusive girl and others. He is then informed that if he had been more familiar with New York, he would have recognized the villains as figures from the New York stage, a teasing reminder that Fairbanks had his stage roots in New York.

After eyeing the girl carefully, Steve announces, "So it's a joke, is it? Now I'll play my cards." The stockyard cowboys have now entered the mansion and Steve turns the tables on the dinner guests by saying that he is the bandit known as Black

Burke. There is a cut back to the image of Black Burke who lowers his bandana to show that he is Steve O'Dare as he winks to the audience and we cut back to a winking O'Dare with his guests. Comparing himself to Lochinvar, he literally sweeps the girl off her feet and takes her out with him. But once outside, with both laughing, he asks her, "Will you go through with this Lochinvar stunt?" And they ride off on a horse together.

Shortly thereafter, Steve is seen on the deck of a ship, writing a letter to his friend, conceding that Russell has won the wager: Steve has been given the thrill of his life. He also acknowledges that he is not the bandit and has never stolen anything except a wife. Before he sticks his head through a porthole to kiss her, he acknowledges, "After all it isn't where you are that counts, it's whom you're with."

There is a potential aesthetic danger when a big movie star is caught literally and figuratively winking at his audience. It suggests that his celebrityhood is the main thing and that the film is just a tawdry vehicle to direct audience affection to the star. But here the star and film are one; *Manhattan Madness* is a kind of game that engages and teases the audience. It likely grew out of Fairbanks' fondness for pranks and practical jokes. It was said that he could appreciate being both the instigator and target of such tomfoolery and here it is carried tit for tat.

Dwan, who was very familiar with Fairbanks' jokes, could appreciate both their emotional and intellectual playfulness. There is some affinity here to the "intellectual game" films of French director Jacques Rivette. There are some tip-offs to the audience in character names such as Cupid Russell and Count Winkie. We can never be sure if Black Burke is a real character who Steve has heard of or an alter ego figment of his imagination.

A key part of the film supposedly had its origins in Fairbanks' friendship with an old cowboy named Jim Kidd. One day they were riding on the Mojave Desert and Fairbanks asked how he liked it out there. Kidd replied, "It don't make much difference where you are, it's who's with you."

The film also had a decidedly unpleasant moment for Fairbanks: He was almost blinded when a blank cartridge was exploded in his face at close range.[85]

In his Westerns with Fairbanks, Dwan had taken him through the serious (*The Half-Breed*) to the comic (*Manhattan Madness*) to the in-between (*The Good Bad Man*). But it was *Manhattan Madness,* with its dexterous development of the East-West contrasts and competitions, first seen in *The Lamb*, that would serve as the blueprint for Doug's future Westerns.

Manhattan Madness was the last collaboration between Dwan and Fairbanks at Triangle. Behind the scenes, events were transpiring that would rupture their association. These events also had ramifications that would change the industry and, in ensuing years, affect the business dealings of both men.

Triangle in Trouble

In June 1916, during a stopover in Chicago when Fairbanks was on his way to New York to continue shooting on *Manhattan Madness,* he told Genevieve Harris of *Motography* about his current plans at Triangle. "Well, the latest about us is that we are going to produce a serial picture which will reach around the world. We are going to adventure straight through every country. This is the idea." Harris says that Fairbanks outlined the plot with "his characteristic vigor and enthusiasm." He elaborated further,

> I'm to play the role of a young American who has a love affair in this country, gets "turned down" and goes to Europe. First he goes to Holland. There he meets a girl who reminds him of the American girl (the same girl will play the parts, you see), and he falls in love with her. Then he goes to France and meets a French girl, also just like the American and so on. That's the general idea. We haven't decided on the girl yet. We wanted Norma Talmadge but the company had other plans for her. We may take Jewell [sic] Carmen, but this hasn't been decided. John Emerson and Alan [sic] Dwan will be the directors and they are already negotiating abroad. And in each country the chap will have some adventures, characteristic of the place. The whole thing will be in light comedy drama style.

Fairbanks appeared unfazed by the fact that a world war was now raging throughout Europe. "We took a little trip to Mexico to finish our last picture. We got a little taste of war there."[86]

It is not clear if this lunatic project was ever seriously considered or just one of Fairbanks' more adventurous pipe dreams. By the time he arrived in New York, Fairbanks was more reasonably talking about making pictures in South America and then making a tour of Europe, after the end of the war.[87]

But Triangle would have been hard pressed even to finance the South American proposal. If Fairbanks was itching to get into a serial, the Triangle Picture Corporation was now involved in a real-life cliffhanger that would determine the survival of the company.

The troubles of Triangle had become evident by early 1916. The company was top-heavy with highly paid stage talent, most of whom were not proving adept in front of the camera or in attracting audiences. Although Triangle budgets were not as lavish as their publicity suggested, they were still more than double the production cost of the competition.[88] Triangle's policy of demanding its theaters only show Triangle programs was also backfiring and causing resentment.

As Triangle's financial problems mounted, Harry Aitken became convinced that the solution to his problems lay in a merger with another production company. He pinned his hopes on enticing Adolph Zukor to join his Famous Players Company with Triangle.

Zukor was the most powerful figure in the film business at the time and someone who would not let any obstacle deter him from his objectives. Aitken gambled that he could convince Zukor that a merger with Triangle was in his interest. Zukor *was* interested in Aitken's Wall Street connections and in how the rival organization operated so it was worth the effort to consider the merger plans. In order for Zukor to assess the full value of Aitken's property, it was necessary for Aitken to open his books to him. This was a risky maneuver but Aitken must have felt he had no choice if he was putting all his hopes on a merger.

As negotiations dragged on, Aitken, with some wishful thinking, decided he could hurry things along by issuing a press release stating that a merger with Zukor was imminent and even giving an approximate date (April 26 or 27) for its completion. This did not occur and instead on June 27, Famous Players announced its merger not with Triangle but with the Lasky Feature Film Company.

The Triangle Film Corporation was now in a deep hole.

After this deal fell through, Dwan was in the process of making his next film. Characteristically, having worked primarily with Fairbanks over the first half of the year, Dwan now turned to a female star. It was the same actress Fairbanks said he wanted for his globetrotting serial, Norma Talmadge, whose sister Constance was also starring in movies for Fine Arts. Norma had been appearing in films since 1910 but her career was now burgeoning into major stardom. Coincidentally, as with Fairbanks, she had just appeared in a film directed by John Emerson (a comedy called *The Social Secretary*) before she went to work with Dwan.

Dwan's film was shot at the Riverdale studio in Yonkers. *Fifty-Fifty* (the title referring to the relationship between men and women) opens in the Washington Square section of New York in Greenwich Village. Lampooning its reputation as a bohemian center for artists, the film opens at O'Malley's, where the "highbrows" meet "with the purpose of giving Art a boost and solving the riddles of the universe." One riddle that the aspiring intellectuals cannot solve is the character of a young woman, Naomi (Talmadge), who is nicknamed "the Nut." She is by profession a china painter but on this occasion is trying to impress as a "Popular Dance Artiste." So we see her coming down a flight of stairs in a grass skirt and barefoot, giving her rendition of the hula and striving to be wild and free.

Naomi is constantly trying to impress and her pretensions as a bohemian mask her naiveté and desire for acceptance. But Naomi manages to attract the attention of lonely businessman Frederic Harmon (J.W. Johnston). Dwan is at his most effective when he keeps his camera on the couple, letting their expressions and body language reveal their predicament: two people of different worlds, not fully understanding each other's needs but pulled to each other by their mutual loneliness. Talmadge is quite touching in conveying her vulnerability.

The couple hastily decides to marry. They appear happy for a year until they have a child. Then Naomi, the "free spirit," becomes totally wrapped up in domesticity and the child. After six months of this, the husband begins to feel that he has lost his wife's interest and takes up with another woman.

Fifty-Fifty works well as a sensitive and sophisticated study of a floundering marriage until various melodramatic contrivances come into play. Since the film was co-written by Robert Shirley and Dwan, the director must take some of the blame for this. Critics picked up on the film's schizophrenic quality. In *Motography*, Thomas Kennedy wrote, "[It] starts promisingly and ends sweetly. If the picture fails to please picturegoers the blame must be placed upon the story, which is filled with unconvincing turns and twists."[89] Julian Johnson in *Photoplay* wrote, "Clumsy and rambling, dramatic and lifelike; there is a qualification of *Fifty-Fifty*, the best though most loosely put-together Triangulation born last month.... Mr. Dwan has handled these episodes with a sure and masterly touch. It is hard to realize what would have happened to this disjointed scenario, in which lifelikeness and melodramatic absurdity stalk hand in hand, in a less talented grasp."[90] Still, Johnson later cited *Fifty-Fifty* as well as Dwan's *Betty of Graystone* as among the notable films of the past year.[91] Despite its flaws, *Fifty-Fifty* was a hit at the box office.

In an unpublished 1979 interview conducted by film historian Joe Adamson, Dwan says that Triangle could not provide him with the funds to finish *Fifty-Fifty* and he had to seek more financing elsewhere. This seems questionable since *Fifty-Fifty* went out as a regular Triangle release. Dwan also said that Triangle was considering closing its New York studio and that Griffith was pressing for that.[92] When Dwan shot and completed *Fifty-Fifty* in the summer of 1916, Triangle, as indicated earlier, was indeed in bad financial straits and may well have been considering such a move.

Like Dwan, Talmadge preferred to continue working in the east. She had told *Motion Picture News*, "If I had my way, I'd like to spend about four months in Los Angeles and eight in New York, so you see I like the east four months better than the west."[93] More importantly, Talmadge's contract of $500 a week with Triangle was set to expire on September 27 and she was reportedly asking for a new yearly contract of $1,000 per week.[94] Of course, Triangle was not in a good position to be granting 100 percent raises.

Dwan explained to Brownlow that at this time he was trying to put together a company with Talmadge as star and himself as director. He contacted Marcus Loew, a major chain theater owner. Loew's business manager Nicholas Schenck referred Dwan to his brother Joe, who was the company's booking manager engaged in employing vaudeville acts. Dwan recalled that Joe Schenck "said he'd help me get financing for my outfit with Norma Talmadge if I'd do him a favor and make a picture with a star he had, first. Well, that sounded fair enough, it would only take a week or two to do that, so I said, 'Who is she?' Her name was Evelyn Nesbit."[95]

Nesbit was notorious for her involvement in one of the major scandals of the young century. Her husband, millionaire Harry

K. Thaw, was filled with resentment of the celebrated Stanford White, the distinguished architect who had made Nesbit a "fallen woman." On June 25, 1906, during a musical performance at Madison Square Garden, Thaw shot and killed White before hundreds of shocked patrons. Nesbit's life was later dramatized on screen in the 1955 movie *The Girl in the Red Velvet Swing* where she was played by Joan Collins (with Nesbit serving as technical consultant) and later depicted as part of the swirl of interlocked dramas in the 1981 film *Ragtime*, based on the E.L. Doctorow novel. Nesbit became a celebrity and for a few years, a silent film star.

Dwan's account is corroborated in the trade stories of the period which announced the formation of the Norma Talmadge Film Corporation with Joseph Schenck as its president. It was also reported that Dwan would be directing features for both Talmadge and Nesbit. The films would be released through the Lewis J. Selznick Service.[96]

For Talmadge, Schenck was able to acquire the rights to Monckton Hoffe's play *Panthea* which was a sensation in both Europe and America. In early November, shortly after *Fifty-Fifty* was released, shooting commenced on *Panthea* at the Biograph Studio (leased by Selznick) on East 175th Street in New York City.

Serving as assistant director to Dwan and doubling as actor was future film director Erich von Stroheim, who had also served double duty for Fairbanks in *His Picture in the Papers*. Most of the principal characters in *Panthea* were Russian, and von Stroheim professed to Dwan to know a great deal about Russia. As for his acting, Dwan remembered that he had cast a number of exiled White Russians in the film, "doing various things, persecuting our leading lady Norma Talmadge.... I needed a lieutenant to put them around. So I select von Stroheim. He had the cut hair, he had the shaved hair because he was a Prussian.... He looked like he just escaped from a German war camp or something."[97]

Dwan recalled that Stroheim was a bit too authentic and took to cracking a whip at his charges. They had enough of that one day "and finally they started to beat hell out of him."[98] Dwan at that point said he stopped using von Stroheim as an actor (von Stroheim did continue to work as Dwan's assistant).

Panthea was a wildly operatic melodrama that had been a stage smash starring Olga Petrova, who, ironically, was now also under contract to Selznick. Panthea (Talmadge), a brilliant young Russian pianist, is coveted by a baron who has her falsely arrested for revolutionary activities so that he can secure her release on terms favorable to him. With the help of a former schoolmate, now a soldier, Panthea escapes to England. There she falls in love with a young composer, Gerald (Earle Fox), whom she marries. Gerald is obsessed with getting his opera produced. The couple moves to Paris where Panthea again runs into the Russian baron. Because her husband is losing his sanity due to his opera remaining unsold, Panthea agrees to sacrifice her virtue to the baron if he will ensure that the opera will be produced. Although the opera is a resounding success, when her husband learns of her action, he hates Panthea for it. The baron succumbs to a bad heart before Panthea can return the favor but his agent takes Panthea back to Russia. The film ends with Gerald joining Panthea in her Siberian exile and telling her that his father is now using his political influence to get them back to England.

Panthea had its premiere in New York on January 6, 1917, playing at both the Rialto and the Loew theaters. Up until that time, the Rialto only played an exclusive first-week engagement of a feature film. Since Joseph Schenck was the booking manager for the Loew theaters, he was the likely cause of having the Rialto suspend its exclusive policy for *Panthea*.[99]

For the most part, *Panthea* was lauded excitedly in the trade reviews, which did not skim over its sensationalistic aspects. *Variety* observed, "Too much praise cannot be bestowed upon Allan Dwan, director and Roy Overbaugh, cameraman, not to mention the star and the entire acting organization. As a

Norma Talmadge, as Panthea Romoft, surrounded by men who wouldn't help her. Talmadge was under Dwan's direction for the second and final time in *Panthea* (1917) (courtesy Academy of Motion Picture Arts and Sciences).

production it is almost too realistic in the first part, which is a prolog to what was originally the legitimate presentation." But *Variety* also noted that some of the less wholesome elements of the original play had been toned down, such as the composer already being married when Panthea eloped with him.[100]

Julian Johnson was even more enthusiastic in *Photoplay*. "It is one of the best photoplays in screen history, and if there were more like it every interpretative art would have to cinch its figurative belt and prepare to fight for existence.... The direction is Allan Dwan's, and he manifests the same leisurely, perfect passion for detail that he showed in *Betty of Greystone* [sic]."[101]

Several of the reviews, including Johnson's, cited the film's "artistic lighting." According to Dwan,

> I wanted to show Panthea playing a piano for three connoisseurs who were judging her talent while her old music master nervously stood waiting in the doorway. We had no set provided for this and no money to make one, so I made a set out of nothing — and it was one of the best scenes in the picture. I put a window frame way up high and shone a very powerful light from it right down onto her at the piano. And I sprinkled aluminum dust in the light so you could see the beam coming down — it was a terrific effect — and I threw a very faint light on these three men's faces listening, and in the doorway (which was also just a frame) was her professor. And it became a big set — all of it in one shot. Anyway, this effect intrigued everybody who saw it, and my reason for doing it was to save money. The old economic angle. Art is economical. Whoever invented spending millions of dollars has ruined the picture business.[102]

Critic and producer Kenneth MacGowan, who saw the film at the time, commented many years later on Dwan's use of light and shadow repeated in a dining scene; he saw it as "only one of a number of excellent effects that he achieved by wedding economy of materials with imagination. This was a clean break with the heavy, solid scenery and sculptured lighting of DeMille and Ince, which stemmed from the realism of Belasco. Dwan was adding to the new stagecraft the fresh and potent power of the lens."[103]

The chief dissenter among the reviewers was *Wid's* which did not consider Talmadge up to the role and found some of the melodrama distasteful and ineffective.[104] (Contemporary viewers may never get a chance to make their own assessment. *Panthea* was revived for a showing at the 1958 Venice Film Festival but the print shown has been unaccounted for since that occasion.)

Panthea proved a smash hit, enticing overflow crowds at the theaters. Film historian Jeanine Basinger wrote, "*Panthea* was Norma's most successful film of 1917, and it is clearly the film that made her a true star."[105]

Dwan and Talmadge were set to continue working together but Dwan quite suddenly found a problem with their working relationship. During the shooting of *Panthea*, Norma one day showed up an hour late. Dwan, concerned that his star might be sick, sought her out in her dressing room. Talmadge was in tears. But they were joyful ones because she explained that she had married her producer Joe Schenck that morning.

Dwan assured her that this was fine but later told Schenck, "You get yourself another director, because I'll go up against any kind of opposition in this business, but I'll be damned if I'm going to buck pillow talk. You two people would have me tied to the mast."[106]

Dwan's departure followed not long after completion of the film and was announced in the trades shortly before *Panthea* opened.[107] Further severing his ties, Dwan sold his one-quarter interest in the profits to *Panthea* to Lewis Selznick not long after it opened.

And what of the film Dwan was supposed to have made for Schenck with Evelyn Nesbit? The answer to that would not surface until years later.

Meanwhile, recent upheavals within the film industry would create another business opportunity for Dwan. After the Lasky Feature Film merger with Famous Players, there was a clash between Zukor and Lasky's former brother-in-law, Samuel Goldfish, who was chairman of the board. Goldfish was forced to resign. He then decided to start his own film company and formed a partnership with two brothers who were theatrical producers, Edgar and Arch Selwyn. Using the first syllable of Goldfish's name and the last syllable of the brothers,' they called the company Goldwyn Pictures. Dwan has said that he had suggested the principals use the alternate syllables and call the firm "Sel-fish."[108] Dwan was not the only one to think of this bon mot and it is impossible to reckon who was first. Writing in 1925, Terry Ramsaye noted that this was a stock joke in the motion picture industry.[109] Goldfish later changed his name to Goldwyn, sparing future generations the dissonant sound of Metro-Goldfish-Mayer.

Goldwyn signed long-established stage stars Maxine Elliott and Mary Garden. (Some unimpressed Hollywood sources responded by referring to Goldwyn's as the "old ladies' home."[110]) For his first film with Elliott, Goldwyn was taking no chances and lavishing all the care possible. The noted writers Irvin S. Cobb and Roi Cooper Megrue were hired to prepare the script. Hugo Ballin, the distinguished painter and muralist, who had studied in Rome, would design the sets. And Dwan, fresh from his success with *Panthea*, was given charge of the production as director. Shooting began on February 19, 1917, on the film titled *Fighting Odds* at Dwan's old haunt, Fort Lee, New Jersey. Goldwyn was spending freely and in the words of his biographer Scott Berg, "a bright hotshot director — such as Allan Dwan — would be hired on a picture-by-picture basis at one thousand dollars a week."[111]

Dwan's prosperous state of affairs was a sharp contrast to the condition of Triangle when he left it, financially dangling from the edge of a cliff. Triangle, however, would be pulled back from the precipice not by the dramatic rescue of a merger but by the application of common sense business practices that had heretofore been avoided.

In October 1916, prodded by accumulated debts and demanding creditors, Harry Aitken made two moves to achieve solvency. He backed away from only using theaters contractually bound to Triangle and allowed independent exchanges to carry his films. But by this point, there were not enough exchanges interested in Triangle product to eliminate Triangle's considerable debt.

Aitken then put his entire exchange system up for sale. By November, it was purchased by William W. Hodkinson, who had formerly run Paramount (Zukor's distribution company). With the $600,000 paid by Hodkinson, Aitken now had enough money to pay his creditors and keep production going. The survival of Triangle was now assured into 1917 and possibly beyond.

But these moves, while avoiding calamity, did not mean profitability. With Hodkinson's advice, Aitken re-arranged his method of payments to Griffith, Ince and Sennett from a flat rate to a percentage basis. The three producers, however, understood too well that in sharing the risks, they would be getting less money.

Griffith had already felt the disappointment of his backers at Triangle in previews of *Intolerance.* Using his profits from *Birth of a Nation,* Griffith then bought out those backers and released the film on his own. Thus, the film that had consumed so much of Griffith's time at Fine Arts never went out as a Triangle release.

Douglas Fairbanks was also getting restless. After *Manhattan Madness,* he shot another film in the east, *American Aristocracy,* directed by Lloyd Ingraham and written by Loos.

Fairbanks' next feature was *The Matrimaniac*, which co-starred Constance Talmadge and was directed by Paul Powell. While shooting proceeded in October, Fairbanks cabled Harry Aitken that he wanted Emerson (then on loan-out to Famous Players) to direct his next feature and Loos to write all the intertitles for his future films. In earlier interviews, Fairbanks had made it clear that the two directors he preferred at Triangle were Dwan and Emerson and now only Emerson was available. Since Loos was already in Los Angeles at the time, Anthony Slide considers it highly probable that she worked on *The Matrimaniac,*[112] which now looks like one of his best films at Fine Arts.

Fairbanks not only wanted to call more of the shots but was restive about the amount of money he was making. While he was being paid handsomely, an estimated $500,000 per annum, he felt it was meager compared to the millions his films were making for Triangle. He was, no doubt, aware of Triangle's financial problems and that the profits from his films were being used to offset some of the company's losses. The idea became fixed in his mind to start his own production company and he consulted with his brother John to assist in the organizational planning.

A worthwhile model had been provided for Fairbanks with the founding of the Mary Pickford Film Corporation, organized in August 1916 for the purpose of producing only films in which she appeared. And while Pickford remained under contract to Famous Players, her films would not be released through Paramount, their regular distributor, but through another new company called Artcraft. Thus, her films would be released independently by a company created "to present and distribute motion picture attractions that will be the highest attainment of the cinematographic art."[113] (The high-toned language here almost sounds like the early Triangle press releases.) Although it was not publicly announced, Adolph Zukor was the man who owned the operation. While Aitken may have felt betrayed by him, Zukor's refusal to merge with Triangle was a sound business decision. Triangle's greatest assets were its major stars (Fairbanks and Hart) and its three producers. Why take on Triangle's debts and other financial problems when these individuals might simply come to Zukor on their own, especially given Triangle's precarious state?

As a prestigious entity with some apparent independence, Artcraft provided some lure for Triangle's major figures. This appeal was underlined in a statement made by Artcraft president Walter E. Greene in the fall of 1916 that the company did not exist to release only Pickford's films; "The aim and object of Artcraft is to handle the headliners of motion pictures."[114]

Fairbanks completed one more picture for Triangle, *The Americano*, a serviceable light adventure, and then headed back east for the Christmas holidays. En route he received news of his mother's death. This severed his last connection with the east. It also intensified his relationship with Pickford, in whose arms he sought consolation.

Fairbanks was ready to move ahead in establishing his own company but there remained the problem of his Triangle contract. A solution was apparently found going back to his beginnings at Triangle. Fairbanks' contract had stipulated that all his productions were to be supervised by D.W. Griffith. Griffith had supervised only two Fairbanks films at most.

Soon after Fairbanks' complaint was reported in the trades[115] in February 1917, it was announced that he had formed his own company and had signed with Artcraft to release his productions. He was joined by Emerson, Loos and other former Triangle personnel including cinematographer Fleming and von Stroheim, who was listed as a location scout. An injunction was brought against Fairbanks by Triangle which noted that he had specifically asked for Emerson to direct him[116] but this was eventually settled out of court with Fairbanks compensating Triangle with an unspecified sum.

Fairbanks' first film with Artcraft, *In Again, Out Again* ridiculed pacifists with Doug playing the pugnacious red-blooded American, appropriately named Teddy. It was released on April 30, 1917, a little over three weeks after America entered World War I.

As for that other war, the one in the film industry, there was a steady march of former Triangle principals toward Adolph Zukor's companies. (It was formally announced that in August,

Artcraft would be absorbed by Famous Players–Lasky.) Griffith, Ince, Hart and Sennett all followed Doug's lead from earlier in the year, going over to Zukor. In addition to Artcraft, the Hungarian-born mogul now also controlled Famous Players–Lasky and Paramount. But of the former Triangle figures mentioned above, only Sennett had not signed an agreement with Artcraft, which like a huge net was catching those who had jumped the Triangle ship. Or as Terry Ramsaye observed in a manner that would have been more pleasing to Dwan, "The Aitken triangle was absorbed into the Zukor polygon."[117]

The King of Yonkers

Following the U.S. Congress' Declaration of War on April 6, 1917, there was a considerable transition in thinking and outlook for moviemakers as for all of America. On April 14, 1917, the Committee on Public Information was created in Washington, D.C., as the government's official propaganda organization. Its director George Creel sent a letter to the National Association asking that the film industry be organized with the CPI. To facilitate the goals involved, a special War Co-operation Committee was appointed with William A. Brady as president and D.W. Griffith as chairman. The director of the pacifistic *Intolerance* subsequently journeyed to Europe where he filmed the feature *Hearts of the World* with a strongly propagandistic war message.

To help finance the war, the film industry also embarked on a series of drives to sell Liberty Bonds. Film trailers and short films were sent to theaters to urge the public to support this effort. Later, various film stars made personal appearances to sell the Liberty Bonds. Douglas Fairbanks, who had once cavalierly talked of touring through war-torn Europe to make a film serial, made coast to coast tours of the U.S. to help the cause.

America's entry into the war came as work was completed on Dwan's *Fighting Odds* for Goldwyn. His star, Maxine Elliott, enthusiastically involved herself in the bond-selling cause. Dwan recalled, "She was a fine woman. And I enjoyed her socially. She used to insist that I go to a lot of functions that were going on at the time. The war was on and they were selling bonds, but it was damned expensive so I cut it out because I'd go to the theater with her and be sitting in a box with her ... and the drive would come on and immediately she'd introduce me and I'd have to buy five thousand dollars' worth of bonds. So after I bought several five thousand dollars' worth of bonds, I said 'That's enough' and I quit. I quit going out with her because it cost too much money."[118] Elliott's prodigious efforts on behalf of the Liberty Loan were also noted in the press at the time.[119]

Elliott's commanding strides were not being reflected in her film output. *Fighting Odds* was still unreleased even as she completed a second film for Goldwyn, this one helmed by theater director Arthur Hopkins. The Goldwyn organization was feeling some trepidation about Elliott's work and there was even some hesitation about which film to release first. But Dwan would now find an opportunity at the same Triangle company that he had left in such turmoil and which was now in new turmoil.

In March, Griffith announced that he was leaving Fine Arts and within days had signed with Artcraft. The studio was thrown into upheaval as other personnel left including Lillian and Dorothy Gish, Robert Harron and Lloyd Ingraham, who were under personal contract to Griffith. Shortly thereafter, Triangle announced that future Fine Arts films would be produced by Thomas H. Ince at his Culver City studios.

But Griffith had been in name and spirit, if not usually in deed, the hub of Fine Arts and the studio name would not long survive his exit.

While the aesthetic legacy was now open for future debate, the pressing task for Triangle was to make the most of the remnants of Fine Arts. Toward this end, Dwan was named supervisor of production for Triangle at the Riverdale Studio in Yonkers, New York. While this facility had been used before by Fine Arts, it was apparently now undergoing renovations. According to *Motion Picture News*, "The new construction work at the Yonkers studio is rapidly being completed and within the next few days, production will commence there under Allan Dwan."[120]

Triangle tried to put the best face on the loss of Griffith and fortunately had a producer of Ince's status to fill the void. But while Ince was clearly the major figure, the press releases made a point of linking his name with Dwan's to strengthen the impression that Triangle's production apparatus was now in good hands. A statement issued by W.N. Seligsberg, secretary of Triangle, said that the appointments of Ince and Dwan had "aroused so much favorable comment that we feel sure these moves have met the desires of our patrons in all parts of the country." He added, "Allan Dwan is also a man who has proven his worth by the production of features of remarkable box-office value. Many of the most successful Fine Arts plays were done under his direction, and like Ince, he has the unusual faculty of getting splendid results out of associate directors, working under his supervision."[121]

A later statement by Hodkinson (now president of the Triangle Distributing Corporation) outlining Triangle's plans gave even greater emphasis to Dwan's importance. "The recent changes in the arrangements of our producing company guarantee to the exhibitor that the Triangle program will maintain uniformly the high standard which the names of Ince, Sennett and Dwan assure to our entire product."[122] Dwan now appeared to have replaced Griffith as the third point of the Triangle.

But while Dwan's name was of value to Triangle, he had only a pittance of the resources that Griffith had when Triangle began. When pressed for a statement regarding his immediate plans shortly after his appointment, Dwan said, "Vital, interesting stories, full of constructive ideas and brimming with human characterization is the ideal we have set for accomplishment at the new studio." Regarding future stars for the company, he commented, "We shall be extremely conservative regarding the exploitation of new stars, and shall make no effort to force personalities into popularity that have not been earned by genuine accomplishment."[123]

In fact, with the exodus of actors from Triangle that had begun in 1916 and only accelerated in recent months, there were slim pickings for Dwan to mold into stars. The emphasis on stories and "human characterizations" was a sensible outlook given Triangle's now limited production values as well as being consistent with Dwan's filmmaking philosophy. But could this philosophy be broadened into something more concrete for Dwan's writers and directors to develop?

More details were available when Dwan was interviewed by *Moving Picture World* a couple of weeks later. He now explained, "We are going to make serious pictures here, pictures that pulse with the problems of today. We are going to accentuate the values of ideals in industry and business, to attempt to show how men and women may be honest and highly successful too. The tendency in business today is toward the idealistic, and we are going to try to do what we can to help it along."[124]

Some of this emphasis toward the "serious" and "idealistic" could be attributed to the atmosphere of the time as the country now was facing the challenges of being a nation at war. Again, this is at variance with the image of Dwan as a strictly commercial filmmaker, but of course he was also trying to find a format that would make his films appealing within their budgetary constrictions.

Dwan had two companies working for him at the Riverdale studio. One was headed by director Art Rosson, whose association with Dwan went back to being his assistant director at Universal. The other was under rookie director Albert Parker, who had played the villain in *American Aristocracy* and who had more recently appeared in Fairbanks' latest *In Again, Out Again*. Not long thereafter, it was also officially announced that the films made at the Yonkers studio would not be called Fine Arts features but simply Triangle Productions.[125]

Rosson had already co-directed (with his brother Richard) his first film *Her Father's Keeper* at the Yonkers studio. It was released just weeks after the announcement of Dwan's arrival and the trades said that it was made before Dwan began his stint as supervisory director.[126] But it may have served as a prototype for Rosson's next films under Dwan's supervision.

The film received good reviews and was light fare while also being topical. Dwan might have also been struck by *Wid's* evaluation of the leading man in the film: "Jack Devereaux looks like a real 'find.' He is the only man outside of 'Doug' Fairbanks that I've seen who puts over the buoyant-enthusiasm personality on the screen without having it appeared forced. He'll win any audience before he has gone six scenes...."[127] Shortly after the release of *Her Father's Keeper,* it was announced that Dwan wanted the Irish-born, twenty-eight-year-old Devereaux to appear in future productions at the Yonkers studio.

Devereaux next starred in *The Man Who Made Good,* directed by Rosson and appearing in May; it was the first Triangle film credited to Dwan's supervision. It was scripted by Robert Shirley, who had also done *Her Father's Keeper.* The reviews were modestly favorable. Peter Milne in *Motion Picture News* called it a "light and interesting story of business and romance...."[128] *Variety* thought it only "fair"[129] while the *New York Dramatic Mirror* saw it as a "refreshing little domestic comedy about a young husband who refuses to accept poverty as his lot and who forces the world to recognize his worth through sheer pluck and initiative. The most original and delightful feature is that his little wife, instead of folding her hands and watching him work, starts out to do her bit to help the family fortunes in the sanest and most modern way imaginable." (She gets a job.[130])

Dwan (center) working in his Yonkers studio in 1917. The man on the right is Arthur Rosson, who directed several films at Triangle while Dwan was supervisor. The man on the left is unidentified (Robert S. Birchard Collection).

But the next picture *American—That's All*, where Devereaux was again paired with Winifred Allen as his leading lady, was almost universally panned by the trades. Dwan, Rosson and Shirley may have gone once too often to the well of depicting Devereaux as the young man trying to make good. *Wid's* was particularly damning, calling it a "badly forced attempt at comedy quite unfunny." The same reviewer who had seen Devereaux's affinity with Fairbanks now groused, "Jack Devereaux got away to a good start in his first Triangle release, but he has failed sadly to keep up the stride he hit, because in his last picture he was somewhat mechanical and in this one he was awful." Even more disparagingly, *Wid's* added, "This, as an instance of supervised production, certainly does not speak well for the methods, or else it proves that while Mr. Dwan is a very good director himself, he isn't nearly so good as a supervisor."[131]

A more provocative film had been shot by the Parker unit and was released July 1, *Her Excellency the Governor*. This was before women in the U.S. were empowered to vote by the Nineteenth Amendment in 1920, though some states had granted that right.

The film chronicles the relationship between two budding politicians, Jack Barclay and Sylvia Marlow. They meet at law school where they have their first kiss and then again, years later, in a courtroom where they are lawyers on opposite sides of a lawsuit which Barclay wins. It sounds like it might have had the dynamics of a Tracy–Hepburn comedy but there is another element, that Jack becomes increasingly influenced by corrupt politicos as he rises to mayor and then to governor of a Midwestern state. Seeing this, Sylvia refuses to marry him. After he vetoes a child labor bill, she joins a suffrage slate running against him. Barclay as governor wins re-election against this tide with Sylvia being elected lieutenant-governor. When Barclay, now being swayed by a sinister faction that wants him to veto an appropriations bill, the lieutenant-governor tricks him into leaving the state at a critical time. While he is away, she signs the bill. While initially angered about being duped, Jack soon comes to his senses and realizes that Sylvia has saved him from shameful behavior. The corrupt boss is kicked out and Sylvia is now ready to accept Jack as her husband.

It would be fascinating to see this film but, like the rest of Dwan's supervisory efforts at Triangle, it isn't known to exist today. In fact, as Kevin Brownlow notes in his book *Behind the Mask of Innocence*, only a handful of the pro-suffrage films have survived.[132]

The critical reaction to *Her Excellency the Governor* was mixed. Of course, it helped if the trade reviewer was sympathetic or saw commercial potential in what it advocated. The *New York Dramatic Mirror* concluded, "Exhibitors should feature the unique political idea in this play and use to the full advertising value in so live an issue as woman suffrage."[133] Louis Reeves Harrison in *Moving Picture World* thought it a "high comedy of political life."[134]

Variety and *Motion Picture News* considered it only "fair" and *Wid* summed it up thusly: "Impossible and very unsympathetic plot made fairly interesting."[135] These reviews complained of what they considered plot credibility problems, such as the entire suffrage ticket winning except for the top post. They also found the distasteful quality of the male protagonist a hindrance to accepting the romance, particularly when the governor came close to treason by wanting to block the appropriations bill. On the other hand, it is likely that the filmmakers sought to make the suffrage cause more sympathetic by allying it with the war effort.

Wilfred Lucas was credited with doing the best he could as the unsympathetic governor but the critical kudos went to the leading lady: "Very bright, cheering and almost inspiring is the portrayal of a modern woman by Elda Millar. She looks the part of an intelligent and entirely competent woman of today, without sacrifice of the feminine, a clean-cut and charming conception."[136] Millar was also referred to as Mrs. De Wolf Hopper, having married the famous stage actor and one-time Triangle star. Eventually she dropped Millar in favor of her married name and changed her first name as well, becoming known as Hedda Hopper. Under that sobriquet she became one of Hollywood's most powerful gossip columnists.

Her Excellency the Governor may have stimulated Dwan to find more hard-hitting material for the Triangle films. It was reported that for the next film to be directed by Parker, Dwan sought the cooperation of John J. Dillon, commissioner of foods and markets of the State of New York. The story concerned corruption in the food industry among middlemen who greatly inflated the price of food for the public. Dillon agreed not only to cooperate but also to appear in the film. The resulting picture, *The Food Gamblers*, may have been the most fascinating of all the films supervised by Dwan at Triangle.[137]

The head of the United States Food Administration, Herbert Hoover, believed his board's efforts could be helped by the motion picture. Consequently, when a film appeared in July 1917 called *The Public Be Damned* that attacked the food trusts, Hoover publicly endorsed it. *The Food Gamblers*, which was released in early August, followed so quickly on the heels of the earlier film, it is not clear if it could have been inspired by the first movie. Dillon's support for the film also presented him with an opportunity to advocate his solution to the problem, state control of food distribution. According to one review of *The Food Gamblers*, "All the situations have their basis in fact and were suggested by the words of Food Commissioner Dillon...."[138]

Romance was injected into the story with the principals again being played by Elda Millar–Hedda Hopper as a crusading reporter and Wilfred Lucas as Henry Haven, a food commissioner who also heads the food gamblers. The script was still another effort by the workhorse Shirley and it was directed by Parker. The film also incorporated elements of the modern docudrama, sensational melodrama and a touch of Gothic horror.

When a food riot takes place on the East Side, June, a reporter from the *New York Globe*, is sent to investigate. Probing the reasons for the exorbitant cost of food, she interviews various people including shopkeepers and farmers. When she speaks to Commissioner Dillon, he shows her a complete diagram tracing the distribution of food through various corrupt channels down to the consumer.

June writes an article that prompts the food gamblers to arrange a meeting with her at Haven's office. While Haven is smitten with her, one of the other gamblers unsuccessfully tries to bribe her.

Depicting the practical effects of the gamblers' enterprise, there is a scene showing an Italian baby in an East Side apartment dying for lack of proper food. The child's father is played by Eduardo Ciannelli[139]; the father works in Haven's commission house, and he is arrested for stealing some fresh vegetables from the facility. After serving a thirty-day sentence, the Italian returns and finds his baby is dead and his wife driven to madness. The Italian then goes to Haven's office, gags the watchman, knocks Haven unconscious, drags him into a storage ice box and locks him in. The Italian then returns to his home and hangs himself. After three days, a note left by the Italian is discovered revealing that Haven is locked in the icebox. Haven, having learned the horror of starvation, is found in dire shape. As a result of his ordeal, he has changed and will aid June in trying to get a food bill through the legislature.

Haven tells his former colleagues that he will expose their corrupt practices. A few days later, he is shot by a gunman employed by the food ring. The final scene is set in the Assembly Chamber where members of the food trust are set to argue against the bill. As they begin, Haven (brought into the chamber in a wheelchair) accuses the food gamblers of attempted murder because of their fear of exposure. His ex-colleagues are put under arrest. Haven then makes an impassioned plea for the legislature to wipe out the food gambling and, with June standing beside him, confesses his own guilt. According to the *Variety* review, at the close of the film there is a direct entreaty to the audience to write to their Congressmen and Senators to enact reform.[140]

Probably the most celebrated of the films Dwan supervised in Yonkers was *The Food Gamblers* (1917), directed by Albert Parker. From left to right in this shot are Hedda Hopper, Russell Simpson and Wilfred Lucas. Hopper is already wearing one of the ornate hats that would become her trademark (courtesy Academy of Motion Picture Arts and Sciences).

All this in a five-reel film that, according to *Wid's*, ran 63 minutes.[141]

The film elicited a favorable and even excited critical response though there were some reservations. *Photoplay* was among the least impressed and while conceding "it is propaganda stuff that strikes a chord of public sympathy," judged it "a mediocre picture."[142]

The *New York Dramatic Mirror* said the film "presents a powerful appeal for the abolishment of food speculation.... It gives a graphic picture of the suffering in the slums where starvation has driven the inmates of the tenements to desperation."[143] *Variety* proclaimed, "No matter what shortcomings the film may have on its production end the theme sure makes a strong, vigorous appeal for the common people to rise up in their wrath.... The dramatic action is carried with sufficient intensity to sustain the real vital importance of the subject. The ever ridden, harassed common people will give this film three lusty cheers."[144] *Wid's* praised the film as "far superior to the production *The Public Be Damned*."[145]

While *The Food Gamblers* was likely not a

major hit, statements in the trades from exhibitors suggest that it may have done fairly good business. This, combined with the film's provocative nature, which generated favorable publicity for Triangle, seemed to encourage the company to back Dwan's proclaimed agenda of "serious" pictures. In stories appearing in *Motion Picture News* and *Moving Picture Weekly*, it was reported, "Allan Dwan who supervises all Triangle productions made in the East is gradually putting into operation a policy of picture making, whereby he aims to specialize in pictures treating of timely issues touching on the every-day life of American people."[146] Of course, *The Food Gamblers* was cited as an example of this policy.

At this point, however, most of the eastern Triangle films already in the pipeline and awaiting release were not in the same relevant mold as *The Food Gamblers*. One substantial film that did emerge was *Cassidy*. The film was based on a *Cosmopolitan Magazine* story by Larry Evans. With a professed Dickensian view of squalor, *Cassidy* told of the last hours of a derelict suffering from tubercular lungs and stranded in San Francisco far away from his native "N'Yawk." To get the necessary funds to return home, Cassidy unwisely chooses to rob a house belonging to the district attorney. After apprehending him and learning of his plight, the D.A. mercifully lets Cassidy go and supplies him with the money for his journey home to die. The attorney had been up waiting for his daughter to return on a midnight train from boarding school.

Stopping at a nearby saloon, Cassidy learns that a white slave ring has mistakenly taken her off the train. Returning the D.A.'s favor, Cassidy rescues the girl and brings her back to her home. Badly wounded, Cassidy makes his way to the railroad station where he dies.

The film was directed by Art Rosson and his brother Dick played the title role in a way that won kudos from the critics. "Dick Rosson gives a performance as Cassidy that brings out all the horror of his life. He paints a graphic picture of the young man that effects [sic] one deeply."[147] Helen Rockwell of *Motography* viewed *Cassidy* as "sordid from beginning to end, but it is real, it is gripping, it is vital."[148] *Motion Picture News* considered it "a very fine picture"[149] and *Photoplay* praised it as a "well played, well constructed drama."[150] Some reviewers also took note of the atmospheric downpour of rain in all the exterior scenes.

Aside from its lionizing of self-sacrifice, *Cassidy* seemed more tenuous in its connection to the current war than either *Her Excellency the Governor* or *The Food Gamblers*. But in the film company's publication *Triangle Magazine*, it was suggested that the film could be promoted in newspapers because it "might be connected up with the draft situation in New York where, in the tenement districts of the East Side, it was found impossible to get enough men who could pass the physical test. Cassidy is one of these."[151]

Thus, *Her Excellency the Governor*, *The Food Gamblers*, and *Cassidy*, while all containing melodramatic plots, created a much more complex and probing portrait of a nation at war than one would expect from wartime propaganda films. They carried the implication that America could not just celebrate its values but must protect them by reform. But there was a difference in spirit from the rabble-rousing tone of *The Food Gamblers* to the stark tragedy of *Cassidy*.

Exhibitor reports in the trade papers suggest, perhaps not surprisingly, that *Cassidy* was a commercial flop. Possibly because of this, it appears to have been the last of the important productions at the eastern studio. Dwan's interest and power as a production supervisor might have also been dwindling against the background of continuing crisis at Triangle. Ince and Sennett had by now also left the company.

Released a week after *Cassidy* on October 28, *The Man Hater* (based on a *Saturday Evening Post* story) was a wholesome character study of a young woman (Winifred Allen) who judged all men by her drunken father until she gradually learned to love her husband. Directed by Al Parker, it was made with a light touch and seemed to please the critics.

Two other "message" films followed that appear to be unexceptional. *A Case at Law*, a plea "for the suppression of the so-called liquor problem,"[152] starred Dick Rosson as a drink-crazed youth.

At Dwan's insistence for realism, part of *For Valor* was shot at Camp Borden, a Canadian military base about eighty miles from Dwan's birthplace in Toronto. The plot concerns a young woman (Allen) who makes extraordinary sacrifices to get her self-centered brother to enlist. He then goes on to become a war hero. The brother was played by future Griffith star Richard Barthelmess. Both films were released in late November, well after Dwan had left Triangle.

Another film directed by Parker under Dwan's supervision, *From Two to Six*, was not released until February of 1918. This had a German spy plot which was solved within the four-hour period indicated in the title.

Dwan's proposed agenda of realistic and relevant films for a financially strapped studio sounds similar to the 1930s strategy that Warner Brothers employed of grabbing stories from the headlines for much of its product. Dwan, however, had a much more limited stable of talent at his disposal. He may have also lacked a bread and butter genre like the gangster film or the road movie to mesh with commercial concerns. The closest approximation may have been his Horatio Alger–type stories starring Jack Devereaux which seemed to have lacked breadth. In any case, Devereaux never became a rival to Fairbanks. After marrying Louise Drew, daughter of John Drew, making him a relative of the Barrymores, Devereaux's days as a leading man ended.

An editorial by William A. Johnston in *Motion Picture News* in early 1918 may have summarized the industry's feelings on content during the war years. Extolling light entertainment, it pronounced, "Serious drama will not be popular — by all the signs of the times." Johnston later elaborated, "This recommendation of light happy plays may be antagonistic to certain artistic ideals. But we fear very much that the exploitation of these ideals will have to be left to an after-the-war era. These stringent times in general and especially for the motion picture industry indicate the due necessity of feeling and filling the market demand."[153] Dwan had surely learned this industry sentiment of what the market could bear during war. That sentiment appeared to have stuck in his mind when another world war loomed on the horizon.

The upheavals continued at Triangle. H.O. Davis became general manager, emphasizing low-budget programmers in the schedule. Dwan left Triangle for a promising offer in the fall of 1917. After his departure, trade stories on Triangle policy saw a shift from stressing serious pictures to that of the studio running a "diversified program."[154]

The Food Gamblers was probably the film that had the greatest impact during Dwan's tenure as supervisor in Yonkers. It was ironic that this came under the leadership of the man who had replaced Griffith at Triangle. Its plot seemed a realistic elaboration of Griffith's 1909 *Corner in Wheat*, the film that many regard as the cinema's first work of art.

Dwan and Fairbanks: In Again, Out Again

Fairbanks' second Artcraft film was a comedy–Western done in the mold of *Manhattan Madness*, playing on the comic possibilities of the East-West dichotomy. But whereas shooting on *Manhattan Madness* had begun in the west and finished on the East Coast, the new film *Wild and Woolly* began in Manhattan before moving on to Arizona and California. Its plot concerns a young son of a railroad tycoon obsessed with the idea of being a cowboy. He finally gets an opportunity to go West, not realizing that his idea of the West no longer exists anywhere but in books and his imagination. Combining comedy and action, this was one of Fairbanks' best Artcraft productions.

The task of having a new Fairbanks film ready, roughly every two months, was an enormously demanding one for a single director and in May of 1917, Joseph Henabery was hired as first assistant. Henabery later recalled, "Fairbanks and [Emerson] realized they had to produce pictures more quickly to fulfill the contract. They decided that could be accomplished if Emerson confined himself to shooting with Fairbanks, while another director helped plan production and shot episodes in which Doug did not appear. Later, such jobs were called second-unit directors."[155]

Emerson would become Fairbanks' leading director for one year. In his twin bio of Pickford and Fairbanks, Herndon refers to Emerson as "sycophantic" but some earlier books tend to emphasize the Emerson–Loos contribution at the expense of Dwan.[156] In Lahue's book on the history of the Triangle company, Dwan is cited only for accepting production responsibilities in Yonkers and is not even listed in the index.[157] No mention is made of his directing eight feature productions for Triangle while Lahue maintains that of the Fine Arts films, "[o]nly the Fairbanks films made in collaboration with director John Emerson and writer Anita Loos are still remembered."[158]

Dwan is even more of a non-person in Loos' various memoirs. In one, Loos describes Emerson's screen debut in the adaptation of *The Conspiracy* as if he had made the film for Griffith's Fine Arts without crediting a director.[159] Of course, it had been made for Famous Players under Dwan's direction. In another volume, Loos says that after the success of *His Picture in the Papers*, Griffith "assigned John Emerson as Doug's permanent director, and put me on as sole writer for the Fairbanks unit."[160] Loos may have been confusing the Triangle period with Emerson's stint at Artcraft but this claim has the effect of wiping out numerous Fairbanks films with other directors. For the record, after *His Picture in the Papers*, Fairbanks made four Triangle films with Dwan, two with Cabanne (who had already directed Fairbanks' first two films), and one each with Lloyd Ingraham and Paul Powell. Emerson directed only one other feature with Fairbanks at Triangle, *The Americano* as well as the oddball two-reeler *The Mystery of the Leaping Fish*.

Emerson and Loos were undoubtedly critics' darlings for the satirical aspects they brought to the Fairbanks films. This continued with two other 1917 features, *Down to Earth* which mocks hypochondriacs and *Reaching for the Moon* which spoofs "New Age Thought." Sandwiched between these films was a Western, *The Man from Painted Post,* which gave Henabery his chance to direct Fairbanks. Henabery conceded that unlike other Fairbanks films, it had no theme or moral but it proved the biggest moneymaker of the Artcraft productions.[161] It may have also suggested that audiences were growing more interested in seeing Fairbanks in straight action films.

Henabery recalled that after the film was made, "Emerson and Loos came back to Hollywood from New York [and] I sensed that things were not good between them and the Fairbanks people...." Henabery did not know the reason for the discord but it may have had to do with the way in which Emerson and Loos were promoting themselves as the brains behind Fairbanks. Emerson had hired publicity agents, not a common practice for directors. Loos wrote of this period, "But worldwide acclaim had made Doug touchy; his male chauvinism had been bruised when the *Ladies' Home Journal* published my picture with the caption 'The little girl who made Doug Fairbanks famous.'"[162] Fairbanks may have been chauvinistic and Loos had certainly helped his career but he was already famous on stage and screen before he made films with Loos and Emerson. Adding to the strain was the fact that Fairbanks now clearly preferred the West Coast while Emerson and Loos wanted to stay in New York.

There were also practical concerns that affected the working relationship. Henabery noticed when listening to a script being developed by Emerson that not much consideration was being given to cost and he regarded Emerson as one of those ex-stage directors with little concern for the technical aspects of film-making.[163]

In the fall of 1917, it was announced that Dwan had signed to work as one of Fairbanks' directors and that he would be alternating with Emerson. But Emerson never directed another film with Doug. By January, Emerson and Loos left Fairbanks and Artcraft to make films in the east for Jesse Lasky. Loos said that when they left, "Doug was relieved to be rid of us."[164]

Characteristically, she made no mention of Dwan and said that Fairbanks "replaced John with Vic Fleming as director."[165] In fact, Fleming would soon be joining the armed forces and would not be promoted to director until almost two years later.

On October 7, about the time that Dwan signed with Fairbanks, Goldwyn at last released *Fighting Odds*. Some reviewers recognized that the film was a re-written version of the screenwriters' unsuccessful play *Under Sentence*. The plot concerned James Copley, an automobile manufacturer who shares his stocks with his employees. He is persuaded to join a conglomerate against the advice of his wife (Maxine Elliott), whose views have always guided him. Copley discovers that although he is given the title of president, he is a figurehead who no longer controls his plant, and is made the patsy when he signs a doctored statement of the company's financial resources. This leads to his conviction and imprisonment with his wife vowing to clear him, which she resourcefully proceeds to do with the assistance of the district attorney.

While *Variety* praised *Fighting Odds* as a "strong story of modern finance," the reviews were generally unenthusiastic. Critics did not regard the plot as credible or original and perhaps dismissed the male protagonist as a "boob" for being duped by a large combine. The critics also appeared conscious of Elliott's age[166] and, while generally respectful, expressed approval of the paucity of her close-ups.

Samuel Goldwyn remembered the film as an "abject failure" and said that no Goldwyn film was ever attacked so ferociously. He noted ruefully that its commercial failure was "so conspicuous that it resulted in the cancellation of other pictures of ours."[167]

An incomplete print of *Fighting Odds* survives at the Museum of Modern Art (three of the film's five reels). It reveals a somewhat better film than the one described above. It's thematically consistent with the pictures Dwan subsequently supervised at Triangle; the business owner victimized by the conglomerate is clearly portrayed as a progressive figure. The villainous tycoon was easily identifiable to the *Variety* critic as a "Wall Street financier." The critics might also have seen too many films featuring corrupt businessmen and by October 1917, with the nation now at war for six months, "institutions of America, including Wall Street and its supports, were now objects of red, white and blue veneration."[168]

It was probably also disturbing to see a male figure so dependent on his wife for wisdom and support and *Fighting Odds* might have qualified as a nightmare scenario for all those decrying a "feminized" America. Again, Dwan could embrace both the resurgence of masculine energy in the Fairbanks films and the rise of feminine power in other movies. He is successful in *Fighting Odds* at depicting the strength of the couple's relationship and their functioning as a team. Particularly effective are the scenes in which the troubled Copely is with his wife. Henry Clive (as Copely) and Elliott exhibit a pantomime that captures the intensity of their bond through this crisis. Through editing and especially the blocking of their movements, Dwan sensitively shows the magnitude and feeling of their commitment to one another. While the female figure is clearly dominant, this is a relationship where each partner has a deep need for the other.

Unfortunately, the melodramatic device of having Mrs. Copley pose as a femme fatale to trick the financier into revealing secrets seems to justify critical objections of credibility. Wasn't the financier who studied his victim likely to have seen a picture of his wife who attended society functions with him? Dwan at least gets some mileage out of the makeover process the heroine undergoes as she sees her new image in a mirror for the first time. Most of the footage for this latter part of the film is missing. Wid ungallantly wrote of Elliott's character, "[S]he hardly needed any assistance when she went calling on this guy at his home because she looked big enough to bat him over the head with something and walk away with everything he owned."[169]

The film Elliott made for Goldwyn immediately after *Fighting Odds*, *The Eternal Magdalene* was not released until the spring of 1919 and quickly passed into oblivion, as did her film career.

Dwan signed his one-year contract with the Douglas Fairbanks Pictures Corporation in New York on September 20, 1917, to take effect on October 15. He was to collaborate on scripts as well as direct five films for a sum of $100,000. Dwan was then living in the Westchester County town of Harmon, which had made for an easy commute to the Yonkers studio, but he would have to move to Los Angeles to work with Fairbanks.

Dwan recalled riding by train to meet Fairbanks in California when he received a telegram from the star to rendezvous with him in Salina, Kansas, where they would take a train back to New York.

Upon following the telegram's instructions and meeting with Fairbanks, the star provided Dwan with this explanation: "I had to get out of Los Angeles for a while. Your friend Owen Moore says he's going to shoot me, if he's sober enough to point the gun."[170] Moore had starred in two of Dwan's films and had renewed his marriage vows with Mary Pickford on the day of Dwan's wedding in San Juan Capistrano. And therein was the problem.

Moore had become a hopeless alcoholic and Pickford had

found a happy relationship with the also-married Fairbanks. News of the affair had begun to leak out. While studio executives dreaded the impact if the affair became public, a greater problem had presented itself: The jealous Moore was now threatening to kill the "climbing monkey" who had taken his wife's affections.

As Dwan recalled, Fairbanks needed to find locations outside Los Angeles for his next film and needed Dwan to help him concoct a story. Doug's brother John accompanied them on the train trip, bringing along books, magazines and scripts. A magazine story that caught Doug's interest, "D'Artagnan of Kansas," was about a young man filled with the romantic ideals of the hero of Alexandre Dumas' *The Three Musketeers*. The story took him to the Grand Canyon, an appealing and picturesque location. Dwan suggested the addition of the Canyon de Chelly in New Mexico. Dwan and Fairbanks then proceeded to put the scenario together.

Apparently, Fairbanks still felt comfortable spending one more night in Los Angeles because he held a banquet there for Dwan on October 26[171] and made a ten-minute speech extolling the director. Various members of the company provided entertainment, which included a boxing exhibition. The evening was capped with a screening of *Manhattan Madness*. The next day, the company left to begin shooting in Arizona.

At the Grand Canyon, they were able to exploit one site to show Fairbanks dangling over a mile-high abyss. In fact, there was a ledge (unseen by the camera) to provide Doug with protection.

At the Canyon de Chelly, the cast and crew were encamped under a sandstone cliff. The Indians in the area would not come near them, saying that this part of the canyon was haunted. While dismissing this as superstition, Dwan still hoped to get the Indians to work on the film, so he placated them by moving the operation to the other side of the canyon. That night, Dwan said, the entire cliff fell on where the tents had previously been pitched.[172]

After the location shooting was completed, the company returned to Hollywood to shoot additional scenes. If Moore had ever been a threat, he apparently was no longer one now.

Some observations should be made about Dwan's role in supervising Fairbanks stunts, especially as they were so prominent in *A Modern Musketeer*. In a 1920 magazine article, Dwan wrote, "I had learned to do a little scrapping in college as well as having done some wrestling and played football. I told Fairbanks that I could teach him how to do the stunts which have since made him famous, and he was willing."[173] This sounds like an astonishing bit of braggadocio but while somewhat exaggerated, it was not too far off the mark. In fact, a trade story reporting Dwan's signing with the Fairbanks Pictures Corporation noted, "At college, Mr. Dwan was a holder of wrestling championships, and many of the athletic 'stunts' which have made Douglas Fairbanks' pictures so strikingly original were the result of consultations and tryouts by the two athletes, Fairbanks and Dwan."[174] This statement most likely was approved by, if not originating from, Fairbanks' company.

During the making of *A Modern Musketeer*, when Doug had to jump from one house to another (actually just facades), Dwan kept the distances shorter than what he knew Fairbanks could achieve. When Fairbanks protested that he could jump farther, Dwan explained that the important thing was not the distance but showing the ease with which Fairbanks could make the jump. Similarly, for the scene where Fairbanks climbs the steeple, Dwan had concealed handholds placed closer than was necessary.

Dwan summed up this philosophy to Kevin Brownlow: "Of course, when Doug did any of his stunts he was essentially graceful, that's one thing he struggled for and I insisted on, there was never to be any evidence of effort on his part...." Contrasting his own athletic skills with Fairbanks, Dwan said, "I did it by sheer muscular push while he did it gracefully, if I struggled through the air, he floated through the air and everything we did was based on measurement of his reach."[175]

A Modern Musketeer was the last Artcraft release of 1917, opening on December 31. Once again a Fairbanks film was selected to open a new theater in New York City owned by S.L Rothapfel. This time it was the Rivoli at Broadway and 49th Street. It was announced in February that Mrs. Woodrow Wilson attended a motion picture theater for the first time by going to see *A Modern Musketeer* at Loews Columbia in Washington, D.C.

The first images of *A Modern Musketeer* were certainly something different as Fairbanks appeared as Dumas' D'Artagnan of three centuries ago. Doug was introduced in a close-up acknowledging the audience and gesturing to his long curls and mustache. He had never appeared in any costume, not counting his Western getups which still could be deemed contemporary. Comporting himself in a tavern, D'Artagnan is dazzled by a mysterious lady who drops a handkerchief. His labor to retrieve it sparks a brawl and swordplay that seems to involve everyone in the tavern. The fight proceeds over a stairway, roof beams and tables as D'Artagnan takes on all comers. As D'Artagnan exits out a window before an advancing mob, a title asks if we will ever see his like again in his pursuit of chivalry.

We then see D'Artagnan in medium shot dissolve into the image of a modern man who walks up to the camera and into close-up, revealing Doug and his signature smile. The prologue we have witnessed is but one of three beginnings to the film, each related to the other and gracefully intertwining like a paper folded into three parts. In fact, all three may be regarded as prologues, each zigzagging in time from the previous one, after which the story proper begins. In the process, the Fairbanks hero is clearly seen as a confluence of past and present.

With each episode, the narrative becomes increasingly outrageous. If the first seems wildly exaggerated, the second ends in absurdity, and the third borders on the surreal. The second segment is a parallel to the first with Doug in modern dress as Ned Thacker of Kansas, spying from his window what looks

Fairbanks makes his entrance as D'Artagnan in *A Modern Musketeer* (1917) (Allan Dwan papers. Collection number 3566. American Heritage Center, University of Wyoming).

Our first glimpses of the infant reveal that he already seems to be showing the delight of the Fairbanks smile.

Ned does indeed grow up with flowery ideas of chivalry that we are shown in ensuing scenes create misunderstanding and chaos until Ned decides he doesn't want to be in Kansas any more. It is then appropriately in reaching the far west that Ned ceases to be a buffoon and becomes the hero. It was another occasion where, in playing an eccentric character, Fairbanks found a good vehicle for both action and comedy.

Much of the sparkle of the film dissipates when the story moves from the wistful comedy of Kansas to the crude melodrama of the West. Fairbanks still impresses with his feats of athletic daring against the scenic wonders of Arizona's great canyons. But the schism between Doug the comedian and Doug the action hero is more apparent.

like a woman being abused by a man. Ned leaps out the window and onto a telephone pole that takes him to the ground. He follows the apparent miscreant into a saloon where, paralleling D'Artagnan's experience, Ned then finds himself getting into a scrap with all the denizens therein. Of course, with much leaping about, Ned subdues them only to find that the "offended" lady is appalled by Ned's action and immediately goes to the aid of her man. Conveying the quixotic nature of Ned's behavior (and by extension of the whole spirit of Fairbanks), the scene is virtually lifted out of Cervantes, adding Doug's variations. Leaving the saloon, the issue of modern woman's rights is brought to Doug's attention but he insouciantly returns to his quarters, which has printed on its window shade, "Society for the Prevention of Cruelty to Women."

The question is then raised if there is a "scientific reason" for Ned's chivalry. And so we have a third beginning, a literal beginning since it gives us the details of Ned's birth, as if revealing the origin of a superhero. A montage of a cyclone's devastating effects on a small Kansas community is followed by a scene of a woman about to give birth. She has been reading Dumas' *The Three Musketeers* for the last six months and praying that she gives birth to a son like D'Artagnan. The woman perseveres as the raging cyclone inflicts damage, and so Ned Thacker is born as if the cyclone helped nurture him. Dwan has it down to a mathematical formula as the title reads:

> 2 + 2= 4
> Cyclone + D'Artagnan=Speed.

A Modern Musketeer was embraced gleefully by both the critics and audiences. Peter Milne of *Motion Picture News* proclaimed, "In *A Modern Musketeer*, Douglas Fairbanks in one bound again attains the heights of comedy, heights which have been languishing for an occupant since his former successes."[176] *Variety* said, "For the multitudes of Fairbanks fans, *A Modern Musketeer* ranks with the best of that series of pictures."[177] *Wid's* said simply, "Here is the best Fairbanks that has been turned out since *Manhattan Madness*."[178] Dwan won praise for his direction, scenario and even for his intertitles. Fairbanks seemed to have fared very well without the aid of Loos and Emerson.

Although Loos had helped mold Fairbanks' screen persona, the Loos–Emerson films were generally less dynamic than those of Dwan in developing Doug as a provocateur who challenges normal life, whether as the evangelist of laughter in *The Habit of Happiness*, the outrageous braggart who provokes a conspiracy hoax and then creates his own in *Manhattan Madness*, or the young man who revives the spirit of chivalry in *A Modern Musketeer*. In the process, the romantic image of Doug was steadily advanced.

Perhaps Dwan had seen more deeply into Fairbanks' character and dreams. Fairbanks' first biographers, Ralph Hancock and Doug's niece Letitia, wrote, "Alexandre Dumas' *The Three Musketeers* had been in the back of his mind ever since he could remember. He once admitted that his ideal had always been

D'Artagnan, the fourth musketeer, and that character had not only influenced every picture he made but Doug had consciously or subconsciously lived the role all his life."[179] This was the first of three occasions where Fairbanks would bring D'Artagnan to the screen.

Fairbanks had by now become increasingly involved in giving his time to raise funds for the war effort. In September 1917, Fairbanks and Billy Sunday staged a benefit baseball game for U.S. soldiers. On October 20, shortly before shooting began on *A Modern Musketeer*, Fairbanks made a whirlwind tour across the country, selling $900,000 worth of Liberty bonds and then purchasing an additional $100,000 to make it an even million.

Dwan too was pressed into service when for another charity event, the *Los Angeles Examiner* Christmas Fund, Fairbanks revived his twenty minute stage act, *A Regular Business Man*. Louise Huff and Frank Campeau joined him for this sketch and Dwan directed it (his first credit for stage direction).

Dwan had also become part of Fairbanks' social circle, of which Charles Chaplin was a prominent member. Jeannie Macpherson, now a scriptwriter for Famous Players–Lasky, held a dinner at her home to celebrate the success of *A Modern Musketeer* with Fairbanks as the guest of honor. The entertainment at the event rated coverage in *Moving Picture World*:

> After the repast the guests provided a unique entertainment. Charles Chaplin gave imitations of English music hall artists and a serious imitation of the late Beerbohm Tree. Messrs. Fairbanks, Dwan, Chaplin and [Ottaway] Treen collectively offered a variety show that would have startled the heads of the vaudeville syndicate had they seen it.
>
> Grand opera was accorded a place on the impromptu program, the same quartette rendering selections from *Rigoletto* and *Lucia*, and Chaplin followed with his famous impersonation of Pavlowa which created merriment. John Browne and Alan [sic] Dwan did a thought transference stunt that astonished the audience. A million dollar show.[180]

If "speed" was the catchword for the hero of *A Modern Musketeer,* it could also be said to extend to its director. A blurb in the publicity pamphlet for Artcraft noted, "Allan Dwan, the new Fairbanks director, is noted for speed, and this gives promise of an increased number of releases this year."[181]

With all the pressures to churn out his films, Dwan's "speed" was likely another asset recognized by Fairbanks in selecting his director. Shortly after Dwan agreed to terms, it was announced that Art Rosson would be leaving Triangle to be Dwan's assistant director. Rosson was quoted as saying that after Dwan resigned from Triangle, "I refuse to work with any other man."[182] With the departure of Emerson, the pressures mounted on Dwan. It was decided that while he would write the scenario of the next Fairbanks film, Rosson would direct it under Dwan's supervision.

Fairbanks was preoccupied not only with a new film but with another charity event, a rodeo to be performed for the benefit of the Red Cross scheduled for January 12, 1918. Fairbanks commitment was surely genuine but so was his fondness for playing the wild westerner to the hilt. Back in May of 1917, Al Lichtman, then general manager of Artcraft, and Ben Schulberg, general manager for Paramount, were sent to Los Angeles. According to a story in *Moving Picture World*, when Fairbanks learned of their visit, he arranged for forty Mexicans in Western costumes and bearing guns to meet their train as it arrived at the station. Led by Fairbanks, who was disguised to look like Pancho Villa, the party ordered the Pullman conductor to deliver Lichtman and Schulberg to them. When the two men disembarked, they were greeted with three shots from every gun. The executives were then ushered into a stagecoach and taken to the Lasky studio. "Work ceased temporarily while Cecil B. DeMille and Mary Pickford extended the studio key to the half-frightened Easterners."[183] Lichtman and Schulberg might have caught on to the joke early but from what we know of Fairbanks' propensity for such pranks, he probably did not warn them in advance.

For the more contained Red Cross benefit show, there would be a Mexican raid, an Indian war dance and Doug riding a bucking bronco. This activity converged with the making of the new Fairbanks film, a Western called *Headin' South*. Due to the influence of Treasury Secretary W.G. McAdoo, who must have been pleased by Doug's bond-raising efforts, Fairbanks was able to charter eight Pullmans and twelve baggage cars to carry two hundred cowboys and as many horses from Los Angeles to Tucson, Arizona, where the exteriors were to be shot.

The film was photographed by Hugh McClung and Harry Thorpe. During the shooting, Thorpe became the second Fairbanks cameraman to be drafted.

Headin' South, released on February 25, 1918, was referred to as a "Tale of Two Borders."[184] This was the kind of symmetrical plot typical of Dwan's sense of design and referred to the Canadian and Mexican borders. In this film, a gambler (Frank Campeau) from the Far North, wanted by the law, kills the Canadian Mountie pursuing him and makes his way to Mexico. Organizing an outlaw band there, he becomes known as "Spanish Joe." A mysterious stranger calling himself "Headin' South" (Fairbanks) joins the gang. When the bandits threaten some Mexican women, Headin' helps them escape. In the ensuing gunplay, the Texas Rangers arrive to save the day and it is revealed that Headin' South is actually a member of the Northwest Mounted Police.

Headin' South was regarded by the critics as something of a comedown from *A Modern Musketeer* but generally pleased both them and the public. Carrying a greater emphasis on action, it was summed up by *Variety* as a "lively melodramatic comedy."[185]

In February, in response to a request from Treasury Secretary McAdoo, Fairbanks agreed to participate in the Third Liberty Loan Drive with another trans-continental tour. But in order to make this tour, Fairbanks would have to work day and night to get his next film finished. Ever the problem fixer, Dwan wrote a scenario called *Mr. Fix-It,* based on a suggestion by Ernest Butterworth, that would use mostly interior settings, making shooting both by day and night possible. This time, Dwan would be directing.

After the robust action of the last two films, *Mr. Fix-It* gave Dwan an opportunity to turn again to the gentler side of Doug's nature. The film's publicity noted that it was the title character's theory "that happiness is a habit and that real happiness comes to those who make other people enjoy life," suggesting a spinoff of aphoristic evangelicalism from the first Dwan collaboration.

At England's Oxford University, Dick Remington (Doug) is a roommate of Reginald Burroughs, a wealthy American who has been away from home for so long that his family doesn't know what he now looks like. When Reginald dreads returning home to his three haughty maiden aunts (they sent him to England to be educated because they thought America too democratic), Dick volunteers to go in his place.

Arriving at the Burroughs' New York mansion in Washington Square, Dick asserts himself and proceeds to shake things up. When he encounters a group of orphan children and their big sister in the slums, he moves them right into the Burroughs home. Moving from this bit of cheery social engineering to affairs of the heart, he makes sure that the woman betrothed to him marries the man she loves instead. He then does the same for his "sister," who also has been matched with the wrong man.

Mr. Fix-It also represented an aesthetic challenge for Dwan in that he could not exploit the atmospheric touches he was adept at extracting with location shooting. However, he was able to employ Wilfred Buckland, known for his spectacular settings in Cecil B. DeMille films, to supervise the furnishings for the interiors.[186] It is not mentioned who designed the New York City streets, where near the end of the film Doug battles gang members. In the course of this urban combat, he makes an escape by a clothesline and swings across the street on an election banner.

This virile action scene, like the climax of *The Habit of Happiness*, is the only outburst of fighting heroics in the film. The rest has Doug behaving as more of a benevolent trickster and a sunshine reformer. One might even comment that apart from the aforementioned climax, *Mr. Fix-It* looks more like a Mary Pickford film. But even more than in *The Habit of Happiness*, Doug's gentle side is wrung from the essence of his screen persona.

In *A Modern Musketeer,* Doug's mother expressed the wish that he would always remain a boy and here it is Doug's eternal boyishness that ignites things, starting with the prank of an identity switch. Doug not only identifies with the children in antics like crawling down the stairs with them but shows a strong empathy for their plight, especially in the case of a little girl with a doll. Dwan was successful in showing Doug's nurturing side because he could see the vitality to reshape his environment in Fairbanks' boyish energy and innocence.

In March of 1918, Fairbanks collected over a thousand dollars at a charity ball for the American Red Cross. To get the money, he was compelled to climb up the side of a building, sing "Over There" and box three rounds with Leach Cross, a former lightweight champion. According to Artcraft's publicity news, Fairbanks several times stopped work on *Mr. Fix-It* "to attend Red Cross teas, Y.M.C.A. meetings and War Camp Fund benefits."[187]

With Fairbanks occupied elsewhere, Dwan likely had a greater share of responsibility in post-production after the exhausting shooting schedule. *Mr. Fix-It* was released on April 15, and the critics appeared to appreciate its change of pace. Peter Milne of *Motion Picture News* noted, "All big stunt stuff is absent. It is Fairbanks the strong, healthy athlete and the comedian who laughs everything full in the face who appears throughout the picture. His personality, his pep, and in this role, his ready grasp of human nature make *Mr. Fix-It* a truly great comedy.... Mr. Dwan is probably the ideal director for the star. The tempo of the action, the arrangement of the scenes, the evident spontaneity of every bit of business are always mindful of his genius as a director of the Fairbanks type of picture."[188] *Photoplay* was one of the few dissenters among the specialty press, calling the film "a thin imitation of the sort of things John Emerson and Anita Loos used to create for him with a curious ramble-scramble fight thrown in for good measure."[189] *Photoplay* was probably correct that the fight scene was extraneous to the story but Dwan was drawing more from his previous work with the star than attempting to parrot the satirical edge of Emerson and Loos.

On April 6, the first anniversary of the U.S. declaration of war, Fairbanks, Pickford and Chaplin helped kick off the Third Liberty Loan Drive by appearing on the steps of the Navy Building in Washington, D.C. The first to be introduced was Fairbanks, who gave a speech to the estimated 40,000 spectators which resulted in a heavy sale. Appropriately, the first purchaser was a Roosevelt — not Teddy but the assistant secretary of the Navy, Franklin D. Roosevelt. The celebrated trio would next take their tour to New York.[190] While Fairbanks and Pickford were undoubtedly sincere in their devotion to the country, the loan drive also provided a cover for them to be traveling together. Beth Fairbanks also headed for New York to meet her husband. And at this time, she finally realized that Doug was having an affair. Before the month was over, it was announced that Fairbanks and Beth had agreed to separate.

Dwan may have also been having marital problems at this time. He and Pauline Bush would divorce in late 1919. Were Dwan's workaholic hours at the studio already creating strains in the marriage?

Then Dwan seemed to briefly drop out of sight. In late May and early June, stories appeared in the trade papers that he had recovered from a serious illness but no details were offered.

During Dwan's absence, Joseph Henabery was pressed into service both writing and directing the Fairbanks feature *Say, Young Fellow!* Released in June, it appeared to continue Fairbanks' winning streak. But in July, Henabery became another member of the Fairbanks staff to be drafted.

Having recovered from his mysterious malady, Dwan plunged into the next Fairbanks film, *Bound in Morocco*. In this August release, Fairbanks played an American driving through the desert when he learns of a beautiful girl about to be sold to a harem and decides to rescue her. One critic commented, "It is in my opinion, the poorest picture in which up to date Fairbanks has appeared."[191] While other critics were somewhat kinder, most cited the thinness of the plot. One bit mentioned by most critics (and recalled by Dwan when interviewed by Bogdanovich) was a scene at the end of the movie where a title reads, "One hundred years later" followed by a shot of two tombstones and a lot of smaller ones around it. (Buster Keaton used a similar comic postscript to his characters' romance in the 1927 feature *College*.) *Bound in Morocco* is one of the few Fairbanks movies to have vanished completely.

The next Fairbanks film Dwan directed would have an atypical source. For the first time since *The Lamb,* a Fairbanks picture was based on one of his stage successes, the 1914 play *He Comes Up Smiling*. Frances Marion, who was having continuing success writing for Mary Pickford, wrote the adaptation. The resulting film, ready for release in September, received the best reviews for a Fairbanks film since *A Modern Musketeer*.

The film was cited in particular for its opening. Fairbanks plays Jerry Martin, a bank teller whose duties include looking after the bank vice-president's pet canary. Critics noted the visual simile of the bars on the teller's window and the canary's cage. One day the bird escapes, sending Jerry on a daunting chase with elaborate acrobatics, including climbing up a building and walking on telephone lines. (The first of two reels of the film, recently rediscovered, drew laughs at the 2004 Pordenone Silent Film Festival.) At the end of his chase, Jerry meets a philosophical hobo who encourages Jerry to find freedom for both himself and the bird. In the course of his odyssey, Jerry becomes a hobo and then later, by donning the wrong clothes after a swim, assumes the identity of a wealthy stockbroker as further plot complications ensue. *Motion Picture News* called the film "a knockout."[192] Wid said, "I think most everybody is going to agree with me that this is the fastest and funniest thing Doug had ever done."[193]

He Comes Up Smiling appears to have done well at the box office but it may have been unable to live up to its potential. The film's release coincided with the worst period of the infamous 1918 influenza epidemic in the United States. Theaters were closed for weeks, though in some cases they reopened with the same attractions they had before the closings. And obviously for a time after that, many were still wary about going to theaters.

He Comes Up Smiling was the last of the Fairbanks comedies to be directed by Allan Dwan, suggesting a triumphant ending to their collaboration. But there was to have been another Dwan–Fairbanks teaming that was aborted with apparent acrimony.

For his next film, Fairbanks decided upon an adaptation of the play *Arizona* by Augustus Thomas. *Arizona* had already been produced as a 1913 feature that ran six reels, co-directed by the playwright.

But who directed the Fairbanks version of *Arizona*? Some sources, such as Alistair Cooke's 1940 monograph *The Making of a Screen Character*, list Fairbanks himself as the director; reviewers during the film's release cited Albert Parker, who had joined the Fairbanks organization shortly before filming began. But the August 25 edition of *Wid's Daily* carried an ad that read, "ALLEN [sic] DWAN NOW DIRECTING AND SUPERVISING THE SCREEN PRESENTATION OF *ARIZONA* BY AUGUSTUS THOMAS."[194] As will be shown later, there are other contemporary sources that list Dwan as director or at least commencing direction of the film.

In late August 1918, there were pressures mounting on both Fairbanks and Dwan, aside from the demands of a hectic schedule. Fairbanks and Beth were now separated and it was a matter of time before she would sue for divorce. With Pickford's marriage also tottering, the prospects were strong that word of the affair between Doug and Mary would become public. And there was no way of knowing the impact that would have on their careers at a time when divorce was highly controversial. Fairbanks also remained deeply committed to the war effort and had just completed a short film supporting the Fourth Liberty Loan Drive. (Fairbanks at first denied his separation by saying that it was German propaganda.) The strains in Dwan's marriage may have also been surfacing by this time as he continued working at his frantic pace.

Also, while *Arizona* was a melodrama, it did not seem to lend itself to Doug's type of humor and acrobatics. The story dealt with a matter of honor at a military base and how an officer is compromised when he tries to restrain a straying wife but is forbidden by his code from providing an explanation.

There were many potential areas of contention in determining how to proceed. And at this difficult time, Fairbanks surely did not want a box office disaster. Making a film dealing with an unfaithful wife also seems a curious decision to have been made during Fairbanks' own awkward situation, especially as the affair is not treated sympathetically.

A hint that there was discord in the making of the film surfaced in an item in the December 1918 issue of *Picture Play Magazine*: "Douglas Fairbanks has completed the last production under his contract with Artcraft. [*Arizona*] was made under the supervision of Director Allan Dwan, who has left the Fairbanks organization and joined Marshall Neilan at the Griffith Studios, where both are engaged in supervising the productions being made by Harry Garson, in which Clara Kimball Young and Blanche Sweet are being featured."[195]

The December issue of *Photoplay* was more to the point: "Allan Dwan is no longer directing for Douglas Fairbanks. Dwan began the new Fairbanks picture, *Arizona*, but left when it was half completed. Albert Parker finished it and will be retained to direct the ensuing Fairbanks subjects."[196]

Further corroboration for the above story can be seen in an agreement signed between Dwan and the Douglas Fairbanks Film Corporation in September. Where Dwan's initial contract with the Corporation was to have lasted until October 15, it was here, by mutual consent, terminated immediately. Dwan's compensation was for $100,000 per year with $52,000 to be paid on a weekly basis of $1,000 per week. The balance was to be paid on the basis of $9,600 per film for five films that Dwan would direct. But for the fifth film on his contract Dwan agreed to be paid only $5,000, suggesting his directorial role was truncated.[197] Albert Parker was announced as the director of *Arizona*[198] and years later reaffirmed this credit to Kevin Brownlow.

So how did Fairbanks come to be listed as director by some sources?

The earliest source I have found for this credit is Alistair Cooke's 1940 study *Douglas Fairbanks: The Making of a Screen Character*, written for a Museum of Modern Art retrospective. Not surprisingly, for a volume of that early date, the book contains errors.

Probably because of the circumstances under which the film was made, Parker's name was not used prominently in promoting it. For initial ads, the only creative credit was "Produced by Douglas Fairbanks Film Corporation."[199] It is entirely possible that the researcher involved, not mindful of the confusion to future film historians (or even that there would *be* future film historians), simply used this as the basis for crediting Fairbanks as director. Once this credit appeared in Cooke's book, it was copied by others. Unless an earlier source is found, Cooke's book appears to be the primary source for this error.

Arizona was released on December 8 as some theaters were reopening while others were closing because of a second influenza wave. The reviews were not encouraging and harped on how the play had been denigrated. *Photoplay* considered it a "cheap burlesque."[200] *Arizona* was quickly forgotten.[201]

And what of Fairbanks and Dwan? An item in the January 1919 *Photoplay* suggested a possible reconciliation: "Allan Dwan, who left the Fairbanks company in the middle of a picture he was directing, is handling the megaphone for the new Clara Kimball Young production. When he has completed it, Dwan will return to the Fairbanks organization to resume his direction of Douglas."[202]

But this was apparently wishful thinking on somebody's part. Two months later, *Photoplay* published this rejoinder: "No peace conference followed the split between Doug Fairbanks and Director Allan Dwan, as predicted by the Hollywood board of strategy. It had been rumored that Dwan, who drew a salary of $2,000 weekly for directing the athletic star for a year, would return, but scouts of the intelligence division report that the parting between star and director was such that not even a Wilson speech at a Versailles conference could ever bring them back — except as combatants."[203]

Dwan seemed to disappear from the public eye in the fall of 1918. At that time, an interviewer caught up with him and got this information: "Allan has been taking a four weeks' layoff since his contract expired at Fairbanks', which he spent on the flat of his back with a doctor in attendance and a trained nurse in the offing to see that he took what the Doc ordered.... No, Allan did not have the 'Flu'; just a trifling indisposition superinduced by nine years of steady work and no play — sort of a nervous breakdown."[204] Both workaholic hours and the breakup with Fairbanks may have taken their toll.

A year earlier, when Fairbanks and Dwan went to work on *A Modern Musketeer*, Fairbanks was said to have given Dwan boxing lessons, and the two would engage in sparring matches between pictures. The sparring had now gone into their work but good-natured competitiveness had here eluded Fairbanks and Dwan.

The Return of the King

In early 1919, Fairbanks, continuing to assert his independence, became one of the founders of United Artists, a film company run not by moguls but by Doug, Mary Pickford, Charles Chaplin and D.W. Griffith.

The freedom and responsibility presented by his UA co-ownership led Fairbanks to contemplate a sea change in his style and persona. In his films, Doug had met assorted challenges and fads and always triumphed. Against these challenges of the modern world and through all his eccentricities, he had personified traditional American virtues and common sense of a kind that he preached in his ghost-written inspirational books. But the films often emphasized the process of change. Doug was steadfast but not dogmatic and there was always a playfulness that left him open for something new. That playfulness was also a characteristic that he shared with Dwan, and it helped make them so compatible.

The struggles for Doug to remake himself in these movies can be seen as the struggles of youth. They were also a projection of the inner conflicts of Americans of the time, who were coping with social changes and entering a world war. By 1920, America was coming out of an era of transition while Fairbanks had reached his thirty-seventh birthday.

Fairbanks was now thinking of working on a grander scale but he had to find an identity that would accommodate his ambitions. While the character known as "Doug" would pass through transformations in his films, "Doug" would be supplanted in a larger transformation that Fairbanks needed to undergo. He would be altering his image but finding one that would be so lasting that it would obliterate the earlier one in the public's memory. He must have also grasped that with his brand of physicality, even if this metamorphosis could extend his career, the time was still limited. He would try to compensate with quality.

Fairbanks had also to resolve an aesthetic question: Was he

primarily a hero or a comedian? Of course, heroes could be light-hearted and comic actors could be heroic but there was a question of primacy that seemed demanded by the times. Film reviews of the teens frequently referred to Doug as a comedian. But in recent decades, when film historians and fans discuss silent comedy, they rarely refer to Fairbanks. Nevertheless, he seems to have had a major influence on the comic figures of the twenties. As with the Fairbanks films, but in his own style, Buster Keaton could mix comedy with a sense of awesome spectacle.

But the comic actor of the twenties whose work is acknowledged to most resemble Fairbanks' comedies is Harold Lloyd. Perhaps the greatest difference between the two would be that where Doug aspired to being some kind of superman, Lloyd was an Everyman. More tellingly, Lloyd's "glasses" character was often shown as a member of the middle class in pursuit of financial success. In the twenties, it become widely accepted that there were burgeoning opportunities for those of modest means to attain wealth. The social crisis over masculinity had not ended but had eased with the realization that "office work" could lead to a fortune.[205]

The Doug of the Fairbanks comedies was rarely concerned about money and usually came from a comfortable background. Fairbanks was a shrewd businessman but in his movies he needed to project the totally romantic side of his personality. The foreign settings of the past helped provide the distancing that made his swashbuckling adventures of the twenties more appealing to moviegoers.

Fairbanks entered this phase of his career cautiously. Returning veteran Victor Fleming was promoted to director to helm two films, the richly inventive *When the Clouds Roll By* (1919) followed by *The Mollycoddle* (1920). The plot of the latter seemed a throwback to earlier Fairbanks films with Doug playing an effete figure who will blossom into manly heroism. The main variation here is that his character is descended from hearty American frontiersmen but he has been brought up in Europe where no effort has been made to toughen him. Before the film is over, he will sail to America and bond with his homeland before going on to the customary heroics.

It was with his next film, *The Mark of Zorro,* released later the same year, that Fairbanks would make his foray into swashbuckler adventures. While based on Johnston McCulley's *The Curse of Capistrano*, the story shows both similarities and variations on *The Mollycoddle*. After a sojourn in Spain, Fairbanks' Don Diego Vega returns home to Mexico appearing effeminized by his contact with the Old World. But Spain has not really corrupted him; Don Diego is using his effete side as a front. The masked hero Zorro, Don Diego's alter ego, leaps into action fighting the oppressors. Unsure of whether audiences would accept him in this nineteenth century period piece, Fairbanks had taken the precaution of making his next film, *The Nut* (1921), another contemporary comedy.

The Nut was the last of his silent comedies. *The Mark of Zorro* was a critical and commercial success and Fairbanks continued in that vein with *The Three Musketeers*. In fact, Fairbanks confessed that he had always wanted to make *The Three Musketeers* but was hesitant about doing a costume film. "I was a little timid and I did not wish to risk *The Three Musketeers*, so I put out as a feeler another costume play, *The Mark of Zorro*.[206] Now, it would seem perfectly logical that Dwan, who had directed and co-written Fairbanks' first incarnation as D'Artagnan in the acclaimed *A Modern Musketeer,* should helm this adaptation of the Alexandre Dumas classic. But had the acrimony between the two men settled down to make this possible?

Neither Dwan nor Fairbanks has left an account of their rupture. However, with the relative failure of *Arizona*, it may have dawned on both men that whatever their disagreements, the project was simply ill-suited for Fairbanks.

The thawing in their relationship appears to have been completed by June of 1920 when *The Mollycoddle* was released. Along with Chaplin, Anita Loos and Mary Pickford, Dwan attended a preview of the work print so that they could deliver accolades for the UA publicity department. Readers of the trades were told, probably tongue-in-cheek, that these three individuals were "disinterested persons" as they heaped praise on Doug's newest movie.[207] In December, Dwan, Doug and Mary were among the luminaries attending a private pre-opening performance to the Broadway premiere of *The Mark of Zorro*.

Just as Fairbanks had challenged the majors by helping to form UA, Dwan in the early 1920s was part of another independent combine, Associated Producers, where a consortium of film directors were running their own company. Looking at their efforts in romantic terms, both Fairbanks and Dwan could be seen as fighting the good fight to preserve creative independence in a decade of increasing conglomeration.

In January of 1921, Fairbanks did offer Dwan the opportunity of directing *The Three Musketeers*.[208] Dwan reportedly stated that such an arrangement would be "a very pleasant one" but because of commitments to Associated Producers, which like UA was fighting for its existence, he had to turn down the offer. Fred Niblo, who had helmed *The Mark of Zorro*, directed the next Fairbanks film.

For *The Three Musketeers,* Fairbanks sported a mustache. (In *The Mark of Zorro* a fake mustache was part of his Zorro disguise while his alter ego, the foppish Don Diego, was clean shaven.) The facial hair which had been derided as a European affectation in *The Mollycoddle* would become a trademark feature in the swashbuckler films.

The Three Musketeers, released in late August, was an enormous hit, easily eclipsing *The Mark of Zorro*. Some critics called it Fairbanks' masterpiece. But having achieved all this and the dream of filming D'Artagnan's adventures, where was Fairbanks to go from there?

It was while Fairbanks was contemplating his next move in December 1921 that Dwan was signed to direct whatever project

Fairbanks decided on. At this point, Dwan no longer had any commitments to worry about. His career was very much in flux. It was first announced that Doug's next picture would be an adaptation of Owen Wister's *The Virginian*. Talk then shifted to Fairbanks doing a sequel to *The Mark of Zorro*. In fact, when Dwan signed his contract with Fairbanks, it stated that he was to work on a film "relative to the further adventures of Zorro or any such other subject you [Fairbanks] may determine upon."[209] Later news releases said the next project would be called *The Spirit of Chivalry*, which was vaguely said to deal with characters like Ivanhoe and Richard the Lion-Hearted.[210]

During this time, an intense effort was going on behind the scenes to convince Fairbanks to make a film based on the legends of the medieval outlaw Robin Hood. Dwan recalled that Doug's brothers John and Robert were behind this proposal but that Fairbanks had demurred, saying, "I don't want to play a flat-footed Englishman walking through the woods." When Robert approached Dwan on this matter, Dwan said that he came up with the idea of having an archery expert come to the studio and shoot arrows. This, of course, fascinated Fairbanks, who had to take a crack at it. As he acquired skill, he enjoyed it immensely. Dwan said he then pointed out the kinds of tricks he could perform with his bow and arrows in *Robin Hood*. In an earlier account, Dwan said he first won Fairbanks over by interesting him in the life of Richard the Lion-Hearted.[211]

In early 1922 Fairbanks decided to make *Robin Hood* and threw himself enthusiastically into the project. Fairbanks and Mary Pickford bought a new film studio, the former J.D. Hampton plant on Santa Monica Boulevard. Covering ten acres of ground, it had plenty of room to accommodate the film's elaborate sets.

A formidable technical staff was assembled, including a research team to gather books, documents, engravings and other artifacts to insure authenticity. Future film director Mitchell Leisen, who had worked with Cecil B. DeMille, was hired as costume designer. Another DeMille veteran, Wilfred Buckland, who had worked on *Mr. Fix-It*, was given the title of supervising art director with Irvin J. Martin and Edward M. Langley serving under him.

While Fairbanks was away attending to business in New York, work progressed on the sets. Dwan has noted that historically English castles were not very large but he was determined to make the film sets much more impressive. Together with Robert Fairbanks, who was an engineer, Dwan supervised their construction. Dwan recalls the completed castle as having massive walls over 90 feet high; the interior hall was an amazing 450 feet long. The sets were larger than those used for *Intolerance*.

Doug returned from New York on March 9. One source indicates that by then, he had learned that he was not going to be able to raise financing for this epic project but would have to risk his own money. But he was in for another shock upon his return to California: He was astounded by the size of the sets and then as he toured them grew increasingly uneasy. Fairbanks told Dwan his objections, specified in different books either as "My pictures have always had the intimate touch. We'd look like a bunch of Lilliputians in the halls of a giant if we used that set."[212] Or "My work is intimate. People know me as an intimate actor. I can't work in a vast thing like that. What could I do in there?"[213] Or "I can't compete with those. That's not me. What can I do in those big sets?"[214] According to these accounts, Fairbanks then decides to shelve the picture or is on the verge of calling it off. Dwan then gets Fairbanks to come back to the studio and begins showing him various devices on the sets to enhance elaborate stunts he can perform. Doug is then won over and *Robin Hood* is made.

Although the story varies slightly in different versions, the single primary source seems to be Allan Dwan. There is no real evidence to contradict the story but there are aspects that don't ring true.

Fairbanks' protests that his work depended on intimacy don't sound convincing when looking at his film career. He found that cinema's saving grace compared to the stage was that it provided him with more space to move and perform his stunts. Towards this end, he sought out the West and its deserts. Could the man who used the Grand Canyon as a backdrop really be nonplussed by a nine-story castle? He had also found a way to utilize giant redwood trees in *The Half-Breed* and after *A Modern Musketeer*, he continued to find wide open spaces and imposing cliffs in *The Mollycoddle*. If he could make use of these natural wonders, couldn't he have adapted to his studio-built sets? Dwan and Robert Fairbanks were practical men. They would not have blindly constructed sets as if they were erecting a Tower of Babel without considering them perfect springboards for Fairbanks' stunts. Fairbanks would surely have asked about such plans before canceling his project. This view of Doug's set intimidation also does not square with the Fairbanks who according to one account banged his fist on a table showing his determination to make *Robin Hood*.[215]

This does not mean that the story is essentially false. While it is quite possible that Fairbanks would have approved the dimensions of the sets, he might have been momentarily stymied when seeing how they looked in reality. But if he was hesitating to proceed with the production, it is more likely that this was due to his realization that he would have to use his own money. Fairbanks may have been less anxious about the size of the sets than the size (and budget) of a film of epic proportions.

And the essential part of the story that is true is the ingenuity in setting up aids to the feats of grace Doug would perform. When surrounded on a railing by Prince John's men over a 50-foot drop, Fairbanks was to jump on a burlap curtain and slide down with ease. Dwan was able to demonstrate how this would be done because a playground slide was camouflaged behind the curtain. Fairbanks delighted in that.

Dwan also showed Fairbanks vines attached to the walls that would permit him to climb up to Maid Marian's window. And for the epic task of jumping a 25-foot gap between one wall and another, Dwan had hidden a trampoline that he believed could have propelled him for 40 feet, if so desired. Whatever else, it is clear how this could have bolstered Fairbanks' spirits and faith in *Robin Hood.* If the story may have been slightly distorted, it was because Dwan relished the role of being Doug's "Mr. Fix-It" and wanted to add a bit more drama to it.[216]

There were indeed far more severe problems for Fairbanks than the size of his castle. The year 1921 had been bad economically for the entire country. The film industry had not fully rebounded in the first half of 1922 and was considered to be in a slump. That largely accounted for why Fairbanks had difficulty raising money. But with *Robin Hood,* he chose to face the risks with optimism. Referring to the industry doldrums, he told the press, "It's all due to bad pictures," and then went on to trumpet how *Robin Hood* would be not only the most expensive but most romantic of all his productions.[217]

Confidence in the film industry had been rocked not only by tough economic times but by a public recoiling against indecency in the film world. This boiled over in the 1921 scandal in which comic actor Roscoe Arbuckle was alleged to have raped and accidentally killed a woman.[218] The furor of the scandal reflected mounting resentment over what many considered an excess of tawdry film dramas and the dubious morals of Hollywood celebrities. Doug and Dwan were conscious of this as they promoted *Robin Hood.* One trade story noted, "It is the opinion of Fairbanks and Allan Dwan ... that sordid realism in pictures has just about had its day. Historical romance, stories that are genuine and human without being either drab or 'sexy,' if they are not already, will soon be the most successful, in their opinion."[219]

The script to *Robin Hood* was open for invention since there was no generally esteemed literary source to the legends but mostly a smattering of obscure poems and plays. There was also no shortage of inventors in the scriptwriting. Dwan commented, "Well, if you could call it a script, yes we were all in on it—we used to have conferences in Doug's dressing room."[220] The participants included Fairbanks, Dwan (whose contract mandated work on the script) and apparently whichever other Fairbanks associate dropped by. In the credits these collaborators were melted down into the pseudonym of Elton Thomas who was said to have written the original story. The person credited with adapting the story was Lotta Woods.

In addition to Fairbanks as the title character, the cast of *Robin Hood* included Wallace Beery, the heavy in *The Mollycoddle,* as King Richard the Lion-Hearted and Sam De Grasse as Prince John. The leading lady was the Australian-born Enid Bennett, who was married to Fred Niblo, the director of Fairbanks' first two swashbucklers.

Robin Hood helped ease the Hollywood slump as numerous technicians were required to meet the colossal requirements of the project. United Artists' publicity claimed that 30,000 players participated in the film. And even though that number was likely inflated, the production provided a boon to those seeking extra work. Dwan recalled that they would go downtown in buses picking up people to work on the film. Dwan said he would divide the army of extras into groups of twenty and designate each group with a number. He would then call out the numbers of those groups he wanted to move in a scene. As Peter Bogdanovich later suggested to him, it was like being a quarterback again.[221]

Dwan also worked with innovations such as the use of glass shots. An artist would paint on a plate of glass; when held in the proper perspective before the camera, it would provide the illusion of whatever object Dwan wanted to insert, say a large chandelier. Or it could be used to heighten the already gargantuan sets. To light these sets, Dwan used huge tin reflectors to amplify the sunlight, keeping some corners dark while illuminating other areas. Dwan gave credit to cameraman Arthur Edeson for helping to maneuver this act of literally painting with light. To follow the action and keep the camera moving, Dwan said he also used the kind of construction boom used to move steel beams to the top of buildings. It was a forerunner of the modern camera boom.[222] The very making of *Robin Hood* became a tourist attraction in Hollywood.

Robin Hood was completed in fifteen weeks, which United Artists claimed was a record for a production of such "gigantic proportions." Both Fairbanks and Dwan were credited with the rapid progress which included working Memorial Day and on four Sundays.[223]

There was much anticipation for the opening of *Robin Hood.* Since the story was public domain and a rival could have made a quickie version to cash in and create confusion, Fairbanks had the film copyrighted with the title of *Douglas Fairbanks in Robin Hood.*[224]

Robin Hood did not have its world premiere in either of the coastal environs but in Chicago at Cohan's Grand Opera House on October 15, 1922. Having the film open in his home town must have pleased Dwan, who was in attendance along with Fairbanks, Pickford and George M. Cohan. In Los Angeles, there was yet another instance of a Fairbanks film opening a new theater, in this case Sid Grauman's Hollywood Egyptian Theater, with premiere tickets going for five dollars. The box office sold out two hours after it opened. Grauman said, "The audience of two thousand stood up and cheered for fully three minutes after the conclusion of the picture."[225]

Even in this early era, merchandising was used as part of the publicity machine for Fairbanks' risky venture. Seven-cent *Robin Hood* cigars were carried by the United Cigar Stores. Also used to promote the New York showing were little arrows that could be thrown at clothing and would stick on impact. The arrows carried *Robin Hood* ads.

One arrow went awry in publicizing *Robin Hood* and it was fired by Fairbanks himself. On the roof of the Ritz-Carlton Hotel in New York for the Gotham premiere of the film, Doug posed as Robin Hood for reporters with his bow and target arrows.

A publicity shot of a giant megaphone to help Dwan command the throngs of players in *Robin Hood* (1922). Standing from left to right are Wallace Beery (in costume as King Richard the Lion-Hearted), Robert Florey, cinematographer Arthur Edeson, Fairbanks and Dwan (courtesy Kevin Brownlow).

Demonstrating how far an arrow can go, Fairbanks released one that sailed a block away. It wound up hitting a Polish (or Hungarian) immigrant working in a factory near an open window. Fairbanks agreed to compensate his wounded victim with $5,000 and Dwan believed it set him on a successful business career.[226]

Robin Hood opened in New York at the Lyric Theater on October 30. The crowds were so large that a second performance was arranged for midnight.[227] After the first performance was over, the audience demanded that Fairbanks appear before them. He obliged and, according to a trade story, "told them of the dynamic force which went into the composition of the picture — that everyone concerned worked with a labor of love and enthusiasm. Then he introduced Mary Pickford, who he claimed was responsible for the inspiration. And Mary admitted that she considered it his finest picture. Allan Dwan, the director, came forward, but modesty prevented him from expressing himself beyond an appreciative bow." Dwan was shrewd enough not to try to upstage his boss. The story goes on to observe, "At the conclusion of the first premiere and the five-minute demonstration for Doug and his 'silent partner' the second premiere was given to take care of the over-flow.... And it is not a matter of publicity to state that thousands were turned away."[228]

Robin Hood was indeed a smashing success, breaking theater records across the country. Probably the most often cited critical citation for the film was Robert Sherwood's review in the *New York Herald* which declared, "It represents the highwater mark of film production — the farthest step that the silent drama has ever taken along the high road to art."[229]

Robin Hood was not just praised on the movie pages but in some editorials. The *Seattle Star*, for example, noted, "So often recently the movies have come in for harsh criticism, it is a positive pleasure to discover a film which can be wholeheartedly and enthusiastically applauded." The editorial went on to recognize "that the movie is susceptible, when in the hands of sincere, intelligent men, of being developed as an art."[230]

At a time when the motion picture industry was in economic trouble and in moral and cultural disrepute, *Robin Hood* helped restore public confidence. Its impact has been compared to that of *Birth of a Nation* but unlike Griffith's film, *Robin Hood* was not an anomaly. It was more of a leader of the pack. Dwan told an interviewer at this time of the power of Fairbanks' vision: "Several prominent producers increased their production appropriations when they learned of the manner in which *Robin Hood* was being produced. At a time when retrenchment was the signal word everywhere, he had the convictions and the courage to press forward."[231]

With its success and notoriety, *Robin Hood* set the tone for better appreciation of large-scale productions that were becoming more common. A columnist in *Motion Picture News* wrote in late 1922, "Let us be thankful this Thanksgiving week for an end to picture depression ... for the optimism expressed by the producers, for the production of such sterling photoplays as *Douglas Fairbanks in Robin Hood....*" The columnist followed with numerous other titles which included *When Knighthood Was in Flower, Blood and Sand, Oliver Twist, Shadows, The Toll of the Sea, Grandma's Boy, Tess of the Storm Country, Sherlock Holmes, Lorna Doone, and The Prisoner of Zenda.*[232]

Robin Hood had captured the imagination of the audiences of its era. But how does this film look today?

First of all, it has been totally eclipsed in the popular imagination as the definitive Robin Hood film by Warner Brothers' 1938 *The Adventures of Robin Hood* starring Errol Flynn and directed by Michael Curtiz and William Keighley. This version added both sound and color to its presentation, as well as retaining Alan Hale as Little John.[233] More importantly, it is snappily paced and the flow of action moves at a clip still quite acceptable to today's standards.

But one can prefer this later film and still find much to admire in the Fairbanks version. The 1922 *Robin Hood* may not have been necessarily better but it took some different roads that were rewarding in their own right. For example, when King Richard enters Sherwood Forest in the 1938 film, he is hooded like his followers. When he reveals himself, it is a sacred moment like the Second Coming, and Robin and his roguish outlaw band fall to their knees. Ian Hunter who played Richard, later actually portrayed a Christ-like figure in *Strange Cargo* (1940).

By contrast, in the Fairbanks–Dwan version Richard is played by the eternal roughneck Wallace Beery showing a touch of the uncouth in the way he orally assaults a drumstick and then licks his fingers. He and Robin are depicted as has having been bosom buddies. When with his face hidden by a helmet he proves his mettle to Robin's men in the forest, there is no similarity to the later version where he uncovers his identity to his adoring subjects. In terms of the king's relationship to the populace, none of this is necessarily of greater historical accuracy but it is more human and less sanctimonious.

The silent version does have its defects, such as its stilted attempts at archaic diction, as with Prince John's line to Maid Marian, "Fret not your pretty head." There is also some over-the-top slapstick comedy when at Nottingham some of Prince John's men are disposed of like the Keystone Cops.

But the biggest complaint about the 1922 version has been about its length, specifically its first half where Fairbanks only appears as the Earl of Huntingdon and not his later incarnation as Robin Hood. One Fairbanks biographer even refers to it as "half a good film."[234]

These criticisms are not completely without merit. In fact, some critics made similar complaints when the film was released, including the reviewers for *Variety* and *Film Daily*. But if there are flaws in the construction of *Robin Hood,* there is also a vision and strategy.

The impatience of many modern viewers with the long wait for the appearance of the title character is understandable. But they might also consider that there is a valid and entertaining approach in showing the path the protagonist had to follow to becoming the legendary hero and the practical and emotional strains that drive him to reinvent himself. Like many of the earlier Fairbanks comedies, a transformation is at the heart of the story.

The liberating tone of the film's second half was also clearly designed to set a contrast to the first half where repression increasingly holds sway. The contrast is not only against the emerging tyranny of Prince John but of the stately but rigid medieval world against which Robin's antics will seem brazenly modern. The first time we see Fairbanks as a knight we have an inkling of his desire to breathe more freely from his apparent discomfort with his helmet.

Dwan demonstrates that he is taking pains to recreate the world of the Middle Ages as he opens the film with a poem, a device he relished in those days. The lines from Charles Kingley read:

> So fleet the works of men
> Back to their earth again:
> Ancient and holy things
> Fade like a dream.

This title card is followed by two shots of the ruins of castles. With further titles about restoring the spirit of a bygone age, a shot of castle ruins, overlaid by Dwan's fond imagery of moving clouds, dissolves into a castle in its former pristine prime. Another title acknowledges that Dwan is giving us history in its idealized state, i.e., mixed with legends.

The next images are among Dwan's most magical. A drawbridge descends and a vanished world seems to fall in our lap, as it comes down with medieval heralds on board followed by a full procession including a jester followed by the king. It is as if a portal had suddenly opened up to a past era. The falling drawbridge is also an eloquent cinematic equivalent of a curtain rising on a scene.

Spectacular long shots treat us to all the pomp of a jousting tournament. The audience is then given a medium shot of one of the participants, the Earl of Huntingdon (Fairbanks). This aristocratic characterization of Robin's earlier identity comes not from the medieval ballads but from the Elizabethan plays of Anthony Munday which included the 1598 *The Downfall of Robert, Earl of Huntingdon.*[235]

Though Huntingdon wins the joust, he is "afeard of women" and of accepting their honors, which has him running in flight from more than a dozen fair damsels and seeking refuge in a moat.

Dwan's penchant for the comic aspects of male insecurity mount when at the sumptuous castle with an all-night feast following the tournament, King Richard watches Huntingdon with a weary eye. Richard and his men will be embarking on a Holy Crusade the next morning. While throughout the spacious castle, knights and their maids make their tender farewells, Huntingdon playfully wrestles with his comrades. Richard, who behaves as a fatherly mentor to the young knight, finally has seen enough of this and calls Huntingdon to him to select a maid.

Huntingdon's unease with women is milked comically. But before this complex can become too grating, Huntingdon sees Maid Marian Fitzwalter accosted by Prince John and, following them up the castle stairs, confronts the prince. Huntingdon

A love scene between Robin (Douglas Fairbanks) and Maid Marian (Enid Bennett) in the giant castle of *Robin Hood* (1922) (courtesy Bruce Calvert).

only seems to get hot and excited about women when he sees that they are endangered, like a close cousin of the protagonist of *A Modern Musketeer*. By morning, Huntingdon and Marian have fallen in love.

As Richard and his men march off to the Crusade, Prince John conspires with Guy of Gisbourne to take power in Richard's absence. Gisbourne promises to dispose of both Richard and Huntingdon and is in return promised that he will get Maid Marian.

With the departure of Richard and his farewell celebrations, the castle is steeped in gloom. In one long shot showing the castle starkly lit and full of shadows, John prods his minions to do his skullduggery, commanding them "to do your task and spare no one." As his men leave the frame, the solitary prince is surrounded by broad expanses of empty space, as if signifying all the power that he now claims. Not surprisingly, John's next act is to walk to Richard's throne and to pick up his crown. As John, Sam De Grasse gives a restrained performance as the settings are permitted to amplify his dour personality.

This is not so of Paul Dickey's performance as Gisbourne, which is hammier but augments his toad-like appearance that makes his striving for Marian all the more unpalatable. Gisbourne also helps to foment distrust between Huntingdon and the king. Marian sends word to Huntingdon at the Crusader encampment that John is beginning to usurp his brother's power in a rule of terror. Fearing that if Richard hears of this, he will abandon the Crusades, Huntingdon decides to take matters into his own hands. He tells Richard that he must leave the campaign to return to England but cannot reveal the reason. Huntingdon beseeches Richard, not as a king, but as his friend to give his unquestioned trust. Richard instead suspects that Huntingdon is merely lovesick for Marian and dismisses his plea as a jest. Using a falcon, Gisbourne intercepts a carrier pigeon message in which Huntingdon tells Marian that on some pretext he will be returning to England. When Huntingdon decides to leave without the king's permission, he is felled by Gisbourne's arrow and is brought into the king's tent as a deserter with the letter as corroborative proof. Richard then orders Huntingdon and his squire to be imprisoned in a nearby tower.

The manner in which Huntingdon's rescue mission hinges on unquestioned trust and friendship is a central component of the story and adds to its aura as a fairy tale. Since Doug and Dwan both had a major hand in the script, it is quite possible their own personal falling-out helped inspire this plot device of a tragic misunderstanding between friends. (Seven years later, when H. Bruce "Lucky" Humberstone was in Robert Fairbanks' office preparing to work as Dwan's assistant director on another film, Doug walked in and said, "Who's going to introduce 'Lucky' to the king?" Fairbanks was referring to Dwan. Humberstone thought that he "was very appropriately named."[236])

With his squire's help, Huntingdon escapes the tower and makes it back to England. Meanwhile, in order to escape Prince John's forces, Marian has faked her death. Upon his return, Huntingdon is shown the embankment from which Marian is believed to have fallen to her doom. Raising his sword, he dedicates himself "To God, to Richard and to Her." He creates a new identity, believing that he has lost the life of his lover and the trust of his friend. Huntingdon will now seek his revenge in the guise of the outlaw leader, Robin Hood.

How will Dwan visualize the conflict of the second half? In keeping with the director's symmetrical sense of conflicting spheres, Sherwood Forest should dominate in the second part. With its sense of unfettered freedom, it can be set against the oppressiveness of the castle where torture is openly practiced. There are certainly some splendid touches in the forest: the guerrilla tactics practiced by Robin's men, the grotto at Robin's headquarters that bears Richard's coat of arms, and Robin and his cohorts burrowing through the network tunnel of tree trunks. (Less successful is the manner in which some of his men cavort through the forest. Dwan recalled, "I had those guys running around on their tippy toes. I told them I'd fire the first son of a bitch who let his heel touch the ground. There weren't gonna be any flat-footed Englishmen in that film."[237] The skipping outlaws evoked some derision even in their own time. At a New York showing, someone in the audience shouted, "Denishawn dancers I call 'em, My Gawd ain't they merry!"[238])

But the forest never quite rises to the level of atmosphere one expects from Dwan. As Dwan suggested in his "tour talk" to Fairbanks, the somber castle becomes part of the fun and is transformed into a playground. In his first appearance, Robin romps through the castle, jumping, sliding and evading the prince's men at every turn. The castle itself with its huge windows is easily penetrated and exited, the structure becoming like John's authority, just a huge façade when challenged by Robin and the rapidly growing ranks of rebels.

Dwan also uses the castle set to intensify the love story. Dwan said that because of Doug's limitations in playing a lover, "we had to invent little stunts."[239] And so there is a scene early in the film where Marian uses Huntingdon's shadow on the wall to sketch his silhouette. Later, the sight of the silhouette evokes Marian's feelings for her missing lover. And in the middle of all his hijinks, harassing and escaping John's men, Robin pauses at the silhouette, which conjures up for him the image of his lost love.

Robin subsequently learns that Marian is alive but no sooner are they reunited then she is abducted by the prince's men. Learning of her capture, Robin rushes to the rescue, leaving word for his men to follow after him. In saving Marian from Gisbourne, Robin himself is captured.

Robin is prepared for execution while an intricate editing scheme ties him to an anxious Marian and the forces now entering the castle (unseen by the defenders). A pamphlet of Richard's coat of arms of three lions, which Robin has been dispensing to villagers, has been mockingly attached to him for his execution. Dwan's great visual coup here is the sudden appearance of a shield covering the entire screen bearing the same coat of arms and deflecting the arrows launched to kill Robin. When the shield is removed, we see Richard and Robin reunited.

Dwan ponders matters sitting on Richard's throne on the *Robin Hood* set. Fairbanks stands on his right; the other men are unidentified (courtesy Tracey Goessel).

A poster featuring the precise title of the film, *Douglas Fairbanks in Robin Hood* (1922) (Tracey Goessel).

As the king's men triumph over their enemies, the rout becomes a celebration. John's two henchmen are mounted on ropes and playfully pushed around like human swings. A row of Robin's men sit on the balcony (next to the curtain with the playground slide) hailing Richard's return, their legs dangling over the wall. This long shot recalls a tableau early in the film where young boys sat on trees to watch the opening tournament with their legs hanging from the branches. The victory of Robin's outlaw band becomes a celebration of the boy in all men.

The parallel shots also remind us that it is this zest for Peter Pan–like freedom that makes the division of the film so logical: the exuberance of Robin and his men contrasting with the stiff formality of the first half. Yet, *Robin Hood* is also a work of formal beauty. Aside from the much vaunted sets, it includes such exquisitely composed moments as the long shot of Marian and Prince John meeting in a plaza in the distant background while observed by Huntingdon's watchful squire standing under an arch in the foreground; Marian kneeling before an altar framed like a Christian martyr before Gisbourne breaks into her chamber; and near the end, a doleful John banished outside the closing drawbridge, again spatially isolated but this time stripped of all power. Cinematographer Edeson deserves much of the credit for these visuals as does Dwan's long-established eye for composition.[240]

There is too the restoration of justice but in this version, the victory is more personal than populist. Not only are the lovers happily reunited but there is the twin emotional resonance of a friendship reborn as a bowing King Richard apologizes for ever having doubted Robin.

Perhaps the greatest honor accorded *Robin Hood* came a year after the film's release. In this pre–Oscar era, *Photoplay* had taken up the burden of establishing an award for merit to rival those for literature and sports. The winner of the *Photoplay* Medal of Honor for best film of the year was decided by *Photoplay*'s readers, who were given a list of 50 nominated entries. The process took months but *Robin Hood* was the winner for 1922.

Though Doug and Dwan were triumphant, they would avoid the pitfalls of long-term attachment. Dwan was now in an excellent position to find new employment. But he was also resuming a professional odyssey that had begun with his last departure from Fairbanks.

4. The Pursuit of Independence

But Allan Dwan saw the poetry in electricity and the business possibilities in the movies. So you see it is a bit difficult to classify him.—Adela Rogers St. Johns, "Artistic Efficiency—That's Dwan," *Photoplay*, August 1920

The experiment might prove disastrous—directors as a group were autocratic, headstrong, scornful of their employers, considering themselves artists and their employers mere dollar-chasers—if these wild men should get control of the studios there might be many bad smashes!"—Benjamin B. Hampton, *History of the American Film Industry*

When Dwan resumed his working relationship with Douglas Fairbanks at Artcraft in the fall of 1917, a story appeared in the *Los Angeles Times* under the headline, "Art and Money: Allan Dwan Is a Director with Big Ideas." Dwan was quoted as saying, "Art and money don't mix in motion picture production."[1] But exactly what did that mean?

Paul Hubert Conlon, the author of the piece, saw this emanating from a central conflict in film production. "Since motion pictures came into being there has existed an eternal fight between the moneyed powers who naturally wanted big features produced at small costs, but demanding artistic results from the director, and the directors who insisted upon producing pictures with a sublime disregard for costs."[2]

Citing Dwan's words, Conlon saw greater problems arising in trying to resolve this conflict. Dwan said, "I know of business managers fresh from commercial successes who try to apply the same economic methods to photoplay production. It can't be done. Where a businessman makes his mistake is in trying to skimp and save in small details, meantime losing sight of the bigger costs, such as holding up an entire company for a few days at an enormous loss in time and money. Here is the real waste in motion picture making."[3]

Conlon here champions Dwan as the reconciler of the divergent interests of art and commerce. He wrote of Dwan, "I have met many men in the screen world—producers, directors, actors, and business managers—but none of them have impressed me with such a perfect combination of artistic ideals and common business sense as does Allan Dwan." Summing up, Conlon sees Dwan as "the student—the thinker" while also noting his openness to the advice and suggestions of others.

The central incompatibility cited by Conlon was also noted in an interview with Dwan three years later. "The great problem of the pictures," Dwan told Adela Rogers St. Johns, "is the welding of art and business."[4] But here Dwan appears to give more emphasis and sympathy to the business side: "I am a business man. I have a commercial mind. It is my personal opinion that things that are 'too good' are generally not good enough. A man can make the most artistic picture ever filmed, but if it plays to empty houses it hasn't achieved a thing for Art or for Humanity. This old stuff about not commercializing Art is the bunk."[5]

In writing about the relationship between Fairbanks and Dwan, Tibbetts cites the above passage to demonstrate that "Dwan almost went out of his way to disclaim anything artistic in his work."[6] This seems somewhat at odds with Conlon's portrait of the man who balanced artistic ideals and common business sense. Had Conlon misunderstood Dwan or had Dwan changed?

In interviews, Dwan would persist in projecting this image as a businessman and commercial filmmaker and a good deal, though perhaps not all of this, was true. But one must also pay attention to the context of his remarks. In the interview with St. Johns, he also says,

> The director is the man who has control of the money. The director is the man who can make or break a film financially and artistically. Most directors are not businessmen. Therefore, the films have had to arrange for business managers, for men who, when the director had laid out the thing artistically and outlined the results he could achieve, will find out how it could be done at the lowest cost. These men contract for material, set salaries, tend to all the commercial delay. When harmony can be completely established between these two factions, pictures will become better, because there will be no waste.

By asserting that he is a businessman, Dwan distinguishes himself from those directors who need business managers. We recall that Henabery had noted Emerson's inability and limitation as a director; that he could not factor in costs in the planning of his films. Dwan is making clear that the producer who hires him will not need to hire a business manager as he himself will be controlling costs and eliminating waste. (And Dwan had indeed established a good reputation in that regard.) By doing so, Dwan is also strengthening his own autonomy. It should also be noted that at this time Dwan, as an independent producer and director, was trying to attract investors. What's more,

Dwan is still referring to an artistic-economic balance that must be maintained.

Of course, it is not unusual for directors to publicly stress their commercial interest and downplay their artistic aspirations. But Dwan seemed to be striving to show that he had attained a proper understanding of the balance needed. This posture as the cinema savant may have come from a need not only to impress the industry but to settle his own personal conflicts. As with a number of these interviews, Dwan's scientific background is noted and it is his scientific, analytic mind that is always in evidence in making his pronouncements.

St. Johns seems duly impressed, even intimidated, by Dwan's scientific learning. She considered him one of those "Tech men [who] radiate an efficiency that is fascinating. You feel cast into outer darkness if there is a curl out of place."[7] Dwan has spoken of how he drew narrative construction from mathematics but there was no mathematical formula that can substitute for creative talent. What Dwan drew from science and mathematics was a philosophical point of view and a strong sense of order.

This sense of order helped to analyze and solve problems and to provide control. And this was needed not only against external problems but to control the dreamer within himself. The scientist could provide shape to the dreamer's creative impulses and keep him eminently employable for his technical and economic skill.

One interviewer may have caught something of Dwan's demeanor when she described him thus: "He has a way of proving what he says ... and a goodly portion of sound logic ... some philosophy ... and dreams.... You can tell that he is something of a dreamer by a soft — kindly, almost — look in his eyes. But he wouldn't ever be caught dreaming, when he should be up and doing. He's certainly not that kind."[8]

It can be more strongly argued that glimpses of the dreamer could be found in his movies and it is a frequent "bane" of creative people. Dwan, looking back at his youth, talked of having the "artistic ideal" but that it did not last long. Speaking of this time as if it were a form of youthful indiscretion, he proclaimed, "That first experience made a realist of me and I've kept my feet on the ground ever since."[9] Yet just a few years after the St. Johns interview, Dwan would refer to this period of the early 1920s as one where he was pursuing art and that he had now (again?) learned his lesson. So when was the overt artist, the dreamer ever totally repressed?

At around this time, Dwan also appeared to be swearing off working in the east. Back in 1913, when employed at Universal, Dwan was already referring to himself as a "reformed easterner."[10] But New York and its surroundings had always had a special allure for Dwan since he went to the city to try to fulfill his hopes as a playwright and he had made some of his most important films there. In a future Dwan film, New York would even be described as the "city of our dreams." But now he told an interviewer regarding filmmaking, "The best results will always be obtained in California, to my way of thinking. In Los Angeles there is nothing to do but work — therefore, we work long and willingly. Here [N.Y.C.] you have all sorts of pleasures and amusements which constantly beckon. The temptation to play when we should work is too great.... I always say I come to New York to recharge my mental storage battery. I'll go back filled with ideas, make two or three pictures — then I'll come on again — get more ideas and go back."[11] But Dwan would be again drawn to work steadily in New York ... for practical as well as artistic reasons. The different facets of his personality could both mesh and contradict each other but the scientist in him was always finding solutions.

The period from 1919 to 1921 would be one of great ferment both in the nation and the film industry. Dwan would meet the challenges with his own display of business acumen and artistic ambition, outspokenness and discretion.

Dwan's most likely goal upon leaving Fairbanks' employ in the fall of 1918 was to re-establish his commercial viability apart from the great star. He seemed to have found a plum target when he got the nod to direct Clara Kimball Young in *Cheating Cheaters*, which was said to have commanded the highest price ever paid at that time for a picture to be made from a stage play.[12]

When shooting commenced in early November, the film industry was still reeling from another wave of the influenza epidemic. At Thomas Ince's studio, everyone (except presumably the actors) was wearing a surgical mask as a precaution against the flu. But this was not the case at the studio where a journalist found Dwan shooting *Cheating Cheaters*. Dwan had an impressive cast which included (in addition to Young) Jack Holt, Anna Q. Nilsson, Frederick Burton, Frank Campeau, Nicholas Dunaew, Edwin Stevens, and Tully Marshall. When asked how he was able to assemble such a cast, Dwan replied simply, "Flu. Many of the studios are closed and as all of the players would rather work than not, I had the pick of a big flock."[13]

But the same reporter on another visit found Dwan less happy with his all-star cast, with the director complaining that with so many stars there was less of a center and more jostling by the actors.[14] The journalist thought Dwan was kidding but when he was interviewed about this film by Bogdanovich fifty years later, Dwan was still complaining about his players trying to upstage each other. He told Bogdanovich that he tied a rope to each of the actor's ankles to restrain them.[15] It remains questionable that established stars even in those days would have submitted to such "reins" but the story certainly reflects Dwan's frustration with the actors.

Despite his problems, Dwan's efficiency again prevailed and it was reported that this was the first of Young's films to be finished ahead of schedule.[16] Released by Select Pictures in January 1919, the film dealt with two criminal gangs, each passing itself off as a wealthy family and planning to rob the other. A surprise revelation not made until the end was that Young, playing the leader of one gang, is actually a detective undercover.

And of course, she's fallen in love with a member of the rival gang and will proceed to reform him. The critics were pleased and *Cheating Cheaters* was successful at the box office. It was remade twice by Universal Pictures, in 1927 and then in 1934. Dwan's newest stint had started with a hit.

Dwan kept to his workaholic pace by quickly signing up for another project. Actress Louise Glaum had started her own production company and for its first effort (in which she would star), she had C. Gardner Sullivan provide the story and Dwan supervise the production.

It is not clear if *Cheating Cheaters* was yet completed when shooting was begun on the Glaum picture known as *Sahara* or *Forbidden Fire*. Probably because it followed so closely on the heels of the other film, Dwan acted as supervisor with the actual directing being done by his dependable assistant Arthur Rosson. (Most trade reviews treated Dwan as the director.) For this production, which was said to have cost about $250,000, Dwan was contracted for 20 percent of the net profits. Glaum leased the Thomas H. Ince studios in Culver City. Production was completed in about a month.

The plot is a delirious, exotic melodrama *cum* soap opera. The French heroine Mignon (Glaum) marries an American engineer who takes her to Egypt where he works on a project in the Sahara. The wife becomes bored and abandons her husband and child for a Russian nobleman who has his own palace in Cairo. Some years later Mignon finds that her husband and child are beggars; he's become a drug addict and amnesiac. With medical help, the husband is restored to health. He shoots the Russian count and gradually the family is happily reconciled.

The film won high praise for its technical virtuosity. *Motion Picture News* noted, "The settings are unusually artistic.... Photography and laboratory work on this picture shows a great advancement in the art."[17] *Photoplay* called it a "large, well-made picture of no special originality."[18]

The film was released as a J. Parker Read production. A little over two months after shooting was completed, Glaum and Read were married. They made other pictures together but Dwan moved on.

Dwan and Hearst

Just as *Cheating Cheaters* was being released, Dwan received his next assignment, directing the budding star Marion Davies. The venture represented a reunion of sorts since the script had been written by the team of Emerson and Loos.

Davies was the mistress of America's most powerful newspaper and magazine publisher of the time, William Randolph Hearst, and had been on his payroll since 1917. After the failure of her first starring film vehicle, the vapid *Runaway, Romany*, released in late 1917, Hearst took her career under his wing and promised to make her a star. (Hearst had already been dabbling in film producing.) Davies was destined to reach stardom and prove herself a talented actress but that was years away. Hearst's guidance of her career was not always helpful but, as Davies' biographer Fred Lawrence Guiles points out, "Hearst's promotion of Marion was to last twenty years, and no film star in America would ever exceed her in terms of publicity."[19] But Guiles added, "She would also have to fight Hearst's constant meddling, since he saw her as a lady of quality on the screen, a kind of blond Alma Rubens, while the Marion Davies who became a legitimate star and not a phony one was impish, unpredictable, and eager to prick pomposity wherever she found it."[20]

Davies had already starred in four features and the 30-chapter serial *Beatrice Fairfax* before she commenced her work with Dwan. It was said that Hearst chose directors for Davies based on their suitability to the script, and Dwan's past work suggested he was adept in projecting the wit of Anita Loos on the screen. Loos was a good friend of Davies and likely understood her comic potential when she co-wrote the script that would become *Getting Mary Married*.

Loos recalled that Marion engaged in various hijinks on the set of *Getting Mary Married*, especially as Hearst was away on a business trip when it was being filmed. According to Loos, Davies went on a three-day binge of practical jokes (such as feigning pregnancy and blacking out one of her teeth) that cost the production $10,000 to $15,000.[21] But trade stories of the time suggest that filming, which took place in Manhattan at the Backer studios on 39th Street, went reasonably quickly and was completed within a month. Dwan recalled, "Marion Davies was lots of fun. She stuttered and stammered and it was a little difficult for her to speak at times, but she was fine."[22]

The Library of Congress print of *Getting Mary Married* includes only the first three of the film's five reels. Davies' character Mary is a virtual prisoner in the New York apartment of her dour but wealthy stepfather. Things get even worse when he is accidentally killed and she must live with his brother and his family in Boston. The stepfather's will stipulates that unless she lives with them for a full year and remains unmarried in that time, she cannot collect her inheritance. These insipid and caricatured relatives decide to make life as unpleasant for Mary as possible to induce her to leave. The film gathers some comic momentum but the loss of the payoff reels is a frustration to any viewer. There appear to be an unusually high number of close-ups of the star for a Dwan film and this may have been mandated by Hearst.

Getting Mary Married was released in April. The reviews expressed not so much enthusiasm as relief that the highly publicized Davies had at last appeared in a film of some quality. Striking a tone of simple gratitude, *Motion Picture News* noted, "For once Marion Davies has been furnished with a decent story. The result of this kind act is not only an excellent picture — it is conclusive proof that this player can act...."[23] *Variety* concurred that this was the best of Davies' films and added,

"Mr. Dawn [sic] seems to have gotten the angle on what Miss Davies needs in direction. There is a wonderful improvement in her work in this picture over the preceding releases marketed."[24]

Getting Mary Married proved modestly successful for Hearst and the release of Davies' potential for comedy was no doubt a factor in that success. Dwan recognized that Davies "had a sense of humor and if you gave her anything funny to do, she'd do it funny. She had a great smile. Half the time they didn't pick stories for her with enough humor in them."[25]

Unfortunately, that would be the case with the next Davies film, which Dwan directed, *The Dark Star*. This was another attempt by Hearst to find "classy" material for Davies, the source being a melodramatic novel by Robert W. Chambers about secret papers hidden in a jeweled idol.

The Dark Star also provided the launching of a new releasing format for Hearst. *Getting Mary Married* had been released through Lewis Selznick's Select Pictures, with the production companies being Hearst's International Film Service and the Marion Davies Picture Corporation. Now Adolph Zukor had begun to see possibilities in Davies as a star and agreed to distribute her films through Paramount–Artcraft. The production combination was newly dubbed Cosmopolitan Productions, deriving its name from one of Hearst's magazines, which would provide source material. For the shooting of *The Dark Star*, Dwan would yet again return to Fort Lee, New Jersey, where Hearst had leased the Paragon Studios.

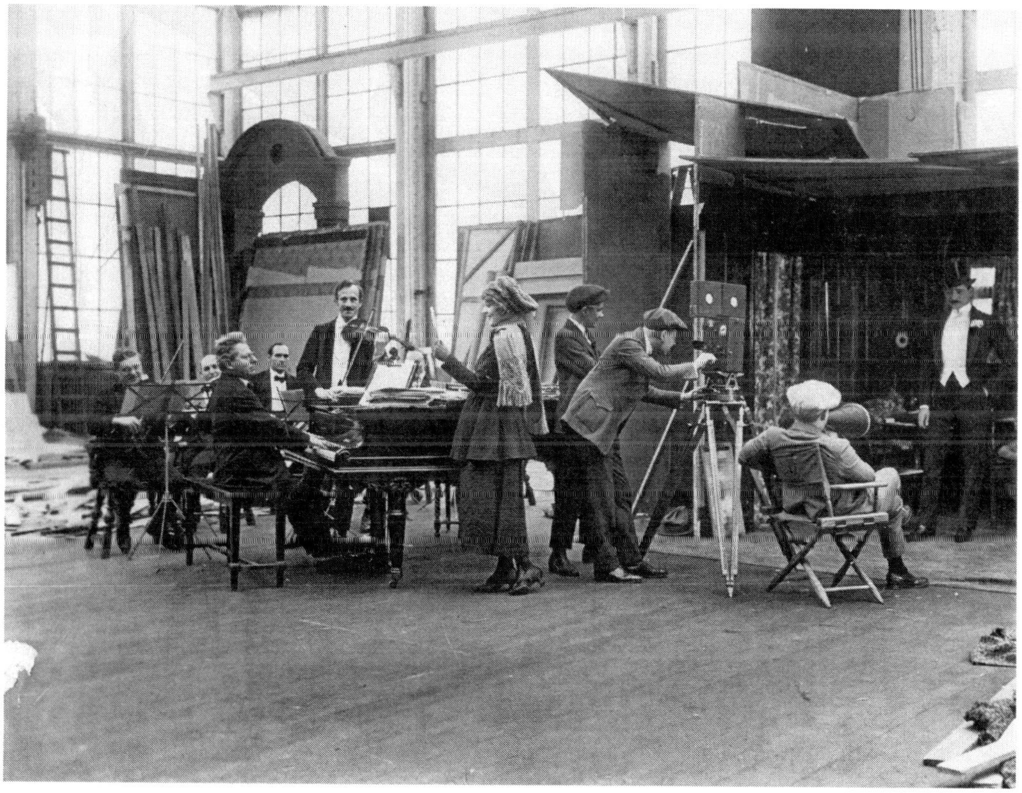

Allan Dwan directing Marion Davies in *The Dark Star* (1919) at the Paragon Studios in Fort Lee, New Jersey (courtesy Fort Lee Film Commission).

The Dark Star would not live up to the hype. *Photoplay* described Davies as "pretty, willing but inert."[26] As for the film itself, the reviewer for *Moving Picture World*, perhaps reluctant to irk Hearst with a complete pan, said he was issuing more of a report than a review. The reviewer noted how the audience at the Rivoli Theater was laughing in derision. He then tactfully suggested that the Rivoli was not the proper venue for the film and that it would work better at neighborhood grind houses.[27] Wid's more bluntly declared the film "[u]nreal, ridiculous ... with laughable errors and expressionless star." Wid also lamented, "I cannot imagine what happened to Allan Dwan."[28]

Years later, Dwan could only explain, "The scenario writer had had a nightmare and put it all down on paper."[29]

Almost immediately after *The Dark Star* was completed, Dwan was negotiating a film deal with another company. But Hearst had grown fond of Dwan's work and did not want to see him go. There followed a frenzied correspondence between Hearst, who was on the West Coast, and his chief financial officer Joseph Moore, who was in New York, on what could be done to retain Dwan. Initially, Hearst cabled Moore on April 23 to move quickly to retain Dwan and advised him to "Keep Zit out of it."[30]

"Zit" was Carl Zittel, general manager for Cosmopolitan Productions. Hearst's admonition suggests not surprisingly that there was conflict between Zittel and Dwan. Dwan had never cared for business managers or supervisors interfering with his work and this must have been a strong reason why he touted himself as a businessman who could make financial decisions.

Moore responded to Hearst with a telegram the next day saying that he had had a long session with Dwan and that the director found Zittel's management "utterly impossible." Dwan was now negotiating with the Mayflower Company and had practically closed the deal. He felt uncomfortable about being approached by Hearst at this time, he explained, because he did not want to appear to be playing one company against another.

Moore then volunteers his thoughts on Dwan, playing on crudely prejudicial terms. "I believe he is thoroughly honest in this; in fact, it is my judgment that Dwan is a man with [the] highest sense of honor, who has been maligned by a lot of tricky Jews, who do not know the first living thing about real, proper business methods."[31]

Moore knows that Hearst is already interested in Dwan but gives him more reasons to bolster his positive view. "Dwan is very fond of you personally and believes thoroughly in you and your ultimate triumph in the movie business, and it is my firm conviction that Dwan is the real genius of the movie business despite everything that has been said to the contrary."[32] This suggests that Dwan had indeed ruffled feathers in the industry with his views on efficient filmmaking but those working with him could find reason to believe that he was right.

By the end of the telegram, however, there also appears another reason why Moore is giving Dwan such a strong sell. Moore suggests that Hearst make Dwan president of Hearst's International Film Service "with a substantial interest in the profits and guaranty of minimum amount that he would earn each year for five years." This shows some gall on Moore's part since that position was then occupied by Hearst himself. Moore also proposes that he (Moore) take over the business end of the company (Zittel's job) and that magazine editor Ray Long take over the story department. Moore argues that he believes that this is the only arrangement that would interest Dwan.

Hearst sent a telegram reply on the same day. While he said nothing to disassociate himself from Moore's anti-Semitic comment, he states flatly that he will not fire Zittel (who was Jewish) and declares him to be "the best business manager that I know of."[33] At the same time, Hearst acknowledges that he does not agree with Zittel in his attitude toward directors. While demurring from the idea of relinquishing his post as president of the International, Hearst is willing to let Dwan take charge of production for the company while Zittel tended to the business sphere.

Hearst is still willing to pay Dwan generously, suggesting up to $25,000 per film, insuring him at least six pictures per year. Hearst says that Dwan could also in this period make a "big" feature film for which Hearst would be willing to pay as much as $30,000. Hearst points out that Dwan could thus earn between $150,000 and 180,000 a year and "be independent of anyone except myself."[34] On the other hand, Hearst notes that profit sharing would be a complicated issue since he already had an arrangement with Zukor on that score. Hearst concludes by telling Moore to have another talk with Dwan and that if he cannot agree to terms, at least have him wait until Hearst can go east to meet him.

In his earlier meeting with Moore, Dwan told him that the "best proposition" would be for him to go ahead and sign with Mayflower and that at the end of one year he could make a "real deal" with Hearst. Now Dwan was being offered the post of head of production, much as he had been at Triangle, only with much better financial resources and most likely a much better salary. He would be working for one of the most powerful men in the country and this magnate would be the only person Dwan would have to answer to.

Dwan made no quick capitulation. In his telegram to Moore the next day, Hearst persisted in trying to find ways to sweeten the deal. To circumvent the problem of profit sharing, Hearst suggests that Marion Davies would be willing to grant Dwan a percentage of her own producing company, or provide Dwan an advance to permit him to start his own company. Hearst emphasizes that this should only be offered if necessary to retain Dwan's services.

Moore apparently had nothing to report back to Hearst. On the succeeding day, April 26, Hearst sent another message asking, "What about Dwan?" And here Hearst makes clear the reason for his passionate pursuit of the director: "I surely want to retain him some way or other for Davies as he is the best man for that star." He uses the word "anxious" twice in the message.[35] While he is trying to phrase his reasoning in impersonal terms, it is clear that this is the concern of Hearst for his lover, the woman whom he promised to make a star. Dwan now appeared to be the director best suited to make that happen and Hearst did not want to lose him. The anxiety involved may have been mirrored Hearst's anxiety at the prospect of losing Marion. Hearst also notes approvingly that Dwan is "a fine honorable gentleman."

But the imperious tone of the last sentence is a reminder of Hearst's emotional interest: "Make him stay," Hearst tells Moore.[36]

This time, however, Hearst would not have his way. Moore's next telegram began, "I have gone over with Dwan thoroughly all the propositions you suggested, and he has decided definitely to go with the other people." Moore thought it useless to try any other proposals and could only hold out the hope that "in

The very formidable William Randolph Hearst was determined to retain Dwan as a director and was willing to offer him a unique position of power.

the event of his new venture's not being as successful as he thinks we will be able to get him back."[37]

The Dark Star was still months away from being released and perhaps if Hearst knew what its reception would be, he might have been less adamant about holding on to Dwan. (Interestingly, Hearst would fight off attempts by the Lasky organization to cut out "vital parts" of *The Dark Star.*) By late July, Hearst was still writing to Moore to try to make some arrangements with Dwan, as well as with Marshall Neilan.[38] But by this time, Hearst says their productions would be too high grade for Davies. Davies would, however, achieve real stardom in the early twenties and at the peak of her career make two of her best films, *The Patsy* and *Show People*, with the renowned director King Vidor.

Why had Dwan decided to decline Hearst's generous offers? There are a number of possible explanations. As Dwan had explained to Moore in their first meeting following Hearst's April 23 telegram, he had practically closed his deal with Mayflower. In fact, the April 19 edition of Wid's Daily had already announced that Dwan had signed a contract with Mayflower. He might not have signed on the dotted line but Dwan may have already felt committed. Still, if nothing had been put in writing, Dwan might have been tempted by the offer.

A stronger reason goes back to his Norma Talmadge experience, when Dwan said that he could not contend with the situation where his lead actress was married to her producer. Dwan had supervised one film with Louise Glaum but never worked with her again after she married her producer J. Parker Read.

At the time, it was well concealed from the public that Marion Davies was Hearst's mistress and Dwan may have been totally unaware of this when he signed to make these two films. But he surely understood the situation by the time he finished *The Dark Star.*

Dwan described Hearst to Bogdanovich as "a nice guy." He also said that Hearst regarded his film productions as "a toy, not his business — and he didn't care much."[39] (Hearst's decision not to forfeit the presidency of International Film Service casts some doubts on that view.) But he acknowledged that Hearst "was very interested"[40] in Davies. The unfortunate selection of *The Dark Star* was an expression of that interest and while Dwan would have to report to only one man, he knew that figure could be quite willful.

The terms of Dwan's Mayflower contract cited in Moore's telegram was for $1500 a week and a fifty percent division of profits. The fixed amount was indeed lower than what he would have gotten from Hearst but if he could choose his own projects and make them successful, he could make just as much, if not more. Dwan also saw the prospect of greater independence.

Dwan's new boss was far removed from Hearst just as the company quaintly called Mayflower was from Cosmopolitan. Isaac M. Wolper, a retail merchant in a Boston suburb, was allegedly inspired by the progress of Louis B. Mayer.[41] This led him to found the Mayflower Photoplay Corporation. Wolper signed the pioneering director George Loane Tucker, who had made *Traffic in Souls* for Universal. Tucker obtained the rights to *The Miracle Man*, a story of a faith healer who brings redemption to a gang of criminals. For his cast, Tucker assembled a group of actors who were not yet stars including Thomas Meighan, Betty Compson and Lon Chaney.

The Miracle Man, released in August of 1919, was an enormous success, earning about three million dollars. While it catapulted its unknown trio of players into stardom, according to Benjamin Hampton it "seriously shook the faith of producers in the star system...."[42] It made them re-evaluate what directors could do without high-priced stars. In Hampton's view, the film "exercised a profound influence in raising the status of directors."[43] In signing with Mayflower, Dwan joined two other well-known directors under contract, Tucker and Emile Chautard. (Chautard was later acknowledged by Josef von Sternberg as his mentor.) This triumvirate would soon be augmented by Raoul Walsh.

Dwan began his work for Mayflower in May. "They gave me carte blanche. I just did as I pleased. I found the story, made the movie, and they distributed it, that's all."[44]

Actually, Mayflower would not be distributing the films it had in production. In August, it was announced that Realart had an agreement to distribute Mayflower films though agreements were also made for each director. Dwan was the first, and his film *Soldiers of Fortune* was the first film released under the Mayflower–Realart arrangement. Realart also seemed to show the same respect for the director's autonomy. Realart president Arthur S. Kane noted, "We hope to have *Soldiers of Fortune* ready for release early in the Fall. However, we have no desire to rush it, and none of the Allan Dwan productions will be issued until Mr. Dwan is satisfied with them in every respect."[45] (Mayflower's contract directors each had their own company and so Dwan had Allan Dwan Productions.)

With *Soldiers of Fortune*, Dwan turned back again to a virile action story. It was based on a novel by Richard Harding Davis, who espoused many of the masculine virtues of the era. Davis had been both a journalist and fiction writer (and, interestingly, in 1895 he joined the staff of the *New York Journal*, a fledgling member of the Hearst newspaper chain). Davis' travels in Latin America had led to the writing of *Soldiers of Fortune* which was first serialized in 1896. As a war correspondent during the Spanish-American War, he had been with Theodore Roosevelt and the Rough Riders at San Juan Hill and had helped to publicize their activities. He continued to write short stories, novels and plays while also serving as correspondent in the Boer War and World War I.

Soldiers of Fortune was prescient not only about the Roosevelt policy of "gunboat diplomacy" but of future American military interventions in Latin America. In the story, Robert Clay, an American civil engineer, heads for the fictional South American country of Olancho to take charge of the iron mines for a man named Langham. General Mendoza, who wants to get his share of the money paid to the government for opening those mines, stages a coup against the president. Clay tries to help those who wish to restore the lawful president to power. He thinks he is in love with Alice, Langham's older daughter, but when the younger sister Hope comes to his aid, shooting some of the general's soldiers, he is convinced that she is the one for him. (Davis liked the idea of a woman accompanying a man on his adventures.) Clay sends a wireless asking for help from an American battleship lying in the harbor. It fires a barrage at Mendoza's forces and "leathernecks" finish the job, rescuing Clay and his cohorts.

Soldiers of Fortune was a familiar property. Not only was the novel widely popular but it was successfully adapted to the stage in 1902 by Augustus Thomas, who had also written *Arizona*. There was also a 1914 film version starring Dustin Farnum. But Dwan gave his dramatization extra punch and verisimilitude.

Perhaps taking a shot at the star system, Dwan told the press, "In this production and the ones to follow, there will be no player starred. I will be devoting my entire energies to presenting big stories in a big way and in engaging players, I will employ the best available actors who are fitted to interpret the various roles."[46]

Norman Kerry, who was reasonably well known for having performed with Mary Pickford but hardly a major star, appeared as Clay. Pauline Starke portrayed Hope and Wilfred Lucas, who had starred in some of Dwan's supervised Triangle films, played President Alvarez. Wallace Beery, destined to be King Richard in *Robin Hood*, impersonated the villainous General Mendoza.

As was usually the case, Dwan sought authentic-looking locations. He told Bogdanovich, "I fell heir to some great backgrounds. I went down and used the fairgrounds in San Diego which were perfect for a small Latin republic.... And I got practically all the people in San Diego working in the picture. There were no unions in those days, so I put an ad in the paper inviting the populace to come out to Balboa Park to see a picture being made. And they came in droves. I put straws hats on them, and when I brought my actors by, I said, 'Wave those straw hats,' and they all waved them. Thousands of people in the picture, all having a good time, eating their lunch and waving straw hats and getting no money, being allowed to see a picture being made."[47]

Dwan's story is borne out by an ad that appeared in the May 28, 1919, edition of the *San Diego Union* advertising a free spectacular show for Allan Dwan Features at the Exposition Grounds at Balboa Park. The buildings that had been constructed for the Panama-California Exposition planned for 1915 (to celebrate the tenth anniversary of the Canal) utilized "a Spanish-Colonial style with colonnades, tiled roofs, patios, and fountains."[48]

Dwan's elaborate battle scenes were shot in the hills and mountains south of Santa Monica. Columnist A.H. Giebler, writing for *Moving Picture World*, visited the locations and observed, "They say that Dwan used an airplane to scout out the location, and I thought that this story was just press agent raving until I saw the place myself. It's the truth. He couldn't have found it any other way."[49] Dwan was assisted in his staging by the ever-trusty Arthur Rosson and future B-movie director James Hogan.

Giebler also reported on the participants in the battle scenes. "Jose Aviles and Lorenzo Lopez, two of the defenders of the hacienda, are old Villa men.... Jose Martinez, for four years Villa's confidential clerk and the only one entrusted with the important duty of cutting the leader's hair, was among the besiegers."[50]

Dwan was also, according to publicity releases, a stickler for research and detail. One trade story referred to the "Dwanesque scrutiny."[51] The same story claimed that Dwan trusted the editing of the film to no one. "He installed a projection room in his summer home so as to give this branch of the work all his spare time."[52] Perhaps thinking not only of his film's hero but of his abandoned career as an electrical engineer, Dwan said he was dedicating *Soldiers of Fortune* to civil engineers.

Soldiers of Fortune was seven reels long, longer than all of Dwan's previous films except for the ponderous *Dark Star*. All of his preparation on the film must have proved invaluable experience for his future work on the epic *Robin Hood*.

Richard Harding Davis had died in 1916 of heart trouble at the age of 52. The New York premiere of *Soldiers of Fortune* at the Capitol Theater honored Davis' memory. Davis had been a vigorous supporter of the Boy Scouts and 5,000 of them stood at attention. Davis' four-year-old daughter Hope, named for the film's heroine, was present for the ceremony. Colonel Theodore Roosevelt, Jr., was invited to address the Boys Scouts on the friendship between Davis and his father, who had passed away the preceding January.

The critics recognized that there was nothing in the film that was unfamiliar but were still impressed by the execution of its elements. *Moving Picture World* reported, "*Soldiers of Fortune* is seven reels of adventure, action and appealing romance without one dull moment."[53] *Photoplay* referred to it as "corking light entertainment, and as easy on the eyes as it is on the mind."[54] While acknowledging that the film was a "splendid production," Wid's Daily appeared more conscious of the stereotypes and clichés involved: "Plenty of mob stuff, action galore, 'greasers' running wild, American cruiser to the rescue with the stars and stripes on top at the finish with the lovers coming into their own. But with all that, thrills, fights 'n everything, it can hardly be termed 'gripping' at any point."[55]

The trades, however, reported that *Soldiers of Fortune* was setting box office records in many cities. Dwan had read the pulse of the times and without Fairbanks had been able to put his own brand on this action picture.

Now seeing the rewards of being an independent producer

with a percentage, Dwan was not likely to be returning soon to Hearst. He was savoring his independence and looking forward to broadening that status.

Hollywood Uprising

In order to understand the significance of Dwan's move towards independence and the reception of *The Miracle Man*, it is necessary to review how forces were operating in the film industry in the last few years and in particular, throughout 1919.

Although this was a period when the government had taken action against trusts, consolidation was continuing in business. In the film business, power was becoming consolidated not just in one corporation but in one man. That man was Adolph Zukor.

Zukor understood how to use different corporations to bolster his profits and outmaneuver his rivals. Famous Players was the company that had been his base. His deal with the Paramount Pictures Corporation provided capital to his company and distribution of his films. When W.W. Hodkinson, the president of Paramount, clashed with Zukor, Zukor managed to get a majority of the Paramount board of directors to depose Hodkinson. Paramount, Famous Players and the Lasky Corporation were then all merged together. Later, Zukor founded Artcraft to bolster his profits and weaken his main rival, Triangle. One profiler of the mogul mused that he was "an illustration of the multiplication table. He amalgamates, He congeals. He is anaconda Adolph, with a versatile appetite."[56]

As early as 1912, when Zukor was advancing the idea of longer films based on stage plays, an article in Hearst's *New York Journal*, probably written by Carl Zittel,[57] praised Zukor as an Everyman with a mind like Napoleon's who was elevating the status of motion pictures. The reference to Zukor's Napoleonic quality would be a fixture of future characterizations.

In 1924, Zukor told *Moving Picture World*'s W. Stephen Bush, "The thought of creating a company which would make longer and better films, features as we called them afterwards, was not born of any dream or vision but came as the result of my observation as an exhibitor."[58] No matter how keen his sense of observation, Zukor knew he was still taking a big chance when he founded Famous Players in 1912 just as when he had converted his Sixth Avenue arcade into a movie theater in 1906. Zukor showed a strong stomach for adversity, as in September 1915 when the Famous Players Studio on 26th Street burned down. Surveying the ruins, Zukor saw his partner Edwin S. Porter looking devastated and lamenting, "Everything I've ever done is gone." Zukor is said to have responded, "Well, we'll start over again. I mean, we know how. We'll just do it in a different place."[59]

In April 1917, the same month that the United States declared war on Germany, the First National Exhibitors' Circuit Inc. was formed. In the words of one early film historian, "Nobody knew it then, but a war, distinctively its own, thereby had been dumped right in the front yard of the industry."[60] By this time, Triangle no longer represented a serious threat to Famous Players–Lasky but First National would waste no time in becoming a formidable rival.

First National had been conceived by Thomas L. Tally, a Los Angeles theater owner. He was allied with another exhibitor, John D. Williams, and their organization acted as a purchasing agent for twenty-six of the largest first-run exhibitors in the U.S.

First National was founded in reaction to one of Zukor's major power ploys. Since Zukor controlled companies representing major sources of production and distribution, he now pursued three keys that would give him a lock over the entire film industry. One of those keys was control over America's film theaters.

Zukor proved successful at block-booking, the practice of requiring that theaters accept not just the films from a distributor they wanted but a huge package of films including minor efforts. In a clumsy way, this had been attempted by Triangle and others but Zukor had proved much more adept at it. He already had in his stable such major stars as Pickford, Marguerite Clark, Wallace Reid, and Harold Lockwood. With the defections from Triangle, he added Fairbanks and William S. Hart to his roster. An exhibitor refusing Zukor's program and thus all of his output would risk losing the fans of those stars to the nearest theater that accepted Zukor's package. Also, since Zukor's studios were churning out over 100 films annually, he had the capacity to fill a theater's schedule for the entire year.

The First National group originally controlled about 100 theaters and in each of the key cities at least one of their houses was a customer of Zukor's films. The association could also issue sub-franchises to other theaters in outlying areas and the organization eventually swelled to include as many as five or six thousand theaters.[61] First National could now threaten Zukor with boycotts of his product. And this organization now had the capital to make their own films and hire their own stars. So Zukor was temporarily checked on this front.

Another key was maintaining a source of story material. This may have been the most elusive of all. With his first venture of Famous Players, Zukor sought to buy up the rights to the popular plays of his day, assuming that there was a ready audience for their adaptation to film. Zukor learned the hard way that this was not always true. The goal of Cosmopolitan Pictures was to scrutinize all the literary properties and authors whose work had been developed for Hearst publications and where appropriate to get film rights for them. In any event, the alliance made between Cosmopolitan and Paramount was not long-lived. Hearst felt he was being cheated by Zukor's distribution practices. After four years, in February 1923 Hearst switched to the Goldwyn organization to distribute Cosmopolitan films.

The third key was control of the major stars and here, as noted earlier, Zukor seemed to be riding high in 1917 and 1918. Also, as suggested earlier, control of the stars was intertwined with success in booking theaters and in making block-booking work. It could also help get higher fees. When Artcraft was founded in 1916, specifically for Mary Pickford, the rental prices on her films were trebled.

First National's method of entering the field was to provide money to independent producers to make films and not be saddled with the costs of building or operating a studio. Instead, they would use their considerable capital to sign stars. And they made a very big catch when they plucked Charles Chaplin from Mutual, the company that Harry Aitken had left in the hands of John Freuler.

As Hampton pointed out, back in 1916 exhibitors had chastised Zukor for granting Pickford a large salary that would increase costs for them. But now Zukor's rival First National had given Chaplin a yearly salary in excess of a million dollars and was bidding high for Pickford, whose contract with Zukor would expire in the autumn of 1918. First National not only offered Pickford more generous financial terms but promised her complete artistic control of her films including "final cut." Pickford signed with First National on November 9, 1918.

First National also signed lesser but still important stars including Lillian Gish, Norma and Constance Talmadge, Anita Stewart and Katherine MacDonald. The days of Zukor's star dominance appeared over.

But a possible new wrinkle to the power struggle for control of the film industry came in the form of rumors that ran rampant in January 1919, during the First National Exhibitors Convention in Los Angeles. The story was that there was to be a merger between Zukor's Famous Players–Lasky and First National. Tally denied the rumors but suspicion developed among the top stars, particularly Chaplin, who hired a detective to investigate. According to Chaplin's autobiography, the female detective worked herself into the good graces of a film executive who told her that he and his associates were planning a forty million dollar merger of all the producing companies which would put the industry on "a proper business basis, instead of having it run by a bunch of crazy actors getting astronomical salaries."[62] The top stars now had to ponder a situation where there would be no bidding for their talents and the size of their salaries would be dictated to them.

In response, Chaplin, Fairbanks, William S. Hart, Griffith and Pickford signed the agreement that would start a new film company, the United Artists Association, and released the news to the press.

The notion that the stars would be running their own studio was met with both cynicism and incredulity and inspired the famous reaction from Richard Rowland, then head of the Metro Pictures Corporation: "So, the lunatics have taken over the asylum."[63]

The starry founders of United Artists knew that to establish their credibility they would need to show that there were important names from the world of finance behind them. During the World War I bond drives, Fairbanks had established a good relationship with William G. McAdoo, son-in-law of President Wilson and former Secretary of the Treasury and then Director General of the Railroads.

McAdoo, having recently become a private citizen, was offered the presidency of United Artists. McAdoo declined the offer but agreed that if they appointed his former assistant on the railroad board, Oscar Price, as president, McAdoo would help in the organizing and be their counsel. The UA founders complied with McAdoo's request and Price became UA's first president.

The names of McAdoo and Price gave United Artists prestige and respectability, but they also needed executives who were savvy in the film business. UA had this in the persons of Hiram Abrams and B.P. Schulberg, both until recently Zukor employees. They had been on board at the outset and there was even a dispute, never completely settled, as to which of the two came up with the original idea for founding the company.[64]

Abrams had become president of Paramount when Hodkinson was forced out. He did not get along with Zukor and resigned the Paramount presidency, a void that was filled by Zukor himself. Abrams now became general manager of UA.

The young Schulberg was an acolyte of Abrams and had followed him to United Artists. But when Schulberg was not granted a percentage in the company, he left its ranks. The press had taken to calling the new group the Big Five after the five founders. However, before the conferences with McAdoo, William S. Hart withdrew, returning to the Zukor fold where he received a pay raise that gave him $200,000 per picture. So they were now the Big Four.

United Artists would distribute their own films with Abrams in charge of sales.

In late January, Zukor was queried about the status of a merger between his companies and First National. Zukor responded as if action was needed to quell a revolution: "Some sort of combination between the bigger producers and distributors, something that would serve to stabilize conditions and discourage the Bolshevik element in the industry, would be very desirable, but so far nothing but idealistic and impractical plans have been proposed."[65] Sounding not particularly interested and extremely suspicious, First National's Williams commented, "The First National is already a strong amalgamation. We own 200 theaters, and are affiliated with 600 more, all first run houses. We will not be dominated by any one."[66]

This time it was Zukor who would not get the merger he wanted.

If it was difficult enough for the trade publications to follow all the twists and turns of this power struggle, it was even more challenging for consumer magazines to explain the significance of all this to movie fans. One magazine article tried to put things in perspective by the author's recollection of watching

A January 30, 1919, front page cartoon in *Wid's Daily* shows Adolph Zukor and other Hollywood power brokers in retreat after the founding of United Artists.

one of United Artists' founders at work. This reminiscence had to do with Fairbanks working with Allan Dwan:

> One of these was the time that I went out on location with him. The day was very hot and Doug had been boxing all morning. They were using Allan Dwan's house "The Outpost" as a location for a hunting lodge.... Fairbanks was dressed in very old clothes. He was stretched out on a couch taking things easy. Notwithstanding the heat, he looked rather cool and comfortable, but his words belied his looks. Too much exercise in the heat had made him so dizzy that he could not work, he said."[67]

Fairbanks starts a rambling conversation with Dwan and begins moving about. Dwan surmises that Doug is feeling better but then Fairbanks again takes on the manner of a sick man whom the author compares to a young boy explaining to his mother why he shouldn't go to school.

> There was a pause. The "invalid" closed his eyes.... Dwan was sitting in a comfortable rocker, his feet on the veranda railing. Obviously, he did not feel any more like working than did Doug. There was a restful silence. Then Doug opened his eyes and fixed them upon Dwan.
>
> "That fellow," he said pointing at him, "used to be one of the most commercial directors in the game, but since he's tied up with me he's changed entirely. We've tried every way to make pictures and *we've found out that when we don't feel like working our work doesn't have any punch in it.* Look at the fellows who are making *pictures*—shall we say works of art?—Chaplin, for instance. Can you imagine him working when he does not feel like it? You *cannot*. But when he *does* work, he accomplishes more in one day than he could in a week of 'efficiency' methods.
>
> "The same applies to Griffith, and to me, for that matter.
>
> "Suppose I had to work under 'efficiency' methods. I couldn't do it—*that's all!*"
>
> And this statement of Fairbanks, made and noted many months ago, seems to me the epitome of the strike of the big five. It is, in effect, a rebellion against the too-much-efficiency, which, in turn, was a rebellion against no efficiency at all.[68]

There was obviously, more involved in the "rebellion" than a war against too much efficiency and the author of the piece, Elizabeth Peltret, acknowledges as much, later in the article. But to stick to the more poetic argument here, the skeptic might question whether Fairbanks and Dwan were ribbing her. The working methods of Doug and Dwan were hardly dilatory and their pace of grinding out films on schedule was impressive.

Doug's friends and co-workers, however, were aware of how Fairbanks combined his adroit sense of production with bouts of mischievousness. One intimate remembered, "Douglas could break up a meeting of directors met to consider a project involving millions, by disappearing through a window, or up a fire-escape; but when the final decision was about to be made it would be his voice and his opinion that decided the verdict."[69] One of Fairbanks' directors, Donald Crisp, complained, "Tell him to do something and he'd take the whole afternoon off and play Doug."[70]

Dwan, the scientific exponent of efficiency, knew how to humor Doug and put up with him and, until that major rupture, could work harmoniously and efficiently with him. Peltret also quoted Fairbanks saying, "We don't use a script at all. Just a few notes-tho [sic], of course, we make a complete continuity. Allan Dwan and I are both thoroly [sic] familiar with the story before beginning work on it, but we believe in leaving much to the inspiration of the moment, so that *our* imaginations may have something to do with the picture, as it were. Otherwise, the action would look cut-and-dried."[71]

Fairbanks and Dwan (seen here in a 1917 photograph) shared a special chemistry and an aversion to the emerging Hollywood factory system (courtesy Kevin Brownlow).

Peltret dwelt on that last line and cited a statement of the "Big Five" that they were against "machine-made entertainment." Consolidation in the industry, whether it was headed by Zukor or someone else, was striving toward the building of many such machines and of making the studios factories.

But at that moment it was Adolph Zukor who seemed to be threatening the greatest domination of the industry since Edison and the Patent Companies.

The rise of First National represented the rebellion of the exhibitors against such domination.

With the founding of United Artists, three major stars (and one major director) were now also resisting Zukor's threat of monopoly.

But what of the other major directors and writers?

Associated Producers and the Directors' Revolt

While there was much concern about Zukor's accumulating power, it was still not clear if the different branches of the film industry felt they had enough in common to unite against him. Outside of United Artists, the question could be asked how much sympathy there was among other creative personnel for the big stars, whose earning power towered over them.

The star system seemed firmly in place at the end of World War I and a solid foundation for future planning. But in the postwar period there soon appeared changes in audience tastes. Hampton notes, "Within two years after Armistice Day, defections in star adoration were definitely reflected in many box-offices and the changing condition began to worry the more acute showmen."[72] It was in the middle of this period that rumors swirled about a possible Famous Players/Paramount–First National merger. While the rival companies were squared off against each other, there was some reason for both parties to worry if preserving the star system was worth all the mounting expenditures of a bidding war.

In their issues of January 4, 1919, both *Motion Picture News* and *Moving Picture World* printed interviews conducted with Richard Rowland, president of Metro Pictures and Screen Classics, in which he attacked the star system. This was the same executive who would make the comment about the "asylum takeover" which would occur shortly thereafter. Rowland asserted that in most instances "the production has made the star rather than the star the production, and that it is now time for the manufacturers of pictures to run their own business in their own way, so that the business can be conducted at a profit." Striking a tone that sounds as if it could be aimed at the playful methods of Fairbanks, Rowland says, "In our opinion, the time has come when motion pictures must cease to be a game and become a business."[73]

The importance of directors was becoming more recognized. Just a few months earlier, that shrewd observer of the film scene, "Wid" Gunning had proclaimed, "The director has come into his own." In the same issue of his publication, he pointed out, "I have preached the importance of the director for four years now and feel considerable personal satisfaction in finding that I was right long ago."[74]

Hampton noted that for years the executives had been located in New York while increasingly most of the production was done in California so that the "director had always been the owner's connecting link with studio operations. Originally, the director had executed or supervised all the details of movie making, writing the simple scenarios required for short films, selecting and directing the players, devising the settings, editing and titling the film. 'The mysteries of the movies' were locked in his brain, and the producer had to rely on his craftsmanship."[75] As films continued to expand in length, writers began to grow in importance as more elaborate scenarios were needed. But directors remained the far more dominant figures. On the other hand, the stars had crept into the directors' realm of power and could command great salaries even as many directors regarded them as mere puppets.

Now there was some question as to whether the smarter move would be to give more power, publicity and money to the directors, the "autocratic, headstrong" group Hampton had described.[76] Zukor was trying a compromise measure, willing to pay larger amounts to directors as well as to screenwriters and the authors of source material rather than to the stars.

The loss of the stars was most likely a driving force in Zukor's alliance with Hearst and Cosmopolitan Productions in getting a corner on source material.

As for finding a director whose name could be as successfully promoted as a star's, Zukor did not have to look far. At his own studio, Cecil B. DeMille had carved out a place for himself as a name director. His 1918 remake of *The Squaw Man*, which he had first filmed four years earlier, was an "all-star" production (that is, with no major star) and proved to be a hit. ("All-star" pictures became increasingly popular; that was one of the ways Dwan tried to publicize *Soldiers of Fortune*.) Like Griffith, DeMille had succeeded in making the director a box office name and he was soon earning more money than most of the stars. But Zukor would need more than one star director.

In February 1919, it was announced that the Mayflower Film Corp. had just closed "probably the most wonderful contract ever made with a director of motion pictures." The contract was made with "George Loane Tucker to produce six special feature productions without any limitations, financial or otherwise, in order that the best possible product may be secured."[77]

Tucker had been originally signed to a one-film contract but when word leaked out about the film special he was preparing, *The Miracle Man*, the large distributing companies began to bid for his services for a series of films. Mayflower than signed him to this six-picture contract and finally came to an agreement with Zukor to distribute the Tucker specials though Artcraft, "the amount involved running into millions."[78]

While not widely known today, Tucker was cited by "Wid" Gunning in 1918 as one of the four best directors in the world following Griffith. (The others were Lois Weber, Marshall Neilan and Maurice Tourneur.[79]) With Tucker now on board, Zukor had a stronger basis for a strategy of using directors to promote films.

Zukor lost no time in exploiting this opportunity in the press. The day after the news of the Tucker signing appeared in Wid's, there appeared an announcement under the heading of "Featuring Directors." Citing the contracting of the Tucker specials, it said that Paramount–Artcraft "is completing an important program in which stars are of secondary importance and the directors are to be featured."[80] The directors listed included Griffith, Ince, DeMille, Tourneur and Hugh Ford.

With the release and huge box office success of *The Miracle Man*, Zukor could move forward with confidence. He was also bringing another new subsidiary into play, the distribution outfit Realart. Just as Artcraft was a vehicle for getting higher rental fees, Realart was founded to get moderate prices for more modestly budgeted quality films with still budding stars such as Mary Miles Minter and Bebe Daniels. Minter was being groomed as a successor to Pickford. (According to Ramsaye, Zukor also founded Realart to provide competition to his former partner Lewis Selznick and staffed the company with some of Selznick's ex-employees.) As noted earlier, Realart became the distribution arm for Mayflower's other "name" directors, Dwan, Chautard and Walsh.

Realart was ostensibly an independent company and for a time Zukor neither confirmed nor denied accusations that it was one of his subsidiaries. But eventually, Zukor did show his hand when it suited his publicity purposes. In November 1919, he told the *Los Angeles Express*, "I decided it was high time that some corporation started in to make pictures with a soul.... Why not make every picture with a soul? That's why I organized the Realart Corporation. That's why I called it Realart."[81]

Realart may be the most pretentious name ever given to a film company but Zukor might have thought it a worthy riposte to his new rival, United Artists. Zukor explained, "There have been some pictures produced that will live forever. These pictures have souls.... Each picture should be a classic. It should be constructed and the story so cleverly told that, like a good book, it will live always." Yet, earlier that year, Zukor had refused to release a film that would be recognized as a genuine classic, D.W. Griffith's *Broken Blossoms*. Ironically, the film was sold to United Artists, for which it made a profit despite its downbeat ending.

That very same month, "the Napoleon of the motion picture industry" encountered still another challenge to his hegemony. After two weeks of circulating rumors, it was officially announced that a group of directors had agreed to form an association upon the expiration of their other contracts. The directors were Ince, Tourneur, Mack Sennett, Neilan and Dwan. Their new company would be called the Associated Producers.

Why had these directors rebelled and banded together just when it appeared that Zukor and other producers were going to give them greater recognition? Two of the directors, Ince and Tourneur, were even to have been included in Zukor's new program of films highlighting the contributions of directors.

Photoplay's "Cal York" claimed to have the answer. "The avowed reason for the new combine was the monopolistic tendencies of the Zukor interests. 'Wiseacres' profess to believe that in the near future, unless something intervenes, Famous Players–Lasky will have a stranglehold on the entire production and exhibition end of the film industry."[82] Of course, it would be less awkward for the directors to leak such widely viewed sentiments to *Photoplay* than to include them in official announcements. In fact, all the participants but Marshall Neilan were contracted with Zukor at the time, Dwan by virtue of his agreement with Realart.

Zukor had embarked on still another new strategy to eliminate his main opposition. He sought advice from attorney Walter W. Irwin, general manager of the film combine VLSE and Hearst's brother-in-law. Irwin suggested to Zukor that Paramount "could destroy First National if it would go into each one of the First National cities and build, or threaten to build, the finest and largest theater in the city...." Irwin took note of the pressure this would create from the exhibitors' bankers who would not want them to fight Zukor.[83]

To obtain the funds necessary to build these theaters, Zukor turned to Wall Street, which had been ill-disposed to invest in motion pictures since the Triangle debacle. In the fall of 1919, a $10,000,000 issue of preferred stock of Famous Players–Lasky was sold and now both preferred and common stock for the company were listed on the stock exchange. Zukor had already started buying up theaters and now had the resources to continue to expand. The fear itself of how many theaters Zukor could buy throughout the country became another weapon in his arsenal.

The directors who comprised Associated Producers recognized that once Zukor gained a monopoly of the industry he would dictate terms, regardless of what viewpoint he was now pontificating.

Some of the concern the directors felt was echoed in a lawsuit filed by Tucker against Mayflower and Famous Players–Lasky in January of 1920. Tucker's *The Miracle Man* had been touted for what a director could achieve without stars and how the industry supported this development. In his suit, Tucker charged that he had not been given the advertising and publicity promised in his contract and sought an accounting of the monies collected for *The Miracle Man*. Tucker charged Mayflower with making fraudulent statements to him of the sums they received from Famous Players. Tucker also asked that the distribution contract between Mayflower and Famous be cancelled for his future productions and that his highly publicized contract with Mayflower be cancelled after the completion of his next film. "Wid" Gunning had also filed an affidavit in Tucker's support and he pointed out that the film's pressbook promoted the idea that *The Miracle Man* was a Paramount–Artcraft picture whereas they had only distributed it and that it was a "George Loane Tucker Production."

The month before the suit was disclosed, it was announced that Tucker had joined the Associated Producers.

Photoplay noted that the coalition of directors was reminiscent of the original arrangement of Ince, Sennett and Griffith for Triangle.[84] The comparison to Triangle, while apt, was not an auspicious one. In their first advertisements in December 1919, the Associated Producers preferred to note that their combination was as "impressive" as that of United Artists. "The principals are Thomas H. Ince, Maurice Tourneur, Marshall Neilan, Allan Dwan, Mack Sennett and George Loane Tucker. These directors are about as well known as any six screen stars, which incidentally, is evidence of the happily increasing tendency of the public to recognize the work of the man behind the camera as well as that of the player in front."[85] The parallels with United Artists were also obvious and raised the question of potential cooperation between the two companies with similar interests. The comparison of the directors' fame to that of screen stars was a bit strained although all six were likely well known to exhibitors.

But exactly how the films of the Big Six were to be distributed remained a vexing question for months. At one point, they seemed close to making a deal with First National. At another time they were seriously negotiating with Goldwyn. "Goldwyn's proposition was to finance the deal on the basis of $150,000 advance to each director to make pictures, but this was 'spiked' by Allan Dwan, who made a demand that Goldwyn abandon its present list of stars and practically turn over the organization to the handling of the 'Bix Six' on [a] 60–40 basis."[86] United Artists also considered handling their films. By late April, it was announced that the Associated Producers were forming their own distribution company.

At a luncheon at New York's Hotel Claridge on February 21, 1920, Thomas H. Ince, acting as spokesman for the group, was already talking about the possibility of Associated Producers releasing independently. Ince had recently arrived from Los Angeles with producer J. Parker Read, Ince's general manager, who had just been appointed general business representative of the Associated Producers. (Read brought with him a print of *Sex*, his latest film, starring his wife Louise Glaum.)

Ince noted that the Associated Producers was open to expansion and that any director, whose production reached the standard that they would establish, could be invited to join the company. He emphasized that all of the directors would be working independently and "we shall vie with each other in surpassing the work of our associates.... We will gamble with every means at our command to outstrip our previous achievements and from this the exhibitor — and the public — will gain."[87]

Dwan was next introduced to speak. In comments clearly aimed at the Zukor organizations and their new financial backers, Dwan said, "Wall Street is a machine. It is not interested in amusement. It is not interested in producing artistic entertainment. It is interested in finance and far above that in politics. It has no place in the motion picture business. Its influence is unhealthy for our industry. One needs to know very little of Wall Street to realize and appreciate that its chief interest is in politics because politics governs financial conditions. The financial manipulators have awakened to the power of the screen for swaying public opinions."[88]

Dwan expressed some concern that such onscreen propaganda might affect the next presidential election in 1924. He then noted the difference between film and the print media: "Wall Street cannot control the press. Publication interests are too diversified, and besides many readers of the newspapers realize that according to the political complexion of the publication so its political news is presented. But everyone who goes to see picture entertainment must see the political propaganda unless they wish to close their eyes."[89]

Dwan's speech sounds rather curious for a director who says he regarded himself as a businessman. Also, there is no record of Dwan raising a similar ruckus when Triangle was established with capital from Wall Street.

However, before considering his charges as opportunism, it should be noted that Triangle used its capital from the financial markets to launch its operations, not as a long-term strategy toward eliminating its competition. Hampton has acknowledged that Zukor's entrance into Wall Street "marked a new era in movie finance," and soon other film companies were listed in the stock exchanges.[90]

The trade press also did not regard Wall Street financing as business as usual. Zukor made a point of denying that such financing would be used for producing and "that in no way did the financial people have any voice in that end of the company's business. The purpose of the new capital was to secure theaters...."[91]

In his speech, Dwan acknowledged that Wall Street money was being used to buy theaters but also believed Wall Street had an interest in production. While Zukor was almost certainly telling the truth that he was only using such funding for theater-buying, the road was now open to Wall Street investment becoming embedded in other areas.

The issue of films being used for partisan propaganda was enough of a concern that in the summer of 1920, *Motion Picture News* thought it was worth an editorial titled "No Politics on the Screen." The emphasis in the editorial was that any such act of propaganda would recoil upon the perpetrators. Citing the newsreel as an example, the editorial stated assuredly, "[I]f any newsreel entered into a campaign of political propaganda the fact would be told to the trade by this publication, for one, in as large a type as we could use. Any exhibitor would be a fool to run such a newsreel...."[92]

Of course, partisanship could be achieved more subtly. According to Ramsaye, Warren Harding's campaign manager Will Hays, in the election of 1920, used his contacts in the film industry to help Harding get plenty of screen time in the newsreels. Ramsaye observed, "The air was full of newsreels, and the newsreels were full of Warren G. Harding."[93] Hays was still remembered by his Hollywood friends when in January 1922, he was formally appointed head of the Motion Picture Producers and Distributors of America.

Unless some future film scholar should prove otherwise, however, it does not appear that Wall Street reaped significant political propaganda in films as a result of its motion picture investment in that time frame. Wall Street's values were already implanted in the national mood of this era. When 1924 came, the Republicans nominated the conservative Calvin Coolidge while the Democrats nominated J.P. Morgan's lawyer, John W. Davis, who also ran on a conservative platform. The Progressive candidate in the three-way race, Robert M. LaFolette, garnered only 16.6 percent of the national vote.

Still, Dwan's concern was in a sense prescient. Dwan did not believe that the print medium was open to manipulation but this was a period in which each major city had numerous daily newspapers (and no radio or television stations existed). So he saw films as the only potential area ripe for media control. But by early in the twenty-first century, with the FCC pondering cross-ownership of newspapers and radio or TV stations, the question of media manipulation would be an even more pressing issue.

Dwan: The Director and His Image

As was his custom, Dwan did not languish long after completing *Soldiers of Fortune*. He soon embarked on *The Luck of the Irish*, a romantic adventure story based on a novel by Harold McGrath. The story concerns the adventures of a plumber named William Grogan. In the process of adopting a little boy he has cared for since finding him in a back alley, Grogan learns he has inherited $28,000. With that bonanza, Grogan decides to take the boy on a trip around the world. On board he sees a schoolteacher (Anna Q. Nilsson) whom he has long admired from afar. She is being pursued by an agent of a former suitor and this leads to various scuffles all over the world involving the heroic plumber. At the climax, Grogan must rescue her from a kidnapping in Singapore.

The story bears a superficial resemblance to the romantic serial Fairbanks had talked of making back in 1916. For the lead role Dwan called upon James Kirkwood, who had seemingly abandoned acting for directing and had been a frequent director of Pickford. Kirkwood returned to acting to stay and would star in three other Dwan films in the early twenties.

Close on the heels of *The Luck of the Irish* and made practically simultaneously was *A Splendid Hazard*, which was also based on a story by Harold McGrath. Dwan was credited as supervisor and Arthur Rosson handled the chores of director, though again Dwan was often referred to as the director. The Griffith star Henry B. Walthall played a Bavarian who discovers that he is descended from Napoleon. "The Little Colonel" of *Birth of a Nation* here aspires to be the "Little Corporal" as he suffers from delusions of grandeur in a plot that moves from France to America to Corsica in a search for hidden treasure.

The Luck of the Irish opened in January 1920 and appropriately was still being widely shown on March 17, St. Patrick's Day. Burns Mantle of *Photoplay* commented, "It is a first class adventure story ... and it hops over the world with the interesting suddenness of a particularly active flea."[94] After a triumphant opening at Grauman's Broadway Theater in Los Angeles, it went on to booming business throughout the country.

With another box office smash, Dwan must have indeed felt he had realized the luck of the Irish. But even in the midst of his success, there was some question as to how his career was evolving. In a generally favorable review of *Soldiers of Fortune*, Julian Johnson of *Photoplay* had written, "I have never ceased to regret Allan Dwan's turn from the spiritual to the material side of motion pictures. In the former he was a public success and an artistic triumph. In the latter he is still — a public success. The public will, and does, like a big, mechanically well-made adventure like *Soldiers of Fortune*. But the public also liked that splendid drama *Panthea*, in which he painted not only vivid action, but the soul of a woman. I wish Dwan would do more *Pantheas*. He can. Perhaps he will. But Dwan is a businessman, I suppose. And he finds that *Soldiers of Fortune* is a better, or at least more expedient, business subject."[95]

Johnson's disappointment may have been influenced by the tenor of some of Dwan's interviews and he may have believed that Dwan's commercial instincts had changed him as a filmmaker. Our own ability to appreciate Johnson's viewpoint is complicated by the fact that most of the earlier Dwan films that impressed Johnson do not appear to exist today. Also, Dwan has proved elusive to many critics given his ability and inclination to shift gears. Another *Photoplay* critic, Burns Mantle, writing of the Dwan–Rosson *A Splendid Harzard*, opined, "Dwan is perhaps our sanest director — yet he is fearless, too and continually presents something new, never traveling the beaten track in stories or action."[96] Even as Mantle's critical words appeared in print, Dwan had embarked on probably the most somber string of features in his career.

Dwan's personal life was also at a crossroads. On October 8, 1919, Pauline Bush sued Dwan for divorce in Washoe County, Nevada, charging desertion and cruelty. The divorce was granted on October 23. Dwan and Bush were among the first Hollywood celebrities to take advantage of Nevada's liberal divorce laws. Bush had taken up residence in the town of Minden, Nevada, following residence requirements. A few days later Dwan passed through the town, lingering long enough to be served the divorce papers, and then matters were expedited by the court. Even in his divorce, Dwan had proved suitably efficient.

One of Doug and Mary's biographers believes Pickford's divorce suit against Owen Moore was modeled on the Dwan divorce as Mary made her Nevada journey for purported health reasons.[97] Pickford and Moore had renewed their marriage vows at the Dwan wedding and now they followed the Dwans in ending their union.

The divorce was amicable enough that property rights and alimony were settled outside the court.[98] Exactly what had caused the couple to part ways is not recorded. Dwan's workaholic pace may have had something to do with it, especially as his wife had cut short her career for domestic life.

In December 1919, Dwan started production on *In the Heart of a Fool*, the first of two films made back to back for Mayflower dealing with divorce and/or broken marriages. Shooting on the next film, *The Scoffer*, was completed by early February. While the complicated plots of the films appear to have little in them that could be considered autobiographical, Dwan's sudden interest in this subject matter was likely not coincidental.

With his acting career revived, Kirkwood would star in both of the films. *In the Heart of a Fool* was based on a novel by former Kansas governor William Allen White and, according to the film's publicity, "more money was spent in preparations alone than average productions cost to produce."[99] The money was said to have been lavished on research and the building of sets. The big action set piece was an explosion and fire in a coal mine, and according to columnist A.H. Giebler who visited the set, this was done with Dwan's careful attention to realism. The film told the tale of five characters and how jealousy, intrigues and the birth of an illegitimate child helped cause two failed marriages. In publicizing the film, Mayflower trumpeted, "Dwan's use of six climaxes is said to in one picture mark a new and courageous departure in dramatic construction."[100] In an unorthodox publicity move, promotion of the film received the cooperation of Catholic societies advocating divorce law reform, the argument being that lax divorce laws encouraged the obvious misalliances depicted in the film.

In the Heart of a Fool was not released until the fall of 1920. The complex structure of the film was noted approvingly by *Motion Picture News* critic Laurence Reid. "In weaving a story from this skein of tangled threads, Allan Dwan has accomplished something which looked well nigh impossible, reading it in cold print. This subject, carrying an assortment of plots and counterplots, based upon eternal triangles, misunderstandings and romantic adventures, is highly complicated but so thorough has been the workmanship that the continuity is simplicity itself and therefore is very easy to follow."

Dwan had spun his triangle groupings into a more sophisticated, if melodramatic narrative. The review suggests that Dwan had found a way of editing his interlocking stories with symbolism in a manner more palatable to audiences than Griffith's elaborate experiment in *Intolerance*. Reid notes that Dwan "establishes the spirit of the original by exploiting the idea that fate plays a healthy hand in guiding humanity into channels of happiness or discontent as the case may be. And he gives emphasis to this by offering brief flashes of an allegorical nature — flashes which show the weaver at his pattern, dropping an empty spool or disentangling the threads which might be compared to incidents in the lives of the characters." Reid concludes his review by saying, "Exhibitors who book it will furnish their patrons with something out of the ordinary."[101] *Moving Picture World* was even more enthusiastic, saying that Dwan "scores one of the greatest triumphs of his directorial career...."[102] Comments on the film by exhibitors were mixed so that it is unlikely it was a big hit, though it may have not done badly.

The title of the film was derived from the libertine character played by Philo McCullough, who believes in his heart that there "is no God." In Dwan's next film *The Scoffer*, it is the idealistic protagonist played by Kirkwood who becomes disillusioned after his wife leaves him and he is framed as being an abortionist who has caused the death of his patient. Kirkwood loses his belief in God and it is regained only when he is performing a crucial operation and a lightning storm provides much needed light. (Dwan found he could make the best depiction of lightning by simply scratching marks on the emulsion of the film.) Still less subtle than *In the Heart of a Fool*, Dwan may have intended this similarly themed film as an accessible fallback if his more experimental film failed. (*The Scoffer* was not known to be currently available in any form but a print was recently discovered by Kevin Brownlow.)

The Scoffer was not released until 1921. *A Splendid Hazard* went out to theaters in the fall of 1920. Trade critics praised Walthall's performance but thought the story far-fetched and said that it would appeal to a limited audience.[103]

As Dwan finished work on *The Scoffer*, he announced that he would soon be ending his association with Mayflower and moving on to Associated Producers. Dwan's contract was set to expire in August, and departing from the company at that time would render it almost impossible to complete the eight films he was originally signed to make for Mayflower. Wolper agreed to let Dwan end his obligations with the completion of one more film. While acknowledging that his relationship with Mayflower had been "most pleasant," Dwan said he was "very anxious to start work on my own productions which will go out through the Associated Producers."[104]

Dwan had yearned for still more independence for some time. He had been involved in a plan a year earlier when he left Fairbanks' employment. Marshall Neilan had proposed reviving the old Biograph studio. According to *Photoplay*, "He and Allan Dwan were to work together though Neilan was head of the scheme. They were to use the Biograph studios in New York and Los Angeles, as stories, market conditions, and seasons indicated, and upon their choicest productions were again to reveal the great name that stood for the first great pictures. For one reason and another, these negotiations were not carried through."[105]

It is interesting to note that Neilan was to be the "head of the scheme." A number of observers argued that Neilan had now outshone his mentor Dwan. It was Neilan, not Dwan, who had been called one of the five best directors working by Wid Gunning. Howard Hawks, who claimed a close association with Dwan, Neilan and the director Allen Holubar, and admired all three, considered Neilan by far the best.[106] (It should also be pointed out that Hawks had worked most closely with Neilan.) But Neilan also had major vulnerabilities.

His biographer referred to Neilan as "the Hollywood version of the Scott Fitzgerald image in a fabulous period of bad booze and good times."[107] Neilan would be absent from his set for days while out carousing and drinking heavily with buddies like John Barrymore, Jack Pickford and Norman Kerry as well as pursuing ardent love affairs. The actress Eleanor Boardman recalled that the cast and crew once had to wait for two weeks after the starting date of a film before Neilan made an appearance.[108] Even the sympathetic Spears concluded that Neilan's films missed greatness because of his refusal to take his work seriously.

Dwan was convivial but not given to excess. Despite their differences in temperament, Dwan and Neilan remained close friends. In one of the milder passages in Kenneth Anger's book *Hollywood Babylon*, Dwan and Neilan are described attending a Hollywood party made up as the bearded Smith brothers of cough drop fame.[109] Fondly remembering Neilan many years later, Dwan said, "Mickey had a pixy heart and only wanted to play with life. Nothing was serious or sacred with him, and yet, he was the salt of the earth."[110]

An interesting contrast between the directing styles of the two men is provided in a magazine article of the mid–1920s. Dwan is referred to as a great "actors" director along with Griffith and Lubitsch. In describing how directors dominated their set, it was noted that DeMille did so physically, Dwan did it mentally and Neilan by "sheer impish personality."[111] Elaborating on Dwan, the author, Dorothy Manners, observed, "A non-committal man personally, holding a strange mental dominance over his players, he sketches the thought of the scene, briefly outlining the frame of the idea over which a competent player may drape the shadings and innuendoes of technique."[112]

Manners (who had worked as either an extra or bit player in *Robin Hood*) described how Dwan shot a scene of a woman being tortured by King John's men. The actress had returned from lunch in a cheery mood and was clearly simulating her discomfort. Dwan had her repeat the scene for hours. Manners describes the scene:

> Aloof, behind his smoked glasses, sitting low in his canvas chair, saying nothing, he watched the feigned emotions of the actress change from simulation into the mental and physical weariness of the character she was interpreting. No longer was the woman merely acting.... Instead of sitting erectly on the bench as she had done in the beginning, she lolled on it, her head bent forward, or her arms — dejection, great physical stress, overwhelming weariness stamped in every line of her drooped figure. Tears she could no longer control streamed down her cheeks. Looking on from the sidelines I felt sure that Dwan would be satisfied with the work she had just done. It seemed unsurpassable to me and probably a lesser director would have been content with it but once more he said, "Again." At the repetition of the direction, when the exhausted woman realized that she was going to have to go through the action again, she gathered her last ounce of energy and threw herself into the work with her ultimate effort. It was magnificent. The awful agony on her face was something to remember. At the end of that take she let her head drop forward instead of slowly lowering it in conscious artistry. There was a paused silence from the group around the

> camera. We were waiting for the director to speak. When he spoke he said, "Great!" rather quietly, and picking up his megaphone walked away, getting lost soon in the shadows of the set.[113]

In contrast, Manners says of Neilan, "He has kidded more great acting onto the screen than many other megaphonians could do in a year of artistic direction. When he wants a little more pep in a scene he calls lustily, 'Let's give it a little more fireworks, boys and girls; this isn't in memoriam,' or if some mannerism of one of his players strikes him as being in any way obnoxious, he immediately takes it unto himself and thereafter proceeds to walk, talk, cough or sneeze directions at the unhappy actor after his own fashion."[114]

Mary Pickford said of Neilan, "I can truthfully say that no director, not even the great D.W. Griffith or Cecil B. DeMille, could wring the performance from me that Mickey did. He invented all sorts of methods to produce the desired expressions and responses. He would dream up running gags long in advance and then at the psychological moment blast them at me."[115]

So Dwan and Neilan, both of Irish descent, were contrasting figures in talent and temperament, with Dwan the more stable one and Neilan the "wilder" figure. Their friendship was like an ethnic variation of the two buddies of Martin Scorsese's *Mean Streets*. As a director, Dwan was methodical and cerebral, Neilan quirky and facetious. (Interestingly, Manners points out that Dwan was at his best doing emotional scenes.) Perhaps "wildness" was also an innate part of Neilan's talent. It was true that after a long absence, Neilan could make up for lost time by working at an extraordinary clip. But Neilan also had a tendency to let assistants finish his work. One of his films carried the curious credit "Directed by Marshall Neilan and Staff."

In this case, Neilan's absence was caused not by his reveling but by his resentment of producer Louis B. Mayer's interference with his production *In Old Kentucky*. Shortly after the first announcement of the formation of the Associated Producers, the November 25, 1919, edition of Wid's Daily published a letter from Neilan complaining of producers who take credit for a director's work under the credit of "under the personal supervision of." Neilan noted that these individuals usually have nothing to do with the actual production of the film. Without mentioning Mayer by name, Neilan attacked the use of this phrase in conjunction with *In Old Kentucky*. A month later, having recently formed his own production company, Neilan proclaimed that the day of the director had arrived.[116] By January, Neilan was complaining of the practices of advertising being injected into films.

In contrast, Dwan could be critical but remained discreet. But when Mayflower was not releasing his films and he considered this a violation of his contract, Dwan took action by taking possession of the negatives of films he had made for the corporation. By June, the differences between Dwan and Mayflower were settled.

About two months earlier, it was announced that the Associated Producers had formed their own distribution company. Oscar Price, who had been just ousted from the presidency of United Artists, was named president of the new company. After one year with UA, relations between the four founders and Price–McAdoo had deteriorated. The two men had done little for the company; their main contribution was the prestige their names lent to the fledgling corporation at the beginning. Now Price could perform the same function for the Associated Producers. For general manager, the more business-savvy Fred B. Warren was selected.

By June, Warren was giving assurances that Associated Producers would be releasing a minimum of 30 productions in twelve months beginning on September. J. Parker Read was now added as another member of Associated Producers.

In order to fulfill their schedule, the members of the organization would have to finish all other commitments and start work soon. Tucker's suit with Mayflower had been settled amicably. But his contract required him not only to finish editing on his current production *Ladies Must Live*, but to shoot four more films for Mayflower. Obviously, that would restrict him for most, if not all, of the one-year period. This may be one reason why another figure, Read, was granted a place in the organization though he was a producer rather than a director.

By July, Dwan had finished his last film for Mayflower, *The Sin of Martha Queed*. Based on a story by Dwan and shot in the mountains of Southern California, it was a strange and contrived melodrama dealing with the effects of the bigotry of a puritanical father. The movie was not released until more than a year later.

Dwan could now concentrate on his first film for Associated Producers, *The Forbidden Thing*, his third film in a year dealing with troubled marriages. On *Martha Queed*, Dwan had found the cinematographer he needed for this project, Tony Gaudio, who would become one of Hollywood's celebrated cameramen, photographing *Hell's Angels*, *Little Caesar*, *The Adventures of Robin Hood*, *The Letter*, *High Sierra* and many more.

Set in a Cape Cod fishing village, the story concerns Abel Blake (Kirkwood), a rugged descendant of the Puritans who is in love with a domestic, Joan, and gives her an engagement ring. When his friends hear of the engagement they take him out to a pub to celebrate. There he meets a sensuous Portuguese woman named Gloria Prada (Marcia Manon). He falls in love and decides to marry Gloria instead. In doing so, he not only breaks the heart of Joan but of his mother, who dies in grief. Joan then marries another man. Neither marriage is happy and Gloria runs off with a circus man. Years pass and Joan has children but tragically her husband dies in a boating accident. Gloria is killed by her circus lover. Ostracized by the community, Blake becomes increasingly despondent and decides to commit suicide by walking into the ocean. But when Joan's little boy follows him, Blake comes back from the brink of death. Later Blake reconciles with Joan and they plan to be married.

Dwan, seated at left, directs his first film for Associated Producers, *The Forbidden Thing* (1920). His ace cinematographer, Tony Gaudio, tends to the camera on far right, while the rest of the film crew provides support (courtesy Kevin Brownlow).

The shooting was reportedly beset by all kinds of problems. Kirkwood was again set to star and Dwan was given assurances the actor would be finished with his previous commitment in time for the beginning of filming. Instead, Kirkwood was not available until three weeks later. Then cameraman Gaudio became ill and was out for a week. Leading lady Helen Jerome Eddy had dental problems that kept her out for a few days and someone accidentally smashed Gaudio's camera. Then one of the company's supply trucks collided with a farmer's vehicle which cost Dwan's unit a good sum of money. It was necessary to work day and night to finish the film anywhere close to schedule.

No print of *The Forbidden Thing* is known to exist. But the George Eastman House does have the key book which contains stills of virtually every scene in the movie. These photographs contain many striking images, at times poetic-looking and sometimes ravishing. They suggest a powerful and lyrical film despite the various plot contrivances. Dwan's hero is stuck on another one of his triangles: his love of the spiritual woman, his mother and the physical woman. After the heavy-handed religiosity of *The Scoffer* and the narrative complexity of *In the Heart of a Fool*, Dwan may have found a simplicity in the characters and story of *The Forbidden Thing* that could express the themes that had gripped him for these last few films.

Simplicity was a virtue that was cited in various reviews. *Photoplay* called *The Forbidden Thing* "[a] simple tale, told as only Allan Dwan could tell it. That is saying a great deal. Dwan is always interesting; he invariably makes his characters living and vitally human beings."[117] *Motion Picture News* said, "One feels inclined to place a gold seal opposite Allan Dwan's name in his first production for Associated Producers. *The Forbidden Thing* which he adapted and directed from Mary Mears' vivid and vital story of a 'faith that would not die' will certainly be classified among the top-notchers. He has constructed the feature in narrative form and has placed remarkable emphasis on its rugged simplicity. The tale is peopled with figures who are actually lifelike—whose joys and sorrows are touched upon with genuine feeling. It is dramatic to the core—but not the drama of the theater but of life."[118]

Variety hailed the film and Gaudio's excellent photography and even noted the painterly details of Dwan's compositions: "Some of the silhouettes are especially fine, and one small scene, that in which the hero standing at his window, looks at his sweetheart's portrait, is capital handling of 'subject' in the painter's sense."[119]

Wid's was also struck by the beauty of individual scenes. "The story is presented as if an old mender of nets was telling the happenings to a young girl, and the shot of this particular point is one of the most beautiful things not only of this picture but of many. It is exquisite."[120]

Wid's called *The Forbidden Thing* as the best Associated Producers production so far. The first had been Thomas H. Ince's *Homespun Folks* starring Lloyd Hughes; according to reviews, it was modeled on the films of Charles Ray. Up to January 8, it had been sold to theaters for a gross of $200,566. It was in Warren's words "a nice little picture but not a big one." Read's *The Leopard Woman* with Glaum had earned $176,501. These films had been released in September and October respectively so had additional time before Associated Producers' report to earn more money than *The Forbidden Thing* which was released in November. By January 8, *The Forbidden Thing* had earned $168,282. By March 19, 1921, it had garnered a respectable $206,251.47. (Shortly after the release of Dwan's film came

Helen Jerome Eddy in Dwan's moody *The Forbidden Thing* (1920), a film that critics found both vivid and spiritual (courtesy Academy of Motion Picture Arts and Sciences).

probably the best picture ever released by Associated Producers, Maurice Tourneur's *Last of the Mohicans.* Warren projected it to gross $450,000.[121])

The Forbidden Thing seemed to complete a cycle in Dwan's work. It may have permitted him to express his most somber thoughts. According to one review, the "forbidden thing" of the title was suicide.

Shortly after *The Forbidden Thing* was completed, Dwan was a guest of honor at a luncheon given for him at Delmonico's in New York, where he mingled with prominent film men and trade press editors. Dwan asked for the cooperation of the editors in keeping the directors informed on what the public wants. After this streak of serious pictures, Dwan may have felt the need to insure that he was in tune with popular tastes. The time was coming when Associated Producers could very much use such commercial insights.

All Fall Down

Recalling Associated Producers many years later, Dwan said of himself and the other members, "We joined, but not very many of us delivered pictures for it. And there were two or three reasons. One was the difficulty in financing because the banks that would loan money were being influenced by bigger corporations to lay off of us and not loan us money. You know, they were making it difficult. So we'd go and get odd banks here and there, and it was difficult. Some of the fellows didn't follow up and get any money and make pictures."[122]

In portions of his interview with Bogdanovich, which were not included in the book, Dwan acknowledges that future director Howard Hawks helped finance one or more of his Associated Producers pictures but is vague about which. Dwan made additional comments on Hawks' financing in Todd McCarthy's book *Howard Hawks*[123] which still leaves the extent of Hawks' contribution unclear.

Hawks' own statements only create more confusion. Hawks told Kevin Brownlow that he "formed a little company and financed Mickey Neilan and Allan Dwan and Allen Holubar...."[124] Holubar was never a member of Associated Producers and does not appear to have had any connection.

As for Neilan, Hawks may have financed some of his films released by First National but Neilan never made any films for Associated Producers. Neilan's biographer Spears says that Neilan's Associated Producers deal fell through.[125] But Neilan was indeed one of the founders of Associated Producers and is not only included in the names of those involved in the incorporation of the company but he was elected vice-president.[126]

An official explanation for Neilan's lack of production for Associated Producers came in an AP full-page ad that appeared in late September 1920: "Owing to Marshall Neilan's contractual obligations with another distributing organization, Associated Producers Inc. will not contract for any of his productions for future delivery until after the completion of the contract."[127] This apparently referred to Neilan's contract with First National. No date was specified for when this contract would expire although it was said to refer to four films. Under the First National agreement, Neilan was already making films independently with his own production company and may have been in no hurry to work under the Associated Producers banner. In 1922, Neilan was sued by AP for failure to pay stock subscriptions and for not fulfilling a contract.

With both Tucker and Neilan tied up indefinitely, the goal of AP making 30 features in its first year was beginning to appear unattainable. Adding to the problem, Sennett would not have a feature ready until February. For his part, Dwan started directing another AP film in November, a light thriller called *A Perfect Crime.* Its stars were Monte Blue (who had doubled for Herbert Beerbohm Tree in *Macbeth*) and Jacqueline Logan, who had come to Dwan's attention as a member of the Ziegfeld Follies. But *A Perfect Crime* is best remembered for a juvenile actress in a secondary role.

Carole Lombard, then known as Jane Peters, was twelve years old when she made her film debut in Dwan's movie. There are two versions of how she got the role. Dwan recalled, "She was a cute little tomboy ... out there knocking the hell out of the other kids, playing better baseball than they were. And I needed someone of her type for the picture. She'd never acted, so we talked to her parents and they let her do it and she was very good."[128] In another version, young Jane was boxing with her brothers in her backyard when Dwan spotted her. (A possible additional factor was that Monte Blue had known Lombard's mother when he was a teenager.[129])

The film tells the Jekyll and Hyde story of a humble bank messenger, who as his alter ego appears as a suave man about town, regaling people with tales of his personal adventures. It is made to appear that the messenger has stolen bank money which has permitted his plunge into high society. In the end, it turns out that he has merely transferred funds to the bank vault. Receiving $25,000 for false arrest and then getting royalties for the publication of a book about his imagined exploits, he wins the heart of his lady love. Most reviewers recognized the film's lack of credibility on several points but found it entertaining. *Photoplay* even thought that Dwan had improved on the original *Saturday Evening Post* story by Carl Clausen.[130] *Motion Picture News* saw the moral of the story as being "the idea that one can become anything he chooses by living the part."[131]

Opening in late February, the film appeared to do moderately well at the box office. Shortly before *A Perfect Crime* was released, it was announced that the up-and-coming director King Vidor would be working for Associated Producers. Vidor did not become one of the members of AP but a percentage distribution contract called for him to deliver four productions during 1921. This would help to keep a more viable amount of films in the pipe for distribution. The films would be shot at Ince's studio. But Vidor's first picture would not be ready for months.

Late in 1920, the membership of Associated Producers had been augmented by the addition of C. Gardner Sullivan, the screenwriter widely known for his work on William S. Hart films. Sullivan was to produce four films annually. Like Read, he was an associate of Ince.

There was another possible avenue to handling AP's product shortage and other problems: a merger with United Artists. As 1920 drew to a close, rumors of such a merger began to circulate.

There were certainly logical reasons that would suggest such a merger. As the only two companies founded by major creative personnel, they were both competing to survive against the Goliaths of the industry. And United Artists, like Associated Producers, was suffering from product shortage. On December 31, 1920, Wid's Daily reported that while Douglas Fairbanks would not comment on the rumors, his brother John admitted that the proposition was being discussed.

While the two companies could be said to have common interests, it was not auspicious that the previous year's negotiations between Associated Producers and United Artists had failed to produce an agreement whereby UA would distribute the films of the former. This would have saved AP the costly expense of a distribution system and would have had the two companies of creative artists joined at the hip.

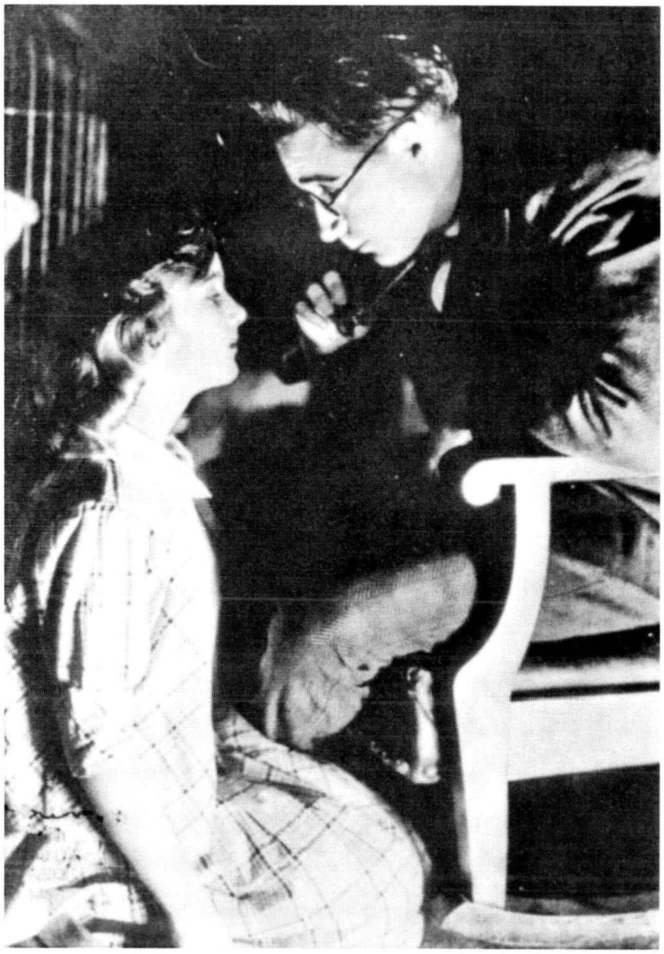

Twelve-year-old Carole Lombard (then known as Jane Peters) made her screen debut in *A Perfect Crime* (1921) starring Monte Blue (courtesy David L. Smith).

There were other practical problems associated with a merger. If all of the members of the Associated Producers became part of the board of directors of the newly formed company, they would have more votes than the original members of UA. Perhaps they would not vote as a bloc but this was still something for Griffith, Fairbanks, Pickford, Chaplin and Hiram Abrams (now president of UA) to ponder. The proposed merger also had echoes of Triangle's attempt to solve its problems with a hoped-for merger with Famous Players.

Despite the various hurdles, a very optimistic story about the proposed merger appeared in the *Los Angeles Times* in early January. Under the headline of "Combine Imminent: Two Stellar Associations to Get Together," the story by Grace Kingsley cited Mary Pickford as its main source. The story referred to the merger as "one of the most important moves ever contempated [sic] in picturedom."[132] It noted that Charlie Chaplin had been one of the dissenters to the merger but that he "has now been completely won over."[133]

The article stated that all of the members of both organizations had agreed that it was in their best interests to get together and that negotiations were underway and would probably be completed in two weeks. Kingsley reported that this statement came from Pickford but did not provide a direct quote. Pickford *was* quoted as saying, "We'll all have one common object and that is to give the world good pictures, and to develop the highest artistic forms possible, whether we make great fortunes or not. In fact, every member of both organizations has been offered large sums to quit the game, or to go over to some other company, but we're all firm. We don't want the art of picture-making tied up. We don't any of us believe that pictures can be made like matches."[134] (Dwan also recalled the offers to get them to abandon independent work. "I know I received a very big offer to quit making pictures. More money to *stop* making pictures than to go and make them for somebody else."[135])

On January 8, the day after the *Los Angeles Times* story appeared, there was a special meeting of the board of directors of United Artists. None of the founders was present but Abrams was there along with UA attorney Dennis O'Brien and three other officers. Among other items discussed were negotiations with Associated Producers which were begun by Mack Sennett. The negotiations involved the joint distribution of the films of United Artists and the Associated Producers. The minutes of the meeting stated, "It was the opinion of those present that they would not approve of the consummation of such negotiations in keeping with the reports which were before the members of the board."[136]

If this did not close the door completely on the merger prospects, Associated Producers would, for its own reasons, prefer to dampen all the merger talk.

On January 14, AP's general manager of distribution Fred Warren sent a letter to Ince and his fellow producers at the company, citing various articles about the proposed merger including the Kingsley piece. He warned them that continuation of the rumor was causing exhibitors to hold off on making bookings until they could be sure which source would be distributing their films.[137]

The rumor mill was not stopped although it took a different turn. In late January, a story in *Variety* cited a "reliable source" referring to a deal that "proposes to form an alliance between the United Artists and three members of the Associated Producers, if some way may be devised whereby the latter can be relieved of their existing contracts with Associated Producers and insure them percentages accruing from pictures now being released by the organization. The three producers whose names are being mentioned ... are Thomas H. Ince, Mack Sennett and Marshall Neilan."[138] Read, who was Ince's associate, would also join not as an individual unit but as part of Ince's contingent.

This would leave Dwan, Tucker and Tourneur to sustain Associated Producers. This source also specified a possible sop to Dwan: that if he felt "left out in the cold," he would be offered the job of directing the next six Fairbanks films. While the authenticity of the story is open to question (especially since like the other rumors it was never realized), its appearance in print was likely to have aroused the suspicions of Dwan, Tucker and Tourneur about the management of their organization.

Overall, the producer-directors were not meeting their production quota. Warren even complained in a letter to Sullivan in December 1920 that when he asked each producer to provide a 30" × 40" photographic portrait of himself, only Dwan honored the request.[139]

Containing the menace of Zukor remained a priority. Warren cautioned Ince against AP joining the National Association of the Motion Picture Industry because of Zukor's domination of the group. Warren believed that in a similar organization three years earlier, Zukor was able to manipulate things in a way that damaged his rival, Goldwyn.

But Zukor was now probably less dangerous than the events he was prognosticating. In October 1920, *Variety* bore a headline in its motion picture section that read, "Zukor Forecasts Period of Depression in Film Trade." Zukor cited the rise in production costs and the decrease of profitability for the exhibitor as major parts of the problem. Zukor, as was often the case, was an astute analyst here.

The problems in the film industry were related to broader economic issues. The Federal Reserve System had aided the Treasury in floating its remaining war bonds in 1919 by keeping its discount rate low for member banks. With increased borrowing, inflation surged. Then to put the brakes on things, the Fed began raising the discount rate in late 1919, up to seven percent by the middle of 1920. The rapid rise of the discount rate now curtailed bank borrowing.

The high rates caused the banks to be especially wary of loans subject to the uncertainty of the movie business. In December, *Variety* reported, "The banking officials of late in the street are turning down all overtures made for loans by the picture people."[140] The article also noted that there "were numerous reports of a general shutdown in production."

While the film industry was hard hit, the impact of tighter money was spreading throughout the country. The U.S. suffered what became known as the Depression of 1920–21. The turndown would be relatively brief but severe.[141]

This would further exacerbate the problems of Associated Producers. The company tried to treat its difficulties in late March by replacing Warren as general manager of distribution with Al Lichtman, who was formerly manager of sales for Famous Players. Warren's parting was acrimonious and on April 2 he sued Associated Producers for $100,000, charging breach of contract.

Warren's complaint also cited that the producers had pledged to provide him with 30 productions and charged them with defaulting on the deliveries of negatives. He noted that between September 12, 1920, and February 27, 1921, only nine films had been presented to him for distribution. The breakdown in how each producer was expected to fulfill his obligations was listed as: Ince at least eight, Tourneur six, Read six, Sennett six, Dwan two, Tucker one (depending on completing his Mayflower films), and Neilan two. Only Dwan had already completed his yearly allotment by February 27.

In May, Associated Producers filed a countersuit against Warren for $200,000 contending that Warren had violated his contract by inducing certain employees to leave for another organization. And most damningly, they maintained that because of Warren's "incompetent, inefficient and extravagant" handling of the distribution system, he had caused the depression of film rentals and the increase of expenses.[142]

Dwan, in the meanwhile was pressing ahead with his next film, *A Broken Doll*. It would be his last film for the Associated Producers.

In recounting his association with Holubar, Neilan and Dwan, Howard Hawks told Joseph McBride, "We made a lot of money the first year, then all of them got a girl. That was the downfall. We lost all that money the next year. Dwan got a redhead who couldn't act. Marvelous gal, good-looking, lots of fun and everything, she couldn't act at all."[143] One of the stars of *A Broken Doll*, Mary Thurman, was most likely "the redhead" who in Hawks' view led Dwan astray. A 1922 news story said that Dwan and Thurman were engaged "according to a rumor current in Hollywood" but no marriage ever came of it.[144] Thurman died of pneumonia in 1925 at the age of thirty.

A Broken Doll was the only Dwan film for Associated Producers in which Thurman appeared. She also had starring roles in Dwan's *In the Heart of a Fool*, *The Scoffer*, and *The Sin of Martha Queed*. She received respectful if not glowing reviews for her previous Dwan pictures and made close to 60 films. She apparently did lack star power because she began to slip to supporting roles not long after her appearance in *A Broken Doll*.

Hawks' account of how three directors came to ruin because they each fell for a talentless actress might have made for a good Hawks movie on filmmaking but it did not have much to do with reality. Certainly the problems of both Dwan and Associated Producers at this time were far more complicated.

A Broken Doll was released in June 1921 and AP's publicity described Dwan's film as "representative of this producer's genius for combining artistic excellence with commercial requirements."[145] In the film, again based on a *Saturday Evening Post* story, Monte Blue plays a ranch hand devoted to the owner's little daughter. When he accidentally breaks her doll, he sets out to get her a new one and in the process meets up with an escaped convict. In the misunderstandings with the law that follow, Blue is arrested but he manages to escape and with the help of the sheriff's daughter Harriet (Thurman) buys a new doll. In the end, all is cleared up and the ranch hand marries Harriet. Reviewers found the story too slight to be of general interest and *Motion Picture News* summed it up as "very doubtful entertainment."[146]

A little over a week after *A Broken Doll* was released, George Loane Tucker died at the age of 49. After all the acclaim and hoopla surrounding Tucker following the success of *The Miracle Man*, he was able to complete only one more film. It was a devastating loss for Mayflower, which had expected four more films from Tucker. According to an internal AP document, he had already withdrawn from the company.[147]

The previous year, Mayflower president Isaac Wolper predicted that large scale film productions of famous poems would be coming into vogue. He said this in conjunction with the release of his forthcoming *The Law of the Yukon*, based on a poem by Robert W. Service and directed by Charles Miller. This proclamation apparently did not impress his colleagues and shortly after that, Wolper was forced out as president of Mayflower and the new management quickly abrogated Miller's contract. Wolper started a new company called Triart but the man who tried to follow Louis B. Mayer's path died not long after in 1922.

Tucker's *Ladies Must Live* and Dwan's *The Sin of Martha Queed* were among the last Mayflower productions to be released before the company faded from sight. In *Martha Queed*, Mary Thurman played the title character, a mountain community schoolteacher whose father, the town's district attorney, always sees the worst in human nature. He compels Martha to marry a man who has compromised her by spreading false rumors that she compromised herself with a "city feller," Arnold Barry (Niles Welch). A hunchbacked man (George

While working on *The Scoffer* (1921), Dwan measures the hand of the actress who had allegedly become the next woman in his life, Mary Thurman (courtesy Kevin Brownlow).

Hackathorne) who has always admired Martha from afar kills the husband. Arnold is accused of the crime and arrested. The hunchback confesses and then commits suicide. Martha can now marry Arnold.

One critic grumbled that the film was "too heavily balanced with depressing shadows"[148] and there were complaints of the plot contrivances. Another praised it for "some of the most exquisitely beautiful photography seen in many a day."[149] The acting was also given high marks. "Mary Thurman plays the heroine with real appreciation for the pathos and sentiment.... Frank Campeau is colorful as the evil gossip."[150] *Variety* condescendingly opined, "It will please all those not familiar with the elementary tutelage of story construction ... 'the general public.'"[151]

The Sin of Martha Queed did appear to do well with audiences. It is one of the few Dwan films of that era to have survived; a print exists at the British Film Institute.

By June, it was being reported that practically all the production and distribution companies were reducing the size of their work force or making salary cuts from 10 to 20 percent. Oscar Price was quoted as saying that Associated Producers had already made some cuts in operating costs.[152]

Still trying to increase the product flow, AP had signed a deal with producer J.L. Frothingham to release four films to be directed by Edward Sloman. Despite all its efforts, Price reported to Ince that Associated Producers had lost $40,000 during the month of June.[153]

Dwan's last film for Mayflower was *The Sin of Martha Queed* (1921), another of his offbeat dramas, this one starring Mary Thurman (shown here with her lover, played by Niles Welch) (courtesy Academy of Motion Picture Arts and Sciences).

By July, a wage decrease had led to a strike on the West Coast by the mechanical departments of some studios.

As summer wore on, Associated Producers appeared to be arriving at a crossroads. An August *Variety* story observed, "The Associated Producers are beginning to line up for a fall campaign of production. Ince, Sennett and Frothingham are ready to go ahead but Marshall Neilan, Allan Dwan and Maurice Tourneur are not certain they want to continue. Allan Dwan now in the east on finances has practically made up his mind that he will not return to the coast but will do his producing here."[154] *Variety* also reported that prior to the West Coast strike, the Associated Producers had held a series of meetings on making changes in their leasing organization. *Variety* claimed the company was now losing approximately $5,000 a day.

In August, Ince and Sennett went to the East Coast to discuss a deal regarding distribution with First National, which was now being officially called Associated First National. Wid's Daily reported, "It is understood that Ince has the entire say-so in the matter and that both Sennett and Lichtman are sitting in with little or no power to form the final decision."[155] By September, the deal was closed with a three-year contract. Ince had in August made an agreement with First National to release eight of his own productions.

Sennett was quoted saying of the agreement, "The bogey of monopoly is gone, wiped out by the merger of the world's great theater organization and this group of independent producers."[156] *Variety* commented more caustically, "The story sent out by Associated Producers on its $50,000,000 'merger' with First National was a splendid piece of press work. It gave the impression of a tremendous amalgamation of gigantic film interests instead of having to explain why Associated Producers did not have sufficient product to continue to maintain its expensive system of exchanges."[157]

Associated Producers had survived as a corporate entity but the idea behind it was dead. The company would hang on a while longer but bore little resemblance to its original promise of an elite corps of directors maintaining high production standards. Dwan, like Neilan, would not participate. Tourneur and Sennett came in for a limited time.

There were many causes for the failure of Associated Producers. Because of contractual agreements and other reasons, the producers were much too tardy in delivering product and never really caught up. Very few of the films that were delivered were of sufficient quality to deliver on the organization's promise of high standards and of the importance of the director. The directors did not have the same cachet with the public that the megastars of United Artists did nor could they attract investment as well. AP's distribution system was too costly and they ran smack into the worst economic climate of the postwar era until the Great Depression.

Ince and Sennett were really more producers than directors. Ince, who served as chairman of the board, appears to have been the real boss from the beginning. This may have mitigated the sense of independence; Tourneur, for example, said he was compelled to make films he did not want to produce. In short, both for the public and for each of its members, Associated Producers did not live up to its promises.

Dwan remained on the East Coast. He was in exile now, not from filmmaking but from its perceived center. In April, he had gone to Hawaii and said he would make his next film there and that it would be based on some of the folk tales of the natives. In November, he was said to be seriously considering a trip to India with Edgar Selwyn and that he would make a picture there if he would go. These may have been pipe dreams but they were also assertions that Dwan could make films outside of the Hollywood studios.

A New York State court decision in December 1921 showed that Dwan had harbored some aspirations toward developing a film center in New York's Westchester County. New York State Supreme Court Justice Donnelly had denied an application by Dwan to give him judgment in a suit of $5,175 on notes. According to papers submitted to the court, Dwan, William Massarene, Margaret Mayo and Edgar Selwyn engaged in a partnership to purchase Croton Point in Westchester for "the establishment of a moving picture and theatrical colony there. After Dwan had put in $5,000 and decided not to contribute further he sold his interest to Massarene for what he had paid with interest."[158] Dwan may have soured on this project but was apparently still publicizing his desire to work in Westchester County. *Photoplay* carried a story that Dwan was going to take a company to Tarrytown to film Washington Irving's *The Legend of Sleepy Hollow*.[159]

As Dwan tried to chart his future course, about a year passed in which he did not shoot a feature film. A purveyor of Dwan's filmography would have difficulty believing that such a gap existed. That was because in this period, *The Sin of Martha Queed* was released more than a year after completion and two other long-delayed Dwan movies appeared, *Superstition* and *The Hidden Woman*. *Superstition* was a Triangle film shot in 1917 that was still not released by the time the company folded; it was sold to Lee Bradford, who distributed it on a state's rights basis. *Superstition* starring Jack Devereaux and Vera Searl is almost certainly a new title for the film *The Jinx Jumper* with the same two stars. It appeared on Triangle's list of upcoming releases but no record of a release or review exists. This film was made during the period in which Dwan was acting as production supervisor and was probably not directed by him.

The other film, *The Hidden Woman*, starred the notorious Evelyn Nesbit. *The Hidden Woman* must have been the film that Dwan had made for Joseph Schenck as part of the deal to finance the Norma Talmadge pictures. Since this would have been made before *Panthea*, the best guess is that *The Hidden Woman* was shot in the late summer of 1916.

Dwan told Kevin Brownlow how after meeting with Nesbit and seeing her limitations, "we cooked up a little story and to keep it out of New York and to keep it from being mouthed about too much, we decided to make it up in the country at a little place she had up there, where she used to live in the summertime...."[160] Brownlow identified this area as Lake Chateaugay, New York, where Nesbit had a cottage by the lake.[161]

The story concerned a social butterfly, Ann Wesley, who after losing most of her assets in bad investments, retires to her bit of land and cabin in the Adirondacks. As in other Dwan films, the lone woman incurs the wrath and gossip of the locals, hypocritical reformers, even though she is trying to do good. In the process, she finds her better self, her "hidden woman," and a long-time admirer comes forth to give her his love and protection.

Released by the obscure American Releasing Corporation

The notorious "girl in the red velvet swing," Evelyn Nesbit, seen at the height of her beauty. Dwan's 1922 film with her, *The Hidden Woman* (the last of her movies to be released), was actually made six years earlier.

(with Fred B. Warren as its v.p.), *The Hidden Woman* was largely ignored by the trade press but did get some mildly sympathetic reviews for its working of the theme of regeneration. The film had been completed in a way that minimized whatever chances it had of success. Dwan said he "never saw any of the rushes, or a foot of the picture, I wouldn't look at it." He left it to Schenck to cut it up and sell it for "a couple of dollars." The film sat on the shelf for years.[162]

Dwan had been "turned off," as he put it, by an extracurricular role Nesbit had asked him to perform for her socially during the making of the film. She had requested a curious favor from him to "referee a party" she was having. When Dwan inquired what that meant, she told him to come over and "I'll show you." Dwan recalled,

> So I went over that night, my assistant went with me, as I didn't want to go in alone, and she was loaded up with these hangers-on, New York people, strange crowd ... they were having an ether party, I never knew what an ether party was, never heard of one, but what they had to be careful of was that nobody that had too much ether would swallow their tongue or pass out. So the referee's job was to look them over and shake them up if they got too far gone. So my assistant and I were pretty busy until about three in the morning waking up these people and tossing them out in the lake to sober them up and getting them over the dreams they were having with the ether.[163]

By April of 1922, when *The Hidden Woman* was released, the whole experience of the Associated Producers may have seemed like an extended ether party where dreams and vast amounts of money had been misplaced.

For Maurice Tourneur, the crash of the party had left lingering effects. Tourneur's second film for Associated Producers, *Foolish Matrons*, had been a flop. Tourneur continued to make films for First National and other companies, but he was becoming disillusioned with the Hollywood system. Back in 1916, Tourneur had written an article for *Harper's Weekly* called, "Movies Create Art" but his disenchantment was evident in 1924 in a piece he wrote for *Kine Weekly* entitled simply, "A Protest." Tourneur wrote, "And to speak of the future development of the art of cinema is futile." Tourneur then asked "Motion Pictures an art? That can never be."[164]

Chris Fujiwara has written that the tone of Tourneur's essay "can undoubtedly be attributed to his disappointment over the failure of Associated Producers and the desultory nature of his subsequent productions."[165] In 1926, after a dispute with MGM during the making of *The Mysterious Island*, Tourneur left Hollywood for good and returned to France.

Still pursuing new film deals, in November 1924 Thomas H. Ince was in discussions with William Randolph Hearst about a producing partnership. Ince joined Hearst and Davies for a cruise on Hearst's yacht, the *Oneida*. During the trip, Ince became suddenly ill. He died two days later on November 19 at the age of forty-two.

The dominant figure among the Associated Producers, Thomas H. Ince, met an untimely death after a cruise on William Randolph Hearst's yacht.

While the official cause of death was listed as heart failure, rumors began to circulate that Hearst had shot Ince in a jealous rage either because Ince was dallying with Marion Davies or that he mistook Ince for the real culprit, another celebrity passenger, Charles Chaplin. Although a gunshot wound would be difficult to cover up and Ince was still conscious when he arrived in Los Angeles, the stories have become a permanent part of Hollywood folklore.[166]

Dwan, however, had had the good fortune to be offered a return to work for Fairbanks. Even before work began on *Robin Hood*, Bert Adler, Dwan's press rep, stated that "because Dwan had joined Douglas Fairbanks for one picture did not mean that the director had given up making his own productions."[167] So Dwan still clung to his dream, at least publicly.

After completing *Robin Hood*, Dwan accepted a job from the same mogul whose threat of monopoly helped inspire the formation of the Associated Producers. But ironically, in submitting to his former *bête noir*, Dwan would find a way to work with relative independence on the East Coast.

This would arise from a chain of events that commenced in Hollywood as Dwan prepared to direct again and waited for a major star who would never show up.

5. Swanson and Swan Song

When you're in New York, you're in the whole world. There's nothing you can't find in New York.... I always had a great respect for it. It's a dirty place, it's this and that, but it's the place.—Allan Dwan to interviewer Joe Adamson, 1979

My general proposition then, is this: In the Original Unity of the First Thing lies the Secondary Cause of All Things, with the Germ of their Inevitable Annihilation.—Edgar Allan Poe, *Eureka*

Rudolph Valentino was, by the middle of 1922, reaping the rewards of a long climb to stardom. An Italian immigrant arriving in America in his late teens, he started in movies in 1914, performing bit parts and extra roles. Given the opportunity to play a leading role, he electrified the public in *The Four Horsemen of the Apocalypse* (1921). Moving from Metro to Famous Players, Valentino was cast in the title role in *The Sheik*. That had proved a sensation but Valentino was prouder of his more recent success *Blood and Sand*, where he felt he had clearly proven his worth as an actor. In his personal life, Valentino had bounced back from a brief and disastrous marriage and had found happiness with art director Natacha Rambova.

Dwan was also in a fortuitous position and had not lost his knack for seizing opportunities quickly. On August 10, 1922, the day after it was announced in *Film Daily* that shooting on *Robin Hood* had been completed, the same publication ran a short item that Dwan had been signed to direct Valentino in *A Spanish Cavalier* for Paramount. This would give Dwan an opportunity to work with the man who had become Fairbanks' greatest rival as the top male screen hero. Filming was to begin on the West Coast in early September.

But on August 30, still in New York, Valentino claimed that the company had breached its contract with him and that he would not be going west and resuming work for Famous Players. This announcement came as *Blood and Sand* was breaking box office records in New York City. Valentino's action must have been especially dispiriting for Famous Players given that they desperately needed their new superstar after the major defections of the last few years.

Ostensibly, Valentino's suit was about how the advertising for *Blood and Sand* was not in accordance with his contract with Famous Players. But this was probably a legal device that permitted Valentino to vent many of his resentments against Famous Players.

While Valentino seemed to be the beneficiary of a string of successes, he was seething about a whole series of incidents, both behind the scenes and squarely in the public eye. After his Mexican marriage to Rambova, a Los Angeles superior court judge ruled that because of a legal technicality, he did not regard Valentino's divorce from his first wife as final. Valentino was jailed for bigamy.

Valentino was incensed that the studio let him spend two days in jail before he was bailed out. He was also disturbed at the way the company lawyers promptly advised him and Rambova to separate and even had them followed by private detectives. Smarting from two scandals already involving studio personnel, the Arbuckle case and the murder of director William Desmond Taylor, Famous Players did not want to risk the further danger of Valentino and Rambova caught co-habitating.

Aside from his sense that he was being treated dishonorably, Valentino, who was earning only $1,200 per week, also had reason to feel underpaid. However, even when Famous Players attempted to placate him by raising his salary to $7,000 per week, Valentino still did not drop his suit against Famous Players.

As Valentino's biographer Emily Leider points out, the actor insisted that "artistic control" was "at the heart of the conflict."[1] In that sense, Valentino's action could be seen in the context of the industry upheavals referred to earlier. Particularly galling to Valentino was that after completing the highly successful *Blood and Sand*, he was thrust into what he regarded as an inferior vehicle, *The Young Rajah*, which did not fare well. Valentino felt that the studio was exploiting his name and cheapening its value by putting him into a slipshod project. Valentino's protest can also be seen as a precursor to the suits by Bette Davis and Olivia de Havilland against Warner Brothers, filed for virtually the same reason.

According to Leider, the studio had pledged that *The Spanish Cavalier* would be shot in Europe and if that did not prove practical, the shooting would take place in New York where Valentino could remain close to Rambova.[2] Instead, Valentino was told to report to California for filming.

For some time, Famous Players clung to the hope that Valentino could be persuaded to make the trek west and resume work while Dwan waited, collecting weekly installments on his salary. As late as February 1923, Famous Players was telling the press, "We are still holding Alan [sic] Dwan, who is ready to do *The Spanish Cavalier*, the script for which was prepared at Mr. Valentino's request by Miss June Mathis. His pictures would have the best production resources that the industry affords, he could have the best scenario writers and directors available, and you may be sure we would give him every possible cooperation."[3]

By this time, Dwan had gone on to other projects and had signed a multi-film contract with Famous Players. It was not until the following summer that Valentino recognized that he would have to resume working for Famous Players.

The Spanish Cavalier was later reworked (without Dwan) as a vehicle for Pola Negri, called *The Spanish Dancer*. Dwan and Valentino would never work together. But with the West Coast production of *The Spanish Cavalier* passing into limbo, a new opportunity was created for Dwan to work away from Hollywood.

Escape to New York

As the story of Dwan's career thus far makes evident, while the motion industry started shifting production to California in the teens, they did not abandon the East Coast completely. With the end of World War I, film companies reconsidered the advantages of increasing production in New York and the surrounding areas.

With lighting equipment becoming more sophisticated, the Los Angeles sunshine became less of a necessity and even in L.A. many films were shot inside studios with artificial lighting. Moreover, many corporate headquarters remained in New York. Thus, if a film was screened for executives in the east and if they wanted new scenes or retakes made, the whole process took more time than if production and executive offices were located together. New York also provided an atmosphere that was more appropriate for some productions.

The flurry of increased production activity on the East Coast included the opening of New York studios by both Fox and Famous Players in 1920. The Astoria Studios built in Long Island for $2.5 million by Famous Players covered more than 140,000 square feet of land and opened in September 1920.

However, in May of 1921 it was announced that the studio was closing down temporarily for reasons of economy, no doubt prompted by the tough financial climate of that year. It was stated that the studio would reopen in January when the rainy season would begin in Los Angeles. But the facilities remained closed through early 1922. Still, in a sampling of industry opinion about the merits of New York and Los Angeles that appeared in the February 1922 issue of *Photoplay*, both Zukor and Lasky affirmed the importance of both Los Angeles and New York as production centers. And Lasky added that the Long Island studio would soon be reopened.[4]

Dwan gave this account of how he got to work at Famous Players' New York branch to Peter Bogdanovich: "And I was having a problem with them [Famous Players] myself. They had put a fellow named B.P. Schulberg in charge and he'd elevated some relatives to supervisors; one of them kept coming down and bothering me and I threw him off and told him not to come back. Anyway, I finally said, 'Look, let me work at the New York studio.' It was idle. They wanted everything out here under one head, but I guess I stood pretty well with them and they finally let me come East."[5]

The implication here is that the eastern studios were reopened to accommodate Dwan. This is patently false, as are other parts of this description.

Schulberg did indeed have a reputation for being heavy-handed in his dealings with Famous Players personnel but in 1922 he was working for another company, his own, Preferred Pictures. Also, the film to which Dwan was assigned, *The Spanish Cavalier*, was stillborn. While he may have incurred some interference in pre-production, Dwan could not have encountered much supervision on a film that was never made.

Even before Dwan had been signed to work with Valentino, at least one Famous Players film, *Missing Millions*, had begun shooting in Long Island. Several other films went into production in the late summer and fall at the Paramount eastern enclave before Dwan started working there. (The tale got even more fanciful in Gloria Swanson's autobiography where she wrote that in order to keep Dwan, Zukor had to build him a studio in Astoria, Long Island. Swanson noted, "He was afraid to refuse him for fear Allan would quit and they wouldn't be able to run the studio without him."[6])

If Dwan had greatly exaggerated the circumstances of his relocation, he was nevertheless correct in seeing it as a personal vindication. He was being paid handsomely just for waiting for Valentino but a prolonged wait was not desirable at a time when Dwan would have wanted to capitalize on his greatly increased bankability after *Robin Hood*. It is likely that Famous Players also wanted to retain this "hot" director whom it had put in such an awkward situation. "I was in a position to say where I worked," Dwan assertively told interviewer Adamson, and the director was most likely telling the truth here.

Dwan's bid at functioning as an independent had failed. But while he was now employed by his erstwhile nemesis Zukor, he had seen an opportunity to gain a good measure of autonomy working in New York, as he had with Triangle. The search for independence in the east that had eluded him only a year ago now came to him while being a part of Hollywood's most powerful company. That there was a good measure of freedom granted him and other directors at Astoria would be attested to by later corporate grumblings.

But for now, Dwan had found his perch and achieved a rapprochement with Zukor. Zukor was not a man to hold grudges, one good reason why he was feared but not hated in his industry.[7]

In his Adamson interview, however, Dwan describes his situation with some offensive words and comments. Describing his problems with supervisors, Dwan says, "The Hebrews is a race, an eager hard-working bunch but they want to take over,

The film tycoon Adolph Zukor as he appeared in 1936. At one time he was regarded as Dwan's nemesis, but after the failure of Associated Producers, he provided Dwan with a production haven in Queens, New York.

they want to be boss.... Lasky took all of his relatives he could find and made supervisors out of them."[8]

The subject of supervisors always aroused deep resentment from Dwan's usually sunny disposition in his later interviews. He goes on to describe a physical encounter with a supervisor he refers to as a "kike." Dwan takes action by then going to Adolph Zukor himself, whom he describes as "my pal."

This incongruousness appears even stranger as he tells his "pal" and Jewish boss, "I can't work with those kikes you got there in Hollywood. Get me out of here. Get me a studio some place else."[9] Zukor listens sympathetically, as if he accepts this as roughhouse ethnic bantering, and then says this gives him the idea to re-open the Astoria studios.

As stated above, this event almost certainly did not happen since Dwan had not been making any films for Famous Players at this time and could not have been harassed by any supervisors, Jews or Gentiles. Dwan is projecting some of his deep resentments as well as his respect for Zukor. He is most likely confusing this time with his earlier experience at Universal (with Laemmle rather than Lasky), as well as with his later conflicts with Schulberg.

At another point on in the Adamson interview, when asked to explain how the film business became divided between West Coast production and East Coast management, Dwan responded, "A motion picture is a combination of Jews and usually they're partners and when they form partnerships, there are divisions," then citing the separation between financing and production. He says he doesn't "give a damn" if anyone finds his statement offensive.[10]

Yet, in the same interview, Dwan talks about how highly he regarded New York City because of its diversity. Dwan then says proudly, "I could make the greatest Jewish story in the world in New York."[11] Dwan's goddaughter Robin Wallace, who is one-quarter Jewish, recalled of her godfather, "He was very accepting of people of all religions, colors and social classes.... If anyone ever started to make disparaging remarks he would become very angry. I never heard him say anything about Jewish people except nice things."[12]

It is difficult to reconcile all these strands with any certainty, especially given the paucity of surviving information from other sources concerning Dwan's innermost feelings. However, the various conflicting comments of Dwan's interview are revealing, especially since whatever else can be said about Dwan's remarks, the 94-year-old does not appear to have been calculating. And again, this whole story is essentially Dwan's fantasy of events.

It's quite possible that Dwan saw himself as very tolerant in his religious and racial attitudes but he was not without lingering prejudices and resentments. These came out in his feelings about the supervisors whom he believes have gotten their jobs because of family connections. He then turns to Zukor, a tough man but a self-made one, whom Dwan regards as his friend. In this fantasy, it is almost as if Zukor absolves him from any possible guilt of anti–Semitism by listening with understanding and then proposing a solution.

Dwan's love of New York City and its various ethnic strands also conflicts with whatever prejudices he may have had. In this interview, he wants to celebrate the lives of Jews on film as much as anyone else and in fact, characters from a Jewish ghetto would play an important role in one his movies shot at Astoria, one for which he wrote the adapted screenplay. He also told Bogdanovich that one of his unrealized projects was a film about the Book of Esther. (It was Dwan's friend Raoul Walsh who would later direct *Esther and the King*.)

Although he never got along with heavy-handed producers or supervisors of any origin, Dwan later had harmonious relationships with Jewish producers such as Sol Wurtzel and Edward Small. (At Fox, he seemed to prefer Wurtzel to Zanuck, the Gentile head of the studio.) In Queens, he would also give a big break to a young Jewish man who showed no discernable filmic talent other than his determination and conscientiousness.

Dwan was signed in late October 1922 to direct a film adaptation of Edith Wharton's novel *The Glimpses of the Moon* at Famous Players' Long Island studio. The contract was apparently signed just as *Robin Hood* was having its initial big city openings to thunderous acclaim, timing that may have produced the best terms for Dwan.

Wharton had already won the Pulitzer Prize for her 1920 novel *The Age of Innocence*. *The Glimpses of the Moon*, her foray into sophisticated comedy, told the story of a young couple who enter into a trial marriage; if either sees the prospect of a more financially advantageous union with someone else, they agree to divorce and let the lucky partner seize the opportunity. Though they are short on means (the husband is an aspiring writer), in the interim they hope to live lavishly by taking advantage of wedding gifts and guest stints with rich friends. While the novel was not as well reviewed as Wharton's more serious books, it was a best-seller and was sold to Paramount for $15,000.

On the basis of its subject matter, *The Glimpses of the Moon* appeared to represent a transition for Dwan to the world of postwar mores and tastes. From the evidence available, even his more serious films of the early twenties contained links to Griffith in milieu and style. Dwan now seemed to be embarking on depicting the high living and prosperity that was the popular image of the twenties.

Robert Kane was then the head of production for Famous Players at the Astoria Studios and he had received credit for helping to cut overhead costs at the studio.[13] This would be helpful since Dwan, perhaps inspired by the effectiveness of the sets in *Robin Hood*, decided that *The Glimpses of the Moon* also lent itself to the use of elaborate sets. According to Paramount's publicity, the sets cost $100,000. Also grasping that *The Glimpses of the Moon* would be sold as a "woman's picture," it was deemed that luxurious clothes would be prominently displayed and that the film would be a "veritable fashion show."[14]

The screenplay was written by E. Lloyd Sheldon and Edfrid Bingham, the former a writer whom Wharton liked and admired.[15] Starring in the film was Bebe Daniels. She had been a leading lady for Harold Lloyd before moving on to dramatic roles for Cecil B. DeMille. The male lead was given to David Powell, who had recently played Boston Blackie in Paramount's *Missing Millions*. Powell would tragically die of pneumonia at the age of 41 in 1925, after having completed a film called *Back to Life*. Maurice Costello, the popular leading man of the teens, was cast in a supporting role. There was also a bit part for Maurice's daughter Dolores, who would go on to become a silent screen star and years later appear in a major role in Orson Welles' *The Magnificent Ambersons*.

Not all of *The Glimpses of the Moon* was shot in New York. Dwan used New York as his base and took his company to Palm Beach, Florida, for three weeks of filming.

There was, however, a major production problem. Three weeks after shooting began, Daniels began to suffer from sudden stabs of pain. The doctors eventually diagnosed the cause as appendicitis. They advised that the operation be performed as soon as possible. Daniels recalled, "Allan [Dwan] threw up his hands, for many thousands of dollars would be wasted if the picture was delayed for weeks while I convalesced. 'Could it wait a week?' I asked and the doctor nodded."

Dwan agreed to shoot the rest of Daniels' scenes in this period and thanked her. During this time, the doctors monitored her condition and were prepared to order an immediate operation if they judged it necessary. Daniels said she was able to finish her scenes and, when not on camera, had an ice pack on her side to quell the pain.[16] She was then successfully operated on, though complications kept her on the "danger list" for days.

The Glimpses of the Moon opened in late March 1923 and was received with lukewarm reviews. The *New York Times* hailed the film for its photography, sets, "sudden changes in atmosphere" and acting. But it also expressed disappointment in Dwan after the triumph of *Robin Hood*, saying that "he had been handicapped by a story which did not lend itself readily to picturization...."[17] The *Times* critic also thought that Dwan had overdone it on the sets. "It would seem that in comparison to those in *Glimpses of the Moon*, for motion picture purposes a fairly comfortable flat would be the Grand Central and Pennsylvania stations joined together as bedroom and sitting room with Madison Square Garden thrown in as a bathroom."[18] Other publications echoed this view, including *Photoplay*, which lamented, "One enjoys the gowns that the ladies wear, and the lovely interiors, but one misses the vital element that was a part of the Edith Wharton story."[19]

Was it in *The Glimpses of the Moon*, rather than *Robin Hood*, where Dwan had indeed lost his characters in the shadows of titanic sets? One dissenting view comes from the film historian Edward Wagenknecht, who called the film "an admirably close-knit and intelligent piece of direction by Allan Dwan."[20]

Exhibitors, however, complained that the film moved too slowly and without punch for their audiences. *Glimpses* appears to have vanished into that vast set of lost films. Fortunately, Dwan had signed a multi-picture contract with Paramount before the movie was released.

According to an *Oakland Tribune* article of December 1922, Dwan would have been engaged to Mary Thurman at this time. However, there is no proof that the report was accurate and even the *Tribune* cited its source as a "rumor."[21] A premature announcement of this kind could even conceivably have ended the relationship. In any case, there is reason to believe that another woman had attracted Dwan's interest by this time.

Film critic Kevin Thomas, who knew Dwan in his later years, believes that Dwan "certainly had an eye for the ladies. He was a short, stocky guy but women really liked him."[22] Thomas also remembers that the director was fond of telling two saucy anecdotes about a particular actress.

That actress was Nita Naldi, who had played the "vamp" role in *The Glimpses of the Moon*. Vamp roles were her specialty and, as film historian Anthony Slide noted, "She lived the outrageous vamp character that she had become onscreen."[23] Naldi supposedly got the part of Dona Sol, the "bad girl" in *Blood and Sand*, through a meeting with the novel's author Blasco Ibanez at a New York dinner party. The two of them got into an argument about the wealth of the Catholic Church, which Ibanez thought should be donated to the poor. Naldi thought his view was Communistic and Ibanez got so angry with her that his false teeth fell out into the front of her low-cut gown. Apparently, he then decided that she was wicked enough to play the character of Dona Sol.[24]

Thomas thought that Dwan "was more than merely fond of Nita." He recalled a story Dwan told about a New Year's Eve party he held with Naldi at his New York apartment. (Since production had started on *The Glimpses of the Moon* in December 1922, this was probably the New Year's of 1923.) This was apparently a studio apartment with an upstairs and a downstairs.

Dwan and Naldi got the "urge" to be alone. Dwan asked her, "How are we going to get rid of all these people?" Nita said, "Leave it to me." Thomas remembers Dwan explaining, "She had a gown, an evening gown that was all front and no back. So she went upstairs ... and turned the dress around, so that she made a grand entrance down the staircase, in effect, topless. And apparently it worked because everybody was so shocked, they fled!"

Another story Dwan told Thomas about Naldi took place during shooting on the beach in Florida (this must have been during the Palm Beach filming of *The Glimpses of the Moon*). "She kept delaying the shooting. And finally, Allan lost patience." An assistant was sent to summon Nita from her "dressing tent" or whatever setup they had on the beach. He was instructed by Dwan, "I want Miss Naldi on the set this instant. I will not wait another second. No excuses." There was indeed no further delay. "And out she paraded and said, 'You wanted me right now.' And he said that she was absolutely stark naked."[25]

Dwan cast Naldi in another vamp role in his next film, *Lawful Larceny*, an adaptation of a hit play by Samuel Shipman. In addition to her modern-day character, Naldi also played Cleopatra in a prologue, so that her vamp might be better perceived as a modern-day Cleopatra. According to Paramount's publicity, Naldi "will wear gowns that will cause Tut-ankh-Amen to turn over in his sarcophagus and breathe the name of his fair Queen Ankhnes-Amen."[26] Clearly this was another film that would indulge in sartorial splendor.

The plot concerns a young husband (Conrad Nagel) left in New York while his wife is traveling abroad. Vivian, a society vamp (Naldi), guides him into an ostensible social club which is actually a crooked gambling house. The husband's losses are so large that Vivian persuades him to give her one of his company's checks for a huge sum of money. It remains for the returning wife to figure out a way to recover the check and set things right.

The key role of the wife was played by Hope Hampton, who received mixed reviews. *Variety* noted that a soft focus lens was used for all of her close-ups. Hampton has been referred to as "untalented" by Anthony Slide.[27] She married a producer and retired before the end of the silent era.

Although *Variety* considered *Lawful Larceny* "a whale of a picture for entertainment purposes" and opined that it "again shows Allan Dwan back in his directorial stride at his best," overall, the reviews were only slightly better than for *The Glimpses of the Moon. Motion Picture News* called it a "mediocre picture, well put together" and observed, "Again we have a moderately well-to-do family living in a house of the dimensions of a convention hall."[28] Dwan may have felt he had found a perfect visual correlative for what would become an American tradition of living beyond one's means. He may have also been using leftover sets from *Glimpses*.

Asked about these criticisms fifty-six years later, Dwan noted that the sets weren't that big. It was the lenses that made them look so large.[29]

Like his previous film, *Lawful Larceny* was perceived as a "woman's picture" and, as with some of his earlier movies, Dwan chose to concentrate on female strength and male weakness. *Moving Picture World* noticed that "both the good woman

On the set of *Lawful Larceny* (from left to right), Conrad Nagel, Hope Hampton, Nita Naldi, Lew Cody and Dwan. Despite her Latin-sounding name and dark looks, Naldi was of Irish ancestry and her birth name was Dooley (courtesy Kevin Brownlow).

and the vamp are strong types while the men folks are but weaklings in their hands."[30] The *New York Times* reviewer referred to the "Amazonian Nita Naldi."[31] *Lawful Larceny* also uses a plot device similar to the one in *Fighting Odds* with the wife posing as a wealthy widow who seduces Vivian's partner into opening her safe and permitting the wife to rectify things.

After the years of the Fairbanks pictures and a high percentage of male-oriented fare, Dwan seemed now more inclined to narratives of female power and a woman's point of view. As Dwan's naughty Naldi stories suggest, he found her intriguing. But on an artistic level, she may have been too limited to inculcate long-range interest. Dwan, however, was clearly receptive to developing the image of a female star.

Finding Female Glory

Mary Pickford once said, "The success of *Robin Hood* and his other Fairbanks movies illustrates what I mean by calling Allan Dwan a man's director. Allan was just right for Douglas, but possibly not for me."[32] Of course, this may have simply been a diplomatic way of saying that Dwan was not one of her preferred directors.

An interviewer on the set of *The Glimpses of the Moon* cited Dwan's attitude.

"'Nobody'll ever believe that the same man directed *Robin Hood* and *Glimpses of the Moon*,' Mr. Dwan chuckled to me as he led me at a breathless pace toward the studio lunch room. 'That was a man's picture and this one is all women.'"[33]

Dwan clearly did not like being pigeonholed as a "man's director" and relished shifting gears. He acknowledged his preference for intimate stories, and women's films offered even greater opportunities in that direction. His survival instincts must have also convinced him that by being adept in handling films for both sexes, he was doubling his availability.

But Dwan had hitherto not bonded with any female star as his collaborator since his work with Pauline Bush. He may have been on the verge of doing so with Norma Talmadge but her marriage to Schenck had cut off that possibility. Dwan had helped launch Marguerite Clark but directed only two of her films in her brief career. He had also left Marion Davies before her talents were fully realized.

Now at Famous Players, Dwan was on a course to work regularly with one of the most vibrant actresses of the silent era. But this course would come through a tangled route.

Gloria Swanson was born in Chicago while an adolescent Dwan was living in the same city. Since she had been born during the first day of Holy Week in the Christian calendar, her father decided to call her Glory but she was christened under the name of Gloria.

Swanson, like Dwan, began her film career at the Essanay Film Company. One of her aunts was an acquaintance of George Spoor, Essanay's co-owner, and she accepted an invitation to visit the studio, with fifteen-year-old Gloria in tow. While there, Gloria was spotted by a casting director and was soon appearing in bit parts playing thirty-year olds with the help of makeup and chic fashion. Swanson acknowledged, "By the time I was fifteen, my mother had turned me into a real clotheshorse."[34] Her sense of fashion and style would become an important accoutrement of her screen persona.

Swanson recalled that while at Essanay, she was tested by Charlie Chaplin for his comic partner but she found his comedic ideas (like kicking each other in the pants) not to her taste. Chaplin was soon asking the studio for someone else.

After moving to California, Swanson signed with Mack Sennett's Keystone Company where she was cast closer to her true age and paired with an equally diminutive partner, baby-faced Bobby Vernon. Swanson joined Triangle in its waning days and appeared in a serious role in *You Can't Believe Everything* (1918) with Dwan's former heavy Jack Richardson as her leading man. Most of the films she made at Triangle were not good but she was fortunate to be spotted by Cecil B. DeMille and was spirited off to Famous Players.

On DeMille's sets, Swanson was swept into a world of opulence that was totally unfamiliar to her but she soon adjusted. She found DeMille her ideal director, and revered him, even when, as in the 1919 *Male and Female*, he had a lion literally breathing down her neck. Swanson was not the center of these films but shared the spotlight with established stars such as Thomas Meighan and Elliott Dexter.

When Jesse Lasky told Swanson that the studio intended to make her a full-fledged star, she was shocked to learn that this meant that she would no longer be working with DeMille. DeMille himself explained to her, "Because studios can't afford to have too many eggs in one basket. You're a star and I'm a star."[35] When Swanson expressed concern that without him the quality of her films might suffer, DeMille assured her by saying that she would be directed by his former assistant, Sam Wood.

Swanson, like Valentino, belonged to the new crop of stars Famous Players was nurturing after the insurgency of United Artists. Both were underpaid but Swanson had gotten the worst of it; she had signed a second contract in January 1919 at the time when Famous Players thought they could bind with First National to impose caps on actors' salaries. Swanson's second contract actually specified that the raise that had been given to her would be deducted in January 1920. Swanson's second husband, the film executive Herbert Somborn, through his lawyer, found enough dubious items in the contract that Swanson was able to threaten Famous Players that she could contest the option of renewal. It was in the ensuing fear of losing Swanson that Famous Players awarded the actress the full star treatment.

Swanson soon saw the routine pattern of her films with Wood. "Sam Wood was all right, but he was a real estate dealer at heart [his earlier profession]. We had been grinding out pictures since *The Great Moment*, and each one was worse than the last.... The only things that changed were the number and length of dresses I wore and the face of the leading man."[36]

Meanwhile, Swanson's marriage with Somborn had deteriorated. She met with Jesse Lasky in September 1921, telling him that she wanted a divorce from Somborn. Since he had left her months earlier, it probably would have been easy to get a divorce on the grounds of desertion. But Lasky told Swanson that this was impossible. Just a week earlier, the Arbuckle scandal had broken out with the death of Virginia Rappe. The studio wanted to avoid anything that might reek of scandal. For Swanson to divorce for the second time (and only a year after the birth of her daughter) could well produce that result. But once again, the need to placate the social reformers would lead to greater complications.

Swanson had fallen deeply in love with Dwan's friend, the irrepressible and irresponsible Marshall Neilan. She managed to arrange a European vacation right after the shooting of *Beyond the Rocks*, rendezvousing with Neilan in Paris where they carried on their affair. But as they prepared to return to the U.S., they faced sobering facts. Swanson would not be able to obtain a divorce for a long time. And any hint of scandal would be extremely detrimental to their careers; Neilan's was already beginning to decline. Swanson told Neilan it was best that he go ahead and marry the other woman in his life, Blanche Sweet, which Neilan did on June 7, 1922.[37] (According to Dwan, Neilan was also carrying on an affair at the time with a teenage Anna May Wong.[38])

If Swanson thought she had put a firm lid on a potential scandal, she found she was sadly mistaken. In March 1923 she received from Somborn a suit for divorce. The document accused her of committing adultery not only with Neilan but with thirteen other men including DeMille, Wood, Lasky and even Adolph Zukor! Somborn also demanded $150,000 for his role in obtaining a better contract for Swanson.

The studio executives were no doubt horrified at the thought of this being made public and confirming the image of Hollywood as a modern-day Sodom and Gomorrah. Swanson saw the suit as simply blackmail.

Swanson recalled that she then received a call from DeMille to meet him at his home. She stated her intention to fight and he advised her to think it over. As she was about to leave, a telegram arrived. DeMille read it and then showed it to Swanson. It was from Will Hays, the designated moral watchdog of the industry. It said that the Swanson suit had to be settled out of court for the good of the industry.

Mulling it over and thinking of her children, Swanson finally capitulated. The studio helped her financially in making the settlement. Swanson would have to make one additional film than she had previously been obligated to do and a morals clause was added to her contract where she could be discharged for "adulterous conduct or immoral relations" and "such charges or any of them are published in the public press...."[39]

All this was bad enough and could have been avoided had the studio permitted Swanson to sue Somborn for divorce a year earlier. But in her autobiography, Swanson said she found herself confronted with another unhappy revelation.

A couple of months later, Swanson was invited to an industry banquet and wound up seated next to Will Hays. For most of the evening, Swanson gave him the cold shoulder until, near the end of the dinner, he asked why she wasn't speaking to him. When Swanson mentioned the telegram demanding a settlement with her husband, Hays denied that he ever sent it. As he assured her that this was the case, Swanson realized that she had been tricked by the studio and that even her beloved director, DeMille, was in on the chicanery.

The next day Swanson stormed into Lasky's office. But once he admitted the forgery, Swanson left.

Swanson now had to consider her next step. She pondered suing the studio but she understood their power to destroy her. At that time, Valentino was carrying on his own lawsuit against Famous Players and she must have seen that it was just tying him up. Swanson decided that with the discovery of forgery, she had some leverage over the studio and that she could use it to get them to let her make better pictures. She told them that she wanted Neilan to direct her.

She brought this news to Neilan and while he liked the idea, he explained that he was in the middle of one film and had already signed to do another. Neilan had earlier told Swanson that she was "being ruined by weak directors like Sam Wood."[40]

So Neilan recommended that she work with Allan Dwan. Aside from praising Dwan's qualities as a director, Neilan said that Dwan was in New York and that Swanson would be better off there. Neilan also observed, "Hollywood is nothing but sunshine and eventually that fries everybody's brains. Just look around."[41]

Neilan phoned Dwan that evening. Dwan said that he had convinced Zukor to a do a movie that he thought would be perfect for Swanson, an adaptation of the French play *Zaza*, which had been previously filmed by Famous Players in 1915 with Pauline Frederick.

After completing her latest opus with Wood, *Bluebeard's Eighth Wife*, Swanson told Lasky that she needed minor surgery and had arranged to have it done in New York City. Swanson recalled that in July 1923 she boarded a train for New York, where she would meet with Dwan.[42] Once she was in New York, Dwan convinced Zukor and Lasky to let Swanson make *Zaza*. Her operation (the ostensible reason for the trip east) could be postponed until after the shooting of *Zaza*. All this elaborate subterfuge appears odd when Dwan had already spoken to Zukor about a property he thought ideal for Swanson. In fact, an item appeared in *Film Daily* on April 17: "Swanson was due here on about the 24th to start work on *Zaza*."[43] So there is no doubt that *Zaza* was already established as the film she would make before she reached New York. Regardless of whether Swanson got to New York by April 24, the July date of departure in her book is surely wrong since it

Dwan's friend, the charming but unstable director Marshall Neilan, in May 1925. After having an affair with Gloria Swanson, he suggested to her that she work with Dwan in New York.

was announced in the trades that *Zaza* was half-finished by mid–June.[44]

It had also been announced by Jesse Lasky's office back on February 7 that upon completion of *Bluebeard's Eighth Wife*, Swanson would make a film in New York.[45] The announcement, which preceded by a month the Somborn lawsuit and ensuing shenanigans, makes no mention of *Zaza* or Dwan. It suggests that a studio ruse had nothing to do with Swanson's decision to work in the east. But the stronger motive for Swanson's move to New York (her dissatisfaction with Wood's direction and humdrum films) would have been established by that point and she was already angry at management for blocking her divorce. Her increasing disgust with the Famous Players executives may have prompted her resolve to remain in the east and find a long-lasting creative collaboration.

In his Bogdanovich interview, Dwan remembered that at the time Paramount "had a grudge against her and weren't handling her well.... Now Mickey Neilan was interested in Gloria and he asked me to get her out of this bad environment too, so I brought her over and put her in *Zaza*."[46] But in a later interview with Adamson, Dwan said, "As a personal favor to me, Mickey Neilan got me Gloria Swanson."[47] In any case, Neilan was a middleman who served both Swanson and Dwan well.

It could also be observed that the same kind of circumstances that had impelled Valentino to avoid working with Dwan, had led Swanson to the same director.

Swanson recounted having dinner with Dwan on her first night in New York. Although Neilan told her that she had met Dwan at one of his parties, she couldn't recall seeing him before. As Swanson described him, "Allan Dwan was easy to forget in that he was inconspicuous in appearance — short, balding, in his late thirties, with a thick waist and a little round pot — but before we had started the first course, I knew that Mickey Neilan was right as usual: Allan Dwan was a genius."[48]

As for the Astoria studio itself, Swanson observed, "It was certainly not another Hollywood. The place was full of free spirits, defectors, refugees, who were all trying to get away from Hollywood and its restrictions. There was a wonderful sense of revolution and innovation in the studio in Queens."[49]

Dwan said that he then had an agreement with Famous Players that if he met the budget, he would receive a bonus for each picture.[50] The bonus agreement would create a problem further down the road but at the time it worked well. Although Dwan took steps to limit the budget, *Zaza* is a handsome film that still looks more opulent than the 1939 remake directed by George Cukor.

Dwan had told the studio that New York would be a better locale to achieve the European background for *Zaza*. Dwan claimed that for atmosphere he used French-speaking extras who couldn't speak a word of English.[51]

On a more practical level, Dwan arranged for his cameraman, Hal Rosson, to see a display of the paintings of Toulouse-Lautrec to visualize the spirit of French cafes. To achieve more novel lighting effects, Dwan said he had Rosson shoot through the scrim of a lady's silk stocking. When they wanted to add more light for an actress's close-up, they had a cigarette burning through the scrim.[52]

Dwan also scouted outside the studio for suitable locations. Swanson said Dwan found a mansion on Long Island that could serve as a French chateau. According to Paramount's publicity sheet, an old general store in Little Neck Bay was transformed into a French home that served as Zaza's love nest. The same publicity sheet referred to a beautiful lake nearby. Dwan said the lake was created by a broken sewer pipe.[53]

Dwan displayed to Swanson and the cast and crew his ability for invention and problem-fixing. When the sweltering heat made studio shooting an ordeal in those pre–air conditioning days, Dwan had giant blocks of ice brought in and used huge fans behind them to provide cool air. Swanson recalled, "*Zaza* turned out to be the fastest, easiest, most enjoyable picture I had ever made."[54]

Zaza was based on a French play by Pierre Berton and Charles Simon. In January 1899, a few months after Gabrielle Réjane starred in its Paris premiere, a version produced by David Belasco opened in New York with Mrs. Leslie Carter in the title role. It was a great success. The play was turned into an opera the following year by Ruggero Leoncavallo.

Zaza is about a provincial singer with great stage ambitions who succumbs to one of her male admirers, Bernard Dufresne.

For a while they live together as she puts her theatrical career on hold. When Zaza learns that Dufresne is married and has a little girl who idolizes him, she breaks off the affair. Two years later, after Zaza has won wealth and fame on the Paris stage, Dufresne comes to see her. Zaza says she loves him as she does someone who is dead and while she will retain sweet memories of him, she never wants to see him again.

Zaza provides an affecting portrait of a woman who suffers greatly in love but pours her life into her art and achieves independence and inner peace. But the character of Zaza also reflects the era of her creation. Raised in poverty by an aunt, she is one of the "poor creatures of chance"[55] who must learn that happiness is not for them. No matter how great her success, Zaza must leave the man she loves to a more respectable woman.

For the 1915 film version, reviews suggest that Famous Players wanted to exploit the "ooh-la-la" quality of the play while toning down its tragic aspect. Dwan may have also shared this concern but with Swanson, he could project an image suited for the more liberated 1920s. The story was updated from the 1890s to the period just before World War I.

Zaza is described in the titles as a former "singing gamine of the streets," who hasn't lost her habit of fighting for what's hers.[56] The first images of Swanson as Zaza are even more telling. Zaza is in her dressing room throwing her clothes, some of which pelt her maid Nathalie. Zaza is in a frenzy and pushes her maid to tears. But Zaza then softens and consoles Nathalie with a candy, showing Zaza's volatility and warmth are intertwined.

Zaza and her fellow artistes can also be seen entertaining patrons by appearing from the stage in swings that fly high above their heads. (The idea of the swing may have been inspired by Dwan's familiarity with Evelyn Nesbit, known for her stage persona as the Girl in the Red Velvet Swing.) To photograph the swings, Dwan had the camera mounted on a platform secured by steel cables that could follow the swing in motion. The vertiginous sensation of the girls' swinging movements enhanced the pleasure-seeking atmosphere of the music hall.[57]

The swing also provided a much more cinematic device for Zaza's "breaking the ice" with Dufresne. In the play, this occurs when he tries to help Zaza rehearse a song. In the film, Zaza's jealous rival Florianne, played by Dwan's former leading lady Mary Thurman, sabotages the swing by cutting into the rope that holds it. As the rope snaps, Zaza goes topsy-turvy, then falls down. Dufresne rushes to her aid. While she keeps her eyes closed, he kisses her, completing the act from an earlier shot when he seemed on the verge of doing so. Dufresne takes her under his care.

Dufresne is played by H.B. Warner who, while not young and virile, brings dignity, charm and kindness to his role. According to Dwan, Warner had not wanted to work for Lasky but was apparently won over by the New York locale.

Dufresne pays for a specialist who saves Zaza from becoming crippled. She continues her convalescence at Dufresne's cottage at the edge of town where he can also lavish his attention on her.

A scene is inserted where Dufresne has a meeting with his wife. According to a title, "Madame Dufresne has always encouraged separation ... but she was ambitious." The diplomat Dufresne has been offered a post in America as charge d'affaires and his wife encourages him to take it for the good of his family. Dufresne agrees. Dwan underlines the distant relationship between the couple by keeping them in separate shots for most of their brief conversation.

Dufresne is here thus a somewhat more sympathetic figure, who is in fact alienated from his wife but bound by family obligations and must say goodbye to Zaza. Rumors then begin to reach Zaza that she is not the only woman in Dufresne's life. From here on, Dwan and his scenarist Albert Shelby Le Vino encase the film in a rich dynamic of emotions, having them intersect at cross-currents and then flowing into a short-term sequence and onto the greater onrush of time. If Dwan is manipulating the audience's emotions, he is doing so more like future directorial masters such as Hitchcock and Kazan with a complex interplay rather than simply tugging and milking the familiar standby devices. Much of this emanates from dramatic high points that were already in the play but Dwan heightens the narrative flow and embellishes them with cinematic bits of business.

Florianne visits Zaza at the home Dufresne has provided for her and ignites things with comments about Dufresne amusing himself with other women until Zaza attacks her and they get into a furious fight. Swanson recalled, "There was a long elaborate fight scene in the picture, for instance, and he made Mary Thurman and me do it in one take. We had to make it good just by our acting.... And Allan convinced us we could. In a minute he could push the most phlegmatic member of the cast to peaks of excitement. He was extraordinary."[58] As the battle rages and reaches outrageous proportions, a wig is ripped off and Zaza's poor Aunt Rosa gets knocked down in the scuffle. Florianne, getting the worst of it, flees in a horse-drawn carriage. The scene ends with Zaza vowing, "I'm going to Paris — and if I find him with another woman, I'll give her worse than I gave Florianne."

The fight (which does not exist in the play) has the audience all pumped up for the encounter with Madame Dufresne, who has been shown to be unsympathetic. Zaza is still full of pluck as she is ushered into the Dufresne home. But then she sees a little girl playing the piano. Upon seeing Zaza, the child introduces herself as Lucille Dufresne. This takes the wind out of Zaza's sails.

As Zaza talks to the child, she begins to melt into tears. In the play, the child has a locket with a cameo of her father but in the film, little Lucille shows Zaza a photograph of her father which is clearly visible, even in long shot. The photograph will be carried over into a subsequent scene. The daughter explains, "This is my papa. He's been away for a long, long time but he's come back now."

When Madame Dufresene finally appears, Zaza says she's made a mistake and leaves abruptly. It is only in the subsequent exterior long shot that we see Zaza's total emotional capitulation as she collapses into the arms of her maid.

Back in her room, Zaza picks up Dufresne's framed photograph. In a scene that won Swanson praise from the critics, she pulls the picture out of its frame. She closes her eyes as she holds it close to her and begins to tear it. As she makes the second rip, she reveals the pain she feels and holds it close to her lips. Dwan underscores how agonizingly long it takes for Zaza to complete this act by cutting to Aunt Rosa talking jubilantly and then back to Zaza still holding the picture to her lips before she drops the pieces to the floor.

H.B. Warner and Gloria Swanson in the memorable finale to *Zaza* (1923).

Later, meeting Dufresne at a large reception, she tells him that because of his wife and child, he has no right to come back to her. She feigns interest in the duke and, standing on a table, she offers a toast to "the little fool who thought she was in love — a toast to the old Zaza!" After Dufresne withdraws, she collapses.

The intertitles refer to the end of Zaza's dreams of love and of the subsequent years in which she becomes a major star beloved by all of Paris. Because of the time period of this version, this also includes her working for the war effort and charities.

In the 1915 version of *Zaza*, co-directed by Edwin S. Porter and Hugh Ford, the filmmakers tried to provide a Hollywood ending by having Dufresne, conveniently now a widower, return to Zaza a year after their breakup. Zaza still seems to discourage him but *Variety*'s Sime Silverman observed, "That's when the caption writer grew more optimistic than the principals seemed to be, although Zaza had a quiet smile by herself...."[59]

The 1923 version overcomes some of this awkwardness by having Dufresene return after a duration of seven years. He is a widower here but the longer time frame makes his wife's death a bit more credible. It also means that Lucille is no longer a child but a young woman. Lucille has become a fan of Zaza and, given what we know of Lucille's early love of music and that Zaza is now a major star, this is hardly a contrivance. But the long duration also has left a mark on Zaza, who has grown as the world has changed, despite her great disappointment in love. The sense that happiness is due her is easy to grasp.

Lucille comes to visit her and, as often with Dwan, a past scene is revisited later in the story. They are again by the piano and recall their first meeting as Lucille talks of her late mother and this time Zaza consoles Lucille. Lucille asks Zaza to sing. While Zaza plays the piano and warbles her song, Lucille disappears. Dufresne enters the room, unheard by Zaza, who has her back to the door. Still in long shot, Dufresne moves closer to the unaware Zaza until he is directly behind her. With that sense of anticipation and incipient joy ever so close, *Zaza* ends.

In his book on Swanson's films, Lawrence J. Quirk complains that *Zaza*'s "pace is rather hurried and the running time (seven reels) too short for full development of the ambience."[60] Actually, Dwan again shows his great economy in storytelling, and his film is rich in atmosphere while running the full gamut of feelings. His final shot, showing a moment preserved at the edge of happiness, seems to glide into eternity.

Of Swanson's performance, *Photoplay* proclaimed, "Gloria Swanson in this picture definitely takes her place among the leading actresses of the screen. She leaves no doubt as to her talent."[61] While there were dissenters from this view and complaints of Swanson being overly boisterous in some scenes, she had captured the imagination of the public. Even the more critical reviewer for the *New York World* confessed, "We have seen no more frenzied crush for tickets at the Rivoli in months than that last night. Miss Swanson must be better than we think she is."[62]

Swanson observed years later of Dwan, "I couldn't wait to do another picture with him. Everything Mickey had said about him was true. Before *Zaza* was half finished, I knew that Allan and New York represented some kind of rebirth for me."[63]

Big Brother

It initially appeared that Gloria Swanson would get her wish and that *Zaza* would be immediately followed with another

Swanson–Dwan pairing. In early September 1923, soon after *Zaza* was completed, Paramount put out a trade ad of their upcoming productions. Among those listed was *The Hummingbird* starring Gloria Swanson, advertised as "an Allan Dwan production." (It had been reported that all the films Dwan directed under his contract would have that credit.)[64] *Zaza* had not yet been released but the ad touted, "After *Zaza*, a box-office knockout, they'll cry for more of Gloria Swanson in French vixen roles.... Filmed by the producer of *Zaza* on the same lavish scale."[65]

While the studio saw box-office magic in a French soubrette encore, Swanson had her own reason for wanting the role in *The Hummingbird*. Her character in that film would be a Parisian gamine who dressed in men's clothes to visit her boyfriend on the battlefront. Swanson wanted to convince the studio that she would be perfect to play the title role in *Peter Pan*, the rights to which Zukor and Lasky had just acquired, and she was sure this vehicle would suit her purpose.

As for Dwan, as *Zaza* got underway, a trade story appeared that he would be transferred to the West Coast as soon as the film was completed.[66] The studio now appeared to relent on that but another change was in store.

At the top of the list in that Paramount production ad was a project called *Big Brother*. It was based on Rex Beach's latest novel which was running serially in *Hearst's International Magazine*. (Hearst's linkup with Zukor was still intact at this time.) The story's regeneration theme was compared to *The Miracle Man*. It was also connected to a national organization, the Big Brother Movement, that was pledged to protect and rear boys from the slum sections who were subject to influences that might lead them to crime. The studio saw huge potential in the project.

It was reported that after seeing *Zaza*, Lasky "was so enthusiastic over this production of the famous Leslie Carter vehicle that he assigned to Mr. Dwan one of the biggest stories of the year."[67]

So Dwan was moved from *The Hummingbird* to *Big Brother*. Veteran Sidney Olcott, whose career stretched back even farther than Dwan's, to the one-reel 1907 *Ben-Hur*, directed *The Hummingbird*. Production of that film was delayed while Swanson finally checked into a hospital for her operation. (The originally announced director of *Big Brother* was Sam Wood, who would again be replaced by Dwan, as he had been as Swanson's director.)

The Big Brother movement was composed of hundreds of prominent men. Its treasurer at the time was Theodore Roosevelt, Jr., and the organization was doubtlessly trying to maintain the same ideals of manhood advocated by his father. According to Paramount's publicity, the members of the movement "have agreed to get behind this picture with every bit of power they possess."[68] While appreciating this boon of marketing assistance, Lasky emphasized to the press, "Neither the novel nor the picture we have made is in any sense propaganda...."[69]

Beach's novel was adapted by future film director Paul Sloane. The story tells of Jimmy Donovan, head of the Car Barn gang. When one of his lieutenants is killed in a shootout, Donovan pledges to take care of his kid brother Midge. In trying to be a "big brother" to Midge, Jimmy tries to go straight but is then arrested for a payroll theft he didn't commit.

Donovan escapes from the police and learns that the real thief is the drug addict Cokie Joe, a former member of his gang. When Donovan makes this discovery, in the memorable words of Paramount's publicity department, "He hastens to the haunts of the hophead."[70] In the ensuing gunplay, Joe is killed. The wounded Jimmy manages to bring back the payroll and exonerate himself. When the Juvenile Court learns of Donovan's heroism, Midge is returned to him.

The popular Tom Moore (a younger brother of Owen) was cast as Donovan and the incorrigible child actor Mickey Bennett took the part of Midge. Cokie Joe was played by Raymond Hatton, often cast as "Bowery types, Mexican bandits, Russian spies, cocain [sic] fiends, and the like...."[71] Hatton would later switch to comedy roles and in the sound era would specialize as grizzled sidekicks to Western heroes.

The plot contained elements with commercial appeal including a resemblance to Chaplin's *The Kid*, which had been released two years earlier. But more significantly, it dealt with the criminal underworld as part of a burgeoning genre that went at least as far back as Griffith's *The Musketeers of Pig Alley* and would reach maturity in the late silent era as the "gangster film."

Audiences of 1923, especially those in urban areas, were familiar with many of the legends of gangland. Paramount's publicity department noted that the Donovan character "will in many respects remind one of Ike the Blood, Indian Louie, Biff Ellison, Chick Tricker, Sardinia Frank, Johnny Spanish and a host of others."

> About a decade ago there were four gangs in the lower section of Manhattan, the one and only doctrine and religion of all being dollars and warfare. The Five Points gang, with 1,500 members, was supreme between Broadway and the Bowery, Fourteenth Street and City Hall Park. Monk Eastman's crowd, with 1,000 members, flourished between Monroe and Fourteenth streets and the Bowery and the East River. The Gas House gang held sway along Third Avenue between Eleven and Eighteenth Streets and the Gophers were in possession of the West Side.[72]

In filming the story, Dwan took advantage of a key resource at his disposal, the streets of New York. Noting the tendency, even in pictures made in New York City, simply to recreate slums on a studio set, Kevin Brownlow wrote of this film, "[W]hen a director had the nerve to insist on filming on location, the difference was so apparent that reviewers drew attention to it."[73]

Indeed, the *New York Times* review of *Big Brother* observed, "Mr. Dwan impresses his atmosphere on all those who see this film. He shows trains on the elevated railroad, above and below, the Queensborough Bridge, street after street of hopelessly squalid dwellings and line after line of freshly laundered flannel and linen hanging on roofs and in open spaces."[74]

At least two descriptions of the location shooting in the film are on record. According to a story in Paramount's press sheet, Dwan was shooting a scene on Avenue A where he wanted to show the neighborhood women busily purchasing vegetables from street vendors. Women crowded around carts which Dwan had selling produce at ridiculously low prices (e.g., potatoes at one cent a pound) As the women fought to take advantage of the prices while the camera was rolling, Dwan had little Mickey Bennett as Midge upset all the carts, sending the women in a mad rush for the fallen vegetables. Dwan impishly commented, "In all my motion picture work I never saw a more realistic scene than this one. Everybody in it acted on natural impulses and they never gave the camera a thought."[75]

A second story was related by Dwan to both Bogdanovich and Brownlow. Apparently for the scene where Midge's brother is killed, Dwan paid two longtime rival New York gangs, the Hudson Dusters and the Gas House Gang, to serve as extras in the dance hall. Dwan recalled this being shot at the edge of Harlem, just across the street from the Polo Grounds. At the time, Paramount's publicity identified this building as the old Manhattan Casino at 155th Street and Eighth Avenue. The rival gang members and their girlfriends had agreed to comply strictly with the orders they were given from Dwan's platform over the dance floor. To light the huge hall, Hal Rosson was using Klieg lights which were then nicknamed "broads." The lights were softened with silk scrims known as "silks." As the dance was about to begin, Rosson decided he needed more light and called out loudly to his staff, "Take the silks off the broads." This was heard by the gangster extras on the dance floor, who interpreted it as an order to rip the clothes off the women. There was pandemonium as the women shrieked and resisted and fights broke out all over the dance floor. The police, who were on the scene to make sure that the gangs behaved, entered the fray waving their clubs. Dwan told Bogdanovich, "Nearly took all the police ambulances in New York to take these guys away to get patched up, and it cost us a little money to buy new dresses but it was worth it. It was the most vivid gangfight I had ever seen."[76] Dwan, however, told Brownlow that when *Big Brother* was to be released, "I was stopped cold by the censors ... because the girls were over-exposed and so that spoiled one of the greatest shots I ever saw come out of the camera...."[77]

Brownlow himself thought the story too good to be true and suspected Dwan of indulging in a bit of the blarney. But he noted that the *Variety* reviewer hailed the direction of the dance fight and contemplated, "[P]erhaps there is some substance to it; perhaps some of the scene survived."[78]

Dwan told interviewer Joe Adamson that while he was in New York, he hated to be confined to the Astoria Studio. He noted that just opposite to Astoria was Blackwell's Island which contained a prison. Dwan recalled, "We always referred to the studio as 'the prison.'" At another point in the interview, Dwan calls the Astoria studios "a mausoleum."[79]

Dwan's gangster drama *Big Brother* (1923) was shot on the streets of New York (Kevin Brownlow).

The inference is clear that for Dwan there was no life in a restricted studio environment. Part of the appeal of New York to Dwan was that it gave so many opportunities to find atmosphere. But his first three films in Astoria show him with limited reach beyond the studio.

Aside from the trip to Florida for *Glimpses of the Moon*, Dwan's ambience in his first two films appears to have been centered on his sets. *Zaza* was richly atmospheric but most of it was interiors. This was entirely appropriate since *Zaza* was about artifice and theatricality.

With *Big Brother*, all accounts suggest that Dwan went to great lengths to gear the film to the reality of the mean streets of his time. According to Paramount's publicity, makeup was employed in the film at an absolute minimum: "Most of the characters in the play are gangsters of New York's Lower East Side.... In Mr. Dwan's opinion the exact characterizations could not be procured with the aid of makeup." According to the release, only Hatton (playing the "dope fiend") wore makeup in the exterior scenes and only two performers including the female lead wore makeup in the interior scenes.[80] The claim may be a bit exaggerated but it does sound like Dwan's methodical approach to material and his preoccupation with realistic detail.

In reviewing the film, the *New York Times* took note of the stylistic change in Dwan's work. "Allan Dwan, the director famous for *Robin Hood* and also for his penchant for appallingly large sets that dwarf the players, has made a picture with an appealing story and stagings of modest proportions that fit the particular sequences like artistic and well-chosen frames."[81] The *Times* praised the film for making its points without sermonizing and concluded, "It is a splendid picture told with unusual sincerity."

The kudos were echoed by other critics. *Variety* called it "a realistic, melodramatic triumph and a really great picture."[82] *Photoplay*'s review said, "Rex Beach wrote a great story but Allen [sic] Dwan has made a masterpiece of it in his translation of words to photography."[83]

In the same issue of *Photoplay*, *Big Brother* merited mention in an editorial by James Quirk. "Right on top of Pike's Peak, with the thermometer below zero, I would take off my hat and make a low obeisance to Allan Dwan for his production of *Big Brother*. He has made a truly great picture."

But Dwan would not repeat his success in having one of his movies win Photoplay's Medal of Honor for best film for a second consecutive year. The 1923 award went instead to James Cruze's Western epic *The Covered Wagon*, starring Dwan's old nemesis J. Warren Kerrigan. (Kerrigan retired from films the following year.) Dwan did receive the compensation of having been cited by *Photoplay*'s poll of five thousand exhibitors as one of the top eight directors of the year, with Dwan finishing just behind Cecil B. DeMille, Griffith, and Rex Ingram and ahead of Neilan, William DeMille, Cruze, and George Fitzmaurice.

Big Brother is among those many films that have vanished and with it, its documentary record of the slums and city streets of its era.

Big Brother was remade in 1931 as *Young Donovan's Kid*, directed by Fred Niblo and starring Jackie Cooper and Richard Dix. Boris Karloff played Cokie Joe.

A Winning Team

The Hummingbird, released in January 1924, received critical accolades and Swanson seems to have gotten along well with director Olcott. The critics noted that for a change, Swanson was not wearing an array of gowns.

The studio agreed to let Swanson and Dwan work together again. Their next project, *A Society Scandal*, was an adaptation by Forrest Halsey of Alfred Sutro's play *The Laughing Lady*. The studio may have been concerned with her fans being disappointed by her masculine clothing for *The Hummingbird* because Paramount insisted that Gloria would be wearing plenty of lavish costumes in her next film.

Dwan retained at least some of the realistic approach of *Big Brother*. Swanson recalled that the trial scenes were shot in a courtroom in Brooklyn.[84] Since the film dealt with high society, Swanson said that Dwan "wanted real, identifiable New York society people in the drama. After a careful look around, he cast the beautiful Morgan twins, Thelma and Gloria, who would shortly become Lady Furness and Mrs. Vanderbilt, in small parts, and the newspapers gasped when the picture was released. Allan Dwan loved flirting with reality in this way...."[85]

According to a trade story, *A Society Scandal* would also mark a stylistic departure for Dwan. The director announced that he would not be using long shots in the film. Dwan apparently wanted to erase his critical reputation for focusing on large sets. Dwan explained, "I do feel that the atmospheric long shot and the spectacular splash has been greatly overdone."[86] He was certainly not swearing off long shots forever but his work with Swanson had turned him to a more intimate approach to filmmaking.

Swanson plays a society woman, bored with her drab and rather stupid husband, who turns her attention to another man. Although the flirtation is innocent, the man leaves her in a situation that looks compromising. At the divorce trial, the husband's lawyer does a convincing job of destroying her reputation. As part of a revenge plot, the woman flirts with the lawyer when she meets him at a party. She arouses his interest and sympathy but when he goes to her hotel room the next day, she rushes out into the corridor in a torn gown shouting that he has attacked her. But as he is being ruined, Swanson realizes she is in love with him.

While the public could not have known it at the time, the lawyer's behavior recalls the blackmail plot of Swanson's real-life second husband. An even more Pirandellian development is that Swanson fell in love with Rod La Rocque, who played the lawyer. La Rocque proposed to Swanson but the romance supposedly fizzled when he saw how Swanson liked to associate with celebrated male friends.[87]

La Rocque was one of two actors in the film considered Latin lovers in the Valentino mode. The other was Ricardo Cortez, who aroused Dwan's ire for overacting. ("You act too much," he told Cortez.[88]) When Cortez fell asleep after numerous takes in which the liquor being served was real, Dwan let him spend the night in the empty studio. After that, Dwan said he got things right on the first take. This is another dubious account but it does show Dwan's disdain for those who would not adhere to a naturalistic acting style.[89]

The film, released in March 1924, pleased the critics but the

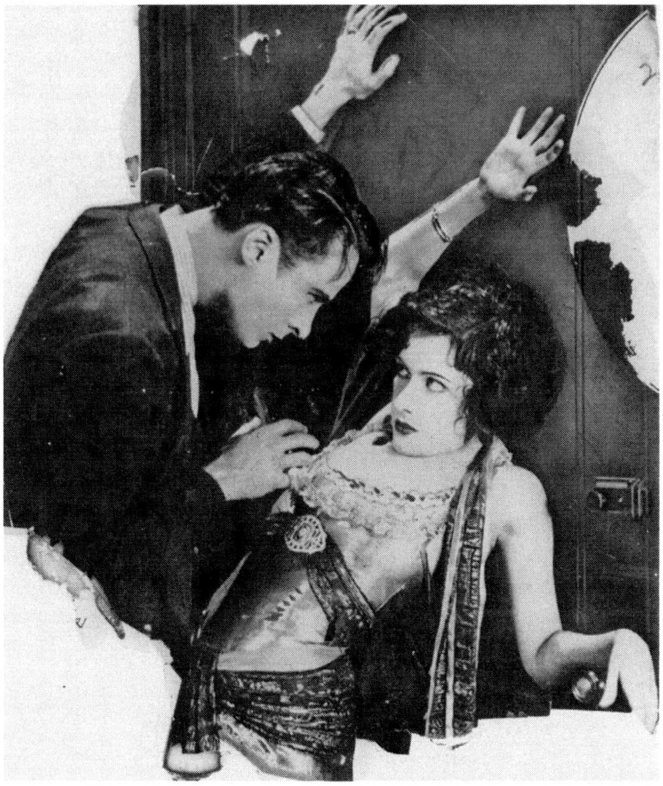

Rod La Rocque and Gloria Swanson in a steamy still from *A Society Scandal* (1924). The two became an item but La Rocque later decided to back off from marrying her.

praise often seemed qualified. *Motion Picture News* observed, "It is excellent of its kind but it won't make screen history.... The picture while artificial is much closer to reality than the usual expose of life among the fast steppers in society."[90] *Variety* summarized, "A little better than the average feature program about sizes it up.... The society atmosphere is consistently preserved. When the upper crusters are shown in action they look the part instead of appearing superficial and actory."[91]

The critics were pleased with Dwan's sense of naturalism, and there was high praise for Swanson. *Photoplay* said, "Gloria Swanson never ceases surprising us these days." After citing her varied work from *Zaza* through *The Hummingbird* to *A Society Scandal*, *Photoplay* concluded of Swanson, "She's growing in stature as an actress by leaps and bounds. She has developed a power of facial expression and breadth of gesture that are strikingly effective. This story ... offers a wealth of opportunity to an actress who really can act, and Miss Swanson never fails."[92]

A Society Scandal turned out to be another hit for Swanson and Dwan. But even before the film was released, the studio had recognized that the two were a winning team. In late January, it was announced that Dwan had signed a new contract with Famous Players to direct five films with Swanson. The studio was probably confident that they had another hit on their hands with *A Society Scandal* but they must have been also pleased that it was completed in what approximated a record for speed at the Astoria Studio, a "trifle over three weeks."[93]

Swanson apparently felt comfortable with setting down some roots in New York. She purchased a home in Croton-on-Hudson, forty miles outside of New York City, so that her children could have country living and she would have easy access to the city. The studio also gave her a second "home" at Astoria, a new moving dressing-room said to be "the most elaborate of its kind so far to be built for a star. Mounted on wheels so that it can be moved to any corner of the studio where Miss Swanson may be working, it is as complete as a deluxe cabin on an ocean liner."[94] This may have been one of the earliest examples of the star trailer.

Swanson wrote that for her next film, Famous Players' sales director Sidney Kent came up with the title *Manhandled* but that writer Frank Tuttle actually suggested the *Saturday Evening Post* story by Arthur Stringer that was to be the basis for the movie.[95] But Tuttle himself has written that when he first met with the director for the film, the story had already been purchased and that Dwan told him that Kent was instrumental in buying the story, which Dwan considered "the most salable property Paramount owned."[96]

For *Manhandled*, Dwan heightened the sense of realism by plunging into the world of working class men and women, particularly one woman. He applied the realistic atmosphere of *Big Brother* to comedy and to a woman's story, while incorporating the ambience for the popular Swanson image to materialize. *Manhandled* became a big favorite with critics and audiences, and for both Dwan and Swanson. But as with Dwan's writing collaborations with Fairbanks, planning the story was done with breezy playfulness.

It was then mid-winter. To get away from New York's cold weather and enjoy a vacation after the completion of *A Society Scandal*, Swanson suggested a trip to Miami Beach with Dwan and Tuttle accompanying her to start discussing the new picture. Dwan brought along a lady friend whom Swanson did not identify in her autobiography.

Tuttle recalled how on the train he and Dwan were invited to Swanson's drawing room. The twenty-five-year-old Swanson there removed her dark glasses "which revealed a glint of unholy mischief in her wonderful eyes."[97] Not long after they began their Florida stay, Swanson suggested they go to Havana. In Swanson's account, this was because the weather in Miami Beach was almost as bad as in New York. In Tuttle's version, it was because someone had been banging and rattling garbage cans below Gloria's window at four o'clock in the morning.[98] In any case, the other members of the party, consisting of Swanson's female assistant, Tuttle, Dwan and his girlfriend, were delighted with the idea, none of them ever having been to Havana. Tuttle recalled, "We blessed whoever had rattled those Miami garbage cans."[99]

While Dwan and Tuttle managed to squeeze in some story conferences, little progress was made during their Havana holiday. The closest they may have come to a story idea came from Swanson's misadventure with some Cuban bigwigs. Convinced that ex-president Mario Menocal and his associate, one Senor De Mesa, were trying to drive her to a trysting place until she furiously demanded to be brought back to her hotel, Swanson said she thought she had found their *Manhandled* plot. "Our little department store salesgirl could get into society and then get abducted — manhandled — by the richest, most dignified, most distinguished man in Cuba, or even by the ex-president, while she's on a cruise."[100] But Swanson said that all her companions, including Dwan's anonymous girlfriend, found that plot too far-fetched.

Dwan and Tuttle arrived back in New York without a treatment but with some notes. The two men were scheduled to meet the eastern studio's new executive producer William Le Baron the day after their arrival. Like a student who had squandered all of his vacation time without doing his term paper, Tuttle told Dwan that he would stay up all night putting together a treatment before their morning meeting with Le Baron. Tuttle said that by morning he had three-quarters of a detailed treatment ready.

According to Tuttle, after reading the treatment Dwan told him, "This is okay, kid. You know we can use some of this dialogue for titles." With Le Baron sharing Dwan's enthusiasm, the script for *Manhandled* was taking shape.[101]

Tuttle wrote that his idea was that "Gloria should work in a department store, and that her leading man — Tom Moore — would be a garage mechanic. They would be roomers in the same cheap boarding house. I felt that Gloria's fans would welcome her as a down-to-earth working girl after all the clotheshorse roles she's portrayed." But Tuttle also acknowledged that he would later have to find an excuse to "dress her up."[102]

Dwan grasped that the plot hinged on firmly planting the characters in a realistic milieu and went to great lengths to construct the proper atmosphere. A working class New York City girl would surely be riding the subway, and Swanson had never ridden the subway in her life. To introduce her to this commuter experience, Dwan dressed the studio's prize clotheshorse in the worst outfit he could find, rendering Swanson unrecognizable. He recalled, "I took her over to what we call the Shuttle, which only runs back and forth from Grand Central to Times Square. Nobody paid any attention to her. I waited for a real pack, shoved her aboard, and left her in there. Well, she rode to Times Square and when she tried to get off, the crowd coming on shoved her back again — and she ended up going back and forth about ten times. She was a wreck — everything she had was ripped off."[103]

Similarly, since Swanson's character worked in a department store, Dwan arranged to get the actress a job at a bargain counter. Swanson wrote, "I borrowed a blond wig from the studio, stuffed cotton in my nose to change its shape, powdered out the beauty mark, and painted on new eyebrows and lips."[104] Swanson crowned her makeover with a five dollar dress and a padded bra. On her first day, Swanson sold toilet soap, eyed the haughty floorwalker so carefully that she could do an imitation of him, and got intelligence briefings in the ladies' room on how to deal with fresh guys. On the second day, a rumor circulated among the sales staff that Gloria Swanson was in the store and the actress then fled at the first opportunity.

According to Paramount's publicity sheets for *Manhandled*, Swanson also prepared for her role by eating several meals at a Bronx boarding house.

While unlike *Big Brother*, Dwan would be making most of *Manhandled* on studio sets, he would reap the benefits of what he and Swanson had learned from their field work. Tuttle occasionally visited the set and noticed that Dwan "had embellished my script with sure-fire directorial touches and Gloria's performance was a joy to watch. She seemed to be having the time of her life portraying a real person."[105]

The opening shot of *Manhandled* shows the weary legs of

Swanson gets battered about in the famous commuter scene from *Manhandled* (1924).

workers going down stairs. The first part of the film is a descent into commuter chaos where in a memorable bit, Swanson's Tessie McGuire, "one of the mob," boards a subway train. Swanson's diminutive size is utilized here as she is battered around the subway car by the sea of pressing flesh and in particular by two hulking males.

Tess' boyfriend, Jimmy[106] Hogan (Moore) is a garage mechanic by day and a taxi driver by night. A Dwan-like problem-solver, he has invented a gadget that will save autos 25 percent on gas. He's confident that once he makes his pitch to a Detroit auto manufacturer, his fortune will be made.

But in the interim, his crowded work schedule limits his time to go out with Tessie, leaving her with little solace after her exhausting day. Swanson evokes much of the feeling of the character by the way she picks up a ukulele and strums it while sinking her head morosely into her chair. In *Manhandled*, Swanson's eyes oscillate between showing flashes of mischief and deep yearning.

Dwan also exploits the boarding house for atmosphere, creating a *Rear Window* effect. Tessie gazes out of her window which is both reflective and transparent, showing her own reflection as well as two scenes through the apartment windows of two families, both saddled with household drudgery. Tessie laments, "Being married ain't any good — not for folks like us!"

The next day, Tessie is back at work at Thorndyke's, a bargain department store where she must deal with hordes of determined shoppers. She also shows plenty of pluck when harangued by a store supervisor. Novelist Paul Garretson, accompanied by the store owner's son Chip Thorndyke, is looking for a salesgirl as a model for one of his characters. Garretson decides that he "wants to cultivate that little Bolshevik" and invites Tess to one of his parties.

Swanson recalled the shooting of the next scene, where again Dwan tried to replicate reality in a studio setting. "Allan wanted a wild New York party scene in the picture, so he set up a real party, as nearly as he could, in the studio. At the rehearsal he told everyone to let go and improvise. He hired Ann Pennington from the Follies for the scene, and she shimmied and did the Charleston like a miniature whirlwind while Allan kept yelling, 'Come on everybody, react! You're there! It's a party!' In the midst of the activity I took a black derby from one of the crew and put it on. Then I grabbed a cane from somebody and started wobbling around in an impersonation of Chaplin. People laughed and clapped, and Allan said to keep it in. The next day, we got a more accurate Chaplin costume for me and shot the whole sequence in an afternoon."[107]

It should be noted that *Manhandled* has been largely circulated in truncated prints in which Gloria's Chaplin imitation is cut. So even some film historians may not be aware that Swanson first performed her impersonation of Charlie Chaplin on film over a quarter of a century before doing it in the 1950 *Sunset Blvd.*

Besides imitating Chaplin's Tramp at the party, Tessie does an impression of a Russian countess that proves so effective it fools a neighbor across the hall, Arno Riccardi (Frank Morgan). Tessie meets a sculptor played by Ian Keith who decides that she would make a suitable model.

Tessie finds herself in a roundelay of polished gentlemen, each of whom warns Tessie that the other is "terrible" with women. She leaves the sculptor after he makes advances. Then on Riccardi's suggestion she becomes a paid fixture in his shop, posing as the Russian countess to help him sell his finery. (Riccardi furnishes her with luxurious gowns which fulfills Swanson's clotheshorse obligations.) When Tessie attracts Riccardi's amorous attentions, she moves on to Chip Thorndyke who literally starts to "manhandle" her and sends Tessie running from his limousine.

Near the end, Tessie returns to her boyfriend Jimmy, who has now sealed his contract with Detroit. But Jimmy is not ready to take her back, as he scolds, "You're like the goods you hated to sell in Thorndyke's basement — rumpled — soiled — pawed over — MANHANDLED!" This bargain basement simile can be traced back to a prologue intertitle: "The world lets a girl think its pleasures and luxuries may be hers without cost — that's chivalry. But if she claims them on this basis, it sends her a bill in full with no discount — that's reality."

Tessie is in a sense getting her comeuppance for her naiveté. Like Zaza, she has indulged in role-playing. But where Zaza enriched her art as she was compelled to extend her acting to real life, Tessie's clever playacting provides her only with illusions that will send her back to the world from which she has sprung.

Tessie decides that she doesn't want anything but Jimmy and in the end, he finally does take her back. So Tessie's fall is cushioned as she gets love and a millionaire anyway. It's a pleasing, if somewhat contrived, ending.

Audiences and critics found little to dislike in this modern Cinderella story. The *New York Times* compared the film to something more contemporary, viz. O. Henry's short stories: "It has the realism, the natural pathos, the contrasting notes and excellent touches of humor which one reads with delight in *The Four Million.*"

"Miss Swanson proves her versatility as a screen actress, this time as a clever comedienne. Her efforts are greatly assisted by the able and restrained direction of Allan Dwan, who has provided fitting scenes for Miss Swanson with the same brilliance he showed in *Big Brother.*"[108] Reviewing the film at the Rivoli, the critic noted, "This is one of the few films which we have heard draw spontaneous applause from the audience, even before the last fade-out."[109]

Kudos for Swanson and her acting range dominated the reviews. *Motion Picture News* marveled that Swanson "is at once the comedienne, the pantomimist, the impersonator and the emotional artiste."[110] The *New York Herald Tribune* noted, "Gloria Swanson does everything that she has never done before. It is a delightful comedy with Miss Swanson in the role of a gum-chewing saleslady."[111] There was also high praise for the subway scene and Swanson's Chaplin imitation. *Manhandled* received the best reviews and box office reception of the Swanson–Dwan collaborations to date.

In the next Dwan–Swanson film, *Her Love Story*, a romance set among Balkan royalty, Swanson's princess falls in love with a captain of the guards. (Ian Keith, the sculptor in *Manhandled*). Her family has him arrested and exiled while she is forced to marry a king. All works out happily in the end.

In her autobiography, Swanson glosses over this movie as "the kind of silly costume picture I was a bit embarrassed to make."[112] Dwan did not remember the film at all when interviewed in 1979. For the most part, the critics were not charmed and the *New York Times* spoke for many in saying, "This picture is far inferior to what we anticipated."[113] One reviewer even chided Dwan for returning to "revel in the towering and broad sets from which he had departed in *Manhandled*."[114]

After completing *Her Love Story*, Swanson sailed for Europe. The actress was furious that she had not been offered the title role in Paramount's *Peter Pan*. Like one of her scrappy characters, Swanson would go to England determined to make her case for the part to *Peter Pan*'s creator, playwright James Barrie.

Paris, New York and Hollywood

Allan Dwan was now a well established director at Paramount. He had even managed to play a part in a grand "art" conference that Adolph Zukor had convened.

Like the robber barons of an earlier day, Zukor had a philanthropic side: It was announced in early 1923 that, for the purpose of "formulating a set of principles for the artistic development of motion pictures, leading novelists, artists, dramatists, educators and others prominent in public affairs in this country and in Europe" were invited by Zukor to attend a conference in New York.[115] This world congress on motion picture arts was held on June 7 and 8, 1923, under the auspices of the Authors League of America. Novelist Rex Beach was chairman of the General Congress Committee.

The conference did have a lively exchange of views, the most vociferous by author Basil King who hinted that the whole Congress was a publicity stunt. King told how he wrote a story directly for the screen which was very successful when adapted as a magazine story. But by the time it reached the screen, after going through studio conferences, it was in a form that was "ridiculous."[116]

Dwan gave his presentation standing between a typewriter and a camera. Dwan told the writers, "This is my medium of expression, this camera; this is yours, a typewriter. If you want successful efforts on the screen you have got to find out just what I can do with this. It does not make any difference what you can do with that unless you know what I can do with this. This child of mine is suffering greatly at present from indigestion because this thing is not giving it the proper food."[117]

Dwan reminded the authors that many of the best features of their stories could not be included on film because of censorship. He added, "We appeal to an elemental mind. We appeal to babies and children and the childish minds of grown-up people. Don't try to elevate us — give us an entertainment.... We want money; this is a money-making business, as well as an art. If it were not a money-making business, it would not be an art because no art starves.... Now do not forget this: I talk now of course from 15 years' painful experience in handling stories and transposing them to the screen...."[118] Dwan now sounded an even more commercial opinion than in his interviews, and many of the writers took him as the voice of the industry. He may well have seen himself in that role. But he also used circuitous logic to affirm that film was an art as it was being commercial. The "15 years' painful experience" included the memory of his work with Associated Producers and the brief wilderness period that followed.

Dwan also articulated his aesthetic views in articles for the *New York Times* in April and May of that year.[119] Like Monroe Stahr, the producer in Fitzgerald's *The Last Tycoon*, he emphasized that writers need to have scenarios that speak in action, not words.

Zukor also offered a $10,000 prize to the writer whose story or play made the best picture produced between September 1, 1923, and August 31, 1924. Dwan was the only film director selected to the committee of judges which included artist Charles Dana Gibson, playwright Elmer Rice, critic Robert Sherwood et al. In December 1924, they gave the prize to author Rafael Sabatini for the film *Scaramouche*.

In mid–1924 Swanson was pursuing her own ambitions. The scriptwriter Forrest Halsey had suggested that seeing J.M. Barrie in England might be her best remaining chance for securing the role of Peter Pan.[120] He also advised her that in France she should try to obtain the film rights to a play by Sardou called *Madame Sans-Gene*. Halsey told her the story about a washerwoman who is elevated to the nobility by Napoleon. Fittingly, Sardou had written the part for Réjane, the same actress who had originated the role of Zaza. In discussing the film with Halsey, Swanson also came upon the idea that the film could be produced in France using the actual locations of the story.

Swanson arrived in London but before she could meet Barrie, it was announced that a newcomer, Betty Bronson, had been chosen by the playwright to portray Peter Pan. Two days later, Swanson moved on to France to pursue her second objective.

Swanson met with the head of Paramount in Europe, Adolphe Osso, who told her that the French would never give the rights to *Madame Sans-Gene* to an American nor would the government permit the use of historic monuments in a film. But Swanson also met with the cinema critic of *L'Aurore*, Andre Daven, who told her that the French could see an opportunity in the project. American films flooded French theaters but with

Swanson as the star, a film that employed largely French talent could sell well in the United States. (The use of an American star in a European film was a little less complicated in the silent era.)

Daven conducted an interview with Swanson that the actress said "was a lesson in diplomatic tact and salesmanship."[121] The French agreed on both counts to what Osso thought impossible. Lasky and Paramount then decided to give their consent to the project. According to Terry Ramsaye, Dwan was set to go to France to direct the film but the French government decided that only a Frenchman could be entrusted to direct scenes involving national monuments and historic sites. Veteran director Leonce Perret was assigned the job.[122]

As part of the deal, Swanson agreed to come back to Astoria to make one more film for Paramount before *Madame Sans-Gene*. That film was *The Wages of Virtue*, adapted by Halsey from a novel by Percival Christopher Wren (who had written *Beau Geste*) and directed by Dwan. Swanson plays Carmelita, a young Italian girl in Algiers who operates a café favored by the men of the Foreign Legion. An American Legionnaire falls in love with her but Carmelita is guarded over by a bullying man to whom she feels obligated since he saved her life.

For the male lead, Famous Players got Ben Lyon from First National on loan-out. Dwan introduced him to Swanson in the studio lunchroom. Lyon was happy to be part of an acclaimed team and asked what Gloria was planning to do next. Dwan responded, "I have a rest after this while Gloria goes to Paris to do her next picture. She's going to make *Madame Sans-Gene* with a French director. You'll like that, won't you, Gloria? And he will probably spoil you so I won't be able to do anything with you afterwards."[123] Lyon remembered thinking, "I felt carried away by all this boy-girl stuff. I had never seen such [a] happy relationship between director and his team."[124]

That same lunchroom, which Dwan recalled as being downstairs from the studio stages, was also the center of some intrigue. An immigrant in his mid-twenties from Austria–Hungary was working there as a waiter. But this man, who commuted from the Bronx, had dreams of working more directly in the film industry. The waiter was Joe Pasternak, who was destined to become a Hollywood producer. He remembered Gloria Swanson as his first prized patron in the Paramount commissary. He worked hard to make sure she got exactly what she wanted ("She liked her salad greens cold and crisp") even to the extent of spreading his tip money around the kitchen to further that cause.[125]

Later, Pasternak traded sections so that he could serve directors who would be in a better position to promote him. Pasternak waited on a number of them but the one he was really drawn to was Allan Dwan. Pasternak recollected, "Allan was an impressive figure of a man, intensely serious, single-minded and single-purposed. He lived motion pictures and regarded everything that did not concern the making of exposed film as an intrusion."[126]

Pasternak then made his move. "When I found out what he liked, I stopped giving him the menu. He would come in, followed by the people with whom he was working on the set, talking pictures, the last shot or the first shot to be made after the lunch break. I'd have ready for him something he'd once eaten with some relish. At first he looked at me darkly, with a who-the-devil-told-you-to-bring-this look. Then he realized that he could go on talking shop without having to think about food, and he appeared to be grateful."[127]

Pasternak, no doubt, ingratiated himself by showing Dwan lunchroom efficiency. He continued to build his case by buying Russian rye loaves in the Bronx for Dwan rather than giving him the usual studio bread. When Pasternak heard that they were looking for someone to play a bit in *The Wages of Virtue* as a wide-eyed wounded Legionnaire watching his comrades go off to battle and weeping because he is too ill to join them, Pasternak sought the part. Dwan agreed to give him a chance.

For an entire day Pasternak tried to induce tears to fall from his eyes but not fresh onions, glycerine drops, smoke or any other backstage trick could make him cry. Only after the day's shooting was over and Pasternak was alone, contemplating how he had blown his big chance, did the tears come.

When summoned the next day, Pasternak could see Dwan's look of annoyance for having wasted an entire day. But while Dwan thought him "lousy" as an actor, the director made clear that he admired Pasternak's hard work, spunk and initiative. He offered Pasternak a job as his "chairman." Only the next day did Pasternak realize that among other things, this required providing the appropriate-sized canvas chair for Dwan with the height required for each shot. His official title was third assistant director.

Dwan had helped launch another Hollywood career: Pasternak would be with him for the duration of the Swanson films at Paramount.

Swanson was back in Paris filming *Madame Sans-Gene* by the time *The Wages of Virtue* was released in November. Critics responded more positively to this film than to her previous effort with Dwan; the *New York Post* went so far as to say that *The Wages of Virtue* was her way of redeeming herself "for giving us *Her Love Story*."[128] Swanson scored points by not wearing "a single striking gown"[129] but there was also genuine praise for her performance. The recreation of Algiers in Astoria was apparently done convincingly enough to impress critics with its atmosphere. *Motion Picture News* judged the film a "thing of pictorial beauty" and cited Dwan's direction as "masterful."[130] *Variety*, on the other hand, thought the film unconvincing and "indifferent."[131]

Dwan did not get a rest after completing *The Wages of Virtue*, quickly plunging into another opus, *Argentine Love*. Swanson had been originally set to star in the film but since she was making *Madame Sans-Gene* the role went to a genuine Latin, Bebe Daniels. While most of the characters were Argentine, the romantic hero was again an American engineer, this time

An autographed picture sent to Dwan in July 1932, "To My Mr. Dwan who changed this boy to Joe Pasternak" (Allan Dwan papers. Collection number 3566. American Heritage Center, University of Wyoming).

played by James Rennie. The film was adapted from a story written for the screen by Ibanez. With two other writers involved, the finished product may have borne little resemblance to Ibanez's original story but Paramount was still keen to exploit his name after Valentino's success in *The Four Horsemen of the Apocalypse* and *Blood and Sand.* The bogus Latin star, Ricardo Cortez (born Jacob Krantz), who resembled Valentino, was also featured prominently in the cast.

Argentine Love was shot in Astoria but again the critics found the locations convincing. Aside from the praise for atmosphere and the performances of Daniels and others in the cast, a majority of the reviews ran from passable to unfavorable. The *New York Times* gave this harsh judgment: "It is surprising that *Argentine Love* should be such a poor picture, as it was directed by Allan Dwan and no matter what the famous Vicente Blasco Ibanez wrote in this special screen vehicle, it was to be presumed that Mr. Dwan could have put some life into it."[132] Released in late December, *Argentine Love* did not turn out to be a box office bonanza.

In his review of *Argentine Love, New York Times* critic Mordaunt Hall speculated, "Mr. Dawn [sic] appears to have had his mind on *The Coast of Folly*—which he is to make in France with Gloria Swanson—when he was producing *Argentine Love.*"[133] It is unlikely that *The Coast of Folly* was ever intended to be shot completely in France although Swanson for a time insisted on it. She would have no more luck than Valentino in convincing Paramount to film in Europe but there were announcements in the trades that Dwan would be shooting exteriors for the film there.[134]

Swanson had completed shooting *Madame Sans-Gene* but remained in France. There were rumors about her spending excesses which were not altogether unfounded. Swanson remembered, "When Allan Dwan wrote details of his arrival in January, I could tell by the tone of his letter that he was worried about me. I had leaked stories to the press that I was remarrying as soon as my divorce was final, and columnists were already hinting that I was marrying a millionaire and quitting pictures. Obviously Mr. Zukor had told Allan to get right over to Paris and find out the truth before I made some awful mistake."[135]

Dwan arrived in Paris with one of the Rosson brothers, Richard, who was serving as his assistant director. Whatever apprehensions Dwan may have had were further fueled when he met Halsey at the train station. Halsey told him that he had arrived just in time and that Swanson was spending money wildly. He added that she had fallen head over heels in love with an Indian maharajah and her foolish behavior with him had become the talk of Paris.

An extravagantly long Mercedes pulled up to pick up the travelers. The back seat was filled with leopard skin rugs and pillows. Swanson emerged from the limousine dressed in gold

Ben Lyon and Swanson in the Foreign Legion drama *Wages of Virtue* (1924).

satin and bedecked with ornate jewelry. She smiled at Dwan and let him give her just a peck on the cheek. She said she would drop the two men off at their hotel to prepare for dinner which would be a formal affair and that they would be called for at eight.

When Halsey picked them up later, Dwan admitted that he was shocked by the change in Gloria. Probably even more startling to Dwan was the size of the mansion to which he was driven. Dwan and Rosson were taken to the library where they were received by Swanson wearing a dress that extended to the floor. She introduced them to her guests, including a throng of visiting royalty.

Swanson's beloved maharajah then entered with a large emerald in the center of his turban. Swanson curtsied to him and as he passed each of the guests, he stopped and waited for them to bow.

The guests paired off and entered the dining room where a sumptuous table gleaming with a hundred candles awaited them. The meal, served on gold-edged plates, went on for two hours. Swanson rose to make a toast to the maharajah and, like nearly all of the conversation of the evening, it was spoken in French. But as she completed her speech, Swanson's friend and colleague Halsey, who appeared to be drunk, caused a disturbance. In tears and rising to his feet, he shouted out in his Southern-accented English, "My God, Gloria, you can't marry this son of a bitch. He's black as the ace of spades." The maharajah threw wine in Halsey's face and, grabbing a knife, chased the screenwriter from the room. Gloria called for calm and asked her guests to remain seated but then a shot was heard from the hall. Halsey re-entered the dining room, wiping blood from his shirt and proclaiming, "There's one dead Indian."

At that point, everyone around Dwan and Rosson broke into hysterical laughter. Gloria then rushed over to Dwan and kissed him "properly." She urged him, "Tell everybody back home I'm not really crazy, will you? And that my bathroom fixtures are not solid gold. That's another house altogether."

The whole thing had been an elaborate practical joke, if perhaps not one in the best of taste. Dwan learned that Swanson was indeed engaged to the man made up as the maharajah except that he was not a maharajah but of French nobility, the Marquis de la Falaise de Coudray. Some of the guests were of actual nobility but others were actors from the cast of *Madame Sans-Gene*.

Swanson recounted this in her autobiography.[136] Dwan told basically the same story to Bogdanovich with some variations. At one point in the proceedings, Rosson aroused Dwan's suspicions by whispering to him, "These bastards are all wearing makeup." Dwan's more macho version ends, "The Hindu began to be abusive, so I swung on him. His [phony] beard went east and his feet went west — he was out cold. And that turned out to be the Marquis de la Falaise de Coudray. After that, things were fine."[137]

In real life, as well as on film, Swanson could kid her image and defuse some of the criticism. She was, like Fairbanks, an inveterate practical joker. In New York, Dwan once had to caution her about her provocative phone calls to strangers.[138]

But her romantic involvement with the marquis was quite real. Swanson wrote that before shooting on *Madame Sans-Gene* began, Daven and Halsey had selected the marquis (whose first name was Henri) to be her interpreter. He was handsome and spoke English well but since his noble family was impoverished, he had to work. The marquis, who at 29 was four years older than Swanson, was also a World War I veteran. He had been badly wounded and received two citations for bravery.

Swanson found Henri not only proficient as an interpreter but indispensable in making all the arrangements necessary for her work and cutting through government red tape. As they socialized, they fell in love. They planned to marry in January. To avoid a circus atmosphere they kept their plans secret from virtually everyone, including Paramount.

But Swanson made a shocking discovery as she prepared for Dwan's arrival: She was pregnant. Had she been able to marry Henri immediately, no one would have been any the wiser. But because her divorce from Somborn was not final, she had to wait a month.

Swanson remembered the morals clause in her contract: If she engaged in relations with men other than her husband and this information was published, she could be fired or, more likely, her status would be restored to her 1920 contract. Swanson would thus lose all the leverage she had worked so hard to attain over the last four and a half years.

Given that the baby's birth at eight months could still have been reasonably considered premature, there may have been no need for anxiety. But Swanson, conscious of how rough the contract game was being played, may have felt she was in a precarious situation. On the other hand, if she did not have the baby, she could start *The Coast of Folly* and finish the remaining films on her contract.

Swanson decided to have an abortion. She wrote that she did not inform the marquis about the turn of events. Her friend Daven made the necessary arrangements.

Dwan returned to America on January 15 but apparently had gotten no exterior footage since it was announced that *The Coast of Folly* would be produced entirely in the U.S. One trade report suggested that a long stretch of Parisian bad weather prevented any shooting.[139]

In another segment of the Bogdanovich interview excised from the published version, Dwan said that after he and Rosson scouted locations, he received a message from London which "insisted that the picture must be done in America and to get Gloria back to America. So I went and told Gloria that and she revolted and said no. So Dick and I were told to come back home."[140] (Dwan's account suggests that the studio was using the story of location shooting in France merely as a pretext to get Dwan to persuade Swanson to return to America as soon as possible.) After he returned to New York, Dwan went to

Palm Beach to make preliminary arrangements for filming *The Coast of Folly*, which was presumed to go into production on March 8.

On January 28, 1925, Gloria and Henri were married. The story made headlines all over the world. The very next day, Swanson went to have her abortion. She then returned to her hotel. Swanson was scheduled to depart for America with Henri in mid–February. But now she stretched out on her bed exhausted.

She stayed in her room for three days. It was then discovered that Gloria was running a fever. It was serious enough that she had to be taken to a hospital. For two weeks, reporters kept a death watch in a café across the street from the hospital. Swanson, however, made a recovery as her marquis whispered in her ear, "You have fooled them all."[141] But she was in no condition to leave soon for the U.S.

The Coast of Folly had to be postponed. The workaholic Dwan was suddenly left without an assignment. This situation helps explain two somewhat mysterious incidents from Dwan's career.

Dwan told Bogdanovich of one film he suddenly had to make on the spur of the moment when the screenplay was only in its early stages and the writer was in Europe. The film was *Night Life of New York*; it was announced in late February that with the temporary scrubbing of the Swanson film, this would be Dwan's next movie.[142]

The film had been originally announced the previous November as *New York Life*. A publicity blurb said it would feature "a cast of big names to be especially selected by Jesse L. Lasky and a story as big as the title stands for, a realistic and ultra-modern photoplay...."[143]

Dwan told Bogdanovich that Lasky had agreed that Edgar Selwyn, Goldwyn's former partner, would write the story and that "certain people would be in it. One day the three of us had lunch and talked about the general idea. Edgar was going to Europe, so the agreement was that while he was away, he'd work on it and soon after he got back, deliver it."[144] With the sudden switch in projects, Dwan's problem was "Selwyn's gone and all I've got is the little conversation we had at lunch...."[145] Writer Paul Schofield must have filled out Selwyn's story in rapid time because Dwan was able to begin shooting in mid–March.

Rod La Rocque, originally cast to repeat as Swanson's leading man in *The Coast of Folly*, was shifted to *Night Life of New York*. Dorothy Gish was set to co-star. The story dealt with Ronald (La Rocque), the son of an Iowa manufacturer. Ronald has a yen to go to New York City; his father has a long hatred of the city since his fiancée jilted him there years ago. Ronald gets into real trouble in the big city when he falls in love with a phone operator (Gish). All works out with Ronald taking the operator to Iowa to marry him while the manufacturer, meeting his lost love, decides to stay in New York.

The eternal problem-solver Dwan used this thin plot as an excuse to follow the characters through all the hot spots of New York night life, filming on the actual locations. Dwan remembered, "We went into real nightclubs and real theaters and real night exteriors — all with available light. That was the first time I used fast film and a wide shutter. Photographed people leaving a theater at night — under the marquee — I had the cameras in a truck so nobody knew we were there — and it photographed brilliantly — with no additional light. Fast film. Eastman made it *that* day, got it down to us and we had to use it *that* night ... it was so sensitive."[146] Perhaps not all of the night club scenes were filmed on location: *Photoplay* reported, "Texas Guinan, famous hostess of El Fey, a popular New York night club, has been engaged with the girls in her cabaret to do their stuff in a replica studio set of the El Fey."[147] Since a large part of the nightclub footage took place at the El Fey, it may have made more sense to film it in the studio.

Dwan claimed, that "within five days — not over that — I had the whole picture shot."[148] *Night Life of New York* was made very quickly but perhaps not quite that fast. In its March 14 issue, *Moving Picture World* said that *Night Life of New York* would begin shooting "next week" In the April 4 issue Dwan was said to be "putting the finishing touches" on the film but it is not clear if that was referring to post-production. Commenting on the speed of the filming, *Photoplay* noted, "Rod La Rocque says that the picture was completed before he knew it was under way. Dorothy Gish says she worked for a week before she knew the name of the character she was playing."[149] Gish's comment suggests that the filming lasted more than one week. The negative cost of the film was a relatively low $177,000.

When *Night Life of New York* was released in July, the critics recognized that the plot looked as if it had been slapped together but were impressed by the performers and "the tour." *Moving Picture World* opined, "Considered as literature, *Night Life of New York* is pretty poor stuff, forced, illogical and inconsequential. But both night life and New York have distinct box-office values, and Allan Dwan has made the most of a sprightly, if impossible scenario.... It moves rapidly [and] shows half a dozen of the best known night clubs in New York.... It gives about $500 worth of night life for whatever admission the theater charges, and it is all authentic."[150] *Photoplay* commented, "More than just a movie — a sightseeing tour of New York. After all the silly burlesques of night life in the big city, Allan Dwan deserves a vote of thanks for presenting Broadway as it really is. All the night clubs and hotels are called by their right names and there are no DeMille settings to deceive you."[151]

Like *Big Brother*, Dwan's *Night Life of New York* provided authentic atmosphere and an invaluable documentary record of a particular aspect of New York City at the time. And like *Big Brother*, all prints of *Night Life of New York* have also been permitted to vanish.

When Selwyn returned to New York, he apologized to Dwan for not yet having the story ready. Dwan replied, "The hell you

Dorothy Gish appears lost in *Night Life of New York* (1925).

haven't — you've got the film finished."[152] Selwyn had received story credit. If the credit had been totally honest it would have instead read, "Based on a lunch conversation."

Another oddity in Dwan's career is that he directed the screen test for film legend Louise Brooks. Brooks, who was then appearing with the Ziegfeld Follies, said to Kevin Brownlow that Dwan "was a great director. He had no business taking tests ... of silly little Follies girls."[153]

According to her diary, Brooks started work on her first film, *Street of Forgotten Men*, on May 20, 1925.[154] Dwan had finished *Night Life of New York* by early April. While he may have had some involvement in post-production work, he was probably available for other duties during part of April before shooting began on *The Coast of Folly*. It was very likely in this time period that Dwan directed the test that brought Brooks to the screen. The test was made at the Astoria studios.

Brooks recalled, "I got up to this dressing room and this guy started messing with my face — oh, he put the most dreadful makeup on me — and I glared at him and we had quite a fuss.... So first Allan Dwan came over–and he knew me — he said, 'What in the name of heaven have you done to your face?' I said, '*I've* done nothing.' He said, 'Well, my God, it looks like you've dunked it in a flour barrel. You have powder all over you. Now fix your face.' So I fixed my own makeup, and put the mascara on and my eyebrows back...."[155] Dwan then told her to run out of the cellar door and run across the room looking frightened when she hears another sound and then run out the cellar door.

"That was the test," Brooks summed up. "But he was so sweet to me, so kind ... he was a great director."[156] And passing that test, the volatile Louise Brooks began her career in films.

Swanson finally felt sufficiently recovered to leave Paris and arrived in New York with her new husband on March 24. Paramount soon packed her off on a cross-country train trip to the West Coast so she could attend the Hollywood premiere of *Madame Sans-Gene* with much hoopla.

Swanson's mood was not good and she recalled being racked with guilt for aborting her child for the sake of her career. Returning to America and to Hollywood had not helped; "weak, run-down, confused, full of guilt and bitterness, I dreaded

Louise Brooks, the legendary silent film star and beauty, passed her screen test with some help from Allan Dwan.

nothing so much as making four or five more films in rapid succession, especially in Hollywood."[157]

By mid–April, Swanson realized the futility of continuing self-pity and that the best way to resolve her problems was to get back to work. She then called Dwan and asked him to lunch so they could discuss doing *The Coast of Folly*.

Swanson assured Dwan that she was fine and wanted to really concentrate on her acting. When Dwan asked what she meant by that, Swanson explained, "From now on, I want to be proud of pictures I make or I want to stop making them. From now on, I want every picture I'm in to interest me. *The Coast of Folly* is a good place to start. I've never played two parts in a picture before, and the old countess will be my first real character part. From now on, I want people to judge my performance, not my personality. I don't want to belong to the public or be dictated to by the studio...."[158]

Dwan cautioned her that the public would want her to stay the way they liked. Swanson snapped back, "Look who's talking. Who taught me to fight the studio in the first place? You and Mickey [Neilan]. The average career lasts five years, I've been already going for ten. It's time to enlarge or quit."[159]

Swanson had put her finger on Dwan's own dual nature. He had gotten his perch on the East Coast and a measure of autonomy. Having won those concessions, he seemed content to appear the company man. He had provided the creative energy for Swanson to reach the peak of her stardom but both director and star were worn down by the grind of the schedule that insured that routine films were part of the mix.

Dwan was also seeking to discourage Swanson from talk of quitting. He knew, and he told her, that for her new contract the studio was "on the brink of offering you the moon."[160]

Contract renewal with Famous Players had also been a question for Dwan. *Variety* noted, "Dwan, it is known, is looking for considerable increase in salary. Whether Famous is going to give it to him is now a question. The director is said to have originally mapped out the director-to-exhibitor-plan which has Senator James J. Walker interested in it. It is possible that in the event that Famous does not renew the contract with Dwan that he will be found at the head of the first producing unit the Walker organization would have...."[161]

State Senator Walker, who was referred to as a good friend by both Dwan and Swanson, was considering launching a producing organization on a cooperative basis with exhibitors. Dwan may have been still considering another independent plan or the possibility of using this option as a bargaining chip with Famous Players. He may have also grasped that despite Walker's interest in show business, he was more concerned with furthering his political career. In mid–March, Dwan signed another one-year contract with Famous. Walker decided to run for mayor of New York City and was elected, later becoming known as the flamboyant and notoriously corrupt "Beau James."

Since most of the *Coast of Folly* story was set in Florida and New York with possibly some in Europe, it's not clear why it was ultimately shot on the West Coast except that Dwan had reported to Hollywood and Swanson was still there after attending the premiere of *Madame Sans-Gene*. According to the *Variety* review, *The Coast of Folly* was all interiors. Even if this was an exaggeration, it suggests that outdoor scenes, if any, were perfunctory. *The Coast of Folly* was the only Dwan–Swanson silent shot on the West Coast.

Of Swanson's return to filmmaking in the U.S., Joe Pasternak recalled, "[A]fter her marriage, Gloria became very conscious of her rights and privileges. She informed the crew that she no longer wished to be called 'Gloria' or 'Miss Swanson' as we had been doing. She was to be addressed as 'the Marquise,' or better 'Madame la Marquise.'"[162] Swanson, however, charged that this was Dwan's doing as part of his revenge for the maharajah evening. "One day he made everyone on the set address me in full, whenever they spoke to me, as Madame la Marquise de la Falaise de la Coudraye, and he made sure that same day that plenty of columnists were present to record the new Swanson image."[163]

Swanson may not have shown airs in that way but she was still capable of acting imperious. Dwan recalled to Adamson how he told Pasternak never to take "no" for an answer from performers when it was time for them to be on the set and Swanson was the toughest to get there. One day while he was waiting for his star, Dwan said Swanson approached him angrily, saying, "I'm going to kill you" and complained of him "siccing" Pasternak on her.[164]

Dwan asked what Pasternak did to her. She responded that when she ignored his calls to report to the set, Pasternak got down on his knees and cried, "Please, Miss Swanson, if you don't come down, Mr. Dwan will fire me." Dwan was amused enough by this that he asked Pasternak to come over and re-enact the scene before them, which garnered some unusual looks from the crew. Dwan said he then gave Pasternak other duties to perform in lieu of calling the actors.

In the course of the film, Swanson does an imitation of Mary Pickford as Pollyanna. As *The Coast of Folly* was in production, an item in *Photoplay* highlighting changes in Hollywood noted, "Mary Pickford now acknowledges that the crown has passed to Gloria Swanson. It's the popular decree written in the indisputable letters of the box-office."[165] Swanson, like Pickford before her, was concerned with being stereotyped. Swanson, however, felt that with this film, she and Dwan "were doing the industry proud with our work. We set a pace we hadn't kept since *Manhandled*, and we both came out of it feeling years younger."[166]

The plot has Swanson playing Nadine Gothaway, who in 1905 deserts her priggish millionaire husband and disappears in Europe. She also leaves behind a small daughter who stands to inherit all of her father's money. But he makes the inheritance conditional on her not being involved in any kind of scandal. Twenty years later, the daughter Joyce (also played by Swanson) is involved with a married man, and his wife's divorce suit threatens to expose Joyce. Her mother, who married a count and now lives in France as Countess De Tauro, learns of this and decides to come to her daughter's aid.

In more ways than the audience was aware, the plot bore similarities to Swanson's real life with the tricky will paralleling the morals clause contract. Most critical attention fell on Swanson's dual role as mother and daughter. Hall in the *New York Times* wrote, "While viewing Gloria Swanson in her new film, *The Coast of Folly*, a somewhat unconvincing and unimaginative effort, one is impressed by the lofty aspirations of the popular actress ... making a bold bid to be known as the Bernhardt of the screen." One problem that troubled Hall and other critics was that Joyce's mother, following the logic of the story, should be between the ages of forty-five and fifty years of age in the modern scenes. Hall noted, "Miss Swanson is singularly well made up as the Countess. She looks old, but always Miss Swanson, and at times she exaggerates the walk of the elderly woman, making it appear that of a woman of 80 instead of 50." Hall concluded that Swanson "would do better to keep to those roles to which she was so well suited."[167]

Some critics were impressed by Swanson's portrayal of the countess but others echoed Hall's sense that the performance needlessly exaggerated the character's age. In his review, *Variety*'s founder Sime Silverman opined, "Miss Swanson as the old woman is very bad."[168] Then writing as if he knew that Swanson had acquired too much power, he added, "And it must

Swanson as the young heroine in *The Coast of Folly* (1925), with leading man Anthony Jowitt.

be very bad for a director necessarily directing a star who may insist upon this or that. Surely Allan Dwan never called for the many close-ups of Miss Swanson as the aged adventuress."[169]

Dwan may very well have indulged Swanson in those scenes. At 26, Swanson was certainly not the last glamorous actress who thought that she could prove her talent by hiding her attractive looks under old age makeup and acting as crotchety as possible. The virtues of the apparently lost *The Coast of Folly* may well have been obscured by the attentions aroused by the novelty of Swanson's twin roles and her determination to show that she could play "old."

As for the film's box office fate, as Dwan observed, "It wasn't a blockbuster but it was a good commercial picture."[170]

Swanson may have pushed her sense of star power too far. An item appeared in *Variety* concerning what happened following the shooting of *The Coast of Folly* after Dwan left for New York and Swanson remained in Hollywood: "A day or two later, Miss Swanson instructed [Richard] Rosson to call the people for some retakes. The assistant did not think there was any harm in it and did so. Instead of retaking a scene Miss Swanson personally directed and appeared in a new sequence which was added to the picture. When word of what had happened reached Dwan, he immediately discharged his assistant, claiming that the latter was only subject to his orders and not those of any star."[171]

It was an indication that there might be more troubles ahead.

Stage Struck

Swanson and Dwan had not equaled the success of *Manhandled* but they wasted no time in moving on to their memorable next project. Swanson wrote, "While Allan and I shot the last of *The Coast of Folly*, we were already ahead on our next script, a funny, wistful story about a small-town waitress who dreams of becoming a famous actress...."[172] Dwan may have drawn some inspiration for the film from his own early stage-struck years. Aside from whatever Dwan and Swanson may have contributed uncredited, three writers including Forrest Halsey were involved in the penning of what would become *Stage Struck*.

In the interim, Dwan had been asked by Famous Players to feel Swanson out about accepting a new contract. They were prepared to offer her as much as $22,000 a week, which would be more than a million dollars a year. Before making her next film, however, Swanson chose to sign with United Artists, where she could produce her films and make as many of them per year as she wished. She would still have to make three more pictures to complete her Paramount contract.

Two weeks after that, Swanson said she saw Chaplin's new film *The Gold Rush*. She marveled at the masterpiece he had created and felt inspired for her own future efforts at both starring and producing. She wrote wistfully about her ill-fated attempt at teaming with Chaplin just a decade earlier.

Perhaps her admiration for *The Gold Rush* also provided Gloria with some inspiration for her next film since she would make a more extensive effort at physical comedy in *Stage Struck*. For atmosphere, Dwan wanted to evoke small town America and was in search of a riverboat for a key scene. Famous Players' location manager Arthur Cozine and art director Van Polglase set out to find the proper setting and were said to have combed the Ohio River Valley for two hundred miles before deciding on the town of New Martinsville, West Virginia. They found the riverboat *Water Queen* and had her pushed nearly two hundred miles so that she could be moored to the bank in front of the Rearview Hotel.[173]

But Dwan planned to use New Martinsville not just for the riverboat scene but to shoot most of the picture. In August, when all was ready, a caravan consisting of Dwan, Swanson and the rest of the cast, and a company of about one hundred minor players, extras and crew, made the trek to New Martinsville. Joe Pasternak had been sent ahead to help in the preparations.

For one of the roles in this comedy, Dwan had selected his friend and fellow Notre Dame alumnus Ford Sterling, who had years ago played the captain of the Keystone Cops. Dwan remembered that Sterling was not in good health and that one reason he came was that he wanted to see New York. Sterling was visibly upset when not long after arriving in New York, Dwan took him to Penn Station and told him, "We're going to West Virginia." Sterling protested that he had bought tickets for a show that night. Dwan assured him he could see all the shows he wanted when they got back but Sterling was not mollified. Dwan then took him through the company's portion of the train which included "two carloads of these beautiful dames" whom Dwan had selected for small parts and extra roles. Dwan said that shortly thereafter, Sterling not only forgot about his missed show but about his health problems.[174]

Virtually New Martinsville's entire population of 4,500 was there at the station to greet the arriving company. Banners were unfurled and the New Martinsville Silver Coronet Band greeted the film people. Dwan said, "We were very much like the shows that came into town."[175]

But no show ever brought this many people to New Martinsville. The hotels could not accommodate everyone so private homes were made available. Dwan said he shared a suite with Pasternak in a hotel that had only one bathroom. The director said that plumbers had to turn one of the closets into "a first class bathroom."[176]

Swanson recalled the town reception: "They paraded us and the whole crowd through the August sun, and then the little cavalcade, with the townspeople walking behind and at the sides, turned down a tree-lined street to the big old house that would be our home for the next two weeks."[177] A residence which sat on the riverbank opposite the Rearview Hotel was turned over to Swanson. With her was her husband the marquis and costume designer Rene Hubert, whom she had brought over from France.

Swanson seated before the camera during production on *Stage Struck* (1925). Dwan, sitting on top of the camera dolly, and members of the film crew seem to be amused listening to her comments.

be bought from a number of the locals. Result: One morning Dwan had no first assistant. Always precise, businesslike, Allan would not stand for this nonsense. He promoted me to first assistant on the spot."[180]

Thousands of people came from surrounding communities and even other states to watch the picture being made. Twelve hundred people arrived in New Martinsville on the riverboat *Vern Swain* that for one day was renamed the *Gloria Swanson*.

Production began on August 18 with the shooting of scenes on the local wharf and on the floating theater, the *Water Queen*. For the shooting of a picnic scene, New Martinsville's Mayor Frank Wells Clark requested businesses to close so that the whole population could swell the numbers Dwan needed for the sequence.

Swanson was puzzled by the behavior of three maids who were brought in to work in her home. The two dining room maids stood gaping as the meals were served by the butler. The upstairs maid was a "howling beauty."[178] The maids appeared in every room listening intently to Swanson and the two men. The Marquis and Hubert took to speaking in French making risqué comments about the very attractive but not very competent maids.

Swanson investigated and learned that the "three maids" were actually society girls who had used their influence to obtain positions to get an intimate view of Swanson. One of them, Eugenia Adams, was the daughter of the president of the Kiwanis club of New Martinsville, a major player in the selection of his town for the film. Adams was also a college graduate who had majored in the language spoken by the two Frenchmen. Swanson discharged them after three days but they were now supplied with plenty of stories for their friends.

The hospitality extended towards Swanson seemed unending. She remembered, "Every hour, it seemed, someone appeared at the front door to present us with a cake or a jar of pickles...."[179] So many curiosity seekers gathered that the approaches to her house had to be roped off.

According to Pasternak, a more serious problem arose. "Prohibition had fallen over the country. Dwan's first assistant and several others in the company discovered that corn likker could

Renita Ashley, one of the bit actresses in the film, observed, "The city was movie mad. The townspeople vied with each other for chances to appear as extras, and so enthusiastic were they and so well did they respond to direction that Mr. Dwan sent half his extra people home after three days. He didn't need them."[181]

There was even more enthusiasm for performing on the *Water Queen* theater which seated eight hundred people. Ashley wrote,

> One night an audience was wanted. There were at least three thousand volunteers. So everybody in the company who knew anything about makeup got busy, and five hundred of the townspeople were made up and used in the scenes. And how they acted! They cheered, they applauded, they were sad, they were gay. When the call came for a panic in the audience they climbed over seats and rushed for windows, as if they had been rehearsed for days. Even the mayor was made up, and Dr. Adams did a comedy scene with one of the actresses representing Little Eva. And they left the boat at midnight, not one having deserted, still cheering for Miss Swanson and Mr. Dwan.[182]

With such a grand spectacle going on in the town, there was little audience left for the local movie theater. Gloria heeded the pleas of the theater manager and agreed to make an appearance there so he could have at least one good night. This was the same evening that Swanson, her husband and Dwan were to have dinner with West Virginia Governor Howard Gore. Swanson kept her promise: After the dinner, she left for the theater with the governor and at the theater they both made speeches. The film shown following the speechifying was *Manhandled.*

Onlookers also got a chance to see how Swanson performed before the camera. In one scene, Swanson's waitress boards the showboat looking for a job. When the manager shouts at her, she loses her footing and goes sliding down a soaped aisle between iron seats. Ashley saw that "she banged into the iron legs of the seats until she was black and blue, lame and sore from head to foot. And she did that slide seven times in one afternoon before Mr. Dwan was satisfied. She was so bruised and lame that her husband and M. Hubert had to carry her up the hill from the boat. But she never whimpered, she never stopped smiling; she never hesitated when Mr. Dwan said, 'Once more.'"[183] The *Water Queen* had its own stock company of hardened actors who watched approvingly as Swanson stoically pursued her craft.

Production apparently went smoothly and by August 27, the local paper, the *Wetzel Democrat,* announced that Swanson and her company were departing for New York. Pasternak said that he was able to help pare three days off their out-of-town shooting schedule. Among the "Gloriagrams" appearing in that issue of the *Wetzel Democrat* was, "It makes no difference how many times one sees Gloria, they always want another look."[184]

After leaving the screen-struck community and returning to Queens, Pasternak said, "Dwan was generous in my behalf, telling everyone how I had taken charge, how I had been able to speed production, and how invaluable I had proved. I expected a bonus."[185] Things seemed promising for the former waiter, who was also enjoying a new romance.

Pasternak was arranging for the company to shoot its final scenes on the studio grounds when he was summoned by the front office. Dwan wished him luck and urged him to ask for a raise as well as a bonus. Pasternak was shocked to learn that he was being abruptly dismissed and told to clear off the lot.

Pasternak rebounded and just four years later produced his first film. However, in his 1956 autobiography, he was still asking, "All I can say, across the years, is that I still don't know and I hope Allan will tell me one day just why I was fired."[186]

Dwan gave his answer in his 1979 interview with Adamson: He said that when he learned of the firing, "I got sore as hell." He found out that Zukor himself had ordered Pasternak's termination. The director then stormed into Zukor's office, saying, "Adolph, I want to talk to you." Zukor came out of a meeting and from Dwan's demeanor looked concerned that there might be some major problem at the studio. Dwan then asked why Pasternak was fired.

Zukor replied, "I had to fire him. He was fucking my girl." Pasternak had stumbled into a relationship with the married executive's mistress! Dwan said, "I couldn't beat that. I begged off."[187]

The scenes shot on the lot were photographed in the two-color Technicolor process. One of these was the dream sequence that opened the film. Paramount's *Wanderer of the Wasteland* from the previous year was the second feature to be shot in Technicolor (the first was the 1922 *Toll of the Sea*). *Stage Struck* was one of a handful of 1925 features (including *The Phantom of the Opera*) that were made largely in black and white with some portion shot in color. The cinematographer was George Webber, who had taken over shooting the Swanson films beginning with *Her Love Story.* Swanson even insisted on bringing him to France to shoot *Madame Sans-Gene.* The sets weren't really suited for color; Dwan claims he had magenta put in front of the lamps to change the colors of the walls and that this strengthened the dream effect.[188]

The film opens with the intertitle, "The greatest actress of all time." There is a close-up of Swanson in color and then a view of throngs cheering from balconies. Another title notes, "No role too difficult — each a triumph adding new luster to a name already glorious." The reference to Gloria herself seems unmistakable especially when a curtain opens and Swanson is seen in long shot in one of her over-the-top costumes, capped with a white headdress.

Subsequent images are increasingly outrageous as we see crowned heads of Europe heaping honors on her. The fantasy comes to a climax in a giant dining hall with a golden floor. Then Swanson steps out into the center of the dining hall, making it her stage. Telling her audience, "You shall forget there is any actress in the world but me!" she transforms herself into Salome and suddenly has jutting-orange hair. She is carrying a tray which a medium shot reveals bears the head of John the Baptist mixed with grapes and other paraphernalia. There is a dissolve to Gloria as a waitress holding a tray with a plate of beans. This shot is also in color but when the plate drops from her tray it dispels her reverie as the film turns to black and white and a voice calls out, "Hey, Jenny, wake up!"

In *Zaza,* Swanson was encased in a story which presented the theater as life. In *Manhandled,* a working class woman drifts from hard-bitten reality into the role-playing games of high society. The problem-solver Dwan was finding ways to incorporate the Swanson image into films while permitting her to deviate from it in her roles.

In *The Coast of Folly,* when a woman designated as "Clothes Horse" at a costume party is asked who she's supposed to be, she replies, "Gloria Swanson." Dwan takes this far beyond in-joke status in *Stage Struck.* The idealized Gloria in this film contains both the excesses of her image carried to an outlandish degree and the perfection Swanson herself pursued ("the greatest actress of all time"). In Dwan's thespian transmigration of souls, the "dream Gloria" is the image that the waitress Jenny Hogan longs to become, and Jenny is the character which Swanson can incarnate to escape her image.

Like *Manhandled, Stage Struck* is grounded in a harsh reality, which in this case contrasts sharply with the opening fantasy.

The equivalent to the subway scene in *Manhandled* here is the early scene where Jenny has to cope with the hurly-burly of lunch hour as an onslaught of working people need to be fed. This gets Swanson enmeshed in all kinds of physical gags.

But there is also a whimsical side to this environment, perched in a realm somewhere between the worlds of Chaplin and Fellini. In the restaurant, Jenny can observe the masterful grace of her boyfriend Orme who flips pancakes and whom Jenny regards as a "genius." (It's a revelation of Jenny's mindset that in her fantasy the great dining hall turns into a theater.) Jenny tries to learn acting through a correspondence course. The realization of her acting ambitions is pursued in the carnival activities around a riverboat, where Jenny exacts a promise that she will be permitted to make a recitation in the ring after participating in a boxing match.

In the publicity material for *Stage Struck* that appeared before it was shot, it was stated that the aspiring actress "comes to New York resolved that she must make great concessions to win stardom, and that her moral code will need revising.... Of course, she finally wins her way, but she reaches her goal on merit. And with the fulfillment of her ambition comes a great love."[189] Again, this has a parallel with a situation in *Manhandled* as described in the intertitle, "So Tessie climbed out of Thorndyke's basement, happy in the thought that she was keeping pace with Jimmy in his struggle to rise in the world." In both instances, Swanson's character can be seen chasing the same upwardly mobile dreams as the male protagonists of the 1920s. In *Manhandled*, her efforts fizzled before the lecherous designs of a male-dominated social world.

In *Stage Struck*, the above scenario was the road not chosen. Instead, Swanson's Jenny was interested in an acting career only because Orme, the object of her affection, loves actresses. But this choice, while imposing some limitations on Swanson's character, was not completely regressive. The classic comic triumvirate of Chaplin, Keaton and Lloyd in their films often aspired to a position or achievement, chiefly as a means of winning the heart of a woman. What distinguishes Swanson in *Stage Struck* is that she is a dreamer with spunk. She fights with as much determination and courage as Charlie, Buster and Harold to do whatever is necessary, to win the one she loves. And she pours herself totally into the bits of physical comedy whether struggling with a tray of dirty dishes or entering a boxing ring.

As the "local girl" disguised with a stocking over her face and given the moniker "Kid Sockem," the petite Swanson must confront the six-foot Gertrude Astor, who is billed as Kid Bellows. The waitress heroine has been given instructions to let her rival knock her out and that then she can take off her mask and do a dramatic recitation. But when Jenny sees Orme in the audience, encouraging Astor, who is also the riverboat's star actress, she takes up the fight in earnest, refusing to go down.

All seems to go wrong for Jenny, including a botched suicide attempt, but in the end she still wins Orme. Their ambitions

Swanson portraying Salome in the waitress' daydream in *Stage Struck* (1925).

are more realistically modest than the inventor's in *Manhandled* and they open their own diner which Dwan lovingly displays in a concluding color sequence. Dwan recalled of his New Martinsville sojourn, "We had a grand time down there,"[190] and he brought back a winningly comic piece of Americana. In her autobiography, Swanson recalled of working on the film, "The script called for broad comedy, which I hadn't played in years."[191] Referring to her work with her co-stars, she declared, "[T]ogether under Allan's direction we achieved moments even Buster Keaton could have been proud of."[192]

But Swanson may have had different feelings about *Stage Struck* when it was ready for release. Her reservations about "broad comedy" from the days of Sennett and her first encounter with Chaplin may have come back to haunt her when she saw the completed film. Shortly after the picture's release, *Variety* carried this story under its column, "Inside Stuff On Pictures":

> Gloria Swanson is said to have proposed to Famous Players that she buy the negative of *Stage Struck* and that they shelve the picture. The star of the film did not like the picture ... adding she felt that it might injure her in the future. Famous is reported to have answered that its pictures are made to exhibit, not to shelve...
>
> Not alone did Miss Swanson not care from reports for the picture when completed but she is said to have been dissatisfied with the way it was made.

> When *Stage Struck* was first shown at the Rivoli, New York, it was a gag among the film men, who knew it had been rushed through in three weeks and looked it. Alan [sic] Dwan, is said to have worked fast to secure a bonus F.P. had offered for quick time and low production cost.[193]

There is no record of Swanson having denied (or confirmed) this story. But there is documentary evidence that Swanson was dissatisfied with the Famous Players policy of awarding Dwan a bonus for completing his films quickly. Swanson had not publicly announced that she had signed with United Artists on July 15 and in late September, Famous Players drafted a proposition for a new contract with their star. The proposal contained provisions obviously intended to satisfy her various complaints, such as cutting down the number of films for her to make per year from four to three. Among the provisions was one that read: "That no bonus or other inducement be offered to any director directing Miss Swanson's pictures to induce him to hasten completion to the detriment of quality."[194]

It's not clear if Swanson had complained specifically about *Stage Struck* since the bonus arrangements may have been in effect from the beginning of Swanson's films with Dwan. Curiously, the following passage appeared in *Photoplay* around the time *Stage Struck* was released:

> Gloria Swanson has gone to Paris for a brief vacation. She finished her work on *Stage Struck* in record time in order to accompany Henry — formerly the Marquis de la Falaise — back to the old home. It seems that Henry's passport had expired and Henry had to go back to get a new one. He didn't want to leave Gloria and Gloria didn't want to be separated from him and so Allan Dwan's company went on a rush schedule in order that Gloria might make the trip. As it was, her sailing was postponed for a week while the picture was being finished.[195]

Swanson as Jennie the waitress in *Stage Struck*, demonstrating her stage acting aspirations to her little dog.

When asked about the *Variety* story in a 1979 interview, Dwan just said jovially that none of his films with Swanson took more than three weeks to shoot.[196]

Variety had used its column story to further assail a film it had already attacked venomously in its review weeks earlier. Drawing on his knowledge of the shooting schedule, Sime Silverman fumed, "The inside of this Allan Dwan–directed comic is said to be that it was made in three weeks, whereby Mr. Dwan drew down a bonus. Just as a matter of opinion, F.P. should have paid Dwan more if it had not been made at all."

In further comments dripping with sarcasm (and using Ford Sterling's Keystone association as fodder), Silverman added, "And what took three weeks to make? Perhaps it needed a week or so to build the Ohio River.... Watching the picture after the second of the six reels, you try to figure out how this ever got past for over two reels. It's one of the old time Keystone models padded out. Ford Sterling has a role in it, and it must have been Ford who recalled the gags...."[197] The rapid-shooting schedule which Dwan had used for all of his films with Swanson may just have provided a convenient excuse for some critics and even Swanson herself to say they disliked the film. And Silverman really didn't need Sterling to make the connection to Keystone since Gloria had worked there herself. This omission may have been intentional as a number of the reviews attacked the film for being unworthy of Swanson's image.

This verdict was submitted by publications ranging from the *New York Times* to *Movie Magazine*. The *Times* decided, "Miss Swanson is active and amusing, but this is hardly a worthy subject for her capabilities. It is a production which undoubtedly will enjoy a certain success in the hinterland, but such might also have been the case if Miss Swanson had chosen to appear in a well-written comedy."[198] *Movie Magazine*, which liked the film better, still concluded, "*Stage Struck* ... is, we think, an unworthy vehicle for Miss Swanson's capabilities."[199] Some of the negative reviews noted that the film played well with audiences, as if it were their task not to let Swanson be swayed down the wrong path by popular appeal.

The reviews were highly polarized, mostly along the "slapstick" issue. Epes W. Sargent of *Moving Picture World* put matters in perspective when he observed,

> When you start to take stock of the things to be thankful for next Thursday, add *Stage Struck* to the list. It is not Gloria at her best, perhaps, but it is Gloria at her most profitable. When you see Gloria as the "Masked Mystery"

> spar a round with the vampish leading woman of the floating theater you will forget her high-hatting in *Sans-Gene* and *The Coast of Folly* and welcome the return of the screen's cleverest woman comic."
>
> This is not in disparagement of Miss Swanson's more ambitious work. She has her moments of real dramatic fire in her dramatic roles and you can't blame her for wanting to exhibit that talent, but when she stoops to the cap and bells she is genuinely funny in her own right and by the grace of the gag men. There are many clever dramatic players who cannot do comedy. Miss Swanson is at her entertaining best in plays such as this and *Manhandled*.[200]

Even more enthusiastic about the direction Swanson had taken, *Photoplay* exulted, "This makes Gloria Charlie Chaplin's nearest rival. Charlie got himself called a genius and taken very seriously when he mastered the trick of pathos behind the gag. In *Stage Struck* Gloria has learned the same lesson. If Charlie is a genius, this picture makes Gloria a genius too. And besides, Gloria also has beauty and IT."[201]

It is likely that gender prejudice played a role in the way *Stage Struck* was belittled as slapstick while male actors doing physical comedy got the kudos. Though *Stage Struck* was not in the same class as *The Gold Rush* or *Safety Last*, it was still a very creditable rival. (Just six years later, Chaplin also used a comic boxing match as a high point in *City Lights* but *Variety* and other publications would not take him to task for appropriating a device that Keystone had pioneered almost twenty years earlier.)

A stronger factor for the negative reaction was the shadow of the Swanson image even as Dwan had used Pirandellian stratagems to keep it at bay and tease its grandiose ambitions. *Stage Struck* was inevitably seen in context with *Sans-Gene* and *The Coast of Folly*. While descriptions suggest these were more middlebrow efforts rather than high art, *Stage Struck* was perceived as having lowered the standards which Swanson had recently set.

Stage Struck did well enough commercially to make the *Motion Picture News* Box-Office Honor Roll for 1925, the only Swanson film of the year to do so. (It earned $624,000 in domestic sales and was budgeted at $428,000.) It was also the last Swanson film on Dwan's contract. Dwan and Swanson would make no more films together at Famous Players–Paramount.

Swanson recalled that before she left for Paris at the close of shooting for *Stage Struck*, she invited Dwan to dinner at her new $100,000 penthouse in New York. As her husband poured the wine, Dwan told her that Lasky had asked him to recommend someone to direct her next picture.

Swanson wanted to know if assigning a new director to her was a punishment as it was now known that she had signed with United Artists. She said that Dwan remained silent for a moment, then said, "I'm going to suggest Frank Tuttle."[202]

Dwan told interviewer Adamson that Swanson "liked to be bossed."[203] As several examples below indicate, this was certainly not true when she returned from France in 1925. In her autobiography, Swanson suggests that Tuttle was too much of a novice to be an effective director and that she had to go "over his head ten times a day. I redirected scenes ... made changes in the script and consulted with all the technicians."[204]

Ironically, the film they were working on, *Untamed Lady*, based on a novel by Fannie Hurst, was a modern-day version of *The Taming of the Shrew*.

While limited in experience, Tuttle had actually been directing films even before he worked on the script for *Manhandled* and had made ten movies before *Untamed Lady*. In Tuttle's autobiography, written before Swanson's but published after, he said that before *Manhandled* was released, "Gloria made a point of declaring, in front of Paramount's bigwigs, that if I started directing again she would be happy to work with me."[205] In his book, Tuttle is discreetly silent about directing Swanson.

Of the final film on her Paramount contract, *Fine Manners*, Swanson wrote, "Richard Rosson turned out to be a delightful surprise. Since he had learned his directing from Allan, he was a superb technician."[206]

Actually, Tuttle had again been assigned to direct Swanson. But he soon dropped out because of "influenza." He was replaced by Lewis Milestone, the future director of *All Quiet on the Western Front*. According to trade reports, he too became ill and had to leave. It was then that Richard Rosson became the director but he also became another "sick-room candidate." According to *Variety*, Swanson herself was now directing the film.[207]

The epidemic appeared to continue when it was reported that Swanson was stricken with an attack of the grippe.[208] But *Photoplay* said later, "Gloria has recovered from her nervous breakdown and gone back to work ... on her new comedy *Fine Manners*."[209]

Illness, of course, was a frequent euphemism used to disguise a director quitting or being fired so *Photoplay* probably more honestly reported that "after the Marquise Gloria had tired out two directors on *Fine Manners*, Rosson was called."[210] Rosson got the directorial credit for the film. (Given that he was the assistant director fired by Dwan for doing Swanson's bidding, he was probably pliable enough to take the job.) And no one would get a bonus for wrapping this film quickly. The production of *Fine Manners* took four months.[211]

Swanson was undoubtedly eager to take the producing reins of her films at United Artists. Her work with Dwan at Paramount was perhaps best commemorated at that dinner before her departure for France. As she remembered it:

> "At least we got to do *Stage Struck*," Allan said after another pause.
>
> "And *Zaza* and *Manhandled*," I said.
>
> "That's right," said Allan raising his wineglass. "We did a lot for Paramount from Manhattan to New Martinsville, in black-and-white and color. Let's drink to us, Gloria."[212]

Farewells and Flourishes

With the end of his working relationship with Swanson, the recent stability of Dwan's career began to unravel. Various forces were at work that would first cause him to leave the studio he had operated at since 1922 and then to quit his cherished eastern home base. In the next few years, the silent film medium itself would begin to vanish.

While Famous Players had continued to weaken First National by siphoning off theaters, the prospect of monopoly was no longer in its grasp. After various merger rumors, in April 1924 Metro-Goldwyn-Mayer was formed. Like a long-awaited cataclysm that would change the landscape forever, a powerful rival had emerged in MGM, pioneering management techniques that other companies soon sought to emulate. Further competition was provided by the surging Fox Film Corporation.

Almost as soon as he completed the editing of *Stage Struck*, Dwan was assigned the adventure yarn *Sea Horses*. On the West Coast, production began in November 1925.

Sea Horses (the title refers to a dangerous reef off the harbor of Panda in Portuguese East Africa) was ready for release in March 1926. A number of the critics complained that the pace was too slow but that it was saved by a rousing finale which featured a ship caught in a typhoon. The cast included Jack Holt as the ship captain, Florence Vidor and William Powell but the reviewers gave top acting honors to George Bancroft in a supporting role. An unconvincing studio set and use of miniatures led Wid's to suspect that Dwan "was held down on production costs."[213]

Dwan remembered little about *Sea Horses* beyond the typhoon and that his star Holt had too much to drink one night and swallowed a bridge of about four teeth. There was concern that Dwan's nautical production might have to be halted for surgery to extract the bridge, but it finally sailed out of Holt's system.[214]

The *Variety* review noticed something new about the film: "As an item of interest to the trade, B.P. Schulberg and Hector Turnbull are listed as associate producers at the 'West Coast Studio,' a phrase which hasn't previously appeared on the F-P titles."[215]

In discussing his years at Famous Players, Schulberg's is the name that stuck most in Dwan's craw. After an absence of seven years, Schulberg was called back to Famous Players by Zukor in the fall of 1925, shortly before Dwan started work on *Sea Horses*. Schulberg had left Famous Players with Hiram Abrams to help organize the nascent United Artists, which then thwarted Zukor's plans to control star salaries. Again, Zukor maintained he didn't believe in grudges. He was more concerned about the competition from MGM and was seeking a strong executive in the mold of that studio's Irving J. Thalberg. Zukor considered his partner Lasky "a wonderful man, but he's almost too nice. He would never hurt anybody. He's a gentleman. But as a result, I feel some of the people in our studio are taking advantage of him. We've got a lot of pigheaded stars and directors in the studio who think they can run everything to suit themselves."[216] Zukor assured Schulberg that Lasky supported his return and would not interfere with his efforts to impose more discipline.

Within a month after Schulberg's signing, Lasky announced that as part of a new reorganization plan, Schulberg and Turnbull would become production heads of the Lasky studio in Hollywood while William Le Baron would be in charge of Long Island production. Walter Wanger remained as general manager of production.

Florence Vidor looks appalled at how dissolute her husband (William Powell) has become in *Sea Horses* (1926). Star Jack Holt can be seen strutting down the stairs at right (courtesy Bruce Calvert).

Schulberg's ascension in Hollywood likely only intensified the competition between West Coast and East Coast production. Referring to that rivalry, Dwan recalled, "People in Paramount [west] hated our guts. There was disagreeable enmity between us and the West. Schulberg was the one I objected to most...."[217] The British writer-director Ivor Montagu described Schulberg as a "strongly relaxed man, who resembled an amiable efficient crocodile smoking a cigar."[218]

Schulberg soon made his own plans for Dwan. Famous Players had purchased Rex Beach's story *Padlocked* (then being serialized in *Hearst's Cosmopolitan Magazine*) for a reported $90,000. In January 1926, Schulberg announced that *Padlocked* would be directed by Dwan. It was indeed a vote of confidence that Schulberg named him to helm such a valuable property. But although the story of *Padlocked* was set in New York and the surrounding area, Dwan was to film it in Hollywood under Schulberg's watchful eye. It is highly doubtful that this would have been Dwan's choice of locale.

For *Padlocked*, Beach departed from the male action ethos for a story involving morals and the generation gap. The plot concerned an overzealous reformer whose bigotry is injurious to his daughter and helps destroy his wife. His moral blindness also leads him into a second unhappy marriage.

Dwan had made films before about the destructive effects of Puritanism but this theme had a new meaning in the emerging culture of the Jazz Age. Dwan noted that in the original story, the seventeen-year-old Edith Gilbert, the reformer's free-spirited daughter, was a talented singer but to make it more apropos for a silent film, this was changed to a cabaret dancer.[219] He could have added that popular dance, especially the dances fashionable in the twenties, was more of a bellwether of moral conflict between the generations.

Lois Moran, who had been lauded for her performance as the daughter in the recent *Stella Dallas*, was selected to play Edith. She was approaching her seventeenth birthday and had studied dance in Paris. The choreography was done by Ernst Belcher, known as "the Dance Master of the Movies." He provided Moran with two original dances that were variations of the popular Charleston.

Moran and Dwan got along quite well. Moran later wrote of Dwan in her journal, "He is young, short and more round than stocky with a brusque, shy manner. He is sentimental but ridicules sentiment[.] Talks little but excellently when he does and above all, knows his business." Regarding his working methods, she observed, "He sketches the scene roughly — then lets the actor give his interpretation of it — then corrects, changes, or leaves intact the result according to how satisfactory it is[.] He will accept nothing but the very best from both the actors and his assistants — and they all either adore him or fear him — I do the former."[220]

Moran and Dwan maintained their friendship after the filming was over. They worked together again just before Moran began her association with a man who was one of the iconic figures of the decade and a literary giant.

Also in the cast of *Padlocked* was Noah Beery (Wallace's brother) as the reformer and, in two small roles, future stars Richard Arlen and Douglas Fairbanks, Jr.

The reviews for *Padlocked* were mixed. *Photoplay* raved, "To every critic of the movies, to every person who claims the cinema knows neither art nor intelligence, we recommend *Padlocked* as a cure."[221] But the reviews were more typically equivocal or disapproving. The *New York Post* groused, "*Padlocked* is only moderately entertaining, and its big moral lesson is a trifle stale."[222]

Padlocked may have also had its visual beauties. Epes Sargent in *Moving Picture World* marveled that in the corridor of a reformatory was "a scene that has the composition and lighting of a painting. The society and cabaret settings are sumptuously done, but that corridor is an art gem. It is the sort of thing that a certain type of commentator regrets that American directors are unable to achieve. Mr. Dwan seems to have done it."[223] Dwan may have had some valuable assistance in that scene since this was one of the early works of the great cinematographer James Wong Howe.

While Lasky gave Schulberg a free hand, Schulberg departed from Lasky's management style. Lasky believed in minimal interference with talent and he saw the film director as "supervising architect of every phase of production, from writing to cutting, rather than have him serve merely as foreman on the

Lois Moran, who would become a muse to F. Scott Fitzgerald, as the young dancer in *Padlocked* (1926).

rough construction job."[224] Schulberg was dismayed to find that Famous Players had "lost control over the producing units of the studio. Every such unit — the Cecil B. DeMille unit, the Raoul Walsh unit, the James Cruze unit, the Allan Dwan unit — ran itself as though it were a completely independent business. Combinations of stars and directors would dictate to the company what they would or would not do, how a picture would be fashioned, how it would be cut, how much it would cost."[225]

Dwan exercised even more autonomy, ensconced on the East Coast where according to Louise Brooks, "the writers, directors and cast were free from all supervision."[226] But the director had compiled a strong commercial track record. He had also made his films quickly and economically. To Dwan, no doubt, his independence was part of a bargain that he had faithfully kept. To Schulberg, that was beside the point. Schulberg saw his mission as operating a factory churning out fifty-five to sixty films a year. In the words of his assistant and future producer David O. Selznick, "[H]e was a remarkably efficient man and he ran his factory well."[227] Dwan felt he did not need anyone to teach him efficiency. As for serving in a factory, while Dwan was methodical in his planning, he said of his films at Famous, "We never made a picture that wasn't fun."[228]

The sense of competition between East and West Coast production yielded benefits that were undoubtedly visible to the management at Famous Players, especially as each provided different atmospheres for their films. But with Schulberg's placement in Hollywood, that competition began to reflect a rivalry between Schulberg and Wanger, the general manager of production, who favored New York.

In early 1926, plans were announced for a major expansion of the Famous Players production facilities in Hollywood. They would be ready for operation by the fall. To any keen observer of studio operations, this could have been a tipoff that the Long Island studio would become expendable. In late May, a little over three weeks after construction began on the new facilities and while he was still at work on his next film, Dwan signed a contract with the Fox Film Corporation.

Filming started on May 8 on Dwan's production *Tin Gods*, his last at the Astoria Studio. Among the scriptwriters adapting the William Anthony McGuire play was Paul Dickey who had played Gisbourne in Dwan's *Robin Hood*. The star was the very popular Thomas Meighan.

The plot concerned an engineer, Roger Drake (Meighan), whose wealthy wife (Aileen Pringle) pursues a political career. Because their nurse is distracted while the wife is making a speech on the radio, the couple's young boy falls out a window to his death. The demoralized husband leaves his wife and accepts a commission to build a bridge in South America. But once there, Drake neglects work in favor of drowning his troubles with liquor. When he grows ill, a dance hall girl Carita (Renée Adorée) nurses him back to health and falls in love with him. Drake's wife seeks him out, having lost her election because of their estrangement. The engineer tells her that she can at last give him a chance at real happiness. Carita, hearing only that part of his speech and not the portion where he says that happiness can come from giving him his freedom, jumps to her death off the bridge the engineer had constructed.

There may have been some personal touches in the film aside from the fact that the protagonist was an engineer. Hall in the *New York Times* noted that that Meighan's character had a "habit of keeping a check rein constantly on his emotions" and in the wake of two major tragedies, suggesting that he was "a strangely unemotional person."[229] Dwan was known for his emotional restraint both in his personality and in his work. The death of the child which puts Drake on the skids also recalls the "lost father" of Dwan's earlier films, though the device was less used in his Swanson films.[230] There was also a horrible symmetry to the way both of the beloved figures in Drake's life fall to their deaths.

The reviews for *Tin Gods* were mixed, though there was strong praise for Adorée's performance as Carita. The critics were disturbed that the romance had such a tragic and seemingly uncommercial finale. Some reviewers, like Sargent of *Moving Picture World*, felt the picture was strengthened by the unhappy ending.[231]

There were also complaints that the bridge used on a studio set looked unconvincing. Both *Padlocked* and *Tin Gods* appeared

Thomas Meighan appreciates consolation from Renée Adorée in *Tin Gods* (1926), Dwan's last film for Paramount, shot at the Astoria studios.

to have done respectable though not electrifying business at the box office.

In early March 1927, Wanger lost his battle to continue feature film production in New York. The closing of the Astoria studio for feature production (shorts would continue to be made there) was a vote of confidence for Schulberg's efficient cost-cutting methods. Ironically, the East Coast studio had reached its high of 40 percent of Paramount's output, including 26 features, in its last full year of production.

Dwan never again worked for Paramount, the studio at which he had first toiled in its struggling days in 1914 and which he had steadied with the Swanson hits of the 1920s. Dwan said that during the sound era he tried to purchase the rights to *Manhandled* but the company refused. Paramount never did remake the film but they used the title for a 1949 *film noir* starring Dorothy Lamour and Dan Duryea.

When Fox signed Dwan, they were said to be looking for directors of the "highest standing" and they would soon put together an impressive roster of "megaphoners."[232] (Dwan's friend Raoul Walsh had preceded him in leaving Paramount for Fox.) Given the new mood at Paramount emphasizing supervision, Dwan was understandably attracted to a studio that valued the status of the director.

The initial report on Dwan's signing said that he was expected to work in Hollywood, since Fox was no longer using its New York studio.[233] But on June 2, just a week after Dwan joined the company, Fox announced that it was reopening its Manhattan studio at 850 Tenth Avenue.[234]

Earlier in this chapter, it was chronicled how Dwan's claims that the Astoria Studio was reopened on his recommendation did not hold up under scrutiny. Could Dwan have confused the two studios in his recollections, and it was Fox that reopened its New York production center at his suggestion?

The salary terms appear to have been generous. A confidential memo prepared for Universal president Carl Laemmle in November 1926 listed most of the top directors in the industry and what they were earning. According to this memo, Dwan was making $50,000 per picture. Only three other directors on the list (James Cruze, George Fitzmaurice and Henry King) were making as much and just two (Lubitsch and von Stroheim) were earning more.[235]

In late July, the first Fox film begun at its New York studio in twenty-four months was Dwan's *Summer Bachelors*. As with his films at Paramount, Dwan used the eastern studio as a base: After completing interior scenes, he moved his company to Southampton and Newport to shoot the other locales of the story. The cast included Madge Bellamy, Allan Forrest, Matt Moore, Charles Winninger and Walter Catlett.

Bellamy, who often projected the image of "beautiful but dumb" in her comedies, also had a reputation of being difficult to direct. Bellamy recalled Dwan using sarcasm to get the best out of her. "He would say, for instance, 'To the left, you see your love approaching. You fear that he doesn't love you any more. He comes up and kisses you tenderly. You burst into tears of happiness and relief— if you can manage it.'"[236]

Summer Bachelors is about a group of husbands who seek other diversions when their wives leave them for vacation. Bellamy plays a young woman who enjoys being around them because she doesn't want to get married. As one reviewer noted, "This idea has its risqué possibilities but most of them have disappeared in the cutting room."[237] Bellamy falls for one young man whom she believes to be married to but isn't. A bizarre contrivance has her put into a trance by a self-hypnotizing crystal and in her hypnotic state, she marries this man she loves. She only learns the truth later. The critics recognized it as frothy and undemanding entertainment, praising Bellamy and her fellow actors. When it was released in December 1926, the *New York Times* noted that "it succeeds, at least temporarily, in dispelling thoughts of the frosty weather."[238]

Summer Bachelors had been heavily promoted by Fox and fared satisfactorily at the box office. Dwan was next assigned to a project that was designated by Fox as one of its five giant specials of the season, an adaptation of an old warhorse of the stage, *The Music Master*. Like *Zaza*, the play had been produced by David Belasco and was introduced on Broadway in 1904. David Warfield, who had played the title role in the first and in subsequent productions, turned down a reported salary of $5,000 a day to appear in the film version. Veteran actor Alec B. Francis was then enlisted to play the elderly music teacher.

The project had been earlier assigned to Victor Schertzinger but was turned over to Dwan shortly after he joined Fox. Lois Moran was signed to play the female lead and according to her biographer, Richard Buller, was assured that her friend Dwan would helm the production.[239] Neil Hamilton was loaned by Famous Players to Fox for the romantic male lead. Dwan cast eighteen-year-old Helen Chandler in her first film; other supporting players included Walter Catlett and tennis great William T. Tilden.

Great care was taken with the production, which began shooting at Fox's New York studio on November 1, 1926. *The Music Master* was adapted for the screen by Philip Klein, son of the play's author Charles Klein, who had died in the sinking of the *Lusitania*. George Webber, Dwan's cinematographer on the later Swanson films, was brought back to shoot the picture. By early December, interior scenes were completed at the studio, and Dwan then had exterior shots taken in Philadelphia.

In the story, Francis' character Anton von Barwig is a symphony conductor in Vienna. His wife, feeling neglected, runs off with another man, taking with them her little daughter. In a search for his loved ones that takes years, von Barwig comes to New York City and works as a humble music teacher and pianist in a medicine show. He recognizes one of his students (Moran) as his daughter but since she is in line to marry a man of social standing, he is urged by her adoptive father not to reveal her secret. However, the Music Master will be rewarded for his sacrifice.

For Moran, this part had similarities to her role in *Stella Dallas*. For Dwan, it was another opportunity to explore the drama of the "lost father." Critics appreciated the performances of Francis and Moran and the faithfulness to the play even if some missed Warfield's voice. *Variety* called it a "beautifully done sentimental story, set in exquisite taste, acted with admirable restraint, and containing honest heart throb.... The picture is done with amazingly few titles, best evidence that the director's hand was sure...."[240] Overall, *The Music Master* earned Dwan his best reviews since the Swanson films.

Around the time that *The Music Master* was released in early 1927, Moran met novelist F. Scott Fitzgerald during his first trip to Hollywood. This began a long relationship between Moran and Fitzgerald. Much to the consternation of his wife Zelda, Moran also became something of a muse to Fitzgerald.

Fitzgerald had worked with Dwan doing intertitles for his Edith Wharton adaptation *The Glimpses of the Moon*. As with most of Fitzgerald's writing in Hollywood, his contributions did not appear in the finished film. Dwan's association with Fitzgerald, however, did find its way into his fiction. According to Fitzgerald's notes, a party given by Dwan in Long Island was the model for one of the grand parties depicted in his classic novel *The Great Gatsby*.[241]

Fitzgerald's fascination with Moran may have also brought him again to use Dwan as an inspiration. The actress in Fitzgerald's short story "Jacob's Ladder," published in the *Saturday Evening Post* in August 1927, is generally considered to have been based on Moran. The film director in the story, the Irish-American Billy Farrelly, who has a studio in Long Island, is also considered by Buller to be based most strongly on Dwan as well as other directors for whom Moran performed. Fitzgerald used this story as a basis for his novel *Tender Is the Night*; Moran acknowledged in an interview in the 1950s that she was the model for the character Rosemary. The film director in the novel has been said by scholars to resemble most closely Rex Ingram but Buller believes that he may have also been based on Dwan and Herbert C. Brenon, both of whom were friends of Moran.[242]

Veteran actor Alec B. Francis played the title role in Dwan's *The Music Master* (1927).

In a trade ad appearing in September 1926,[243] Fox included photos of an impressive roster of directors in its employ including Dwan, Raoul Walsh, John Ford, F.W. Murnau, Harry Beaumont, Frank Borzage, Howard Hawks and John Griffith Wray. But one of Dwan's most impressive contributions to Fox appears to have been made anonymously. This involved the development of the sound film.

The roots of this experiment go back to Dwan's tenure at Paramount. In his interview with Bogdanovich, Dwan described how for a show at the Lambs' Club known as the Lambs' Gambol, Dwan used Lee De Forest's sound laboratory to make a short film. Actor Thomas Meighan, who had become "shepherd" of the Lambs Club, tried to suspend the rule that barred women from membership or performing at any of the gambols. In the face of intense opposition from members, Meighan was forced to retreat. Dwan's impish solution was to shoot a sound film skit featuring Meighan and Swanson, with the latter singing and crashing the "No Women Allowed" club.[244] The film showing was cited by *Variety* in its April 29, 1925, issue covering the event.

This was just a stunt but in the same discussion, Dwan also recalled making a Fox sound newsreel at West Point that "set them all on their heels."[245] Such a film was indeed made.

Fox and Warner Brothers were the two film companies working to develop a viable synchronized sound system for their pictures while the other corporations had taken a wait-and-see approach. Fox bought the rights to a sound-on-film system developed by Theodore Case while Warners' was using the Vitaphone system which required the use of disks. Fox would call his system Movietone. Without disks, Movietone needed less equipment and was more mobile.

In 1926, Warners had released a Vitaphone feature, *Don Juan*, with a music track and sound effects. In that same year, there were numerous Vitaphone shorts in which vaudeville acts could be seen *and heard* performing onstage. Fox also released sound shorts made earlier as tests that included vaudevillian Chic Sale doing monologues and soprano Raquel Meller singing.

But in late April 1927, critics and audiences saw onscreen something that they had never seen and heard before. Under the heading of "New Vistas," a report in *Film Daily* prognosticated, "Broadway is slated for a thrill. Movietone has filmed a review of West Point cadets. It is astonishing."[246] On Friday, April 29, this newsreel was previewed at the Roxy Theater in New York. The full title was *The Military Academy at West Point*. A trade report noted,

> For the first time in screen history, a news event has had its sound recorded simultaneously with the photographing of its action — a review of West Point cadets photographed by Fox News and Movietone...
>
> The subject opens with a bugler sounding a call — a West Point officer speaks a brief introduction, and we go into a snappy musical of arms, executed with typical West Point precision. We hear the commanding officer bark his command — the slap of hand against rifle as they are carried out. A military band plays in the background — the strains of a march burst forth — the cadets march before it, and for a moment the volume dies down as the West Pointers blanket the sound — they pass and it pours from the loud speakers again. A band, near the horizon, its members mere specks, marches straight towards us — faintly we hear the strains of the official West Point march — on it marches straight into the camera, the music growing in volume with every step — until the band stops before us and the music booms forth from the screen.[247]

Sid Silverman in *Variety* noted that the significance of the sound in this footage jolted even the Fox personnel, adding, "The entire Fox unit believes in it and the newsreel unit was gnashing its teeth because it didn't have a machine to catch the blowing of the levees to save New Orleans. Its outdoor possibilities are limitless...."[248]

It was, according to *Film Daily*, "the first talking picture taken out of doors" and it caused a "sensation among the trade and newspaper representatives present."[249]

Dwan's name was never mentioned and it's unlikely that even if a print of this newsreel should ever turn up, his name would appear on-screen. Dwan may have exaggerated, misremembered or even invented stories but he was not likely to have taken credit for a film in which he was not involved. The film was long forgotten by the time he mentioned it to Bogdanovich and there surely was a reason that he recalled it. It's also logical that Dwan would have been involved in making the film since he was one of the few directors who had made a sound film and was in New York under contract at the time. Most notably, Dwan loved taking his crew away from the studio and on location. Also, as with tracking shots and Technicolor cinematography, Dwan was fascinated by new technologies.

But the *West Point* film was made by no mere technician. Rather than being concerned with the perfection and stability of the sound which would render the scene static, the newsreel was made by someone who had an understanding of the dramatic value of changing the levels of the sound to accompany the images. Audiences had never experienced anything like that.

There was "an unexpected reaction" to this film: "Fox's vice president and general manager, Winfield R. Sheehan, was inspired by the enthusiastic response and immediately began exploring the possibilities of talking newsreels."[250] Dwan returned to making silent features.

The West Point newsreel was apparently made after Dwan had completed another feature film following *The Music Master,* which would not be released until September. That movie was *The Joy Girl,* another Cinderella comedy. In January, production was delayed while the star Olive Borden finished a Fox film on the West Coast and leading man Neil Hamilton recovered from an illness. But the most famous casting story for *The Joy Girl* was about a supporting player.

Dwan told Bogdanovich that as he was preparing to cast *The Joy Girl,* he was having lunch with his studio manager at the Ritz Hotel when he spotted actress Marie Dressler sitting alone at a table. Dwan said he sent her a note to the effect that he was a film director and admirer of her work and would like to cast in her in a film he was about to start shooting. Dwan was then told by the bellboy that Dressler would like to see him in her room.

When they met, Dressler asked him if he meant what he said in the note. When Dwan responded affirmatively, he said Dressler told him, "Well, you've saved my life, son.... I just had my last meal downstairs and I was going to go out that window, I'd reached the end of my strength. The world was through with me and I was through with the world. But this looks like new hope."[251]

Dwan said that he not only cast her in *The Joy Girl* but provided her with letters of introduction, got her a good agent and paid for her way to Hollywood. She was soon hired by MGM where she reached the pinnacle of her fame. Dwan said, "But she never forgot — every time she was interviewed, she always told them I was responsible for her career in pictures. I wasn't — it was just that *moment.*"[252] (Prior to Dwan's offer, Dressler had not been in a film since 1918.)

Dressler's biographer Betty Lee has cast doubt on Dwan's version of the story and notes that Dressler gave a different account: "I got a telephone call from Allan Dwan, one of Hollywood's topnotch directors. He wanted me to play a small part in an Olive Borden picture he planned to screen in Florida. I was not at all keen about it.

'Most important offer of my life!' I scoffed. 'Why, it's just a bit, I'll be lost in the shuffle.'" But on advice from her friend Nella Webb, Dressler took the part.[253]

Lee cites five witnesses to Dressler's version of the story. Also, on the date Dressler said she received Dwan's phone call, January 17, Dressler was no longer living in the Ritz but sharing an apartment with her friend Webb. Lee also found "irrefutable evidence" that Dwan's story of paying Dressler's way to California and providing her with letters of recommendation and "taking care of her" to be "seriously flawed."[254] It might be added that Dwan's narrative, where Dressler tells him that she was just about to commit suicide when she received his message, also sounds like a bit of the blarney.

But the important thing, as Lee conceded, was that Dwan did "open the doors to the future for Dressler and certainly on that historic January 17, as Nella had confidently predicted."[255] After learning of Dressler's situation, her friend Frances Marion, now a highly successful screenwriter, was able to convince Irving Thalberg to give her a role in *The Callahans and Murphys.*

And this began Dressler's career at MGM, leading to an Oscar for the 1932 *Emma*.

When Dwan had his *Joy Girl* cast ready, he assembled them at Penn Station on February 5 for a trip to Florida on a train designated as the *Joy Girl* Special. Dwan had set a schedule for ten days of shooting exteriors in Palm Beach. Production then continued in New York and wrapped in March.

The Joy Girl, like *Stage Struck*, also had sequences shot in Technicolor, both at the beginning and end. The color preface was said to have "depicted the luxurious existence at Palm Beach."[256] A print of *The Joy Girl*, albeit with Czech intertitles, survives at New York's Museum of Modern Art but without color sequences.

In the plot, Borden's Jewel Courage is a designing young woman who tries to pass herself off as part of the wealthy set in Palm Beach to snare a rich husband. The man who gets her interest is actually a chauffeur to a millionaire and is posing as his employer. When his boss John Jeffrey Fleet (Neil Hamilton) discovers this, he decides to continue the masquerade and act as if he is the chauffeur to see if he can win the girl without his millions. Jewel and the actual chauffeur find out too late that neither of them is what they pretended to be to the other but their marriage is annulled because of the chauffeur's previous marriage. Jewel goes into business and, proving successful, she realizes that she really was in love with the "chauffeur," whom she is happy to learn is the real millionaire.

A number of critics did not find the heroine particularly sympathetic. One of the images that stands out in the movie comes when Jewel and the chauffeur learn the truth about each other, and some loose change is tossed on a bed. A shot of the coins on the bed conveys the sense that for all her pretensions, Jewel has been dealing in low-scale prostitution. There is also some pathos in watching Dressler's wealthy widow striving for the attentions of a young man on the make. *Variety* complained that Dressler didn't indulge in "surefire low comedy" and "doesn't do any mugging"[257] but Dressler's straight playing was right on the mark. Under the veneer of a Cinderella story, *The Joy Girl* did have some brittle edges. The film fared well at the box office.

There is some reason to believe that Dwan took more of a personal interest in his next film, *East Side, West Side*, based on a novel by Felix Riesenberg. Dwan wrote the adaptation for the film, which was a melting pot story set in New York City.

The plot involved the linking of a young man of Irish extraction with a Jewish family. A number of movies had already exploited the relationship of Irish and Jews, as well as the very popular play *Abie's Irish Rose*. Though such plotting was usually done for comedy, this was becoming a time of ethnic sensitivity, especially as New York's Governor Al Smith, an Irish-American and a Catholic, already seemed in line for the Democratic presidential nomination for 1928.

East Side, West Side was scheduled to use as locations the Bowery, Fifth Avenue, Harlem, Morningside and Washington Heights. According to one blurb, apparently put out by the studio after filming began, "Al Smith's birthplace will be seen in *East Side, West Side*. It was by chance that a Fox cameraman got a shot of the governor's first home. They were shooting exteriors near the Brooklyn Bridge, when informed that Al's initial house was within range of the cameras."[258]

Within the Fox studio, one set representing a ghetto street was "one of the largest sets built in a studio. It was designed and built by Sam Corso."[259] Dwan used Jewish residents from the East Side as extras for the studio scene. According to one report, Dwan's instructions had to be repeated in Yiddish to be understood.[260]

At the time, it appeared that Dwan could continue working in this fashion. Fox announced in March that in the 1927–28 season, twelve films would be made at studios in New York "which will be directed by Allan Dwan among

Neil Hamilton surveys the plush Palm Beach setting in *The Joy Girl* (1927).

others."[261] But in June, while *East Side, West Side* was being shot, there was an announcement that Fox had in the last year spent more than three million dollars in improving its West Coast studios, including the erection of three stages "large enough to house a regulation baseball field."[262] Again, the expansion of the Hollywood studios would make the New York facilities less valuable.

Dwan probably did not then know that *East Side, West Side* would be his last feature film made in New York City. But quite appropriately, in this film he would make the city as much a star as his individual characters. It opens with an establishing long shot panning the city skyline and the Brooklyn Bridge. A young man on an old barge eyes the skyline. John Breen asks his mother why he can't get a job in the city. He is tired of hauling bricks for others to build. Dwan catches the mood of those at the edges and lower rungs of society who seem shut out from its main activities and can look at them only from afar. John is in fact tied to his family on the barge though it is not exactly *his* family since, ever the voyeur, he peeks in the cabin window and hears his "parents" talking about his real father, who lives in the city.

The young man is played by George O'Brien, who had established himself as an action star in films like John Ford's 1924 *The Iron Horse*. O'Brien recalled, "One of the greatest experiences I ever had was coming back [to New York] and doing *East Side, West Side*, with a man who did have that kind of reputation, not for swearing at you, but for being rather brittle and sarcastic, Allan Dwan. The first morning I came in 15 minutes early: He came in and I said, 'Allan, how are you?' and he said 'George, I'm delighted.' And we hit it right off. I listened and paid attention, because I saw this man had it."[263]

At the time, O'Brien had just completed *Sunrise*, which explored a wholly different side of his personality. The classic *Sunrise*, directed by F.W. Murnau with its dichotomy of city and country life, captured some of the ambivalent feelings of the period about emerging modern cities, as would King Vidor's celebrated *The Crowd* which was being shot in New York about the same time as *East Side, West Side*. Given what seems John Breen's trapped adolescence aboard the barge, the city in Dwan's film appears to represent life itself, at least the part of it which provides a passage to adulthood. It is also the materialization of dream images.

John is literally thrown into city life, like a savage act of rebirth, when the barge collides with another craft and sinks. John loses his mother and foster father. In what seems like a caricature of urban life, as soon as John finds himself in the city, he is pursued by a gang of toughs. He finds refuge with a Jewish family, the Lipvitches, who "adopt" him.

When John shows real pugnacity in handling the neighborhood ruffians (which Dwan highlights with an overhead shot), he considers a career as a boxer. As John works out at the Samson Club, wealthy visitor Gilbert Van Horn (Holmes Herbert) asks how he got what then seemed the unlikely name of "Fighting Lipvitch." (O'Brien, a former boxer, had already played pugilists in at least two other features.) In the film's most spectacular contrivance, Van Horn realizes from the story that John is his son. (Van Horn had been a junior in college when he married the Irish maid. His parents had the marriage annulled. His former wife bore a son and kept him when she remarried.)

We are back in the realm of Dwan's lost-father figures. Our protagonist, half working class Irish and half patrician Dutch, lives with a Jewish family and does not know his real father. It is possible that the confusion surrounding his ethnic identity was intended to reflect the emerging citizens from the city, a mixture of relative newcomers also trying to assimilate with the country's older ethnic groups.

Van Horn takes an interest in John without revealing his true relationship to him. When Van Horn asks John what he would do if he found his real father, John replies, "I'd kill him," sounding much like Passin' Through in *The Good Bad Man*. The repetition of this device suggests a Freudian concern with patricide though Dwan makes little more of it here, save to keep Van Horn's parentage concealed. Van Horn emerges as an ideal father to John by keeping his paternity secret.

Later, from a high rise building, John and Van Horn watch the ticker tape parade for Charles Lindbergh. John confides to Van Horn that he'd give his soul to do something like Lindbergh's feat. "I used to dream of New York," he tells his prospective mentor. John tells Van Horn that he would like to become a builder. (Skyscrapers and ambitious dreams are intertwined in the film.) Van Horn helps John abandon boxing to obtain an education in engineering. There are also romantic complications when the Lipvitch daughter Becka lets John go for the sake of his career as he can now meet society women.

A more tragic plot twist is that Van Horn perishes at sea in an ocean line disaster. Dwan makes death more tangible by having water claim the lives of all three of John's parental figures. John himself plunges into despair and confusion. The titles invoke New York as a "city of illusions" and of "false hopes" as if it was a modern Babel.

John is restored to equilibrium when Becka finds him and the misunderstandings between them are cleared up. Dwan has seized an old plot device for resolution but has not transformed it to the dramatic level of the situation. In *Sunrise*, Murnau had taken a marital reconciliation and raised it to the stature of a religious epiphany that overcame the impersonality of the city and elevated its pleasures.

One of Dwan's greatest strengths was his unpretentiousness but here he shows his limitations in not rising to the occasion as would Murnau and Vidor. But *East Side, West Side*, for all its limitations, remains a fascinating film. Though he falters at the center, Dwan, in his location shooting, envelopes his characters with the power of the metropolis forever growing around them, in much the same way as the characters would be surrounded by the ever-expanding railroad in Sergio Leone's *Once Upon a Time in the West*. Toward the end of *East Side, West*

George O'Brien and Virginia Valli atop a skyscraper in *East Side, West Side* (1927), Dwan's last film shot in New York and his valentine to the city (courtesy Academy of Motion Picture Arts and Sciences).

also reported that Dwan "expressed his regret at the passing of Eastern production, but asserted it is likely that a year hence will find the producers returning to New York."[266]

Dwan's comment about the future was more accurate than he may have realized and feature production would soon return to Astoria. But at the moment, filmmaking in the east had all but dried up. At United Artists, Swanson had insisted on continuing to work in the east with her first film, *The Love of Sunya*. But after that, she thought it better to take advantage of new facilities offered to her in California. She remembered, "Much as I loved New York and mistrusted Hollywood and wanted to be a rebel like Allan Dwan, the agonies of producing totally on my own in a rented space with an inexperienced crew convinced me that Hollywood was worth a try."[267]

Dwan now did something that forestalled any other decision. He had decided to remarry.

Side, New York is shown at its zenith when Dwan's camera tilts up a skyscraper where John and Becka are perched on top. The lovers ask, "We tear down and build up. When is it going to stop?" John, now the architect, answers, "When we have our perfect city, the city of our dreams." Dwan's hero, who has suffered through much disorientation in his identity quest, now accepts New York as part of a neverending climb, while clouds are seen moving majestically overhead. With *East Side, West Side* Dwan had given a fitting valediction to New York City.

The film got respectful reviews and did well financially. But in late July, shortly after shooting had been completed, Fox "let out" the technical crew of its New York studio with no future productions scheduled.[264]

With the expiration of his contract, Dwan was left to ponder whether he should remain with Fox and how to preserve his niche in the east and, more importantly, his independence.

A couple of days after Fox's decision, Dwan told members of A.M.P.A. that the availability of funds from bankers to finance independent units if major salary reductions had gone into effect, stopped the producers from enacting such plans. Dwan believed that the possibility of such independent financing prevented the studios from enacting the reductions. Dwan told the group, "The only employees hit by the retrenchment were stenographers and others who are not highly paid."[265] Dwan was again sounding like a defiant independent. It was

Little is known about any other romantic liaisons Dwan may have had between his marriage and after Nita Naldi, except for an observation made by Louise Brooks. She remembered Dwan "in his apartment up on 85th Street. This little fat man with the gorgeous Follies girl, Helen Lee Worthing, loaded with cocaine, twining her long legs and her flaxen hair round him. She adored him; everybody did."[268]

Dwan's bride was a dark-haired beauty who had also worked in the Ziegfeld Follies, Marie Louise Shelton. While this was the name on her marriage certificate, she was often referred to as Betty Marie as well as just Marie Shelton. A native of Atlanta, Georgia, she was twenty-five years old. Dwan was forty-two. Shelton had a small part as Swanson's friend in *A Society Scandal* and also played a model in *Manhandled*.

Dwan and Shelton were wed on August 16, 1927, in Malone, New York, near the Adirondack Mountains. They may have been traveling together for some time. In January 1927, a Florida newspaper reported that while scouting locations for *The Joy Girl*, Dwan was staying at the Flamingo Hotel in Miami Beach with Marie Shelton, his "scenario writer."[269] Since Shelton never received a screenplay credit, this was likely a cover for purposes of respectability.

Both bride and groom had been previously married but the usually efficient Dwan, unlike Shelton, did not have his divorce decree with him. The wedding was delayed for twenty-four hours while Dwan wired his lawyer so he could comply with state law. A certified copy of the decree was received in Malone the next morning.

The couple honeymooned in Europe. Dwan contacted Joe Pasternak, who was now working in Universal's German branch. Dwan was looking for a tour guide and Pasternak recommended a twenty-one-year-old German friend who was toiling as a ghostwriter of screenplays. That friend was future American film director Billy Wilder, then living in Berlin. Wilder recalled, "Except for the train ride from Vienna, I had never been outside Berlin. But when I was offered 100 marks a week, I put that small problem out of my mind. I purchased a Baedeker and studied it."[270]

Wilder was able to provide the honeymoon couple with *faux* lectures from Dresden to Munich to Baden-Baden; he said that Dwan cut the talks short so they could get back to the bar. Because of Prohibition, Wilder said, Dwan wanted to come to

Marie Louise Shelton, a former Ziegfeld girl, became Dwan's second wife in August 1927 (courtesy Academy of Motion Picture Arts and Sciences).

Europe to "catch up on his drinking. Four double martinis went down like water. His young wife tried to keep up. I only drank lemonades. I was on duty."[271]

Unfortunately for Wilder, at Heidelberg, they encountered an English touring group and when their bona fide guide heard Wilder's nonsense lectures, he told Dwan the truth. Wilder's tour guide career then came to a quick end. Wilder claimed that Dwan shouted to the English group, "Never trust a son of a bitch who doesn't drink."[272]

Pasternak has also given his own account in which he "remembers Dwan phoning him from Heidelberg and screaming that Pasternak had given him a terrible guide. He had gone on the make for his new wife and she was falling for him. He was a fine dancer and Mrs. Dwan loved to dance and when he got back to Hollywood, he was going to get Pasternak's ass for this mistake...."[273] The yelling sounds very uncharacteristic of Dwan, suggesting an older man's insecurities.

Dwan's European vacation may have been conducted for a business reason as well as a honeymoon and all the alleged drinking. A trade story that appeared in late July noted that Dwan "is said to be looking toward Europe for future affiliation. He is expected to shortly announce decision to sail for the other side, and later, a contract with an English company."[274] Because of the looming quota law in the U.K. which mandated that a certain percentage of films released had to be made domestically, the British were said to be offering high salaries for American film players and directors. Sidney Olcott, John Robertson and Albert Parker were among the American directors leaving to work in Britain in late 1927 and early 1928.

Dwan kept the opportunities in the U.K. in mind for another day but at this time, he decided against working abroad. In September, it was announced that Dwan had signed a five-picture deal with the producer Robert T. Kane, who had his own unit making films for First National. The deal reunited Dwan with Kane, who for a time was in charge of general production duties at the Astoria Studios. Also in Kane's unit was another Astoria exile, scriptwriter Forrest Halsey.

Kane had been one of the last holdouts to cling to working on the East Coast but now he too was obliged to go west to work at First National's Burbank studio. At least Dwan was now with fellow diehards who were reluctantly making the trek to California. He was also under contract to Kane and his independent unit, not to First National, so while Dwan lost his eastern enclave, he remained something of a maverick.

Dwan's first film for Kane would be *French Dressing*, a sophisticated comedy-drama starring H.B. Warner, Lois Wilson, Clive Brook, and Lilyan Tashman. In the story, a prim Boston wife (Wilson) heads for Paris to get a divorce after catching her husband in an innocent flirtation. But her friend (Tashman), the object of his attentions, follows her to Paris and introduces the wife to the world of high fashion, hence the title. As the wife blossoms into a "bird of paradise," she catches the interest of a debonair Frenchman (Brook). The husband (Warner) also arrives in Paris to try to sort things out.

The reviews from the *New York Times* on down were sparkling. Dwan had penetrated Lubitsch territory with perhaps a few touches of his own. Reviewers were delighted by the action being carried by the deft playing of this quartet. *Film Daily* praised Brook for "doing an Adophe Menjou to a brown turn."[275]

Variety touted *French Dressing* as a "[v]ery smooth comedy of high life, of genteel atmosphere, great pictorial beauty, with appeal to all classes of fans." In the same review, *Variety*, which had previously disparaged Dwan's rapid schedules, now lauded the efficiency of the production without citing Dwan by name. "The inside facts of the production are that it was just 14 days in actual studio work, sets and all other details being ready to hand when the shooting began. And still there is no sign of roughness or haste. The picture couldn't be smoother in its suave ease if it had been stretched over two months instead of two weeks.... The film is said to be one of the most economical in negative-cost Kane has ever released. For its kind it is one of the neatest pieces of work Kane or anybody else has sponsored."[276]

Variety also praised the film's aesthetic economy: "It takes two close-ups and one brief title to convey a world of unexpressed drama, where the ordinary 'movie' technique would have had two artificial actors generating high-power scenes all over the place. That's one of the distinctions of this picture — it gets much of subtle suggestion by indirection."[277]

French Dressing premiered in New York on December 10 and became a hit with audiences.

Dwan's contract with Kane called for making five films within one year. To meet that goal, Dwan directed some films and supervised others. As the *Variety* review indicated, Kane was also interested in speed and efficiency and both Dwan and Kane could draw on their experience at Astoria. They may have also both been in a hurry to complete their contract obligations because they completed four films within less than three months.

Their second collaboration was *The Whip Woman*, directed by Joseph C. Boyle though listed as an Allan Dwan production. It was based on a script by Halsey and Leland Hayward and starred Estelle Taylor, the wife of boxing heavyweight champion Jack Dempsey. The cast also included Antonio Moreno, Lowell Sherman, Dwan's one-time star Hedda Hopper and a teenage Loretta Young in one of her earliest roles. The film was shot back to back with *The Mad Hour*, also directed by Boyle and starring Sally O'Neill. Shooting was completed on the second film by January 3, 1928, with the two pictures being released respectively in February and March.

The Whip Woman, set in Hungary and telling the story of a young woman who keeps all men at bay with her whip until she falls for the hero, was greeted with open derision by critics and audiences. The *New York Post* stated, "[I]t is here personally pronounced one of the two or three worst films we have ever seen."[278]

The Mad Hour, based on an Elinor Glyn story, fared only somewhat better. *Photoplay* observed, "Elinor Glyn gives us another moral on the folly of jazzmania. Just how Madame Glyn thinks that a daughter of a taxi driver is clever enough to entrap the son of a multimillionaire into marriage via the gin route and dumb enough to sign him away, lose the custody of her baby and go to his jail in his honor, is beyond average comprehension."[279]

After these "supervisory" efforts, Dwan next directed for Kane a film originally titled *The Headliner*. Based on a Ben Hecht story, it's notable for, among other things, being set in New York City although shot in California. In the opus finally titled *The Big Noise*, Dwan not only recreated the subway and city streets but a mirthful trip to Coney Island. Veteran comic actor Chester Conklin plays John Sloval, a tired subway guard who accidentally falls onto the tracks as a downtown express is heading his way. He is rescued just in time and has little more than a slight scratch on his head to show for it.

The story is covered in a tabloid, the *Daily Mail*, in just four lines. But the city editor, seeking an issue for the paper's mayoralty candidate, quickly seizes on it and transforms Sloval into a "subway hero" who was ready to sacrifice himself to save others. The papers rail against the subway corporation while the tabloid's mayoral candidate quickly gets himself photographed visiting Sloval recuperating in a nursing home.

Dwan and his associates apparently pulled out all the stops in this satirical portrait. According to the *Washington Post* reviewer, "Ned Sparks, who plays the part of the mayor, would make an excellent double for Mayor 'Jimmy' Walker himself."[280]

If *East Side, West Side* was Dwan's valentine to New York City, *The Big Noise* may have been more of an irreverent Bronx cheer. One trade publication advised trying to sell it as a "true slice of big city life."[281] The *Washington Post* noted that the "picture is, in motif, comparable to both *The Crowd* and *Chicago* [the 1927 ancestor of the 2002 film musical] although dealing with entirely different situations."[282] Some critics also saw pathos in Sloval's "transition from a 'whisper' to 'big noise' and back again,"[283] or in more modern parlance, his fifteen minutes of fame. Citing the film as "genuinely human," Laurence Reid of *Motion Picture News* perversely noted, "There is a background of something which might register as utter futility of life. And this note is what makes it click so well."[284]

While *The Big Noise* collected good reviews, it disappeared quickly from theaters and seems to have now vanished completely. In fact, only one of Dwan's five films for Kane remains extant today and that is *Harold Teen*, based on a popular comic strip. Arthur Lake, later to be typecast in films and television as another comic strip character, Dagwood Bumstead of *Blondie*, played the title role. This film was not helmed by

Dwan appears to be adjusting the head bandage for Chester Conklin, as the film's nurses watch, in this publicity still from *The Big Noise* (1928).

consisting only of viewing the rushes and discussing them with Kane.

At this time, Kane was First National's only independent producer, and the studio may have been ready to end this arrangement with the termination of his contract. In early 1928, the trades reported that Kane intended to make a film called *Satan's Bushel* with Dwan directing. There were further reports that Kane was trying to have the film released through United Artists and was considering having it produced at the Cosmopolitan Studio in New York City. But the proposed deal with United Artists did not go through.[286]

With the end of his contract with Kane, another association ended for Dwan and he had to look elsewhere for work.

Dwan but by the young director Mervyn LeRoy, who would go on to a long and successful career extending into the 1960s with films like *Little Caesar, I Am a Fugitive from a Chain Gang, Gold Diggers of 1933* and *Gypsy*. But that career almost ended prematurely with *Harold Teen*.

In the film, the story's comic-strip teenagers set out to make a movie. Given their ineptness, LeRoy decided that they would mess up everything so badly that they would shoot their movie upside-down. But the studio bosses and Kane didn't get the joke and assumed that it was LeRoy who was the inept filmmaker. Kane refused to buy LeRoy's explanation and told him that he would be removed from the picture. LeRoy recalled, "I probably would have been kicked off that picture — and it would have been tough to get another one, with that sort of blemish on my record — except for the kindly and timely intervention of Allan Dwan.... For some reason, he had seen my upside-down rushes. He got the joke right away and went to bat for me. He told Kane and the others that he thought the upside-down scene was very funny and was exactly right for the film's characters. They had a great deal of respect for Dwan's judgment so they let me finish *Harold Teen*."[285]

When the picture was previewed, audiences laughed heartily at the upside-down scene. *Harold Teen* proved to be a major hit.

The fact that LeRoy had either forgotten or did not know of Dwan's involvement in the production suggests that, as co-producer or supervisor, Dwan had a very light touch, perhaps

The Iron Mask

In May 1928, Dwan took over as director on a troubled MGM feature, *Tide of Empire*. The film was actually a Cosmopolitan production being released through MGM. Dwan did not sign a long-term contract so that once he completed the film, he was again a free agent.

And once again, when at a crossroads, Dwan was called back by Douglas Fairbanks.

Almost immediately after completing his feature *The Gaucho* (1927), Fairbanks began preparations on a film that was intended as a sequel to *The Three Musketeers*. On June 25, 1928, Dwan signed a contract to direct Fairbanks' next film as well as to collaborate in developing and writing the scenario. The project was referred to in the contract as *The Further Adventures of D'Artagnan*. Dwan's fee for the film remained at his high of $50,000.[287]

As with *Robin Hood*, Fairbanks put screenwriting chores in Dwan's contract, so he must have expected a major contribution from Dwan in that department. Dwan said that the "Elton Thomas" in the writing credits represented "twenty people. It was everybody who said, 'Let's do this,' and 'Wouldn't it be great if we did that?'"[288] Dwan said he brought in writers that Fairbanks knew well such as Tom Geraghty (who had also worked on some of Dwan's First National films). But it is likely that Fairbanks and Dwan made the biggest contributions, at least in terms of structuring the scenario.

Fairbanks had made four features since he had last worked with Dwan and he was no longer playing the guileless youth of *Robin Hood.* In *The Gaucho,* Fairbanks' bandit hero has clearly been around for a while and has become so well known that he mockingly autographs his "Wanted" poster. In a scene evoking Poe, Fairbanks is celebrating when a shrouded, leper-like figure known as the Black Doom enters his hall. Fairbanks says that if he was in that man's place, he would find some lonely spot and kill himself. In an act of reprisal, the outcast later touches Fairbanks bleeding hand and advises him to follow his earlier suggestion. Fairbanks watches in horror as his hand becomes infected and dead to all feeling, realizing that he will soon become as afflicted as the Black Doom figure. Fairbanks' bandit keeps his affliction secret save for one devout woman, who will lead him to spiritual salvation and a miracle cure.

The scenario of *The Gaucho* also went under the collective pseudonym of "Elton Thomas." The bandit's dread of seeing his hand and then his entire body debilitated may well have mirrored Fairbanks own anxiety at the coming of old age.

Such concerns spilled over into *The Iron Mask* as in the guise of D'Artagnan, Fairbanks permitted himself to age to something like his actual years. The mysticism of *The Gaucho* also surfaced in *The Iron Mask* but in far more graceful form.

As Fairbanks headed towards his forty-sixth birthday, he recognized that his days as a swashbuckling stunt-performing star were numbered. Dwan recalled, "Doug seemed to be under some kind of compulsion to make this picture one of his best productions. He had always meticulously supervised every detail of his pictures, but in this one I think he eclipsed himself. It was as if he knew that this was his swan song."[289] Fairbanks made no more swashbucklers after this and it is clear to anyone watching the film that this was intended as his farewell to that heroic image.

Maurice Leloir, the French painter and watercolorist, renowned for his 1894 publication of illustrations for *The Three Musketeers,* was in his seventies summoned by Fairbanks to America for a reported $40,000.[290] Leloir, who was also founder and president of the Costume Society, was selected to design the costumes for *The Iron Mask* and to oversee the production for period authenticity. A rich assemblage of artists were hired to design the sets including Wilfred Buckland, Ben Carré, and Laurence Irving, the grandson of the great English actor Henry Irving. Expert assistance was also rendered by Fred Cavens, the Belgian fencing master.

The Iron Mask was based on several books that continued the adventures of D'Artagnan and his companions from *The Three Musketeers,* including the third section of Alexandre Dumas' novel *The Vicomte de Bragelonne* which is known as *The Man in the Iron Mask.* The memoirs of D'Artagnan, Richelieu and De Rochefort were also cited in the credits. As it was a sequel to his 1921 *The Three Musketeers,* Fairbanks attempted to retain for *The Iron Mask* as many actors as possible in the same roles despite the lapse of eight years. Two of the actors playing the Musketeers in the earlier film, including the late George Siegmann, had to be replaced. Stanley J. Standford and Gino Corrado filled the void while Leon Barry reprised his role as Athos. Marguerite de La Motte returned as D'Artagnan's love interest Constance. Barbara La Marr, who had previously played Milady de Winter, had died in 1926 and was replaced by Dorothy Revier. Nigel de Brulier again very ably impersonated Cardinal Richelieu. Adolphe Menjou, who had played Louis XIII in the first film, was now too big a star for this small part so Rolfe Sedan took the throne.

A new character for *The Iron Mask,* in fact a double role, was that of the young king Louis XIV and his usurper twin brother. That part went to twenty-year-old William Bakewell, who had already made numerous films including two for D.W. Griffith and the Kane–Dwan *Harold Teen.* In his autobiography, Bakewell expressed his gratitude to Dwan for suggesting him for the part to Fairbanks.[291]

In the fall of 1928, as *The Iron Mask* neared completion, the "talkie" revolution was going full stride in Hollywood and more films were being shot or re-shot in sound. Dwan said he advised Fairbanks, "We'd better beat them to the punch."[292] A prologue was filmed where Fairbanks made a poetic speech introducing the picture, plus another speech at the film's midpoint.

Few were granted admittance to the set as extra care was taken with a technology then in its infancy. Bakewell recalled, "The techniques of sound were so new that each shooting of the speech was as nerve-wracking for Doug as today's count-down for the atomic bomb. Finally, after tedious take-after-take and countless glasses of water to lubricate his nerve-dry throat, the mission was accomplished and the film was in the box."[293]

But how well had Fairbanks recorded? For many years, the sound sequences in *The Iron Mask* were unavailable. Then in 2000, a version restored by Photoplay Productions in collaboration with the Museum of Modern Art and Douris Pictures was made available. We can now hear Fairbanks speak in a rich baritone. But how do we square that with Fairbanks' extant sound films where he appears to have more of a tenor's voice?

In his Bogdanovich interview, Dwan acknowledges that Fairbanks "had a high voice"[294] but doesn't explain how that was rectified on the soundtrack. But he later admitted to Brownlow that after listening to Fairbanks record, they "got a deep voiced fella, hired him to do it, so we did the epilogue with him."[295]

Was it really a voice other than Fairbanks' that audiences heard in 1929?

During the writing of this book, Brownlow was queried about Dwan's claim. He said that long after he interviewed Dwan, he met the sound engineer of *The Iron Mask,* Ed Bernds. Bernds assured Brownlow that it was indeed Fairbanks' voice that was used in the prologue and midpoint of the film. Brownlow also believes it would have been extremely difficult for a substitute to recite the long poem while Fairbanks mouthed it without going out of synch (although Fairbanks' voice *does* go out of sync slightly). And regardless of the register, the voice here does sound like that of Fairbanks.[296]

Bernds, the sound engineer (and future film director), also for a brief time had a chance to watch the filming of *The Iron Mask*. He later commented, "It was a noisy, crowded set; there seemed to be a dozen things happening at the same time. I tried to discern whether there was some sort of order in this chaos. My attention was drawn to a man who seemed to be in charge. He shouted orders in a strong, commanding voice, and men obeyed him; I learned that he was the boss electrician, called, appropriately, the gaffer. Then I saw that another man exerted a great deal of authority: Lucky Humberstone, the assistant director. Finally, I discovered that the gentleman sitting quietly in a canvas chair was the director, Allan Dwan."[297]

The experience left Bernds with the impression that Dwan was a "passive" director though he may have been watching little more than extras in crowds being prepared for filming.[298]

But Bakewell, who was on the set far longer than Bernds, had an altogether different impression of Dwan. He remembered, "Dwan could be a bit of a Napoleon on the set. Allan was a little fellow, but solidly built, and he carried himself rather majestically. There was never any doubt that he was in charge.... Few directors knew more about their job than Allan Dwan."[299]

Talking about his role in the film, Bakewell added, "The part was an actor's field day and Allan helped me tremendously, despite his slogan, 'I don't talk to actors' (uttered with a caustic tongue-in-cheek). As a matter of fact, he usually transmitted all orders to the cast via his assistant Bruce 'Lucky' Humberstone...."[300]

Bakewell recalled an incident where actor Ulrich Haupt (who played the villainous De Rochefort) asked Dwan for a conference regarding a scene they were about to film. "Allan completely ignored the request but sent 'Lucky' to him with his instructions. This infuriated Haupt, quite understandably, and he took it as a personal affront. A hush fell over the set as it looked as though he were going after Dwan. But the imperturbable director glared him down and Ulrich retreated to his dressing room muttering in his crepe hair beard until he cooled off. Had the incident really become physical, I think Allan could have measured up since he was quite sturdy and once played football for Notre Dame."[301]

In a 1978 interview, H. Bruce "Lucky" Humberstone, in essence, confirmed Bakewell's story of Haupt backing down from Dwan.[302] The choice of Humberstone as assistant director had been imposed on Dwan by Fairbanks. Humberstone, the future director of numerous Charlie Chan films and the early film noir *I Wake Up Screaming*, had also held that position during the shooting of *The Gaucho*. Before shooting began, Dwan told Humberstone, "I don't hold anybody else in the crew responsible for anything but my assistant ... I don't talk to anybody else but my assistant and that's you."

So Bernds did not see the authority Dwan exercised through keeping his actors at arm's length and having his assistant make sure the crew members were all performing their tasks. This left Dwan free to concentrate on more creative matters. Humberstone said that "there were so many things I learned from Allan Dwan that became valuable to me in my days of directing. He's an unbelievable guy." But Bernds' belief in Dwan's "passivity" would resonate at another time years later.

Humberstone did not believe that there was a complete script for *The Iron Mask* but more of a "story outline." Humberstone recalled that both Dwan and Fairbanks contributed ideas as the film was shot. "I would say that Fairbanks contributed to it equally as much as Dwan except that Dwan was the man that had to put it all together and have it make sense."[303]

Dwan and Fairbanks seemed to have come full circle in filming *The Iron Mask*. Both had been steeped in the drama of the period going back to *Richelieu*. They had first treated the character of D'Artagnan in *A Modern Musketeer* and this was the only character Doug would play both in comedy and swashbuckling drama. Dwan had not been available for directing *The Three Musketeers*, but with D'Artagnan in this film, Fairbanks would round out his cycle of spectacles. As the authors

Douglas Fairbanks playing D'Artagnan for the third and last time in *The Iron Mask* (1929).

of *The Fourth Musketeer* noted, D'Artagnan had always been Fairbanks' favorite role.[304]

Myron Meisel said of *The Iron Mask*, "Dwan's visual style achieves maximum emotional effects with minimal manipulation."[305] Dwan captures the essence of Louis XIII by frequently showing him in long tracking shots. With his measured, regal gait, his power seems to sweep over all the space before him.

There is room in the complicated plot for only one long romantic scene between D'Artagnan and his lover Constance but it is done beautifully. The scene ends mischievously with D'Artagnan making a sly sexual innuendo about Constance being pregnant which the silent medium can convey innocuously. But perhaps the most striking moment occurs when, seeking refuge from prying eyes, D'Artagnan whisks Constance across a garden wall. As D'Artagnan bounds over the wall and taking her hand leads Constance to follow him, the moment is captured in two seamlessly edited shots as Constance seems to float through the air in a sense of rapture. It was part of the romantic grace that Dwan said he always wanted Fairbanks to project.

The Three Musketeers opened with a chess game but *The Iron Mask* even more strongly conveys that in the court intrigues, nearly every life is reduced to a pawn in the struggle for power. After Cardinal Richelieu learns that the Queen Mother has given birth to twins, he does his utmost to preserve the secret. Since Constance, as the queen's seamstress, is one of the very few who know, he has her taken to a convent for confinement.

The forty-five-year-old Fairbanks did very few stunts in this film; the most notable one came in a failed attempt to rescue Constance. As D'Artagnan, Fairbanks catapults from a tree to a window sill. Though Fairbanks swung from a horizontal bar concealed in the branches and the stunt was meticulously planned, it was still an impressive act. A gymnastic coach observing the action observed, "That's one hell of a move. It would challenge a champion gymnast today."[306]

The Musketeer motto and "mystic phrase,"[307] "All for One and One for All," is reprised throughout the film, which seems rooted in its own cosmology of primal units that are torn apart and need to coalesce. For a swashbuckler, *The Iron Mask* is uncharacteristically very much a story about the pain of loss and separation; D'Artagnan early on losing his beloved Constance to a murderer, the Musketeers being bound by threat of death not to meet again, the Queen Mother unable to see one of her sons for more than two decades. A prince sent into forced exile soon after birth, grows with evil ambitions while the passage of time also unites old enemies D'Artagnan and Richelieu in defense of France. In a story that spans twenty-four years, flashbacks abound for reasons of longing, nostalgia and the penetration of a mystery that haunts D'Artagnan.

The young Louis XIV and aging D'Artagnan each wear half of a coin around their necks. The medals make a perfect whole when they are joined together. The medals were given to them when Louis was still a child by Richelieu, who enjoined D'Artagnan to keep the prince under his protection and to preserve the French state. The coin halves also begin to signify the emotional bond between the two as we see, twenty years later, the camaraderie that has developed between Louis and D'Artagnan. When the king's half of the doubloon is shown in Louis' desperate message on a prison plate, it confirms to D'Artagnan the king's identity. But the imagery also conveys

Enormous shadows are part of the sinister visual scheme for the scene in *The Iron Mask* (1929) where Louis XIV is confronted with his evil twin, who bestows the iron mask on him.

the danger of shattered unity that leads to chaos and violence. The throne itself is actually split as Louis' twin has usurped the crown and imprisoned his brother, concealing his face with an iron mask.

D'Artagnan is the narrative's depository of memory, and all but one of the flashbacks in the film emanate from him. (That one flashback turns out to be false and is corrected by a subsequent flashback from D'Artagnan.) Not only does he protect the king but, regaling him with stories of the Musketeers, he has become their chronicler and poet. It is also through his memories of dying words that D'Artagnan unravels the danger to Louis.

It is fitting that in calling the Musketeers back together to rescue the king, D'Artagnan leads them to their greatest exploit and also to death — immortality in both senses of the word. As in *Robin Hood*, a great friendship that was lost is restored and perhaps that was another reason Fairbanks recalled Dwan for this project. When the Musketeers free the young king and fight their way out of the River Castle, the action is perhaps the most stirring of all Fairbanks features. The flight to freedom in which one by one the Musketeers "pay their toll" to the next world recalls the pursuit by Death of *The Little Match Girl*, the Jean Renoir film released the previous year.

It is difficult for any analysis to do justice to the interlocking emotions and relationships involved in *The Iron Mask*. D'Artagnan loses his lover and friends but then finds himself becoming a surrogate father to Louis XIV. The Queen Mother has longed for her lost son but recoils in horror at what he has become when he finally returns. Time itself is almost a perverse character in the film.

Time is an integral element in *The Iron Mask* as space was in *Robin Hood*. When *Robin Hood* was planned, Dwan and his collaborators devised a broad canvas for Doug to enact his stunts: a titanic castle and drawbridge, a jousting field and Sherwood Forest. With time at last confronting Fairbanks with his limitations, *The Iron Mask* is a more contemplative film.

The Iron Mask is also a film of great visual beauty not only because of the splendor of its meticulously recreated sets and costumes but because it contains some of Dwan's most artistically composed shots, arguably even besting *Robin Hood*.[308] In the final sequence with his Musketeer comrades all killed, a mortally wounded D'Artagnan staggers into the Palace Garden to meet his end. Dwan visualizes D'Artagnan's journey to Eternity with heightened theatricality as he frames it like a screen image through a large doorway. In an impressive use of depth of field, D'Artagnan's crumpled figure is seen in the distant background under huge, dark clouds.

In a tighter shot, D'Artagnan stumbles, then raises his arms and shouts, "Ho-la!" — the musketeer call to each other for help. Superimposed on the sky, the images of Aramis, Athos and Porthos appear, all exhorting D'Artagnan to join them. As D'Artagnan dies, they render their last act of assistance, pulling him over to the other side. The Musketeers are reunited once more, this time forever. There are two cuts back to the tragic scene below, first a medium shot of the king bending over the body of D'Artagnan, then a long shot of the king and all of his courtiers in mourning and making the sign of the cross. The Musketeers, towering figures in the sky, look down with smiles and amusement. It was the Fairbanks smile, shared with others and broadened to metaphysical resonance. There is an appeal to all that is transcendent in human beings as the Musketeers march off to greater adventures in the beyond. As their images ascend farther into the sky and then dissolve, the ending title is "The Beginning."

There was indeed a "beginning" occurring in Hollywood ... and an ending. Sound was coming in and the days of the silent film were numbered.

When *The Iron Mask* was released in early 1929, it was part of the vanishing breed but some of the early responses greeted it as a relief from the stilted talkies. On its front page, *Film Daily* proclaimed, "It flashes across the screen like a streak. Loaded down the very gunwales with action is Doug's latest. In these days of sound, when talking pictures mean slow moving pictures, it is like coming home to roost to sit through a production that gets under way from the opening shot and whoops it up all the way to the finish."[309]

Other reviews were as enthusiastic. *Photoplay* hyperventilated, "Action, action, action — more action. That tells the story. It is adroit. It is imaginative. It is resplendent.... There is the characteristic Fairbanks breadth and sweep and stunts. And it is his best job of story-telling."[310]

The Iron Mask opened at the Rivoli Theater in New York on February 21.[311] There were midnight shows daily and a new Rivoli record was set with over $62,000 earned in its first week.[312] United Artists advertised that it also set opening records in Los Angeles, Seattle, Detroit, and Indianapolis.[313] In the end, *The Iron Mask* grossed $1.5 million, a $100,000 improvement over Fairbanks' previous film *The Gaucho*, but far short of the two million–plus earned by *Robin Hood*.[314] The further entrenchment of the sound film probably kept *The Iron Mask* from more sensational earnings.

Fairbanks had made his last swashbuckler but he would not be comfortable in any other form or genre in the sound era. The open-air sets of the silent era were now replaced by the much more restricted soundstages.

Laurence Irving, who had worked on the set design of *The Iron Mask*, recalled visiting the soundstage with Fairbanks. "We walked down and the doors of the big studio were open, and instead of seeing a nice bright place where everybody was extremely happy working, it was a ghastly sort of cave hung with blankets, no lights, the whole of the floor covered with serpentine wires and cables, and then these menacing microphones...

"As he took this in, Douglas laid his hand on my arm, as he often did when he spoke to me, and he said, 'Laurence, the romance of motion picture making ends here.'"[315]

Five years after the appearance of *The Iron Mask*, Fairbanks' last film was released. A little more than ten years after *The Iron Mask*, Fairbanks was dead.

When Bogdanovich asked Dwan what he thought of the potential of sound, he said, "[I]t was the end of a fine art."

Dwan's objections to sound were both aesthetic and political. Like other critics, he thought sound films too much like the theater. "They're a different thing — an extension of the theater — with more and bigger sets, more expanse, but otherwise the same, because everything's based on what you say or what's the sound. And I liked pictures as pictures in motion. We used words for titles, but we always got the best effect from *doing* something rather than saying something, and we said as little as possible."[316]

Even more to Dwan's dislike was that talking films mandated more detailed scripts that had to be adhered to and that the studios could scrutinize. For Dwan and his collaborators this was a fundamental change from the silent days, "[b]ecause then we were actually creating it ourselves. When the job was being handed to us on paper and the rules were laid down and our stuff was being inspected daily by executives, we became just members of the crew. And the fun went out. We did our job as we saw it, but we always had a mentor over us saying, 'I like it' or 'I don't like it.' So I still enjoyed making pictures, but it wasn't the same thing. You didn't have to exert yourself. We used to mold a scene the way we wanted it, but we couldn't after we got scripts."[317]

Film historian Richard Koszarski concurs to some extent with Dwan that more power flowed to film directors in the silent era. "With producers exercising little authority, studio chiefs preoccupied with business and contractual matters, and the value of a screenplay not yet established at the level talkies would allow, much creative power was concentrated in the hands of a relatively small group of filmmakers capable of conceiving, orchestrating, and executing specific projects."[318]

This is Koszarski's introduction to a chapter on these filmmakers, and as he notes, "Most of these examples are drawn from the ranks of directors...."[319]

The transition to sound complemented the ongoing process by which the film companies meant to transform their studios to efficient factories. Scripts with all the dialogue delineated were more effective blueprints for executives to scrutinize than scripts which depended largely on images and emotions to be projected onscreen.

In the politics of screen power, the change to sound also strengthened the studio's hand against creative personnel. Dwan recalled, "[W]e found ourselves really struggling for existence because the executives thought we were no longer needed — that silent picture makers didn't know anything about dialogue or sound. So they imported directors from the theater to do the directing."[320]

Actors were still more endangered, especially as early sound equipment did not always provide an accurate recording of their voices. Even writers were affected as the studios assumed playwrights could script better dialogue.

The Iron Mask was probably Dwan's most accomplished film of the silent era and its ending was a magnificent sendoff to the silent cinema and to Fairbanks. It was also the capstone of a working relationship between Fairbanks and Dwan that had gone back thirteen years. Fairbanks had typified a special kind of freedom onscreen that suggested that anything was possible. To Dwan, as well as to Fairbanks, that freedom was now gone.

The prologue that Fairbanks spoke in *The Iron Mask* began with these words:

Out of the shadows of the past
As from a faded tapestry
Of Time's process slow and vast
I step to bid you bear with me
That while your fancy I engage
To look upon another age.

Another age was now fading into the shadows. It was not clear how Dwan would cope with this new era or even if he would survive.

Part Two

Keep Your Head Down!

If you get your head up above the mob, they try to knock it off. If you stay down, you last forever.—Allan Dwan, quoted in *The New York Times*, May 7, 1950

6. Fox and Trot

Peter Bogdanovich: *"I'm surprised you survived."* **Allan Dwan:** *"Well, I'm sometimes surprised too."*
—Bogdanovich and Dwan discussing the director's career in *The Last Pioneer*

In 1929, Dwan returned to work for the Fox Film Corporation and continued to make films for them, along with other studios, in the early 1930s. Dwan told Bogdanovich that then, while globetrotting in Europe, he stopped in London and accepted an offer to make a film. He made *two* more films there and then returned to the U.S. He said he found that he had been forgotten in the States and had to establish himself all over again. It was, however, not too long before Dwan was back working at Fox but under very different circumstances.

A closer scrutiny of those years suggests that they were far more difficult than Dwan acknowledged.

Nineteen twenty-nine did not begin auspiciously for Dwan. On January 2 his brother Leo Dwan, who was now Allan's business manager, was involved in an auto crash that killed Leo's twenty-eight-year-old wife. Leo recovered in a hospital in Santa Barbara.

Dwan returned to Fox later that same month. His first film for them was *The Far Call*. Still to be released was *Tide of Empire*, which was filmed before *The Iron Mask*. It went out on March 23. Including *The Iron Mask*, which was released in February, a total of five Dwan films appeared in 1929. Three of the five films concerned romances that crossed cultural and geographic barriers. And the first of these was *Tide of Empire*.

As a film project, *Tide of Empire* had a trouble-plagued history. It was based on a 1927 novel by Peter B. Kyne, who is probably best known for his book *The Three Godfathers*, which was made into several film versions (including two directed by John Ford). *Tide of Empire* deals with the California Gold Rush and the influx of Americans into "Hispano-California" as seen through the eyes of an Anglo-Irish adventurer named Dermod D'Arcy. It is a sprawling, episodic and confused book. Early in the novel, D'Arcy bemoans the fate of the kind Spanish landowners he meets, noting that they are "a wonderful people doomed to oppression and extinction as surely as the Indian." D'Arcy ponders how helpless they will be "in the hands of the eager, greedy, empire-building Anglo-Saxon...."[1]

This conflict is soon altered from its opening description as both the author and his protagonist show increasing contempt for the Spanish aristocrats. D'Arcy views them as lazy, impractical, unimaginative, hypocritical and frozen in the traditions of the fifteenth century. (Little sense is conveyed of a larger Hispanic population beyond the decadent aristocrats.) While D'Arcy falls in love with the Spanish senorita Josepha Guerrero, she becomes almost indistinct in the last third of the novel where Kyne appears to be much more comfortable extolling the democratic camaraderie of D'Arcy and his fellow miners in their haven of Happy Camp.

The book is particularly schizophrenic in the area of racial tolerance. D'Arcy upholds the rights of foreigners (such as the Chinese Jim Toy) in his camp, against a xenophobic mob of Anglos. On the other hand, Josepha's wastrel half-brother Romauldo becomes increasingly demonic each time he appears in the novel. This is attributed, several times, to the fact that his blood was not "pure" and that his mother was one-quarter Indian, as if his evil was a kind of genetic disorder. In contrast, it is noted that Josepha's Spanish lineage was pure Castilian and her mother was half-English. In an absurdly racist musing, D'Arcy tell his sidekick, "My heart aches for Josepha, Bejabers. An English soul in Hispano-Californian surroundings. How she must suffer!"[2]

While released by MGM, *Tide of Empire* was a Cosmopolitan production, which meant that William Randolph Hearst would serialize the novel and back the film with loads of advertising. In the first screen treatment by Waldemar Young, an attempt was made to preserve as much of Kyne's novel as possible through condensation and rearrangement.

In that draft, completed in late November 1927, Romauldo was still the villain. In a new treatment ready in December, Romauldo's character is modified and while he is still a thief, he is permitted to escape at the end. It should also be noted that while stereotypes had not disappeared, Hollywood was now responding to criticisms of its depiction of Latinos. For example, scenes were cut and titles removed from the 1918 release of the Dwan-supervised *Headin' South* after complaints were made by the Mexican consul in New York.[3]

As work began on the *Tide of Empire* script, Jack Conway was assigned to direct the film under the title *The Argonauts*. The title was back to *Tide of Empire* when the film was ready to go before the cameras on February 18, 1928, with Al Rogell, who specialized in Westerns, now set to direct. MGM's rising star Joan Crawford was cast as the Spanish senorita and Norman Kerry as D'Arcy. But script problems remained. After three days, the production was shut down for a script conference. The delay lasted for over two months. Before the end of March, Rogell was out and Dwan was brought in as director.

On March 21, Burton King wrote a memo to the producer Hunt Stromberg recommending more script changes and incorporating suggestions from Dwan to streamline the scenario.[4] A new script was finally approved by Stromberg on April 23, 1928.

Dwan was also assembling a new cast. By mid–April, Renée Adorée, who had previously appeared in Dwan's *Tin Gods*, replaced Crawford in the role of Josephita Guerrero. Shortly thereafter, it was announced that James Murray, the star of King Vidor's *The Crowd*, would be the leading man. But before production began, Murray was replaced by George Duryea, who would later be more famously known as Tom Keene. With the signing of William (Buster) Collier to play Romauldo on May 3, Dwan said he could now start shooting. Production began the next day.

The shoot did not go smoothly. In fact, this would be one of the few films Dwan directed where he fell behind schedule. When the film officially wrapped on June 15, it was a week behind schedule but Dwan still had to do more re-shooting after that. By the time all filming had been completed on June 27, the deficit figure had increased to thirteen days.

Part of the problem may have had to do with various logistical difficulties and the shooting of additional scenes not in the original script. But it was also because of the condition of Adorée, whose health would become increasingly fragile and who may have been pushed too far by the studio. On May 14, Adorée had to shoot a retake for *Forbidden Hours* at 8 A.M. She could not make it to that set until 8:40. By the time she changed and was on Dwan's set it was close to 10 o'clock. Her frequent lateness increased to longer durations and on some days she was too ill to work at all. According to the June 8 Daily Production Report, Adorée was on the set at 7:20 but had to lie down with a doctor and nurse in attendance. According to the doctor's report she was on the verge of a nervous breakdown. The production report indicated that Adorée would still be able to continue work later in the day.[5]

Tide of Empire was released with a soundtrack that contained sound effects and music, including a romantic song, "Josephita." Little notice was taken of the film; it was not reviewed by the *New York Times*, *Variety* and other trade journals. While the picture may have been overlooked in the increasing tide of talkies, in some of the few publications where it *was* critiqued, such as *Photoplay* and *Film Daily*, the reviews were good.

Tide of Empire is surprisingly cohesive, considering its picaresque source. It impressively compresses much plot and action into a 73-minute running time, giving it the feel of a mini-epic. Unlike the novel, the film begins from the viewpoint of its Spanish protagonists. The Guerreros are shown as a religious family with vast land holdings but also generous to the poor. In an early scene, after Romauldo has squandered the money he obtained selling the family sheep by gambling, his sister Josephita aids him by lifting the purse of her sleeping father Don Jose, taking out just enough money to cover the lost "sheep funds." (Romauldo is depicted as weak rather than wicked and no mention is made of his ethnic origin.) Don Jose is played by George Fawcett, Dwan's grouchy millionaire in *The Habit of Happiness*. Don Jose opens his eyes long enough to see what Josephita has done with the money but he plays along, as if nothing has

A still taken during the first days of shooting of *Tide of Empire* (1929) before the film was shut down and re-cast for production months later. Joan Crawford (left) originally played Josephita and Norman Kerry (right) was first cast as the male lead. Nigel De Brulier stands between them as Josephita's father (courtesy Academy of Motion Picture Arts and Sciences).

happened. There is a reference in the titles to the life of the dons being "one long siesta in the sun."

This is all shattered with news of the discovery of gold as Americans begin to flock to California. In early 1929, Americans were still optimistic about the inexorable march of an empire accumulating wealth and they could empathize with movies about gold rushes. In this film, we also see the toll it takes on the native population. It is personified in a montage of cowboys and stampeding cattle superimposed over the faces of Don Jose, Josephita, and Romauldo. Gringos are seen stealing pigs from the Guerrero estate. When Romauldo tries to stop them, he is whipped.

It is not long after this that Derry D'Arcy (Keene) enters the story. He is also seeking gold but shows greater sensitivity to his Hispanic hosts and can even address them in their native language. But when the Guerreros try to reverse their declining fortunes in a horse race with Romauldo on their prize horse El Capitan, they are defeated by D'Arcy's unbeatable horse, Pathfinder. With his victory, D'Arcy wins the Rancho Chico, the Guerreros' estate.

D'Arcy is quickly captivated by Josephita and decides that he will return the land to the family. D'Arcy sends Josephita a note of transfer of the land back to the Guerreros. But before she can inform her father, he has died of grief.

Josephita carries D'Arcy's note back to the gringo town and awaits D'Arcy in her hotel room. When notified, D'Arcy, unaware of Don Jose's death, blissfully misinterprets the reason for Josephita's visit. The ensuing scene is stirringly operatic; Dwan's use of editing, spatial relationships, blocking, camera placement and even sound as well as the talented playing of his principals all contribute to the effect.

When D'Arcy's sidekick Bejabers (James Bradbury, Sr.) informs Derry of her arrival, he does a mock flamingo; castanets on the soundtrack add to the jocularity. In long shot, D'Arcy bounds up the hotel's interior steps so quickly that in the next shot he bangs into the door. When the door opens, there is an exchange of close-ups of Josephita and then D'Arcy. D'Arcy is literally huffing.

Then in two-shot, Josephita hands him back the note in a businesslike manner and tells him it comes too late. After another exchange of close-ups, she adds that her father has died. She then walks away.

In another two-shot, Josephita is standing in a doorway and the deflated D'Arcy is some distance behind her. He moves towards her, asking, "How can I tell you how sorry I am?" After a tighter two-shot, Josephita tells him not to try.

And so this *pas de deux* of pride and regret continues until they move out to an outdoor balcony where Josephita can look over the teeming crowd of people and accuse them and D'Arcy of having stolen her people's lands and killed her father. D'Arcy, in both senses of the word an apologist for Empire, continues to tell her that the tide of empire can bring good as well as cruelty.

Meanwhile, Romauldo has run into a gang of gringo outlaws who take a liking to his horse El Capitan and force Romauldo to ride with them. The gang plans to rob the Wells Fargo stagecoach in town but their raid is repulsed and the outlaws are quickly gathered up to be tried and hanged. A wounded Romauldo, who has no way of proving he was not part of the gang, seeks refuge. D'Arcy and Josephita hide him. But he is discovered and hauled away by the mob to be hanged. Josephita desperately protests that Romauldo is all she has left.

D'Arcy pretends to go along with the hanging but instead

A scene from the completed *Tide of Empire* (1929) with Renée Adorée as Josephita trying to keep a lynch mob from seizing her brother (played by William Collier, Jr.). Josephita's would-be lover (George Duryea) stands at far right, appearing helpless to stop the mob (courtesy Academy of Motion Picture Arts and Sciences).

Buster Keaton's gag appearance in *Tide of Empire* (1929) was cut but this photograph is a surviving souvenir of the occasion. From left to right are Natalie Talmadge, Dwan, Constance Talmadge, Keaton, Renée Adorée and William Collier, Jr. Keaton was then married to Talmadge (courtesy Kevin Brownlow).

helps Romauldo to escape on his horse Pathfinder. When Pathfinder manages to jump over a chasm between two cliffs, the pursuit ends.

D'Arcy has found his method of restitution (a reversal of the earlier horse race) and he and Josephita embrace. *Tide of Empire* may be a relatively minor film and its politics simplified but it is still a work of heightened feeling.

Also notable in the film was an early use of the zooms lens. Dwan uses it twice, first to show a wagon coming into the town as a milestone of its development; then a shot of the Wells Fargo stage which will develop a link between west and east. On both occasions, Dwan zooms out, rather than in. (According to Dwan, as a gag, Buster Keaton appeared in the film as a bum being thrown out of the saloon. The scene was cut but a photo of Keaton on the set survives.)[6]

But more memorable was Adorée's adept playing under great strain. As *Photoplay* noted, "Adorée as the fiery senorita again proves herself a trouper of the highest caliber."[7] Only three more Adorée films, including two sound films, appeared after *Tide of Empire* was released. She died of tuberculosis in 1933 at the age of thirty-five.

Dwan's next three films for Fox all had exotic locales and one wonders if they were inspired by the trend of ethnographic documentaries. The first of these, *The Far Call*, set in an island in the Bering Sea, was, strangely enough, based on a story in *Good Housekeeping* by Addison Marshall. In a return to his usual efficiency, it was reported that Dwan completed *The Far Call* ten days ahead of schedule.[8]

Like *Tide of Empire*, *The Far Call* had a soundtrack but available records indicate it consisted of only music and sound effects. A young sailor (Charles Morton) lands on St. Paul's Island, intending to lead a pirate raid on the seal hatcheries. But when he meets the governor's blonde daughter (Lelia Hyams), he learns that he is the lost son of an old and respected St. Paul pioneer (another variation on the lost father theme). Morton changes his mind about the raid but this view is not shared by his associate, London Nick (Ulrich Haupt, the villain of *The Iron Mask*.). Morton then leads in the triumphant battle to defend the baby seals against the pirates. As with *Tide of Empire*, there were few reviews but those that appeared praised the vivid action sequences.

Dwan's next film, *Frozen Justice* was set in the same frigid zone. Shortly before Dwan's first tour with Fox, the film was announced as a John Ford project in early May of 1926. A press release stated, "John Ford will take a company to Alaska and spend a year, if necessary, to make this photoplay of epic proportions. No expense will be spared to put into the picture all the dynamic conflict, masterful narrative and dramatic power which the author, Ejnar Mikkelsen, created in his book."[9] Apparently, there were second thoughts on sparing no expense with a year long shoot in Alaska. Prior to Ford's involvement, the story had also been considered a project for director F.W. Murnau.[10]

In March of 1929, Fox announced that it would discontinue making silent features and that henceforth it would make only talking and musical Movietone films. Dwan had experimented with sound as early as 1925 and had made the landmark West Point sound film. He could have been one of the trailblazers in that area but he had refrained from making talkies, until perhaps now he was forced to by the terms of his contract. (*Frozen Justice* was one of the films for which Fox provided an alternate silent version for theaters not yet wired for sound.) The production of *Frozen Justice* did not entail bringing cumbersome sound equipment to northern locations, although it incorporated some second-unit Arctic photography from Charles B. Clarke. Dwan's cameraman of the Swanson days, Harold Rosson, shot most of the film in a studio.

The film tells the story of a half-white Eskimo woman who runs away from her husband and heads for civilization with a white sea captain. Lenore Ulric, one of David Belasco's biggest Broadway stars, had made some early silent films; she was signed for the lead in her first talkie role. Paul Muni, who had just completed *The Valiant*, which would earn him an Academy Award nomination, was initially mentioned as the male lead but this did not transpire. Instead, Robert Frazer would play Ulric's Eskimo husband Lanak. The role of the unscrupulous sea captain would go to Ulrich Haupt. (This may be the only film in history to feature an actress whose last name is Ulric and an actor with the first name Ulrich.) There was also a plum role for theater veteran Louis Wolheim.

Dwan recalled to Bogdanovich that on *The Far Call* the studio employed a theater director and he was told to "watch what he does and learn what you can from him." Dwan observed that "just the reverse occurred — he'd turn around and say, 'What do I do now?'"[11] However, since there was apparently no dialogue in *The Far Call* and no one credited with assisting Dwan in that capacity, Dwan was most likely referring to *Frozen Justice*. Here, Elliott Lester was given the peculiar credit of having "staged" the film. He later performed the same function on Murnau's *City Girl* and Dwan's subsequent *South Sea Rose*.

Like *Tide of Empire*, *Frozen Justice* was set during a gold rush, the Klondike rush of 1898 and '99. To capture the flavor of a gold rush town like Nome, where it seemed every other building was a dance hall or saloon, Dwan had the sound technicians mount the microphone on a boom which would pick up the sounds of different establishments as the camera moved from one to another. A silent fragment of the film exists in the Library of Congress and one can observe the beautiful, sinuous movements of the camera as it moves down the Nome street, weaving in and out of various dance halls and saloons.

The well-traveled streets of Nome provide a contrast to another area, the snowy desolation of the heroine's Eskimo home. Ulric's heroine, Talu, is caught between these two different worlds, dissatisfied first with her Eskimo village and then disillusioned with her honky-tonk existence in dance halls. In the finale, the captain takes Talu away in a sled, with her Eskimo husband in close pursuit. There is a break in the ice and the sled falls in the chasm. Talu, mortally injured, is rescued by her husband while the captain is crushed by two huge cakes of ice. Talu dies in her husband's arms, another of the era's tragic half-breed figures.

Critics were universal in their praise for the sense of atmosphere Dwan established but were less pleased with the story. Richard Watts, Jr., in the *New York Herald Tribune* opined, "As long as *Frozen Justice* stays in Nome it remains excellent.... The rest of it, though seldom particularly dull, is less impressive. The scenes in the Alaskan wastes, which include Eskimo villages, ice crushes, Arctic storms and incidental spectacles, are well staged, considering that they are all studio effects, and the acting is reasonably lively. It is in the story that *Frozen Justice* is chiefly deficient.... The conclusion dares to be tragic and the pace manages to remain fairly lively, but the picture must rely on its Nome episodes and Miss Ulric for the fact that it is a pretty good program production."[12] *Variety* regarded the film as "moderately good" and thought, "The cracking glacier sequence, in which Talu and the captain are killed, is a peach."[13]

Ulric was the centerpiece of many of the reviews and she was considered sultry and exotic though there was some consternation at how quickly her accent and unease in English vanished after a short time in Nome.

Frozen Justice had its New York City opening on October 25, 1929, at the Roxy Theater with Ulric and Dwan making personal appearances. Four days later on New York's Wall Street came the great stock market crash that presaged the Great Depression. There was subsequently less of a market for movies celebrating gold rushes.

Dwan's next film was a reprise with Ulric, but this time turning away from the cold to a tropical climate. It was announced that *South Sea Rose*, Tom Cushing's play that was originally known as *La Gringa*, would be filmed even before it became a stage play. Ulric had been slated to star when it was still planned for the stage. The film gave Ulric another opportunity to sing: she warbles the popular number "They Call Me South Sea Rose."

Ulric plays Rosalie Dumay, a French orphan brought up on the South Seas island of Tongawara. She is believed to be an heiress to a great fortune in France held by her uncle. A young trading captain (Charles Bickford) marries her for her money and brings her back to his staid New England village. But his love for Rosalie becomes genuine when his jealousy is roused by her dallying with the local doctor.

Critics found *South Sea Rose* more pleasing than the heavy drama of *Frozen Justice*. Mordaunt Hall in the *New York Times* acknowledged, "[It] may not be a well-knit or always a believable comedy, but it has some good fun coupled with competent acting. The idea of a vivacious French girl, born in the South Seas, disporting herself in the shortest of skirts before strait-laced women in a New England community and finally giving an exhibition of how the hula-hula ought really to be danced brought forth a hearty wave of merriment from a Roxy audience...."[14] *Photoplay* championed it as one of the six best pictures of the month, noting that it had "[g]reat comedy and a wonderful storm at sea...."[15] *South Sea Rose*, which was released in December, was also popular with audiences.

South Sea Rose marked Dwan's last feature-length collaboration with Hal Rosson, who shot three of Dwan's 1929 films and whose work with the director went back to 1915. It was also the end of Dwan's close association with the Rosson broth-

Poster of *South Sea Rose* (1929) featuring Lenore Ulric as the title character.

ers. Hal went on to shoot such classics as *The Wizard of Oz* and *Singin' in the Rain*, with his final film being Howard Hawks' *El Dorado*. Arthur was credited as co-director of Hawks' *Red River* for his second unit work.

The Return of the Queen

Just as Dwan had eventually reunited with Fairbanks, he also had hopes of working again with Swanson.

In the spring of 1927, Dwan sent Swanson a manuscript called *Venus* for consideration but Swanson declined, saying she had already settled on projects for the next two years.[16]

Most probably, Swanson did not care for the play but preferred not to offend Dwan.

She was, in fact, now shopping for her next project. Her first film as an independent producer at United Artists, *The Loves of Sunya*, had barely managed to break even. In her autobiography, Swanson said she had then decided she would settle on nothing but the best; "If I failed, I could go back to working for someone else. But before I failed I wanted to make my *Gold Rush*."[17]

At UA, Joseph Schenck tried to persuade Swanson to appear in an adaptation of the romantic comedy play *The Last of Mrs. Cheyney* and even promised to "to pull corporate strings to get Allan Dwan to direct it."[18] But Swanson wanted something more ambitious. She said that when she and her husband Henri started screening recent Hollywood films, the one that seemed to stand out above all others was *What Price Glory.* Swanson wanted to meet its director, Raoul Walsh. She was already aware that Walsh had directed *The Thief of Bagdad* and that he was friends with Fairbanks and Dwan.

Walsh suggested to her as a project the Somerset Maughm short story *Miss Thompson*, which had become the highly successful play *Rain.* To appease the censors, the minister of the story was changed to a non-cleric reformer. Swanson would star as Sadie Thompson, the prostitute, who would become the object of attack and obsession by Davidson the reformer, played by Lionel Barrymore. Swanson made it clear that she wanted Walsh not only to direct but to play the part of the Marine sergeant who falls for Sadie.

According to some press reports, Swanson remained volatile during the making of *Sadie Thompson*. An article in *Variety* stated, "Raoul Walsh and Gloria Swanson are reported in clash over the production of *Sadie Thompson*.... He has objected to Miss Swanson's attitude on directorial procedure and threatened to walk out, with Miss Swanson promising to be good if he'd remain."[19]

Photoplay added another wrinkle to the story: "If there was any truth in the rumors that Gloria Swanson and her director, Raoul Walsh, were interested in each other, here's good proof that it's all off now, for they tell me he has walked off the set twice recently. Not a question of who's wearing the pants, but who's holding the megaphone on *Sadie Thompson*."[20]

Released in January 1928, *Sadie Thompson* was a triumph both with the critics and at the box office. Swanson was nominated for an Academy Award for Best Actress at the very first Oscar presentation but lost to Janet Gaynor for *Seventh Heaven*.

Swanson remarked of Walsh, "No wonder he and Allan Dwan were close, I thought; they were totally kindred spirits."[21]

According to Dwan, he also provided some writing help to Walsh on his pictures. There is a scene in Walsh's 1929 *The Cock-Eyed World* where one of the Marines escorting a beautiful young woman approaches star Victor McLaglen and tells him,

"I brought you the lay of the land." The Marine then pulls out a map and holds it before McLaglen as he points to it. This bit of sly tweaking of the Production Code just barely got past the censors, as Walsh later recalled. Dwan told Bogdanovich, in one of the passages not included in the interview book, "I used to give him [Walsh] those lines, occasionally.... 'The lay of the land,' I gave him that."[22]

Dwan added, "I used to go around and watch Walsh and try to feed him stuff. I wouldn't dare do it myself. And he was fine for that. He loved it. Any little suggestions."[23]

There is no source to confirm that Dwan fed Walsh those lines (but it *is* quite possible, especially since both men were working for Fox at the time). The interesting implication is that Walsh was a bit wilder as a director than Dwan. Dwan preferred to remain more cautious but enjoyed supplying Walsh with (literally) raw material. Dwan acknowledged that Walsh sometimes visited Dwan's sets as well but does not mention any contribution Walsh may have made to his films.

With United Artists, Swanson had achieved independence. But she was not adept at controlling her business affairs, and as editing proceeded on *Sadie Thompson*, she was in debt for more than half a million dollars, even after she sold off assets such as her property in Croton-on-Hudson. In California, Swanson owned leaseholds in Malibu and for advice she turned to Dwan, who was one of the first members of the film industry to build his home in that exclusive area. Dwan recommended that she speak to his then-producer Robert Kane, who not only was interested in Malibu property but might give her some good financial guidance. In their ensuing discussion, Kane set up a lunch appointment for Swanson with a man regarded as a financial wizard, Joseph P. Kennedy.

Thus, Dwan had indirectly helped arrange that fateful meeting.[24]

Kennedy was a banker, film distributor, Wall Street consultant and, of course, the father of a future U.S. president. After her second meal with him, Swanson was convinced she had found "the right business partner to straighten out my career."[25] He took over Swanson's business affairs and also became romantically entangled with the star whom Terry Ramsaye had dubbed "the reigning queen of the movies."[26]

Kennedy had studied the movies as an industry and saw in them a new corporate business with a potential that had not been properly evaluated. Kennedy told Swanson, "I studied business at Harvard. I'm just applying the principles I learned there to the movie business because I'm convinced that most people in the movie business don't know how to do that."[27]

Dwan thought he found mathematical principles in movies so he could understand how to make them. To Kennedy, unlocking the mysteries of the movies was part of gathering data for a broader agenda. Kennedy told Swanson that the "trick" and "challenge" of motion pictures "was to make a fortune in them and also exploit their economic and political potential."[28]

Swanson noticed that Kennedy kept repeating the word "important" in discussing the prospective film of their future collaboration. Kennedy explained to her, "If he became involved, he would hold out for an important story as well as an important director."[29]

The next step he saw for them in achieving his ends was to make a prestigious film directed by Erich von Stroheim!

Von Stroheim was known for his profligacy but Kennedy assured Swanson that two producers would keep him under control. Swanson seemed sold. It is interesting to note that while the studios had in the last few years worked increasingly hard to develop a factory system, a keen observer like Kennedy still recognized that to make a film regarded as important he would need an "important" director.

Kennedy knew about movies but did he know enough about making a movie?

As one author noted, "He had made money by manipulating film companies, not by scoring at the box office."[30]

Von Stroheim had written a story especially for Swanson. The plot seemed a perverse play on Swanson's past Cinderella stories but von Stroheim's previous film, *The Wedding March*, had also used the same device. In *Queen Kelly*, Swanson begins as an innocent convent girl who is kidnapped by a prince and then chased out of the palace by a raving, whip-lashing queen. She finds herself transported to Africa where through a sequence of events she becomes the "queenly" madam of a brothel. In the end she is reunited with her prince who makes her a true queen.

When Kennedy and Swanson started talking about the von Stroheim project, Kennedy was in the unique position of running two (small) film studios simultaneously, FBO and Pathé. (He was able to give the marquis a job in Pathé's Paris office, thus both finding employment for Swanson's husband and getting him out of the way.) As *Queen Kelly* was about to go into production, Kennedy was among the participants completing the merger that would form RKO-Radio Pictures.

After lengthy preparation, filming on *Queen Kelly* began on November 1, 1928. It ended in total fiasco less than three months later. Swanson had become concerned as hours of footage piled up with no end in sight while von Stroheim persisted in adding increasingly raunchy touches unlikely to pass the censors. More importantly, Swanson found her performance overshadowed by the sets and other players. On January 21, Swanson's patience ran out when in one scene Tully Marshall, under instructions from von Stroheim, drooled tobacco juice on Swanson's hand. Swanson turned and walked off the set. She phoned Kennedy in New York and told him to come to California to make decisions.[31] Von Stroheim was then sacked by Kennedy.

Even a source sympathetic to the director, film historian Richard Koszarski, has concluded that it was "von Stroheim's well-documented excesses, both financial and directorial, which brought the picture down on top of him."[32]

Queen Kelly had been heavily advertised as a forthcoming United Artists production. Stuck with an uncompleted and perhaps unreleasable film and the loss of well over $700,000, Kennedy and Swanson were confronted with the possibility of a public debacle.

The shock of seeing her financial savior and industry savant humbled by failure shook Swanson's confidence. She was also now deeply in debt to Kennedy. In desperation she improbably sought out the Paramount executive she had believed guilty of forgery, Jesse Lasky. It was as if she had come full circle to her beginnings as a star.[33] This was a fruitless turn as Lasky was unlikely to help the star who had abandoned his studio and its lucrative offers. Nor would he want to antagonize Kennedy.

Kennedy wrote to the marquis in Paris ascribing Gloria's action to her "overwrought condition and the discouragement over the whole situation." He said that Gloria had been close to a nervous collapse and had to be hospitalized, adding, "We had a very drastic showdown after the Lasky incident, and I insisted that some sort of a finish must be made because there was too much money at stake and too much loss of prestige if the picture was not finished."[34]

Matters seemed to be resolved but it was demonstrated that, pushed into a precarious financial situation, one of the two partners could abandon the other, despite the intimacy of their relationship.

There were various attempts by Swanson and Kennedy to complete *Queen Kelly* as an all-talkie and even as an operetta, but none proved satisfactory. One director who was approached about the salvage operation, Edmund Goulding, advised Swanson to shelve the picture and start another one.

Goulding and Swanson, with the help of actress and dialogue writer Laura Hope Crews, wrote the script for the new film in three weeks. It was then shot under Goulding's direction in twenty-one days. Goulding even wrote the music for a song for her to sing, "Love, Your Spell Is Everywhere."

The film was the 1929 *The Trespasser* and it proved to be a hit that won Swanson her second Oscar nomination. In her autobiography, Swanson noted that although he provided financing for *The Trespasser* because it was really her project rather than his, Kennedy did not want his name to appear in the credits. Film historian Cari Beauchamp has pointed out that not only does "Joseph Kennedy Presents" appear at the beginning of the picture but that Kennedy heavily promoted and marketed the film.[35]

In the meanwhile, Swanson had soured on Goulding when he remained adamant that *Queen Kelly* could not be salvaged. Kennedy, probably still fuming over his financial losses, reneged on an oral promise to Goulding to make him a partner. When Goulding threatened a lawsuit, Kennedy successfully countered by threatening to expose Goulding's bisexual lifestyle.

Kennedy did indeed remain committed to finding a successful project for Swanson whether out of pride or business reasons. He commissioned screenwriter Josephine Lovett to write a comedy for Gloria that would be a worthy follow-up to *The Trespasser*.

In early 1930, while Kennedy was having dinner with Swanson, he presented her with a bound copy of Lovett's screenplay, *Purple and Linen*. Swanson recalled that when later that night she and her friend Virginia Bowker read the script, "they were aghast. It was absolutely terrible."[36] Swanson said that she "didn't have the heart to tell Joe, so I asked him if I could let Allan Dwan read it, and he said to go right ahead."[37]

After the firing of von Stroheim, Swanson said that she sought help on *Queen Kelly* but that all the directors she really trusted (Neilan, Dwan and Walsh) were on location or too immersed in their projects. According to one source, it was Dwan who "steered" Swanson to Edmund Goulding.[38] Dwan was, in a sense, the anti–von Stroheim. He was the director known for fixing problems rather than creating them, for keeping on budgets and ahead of schedule. Yet Dwan was hardly lax in his maintenance of quality. In fact, he shared with von Stroheim an obsession with detail. As the reference to the torture scene in *Robin Hood* indicates, he could order numerous retakes when he was not satisfied. But with his vaunted scientific sense of calculation he kept things in proportion. When Swanson phoned Kennedy regarding von Stroheim, she bellowed, "Our director is a madman."[39] It was back in 1919 that *Photoplay* called Dwan "perhaps our sanest director."[40]

Swanson recognized that Kennedy, who had so much to teach her, was also "the classic example of that person in the arts with lots of brains and drive but little taste or talent."[41] Yet for both personal and professional reasons she wanted him to succeed.

Dwan and Swanson had remained in touch socially. On February 5, 1930, Dwan sent her a telegram expressing his regret that they could not get together on some unnamed project. But Dwan added,

> THERE IS NOTHING I WOULD RATHER DO THAN WORK WITH YOU AGAIN STOP PLEASE ACCEPT MY LATE BUT SINCERE CONGRATULATIONS ON THE TRESPASSER STOP LETS DO MANHANDLED AGAIN AS A TALKIE LOVE AND KISSES=
> ALLAN DWAN[42]

A month later Dwan found himself working together with Swanson in a way he never envisioned.

Dwan read the script and agreed completely with Swanson on its merits. He was willing to oblige Swanson by coming to meet Kennedy at her bungalow and stating his opinion. Dwan explained that the script was awful and advised Kennedy not to buy it. Kennedy told the full truth, that he had not only bought the screenplay but commissioned it.

Swanson now wanted to spare Kennedy another failure. She remembered, "I signaled Allan frantically and implored him to take it home, read it again, and see if he couldn't come up with some ideas to liven it up. Allan looked daggers at me and said he couldn't promise anything, but that he would try."[43]

Swanson phoned Dwan that night. "Please, Allan," I said. "Remember, we started with nothing a couple of times when we worked for Paramount."

"Nothing would be preferable," Dwan said.[44]

Swanson remained insistent, emphasizing the importance of Kennedy succeeding with his idea even if nothing was left of the idea in the film that materialized.

The next day Dwan returned for another meeting with Swanson and Kennedy. Dwan put forth some ideas and suggestions for saving the script and sprucing up the humor. This did have the effect of inducing some chuckles from Kennedy. He turned to Swanson and said reassuringly, "You see, Gloria, just a few changes and it will be fine."

Dwan also told Kennedy he didn't think much of the title. The disappointed Kennedy pressed Dwan for a new title. Dwan suggested, "Let's make it first and then name it. It'll be less confining to work that way."[45]

Kennedy wanted to discuss money but Dwan said that it was too early for that. Dwan proposed that he would round up a few actors and they would act out some scenes in front of Kennedy. If he was pleased, they could then write up an agreement.

With Swanson's help, Dwan assembled a group of actors and they improvised several scenes and honed them to a satisfactory level. When the actors performed before Kennedy and his four Irish-American underlings whom he called the Four Horsemen, they all laughed uproariously. Dwan was given a green light to start the film.

In his own account to Bogdanovich, Dwan makes no comment on the script being dreadful, only that Swanson called him over to discuss the project with her and Kennedy, that he made a few suggestions and then agreed to do it.[46] However, the fact that Kennedy assigned two more writers to the project suggests that there were at least some problems with the screenplay.

Kennedy also remained adamant about the importance of having a title despite the fact that he had earlier acquiesced to waiting until the completion of the film. It was decided to invite a group of writers to dinner and elicit suggestions from them. Dwan says that this was his idea[47] but Swanson puts it under the umbrella of a collective "we."[48] As Dwan and Swanson told the film story and cited bits of dialogue about the tale of Swanson's meandering widow, someone exclaimed, "What a widow!"

Dwan then turned to Kennedy and said, "There's your title."

According to Swanson, Kennedy (who was laughing and hitting his thigh) called out, "Find out who said that and give him a Cadillac." The winner was Sidney Howard, the Pulitzer Prize–winning playwright and future credited screenwriter of *Gone with the Wind*. When Dwan told his version of the story to Bogdanovich, he added, "I tell you that just in case you think it's a sane business."[49]

Perhaps partially because the script of *What a Widow!* was being re-shaped by improvisations, Dwan decided on doing something novel in preparing a feature film: "[T]o avoid uncertainty or another trap, I suggested something that had never been done, and may never be done again. I got the nucleus of the cast together and went on some standing sets and photographed the entire picture in two days — every scene in master shots, with all the dialogue — but without costumes or makeup or any of the extras, and none of the action. It didn't cost much under those conditions. We cut it together and that way we could see and hear the flow of the story — and were able to correct the parts that were weak."[50]

Dwan conducted this dress rehearsal film very early in the proceeding because it was reported in *Film Daily* in mid–March (the article said the shooting took three, not two days).[51] *Photoplay* also carried this story, again citing three days, and noted, "This novel experiment is the idea of Joseph P. Kennedy, in general charge of Gloria's productions. He believes it will save time and money in the long run."[52] Given Kennedy's inexperience and ignorance of production methods, it is questionable that he was responsible for this strategy.

Dwan said that because they were able to look at this "pilot" film, the actual shooting was easier and proceeded more quickly. Dwan said that watching the film also provided ideas for characterizations and other bits of business. But Dwan never used this technique again because "I never found any occasion where it was necessary or where anybody would stand for it."[53] (Over fifty years later, director Francis Ford Coppola would shoot a "dress rehearsal" on video for his film *One from the Heart*. That movie proved to be an epic flop.)

In Dwan's interview with Koszarski, unlike his earlier one with Bogdanovich, Dwan says that he and Kennedy had come into conflict. He claimed he told Kennedy, "Look, we're going to make it my way ... or I'm not interested." Dwan said that Kennedy responded, "Okay. You make it your way and if we don't like it we'll make it over." In this version, the pilot film was Dwan's way of making sure that the course he had chosen was correct.[54]

Dwan's partners in this enterprise were also making their contributions.

Since this was to be a frothy comedy, Swanson was back to playing the clotheshorse. She proudly recalled, "The real hero and star of the picture from the beginning was Rene Hubert. He designed a whole wardrobe for me, including all my jewelry except for a jeweled fan that held lipstick in the handle, which I designed myself. When Allan saw it, he opened a scene with a marvelous close-up of me reflected in it."[55]

But besides employing her trusted costume designer, Swanson brought in another important collaborator. In her travels in Europe she had an opportunity to view the latest in *avant garde* art styles. In 1929, Swanson met the Chicago-born architect Paul Nelson, who had done much of his work in Paris but was visiting the Pathé studios with relatives. She kept him in mind for her next project. Nelson's enthusiasm for modern design must have registered with Swanson, who probably saw this as helping to give her film a totally up-to-date look. *What a Widow!* was Nelson's one and only contribution on film.

Nelson's innovative designs were also exploited in the film's publicity which referred to him as "Paul Nelson, Paris."[56] In its column "Inside Stuff— Pictures," *Variety* noted, "New mode in set construction and motion picture backgrounds will reach the screen when Gloria Swanson's *What a Widow!* is released." The column added the dubious credit, "Joseph P. Kennedy noticed Nelson's work in Paris and took him to Hollywood expressly for the Swanson picture."[57] (Two letters from Nelson to Swanson in the Ransom Collection, appearing almost twenty years apart and expressing the architect's gratitude to the actress for giving him his start, appear to confirm that Swanson was chiefly responsible for bringing Nelson to the project.[58])

Other film studios took their cue from Swanson's move. Two weeks later, the same *Variety* column noted, "Major studios believe that while motion pictures have made rapid strides in the advancement of technique in most every phase, set designing has been overlooked. A number of studios are concentrating on new ideas in sets. With Gloria Swanson taking the first step in using modernistic backgrounds, Paramount promises revolutionary stage settings in its forthcoming *Paramount on Parade* revue."[59]

Donald Albrecht, who studied photographs of Nelson's sets for Swanson's film, observed, "The use of open, flowing space in the sets for *What a Widow!* illustrates one of modern architecture's most significant contributions to film — namely, the vivid rendering of three-dimensional space on the flat, two-dimensional movie screen.... The simplest of these [optical tricks] is the placement of walls, screens, or other large objects in the foreground of the picture. Functioning as frames, these elements heighten the perception of distance between foreground and background."[60]

Given how Dwan handled the sense of space in the vast sets of *Robin Hood* and his penchant for large sets in his lost films of the early twenties, one can only wonder what spatial schemes a more mature Dwan would have constructed as he followed his merry widow and her suitors across Nelson's sets.

There was one contribution to the film's sense of modernity that more assuredly came from Kennedy. At a climactic point in the movie, Swanson's heroine, the liberated widow Tamarind Brooks, realizes the man she loves is about to leave Paris for New York. She makes a dash to get on the Dornier DO-X airplane in which she and Owen Moore are married as the plane flies past the Statue of Liberty.

The Dornier DO-X made its first transatlantic passenger flight late in 1930. So *What a Widow!* portrayed this as the normal means of travel just before it began. Kennedy was able to get the Fokker Aircraft Corporation to give him footage of the DO-X in flight over Lake Constance, Switzerland, and to lend his company a model of the interior to depict Swanson flying to New York. The pilot of the plane was also hired to play himself.[61]

While *What a Widow!* was being attired in chic trappings, Dwan cast as Swanson's leading men two actors who were something short of being new and fashionable. Pickford's first husband Owen Moore was still handsome and dapper at age 43, while veteran character actor Lew Cody was forty-six. Their experience was probably needed, given all the improvisation involved in putting the new script together. And six much younger men were also being cast as Swanson's lovesick admirers.

Swanson said she already saw problems developing. "As shooting progressed, the mood of the initial improvisations proved hard to preserve. Polishing silly, spontaneous madness is difficult going at best, and Allan had a number of handicaps to cope with. Owen Moore was not well at the time, and Lew Cody could not remember his lines, so we had to re-shoot

Paul Nelson's modernistic sets for *What a Widow!* (1930) helped to create a change in Hollywood art direction.

many of the scenes, and each time we did, we lost some of the original bounce. In addition, while it was no small coup to have Vincent Youmans as our songwriter, the songs he came up with were never going to make anyone forget 'Tea for Two.'"[62]

What a Widow! may have undergone one of the great salvage efforts for an independent film, especially one that had to be salvaged before it was made. It was certainly something new to Dwan's experience. While he may have been nudged into the project, he seemed to look back fondly on the rescue effort and remembered *What a Widow!* as a "successful picture."[63] Unfortunately, this was not the case. The public response to *What a Widow!* was only "lukewarm."[64]

Overall, the reviews were not bad. Even in the case of the largely negative review from the *New York Times*, it was noted that the critic was seeing what a theater executive told him was a bad print where the voices of the players were often indistinct, and when Swanson sang there was "poor synchronization." The *Times* judged it "a comedy of sorts, a farce that sinks to slapstick.... It is a farce that would have been far more effective had it been done in a more sober fashion."[65]

Several of the reviews also cited the slapstick elements but somewhat more sympathetically than the *Times*. Ironically, the reviewer who fumed most vociferously about slapstick in *Stage Struck*, *Variety*'s founder and owner Sime Silverman, gave *What a Widow!* one of its most enthusiastic reviews and did not mention slapstick at all. Silverman cited the film's "rapid moving scenes. They will tell the foreigners that none of them has anything on Alan [sic] Dwan for swift or subtle kaleidoscopic direction."[66] One critic complained, "Some of the scenes are so fast that the dialogue is indistinct."[67] Was Dwan anticipating how sound would be exploited in the 1930s with fast-paced dialogue?

The shortcomings of the film may have also been exacerbated by changing times. The story of how a young widow sails to Paris with five million dollars to spend and plenty of time to involve herself in dalliances (which to please the censors are all innocuous) may not have been the right choice for a country just beginning to feel the brunt of the Great Depression. Richard Barrios has commented, "Though audiences still loved Swanson and applauded her singing, a trifling piece of slapstick about empty-headed socialites, seemed in the bleak autumn of 1930, as out of step as a film could be."[68]

No print of the film is now available. The soundtrack is preserved at UCLA but is not available to researchers. The trailer is held by the Library of Congress.

The merger plans that resulted in the formation of RKO-Radio Pictures earned Kennedy a financial bonanza but he would have no place in the new corporation. Although it was not reported in the press, his colleagues were well aware of his ruthlessness and his penchant for betrayal when it came to gaining power. So he was frozen out of the new management structure.

There were now far fewer companies left in the film business and Kennedy knew he was a builder and promoter, not a long-term administrator.[69] There were also family and social pressures to end any threat to his marriage. It was time to pull up stakes. Kennedy left Hollywood for good in April 1930 before filming began on *What a Widow!* His business and personal involvement with Swanson was abruptly ended.

It wasn't until months after Kennedy's departure that Swanson learned how Kennedy had manipulated her company Gloria Productions to pay for his own corporate expenses. Apparently even the Cadillac awarded to Howard had been charged to her expense. She was now in debt for $1.5 million, triple the amount she owed when she first met Kennedy.

Gloria Swanson faces one of her young suitors in *What a Widow!* (1930). This film set her off on a path of irrevocable decline.

Swanson believed she had made *What a Widow!* to help salvage Kennedy's ego. Perhaps Kennedy had intended the project as a parting gift. Its failure put Swanson's film career on a downward spiral from which it never recovered.

Dwan may not have been seriously tarnished by *What a Widow!* but his career seemed to be ebbing in importance. The film's failure did suggest that both the industry and country were changing and that this period of transition would be treacherous for veterans of the film industry.

Despite Goulding's advice, Kennedy and Swanson had not given up on *Queen Kelly* but as *What a Widow!* was being readied for production, Kennedy finally announced that work on *Queen Kelly* would not be resumed.

Incredibly, in 1956 Swanson went back to von Stroheim and with his help had re-enlisted her *Queen Kelly* co-stars Walter Byron and Seena Owen to complete the film. This time, Kennedy declined to supply the financing.[70]

Kennedy was most likely completely fed up with the project and may have soured on ever producing a film completely on his own. He had turned to two directors, one mad and one sane, and neither was able to deliver the hit he craved.

Downfall

After the highly complicated exercise of making an independent film for Swanson and Kennedy, Dwan returned to studio work, perhaps eagerly. On June 24, 1930, he signed a one-picture contract for $20,000 with Warner Brothers. The term of employment was said to have begun on June 18 so Dwan was apparently working on the film even before the contract was signed.[71]

The film was to be released under the aegis of First National. The one-time main rival to Paramount had been weakened as Adolph Zukor siphoned off their theaters. Warner Brothers purchased the firm and assumed total control by 1929. Some film projects were then designated to go under the Warner Brothers banner and others with the First National brand. Although A and B films appeared under both designations, the more prestigious films generally went out under the Warners name.

Based on a short story by Ben Ames Williams (who later wrote the novel *Leave Her to Heaven*), Dwan's *Man to Man* was released in December 1930. It's one of the films that demonstrate the Dwan paradox. On some levels a minor and even routine film, it is executed with deep conviction and with the stylistic intricacy befitting a masterpiece. Dwan's sense of personal involvement is evident in what is another "lost father" saga and what was billed in the company's press sheets as a "powerful drama of a prodigal father."[72] Film historian William K. Everson believed that Dwan "seems to be exhibiting far more personal interest in this film than in some of his bigger silent vehicles with Fairbanks and Swanson."[73]

The plot is simple. Michael Bolton (Phillips Holmes) is a popular star athlete at Southern College. When a news story appears in the papers about a prison convict who did not join his fellow prisoners in an escape, one of the students jokes that since the convict's last name is Bolton, he must be Mike's father. Mike at first denies this but then confirms it is his father. When Michael finds himself ostracized, he quits college and returns to his home in the small town of Hardinsville, Kentucky, where he gets a job as a bank teller. When his father is pardoned and returns home, Michael is respectful but cold. Later, when $2,000 in bank funds are missing from Michael's cubicle, both father and son are implicated.

Everson commented on the film, "Many of the compositions are quite lovely, and there is one really beautiful shot of two lovers, sitting in their roadster at dusk, while a locomotive roars by in the background...."[74] But even more striking is the entire sequence of which that shot is only a part. Michael is telling his girlfriend that it is unlikely that he will be elected class president as she expects and he reluctantly reveals the secret that his father is in prison for killing a man. After initially looking shocked, the young woman tells him that it doesn't make any difference.

There is a cut to a college newspaper story on how the popular athlete Bolton failed to be elected president of his class. In the next shot, we see that Michael is reading the story on a train. He looks out the window and sees a car parked with a boy and girl; a tighter shot reveals that his girlfriend is with another man. There is a cut to a dejected-looking Michael closing the train window shade.

The whole manner in which Michael and his girl are seen in the foreground and the train in the background, edited with the bridging device of the newspaper so that we next see Michael in the train looking out at his girlfriend in the car with someone else, is an astonishing bit of business. Without a single word being uttered, Dwan has explained why Michael is leaving college and the editing conveys his emotional dislocation and literal reversal of fortune.

When Michael is taken to the bank by his Uncle Cal (Russell Simpson), the camera follows him down the street in a long tracking shot. As Dwan had claimed he had done a year earlier, a microphone must have been attached to the boom because we can hear Cal and Michael exchanging words with people passing by. Some early sound films had sequences employing long tracking shots to relieve the tedium of static dialogue scenes but few in 1930 may have had synchronous sound.

George Marion, who had earlier that year played the father in *Anna Christie* to Greta Garbo's Anna, is his father's old friend, the banker Jim McCord, who hires Michael. He tells him to be proud of his father since he killed as a matter of honor; he was avenging the other man's fatal shooting of his brother. Jim explains that longtime residents of Hardinsville believe that Michael's father had done nothing wrong.

When Michael's father, "Barber John" (Grant Mitchell),

steps off the train, he looks in vain for his son to be waiting for him. John's arrival, as he is greeted by various gents, is also filmed in long tracking shots. Dwan treats the tracking shots in *Man to Man* as motifs that gain in importance as the film progresses. While Michael accompanies his co-worker at the bank, Emily Saunders (Lucille Powers), in a long walk to her home, she shows her interest in him.

Phillips Holmes as Michael was excessively awkward and tentative. But there are also genuine flashes of sensitivity and pain in his performance that are astutely caught by Dwan's camera. Meeting his father at home, Michael is non-committal and standoffish. But when John casually says he kept in practice by working as the prison barber, the extremity of Michael's facial reaction and head movement convinces John that his son is ashamed of him.

After Michael leaves, John confides his feelings to Cal, who is angered by the boy's behavior. John counsels patience while admitting his sense of hurt that his son is ashamed of him. Mitchell would go on to play figures of authority in countless movies as judges, businessmen and harried fathers, roles where he often appeared as less of a character than as a fixture. But this was one of his early films after he came to the movies from a strong stage career. His work in *Man to Man* is, as Everson put it, a "really moving and sensitive performance"[75] that anchors the film.

What makes the conflict in *Man to Man* especially gripping is how Michael persists in acknowledging his ties to his father to friends and strangers. In the opening scene after some hesitation, he is emphatic in proclaiming, "I *am* his son." Later when a sore loser playmate at the Hardinsville town picnic makes a derogatory comment about his father, Michael demands that he take it back and resorts to his fists when the roughneck refuses.

Michael's shame of his father clearly coexists with feelings of love and pride for his dad. A big part of Mike's problem, as he confesses to Emily, is that despite all the outpouring of sympathy for his father, Michael feels that behind his back the townspeople are expressing far different feelings. Mike is still smarting from the turnabout in popularity he experienced at college and he has come to see most people as fickle.

Shortly after Barber John's return, there is a medium shot of Mike sitting before the bars of the bank teller's cage. At first this seems like a heavy-handed reminder of his father's prison record. But Dwan conveys that Michael is physically as well as emotionally imprisoned. The view from his cubicle extends across the street where he can see his father's barber shop, which has now reopened. This view will always be before him as he works.

This touches on another aspect of Dwan's work both in style and theme: voyeurism. In a sense, it complements the obsession with the lost father. If someone must conceal his paternal identity and his feelings, then he must often be content to look at the object of his issue and affection from afar or clandestinely.

In *Man to Man*, it is Michael who does most of the looking. Much of this has to do with his repressed feelings for his father as well as his sense of stasis over what to do. Michael seems paralyzed at the front door of the bank when his father's carriage rides by on his return. Returning home much later, Mike cautiously looks in the window to see his father with Uncle Cal before entering the house. In the scene by the railroad bridge, Michael went from being in the driver's seat with his girl to watching her with a new boyfriend from a train window. In the very opening of the film, it appears we are at a track meet watching Michael racing over hurdles only to have the camera zoom back at the end of the sequence and reveal that Michael and his fellow students are watching the event on film, an augury that Michael will soon be reduced to a passive status.

Barber John comes into the bank at one point and, going to Michael's window, asks him for change. Michael has to go to get it at another window. While waiting, John accidentally drops his cigar into Michael's cubicle. John extends his arm as far as he can through the teller's window trying to retrieve it. On returning, Michael looks suspiciously at John's arm dangling through the window but we have seen that he has done no more than reach his cigar. When Michael tabulates his accounts at the end of the day, he discovers that $2,000 is missing.

Michael becomes convinced that his father took the money. The other teller, Vint Glade, tells the inspector of Michael's father extending his arm through the window. Confronted by that information and knowing that his father could now be sent to prison for life as a "two-time loser," Michael signs a

Before he became embedded in small, stereotyped roles, Grant Mitchell (seen here in a 1938 photograph) demonstrated the strong acting skills that had served him on stage in Dwan's *Man to Man* (1930).

confession that he stole the money. He does so despite having had a nightmare vision of his father appearing before him and chortling, "I took the money but you'll get the blame. You were ashamed of me because I went to prison. Now you'll go to prison." (The dream also suggests Michael's sense of guilt for his shame.) When John finds out that his son is being accused and that his reaching through the bank window is being discussed, he confesses to the crime and explains away his son's confession as a young man trying to protect his own father. Michael, who has tried to get away, is brought into the bank, where he continues to insist that he committed the crime. Father and son engage in a bizarre duel of guilt and love as both try to confess. Befuddled authorities decide to arrest both of them and take them to the jail.

Outside of seeing the film, it is difficult to describe the power and majesty of the tracking shot showing father and son being marched to the jail together with the gesture of the father extending his hand to his son's shoulder. This is a film with such stylistic conviction that one begins to grasp the universality of the tortured mixture of pride and shame a son can feel for his father.

The rest of the movie seems anticlimactic, including the denouement as Emily hatches a scheme that will expose Michael's co-worker Vint Glade as the thief. The sequence is leavened with comedy, including some racial humor, though mild for its time. The old vaudevillian Otis Harlan proves most nimble here and as prone to malapropisms as his black friend played by Johnny Larkins. Portraying Vint, who is tricked into confessing, Dwight Frye degenerates into hysteria, showing some of the traits that would typecast him in Universal horror films.

Another interesting aspect of *Man to Man* is its resemblance to Dwan's 1915 *David Harum*. It has the small town atmosphere, the long tracking shots of men walking, the plot of the young romantic hero being framed for a bank crime; there is even a joke about horse trading. Dwan has not merely tried to recycle old tricks and plot from a former success. Rather it appears that when confronted with the story "Barber John's Son," Dwan took his experience from *David Harum* and showed how every device and plot line could be improved on and deepened, as if that had been gestating in his mind for years. *Man to Man* is a richer film than the classic *David Harum*.

Man to Man is the first of four consecutive well-crafted and largely unrecognized films made by Dwan in this period. The second, the World War I drama *Chances*, was also made at Warner Brothers, while the next two, *Wicked* and *While Paris Sleeps*, were made at Fox. There are interesting thematic and stylistic connections that can be made through all four films.

Man to Man must have done well enough that Warners agreed to sign Dwan to another one-picture deal on January 5, 1931, again for $20,000. Dwan's employment was specified to begin on January 19 and since his contract left open the possibility of "assisting in the preparation of the story" he may have had some input in the final draft of the script which was completed on January 23.[76] The genesis of *Chances* was also related to the search to find a suitable vehicle for Douglas Fairbanks, Jr.'s first major starring role. At the time, Darryl Zanuck was supervisor of production for Warners. Fairbanks pestered Zanuck for the opportunity. Fairbanks recalled,

> We even had a long, drawn-out argument about my first real "starring" picture. One story after another was discussed and discarded. Eventually, after being told there was a limit to my new powers of approval, I was advised the movie would be *Chances*, another Great War picture — this time with an English setting. A bittersweet romance about two brothers in love with the same woman, *Chances* recalled *The Dawn Patrol*. Again, there were French battlefield scenes and again, my brother was killed in action.[77]

The Dawn Patrol was a hit of 1930 with Richard Barthelmess playing Fairbanks' close friend, not his brother. *The Dawn Patrol* had been directed by Howard Hawks and he was originally assigned to do *Chances*, based on a best-seller by A. Hamilton Gibbs. Hawks, however, told the Warners brass he thought the novel was "lousy"[78] and would make a terrible film. Refusing to budge, Hawks was relieved of the assignment.

Though sharing some similarities with *The Dawn Patrol*, *Chances*, as directed by Dwan and scripted by Waldemar Young, is not a war film in the same sense as the Hawks picture. As was sometimes the case with Dwan, he would straddle two genres in one film. *Chances* does not tip the balance to either the war film or the wartime romance. The film may be said to have four acts, with two each alternately taking place on leave and in the combat zone, followed by a brief epilogue.

The plot device of two brothers (or any two buddies) falling in love with the same girl was hardly new or complex but Dwan had an asserted aptitude and interest in developing relationships into triangles. If the device is familiar, it nevertheless achieves an unusual intensity in *Chances*.

The film opens in a fog-enshrouded city under the title "London 1914." A policeman upbraids a newspaper vendor for striking a match, since no lights are to be displayed for fear of zeppelin attacks. The fog seems an apt metaphor for all the confusion and misunderstanding that follows in the story. As brothers Tom (Anthony Bushell) and Jack Ingelside (Fairbanks) walk down the street, Jack almost collides with a young woman walking in the opposite direction. Jack finds the lady fetching and wants to get acquainted. She is amused as she insists that they actually do know each other but Jack doesn't remember. She assures Jack that they will meet again. Tom has kept walking and has not heard any of this.

When the brothers enter their mother's home, Jack is amazed to see the young woman sitting in the drawing room. Jack still doesn't recognize her but Tom knows her instantly: She is Molly Prescott (Rose Hobart), a childhood friend whom Tom always liked but whom Jack remembered as a "horrid little girl." Molly has been away studying painting in France. Molly drops a few hints of their earlier meeting while Jack signals to her frantically not to reveal that he tried to pick her up the night before. Jack is relieved that she keeps his secret and he escorts her out. Tom tells his mother how beautiful she is and how he is still smitten with her. Tom contrasts his attitude with Jack's: "Jack's the ladies man in our family. They're all alike to Jack. He never takes one of them seriously."

There is a cut to a lateral tracking shot of Jack walking Molly through the garden; again Dwan's moving camera helps to weave the spell as Jack's interest in Molly deepens. When Molly tells Jack she wants to paint a landscape of one of the cliffs near the sea at dawn, Jack leaves to meet her at sunrise without telling anyone.

Later that night in the garden, Jack tells Molly that his love for her is genuine. But inside the house where a dance party is being held for the Red Cross, Jack learns from his mother that Tom is in love with Molly and has been for years. She tells Jack that Tom is "so sensitive. If she refuses, it will break his heart." Jack then intentionally displays his interest in another woman in front of Molly, and succeeds in breaking her heart. When Tom asks Molly if she will marry him and will wait for his return, she agrees out of spite.

Hobart with her dark brooding eyes is excellent as Molly. But her pain is most powerfully expressed when Dwan has her move to a staircase and just stand there with her back to the camera, concealing her face from everyone. As Jack, Fairbanks seems a bit callow at times but overall rises to the occasion.

Ten acres of ground from the Warner Brothers–First National ranch in Hollywood were used for the battle scenes. It was the first time Dwan made use of a twentieth century battlefield. With the help of technical experts, he depicted the fighting against what seemed a perpetual night.

For the scenes of the home front, Dwan used both interiors and a studio garden. He also had an opportunity to break out of the studio environment: For the scenes of Molly and Jack at their dawn rendezvous in Cornwall and for a later meeting at a beach in Calais, Dwan needed a picturesque area by the sea that could double for both locations. Dwan knew just such a place. The scenes were filmed at Santa Barbara where Dwan had concluded his career at Flying A.

The beach scene at Calais is particularly beautiful. It occurs after Jack's success on a dangerous assignment gets him seven days' leave. Molly confesses to Jack that she accepted Tom's offer only because she wanted to show Jack that she "didn't care." She also admits that she has stopped writing to Tom because she doesn't love him. It is Jack who must tell the truth directly to Tom. Molly also gives Jack a photo of herself with an inscription on the back: "Keep me with you always and I'll try to keep you safe."

For the transitions between home front and battle front, Dwan uses montages of moving wheels, e.g., on Jack's return, locomotive wheels dissolve into truck wheels which dissolve into auto wheels and then dissolve into motorcycle wheels. It is as if he is indicating a whole evolutionary process in moving from one theater to the other.

In the film, it almost appears as if they are parallel worlds. At home, Jack and Tom spend time with their mother. On the war front, the two brothers are seen at headquarters where they often share the table of their commanding officer Major Bradford (Holmes Herbert) who acts as a stern but understanding father figure. (The character of Bradford is said to have been based on the author of *Chances*, A. Hamilton Gibbs, an officer in the artillery in World War I.[79])

Something of the gap between the two worlds is expressed in an exchange between Jack and Tom, when Jack returns. The dialogue is taken almost verbatim from Gibbs' book. Jack tells Tom that how he is unable to tell their mother what is really happening at the front. Tom responds, "I see what you mean. One doesn't realize that every letter home is really a lie from start to finish. I suppose it's just one more thing we'll have to compete with when this is over. It's a great war!"

Tom clearly has concerns about the long-range effect of the "noble lie." War has bred such lies. But the "noble lie" was what Jack had attempted without thought to the consequences and the inability to sustain it.

It is perhaps not coincidental that this has the opposite effect of the climax of *Man to Man* where two noble lies help rectify things. It was as if Dwan wanted to show there was another side to the effects of noble lies in different circumstances. The truth emerges when at the front, Tom mistakenly puts on Jack's coat and discovers Molly's picture. He thinks that Jack has just forgotten to give it to him. But when he confronts Jack with his negligence, Jack insists that the picture is his. Tom, at first

Rose Hobart and Douglas Fairbanks, Jr., are the wartime lovers deceiving Fairbanks' brother in *Chances* (1931).

perplexed, gets the point. He dismisses Jack's plea that this came from a misunderstanding and feels that Jack and Molly have both "chucked" him and Jack has done him a "mean and dirty trick." This occurs just before they are being called out to face an attack.

The final release print of *Chances* also carried its own "noble lie." In his interview with Bogdanovich, Dwan remembered, "[T]here was one little scene in it that was made after I'd gone. In the story, the British retreated — there was a rout. And there was a squawk about it because they said the British market would be shot to hell — they wouldn't release it there if the British army retreated. So they had to put in a scene between a couple of officers in which they decide to *pretend* to retreat. And then go on with what I'd shot — which was a retreat during which they'd turn and resist — but the hell was knocked out of them — nobody had a victory."[80]

Evidence suggests that Dwan's account is correct. It was announced on March 9 that shooting on *Chances* was completed.[81] Warner Bros. script records at USC show that a retake was ordered for a scene at headquarters on April 11, 1931. In it, the brigadier orders Major Bradford, "Retreat ... and the more disorderly you make it the better."[82]

According to William K. Everson, a few clips from Richard Barthelmess' silent *The Patent Leather Kid* were used in the battleground finale but most of the battle footage was clearly shot for this film.[83] Under heavy fire, the artillery unit must make its way on horseback dragging the cannons with them. Crisply edited, it is a memorably nightmarish ride made against billows of smoke and a black sky, with bombs illuminating the scene like lightning. There is a chilling dissonance seeing men with World War I helmets riding horses on a twentieth century battleground as if a great cavalry detachment had been recruited into the wrong century. It is a scene that says much about the First World War, and the facile insertion of discussing a "planned retreat" does not take away its sting.

The men then dismount to put their artillery into action but Major Bradford soon calls on them to fall back into the trenches. In a situation like this, entailing a triangular relationship, the usual movie convention would be for the character who loses the girl to sacrifice himself for the one who is loved by the heroine and indeed that is what happens in the novel.[84] While tragic, this leaves everything properly squared morally. But what happens in the film *Chances* is that while the other men, including Jack, scurry for cover, Tom remains on the battlefield, as if his discovery has left him in a daze. Jack races out to try to get Tom to take cover but he is already hit. Tom at least recognizes him as "his pal." Jack carries him over the barbed wire and urges him on as they both collapse into a foxhole.

Chances symmetrically concludes where it started, in a London fog. Molly meets Jack who is walking with a limp. Tom is dead but Jack at least has the satisfaction that Tom told them they were pals again at the end and that "it would be terrible without that." Unspoken is the fact that he may have perished because of the shock at the way the noble lie was revealed to him. Molly must light Jack's cigarette for him because he has lost the use of his left arm; a policeman calls out, "Put out that light." Together Jack and Molly walk into the fog, trying to make the best of things.

There were good, but not spectacular reviews for *Chances*. The *New York Times* called it a "thoroughly human story of war and love.... It rings true in every episode, nothing being overdone, for which [Dwan] deserves much credit."[85] In assessing Dwan's career, critic Myron Meisel refers to *Chances* as "among the most remarkable of all World War I films."[86] Part of this may be because *Chances* is not concerned with just the war. Dwan again paradoxically shows the intense feelings of his characters while also exercising emotional restraint. Consequently, the film registers their intensity while also methodically showing how they deal with everything love and war have thrown at them. The title *Chances*, which Gibbs may have selected for its Hemingwayesque terseness, seems highly appropriate. (The novel's inscription reads, "...through all the chances and changes of life 'till death do you part.")

The film clearly was not a big war epic in the manner of *All Quiet on the Western Front* or *The Big Parade*. Fairbanks was grateful to have his father's favorite director shepherding him but he recalled, "The picture, in spite of dear Allan's patient and paternal guidance and the expensive production given it, did not have a story of power and sweep to match its background, nor a part that demanded anything unusual from me. It was good, but not good enough. Today it is still affecting though a little dated."[87]

At the company party at the conclusion of filming, Fairbanks said he received an unusual gift from Dwan: one of the few remaining copies of Napoleon's actual death mask. "How he got it or from where, he would never tell, but ... I prized it and the thought beyond words."[88]

It was also perhaps an appropriate gift from someone who, according to Billy Bakewell, could be a real Napoleon on the set.

While all of these films are relatively short features, under 75 minutes long, *Wicked* is the shortest, clocking in at just slightly under an hour. If more of a programmer (and also qualitatively the least of the four pictures), it is nonetheless a brisk and absorbing film. Like *Man to Man*, the story deals with the protagonist being sent to prison and its aftermath. Ironically, while this film was made at Fox and *Man to Man* and *Chances* at Warners, it is *Wicked* that looks much more like the prototype of film that was starting to roll out at Warner Brothers, the sensationalist expose of injustice including the plight of the unfairly imprisoned. Dwan's films also ran at the breakneck speed that would be favored at Warners, and *Wicked* was a prime example. Bogdanovich commented admiringly to Dwan in their interview, "The pace is terrific — there's an attempted robbery, the girl's husband is killed, she's arrested, we find out she's pregnant, and they've got her in front of a jury — all before the first reel is over."[89]

Margot's sentence in prison is interrupted so that she can give birth to her baby outside the prison walls. She signs away her maternal rights so that her daughter Antonia can be taken to a children's home while Margot returns to prison. After she is pardoned two years and five months later, she goes to the home only to find that her daughter has been adopted. Margot desperately tries to find who has adopted her daughter.

Wicked is another hybrid genre film, moving from prison-injustice exposé to women's film. It's also a mother-and-daughter prison film that parallels the father-and-son drama of *Man to Man*. But given Antonia's age, there is little basis for interaction.

Dwan was usually less successful (and perhaps less committed) when he attempted to depict the plight of a "lost mother." But he is also acting under the strain of compressing two different storylines into less than an hour and pleasing an audience already depressed by the goings-on. Although the film was fairly well received by the critics, there was also some fatigue from all of the heroine's travails. The *New York Times* complained, "[T]he greater part of the film is somewhat distressing and Allan Dwan, the director who did such excellent work on *Chances*, has reached out too often to pile on the agony."[90] *Variety* thought it was "too depressing."[91]

And so a *deus ex machina* appears in the person of Scott Burrows, played by Victor McLaglen, as an old beau of Margot's. He comes to her from Australia, six months into her sentence, promising to do all he can to get her out of prison. Burrows also resolves the adoption issue by appealing to the adopted parents that they are too old to have the child, permitting Margot to take charge of her daughter. Burrows then marries Margot and takes her and Antonia to Australia. Dwan acknowledged to Bogdanovich that he "had to compromise, put on what they called a happy ending."[92]

Dwan's next film, *While Paris Sleeps*, was one of his most unusual. Not only is it the best of his films of the early 1930s, it's perhaps his best film of the decade. Dwan told Bogdanovich that its success was "a design and an accident — it just worked out. A lot of pictures are accidental. No matter how hard you work on them, accidentally something good comes out of them — or sometimes something bad too."[93]

Although an element of serendipity was involved, the key word in Dwan's description is "design." Dwan had started his directorial career by making films on location and grasped what actual locations could contribute to a film in atmosphere, realism and, most elusively, dramatic truth. He consistently sought to enhance his films with those qualities that could be provided by location shooting. As the studio system evolved, Dwan developed different strategies. For *East Side, West Side*, he used his intimate knowledge of New York City to reproduce a good chunk of it in the studio, where it could be controlled, in what was acknowledged as one of the largest sets created in a studio. At the same time, the film benefited by scenes shot on actual city spots.

The pressures and practical reasons for studio shooting increased further in the early sound era of the 1930s. It was reported that the largest interior set ever built at First National was constructed for *Chances*: "It represents both the interior and exterior and garden of a large English country home, and fills the entire stage...."[94] For that film, Dwan also had the huge battlefield at the Warner Brothers–First National ranch and was still able to use at least two location scenes.

For *While Paris Sleeps*, Dwan and Fox took a different step. Part of a city was recreated on the studio lot, with a particular emphasis on the seamy side. A few years earlier, Fox had shown its expertise in reconstructing Paris on a back lot for Frank Borzage's 1927 *Seventh Heaven*, which had proved a big hit.

The press notes for the film state that Dwan and Basil Woon, its sole credited writer, met in Paris a few years before they made the film and that together they had looked the city over with a possible film in mind. Woon, an Englishman, apparently knew the city well. He was married to a Frenchwoman, had lived in the city for fifteen years and written a book called *The Paris That's Not in the Guide Books*.[95] In his Bogdanovich interview, Dwan said that he "saw a lot of France before I made the picture. And out-of-the-way places too. I avoided the big popular cafes and prowled down into the other sections of Paris. And it might be that some of that smoky atmosphere stuck."[96]

So Dwan knew the kind of louche and sinister ambience he wanted but didn't know how well it could be constructed on film, as this was not an approach he had tried before. Credit must go to the art director of *While Paris Sleeps*, William Darling, and to the cinematographer Glen MacWilliams for providing the right shadowy lighting to give the proper look to the sets and evoke the mood required. Dwan was fortunate in their craftsmanship but he also deserves credit for conveying to them just what he needed. William K. Everson observed that the film's "stunning pictorial impact — superb sets, lighting, camerawork and art direction — give it the gloss of von Sternberg at his best."[97] *While Paris Sleeps* has been cited as a precursor of the fatalistic, dark French films of the late 1930s such as Marcel Carne's *Le Quai des brumes*. To a lesser extent, it might also be said to anticipate the Hollywood film noir of the next decade.

The press sheets proudly noted that *While Paris Sleeps* was shot "in entirety at Movietone City, Beverly Hills, Calif., with many scenes brought especially from Paris for the production."[98] The latter was probably a reference to a few stock shots of the city.

The plot is what might be called the quintessential "lost father" story. Victor McLaglen plays Jacques Costaud, a winner of the Croix de Guerre in the First World War, now serving a life sentence for killing a man in a brawl. When he learns that his wife is dying and that his daughter Manon is in potential danger, he escapes from his penal colony in French Guiana and manages to return to Paris. His wife is now dead and Manon is impoverished since the money he left to provide for his family was withheld from them by the man entrusted with the funds. Costaud learns that Manon is working in a sleazy café and that the gang running the establishment is planning to sell her into prostitution. Costaud takes the gang on single-handedly to free Manon and her boyfriend from the criminals so that the boyfriend can marry her and start a new life in the country. Costaud chooses not to be taken alive by the police.

Dwan expertly sets the mood for the story in one of the French penal colonies in Guiana now remembered as Devil's Island. It begins in complete darkness while the sounds of barking bloodhounds are heard. Darkness suffuses much of the film, just as the barking bloodhounds foretell that Costaud will be relentlessly pursued. As their lanterns illuminate the scene, we see a line of prison guards following the bloodhounds. The camera boom moves towards the guards, glides past them and then moves down an embankment to reveal two prisoners hiding in the brush. One of them is Costaud. When they try to move on, they are spotted by the guards, who open fire. Costaud's companion is killed but Costaud dives into the river. The guards fire into the water and, not seeing the prisoner surface, assume that he is dead.

The prison warden and doctor discuss the report that Costaud has been killed. It is noted that Costaud, who had already served fifteen years, had received a letter from his dying wife. The warden concludes, "It's always a blessing when a man who is dead mentally, dies physically."

The opening camera movement downward foreshadows a story that is quite palpably a descent into an underworld for the purpose of rescuing an innocent. Costaud has escaped one hell to enter another, moving from a jungle hell to a civilized one. If he is essentially a dead man walking, he will struggle a little while longer to save his daughter before he disappears from the earth.

Camera mobility is a major part of the style of *While Paris Sleeps* but here there is less emphasis on lateral tracking and more on the camera moving into the frame. This is more of a quality of gothic cinema where the camera is leading us into unknown places and penetrating the faces of a rogues' gallery of characters.

Bright lights in the next scene signal that we are now in Paris but this scene, like much of the rest of the film, is set at night. After a glimpse of landmarks such as the Arch de Triumph, we are shown the Eternal Flame at the Tomb of the Unknown Soldier, where Costaud's daughter Manon (Helen Mack) is laying a wreath to her father because she was told his body was never found. In another part of Paris, we see Costaud, who has somehow made his way across the ocean. Costaud glances at his wife's letter, which says that Manon was told that he died a hero.

We are again in the realm of *Man to Man* and *Wicked* where the shame of a parent's prison record has created problems for the offspring. (The protagonist cannot reveal his true feelings, recalling *Chances*— as does Costaud's service in the First World War.) But why the emphasis on imprisonment through three films in this period, made with different writers and at two different studios? When *While Paris Sleeps* was shot in late 1931, the country was in the worst throes of the Depression and audiences were in the mood for downbeat fare such as horror and gangster movies. Still there was hardly a glut of parent-in-prison films.

Given the sense of conviction conveyed in these movies, they probably expressed some of Dwan's personal concerns. Possibly they reflected some festering resentment toward the end of the silent era and the studio-bound restrictions (imprisonment?) of filming with sound. If that was the case, *While Paris Sleeps* may be the Dwan film closest to the aesthetic of the silent film. Dialogue is sparse and absent for long stretches.

Parallel editing is used to join the movements of Costaud and Manon. At one point, the characters are perversely prevented from meeting when Costaud is unknowingly standing outside her door and Manon first appears ready to walk out, but then decides to sit down and eat instead.

Manon had returned from her visit to the Unknown Soldier's tomb only to learn that a man has been given her room because she cannot pay the rent. Manon protests that she doesn't know what else she can do to find a job. We know we are in a seedy part of the city when the landlady replies, "If I had a face and figure like yours, I wouldn't ask silly questions."

The landlady tells Manon she cannot get her belongings unless she pays her rent. Desperate to reclaim her things, Manon sneaks upstairs and then walks on a ledge to get to her apartment window. The striking long shot of Manon's perilous advance on the ledge, where we also see silhouettes of two of the female tenants through the shades of their windows, has a perverse beauty.

After she climbs into her apartment, Manon quickly retrieves her most prized possession, her father's medal, the Croix de Guerre with three palms. Manon is soon discovered by the male tenant, Julot (Jack La Rue). He first allays her concerns and then tells her that she can sleep in the room if she wishes. When she looks chagrined, Julot explains that he works all night. Julot later tells her that he can get her a job as a cashier in a local café, the Casque d'or.

There are sinister goings-on in the café, which is located next door to a pastry shop. Julot brings a police informer, Mouche, from the café and into the basement of the pastry shop to the gang headquarters in the bakery under the shop. Dwan makes the most of the atmosphere with silhouetted figures and menacing shadows in an evocation of a horrific and literal underworld. As Mouche is taken down to the bakery, he is momentarily encased in total darkness as if presaging what's to come. Mouche is told he must pay the penalty for his acts: Screaming and pleading, he is lifted up to be thrown into the furnace, although there is a cut before this occurs. Fox's publicity claimed that the "torture bakery ... had a counterpart in real life, and was the main element in a recent news story depicting gangdom at its worst."[99]

The café is a front for the gang luring young girls into white slavery (they are shipped to South America). Manon is an intended victim but has two allies. When she begins her first day of work, she is pleased to meet the café's accordion player, Paul Renoir. (Talk about an artist figure!)

Of course, Paul and Manon are attracted to each other and he takes her on a boat ride. When they pass the old royal palace, Paul is quick to point out that that was where D'Artagnan used to live and that he was a Gascon like Paul is. This may be simply an inside joke (and Dwan's films sometimes do make references to other Dwan films) since Paul is played by William Bakewell, who portrayed Louis XIV in *The Iron Mask*. But it also notes something of a historic comedown as in this world and age; the man who can retain D'Artagnan's romantic vision is now a scoffed-at troubadour. ("Did he play the accordion too?" Manon teasingly asks.)

Costaud proves more effectual at protecting her from an ardent admirer than Paul, who gets knocked aside in a café scuffle. But like other Dwan protagonists, Costaud is reduced to looking at her. That look in these surroundings cannot avoid seeming lecherous. When he tries to approach Manon, she flees, assuming the worst and telling him that he is making a "mistake."

Like many other Dwan films and particularly the ones shot in the 1930s, *While Paris Sleeps* is made with extreme economy and packs all its incidents into 68 minutes. But Dwan still manages to find time for scenes and moments that do more to establish mood than to advance the plot. During the time that he is looking for Manon, Costaud approaches a young woman whose face is obscured under an umbrella. A close-up at first suggests another innocent beauty but then the manner in which she smiles and cocks her head towards a possible rendezvous spot tells otherwise. Costaud recoils, probably recognizing how quickly his daughter might be put in a similar position.

After Paul has helped Manon escape the while slavers and has her in his room, Costaud enters and says that he was a friend of Manon's father's. While Costaud sometimes sounds more like he's talking to himself, he promises Manon and Paul that in repaying a debt he will provide money for them to get away from what Paul calls "this sewer."

In the onrush of melodramatic events that follow, Paul is captured by the gang and used to lure Manon to come to the bakery. The white slavers threaten to kill Paul if Manon does not go to South America. Meanwhile, Costaud has been arrested and is being taken to a police station. He muses, "I killed five men in a shell hole and got a medal. I kill one man in a brawl and got life." Costaud manages to escape and makes his way to the labyrinthine bakery hideout. He takes on the gang, freeing Paul and providing him with the money promised. Rather than be re-captured by the police, Costaud chooses death by explosion. The flames from the inferno dissolve into the Eternal Flame before which Manon stands honoring her father, who was an unknown soldier in a way she will never grasp.

It may be pushing the envelope a bit much to call *While Paris Sleeps* an elegy to the veterans of the First World War and their falling on hard times. But it did fit the era. *While Paris Sleeps* was released in May 1932. That summer, thousands of unemployed World War I veterans marched on Washington, D.C., demanding the bonus they had been promised for their duties. The bill awarding their bonus failed to pass Congress; in July, when they continued to protest, they were driven out by the U.S. Army and their shacks were burned.

Jack La Rue has some sinister designs on Helen Mack in ***While Paris Sleeps*** **(1932).**

While Paris Sleeps is a nightmare fantasy of its depressed time, anchored in sordid reality. But there is also a timelessness in the travails of its protagonist who could evoke Victor Hugo's Jean Valjean of *Les Miserables*.

The film that was released in 1932, however, was not exactly the film as Dwan originally shot it.

On January 22, 1932, after having seen a print of *While Paris Sleeps* in a laboratory projection room, Jason Joy of the Motion Picture Producers and Distributors of America wrote Fox executive Al Rockett that the film was in violation of the Motion Picture Code which stated, "White slavery shall not be treated." Even the noble sacrifice of the father in the story could not mitigate this. Joy apologized for jeopardizing the company's investment but pointed out that had the script been submitted to the MPPDA in advance (which it should have been under the provisions of the code), the company would have been alerted before the film went into production.[100]

Will Hays backed up Joy's position and added that the film might also arouse protests from South America for the reference to sex traffic there. In another letter, Joy told Hays that he had learned from an "authoritative source" that before he wrote his letter, someone at the studio had already raised the matter.[101] So studio politics might also have become an issue here. By early February, Joy reported that Fox had agreed to shoot revised scenes to remove all suggestion of white slavery and the work of the procurer.

Actually, the white slavery aspect was not removed from the story. With ingenuity that suggests Dwan's hand, there is a scene in which the character Kapas tells Manon that he wants her to become a model in his dressmaking establishment in South America and that the wealthy men there treat his shop as a matrimonial market. Kapas tells Manon that she should be ready to leave on a ship that night. Paul, who enters the café at this point, tells Manon not to listen to them (he knows what Kapas and Julot are really up to). A brawl ensues before he can say anything else.

The MPPDA was satisfied that the white slavery angle was "well disguised"[102] though they insisted on pruning a bit more dialogue, such as "She must come willingly."[103]

While Paris Sleeps still provoked a letter of complaint from the French embassy, which also protested the depiction of France in other Hollywood films. Of Dwan's film the letter noted, "In effect, this film, the locale of which is the underworld of Paris, creates for Paris a most deplorable propaganda in other countries...."[104]

While Paris Sleeps seemed to have had something to offend everyone.

More than any of Dwan's other films, *While Paris Sleeps* was intense melodrama, even crude melodrama by the standards of the time. It was not likely to be shown at prestigious theaters. Robert Landry's review for *Variety* noted, "Originally booked for the RKO Hippodrome in New York, but with that house suddenly shuttered for the summer this Fox programmer sneaked in for its metropolitan bow at Loew's New York daily grind. Film is not as bad as that might suggest. At the same time no difficulty is encountered in comprehending why the Roxy didn't want it. What *While Paris Sleeps* has in abundance is action and melodrama and that has merit these days. Accordingly, it may be put down as a successful picture outside the deluxers."[105] Landry had no problem in detecting that the film dealt with white slavery. He noted that the killing of Mouche was "[j]ust a trifle brutal even for this era of stark realism...."[106] Other reviews also saw the film as a tough though unbelievable melodrama.

Another box-office liability was the lack of stars though Victor McLaglen registered strongly as an avenging and world-weary Samson having burst free from his shackles. Dwan had been more fortunate in leading ladies with Rose Hobart (*Chances*) and Elissa Landi (*Wicked*). Helen Mack conveyed the doe-eyed innocence essential for the role of Manon but lacked the vibrancy that could have made more of the part. Further down in the credits, cast as the landlady was Dot Farley, a star comedienne of the early silents who was Dwan's fellow employee at Essanay in 1910.

As the above description indicates, even the edited *While Paris Sleeps* was quite suggestive. In May 1938, the MPPDA, now under Joseph Breen, denied a second request to permit the film to be re-released, the first query having been made a few months earlier. *While Paris Sleeps* may have been one of the pre–Code films headed for oblivion but it was saved thanks to the efforts of the archivist Alex Gordon and film historian William K. Everson.[107]

There may have also been consequences for Dwan. It was previously mentioned that Jason Joy knew that someone at the Fox studio had raised warnings about *While Paris Sleeps*. It was a costly business to re-shoot scenes but Fox capitulated and did so. In a letter to Hays, Joy wrote with satisfaction, "There was no discussion. The Studio accepted our decision as final, but they severely censored the personnel for having allowed the picture to reach its completed form without first having checked with us."[108]

Note that Joy refers to "personnel" and not just one individual so it's quite possible that as director, Dwan also shouldered some of the blame. Dwan, who had tried to be both independent and careful, here may have gone too far. Perhaps he had been emboldened by the relative laxity of code enforcement at this time. Joy's letters, of course, don't reveal *how* angered the studio bosses were at the supposed transgressors. But after making two films each for Warners and Fox, Dwan's next directorial effort was at lowly Columbia.

There is another story about Dwan dealing with adversity during the filming of *While Paris Sleeps*. Screenwriter Basil Woon recalled that just when they were about to shoot a scene, an assistant director informed Dwan that there was a fire at Malibu Beach where Dwan had his home. Woon recounted,

> Dwan, like many of the bigger men in Pictures, had just lost a great amount of money in the stock market. If his home was wiped out, it would pretty much wipe him out too.
>
> He thought of all this, as I say, but not for more than thirty seconds. Then he smiled a twisted smile.
>
> "Well," he said, "if it's on fire I guess I can't do anything about it." His eyes returned to the set, to the job on hand. His voice regained its authoritative ring. "Roll 'em!" he roared. "ACTION."

Dwan would later learn his house had been spared by the fire.[109]

While Paris Sleeps seemed to sum up a whole period of Dwan's career where his films were more somber than usual. They may have constituted his darkest string of melodramas since his work at Universal in 1914. It may have been time for Dwan to do something more uplifting. He may have thought he found it in a project at Columbia called *Faith*.

Faith was inspired by the Bank of America. Originally known as the Bank of Italy, under the leadership of A.P. Giannini working closely with his younger brother Attilio, it had helped bankroll the nascent film industry. By 1932, the senior Giannini was a board member of Columbia Pictures. But by this year, feeling the brunt of the Depression, the bank itself was in trouble, having lost deposits totaling $254 million in 1931. There was a danger that the bank would go under and Columbia with it. According to film historian Joseph McBride, "*Faith* was an attempt to propagandize for the liberal lending policies the Gianninis stood for and to help ensure that their bank would survive and maintain its character."[110] Screenwriter Robert Riskin met Attilio Giannini and reportedly used him as the model for the banker hero in *Faith* played by Walter Huston.

Things did not go well for Dwan on the set of *Faith*. His cameraman Joseph Walker and sound mixer Edward Bernds were part of a regular crew used to working with director Frank Capra. They were not impressed with what they saw from Dwan. Walker remembered, "Dwan didn't seem to know what he wanted out of it."[111]

Bernds, it will be recalled, had worked as a sound engineer on *The Iron Mask* and had already formed a negative opinion of Dwan. In his memoirs, Bernds wrote, "In 1928, Dwan had sat impassively on the set of *The Iron Mask*. In 1932 he sat impassively on the set of *American Madness* [the revised title of *Faith*]."[112]

We know that Bernds' observations of Dwan's direction on *The Iron Mask* were contradicted by Bakewell and Humberstone, who found much dominance in Dwan's "passivity" on the set. Bernds' conception of what made for a forceful director may have been based on very limited observations. But he did make some points on what went wrong with Dwan on *Faith*:

> He chose camera setups, then accepted whatever the actors gave him in performances. With excellent actors, that approach sometimes worked well, and Walter Huston was certainly an excellent actor, but in this case it did not work at all. Something was needed to spark intensity, to make the problems posed by the story believable.... After several days shooting, Harry Cohn came to the same conclusion. He shut down production and dismissed Dwan.[113]

Harry Cohn had fought a hard-bruising battle for control of Columbia. *Faith* was to be Columbia's first major production after he won that battle and he did not want it to fail. Possibly Cohn and Dwan did not get along. Walker pointed out that Cohn often removed a director after a few days of shooting just to shake things up and keep people from getting complacent.

Dwan was fired after three days of shooting in late March. Roy William Neill directed for one day until Frank Capra was able to get to the set, after Cohn had removed him from another film. Capra decided to scuttle all the previous shooting and start from scratch and even had the set rebuilt. A story had been issued to the press that Dwan had become ill and therefore needed to be replaced.

What had happened to Dwan? There is no record of him having been fired since his experience at Flying A in 1913.

As Dwan once explained, it was his tendency not to interfere too much with actors' work but he was also known to convey his dissatisfaction with a performance and had even been considered in the silent era a great actors' director. Had he grown too complacent? Had the experience at Fox with *While Paris Sleeps*, where he had allegedly gone too far, made him more reticent to assert himself on this film? Were his detractors on the set biased because they were not familiar with his method of directing?

We will never be certain of the answers but Capra did make a major success out of *American Madness*. The film was a turning point for both directors. For Capra, it helped establish the themes he would invoke and develop in his subsequent populist films and for which he would be identified. For Dwan, it was, at least for a time, the end of his status as a major director.

Both men came from immigrant stock. Both had come from scientific backgrounds and both probably exaggerated their accomplishments in those realms. But Capra, at thirty-five, was still a young director with a bright future. Nearing his forty-seventh birthday, Dwan already seemed an aging pioneer from an earlier era. Unlike Dwan, Capra regarded the coming of sound as "an enormous step forward."[114] Thus, Capra may have been better disposed to handle a project as rhetorical as *American Madness*.

Although still well paid, Dwan had been slipping for some time and that seemed to accelerate in the sound era. He had experimented with sound in 1925 and in early 1927, and had the technical know-how to make a major impact with a good early sound feature. But he resisted making sound films until they were becoming commonplace. Since 1930, only *Chances* had won him strong reviews and even that film was not a major success.

With this firing, his career seemed to plummet and no job was now in the offing. In 1978, interviewer Howard Mandelbaum asked Dwan about his firing from *American Madness*, and he declined to comment.[115]

But in a section of the Bogdanovich interview not included for publication, Dwan did perhaps subconsciously reveal his feelings about the matter. In a middle of a discussion about Florenz Ziegfeld and his love for elephants, Dwan does an odd segue to talking about the Broadway star Marilyn Miller, who had made a few films:

> Remember Marilyn Miller, the star. She was a great friend of mine, of ours. And she had a houseful — she wasn't doing well out here. And she had all kinds of elephants around her house. Little elephants. Statues. And a lot of them had their trunks down, doffers down. And I said, "You get rid of every one of those elephants with their trunks down. They're bad

luck. An elephant must have its trunk in the air. If it isn't, it'll bring you bad luck. So get rid of them."[116]

Miller, the famed Broadway musical star, had made the transition to Hollywood with two early musicals, *Sally* (1929) and *Sunny* (1930). By the time she made her last *Her Majesty Love* (1931), the genre had become moribund; there was a year-long gap between *Sunny* and *Her Majesty Love* in which she returned to Broadway.

So Miller's phone was not ringing in this period. This would have been the time which Dwan described that Miller "wasn't doing well out here." It would have been some time in 1931 but the description Dwan gave also sounds oddly prescient of the months after his firing when he was not working. He continued,

> And we'd all had some cocktails.... We got a clothes basket and gathered these things up, about 15 of them or so. Elephants with their trunks down.... And we got in the car with the top down, an open car, and we drove to every studio here, and I threw an elephant over the gate of every one of those studios until I got over on Gower Street. And at Columbia Studio there wasn't any gate I could throw it over, but there was a light in the executive offices above the entrances. Now it happened to be Cohn's office and at the time he's having a conference with some big directors and amongst them is Frank Capra who told me the other end of the story. So I took one of those things, a black jade one, and I threw it through that window. Crash! And there they are and in — boom — and it lands in the middle of the floor. A black object. And these guys dove in all directions. Ran screaming out of the studio that somebody was bombing them, and we, in the meantime had driven off. But Capra told me the effect — they were sure it was a bomb — they'd been bombed — and Cohn crapped in his pants, ran into a wall, cut himself trying to get through a glass door trying to get out. And it was only this elephant. And we went everywhere — Universal and all over the place and got rid of these elephants.
>
> And about two days later she got an offer from Warner Bros. to come in and do a picture. She hadn't gotten a thing up to then. She was just desperate about what's going to happen to her. Nobody seemed to want her. And all of a sudden — bang — it came. Because it was the bad luck.[117]

It is not surprising that this strange episode was not included in the interview book but in view of the *American Madness* firing, it becomes more pertinent and even fascinating. How much of this story was embellished or changed in time or happened at all, are factors to contemplate. Most importantly, it was something that Dwan wanted to talk about, even volunteered, while he made no mention of his firing from *American Madness*.

What is striking is that it is only at Columbia that Dwan actually throws the elephant through a lit window, although the lack of the gate at this Poverty Row studio is a practical explanation. But why throw an object through a lit window where people are presumably present and it might possibly hurt someone? This sounds strangely uncharacteristic and reckless from a man who had the responsibilities of a director. But then going on this drunken spree also sounds unusual for Dwan.

And it seems to be curiously apropos that the only person hurt at the Columbia office is Cohn, who figuratively or literally soils himself and then cuts himself on a glass door, we assume leaving him bloodied. How coincidental it also seems that the man who witnesses this and reports it back to Dwan is Capra, who had replaced him on *American Madness*. Was this like Dwan's tale of immediate ruin for Samuel Hutchinson at Flying A, a fantasy revenge?

Dwan might have also identified with Marilyn Miller being "desperate about what's going to happen to her." Would he now be a washed-up silent film director in the midst of the Depression? Was it all, as he said about Miller, "bad luck"?

Finally, there is the odd reference to the Columbia executives concluding that a bomb had been thrown at them. Did this also reflect a hidden desire on Dwan's part? Did the man who saw himself as a businessman director now have fantasies of throwing bombs at the studios?

Throughout the country at this time, many others may have felt a change that pulled their outlook from Faith to American Madness.

Exile to England and Return

Dwan seemed once more to have been cast adrift.

His sudden dismissal at Flying A almost twenty years earlier had been jolting and "terrifying" but Dwan knew it had not been the result of any failure. He was soon hired by Universal.

In 1920, he had joined in a challenge to the Hollywood system as part of the Associated Producers. He flirted with mounting independent production on the East Coast but that plan was stillborn and his tenure with Associated Producer ended in disillusionment. For months he was idle, remaining in exile from the Hollywood industry, not wanting to return to the West Coast production he had helped pioneer.

Dwan then found a niche with Famous Players–Paramount, working almost exclusively on the East Coast and with virtual independence within the studio system. Dwan had found commercial success there, particularly in his films with Swanson. He could be comfortable feeling both "in" the system and "out" of it. But after five years both with Paramount and Fox, he lost his East Coast bastion.

With his firing from *American Madness*, Dwan was confronting the greatest crisis to his career. He then found a way to keep his career going by working abroad. Years later, he would discuss it casually.

Explaining how he came to work in Britain, Dwan told Bogdanovich, "I used to go to Carlsbad every year.... On my way, I stopped off in London and somebody asked me if I was available to make a picture. Nothing much was happening over here, and I thought it would be fun to try, so I did. And I liked it, and stayed to make three."[118]

The above may be an accurate description of how Dwan came to work in England, especially if we interpret the line "Nothing much was happening over here" as a euphemism for "Nobody was hiring me." Dwan's firing at Columbia had taken place at a particularly unfortunate time when studios were incurring losses and cutting back.

Dwan's trip to England seemed to go almost unnoticed in the trades and he received the barest of press coverage. A reference to Dwan shooting his first British film, *Her First Affaire*, appeared in *Variety*'s London Chatter column in early November, over seven months since his firing from *American Madness*.[119] Made for St. George-Sterling, *Her First Affaire* is best remembered for the discovery of a new star, a discovery made by Dwan himself. This is how Dwan recounted the story in *The Last Pioneer*:

> I went up to an agent's office to get some actors. I wanted a girl about 14 years old who, in the story, was going to have her first love affair. And the woman they brought in for the part was around 35 years old, though still a girlish type. And she had her daughter with her, just because she didn't want to leave her home ... and I'm looking at the kid. I said, "What about her — can she act?" "Well our family have been actors but no, she's not an actress." "Well," I said, "that's who I want — I want her." Well, they were shocked — *everybody* was when the word went out I was insisting on this girl whose mother had come for the job. Finally they bent over my way and I got her. She was Ida Lupino.[120]

There is no question that Dwan gave Lupino her big break to stardom but there are some problems with this story. First, the character of the girl in the film is not that of a fourteen-year-old but a woman considering marriage. Lupino, however, was indeed a fourteen-year-old at the time.

Lupino did come from a theatrical family whose roots could be traced to émigré Italian puppeteer Giorgio Luppino who had fled to England in the seventeenth century for political reasons. Ida's parents Stanley and Connie Lupino were actors as was her uncle, Lupino Lane, who had worked with Ernst Lubitsch.

It was in fact her uncle, when directing a film called *The Love Race* starring Ms. Lupino's father, who insisted that Ida have a bit role. The part was so small that it was uncredited but not surprisingly, it roused Ida's interest in acting. In January 1932, she was enrolled in the Royal Academy of Dramatic Arts. When the Royal Academy staged a production of *Heartbreak House*, George Bernard Shaw himself selected Ida to play the role of Ellie. Lupino had shown that she could look adult beyond her years. But she made screen tests at several studios to no avail. She was rejected as being "too young and innocent."

So Lupino already had acting experience and was pursuing a film career before she was selected for the lead in *Her First Affaire*. In 1933, a British film magazine reported that it was after Dwan saw her in *Heartbreak House* that he decided he wanted her for *Her First Affaire* and contacted Ida's agent.[121] Had Dwan not given her the lead in *Her First Affaire*, Lupino might have waited for years to get a major role in films or might have never gotten her break.

When she met Dwan, the would-be starlet repeated to the director comments she had heard that she was too young for the role. Dwan adamantly insisted she read for the part anyway. A screen test was arranged. After it was over, Ida was amazed to learn that Dwan had chosen her.

Another variation of the story appeared in a *New York Times* article about Lupino in 1941. Here, producers were discouraging young Ida from a career in films or on the stage when Dwan "espied her in an agent's office and hired her on the spot for the feminine lead" in *Her First Affaire*.[122]

Dwan shot the film with his usual rapidity and it was ready for a trade screening by December 1932.

In the picture, Lupino plays Anne, a young woman fascinated by the sexual freedom philosophy of popular middle-aged novelist Carey Merton (George Curzon). There are some mildly amusing incidents including a masked ball as Anne becomes infatuated with the writer. In the end, things are resolved when Anne's jealousy is aroused by the attentions of the novelist's wife extended to her boyfriend and she realizes she does not really believe in the free love principles. Apparently neither does the author when he learns of his wife's involvement with Anne's beau. As with some of Dwan's silent films, sexual morality is teased but then upheld in familiar fashion to the satisfaction of the censors.

Variety may not have been far off the mark when, after conceding that the film was "capably produced and directed," noted that "the story is too machine-made in its unfolding...."[123]

Dwan said of Lupino, "I'll make a level bet she will not remain in this country a year."[124] Lupino's first Hollywood movie, *Search for Beauty*, was released in early 1934.

Around the time that *Her First Affaire* came out, the British trade magazine the *Kine Weekly* alerted its readers that "Allan Dwan, the famous American director, who is at present, in this country, is contemplating the formation of a production unit of his own to make British pictures. Although unable to give any details at the moment, Mr. Dwan told the *Kine* that he anticipated going forward with the project early in the New Year." The story added that the company was in formation and "that the financial end has been assured."[125]

So even in England, Dwan had not abandoned his hopes of going independent again. Although it was observed that the financing had been assured, the timing of the announcement with the release of *Her First Affaire* suggests this was done with the hopes of spurring investment if the cash men found the film appealing.

In the meanwhile, another enterprising producer, this one having been fired from Fox in the U.S., had formed a company that would employ Dwan. Alexander Korda was founder and managing director of London Films, which came into being in February 1932. Korda had directed films for Paramount in Europe, including the celebrated *Marius* in France.

When help was needed to boost the foundering British film industry, the British government passed the Cinematograph Films Act of 1927, more popularly known as the Quota Act. It required that a certain proportion of the films released in Britain had to be British in origin. Paramount, like other American companies, therefore produced some films in the U.K. Many of the films made as a result of the act came to be known as "quota quickies" because they were speedily ground out to conform to the terms of the act. Paramount, however, had produced more expensive films.

At the time that London Films was founded, Paramount had decided to reduce its own operations in the U.K. and gave Korda's company a contract to make five Quota films. Three of these films were assigned to Hollywood directors including Dwan, Rowland V. Lee and Robert Milton. So while Dwan never worked directly at Paramount again, his new film did have a connection with his home studio of the 1920s.

Dwan's project was *Counsel's Opinion*, which like *Her First Affaire* was based on a play and again offered a risqué plot that was happily resolved without discomfiting the censor. The story involved a divorce lawyer named Logan (Henry Kendall) who after a charity ball cannot find his way home in the fog and is forced to put up at a hotel. There is a shortage of available rooms and a young woman forces Logan to share his suite with her. It's all done innocuously but the next day the lawyer learns that one Lord Rockburn is considering a divorce because of his wife's conduct after the ball and is seeking counsel's opinion from Logan. Logan is convinced that Lady Rockburn was the woman who shared a room with him and that he might be a co-respondent in the case. In the end, Logan's dilemma turns out be just a misunderstanding and the lady in question, another of Dwan's stray widows, is free to marry Logan.

Ida Lupino became a precocious star at age fourteen, thanks to Allan Dwan.

The film was not well received by London's *Observer*, which commented, "[T]here is perhaps more naiveté than usual about this comedy of a divorce counsel who imagines himself mixed up in his own case. The director is an American, Allan Dwan, who must either have come or gone away with odd ideas of British humor."[126] British filmgoers, however, were more generous in their estimate of the film. Star Henry Kendall recalled, "The film was a great success and I believe made a lot of money for Korda.... This picture put me right on top as a British star...."[127]

The female lead was played by Binnie Barnes. Dwan must have found her congenial to work with as she would later appear in four more Dwan films on the other side of the Atlantic. Five years later, Barnes had a supporting role in Korda's color remake of *Counsel's Opinion*, *The Divorce of Lady X* with Merle Oberon and Laurence Olivier.

Around the time that *Counsel's Opinion* was released, on March 30, 1933, the *Kine Weekly* had a grim report: "In Hollywood the eight-week slashes in salaries affect stars, directors, writers, supporting players, technicians and office employees. The unions are standing out. Cuts are 50 per cent."[128]

In 1932, the Big Eight (Paramount, MGM, Warner Bros., Fox, RKO, Universal, United Artists and Columbia) had suffered a net loss of $26 million. The film companies hit bottom in early 1933 with three major corporations, Paramount, Fox and RKO, going into bankruptcy or receivership.

Newly elected president Franklin D. Roosevelt's economic recovery plan mandated the kind of salary cuts now being administered. But help was also on the way for the film industry: FDR's National Industrial Recovery Act, which went into effect in June, was to promote recovery by sanctioning certain monopolistic practices in American industry. In the film world, this would help the Big Eight tighten their control over the market. As the year wore on, for various reasons Hollywood began to regain its footing.[129]

As Dwan prepared for his next film, his casting opportunities were boosted by a new influx of American stars. Arriving in Britain in May were the celebrated married couple Ben Lyon and Bebe Daniels, each of whom had worked for Dwan prior to their marriage. Also coming to England were Sally Eilers and Thelma Todd. Fox and the British company B.I.P. jointly held a reception for the newly arrived stars at the Dorchester Hotel and Dwan was among the luminaries in attendance.

Lyon and Eilers were soon set to star in a B.I.P. project for Dwan called *I Spy*.

Production began in May. Dwan appeared to be again demanding regarding interior sets. Over two hundred yards of railroad track including a Ruritanian station were said to have been built on the Elstree lot for the film. While Dwan worked on the picture, still another American director, Sam Taylor joined the exodus to Britain.

I Spy was a burlesque of espionage melodramas, with Lyon portraying a playboy who is mistaken for a master spy. His fate becomes intertwined with that of an American actress (Eilers) posing as a countess in trying to pay a hotel bill. Misunderstandings and danger follow them in this comedy-thriller until they manage to escape.

I Spy opened at London's Hippodrome on August 3. *Variety* thought that the "two American stars are well directed by the American producer" and that the film would have a "good chance in the States."[130] It was later released in the U.S. under the title *The Morning After*. A more recent appraisal comes from David Quinlan's 1984 book *British Sound Films* which describes *I Spy* as "pretty awful."[131] It did not lead to any further breakthroughs for Dwan in England.

Ben Lyon and Sally Eilers starred in Dwan's British *I Spy* (1933), released as *The Morning After* in the U.S.

On June 25, just as Dwan was finishing work on *I Spy*, his mother died in Hollywood after what was described as a "lingering illness."[132]

Dwan's hopes for establishing an independent production company in Britain never materialized. In late October, it was announced that he would be returning to Hollywood in a few weeks.[133] The expatriate director may have become convinced by this time that conditions were improving in the American film industry. (Of course, it can be argued that since Dwan was still a Canadian citizen, he was an expatriate in America, not England, where he was considered a British subject.)

He was fortunate to have found some work relatively quickly. But then it seemed that just about everyone available with directorial experience worked on the MGM film that was finally titled *Hollywood Party*.

Hollywood Party had its genesis in the format of the all-star revue films at the dawn of the sound revolution and was originally to be titled *The Hollywood Revue of 1933*. But by now the concept of simply stringing together various musical numbers and comedy routines like a vaudeville show seemed dated. So everything would be tied around the pretense of a plot.

MGM decided to parody its colossal hit of the previous year, *Tarzan the Ape Man*, by having comedian Jimmy Durante play a movie star whose screen persona is a jungle lord ("The Monarch of the Mudlands") called Schnarzan. Unfortunately for Schnarzan, he has a screen rival called Liondora. Liondora and his producer are set to bolster the realism of their jungle epics by purchasing lions from the famed explorer Baron Munchausen (radio personality Jack Pearl). Durante/Schnarzan tries to beat them to the punch by holding a huge party in honor of the baron where he can buy the lions before Liondora can.[134]

The party (and the film) was envisioned as providing a showcase to various MGM stars such as Joan Crawford, Jean Harlow, Marie Dressler, Clark Gable and others. As a kind of inside joke, Lupe Velez, who married Tarzan star Weissmuller during the time *Hollywood Party* was being shot, played Schnarzan's onscreen jungle mate and off-screen jealous lover. Weissmuller himself appeared in a water ballet with swimming chorines. Lavish musical numbers were planned and the celebrated team of Richard Rodgers and Lorenz Hart provided both script ideas and songs. The film even included a Technicolor cartoon produced by Walt Disney.

There were grand ideas but apparently not a great deal of careful planning nor a suitable script when filming began in August 1933. Edmund Goulding, Swanson's one-time screen savior, was assigned to direct but quit. He was replaced by Russell Mack. Mack was soon replaced by Richard Boleslavsky. The unfortunate Boleslavsky had been earlier involved in the unsuccessful attempt to salvage *Queen Kelly* which had suffered from indulgent directorial control. Here, Boleslavsky was mired in a production where no one seemed able to exercise *any* control.

In mid–January 1934, Dwan was called in "to direct the added scenes on Harry Rapf's MGM production of *Hollywood Party*, which started as just a picture and grew to special calibre."[135] Again Dwan was asked to play the role of problem-solver. He recalled to Bogdanovich,

> Every star on the MGM lot was in this picture and every director on the lot had done a piece of it. But when they tried to put it together, it just wouldn't jell. It was nothing. So I was invited over by Eddie Mannix to look at it and to see if I could do anything with it. So I went into a projection room — nobody else was there — and they started to run this movie for me. Thousands of feet of film, all disconnected stuff. Even Mickey Mouse was in it. And after a while, I was conscious of people coming in and sitting down close to me, but I couldn't see who they were.... Finally it ended, and they hadn't even turned the lights up when somebody beside me — who turned out to be Mannix — said, "Well, what do you think of it?" And I said, "It's a nightmare." And from behind, a pair of arms were thrown around my shoulders and a voice said, "A genius! At last we've got a genius! Now we've got something." And the lights went up and it was Louis B. Mayer ... he said, "That's just what it is — it's a nightmare — we make it a nightmare." He looked at me. "How are you going to do it?" Jimmy Durante was in the footage and I couldn't think of anything else real quick, so I said, "Durante has a dream. He dreams all this stuff, so it's mixed up and it doesn't have to tie together because it's a dream."[136]

Looking at all the loose footage and describing it as a dream may not have been very original but it was perhaps the only logical way to put the loose ends together. Dwan went on to explain that Durante has the dream while waiting for his wife to get dressed for a party. According to Dwan, the casting director came to him after a conference about who would play Durante's wife, asking Dwan who he thought should have the role. And Dwan said simply: Durante's wife. And indeed it is Mrs. Durante who plays Mrs. Durante. Dwan concluded, "And I went out and made the additional scenes that would tie this together — worked two or three days on it — and they gave me a nice fat check."[137] For the film, Dwan was also briefly reunited with his old cinematographer Hal Rosson.

These additional scenes did not prove sufficient to end the *Hollywood Party* nightmare for the studio and by March, Charles Reisner was assigned to direct other sequences. Roy Rowland was also alleged to have directed some scenes. George Stevens directed scenes involving Laurel and Hardy. Appropriately, as masters of chaos they release the lions, bringing the film to a climax.

In late April, after a preview in Atlanta, *Hollywood Party* was sent back to the studio for more cutting. After all the long months of shooting, *Hollywood Party* was released in May with a lean seventy-minute running time. *Variety* described it as a "big short."[138] There was no sign of Crawford, Harlow, Dressler,

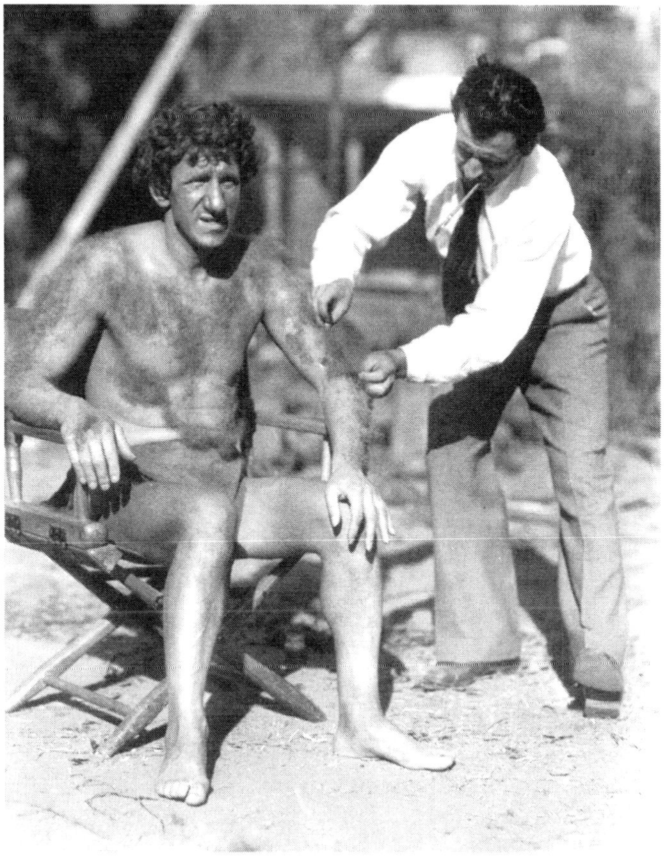

Jimmy Durante prepares for his role as Schnarzan in the film within a film within a dream, which was *Hollywood Party* (1934). A make-up man adds to Durante's hirsute appearance.

Gable or Weissmuller although Laurel & Hardy were included along with Charles Butterworth, Polly Moran, Robert Young and Ted Healy and the Three Stooges. No director was listed. The Disney color cartoon *The Chocolate Soldiers*, introduced by Mickey Mouse, garnered the most praise. Other highlights included the rendition of the title song by Frances Williams and Laurel & Hardy's confrontation with Lupe Velez. But the film often seemed tedious and underdeveloped. It lost MGM half a million dollars.

So Dwan's brief participation in *Hollywood Party* would not help his résumé. While the firing from *American Madness* may have been forgotten, so were the director's achievements. Dwan described the situation: "And a very funny thing — having been out of the country three years, I was forgotten — they didn't remember me around here. They forget you quick in the picture business — overnight."[139]

Actually, Dwan had only been gone for one year but it must have seemed to him like more. He professed to be amazed by the changes that had taken place in personnel. "You found everything changed. First of all, during the disasters, corporations changed hands, new executives were in and new systems — everything was altered. Fellows who were your prop men were now running the studio. Your position was gone.

You had to re-establish yourself, begin all over again. It was difficult. And embarrassing."[140]

Dwan's comments may have been only slightly exaggerated. The film industry was indeed undergoing a transformation and some of the major stars and directors of the 1920s were falling by the wayside.

Both of the great silent stars whose names had become intertwined with Dwan's were beginning to fade from view. Each had also made a film in England around this time.

Gloria Swanson's career had continued to slip. Swanson was now married to an Englishman, Michael Farmer, and by virtue of that marriage, she was an English citizen and could form a production company in England. Production costs were also lower in the U.K. and because of the quota system, the film was assured of good distribution there. A youthful Laurence Olivier was set as Swanson's leading man in the film entitled *A Perfect Understanding.*

The film went over-budget and Swanson had to sell her stock in United Artists and then borrow an additional $100,000. *A Perfect Understanding* was not well received by the critics. It grossed only $170,000 and ended Swanson's career as an independent producer.[141] Swanson next appeared in a film for Fox, *Music in the Air,* released in late 1934. Although this was a better picture, she was less prominently featured in favor of the younger leads. When *Music in the Air* flopped at the box office, Gloria Swanson's movie-star career was over.

Of course, in 1950 Swanson electrified audiences with her performance in *Sunset Blvd.* and received her third Oscar nomination. Even that classic did not spur her movie career.

Douglas Fairbanks' career as a movie star was also ebbing away but Fairbanks was not struggling to hold on. He was impressed with the British cinema, especially with Alexander Korda's *The Private Life of Henry VIII.* Fairbanks was trying to arrange some ambitious production and distribution plans around Korda's London Films. He played an aging Don Juan for Korda's company. There was even talk of Doug and Doug Jr. starring in a new Zorro film but nothing came of that. Fairbanks Sr. was past the age of the kind of robust physical acting he enjoyed.

The Private Life of Don Juan, released in 1934, proved to be Fairbanks' last film. There was some bitter irony in his role since he had strayed from Mary Pickford and was seeing Lady Sylvia Ashley, whom he would eventually marry.

After *Don Juan,* Fairbanks planned to devote himself to production and to advancing his son's career. But the great swashbuckler died just five years later, in December 1939, at the age of fifty-six.

Dwan had personally drifted away from Fairbanks as they worked in different spheres. Dwan recalled, "Occasionally, I'd see him in England. Bump into him here and there. But not very often."[142]

The years 1933 and 1934 proved to be something of a clearinghouse for major silent film stars who had begun to fade in the sound era. John Gilbert's last film was the 1934 *The Captain Hates the Sea.* Clara Bow's last picture was the 1933 *Hoopla.* Mary Pickford's last starring film was the 1933 *Secrets.* Lillian Gish capped her career as a film star with the 1933 *His Double Life.* She did return to films in the 1940s but as a supporting actress.

But there were also directors who did not survive the transition to sound for long, or at least at the same level of success they enjoyed in the silent era. Fred Niblo had directed two of Fairbanks' swashbucklers, *The Mark of Zorro* and *The Three Musketeers,* as well as MGM's 1926 super-production *Ben-Hur.* By 1930 his career was in eclipse and, like Dwan, he went to England in hopes of spurring a comeback. His last films were released in 1932.

James Cruze had been a major director in the 1920s, winning his greatest fame *The Covered Wagon* (1923). But after the disastrous reception of the 1936 *Sutter's Gold,* his career hit the skids. His last films, made for Republic Pictures, appeared in 1938. In the case of Malcolm St. Clair, as critic Andrew Sarris put it, his silent films "fizzed" and his sound films "fizzled."[143] St. Clair was able to continue making films until 1948 but from the mid–1930s on, he was a "B" picture director. Herbert C. Brenon, who had made such silent classics as *Peter Pan, A Kiss for Cinderella* and the 1926 *Beau Geste,* steadily declined in the early 1930s. In 1935 he went to England (a common theme here) where his last films were released in 1939.

Things also grew worse for Dwan's friend Mickey Neilan, who had already been in decline in the 1920s. In 1930, Pickford's "favorite director" was signed to helm her film *Secrets.* But there were problems with financing, with the script and, possibly, with Neilan himself. Pickford stopped production midway and burned the negative after accruing a loss of $300,000. The film was later made from scratch with Frank Borzage directing.

Neilan was now drinking heavily but his career staggered on for a few more years. His last three films were released in 1937, all quickie musicals starring Pinky Tomlin, made for a small independent company.

As the careers of these established directors rapidly sank, prospects could not have seemed good for a veteran like Dwan to re-enter the industry as a director. After his brief stint on *Hollywood Party,* he was not contracted to direct any further films in 1934.

Dwan decided to gamble on his abilities as a writer to get him back into the business of directing. He wrote a story called *Baa Baa Black Sheep* and sold it to Fox in February 1935 for $5,000.[144] According to Dwan, Fox liked the material for Claire Trevor, who was being groomed for stardom by the studio. Dwan insisted that he wanted to direct the film and cited the arrangement as the beginning of what is known as a "package deal." His desperation was evident in the way Dwan described his stratagem of using a story to come back as a director: "They want somebody *with* a good piece of material — unless they've sent for you, and they weren't sending for *me.*"[145]

What kind of a story did Dwan come up with and how did he calibrate it for box-office appeal? The story for the film eventually called *Black Sheep* is interesting on a number of levels, including Dwan's sense of both calculation and personal reflection. His protagonist was a gambler, just as Dwan was playing for high stakes now. Gamblers would appear prominently in several of Dwan's films in the latter half of his career.

In a change of pace from his somber melodramas of the early thirties, all of Dwan's English films had been essentially comedies and *Black Sheep* would be a light-hearted crime film. *While Paris Sleeps* may have weighed heavily on Dwan's mind because he would both adapt and invert a number of its elements in *Black Sheep*. While *Black Sheep* was light and *While Paris Sleeps* was dark, both films had the "lost father" story at its center. Where in *While Paris Sleeps* the offspring was a woman, in *Black Sheep* it was a young man. *While Paris Sleeps* was set among the lowest dregs of society; *Black Sheep* dealt largely with the upper crust. *While Paris Sleeps* begins in a Guyanese jungle and then shifts to Paris, but we never see how the protagonist goes from one place to the other. Nearly all of *Black Sheep* unfolds on an ocean liner crossing the Atlantic.

Finally, regarding the casting of *Black Sheep, While Paris Sleeps* starred Victor McLaglen, who was one half of the Quirt–Flagg duo who appeared in Walsh's *What Price Glory* and its sequels. In an interesting mark of symmetry, the star of *Black Sheep* was Edmund Lowe, who represented the other member of that team.

Dwan's story was adapted into a scenario by Allen Rivkin. Dwan said that a big ocean liner had been built on one of the Fox lots for another picture and it was then used for *Black Sheep*. Again, he had found a way for the studio to save money.

Black Sheep opens with a long shot of the S.S. *Olympus* and then proceeds into a series of interior shots. A sign proclaims "Ballroom" and, after we glimpse the ballroom, through a series of vertical wipes and dissolves, the camera stays on the move as we get a tour of the entire ship. Signs for the different ship sections rush by, including "Smoking Room," "Promenade," and "Second Class Smoking Room," as if we were being introduced to the various characters in the story. Of special interest is the sign declaring "Second Class Passengers Not Allowed Beyond This Point." The camera moves down the stairs below the sign, emphasizing the difference in social strata. The tour finally settles on a sign reading "Beware. Passengers Are Warned to Take Precautions Against Professional Gamblers." In the opening seconds, the viewer is thus acquainted with the whole world of the ship and the rules that govern it.

In the ballroom, the protagonist John Dugan (Lowe) is watching the individuals around him who do not look like promising participants for a card game. Given that we have just seen the warning about professional gamblers and that Dugan is marking time playing solitaire, the audience is led to suspect that he is a gambler.

Dugan's concentration is interrupted by the incessant flickering of a cigarette lighter. He finds that the source is Jeanette Foster (Trevor). They quickly get acquainted and Dugan learns that she shrewdly uses a cigarette lighter without fluid to meet interesting people.

Dugan invites her to "see how the rich people live" and lifts Jeanette over the barrier to first class. In the bar, they watch as a young man is fleeced at the gaming tables by two oilmen who are sharp poker players. (One of the oilmen is portrayed by Eugene Pallette, who was once a player at Flying A.)

Dugan takes the young man, Fred Curtis (Tom Brown), under his wing and helps him get his checks back. Fred has still other troubles since the woman he has been escorting is blackmailing him with his I.O.U.s to get him to help her sneak stolen jewelry by customs. Dugan is reluctant to go too far to help the young man until he sees a picture of Fred's mother in his room. Dugan later confides to Jeanette that this woman was his wife and he realizes that Fred is his son, not an extraordinary coincidence in a Dwan film.

In a drunken stupor, Dugan tells how he married this society woman and they tried to live on his meager salary as a runner for a brokerage firm until her mother interfered and persuaded her to leave Dugan, even though she was then pregnant. Dugan's wife died after childbirth and the boy was raised by his grandmother to believe that his father was killed in World War I. Meanwhile, Dugan, returning from the war, finds that his only skill is in playing poker and so becomes a gambler.

The plot device recalls the patrician family with its class snobbery in *East Side, West Side* as well as *While Paris Sleeps*, where the living lost father becomes a dead war hero to his offspring. There is also the interesting aspect of Dugan's psychology since he has chosen a profession that compels him to keep mingling with the upper classes and he is continually being expelled from their midst, as if always re-living the experience of his youth. Early in the film, it's the detective Mather who catches him in first class and ejects him.

Mather (great Puritan moniker) is Dwan's hapless voyeur in this film. He is always on the lookout for Dugan, spying through a window or bursting through doorways, but he can never properly ascertain what's going on. Mather resembles the police in the Boston Blackie films of the forties who are continually outwitted by the supposed criminal who turns out to be no less virtuous than they are. Since Mather is something of a Keystone Cop, Dwan selected the former chief of the Keystone Cops to play him, his friend Ford Sterling.

The opening shots of the film give a full sense of the great breadth of the ship *Olympus* but as the story unfolds, there are increasing attempts to restrict the space in which Dugan can move, so that he must literally know his place. Not only is he banished from first class but at one point, by command of the captain, Dugan is to be locked in his room for the duration of the voyage. Thanks to a passkey, Dugan is still able to go about his business. But still greater confinement is ahead. While snooping in one cabin, Dugan is almost caught and has to hide behind the entrance door. Dwan astutely milks the scene at some length for suspense as Dugan is frozen in that spot. Dwan shoots Dugan from an angle so that we can see him while the other characters in the shot can't, until he can find an opportunity to escape. (Dugan's confinement also evokes the imprisonments featured in Dwan's early 1930s films.)

Restriction of movement is a severe violation for a Dwan character and film but Dugan uses his room arrest to serve his ends. Earlier, at a card game, Dugan was able to bilk two card sharps by having Jeanette win the bulk of the money after Dugan was out of the game. Dugan could be most manipulative when he appears passive, something that Edward Bernds at Columbia should have recognized in Dwan.

As a vehicle for Claire Trevor, Fox certainly got its money's worth out of *Black Sheep*. As Jeanette, she could show her sass by holding her own against Dugan and operating in sync with him. When Dugan says of the woman blackmailing his son, "This dame is too smart for him," Jeanette snaps back, "Aren't we all?" There were also occasions for Trevor to convey her softer side without losing her sense of control. In one scene, she maternally tucks Dugan in bed after he passes out from a binge.

Dugan (who is played expertly by Lowe) works out his stratagem so that at dockside when the *Olympus* arrives, the shady lady is outwitted. Dugan even meets his mother-in-law and is able to assure her that he hasn't revealed his identity to his son. Having now reconciled that part of his life, Dugan can leave the gambling business that repeats it and tie the knot with Jeanette.

Black Sheep is clever and engaging, if not particularly original. The film did not make any big ripples with the critics but Fox seemed to be satisfied with the results. Dwan, the former "black sheep," was now welcomed back to the fold with a Fox contract. His career had been saved but he would be entering a division at Fox that was not of the highest esteem.

At the age of fifty, Dwan was about to become a B-movie director.

B-Movie Maestro

Claire Trevor has been referred to by her biographer Ray Hagen (*Killer Tomatoes*) as "Brass with Class." Although she played her share of tough dames, she still exuded a sense of intelligence and integrity that won her respect. She had studied art at Columbia University and then spent six months at the American Academy of Dramatic Arts before abandoning it to seek stage work. Trevor starred in two Broadway plays but after signing a contract with Fox in 1933, she had become ensconced in B films. She did, however, have an admirer among the Fox executives. This would be the genesis for her next film with Dwan, *Navy Wife*.

In a section not included in Bogdanovich's published interview, Dwan recalled, "Claire Trevor was with Fox, an actress, and she'd gone to Honolulu on a vacation and was going to be there three or four weeks or something. And Sol Wurtzel, who had a terrific yen for her, said to me, 'You got any ideas for how we could do a Honolulu picture?'" When Dwan asked him who was to be in the picture, Wurtzel replied, 'Well, if we could think up something Claire Trevor would be interested in ... she's in Honolulu and we could go and grab a few scenes.'"[146]

Edmund Lowe requires the assistance of Claire Trevor in *Black Sheep* (1935), however much he may appear to protest here to the steward, John Rodgers. The film restored Dwan to his status as a Hollywood director.

Dwan said he came up with the idea that Trevor was a navy nurse and Wurtzel seemed pleased. Dwan said, "I think that was the basis—just go over and knock off some scenes with her as a nurse and figure out why she's a nurse and take it from there.... It was that kind of thing. No script or anything."[147] This anecdote suggests Dwan could still make films by location inspiration as he did with Flying A.

The amount of footage shot was probably relatively small. A June 1935 story in the Hollywood Reporter confirmed that exteriors "were filmed at Hawaii during Miss Trevor's recent vacation to the island." But the article added that most of the cast (including Ralph Bellamy, Jane Darwell and Warren Hymer) had just been selected and that actual shooting would not start until July 15.[148]

The film was originally titled *Beauty's Daughter* and credited with being based on the novel by Kathleen Norris. Dwan told Bogdanovich that the novel "had nothing in it that we used" but that since Fox owned the property, the credit was added to give the film "dignity."[149]

After a bathetic opening set at a San Diego naval hospital, in which Trevor's nurse sings "Swing Low, Sweet Chariot" as a last song request from her expiring patient, *Navy Wife* mercifully turns to low comedy following three sex-starved sailors returning to port. The sailors ride off on motorcycles, two of them with attached sidecars for their girlfriends. In an outlandishly cartoonish sequence, the coupled motorcyclists both crash while simultaneously trying to drive and attend to their girlfriends. The third cyclist (played by Hymer, who specialized in portraying pea-brained tough guys) also cracks up. Hymer's "accident" is intentional because he wants to be hospitalized so he can be treated by Trevor.

After their release from the hospital, the sailors are back dating their girls, one of whom now sports an eye patch. This is the kind of raucous, hearty and not very tasteful kind of humor one associates with Raoul Walsh and the eye patch may have been a gag tribute to Walsh, who also wore a black patch after losing one eye in a 1929 road accident. Hymer takes his moronic quest for repeated hospital stays to a pathological level and eventually becomes Trevor's limping houseboy in Hawaii.

The drama centers on Trevor's vulnerability as the daughter of divorced parents. But she falls in love with a widowed naval surgeon (Bellamy) who has an invalid daughter. When the entire group is transferred to Hawaii (in those pre–World War II days, it was necessary for a title to identify Pearl Harbor as a naval base in Hawaii), Bellamy proposes marriage and Trevor accepts.

Bellamy seems undemonstrative in affection for Trevor and she suspects that he is still in love with his dead wife and needed his former nurse only to care for his daughter. In a traditional "woman's film," they would have bonded as Trevor would have taken the initiative in getting the daughter to walk.

However, the aesthetics of the B film mandated returning to action when possible. While treatments restore the girl's ability to walk, Trevor believes that Bellamy is seeing another woman. All is resolved with a spy plot absurdly inserted into the final reel. The other woman turns out to be a master spy and in a slambang finale she shoots Bellamy, who was working for naval intelligence. He survives and is sufficiently recovered to show his love for Trevor by the fadeout.

Trevor's characterization is short-changed by this mishmash but Dwan has provided her with some good moments. One is at the San Diego hospital where an inveterate practical joker tells Trevor that Bellamy has been transferred to another base. Trevor is crestfallen but tries to hide it. Once outside, she receives a letter from Bellamy that explains that he has gone to Santa Barbara to spend the weekend with his daughter. Trevor appears touched both by the contents of the letter and the fact that Bellamy sent it to her. As the camera tracks in to a close-up, Trevor's face seems to register the look of love. Then we hear the laughter of the practical jokers and Trevor's expression changes to one of defensiveness. Her insecurities take over as if succumbing to love is a humiliation.

Claire Trevor and Dwan fill up on water in this gag shot from the filming of *Navy Wife* (1935).

Just as *Navy Wife* was going into production in Hawaii, there was a major development with the Fox Film Corporation. On May 29, 1935, Fox merged with Twentieth Century Pictures.

Darryl F. Zanuck had helped found Twentieth Century three days after he left as chief of production at Warner Brothers in April 1933. Zanuck proved adept at making hit films for his nascent company and was helped by timing; soon after Twentieth Century was founded, the movie industry experienced an upturn in business.

Management at Fox had proved much less successful. (William Fox had been driven out of his company in 1930.) Fox needed a more forceful studio head and Zanuck needed a studio. Twentieth Century did not own studio property and rented space from the Samuel Goldwyn Company.

Winfield Sheehan resigned as Fox's production chief in July and Zanuck aggressively took the reins of power. After Sheehan's departure, Zanuck began replacing the other Fox executives with his own people.

But there was one notable executive whom Zanuck could not depose. Sol Wurtzel had an iron-clad contract that protected him from suffering the same fate as many of his colleagues. He had also produced some very successful films for Fox, including its biggest hit of 1935, John Ford's *Steamboat Round the Bend* starring Will Rogers. Zanuck made Wurtzel executive producer of all B pictures at the studio. The Sunset-Western lot on the studio was the designated area for B-movie production.

Wurtzel had an annual budget of $6,000,000 to make 24 films, with the budgets usually running from $150,000 to $200,000 per film. The stable of directors included besides Dwan, Malcolm St. Clair, George Marshall and Alfred Werker. Among the young rising directors in the unit was H. Bruce Humberstone, Dwan's assistant director for *The Iron Mask*.[150]

Late in 1935, Twentieth Century–Fox's publicity department's brief biography of Dwan described him thus:

> Jovial and congenial, he always put his company at ease and at the same time maintains a rigorous discipline which enables his companies to accomplish a great deal of work. He is an omnivorous reader, plays a good game of tennis, and drives his own car despite having a chauffeur.... He doesn't smoke and is always faultlessly attired. He has five cats and one dog as pets.
>
> Dwan is married but has no children. He is five foot seven and a half inches tall, weights 200 pounds and has grey hair and brown eyes.[151]

Again, Dwan's efficiency was duly noted. He would need it for B-film work. Two to three months would be spent in preparation for the Fox Bs but only three weeks of shooting. The running time for B films of this time ranged from fifty-five to seventy minutes. Dwan had already been making A films in that range and could keep things moving. This he would do as the assignments came fast and thick.

Dwan's survival in the industry (and any hope of upgrading his status) depended on his ability to make something interesting, if not first-rate, out of these second-feature scenarios. Bogdanovich noted that Dwan "was assigned a series of scripts that would have made a lesser man throw in the towel."[152]

Here are the films and how Dwan contended with the challenges:

Song and Dance Man, based on a play by George M. Cohan and filmed previously in 1926 with Tom Moore and Bessie Love, was released on March 13, 1936. The story concerns a song-and-dance team consisting of Julie Carroll (Claire Trevor again) and Hap Farrell (Paul Kelly). Hap blows their money by gambling and then, eager to demonstrate to his chums that he is the "best little song and dance man in the world," sprains his leg. Knowing that they now won't have the money to pay the rent, Julie goes out to try to pawn Hap's revolver. The pawnshops are closed. When Julie meets a millionaire playboy, she tries to sell it to him. The playboy, Alan Davis (Michael Whalen), thinks she is trying to rob him and knocks her out.

In this realm of film fantasy, after Julie revives and tells Alan her story, he is soon arranging for her to have an audition. Hap thinks the audition is for both of them but he is soon put straight that it is just for Julie.

Alan warns Hap that he is bringing Julie down and Hap puts on a drunk act to instigate a breakup with her. He then disappears but later returns when Julie almost loses her place in the show because the director wants to give the role to his girlfriend. Hap muscularly sets things straight while Julie and Alan head for nuptials.

Dwan was fortunate (or shrewd) in getting Paul Kelly for the male lead. If Whalen's character and many of the other elements in the backstage story are pure Broadway and Hollywood fantasy, Kelly shows the grit that makes him believable as a trouper and gives the story some grounding in reality. Ruth Donnelly as the landlady also provided wisecracking support, as when Julie and Hap enact one of their more pitiful routines and she muses, "They haven't got any more future than a cake of ice."

Late in the film, Dwan and his cinematographer Barney McGill have a lovely background shot of weary chorus girls sitting on the floor with their shadows looming behind them, as if suggesting how Degas might have pictured Broadway stage girls. When Hap punches out the director and takes over the show, the dance number is staged vigorously in a swooping crane shot.

The film's modest virtues were not appreciated by critics who groused how archaic the vaudeville setting was. Yet the story seems to some extent to be about the fading away of the old song-and-dance men before the ambitious demands of the Broadway stage.

Dwan's next film, *Human Cargo*, which went into general release in June, was one of the best of his eight B movies for Fox. Myron Meisel writes of the film, "As an impressive lesson in the craft of effective storytelling in 66 minutes of total directorial control, *Human Cargo* would be an exemplary object of study in any filmmaking class, a compendium of apposite narrative choices. It is fast, efficient, and deftly realized — it represents what television technique could be and rarely is."[153]

Human Cargo, based on the novel *I Will Be Faithful* by Kathleen Shepard, dealt with a social issue that has become even timelier, illegal immigration. The film opens with a news story written by Patrick "Packy" Campbell, bearing the headline, "7 Aliens Dumped in Reservoir." The story refers to a figure of 10,000 aliens a month being smuggled across our borders and how this operation is run by international racketeers. The criminals blackmail the aliens, threatening to reveal their secret. The story concludes that, when faced with capture and arrest, "these racketeers think nothing of destroying the evidence by sacrificing the lives of hundreds of Human Cargo."

This being a B film, this issue is dealt with as one of the pursuits of an ace reporter, Campbell, played by Brian Donlevy, another actor being groomed for bigger things. Trevor again co-stars, this time as rookie reporter Bonnie Brewster, aspiring to become Packy's rival.

Packy has found a key witness, an illegal immigrant named Carmen Zoro, played by seventeen-year-old Rita Cansino, later to be known as Rita Hayworth. In his Bogdanovich interview, Dwan said that she and her father "had an act — we saw them down in Tijuana. That's where we engaged her."[154]

Dwan might well have seen Cansino-Hayworth perform with her father but before *Human Cargo* was made, she was already under contract to Fox and had appeared in four films in 1935. Actually, *Human Cargo* was more of a last for Cansino than a first. The teenage actress had been signed by Winfield Sheehan of the old Fox regime. Zanuck was less impressed with her and would not renew her contract. *Human Cargo* was the last Fox film in which she appeared before she made a new start at Columbia and within a year become known as Rita Hayworth.[155]

Dwan said that on the set, "she'd get so nervous — she'd cry — very frightened about working around the others who seemed to be more pro.... But she soon got over it, and got along pretty well."[156] Hayworth's fright may have aided her performance as her character Carmen reluctantly becomes a government witness and is in a state of terror about being killed by the racketeers. The sense of fear is palpable and Dwan adds to the suspense with crosscutting as Campbell arrives, snooping to find out what will happen.

Carmen is murdered before she can tell the vital facts to the D.A. It is to the credit of Dwan and his collaborators that at least temporarily, we forget that this is the old cliché of the character being killed just before revealing the culprit. We feel the impact of the loss personified in a close-up of Trevor looking totally devastated. Campbell enters and tells her, "Snap out of it — it's all part of the job."

The killing of Carmen is in many ways the heart of the film. Carmen's death makes tangible what we saw cited in the newspaper, how human beings are exploited and then become disposable. The rest of the film may be fanciful but the point is made and the audience's emotional commitment to the crusade is sealed.

The mood lightens when Campbell and Bonnie go undercover and pose as immigrants with not very convincing French accents, trying to get across the Canadian border. They wind up on a boat full of passengers from different countries but are discovered by the gang. Of course, they manage to get out and eventually are able to expose a prominent civic leader as the gang boss.

Human Cargo won some good notices. The *Hollywood Reporter* review stated, "Familiar story material that is so skillfully woven into screen entertainment as to lift it out of the rut into a rating of first class B product that should be good box-office on the duals, despite its lack of draw names."[157] But *Human Cargo* was still a B with its share of clichés and could still be dismissed by some critics as "an assembly job of trite situations."[158]

Dwan's next B film, *High Tension* was made without Trevor but had Donlevy returning to play another roughneck, this time a cable layer–deep sea diver, Steve Reardon. He's always providing daring and successful service whenever there's a crisis with underwater cables to keep the company going. Reardon and his boss Willard Stone (Robert McWade) are continually sparring. Steve has an even more volatile relationship with his girlfriend Mac (Glenda Farrell), who uses Steve's exploits for her romantic adventure novels about a deep sea diver. Midway through the film, Steve also gains a friend in Eddie Mitchell, whom he helps train to become a cable engineer. At the film's climax, Eddie, who has become the company's superintendent in Hawaii, desperately needs Steve's help.

High Tension, which was released in July, belongs to the subgenre of films that were made in the late 1930s and early 1940s like *Slim* and *Manpower*, featuring ordinary men who perform dangerous jobs so everyday life can continue with all of its modern standards and connections intact. Donlevy's Steve Reardon is a more elite character but still in that mode.

Claire Trevor, this time in peril because of her duties as an investigative reporter, is menaced by, from left to right, Morgan Wallace, Edward Cooper and Harry Woods in *Human Cargo* (1936).

Discussing his B-film service with Bogdanovich, Dwan noted that while the projects were assigned to him, "I still worked on the scripts — always with two things in mind — budget and speed, tempo. I'd eliminate stuff that was extraneous and speed up stuff that was written slowly. A writer stretches a story out, and you've got to fix it up. Make it move."[159]

High Tension is Dwan's fastest-moving film of the sound era and may move as rapidly as any B film made in the 1930s. An enormous amount of activity is packed into just 63 minutes, the shortest of all Dwan's B films for 20th Century–Fox. More importantly, Dwan maximized this pace to match the story. The opening is virtually a montage of different people complaining that their cable service (in those days that meant to transmit cablegrams and telegrams across the ocean) has been cut off and that they need it restored immediately. This is ultimately conveyed to the boss of the cable company, Stone. Stone is trying frantically to contact Reardon, who is out on the company ship the *Trident* to make repairs.

The rapid-paced editing of the first moments of *High Tension* comes to a halt when Reardon is seen in his diving bell 100 fathoms down, reading Mac's accounts of his heroic exploits in her book *The Son of Neptune*. (While lacking Trevor's sense of vulnerability, Farrell is even brassier and more combative.) When he finally picks up the phone, Stone excitedly talks about all the money that's being lost. Reardon explains that it will take six hours to repair the cable. When Stone threatens to fire him if the cable isn't repaired in two hours, Steve says he'll quit. Stone backs down. When an underling suggests that Reardon should be replaced, Stone gives him a litany of all the incredible feats Steve has done to keep the cable system functioning.

High Tension is, in its modest way, a celebration of a new modern world where everything moves with astonishing speed but is still struggling to keep up with raised expectations. (One might find an interesting parallel with the emergence of the Internet.) Late in the film, Mac in San Francisco decides she wants to go see him in Hawaii; she appears in Hawaii in the next sequence, explaining to Steve that she took the China Clipper which took her just 14 hours. Steve himself is a dynamo of energy and speed, often entering scenes unexpectedly and at one point, coming into the office riding a bicycle. (His incessant movement recalls that of Fairbanks.) The ratatat dialogue often matches the pace of the editing.

With its focus in the power of technology and engineering skill, *High Tension* may have been a more personal film for Dwan than the other Bs. When Steve meets Eddie Mitchell, Eddie tells him that he's been to Cal Tech where he studied "football mostly, a little engineering on the side." Eddie has not found work in his field but Steve tells him that he can make a "real engineer" out of him working with underwater cables. Eddie is Dwan's first featured engineer in the sound era and his description carries some suggestion of Dwan. The role of Eddie is played by Norman Foster, who Dwan claimed helped him write *Black Sheep* without taking credit. Dwan elaborated, "I was helping him become a director at the time."[160] *High Tension* was, in fact, the last film Foster appeared in before his first directorial effort *I Cover Chinatown*, in which he also starred. Thereafter, his career consisted almost totally of directing. So Steve's mentoring of Eddie may have had a real-life parallel in Dwan's mentoring of Foster. (Another film parallel may have involved Stone's underling Tuttle, who is always suggesting that his brother-in-law could take over Reardon's job, recalling the studio nepotism that Dwan despised.)

The competitive spirit is not just the sparkplug for the characters but their life blood. Steve prepares Eddie for working in a diving bell by advising him that he will be finished if the bell's cable breaks, then tells him that he can get in if he has "the nerve." Stone consistently makes demands on Steve but knows to back down when Reardon threatens to quit.

High Tension stands among the best of Dwan's Bs and received good reviews. *Variety* rated it as a "[s]peedy, actionful comedy, which looms as strong fare on any dualer [double-bill] and may get by in some single spots." The writers Lou Breslow and Edward Eliscu were cited for dialogue "that almost

Brian Donlevy, Theodore Von Eltz and Norman Foster all keep things moving in Dwan's energetic *High Tension* (1936).

crackles with vitality and humor." The review also noted, "Allan Dwan has directed with consummate skill, always with an eye for the unconventional."[161]

Trevor was back in Dwan's next B film, *15 Maiden Lane*, this one out by late October. She plays an amateur sleuth who matches wits with a jewel thief (Cesar Romero). The title refers to New York's diamond district. While this film exists, prints are rare and this is the only Dwan B at Fox I have not seen. *15 Maiden Lane* was one of the numerous films cited (along with *Human Cargo*) in John Cocchi's book *Second Feature* as notable examples of B movies. Cocchi wrote, "Oddest element of this Sol M. Wurtzel production is that Romero completely steals the film; he's graceful on the dance floor as he twirls Trevor on the slightest provocation; as the gang leader he's not only charming and resourceful, but also a ruthless killer."[162] There were modestly good notices as from the *Hollywood Reporter*: "It all adds up to better-than-average fare of its kind thanks to the slick, tongue-in-cheek direction of Allan Dwan, and will find its satisfied following in the duals."[163]

For his first year as a B filmmaker, Dwan had provided a steady stream of modest but solid entries. His record began to falter in 1937, possibly because he was given more serious material that did not prove as easily adaptable to the B-picture format.

The first of these was *Woman-Wise*, which starred Michael Whalen as a sports editor, Tracey Browne, at odds with a dishonest boxing promoter. A subplot involves Browne taking on the spoiled son of his boss as his assistant and trying to make a man of him. Although the film touches on the interesting issue of old fighters being exploited by certain promoters and managers, it gets bogged down in its plot complications and becomes tedious. For what it's worth, the film did get mildly sympathetic reviews from the *New York Times* and *Variety*.

Dwan's next film, *That I May Live*, released in April, about an ex-con trying to go straight, was more of a disaster. Dwan told Bogdanovich, "I saw that again recently — it was horrible."[164] The story is so weak and naïve that the *New York Times* reviewer averred that there was "much stronger stuff" in the latest episode of a Dick Tracy serial.[165]

But Dwan's next film, containing a story with a provocative social theme treated with fairy tale lightness, came out better than one would expect. *One Mile from Heaven* may not be the best of Dwan's B movies at Fox but it is the most interesting.

The film was adapted from a story by Judge Ben B. Lindsey, a noted social reformer. It was said to be based on an actual case in Denver in which Judge Lindsey was informed that a black woman was raising a blonde child whom she claimed was her daughter. It was learned that the woman, referred to as "Mammy Jackson," had worked for a midwife and that her duty was to burn in a furnace the bodies of babies born dead, as was the case with the child of a Chicago debutante. But when Mammy Jackson heard the infant meow like a sick kitten, she realized the baby was alive. Jackson then kept the child and raised her as her own. When the case became publicized, the real mother, now married, stepped forward to claim the child and wanted Mammy Jackson to live with them too.

Lou Breslow and John Patrick, who had worked on the scripts of *High Tension* and *15 Maiden Lane*, did the screenplay for *One Mile from Heaven*. In their take on the story, Claire Trevor, playing a feisty reporter in New York City, discovers the black mom rearing a white daughter.

Trevor, as the reporter Lucy "Tex" Warren, irritates the three men in the court press room by beating them at poker. For revenge, one of them arranges that she get a bogus phone call from her paper telling her to go to a lot in Harlem where a dead body has been found.

Tex finds nothing of the sort and realizes she's been conned. But then she hears the sound of tap dancing. Dwan shows shots of dancing legs which sound a clarion call to the children of the neighborhood. It is revealed that the tap dancer is the policeman on the beat, known as Officer Joe, played by the legendary tap dancer Bill Robinson. Tex then sees the only other white person in the group, a child named Sunny (Joan Carol). She is carrying her cat Duchess in a bird cage to make sure she is protected from one of the neighborhood dogs. It is an *Alice in Wonderland* kind of image which signals that we will be seeing a different kind of world.

Tex is astonished to see that Sunny's mother is a black woman named Flora Jackson. Smelling a story, Tex arranges to meet Flora. Flora insists that Sunny is her child and tries to discourage Tex from asking questions, but Tex is persistent. Officer Joe is close to Flora and backs her up.

Tex's story rouses the interests of her rival male reporters. While interviewing Flora at her home, they steal a photo of Flora and Sunny, which is printed in the newspapers. Reading a newspaper, a convict remembers Flora's face from the time when gangster Cliff Lucas dropped off his child with her. Lucas was later killed by the police and the mother believes that her child died in an accident. The mother Barbara Harrison (Sally Blane) has married a rich oilman and the gangsters believe they can extort money from her by revealing that her child is still alive and they can return her to Barbara.

One Mile from Heaven is a B movie with a parallel structure, where the somber main plot has the two women, Barbara and Flora, threatened by ruthless criminals, matched with the comic subplot of Tex trying to outwit the male reporters.

Flora is played by Fredi Washington, a light-skinned black woman best known for playing the rebellious daughter of Louise Beavers in the 1934 *Imitation of Life*. In his book *Cult Movie Stars*, the author Danny Peary referred to her as "[p]erhaps the only actress who couldn't have a movie career because she was too beautiful."[166] She was too striking to be cast as a maid but as a romantic figure she could not be paired with the leading white stars. For *One Mile from Heaven,* the solution was to match her with Robinson, who could lighten up the drama with his dance routines.

Although *One Mile from Heaven* was not a traditional woman's film, it was aimed at female viewers and it's the women characters who solve the problems. It's Tex who tails the gangsters and is able to report them to the police. At the court hearing, the judge rules that the child must be given to her rightful mother but it's Barbara who insists that Flora will not be separated from Sunny and that she will come to live with the wealthy Harrisons as their nurse. (There is also a marvelously effective long take of Flora talking about her child sitting in her lap. Sunny gradually and subtly reacts emotionally to what's being said.) And as a final comedic touch, Tex outsmarts the male reporters trying to scoop her and lands them all in jail.

Howard Hickman, Joan Carol, Fredi Washington and Bill Robinson in *One Mile from Heaven* (1937), one of the few 1930s B movies to deal with a racially sensitive issue.

Dwan may not have been a feminist but his films sometimes took a female viewpoint. In race relations, while there is no reason to bracket him as a progressive, he did seem to have a more humane touch in the Hollywood brand of racial humor. If in *Man to Man* Johnny Larkins seems buffoonish, he is matched by the white comedian Otis Harlan. In *High Tension*, the incomparable Hattie McDaniel, playing a maid named Hattie, does her share of clowning but, foreshadowing her later role in *Gone with the Wind*, also gives the white heroine some sage advice about pursuing her man. With *One Mile from Heaven*, Dwan and Wurtzel played a delicate balancing act. *Variety* opined, "They skate on pretty thin ice in this picture.... Film has the advantage of being away from the stereotyped run of pictures, but whether the theme fits into the popular groove is something to think about."[167]

In the more comedic part of *One Mile from Heaven* (1937), reporter Claire Trevor has the last laugh in outsmarting her male colleagues (left to right) Chick Chandler, Russell Hopton and Ray Walker. Fred Kelsey plays the cop.

The final scene has the Harrisons hosting a party at their estate for the children of Sunny's Harlem neighborhood. The fact that Flora must still be at least nominally employed as a nurse still smacks of servitude but that may have been the most practical solution in the context of its time. (Even more interestingly, to keep Flora and Joe together, Joe's patrol beat has been moved to the Harrisons' upscale neighborhood.) The final images of Joe dancing triumphantly at this celebration of blacks and whites, cutting across barriers of both race and class, may have been a utopian vision of hope in the midst of the Depression.

There was less hope for Fredi Washington. Even though *Variety* characterized her performance as "splendid," *One Mile from Heaven* was her last film. She returned to the stage.

For Claire Trevor, however, her period of B-movie internment was coming close to an end. Wurtzel sent her a telegram in which he said that Joe Schenck had considered the film "one of the best pictures he has seen in a long time and that you gave a fine performance."[168] She was soon appearing in *Dead End* which would win her a Best Supporting Actress Oscar nomination.

There would also be some good news for Allan Dwan.

Shirley Temple and the Height of Energy

Dwan's days in the B-movie wilderness came to an end when Darryl F. Zanuck offered him the opportunity to direct *Heidi* with the great child star Shirley Temple. It had been over five years since a major Hollywood film had been released with Dwan's name as director. Another silent director, Malcolm St. Clair, twelve years younger than Dwan, *never* emerged from Fox's B-movie serfdom. But Dwan had not only returned from his latest place of exile, but would be directing 20th Century–Fox's biggest star.

Temple started her movie career with the small independent company Educational Films in a series of shorts called "Baby Burlesks." These pictures had small children mimicking adult stars in parodies of their films. Temple's mother Gertrude, realizing that Shirley's future was limited in these movies, made the rounds of the studios with Shirley, getting her into feature films. Her breakthrough success came at the age of six in the Fox feature *Stand Up and Cheer* (1934). Except for two loan-outs to Paramount, *Little Miss Marker* and *Now and Forever*, all of her remaining films in the 1930s were at Fox. Little Shirley rapidly became the company's second biggest star. When Fox's top star, Will Rogers, was killed in a plane crash in August 1935, Temple's importance to the studio increased exponentially and she rose to the occasion with continuous smashes at the box office.

Shirley had been signed by Winfield Sheehan but she was one holdover from the old regime Zanuck would keep firmly in place. After taking command of Fox, Zanuck hastily assembled a story conference with his best writers making their top priority to develop projects for Temple. They were to follow a basic formula whereby she would melt the heart of some curmudgeon and give her target a newfound appreciation of human beings. However, many variations would have to be found to keep the films interesting. Nineteen writers were assigned to an entity simply called "Shirley Temple Story Development." As Temple biographer Anne Edwards described it, "The work on Shirley Temple projects was a veritable factory."[169]

But to a much greater extent than it was for Fairbanks, time was a ticking bomb for Ms. Temple, as each year she moved closer to adolescence. Fortunately, the little actress showed that in addition to her charm, she could also sing. Beginning with *The Little Colonel* she demonstrated her considerable Terpsichorean ability by dancing with Bill Robinson.

As Shirley approached her ninth birthday, she was losing her baby look. Zanuck realized that he would have to go beyond his Pollyanna formula to keep Temple at her box office pinnacle. He decided to star her in films based on popular literary classics that would put greater emphasis on Shirley's dramatic skills.

First up was Rudyard Kipling's *Wee Willie Winkie* for which the child protagonist was changed from a boy to a girl. Also in line with this upgrading of story material, Zanuck selected a major director, John Ford, to helm the picture. Ford was not yet the director of legend but he had already won an Oscar for *The Informer* and had directed *The Prisoner of Shark Island*, one of the most important Fox films of the previous year (1936).

The result was a thoroughly charming girl's own adventure film, which in the words of critic Andrew Sarris contained "extraordinary camera prose passages from the wide-eyed point of view of a child."[170] Much to the relief of Zanuck, it also grossed $1,250,000 domestically. In her autobiography, Shirley Temple Black said she regarded *Wee Willie Winkie* as the best of her films. Ford had initially been cool to Shirley but she won him over.[171]

Zanuck next turned to the children's novel *Heidi* by Johanna Spyri, and plucked the veteran Dwan from his B-movie stable. Dwan remembered getting the assignment this way to Bogdanovich: "Shirley Temple was starting to slip. They hadn't made very good stuff with her, and *Heidi* was an effort to boost her back, and it worked."[172]

He elaborated more on this with Temple biographer Robert Windeler: "She'd had her peak and was sliding [in 1937]. Zanuck would like to have made a trade, but nobody was interested, and I liked to avoid children, especially those who were over. In a kind of left-handed way, he gave me *Heidi* and said, 'See what you can do with it.'"[173]

Dwan is clearly incorrect in saying that Temple's career was slipping. On the contrary, her films were continuing to show box-office strength, even given the fact that the hit *Wee Willie Winkie* had not been released at the time Dwan was offered *Heidi*.

But while it was literally true that Temple had shown no sign of fading at the box office, there was still considerable concern over how she would weather the coming transitional years and this had prompted Zanuck's reassessment over how her future should proceed.[174]

The child star herself was aware of this tension in the air and this is what Dwan had grasped. Over fifty years later, Shirley Temple Black wrote, "Dwan's comment that I was passé, however, neatly epitomized the ambivalence behind studio doors.... On the one hand, I was ranked number one at the box office

Darryl F. Zanuck fostered the merger that left him running Twentieth Century–Fox. Even in his leisure activities, Zanuck looks quite the commander.

for a third successive year. On the other hand, some clairvoyants, even my director, believed I would soon disappear from the scene. I was central in an odd sort of split screen, dominant and moribund all at the same moment."[175]

It is not difficult to spot a lingering sense of hurt as Black remembered the kinds of doubts Dwan epitomized, despite her having achieved such remarkable success. But it is to her credit that she took those doubts as a challenge which she would have to meet.

Regarding Dwan, she wrote, "As had been the case with *Wee Willie Winkie*, during the making of *Heidi* I had a director who was skeptical if not annoyed at the prospect of working with me. As *Heidi* progressed, however, Dwan's initial attitude of resignation warmed perceptibly."[176]

One can surmise that having survived his B-movie tenure, Dwan was suspicious that Zanuck was leading him into another trap, risking the brunt of failure if he could not deliver the goods with a child star who may have already passed her prime. Henry King, one of Fox's ace directors, had already declined to direct *Heidi*.[177] But Dwan, like Temple, must have recognized, however reluctantly, that there was also a golden opportunity in rising to the challenge. He could once again emerge as the problem-solver.

The manner in which Temple ultimately won the hearts and respect of the curmudgeonly Ford and Dwan sounds much like a Shirley Temple movie. But unlike in her earlier films, she had not done it through sweetness and guile but through her professionalism and hard work. She recalled that in confronting the developing skepticism about her future, she decided that her "only objective was to elevate my ability to the height of my energy. What really mattered was daily professionalism, sustained interaction among our total crew, the rhythm and celebration of work in everyday life."[178]

Elevating ability to the height of one's energy sounds like the kind of mathematical formula and ambition Dwan would have relished, like "Cyclone + D'Artagnan = Speed." Referring to his work with Shirley, Dwan acknowledged, "I had to use that energy 'cause it was bouncing all over the place."[179]

Dwan later fondly remembered Shirley: "She was fun all the time. Very often she'd have other children around, we had to have discipline on the set, so I created a police department and had some badges made. She was the Chief of Police. I was only Captain. And everybody around her had to wear a badge and salute, and the Chief had to keep discipline — so she behaved herself."[180]

Black recalled having originally organized her "police force" in 1935 where members could be fined for infractions such as forgetting their lines. The director David Butler had supplied the force with Junior G-man badges from a toy store. But she remembered of Dwan, "In the end, it was he who gave identity to my police force by replacing my 'Junior G-man' badges with gilded ones engraved with the name of my force."[181]

In interviews, Dwan showed that he thought he and Shirley worked as collaborators. Dwan recalled for Windeler, "Shirley helped invent the dream sequence where she's in Holland because she thought that way — she knew it was a good spot for a musical number."[182]

This is the musical sequence where Shirley and a group of other children sing, "In My Little Wooden Shoes." Black recalls that the musical sequence was written in the middle of the shooting. Supposedly the scriptwriters, as well as Dwan, credited Shirley with the idea of the wooden shoes.[183] But in her autobiography, Black did not welcome the credit accorded her for the sequence. In fact, she felt that Dwan had "blamed" her for the invention and regarded his account as "muddleheaded."[184]

The reason for Black's discontent on this score is that she regarded the musical sequence as marking "the collapse of any studio resolve to build on the purely dramatic momentum first evident in *Wee Willie Winkie*." She also adamantly denied what she said was the studio claim reported elsewhere that her mother requested the inclusion of a musical number.[185] Regarding Dwan's comment "She knew it was a good spot for a musical number," Black responded, "*Any* spot is good for a musical number...."[186]

With all due respect to Black's experience in the musical genre, this is not precisely true although it may have been true of most of her early vehicles. But *Heidi* is a very carefully structured film, especially in its balance of comedy and drama, and there are clearly many passages that would have not been appropriate for a musical number and certainly not in most of the last reel unless the song was darkly operatic.

In the novel, the orphan Heidi has been raised by her Aunt Dete in the Swiss village of Mayenfeld but Dete now wants to concentrate on her career and so takes the child to the neighboring village of Dorfli at the base of the Alps and hands her over to her grandfather. Heidi finds happiness there. Dete returns one day to take Heidi away, this time to Frankfurt, Germany. Dete has been paid to bring Heidi to stay with a wealthy family and give comfort to Klara, the daughter who is paralyzed. Heidi is unhappy in the city and with the strict discipline enacted by the governess Fraulein Rottenmeier. She becomes homesick for her home in the Alps. Thanks to a sympathetic doctor, the diagnosis is that Heidi must return to her Swiss village.

Dwan said of *Heidi*, "[I]t was a very grim, heavy story.... Mean old housekeeper and aunt who sold her down the line. All those awful things, like *Uncle Tom's Cabin*.... So we made it funny."[187]

Actually, while the material was lightened, at times *Heidi* also had its share of Victorian melodrama. But lightness does not seem to have been paramount in Darryl Zanuck's mind as he reviewed the first draft of the screenplay of *Heidi* completed on January 29, 1937. It was recorded that "Mr. Zanuck feels that *Heidi* has the possibilities of being a great moving picture of the *David Copperfield* school." At another point in the same report, Zanuck says that the grandfather's search for *Heidi* "can be as significant and as powerful as the man-hunt in *Les Miserables*."[188]

Still later, Zanuck appears to see the grandfather, Adolph Kramer, to be as tested as Job. He is a man who has lost his faith until the arrival of Heidi helps bring it back to him. Then when she is missing and he can't find her, he again denounces God until he is again brought back to his faith by the miracle of finding Heidi.

All this sounds a bit ponderous for a Shirley Temple movie, not to mention that the dramatic emphasis on the grandfather might have him overshadowing Shirley. (Shirley is still called upon to suffer a breakdown in the story.) Without sacrificing Zanuck's dramatic ambitions, there was a need to find some balance.

By the time that Zanuck discusses the script treatment of April 30, he is citing Dwan for giving his input and of having the opening scenes reflecting Dwan's suggestions. The emphasis is still very dramatic and Zanuck is deeply involved with developing the scenes of the grandfather's search for Heidi in the last part of the film.

Some background scenes were shot in Switzerland by director Otto Brower; according to *The Hollywood Reporter*, he was originally assigned to direct the film.[189] It is doubtful that a director of his stature (directing mainly B Westerns) was seriously considered by Zanuck. Dwan recalls Lake Arrowhead, California, as the location depicting the Alpine scenes and also acknowledges Zanuck's loosening the purse strings to provide a classier production.

In the film, as in the novel, Heidi's grandfather is known as a misanthrope who has severed his connections with the people of Dorfli and lives in a hut in the mountains. Having been alone for so long, he accepts Heidi only reluctantly and remains coldly taciturn and even menacing. Looking at the grandfather from Heidi's point of view, Dwan has him appearing threatening in a series of Hitchcockian shots, settling on a close-up of a knife he is holding. Heidi braces herself before realizing that he is using the knife only to cut some bread.

Heidi gradually wins over her grandfather by her cheerfulness and her ability to adapt to situations. When her chair proves too small to permit her to eat from the table, she puts her food on the chair and sits on the floor. The musical sequence "In Our Little Wooden Shoes" is triggered by the scene where the grandfather is reading to Heidi a section in a storybook taking place in Holland. The musical sequence is Heidi's dream and ends with her asleep and being put to bed by her grandfather, further cementing their relationship. It also heightens the fairy tale atmosphere of the story.

But there is also a tragic dimension to the character of Grandfather Kramer. His son Tobias refused to heed his father's warnings not to marry a girl from Mayenfeld. After he married her anyway, the father disowned Tobias. When the villagers sided with the son, Adolph Kramer began to shun all human contact. With Tobias and his wife both now dead, Heidi rekindles Kramer's feeling of family.

It should have been easy for Dwan to empathize with Kramer's isolation after the director's own years away from the mainstream. And Dwan surely recognized Kramer as another "lost father." When the village minister visits Adolph and tries to prod him to come to church, Kramer resists.

The grandfather will finally expunge his feelings in a catharsis brought on by Heidi's request for Sunday school instruction. He opens a book that contains his son Tobias' signature from his childhood. In Heidi's attempt to read the New Testament parable of the Prodigal Son, Kramer is transported to seek a spiritual reconciliation with Tobias. When Heidi stumbles over the words, she gives the book to her grandfather to read. She sees that he can recite the story without looking at the book.

When she asks him if he knows it by heart, he emphatically repeats the phrase, "By heart." The story of the Prodigal Son here becomes the tale of the Prodigal Father.

In the transcription of Zanuck's conference on the April 30 draft of the screenplay, Zanuck had a "Note to Mr. Dwan" in which he suggested that "you get great big head close-ups of Heidi in thoughtful interested reactions. Also large heads of the old man reading."[190]

For the most part, Dwan ignored Zanuck's suggestions. Most of the scene is in medium two-shot although Dwan does cut briefly for a tighter shot of their two heads but only to emphasize the moment when the grandfather says, "By heart." While Kramer is looking ahead as if having a vision, Heidi is looking intently at her grandfather and moving closer to him. The interplay inherent in the two-shot is used by Dwan to show the relationship developing to another level where Heidi acts as a conduit to Kramer's son, thereby leading her grandfather back to the community and to religion. The next scene has Heidi and her grandfather entering the church where Adolph will be embraced by his erstwhile enemies.

The second part of the film begins when Dete returns to Kramer's hut and, finding Heidi alone, tricks her into coming with her, promising to bring her back later in the day. In actuality, Dete is delivering her for cash to a wealthy family in Frankfurt.

This sets up another of the oppositions of locale that Dwan exploited so well. In Dorfli, Kramer begins his agonized effort to find Heidi, realizing he cannot live without her. Heidi now moves from the majestic splendor of her grandfather's mountain home to the narrow streets of Frankfurt. A title page clues us in that for Heidi, Frankfurt is "like a great noisy cage."

As Heidi, Shirley Temple melted the heart of her bitter, hermetic grandfather (Jean Hersholt). A similar process was repeated in numerous Temple movies but *Heidi* (1937) was one of the most memorable.

The Sesemann household is ruled by the corrupt governess, aptly named Fraulein Rottenmeier (Mary Nash). The Sesemann daughter Klara (Marcia Mae Jones) lost her ability to walk in an accident months ago and it is Fraulein Rottenmeier's intention to keep the girl in an invalid state as long as possible, until she can convince the widower father (Sidney Blackmer) that her services are indispensable. Herr Sesemann's business causes him to be absent from his home for long stretches of time and the governess uses all her influence to convince Klara that she is weak and helpless.

This is another house of gloom, reminiscent of the miserable household in the Fairbanks film *The Habit of Happiness* of twenty years earlier. Heidi challenges things not overtly as an apostle of optimism like Doug, but as the rustic child who sees through all the pretensions of the city folk.

Far more than the musical sequence, the scenes at the Sesemann home bend the film toward comedy. Having been reared with her grandfather's appreciation of the mountains, Heidi is a child of nature who talks to Klara of goats as if they are human beings. Klara is enchanted and amused by Heidi, but Fraulein Rottenmeier becomes her instant enemy. This was not the first or the last time Dwan would project the romantic view of the child of nature confronted with the hypocrisy of the civilized world, going at least as far back as Marguerite Clark in *Wildflower*. Rottenmeier scolds Heidi with comments like, "You are not in your barbarous hut in the Alps now but in a cultured home."

Far from being intimidated by the conniving governess, Heidi is soon mimicking and ridiculing Fraulein Rottenmeier to Klara's delight. This is an opportunity to show another side of Shirley's persona. She turns the household upside down, mocking the governess' sense of etiquette while Fraulein Rottenmeier's skills as a teacher are likened to that of a monkey that has entered the house after escaping an organ grinder. Authority looked even more ridiculous when exposed by a child. As with the screwball comedies of the era, making established orders look ludicrous, Shirley could reflect the rebellious spirit of the 1930s.

After the broad humor of the monkey scene, the film's comic element recedes. It's still displayed in bits, especially by Shirley Temple regular Arthur Treacher, though his English butler Andrews seems a little out of place in Frankfurt. The mood slowly shifts to the dramatic, highlighted by Heidi and Klara's Christmas gift to Herr Sesemann on his return. With Heidi's help, Klara has begun to walk again and Shirley has again proved the champion problem-solver.

Sesemann realizes that his daughter would be better off without Fraulein Rottenmeier, and dismisses her after she abuses Heidi. The Sesemanns are well intentioned but disturbingly patronizing in their desire to adopt Heidi into the household. Klara insists that she wants to keep her as if referring to a pet, and Sesemann cavalierly dismisses her grandfather's claim to Heidi by saying that he's heard stories that Kramer is a terrible man.

Grandfather Kramer arrives in Frankfurt and there will be much crosscutting between his odyssey and the Sesemann family. As Zanuck wanted, this will be an elaborate and heart-wrenching search and Kramer's obsessive behavior outside of his native habitat, checking everywhere in Frankfurt for Heidi, will land him in jail, or at least in a detention room since the jails are filled on Christmas. This segment is dominated by the grandfather's angst and the opportunity is manfully seized by Jean Hersholt in that role. (In one of his reports, Zanuck mentioned that Spencer Tracy and Paul Muni had been considered for the part.) All that survives of Zanuck's grandiose religious vision is a vocal appeal to God by the imprisoned Kramer.

The bitter Fraulein Rottenmeier has now kidnapped Heidi and is leading her to one of the great Victorian horrors, being sold to gypsies. Kramer escapes from the detention hall and eventually finds Heidi fleeing from Rottenmeier. The renegade governess calls on the police, claiming that the old man kidnapped her child.

The matter is hashed out in a police station where the police appear to believe Rottenmeier and are intent on putting Kramer in jail despite Heidi's tearful pleas and her angry hysteria about being taken away by Rottenmeier. While the storyline is too diffuse to have anything like the intensity of Chaplin's *The Kid,* the scene has a genuine charge of emotion. On the advice of one officer, Heidi's request to contact the Sesemanns is finally accepted by the police.

There is no follow-up scene to show how matters were sorted out or how Fraulein Rottenmeier got her just deserts. Nor is there the concluding scene that Zanuck insisted upon after reading the April 30 treatment, that of Heidi and her grandfather walking home together and into "a beautiful sunset shot of the Alps." Instead the finale resembles the "utopian" ending of *One Mile from Heaven*. At the grandfather's hut, he and his neighbors greet the Sesemanns and Andrews. There's a festive meal as country folk and city folk, rich and poor, Swiss and German, gather together in celebration. It was the kind of optimistic vision that could appeal to the hopes of the film's audience, especially that of Depression Era America.[191]

Heidi could have been made into a purer version of the novel without the excesses of Zanuck's pretensions. But the film that exists, while thoroughly a Hollywood creation, represents a marvelous balance, building on the commercial expectations of a Temple film and fitting into a dramatic context with reasonable faithfulness to its nineteenth century story. In the final shot, a close-up, Ms. Temple talks directly into the camera ("And please make every little boy and girl as happy as I am"), as if taking leave of her character and melting into Shirley, who assures her audience of her presence with the kind of ingratiating smile once displayed by Douglas Fairbanks. The *New York Times* review said that this close-up brought the audience to their feet.[192]

Shirley the celebrity still overwhelmed her characters. Fairbanks avoided this fate when he morphed into the various guises of his swashbuckling characters. But for Shirley Temple, there did not appear to be such options.

Heidi was originally released in October 1937 in a three-tone tinting process that consisted of a combination of sepia, amber and copper tones for daylight and blue, orange and copper tones for night. The aforementioned *Times* review noted "a soft sepia (and blue) tinting to accentuate its dream world quality...."[193]

Variety thought that the film had appeal for adults as well as children and that it would be good for at least the average Temple draw if not better.[194] *The Hollywood Reporter* raved, "The new Shirley Temple picture is among her very best, which means that it is grand entertainment...."[195] *Heidi* remains perhaps the most beloved of the Shirley Temple films.

Zanuck had shored up Temple's stature and even boosted it with the combination of *Wee Willie Winkie* and *Heidi*. But it had come at a price. While *Heidi* earned a zestful one million dollars in rentals, it had been budgeted at $600,000 which meant that its profit was moderate.

The next Temple film, which Dwan would also direct, would be more conventional and more modestly produced. One stratagem that Zanuck had used was to remake Mary Pickford films such as *Poor Little Rich Girl* and Fox would revert to that formula in next starring Shirley in *Rebecca of Sunnybrook Farm.*

However, almost none of the original story beyond the title survived in the modernized version. Fox had made a more faithful remake in 1932. The Temple film was so radically different that the screen credit read that it was only "suggested" by Kate Douglas Wiggin's book.

Dwan recalled, "And I had Raymond Griffith again so I was able to say, 'Let's go after this with an updated attitude — put some music in it — give Shirley something to sing — let's get radio in.... And we injected all that."[196]

Raymond Griffith, who had been the famous dapper comic film star during the silent era, was the associate producer on both *Heidi* and *Rebecca of Sunnybrook Farm*. According to Dwan, he was a good friend of Zanuck's and may have helped pass ideas from Dwan to the film mogul. However, Zanuck was not shy about putting music in a Shirley Temple film.

Dwan also acknowledged that he had to sometimes work through Shirley's mother Gertrude, who had great influence over her daughter. But he also enjoyed working directly with Shirley and marveled at her remarkable memory, noting, "You'd just tell her once and she'd remember the rest of her life...."[197]

Mrs. Black did have one unpleasant memory of Dwan on the set of *Rebecca of Sunnybrook Farm*: "Some directors need a private buffoon at hand, a sort of clown type to act as a lightning rod when tempers flared. Dwan had a script supervisor, a man who wore horn-rimmed glasses and a fixed grin regardless of what happened to him. If Dwan became exasperated over something, he would knock the script folder from his hand. Instead of flaring back, time and again he simply stooped to retrieve his scattered papers, staring up with the moist, mute apprehension of a whipped dog. Once or twice I saw Dwan punch him on the upper arm or grab a pinch of flesh and twist.... The situation always struck me as odd. Why the man never fought back escaped me."[198]

While Dwan could be a hard taskmaster, this is one of the few reported occasions of sadism since his days with Kerrigan. This harshness may have surfaced at Fox because of Dwan's long wanderings out of power. Don Ameche, who worked with Dwan the following year on *The Three Musketeers*, said Dwan was "like Henry King, a really severe man, and inclined to pick on people a little bit when he found someone he could do that to."[199] Dwan's goddaughter Robin Wallace has also said that her godfather acknowledged that he was a harsher director when he was younger but that he mellowed with age.[200]

The revamped plot of *Rebecca of Sunnybrook Farm* has Shirley playing still another orphan, Rebecca Winstead, who is taken by her stepfather Harry Kipper (William Demarest) to audition for the "Little Miss America" contest sponsored by Crackly Grain Flakes. Rebecca's singing quickly puts her over but through a miscommunication she is told that she has failed. With no hope of deriving income from the child, Harry leaves New York City and takes Rebecca upstate to leave her at her Aunt Miranda's farm. By the most improbable of coincidences, living next door to Aunt Miranda is Tony Kent (Randolph Scott), the radio advertising executive running the contest. When he hears Rebecca sing, he immediately recognizes her voice as his selection for Little Miss America. Rebecca also introduces Tony to her cousin Gwen Warren and a romance soon flourishes.

Because her sister ran off with an opera singer and they became destitute, Aunt Miranda despises show business and forbids Rebecca to sing on the radio. But Tony and Gwen work out a plan to sneak Rebecca from her home one night to Tony's house where a special hookup permits the radio program to originate from there. When the newly married Harry hears Rebecca's voice on the radio, he and his wife Melba decide to cash in by asserting Harry's legal rights as her guardian. But Rebecca uses a clever ruse to make Harry and Melba think she can no longer perform. For $5,000 they then agree to let Tony take Rebecca back to Aunt Miranda.

While this seems ostensibly another city vs. country values story, the film shows little conviction in that regard. Most of the farm scenes are shot on sound stages and Shirley's one big pastoral chore, chasing a little pig, is just a lead-in to her first meeting with Tony.

Rebecca's only expression of joy at being on a farm is a brief number sung with Bill Robinson, "An Old Straw Hat." There are no exterior shots of the city and except for a very brief scene in Harry's apartment, the only city scenes are set in radio studios. *Variety* opined that a more fitting title for the film would have been *Rebecca of Radio City*.[201]

This *Rebecca of Sunnybrook Farm* has more plots and subplots than a Shakespearean tragedy but most are resolved matter-of-factly or just disappear. The lack of dramatic resolutions may be one reason why *Variety* decided, "Allan Dwan's direction is nothing to brag about."[202]

Bosley Crowther in the *New York Times*, referring to Shirley Temple, declared that "any actress who can dominate a Zanuck musical ... with Jack Haley, Gloria Stuart, Phyllis Brooks, Helen Westley, Slim Summerville, Bill Robinson, et cetera, can dominate the world."[203] But there is a flip side to Crowther's statement. While Shirley is the hub of the story, the film never gets too mired in her predicaments but can keep turning to scenes highlighting Demarest doing his pratfalls, Westley and Summerville still caught up in Miranda's quarter-of-a-century-old vendetta against Homer for missing their wedding, Haley and Brooks doing a charming duet of the ballad "Alone with You" or Franklin Pangborn contributing a droll bit in a cameo. While there are no great moments, there is a profusion of amiable characters animated by expert actors and music contributed by several songwriting teams. Pacing rather than structure is important for Dwan here and in an 81-minute time frame, he keeps the action moving pleasantly without dawdling over plot points.

Shirley, of course, has the most prominent role in the film's radio broadcast as she sings "Come and Get Your Happiness" which incorporates some of the rural values into it. There is a somewhat surreal moment as Rebecca, who is making her radio debut, tells her listeners that she is going to sing "some of the songs I've introduced to you." Shirley then sings a medley of songs she's popularized onscreen including "The Good Ship Lollipop," "Animal Crackers," "When I'm with You," and "Goodnight My Love!" So this time, the film character becomes the celebrity Shirley Temple well before the ending, though she will revert back to character. This suggests the format of variety TV shows where the star could step in and out of character during sketches.

Rebecca introduces the last song on the broadcast by saying, "The clock is ticking the hours away. My moment with you is now ending." Shirley Temple was riding atop popularity polls but it was difficult to escape the imagery of time running out. Still, while much of Shirley's performance was limited to her usual bag of tricks, her star power was evident in kudos from the *Times* and elsewhere. *Rebecca* proved even bigger than *Heidi* at the box office, accruing $1.25 million in rentals.

Dwan told the authors of one Shirley Temple book that she excelled in scenes portraying anger. "She could get so mad; she'd tear the set down. There was probably a good deal of suppressed anger in her, and acting gave her a chance to express herself. I believe she was dying to do something tragic or dra-

Bill Robinson and Shirley Temple commence their dance number "An Old Straw Hat" in *Rebecca of Sunnybrook Farm* (1938).

matic."[204] But her opportunities to do something new at Fox were dwindling.

Dwan collaborated again with Temple at a more fateful time.

Suez: The Price of Fame

Dwan's next assignment at Fox came unexpectedly when in mid–December 1937 he was called upon to replace Sidney Lanfield a week before production was to begin on the comedy *Josette*. According to a story in the *Hollywood Reporter*,[205] Lanfield was stricken ill and was to be hospitalized for at least four weeks. Simone Simon was set to star with Don Ameche and Robert Young, the latter having been loaned to Fox by MGM.

Josette was a trifling romantic comedy about two brothers (Ameche and Young) in New Orleans out to prevent their father from marrying a much younger woman. The brothers think the nightclub chanteuse played by Simon is their target, but unknown to them she is only appearing under the name of "Josette" while the real Josette has gone off to rendezvous with their father in New York. Clearing up the accumulated misunderstandings so that Ameche and Simon can clinch their romantic destiny proves more tedious than mirthful.

According to the *New York Times*, Dwan then landed a Fox assignment that hardly seemed more promising, working with the Dionne Quintuplets in an exercise called *Five of a Kind*. But before he could begin work on the film, Dwan was called away by Zanuck for a much more important project.[206]

Zanuck had decided to film an expensive historical epic on the building of the Suez Canal, and Dwan was given the plum assignment. The movie was to be called *Suez* but one man had been the driving force behind the building of the canal, the French diplomat Ferdinand de Lesseps (1805–1894), and the film would be essentially his story.

Lesseps came from a family with a history of service in the diplomatic corps. In 1849, he was disgraced for having exceeded his instructions in a political incident in Italy and his diplomatic career came to an end. His troubles deepened when in 1853, both his wife and one of his sons succumbed to scarlet fever.

These personal losses left a void in his life and Lesseps poured all his energy into the prospect of building a canal in the Isthmus of Suez. In July 1854, he learned that his old friend Said had acceded to power in Egypt. Going to Egypt, he convinced Said of his vision of the canal and of its potential for prestige and profits for Egypt. Said granted Lesseps the exclusive power to form and direct a company to construct a canal on the Isthmus of Suez.

Lesseps returned to France to form his company and to promote the canal project. Louis-Napoleon, a nephew of the famed Bonaparte, had begun a Second Empire for France and would reign as Napoleon III. Lesseps needed to win, if not the emperor's full support, at least his sympathies towards his project. Lesseps had a trump card in that Louis-Napoleon was married to his cousin Eugenie de Montijo. Officially, Napoleon did not initially support the canal. The British opposed it and he had no desire to create a breach with them. But through his connection with Eugenie, Lesseps learned that privately Napoleon thought the canal was a splendid idea and would do nothing to interfere with Lesseps' plans.

Lesseps sold shares in his company to raise capital for the building of the canal, which began in 1859. He encountered various problems but proved fully adept at diplomatic strategies and raising more money. The Suez Canal was finally completed in 1869, just as funds for the project were about to run out.

Even in its planning, *Suez* the movie was a mammoth undertaking. There were six treatments of the story, the first two by Sam Duncan. The 20th Century–Fox files at USC contain almost a hundred pages of comments about the treatments from Zanuck and other studio personnel.

One feature that was present from the very first treatment (completed on March 29, 1937) was that Lesseps would be caught romantically between two women. Historical issues were also raised in the reactions to the first treatment, most notably in the depiction of Great Britain.

On the cover of the first treatment, Zanuck scrawled in pencil, "Epic possibilities — new — thrilling — how much authentic?" Zanuck also asked, "How much English resentment?" and then further down gave his view on the amorous aspect of the film: "Romance is nothing —flat —" followed by suggestions on how the romantic element should be built up.[207]

Zanuck knew there were ways to modify British intransigence so as not to make it offensive while still providing a major hurdle for Lesseps to overcome. In the finished film, British opposition is personified first by the avuncular Nigel Bruce playing a fictitious character. Outside of the political arena, Bruce's character is shown as a good friend to Lesseps' father (Henry Stephenson). When Lesseps goes to London to seek help, he is met by an antagonistic Prime Minister William Gladstone (played by George Zucco sporting a wig). Actually, Gladstone was on record for having attacked the British government's disapproval of the canal and in one treatment of the script was depicted as Lesseps' savior. However, Zanuck insisted on changing the sympathetic British figure to Benjamin Disraeli, claiming it would add importance to the story.

In the closing reels, Lesseps would be portrayed as being at the end of his rope, having run out of funds to complete the canal. The scene would then shift to England where Disraeli, who had pledged his support to Lesseps, appeared to be losing his bid to be elected prime minister. But the tide suddenly turns and, summoned to form a new government, Disraeli announces that he is going to put Queen Victoria in business as part-owner of the canal.

Disraeli did, in fact, purchase a major share (44 percent) of the canal company for his country but this happened six years after the canal had been completed and he purchased the shares not from Lesseps but from the Egyptian pasha who had fallen deeply into debt. According to a recent history of the Suez Canal, its purchased shares completely changed Britain's perspective on the importance of the canal. "By the beginning of the twentieth century, the Suez Canal had become the fulcrum of the British empire and an excuse for imperial expansion. As the volume of trade increased, the British government began to treat the canal as the most vital, and vulnerable, point in the whole empire."[208]

Jason Joy, the former MPDAA member, now a Fox executive, had written to Zanuck, "It will be much easier for these audiences [those of Britain and its dominions] to believe that the project was temporarily blocked for individual reasons than that their political leaders were too dumb to fore-see the advantages it would give them."[209]

Philip Dunne and Julien Josephson handled the future versions of the script. Dunne thought that there was too much plot and that the script had to be both simplified and made more authentic. He was also the first to suggest in writing that Tyrone Power play the lead although he qualifies it by asking Zanuck "if you think he could carry what would amount to a one-man show...."[210]

Dunne also eschewed the happy ending of the second treatment and thought that the drama of the film was in Lesseps sacrificing everything he has "until finally he has nothing left but his victory over the isthmus."[211]

There was indeed something to be made of Lesseps' obsessive championing of the canal, which was more of a one-man show than, say, T.E. Lawrence's leading the revolt in the desert. But Zanuck would not part with the concept of Lesseps' romantic quandary with two women which his instinct told him would be far better for the box office. And he remained committed to the importance of Lesseps' hopeless love for Eugenie. In their time, there was much speculation on how much Lesseps' closeness to his cousin, the empress, helped him to get approval from Louis-Napoleon regarding the canal. Historically, what we know is that in the 1860s, "Lesseps and Eugenie Montijo became quite close, but before that their relationship was something of a mystery. He had watched her grow up during his years in Spain, and she wrote him repeatedly during her quick courtship with Louis-Napoleon to seek his advice. After that, they maintained a correspondence, but the few surviving letters do not suggest more than a polite familial fondness between them."[212] Zanuck insisted on a scenario that would have Lesseps and Eugenie in love until Eugenie begins receiving the attentions of Louis-Napoleon.

Reviewing the first treatment by Dunne and Josephson, Zanuck was delighted by the injection of a new character as Ferdinand's second love, Toni Pellerin. In Duncan's treatment, Lesseps' second romantic interest was the daughter of a consul. Toni had a more plebian origin (the granddaughter of an army sergeant). Her actual parentage is not established but living in the desert, she is a delightful tomboy who has never been educated. Zanuck's one complaint about her was that the treatment kills her off, which he thought was a commercial liability for the film. Meanwhile, Zanuck continued tinkering with Eugenie's character.

By early February 1938, with the first drafted script, Zanuck was still trying to achieve the desired balance in Eugenie's personality. He complained, "The character of Eugenie must be changed. There is no reason for her to be a heavy. She should be as good, in her own way, as Toni — and as we will show, she is loyal to Ferdinand all the way through. She loves him, will always love him, only she has chosen the ambitious road for herself and she will stick to her decision."[213]

One difficulty appears to be that Zanuck never wants Eugenie to behave as if she is ambitious or power-hungry but prefers that to be lightly suggested. Zanuck became preoccupied with revising an early scene in which Eugenie turns down Lesseps' marriage proposal and he departs. It was only after reading the final script that Zanuck felt he had come up with a solution to ending the scene. After Ferdinand has left, the maid and the milliner arrive with dresses and hats but Eugenie chases them away. As Eugenie lies on the couch sobbing, the camera pans to a pedestal on which is displayed the Empress Eugenie hat. Zanuck had found a visual correlative to symbolize Eugenie's vanity and thirst for power even as she is in tears.[214]

Dwan had already begun contributing some input which Zanuck acknowledged in his conference to the previous treatment. It's possible that Dwan or someone else helped Zanuck finally wrap up that scene though no one is credited. In the conference notes for the final script, Zanuck recommends some of Dwan's suggestions though none of them represent major changes. At one point, Zanuck refers to Dwan's notes[215] but they do not appear to have survived in the present collection.

Of course, shaping the characters on paper was one thing but realizing them in the flesh was quite another. For the principal roles in *Suez* there were two major stars, Tyrone Power as Ferdinand de Lesseps and Loretta Young as Empress Eugenie, as well as a French actress being groomed for stardom, known only as Annabella. (She was born Suzanne Charpentier.) Before being signed by Fox, Annabella had starred in the French classics *Le Million* (1931) and *Le quatorze juillet* (1932).

Young, then a reigning Fox star, had a reputation for sanctimoniousness. According to her biographers, she did indeed avoid the easy route of the casting couch. But while she prided herself on her strong moral values and Catholic religiosity, she had given birth to a child conceived out of wedlock with Clark Gable, which was kept secret for decades though rumors abounded.

In 1928, Young had performed one of her earliest acting chores as a teenager in the Dwan-produced film *The Whip Woman*. Although that part led to her getting a role in *Laugh, Clown, Laugh*, a major step-up since she co-starred with Lon Chaney, the Dwan film is not included in the listing of her films in her autobiography.[216]

Dwan's recollection of Young in the role of Eugenie sheds some light on her handling of the part. Dwan said he regarded Young's role as Empress Eugenie to be "typecasting" since she conveyed a sense of royalty. "Loretta was always above everything, you know. And she used that quality as Eugenie, of having complete control over her situation and being vastly superior to everybody. It came naturally for her to make you feel that everyone she came into contact with was far beneath her."[217]

Leaving aside the issue of the fairness of Dwan's comments, Young did convey the sense that Eugenie never sees anything wrong with her behavior, that even after dumping Lesseps for a tyrant, she is still being generous to him. That may also be the key to her character, who feels she can downplay her ambitions by always appearing to be acting in a spirit of generosity. It was also in keeping with Zanuck's conception of the character, whose selfishness is never overt.

After rioting has broken out in France, Eugenie goes to Ferdinand as an emissary from Louis-Napoleon, telling him that if he can persuade his father and other members of the nation's assembly to adjourn, Louis will act responsibly and preserve democracy. When Lesseps succeeds in convincing the assembly to do so, Louis-Napoleon responds by arresting all in the assembly he considers his enemies including Lesseps' best friend, but not Lesseps himself. When Louis confesses that he has used Lesseps, Eugenie reminds him that he has also used her, since she believed his assurances. In most Hollywood movies, this would be the scene where the heroine would realize the perfidy of her boyfriend and turn back to the hero. But later Lesseps is startled to learn that Eugenie has married the now emperor Louis-Napoleon. This may be closer to real life but no explanation is offered for Eugenie's decision.

Annabella confessed to being intimidated by Young's "aura of glamour" with a regal authority so strong that all heads turned when she came on the set.[218] But then something unexpected happened: Annabella and Tyrone Power fell in love. The following year they were married.

Young was already concerned that the studio was using her to boost Annabella's career and was prepared to stand her ground. When Zanuck complained that a scene had to be reshot because Young stood out so much, she supposedly replied, "That is what I intended." Young also tried to enhance her appearance by working with the costume designer to provide her with "the largest hoop skirts ever" and letting her fingernails grow long despite Zanuck's protests.[219] The Eugenie hat she wore and which figured prominently in one scene further added to Young's glamorous image. Heavily promoted, it became quite fashionable.

But no amount of fashion could hide the fact that Young was not the center of attention here. She had already dealt with Power's presence in four films but the challenge now was beyond her control. Power's biographer, who had interviewed Dwan and Annabella, observed, "If queenly ambitions and different social stations kept Eugenie and De Lesseps apart in the movie, on the set the thing that really kept them apart was Annabella and Tyrone's obvious delight in her. Allan Dwan seized upon this at once and in the final shooting script, he got it onto the screen."[220]

The situation left Young terribly insecure. She appealed to Dwan for support. He assured her that her performance was fine but he did not become the confidant she may have been seeking. He, no doubt, grasped that some of that insecurity suited the onscreen rivalry of the two women.

Dwan had other things to occupy him in the making of *Suez*. *Suez* was released when Hollywood was having a cycle of disaster movies. There had been the great fire in Fox's own *In*

Loretta Young taking her role as the empress very seriously in *Suez* (1938).

Old Chicago, the earthquake in *San Francisco*, the plague of locusts in *The Good Earth*, and the climactic storm in *The Hurricane*. The climax of *Suez* was an enormous sandstorm which destroys much of the work on the canal. Dwan said that he used about a hundred huge airplane prop fans to produce the wind. That wind was strong enough to knock people off their feet but what made the job really onerous for the actors was that the blowing sand could cut the skin off people. As the leads in this sequence, Power and Annabella bore the brunt of this and the sand made their eyes red and swollen. Once Dwan discovered the problem, he found another of his clever solutions. Truckloads of ground-up breakfast cereal were ordered and then thrown in front of the propeller blades to provide the same cinematic effect as the sand.

According to screenwriter Dunne, Dwan had nothing whatever to do with the script of *Suez* and that he did not even meet the director until the film was well into production. He saw himself and Dwan as both serving their respective places "on the assembly line."[221] Actually, we know from the script conferences that Dwan was providing Zanuck with some feedback in the late stages of the script treatments. However, this was a project so huge that Dwan's role was probably more limited than for any of his other Fox films. Dwan commented, "Zanuck cooked up the idea of making it, they developed it and he assigned it to me."[222]

Knowing Dwan's background, one would think that the story of such a major engineering feat would hold special appeal for him. When asked by Bogdanovich about *Suez*, Dwan replied, "Well, I liked the human story. Whether the canal was built or not was of no importance to me."[223]

This sounds odd given that the whole story is about Lesseps' efforts to build the canal. But in the framework supplied by Zanuck and the scriptwriters, the struggle to build the canal proceeds in the vortex of personal relationships. And Dwan nearly always found those interlocking relationships, especially the triangle, to be at least as interesting as any other aspect of the plot.

Annabella's Toni, the other female component, is introduced in the story after Lesseps arrives in Egypt with a shot showing solely her bare legs and feet running out of the water, suggesting that she is naked. This is confirmed as she runs back into the water when Lesseps arrives. She refuses to come out until he turns his head away.

After reviewing the final script, Joseph I. Breen, working as censor for the Association of Motion Picture Producers, wrote to Fox that it should not be suggested that Toni is naked when with Lesseps, noting that even suggested nudity "must not be shown."[224] The suggested nudity was still shot and remains in the film.

Thereafter Toni is dressed as a boy in dungarees, with her hair short and pushed back under a fez, a stark contrast to the fashion plate Eugenie. Apparently raised in the desert with almost no formal education, she is something of a child of nature, almost like a grown-up Heidi. Like Heidi, she has no mother and father but lives with her grandfather. Though untutored and unsophisticated when Ferdinand has his first major crisis, Toni, like Shirley Temple, will comfort him and explain just what he must do.

The historical Lesseps was a highly skilled negotiator and promoter, and a shrewd observer in assessing everything necessary to be done to get the Suez Canal built. Perhaps Ronald Colman, with his oratorical skills, might have been suitably cast as Dunne at one point suggested. It seemed more problematic how the youthful but guileless Tyrone Power might convey Lesseps' experienced salesmanship.

Whatever Power's limitations and the need to conform to his image, the actor would not find much support in the script. After reading one draft, Zanuck complained that Lesseps' character would have to be changed, that he was too much "a man of destiny" with other people paving the way for him. His movement appeared to end with his visionary idea and Zanuck grumbled that "he doesn't seem to have any drive of his own."[225] Subsequent drafts did little to change this shortcoming. Zanuck seemed to lose interest in pursuing the subject and tellingly sometimes referred to Ferdinand as "the boy."[226]

In the film, the key scene in this respect is when Eugenie tells Toni that she must look out for Ferdinand because he is a dreamer. Perhaps this may have been the reason why she forsook him for Louis-Napoleon but she is still touched by the altruism and grandeur of his vision. He is clearly a "great man" and, as in other historical films of the period, the women in the great man's life must help him realize his destiny. Given the situation here, the women have to go into overdrive to get the job done, though Toni does most of the lifting. Despite the story centering on Lesseps, *Suez* arguably continues the arc through Dwan's *One Mile from Heaven* and the two Shirley Temple films as more of a female-driven movie.[227]

Tyrone Power carries Annabella during the climactic sandstorm in *Suez* (1938).

Toni herself seems to incarnate the idea of the canal. The first time Ferdinand sees her, she is emerging from water in the desert. It was after she took refuge with Ferdinand in some ruins during a rainstorm that Lesseps is inspired with his vision of the canal. A seeming augury of destiny, Toni sees a rainbow just before Ferdinand gets his idea. (This may have some basis in fact as Lesseps recalled seeing a rainbow just before he raised the issue of the canal with Pasha Said although Lesseps here may have been as fanciful as any Hollywood scriptwriter.) It is also Toni who, as the cyclone rages through the sands, rescues Ferdinand from destruction at the cost of her own life. (Zanuck had changed his mind about the tragic ending.) It is just before the storm erupts that Lesseps acknowledges that Toni has been his "guide, philosopher, and friend" as well as his "good angel." It seems sadly appropriate that she is destroyed fighting what is called the "devil wind." Michael Henry Wilson has pointed out that in Dwan's films there are a number of characters who serve a mystical purpose and are directly or by name referred to as "angels."[228]

Close-ups in *Suez* play a more important role than usual in a Dwan film. After the cyclone, there is a long take of a close-up of Lesseps despondently musing on how, in trying to bring something wonderful to the world, he has only brought destruction. It is his last expression of despair before the next scene reveals that help will be coming from Britain.

Power makes most of his soliloquy from his right profile. In the final shot of the film, Lesseps is looking over the canal from the same hill where he first conceived of the project. It is a close-up of his left profile. As he is alone, he says nothing, but only hears the words of Toni predicting his victory, as if she brought out this flip, triumphant side of his personality.

It is quite apparent that Toni's character belongs much more to a Hollywood fairy tale than to reality; this is one of a number of reasons that *Suez* is unconvincing as history. Frank S. Nugent in the *New York Times* saw it as "a ponderously implausible description of how the Suez Canal came to be built by a dark-haired juvenile through the inspiration of a regimental sergeant's granddaughter and his unrequited love for the Empress Eugenie."[229] The film nonetheless accrued a winning two million dollars in rentals and received three Academy Award nominations including cinematography, sound and original musical score.

Power's biographer Fred Lawrence Guiles took the view that *Suez* was "an epic drama with a very modern look about it. It has no happy ending, and its drama's building blocks are frustrations, both external and emotional."[230] The point that the characters lose all they value personally in pursuit of their ambitions is somewhat banal but still affecting.

Interestingly, the historical de Lesseps, who had lost his wife before he became involved with the canal, remained unmarried in the years that followed as if work on the canal consumed his whole life. But just a few days after the Suez Canal was opened, the sixty-four-year-old Lesseps (forty years older than Power was when the film was released) married a twenty-one-year-old woman. He must have been still quite vigorous since they lived together for twenty-five years during which his wife bore him twelve children.

In one of the last sequences of the film, as the completion of the canal is being celebrated, Ferdinand mounts the stairs to the empress' throne as she presents him with a ribbon of the Commander of the Legion of Honor. She tells Lesseps, "You've won," and he replies, "Yes, I've won. And I've lost — everything I'd learned to hold dear." Eugenie answers ruefully as if speaking for both of them: "Perhaps that is the price one pays for fame."

Despite the success of *Suez*, Dwan did not feel he was getting his measure of fame and power. He believed that Zanuck was unfavorably disposed to him because he had worked under Sol Wurtzel and had been a part of the old Fox regime before Zanuck took power. In seeming gratitude for *Heidi*, Zanuck had given him the prestige assignment of *Suez*. Dwan said that after the sneak preview of *Suez*, the only comment he got from Zanuck was a grudging, "Nice picture." He did not get any more projects of comparable importance. Dwan told Power's biographer that his tenure at Fox was chiefly marked by "Zanuck's complete indifference."[231] To another interviewer, Dwan described his relationship with Zanuck as "mutual hatred."[232]

While he had escaped the B unit, Dwan was not restored to the same stature he had in the silent era. In the coming years, Dwan would reconsider the value and usefulness of fame.

Fox, in the meanwhile, would learn the price of a lawsuit. Paul de Lesseps, one of the twelve children Ferdinand had fathered with his second wife, sued Fox for showing the private life of his father in a matter that was "false and derogatory."[233] Lesseps was joined in the suit by the Marquis de Casa Fuerte, who represented himself as Empress Eugenie's grand-nephew. The first phase of the suit was to seize French prints of *Suez*. A French judge ruled against this in an order made in his chamber on January 18, 1939. While conceding that great liberties were taken with the truth in the film, it was noted that the film was not presented as a documentary work but as a romanticized story of the building of a great French masterpiece. Also, neither Lesseps nor Eugenie were shown as having been moved by "base or petty sentiments." While Eugenie did sacrifice love for ambition, she was not depicted in an odious way (Zanuck may have had the threat of a lawsuit in mind when he molded the character) and was beyond reproach as a wife.

It was further noted that, unlike Paul de Lesseps (who according to one Fox source had written his own screenplay about his father), the rest of the Lesseps family had approved of *Suez*. The judge observed that the family had recognized that depictions in novels, on stage or screen were, to paraphrase a line from the film, "the price of glory that famous people have to pay."[234]

Frontier Marshal: Tombstone to Tombstone

In his later years, Dwan was adamant in his feeling that he was treated badly or indifferently by Zanuck. He felt that he did not receive proper credit for the success of *Suez* and he was not given assignments of similar prestige after that. In fact, on two occasions he was back to working with Sol Wurtzel, the B-movie impresario. Dwan certainly had not won the status he felt he deserved as one of the studio's top directors.

Dwan should have felt some reason to feel grateful to Zanuck for lifting the director from the B-movie stable. In early 1939, Ed Sullivan, then a syndicated columnist, observed, "Dwan has staged a miracle comeback at 20th Century–Fox."[235] Even allowing for the hyperbole of columnists, Dwan's rebound *was* impressive.

On February 2, 1939, Dwan signed a $2250-per-week Fox contract.[236] It granted Fox the option of signing Dwan to additional yearly contracts with the weekly rate increasing $250 per week for each of the succeeding four years. According to a Treasury report publicly released to the Associated Press, Dwan's earnings for 1937 were just shy of $70,000.[237] With his yearly salary now totaling $117,000, Dwan was clearly making headway at Fox, at least commercially. Perhaps Zanuck's hands-on approach to production was a stronger factor why Dwan did not feel comfortable with his boss.

Three films directed by Dwan were released by Fox in 1939. The first two, both comedies, will be discussed in the following chapter. The last of the trio was *Frontier Marshal*, which like *Suez* dealt with actual events and was the first film to use the name of its Western hero, Wyatt Earp.

On October 26, 1881, the most famous gunfight of the Old West took place in Tombstone, Arizona. Although it would become widely known as the Gunfight at the O.K. Corral, it actually took place in a vacant lot across the street from the corral. There had been long-simmering tensions between the Earp brothers on the one side and the Clanton clan, the McLaurey Brothers, and a faction known as the "Cowboys" on the other. Although Wyatt had served as a lawman in various capacities over the years, it was Virgil Earp who was the U.S. marshal in Tombstone. When trouble threatened, Virgil deputized his brothers Morgan and Wyatt as well as Wyatt's friend, the notorious gambler Doc Holliday. The immediate spark to the confrontation was Virgil's arrest of two friends of the McLaurey brothers for a stagecoach robbery but this became entangled in other standing issues.

The gunfight that erupted left three men dead, brothers Frank and Tom McLaurey and Billy Clanton. Virgil and Morgan were wounded though not seriously; Holliday's hip was grazed by a bullet. Of the Earp party, only Wyatt was not hit.

In his later years, Wyatt settled in Los Angeles, becoming another of the visible remnants of the Old West. He often visited film sets and Dwan remembered him as a "one-eyed old man." Dwan recalled, "He was a visitor to the set when I was directing Douglas Fairbanks in *The Half-Breed*. As was the custom in those days, he was invited to join the party and mingle with our background action. I think there was a trial of some kind. A group of people demanded that the half-breed be sent out of town. In that group was Earp; he only stood there and nodded his head."[238]

Earp historian Jeff Morey and film historian Michael Blake have independently examined *The Half-Breed* and found "no one who even remotely resembles Wyatt Earp in the courtroom scene."[239] Earp biographer Allen Barra said of the same film, "There is an extra who is an old man with a white mustache sitting in the crowd, but it doesn't look like Earp. It appears to be the legendary Texas John Slaughter, who was at least as well known out West in 1915 as Wyatt Earp and who also had friends working in Western movies."[240]

Earp may have appeared in another scene and/or in a long shot where he was not recognizable, or perhaps the scene was not used. Earp may have actually declined Dwan's invitation. It's also possible that Dwan confused him with someone else, especially since Earp was never "one-eyed" as Dwan recollected. There were certainly plenty of other famous Western figures still around at the time.

After a failed effort by a family friend to write the Earp story, Wyatt was contacted by writer Stuart Lake in January 1928. But in the latter part of the year, Earp's health began to fail. Earp and Lake continued to correspond until Earp died on January 13, 1929, two months before his eighty-first birthday.

Lake continued to work on the book, now with Earp's widow Sadie overseeing the project. Sadie wrote to Lake that the book "must be a nice clean story."[241] However, to do that involved suppressing information about the kind of rough 'n' tumble life Earp led. Sadie certainly would not want it revealed that she had once lived with Earp's rival Sheriff Behan or that before their union, Earp was living with a prostitute who died of a drug overdose after Wyatt left her for Sadie.

Published in 1931, Lake's book *Wyatt Earp: Frontier Marshal* resonated with both the critics and the public. In October 1932, he sold the film rights to the Fox Film Corporation for $7,500, which he split with Sadie. The resulting film was a low-budget effort produced by Sol Lesser and directed by Lew Seiler. Because of Sadie's objections, the hero played by George O'Brien was called Michael Wyatt. The film vanished quickly, receiving very little notice.

In 1939, Fox decided to try again with the same material. Aside from some notable big-budget exceptions such as *Cimarron* and DeMille's *The Plainsman* and some offbeat entries such as *Law and Order* (another version of the Earp story without using the actual names), the Western was largely the preserve of the B film in the 1930s. Audiences and especially urban audiences could not take the genre seriously. The Western's celebration of national progress and "tide of empire" must have seemed particularly out of sync for theater patrons of the Depression era. But in 1939, the Western seemed to be making a comeback. John Ford's classic *Stagecoach* was part of a field that also included Warners' *Dodge City*, Paramount's *Union Pacific* and Universal's *Destry Rides Again*. Fox had invested over a million dollars in its Technicolor production *Jesse James* starring Tyrone Power and Henry Fonda. The film opened to strong box office, which may have stiffened Fox's resolve to produce another Western.

Fox seemed to be hedging its bets by making the second film a B Western, cranked out by Sol Wurtzel's unit. But while *Frontier Marshal* was to cost a projected $500,000, less than half the budget for *Jesse James*, this was also more than twice the usual amount spent for a B film. So *Frontier Marshal* may have been more of a lesser "A" than a B movie. With this film, Dwan returned to the genre he helped pioneer: It was his first talkie Western.

Sam Hellman did the first treatment for this new *Frontier Marshal*, which was completed on February 21, 1939. What seems remarkable about this outline and Hellman's first script draft is that it begins with the Earp figure (called Dave Wyatt at this stage) being "a reckless young man ... lawless and undisciplined, and a fugitive from justice."[242] At the beginning of the story, he is wounded and left for dead by a posse but is found and nursed back to health by a mission priest who sets him on the road to reform.

The real Wyatt Earp was indicted for horse stealing along with two other men in Missouri in 1871 (the charges were later dropped). The script, however, placed Earp's fugitive experience in 1880 when he was already in Tombstone.

Whatever the merits of this approach, there was no chance that with this kind of script they would be able to call their character "Wyatt Earp." Perhaps because of this, Hellman was asked to do a revised story outline based on a discussion he had with Wurtzel and Dwan on April 20. Unlike Zanuck, Wurtzel was not known for providing more than the most general of concepts so it's likely that Dwan had much more to do with helping Hellman re-shape the script.[243] In fact, Hellman told Wurtzel that after their meeting, he had a later talk with Dwan on making further changes.[244] The revised outline jettisoned the idea of the Earp figure being an outlaw turned lawman. The rest of the script treatments followed suit and the hero was now called Wyatt Earp. The story took place in Tombstone and centered on the events leading to the O.K. Corral gunfight.

Dwan recalled that when he made *Suez* at Fox,

> I put about a million tons of sand on the back lot to make a desert. Wagon-loads and wagon-loads came up from the beach and filled the place with sand for over a half-a-mile wide. And at the time someone said to me, "Well, what are we going to do with this sand when you get through?" I said, "Well, some sucker will have to move it out of here." Now, when *Frontier Marshal* came along, I induced Zanuck to let me build a western street back there. And in order to do it, the sand had to be moved. So *I* was the sucker! By the way, normally, building a western street would have been prohibitive — two or three hundred thousand dollars. I told Zanuck I'd put one up for twenty thousand if he'd let me have carte blanche and do it my way. I knew where there were all kinds of western fronts around that lot that had been put there way back in the time of Tom Mix — I'd used them in the old days.[245]

Dwan went on to explain how he used a regular moving company rather than studio personnel to put up the fronts and shove the sand out of the way.

Most of *Frontier Marshal* was shot in the studio back lot but Dwan also took his crew to Lone Pine which had provided good locations since the silent era.

But Dwan and Fox now faced a more formidable challenge. On June 13, shortly after shooting got underway, Dwan received a visit from Mrs. Earp, who was not happy about the *Frontier Marshal* script. Dwan referred her to Fox executive Jason Joy. Sadie poured out her objections to Joy, leaving him "upset." Shortly thereafter, she fired off a three-and-a-half page letter of criticisms to Wurtzel.[246]

Mrs. Earp complained that the film was not the full-fledged biography Lake had presented in his book. It dealt with only one episode in his career and even that one was not done accurately. ("All that I can see in the script is fiction, very commonplace fiction."[247]) She also thought the script injurious to Wyatt's character: "[T]he script author has made Wyatt Earp a character of low degree, a frequenter of saloons, a brawler, an associate of cheap individuals, a bum and a coward." She saw her husband as having been "selected and created by a Providence that raised Him up a man in his place and in his hour in the winning of the West."[248] She wanted to rescind her permission for the use of her husband's name.

Wurtzel had a sound basis to feel that the script had not denigrated her husband and that her comments smacked of hyperbole. She did, however, have a valid point that the script, like most movie scripts about historical characters, was not accurate. It was a similar argument to the one in the *Suez* suit so it was important to establish that Fox was not making pretenses to historical truth. Zanuck had told Wurtzel that he wanted under the on-screen title the line "The Story of Wyatt Earp." Wurtzel suggested that the tagline be dropped and Zanuck concurred. (Zanuck initially wanted to substitute "The Saga of Tombstone, Arizona" but that too was eliminated.[249])

George Wasson, Fox's legal counsel, wrote in his first draft of a response to Sadie, "[Y]our letter indicates that our desire to show Wyatt Earp only in a favorable light and yet have a picture filled with action and romantic interest, and our desire not to tread upon too personal a ground in our treatment of his character, has led us into a position where you state we have not portrayed his life...."[250] Wasson's point was that by adding fiction to the story, they were romanticizing Earp and not going into areas Sadie might not like if they were more accurate and complete in telling his story. The implication was that demanding both an idealized Earp and a truthful one was being unreasonable. This probably sounded too contentious to Wurtzel and another letter was sent that simply stated that the film would contain nothing derogatory to any person portrayed in the picture.

Dwan preferred dealing with a purely fictional character. "We never meant it to *be* Wyatt Earp," he insisted. "We were just making *Frontier Marshal* and that could be any frontier marshal."[251] Nevertheless, while much of the movie was fiction, there was enough truth to bind it to the Earp story. Although he did not realize it, with this film Dwan was helping to establish some of the basic screen myths about Wyatt Earp and the story of the O.K. Corral gunfight.

Frontier Marshal opens with an irreverent montage of the founding of Tombstone and its early history. As a miner is seen laboring among the rocks, subtitles tell us, "'All you'll find is your tombstone,' they told Ed Schieffelin in 1877 when he went prospecting into the savage Apache mesas of southern Arizona...." As he is seen reaping some benefit from his mining, the title continues, "Instead Schieffelin uncovered a lode of silver, fabulous in its richness." The montage then shows the rapid exodus to the area and how a "mushroom metropolis sprang up overnight." As we see both a house-raising and shootings breaking out, a title informs the viewers, "And thus was born the appropriately named city of Tombstone." The editor of the town newspaper, the *Tombstone Epitaph*, says it has become a race: whether the city or the cemetery will be larger.

This sets the scene for the opening conflict, a rivalry between the two saloons of Tombstone, the Bella Union and the Palace of Pleasure. The latter is operated by Ben Carter (John Carradine) who is in league with Curly Bill (Joseph Sawyer), a stagecoach robber. Unlike Carter, Curly Bill is named after a real Tombstone personality, Curly Bill Brocius, a Clanton ally who was eventually killed by Earp in his vendetta. It's hard to argue that the film is not derogatory to Curly Bill but his last name is not used and he probably did not have any surviving relatives who could threaten Fox.

Carter is concerned that the arrival of Chicago chorus girls is giving the Bella Union an edge over his Palace of Pleasure. At Curly Bill's prodding, Indian Charlie, who is known to have trouble holding his liquor, is given some whisky and sent to the Bella Union where he is likely to stir up trouble. Charlie is played by the former Fairbanks regular Charles Stevens. Since he was not a Fox contract player, it's possible that Dwan had something to do with his casting. Stevens, who claimed to be Geronimo's grandson, got a lot of mileage out of this characterization as he would play virtually the same role in the 1942 *Tombstone, the Town Too Tough to Die* and John Ford's 1946 remake of *Frontier Marshal, My Darling Clementine.*

When Charlie's drunkenness predictably turns to gunplay, the mayor (Harry Hayden) orders the marshal (Ward Bond) to apprehend Charlie. Fearing that he will be gunned down, and protesting that he has a wife and kids, the marshal refuses. As they wrangle, an off-screen voice is heard saying, "A nice lot of law you got here." The mayor and townspeople look up as if seeking divine guidance and we see Earp (Randolph Scott) from a low angle, towering over the situation as he looks down from a hotel balcony. Earp says that he is just a visitor trying to get a good night's sleep but can't with all the noise: "What kind of town you got here?" Offered the opportunity to do something about it as marshal, Earp climbs down like a godlike hero, descending from the heavens to aid the mere mortals below. (This should have satisfied Sadie, showing that her husband and Providence were indeed linked.) He fearlessly takes a gun, heads for the saloon and, after grazing Charlie with a bullet, drags him by his heels to the awaiting populace. Earp remains reluctant to take on the job of marshal but after being roughed up by Curly Bill and his men later that night, he changes his mind and accepts the badge.

As in *Black Sheep* and *One Mile from Heaven*, card-playing has an important establishing role, especially when someone is caught cheating. In this case, it's Jerry, the singer at the Bella Union. When she responds to Wyatt's accusation by slapping him, he dunks her in a water trough. This sets up the scene when her boyfriend Doc Halliday comes gunning for Earp.

In her letter to Wurtzel, Mrs. Earp expressed her disappointment that the film script was not really Lake's story of her husband and added, "Neither is it the story of 'Doc' Holliday, who in the script version has been made a prominent character in the plot."[252] Sadie's lament could resound through *Frontier Marshal* and future film versions of the story where Doc seems to steal the picture from Earp. In fact, the relationship between Wyatt and Doc is a large part of what makes the Earp legend so enduring, a relationship as strongly mythological as any friendship in American literature. Audiences remain fascinated by this seeming bad man who becomes a "good bad man" in his attraction and dedication to a man of law and order. In this myth, Holliday is bound to Earp by his innate sense of honor, which carries him beyond his vices. He may also recognize in Earp a goodness that is something he has lost. That is one reason why the script of Earp as a fugitive from justice would not have worked as well. The relationship cuts deeper because of this fundamental contrast between the two.

There is also fascination with the character of Holliday himself, of why this genteel, educated man from a respectable family has fled to the west. Holliday's latest biographer Gary Roberts has suggested some answers but the solutions remain murky. For the purposes of myth, the question can be left to each storyteller to answer. Earp biographer Allen Barra thought that the best summation of Holliday's life came in the 1905 novel *The Sunset Trail* by Alfred Henry Lewis in which Doc appears as a character. Lewis had edited Bat Masterson's Human Life profiles so Masterson, who knew Holliday, may have been the source of the line. Holliday says, "I mixed up in everything that came along. It was the only way I could forget myself."[253] It sounds similar to D.H. Lawrence's belief of why people came to America: "That's why most people have come to America and still do come. To get away from everything they are and have been."[254]

Frontier Marshal is the first Western that truly establishes the relationship between Earp and Holliday, whose name for some unfathomable reason is spelled "Halliday" in the script and picture. Dwan is drawn to him as an outcast and gambler though he has precious little time to gamble on cards in the film. Halliday (Cesar Romero) is first seen in the movie entering the Bella Union. There is a close-up of Doc surrounded by darkness with shadows permeating his face, as if darkness defines him. With the exception of an unsuccessful stagecoach robbery, all of the violence in *Frontier Marshal* after the opening montage takes place at night. Doc Halliday's figure of ambiguity appears to be the film's heart of darkness.

In the early stages of scripting, Wurtzel and Dwan appear to have been left alone to supervise Hellman. Records show that Zanuck held a conference after the second draft screenplay of May 10. He was contemplating casting Romero in the role of Halliday and wanted the dialogue changed with lines more appropriate for "a sullen guy rather than a flowery gentleman."[255] Zanuck also had all references to Halliday having tuberculosis removed. He preferred that Halliday's disease remain unspecified while it was still conveyed that he hasn't long to live.

Although Zanuck had another conference after the next script treatment, it is fair to say that Dwan appeared to have much more freedom on this film than on *Suez*. In between the two Zanuck conferences, at least three more memos and script changes passed between Hellman and the team of Wurtzel and Dwan.

After his dramatic entry, Halliday appears keen on provoking a fight. He approaches Earp complaining that he doesn't like the way he is running the town. But before he can go further, Halliday succumbs to a coughing fit. While he is indisposed, Blackmore, a shady gambler, tries to shoot Doc. Earp thwarts Blackmore. A grateful Doc forgets about quarreling and proposes that he and Earp drink together. A friendship is born.

At the bar, Earp and Halliday talk about their firearms and start comparing the sizes of their pistols. The homosexual implications may be the ultimate joke on the dubious accounts of

Cesar Romero (center) as Doc Halliday is the object of affection of dance hall girl Jerry (Binnie Barnes) in *Frontier Marshal* (1939). Randolph Scott as Wyatt Earp (left) looks on.

Earp's Buntline special. The depth of the friendship between Earp and Holliday may have created some suspicions of homosexuality. But here, Dwan is more likely emphasizing the need for both men to sound off some macho bluster. Their sense of insecurity becomes apparent when both are pressed into a situation with two women. Indeed, Jerry walks in the Bella Union to find the men engaged in their phallic "gunplay."

Jerry is enraged that Halliday has become friendly with Earp instead of chastising him. Jerry is played by Binnie Barnes, Dwan's leading lady in his British *Counsel's Opinion*. Other actresses such as Claire Trevor and Barbara Stanwyck were suggested for the role but while less high-powered, Barnes is an apt choice. She is an attractive but large woman suggesting the kind of toughness needed to survive on the frontier. Her English accent also marks her as an outsider, an immigrant. (Doc's actual woman at the time, Katie Elder, whose real last name was Harony, was a Hungarian immigrant.) Jerry's love for Doc is real but the film makes clear that his involvement with her is more of a sexual dalliance.

The catalyst in upsetting the established emotional relationships is the arrival of Sarah Allen (Nancy Kelly), the woman from Doc's past who knew him when he was a respected Illinois doctor (an obstetrician tenderly delivering babies!). Here the film pinpoints Doc's reason for his metamorphosis into a Western gunman. When found to be suffering from a disease likely to be fatal, he decided that he would be "taking advantage" of Sarah to permit her to marry him. Doc tells Sarah that he is now a changed man and encourages her to believe that Jerry is the woman he loves.

Wyatt watches what's happening closely; there are recurring shots of him silently observing the whole drama at the bar. Earp intervenes when Doc's self-loathing begins to turn violent. (Saying "I don't like you," he shoots his reflection in the saloon mirror.) Earp knocks out Halliday before he can shoot the bartender and takes him to his room. When placing the unconscious Halliday in bed, Wyatt sees that in his wallet Doc carries a photo of Sarah and realizes that despite his protests, he still loves her.

Wyatt is becoming one of Dwan's voyeurs. He tells Sarah of his discovery and pleads with her to stay, which she does. But Earp is also showing his own admiration for Sarah. When he tries to persuade Jerry that Doc really loves Sarah, not her, it prompts Jerry to say, "If you like that dame so well, why don't you grab her for yourself?" As Hellman wrote in his revised outline, "Also we find that Earp himself has fallen under the spell of Sarah's charm and quality. He is not in love with her — his loyalty to Halliday would prevent even the thought of it — but it is quite obvious that Sarah is something strange and marvelous in Earp's eyes."[256]

Thus, we do not just have a repeat of a protagonist caught between two women (*a la Suez*), but a perverse quadrangle. Jerry loves Doc who feigns loving Jerry while running away from Sarah whom he really loves. Earp admires Sarah from afar and may even be said to be loving Sarah vicariously through Doc. (Earp's distanced admiration for Sarah could avoid offending Sadie Earp who, according to Dwan, did not want Earp given a love affair with Sarah.)

In an effort to get rid of Earp and his meddling, Jerry informs Carter that she heard the mayor telling Earp to ride shotgun on the stagecoach carrying a silver shipment that will leave a day early to fool the stage robbers. All she asks for her information is that Earp be killed by Curly Bill and his stickup men. The plan goes awry when in an effort to get away from Sarah, Halliday also decides to ride in that stagecoach. Jerry knows that Carter and Curly Bill hate Halliday as much as Earp and would just as soon kill him as well.

Locked together in the cramped quarters of the stagecoach and away from the public view, Earp takes doleful looks at Doc, while Doc for the most part looks away from him. Doc is leaving Tombstone because Earp convinced Sarah to stay. Earp apologizes but extols Sarah. Then Earp continues in lines uncharacteristic of a Western hero: "All I ever knew about love was what I've seen around dance halls and places like that. But it can be entirely different. Altogether different."

The lines suggest that Earp had been even more cynical about love than Halliday (who had been engaged) and that through the friendship with Doc, his romantic feelings have been awakened. This exchange is interrupted when the stagecoach is fired on by Curly Bill's men. In the ensuing melee, Earp and Halliday again team together, Carter is killed and Doc receives a minor arm wound.

Given that the film is only 71 minutes long, the allocation of so much time to the emotional relationships means that much of the plot and action has to be squeezed into a relatively small time frame. But when he needs to, Dwan keeps the action moving briskly, especially with his mobile camera. Also, as with the stage attack, the film's lingering on dramatic moments makes the intrusions of action sequences more startling.

In a later gunfight in Tombstone, the bartender's little boy is caught in the crossfire. Doc is called upon to operate on him in the makeshift conditions of the saloon. In the role of assisting Doc, Wyatt is seen in two separate shots holding up a mirror. These shots are not only a riposte to Doc's shooting of the mirror image of himself but convey that Earp has also figuratively been holding a mirror up to Doc.[257]

After a successful operation, Halliday concedes to Sarah that it feels better to give a life than to take one. But as soon as he walks out of the Bella Union, Doc is shot to death by Curly Bill and his men. The shocking denouement seems more like a mob rubout in a gangster film. It is followed by Curly Bill's line that will be uttered many more times in Western films: They will be waiting for Earp at the O.K. Corral.

Although Earp courageously volunteers to face the gunmen alone, he also shows the wiliness of a number of Dwan heroes and gets the drop on them from behind. Earp succeeds in killing all of the outlaws except Curly Bill, who manages to get back to the town street near the Bella Union and find a rifle. Then for perhaps the only time in a major Western, it's a woman who ends the Gunfight at the O.K. Corral as Jerry picks up Doc's pistol and blasts Curly Bill.

In the end, it is Sarah who decides to set down roots in Tombstone and Jerry who leaves as the town is becoming too civilized for her. Wyatt is last seen walking back to Sarah's hotel and straightening his tie, suggesting that he is trying to look his best for her.

Zanuck suggested the very last scene: As Jerry's stagecoach passes Boot Hill, she tearfully says, "Goodbye, Doc." The last shot tracks in to Doc's tombstone which declares him a "Beloved and Respected Citizen of Tombstone." In the script conference notes, it is stated, "Mr. Zanuck thinks that this ending will give us the feeling of the whole country and it will give our picture more importance."

Dwan was likely pleased with Zanuck's suggestion, as it provided a neat symmetry with the opening montage. Doc's death and the elimination of the Palace of Pleasure gang appear to settle the question of whether the cemetery will grow faster than the town of Tombstone.

But closing the film with the imagery of the tombstone also suggests a circularity that provides a balance against the concept of the West as a movement of progress. (We assume that Jerry will find a town as untamed as Tombstone was.) And ending the film with Doc's tombstone has the effect of lionizing him and suggesting that he, not the frontier marshal, is the key character. The flawed Halliday and Jerry are also arguably more sympathetic figures than the strait-laced Earp and Sarah. Looking at the major Westerns of 1939, both *Union Pacific* and *Dodge City* are essentially championing the triumph of civilization. *Jesse James* and *Stagecoach* are more populist films showing distrust of the power and hypocrisy of established orders. *Frontier Marshal* and *Destry Rides Again* seem to fall in between, both clearly on the side of law and order but with some sympathy to the "wild" characters swept away by civilization.[258]

Dwan shot *Frontier Marshal* with his customary efficiency. A *Hollywood Reporter* article said that by completing the film on July 8, he was finishing six days ahead of schedule with a savings of approximately $40,000 on the $500,000 budget.[259] The savings might have been a little less since a subsequent story said the film was actually finished on July 11.[260] Even more impressive is how rapidly post-production was completed (including titling, editing and music scoring) since the film was ready for viewing on July 28.

Frontier Marshal received good reviews. Bosley Crowther in the *New York Times* said, "With a grand cast and an excellent job of directing by Allan Dwan, Mr. Earp's screen biography becomes entirely worthy of its fabulous subject.... *Frontier Marshal* is a cracking good Western, and in the movies there's nothing much better than that."[261]

The film has been viewed less favorably in more recent times. As succeeding Earp films have gone deeper into the myths and history, *Frontier Marshal* appears threadbare; it does not include the other Earp brothers or the Clantons. However, *Frontier Marshal* is important for helping to establish some of the basic myths, especially as the studio had to deal with Mrs. Earp and potentially the relatives of other figures who might come out of the woodwork if they saw some reason to take umbrage.

Six years later, Fox decided to remake the film with John Ford helming the project and the result was the classic *My Darling Clementine* starring Henry Fonda as Earp. Dwan's version was screened for Ford on October 31, 1945. Much of the *Frontier Marshal* storyline was transferred to the remake but Ford and his principal screenwriter worked their own variations on different aspects of the plot. In *Frontier Marshal*, Eddie Foy, Jr., played his father who had actually toured the West as a musical comedy star; in the Ford version this was changed to a Shakespearean actor played by Alan Mowbray. The decision in *Frontier Marshal* to turn Doc Holliday's real-life dentist into a surgeon was duplicated by Ford with both films having Doc perform a dramatic operation.

Jerry (Binnie Barnes) bids her final farewell to Doc Halliday in *Frontier Marshal* (1939).

In Ford's film, Dwan and Hellman's colorful romantic quadrangle provided the basis for a poetic ritual by which a civilized man fell to ruin on the frontier while a frontiersman reinvented himself as a champion of civilization.

It should be pointed out that the character of Linda Darnell's Chihuahua in *Clementine* is more of a stereotype than Binnie Barnes in the role of Jerry, who not only provides a tougher and more realistic character, but is probably the most passionate figure in the quadrangle.

Still, Dwan's film, for all its virtues, pales as a more nascent development of the Earp myth alongside Ford's classic.

Or as Ford told Fonda regarding the earlier movie, "Shit, I can do better than that."[262]

7. Escape Into Comedy

A humorist is a moralist disguised as a scientist something like an anatomist who practices dissection with the sole object of filling us with disgust; so that humor, in the restricted sense in which we are here regarding the word, is really a transposition from the moral to the scientific.—Henri Bergson, *Laughter*

Dwan's preoccupation (one might even say obsession) with dealing exclusively with comedy in the years between 1940 and 1946, sets him apart from nearly every director of any stature in that period. Even champions of lightweight material like George Marshall turned out some action dramas during those years. Dwan's skein extends even longer if we consider that two of his three films of 1939 were comedies.

Preston Sturges is virtually the only other major director who cranked out comedies so relentlessly during that period and even Sturges created one somber film, *The Great Moment*, in that time frame. Although similarities to Sturges appear in some of Dwan's movies of that period, only one of his films, the 1946 *Rendezvous with Annie*, can truly be compared to Sturges' work.

Where Sturges produced satires, Dwan is best remembered in this period for the farces he made for producer Edward Small. Four of the five Small films are cited as farces but throughout the early and mid–1940s, Dwan dabbled in different forms of comedy. If Dwan the businessman was looking for what forms of comedy seemed most commercial, Dwan the scientist was seeking out the different variations in film comedy. Two of his films in this period may be called comedy-dramas while other films explored the alchemy that could change a film from one categorization to the other. Dwan treated comedy not just as a genre but as an ingredient, or perhaps as a weapon that needed to be used strategically to give the spark to his story.

Referring to the films made for Small in the last two years of World War II, Dwan has emphasized that he made them as morale boosters for the troops. There is no reason to doubt Dwan's sincerity and in fact, just before he made the pictures for Small, he had directed a film about entertaining Allied troops. Dwan may have also reflected on his filmmaking philosophy during the First World War in which he tried to bring pertinent moral and social issues before the public. The public did not seem to buy that at the time and Dwan may have decided in retrospect, what people needed most in war time was laughter.

Dwan had already been tinkering with comedy for two years before war came.

Dwan's involvement with the 1939 musical comedy version of *The Three Musketeers* evokes the widely quoted line by Marx: "History repeats itself, first as tragedy then as farce." Although Dwan had worked with Fairbanks on his first portrayal of D'Artagnan in *A Modern Musketeer*, he was unable to accept Doug's invitation to direct *The Three Musketeers*. But he did direct the sequel *The Iron Mask* with an ending that mixed triumph and tragedy. With this new version of *The Three Musketeers* co-starring the Ritz Brothers, Dwan would have to find the humor in the same material.[1]

The film was to be a vehicle for the Ritz Brothers and Zanuck complained that in the first script treatment by Sam Hellman they were being used more as comic relief rather than as the stars.[2] With more emphasis on the Ritzes than on Dumas, at one point the title was changed to *One for All*. Morris Musselman took over from Hellman in the script-drafting. Various gags and comic storylines were inserted. Julian Johnson, the one-time *Photoplay* critic now working for Fox, wrote to Zanuck regarding Musselman's treatment, finding most of the comedy in the early scenes to be "more or less routine and tiresome." Johnson then noted, "But from the moment the Ritzes take D'Artagnan to Bernajou's house and he is given Constance's room, I felt the story picking up speed, and from then on, it was interesting, amusing and exciting to the end. Analyzing this from the story standpoint, I would say that old Mr. Dumas is the answer."[3]

In his response the next day, Zanuck appeared to concur with Johnson that there was too much of the Ritz Brothers and reversed his earlier dictum. He now contended, "The Ritzes are much more effective when they come on every now and then and do a sock piece of entertainment, than when they try to sustain a plot."[4] The title was back to *The Three Musketeers* and another writer, William Drake, was brought in to work on the "straight" scenes. On a separate track, Sid Kuller and Ray Golden (who had past experience writing for the Ritz Brothers) turned over their material to Musselman, who worked it into the script.

Dwan was now free to put the emphasis on the story. Only one member of the cast of Dwan's *The Iron Mask* appeared in the new version of *The Three Musketeers*: Gino Corrado, who played Aramis and had now become a ubiquitous bit player, performed uncredited as a member of the cardinal's guards, who confront the Ritz Brothers in a tavern brawl.

While the Ritz Brothers did not occupy center stage, they did more than provide comic relief against a straight romantic plot. Much of the humor derives from the Ritzes' interaction with the other characters (especially D'Artagnan) as opposed to just doing their own schtick. Also, there was not really a "straight dramatic" plot because the film was also being done as a musical.

There are numerous reasons why Fairbanks' *The Three Musketeers* and (especially) *The Iron Mask* are among the best, if not the best versions of Dumas' Musketeer novels. But one advantage is that the films were silent and that D'Artagnan's romantic escapades took place in a stylized world where words and dialogue would not be an encumbrance. In script memos for Fox's *The Three Musketeers,* there was some concern about how the audience would react to the dialogue, especially D'Artagnan's flowery sentiments.[5]

It should also be remembered that long before he made *The Iron Mask*, Dwan had directed Fairbanks in *A Modern Musketeer* and in his first crack at D'Artagnan, he had already suggested the comic potential of the character through his American Midwestern imitator. Dwan had also evoked the spirit of D'Artagnan in the aspirations of the Gascon-born Paul Renoir (Billy Bakewell) in the modern-day *While Paris Sleeps.*

D'Artagnan is first seen in the movie riding his old steed Cherie, who has clearly seen better days, while Gascon warbles a tune as if he was a singing cowboy. (The British title of the film was *The Singing Musketeer.*) The moving camera follows the mood and tempo of Cherie's laconic pace. (Later, Dwan's tracking shot adds some zip to D'Artagnan singing the *Musketeer Song* with the Three Lackeys [the Ritz Brothers] as the camera energetically moves before their strident pace through winding streets.) D'Artagnan is both amiable and boastful, announcing that he is the best swordsman in Gascony, which he demonstrates by besting an insipid cavalier.

A title card introduces us to the Coq D'Or, the tavern where assignations for duels are often made. The Three Musketeers arrive there, each having been challenged to a duel for some triviality at which D'Artagnan had chosen to take offense. While waiting for D'Artagnan, the Musketeers challenge the three lackeys to a wine-drinking session. The Musketeers wind up under the table when it's over.

After the Musketeers are put to bed, the lackeys steal and don their uniforms, hoping to impress the women. D'Artagnan bursts through a window apologizing for his lateness and offering to fight all three at once as he takes the lackeys to be the Musketeers despite their pitiful protests. When attacked by the cardinal's guards, D'Artagnan and the lackeys join forces, thus establishing their friendship.

Like the would-be D'Artagnan of *A Modern Musketeer,* this hero's lofty sentiments often outpace his common sense. The challenged "Musketeers" consider him either a madman or a fool. But Dwan and the scriptwriters have just stretched the character a bit to emphasize the recklessness and vulnerability of his romanticism.

As D'Artagnan, Don Ameche lacks the charisma (to say nothing of the physical agility) of Fairbanks. Critics have likened him to Power in his blandness as a Fox leading man. But Ameche has a charm and energy that was conspicuously missing in Power's performance in *Suez.* The charm may at times seem surface-thin but it serves him well in portraying the brash D'Artagnan. There is also his look of rueful discomfiture when he is caught trying to flatter a lady with fanciful lines that are not his own.

D'Artagnan had challenged one of the Musketeers because of the effeminate look of his hat. This suggests something of D'Artagnan's male insecurity bordering on homophobia. As with some of Dwan's other insecure men, he will experience humiliation at the hands of a woman, in this case the Amazonian Milady de Winter, zestfully played by Binnie Barnes. She proves a far more dangerous adversary for D'Artagnan than the pompous De Rochefort portrayed by Lionel Atwill.

The atmosphere of perpetual intrigue and spying from the more dramatic versions of the story is again just slightly more exaggerated for the musical comedy. Voyeurism may require some effort as with the concierge Naveau (John Carradine), who has a hole in his floor so he can eavesdrop on what's going on in the room beneath him. On the other hand, D'Artagnan just has to lie in bed to see a whole adventure unfold before him as Constance (Pauline Moore) enters his room to arrange a rendezvous between the queen (Gloria Stuart) and the Duke of Buckingham (Lester Matthews). D'Artagnan commits a greater act of bungling than any of the three lackeys through his tardiness in leaving the room and his instant bellicosity towards Buckingham. He causes a ruckus that awakens Naveau, who watches the whole scene through his spy hole. Naveau reports to Richelieu the queen's love affair with Buckingham and that she's given him an emerald brooch as a keepsake. Richelieu, who is eager to undermine the queen, has De Rochefort send Milady de Winter on a mission to get possession of the brooch.

D'Artagnan instantly falls in love with Constance; even the heroine remarks on the rapid-fire pace of his emotions. D'Artagnan sings her the ballad "My Lady," gracefully filmed with D'Artagnan literally refusing to be locked out of Constance's life. Its overblown sentiments accurately match D'Artagnan's character. While no classic, the song is quite serviceable and charming. (The song later is dramatically passed from Constance to D'Artagnan during her imprisonment in the cardinal's chateau.)

The Ritz Brothers, with their cross-eyed looks, mugging, and storehouse of bad puns, are used in careful and effective restraint. Their cringing cowardice induces some laughs but they also act as Sancho Panzas to D'Artagnan's quixotic ranting. At one point they almost seem to be playing straight men to him when he utters the lines, "To die for the queen is to die gloriously. This is indeed our lucky day," and they all profess agreement while looking for a way to get out of this.

The lackeys reluctantly rescue D'Artagnan when he is bested by de Winter. In the film's funniest scene, when Milady deposits an important secret document into her cleavage,

D'Artagnan leaves it up to the lackeys to be the "problem-solvers" and get the document while still behaving as gentlemen. How do they do this? Suffice it to say that it leaves Milady having a very bad hair day. Dwan himself claimed that he was the source for this scene.

The last part of the film, while nicely atmospheric, is done conventionally with D'Artagnan providing the necessary derring-do. Though lacking the budget and pictorial splendor of Dwan's Fairbanks swashbucklers, there is in this section a beautifully composed shot, moodily lit and deftly using depth of field which shows D'Artagnan and Constance at the top of a grand staircase watching the turn of events that occur below when Milady arrives to warn the cardinal's men.

There was a script plan to bring back the original Musketeers at the climax, where they would substitute for the Ritz Brothers in winning the day. This was not done and perhaps did not fit in with the brisk pace set for the film. The real Musketeers do appear behind D'Artagnan in the concluding Musketeer parade where the Musketeers are at last seen actually bearing muskets.

The film was generally well received. *The Hollywood Reporter* called it "surefire entertainment of the kind that breeds word-of-mouth ticket selling."[6]

Dwan made one more film for Fox with the Ritz Brothers, a comedy-thriller called *The Gorilla* that is regarded by most critics as a very minor effort. One of the few champions of the film is Michael E. Grost, who has a website devoted to classic films. He considers *The Gorilla* in some ways an experimental film "taking apart narrative structures the way Alain Resnais would do with *L'Anne dernier a Marienbad.*"

The three Ritz Brothers gleefully take up Binnie Barnes' challenge in *The Three Musketeers* (1939).

The Gorilla was based on a 1920s stage play which was likely inspired by such antecedents as *The Bat* and *The Cat and the Canary*. *The Gorilla* had previously been filmed in 1927 and 1930 and the emphasis in both versions was on comedy. (There was also a woefully bizarre 1937 variation, *Sh! The Octopus*, which was basically the same story but with an octopus substituted for the gorilla.)

Dwan made some comments about the problems of working with the Ritz Brothers when discussing *The Three Musketeers* with Bogdanovich. According to actor Edward Norris, the annoyances with the Ritz Brothers were at least as bad on *The Gorilla*. "They were always calling their bookies, playing the horses. Half the time one of them was on the phone. Dwan tried to keep a tight reign [sic] but it was difficult." Norris also complained that the brothers had a habit of taking the good dialogue away from the other actors. "When they got through with the script, there was nothing for Anita Louise and I to do."[7]

Dwan might have accepted the Ritzes' pilferage of lines because their parts needed beefing up. According to a *Hollywood Reporter* news item, the Ritz Brothers walked out on the scheduled starting date and were gone for five days. This was allegedly because of a script conflict.[8] Given the fact that the Ritzes all looked and behaved similarly (except for Harry's dominance), their behavior could be grating without the impetus of good gags and dialogue. They were more like a comic chorus than a comedy team, which is why they functioned better in the background.

Part of the cinematic challenge of material like *The Gorilla* was to turn a house into a labyrinth of threatening horrors. Except for an opening montage of newspaper headlines and four relatively brief shots outside of the Stevens mansion, all of the film takes place inside the mansion or its garage. The opening shot after the montage is one of the few exteriors. The camera moves in on a railing atop the mansion, which is clutched by what looks to be a simian arm. The camera carefully does not reveal more than an arm and then moves down to an open window where, inside, Kitty the maid (Patsy Kelly) is reading *Romeo and Juliet*. The arm enters the window to leave a paper with a message to the owner of the house Walter Stevens (Lionel Atwill), "You Are Next to Die." Stevens invites his niece and her fiancé to be with him the next night, as well as three detectives (the Ritzes) for protection.

The next night (of course a rainy one) will be marked by all kinds of strange events including eerie disappearances, warnings from the killer through the radio and the appearance of a real gorilla, which we later learn had been set loose from its trainer. Dwan maintains a sinister atmosphere with the dexterous use of well-designed sets and astute lighting and camerawork by cinematographer Edward Cronjager. In one master shot of a large room when lightning flashes, a human figure can be seen for an instant in front of a window in the distant background. At times, the film seems to forsake narrative continuity in favor of a succession of moments of characters stumbling into one strange set of situations into another. One can understand something of Grost's point that this almost seems like experimental filmmaking. The problem is that even in these moments, the atmosphere is being sustained by some very shopworn devices such as secret passageways, a marauding monster, dark rooms with sudden surprises, etc. Thus, even when they are effective, they remind us of the artificiality and conventions of the genre. As the *Hollywood Reporter* review noted, it includes "sliding panel hocus pocus, plus a sizable quota of nightmare-exciting ape close-ups."[9]

If the concept is crude, the execution is often good. Some of the shots of the gorilla are actually quite menacing and not at all farcical as many examples of the simian makeup of the time would suggest. The problem with *The Gorilla* is that the background is fine but the foreground is missing. As Zanuck realized when they tried to put the comedy team at the center of *The Three Musketeers*, the Ritz Brothers could not carry the story. In *Variety*'s review of the 1927 film, it noted, "The play had its punch in its flow of the wisecracks from the two detectives."[10] With the Ritz Brothers, the two detectives have been increased to three with Harry Ritz playing the new character Harrigan but with a paucity of amusing lines. Patsy Kelly gets off a few good wisecracks, though hardly enough to salvage things.

The film also seems to turn logic on its ear in its final "explanations." Joseph Calleia, playing the mysterious stranger who has been popping in and out of view in the house, suddenly announces that he is Detective Caletti, an investigator for the Securities and Exchange Commission! He explains that Stevens is the gorilla and that his crimes are attached to his shady financial dealings. He displays the phony gorilla sleeve used to frighten people and follows the wire from the radio to expose Stevens in a secret room. That Stevens is tied up and gagged does not seem to faze Caletti.

Somehow, everyone buys this reasoning until Caletti is about to leave and Harrigan shakes his hand, realizes that it is phony and pulls it off, revealing a hairy ape hand. The stranger admits he's the gorilla but wrests the gun away from Harrigan. However, as soon as he steps outside, the butler Peters (Bela Lugosi) is there to put a gun at his back.

It is then Stevens' turn to explain that he and his investigator A.P. Conway (Paul Harvey), another character wandering in and out of the house, cooked up this scheme to trap the real killer. (Stevens was actually the killer in the first film version.) But this does not explain why early in the film, in private, Stevens phoned Conway (pretending to be one of his creditors) to appeal for more time to pay his debts. Nor could the various secret passages in the house have been constructed at a moment's notice.

For that matter, the final apprehension of Caletti by the butler Peters also seems weird. Several times during Caletti's speech, Dwan perversely shows Peters standing with the other characters. How and why he suddenly slipped away so that he could appear outside the house with his hat and coat on is not revealed. But if it seems illogical, it is not inconsistent. Several times in the course of the film, Peters suddenly appears in rooms that have been locked from the inside. Both Atwill and Lugosi seem to have been cast as red herrings but Lugosi's Peters appears to have been given some special powers. (Or are there even more secret passages in the house than we have seen?)

From one script conference we have this note. "However, in regard to certain fallacies which Mr. Dwan brought to light, Mr. Zanuck was of the opinion that in a picture of this type, the audience knows what to expect and they do not expect the same legitimacy

The Ritz Brothers, flanked by Anita Louise and Edward Norris, have difficulty contending with all the dangers in *The Gorilla* (1939).

as in an ordinary story. Therefore, we must be content with the foundation as it is...."[11]

The finished film seems to be spoofing the idea that any of the story's logic could hold up. As Kelly's Kitty notes, "Even the gorilla doesn't know who the gorilla is." Given the film's contrivances, it is not an attack on logic but an acknowledgment that the illusions provided in the film could never make sense. While *The Gorilla* may be missing the requisite humor, Dwan's playful gaze remains visible.

Finishing Up with Fox

Although it was produced by Zanuck, *The Gorilla* looked much more like a B film than did *Frontier Marshal*. For his next film, Dwan was again working with Wurtzel in a project that looked more like typical B material.

The Sweetheart of Turret One was sold to Fox by Samuel Goldwyn. The original story was by Frank "Spig" Wead, the former naval officer who later worked with John Ford and whose life would be depicted by Ford in *The Wings of Eagles*. Three additional writers contributed to the script including Lou Breslow, who had worked on some of Dwan's better Bs including *High Tension* and *One Mile from Heaven*.

The original Wead story concerned a young woman's attempt to take care of an orphan ("The Skipper") with some assistance from the sailors in the area around San Pedro Harbor. Scrappy, one of the sailors involved in the "Papa Watch," finds himself falling in love with June, the lady caring for the child. Scrappy is very reluctant to get involved and puts in for a transfer to China so he can continue to lead a free life. But the Skipper begins to get under his skin and Scrappy finally proposes to June.[12]

Wead's story may have reflected some of his own difficulty in reconciling his naval career to his family duties. The story, however, is a fairly straightforward and sentimental tale. But this was one of those rare cases where a story actually became more complex in the transformation to film, an even rarer event for a B picture.

Part of this may have been attributable to the comic payoff at the climax which requires a baby somehow to wind up on a battleship. It's possible that a lot of thinking went into establishing the circumstances that led to this odd development. The film that emerged from this process had a good deal of somber, even disturbing material, while still leading to a comic climax. There is no record that Zanuck was involved in the planning of this film and it's likely that Dwan was able to operate as usual with Wurtzel giving him a free hand in shaping the screenplay.

As part of a package deal, the services of actor Jon Hall were sold to Fox along with the screenplay. Hall had not acted in thirty-six months for Goldwyn but remained on full salary, having made his last appearance in *The Hurricane* (1937), directed by John Ford. The female lead for the film, finally titled *Sailor's Lady*, was given to Nancy Kelly, the Sarah of *Frontier Marshal*. Dana Andrews, who was under a shared contract with Fox and Goldwyn, played the role of Scrappy.

In the completed script, Scrappy is no longer the central character. Hall is the male lead, Danny Malone, who is planning to marry his sweetheart Sally Gilroy (Kelly). Just before the sailors are to embark on shore leave, Scrappy gets the news that his pay is being garnished for back alimony and all that he will get from his paycheck will be four dollars. The embittered Scrappy now says he will do all he can to prevent his pal Danny from getting married and plants an item in Danny's duffel bag so he will be denied liberty. Danny manages to sneak off the ship using another sailor's pass.

Danny has been sending Sally money to put a down payment on a house for their impending marriage. Danny is startled to find that she has put a payment on a house in a neighborhood that seems a bit extravagant for him (officers have homes nearby) and is surprised to see that she has not spent the money on furniture. But what really astonishes Danny is that he finds that Sally has a baby girl in the house. "It couldn't be ours," he tells her. (The film had to stay within censorship limits.)

Sally explains that a couple they knew was killed in an auto accident, making their baby an orphan. Sally said that when she was asked to take care of the infant for a time, she fell in love with the child and wanted to make it her own. Danny protests that he would prefer a chance to save up for a year before having a child and doesn't want "a second-hand family." Sally, however, is adamant and appeals to Danny not to begrudge the baby a home.

Meanwhile, two other couples who are friends of Danny and Sally are waiting for them, including Scrappy and his girl Georgine (Kay Aldridge). When Scrappy learns that Danny can't go out with them, he decides to do his pal "another favor" and reports his absence from the ship to the navy. Just as Sally is trying to explain to a nosy neighbor, Miss Purvis, what a good father Danny will be, the shore patrol comes and arrests Danny at the front door.

The plotline involving three couples (one of them, Joan Davis and Wally Vernon, are there for comic relief) was the kind of structure that Dwan favored. Danny is caught between the pull of his buddy (Scrappy) and the unyielding maternal instincts of his girlfriend. Scrappy not only commits the betrayals listed above but also has some sailors deliberately agitate and insult Miss Purvis and then cause a confrontation with Sally. Scrappy claims to be doing all this in the name of friendship but these acts seem malicious enough to suggest Scrappy's jealousy at Danny's relationship with Sally. Danny is oblivious to Scrappy's part in sabotaging his impending marriage and regards him as his closest friend. When Scrappy emphatically refers to Danny as his pal ("Anything for a pal") as he prepares his next deception, the relationship takes on an eerie resemblance to Iago and Othello.

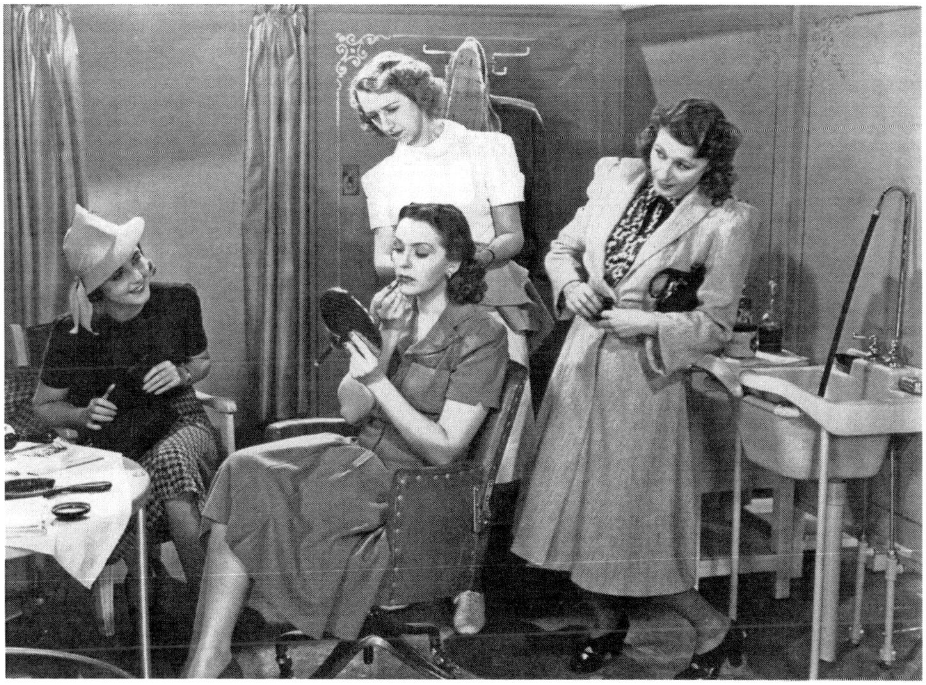

Kay Aldridge, Nancy Kelly (both seated) and Joan Davis (right), prepare to take on their Navy boyfriends in *Sailor's Lady* (1940). The beauty operator is Marie Blake.

While Sally's desire to provide a home for the orphan Skipper may show her generous spirit, her behavior also suggests an intense maternal obsession, wanting to be a mother even before marriage. Her groom-to-be also may be developing some resentments and having second thoughts. When Danny discovers his steak is too dry, Sally explains that she squeezed the juice out of it to give it to Skipper; then blithely suggests that she can make up for this by opening a can of beans for him. The house itself looks eccentrically baby-centered. Bereft of virtually all furniture except for a small table and chairs, it has a look of Spartan bareness although it does have a playpen, crib and perambulator. (Sally notes, perhaps with some satisfaction, that Danny will not be able to invite his buddies over to the house for some time.) By contrast, Danny's ship quarters seem homier and a focal point of camaraderie.

Danny is the pivotal figure caught between Sally's strong nesting instincts and Scrappy's dirty-tricks campaign for bachelorhood and buddy primacy. But *Sailor's Lady* has another male character, who is also a pole apart from Danny, the sailor Rodney, played by Larry "Buster" Crabbe. The first time we see Sally waiting for Danny at the dock, Rodney is there to remind her that he is part of the base force and more reliable than Danny and the other sailors. Touting himself as the dependable male, Rodney uses every opportunity to present himself to Sally as a preferable marriage choice. There is more than a touch of sanctimoniousness to Rodney. When Danny kids him about wearing his halo, Rodney protests to the parish priest, Father McGannn, that Danny has made a sacrilegious remark. (*Sailor's Lady* is one of relatively few Dwan films to make reference to his Irish-Catholic origins.) Sally doesn't seem to like Rodney but he remains a viable alternative during her difficulties with Danny.

The moment of truth for Rodney (and even more so for Sally) is when he turns up at the house to elope with Sally at the same time that Danny has returned to iron out his problems with her. A fistfight breaks out between the two men. In pursuing what he wants, Rodney will not relent to Sally's appeals any more than Danny. Sally tries to intervene and becomes entangled between the two brawling men.

In the scuffle, Sally is whipped around the men and for a moment, it appears that the sequence will suddenly be lurching into slapstick comedy. But in the next shot, we see Sally thrown down to the floor and knocked senseless. With its effect of brutalizing a woman, the fistfight takes on a menacing quality. The mood seems to accelerate to outright horror when Danny is sent reeling into Skipper's room and crashing into her playpen. The next shot shows Skipper safe in her crib. Sally's outrage about what is happening becomes quite palpable. Using a piece of the wrecked playpen as a club, she beats the still squabbling men out of the room.

First teetering on exhibiting more robust humor, the film has taken a move towards serious and even disturbing drama. Disgusted by the behavior of all the sailors she has encountered while Miss Purvis (played by Mary Nash, the Fraulein Rottenmeier of *Heidi*) pursues Skipper's case to juvenile court, Sally knows she is on the verge of losing the infant. But it's at this juncture that *Sailor's Lady* makes its pirouette into comedy. This begins with a reckless act that's almost as disturbing as what preceded it. Sally joins a tour group that's being taken aboard Danny's ship, the U.S.S. *Dakota*. She leaves Skipper in one of the ship's cabins and then departs with the rest of the group. Sally leaves a tag on the baby stating that she is the responsibility of the First Division (Danny's group).

Sally doesn't want the baby to be with her when Miss Purvis arrives to take her away. It's also her challenge (or, as Scrappy puts it, her revenge) on the sailors and the navy. In an early scene in the film, Sally's friend Myrtle (Davis), talking of the problems in interesting their sailor boyfriends in marriage, muses, "The Navy's all they have and all they want, guns, boats and buddies." Now out of both desperation and anger, she has left it to the men and the Navy to show how they can take care of a baby.

The *Dakota* is about to engage in combat maneuvers and the sudden discovery of the baby on board throws the officers

Buster Crabbe (center) challenges Jon Hall for Nancy Kelly's affections in *Sailor's Lady* (1940), precipitating a destructive brawl.

into a tizzy. Following the bureaucratic chain of command, the *Dakota* begins signaling the other ships to get instructions on what to do about the baby on board. The editing becomes frenetic as the messages pass through each ship all the way to the authority of the admiral. (One somber note is that one of the ships the *Dakota* is communicating with is the *Arizona* which would be sunk at Pearl Harbor a year later.) It's finally conveyed that a destroyer will pick up the baby the next night.

Danny and his shipmates have to scurry to take care of the baby, including improvising an equivalent to diapers at changing time. As the big guns sound off during maneuvers, Skipper wakes up crying hysterically. The ship's commander, Captain Roscoe, is deeply absorbed into the war games and his ship's firing is proving most accurate. But on the advice of the ship doctor, the captain reluctantly orders firing to stop. Roscoe now feels that his performance in the exercise has been fatally compromised. And what's more, the child is still crying! A Marine checks the child and finds that the cause of the crying is an open safety pin. There is a cut to a close-up of the mortified doctor.

In the judgments for the maneuvers, it is determined that Roscoe ordered a ceasefire at precisely the correct time. It was determined that the firing had already taken their maximum effect and to continue would have been wasteful. Roscoe apologizes to the "young lady" for blaming her for his anticipated loss when she has helped him win the day.

There is then a cut to the Church of the Good Shepherd where Danny and Sally are getting married with Skipper in tow. Logically, this does not seem right. Wouldn't the juvenile court remove the child for Sally's irresponsibility in leaving her on a battleship? Perhaps Roscoe, in his delight at winning the maneuvers, helped cover this up. The viewer is free to provide his own explanation since Dwan omits any kind of bridging scene between the *Dakota*'s return and the wedding.

If it doesn't make sense logically, it does make sense dramatically. The lady has tamed the Navy to domesticity with the collaboration of a female child. (It was apparently important to the story that the child be a girl since Skipper was actually played by one Bruce Hampton. Perhaps the fact that a boy had to be dressed as a girl could be added to the sense of male humiliation.) It's also added as a sweetener and act of gender reconciliation that the baby helps the *Dakota* win the combat maneuvers.

As in other cases, Dwan no doubt would say that he appreciated the scenes of male humiliation for their comic value. But these situations, which persist in his other films, are here given a weightier dramatic context and a stronger relationship to everyday life.

Later in 1940, Dwan made a film for Universal called *Trail of the Vigilantes*. Dwan said the original intention was to make a serious Western film. He recalled, "I went with a company clear up to a location in the mountains and started it, and I hadn't made three scenes before it struck me that this was not a good drama and that if it were made into a drama, it would be a miserable thing. I hadn't paid much attention to it in script form, but when I got these actors in front of me, I saw that the situation was humorous, not serious. So just on a hunch I closed up the company and took them back to the studio."[13] Dwan said that his action shocked Universal and they considered replacing him. Concerned about its investment, the Universal execs apparently had enough respect for Dwan's judgment to ask him what he would do. Dwan said he replied, "Well, let me pick a writer and go to work." Dwan got hold of a writer and "in a few hours we adjusted the script into the same story with a tongue-in-cheek approach as comedy."[14]

Trail of the Vigilantes has been fondly remembered by Western fans for its kidding of the genre. Dwan's story has only added luster to its reputation. The eminent film historian William K. Everson, however, doubted Dwan's claim that the film started as a serious one. In Everson's view, "This seems an extremely unlikely premise and also an impractical one," as he pointed out the "increases in budget and shooting" that would be prompted by the change. Everson also maintained that the "film wasn't of sufficient importance to rate an in-production change of status...."[15] Everson also noted that *Trail of the Vigilantes* was following in the path of other tongue-in-cheek Universal Westerns such as *My Little Chickadee* and *Destry Rides Again*.

Production records for *Trail of the Vigilantes* provide some evidence of what happened. According to the Assistant Director's Daily Report, shooting began on October 5, 1940. On the report of October 11 there is a notation, "We were advised to disregard original script, as story is being revised...."[16] The report also specified that 5½ pages were shot that day from the new script while previously 11¼ pages had been shot from the old script. So it was after six days of filming that shooting began on the new script. The report also states that the film had been in production for seven days so there was apparently no shut-down though the pace was much slower before the script change.

There is also a memo on how one of the supporting actors, Paul Fix, would be paid. The memo notes, "As you will remember, it was very uncertain how the character he was playing would appear in the script which was being written as we progressed."[17]

So it's clear that *Trail of the Vigilantes* underwent major rewriting after production began and Dwan's explanation that he was tilting it more towards comedy seems reasonable. The picture's estimated budget was $460,000, so as Everson says, it was a minor A rather than a B film. It involved enough money that Universal had reason to be concerned by Dwan's warning that the film would not work as written. The key factor in persuading Universal to accept the rewrite may have been Dwan's acknowledged ability to work quickly and efficiently, even when making changes. Universal's records show that despite the script overhaul, *Trail of the Vigilantes* went only ten days over schedule and that the probable final cost of the film was $10,000 less than the estimated budget![18] Dwan's celebrated efficiency clearly bought him a larger measure of artistic freedom.

Dwan was signed by Universal for $20,000 to direct *Trail of the Vigilantes* and this must have been arranged as a loan-out since Dwan was still under contract to Fox. According to Blackie Seymour in an article on the film's female star Peggy Moran, Dwan was given the job when the original director took ill.[19] In a phone conversation with the author, Seymour said he learned this from either Moran or Andy Devine, both of whom he spoke to extensively. This might explain what ne cessitated the loan out, especially as Dwan had a reputation for taking control quickly. The article also says that Dwan dropped the selected cast and crew but this sounds more questionable.

The starring role went to the sophisticated Franchot Tone, who had never appeared in a Western before and never would again. Filling out the ranks of cowboy heroes in the film were Broderick Crawford, Andy Devine and *Destry Rides Again*'s Mischa Auer. Nancy Kelly was considered for the female lead but the part went instead to Peggy Moran.

Everson does make a valid point that *Trail of the Vigilantes* is both a comedy and action film but that can also be seen as an indication of how seamlessly Dwan interlaced the plot with the comedy and that he could retain the central plot while hanging various odd bits of business around it.

The opening scenes suggest a parody of the beginning of *Frontier Marshal.* As with the latter film, there is a prologue, putting the story in a historical and portentous context: "Before the turn of the century, death and violence rode the western range." The ensuing montage charts the growth of power of the vigilantes. The montage is shown framed in the page of a book, as if illustrating the prologue's faithfulness to history. Dwan saved money on the montage by using stock scenes from Universal's Ken Maynard Western *Smoking Guns* and the recently released *Diamond Frontier.*[20]

Full screen is then restored as the film cuts to Kansas City where an Eastern investigator, Tim Mason (Tone), is being asked to go undercover out West and find out who was responsible for the killing of a newspaperman trying to find the source of an epidemic of cattle rustling. Mason at first protests — he was intending to go to New York City (as Dwan often preferred to do) — but is finally convinced to take on the assignment. Mason, as played by Tone, is a dyed-in-the-wool Easterner who when riding high, spouts lines like, "Just a demonstration of Eastern mind over Western matter." Such a line has the satirical glint of the intertitles in the Fairbanks films and recalls the comic variations worked there on the East-West rivalry. But then the assertion of eastern brains over western wiles goes back to one of Dwan's earliest films, *Rattlesnakes and Gunpowder.*

Along with these threads, the *Frontier Marshal* parody-parallel continues when Mason arrives in a Western town, not with the grim name of "Tombstone" but "Peaceful Valley" — or so says the train conductor as bullets whiz around him. As in *Frontier Marshal,* the trouble is brewing from the saloon but the drawback is not the sheriff's cowardice (although that is later amply demonstrated) but that he is incapacitated. The sheriff, the under sheriff and deputy are found handcuffed in various contorted positions while the perpetrator of their constraints is carousing in a saloon using a patron as a human bowling ball. Mason (to become known to everyone as "Kansas") confronts the rascal Swanee (Crawford) and his pal Meadows (Devine). After some scuffling and then joining forces to confront the sheriff, the three become friends. Kansas is invited to join Swanee and Meadows in working as a cowpuncher for John Thornton (Charles Trowbridge), giving him an opportunity to pursue his undercover work.

Much of the humor in *Trail of the Vigilantes* comes from the characterizations which provide the basis for physical gags. Kansas, determined to prove that he's no longer a tenderfoot, tries several times to imitate the cowboys in their athletic ways of mounting a horse, with persistently painful results. Peggy Moran, as Thornton's daughter Barbara, is the pursuer in her romantic interest in Kansas, often trying to entrap him by doing things like lassoing him off his horse. Meadows comes from a long line of valets and compulsively behaves as a servant towards his friends. Most colorful of all is Mischa Auer's Bolo (or whatever he calls himself at any given instant), an exile from everywhere who claims to have been a matador, gaucho, Cossack and in less convincing guises an American Indian and a Southern gentleman lawyer. His physical feats are sometimes impressive while at other times less successful. (When almost seriously injured during one of his exploits and asked what he was trying to do, Bolo answers, "I haven't the slightest idea.")

Physicality is a hallmark of the production and while Dwan did not have a Fairbanks as star, the activity is spread out among the characters with stuntmen doing yeoman service. (Many of Auer's stunts were filmed in extreme long shot.) Tone's Kansas is at his most Fairbanksian when comically hanging from a chandelier and working his way to get to a balcony where the heroine is held prisoner in one of the rooms. The villain (Warren William) goes down like a failed Fairbanks in a spectacular fall when jumping from a building to a tree branch. Everson notes that *Trail of the Vigilantes* was "something of a landmark film in bringing about reforms and upgrading of salary scales and union regulations relating to stuntmen. Tom Steele (doubling especially for Warren William) is the leader of the crew of stuntmen employed in the film."[21]

Among the Western elements lampooned are chase scenes, of which there are several; they go on for long stretches with over-the-top stunts. Universal shrewdly re-used one of the chase scenes in two of its later features, *Road Agent* (1941) and *Gunman's Code* (1946). Other footage from *Trail of the Vigilantes* was recycled in the Universal feature *Rustler's Roundup* and the serial *The Scarlet Horseman* (both 1946) and in a 1950 featurette, *Western Courage*.[22]

As Dwan had known since at least the Fairbanks films, comedy did not necessarily destroy the audience's interest in the straight plot. When the heroes try to rescue Barbara by entering a town full of outlaws, the film soars with both humor and excitement. Everson wrote, "While amiable rather than overwhelming in its comedy material, *Trail of the Vigilantes* must certainly be considered a major success in the then very rare forays into western spoofing, and is equally certainly superior to such later and more ambitious works such as *Blazing Saddles*."[23]

At the time, *Variety* observed that the film had "a liberal dash of straight-line and sideline satire directed at Westerns in general. Picture is a fast-actioner with plenty of broadside comedy, and rates as a strong programmer...."[24]

Blackie Seymour commented that the movie was crammed with both humor and action "at a pace rarely if ever equaled today. *Trail of the Vigilantes* was possibly the fastest-moving western ever made."[25] According to Seymour, Dwan's fast pacing was abetted by extensive work in the editing room. Seymour owned stills of several scenes not included in the final cut.

In *Sailor's Lady*, Dwan pushed the dramatic elements to the forefront and found the comedy in the final act catharsis. For *Trail of the Vigilantes*, Dwan saw it fitting to bask the dramatic story in comedy while preserving the action plot. For two films in one year, Dwan found the essence of comedy in each by going into two almost diametrically opposed directions.

Between those two films, Dwan was involved in a more pressured situation where he would have less leverage, working once more with Shirley Temple on *Young People*. The film was based on an outline written by Zanuck.

Since they had last worked together, Shirley had appeared in one of her best films, the Technicolor *The Little Princess* (1939). Shirley was actually permitted to have a father in this one, though he was offscreen for much of the film while Ms. Temple was again menaced by Mary Nash.

She had both parents in *The Blue Bird*, an elaborate Technicolor fantasy that departed from formula by having Shirley

Franchot Tone, or perhaps a stunt double (hanging upside down), learns from Broderick Crawford (center) and Andy Devine (right) that there are some peculiar things going on in Peaceful Valley in *Trail of the Vigilantes* (1940).

play a spoiled child, at least at the beginning of the movie. Based on a play by Maurice Maeterlinck that had earlier been adapted into a 1918 film directed by Maurice Tourneur, *The Blue Bird* was released in early 1940. Seen as Fox's answer to the recently released *The Wizard of Oz*, the film was probably too gentle and ethereal to succeed with the audiences of the day as Shirley enters a world that contains dead grandparents and unborn children. It flopped with both the critics and audiences of the period, breaking her string of box office successes. (The film also had its admirers and was well received at the 1965 San Francisco Film Festival with the star in attendance.)

In late 1939, as he planned Shirley's next film, Zanuck had more pressing concerns than posterity. Zanuck wrote an outline tentatively called *The Come-Back* or *The Girl Who Came Back,* which he intended as her next vehicle. Both titles suggest that Temple had suffered a setback though the outline was completed in October, well before *The Blue Bird* had been released. It's possible that Zanuck may have been only thinking of the characters in the story but perhaps the very fact that Shirley was getting close to leaving childhood was the setback that troubled him. She would celebrate her twelfth birthday that coming April.

In preparing the outline, Zanuck screened the various musical numbers that Shirley had performed for Fox over the years and had them assembled together for use in this film. It was noted that in viewing these pictures, "Mr. Zanuck realized that Shirley had almost tripled in size since her first pictures and it would be sensational if we could see her actually grow up in front of an audience from a little kid who could hardly walk, to the young lady she is at the present time. If we could get a story of this kind, we would have a sure-fire hit for her."[26]

To a greater extent than before, Shirley Temple the personality was invoked to tower over the character she was portraying. Zanuck was betting that audiences would make the familial connection with Shirley as they were reminded how she grew before them, as if she was one of their own. It was hoped that they would then feel emotionally committed to following her to the next stage of her growth.

Formula elements reappeared. Once more, Shirley was an orphan, this time being adopted by a vaudevillian couple and raised to be part of their act. Again, there was a farm. (Zanuck noted to his writers, "See *Rebecca of Sunnybrook Farm* and *Poor Little Rich Girl* for ideas of this nature."[27]) The family retired to the farm but grew bored and restless and sought to return to the stage. They then found that show business had changed and that radio and motion pictures had supplanted vaudeville. Shirley saves the day by becoming a star in radio, or the musical stage or perhaps in movies!

The irony and redundancy of that concept must have dawned on everyone including Zanuck and that resolution was abandoned. It was then decided that the rowdy vaudevillians would clash with the staid residents of the New England town in which they chose to settle.

The script was also to have Shirley and her adopted parents identify with young people at odds with their conservative elders. Zanuck envisioned the film as having the same kind of appeal as *Babes in Arms*.

Zanuck was especially insistent on one point: that the film be made for $600,000. While this was hardly cheap, it did show that at a critical time in Temple's career, Zanuck felt a need for retrenchment. *The Little Princess* had been budgeted at $700,000 and *The Blue Bird* was done for $1,000,000 and Zanuck felt the time had come to hold the line. It was revealing of how he viewed the prospects of his star when Zanuck observed, "We must not kid ourselves; if we spend any more than this we are in dire trouble...."[28]

Sidney Lanfield was originally assigned to direct *Young People* but he was shifted to another film and replaced by Dwan. There may have been hopes that Dwan would help rekindle the box office prowess of his earlier films with Temple, *Heidi* and *Rebecca of Sunnybrook Farm*.

In her autobiography, Mrs. Black remembers approaching the project with little enthusiasm and said that the script by Edwin Blum and Don Ettlinger "made cheerless reading."[29] She recalled *Young People* being scrapped in favor of another film called *Schoolmates*. On April 2, *Schoolmates* was suddenly dropped and *Young People* was reinstated. The poor box office returns on *The Blue Bird* may have had something to do with the increased concern about how to approach Shirley's next film.

As Zanuck had planned, scenes from two of Shirley early films were incorporated into the action, making it appear that they were performed with her vaudeville adopted parents Joe (Jack Oakie) and Kit Ballantine (Charlotte Greenwood). Inserted are Shirley's hula dance from *Curly Top* and her singing of "Baby, Take a Bow" from *Stand Up and Cheer*. New songs were written by Mack Gordon and Harry Warren. We get our first glimpse of the more mature Shirley singing the elegantly snappy "Fifth Avenue." Decked out in top hat and tails, a much taller Miss Temple appears to be on the brink of adolescence. The song also sets a demarcation line because the Ballantines will soon be forsaking New York and their other big city spots for life on the farm.

Determined to find a place where they can settle down and where daughter Wendy can finally have a normal upbringing, the Ballantines head to the New England village of Stonefield, where they have purchased a farm. Their driver gives them an understated summary of the town when he says, "This ain't no New Deal country."

Young People is unusual for a film of its time to the extent by which conflicts are identified by specific political labels. Although the New England state is never identified in the film, the script conferences place it in Vermont, the birthplace of Calvin Coolidge and at that time a bastion of conservatism. Indeed, Coolidge exemplified the terse way in which the Stonefield residents respond to questions.

At the town meeting, the film cites Mike Shea (George Montgomery), the editor and reporter of *The Stonefield Democrat*, as the leader of progressive forces in the town and opponent of the forces too mired in tradition to consider any new ideas. Hester Appleby (Kathleen Howard), the real power in Stonefield, quickly conveys her snobbery to Kit, who decides that Hester "must have been weaned on a pickle." The real purpose of the political element is to set up the conflict between old and new, an intergenerational conflict.

Shirley Temple has a decidedly elegant look in top hat and tales (as do Jack Oakie and Charlotte Greenwood playing the vaudeville couple who adopt her) in *Young People* (1940). The movie's box office failure effectively ended Shirley's tenure at Twentieth Century–Fox.

Zanuck certainly didn't identify himself as a liberal but in one memo he observed, "There is no town in the world today that doesn't have YOUTH and youth of today is very liberal-minded and progressive."[30] This would help provide the film with opposing forces and in Zanuck's view help young people identify with the characters.

The problem with Zanuck's vision is that the camaraderie of youth is never realized in the movie. Most of the children are much younger than Wendy and she forms no bond with the ones closer to her age. Wendy, with the encouragement of her parents, prepares her fellow students for a big musical number for the school recital. They perform the song "Young People" but the disparate group is torn apart when the parents are appalled by the pseudo-sophistication of the lyrics and the kiddie conga dancing. With Hester's helping hand, the family has now alienated most of the townspeople.

For most of the film up to this point, Shirley has retained her relentlessly cheery nature, which seems more than a little cloying for a budding adolescent. The greatest challenge to her emotional equilibrium is when she learns from one of the spiteful children that she is adopted, something that the Ballantines could never bring themselves to tell her.

Wendy's ensuing confrontation with her adopted parents in the family car on a dark, rainy night makes for credible drama. Then Wendy begins to sing "I Wouldn't Take a Million." The song had earlier been sung by Joe to show that his daughter is priceless and Wendy now returns the compliment to her adopted parents. This has the kind of twisting dramatic effect that Dwan was able to invoke in *The Three Musketeers* by having a song once performed, then re-sung by a different actor in a different situation to add a different dramatic layer of meaning. But it seems a miscalculation that Shirley begins to sing it with her usual perkiness instantly restored, as if it never left her.

On the other hand, Shirley had been an orphan throughout so much of her film career that it seemed a little late to get worked up about it now.

The torrential rain is the first sign of the hurricane, the cataclysm that will provide the film's climax. The Ballantines help gather up the children who had been out picking berries and get them into a warm house. When one child is missing, Joe goes out to look for him. While it's brave of Joe to take the risk of going out in the hurricane, the act of simply finding the child and bringing him back to the house is too cinematically understated to provide the big climax anticipated. An angry Wendy gets to upbraid Hester, telling her, "You're mean and full of vinegar." Signaling her reformation, a chastened Hester then takes Wendy into her arms. Another sourpuss had been snagged by Shirley.

Dwan was unable to overcome the completely formulaic manner in which things are resolved. Suddenly, Hester and the townspeople are won over and endorsing something called "Progress Week." It may have worked better if it was shown that Hester and the townspeople had found a greater respect and affection for the Ballantines, while disagreements would remain. Despite some spirited moments, *Young People* did not work as a transitional film but as more of a dead end.

Young People was an even bigger financial flop than *The Blue Bird*. The final rupture between Fox and Temple would occur before the film was released. Mrs. Black remembers the problem, beginning when Zanuck wrote to her mother, telling her to have Shirley ready to start *Lady Jane* one week after the completion of *Young People*. When Shirley's father protested that her 1935 contract called for four weeks between films, relations began to sour between the Temple family and Fox. *Lady Jane* was withdrawn as a project and, as the studio circulated rumors of Shirley's retirement, it became clear that no more Temple films would be made for the one-year duration of her contract.[31] Concerned about letting her career languish led the

Temples to buy out the contract. Shirley moved on to MGM to make her next film but she would never be a top box-office star again.

By the time *Young People* opened that summer, some critics had assumed that the film with its retirement plot had been made to mark Shirley's exit. The twelve-year-old was given a farewell party by Fox that was not over-generous in gifts. Shirley's former co-star Jack Oakie groused, "The kid who had coined millions for the industry received a chill from the studio to go down in movie history."[32]

Dwan also would not remain at Fox much longer.

Dwan's final film for Fox on his contract, *Rise and Shine* did not have the aesthetic complications of his three comedies of 1940. It was based on James Thurber's "My Life and Hard Times," but most of Thurber's account was left unused as the screenplay concentrated on "Boley" Bolenciewicz, a star on the college football field but short on brain power. Because the Conference Investigating Committee is beginning to check on the intelligence ratings of college athletes and Boley needs a quiet place to get all the sleep he needs, Clayton College has him dispatched to the home of one of its instructors, Prof. Murray. What is concocted from this plot is a blend of college musical and screwball comedy.

Adapting the screenplay was Herman J. Mankiewicz, who also co-wrote *Citizen Kane* with Orson Welles. *Kane* was released the same year as Dwan's film so *Rise and Shine* may be remembered as Mankiewicz's "other film of 1941."[33] Conference notes indicate that Dwan and Mankiewicz worked together in polishing up the *Rise and Shine* screenplay.

Cast in the lead as Boley was Jack Oakie, fresh from his success in Chaplin's *The Great Dictator*. Playing the Mussolini-inspired Napoloni, Oakie had been cited with an Academy Award nomination for Best Supporting Actor. Ironically, the man who beat him out for the Oscar, Walter Brennan in *The Westerner*, was loaned out from Goldwyn to co-star in *Rise and Shine*.

Oakie had played football players in college musicals for Paramount until the mid–1930s when he was deemed too old for such parts. The fact that Oakie now really looked too long in the tooth to still be in college added to the fun of his portrayal of the likable but thick-headed athlete.

The Murray family turns out to be a collection of screwy characters. The professor (Donald Meek) is constantly practicing magic tricks and often greets visitors by pulling eggs out of their ears. Brennan's Grandpa is old enough to have been a drummer boy in the Civil War but still has a fierce libido, which he is ready to demonstrate with every woman he meets. The mangy family dog, Mugs, also shows strange behavior. Even a straight character like the professor's daughter Louise, played by seventeen-year-old Linda Darnell, has to pitch in and sing "Rockabye Boley" to get the dimwitted Oakie to go to sleep. In his *New York Times* review, Bosley Crowther suggested that the film could have been subtitled, "You Can't Take It with You to a Football Game."[34]

But the parade of oddball characters doesn't end there. A notorious gambler and gangster known as the Menace (Sheldon Leonard) is interested in Boley's potential to determine the outcome of some major games and sends out a group of underlings to keep a check on him by moving next door to the Murrays. This squad includes the perpetually pompous and larcenous Raymond Walburn as Colonel Bacon, his wise cracking wife Mame (Ruth Donnelly) and the strait-laced character Jimmy McGonigle (George Murphy). They are later joined by the Menace's flunky, Seabiscuit (Milton Berle), nicknamed for his omnipresent horse laugh.

Despite the profusion of fun characters, *Rise and Shine* never goes over the top or strays far from its plot. Dwan and Mankiewicz keep most of the humor anchored around Boley, regardless of who is providing the mirth. At ninety-two minutes, *Rise and Shine* is Dwan's longest film since *Suez* but once the plot is set in motion, Dwan's flair for well-paced action is in evidence.

As the dim-witted football college star of *Rise and Shine* (1941), Jack Oakie (lying on the ground) was expected to win the big game against Notre Dame. Linda Darnell and George Murphy express their support from the sidelines.

Songs provided by Leo Robin and Ralph Rainger were interspersed throughout the film, some for comic effect. George Murphy had been borrowed from MGM for his dancing talents though there was no musically inclined leading lady to accompany him, singing or dancing. The most engaging song in the score, the romantic, "I'm Making a Play for You," was sung by Murphy to Darnell when both are riding bicycles.

Dwan and Mankiewicz also found ways to skirt the censors. Murphy's Jimmy McGonigle succumbs to the Dwan penchant for voyeurism as from his window, he watches Louise in Boley's bedroom. The shots observed from Jimmy's point of view create the impression that she is sleeping with Boley while the audience knows she is just trying to induce Boley to go to sleep. Similarly, there are some suggestive wisecracks turning up at the college's lovers' lane of parked cars as when one girl complains to her boyfriend, "What do you think I am, a giraffe?"

Dwan may have been responsible for the fact that Clayton College plays its climactic game against his alma mater, Notre Dame. Malcolm St. Clair, one of Dwan's rivals during the silent era, did second unit work shooting football scenes at the USC campus and the Los Angeles Memorial Coliseum as well as other footage near Chino, California.

Rise and Shine was reasonably well received and fondly remembered by some. In his autobiography, Oakie remembered the film as one of his favorite pictures.[35] In his book on Twentieth Century–Fox, author Tony Thomas cites *Rise and Shine* as "the most amusing of all college musicals."[36] In *Rise and Shine*, Dwan was able to breathe some life into two subgenres, one that had largely faded (the screwball comedy) and one that would soon be fading (the college musical).

Two days after *Rise and Shine* opened in New York, Pearl Harbor was bombed by the Japanese and World War II came to America. While the mood of the country had turned somber, comedy films would have a new value.

Radio and War

Dwan cited MCA as the chief mover in getting him involved with a trio of films in the 1940s. The Music Corporation of America was founded in 1924 and was originally a music booking agency in Chicago. MCA booked prominent musical artists and then in 1939 created a movie division and moved to Los Angeles.

Dwan recalled that in the early 1940s, MCA called and asked him if he would be interested in making a picture with some of their clients. Dwan explained that he had just signed with Berg and Allenberg. He said that MCA then bought him from those two agents.[37] MCA's Lew Wasserman, who would become a major power broker in the entertainment industry, became Dwan's personal agent. MCA saw that one way of building an empire was by building packages.

Dwan recalled, "Instead of just representing people, they put people together. They had Edgar Bergen and 'Fibber McGee and Molly'—big radio stars—and they bought me away from my agent so I'd be one of their clients and part of a package, and so when they went to RKO, they supplied the whole works—stars, director and everything. That was their method."[38]

Fibber McGee and Molly were not the names of the performers but of characters on a radio show. The fictional married couple was played by an actual married couple, Jim Jordan and his wife Marian. They were so linked with their radio characters that in the opening credits of the film that Dwan would make, they were identified not by their real names but as "Fibber McGee and Molly." Edgar Bergen also had a popular NBC radio show, serving up comedy as a ventriloquist with his alter ego dummies Charlie McCarthy and Mortimer Snerd. Yes, the idea of a ventriloquist on the radio does seem odd but it did work. Having radio stars making movies was one way of using their popularity to exploit another medium. Both Bergen–McCarthy and Fibber McGee and Molly had made films before but combining them in Dwan's *Look Who's Laughing* through their links with MCA sounded like a promising idea to maximize profits.

While the screenplay was credited to James V. Kern, precautions were taken that the characters would be true to their radio personalities. So intermingled with the Kern screenplay was material for the McGees written by Leonard L. Levinson and Don Quinn and for Bergen by Zeno Klinker and Dorothy Kingsley.

Look Who's Laughing went into production on May 12, 1941, with a budget of $396,131. But perhaps due to Dwan's efficiency, by January of the following year the total negative cost of the film was listed as $357,928.35. Dwan's MCA deal must have been to his liking since he was paid $30,000 whereas on *Trail of the Vigilantes*, made just months earlier, he had earned $20,000.[39] Lucille Ball, then a rising star at RKO, was added to the radio stars in the cast.

The plot had Bergen, after the close of his radio season, leaving on vacation in his private plane, accompanied by Charlie McCarthy. When Bergen gets lost and the plane runs low on fuel, he is forced to land in Wistful Vista, the home town of Fibber McGee and Molly, thus intertwining him with another radio world. Although references are made to Bergen being a ventriloquist, Charlie McCarthy is treated as an independent if adolescent character who talks without Bergen around.

Fibber McGee is seen as something of an eccentric, a part-time inventor with big dreams, while Molly helps to fix his feet to the ground. He is also a personification of the little guy. In the film's sub–Capraesque plot, he is trying to keep the town's airstrip from being sold to the local real estate developer so that it may instead be bought by Horton Aircraft. Horton is looking for a locale to build a new factory that will provide many jobs to the community.

Look Who's Laughing has moments of charm or amusement. When the citizens of Wistful Vista come to appeal to Bergen to do his ventriloquist act, he explains that Charlie McCarthy has already retired for the night. When Bergen sees that a little girl has a headless doll, he draws a face on his hand and then uses that hand as its head for his verbal exchanges with the doll. McGee has rewired his house but with such wacky results that his refrigerator opens when the doorbell rings. He has also invented a dishwasher that shoots the dishes out like a geyser. As Molly, Marian Jordan is given a chance to show her mimicry by supplying the voice to a young girl on the phone who wants to date Charlie McCarthy.

These intermittent pleasures are modest. There is also a tedious romantic subplot in which Bergen must be prodded to recognize that he is in love with his assistant (Ball). Despite Dwan's attempts to keep things moving, *Look Who's Laughing* is a long 78 minutes. The film is probably best enjoyed by fans of the radio performers and those willing to soak up the small town atmosphere without expecting much in the way of comic payoff.

It may have been because of those many radio fans that *Look Who's Laughing* proved to be one of RKO's most profitable films of 1941. RKO's new president Charles Koerner became a strong believer in movies with radio personalities and another Bergen–McGee film, *Here We Go Again*, with Dwan once more at the helm, was readied for the next year.

Given that these films were visualizations of radio comedy series, they have the look of prehistoric sitcoms. Ironically, one of the stars of *Look Who's Laughing*, Lucille Ball, was to become the greatest star of TV situation comedies. In *Here We Go Again,* there was another icon of the sitcom future, Gale Gordon, who would appear in one of the early TV hits, *Our Miss Brooks*, followed by various incarnations of Ball's comedy shows. In *Here We Go Again*, Gordon plays Otis Cadwalader, an old flame of Molly McGee.

There is less of a fixed plot in *Here We Go Again* than in the previous film. The story rambles from the McGees celebrating their twentieth anniversary to their checking in at an upscale hotel beyond their means to Cadwalader using McGee to get Bergen to invest in a formula substitute for gasoline.

While the plot meanders, Bergen's romance with singer Ginny Simms permits the entrance of some songs including a tune warbled by Charlie McCarthy, "Delicious Delirium." The sequel also has more of a surreal feel to it as Charlie can now be actually seen moving around in long shot. Charlie's mobility is provided courtesy of the uncredited Jerry Maren, who played one of the Munchkins in MGM's *The Wizard of Oz* and here doubles for Charlie. The flamboyantly extroverted McCarthy, usually dressed in tails, top hat and monocle, always seemed a contrast to the more reserved Bergen. Seeing this alter ego now running about is a bit disconcerting, as if providing a preview of *Dead of Night* with its demonically rebellious dummy. An addition to this film is Bergen's other dummy creation, Mortimer Snerd, a moronic bumpkin, intended as a contrast to Charlie's urbane sophistication.

The film ends with a chase on a dangerous mountain road. Just when it seems everyone is safe, an explosion appears to engulf nearly all of the principals. In this ghoulish finale, Charlie is seen asking, "Wow! Anybody want to adopt an orphan?"

When RKO's *Journey Into Fear*, co-written by Orson Welles and featuring him as a supporting player, was judged too confusing by the critics, the studio pulled it and replaced it with *Here We Go Again*, which was a "box-office natural."[40] *Here We Go Again* was hardly more coherent but at least the characters were familiar. (Dwan said he checked out the various sets on the lot and decided to use Welles' sets for *The Magnificent Ambersons* in *Here We Go Again*.)

Between these two films, Dwan shot the 1942 *Friendly Enemies*. Dwan had gone to work for independent producer Edward Small. As Dwan recalled, they were originally supposed to start with an adaptation of the play *Up in Mabel's Room* but Small found a problem in "clearing it properly."[41] Since he already had Dwan and others under contract,

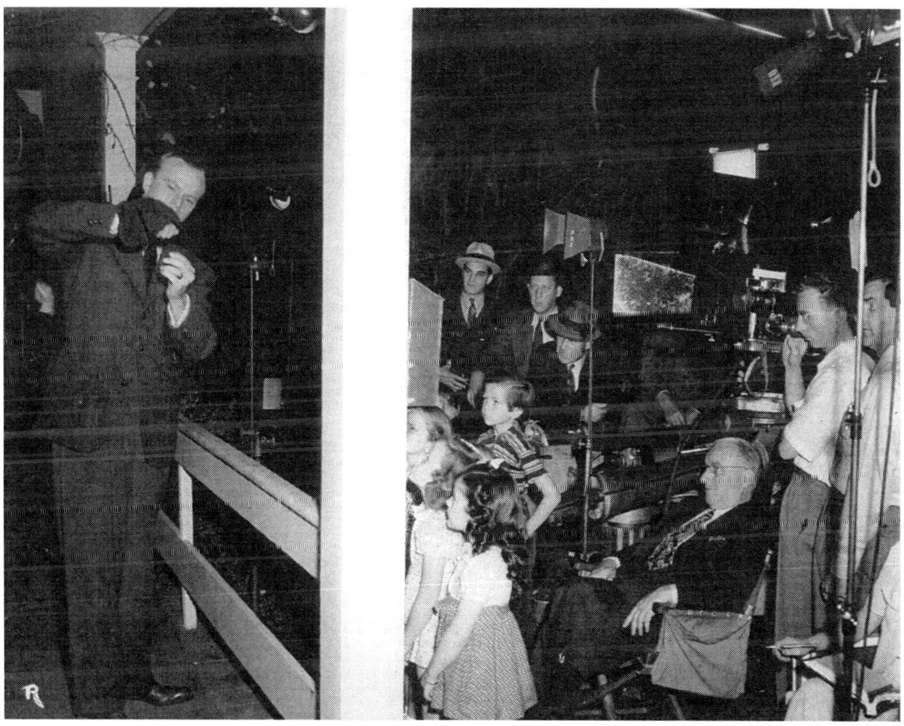

In a charming scene from *Look Who's Laughing* (1941), Edgar Bergen uses his hand to provide the head to a little girl's doll while Dwan watches from his chair with keen interest, as do a gathering of spectators, including members of the film crew.

Small was bound to pay them for their time even for doing nothing. Dwan says that he then asked Small what other material he had available. Among those projects was a play called *Friendly Enemies.* Dwan read it and said he quickly determined that it could be adjusted to a film script without a major rewrite and claims he was ready to start production in a week. "The following Monday we started to shoot *Friendly Enemies* with a good script and with a good cast on a set inherited from Paramount. And we made it in about nine days."[42]

Records from the Edward Small collection at USC indicate that *Friendly Enemies* was indeed put together quickly, though not quite as rapidly as in Dwan's account. The project was cleared by the censors on January 15 and a shooting script was completed by February 2 (a Monday). Production began just three days later while the script was being continuously revised on February 10, 12, 16, 17, 18 and 25. The rights to the play, which were purchased for $22,000, were cleared on February 26 while the film was being shot. The film was in production for twenty-one (not nine) days but this was still three days ahead of schedule.[43]

Dwan also said that he derived his satisfaction from the "challenge" of making the film. This kind of by-the-seat-of-your-pants filmmaking may have reminded him of the free-wheeling methods of the silent days. And it also gave him a level of control since no one would want to hamper a production shooting on such a tight schedule. His ability to put together projects so quickly and cheaply, no doubt kept Dwan highly employable. And it could make it easier for him to finance projects of his choice.

For *Friendly Enemies,* Nancy Kelly was loaned out from Fox while James Craig was borrowed from RKO. Although Dwan added some exteriors to the film, he did not undermine the theatricality of the source. He maintained a strong sense of spatial unity. Rather than cutting, he would show characters continuing their conversation as they walked from one building to the next.

The film's style may have reflected the need for economy and possibly the influence of Orson Welles. For the more serious parts of the film, depth of field shots provide long, dramatic entrances for characters from the distant background. In Dwan's long shots, the central character Karl Pfeiffer is sometimes surrounded by large empty spaces emphasizing the protagonist's isolation from his family. The latter was not necessarily a Wellesian influence. Dwan used such compositions with the large sets of *Robin Hood.*

Friendly Enemies was a World War I era play by Samuel Shipman and Aaron Hoffman that, while revived because of parallel events in World War II, must have seemed old-fashioned even in 1942. Seen today, it is on a number of levels a historical curiosity.

Film *and* play concern the patriarchs of two well-to-do German-American families, both of whom emigrated from the old country and built their fortunes here. One, Heinrich Block (Charlie Ruggles), is fully assimilated, while the other, Karl Pfeiffer (Charles Winninger), remains loyal to his old country and feels that U.S. intervention on behalf of the Allies is based on lies. The two, of course, are old feuding friends.

The play dates back to the days when ethnic humor and funny accents were surefire laugh-getters in vaudeville. The burlesque accents are jarring for a film, even a comic one, with such serious concerns. (There was a 1925 silent film version that starred the comedy team of Joe Weber and Lew Fields.)

The pivotal plot crisis lurking under the drawing room comedy is that Pfeiffer's son William (Craig), who is engaged to Block's daughter (Kelly), has enlisted in the U.S. Army and virtually all of the other characters are searching for a way to

James Craig, Nancy Kelly, Charles Winninger, Ilka Gruning and Charlie Ruggles in the melting-pot comedy-drama *Friendly Enemies* (1942).

break the news to Karl. Unlike the lost fathers in Dwan's films, it is the one who is present and conspicuous who has been unable to influence his son.

The other major plot thread is that Karl has contributed money to a group which he has been told will help counter lies about Germany, but which is in reality a fifth column organization.

These plotlines will converge when the transport conveying his son's division is bombed by the saboteurs. In a rather unbelievable plot revelation, the German front man Anton Miller (Otto Kruger) actually phones Karl to tell him what his money has really been used for. The reason for this lapse in verisimilitude is pure theatricality so that Karl gets this shocking news in front of his friend Heinrich and his daughter.

The moment of truth is when Karl finds there is no better word to describe the Kaiser and his generals as "Huns." After that, he can proclaim himself a "real American." The fact that his full assimilation is signaled when he starts to use a slur to describe his former countrymen is startling but a reflection of the time when the play was written. In 1942, the *New York Times* reviewer found the use of the term "an irrelevant and childish epithet in this year of crisis."[44]

The film moves from comedy to near tragedy and then to comic melodrama as Bill is found safe and sound. For the final act, Karl and Heinrich trap the head of the saboteur ring. Though the emotive mechanics are obvious, the old-time machinery is well operated by Dwan.

The character of Karl Pfeiffer, as played by Winninger, is most affecting and comes closest to transcending the play's dated melodrama. Winninger had been originally cast as Block but was then shifted to portraying his rival. Like his character, Winninger's real first name was also Karl, adding a Pirandellian layer of reality as Block keeps trying to change his name to Charlie. Short and feisty but with a chubby, cherubic face, Winninger is touchingly pathetic, at first in comic befuddlement and then in bereavement as the pains of international and family tragedy overtake him. Karl's anguish at separating himself from his roots might even be more understandable today than it was in 1942. While Pfeiffer is misguided, he is also the character who most deeply yearns for peace. It can also be more easily acknowledged today that some of what was said about Germany during World War I was indeed propaganda rather than truth.

Friendly Enemies opens with the credits set over a drawing of the Statue of Liberty. It ends with a montage of newsreel clips showing the conclusion of World War I intercut with shots of the characters, including William, returning from the war safely. The final shot, which was not indicated in the shooting script, is that of the American flag. But this is arguably more than a morale-boosting, flag-waving finale with the country again at war. The American flag has been revealed to be Karl Pfeiffer's destiny, finally reached long after his immigrant beginnings. The importance of this image from the director of the future *Sands of Iwo Jima* and *Silver Lode* should not be underestimated. (The Canadian-born Dwan also had a long journey towards citizenship. His naturalization occurred just three years earlier when he became a U.S. citizen in November 1939 at the age of 54.)

Despite being derided by critics for being outdated, according to Small, *Friendly Enemies* turned a profit.

Dwan still had one more film to make with radio stars as part of his arrangement with MCA and RKO. Originally, Edgar Bergen was again to star, this time matched up with bandleader and comedian Kay Kyser. But Bergen decided to bow out to devote more time to his radio show and camp appearances, so the picture was basically a Kay Kyser movie. (Before the film was made, Kyser already had made a commitment to appear before an army camp and this appearance was incorporated into the film.) For support, Kyser would have Joan Davis and Mischa Auer. The movie was also to feature a new young star, Marcy McGuire, touted as RKO's "Mickey Rooney."

For this film, eventually to be called *Around the World*, Dwan was paid a flat rate of $50,000, a nice improvement on the $30,000 he had been paid for his first RKO picture, *Look Who's Laughing*.

By the end of 1942, when *Around the World* was being planned, America had been at war for over a year. It was decided that the story would focus on Kyser's efforts to entertain Allied forces all over the globe, further popularizing the concept of the United Nations. The film had a written prologue that began with the words, "To every battle front where men and women of the United Nations fight — civilians from all walks of life are contributing their honest efforts to the struggle. Among these, the brightest stars of Hollywood and Broadway do their bit — we welcome you to come along on this tour of the global conflict...." There are recurring stock shots of a plane in mid-air while titles identify what countries the group is going to. But it is all too clear today, and perhaps even then, that the cast almost never leaves the RKO back lot. (Some footage was shot at Lone Pine.)

Most of the cast members play themselves as the entertainers on tour. The main plot element is the appearance of an aspiring starlet, teenager Marcy McGuire (using her real name), who wants to hitch up with Kyser's gang so she can join her father who is in the military in Washington, D.C. Kyser declines to take her on but Marcy circumvents this by hiding in a crate and stowing aboard a plane.

This ploy is only a part of the hokey humor of the film, which employs lots of puns and other bits of corny material. Leaving Australia at the beginning of the film, Kyser suggests that they cross raccoons with kangaroos so they can get fur coats with pockets. The script was largely written by Ralph Spence, the author of the play *The Gorilla*. The *Variety* reviewer observed, "Spence digs deep into his memory for numerous aged dialog cracks."[45] Within the first half hour, the film is becoming wearisome although there will be moments of mildly inspired comedy such as a scene where Auer fights a duel using a sword which Kyser has hooked up to emit electricity. Several of Jimmy McHugh's less memorable songs are sung by McGuire, Harry Babbitt, and Georgia Carroll (who in real life later married Kyser). The high spirits of the performers inject some life into the goofy novelty songs "A Moke from Shamokin'," "He's Got a Secret Weapon" and "They Just Chopped Down the Old Apple Tree."

McGuire, who was seventeen years old at the time, recalls that working under Dwan was very stressful. She remembers that he was "not unkind" and perhaps didn't know the kind of pressure he was putting on her.

The film continues along its flighty way until the group encamps in Liberia. Then Marcy is notified that an American general (Robert Armstrong) wishes to see her. She is pleased to learn that her father was able to leave Washington and take a more active part in the war effort. What she and the audience are not prepared to learn is that her father was killed when his transport was sunk by the Japanese.

This revelation is contrary to the entire silly mood of the film and comes across as even a greater shock than the sudden murder of Doc Halliday in *Frontier Marshal.* Marcy has flown from Australia to Asia to Africa and now has learned that she will never reach her father. There were other films from that era with bigger names about stars entertaining the troops such as *Star Spangled Rhythm* and *Stage Door Canteen.* But neither of them had this kind of kick-in-the teeth ending with its revelation of another lost father.

Throughout the film there are scenes where the Kyser band starts to play and perform "Great News Is in the Making" but for different reasons, little more than a few bars are heard in the film. Now having heard the tragic news of her father's death, Marcy is supposed to sing this piece.[46]

She at first rebels against performing, despite the pleas of Kyser and Davis that the show must go on. Seen running away in a long tracking shot, Marcy bumps into the general, who asks her how tough she is. That may not impress her but being stopped there permits her to hear Kyser's introduction of "Great News Is in the Making." Kyser refers to it as a "song of hope and confidence; a song of gratitude and praise and blessings to the men and women of the United Nations around the world." Marcy runs back to perform the song.

McGuire recalled laughingly, but with some frustration, that Dwan "made me laugh when I was supposed to cry and made me cry when I was supposed to laugh." When singing "Great News Is in the Making," "that's when I was crying when I was singing and he was making me laugh and I was hiding behind the scenery to keep the mood that I was crying."[47]

Dwan's methods understandably kept McGuire off balance. But perhaps he was trying to maintain a balance in directing the young trouper, making sure she kept serious during the comedy and didn't take the lachrymose moments too far. (McGuire also pointed out that at least part of the reason that Dwan disrupted her crying scene was that he was laughing so hard at some of Joan Davis' antics.)

In an earlier draft of the script, after the performance of this song, the scene shifted to Brazil and a fast, happy musical number. And there would also be a romantic distraction for Marcy.[48] Since Dwan was the producer as well as director of *Around the World,* he was most likely responsible for having this more pacifying scene cut from the final script.

Around the World ends with the "Great News Is in the Making" number. Dwan does not push the tragic development for its tearjerker potential. It is as if after all the frivolity, he was reminding the audience that progress in winning the war was not going to be made without great sacrifices. *Around the World* was released in November 1943. The following years of 1944 and 1945 would bear the United States' highest casualty totals in the war. *Around the World* indulged in some of the vintage silliness of 1940s comedy but it did not flinch from telling the truth.

The Small Farces

Dwan said that in 1943 he made his own contributions to the war effort working in the U.S. Armed Services photographic division, which organized and trained units throughout the country to cover the war.[49]

Marcy McGuire (center) gets consolation from Kay Kyser and Joan Davis after receiving devastating news in *Around the World* (1943). As of this printing, Ms. McGuire is still writing songs (courtesy Marcy McGuire).

The comedies that Dwan had made from 1939 to 1943 all had a hybrid quality. They were either bona fide comedy-dramas (like *Young People* and *Friendly Enemies*), less orthodox mixtures of comedy and drama (*Sailor's Lady*, *Around the World*), mixtures of genres such as *The Gorilla* (comedy-horror) and *The Three Musketeers* (swashbuckler–musical comedy), mixtures of sub-genres (*Rise and Shine*), or mixtures of media (*Look Who's Laughing*, *Here We Go Again*).

There was no such ambivalence in the four films Dwan made for producer Edward Small that were released in 1944 and 1945. These were all out-and-out farces. Dwan later commented, "My main reason for doing all those farces was because I knew they'd be seen by a lot of kids at war and in army camps, and they'd cheer them up. That whole series was made with them in mind. I didn't give a damn what the people who bought tickets saw or liked. I was thinking about those kids."[50] Dwan's statement also suggests that he and Small had come to an agreement that this was the kind of entertainment wartime audiences would be eager to see.

Although Small had served as a staff producer for the majors, most of his work was in independent production since 1932 when he founded Reliance Pictures (along with Joseph Schenck and Harry Goetz) which released through United Artists. In 1938, he re-formed his operations to found Edward Small Productions and again released through UA. Although by necessity he had to be economical, Small was resourceful enough to provide respectable product that could compete with the majors.

Abroad with Two Yanks (1944) with its two feuding Marine buddies sounds like a borrowing from Raoul Walsh's series of Quirt and Flagg movies that started with *What Price Glory*; the similarity was duly noted in the *New York Times* review.[51] But *Abroad with Two Yanks* was far from ready-made when production began. Dwan told Bogdanovich that a lot of the film was off-the-cuff: "You'd be surprised how little script we had."[52]

Dwan's account is corroborated by Small in his unpublished autobiography. Dennis O'Keefe was to have one of the two lead roles and Small borrowed William Bendix from Hal Roach to play his Marine rival. According to Small, the loan-out deal for Bendix had a strict cutoff after the stipulated weeks. Small wasted no time setting a start date for the film, which meant that the entire cast and crew would go on salary that day. But Small ruefully noted, "There was a slight problem. I didn't have a shooting script."[53]

Small had also borrowed Lewis Seiler from Fox to direct the film but Seiler was not happy with the situation and Small sent him back to Fox. Small then turned to his "old friend, Allan Dwan," whom he knew was experienced in handling every kind of filmmaking problem. Small noted, "Allan also had a good mechanical mind, which was going to be handy in bolting together all the bits and pieces of a script that wasn't yet born."[54] Small hired the comedy writing team of Charlie Rogers and Wilkie Mahoney "to do the shooting continuity as fast as we could manage." According to available records, Small employed a total of thirteen writers to adapt the story by Fred Guiol.[55]

Small's problems were compounded by the discovery that there was no material to construct sets. Small had an agreement to use the RKO-Pathe lot and a set was found that could be converted into a living room. So a scene had to be written taking place in the living room and this was the only scene ready the day shooting began. Small recalled, "Allan Dwan and I made a pact. Neither of us would let the actors or crew know what was happening, for they would have panicked along with us if they found out what was going on behind the scenes."[56] Making matters still worse, Small had developed abscesses in both of his ears and the infection made him temporarily deaf.

Small said he made an arrangement with Dwan that the new scenes for each day's shooting would be delivered by 2 P.M. Dwan remembered, "Small had writers sitting with him while I was shooting. And around two or three in the afternoon he'd send down the pages that were supposed to have been shot that morning, but I'd already shot what I wanted to shoot and we'd just file the script away. So I was always off-the-cuff and he was about a day behind me with the script all the way through."[57]

Small does not mention improvisations or writing by Dwan. He notes, "Allan marveled that in the writing the characterizations of O'Keefe and Bendix always correctly motivated their comedy situations."[58] The plot of *Abroad with Two Yanks* follows a straight line of the two characters engaged in a battle of one-upsmanship in attracting the attentions of a certain young lady, making both rapid writing and improvisation easier to maneuver.

Small recalled that despite all the problems, the picture was filmed so precisely that only 250 feet had to be cut from the total footage shot. Small wrote, "In the morning [while waiting for that day's script], Allan rehearsed and faked a lot of shots we didn't need, just to keep up the pretense of activity."[59] If Small's statement about the "250 feet" is correct, most of what Dwan shot must have gone into the film, with or without the help of Small's writers.

As Small described the two characters, they were "a couple of football players, friendly rivals, who wound up in the army together. One character was sharp and aggressive, a live-by-his-wits type. His pal was the opposite — a slow thinker, sometimes dumb, but always likable."[60]

O'Keefe played Jeff Reardon, the sharpie, and the rotund Bendix was selected for the other character, Biff Koraski. Koraski could have been played like Jack Oakie's "Boley" Bolenciewicz, a likable dimwit and, as the name would suggest, an ethnic stereotype. But Biff is a little bit out of that mold and shows a penchant for poetry. Hearing him recite, Jeff cracks, "That's what happens when a college football player goes to his classes."

Like *Around the World*, *Abroad with Two Yanks* opens in Australia with the Marines (not the army as Small wrote) landing fresh from recent campaigns against the Japanese. Biff and Jeff find themselves in competition for the attentions of an Australian lady, Joyce Stuart (played by American actress Helen Walker, whose accent is explained by her education in the U.S.).

While the action is farcical, Dwan and the scriptwriters recognized that at least one of the characters must have some grounding in reality. Biff, the football player with the poetic aspirations, may have appealed to Dwan but he could have identified with the quick resourcefulness of both characters. It is perhaps fitting that the sharpie and handsome Lothario type, Jeff, is more one-dimensional and for a time is made to feign madness. Biff, however, is given an opportunity to talk about his working class origins and how his father worked in a coal mine. In long continuous tracking shots, reminiscent of Sturges in *The Miracle of Morgan's Creek*, Koraski recites poetry and then bares his heart in a proposal to his intended love, Joyce, only to learn that she finds his proposal "terribly flattering." (While the Sturges tracking shots showed much of the small town setting, Dwan by necessity had to have his actors circling the one big set.)

In the open warfare between Marine buddies in *Abroad with Two Yanks* (1944), William Bendix restrains Dennis O'Keefe from pursuing his female objective by imprisoning him in a big bird cage (while freeing the bird).

Having worked hard to establish Biff's feelings, Dwan then drops them and any pretense of sentiment. It is now open war between Biff and Jeff although Biff is fighting not for himself but on behalf of Joyce's longtime Australian admirer Cyril (John Loder). The action becomes increasingly cartoonish and with Dwan's pacing takes on a manic energy. The scene where Biff locks an unconscious Jeff in a giant bird cage (while freeing the bird) to restrain him from further romantic adventures as Biff sings "He's Only a Bird in a Gilded Cage" might be said to anticipate Frank Tashlin.

In the second half of the film, Dwan makes some gibes at the masculine ethos of the Marines when Biff tries to show Cyril how to dance more intimately with his partner. Later, Biff and Jeff don women's clothing to participate in a "Marines Follies" show but both go AWOL, still in drag, to continue the pursuit of Joyce. Joyce is so used to Jeff's erratic behavior that she is not flustered at seeing him in female attire although after kissing her, she does complain that he's getting his lipstick all over her face.

A tolerance for very broad comedy is necessary to appreciate the final reels of *Abroad with Two Yanks*. It should also be conceded that these sequences are executed with gusto and it can be difficult to resist the comic cruelty of the horrified looks of women watching one "lady" (Biff) applying a football tackle to a supposedly pregnant woman (Jeff). The film proved a hit with the audiences of the day.

Small and Dwan had first tried to film *Up in Mabel's Room* in 1942 when it was scratched in favor of *Friendly Enemies*. In January 1942, Dwan, Small and the two writers met with the censors, who considered the material "very questionable." The censors reported, "Mr. Small seemed impressed with the seriousness of the problem...."[61] Small was apparently "impressed" enough to realize that the film would not get approved by the censors.

Some time later, the censors relented when they became convinced that the plot would not live up to the suggestiveness of the title. Small then hired Ray McCarey, the younger brother of the more celebrated director Leo, to direct the film. But just as the picture was about to go into production in October 1943, Small fired McCarey and replaced him with Dwan. A *Hollywood Reporter* story cited the dismissal "as a result of differences of opinion on the film's casting and storyline."[62]

Over the next few weeks with Dwan at the helm, the script underwent a complete rewrite. Before the film was ready for production, one of the announced stars, Joan Bennett, exited the project. There were some Dwan veterans in the eventual cast including O'Keefe, Marjorie Reynolds, Mischa Auer, Lee Bowman, Charlotte Greenwood, and Binnie Barnes. Production began on November 24 but was suspended for three days in December when Auer suffered a serious illness that required his hospitalization. Auer returned on December 30 to complete his role.

While the censors had permitted the project to be filmed, they were still watching suspiciously. In a letter from Joseph Breen, it was "suggested" that the film "omit the one element of Alicia thinking that Garry is the father of an illegitimate child."[63] The filmmakers were able to convince Breen to leave the gag in but Breen continued to ask for changes during filming as late as December 1.

Released in April 1944, *Up in Mabel's Room* proved a hit at the box office, accruing $1,753,301 in rentals. After deductions were made for production and distribution expenses, Small's company had a net profit of $647,969.20.[64] Small then wanted to adapt another play, *Getting Gertie's Garter*, co-written by *Mabel's Room* author Wilson Collison, with a plot so similar it verged on a remake.

Small had first tried to obtain the rights to *Getting Gertie's Garter* even before *Mabel* was filmed. True to form, the Hays Office was dubious of a picture with a title of that nature. A May 1942 inter-office memo in Small's company indicated that the Hays Office had rejected the title and that the deal to acquire the rights to *Getting Gertie's Garter* would probably not go through. As late as January 1945, the censors remained adamant that the title not be registered. But Small was now confident that he would prevail, noting that they "had the same situation on *Up in Mabel's Room*, as they had the idea that we were going to make the wrong kind of picture. When they learned that we intended making a picture acceptable in every way from the standpoint of the code, they were willing to register the title."[65]

Small purchased the rights to *Getting Gertie's Garter* on March 28, 1945. Breen approved of the shooting script on May 11, but included his usual list of "minor items" that required correcting.[66] The issue of the title remained unresolved until June 22, when the film was already in production, and Will Hays personally approved of the title. But in his letter, Hays cautioned "that extreme care will be exercised in the advertising and exploitation in connection with the title and the picture."[67]

O'Keefe plays the harried husband in both films while Binnie Barnes was the only other holdover from *Mabel*. Although nine writers were paid for toiling on the script of *Getting Gertie's Garter*, only three contributed enough to be credited, including Dwan, who received top credit. (It's also likely that Dwan had some input on the rewriting of *Up in Mabel's Room*.)

Voyeurism, which had been lightly touched upon in *Abroad with Two Yanks*, was a major preoccupation in *Up in Mabel's Room* and *Getting Gertie's Garter*. Based on separate old plays, these two films recount very similar plots of a married man trying to retrieve an incriminating piece of intimate apparel from an old flame. In both films, his frantic obsession spreads like a virus to other couples who observe him. A series of incidents and misunderstandings set off additional jealousies and suspicions. The faith and trust of couples in each other becomes sorely tested in the process as things quickly snowball.

Unlike the plays which took place entirely in one locale, each of the films is divided in two sections, a prologue set in an urban workplace and home and the main action which takes place on a country estate that includes a two-story house with enough second floor rooms to accommodate numerous guests. While this conforms to the kind of split location structure Dwan sometimes favored, it was also used in romantic comedies of the 1930s, for example *Bringing Up Baby*. When the action switches from the city to the country, it is as if we are transferred to a magic forest or house of illusions, where all kinds of confusion must be spread before the truth can be recognized.[68]

Both films are marked by frenetic action with characters sneaking in and out of bedrooms and even in and out of windows. Dwan is able to enhance the bustle and naughtiness of the plays by taking his camera under beds and on window ledges.

Up in Mabel's Room is the funnier and warmer of the two

The married couple Dennis O'Keefe and Marjorie Reynolds start off the day with each grabbing the wrong pair of shoes. It's just the first of many mix-ups in *Up in Mabel's Room* (1944).

films but *Getting Gertie's Garter*, which also gets its share of laughs, is edgier.[69] The distinctions between the two films include differences in visual design, characterizations and especially in casting. These factors are particularly notable in the dream sequences inserted into each film. In *Mabel's Room*, the protagonist's former girlfriend can be seen in a department store window displaying the underwear her beau gave her with his name inscribed. O'Keefe is walking by with his wife when they notice a crowd around the window and the item on display. O'Keefe's wife is mortified and the husband's exposure is magnified by the fact that he's seen wearing no pants.

In this farce, O'Keefe's wife is played by Marjorie Reynolds, whose character is depicted as sweet but tied to her mother's apron strings. By contrast, in both look and characterization, Sheila Ryan as O'Keefe's wife in *Gertie* is made of sterner stuff. The dream in *Gertie* is darker and weirder, almost fetishistic. O'Keefe is on trial. His wife appears as a threatening giantess who is Justice personified, holding the scales on which O'Keefe sits. O'Keefe's "tell-tale organ," his right ear, which operates as a kind of polygraph (it wiggles when he lies), assumes a titanic proportion as it betrays him. At the end of the dream, O'Keefe is found guilty and is strangled by his erstwhile avuncular lab assistant (Don Beddoe).

O'Keefe's one-time paramour in *Gertie* is played by Marie "The Body" McDonald. (The publicity moniker failed to catapult her career). Unlike the serene Gail Patrick as the eponymous Mabel, McDonald's status is not secure and she could be seriously compromised if the truth is not properly revealed. Her boyfriend is played by stalwart B actor Barry Sullivan who, while appearing quite amiable, clearly has the potential to be more menacing than the mild-mannered Lee Bowman, who was Mabel's fiancé. Even among the servant characters, where Auer was a merry mercenary always upping the price for his underwear raids, J. Carrol Naish is more of a sinister blackmailer. *Gertie's Garter* also had no benevolent unattached character like Charlotte Greenwood's Martha in *Mabel's Room* who would try to reconcile some of the crises.

Dwan was more apt to show characters framed in windows in *Gertie's Garter*; even in interior shots, characters who are co-conspirators in the film's dizzy alliances are grouped in the foreground away from the other characters. There is more spying than hiding in *Gertie's Garter* until a climactic farcical setpiece where everyone seems to be hiding or searching through a barn. In the aftermath in the house, the characters try to maintain dignity and moral superiority, while strands of hay can be seen sticking to their hair and clothes.

In *Mabel's Room*, Dwan and his colleagues adhered to the censors' dictum that the husband's pre-nuptial dalliance would be shown as innocuous. But in the romantic final scene in *Gertie's Garter*, when O'Keefe assures his wife he's never kissed Gertie "like that," his right ear starts to wiggle.

When a preview audience was queried as to whether the action in *Gertie* was clear, one respondent commented, "No, but that's okay." Another also responding negatively but added, "The confusion made the fun."[70]

The best known of Dwan's farces with Small is the 1945 *Brewster's Millions*, which is based on the 1902 novel by George Barr McCutcheon and the 1906 play by Winchell Smith and Byron Ongley. The story concerns a young man who inherits a million dollars only to learn about a provision in the will that stipulates that he will get *seven* million if he spends all that he has thus far inherited in one year. This old theatrical war-horse, which had also been filmed several times previously, taps into American fears (and fondness) of reckless spending and investment.

The play's relevance for audiences may have diminished in recent years and even the 1985 version with Richard Pryor and John Candy (in which the protagonist has to spend $30 million) now seems outdated. To match current standards of financial wealth, the story might have to be re-titled *Brewster's Billions*. Reality may have even outstripped fiction in recent corporate shenanigans where executives seem to have followed the screwy

Marie "The Body" McDonald, Barry Sullivan, Dennis O'Keefe and Jerome Cowan are just some of the players ensnared in the confusions and misunderstandings in *Getting Gertie's Garter* (1945).

logic of the play by earning millions while driving their companies into the ground.

All this is worth noting as a way of pointing out that besides the considerable skill of Dwan and his collaborators, *Brewster's Millions* is given an added poignancy and edge by its 1944 setting as Americans, who had just endured a long depression and the spending restrictions of wartime, were on the eve of the greatest and longest national economic boom. Particularly resonant is the recurrent use of the Depression era song "We're in the Money," which changes meaning as Brewster gets deeper into the nightmare of financial entanglements.

In *Brewster's Millions*, Montague Brewster (O'Keefe again) is an Army veteran recently discharged after having been wounded in combat. In this version, by the terms of his uncle's will, to get seven million dollars, Monty must spend the one million in a mere two months, from August until his 30th birthday on October 13. The will also has very specific clauses making his task harder; for instance, the amount he can give away is limited and he must not accrue any assets.

Brewster's Millions ostensibly differs from the other two Small farces based on stage plays in that its anxieties center on money rather than sex. However, there is also a provision that forbids Monty from marrying during this two-month period. Because of his military service, Monty has been waiting for two years to marry his sweetheart Peggy. Given the mores and censorship of the period, this condition adds considerable sexual and romantic tension.

Monty must also swear not to reveal the provisions of the will to anyone. So as with the other two farces, the protagonist is restrained from telling anyone the truth. Much of the comedy must thus emanate from a very repressed and frustrated hero.

What Donald Phelps has said about all the stage-to-film Small comedies is especially true of *Brewster's Millions*: "Dwan reduced the conventions of second-rate stage humor to pure speed: these comedies are fantasies of speed and maneuver...."[71] In his perceptive essay on Dwan, Kent Jones contrasts the marathon pace of *Brewster's Millions* with the other films by noting *Brewster's Millions* is "a straight line all the way, a race against the clock movie...."[72] This is true to the extent that *Brewster's* has a clear starting point and finishing line. But even in the more linear financial world of Dwan's 1945 film, the protagonist must cope with some wild zigzags to get to his goal. Also, since Monty's girlfriend and war buddies become part of his new "finance corporation," they try to push the company in one direction (profit) while Brewster pursues complete ruin. This all plays a part in the film's distinct rhythm.

As head of the corporation, Monty initially feels he can keep everything under control, trying to conceal his delight that with 54 days to go he has already squandered one-third of his million. The camera occasionally catches Brewster smiling at his exasperated friends, as if he feels he is playing a prank on them. But about midway through the film, things become unhinged for Monty with three financial scenarios going amok in one scene. Brewster tries to placate the worried Col. Drew about his apparently failing bank by giving him a deposit of $250,000. (This part of the scene plays like a capsulized parody of *American Madness*.) At the same time, Monty is trying furiously to reach the Lumber & Fuel Company by phone when he learns that the once diving stock has reversed course and is now earning him thousands. The still very new medium of television is brought into the scene so Brewster will see the horse he bought to lose, instead ride to victory at the race at Belmont. The flip side of Brewster's surreptitious smiles is visualized when we see his three chums in the foreground cheering on Monty's horse while behind them, Brewster is frantically gesturing for the horse to slow down. Dwan orchestrates all these dramas like a three-ring circus playing in one large office. By the time it's over, the bank has been saved and with these other "reversals," Brewster has regained all the money he's lost and made an unwelcome $25,000 profit.

The next scene has Monty locking himself in his room and features an animated sequence where the "Man in the Moon" on his notepad begins to address him. With the Man in the Moon mouthing some bad puns, the scene is less imaginative and amusing than the dream sequences in *Mabel's Room* and *Gertie's Garter* but it serves a stronger dramatic purpose.

As Brewster, Dennis O'Keefe learns it's far more difficult than he thought to get rid of one million dollars in *Brewster's Millions* (1945). Business partner Herbert Rudley shows him the latest ticker tape.

Through his "conversation" with the Man in the Moon, the audience grasps the full sense of horror and anxiety that has begun to overcome Brewster in realizing the difficulties in blowing a million dollars. Also, since his friends spy on him through a keyhole, they begin to have their first suspicions about his sanity.

From here on, the race to the finish intensifies at a mounting tempo. Brewster backs a musical "turkey"; Dwan said he resisted pressure to include a number from the show in the film because it would upset the pace he had set for the picture.[73]

Dwan brings the proceedings to a crescendo at the climax including the last-minute hitch provided in the play. Phelps writes that this kind of comedy is "not so much funny as exhilarating; the laughter is that of excitement and relief, paired as at a hockey game or horse race."[74]

Despite the film's relentless pace and O'Keefe's broad clowning, the film maintains its warmth and humanity thanks to excellent use of secondary players such as Auer, Joe Sawyer, Herbert Rudley, June Havoc and most prominently, Eddie "Rochester" Anderson. In April 1945, the Memphis Board of Motion Picture Censors banned showings of *Brewster's Millions* because Anderson's character had "too familiar a way about him" and that the film presented "too much social equality and racial mixture." Viewing the film today, the treatment accorded Anderson in the film seems a little short of the standards described. But enough of the charm and vibrancy of Anderson's personality comes through to make the censors' discomfort understandable.[75]

Dennis O'Keefe tries to explain his predicament to Nana Bryant while Eddie "Rochester" Anderson looks on in *Brewster's Millions* (1945).

Rendezvous with Annie

Dwan's next film, the 1946 *Rendezvous with Annie* was made at Republic Studios but because it shares affinities with the comedies just mentioned, it is covered here rather in the chapter on Dwan's Republic years.

While it shares the wartime setting of some of the earlier films and has a plot as ingenious as *Brewster's*, there are also distinct differences here. *Rendezvous with Annie* is ten minutes longer than *Brewster's* and speed is less of a factor (despite its own plot deadline) in this intricate narrative that borders on the Kafkaesque. It is like the Small films, pure comedy rather than a hybrid, but there are layers of disturbing feelings as well as some stylistic eccentricities for a comedy. It is as if after seven years of experimentation, Dwan found a complete integration of substance with comedy.

The story involves a London-based Army clerk who uses a three-day pass to go AWOL by flying back to the U.S. for a brief sojourn with his wife in New Jersey, courtesy of a couple of Air Force pals on a quick mission to the U.S. In the process, he obviously does all he can to keep his visit secret. But his excursion gets him into far more trouble than he ever imagined.

Rendezvous with Annie is the best of Dwan's 1940s comedies although it has been rarely screened in recent decades. Despite its comic shenanigans, it strongly conveys the intensity of its protagonist's feelings to return to his wife and home, feelings that audiences must have keenly identified with one year after the end of World War II. The longing of men at war for home has been evoked by storytellers going back to Homer but modern technology had found new possibilities and adventures for the long journey home. Indeed, the *Hollywood Reporter* surmised that "the story idea probably stems from that news item about the G.I. who twice flew the Atlantic in order to spend a single night at home."[76]

The film also takes on a broader canvas than the self-enclosed worlds of the Small farces. In *Rendezvous with Annie,* the protagonist's fear of exposure involves much more than his wife. The community at large, as depicted in the hero's small town, plays a significant part and nudges the film into the realm of satire.

The preoccupation with small-town ethos also brings Dwan closer to Sturges and there are interesting similarities between *Annie* and *The Miracle of Morgan's Creek*. Both involve a momentous birth and an apparent violation of sexual mores. Both also star an actor whose first name is Eddie but there is a tremendous difference between Dwan's Eddie A(lbert) and Sturges' Eddie B(racken).

Albert also represents a change from Dwan's previous leading man in the other comedies, O'Keefe, whose style like Bracken's is frenetic though Bracken was the more gifted farceur. O'Keefe's mugging verges on the cartoonish but Albert's mellowness establishes him as a very real and empathetic figure.

The film is based on a short story by Mary Loos (Anita's niece) and her husband Richard Sale, who also collaborated on the screenplay. Like *Miracle*, most of the story is told in flashback but the flashback structure in *Annie* is actually more intricate. Jeffrey Dolan (Albert) is in a jail cell when Dolores Starr (Gail Patrick), who barely knows him, comes to visit and offer her help but confesses she knows little of his predicament. Dolan tells her his story.

Dolan begins by explaining that he was an Army corporal and clerk in London and the first flashback scene shows a grumbling Dolan getting a three-day pass instead of the furlough he requested. He longs to go back to America to be with his wife Annie, whom he hasn't seen for eighteen months. An air raid siren breaks up the bickering.

As the film cuts to the building's bomb shelter, Dolan's homey, off-screen narrative voice resumes. "There's one thing about bombs ... they make you meet a lot of nice people in a hurry. We Americans and British got to know each other very well in that sub-cellar. I often sat with a jolly old gentleman. I didn't know his name so I thought of him as the 'old duffer.'"

It's clear that the old duffer (C. Aubrey Smith), a civilian, and Dolan have a strong rapport; Dwan's camera embraces them in two-shot for virtually the entire scene. Script, acting and direction are all beautifully coordinated to give this seemingly mundane sequence a magical warmth.

Jeff rhapsodizes to his English friend how wonderful and intelligent his wife Annie is and how she is running his mill business while he is away. Queried about his wife's cooking ability, Jeff goes into a long exposition on Annie's wonderful chocolate cake "that cannot be duplicated anywhere in the world." He describes in loving detail each bit of her preparations and, using the old gentleman's hat as a bowl, pantomimes each of Annie's delicate movements to get the cake just right. Near the end of the description, there is a cutaway to a single reaction shot of a bystander to heighten the illusion (and leaven it with some humor). The scene rises to a doting level of culinary sensuousness that reveals the extent of Jeff's love for his wife and his yearning for home.

Jeff still has chocolate cake on the brain in the next scene where he runs into two of his pilot buddies who have been assigned to a special mission to the States. He has to disappoint them with the news that he has no more of the cake left from Annie's last shipment and then reiterates the sad saga of his three-day pass. The pilots quickly concoct a scheme to get Jeff a brief visit with his Annie. They are scheduled to arrive in New York at 9 P.M. Since Dolan's home is in Woodville, New Jersey, this would give Jeff enough time to take a late train to Woodville, meet Annie, spend a night at home and then take a train back to New York the next morning for the flight back to London. Of course, if the plot were uncovered, Dolan could be court-martialed for going AWOL.

Not surprisingly, in his journey, Jeff does begin to encounter some potential traps that could give him away. When the plane stops in New Foundland, Jeff runs into the spit-and-polish General Trent (William Frawley). He also has to get by the traffic clerk (played by co-writer Sale) since his name is not on the flight manifest.

Having survived these pitfalls, Jeff must still accompany the pilots to the Bongo Club, a nightclub where one of the pilots wants to see the singer Dolores Starr, to whom Dolan is now telling his story. A photographer snaps a picture of them at their table. Jeff also encounters the mayor of Woodville, Everett Thorndyke (Raymond Walburn). Dolan denies his identity to Thorndyke though his name is plainly visible on his dogtag.

Finally, Dolan is able to phone Annie (Faye Marlowe) and tell her that he is taking the midnight train to Woodville but that no one else can know this. Dwan shoots their reunion in a street outside the train station in one long take in long shot in an understandably deserted area. The setting looks more appropriate for a murder in a film noir than for a romantic meeting. There is only one lit area in the center of the shot and both spouses emerge from opposite dark corners of the frame. The lovers move to the center, stand before each other for a few seconds and then embrace.

It is not only a sense of counterpoint that gives strength to the scene but the feeling of lovers who in dark isolation have briefly found solace outside the world of war and troubles. Kent Jones has aptly likened this scene to that of Teresa Wright comforting Dana Andrews after his nightmare in *The Best Years of Our Lives*, which was released the same year as *Annie*.[77] As Jeff first appears in this shot as a shadow, there is also some sense of portent of the consequences of his phantom-like visit.

The next morning, Annie drives Jeff to the train station with the all-important chocolate cake wrapped in the day's newspaper. Annie proclaims, "I'll always remember this as the most wonderful anniversary we ever had," but Jeff cautions her never to mention this visit in letters or that he would face a "firing squad." Back in London, Jeff presents the old duffer with what's left of the cake, saying he had been on a secret mission which brought him back home. He also lets the old man see the date of the newspaper.

Since we know that Jeff is already in jail, the viewer watches *Annie* waiting in dread the slip-up that will betray him. It is both a relief and a puzzle that the narration ends with Dolan having evaded detection. Jeff explains to Dolores that he must tell her the whole story and so begins a second narration.

When the war in Europe ends nine months later, Dolan returns but decides to surprise his spouse and sends no advance word. On his arrival, he is told by his weeping housekeeper that his wife is at the hospital. Upon seeing his newborn son,

Faye Marlowe presents Eddie Albert with the all-important chocolate cake in *Rendezvous with Annie* (1946).

of the film therefore has a symmetry with the first half as Jeff revisits each of the situations he cunningly bypassed the first time. In the process, he also finds the unreliability of memory and people.

His visit to Gen. Trent in Washington, D.C., proves fruitless. Jeff also finds that he had forgotten that in the photo snapped at the Bongo Club, he had ducked under the table. His two pilot friends are now career military officers and would endanger themselves by revealing what happened. And in the cruelest cut, Woodville's Mayor Thorndike refuses to acknowledge that he saw Jeff at the nightclub because the mayor was with a woman other than his wife. The mayor also sounds like he's blackmailing Jeff to stay quiet to secure a pending re-conversion loan for his mill. Jeff, who rhapsodized on how much he loved Woodville in the first half of the movie, now rails against the "injustice of this town."

Jeff softly exclaims, "I'm a father" to which a nurse deadpans, "It's a miracle." The line again invokes Sturges' *Miracle of Morgan's Creek* but here the "miracle" is not the solution but the beginning of problems.

Jeff remains oblivious to the implications of no one in Woodville knowing that he has been home in the last nine months. But then there appears in the plot another screwy will, this time pronounced by one Mr. Snodgrass, played by crusty old Will Wright. Jeff learns that his Uncle Harry has left $500,000 to Jeff's son "if and when he is born." It finally dawns on Jeff that his fatherhood is suspect. His explanation is not accepted by Snodgrass who demands proof of his return home. By the provisions of the will, Jeff has "until a week from Monday" to prove his paternity.

Jeff is the most bizarre of Dwan's lost father figures. The issue of paternity is not a problem between husband and wife but is one of public perception. Cast into a great nightmare of male insecurity, Jeff shows little preoccupation with public humiliation but is steadfastly determined that they "can't pull this on my son." Homer's war veteran Odysseus at least got to confront flesh-and-blood suitors to his wife. Jeff has to deal with a phantom imagined by the populace. While the film shows the fickleness of the townspeople, Jeff is also responsible for his predicament and will be repeatedly frustrated by the effectiveness of his own cover-up.

Jeff's quest also invokes Dwan's penchant for circularity of narrative and locales as he must return to each of the places and people he encountered months before. The second narration

The noir shot and other dramatic devices in the first half of the film now take on a new context in a feature that might be described as farce noir. Many of the exteriors (including his arrival by plane and by train) were at night. There were scenes of Jeff confronted by dangers that appear threateningly in front of him (the two MPs at the airport) and that linger menacingly behind him (an MP waiting outside the phone booth while Dolan called his wife). These elements become even more apparent in the second half of the film. Jeff has committed a "perfect crime" and is caught in a trap of his own making. And in trying to prove his "innocence" (i.e., that he had sex with his wife), Jeff becomes involved with a femme fatale who was first seen in the movie singing in her act to her four onstage boyfriends.

Jeff's visit to Dolores Starr results in him getting into a scuffle with her husband, who had become threatening. Dolores doesn't remember seeing Jeff on the fateful night, but when she gratefully kisses him, another photo (and not an exculpatory one) is shot for the newspapers.

The next day from his hotel in New York, Jeff talks to Annie over the phone. Dwan captures their conversation in a split screen, an effect that seems so seamless that the frames of the windows of Jeff's hotel room overlap with the door frame of his home. Jeff and Annie both hold their copies of the newspaper with the "scandalous" photo before them from their respective ends of the screen, the papers meeting in the middle. The spatial unity of the split screen celebrates Jeff's bond to Annie and his home but then perversely becomes the setting for an

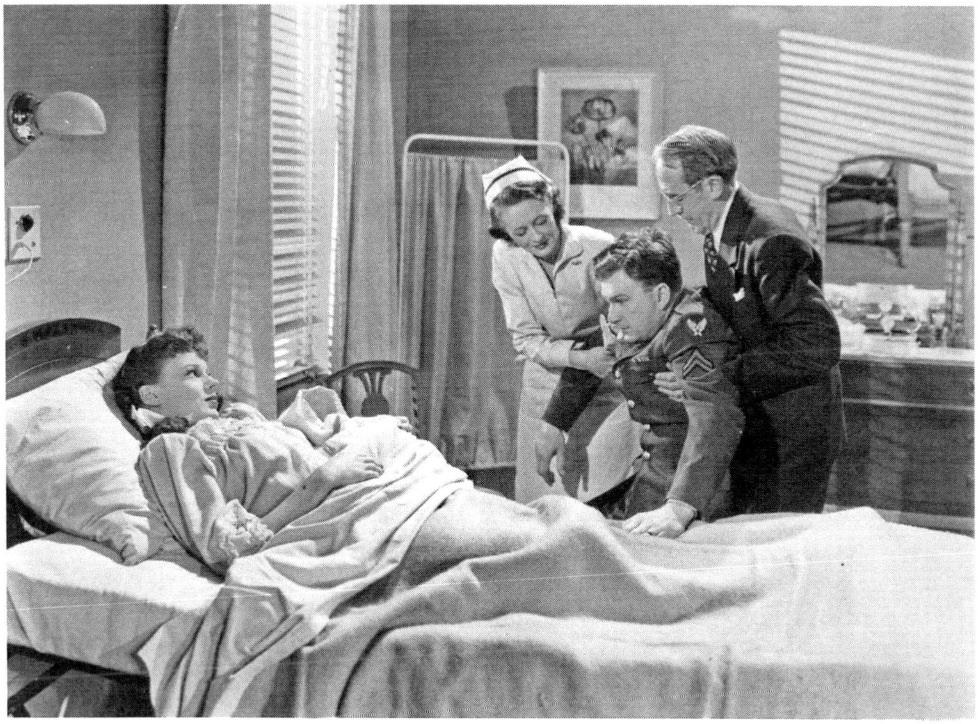

In ***Rendezvous with Annie*** **(1946), a nurse (Mary Currier) and doctor (Housely Stevenson) lend support as Dolan (Eddie Albert) is overcome when he learns his wife Annie (Marlowe) is presenting him with a son. Dolan doesn't yet know the crisis this birth will create.**

argument that drives them apart. The bedrock of the relationship between Jeff and Annie seems to be floundering as the split screen breaks into separate shots of Annie and Jeff.

However, this same newspaper contains a picture of the diplomat Sir Archibald Clyde, whom Jeff recognizes as "the old duffer." Sir Archibald is visiting New York so Jeff dashes off to see him, remembering that he confided his visit to him when he gave him the chocolate cake wrapped with the Woodville newspaper. But at Sir Archibald's hotel, Jeff recognizes the reporter who got him in trouble and they get into a fracas, landing Jeff in jail in what is suspected to be an assassination attempt.

This may be the most disappointing part of the film. After much of the genial comedy of frustration, a more imaginative and uproariously dynamic scene should have capped the movie as the cause of Jeff's incarceration. But the final sequence is fully in keeping with the mellow mood of Jeff's character and the film's shaggy dog story. Through Dolores' influence, the police free Jeff and bring him to his home in Woodville. The final scene is like a curtain call with many of the characters of the story present. Dolores is there with her husband, as is Sir Archibald, who is chatting with Mr. Snodgrass. Sir Archibald vouches for the proof of the August 13, 1944, newspaper wrapping on the chocolate cake but Snodgrass refuses to regard this as proof, arguing that one of the fliers at the base could have brought back the cake and newspaper.

But like the noir femme fatale who sometimes turns out to be the hero's savior, Dolores is the "angel" who arrives to set things right. This time Dolores blackmails Mayor Thorndike, who has just arrived, with a blowup of the Club Bongo photo (shades of Michelangelo Antonioni!) that shows Thorndike in the background seated with an incriminating blonde.

Thorndike tells Snodgrass that he and Jeff were together at the club that night, which Snodgrass accepts as proof. Jeff and Annie are reconciled and everyone can sit down to enjoy what Sir Archibald calls "the best chocolate cake in the universe."

Rendezvous with Annie makes some jabs at small-town mores and military officialdom but is far less incisive than Sturges' *Miracle of Morgan's Creek*. It also goes more for smiles and bewilderment than for the belly laughs of *Morgan's Creek*.

But the marvelously engineered structure of *Rendezvous with Annie* adheres to a more classical style of storytelling. The pilots who convince Dolan to join their mission are wisecracking tricksters who often communicate with Jeff by talking to each other, leaving Jeff off balance and befuddled like someone not let in on a joke. Their banter is a non-stop flow of jokes, bluffs, and schemes and in flight they can conjure up a storm to distract a disciplinarian general (though it affects Jeff worse). In the process, they plunge Jeff into an odyssey of trepidation, joy, disillusionment and reconciliation and possibly do it all just for a sample of chocolate cake. But their capriciousness is also the wind of fortune that enables Jeff to gain an heir to unlock his uncle's zanily contorted will.

For his attempt to circumvent authority, Jeff's penance is his quest which confronts him with all of his uses of deception that now endanger his son's inheritance. It forces Jeff to again leave Woodville and even to see it in less idealized terms. And beyond the deep frustration and anxiety he experiences, the ensuing press exploitation threatens what is dearest to Jeff, his relationship with Annie and his son.

As a visual correlative, the chocolate cake has moved from being an expression of his yearning for home to the mercurial inspiration for his being whisked across the Atlantic to a celebration of the event with the only person with whom he shared his secret in London. In reuniting Jeff with his old friend and bringing him to his home with a couple of other newfound pals, the cake takes on a glow of communal spirit. But all the friendships, as well as the ordeals, have flowed out of Jeff's love for Annie. Rarely has the clichéd Hollywood ending of the shot of lovers kissing seemed so appropriate.

There was a parallel struggle to Jeff's odyssey in Republic Pictures' efforts to get *Annie* made. In August 1945, after reading a seven-page synopsis of the story, Joseph Breen told Republic, "This story appears to us to violate those provisions dealing with the 'sacred intimacies of married life,' which are not treated properly in the story; and further supposed or alleged illicit sex and illegitimacy are treated for comedy purposes, which likewise is a Code violation."[78] Breen was apparently ignoring that "alleged illegitimacy" was used in *Up in Mabel's Room* but he may have regretted passing that. Also, in this proposed film, "illegitimacy" was the central issue.

Like Edward Small, Republic did not give up on trying to convince the censors to approve the script. An important development occurred in October when Dwan joined the discussion with Breen. Ever the problem-solver, Dwan found a way out of the impasse. Breen wrote, "We repeated our objections to the story, as expressed heretofore on numerous occasions to Republic. Mr. Dwan, however, injected into the story a new element, which, possibly, will make it acceptable under the Code. He proposes to establish it that, according to the will of the young man, Jeff, a legacy of $100,000 is to be paid to his first-born son."

Breen noted that now Jeff's quest to prove his son's legitimacy was "motivated chiefly by his desire to secure the legacy for his son." In Breen's opinion, this was acceptable, unlike Jeff being "motivated by his desire to establish the fact that it was he who slept with his wife and not someone else."[79]

So in the eyes of the censor, for the protagonist to establish the "legitimacy" of his son's birth in order to prove the faithfulness of his wife was a vulgar motive. But to do so in order to earn inheritance money for his son was not. Dwan's understanding of the censors' mentality permitted him to make the crucial suggestion that got the film made. In doing so, his exposure of the censors' mindset may have said almost as much about acceptable attitudes on sex and money as his farces did.

8. *The Sands of Republic*

This is the poorest soil I ever saw. What does anyone want to take an island like this for?— Line from the 1949 *Sands of Iwo Jima*

It is very difficult to articulate the intelligence Allan Dwan can bring to bear on an idiot project.— Myron Meisel, *American Directors*

Myron Meisel has written of Dwan's tenure at Republic "as most problematic in terms of material. It is with these Republic films that one's love for Dwan is put to its most rigorous test. Here the players are generally hopeless, as the scenarios disintegrate."[1] Founded in 1935 as an amalgamation of several small independent companies, Republic became known for its grinding-out of B movies and serials and was derisively called "Repulsive Pictures."

Yet it was at Republic that Dwan made his most famous movie, the 1949 *Sands of Iwo Jima.* The film, like the battle, may have been a victory at a studio on unfertile terrain. Dwan recalled with disappointment that after the film's huge success, Republic's owner Herbert Yates was not inclined to spend that kind of money again on a film.[2]

If Republic was like a desert, then Dwan may have found his Sphinx in Vera Hruba Ralston, the Czech ice skater turned actress. Yates, who later married her, was determined to make Ralston a big star despite her major limitations. Dwan, the perpetual Mr. Fix-It, would get his chance to solve the riddle of making successful films with Ralston as he was compelled to have her star in three of his movies. He later referred to making these pictures as "penances."[3]

But the above paragraphs do not tell the whole story of the situation at Republic at the time of Dwan's tenure. If Republic specialized in B movies and action films (especially Westerns), it also had highly skilled personnel in that area. For example, Republic's makers of special effects, the Lydecker Brothers, Howard and Theodore, were considered among the best at the time. Talented performers like Joan Leslie would find opportunities at Republic not available at the major studios where they were overshadowed by the big stars. By 1946, economic pressures were also arising that would push Republic towards making more "A" features. Film rental fees were not keeping up with rising production costs and a Federal consent degree was ending block-booking, requiring films to be sold individually.

As they tried to upgrade their product and boost studio prestige, Republic signed Oscar-winning director Frank Borzage, who made three films at Republic including the classic *Moonrise* in 1948. Yates also permitted Ben Hecht to direct the arty and bizarre *Specter of the Rose* in 1946 and granted a contract to Orson Welles to shoot *Macbeth* at Republic. The studio also tried to sign John Ford, returning from World War II, in September 1945. Ford instead went to Fox but he would eventually make films at Yates' studio including his Oscar-winning *The Quiet Man.*[4] And in September 1945, Republic succeeded in signing Allan Dwan. Dwan recalled that he was invited to Republic by his old friend James R. Grainger, who was vice president and sales manager at Republic. (Grainger had been head of Fox's sales department when Dwan signed with the studio in 1926.)

By the terms of his contract, Dwan was set to receive $1,000 a week for a guaranteed 52 weeks per year, plus five percent of the net profits of all his pictures. Dwan also had the right to be credited as associate producer on all his Republic pictures.

Dwan's tenure at Republic started auspiciously with *Rendezvous with Annie.* Mary Loos happily recalled that the film was "a success, and really a classic" although even at the time of her 1990 interview, she bemoaned that it was too rarely being shown. Loos married her script partner Richard Sale in December 1946 and Eddie Albert sang "September Song" at their wedding. She recalled Dwan as a "beloved man, who was very dear to us and also very important in our life." She said that because Dwan bought *Annie* as his first picture at Republic, "This made us a writing team."[5]

Loos and Sale also worked on Dwan's next Republic opus, a musical called *Calendar Girl.* The film is set at the turn of the century in an idealized Greenwich Village, where a kindly landlady helps all the struggling artists in her building. The movie might be seen as a nostalgic celebration of Dwan's love of New York City.

Calendar Girl has a graceful beginning with the young heroine literally opening the window to the story as she sings her first number and Dwan's camera follows her down a stairway. The songs by Jimmy McHugh and Harold Adamson are pleasant but also instantly forgettable. The leading players are similarly pleasant but somewhat bland, as is the picture. Victor McLaglen appears as the buffoonish father of the heroine but at least he gets to live in a nicer neighborhood than the one in *While Paris Sleeps.*

Dwan attends the 1946 wedding of his scriptwriting team, Mary Loos and Richard Sale. The bride has her arms around Dwan; Ilona Massey can be seen seated at the right. Mrs. Dwan is in the upper right corner. Eddie Albert is directly behind Loos (Allan Dwan papers. Collection number 3566. American Heritage Center, University of Wyoming).

Northwest Outpost, released later the same year (1947), was a far costlier musical venture. Composer Rudolph Friml, celebrated for his operettas from early in the century, was paid $62,000 for the score that included seven songs. Dwan said that more credit for the score should have gone to musical director Robert Armbruster, who was paid only about a tenth of Friml's salary. Dwan remembered, "I don't think Friml wrote three notes for the whole show.... Armbruster had to play phrases on the piano or have [Friml] play little phrases out of some song he hadn't finished and Armbruster would pick it up and finish it."[6] The music is less than entrancing.

Set in the 1830s, *Northwest Outpost* was a frontier operetta starring Nelson Eddy (in his last theatrical film) that was one of the dozen most expensive pictures shot at the usually lean Republic, costing $1,224,258. It exceeded the budget by $204,551.[7]

The setting has its basis in fact. Fort Ross, at the mouth of the Russian River north of San Francisco, was a Russian colony until 1842. Eddy as an American cavalry captain working for the Russians is without his celebrated co-star, Jeanette MacDonald. Her place is taken by the exceedingly beautiful Hungarian Ilona Massey. She had appeared previously in two movies with Eddy but the emotional chemistry between them does not gel here. Worse still is the contrived plotting. When Massey was in Russia, an officer (Joseph Schildkraut) accused of conspiring against the czar was sentenced to life imprisonment. Knowing that Massey's father, a general, could also be implicated in the plot, Schildkraut keeps his silence when he blackmails Massey into marrying him. Why a man entering life imprisonment would blackmail a woman into marrying him may defy rational explanation. However, by the time he arrives as a convict at Fort Ross and again meets Massey, Schildkraut has come up with a more sensible blackmail scheme: He will inform on her father if she does not help him to escape.

This improbable operetta also has its share of jaw-dropping scenes — for example, the members of a Russian chain gang singing a dirge about their weariness and longing for love, a scene as campy as the "Prisoners of Love" song in *The Producers*. But Dwan did provide some interesting visuals including the pageantry of a Russian Orthodox Easter service. Dwan confessed that he did make fun of the plot and the climactic scene has virtually all the principals winding up on a Chinese junk where the issues are resolved.

Dwan's next film *Driftwood* also had a Russian connection as the actress playing its child protagonist was the daughter of Russian immigrants. There were, however, no ethnic aspects to this film which starred Natalie Wood, who was approaching her ninth birthday as filming began on May 15, 1947. Dwan, known for his alertness to new talent, was intrigued by the child. He remembered, "She had a real talent for acting, an ability to characterize and interpret, and that was a pleasure."[8] Mary Loos, who co-wrote the film with Richard Sale said, "Like all of us, Dwan fell in love with Natalie."[9]

Natalie had already made her signature film as a child star, *Miracle on 34th Street*. Young Miss Wood was then under contract to Fox but a loan-out deal to Republic was arranged for this film. Wood's biographer Gavin Lambert said that *Driftwood* "allowed Natalie to reveal more depth of character than in most of her major studio productions. Fiercely independent-minded, but at the same time eager to trust other people and consequently very vulnerable, Jenny was the childhood role closest to Natalie's childhood self."[10]

The original story, *Heaven for Jenny*, had been written by Loos and Sale for *Liberty Magazine* in 1945. Producer Arnold Pressburger optioned the story and commissioned a screenplay adaptation by the authors for a film to be directed by Leonid

Moguy. When Pressburger was unable to get the film made, he sold it to Republic. An important collaborator for Dwan on *Driftwood* was cinematographer John Alton. Alton was soon to leave Republic but would later work with Dwan on numerous occasions.

Driftwood is a flawed and sometimes exasperating movie. But it is also a lyrical piece of Americana, among Dwan's most touching and poetic films. Like much else at Republic, it was filmed quickly (three weeks).

The film opens in Bullfrog Springs, a southwest gold rush town turned ghost town, inhabited only by the Reverend Hollingsworth and his great-granddaughter Jenny. In the opening shot, the camera pans past a graveyard to a tilted sign on a church inviting people to come and be saved by Hollingsworth. The camera continues to pan right and then moves into the church, which is virtually in ruins. In addition to Alton's low-key lighting, the compositions of these first shots are marked by jagged diagonal lines made by dilapidated pews and other objects. The effect is almost expressionistic, suggesting something of the otherworldly existence in which Jenny has been raised. The minister is played by H.B. Warner, who had previously worked with Dwan in *Zaza* and *French Dressing* but perhaps the operative reference here is his having portrayed Christ in DeMille's 1927 *King of Kings*. He is stricken as he delivers verses from Jeremiah and soon dies. But the Reverend Hollingsworth has left instructions to Jenny to go to the nearest town, Panbucket (which he refers to as "Sodom and Gomorrah").

Jenny is an innocent, a child of nature thrust into the hotbed of civilization like other Dwan protagonists. (When one character refers to Jenny as a "wildflower," it's a good reminder that this line extends back to Marguerite Clark.) Jenny has been taught to fear airplanes which she identifies as "Beelzebub." A plane crashes as she makes her way through the wilderness but it leaves her with a surviving dog, a collie that she adopts as her own.

Jenny is found and picked up by Steve Webster (Dean Jagger), the town doctor, who drives her into Panbucket. When the sheriff can't accommodate her immediately, she spends the night at Steve's house. The next morning, she meets the acerbic Murph (Walter Brennan), who had adopted Steve when he was a child.

The plot suggests that Jenny may blossom as a Shirley Temple figure like Heidi who will mend everyone's problems. But Jenny's path is more convoluted. Remembering the Biblical phrase (Psalm 91:4) that "truth shall be thy shield," she believes she has been commanded to speak the truth to everyone. Thus, when Murph tells her that Mathilda (Charlotte Greenwood), the unmarried aunt of Steve's girlfriend Susan (Ruth Warrick), has been waiting for a man for thirty years, she doesn't hesitate to mention that to Mathilda when she meets her. Jenny's troublesome truth-telling is quite unrestrained and causes havoc. This appears to contrast with the hiding of the truth which was at the center of three of the Small farces and *Rendezvous with Annie*. But the story will turn on revelations that Jenny actually tried to conceal.

The characters that Jenny comes into contact with are an appealing gallery of likable people who have run into roadblocks resulting from their limitations. They may be as much "driftwood" (the term Murph applies to Jenny) as she is. Steve is a doctor with ambition but he's met with hostility in the town by the mayor (Jerome Cowan), who refuses Steve's proposal to build a hospital and brands Steve a "radical." Steve struggles to make ends meet while he continues to find a cure for spotted fever. Steve can't make enough money to feel he can marry Susan, and her aunt considers Steve "an unsteady, impractical dreamer." One suspects that Dwan felt some affinity with Steve as a more negative version of himself, the man of science who is not permitted to solve problems and who may have let the dreamy side of his nature dominate.

Irene Rich, Victor McLaglen and Jane Frazee in Dwan's period musical *Calendar Girl* (1947), set in New York's Greenwich Village.

Susan, a schoolteacher, is also frustrated by Steve's pride, which will not permit him to accept her earnings as a way of launching their marriage. Mathilda still broods over a broken marriage proposal of thirty years ago. Murph, marvelously played by Brennan, seems the most self-assured of the characters but he may be less than candid when talking of his satisfaction with not having married.

In its vision of characters stymied by small-town myopia, *Driftwood* parallels Dwan's earlier *Young People*. Panbucket also reflects the way the characters acknowledge a "glass ceiling" and accept a restricted place for themselves. Abner Green (Francis Ford) is incarcerated for failing to pay alimony. Abner is a "happy man" when he's in jail but we're told that "when out [of jail], a woman takes him to the cleaners." Jail has become not only a permanent home for him but in a town in which we see little sense of community, the jail has become a social club where Murph and even the judge come to play cards with Abner.

Steve waits for a grant for the research facilities he needs and meanwhile uses the porch of Murph's house as his laboratory. Aunt Mathilda points out that only the porch belongs to Steve and that the rest of the house is Murph's.

Conversely, except for one brief medium shot of Susan on the phone, we never get to see the interior of Aunt Mathilda's house. As if reaching a skirmish line, all conversations with Mathilda, Susan, and Steve stop at Mathilda's front porch. Of course, Dwan and Republic saved money by not using another interior. But Dwan's efficiency was also a part of his sense of dramatic restraint, being expressive via what he *didn't* show. Until the late scenes at Murph's house, we never see Steve and Susan in a home together.

Driftwood does have its flaws. The mayor and his bratty son (Teddy Infuhr) are a bit overdrawn. A courtroom trial of Jenny's dog is overly manipulative, leading to a weepy "Please don't shoot my dog" climax as no one bothers to check until the end of the trial to see if the victim was actually bitten.

Young Natalie Wood first encounters the collie who will become her protector in *Driftwood* (1947).

One of the interesting aspects of *Driftwood* is how science and religion are linked together as allies. Some of this emerges from the unlikeliest plot development this side of Dickens. The dog that improbably survived the plane crash and appeared before Jenny in the desert turns out to have been from an experimental center. Because of its fluke immunity, the dog's blood provides the basis for a serum against spotted fever. The dog is thus available at a crucial time when a spotted fever epidemic breaks out in Panbucket.

On the one hand, the Reverend Hollingsworth's distrust of modern science and his linking the plane to the demonic is debunked. But the madly improbable appearance of the dog (whom Jenny names "Hollingsworth") at a crucial time suggests a miracle. However, because Jenny does not tell anyone of the dog's origin and hides evidence, the dog's status is not discovered until it's almost too late and Jenny herself has been stricken with the fever.

To learn how to use the serum from the dog's blood to save Jenny, Steve needs the help of a medical specialist, Dr. Adams. But also arriving at his house is the Reverend MacDougall, who brings his grandchildren to be vaccinated by Steve. This reverend, played by Dwan's former silent film star James Kirkwood, states his credo, "If a thing can be done, science can do it. If it can't be done, faith can do it." His grandchildren pray for Jenny, and she is seen recovering in the next scene.

The reconciliation of the townspeople with Steve and his friends is more convincing than the similar reconciliation in *Young People*. The townspeople, who had previously ignored his recommendations to be vaccinated, now flock to Murph and Steve's house with their children. A new sense of his value to the community helps Steve decide not to leave Panbucket, as he previously planned.

The struggle to fight the epidemic brings all of the four main adult characters together.

Jenny, who had earlier been their problem, becomes part of the fabric that now makes them a family. With this film, we begin to see bits of a peculiar mysticism that will appear in a number of Dwan's later movies.

Dwan's next two films, both released in 1948, are also structured as fables. According to Dwan, *The Inside Story* was an idea he said he cooked up with Loos and Sale (though based on a story by Ernest Lehman). "At that time there was a lot of financial trouble going on in the world, and I thought it would be a pretty good idea to hit the topic in some way, and to enlighten people that the worst place for money to be was in a bank — that money ought to work. I tried to show what a thousand dollars would do if it moved fast enough, from person to person."[11]

While the nation's postwar economy was headed for an enormous upward path, there were some hitches ahead, including a brief recession that began in 1948. (It actually started months after *The Inside Story* was released.) The fear that the nation would lapse back into the Depression was still quite palpable when the film was made and this is interwoven into the plot. It opens in the present day (1948) with one character, fearing the worst, putting his money into his security box, while another known as Uncle Ed (Charles Winninger) keeps only bonds in his box and asserting the importance of keeping money in circulation. To make his point, Ed begins telling the story in flashback, which goes back to March 1933, shortly after FDR took office.

The Inside Story may be seen as a Depression era allegory. The idea that the community can regain wealth by spending an allotted amount of money actually harkens back to *Brewster's Millions*. The film is pivoted on the premise that the passage of one thousand dollars through one town will reap many benefits though the funds didn't actually belong to the person who sent the money on its way.

It is interesting that the film is set in a small town in Vermont, the state that was lampooned for its diehard conservative ways in *Young People*. Uncle Ed, proclaimed in a written prologue as typifying the everyday person, spouts the kind of aphoristic, not-letting-you-know-any-of-my business lines that were used in *Young People* to describe the taciturn New Englanders. But Uncle Ed does it with a twinkle in his eyes and a sense of fun that gives it a whole new perspective.

The parting of the thousand dollars arises from a strange confluence of factors including a check that cannot be mailed because of the government-proclaimed national bank holiday and a recipient delayed in appearing at the agreed rendezvous place, the Silver Creek Inn, because his wife is having a baby. (Another miracle birth?) The man sent from New York City with the check (Roscoe Karns) is so frightened by the appearance of two bootleggers (Allen Jenkins and William Haade) that he asks Uncle Ed to place the check in the inn's safe. Completing the circle of ensuing confusion, the absent-minded Uncle Ed fails to mention the presence of the thousand dollars in the safe when the hotel's owner, Horace Taylor (Gene Lockhart), relieves him at the front desk.

So when Taylor's leading creditor, Jay Jay Johnson (Will Wright), comes into the inn insisting that Taylor pay him the money he needs to save himself from foreclosure, Horace uses the $1,000. Because Uncle Ed placed the money in an envelope belonging to Taylor's prospective son-in-law, Horace believes the aspiring painter had repaid his debt to him. Only when Uncle Ed returns from his lunch break does Horace learn that the money he has paid to Johnson wasn't his. And so the chase is on to retrieve the check before the rightful claimant arrives.

Although primarily a comedy, *The Inside Story* does not shirk from showing some of the quiet desperation of the period. Audrey O'Connor (Gail Patrick) works in New York City and returns every two weeks to Silver Creek where her lawyer husband Tom (Robert Shayne) waits impatiently since he has nothing to do. Dwan's camera watches through a window when Tom pulls out a gun and contemplates using it on himself.

While male insecurity is a recurrent quantity in Dwan films, perhaps the most intelligent and benevolent character in this movie is the matriarch of the town's wealthiest family, Geraldine Atherton (Florence Bates). She pressures Jay Jay to pay up his rent (she is therefore another of the instigators of the circulating thousand) and then gives the money as a retainer to Tom for future work, thus boosting his pride.

So even before Horace begins his search, the money has already passed through three different people. Horace's task has some similarity to the chasing of female apparel in the Collison–Small farces. But if Taylor is frenzied, the pace of this film is not, even though the chase period elapses between noon and 9 P.M. when the situation must be resolved. There is time for dawdling, for a woman to cite some of the nation's greatest depressions, for a man to regain some of his pride, for a dowager to enjoy a dinner with two gangsters, even for someone to resist any distraction from his favorite dessert. The interlocking concerns of a broad array of characters seem to look forward to Robert Altman. Michael Henry Wilson has noted that for Dwan, "the ideal story is an ensemble piece" and he observes that "the microcosm illustrates our mutual interdependence — as with the chain of debts that link all the characters in *The Inside Story*."[12]

Lockhart's Horace in his bluster seems to elicit less sympathy than one would expect. The counterweight is Winninger's Uncle Ed, constantly pulling up his eyeglasses and unable to recognize familiar faces popping in front of him. That someone

Gene Lockhart leans on Charles Winninger for support while he chases the circulating $1000 in *The Inside Story* (1948).

Ensemble casting was an important element in *The Inside Story* (1948) and here appearing clockwise around the table during a script conference are Florence Bates, Charles Winninger, Roscoe Karns (standing), Dwan, Allen Jenkins, Gail Patrick and William Haade.

as unobservant as Ed should be the narrator seems inexplicable. But a closer look at Uncle Ed, as Winninger portrays him, also shows his hidden virtues. There is a mystic benevolence in his forgetfulness that helps spark the thousand dollar run; a quality of unflappability and resilience in his insouciance and an infecting sense of good spirits even when tied to the corniest sense of humor. As his narration reveals, Uncle Ed may seem myopic but he does grasp the long view of things. In the meanwhile, Dwan's accidental stimulus has rescued Horace's business, kept Jay Jay in his store, helped save a marriage (and possibly a life), and kept a future marriage on the tracks.

The stakes are raised considerably in *Angel in Exile,* which follows the path of not one thousand, but one million dollars in gold. The objective in *Angel in Exile* is not to circulate the money but to launder it by putting it into a mine. Charlie Dakin (John Carroll) has just been freed after serving five years in prison. With his cohort Ernie Coons (Art Smith), he works on an ingenious scheme to turn their stolen loot into the bona fide profits of a mining venture. But hard on their heels are their two former partners in crime, Max Giorgo (Barton MacLane) and Carl Spitz (Paul Fix). The less savory duo also want their cut and seem to have their own ideas about how many parties will be around at payoff time.

Dakin decides that he can use the impoverished village of San Gabriel to hire men he needs to work in the mine, giving it an extra veneer of legitimacy. San Gabriel's schoolteacher, Raquel Chavez (Adele Mara), is taken with Dakin's charm and his offer of employment to the people, seeing him as a force for good.

Predictably, Carroll's amiable huckster falls for Raquel and for the plight of her people. At a critical time when an epidemic breaks out in the town (this time it's typhus), Dakin joins Raquel's father, the village doctor (Thomas Gomez), in nursing the sick. Dakin tells each of the patients that he has seen the Blue Lady, a Mexican legend about the ghost of a devout woman, and describes her to them. The con man's benevolent con job (?) works and all the sick people he's visited recover. Dakin returns to the mine for a final showdown but first instructs that reward money for the stolen gold should go to the people of San Gabriel.

Angel in Exile was co-directed by Philip Ford, Francis Ford's son (and John Ford's nephew), who put in one week's work while Dwan was ill. *Angel* is basically a simple tale of conversion but there is conviction in its decency and sense of atmosphere. Certain images stick in the mind such as Dakin first entering San Gabriel following a flock of white sheep (with himself as another of Dwan's black sheep?); the two gangsters flipping a coin to decide who will be the shooter, seconds before gunning down their victim; and Raquel seen through the upper frame of a well, riding to be at Dakin's side during the resolution.

Sands of Iwo Jima

Another look at the World War II battle of Iwo Jima was on view in 2006 when Clint Eastwood's film *Flags of Our Fathers* was released. In her review, the *New York Times* critic Manohla Dargis, praising Eastwood, noted, "[H]e floods his scenes with raw emotion that serves as a rebuke to gung-ho fictions like *Sands of Iwo Jima*, a 1949 bad joke in which John Wayne hands an American flag to the real Ira, Doc and Rene so they can raise Old Glory once more...."[13] The names Dargis cited refer to Ira Hayes, John "Doc" Bradley and Rene Gagnon, the two Marines and Navy corpsman who helped raise the American flag over Iwo Jima in the iconic photograph taken by Joe Rosenthal. *Flags of Our Fathers* was based on a memoir of the same name by Bradley's son James, who co-authored with Ron Powers.

Much of the context had changed in the time elapsed from Dwan's 1949 film to when *Flags of Our Fathers* appeared fifty-seven years later. *Flags of Our Fathers* is in many ways a more thorough and truthful account of the events surrounding the Iwo Jima battle but the plots for both films center on a father-son relationship. In *Sands of Iwo Jima,* the relationship is figurative; in *Flags of Our Fathers* it is literal. Yet ironically, the relationship registers more weakly in *Flags of Our Fathers*: For much of the film, the son is a shadowy, cryptic figure (unlike in the book).

During World War II, Iwo Jima was the vital link in the chain of islands the U.S. seized from Japan and it was to serve as a base for bombing the mainland. The Japanese regarded Iwo Jima as part of their homeland and, with twenty-two thousand men ensconced in blockhouses and a network of tunnels and caves, they were prepared to fight savagely in its defense. The Marines landed on the island on February 19, 1945, and in the first eighteen hours, 2,312 Americans were killed or wounded. When informed of the casualties, President Roosevelt is said to have gasped in horror.

By February 23, the Marines managed to capture Mt. Suribachi, the extinct volcano which was the highest point on the island. To the sound of cheers and shouts from Marines and from the men on the fleet offshore, the American flag was raised on Suribachi. Because that flag was too small and the Marines wanted to be assured that it would be saved as a memento, a second, larger flag replaced it. Rosenthal, an Associated Press photographer, managed to get to Suribachi in time to photograph that second flag-raising, though it seemed anticlimactic.

When that photograph was published in newspapers across the country on February 25, it electrified the nation. People may not have grasped the classic triangular lines, the diffused sunlight or any of the other aesthetic qualities that made the picture so powerful. What they felt was an onrush of pride and triumph after five days of dire news of high casualties.

News stories appeared about the intense enemy resistance the Marines met as they scaled Suribachi. In fact, they encountered no resistance at all. On the other hand, the flag-raising was seen as bringing the battle to a neat conclusion. Most reporters vacated the area shortly thereafter. The battle, however, continued for another thirty-one days. By the time it was over, the Americans had suffered a staggering 26,000 casualties, including 6,821 killed or missing.

Half of the six flag-raisers were killed on Iwo Jima. Survivors Bradley, Hayes, and Gagnon were sent home for a special mission. As during World War I, the government was using bond drives to help finance the war. But this time, it was the three flag-raisers, not movie stars like Chaplin, Fairbanks and Pickford, who were needed to spearhead the drive. Acclaimed as national heroes, they helped the latest bond drive, known as the Mighty Seventh, reach its monetary goal — and then double it.

Four years after the war, Bradley, Hayes and Gagnon were again called into the spotlight to appear in a movie.

Sands of Iwo Jima was the brainchild of Republic producer Edmund Grainger. Feeling that a major film had not been made about the U.S. Marines, Grainger (inspired by the flag-raising at Iwo Jima) wrote a forty-page treatment that he registered under the title *Sands of Iwo Jima.* He then turned to writer Harry Brown, whose credits included the acclaimed 1945 World War II film *A Walk in the Sun,* to develop the treatment into a screenplay.

Grainger also sought out and received the cooperation of the Marines. His request came at a time when the Marines were seeking to bolster their image as their very existence was the subject of debate. From the first treatment, Grainger had ended his story with the flag-raising on Suribachi, so the Marines could again use their trump card of the three survivors of that event to publicize the Corps.

For the lead in the film, Grainger first considered Kirk Douglas. When negotiations with Douglas' agent stalled, Grainger decided to look closer to home and picked John Wayne, who was then working at Republic. There has been some dispute on how Wayne got the part and whether Republic's boss Herbert Yates considered him prominent enough for such a major role, although Wayne had starred in the big-budget *Wake of the Red Witch* for Republic a year before *Sands* was filmed.[14] Dwan told Bogdanovich that Yates had said he wanted to save Wayne to co-star in a film with Vera Ralston. Dwan said he encouraged Grainger to "fight" and to get Wayne to meet with Yates. Yates then relented.[15]

Wake of the Red Witch was classified by Republic as a Premiere production, a category to be used for Republic's most expensive and prestigious films. *Sands of Iwo Jima* was also placed in that class and was originally budgeted at $937,000. Dwan recalled that it was his friend James Grainger, Republic's director of sales and Edmund's father, who first approached him about directing the film. Dwan was excited enough by the project to relinquish his right to be associate producer to Edmund even though that entailed waiving his usual five percent share of net profits.

In addition to helping insure authenticity, Marine cooperation also provided Republic with facilities and services that helped keep costs down. This included archives of documentary battle footage, technical assistance, and the use of the Marine base at Camp Pendleton, conveniently just 100 miles south of Los Angeles.

In her review of *Flags of Our Fathers,* Dargis noted how in *Sands of Iwo Jima* Hayes, Bradley and Gagnon raised the American flag "this time over the sands of Southern California." But this was not the first time the three men had gone through a simulated Iwo Jima battle in that location. For six months in 1944, along with 21,000 men, they had trained at Camp Pendleton in preparation for their assault on Iwo Jima. So in a sense,

A con man ingratiates himself with the populace of a small Mexican village in *Angel in Exile* (1948), featuring (from left to right) Thomas Gomez, Adele Mara, John Carroll and Alfonso Bedoya.

it was the second time that Camp Pendleton had substituted for the bleak island.

While most of Republic's Iwo Jima battle was staged at Pendleton, the beach landings took place at nearby Camp Del Mar, the Marines' amphibious base, with the help of "over 1,000 marines, two squadrons of Corsair planes from the Marine Air Station at El Toro; thirty amtracs, cruisers, destroyer escorts and L.S.T.s invading a mile and a half of beach."[16] Grainger later recalled, "We had to coordinate all that and train the Marines, not so much in the landing techniques, but in the movements of the boats so that the cameras could follow each boat."[17]

Because the script for *Sands of Iwo Jima* was fashioned to have the Suribachi flag-raising, which occurred relatively early in the battle, at the conclusion of the movie, only a limited part of the film was set at Iwo Jima. The title may thus sound like a misnomer but Iwo Jima provides the climax to the story.

The earlier battle of Tarawa also had to be recreated at Camp Pendleton. David Shoup, commanding general of the First Marine Division at Camp Pendleton during the shooting of the film, was a veteran of Tarawa. Shoup told film historian Larry Suid that the sets copied from actual footage from the battle were "very, very accurate.... [I]t was a fearsome thing to look at because, having experienced the battle, goddam, I didn't want to go through it again."[18]

Shoup played himself in the movie, communicating by walkie-talkie with Jim Crowe, one of his actual battalion commanders. Shoup said he objected to using the words in the script, which were not faithful to what he had said during the battle, so it was changed on the spot. "After they heard Jim and I say what we actually said, they were very happy to use our actual words."[19] (Despite this striving for accuracy, the exchange still sounded a bit stilted.)

Sets were assembled and then torn down when a scene was finished. But they had to be sure that the scene was shot properly before that was done. Each day the rushes were scrutinized.

Captain Leonard Fribourg was the technical consultant when the crew and actors came to Pendleton in July of 1949. He remembered, "If the rushes met the approval of Grainger, particularly Dwan, and of Wayne, then we would proceed. Only a couple of times did we have to go back and reshoot stuff."[20] Fribourg's emphasis on the importance of Dwan's judgment suggests the kind of authority he wielded here, which was probably greater than was true on his other big-budget sound film, *Suez.* In a 1994 interview with Leonard Maltin, actor Richard Webb recalled, "Allan Dwan always had command of the picture. He had control of every actor in the thing."[21]

Dwan worked closely with Fribourg to establish authenticity in details. Fribourg remembered, "In every scene where the military was involved, Mr. Dwan would never roll the camera unless he got my approval that everything looked right when he was starting."[22] Fribourg said of Dwan, "I think he's one of the finest men I ever met. I really believe that. And he says what he thinks. He doesn't try to play a game."[23]

There was another formidable figure whom Fribourg admired and that was the star, John Wayne, who played Sgt. John Stryker. Fribourg recounted, "Wayne wanted to play Stryker so bad he could taste it. He read the story and said, 'Stryker is Wayne.'" Fribourg said that he answered Wayne's questions about being a Marine but that Wayne became particularly interested in a warrant officer whom he thought typified Stryker. Wayne spoke to the man and observed him keenly. Wayne also became friendly with the man who led the Marines up Mt. Suribachi, Lt. Harold G. Schrier, and listened to him relate his experiences. Schrier played himself in the film and, unlike Shoup, was more of a natural actor. When giving orders to Wayne in the picture, Schrier would be strikingly terse and businesslike. While Wayne prepared to play the tough sergeant, Fribourg also played the role in a sense, drilling the actors in Wayne's movie squad in "a miniature boot camp."[24]

Some of this toughness was also demonstrated by Dwan. Future producer and TV executive William Self, playing one of the Marine recruits, recalled a scene in a foxhole when he was shocked to be suddenly hit with mud in his face. "Allan Dwan had thrown the mud at me. He said, 'You forgot your line.' And I said, 'Mr. Dwan, I don't have a line here until so-and-so says such-and-such.' And he said, 'Oh, that's right. You're right. I apologize.'" But Self said that most of the time Dwan, while rough, was polite.[25]

Dwan also continued to keep his assistants on their toes. Andrew V. McLaglen, a future director and the son of Dwan's former star Victor, served as second assistant on *Sands of Iwo Jima*. He remembered that Dwan refused to tell his assistants in advance what the next shot would be. So the various assistants would sometimes steal Dwan's copy of the script when the director wasn't around. "That was just more fun for us: 'Who's going to steal it this time?' It was usually the unit manager who was also a friend of mine.... At just the right time, whether Allan went to the bathroom or whatever he did, we would look at the script. And we were having a game!" McLaglen remembers Dwan affectionately as a "tough old bird.... There were never any bad words said about Allan."[26]

The elusive script had also undergone some changes: Wayne brought in his friend and associate James Edward Grant to re-write it. That Wayne had the power to do this suggests that Yates acknowledged the importance of his star. Wayne believed that Grainger wanted to stick to old clichés and so he brought in Grant "to improve the personal story and the intimate scenes of the picture."[27] Wayne also stated, "Mr. Dwan did become irritated at times with Jimmy before the picture was completed because Mr. Grant wasn't given time to re-work the script before production started."[28] Production began in July 1949 and the shooting script shows that numerous revisions were made, some with August dates.

Wayne's description also suggests a rift with Grainger who, he claimed, held up delivery of Grant's revisions to Dwan. Matters would come to a head when one scene aroused the ire of Fribourg. In this scene, Sgt. Stryker's men were being taught to use their bayonets and one Marine was performing abysmally. Stryker challenged him and hit him with a horizontal butt stroke of his rifle. Fribourg told his interviewer Larry Suid that watching the rehearsal, "I almost fell off my chair."[29] He immediately said that a Marine sergeant would never do this as a training demonstration and demanded this scene be stricken, despite Dwan's protests. Dramatically, this was an important point because it showed that while Stryker's intention was to toughen up his men for combat, he was capable of going too far in ways that would alienate them.

As Fribourg recalled, this was the only time a dispute had to be resolved in Washington. The Marines overruled Fribourg and permitted a modified version of the scene, which would be later followed with a comic follow-up in which the Marine is instructed properly by Wayne with the help of the Mexican Hat Dance.

Wayne said that Grainger was "evidently afraid" of the bayonet scene and tried to eliminate it. Wayne went over his head to Yates, who then ordered Dwan to shoot the scene. In this convoluted way, Dwan finally got what he wanted. Wayne acknowledged that he had connived to get his way and described himself as "a sort of 'Richelieu' of Republic," a description that no doubt would have amused Dwan.[30]

Despite the cooperation of the Marines, *Sands of Iwo Jima* still went $460,550 over budget. Its final negative cost was $1,397,558.[31] During shooting, Grainger told a reporter, "Without Marine cooperation the film would have cost at least $2.5 million."[32] *Sands* was not the costliest Republic production up to that time. Both Frank Borzage's 1946 *I've Always Loved You* and director Lewis Milesone's *The Red Pony* cost more, though *Sands* had the greatest cost overrun.[33]

Sands of Iwo Jima was set for general release in March 1950 but to qualify for the 1949 Academy Awards, it was given December play dates in key cities. A December 14 premiere in San Francisco was kicked off with plenty of hoopla. A parade was led by a 150-piece Marine Corps band, a color guard numbering 500 and a long motorcade that included then governor and future Supreme Court Chief Justice Earl Warren and Republic's president Yates. One thousand Marines paraded two weeks later when *Sands* opened at the Carthay Circle Theater in West Los Angeles on December 28.

The reviews were very good but there was also strong competition from two other war movies that opened that year, MGM's *Battleground* and Fox's *Twelve O'Clock High*. Of Dwan's picture, the *New York Times* noted that it "has undeniable moments of greatness" but cited various clichés that detracted from the movie. The *Times* lamented, "*Sands of Iwo Jima* could have been a great war film instead of just a good one."[34] The film succeeded in getting four Academy Award nominations including story, sound, editing and Wayne's first nomination as Best Actor. But it won none on Oscar night. It did, however, rack up handsomely at the box office, and eventually took in $4,227,407 in gross receipts. Following closely on the heels of *Red River* and *She Wore a Yellow Ribbon*, *Sands* helped catapult Wayne to superstardom.

Ironically, *Sands of Iwo Jima* is narrated by a relatively minor character in the story, Corp. Robert Dunne (Arthur Franz). Since Dunne serves as a persistent sounding board and is a teacher, he is well qualified to provide needed exposition in his voiceovers.[35]

The film opens at Camp Paekakariki in New Zealand. The story is spread across four locales, New Zealand, Tarawa, Hawaii, and Iwo Jima. Each location provides its own narrative thrust so they can be said to serve as four acts for the drama. The amount of running time devoted to the campaigns at Tarawa and Iwo Jima is roughly equal, each about 22 minutes long.

Sgt. John M. Stryker (Wayne) is the hard-bitten non-com

heading a squad of replacements entering the scene as the film begins. Since only Dunne and Pfc. Bass (James Brown) are holdovers, we assume that the rest of the squad had been killed or wounded at Guadalcanal or some other battle. One of the replacements is Al Thomas (Forrest Tucker), who served with Stryker before and hates him for having turned him in for some infraction. While the Stryker–Thomas rivalry is used fleetingly, much of the early part of the film is expended with some tiresome and clichéd service humor (the perpetually squabbling Flynn brothers, for example).

For his role as Sgt. Stryker in *Sands of Iwo Jima* (1949), John Wayne received advice from several Marines including Lt. Harold G. Schrier (left) who led the Marines up Mt. Suribachi and played himself in the film.

Among the new recruits is Pfc. Pete Conway (John Agar) whose father, a colonel, had been killed at Guadalcanal. Stryker tells Conway that his father had been his C.O. on Guadalcanal and makes an offer of friendship that he has made to none of the other recruits. But Conway rebuffs him. Conway later tells Dunne that after his father was killed, he felt obliged to join the Marines as the men in his family had always done. But he complains that his father had always thought him too soft.

With Wayne as the tough sergeant with the heart of gold and Agar as the young man who must prove himself, both characters might also be seen as clichés. But there is another component to Wayne's Stryker. His wife had left him and taken their infant son (named Sam, after Conway's father). With the child now ten years old, Stryker vainly waits to receive a letter from him but for all purposes he has lost his son and family. It is as if *Rendezvous with Annie* had a much darker ending where Dolan's paternity was finally denied by everyone including his child.

Like two lovers who had both lost their mates, Stryker and Conway are each painfully reeling when they meet and see in each other a chance to resume the father-son relationship that had been taken away from them. Stryker becomes unusually solicitous for a sergeant to establish a relationship with a private; Conway repeatedly goes out of his way to antagonize the man who commands him. But he makes it clear that he sees Stryker as a prototype of his father and in one scene says that when Stryker talks about him, he hears his father speaking.

Despite his expressions of contempt towards Stryker and by extension his father, Conway tells his fiancée Allison that he has to prove something to somebody who's "dead now." So Conway clearly needs Stryker as a living father substitute.

The father-son relationship was also obviously something that Wayne and his scriptwriter Grant were comfortable emphasizing. The previous year in *Red River,* Wayne had made a breakthrough playing a tyrannical cattleman with a rebellious adopted son portrayed by Montgomery Clift. In his very next film for Republic after *Sands,* the cavalry picture *Rio Grande* directed by John Ford, Wayne plays an officer who like Stryker is divorced and hasn't seen his son in years. Having flunked out of West Point, the son then enlists to serve as one of Wayne's troopers. Wayne continued to play a mentor role to young actors in a number of his films, especially towards the end of his career.

Dwan could not have written a plot more suited to his preoccupation with the lost father figure and this may have been one of the reasons why the script quickly caught his interest. The apparent justification for the emphasis on the Stryker–Conway relationship is crystallized in a scene in which Conway sits up late at night in his tent talking to a dozing Dunne about Allison, his newfound love, and why she seems so important to him. Stryker is still awake in his own tent and as ever is vigilant to what Conway says or does. "I think it's because when you get out here ... you realize, away down inside you ... that maybe something's got your number on it. And you want to leave a little piece of yourself behind. It doesn't matter whether it's a boy or a girl — just as long as you know you won't be forgotten." It must have been easy for the childless Dwan to empathize with the eavesdropping Stryker, who has also been denied a filial link.

In her book on World War II combat films, Jeanine Basinger suggests that the father-son relationship enacted by the two characters is used to demonstrate how the Marines propagate their own sense of family.[36] For Dwan, it was part of a continuing examination of how far and how painfully individuals would reach to fulfill their sense of fatherhood. Interestingly, Stryker's efforts to extend himself to Conway are balanced by his insistence on hiding his emotions from the rest of his men. When after the battle of Tarawa, Stryker asks Dunne to get some sake out of his bag and distribute it to his squad, he tells Dunne to tell them that he got it "off a dead Jap."

Stryker's most painful attempt to achieve a rapport with Conway comes late in the film at a bar in Hawaii, where Conway is celebrating the birth of his son in New Zealand. Stryker kids him about how he'll feel when his son doesn't write to him and Conway snaps back that won't happen because he'll be with him. Sounding at his most priggish, Conway tells him, "I won't insist that he be tough; I'll try to make him intelligent — and I won't insist he read the Marine Journal of Tactics; I'll get him a set of Shakespeare. In short, I don't want him to be Colonel Sam Conway or Sergeant John Stryker — I want him to be intelligent, considerate, cultured and a gentleman." In the end, Stryker does not become quarrelsome; he just tells Conway to "beat it." But after Conway exits, he refutes his subordinate's observation that Sam Conway could not have been proud of his son, insisting, "It's something inside a guy ... he's always proud of a kid."

On the one hand, Stryker may be thinking about his own son. But he is also cognizant of how Conway has faced him directly and refused to back down, almost daring him to strike him. In fact, in an earlier scene, at the risk of court martial, Conway had tried to hit the sergeant but Stryker deflected his attack. Even as Conway protests that he does not have to be tough, he is doing all he can to impress on his surrogate father just how tough he is.

Dwan changes the order of scenes in the script to show how Stryker saves Conway's life in a training exercise gone awry after this incident but Conway is still not won over. Later, there is a scene which in the final shooting script simply called for a master shot of the squad being briefed shipboard about their impending landing on Iwo Jima. But in the film, in a more intimate medium shot, Conway asks about the effects of aerial bombardment in softening Japanese resistance. Stryker sitting alongside him stares at Conway as he asks the question. Even as the officer answers, Stryker's gaze remains strangely fixed on Conway, not on the man briefing them, and Dwan's camera remains for a time fixed on the two men. Wayne's soulful stares at Conway are far more eloquent than some of the dialogue in expressing Stryker's feelings.

The very act of looking is a motif in the film. It is in the look and face put on for others to see that these men can convey their strength and resolve. After landing on Tarawa, the Marines, entrenched behind logs on the beach, endure a steady bombardment. One baby-faced Marine (Dick Jones), standing next to Stryker, panics and begins to run. Stryker's voice is heard calling out in desperation, "Stay here, kid!" as in long shot we see the young Marine cut down. After another Marine is killed, there is a cut to a close-up of Stryker evincing to the other Marines his imperturbability by casually popping a cigarette into his mouth.

A look can also show cracks in the façade when later in the battle, Stryker is struggling to trigger a satchel bomb next to a Japanese bunker. There is a cut to a close-up of Conway watching from the trenches, shouting, "Throw it!" and clearly looking rattled. Is he just concerned about the success of the operation or is he showing the first sign of his true feelings about Stryker?

Wayne continued to exude the brooding quality he projected in *Red River* and in *Sands*, this is repeatedly conveyed by the way Stryker stares into the distance rather than looking at any particular individual. In a close-up, Stryker shows his hardened features and steely resolve when he refuses to let Conway rescue a wounded Marine calling for help, lest the squad's position be revealed to the Japanese. In a subsequent close-up, when he is not facing Conway, but looking out at the direction of the Marine's cries, we see the sweat and tension on Stryker's face. Later, on the ship, after he tells Dunne not to reveal that the sake being distributed to the men comes from their sergeant, Stryker is left at the railing staring out to sea, stressing both his isolation and concern about the dangers to come.

After his devastating confrontation with Conway in the Hawaiian bar, Stryker does not look at his buddy Bass (James Brown) standing next to him at the bar. Instead, Wayne's Stryker stares blankly ahead until a wistful look comes to his face and he utters the line about "always being proud of a kid."

On Iwo Jima, the two men become reconciled only when Conway saves *Stryker's* life. It is when Conway receives Stryker's praise and gratitude for what he has done that Conway feels he has received fatherly acceptance. His hostility melts away and Conway can then tell Stryker that he intends to name *his* son Sam after his father.

Earlier, in Hawaii, Stryker experienced his own epiphany when he encountered a woman of the night caring for her child, who had been abandoned by his father. Her parental plight convinces Stryker to drop his self-pity and drinking binges. The situation also permits Stryker to assert his fatherly role by helping to feed the baby and then giving the woman financial support without taking anything in return. (Despite repeated demands from Joseph Breen and his colleagues that the woman not be depicted as a prostitute, the filmmakers did not capitulate to the censors although they did make modifications.[37]) There was also a reconciliation between Stryker and Thomas which foreshadowed the resolution of the more important relationship.

Wayne's heroics really captured the public's attention, and his image in that film would resonate for years to come. Political figures like Newt Gingrich and Pat Buchanan claimed to have been inspired by Wayne in *Sands of Iwo Jima*. In his book *Born on the Fourth of July*, Ron Kovic said, "John Wayne in *Sands of Iwo Jima* became one of my heroes."[38] This encouraged Kovic to join the Marines in 1965; he came back from Vietnam paralyzed and deeply disillusioned. But the source of the inspiration sometimes itself became overblown. In another Vietnam memoir, *A Rumor of War*, Philip Caputo said he envisioned himself "like John Wayne in *Sands of Iwo Jima*, and then coming home a suntanned warrior with medals on my chest. The recruiters started giving me their usual sales pitch but I hardly [needed] to be persuaded."[39] As one Wayne biography points out, Caputo had forgotten that Wayne's character was killed in *Sands of Iwo Jima*.[40]

The image of Wayne at Iwo Jima as some kind of superhero annihilating hordes of Japanese remained lodged in the popular imagination. But Dwan's heroes were rarely larger than life except perhaps in the Fairbanks swashbucklers, and even there he would remind viewers of the vulnerability and mortality of his hero. In *Sands*, Stryker was closer to the average man, a flawed man who was aware of his limitations. One commentator on the film who acknowledged that was John Wayne himself.

In a letter to the film historian Suid, Wayne wrote, "[Y]ou stated that I slaughtered thousands of Japanese.... I did not once shoot one Japanese in *Sands of Iwo Jima*."[41] Wayne's statement is not really accurate. He did shoot one Japanese soldier on Suribachi towards the end of the film. Earlier he had thrown a satchel bomb into a pillbox at Tarawa and at Iwo Jima he threw a hand grenade at an underground source of gunfire. But Wayne's point is clear and valid. He was not performing super heroics when he was playing Stryker but an Everyman trying to get a tough job done.

The movie appearance of the three real-life flag-raisers was brief, receiving the flag from Wayne and then raising it in long shot on Mt. Suribachi. *Sands of Iwo Jima* repeated some of the misconceptions of the initial news coverage of the battle such as not showing two flag-raisings and depicting the climb up Suribachi as a deadly exercise.

Rosenthal's photo remains a powerful iconic image. However, it was not the act of raising the flag that was seen as heroic but rather how the picture symbolized the group triumph of the many valorous acts the U.S. Marines performed on Iwo Jima. If a photograph captures a moment, a motion picture must commemorate a broader, though still limited, canvas of activity. It is significant that in later years, the above figures cited a fictional character, Wayne's Stryker, rather than the flag-raisers as their sources for inspiration from Iwo Jima. It was Wayne who projected the indelible image of the American fighting man. And as noted, Wayne's image in the film, like those of the real flag-raisers, became distorted in myth.

The film itself manages to puncture part of that myth. In a dialogue exchange included in the film but not in the final script, Conway tells Stryker that he is "indestructible." Stryker suggests that he stay close to him and a little bit of it might rub off. Conway says that he has been haunted by a voice that tells him that he will die in combat. (In Bradley's book, two of the flag-raisers who were killed had told friends of having just the same feeling.[42]) Stryker discounts that and denies that he has ever felt that way. But shortly thereafter, as Stryker recites the unfortunate line, "I've never felt better in my life," and sits down to smoke a cigarette, he is suddenly shot to death. A letter to his son, found on Stryker's body, reveals that he too had the feeling that he might not walk away this time.

Even this death scene has created myths. In the December 1985 issue of *American Film*, a letter to the editor sought to correct a statement made by film historian Basinger in an earlier issue on the death of Wayne's Stryker in *Sands of Iwo Jima*. She had written that he had been shot in the head. The letter-writer insisted that all real movie fans knew that Wayne's Stryker got his fatal wound in the back.[43] Indeed most film fans spoken to by the author agree with that assessment.

But the editors of *American Film* showed poor judgment in not consulting Basinger before they published that letter. In the January-February 1986 issue, *American Film* published Basinger's own letter which noted that viewers can see that when Wayne is shot, "The velocity knocks him backward as the cigarettes fly into the air and his hands rise involuntarily to his chest. If he had been shot in the back, he surely would not have been driven backward by the impact of the bullet." Basinger also notes that the private who kills Wayne's assailant moves downhill in front of the group of Marines, not behind them. Basinger acknowledges that Wayne was shot in the chest.

So what created this confusion? Basinger pointed out, "Later, an insert shows Wayne's body, face down with an exit wound. Stills that reproduced this image of Wayne have caused people to believe that he was shot in the back. Allan Dwan told me years ago that preview audiences did not believe Wayne was really dead, and they added the shot even though it caused some confusion...."[44] So preview audiences may also have been convinced that Stryker was "indestructible."

A good bit of newsreel footage is used during the assault on Iwo Jima and this only intensifies as the patrol heads for Mount Suribachi. There are a number of jarring mismatches both in film stock and style. As these proliferate, one begins to question whether the newsreel footage is serving as background to the fictional narrative or if the actors and their props are serving as mediators to the actual footage. This blending of the real and the fictional serves as an appropriate lead-in to the fusing of the characters of the story with the actual flag-raising and with some of the real-life figures participating in the drama.

There then appears Stryker's letter to his son, which is picked up by Stryker's former nemesis Thomas and read by him. (In the final shooting script, it was read by Conway but the change permits us to see Conway's reactions.) The letter is the last of the many Stryker has written that he gallantly assumes "have never reached" his boy. The letter contains words of advice ("Always do what your heart says is right") but it is also an acknowledgment of Stryker's shortcomings: "[W]hen you grow older and get to know more about me, you'll see that I've been a failure in many ways. This isn't what I wanted but things just turned out that way. If there was only more time I...." As the

John Agar and John Wayne in a tense scene from *Sands of Iwo Jima* (1949).

letter is read, the emotions are registered in reaction close-ups of the other members of the squad crouched around Stryker's body. Each must contemplate how he has judged Stryker and the things he never knew about him. When the letter ends in mid-sentence, Conway takes it, promising to finish it.

At this emotional moment, the flag-raising begins. The flag-raising is almost like an answer to the pained despair of the letter. As with the reading of Stryker's letter, close-ups of each squad member are projected, intercut with long shots of the flag-raising. (The fact that Dwan took the time for close-ups of all these characters again suggests he was "editing in the camera.") As they look up, each Marine appears as if he is being roused from his grief. In the next round of camera shots after the raising (including a two-shot with the close-ups), each Marine appears mesmerized and uplifted by the sight of the Stars and Stripes. In the remaining shots, except that of Conway who seems to assume command of the group, the Marines again meld into a single unit. There is once more a mystic power at work on the audience's emotions as there was at the conclusion of *The Iron Mask.*

In his book *John Wayne, Actor, Artist, Hero,* Richard D. McGhee writes, "[S]omething passes from Stryker.... It charges the energies and expressions of his men...."[45] The concept that something passes from one Marine and reanimates itself in others is easily grasped as part of the mystique of the Marines' *espirit de corps*, certainly a key point the Marines wanted conveyed by the film. As the flag is raised, the "Marine Hymn" is played on the soundtrack, first softly, then building with accumulating force as the Marines walk away. McGhee asserts, "Stryker is transformed into the American flag." And indeed there is symmetry in the way the letter-reading and flag-raising sequences are shot.

But McGhee's claim suggests a virtual resurrection and has the effect of almost deifying Stryker.[46] Dwan, however, seems to envision Stryker becoming a part of something greater just as in *When Paris Sleeps*, Jacques Costaud's conflagration dissolved into the Eternal Flame of the Unknown Soldier. A more realistic perspective of the character is to see Stryker not as transformed into the flag but absorbed by it. Even as he acknowledges his shortcomings, it is Stryker's reaching out to posterity and to the son he never knew that moves us. With his death, that reach to posterity is incarnated in the flag which encompasses a patchwork of individual struggles and hopes that are passed from generation to generation. In this view, the flag is not a sacred object but a living symbol that needs to be continually replenished. The passing of the torch need not be restricted to a biological child and it is Conway who begins assuming Stryker's demeanor and his stock phrase of "Saddle up...." Not only has Stryker become a surrogate father to Conway but both of them claim linkage to Conway's father Sam, as each has named his son after him.

Stryker, like other Dwan paters, has no remembered relationship with his offspring. But in Dwan's films it is the detachment of paternity that permits it to be ennobling. It is the father who must prove his worth even if it will never be known to anyone but himself. He may feel overwhelmed by his own failures but he must lay out opportunities for the next generation. It is, in fact, Stryker's sense of failure that compels him to seek Conway out as his last opportunity at fatherhood.

The final shot in the shooting script was to have been the Suribachi flag waving defiantly. *Friendly Enemies* had ended with a shot of the flag but Dwan probably grasped that the flag had already served its purpose in the film. Instead the Marines walk towards the gunfire and disappear into a mist and uncertain future. While the film may give the impression that the battle is essentially won, it still appears that there is much mopping up to be done as Conway proclaims, "Let's get back into the war." We don't know if Conway's premonition of death will prove correct or how many more members of the squad will be killed. But Conway has assumed Stryker's role and he too now has a son, who will have to decide his own form of continuity.

Wayne's iconographical and star-studded status makes it more difficult to imagine Stryker as an average man. What would have been the difference had he been played by someone like Van Heflin? The reading of the letter would have been far more painful and the film would almost certainly have been less popular.

On the other hand, the casting of Wayne, like that of Fairbanks in *The Iron Mask*, made the character more inherently transcendent. The dramatic moment in this film is also a microcosm of what had happened historically. Like the American people, jarred by the devastating large losses in the final year of the war, the Marines of the movie *Sands of Iwo Jima* find similar solace in the flag-raising.

Wayne's portrayal of Stryker was undoubtedly colored by the fact that in the immediate years after *Sands* was released, he became a symbol of American power. But the clash of Wayne as Superhero and as Everyman in *Sands of Iwo Jima* may also reflect the conflicted feelings of the memory of war.

Rendezvous with Ralston

Dwan's wife Marie died on March 13, 1949. The couple was watching television when Dwan noticed that Marie appeared to have fallen asleep. When he went to awaken her, he discovered that she was dead. Mrs. Dwan was only forty-six years old but she had apparently been in poor health for years. Among other problems, she had suffered from a cerebral embolism and thrombosis for three years and from portal cirrhosis of the liver with ascites for six years.[47]

Columnist Louella Parsons said she received the news of Marie's death from the wife of director Robert Z. Leonard, who told her that Dwan was in a state of near collapse.[48] Marie's death occurred not long before pre-production planning began on *Sands of Iwo Jima*. Dwan was likely able to assuage his grief by pouring himself and his energy into this major production.

But after the heady success of *Sands of Iwo Jima*, Dwan would be back to confronting more mundane problems at Republic. This would come in the challenge of a leading lady.

Czech actress Vera Ralston, a former Olympic figure skater, had appeared in a couple of American films that included her in skating scenes in the early 1940s. By the mid–1940s, she was playing straight dramatic roles for Republic. As Randy Roberts and James S. Olson noted, "At exactly what point in their relationship Ralston and Yates became lovers is unclear, but it was probably early on, for almost from the first he evinced willingness to promote a career that every objective observer agreed was doomed."[49]

Joseph Kane, who directed Vera in eleven Republic films, recalled, "She got so that she understood English. She could talk all right, but she never was a very good actress. She was fair, but her main difficulty was she was often miscast.... She was in the same sort of position with Yates as Marion Davies was with William Randolph Hearst."[50] Thus, Dwan now found himself in a position that he had tried for years to avoid.

Wayne's biographers Roberts and Olson believed that Yates planned to use Wayne to advance Ralston's career.[51] After making their second film together, *The Fighting Kentuckian*, Wayne felt Ralston's casting had hurt the movie. Wayne said of Yates, "I respected him in many ways and he liked me. But when it came to the woman he loved — his business brains just went flyin' out the window."[52] Dwan made a similar comment in sizing up the predicament. "A man goes nuts about a woman — what can you say? It's a hopeless situation."[53]

Ralston co-starred with John Carroll in two Dwan Westerns. Carroll had already made three films with Ralston and was reportedly her favorite co-star.[54] Dwan made clear to Bogdanovich that he did not consider Carroll a bargain either.[55]

While the second of Dwan's two Ralston–Carroll films was in production, an item appeared in Hedda Hopper's "Looking at Hollywood" column: "My hat's off to Allan Dwan, director, who took a slub at John Carroll. Carroll's younger, bigger and huskier than Dwan but Allan's spirit is that of a mountain lion. The incident took place because Carroll muffed his lines and refused to read them from a blackboard."[56] Dwan did speak in his later years of assaulting uncooperative actors and the story is at least in the realm of possibility.

Surrender, Dwan's first Ralston film, shared the wild, fatal romanticism of Westerns like *Duel in the Sun* (1946) and *Colorado Territory* (1949) as well as the noir mood and style of oaters like *Pursued* (1947) and the 1948 *Blood on the Moon*. Its opening nocturnal scene is indeed noirish with a group of rivals of the protagonist, Gregg Delaney (Carroll), awaiting his return in a street in the town of La Mirada. Delaney manages to evade them and run for his life to seek a hiding place. Dark alleyways and menacing shadows keynote the atmosphere. Catching his chief rival Barney Gale from behind, Delaney is able to dispatch him with a knife concealed in his cane while Gale's gunshot goes awry. The killing is visualized onscreen by their shadows.

This scene establishes the look of the film. Except for two brief scenes, all of the exterior shots in the picture are set at night. The opening scene is also a microcosm of the movie: Different forces will continue to seek out the life of Gregg Delaney.

One force is the sheriff, William Howard, played forcefully by Walter Brennan. Howard is a former rustler "who has seen the light." In his self-righteous zeal, he can only believe the worst about Delaney, another of Dwan's gambling figures, who here runs the Crystal Palace Bar and Casino. As Gregg notes, Howard would never believe that Gale's killing could have been in self-defense and is convinced that Gregg is responsible for bringing evil into the town. Gregg's close friend, the newspaper editor Johnny Hale (William Ching), compares Howard to Javert, the obsessive police inspector in *Les Miserables*.

The other power is, again in true noir fashion, a femme fatale, Violet Barton (played by Ralston). Violet uses her beauty to manipulate men. Once can imagine Marlene Dietrich playing her with glamour and style. Ralston is attractive but no dazzler. She is referred to as a trollop and Ralston's character does appear common and vulgar. At first, she seems to be attracted to Gregg but as a result of a misunderstanding, she finds herself paired with Johnny. After finding that Johnny is rich, perhaps out of capriciousness she stands up Gregg, who is smitten with her, and marries Johnny. She may also be spiting her long-suffering older sister Janet (Maria Palmer), who loves Johnny.

Violet is, not surprisingly, a lady with a past. That includes a previous husband to whom she is still legally married and who has just finished serving a prison sentence that Vi escaped serving with him. He is played with oily élan by Francis Lederer. Vi disposes of him in Delaney's office using Gregg's knife. But it is Johnny, and not Gregg, who returns to the office first and he becomes implicated in the murder.

Johnny is ready to take the rap for his friend Gregg, while Sheriff Howard has determined that Gregg is the murderer. Devoted to Hale for having saved his life during the Civil War, Gregg frees Johnny and takes him to his estate close to a trail leading to the Mexican border. Sorting things out, it doesn't take long for Gregg to learn that Violet is the murderer. For reasons that must have stumped audiences of the time, given how she has tormented all the cast members, Gregg decides not to turn Vi over to the law and concedes that he loves her, declaring, unconvincingly, that they are alike.

The wily Sheriff Howard has anticipated their flight to Mexico and has set up a trap to intercept Gregg and Vi before they reach the border. Dwan impressively stages the climax as Gregg and Violet find themselves surrounded. Howard mounts the highest hill in the area where, like an all-seeing deity, he can look down on everything that's going on. Gregg and Vi take refuge in a ditch, and Gregg keeps the posse at bay. When Howard sees Gregg kill one of his deputies, he fires down into the ditch, fatally wounding Gregg. Violet now has a chance to surrender and possibly to survive by blaming Gregg for the murder. But as if almost on a whim, she takes Gregg's gun and starts firing at the deputies so that they return her fire and she can die with Gregg. As if emulating the final scene in *Duel in the Sun,* the camera cranes back, moving away from the two bodies joined together for eternity while a chorus warbles the title song on the soundtrack.

While this final gesture is not without effect, it would have worked much better had Vi been portrayed with more style and charm, which would have drawn us to her despite her evil deeds. While *Surrender* may seem too grandiose and operatic, it might have worked with a more charismatic leading lady.

This was not the kind of film Dwan cared for. He later said, "I know I made one great classic at Republic to please Yates, in which both the leading man and leading lady die in each other's arms in the last scene and the camera pulls gently away from them lying there in the mud. And I think the picture's still lying there."[57]

With the same stars, Dwan made another film more to his liking. Dwan told Bogdanovich that he liked the background of Virginia City and the period in which people were making their fortunes out of silver. "Making allowances for the cast — Carroll and Vera Ralston again — it was a pleasant picture. Of course, she tried very hard and was a very nice girl."[58]

Dwan was clearly more comfortable with this assignment. There are more elements that we associate with other Dwan films. There is also an interesting symmetry with *Surrender.* As with the parallels between *Young People* and *Driftwood,* Dwan seems to be re-working the material of an earlier movie to make a more successful film.

That film, *Belle Le Grand,* opens with a courtroom scene in Natchez, Mississippi, in 1850 as the state is making its final argument The camera is fixed in the jury box as the prosecutor seems to be leaning into the viewer. He tells the jurors that "you have been chosen to sit on judgment on a murderess."

The alleged murderess Sally Sinclair is played by Ralston, almost as if she survived in some parallel universe to stand trial for the murder committed in *Surrender.* The circumstances are different, however, as it is her husband, a riverboat gambler, who committed the murder and fled. She was at worst an accessory and possibly not involved at all.

The impact of the "jury shot" is also to make the viewer himself feel he is being asked to scrutinize Sally. This seems a daring thing to do but the overall effect is to make the viewer more sympathetic to her.

The subsequent scene has Sally returning from five years in prison. She is followed by the camera in one marvelously sustained shot: an abject and pathetic figure moving slowly through a fog, shot in soft focus, to the dirge-like music of "The Old Folks at Home." While this suggests another somber, if not maudlin film, it is here that the movie makes its pirouette. Sally decides that she will become the "only thing the world will let me be," a gambler. Her fall becomes her rise as there follows a montage of card games and roulette wheels. When it's over in 1870, Sally is prosperous and known by the name Belle Le Grand.

The story resumes in San Francisco where Belle is visiting the stock exchange. It's there that she runs into John Kilton, played by Carroll, who again has William Ching portraying his best friend. Kilton is using his mining venture to play the stock market.

The plot is pivoted on a series of opposites from the previous film. Where Carroll was stalked by fate and a vengeful sheriff in the first film, here he is known as "Lucky John" and early in the film he survives a shooting when the bullet hits his watch instead of his body. His chief rival (who is not on the right side of the law) is persistently outsmarted by Kilton.

Kilton's nemesis is Montgomery Crane (Stephen Chase) who as Charles La Farge was also the husband who left Belle in the lurch at the beginning of the film. This time it is Belle who has the power to blackmail the husband but chooses to keep him on a short leash.

Where Ralston tormented and bullied her sister in *Surrender,* in this film Belle has paid for her much younger sister's board and education and she has now blossomed into Nan Henshaw, the young opera singer, portrayed by 21-year-old coloratura soprano Muriel Lawrence in her film debut. Since Nan was too young to remember what her older sister looked like, Belle has become her secret benefactor and protector. The unknown older sister functions here as a variation of Dwan's lost father figure.

Virginia City, the location of the mine, is the seat of the action and a colorful place. As the self-proclaimed "Queen of the Comstock," the middle-aged Hope Emerson plays the Amazonian-sized Emma McGee, who dwarfs her milquetoast husband (John Qualen) and most of the other males in the film. Emma is a sweet but tough gun-toting gal who evokes memories of Dwan's Calamity Anne. She and her husband are Kilton's partners in the Queen Midas silver mine.

Ralston looks relaxed and assured in her role and is engaging. Early in the film, when Belle entered the stock exchange, she was asked if she intended to play the market and replied, "Why not? Gambling is my business." *Belle Le Grand* is lively in showing the similarities (and differences?) between gambling and stock-speculating and the respective montages of gambling and of the stock market seem to rhyme.

With its opera sequences and resplendent sets, *Belle Le Grand* could almost pass as an MGM Western of a decade earlier. (Carroll is remembered as a second-string Gable.) Dwan undoubtedly took pleasure in being able to recycle the Universal sets from the 1943 *Phantom of the Opera.* The film also has an elegant score by Victor Young.

But the picture worked at its center with Ralston and Carroll as the two power brokers whose romance advances in exchanges of generosity and strategic moves. They are not doppelgangers as in *Surrender* but in this pleasant if relatively minor effort, are fellow "weeds."

The remaining films Dwan made at Republic are like a Noah's Ark breakdown of genres: two musicals, two war films and two Westerns. The six films are also evenly divided between color and black and white. Since the next film is a war picture that co-stars Ralston, it will be discussed here. A war film Dwan made for Allied Artists will take the place of the Ralston picture in the pairings of the next section of this chapter.

While Dwan's sense of playfulness and better casting helped

A group photograph of some Republic studio personnel shot during the time *Northwest Outpost* (1947) was being filmed. In front row from left to right are Nelson Eddy, Maria Ouspenskaya, Vera Ralston, studio head Herbert Yates, Ilona Massey, director Frank Borzage and Elsa Lanchester. Dwan, wearing glasses, can be seen in the second row, just behind Massey (Allan Dwan Collection, Box 2, Photograph Folders, American Heritage Center, University of Wyoming).

relieve some of Yates' pretensions regarding Ralston, the director faced a more somber project with her in his next film. *The Wild Blue Yonder* tells the story of the B-29 bomber that played a crucial role in defeating Japan in World War II. Along with Ralston, the movie starred Wendell Corey and Forrest Tucker. As with *Sands of Iwo Jima*, it told a largely fictional story against a backdrop of historical events.

Dwan directed the screen duo of John Carroll and Vera Ralston for the second time in *Belle Le Grand* (1951).

More humor was injected in this film, permitting Phil Harris to sing his hit novelty song "The Thing." Dwan even inserts a joke that refers to *Rendezvous with Annie*. There's also a standard plot involving a woman courted by two pilots; of course, only the one who wins her affections will survive. Ralston plays a nurse who suffers from memories of the past. Had her feelings registered the pain of war convincingly, the plot might have transcended its clichéd origins. But Ralston's inexpressive appearance conveys little of the character's emotional baggage and one can only imagine Dwan's exasperation.

The film does flirt with some real issues and factual events. Air Force Lieutenant General Curtis LeMay, who played an important part in the story of the B-29 bomber, was portrayed by Republic director William Witney. Two plot points in the film, LeMay's insistence that bombers fly at dangerously low altitudes to insure more precision bombing and the problem with bomber crews who used dubious excuses to duck out of missions, were both discussed over fifty years later in Errol Morris' 2003 Oscar-winning documentary *The Fog of War*. (The man at the center of that documentary, Defense Secretary Robert McNamara, had worked with LeMay during World War II and again during the 1962 Cuban Missile Crisis.)

Although by Republic standards, *The Wild Blue Yonder* was an ambitious film, its rewards are modest.

At this time, Dwan's thoughts were still with his deceased wife but actor Richard Erdman found Dwan's way of commemorating her on the set distasteful. Erdman recalled, "Every morning he'd come in with these little poems to his dead wife and he assembled some of the cast around him and sat in a chair and started reading his poems to his dead wife. I found it shocking and stupid and vulgar."[59] Erdman was also unhappy with other aspects of Dwan's behavior. He said that Dwan "started pissing me off" in his treatment of a young actor named Terry Kilburn, inferring that he was gay and "being rather rude about it."

Erdman finally had a confrontation with Dwan. Erdman was in a mockup of a plane that was on a big ramp about twenty feet from the floor. Dwan was across the soundstage in his chair. Dwan sent his assistant Richard Moder to go up to Erdman to give him his instructions for the scene. Erdman was not happy being directed by proxy. Erdman told Moder, "I think he [Dwan] should direct the actor. I'd appreciate it if he did that." The exchanges went back and forth until Moder told Erdman that Dwan was very upset and "said some rather rude things." At that point, Erdman left the set for his dressing room and said he would not return until he received Dwan's apology.

The next day Erdman was told that Dwan wanted to see him. Dwan was "not looking at all apologetic." Dwan said they had a disagreement and Erdman corrected him: "No, we don't. What do you want me to do? Just tell me what you want me to do." Ironically, Dwan told Erdman that he wanted him to look happy in the scene. With that the matter was settled but Erdman remembered Dwan as "a contemptible man."

While Erdman said that he enjoyed being with most of the cast and that they got along well, that did not extend to Ralston: "Wendell hated her." Erdman felt that Ralston remained distant from the other cast members.[60]

Other Republic personnel felt more generously towards Ralston. Joan Leslie remembered, "I worked with Vera. We became friends. I liked her very much even if she did learn her lines in Czechoslovakian."[61] Kane, Ralston's most frequent director, said that she never took advantage of her position to make things rough for anybody. He remembered her as "very nice to work with ... always very cooperative, worked very hard, tried very hard."[62] Dwan concurred on these last points and added, "She just hadn't been trained to be an actress long enough to be a star."[63]

Dwan's comments about Yates were less generous. Dwan told Howard Mandelbaum that he regarded Yates as uncouth and that the mogul spat into waste baskets. He also claimed that Yates would be given injections to boost his virility before going home to Vera.[64] Dwan's acerbic remarks likely reflected his resentment of Yates' artistic abuse of the executive-actress relationship.

Ralston and Yates were finally married in 1952. While they were on their honeymoon, the annual shareholders meeting for Republic was contentious. Among the items under scrutiny was how Ralston affected the company's performance. In 1956, investors sued Yates for his favored treatment of Ralston, alleging that by then eighteen of her films had flopped. Undaunted, Yates had her star in six more Republic films before the company folded in 1958.[65] The reasons for Republic's demise were more complex than the failure of one star but Yates' obsession had done its damage at a time when the film industry and particularly his company were in precarious shape.

Two by Two

The first of Dwan's two Republic musicals was a biography of composer Stephen Collins Foster. Numerous accounts show that Foster had a sad and brief life, dying at the age of thirty-seven. Dwan depicted his story as a comedy.

Earlier film versions treated Foster's life more solemnly, including the 1935 *Harmony Lane* made by the independent Mascot company and the 1939 *Swanee River*, the latter a big-budget affair at Fox with Dwan's former star Don Ameche as Foster and Al Jolson as E.P. Christy, who popularized some of Foster's songs.

The title for Dwan's film, *I Dream of Jeanie*, came from one of Foster's songs which had not sold particularly well in Foster's lifetime. But in the early 1940s when a dispute between radio broadcasters and the American Society of Composers, Authors and Publishers (ASCAP) encouraged the playing of songs in the public domain, *Jeanie with the Light Brown Hair* (the proper title) suddenly became a hit.[66] That impetus and the fact that in Dwan's words, "the stuff was free" probably sparked Republic's interest in producing a Foster musical biography.[67]

The film opens with some of Dwan's most playful editing since the beginning of the 1917 *A Modern Musketeer*. The first shot is that of an aged black patriarch singing to his group of children (to the tune of "Oh, Susanna"), "In 1849 a young man wrote a song. The song it made no sense at all but it moved the world along." (Those lyrics were written by Dwan.)

Eileen Christy, unlike her snooty sister in the film, enjoys the music of Stephen Collins Foster, played by Bill Shirley, in *I Dream of Jeanie* (1952).

There is a cut to minstrels dancing in city streets to celebrate that same tune and then a cut to a pipe organ on a riverboat also playing "Oh, Susanna!" making the melody seem ubiquitous. The camera tracks in to a woman on the boat, clearly vexed by the song and exclaiming, "If only I could get my hands on the dreadful man who wrote that song!" Under the title of "Cincinnati" there is then a cut to an interior. Young Stephen Foster is seen working in a bookkeeping office playing a flute and waiting for his girlfriend to arrive when her riverboat docks. The audience is led to suspect that it is the same woman being driven mad by "Oh, Susanna."

This opening montage establishes the impression of a documentary record intertwined with a sense of the ridiculous.

The career of Stephen Foster began at the dawn of celebrityhood for show business figures in America. By the time the film was made, Dwan had found time to reflect on his own flirtation with fame in the first part of his career. A *New York Times* interview with Dwan found the director not savoring the success of *Sands of Iwo Jima* and preferring to be away from the limelight. He commented, "After a picture like *Iwo Jima*, I get kind of nervous. If you get your head up above the mob, they try to knock it off. If you stay down, you last forever."[68] Dwan reiterated that sentiment throughout the latter part of his career and in retirement. When he was at Fox in the 1930s, he may have yearned for some of his lost fame. Now, he believed he was better off without it. He was one of cinema's pioneers but he was a pioneer in exile from his former prominence.

In *I Dream of Jeanie*, scripted by Alan LeMay (who later

wrote the novel *The Searchers* on which Ford's classic was based), Foster is beset by problems having to do with the lax copyright laws of the time involving composer rights. Steve is a humble lad who is happy to have his songs printed as sheet music even if he doesn't get credited for them. In the film, he is under siege by his publisher and by E.P. Christy for not giving them exclusive rights to "Oh Susanna!" even though they paid him nothing for it.

The film's Stephen Foster can be quite exasperating, though one recognizes that his joy is in creating the songs rather than reaping benefit from them. (Steve prefers to live in a stable where playing his music will not disturb anyone.) However, the success of his songs becomes a total embarrassment to him when he learns that the woman he loves, singer Inez MacDowell (Muriel Lawrence), sees them as vulgar and prefers the classics. Inez has musical aspirations of her own and Steve is eager to help her even if he is not a very good accompanist.

Steve's full appreciation of the "catastrophe of success"[69] comes at Inez's recital when Christy interrupts the recital carrying all the music he has found in Steve's room. The celebrated singer announces to the startled audience that he will be giving the premiere performance of the songs of a great American artist, Stephen Foster. Inez runs off with Steve in pursuit. Trying to console Inez, Steve remains out of the recital room and sits with Inez on the stairs. After Christy performs "My Old Kentucky Home" to great applause, there is a cut back to the couple on the stairs with Inez griping to Steve, "You never lived in Kentucky." It was true that in his early songs Foster romanticized a South of which he had seen little. As the songs and applause continue, a cut back to the stairway has Inez now complaining to Foster, "How many of these things did you write, a million?" Arguably the funniest part of the film is the paradox of watching Steve sink into ever deeper humiliation as his songs are performed and acclaimed. Steve later promises to Inez that he will stop writing popular songs but later, as he is getting Inez tickets for a Jenny Lind concert, they are astounded to see a parade of minstrels cavorting in the streets playing Foster's music and carrying his song titles on banners.

Meisel has written that "even an irretrievably foolish film such as *I Dream of Jeanie* is directed with such controlled confidence...."[70] The "foolishness" of the film includes such tired gambits as Steve being so hopelessly in love with Inez that he does not notice that her sister Jeanie (Eileen Christy) is the one who really loves him and whom he is really attracted to. Despite the fact that Inez is appalled by his music and has told Steve that she is in love with someone else, Steve persists in wooing her by serenading her with "Beautiful Dreamer" outside her window. There is nothing exceptional in the staging of this scene except in its startling directness and quixotic nature. Bill Shirley, who plays Foster, had a stirring tenor voice and whatever the dramatic limitations of the performers, the songs are sung quite well. Predictably, Steve's appeal does not move Inez.

Foster, who had up to now appeared obliging and carefree, suffers something of a breakdown, ripping up his music and running out of his room in confusion. It is not his beloved but Foster himself who is the "dreamer," a part of Dwan's own makeup that he felt had to be always locked under control.

Heretofore in the film, Dwan had used the Republic Trucolor process blandly. But as Steve races though the woods, the dark greens of the forest become almost expressionistically menacing. Steve now hears his music as a cacophony of dissonant sounds like a Charles Ives composition. The price of fame has become the horror of fame and Steve runs in terror. He stops as he reaches the Ohio River with a rowboat offering a possibility of escape into reddish brown waters. At such a point, *I Dream of Jeanie* begins to resemble the "artist's" paranoia of Arthur Penn's later *Mickey One* in its dwelling on the terror and guilt of fame although the Dwan film is too anchored in its narrative, however silly, to look arty. Like *Rendezvous with Annie*, *I Dream of Jeanie* is something of a nightmare comedy.

The journey down the Ohio River, where Steve gets to see the real South, might have been played as a Huckleberry Finn odyssey but this would have gone beyond the scope of a Republic production. It's time to wrap up things: After Steve is found, the inspiration of Jeanie helps him complete (what else?) "Jeanie with the Light Brown Hair" and the movie ends with everyone on the riverboat somehow being able to sing the just-written song.

I Dream of Jeanie also includes a scene where Steve helps take care of an injured black child and tells the boy's concerned mother (Louise Beavers) that he has learned everything he knows about music from the black populace (although he addresses them with the unfortunate phrase, "you people"). This rightful acknowledgment of the source of Foster's music may have been also intended to balance the scenes of singers in blackface. Blackface was indeed the convention of minstrel music at the time and the film's depiction of it is historically accurate. Dwan does tweak the convention a bit as when guest star Rex Allen appears as a minstrel of the time who is presented as "Rex Allen."

Republic held the June 1952 world premiere of *I Dream of Jeanie* in Pittsburgh with plenty of hoopla as fifty concertizing minstrels entertained crowds at a riverbank. The picture's stars Christy, Shirley, Lawrence and Ray Middleton performed on stage for an hour at the Fulton Theater before the film began.[71] Middleton, who created the role of Frank Butler in *Annie Get Your Gun* on Broadway, contributed the strongest dramatic presence to *I Dream of Jeanie* in the role of Christy. Middleton would be summoned again by Dwan for a subsequent Trucolor musical for Republic, the 1953 *Sweethearts on Parade*, joined by his *Jeanie* co-stars, Shirley and Christy.

Sweethearts on Parade followed quickly on the heels of *Jeanie*'s opening, going into production on July 31, 1952. Again the music was drawn largely from songs in public domain. But this was a far more eclectic score embracing everything from traditional American folk tunes to Johann Strauss to Bel Canto Opera. There was mercifully only one blackface number here,[72] used for the Stephen Foster number *Nellie Bly*, but it is vigorously performed and choreographed.

Both Meisel and Bogdanovich praise the *Sweethearts* dance numbers while dismissing the film. This author's contention is that while *Sweethearts on Parade* may be no masterpiece and is flawed, it is a more satisfying and interesting film than has heretofore been acknowledged and certainly a more ambitious film than *I Dream of Jeanie*. In both dramatic and musical structure, *Sweethearts* is striking in concept and quite often in execution. Unfortunately, *Sweethearts on Parade* is among the most difficult Dwan sound films to see in quality form, as it survives in mostly faded color prints. The color may not even have been given the proper treatment originally as the *Variety* reviewer complained of Republic's Trucolor process that it "wasn't very true, changing colors in mid-scene upon occasions."[73]

Sweethearts on Parade may be seen in the context of two other films of the period, Henry King's 1952 *Wait 'Til the Sun Shines Nellie* and John Ford's 1953 *The Sun Shines Bright*, the latter also filmed at Republic. Both films draw their titles from songs of bygone times and feed on an atmosphere of nostalgia.

Sweethearts on Parade actually begins with the song "Long, Long Ago" but with new lyrics written by Dwan: "Let's Journey back to Yesterday.... And Live Again the Simple Way of Dear Old Kokomo...." Against these lyrics, the opening montage paints an idyllic portrait of "An Indiana Soft June Day Some Eighty Years Ago."

Dwan was possibly drawing from his own memories of the nineteenth century Midwest. Dwan had added his own lyrics to a couple of the songs in *I Dream of Jeanie* but his contributions were more numerous in this film. Composer Robert Armbuster, who wrote the adapted score, as he had for *Jeanie,* also contributed lyrics. Since the *Sweethearts* score is a patchwork of songs from different eras, the lyrics provided by Dwan and Armbuster help anchor the songs to the narrative. In fact, the majority of the twenty-one songs (and arias) in the film help advance the plot or comment on it.

That plot is another of Dwan's depictions of a lost father. Kathleen Townsend (Lucille Norman) gives music lessons to young people in Kokomo and is loved by the community. Her daughter Sylvia is now coming of age and, while she loves her mother as a pal, she also yearns for a paternal figure. Kathleen is considering a marriage proposal from Kokomo's stuffy physician Dr. Harold Wayne (Clinton Sundberg). But Sylvia's queries set Kathleen off on a reverie. While Sylvia sits dreamily on the porch steps, Kathleen withdraws into a room where she uncovers mementos of her marriage. She finds a photo of her and her husband, Cameron Ellerby (Middleton), from when they sang "Now, You'll Remember Me" in *The Bohemian Girl.* There is a flashback to them singing and then Kathleen telling Cam of her pregnancy. In a voiceover, Kathleen recalls that when she had her child, Cam sang with other prima donnas and had affairs with them. Kathleen then decided to take her baby and leave him but she now has second thoughts on whether she acted wisely. Sylvia knows nothing of her father or what he looks like.

Dwan playfully cuts to the front exterior of the house as the wagons of a medicine show are passing by. Seated on one of the wagons is Cam, who is singing "A Rovin'." He catches a glimpse of Sylvia and sings directly to her, the camera catching his point of view as the wagon sweeps by her. A second wagon carries a young man closer to her age, Bill Gamble (Shirley), whose gaze also fixes on her as she is seen running excitedly into the house in a graceful mobile shot. Kathleen remains within the house, unaware of her husband's "return."

Lucille Norman (left) sees that her daughter (Eileen Christy) has finally met her father (Ray Middleton) in the musical *Sweethearts on Parade* (1953).

The scene may upset some critics as the epitome of fortuitous coincidences. However, it is also logical that Cam in his downward spiral after Kathleen left him would wind up in a wandering medicine show and that Kathleen had not traveled all that far away.

When the medicine show pitches camp, the second of the main locations is established (the first being Kathleen's home). Dwan's aesthetic and budgetary strategy of using two locales is taken to a particularly schematic extreme. The medicine show is the preserve of the two male protagonists, typifying their love of freedom and show business as well as their cultural disreputability. Home belongs to the two women establishing security and respectability as well as their love of refined music. The editing between the two locales is quite methodical. At one point, it even suggests a telepathic connection between Kathleen and Cam, emphasizing the lingering bond between the two, though neither is aware that the other is nearby. The parallel editing shows Dwan both maintaining and playing riffs on the Griffith tradition.

The atmosphere of nostalgia gives way to a rumination on love, time and memory. Bill Gamble's romantic interest in Sylvia provides a youthful parallel to the plight of the middle-aged lovers and will serve as a bridge when Bill takes Sylvia to the medicine show. Bill's friendship with Cam also helps fill in narrative gaps; it's Bill who reveals that Cam has been long preoccupied with something that makes him "live within himself." Bill himself is a bridge figure, being both a talented singer and a certified physician. Like Dwan, he is both a man of science and of the "arts" and claims he found the medicine show provided better employment. But it becomes clear he loves the life he is leading. There is also an element of risk in Bill forsaking medicine for the tent show. It's no coincidence that his name is "Gamble" and that he resembles some of Dwan's gambler figures. The "open road" life of the tent show may have also interested Dwan since it resembles the gypsy caravan existence of his early years with the Flying A Company.

The most impressively staged of the musical numbers is Franz von Suppe's "Young Love," set by a lake with Bill and Sylvia. Dwan orchestrates the scene with lyrical camera movements and poetic cutaways to images outside the sphere of the lovers. Later, Bill takes Sylvia to the medicine show and invites her to sing on an empty stage. Observing Sylvia singing "Ah non guinge" from Bellini's "La Sonnambula," Cam has a flashback of seeing his wife sing the aria. Cam then angrily demands that Sylvia get off his stage, as he lapses into an alcoholic bout of depression. This sets off the chain of events that will lead to Kathleen going to the medicine show and coming face to face with Cam.

One of the more felicitous aspects of *Sweethearts on Parade* is the manner in which numerous minor characters contribute to the story and stand out in their own right. For example, a couple of the chorus girls act as a wisecracking Greek chorus to some of the goings-on. But the most important secondary character is Lolita Lamont (Estelita Rodriguez), a medicine show singer who also does household tasks for Cam. Lolita is in love with Cam but she's not sure if Cam takes her seriously. It's Lolita who foils the sheriff's attempt to close the show because of Sylvia being entertained there by Bill. Her rendezvous with Bill causes the disturbance that puts Sylvia under Cam's care. She appears to be another of Dwan's angels. The Angel Lolita, after learning the truth, goes to Sylvia and tells her that Cam is her father and that he loves her, as does Bill. Lolita says she has revealed this because she believes in Love. Here, the "other woman" may be the most idealistic character in the movie.

At the end of the film, Kathleen and Sylvia abandon the security of their Kokomo home to go off on the open road with Cam and Bill's tent show, not a typical ending for a movie of the fifties.

While not all the song selections were judicious or worked well dramatically, *Sweethearts on Parade* remains one of Dwan's most audacious films. None of its main performers went on to better things in the industry, though Shirley did dub the singing voice of Jeremy Brett as Freddy Einsford-Hill in the 1964 *My Fair Lady*.

Harry Carey, Jr., played the poet James Whitcomb Riley in *Sweethearts on Parade* and, like others, he remembered Dwan as "tough." But he adds, "Only in the sense that he did not suffer fools lightly. There were quite a number of directors back then who could be sadistic, very nasty, but Mr. Dwan wasn't one of those. *But* ... if you hadn't done your homework ... beware. He could really chew a lazy actor's butt off!"[74]

Another performer appreciated Dwan's rigor. Joan Leslie recalls, "I was very comfortable with him. He was a strong leader.... I loved being under his direction because he seemed to show confidence in me." Under her contract with Warner Bros., Leslie appeared in *Yankee Doodle Dandy*, *Sergeant York et al.* in which, as she acknowledges, she played "sweet young things." For the title role in *Flight Nurse*, Leslie would have to

Joan Leslie takes a break with Forrest Tucker from her quest to find her missing helicopter pilot boyfriend in *Flight Nurse* (1953), set during the Korean War.

show sterner stuff. While Dwan had confidence that she could play the character, "he wasn't sure that I could physically do the part that a flight nurse would do under pressure." So he gave Leslie a "peculiar test." Leslie recounted that they "went to an airport and he said, 'I want to see you run to a plane starting with me and running to the plane,' which was half a block away. He wanted to see what I looked like from the back [*laughs*] ... to make sure that I would look like a flight nurse from the front and back."[75] Dwan's method here is reminiscent of when he had Swanson riding in subway cars and working at a department store in preparation for a role.

Although Leslie is strong in her portrayal, *Flight Nurse* is one of Dwan's weaker films at Republic. Alan Le May's script is pitifully disorganized and replete with trite dialogue. The film, shot while the Korean War was still being fought and incorporating news footage, is overly preachy with a voiceover of Leslie reciting the Nurse's Creed. Other ponderous voiceovers also soften the drama. Apparently because the central figure is a woman, there has to be a secondary soap opera plot about the nurse's boyfriend, a helicopter pilot who is missing in action. She embarks on a search for him although it is revealed to the audience that he is already in a military hospital. The result is an artificial structure limiting the scope of the nurse's heroic deeds.

Flight Nurse was inspired by the true story of Air Force nurse Lillian Kinkela, who also served as the movie's technical advisor.

A May 21, 1953, photograph of the real Air Force nurse who inspired the script of *Flight Nurse*, Lillian Kinkela. She served as a technical advisor on the film (courtesy Adrianne Whitmore).

In addition to her service in Korea, Kinkela was one of the most decorated military women of World War II and she went on to win the Korean Service Medal. Asked to comment about inaccuracies in the film, she began by laughingly noting, "I did not run around Korea looking for my helicopter pilot."[76] (Leslie said she was "lovingly" referred to as "Kinky" on the set.[77])

Kinkela said that she got along very well with Dwan but that the script was already completed when Dwan first saw it. Consequently, when she raised various objections, Dwan would explain, "Now, Lillian, that's the way the script was written." Since *Flight Nurse* was Dwan's last film at Republic, he may no longer have had the clout or the inclination to press for changes.

Both Leslie and Kinkela remembered that Dwan did act decisively in the matter of casting. When the actor originally chosen as the nurse's boyfriend seemed too cold and impersonal, Dwan fired him on the spot and replaced him with Arthur Franz.[78]

Fortunately, *Flight Nurse* does have its strengths such as Ben Cooper giving a harrowing account of his being held prisoner by the North Koreans. It's also demonstrated how Leslie's Lt. Polly Davis uses her femininity to bolster the men's courage. When their airplane is forced to ditch, Lt. Davis helps calm the nervous males by coolly putting on her lipstick, a "secret weapon" she had used previously to reassure patients. Davis also feels she is acting as a surrogate for the women at home. In one scene, a series of superimpositions shows Polly's face morphing into the visages of the mothers or the sweethearts of the servicemen.

After depleting its soap opera conventions, *Flight Nurse* does show the more assertive side of its protagonist. Once they are reunited, Polly's boyfriend Mike realizes that while he is physically and mentally no longer suited to continue in the fighting, she has emerged in his words as "Polly the Lady Warrior." They part amiably and Polly returns to her air missions.

When Polly is not exhausting herself searching for Mike, there is something distinctively modern in her unyielding dedication and how she interacts with her Air Force team. Over the years, Kinkela found that "I cry every time I see the movie."

Lilllian Kinkela Kiel died on June 30, 2005, five months after she was interviewed for this book. One obituary referred to her as "an airborne Florence Nightingale."[79]

The last newsreel films shown in *Flight Nurse* are of the American forces at the Chosin Reservoir. This is where Dwan's superior 1956 Korean War drama *Hold Back the Night* begins. Based on a novel by Pat Frank, it chronicled the bleak period in the war in November 1950 when Chinese forces entered the conflict and American troops stationed at the Chosin Reservoir were in danger of being overwhelmed. To break out of their trap, the Americans had to make their way to the Sea of Japan, seventy-eight miles away, in terrain where the temperature would plunge at night to 30 degrees below zero.

Warner Bros. had produced a film, the 1952 *Retreat, Hell!*, directed by the resourceful Joseph H. Lewis, which dramatized the events in fictional form a little over a year after they occurred. *Retreat, Hell!* received the cooperation of the Marines and like *Sands of Iwo Jima* was shot at Camp Pendleton.

In 1953, Allied Artists requested cooperation for a film based on Frank's novel *Hold Back the Night.* The Marines initially refused assistance on the grounds that the storyline was too similar to the recent *Retreat, Hell!* to be of additional public relations value to the Corps.[80] AA shelved the project for a year and then re-submitted their request to the Marines. This time the Marines agreed to provide help for shooting the picture at their cold weather training facility at Pickle Meadows in Northern California. When the film went into production in February 1956, unlike *Retreat, Hell!* where cold weather had to be simulated in Southern California, the cast and crew experienced the real thing.

There had been delays in production which was once scheduled for early 1955 with Thomas Carr directing and Richard Basehart starring. When Dwan took over production, he most likely approved of the new star, John Payne, who had appeared for him in three earlier films at RKO, but knew that Payne was not a big box office name. So Dwan recalled that regarding the budget "it was a matter of trimming"[81] to get the project in shape. Dwan explained his involvement by saying, "Yes, it was a Marine picture, and anything — when you say 'Marine,' I'm on, you know I want to do it."[82]

John Payne is the officer in charge and Chuck Connors his sergeant in Allied Artists' *Hold Back the Night* (1956), the Korean War story of one company making the long retreat from the Chosin Reservoir to the Sea of Japan after Chinese troops entered the war.

Back in 1931, Dwan's *Chances* had run afoul of the British censors with its depiction of a British retreat. Now Dwan was making an entire film that consisted of American forces in retreat. But this would also be told as a tough story of survival and by mid–1956, when the film was released, it had been three years since the Korean Armistice with American troops having fought back to the 38th parallel.

As with *Flight Nurse*, the protagonist provides voiceover narration. Payne's Captain Sam MacKenzie tells us at the outset, "This is the story of a company of American Marines." Then he adds, almost incongruously, "And this is the story of a bottle of Scotch, a remarkable bottle." While the bottle would be there for metaphoric value, the narration makes it clear that these are two parallel stories. One would be told in the present tense, the other in flashbacks, until gradually the two stories intertwined.

Dwan establishes a visual frame of reference for the retreat under the opening credits. In a series of long shots, U.S. Marines are seen marching from right to left as we are told, "The end of the war seemed certain. The only question was, would we capture the North Korean Army before it escaped into China? Or that seemed to be the problem...."

After vast numbers of Chinese troops attack, the Americans are seen moving onscreen in a reverse direction against a bleak, snowy landscape, from left to right for the remainder of the film.

In the first scene, after one of his men has been disciplined for being drunk and disorderly, Capt. MacKenzie becomes anxious and checks his bag for his bottle of Scotch. The bottle is in a leather case marked "1942." Sam tells Lt. Cozzens (Peter Graves) that he has been carrying it around since the last war. In flashback, Sam is shown receiving the bottle as a gift from his girlfriend just as he prepares to go off to war; she tells him to save it for a special occasion. When Cozzens questions Sam further on why no occasion has prompted him to open the bottle, Sam can only say, "It's become like a sort of symbol."

Some time after his men have been forced to fall back from the Chinese onslaught, Sam has his second flashback. This one is set in Melbourne after MacKenzie has returned from Guadalcanal. He eagerly accepts an invitation from a young woman named Kitty (Audrey Dalton) to go to her apartment where he can supply the booze with his bottle of Scotch. The scene seems reminiscent of an episode from *Sands of Iwo Jima* but here there is a twist. Kitty picks up a photo portrait of her M.I.A. husband and, tenderly clutching it to her body, says that each night she listens to Japanese broadcasts to learn if her man is among those taken prisoner. Sam, steadfastly holding on to his bottle, realizes they should not have this idle tryst. Their lovers seem to be represented by the objects that Kitty and Sam cling to. They also decide not to drink the Scotch, which becomes a symbol of sexual restraint.

Sam's past personal crisis fades against the harsh reality as the Marines sustain enemy attack to the sound of Chinese bugles and must begin their march to the port of Hungnam. Another crisis erupts with the accumulation of wounded as the battles continue.

In one of the grittier scenes in *Sands of Iwo Jima,* Stryker prevented Conway from going out to help a Marine even when Stryker recognizes that the wounded man was his friend Bass. Stryker had been warned by his commanders not to do anything to give away the position of his squad. There is an opposite emphasis in *Hold Back the Night.*

In the Korean retreat, MacKenzie is adamant that the Marines observe their axiom of no wounded men being left behind, even when it appears they will have to be carried by the men. In a departure from the novel, Sam is opposed by Lt. Cozzens, who feels that they are being slowed down. Cozzens is derided by MacKenzie as being too much of a machine. He may be seen as a stricter version of Stryker and as in *Iwo Jima,* when one Marine remarks that the disciplinarian knows his business, another Marine rejoins sarcastically, "Like a bank robber." (In *Iwo Jima* the retort was, "So did Jack the Ripper.")

Sam's final flashback shows him after his return home in 1945 and on a drinking binge when he suspects that Anne has another lover. (Sam's bender does *not* include imbibing from the Scotch bottle.) When Anne finds him drunk, Sam protests that in all his years at war he never opened the bottle even when he was offered hundreds of dollars for it in foxholes. The bottle has now come to symbolize not just restraint but Sam's faithfulness. As Sam collapses in tears, he and Anne decide to marry right away.

The bottle has become something of a talisman. Dwan never uses any camera tricks with lighting or eccentric angles to enhance the stature of the bottle. However, the bottle is nearly always seen carefully kept in its protective leather case. It is clear that all the meanings and properties of this "remarkable bottle" have been bestowed by Sam and those who come in contact with it as a means of coping with a crisis.

Ultimately, the situation grows more desperate and the company strength has shrunk to less than thirty men, who now seem too tired to move. In his last attempt to "hold back the night," Sam promises his men to let them all take a swig of his bottle of Scotch ... if they manage to traverse the last seven miles to their destination. In their final engagement, MacKenzie is wounded and is carried away with two other injured men by helicopter. Keeping his promise, the captain leaves the Scotch bottle with the men, who have been told a little of its history.

Deciding that the bottle is their "luck" and may be needed again, the Marines elect *not* to drink the contents and to return it to their skipper. In this story of survival, the bottle takes on values (among others) of determination, endurance and restraint. All would be needed in the "police action" of Korea. Major-General Oliver P. Smith, who played a major role in the actual event, said he preferred Dwan's film to *Retreat, Hell!,* citing it as "very well done, it looked almost like a documentary but it just wasn't."[83] However, *Hold Back the Night* succeeds in tapping a psychological dimension lacking in most documentaries.

The last two films to be discussed are Westerns and they are saved for last because in the next phase of Dwan's career, Westerns play a major role. Dwan's career was returning to the genre that had dominated his beginnings as a director. Both of these Westerns center on women.

Montana Belle was filmed at Republic in 1948 but was released in 1952 under the RKO logo. It was actually produced by Fidelity Pictures, which made a deal to shoot at Republic using the studio's personnel. For the title role, Jane Russell was borrowed from RKO Pictures. Dwan directed as a "friendly gesture" to Republic and agreed not to receive a percentage compensation or associate producer credit.[84] In April 1949, Fidelity sold the completed *Montana Belle* to RKO for $875,000. The film had been budgeted for $650,000 and both Fidelity and Republic shared in the profit.[85] Howard Hughes, who con-

Jane Russell as the outlaw Belle Starr flanked by Forrest Tucker, Jack Lambert and Roy Barcroft in *Montana Belle* (1952). The movie sat on the shelf for more than three years before Howard Hughes decided to release it.

Jane Russell shows a much more entertaining side in feminine attire as her blonde alter ego Montana in *Montana Belle* (1952).

trolled RKO, kept *Montana Belle* on the shelf for over three years, finally releasing it in late 1952.

With scant interest in anything having to do with the actual Belle Starr and the Dalton gang, the film has Bob Dalton (Scott Brady) rescuing the newly widowed Belle from a lynch mob and bringing her to the Dalton hideout owned by Mac (Forrest Tucker) and the Indian Ringo (Jack Lambert). While the Daltons are away committing robberies, Belle forms her own gang with Mac and Ringo and outperforms the Daltons in the newspapers. It is incorrectly assumed that Belle and the Daltons are working together.

Posing as respectable citizens, Belle, Mac and Ringo enter the city of Guthrie and pay a visit to the gambling establishment they had earlier robbed, the Bird Cage, run by Tom Bradfield (George Brent). Unknown to Belle, Tom has been engaged by the Bankers Protective Association for $100,000 to find the Daltons. Although Belle was wearing a bandana over most of her face during the robbery, Tom recognizes her by her eyes. He remains silent, hoping to catch the Daltons through her, and even agrees to take her on as a partner.

Belle is traveling under the name of Lucy Winters, nicknamed Montana, and wears a blonde wig. She decides to stay in Guthrie and use it as a base for her gang's crimes. She makes her decision looking into a mirror with the camera capturing both her and her mirror image. Belle is creating a separate identity for herself as the blonde Montana, wearing dresses instead of Belle's jeans and boots.

In Dwan's hands, *Montana Belle* becomes a lesson in role-playing. As Belle cavorts as Montana in feminine attire, her personality changes. With *Montana Belle*, Dwan worked for the first time in color for an entire feature. Even with the dubious Trucolor process, one can see a pictorial strategy. In the early scenes when Belle is dressed in pants, boots and cowboy hat, greens and browns predominate. Removed from the rustic world, she now appears wearing a bright blue dress, blue feathers and a red floral hat. As Belle, she showed she could shoot and ride as well as any man (actually better) but she seizes new opportunities as Montana.

Star Jane Russell remembered Dwan as "a doll. He even let me sing. I figured that since Calamity Jane [sic] was posing as a dance hall dame, why not let her sing."[86] So Montana sings two songs, in one of which she gamely shows off her bare legs to the male customers of the Bird Cage. Montana revels in her newfound femininity and while dressed in white confides to her cohorts, "I didn't know how wonderful it was to have nice clothes."

Predictably, in this mood Belle-Montana finds herself falling in love with Tom. Tom is another of Dwan's professional gamblers and, despite the deal he has made with the bankers, he has fallen in love with Belle and is willing to gamble on it. He tells Belle that he knows her identity and unfurls his quaint rehabilitation program for her: He will marry her and take her to Mexico, then make arrangements for her to surrender to the law and repay her debt to society.

In a bizarre scene, Tom matter-of-factly tells Matt Tower (John Litel), who engaged him for $100,000 to capture the outlaws, that he is planning a Mexican honeymoon because "Belle and I are tremendously in love...." Tower is puzzled because he thought her name was Montana. Tom then gives the stunning announcement, "My partner and the woman I love is Belle Starr." Tower understandably says, "A couple of things I have to think over here."

This surreal discussion is punctuated by Pete Pivan (Andy Devine) making an entrance through the office window. Devine plays his usual amiable buffoon with the additional characteristic of gleefully selling out people and information for money. He tells Tom that Belle is being coerced to participate in a bank robbery with the Daltons and her two associates.

Russell made *Montana Belle* just after she finished playing another tough cowgirl in the Bob Hope comedy *The Paleface*. *Montana Belle* was released the same year as the Hope–Russell sequel *Son of Paleface*. *Montana Belle* might have its own claim to being *Daughter of Paleface*. Dwan serenely lets the absurdities overflow as the lovers strive for happiness despite the odds. Tom rescues a wounded Belle from the bank robbery and soon they are encamped, blissfully talking about a Mexican honeymoon though a posse is hot on their trail and about to overtake them. The talk turns to Belle doing her time and then enjoying happiness with Tom, although Tom had earlier acknowledged to Tower that the law would give her life. It's reminiscent of the Neil Simon line defining a Joan Crawford movie as one where her lover is sentenced to the electric chair and she promises to wait for him.

Perhaps to a greater extent than *I Dream of Jeanie*, *Montana Belle* can be called a "foolish film" but Dwan clearly has fun showing the difficulty in reconciling the twin personae of Montana and Belle.

In his two Korean War films and in the two cited Republic musicals, one can see Dwan moving toward greater refinement in the second of each pair. "Refinement" may not be a word one would feel comfortable applying to Dwan's *Woman They Almost Lynched* but while raucous and excessive, it gallops further into the gender issues raised by *Montana Belle*.

In *Woman They Almost Lynched*, there are two principal female characters caught in something resembling the Montana–Belle split and inevitably they are drawn to a gunfight. According to Jeanine Basinger, "They are fighting over the issue of what it means to be a woman. In fact, the whole movie is structured on this very issue."[87]

When Bogdanovich asked Dwan how he decided to play the entire film as a parody, Dwan responded, "Well, what else could it be? Again, either you suffer or you don't — take your choice."[88] Despite having Russell as a lady gunslinger, *Montana Belle* was still largely bound by genre conventions which Dwan could only tease in finding something amusing in this potboiler. *Woman They Almost Lynched* would flout genre conventions on a much larger scale, permitting Dwan more incisive effects.

A narrator sets the film in the spring of 1865 with the Civil War having raged for four years. He notes, "In the backwash of that war, a new breed of men had sprung up, Quantrill, Frank and Jesse James, the Younger Brothers...." Onscreen appears a montage of night raiders indiscriminately pillaging as the narrator refers to "one of the darkest pages of American history ... law and order disappeared.... But Border City was different. It had a law of its own...." The montage seems like a distillation of havoc and instability just as the opening montage to *Frontier Marshal* evoked a growing and violent civilization always threatening to contract into itself. In the first scene thereafter, a little boy struggles to get a glimpse of a lynching as most of the townspeople watch in rapt fascination. We later learn that the man is being hanged for having made an "inflammatory speech."

We are a long way from *The Virginian* where lynching was justified to protect property from cattle rustlers. The mayor of Border City explains that half of the city is in Arkansas (Confederacy) and half is in Missouri (Union) and that to keep things from collapsing into chaos, strict neutrality is being enforced with hanging as the penalty for anyone trying to arouse passions for either side. There is only the hangman; no sheriff or courts exist here. And the mayor who took this job is a woman. According to one member of the coterie of women that surround Mayor Delilah Courtney (Nina Varela), "No man had courage enough to take the job." With a first name that evokes emasculation and an appearance that suggests a particularly stern Marie Dressler, Mayor Courtney seems up to the job.

The concept of the lawless Western town is taken to its limit, suggesting an almost post-apocalyptic community with things turned topsy-turvy. Border City's female leadership also provides an appropriate backdrop for the women antagonists in the film.

A stranger to these parts is Sally Maris (Joan Leslie) from Michigan, who is nursing a wounded Jesse James (Ben Cooper) on the stagecoach bringing her to Border City. As one of Quantrill's men, Jesse has been wounded in a brief engagement where they slaughtered a small Union patrol. Jesse is portrayed as an innocent provoked into joining Quantrill's outfit.

Sally comes to town to seek out her brother Bill (Reed Hadley), who owns the hotel and saloon, only to see how he has degenerated in the two years since he last wrote to her. His bride-to-be, Kate, had been kidnapped by the notorious Quantrill (Brian Donlevy). Kate has now been totally won over by the renegade leader. While Sally unpacks upstairs, Kate returns claiming to be Quantrill's wife. When Bill remains aloof, Kate decides to torment him by singing a romantic song, "All My Life," which she croons to various men in the saloon and mockingly to Bill himself. Exploding with rage, Bill cracks and pulls out his gun, threatening to kill Kate. When Lance Horton (John Lund), the foreman of Delilah's lead mine, tries to stop him, Bill turns on Lance. Lance shoots Bill in self-defense. Sally returns to find her brother dead. She and Kate become bitter enemies while Lance now feels duty-bound to protect Sally since he killed her brother. Sally has other ideas.

Failing to find "respectable" work, the wholesome Sally decides to reopen the Lead Dollar Saloon under her management even if it means that she is branded a "honky-tonk queen." The conflict with Kate leads to violence, first in a saloon brawl and then in a gunfight. Adding to the Byzantine plot, Lance is actually a Confederate spy selling some of the lead in Delilah's mine to Confederate forces while she is selling the rest to the Union.

As Kate, Audrey Totter gives the proper tone to this vehicle. Her outrageous performance gives both life and artifice to the picture. She seems perpetually pumped up, always ready to explode, but as brooding as she is flamboyant. In one scene, Cole Younger (Jim Davis) talks of his plan to carry Sally off. Behind him is a curtain and as he talks of Sally being a saloon girl, a form begins to materialize behind the curtain until we see Kate's silhouette. Then she emerges, barking, "I was a saloon girl!" Kate is a kind of shadow of Sally or double image; she was stolen from Bill by Quantrill just as Younger now wants to abduct Sally. Her hatred of Sally may also be fueled by reminding her of what she was before her kidnapping.

The brawl in the saloon is prompted by the news that Confederate troops are nearby. Kate, always ready to provoke with her vocal talents, wants to sing "Dixie," but Lance points out to Sally that with the numbers of Yanks and rebels in the Lead Dollar evenly divided, the song could start a bloody riot. Sally takes the challenge and assaults Kate as she begins singing. Dwan's direction of the drawn-out brawl in some ways typifies his overall approach to the film. At times it veers towards comedy as when a man claiming to be neutral is caught between the combatants. At another point, a punch misses one woman and hits a male onlooker. But the fight scene then veers towards the realistic and the brutal as Sally steps up her attack, pounds Kate's head and drags Kate almost completely across the saloon bar.

Most of the scene was shot with stunt doubles. (Early in the scene Dwan cleverly uses a stairway to limit the view of who's fighting.) But Dwan needed to use Leslie and Totter in close-ups and the gender-bending did create a challenge for Leslie. The actress said she found it difficult to strike a woman: "I had a heck of a time trying to do that. I pulled my punches before I'd get anywhere near her. And Allan would say, 'No, no, you got to hit her. Strike her.' I couldn't do that any more than I wanted anyone to do that to me. Audrey would say, 'Come on, Joan, you can do it.'"[89] (Recalling the scene, Totter said of Leslie, "She's such a sweet person."[90]) She finally appeared to satisfy Dwan. After her victory, Sally collapses into tears, saying, "Brawling like a common hussy."

Sally and Kate must then engage in a gunfight which is shot like the standard Western confrontation, cutting back between Sally and Kate, armed and walking towards each other, with cutaways to observers breathlessly awaiting the outcome. Sally, who was raised to shoot and hunt by her brother, does not outdraw Kate but fires more steadily and maims her opponent. Clutching her wounded hand, Kate also has to listen to Sally's admonishment, "Why don't you try acting like a woman? You were born a woman but look at you. A bloodthirsty female. A disgrace to all women."

There is also Quantrill's memorable comment to Kate, "Why don't you give up? She fights better than you. She shoots better than you. She even talks better than you." Cole Younger, still planning to abduct, Sally adds, "Yeah, I'll bet she even cooks better than you." (Dwan told Bogdanovich that he originally wanted a pause before "cooks."[91])

Leslie said that she was later told that while she and Totter acted out their gunfight in all seriousness, Dwan was laughing uproariously behind the camera. Basinger took the view that "*Woman They Almost Lynched* is not a comedy, at least comedy was not its intention. It is in fact a taut and well-directed oddball western in which women are central to the story. Its shoot-out is a classic example of how a genre shifts its concerns to accommodate a story about women."[92]

Dwan found much humor in sex role reversals but the obsessiveness and intensity in which it persisted in his films suggests that his interest was not entirely facetious, even if he didn't admit it. Sally's take-charge attitude is shown as just as valid as that of the reluctant male lawmen of numerous Westerns, who take up arms to combat the violence they detest. More importantly, no matter how exaggerated or outrageous the situations appear in *Woman They Almost Lynched*, the characters and their feelings are always treated seriously. Andrew Sarris commented, "I can't decide whether it's a question of virality or vulgarity, but either way, this is not the kind of lazy or jaded filmmaking one expects in the lower depths."[93] Nicholas Ray's cult masterpiece *Johnny Guitar* (made at Republic the following year) also indulged in such delirium, including its preoccupation with rival gun-toting women.

Where Sarris is perplexed by the alternatives of vitality and vulgarity, critic Roger McNiven celebrates "Dwan's dual attitudes of parody and pathos ... developed here in counterpoint."[94] McNiven is on solid ground citing Dwan's delight in fusing two seemingly contrary approaches.

The key dramatic turning point in *Woman* is the change in Kay's character from bad to sympathetic. When a Union detachment attacks Quantrill's men in Border City, Kate seeks refuge, which Sally grants her since she fears that if captured, Kate will reveal that Lance is a Confederate spy. Reverting to her former identity (a saloon chanteuse) turns out to be Kate's best disguise from the Northern forces. Where her earlier attempts at singing were cruelly provocative, her singing of "How Strange" commemorates what will become her redemption. (It is one of the numerous plot weaknesses in *Woman They Almost Lynched* that the Union soldiers searching for Kate Quantrill cannot imagine that she might have changed from pants to a dress or that various people including the mayor could have correctly identified her.) But now in women's clothes, Kate seems to have undergone a rebirth. Having been the only woman in Quantrill's gang, she is now back in the company of women with Sally and her chorus girls. Kate sings of an angel within her who is changing her and renewing her.

The "angel" is Sally, who though she had a motive for hiding Kate (to keep her from talking) could have also justifiably shot her. Kate recalls to the women that the last decent person she knew before Sally was her brother Bill. Sally's star-crossed romance with Lance (Northerner–Southerner) recalls the thwarted Mason-Dixon romance of Bill and Kate. As if a cloud had been lifted from her moral vision, Kate acknowledges how she eventually stopped resisting Quantrill and became like him, animated by a hatred that could not be exorcised. McNiven likens Dwan to Jean Renoir as "a classic humanist," noting, "Dwan would always prefer to climax his action films with scenes of transformations of his villains."[95]

Thought not always at the climax, such transformations exist in Dwan's films going back to Jack Richardson in *The Reformation of Sierra Smith* through Fairbanks (*The Good Bad Man*), the grandfather in *Heidi*, Doc Halliday and Jerry (*Frontier Marshal*), Al Thomas (*Sands of Iwo Jima*) and Charles Dakin (*Angel in Exile*), among others.

But there is also a dark side to Dwan's transformations. While individuals can change for the good, human beings collectively can revert easily to a mob or to cruel snobbery. Thus, we have the ostracizing of Betty Lockwood in *Betty of Greystone* and of Michael Bolton in *Man to Man*, the public suspicions centered on De Lesseps in *Suez*, the communities in New England and New Jersey turning against Wendy and her foster parents in *Young People* and Jeff Dolan in *Rendezvous with Annie*, the lynch mobs of *Tide of Empire*, *Montana Belle* and *Belle Le Grand*. In *Woman They Almost Lynched*, just the singing of "Dixie" in a saloon can change convivial patrons to warring factions. Dwan's views about the dangers of raising one's head "above the mob" undoubtedly arose from a deep-seated belief about human nature.

Delilah Courtney tries to maintain neutrality through lynch law but the individual characters in the film rise more gracefully above politics. Lance neglects returning to his Confederate forces so he can make sure the Northern girl he loves is safe. Because she loves Lance, Sally helps this rebel spy escape the Union soldiers. Jesse James is a part of Quantrill's guerrillas but is also steadfastly loyal to the Northern Sally.

Cooper's Jesse resonates most deeply of all the male characters. (Lance is a somewhat ineffectual hero.) During their stagecoach ride, Sally tried to persuade Jesse to quit Quantrill and being an outlaw. After giving it some thought, Jesse decides that it's too late. Unlike Kate, he will not find salvation. But if Jesse remains among the damned, he is also an "angel" to Sally, provides her with his revolver for the gunfight with Kate and even worries about her own moral state when she decides to become a saloon girl.

It is, however, the women who register most strongly in the heroics. Knowing that Lance will be identified as a spy by one man captured from Quantrill's band, Sally places false evidence on her person so that she appears to be the Confederate spy. She's ready to accept a traditional female martyr's role, to be executed not by the Union Army but by Mayor Courtney's lynch rule against violating neutrality. Fortunately, Kate chooses a more flamboyant role, appearing at the hanging on horseback and proclaiming that Lance was the real spy and Sally was just trying to shield him. Asked for proof, she announces that she is Kate Quantrill. This outlandish sequence ends with Kate still in her female attire galloping out of town and the Yankee cavalry in rapid pursuit. Naturally, Kate gets away.

Sisterhood triumphs and the canny politician, Delilah, is suddenly blaming the men for almost hanging an innocent woman. Never one to be bothered by hypocrisy, she had continued to sell lead to the Union Army despite her neutrality rules. Having previously shunned Sally, Delilah now sees her as personifying the nobility of women, ready to sacrifice her life for "a mere man."

Despite the gross exaggerations and caricatures — or more likely *because* of them — *Woman They Almost Lynched* captures the ambiguities and contradictions in its characters.

Michael Henry Wilson has written of Sally and Kate, "Discovering they stand united in the face of men's violence and concupiscence, the two women outdo each other in acts of nobility, and eventually help each other out."[96] The designation of what it means to be a woman that Basinger cited appears to have broadened to entail quite a bit in the course of the film.

The extreme and even cartoonish conditions in Border City raise questions about what it means to be an outlaw or a soldier or a friend in the vortex of such tangled loyalties and alliances. The Lead Dollar Saloon, where so much of the action takes place, is marked by the geographical line dividing the Union from the Confederacy. (All the intrigue in Rick's Café in *Casablanca* seems tranquil in comparison.) That Dwan's characters manage to find their way in this no-man's land is what Wilson calls the "moral beauty" of his films. Even more than usual in Dwan's ensemble casts, very minor characters show their value. Memorable here in a low-key way is Gordon Jones' caustic but amiable Union sergeant counterbalancing the stuffiness of his commanding officer.

In retrospect, Dwan's tenure at Republic seems less problematic than described by Meisel. While Dwan complained of being saddled with stars like Ralston and Carroll, Republic

Joan Leslie and Audrey Totter demonstrating their catfight in *Woman They Almost Lynched* (1953). The scene was effective for both comedy and action despite Leslie's reluctance to hit a woman.

If Republic budgets were often skimpy, Dwan was proficient at making do with what he was given. Republic could also provide strong expertise in some areas. The stagecoach raid by Quantrill's men early in *Woman They Almost Lynched* is full of swirling movement and crisp editing while Dwan's camera is mounted on the moving stagecoach. The scene is also enhanced by first-rate stunt work provided by Republic.

There was a definite lack of sophistication in most of the projects that he was given that kept Dwan from doing top-notch work. Still, a comedy like *Rendezvous with Annie* was, if anything, both more sophisticated and more naturalistic than his rapid-fire farces for Small. And it's difficult to imagine Dwan making quirky films like *The Inside Story* or *Woman They Almost Lynched* for any of the major studios.

Despite the drawbacks and Yates' dictatorial power, some of Dwan's films at Republic were as personal as any he had done since the beginning of the sound era. Far from declining as he approached his sixty-ninth birthday, Dwan's cinematic powers seemed to have been sharpened in his Republic tenure. Moving on to another troubled studio, Dwan's filmmaking prowess would crystallize into some of his best work. It would begin with a Western that was just as tumultuous, if less outrageous, than *Woman They Almost Lynched.*

also gave him an emerging superstar in John Wayne. If some performers were lackluster, Republic also provided Dwan with notable talent like Walter Brennan or unheralded but quality players like Eddie Albert and Ray Middleton. Ironically, on Fox's loan-out of Natalie Wood to Republic, Dwan found a child actress even more talented than Fox's Shirley Temple.

9. Apotheosis with Bogeaus

Then the Lord said to Joshua, "Say to the people of Israel, 'Appoint the cities of refuge, of which I spoke to you through Moses, that the manslayer who kills any person without intent or unwittingly may flee there; they shall be for you a refuge from the avenger of blood.'"—Joshua 20: 1–3.

These all died in faith, not having received what was promised but having seen it and greeted it from afar and having acknowledged that they were strangers and exiles on the earth. For people who speak thus make it clear they are seeking a homeland.—Hebrews 11:13–14

It is one of the ironies of Dwan's career that he made some of his best films near the end of his years as a director working at a dying studio, RKO, the company that Joseph Kennedy had helped to found and at this time owned by another Hollywood outsider, Howard Hughes. As Dwan told Bogdanovich of his work there, "They were token pictures to keep the studio alive...."[1]

In February 1953, Dwan's friend James Grainger left his job as sales manager at Republic to become president of RKO Pictures Corporation. Grainger assumed the appointment when RKO was reeling from almost five years of Hughes' mismanagement.

After Hughes gained control of RKO in May 1948, he assured employees that their jobs were not in danger. Hughes then proceeded to cut 75 percent of the company's personnel. With production already in steep decline because of the meager work force, Hughes insisted that only he could make the key decisions involving the studio's important films. He then proved notoriously difficult to find when those decisions had to be made. He wouldn't even move into the RKO offices but maintained his headquarters at the Goldwyn Studios over a mile away.

When projects did get approved, Hughes would provide *too* much contact, constantly meddling and often calling his producers at two or three in the morning. Not surprisingly, a number of producers exited the studio. In the first two years of Hughes' ownership, RKO lost a combined total of nine million dollars. In 1952 alone, its losses were put at over ten million.

In September 1952, Hughes sold RKO to a Chicago syndicate. Shortly after the sale, a series of articles in the *Wall Street Journal* exposed three leading members of the syndicate as having unsavory and possibly criminal associations. Facing an onslaught of negative publicity, the new owners relinquished their control, putting Hughes back in charge.

This was the situation when Hughes appointed Grainger president. At this time, RKO had made only one feature in the last seven months. As production at the studio dried up, RKO was getting practically all its releases from independent producers by purchase or co-production deals. Hughes' inept bid at total control had resulted in a situation where the studio had little control over most of its product.

It was under these circumstances that Dwan found an opportunity at RKO.

Dwan was assigned to work with one of RKO's independent producers, Benedict Bogeaus. In contrast to Hughes, Bogeaus was a small-scale tycoon with smaller-scale eccentricities and his own flair for the unorthodox.

A *New York Times* profile of Bogeaus in late 1945 noted, "Even amid the film colony's congregation of fabulous personalities Mr. Bogeaus stands out as a fabled character. Since he was born in Chicago forty years ago he admits to having earned and lost at least three fortunes."[2] Bogeaus made his first fortune in real estate in his mid-twenties.

When his investments were hard hit by the Depression, Bogeaus went off to Europe. He pursued an odd assortment of enterprises as he cavorted between America and Europe, claiming that he crossed the Atlantic "forty-eight times on all the best ships afloat."[3] On one excursion, Bogeaus said he bought an interest in a toothpaste cap that snapped itself shut and didn't have to be screwed back on, only to find out later that it didn't work.[4] Returning to Chicago in 1935, he started a radio manufacturing company but that involvement didn't last long. In Belgium in 1939, Bogeaus found a man who had invented "the perfect zipper" and bought the American rights. After the Nazi invasion, Bogeaus claimed that the Germans did not want him to take the zipper blueprints out of the country and pursued him until he caught a boat to South America. When he finally got back to the U.S., he either sold his zipper patents to a Philadelphia firm[5] or abandoned the enterprise because it proved financially impractical.[6] Like Dwan, he sometimes gave more than one version of his fabulous adventures.

Moving to California, Bogeaus went into a partnership with a man who had invented a portable motion picture developing machine which was in demand by the U.S. military. Supposedly for the purposes of this machine's production, Bogeaus purchased the General Service Studio, a movie plant covering a Hollywood block. Bogeaus used the facilities for manufacturing for only a few months. Since he had dabbled in film production during his European sojourns, Bogeaus likely had an interest in using the studio for films all along. The facility was rented to various independent producers but Bogeaus himself decided to begin producing his own movies.

Bogeaus' first four American films, *The Bridge of San Luis Rey*, *Dark Waters*, *Captain Kidd* and *Diary of a Chambermaid* (the last directed by Jean Renoir and co-produced by Burgess Meredith), were all hits. By 1945, Bogeaus was getting extensive coverage in the press as one of what would be a long line of independent producers, having their moment in the media sun, explaining why they had found the success that had eluded so many producers at the major studios. And as with others who thought they had discovered the Midas touch, his streak would come to an end.

Bogeaus did subsequently produce the well-regarded *The Macomber Affair*, based on Ernest Hemingway's short story "The Short Happy Life of Francis Macomber." But by the early 1950s, he was encountering difficulties. In 1951, Dorothy Lamour won a judgment of $84,945.80 against Bogeaus for money not paid to her for work in two films when Bogeaus failed to contest the suit.[7] In August 1952, Benedict Bogeaus Pictures went to Federal court, claiming to be over $220,000 in debt and seeking protection from its creditors. These included Mickey Rooney and Robert Preston, the stars of Bogeaus' *My Outlaw Brother*, who were owed thousands for their work in the film.[8] Bogeaus contended that his company could pay the debts when it received profits from the film. (Bogeaus had sold the General Service Studio facilities some years earlier.) But the financial problems continued in October when Bogeaus was sued for defaulting on a $15,000 promissory note.[9] Legal difficulties persisted into the mid–1950s when United Artists sued Bogeaus who, when trying to raise funds to avoid foreclosure, released *My Outlaw Brother* to television while it was still in theatrical release. Bogeaus followed with a countersuit against United Artists for "mishandling" the film in its distribution.[10]

Bogeaus turned to RKO to distribute his films with the 1953 *Count the Hours*, directed by Don Siegel. But Bogeaus' knack for getting into trouble struck again. Bogeaus assigned Siegel's unit to a set that was not only unsuitable for the script but belonged to another company. After getting kicked off that set, Bogeaus was able to make do by "borrowing" some other sets. Because the crew had not been paid, Siegel was able to finish shooting only by promising to hide the film shot on the last day from Bogeaus until everyone was paid in full.[11]

While Grainger needed the contributions of independent producers to RKO, he did not need more financial headaches to add to the chaos of Hughes' tenure. Since Bogeaus apparently had a co-production deal with RKO, Grainger needed someone to watch the money and he recognized Dwan as a reliably efficient hand. Dwan recalled, "Now Bogeaus was notoriously extravagant in the early days, and they weren't too confident that he could safely handle the kind of budget he'd have to use, so to give himself some security Grainger reached out for someone with experience to work with Bogeaus. And I was elected."[12]

Dwan said that on their first film, he and Bogeaus soon clashed. Dwan said that with the script and production schedule Bogeaus had in place, the film would go way over budget. Dwan tried to pare the script down to a manageable size while Bogeaus fumed with anger. "He was going to throw me off but they wouldn't let him, so we went ahead and made the picture within our budget."[13] Although the picture was set for RKO release, Bogeaus had it shot at Republic, the studio Dwan had just departed.

The film in which Dwan and Bogeaus were engaged was a Western that went under the working title of *Desperate Men*, which was later changed to *Silver Lode*. It would prove successful when released in 1954, but initially it did not seem likely that the two men would ever again collaborate after their budget battle. Dwan recalled that Bogeaus "was disgruntled and angry. 'You'll never work for me again,' and the rest.... He put another director on the next picture, but about a week later he sent for me and I came in and took that one over, and then we started a very friendly relationship.... We stayed together for ten pictures. I went in as a policeman and ended up friendly with him."[14]

Team of Outcasts

Dwan makes it clear both in his Bogdanovich interview and elsewhere that he called the shots on making the Bogeaus-produced films while Bogeaus took care of the business deals. He told the film publication *Bright Lights*, "All the stuff I did at RKO, though Bogeaus' name was on it, he just did what you asked him to."[15]

To Bogdanovich, Dwan made reference to Marcelene, a famous clown at New York's old Hippodrome. His schtick was that while always trying to be helpful he would mess everything up. "So every time Bogeaus would do anything I didn't like, or come around with suggestions, I'd say, 'Well, Marcelene, I'm afraid I can't agree.' And he began to accept it and we had a very good relationship."[16]

Dwan did acknowledge later in the interview, however, that Bogeaus would persist in trying to influence editing. "But we had Jim Leicester, who was a very good cutter, and when Bogeaus would tell him to change things, Jim would run it for him next day and say, 'Hey, I think that suggestion of yours was a big improvement'—and it was exactly the same—he hadn't touched it.... So he was kept under control pretty well."[17]

Leicester is not around to confirm this but the story at least suggests that even Bogeaus' attempts at creative involvement were small-scale. However, this does not mean that Bogeaus had no creative role in the films he produced with Dwan: It was Bogeaus who purchased the properties. If Dwan sometimes disagreed with his selections, overall they provided the framework he needed. There may have also been inherent limitations within each project.

In an interview with Simon Mizrahi of the French publication *Presence du cinema*, Dwan (speaking of Bogeaus) said, "The films I shot with him are combinations of both our sensibilities.... That type of stories, those sets that were similar in all our films, were Bogeaus's doing as well as mine."[18]

Dwan and Bogeaus may have found they had much in common ranging from their Chicago upbringing, their practical interest in mechanical innovation and the hard knocks they had both experienced in reaching this late point in their careers. The fusion of themes in these films suggest that Bogeaus had indeed found things that appealed to Dwan. Bogeaus also provided Dwan with the stability of a regular crew of highly skilled craftsmen who were out of favor with the major studios.

Bogeaus had first employed cinematographer John Alton on the 1953 *Count the Hours*. Dwan had already worked with Alton on the 1947 *Driftwood* and welcomed his hiring. Dwan said, "John Alton was a fine cameraman and we hit it off well. He was good for us because he's wonderful with lights — very economical."[19]

The Hungarian-born Alton joined MGM as a lab technician in 1924. He went to Europe to film backgrounds for Ernst Lubitsch's 1927 *The Student Prince*. After sojourns in France and Argentina, where he further developed his camera skills, he returned to Hollywood and began his American career as a cinematographer at Republic in 1940. He proved one of the foremost cameramen in developing the visual style of film noir. His frequent stints for director Anthony Mann were quite notable in this regard but he arguably did even more impressive work in Joseph H. Lewis' perverse noir classic *The Big Combo* (1955).

Though he is now best remembered as probably the greatest cinematographer of film noir, he won his only Academy Award for the splashy Technicolor *An American in Paris*. (Alton was also a favorite with its director Vincente Minnelli.) All of his RKO films for Dwan were in color. Alton's career was nonetheless blighted by the way he had antagonized executives and unions by his refusal to follow standard procedures. But his cost-cutting methods and innovative skill were appreciated by Dwan and Bogeaus.

The art director Van Nest Polglase had long been a mainstay at RKO; in fact, he had designed the company's "beeping tower" logo. From 1929 to 1942, he was given art director credit on all RKO films (even those done by his assistant). He received six Oscar nominations including one for his work on *Citizen Kane*. His credits also include *King Kong*, *The Informer* and most of the Astaire–Rogers musicals.

Alcoholism had, however, driven Polglase out of RKO in 1942 and continued to plague him in the ensuing years. Dwan told Bogdanovich that Polglase "started to hit the bottle pretty hard and by the time he got off it, people had lost confidence in him. But I'd known him to be a very fine art director [*Stage Struck*, *Look Who's Laughing*] and a practical one, which is the kind I like.... This was a great guy to take one set and transform it into another one for you with very little money. So I approved of him highly when he was proposed. RKO wouldn't employ him but we would."[20] Polglase's most notable work for Dwan was in *Tennessee's Partner*, *Slightly Scarlet*, and the less esteemed *Pearl of the South Pacific*.

This quartet of outcasts would perform very well together and it is perhaps not surprising that Dwan's theme of redemption would appear prominently in their films. Rounding out the crew of regulars were film editor James Leicester and composer Louis Forbes.

There was no similar consistency in the roster of writers employed on these films. The fact that the movies display such thematic consistency appears to confirm that Dwan, as he told Bogdanovich, had much to do with supplying the basic ideas to the writers.

The French critic Jean Lourcelles may have been the first to cite in these films "the idea of a place of refuge ... found and threatened and lost, and which therefore must be recaptured."[21] These exist in all ten of the films Dwan and Bogeaus made together including the two made outside of RKO. In some, such as *Silver Lode*, the Biblical injunction exists to be tested quite literally. In *Tennessee's Partner*, the gambler Tennessee has been run out of a number of states, and card-game shootouts seem a likely cause. In most of the films, the quest of refuge is paramount to the story but even in cases where it is more peripheral to the plot, it casts a wider thematic shadow. In *Slightly Scarlet*, Dorothy Lyons begs her sister for protection but her situation exposes the vulnerability and precarious state of all three of the film's major characters. The need for a place of refuge is both justified and thwarted in these films by the widespread distrust and betrayals.

In the 1950s, the major veteran directors of the silent era like Ford, Hitchcock, Hawks, Vidor, Capra, Walsh, etc., were working on more lavish budgets than Dwan, even if their critical reputations were in disrepair. Both thematically and financially, Dwan's films had more in common with those of the younger directors who were challenging the establishment in the 1950s.

In terms of content, Dwan may have been closest to Nicholas Ray whose films also focused on outcasts and their alienation from society at large. There are even some stylistic similarities. V.F. Perkins says, "Much of the meaning of [Ray's] *King of Kings* is contained in its intricate pattern of looking, glancing and staring."[22] Nevertheless, Dwan was able to portray this alienation with much less of Ray's anguished subjectivity. Dwan's sense of detachment, which permits him to view events in a much wider context, is one of the things that prompts the use of terms such as "serenity" to describe his work. It is this paradox which helps make Dwan's fifties films so fascinating.

Dwan's traditional brand of filmmaking would make little use of the fifties method acting championed by Elia Kazan and others. He was similarly distanced from the sense of subversive outrage evident in the films of Sam Fuller, Robert Aldrich and Phil Karlson, the dark grandeur of Anthony Mann and the fatalism of Don Siegel. Dwan was overall closer to the more ironic works of Budd Boetticher and Douglas Sirk, who still encapsulated worlds of tension and steamy melodrama.

Dwan's major and fully mature films of this period are *Silver Lode* (1954), *Tennessee's Partner* (1955), *Slightly Scarlet* (1956) and *The River's Edge* (1957). All were produced by Bogeaus and except for the last, all were made at RKO.

John Payne starred in three of the four films. His career has been compared to that of Dick Powell's in that he made the transition from musical star (for Payne the 1940s) to tough guy in the 1950s. Payne's characters could exude both charm and intelligence but as with Dwan's first screen hero, Kerrigan, his wily heroics were usually closer to Odysseus than Achilles. Payne was the kind of low-key tough guy who would lower his voice to sound more forceful. In some ways, he may have served as a surrogate for Dwan and the accusation of lack of emotional fire made against his character in *Slightly Scarlet* might have been similarly leveled at Dwan.

Howard Hughes wrecked RKO with his mismanagement. But the chaos he produced also created some opportunities for others.

To refer to these films as a tetralogy seems strained for the works of a filmmaker who always strove against pretension and was still less overtly "artistic" than Ford, Hitchcock and even Hawks. However, these movies not only develop recurrent themes and styles but exhibit a sense of narrative continuity from film to film. Since these pictures also bring Dwan's work to an artistic crescendo, it is more beneficial to discuss them in detail in the final section of this chapter.

Besides the three RKO films cited above, Dwan made five other movies for the studio. Given that these were "token pictures" often intended as second-feature fodder, it is not surprising that the majority of Dwan's efforts were unexceptional. These latter movies included two Westerns and three exotic adventures.

Yet the five minor films that Dwan made at RKO are, in varying degrees, not without compensations. They also reflect some of the themes and plot lines Dwan developed more trenchantly in the films above.

Passion (1954) was apparently the film Bogeaus was about to make without Dwan after *Silver Lode* until he thought better of it. An article in the *Los Angeles Times* states that Harmon Jones was originally supposed to direct the film.[23] Most of Dwan's brief comments with Bogdanovich about this movie refer to his cunning in renting or stealing expensive Spanish sets for use in the picture. Ironically, *Passion* is visually at its most impressive in its exterior mountain scenes. Critic Donald Phelps considered *Passion* (along with *Tennessee's Partner* and *Most Dangerous Man Alive*) his favorite Dwan movies, citing them for their "coruscations of plot, their picaresque chains of incident, through which Dwan traces a skein of narrative logic."[24]

Passion has a written prologue: "Early California ... under Mexican rule ... the timeless mountains and eternal snows looking down on the everlasting struggle of man against man." The prologue recalls the introductions to silent movies, especially those that would assert the metaphoric importance of a tumultuous spectacle that would be the climax of the film.

Despite its exotic appeal, this is basically a revenge Western. In an attempt to control a vast range of territory, the villains try to seize the protagonist's land by attacking his home and in the process killing his wife and father-in-law, with his missing child assumed also killed. When insufficient evidence permits the culprits to go free, the hero (Cornel Wilde's Juan Obregon) takes the law into his own hands and begins killing the murderers one by one. Like John Payne's respectable citizen in *Silver Lode,* Obregon now becomes a fugitive from justice.

A more complex character is that of the lawman Captain Rodriguez, played by Raymond Burr. Some usually reliable reference sources list his character as a bad guy. Though Burr was often cast as a heavy during this time, his character is no villain. Rodriguez, a friend of Obregon, is also pledged to enforce the law. When Obregon kills the first of his family's murderers, Rodriguez lets him escape. But when Obregon continues his spree of vengeance, Rodriguez feels personally responsible for the killings and becomes obsessed with capturing his former friend. He is a Javert haunted by his capitulation to friendship and compassion, a more complex version of Walter Brennan's sheriff in *Surrender* and another demonstration of Dwan's ability to refine previously used devices.

To many of Dwan's admirers it may seem perverse that he would direct a film called *Passion*, given his penchant for detachment. The *New York Times* and *Variety* reviews thought the title inappropriate. The critic Michael Henry Wilson has suggested that the title of the film should be taken in the religious sense. (There are certainly mystical elements in the film, particularly in its closing reels.) Most directors, including a great one like Fritz Lang, would most likely give the greatest conviction to the revenge part of the plot. Dwan's talents register most strongly in Obregon's epiphany against further violence.

The climax employs location photography in the mountain range between California and Nevada. As a storm approaches, the avenger's pursuit of his final quarry Sandro (Rodolfo Acosta), shot on a glacier, conveys the sense of desolation at the end of Obregon's quest. For most of this sequence, shots of moving clouds, sometimes threatening but always majestic, are alternated with stark long shots of isolated figures moving in the snowy mountain landscape. Evoking some of the power of the silent film sagas of Sweden's pioneering directors Sjostrom and Stiller, Dwan's use of the pathetic fallacy (the weather mirroring inner human turbulence) shows Obregon confronting a feeling of a power beyond vengeance.

Obregon and Sandro make it to a cabin where they find shelter and Obregon's demons are exorcised. As Sandro makes a convenient deathbed confession with Rodriguez's arrival, the lawman now says he will testify on Obregon's behalf. Obregon gains a new perspective not only by his detachment from this world but rejoining it with the news that his son has been found alive. He is not just another of Dwan's lost fathers restored. Like the long-suffering Job, he will be rewarded. Juan will not only regain his son but likely a wife who is the identical twin sister (Yvonne De Carlo) of the boy's mother, but stronger and more resilient.

Passion is, as suggested in the last paragraph, still too facile in formula but Dwan and Alton deliver a climax of striking force. It is arguably the best of Dwan's secondary films with Bogeaus.

Dwan's next feature *Cattle Queen of Montana* is fairly routine and at best, a very modestly entertaining film. It looks like the kind of Western Dwan might have made had he remained at Republic. In fact, Republic the next year released the similarly titled *The Maverick Queen* also starring Barbara Stanwyck, helmed by Republic's house director Joseph Kane and possibly the better film. Screenwriter Robert Blees, who was one of three credited scribes on *Cattle Queen*, remembered, "This was a picture that had a lot of trouble ... screenplay trouble. Nobody would accept it."[25]

Cattle Queen of Montana was shot on location in the Glacier National Park area of Montana. It was the first time that Dwan worked with Ronald Reagan and Barbara Stanwyck, each of whom would make an additional Dwan film at RKO. Of the future president, Dwan recalled, "Reagan was a nice man but he's got a temper." While Reagan was a skilled horseman, he was given an Indian horse that wasn't broken and was untrained for films. Despite Reagan's best efforts, the horse would not approach the camera as it was supposed to and instead started dancing sideways. Dwan recounted that as Reagan "went by the camera, he yelled out to me, mad as hell, 'I'm not one of those Hollywood riders who says he can ride and can't ride! This goddamn horse won't do what I tell him.' He's explaining himself to me as he flies by the camera. Of course, we're howling with laughter."[26]

Both Reagan and Dwan professed their admiration for Stanwyck on the film. Dwan remembered her as a "terrific worker and a great friend to the working men on the crew."[27] Reagan recalled how, rather than use a double when she was supposed to be swimming in a lake, Stanwyck went into the icy water herself. He added, "Movie scenes are never filmed in a few minutes. There is always a reason for doing it over and over, then over again. But not one whimper out of Stanwyck."[28] John Alton commented, "She came out blue, but did not hesitate to do another take."[29]

The Blackfoot Indians, who served as extras in the film, were

Benedict Bogeaus, the independent producer who became Dwan's collaborator on ten films. The relationship did not start out smoothly, though.

so impressed by Stanwyck's stamina and ability to ride well and do her own stunts that they bestowed on her their most revered name, Princess Many Victories III. She was also inducted by the braves of the tribe into membership in their Brave Dog Society.

As Dwan's preoccupation with lost father figures receded, women took on greater importance in his films. Stanwyck continued to refine her female ranch boss characterization, reaching its most gripping level in Sam Fuller's 1957 *Forty Guns*, before being packaged for television in the TV series *The Big Valley*. In this film, an Indian attack takes the life of Stanwyck's father and most of her men, just a day before they were to file a claim for their land. An educated Indian, Colorados (Lance Fuller), finds the survivors and takes them into his Blackfoot camp where they can recover and start life afresh. Also slipping in and out of view is an amiable but mysterious gunman (Reagan).

In Phil Hardy's indispensable volume *The Western* (in his Film Encyclopedia series), *Cattle Queen* is described as evoking "a world of easeful innocence far removed from the cynicism and violence that was the norm in the Western of the fifties."[30] The description is a tribute to Dwan's ability to convey a sunny appearance of life even as it is dotted by black holes of deceit. Consider the ring of betrayals in the *Cattle Queen* plot:

- Nachakos, the Blackfoot leading the raids, risks bringing down the wrath of the whites on his people.
- He does so by arrangement with the white Tom McCord, a land grabber who betrays his own people by encouraging Nachakos to attack white settlers.
- After befriending Jonesy (Stanwyck), the gunman Farrell (Reagan) appears to be undermining her as a henchman for McCord.
- Later, it is revealed that Farrell is a government undercover agent who is spying on McCord.
- Jonesy, suspicious of McCord's methods, decides to investigate McCord herself by posing as a friendly guest. In one scene, in McCord's home, she actually exchanges her usual riding breeches for a pink dress! While staying with him, she discovers vital evidence.
- When Nachakos appears to be getting too ambitious, McCord decides to turn on his partner, inciting white settlers against him.
- Growing jealous of Colorados' interest in the white woman (Stanwyck), his Blackfoot girlfriend Starfire (Yvette Dugay) goes over to his enemy Nachakos to deliver Jonesy to an ambush.
- Starfire herself is betrayed when she is killed by Nachakos' men.
- Adding to this atmosphere of distrust is the hostility of the local townspeople to Jonesy's friendship with the Indians.

Dwan's placid depiction of these facts keeps his Western looking traditional but we are never fully engaged with any of the characters, though we admire Jonesy's gutsiness.

If *Escape to Burma* is not the worst of Dwan's RKO films (though I think it is), it is certainly the most disappointing. The *New York Times* reviewer was even puzzled by the title since all the events of the film take place in Burma.[31] With strong leads Stanwyck and Robert Ryan, there was every reason to expect something more worthwhile.

Ryan played Jim Brecan, a man on the run accused of murdering the son of the ruler of the kingdom of Sakar, apparently a part of Burma. This was the first of Dwan's films to be released in the U.S. in widescreen, using RKO's own format Superscope. Dwan exploited the widescreen with long lateral tracking shots to emphasize the sense of pursuit.

In a variation of her ranch-owner roles, Stanwyck plays an American running a plantation in what was then called Burma (now Myanmar). Her concern for her elephants, shown early in the film, makes one curious to see how they are used to do work but that is played down in the rest of the movie. Ryan finds a temporary refuge at Stanwyck's residence. Erotic feelings between them are skillfully shown arising during the excitement of a tiger hunt.

It is all downhill from there. When a British law officer arrives at the plantation, Brecan goes on the run and most of the rest of the film deteriorates into a monotonous chase with other extraneous "police forces" entering the fray and violence breaking out. Alton's cinematography still delivers some stylish but empty touches. An exterior nocturnal shot of approaching bandits (bathed in dark blue) is alternated with an interior shot of the protagonists in a hut around a fire (suffused in green light). In an interview, Dwan acknowledged that *Escape to Burma* looked "good" and noted that he had purloined the sets from Howard Hughes' *The Conqueror* with John Wayne.[32] Actress Lisa Montell recalled that the sets were so huge that "you could put a whole city in there."[33]

Dwan's admiration of Stanwyck grew with this film. He recalled, "The animals loved and obeyed her. The gigantic elephants were like kittens in her presence. She could have been a great animal trainer had she wished."[34] He added, "A director's greatest pleasure is the cooperation of a dedicated star. My sixty years of work would have been blessed by a longer association with her."[35]

Dwan's next film *Pearl of the South Pacific* (1955) was derided by Dwan himself. "It should never have been done. We tried to talk Bogeaus out of that one — I don't know how he got involved."[36] *Leonard Maltin's Movie and Video Guide* sums it up as a "so-bad-it's funny relic of its era."[37]

The film was based on a story by one Anna Hunger. So one could even say that the story was from Hunger. Yet, *Pearl of the South Pacific* is a step up from *Escape to Burma*. And the film, while it may be a minor one and by most standards a bad one, is not without its pleasures and beauties.

Pearl also has its share of banalities about an island paradise. Some of the scenes of Virginia Mayo's bogus missionary Rita trying to seduce the naive George (Lance Fuller) verge on par-

***In Pearl of the South Pacific* (1955), Michael (Basil Ruysdael), the self-appointed white guardian of the island, looks on as Rita (Virginia Mayo, right) stays with an injured boy and his mother. Momu (Lisa Montell) is at the far left (courtesy Lisa Montell Janti).**

ody. (Donald Phelps happily acknowledged, "I got a pleasant start watching Virginia Mayo's hilarious camp of a sea-going doxie impersonating a lady missionary—next to *White Heat*, the best casting I've seen of this second-string Susan Hayward."[38]) And the secret treasure in the film is guarded by a "devil" octopus, which may trigger memories of Ed Wood's beloved monster with rubber tentacles.

Those without affection for the exotic adventure story may sign off on this one immediately. Other viewers might prefer that more of the Polynesian characters in the film speak for themselves rather than have their views filtered through the lips of a white protector.

But the script bears some consciousness of this, and the hubris of the elderly Michael (Basil Ruysdael), the white high priest of the island, is duly noted. (One character ridicules him as the "Great White God.") One aspect of the story that has not dated is the romantic hope to keep inviolate what remnant exists of indigenous people untouched by civilization. As Michael himself points out "Men ... have always sought a happier place than their own, some far-off isle contentment but few have found it." Michael describes himself as a "troubled man" who found the island in his youth. This island is the ultimate haven of refuge that Dwan characters seek.

In this opus, Rita Delaine (Mayo) is one of a trio of adventurers out to swindle the natives of black pearls. Her cohorts include her fiancé Bully Hayes (David Farrar), whom she has embraced out of spite for her former lover Dan Merrill (Dennis Morgan), who has been shanghaied to join them. Dan and Rita carry the memory of their love affair but for Rita it has become a reminder of her lingering hate for him—a hatred that still binds her to him.

Rita tries to establish a beachfront for them as a missionary, especially with the fascination she provides for Michael's son George, who knows nothing of the "outside world." Her arrival interrupts the wedding ceremony of George to his native betrothed, Momu (Lisa Montell).

For a tropical island, there is much emphasis in *Pearl* on interiors. A number of the scenes take place in Michael's spacious residence or in the temple. The treasure of black pearls that the whites seek is hidden in a grotto that can only be reached by swimming underwater through a lagoon. The sense of a self-enclosed world is palpable, if always fragile.

Rita comes to feel remorse for her Eve-like temptation of George to shatter his Eden and promises to stay with George if he sends the white men away with the pearls. There is then a cut to one of Dwan's most contemplative shots where a locale from an earlier scene is revisited. It begins with a high angle view of the crestfallen Momu, wandering around the temple and kneeling to pick up the floral wreath left from her aborted wedding, with the crane then swooping down on her as she prays for George to be kept safe and delivered to her.

The cruel riposte is a cut to a scene in which George is treacherously stabbed. Michael then appears to be dying from a stroke. Rita is taken away to be executed and her appeal to the war chief that "every good thing is being destroyed because of revenge" is ignored.

Michael then emerges with help from Momu and we hear that George too is recovering. Dan has fled the ship which the natives have destroyed with its crew and returns to Rita. With blessings from Michael, they shall all live on the island as one people.

The twin "resurrection" of the father and son may be seen as part of a mystical plan or as a ghastly and ironic set of improbabilities that cast doubt on any secluded paradise surviving. But here a place of refuge and contentment has been preserved.[39]

Dwan followed *Pearl* with another Western, *Tennessee's Partner*, returning to a Bret Harte story for the first time since the 1916 *The Half-Breed* with Fairbanks. The film starred Rhonda

Fleming as well as providing return engagements with Dwan for John Payne and Ronald Reagan. *Tennessee's Partner* was highly touted in the press as being part of a production renaissance for RKO.[40]

But RKO was moving closer to its demise rather than a revival. The day of reckoning was close at hand as Bogeaus prepped his next production *Slightly Scarlet* while shooting wound up on *Tennessee's Partner*.

Slightly Scarlet was based on James M. Cain's novella *Love's Lovely Counterfeit*, first published in 1942. Universal took up the property but was advised by Joseph Breen in 1945 that this story "contains much which is unacceptable under the provisions of the Production Code...."[41] In 1947, Republic's Edmund Grainger, who then appeared interested in filming Cain's book, was warned by the MPAA that "even though he might make a picture which complied with the letter of the Code, if the picture still emphasized the activities of the gangster, it would most likely bring forth public condemnation."[42] The MPAA clearly did not want a return to the gangster films of the pre–Code era.

Bogeaus got control of the property and in early June 1955 announced that it would be adapted to the screen under the title of *Counterfeit*, with Barbara Stanwyck in the leading role. Virginia Van Upp was to write the screenplay and Kurt Neumann was named as the director. July 6 was set as the start date.[43] However, things began to go awry with the project starting with a problem with the screenplay. Bogeaus turned to Robert Blees to write the script but there was a catch. "The problem is, kid," Blees remembers Bogeaus telling him, "I start shooting in three weeks. Take it or leave it."

The writer replied, "I'll do the best I can."[44]

Blees began his task in an abandoned setting where much of RKO's creative talent had vanished. "I remember very, very well. I practically lived at RKO, on the fourth floor of the Writers' Building, and nobody else was there because nobody else was working for Howard Hughes. And I spent my life there." Or so those three weeks must have seemed.

Much of the script difficulty was with the original source material. Blees said he knew that Bogeaus had paid only $10,000 for the rights to *Love's Lovely Counterfeit* because "nobody else wanted it." When Bogeaus said he had a story with James Cain's name on it, the unimpressed Blees responded, "Yes, and it's a lousy novel." But while throwing out much of the book, Blees maintained its framework, noting, "I can write a melodrama about two sisters better than this."

He added, "I wanted to make this as gritty, strong and as sexual as *Double Indemnity*," the 1944 noir film classic which had also been based on Cain's work (and which also starred Stanwyck).

Blees had to report to both Bogeaus and to Hughes' right hand man, C.J. Tevlin, the v.p. in charge of studio operations at RKO. Blees believed that, like Hughes, Tevlin "didn't know anything about the picture business either." Blees said that after his first week of writing, Tevlin conveyed to him a message from Hughes: "Howard says you can't make it this rough." The censorship problem was apparently still haunting the project.

But in the second week, Blees said he received some words of encouragement. "Fuck the censors," Tevlin now told him. "Make it any way you want."[45]

Could it be that Hughes—who had proved so inimical to creative talent at his studio—would now provide a bulwark of support against the censors? Hughes had been down this road before and had locked horns with the censors over his independent productions *Scarface* and *The Outlaw*. *Scarface* was from the early thirties gangster cycle that Breen and his cohorts were determined to prevent from being repeated. Hughes had cuts made and the ending softened to get the Seal of Approval. But in New York, the State Board of Censors still refused to permit *Scarface* to be shown. Hughes was one of the few producers willing to challenge the censors and he filed a lawsuit against New York and other states. After winning the New York case, Hughes restored the footage and the original ending. As recently as 1953, Hughes had again defied the censors by releasing *The French Line* starring Jane Russell without the industry's seal of approval.

Raymond Burr, Cornel Wilde and Yvonne De Carlo in *Passion* (1954). Burr's lawman began as Wilde's friend before becoming obsessed with capturing him.

But the following week the signal from Tevlin had changed again. "Hey, tone it down, kid," he now told Blees. Was this just another example of Hughes' erratic behavior?[46]

Something else, however, was going on behind the scenes. Hughes had received a formidable bid to buy RKO.

RKO's assets had dwindled considerably by this time but they still included a library of about 900 theatrical movies. Thomas O'Neil, the president of General Teleradio which owned six television stations (as well as a 569-radio station network), found the lure of this library irresistible. With thirty bankrupt old movies he had gotten from Bank of America's vaults, O'Neil had introduced a series called *Million Dollar Movie* on one of his stations. A film would run for a week on the station as if it was playing at a local theater but one now in the viewer's home. The concept proved so popular that O'Neil then rented the films to 95 other stations.

The film library was all that really interested O'Neil about RKO but Hughes would not sell it separately. O'Neil would have to pay for the whole shebang to get what he wanted. It is likely that Hughes or his lieutenants must have realized that they did not want to create any controversy that might discourage the buyer.

Meanwhile, there were other problems developing on Bogeaus' project. After the starting date for the film had been pushed back to July 12, Stanwyck announced that she was quitting the production. The initial report was that the "delay in script completion" would create problems for her other commitments. But Bogeaus also said that Stanwyck told him she wanted her role in the film expanded.[47] It was later reported that Stanwyck had to bow out because of a recent back injury.[48] This could have been a face-saving way out of a thorny problem, but one of Stanwyck's biographers does cite that the actress fell down a flight of stairs on June 29, 1955, and cracked a vertebra.[49]

Blees had wanted his script to rival that of *Double Indemnity* and Stanwyck, one of the lead players of that classic film, had until now been set to star in this new Cain adaptation. Not only was that opportunity now lost but Robert Ryan, who had been set as the male lead, broke his leg and he too was now out.

When it was first announced that Stanwyck planned to leave *Counterfeit,* it was also reported that Bogeaus was in negotiations with Arlene Dahl to play the younger sister in the story. With Stanwyck now gone, Dahl had a casting recommendation for the other sister and it was someone who, like her, had red hair. Said Dahl, "Rhonda [Fleming] and I were good friends. But people kept thinking we were one and the same person. So we wanted to do a film together so that people would see we had red hair in common but that was about it."[50]

The same time that it was announced that Fleming was replacing Stanwyck, there also came word that Bogeaus was dropping Kurt Neumann as director in favor of Dwan. Bogeaus' only public comment on the move was, "I signed Dwan because he is a good director, has worked for me before and I wanted him."[51] It was also another case of a producer calling on Dwan when he knew he was in trouble.

Dwan probably did not need much coaxing to choose Fleming to replace Stanwyck since he had just completed *Tennessee's Partner* starring Fleming and John Payne. And both were brought into this film with Payne as the leading man. Also simultaneous with the announcement of Dwan's signing was a new title for *Counterfeit.* It was now to be called *Slightly Scarlet.* Given the timing, Dwan most likely thought of or selected the new title. He had always been fond of red-haired women and

Robert Ryan, Barbara Stanwyck and Lisa Montell are at the top of the stairs in *Escape to Burma* (1955) while Stanwyck's foreman Murvyn Vye stands before the bowing elephant.

now he would have two starring in the same film. (Stanwyck had her hair dyed red for her two color films with Dwan.)

One of those red-haired ladies might have been vetoed for the role. Dahl recalled that early in her Hollywood career she was at the celebrated nightclub Ciro's and she remarked to her escort that a man standing at the bar had terrible body odor and then asked, "who wears sneakers or tennis shoes with a suit?" The topic of her conversation came over to her. "Miss Dahl," he told her, "I overheard what you said and you'll never work for RKO as long as I'm there." When he left, the baffled actress asked, "Who was that?" The reply was, "Howard Hughes." Hughes may have still remembered their run-in but he chose not to block her being cast in *Slightly Scarlet.*[52]

Dahl's recollection of Dwan was much more positive. "He was wonderful. He had a great sense of humor. He was a slight man but he had great strength of character."

Dahl played the sister who was "the bad girl" and she did not have much experience playing that kind of role. She remembered that she and Dwan discussed the character and that she made some suggestions. Dwan deferred to some of them but in other cases, he had his own views on how the character should behave in a given scene. Dahl found him "very generous": In those cases of disagreement, he would shoot the scenes both ways. Dahl compared Dwan favorably to other directors, noting, "Most directors are ushers. They say 'this way' and 'that way' but they don't talk about the background of the character beforehand."[53]

There was, however, one moment when Dwan's dual approaches to the two actresses clashed. Fleming was rehearsing a scene where she was brushing her hair and waiting for her cue from Dahl, who was on the bed. Dahl said something but the expected line did not come. Confused, Fleming asked, "Wait a minute, where's my cue?" Dahl had improvised the line and now apologized for not telling her co-star in advance.[54]

Dahl remembered, "I discussed it with Allan but I didn't discuss it with Rhonda. And he said, 'Don't tell her. I'd like to see her reaction.'"[55]

And so as with Marcy McGuire in 1943, Dwan may have seen the merit in sometimes keeping one of his stars off-balance.

Slightly Scarlet went into production on July 18, 1955, the same day that it was announced in Las Vegas that the contracts were signed for the buyout of RKO Radio Pictures. Referring to RKO's refusal to fight the censors for the script he wanted approved, Blees felt that "the picture would have been better if it hadn't been for Howard Hughes' own censorship problems."

But the battle with the censors on *Slightly Scarlet* did not end with Blees' completion of the script. With the film now in production, the MPAA said of the revised script, which they had received on July 19, "While this basic story seems to meet the requirements of the Production Code, there are several important elements in this script which could not be approved by this office."[56] There followed close to three pages of various objections.

Dwan felt some of the same frustration expressed by Blees. "We were handcuffed. There were things I wanted to do that were very hard to get by. Today without censorship, it'd be easy."[57]

Dahl recalled that the censors were present on the set. Dwan remembered in particular one scene that drew the censors' ire when "a gangster came into a house, looked across the room and there was a couch from which a woman's leg came up with a foot wiggling. And as he walked over, the leg disappeared; he came over to her, looked down and you knew he was looking down at an 'exposed' woman. Then she sat up and they carried on a scene — she was flirting with him and he didn't know who she was. Well, the censors said that leg coming up in the air wasn't allowed. Too suggestive."[58]

Dahl also recalled the fuss that resulted after she took off her stockings. But she remembers a more positive outcome for Dwan. Dahl recounted that the censors had "quite a few meetings with Allan. It was a very provocative scene and Allan finally won out."[59] And the shot of her raised bare leg did indeed remain in the film.

Of course, the lady was seen not to be completely "exposed" after all. The censors did excise the last part of the gangster's line to Dahl, "Maybe you and me will have ourselves a real ball, right here. Or upstairs." The gangster was also forbidden from later recounting, "Too bad you couldn'ta seen us half an hour ago. We were doin' two or three things at once."[60]

There was apparently some give-and-take with the censors that continued almost to the last minute. When the film was granted a Production Code certificate on October 14, 1955, there was also this postscript from Geoffrey Shurlock of the Production Code Administration: "The Certificate is issued with the understanding that the changes agreed upon in our projection room on October 13, 1955, will be incorporated into all prints of this picture to be released."[61] What was decided in the projection room was not recorded.

Slightly Scarlet also provided a suitable challenge for Dwan's cinematographer, John Alton. While Dwan and Alton respected each other, there were differences in style and temperament. Alton took the view that Dwan should have adapted to newer methods. Alton said, "He was a big director at the beginning of the motion picture industry, but he didn't change, he didn't care or bring anything new to it, so that's why he fell off. But he was a good director."[62] Dwan said of Alton, "He was very pompous and aristocratic but he turned out to be a great cinematographer."[63]

Alton could be brilliant but his expressive ambitions could lead to excess. The Academy Award he won for *An American in Paris* was for photographing only the climactic ballet. Director Vincente Minnelli was frustrated with the journeyman cameraman assigned to his picture and felt he would not be up to the task of providing the mood necessary for the ballet.

Minnelli had worked twice before with Alton and called on him to film the long ballet sequence. He said he selected Alton because "I knew he'd approach the light changes in the ballet with the boldness — and the madness — that was needed."[64]

Alton again worked with producer Arthur Freed and Gene Kelly on *Singin' in the Rain*, but was fired after two weeks, perhaps for providing too much "madness." Looking at the rich visuals Alton later provided for director Richard Brooks on *The Brothers Karamazov*, Todd McCarthy observed that "it does provide some telltale clues as to what his dissatisfied collaborators on *Singin' in the Rain* might have been complaining about: Numerous scenes, particularly the interiors, are lit in utterly unrealistic ways, with lighting sources remaining quite unjustified and odd colors, notably purple, green and yellow, bouncing off ceilings or bathing the characters in back light."[65]

Dana Andrews and Don Dubbins are the two seamen seeking a freer world in *Enchanted Island* (1958).

Dwan had permitted Alton to use such effects, to a limited extent, in *Escape from Burma*. But given that the majority of the films he made with Alton were Westerns, it is perhaps understandable that Dwan kept some restraints on Alton. However, with the neurotic subject matter of *Slightly Scarlet*, Dwan, like Minnelli, recognized that Alton's dizzying effects were just what he needed. McCarthy, writing the introduction to Alton's book *Painting with Light*, noted that *Slightly Scarlet* "is a major noir and arguably the best ever shot in color and widescreen."[66]

Slightly Scarlet did not cause much of a stir among American critics of the time who regarded it as just another melodrama. *Variety* thought it did "a fairly effective job of providing crime-doesn't-pay entertainment..."[67] while Bosley Crowther of the *New York Times* dismissed it as "an exhausting lot of twaddle."[68] In France, however, some critics were developing an appreciation of Dwan's films with Bogeaus. Writing for *Cahiers du Cinema*, Jean-Luc Godard rated *Slightly Scarlet* as among the ten best films of 1956.[69]

The new regime at RKO proclaimed that it would revive the company as a production center. In the first half of 1956, "RKO was probably the busiest lot in Hollywood, with thousands of employees turning out features, industrial films, television commercials and shorts."[70] But the resuscitation was short-lived. It soon became evident that General Teleradio lacked the resources and ability to bring RKO back from its moribund state. By the fall of 1957, O'Neil sold the filmmaking plant to Desilu, which would use the studio for television production.

Bogeaus must have encountered problems making films with the new RKO management because in August 1956 he announced that he would be independently producing two films to be released by Twentieth Century–Fox. One of them was to be a remake of his 1944 film of Thornton Wilder's *The Bridge of San Luis Rey*. Bogeaus had announced over a year earlier that the same project would be made at RKO with Stanwyck in the lead. The project may have proved too big to be done at a dying studio. Despite Bogeaus' new announcement, it would not materialize at Fox either.

The other project, *Conquest*, later morphed into a film to be titled *The River's Edge*.

In the interim, Dwan had departed from Bogeaus to make a war film at Allied Artists, the aforementioned *Hold Back the Night* (see last chapter). He now rejoined Bogeaus to direct this new film.

The River's Edge was based on the story "The Highest Mountain" by Harold Jacob Smith; the credited writers were Smith and Dwan's film editor, James Leicester. Dwan recalled that Leicester always wanted to write and that both he (Dwan) and Bogeaus agreed to his script work. However, Dwan noted that "it was a conglomeration job. And we had to put the credit some place so we gave it to him."[71] So while Leicester may have done the majority of the work, his name functioned like Fairbanks' "Elton Thomas" for several contributors, almost certainly including Dwan.

Dwan was impressed by the way that Bogeaus was able to get two major male stars, both Oscar winners, Anthony Quinn and Ray Milland, to star in the project. Shot in Mexico, *The River's Edge* was a taut and stark action drama.

The last of Dwan's RKO films, *Enchanted Island*, based on Herman Melville's *Typee*, is another film set in the South Seas, in the Marquesas Islands. This time Bogeaus' production company was Waverly Productions and for a second time a Bogeaus–Dwan film was shot in Mexico. It was ultimately released by Warner Brothers in 1958.

Dana Andrews, who had worked with Dwan almost twenty years earlier in *Sailor's Lady*, was the male lead. Cast as the leading lady was Jane Powell, MGM's pert musical star. After serving as the studio's perpetual ingénue for over a decade, Powell left with the waning days of the musical at hand. Hoping to re-start her film career, she was excited about her role. "I didn't have to sing. I was to do something different, and even more important, I got to die in the end! If anything was going to establish me as a serious actress, I thought, dying ought to do it."[72]

Powell was to be cast as the native island girl Fayaway. While Dwan felt the Mexican locations could adequately fake a Pacific island, he was otherwise unhappy about the production. As Dwan explained it, Bogeaus wanted to do *Typee* while really getting away from the book because of Allied Artists' interest in the same project and there were also some legal problems that mandated that the film be called *Enchanted Island.* Aside from the difficulties with the script, Dwan's star Andrews had an alcohol problem. Dwan complained, "I suffered through it with a drunken actor and a nice girl who didn't belong in it — Jane Powell — she just looked false as hell."[73] Dialogue was inserted in the script to explain that Powell's blue eyes came from an Irish castaway.

Meanwhile, Powell learned to her chagrin that it was decided that her character wouldn't die after all. Powell said Bogeaus was concerned that her fans didn't want her to die. Powell also noticed Dwan's apparent lack of interest with the project. "Allan Dwan seemed so thoroughly bored that I thought he didn't want to be on the set at all."[74] It must have been a very sad shoot with Dwan's frustration, Powell's disappointment and Andrews' struggle with his own demons. Bogeaus and Waverly Productions later sued Andrews for $159,769 for damages, arguing that his work on the film was "interrupted only by infrequent and occasional periods of sobriety."[75]

One of the themes in the film, frequently expressed in the dialogue, was of the search for freedom, and for both the characters and the filmmakers, it would prove elusive. Given all of the problems, it is not surprising that *Enchanted Island* should have been such a disappointment. What is perhaps more surprising is that the film is not completely without merit, even if it doesn't live up to the praise of its champions in France.

One of the striking characteristics of the novel is how at a certain point, it turns into a series of anthropological observations in which the protagonist comes to identify the way of the Typees as being almost in every manner superior to that of the Europeans and even of other Polynesians. The protagonist's arguments, however, are almost comically undercut by his increasing apprehensions that his genteel hosts may be planning to kill him. Despite his familiarity with the Typees, both his idealization and fears suggests a residual distance he maintains from the natives as well as an unbridgeable gulf between the two cultures. The film finds its own equivalent of this tension with its plot alterations but even the most ideal adaptation of *Typee* would have had to expand the limited dramatics of its story.

While Dwan was disconcerted by the "falseness" of Powell's appearance, the Fayaway of Melville's novel also had blue eyes and light skin and the narrator noted that a number of the Typees shared these traits. Of course, Powell's "girl next door" image might have seemed too familiar. But it's a certain familiarity that assures fugitive seamen Abner (Andrews) and Tom (Don Dubbins) when they first spot her, that her tribe cannot be cannibals because she is a "pretty girl."

Typee or Happar? That is the question asked both in the novel and film. The Happars are the natives known to the white men as placid and friendly; the Typees as vicious, savage cannibals. The delineation sounds like the neatly stereotyped lines drawn by civilized visitors to characterize the natives. Following the lead of Fayaway into the village, Ab and Tom assume that these are the good, noble natives, the Happar. It is only after they spend some time effusing admiration for the Happars do they learn from the annoyed chief that they are the Typee.

Among the most disappointing aspects of *Enchanted Island* is how much of Melville's description of the particulars of Typee life is junked in favor of showing them as the generic South Seas islanders of countless movies with such clichéd ploys as the death-defying dives into the water from high cliffs. Aside from Powell's Fayaway, the only native to emerge as a full-fledged character is the chief Mehevi, whom Ab comes to respect. The part is played by a European, Friedrich Ledebur, who had also played a Polynesian in another Melville adaptation: Queequeg in John Huston's 1956 *Moby Dick.*

Even when Mehevi drops the practice of keeping guards around Ab, the sailor recognizes that he is always being watched, with observers sometimes working surreptitiously from treetops. It is Big Brother at work, even in a primitive village. But the Typees have a legitimate reason for their suspicion. They are concerned that any white man leaving the village will lead those of his own kind back to take over the Typee land. (Their cannibal reputation, whether valid or not, has clearly served them well in keeping out strangers.)

Ab's often expressed desire for freedom finds an outlet in his love for Fayaway. His love for her clearly marks his breakaway from "civilized" views as he differs with Tom's racist disapproval of a union with her.

The one stunning shot in the film occurs after the native wedding ceremony of Fayaway and Ab. The couple departs in a canoe for the small island where they will spend their honeymoon. As the canoe moves through the waters, Fayaway unfastens her tappa robe and stands erect as she spreads it out like a sail. (The camera, of course, discreetly follows the action from behind.) Dwan holds the shot for almost a half minute as the scene is made even more beautiful by the sudden appearance of water lilies, a feature more typical of the Mexican shooting location than of the South Seas.

Fayaway's liberating act is taken from Melville but the effect is enriched by the context, signifying the freedom Ab feels he has won with Fayaway in a marriage that does not occur in the book. On their small island, Ab proclaims, "At last I'm free," and the camera tilts up a nearby palm tree, this time showing no ensconced spies.

But their bliss and Ab's sense of freedom are both dispelled when Ab learns that the natives have killed Tom for trying to escape the island. For making that discovery, Ab and Fayaway are both sentenced to death. The Typees appear divided about the verdict, and Ab and Fayaway are able to escape. Ab's loss of freedom then comes from a more mundane source, as he returns to the captain he once deserted, who now muses, "A married man makes a docile hand."

In a 1971 film *How Tasty Was My Little Frenchman*, Brazilian director Nelson Peirrara Dos Santos told a similar story about a white man, forced to live with cannibals for a year. This is a vastly superior film to Dwan's, particularly in its bleak and despairing view of the formidable wall between radically different cultures. It is to the credit of Dwan's picture that some small understanding of that divide is felt here.

Four Sides of the Triangle

The major films of Dwan's partnership with Bogeaus are uneasy forays into human nature and relationships. Most of the minor films proceeded directly after the success of *Silver Lode*. As if getting into a solid groove, Dwan and his collaborators then pulled off in succession *Tennessee's Partner* and *Slightly Scarlet*, and then, after Dwan directed *Hold Back the Night* for Allied Artists, Dwan and Bogeaus made *The River's Edge* for Twentieth Century–Fox.

The relationships in the films were given an interesting sexual dimension by having the protagonists appear in groupings of three in alternating blendings of genders; in *Silver Lode* the chief sympathetic characters are a man and two women; in *Tennessee's Partner* they are a woman and two men; in *Slightly Scarlet* a man and two women and back to a woman and two men as the only principal characters in *The River's Edge*.

Silver Lode

The Western *Silver Lode* (1954) concerns an apparently upstanding citizen, Dan Ballard (John Payne), who is about to be married on the Fourth of July, when a man named McCarty, claiming to be a U.S. marshal, rides into town with three deputies and presents a warrant for Ballard's arrest for murder. In a rapid succession of events, without showing any proof, the "marshal" is able to turn the initially supportive populace against Ballard.

In its obvious parallel with the McCarthyist witch hunts of the 1950s, *Silver Lode* covers similar ground to Ray's *Johnny Guitar*, released the same year. *Johnny Guitar*'s thematic expanses are broader and its style more baroque but *Silver Lode* is an even more intense and single-minded account of a descent into mass hysteria. In fact, the parallels with McCarthyism would be clear even if the film's villain wasn't named McCarty.

That an allegedly anti–McCarthyist film could emerge from RKO was deeply ironic.

In 1952, Hughes had locked horns with the Screen Writers Guild over his denying screen credit to writer Paul Jarrico, who had taken the Fifth Amendment before the House Un-American Activities Committee. Daring the Guild to stage a strike against RKO, Hughes then mounted his own offensive. He placed one hundred "loyal" studio employees on "leave of absence" while he developed a security system to screen all creative or executive personnel for possible Communist sympathies.

The screenwriter for *Silver Lode*, Karen De Wolf, is alleged to have been a victim of the blacklist. In any case, *Silver Lode* would be her last theatrical film credit, though she would continue to work in television.[76]

Though *Silver Lode* bore superficial resemblances to *High Noon*, it was considered to be just another Western. At the time, little scrutiny was paid to any political message it may have borne.

Dwan told his French interviewer Simon Mizrahi that he didn't regard *Silver Lode* as a political film but as a satire of a hypocritical small town.[77] Howard Mandelbaum said that in his interview with Dwan, the director responded with irritation when he brought up the use of the name McCarty and refused

Dan Ballard's fiancée Rose (Lizabeth Scott) and former girlfriend, the scarlet Dolly (Delores Moran), are the only two people who unswervingly defend him in *Silver Lode* (1954).

to discuss it further.[78] Dwan may have a valid point that the film should not be limited to a political context of its day but that *Silver Lode* shares themes from his earlier films of small-town provincialism and intolerance. However, Dwan controlled the Fourth of July imagery that runs through the film and he clearly understood its implication, that this was what was then happening in America.

Dwan's personal political views are not easy to pin down. In 1942, he was a registered Democrat but by 1944 he had changed to Republican. He remained a Republican at least until 1954, the last year his registration was available.

Silver Lode is one of Dwan's starkest and most resonant dramas. But part of the style of the film derives from the comedies Dwan made for Edward Small in the 1940s.

There is more than sheer perversity or plot reversal involved here. The Small comedies, especially *Up in Mabel's Room* and *Getting Gertie's Garter*, are concerned, however farcically, with the search for truth and need for trust. This leads to characters perpetually snooping on one another and struggling to interpret what they've seen versus their faith in each other.

If anything, voyeurism is carried further here, as it will be in a number of Dwan's fifties films. But some of the action is directly evocative of the comedies. In one scene, Marshal McCarty, looking for Ballard, searches a woman's bedroom, first the closet and then under the bed, places that Dennis O'Keefe's characters hid respectively in *Gertie's Garter* and *Mabel's Room*, leaving the lady (Dolly) to deadpan to McCarty, "What do you think this is, a French farce?" (Dwan had collaborated with De Wolf on the script for *Getting Gertie's Garter.*)

In the same scene, a man sticks his head in Dolly's open window, announcing, "I'm looking for Ballard," and she indignantly slams the window on his cranium. Dwan and his collaborators are undoubtedly suggesting that McCarty's hunt for Ballard is something of a farce but the film is also far more complex and nuanced. McCarty's attempt to arrest Ballard at the opening violates the celebration of both a national holiday (July 4) and a religious ceremony (Ballard's wedding to Rose Evans). A network of patriotic and religious imagery will unfold throughout the film with the elements sometimes overlapping.[79]

Silver Lode opens with a shot of banners reading "Welcome to Silver Lode: A Safe and Sane Fourth of July — Giant Picnic and Parade — Come One and All" while a band plays "Three Cheers for the Red, White and Blue." That the imagery and soundtrack suggests an allegory of America is something not to be taken cavalierly from the director of *Sands of Iwo Jima*. The camera tilts down to reveal a group of children lighting firecrackers. After they run off and the firecrackers explode, they see something that makes them recoil. As stark music breaks on the soundtrack, there is a cut to the movement of horses' hooves and then an ascending tilt to reveal four armed men arriving in town. Not inaptly, Myron Meisel has likened their menacing arrival to that of the gang in *The Wild Bunch*.[80]

Marshal McCarty's quest for Ballard leads him to the Evans home (with an American flag displayed outside). Ballard's wedding ceremony is about to be performed, with Ballard marrying Rose Evans, daughter of the richest man in town, a fact directly or indirectly noted by some jealous townspeople. McCarty accuses Ballard of having shot his (McCarty's) brother in the back after cheating him in a card game. McCarty claims the sum was $20,000, which we hear confirmed as the amount Ballard first brought to town when he was just a "saddle tramp." He has risen to become a rancher and a pillar of the community and the people are righteously shocked by McCarty's accusations. Ballard counters that McCarty was a rustler and dismisses his charges by calling him a "liar." When McCarty demands that Ballard get his horse, the prospective bridegroom begins

Ballard (John Payne) seeks shelter under the flag-draped table in *Silver Lode* while gunman Alan Hale, Jr., tries to finish him off.

a walk to the stable with virtually all the townspeople following.

The religious issues assert themselves quickly. McCarty justifies himself by quoting the Bible's "eye for an eye" passage while the minister, the Reverend Field (Hugh Sanders), counters the reference to "turn the other cheek." The townspeople's escort of the accused Ballard through the streets has the somber mood of a Passion Play march. Ballard restrains his prospective brother-in-law Mitch (John Hudson) and later a cowboy (Myron Healey) who wants to defend him. He tells Mitch, "Put the gun away, we'll handle it legally.... You kill one man, it's not hard to kill a second; the third one's easy," echoing passages from John and Matthew when St. Peter or another disciple tried to defend Jesus: "Put your sword back to its place for all who take the sword will perish by the sword."

Mitch repeats his offer to defend Dan with a gun, as do others. But when Sheriff Wooley is killed under circumstances strongly incriminating Ballard, nearly all of Ballard's followers desert him. Townspeople who marched with him in the streets are ready to put him to death. Only two women remain visibly steadfast in their loyalty throughout the film, the pure, Madonna-like Rose (Lizabeth Scott) and the Magdalene–saloon girl Dolly (Bogeaus' wife Dolores Moran), who was Ballard's former lover.

Near the end of the film, a wounded Ballard makes his way to the church for sanctuary, which is granted by the Reverend Field. When McCarty follows him in there and is then killed in a freakish accident, the reverend proclaims it "an act of God."

Dwan and screenwriter Karen De Wolf do not overwhelm the film with religious imagery; it is clear that Ballard is no Christ figure who will sacrifice himself for the good of the town. Rather, the religious parable highlights an archetypical situation of how a revered figure is first defended by the community and then abandoned as accusations against him are manipulated to gather greater authority.

The scenario reveals fairly early (but not immediately) that Ballard is innocent of the charges. But we never know completely what kind of a man he is. Is he indeed a social climber who abandoned his dance hall girl friend for the richest marriage prospect in town?

Like the Biblical story, the film persists in asking "What is truth?" and how faith should be balanced against the need for evidence. As McCarty presents his charges, some of the townspeople begin to demur that they've "only known Ballard for two years. The marshal seems to know more about him than we do."

Still, there is enough suspicion about what McCarty and his thuggish "deputies" will do once outside the town limits. Sheriff Wooley gathers a posse to accompany them to the California town of Discovery and make sure there are no accidents. McCarty's confrontation with the posse comes as the somber background music of the Passion Play march is overridden by the flute strains of "Yankee Doodle Dandy." The "pilgrims" are again at the center of a town decorated by patriotic banners and the "Welcome to Silver Lode" legend. Faith and patriotism do indeed intertwine here.

Ballard's stature in the community is seen as a reflection of their values. As a stable boy tells Ballard regarding the charges of him shooting a man in the back, "If you did, I'd never believe anyone again."

The greatest hope for Ballard is getting official confirmation of his innocence and McCarty's treachery. He requests a message be telegraphed to Discovery on the veracity of the charges and McCarty's claim of being marshal, but the action is delayed by cut wires that have to be repaired.

Ballard's adversary is named "McCarty" (not quite "McCarthy" as some reviewers have noted) not only to suggest Sen. Joseph McCarthy status as a "witch hunter" but his power as a demagogue. And as energetically played by Dan Duryea, McCarty shows a shrewd ability to shift gears and tactics.

Initially, McCarty tries to hustle Ballard out of town before Judge Cranston (Robert Warwick) can rule on blocking extradition to California. But when threatened with armed intervention by the populace, McCarty tries to soothe them: "If I've been overzealous in my duty, I apologize. This citizen wants his rights. No law officer should let his prisoner feel he's run away with them." Once in the judge's office, he puts his situation another way: "I find it hard to convince the citizens there's anything else besides mob law."

The judge refuses to block extradition but appeals to McCarty to grant Ballard's request for a two-hour delay before departure, which he grants. Ballard uses the time first, to try to have the telegraph messages sent and then enlisting Dolly's help to find a weak link among McCarty's deputies, who will reveal the truth for money. Johnson (Harry Carey, Jr.), who is terrified that McCarty is planning to eliminate him, signals his willingness for a meeting. McCarty uses the extra time to sarcastically belittle Ballard before the townspeople.

In this second act "limbo," Dwan's visual style entails the increasing use of "window shots." McCarty's deputies stare threateningly at Ballard through the storefront window of the telegraph office. More chillingly, we see Johnson framed against a double bar window looking out onto the street at McCarty, who is seeking him. Inside the Evans house, Ballard gazes at McCarty standing outside the front door and at one of his deputies waiting at the back one. The Evans family assists him in evading them. The furtiveness continues as Ballard signals his presence to Johnson outside the saloon window and they meet inside the stable.

The window shots help convey the dramatic sense of foreboding and secrecy that now permeate the atmosphere. From inside the stable, Ballard calls out that Johnson has talked and asks for the judge to be brought to him. But McCarty is able to regain control by ambush and demagoguery.

Realizing that he has little time to act, McCarty enters the barn though the hayloft. He guns down Johnson and then goes out to tell the crowd that Ballard has shot his deputy. Back inside, McCarty tries to make a deal with Ballard to get his money and land. The eavesdropping Sheriff Wooley, now entering the hayloft, hears this but as the people batter down the door, McCarty wheels around and shoots Wooley while the latter wings McCarty. Anticipating McCarty's further gunplay, Ballard picks up the guns of the two victims, only to have the crowd burst in at that point to see Ballard thus armed standing over the bodies of the two men.

This Hitchcockian moment propels Ballard into the appearance of guilt. When he protests his innocence, the previously stalwart Myron Healey character asserts, "A man's got to believe his own eyes." As Wooley's widow sobs, the crowd turns against Ballard. Their attitude is only reinforced when Ballard uses his weapons to keep them at bay and flee. In the ensuing flight, he fires back at McCarty's two remaining deputies and kills them, while also wounding a pursuing Mitch in the hand. Now his fellow citizens are also after him. Again, we see the main thoroughfare of the town with its flag-draped tables. Now these only act to provide cover for the escaping Ballard.

The mood turns strangely festive as hunting down Ballard becomes a major preoccupation. McCarty appeals directly to the citizens: "I'm deputizing every man in this town. Go home and get your guns." Judge Cranston counters, "Listen to me. Mob violence is the death of any town. Let Ballard surrender." The crowd jeers at the judge's remarks and McCarty is able to continue: "You've seen what Ballard is and we'll search for him house by house."

McCarty has now taken control of the very mob violence he attacked when it was against him. Having gained the mob's confidence, he conveniently drops his earlier "concern" for citizens' rights as he insists on the searching of every house.

Through the frame of a window, Ballard is next seen fleeing from the mob as he makes his way to hide in a haystack. But this time the framing is not from any person's point of view. The viewer might recognize the scene as being from the back of the Evans' home but it could just as well be any house in Silver Lode.

Ballard again seeks respite in the Evans home but this time, everyone there except Rose is against him. Like the scene in the stable and recurrent visitations to the Independence Day reviewing stands, the setting of the Evans house is a parallel of earlier scenes and a reminder of the fickleness of people's sentiments.

Encumbered by gun wounds, Ballard makes one last desperate attempt to get to the telegraph office. The stasis of the window shots which left him and other characters staring helplessly is supplanted by a burst of activity as Dwan stages a long and continuous tracking shot following Ballard, occasionally stopping and firing when confronted by various assailants in the distant background. He then resumes his frantic run through the town, hunted by seemingly everyone. There is a last lingering by Ballard at the flag-draped tables now empty of guests or communal feeling.

In what seems his last act of desperation, the exhausted Ballard staggers to the town church where the Reverend Field, absent for some time from the film, welcomes him and offers sanctuary. When the townspeople seem to hesitate, McCarty has one opportune blast of demagoguery to demolish even that protection.

Shortly after Ballard enters the church, a carriage moves through town. Dwan dramatizes its approach with an overhead shot that reveals Sheriff Wooley's body being transported, moving through much of the community and drawing it together.

In *Silver Lode* (1954), Ballard's flight from the mob comes to an end as only the church before him offers the hope of sanctuary.

As the men of Silver Lode remove their hats in respect, McCarty exploits the moment to launch his challenge to sanctuary. His sarcastic oratory is a cheap, demagogic evocation of Mark Anthony's funeral speech for Caesar: "An hour ago Sheriff Wooley was alive. An hour ago Wickers, Kirk and Johnson were alive. Four good men. Family men. But the maker of widows and orphans is alive and safe in there.... What sanctuary was there for the men Ballard murdered? Come on, we're going in."

With that, McCarty has demolished the town of Silver Lode's last restraint on the law and custom and in long shot we see the startling image of armed men filing past church benches and pews.

Convincing the people of the "truth" remains a key in any political battle and one can say that the truth is both a casualty and weapon in these disputes. As Ballard faces his last chance, Dolly and Rose persist in getting Paul Herbert to send the crucial wires. Meanwhile, Ballard is using the bell tower as sanctuary. Even looking out the window is no longer a possibility as people in the crowd take potshots at him.

McCarty enters the bell tower and, ever the consummate politician, having manipulated the crowd below, he privately tries to make a deal with Ballard to let him escape with his life, if he turns over all his holdings to him. But Rose now enters the church carrying a telegraph message announcing that McCarty is an impostor and a criminal. The crowd's mood begins to change. McCarty tries to take Ballard "with him," firing at point blank range. When Ballard thrusts the church bell at him, the bullet ricochets off the bell and kills McCarty.

The minister pronounces this a miracle. Ballard, however, can only bitterly comment on how by failing to believe him, his fellow citizens almost killed him and forced him to kill. As he and Rose exit the church, the townspeople exchange glances at each other or look above until the town loudmouth asks, "How do we know that those telegraphs were real?"

Dwan cuts back to the telegraph office where Dolly and Herbert are verbally sparring and Herbert is lamenting the trouble he will get in for "faking" those messages. But just as he is about to leave the office, a message comes in on the telegraph. And it is an almost verbatim replica of the message Herbert was bullied into writing.

The ostensible "happy ending" leaves us with a number of unsettling aspects. Ballard is saved by a "miracle" but the need for a miracle only underscores the community's willingness to turn into a mob. In his bitterness, Ballard neglects to see how events have turned people against him. The faith of Rose and Dolly is strong enough that they take a risk in forging the telegraph messages. But even in a limited way, they have felt compelled, like McCarty, to manipulate facts. And "facts" with all the means to embroider them aren't necessarily superior to faith. (Dwan told Mizrahi that he was pleased by how the protagonist was initially condemned for false reasons and then pardoned for equally false reasons.[81])

The last shot is another window shot. It's a fairly long take as Herbert gazes outside the storefront window offering a panoramic view of one street, still draped in the flags of the Fourth of July celebration, as Dolly runs to the church. In the foreground, Herbert looks through the window, pondering what will happen next, scratching his head in apparent perplexity. The window shots emphasize a sense of foreboding as characters stare at the action, waiting for what will happen next and trying to size up the situation like viewers watching TV screens which were at the time becoming increasingly popular.

That following year, Dwan made the first of two films for the new medium. In the same year as *Silver Lode*'s release, Sen. Joseph McCarthy was widely seen by TV viewers in the Senate-Army hearings. But their impact was the beginning of the end for him.

Silver Lode is in some ways Dwan's best formal achievement, certainly up to that time. It is also a taut, involving drama with an apparent political and sociological context. As a barometer of the decade's anxieties, *Silver Lode* anticipates such later paranoid classics as Phil Karlson's *The Phenix City Story* (1955) and Don Siegel's *Invasion of the Body Snatchers* (1956).[82] But its tensions and pessimism seem atypical of Dwan, as do its similarity to films by Karlson and Siegel. Of the RKO films, Dwan's own personal favorite was the more relaxed *Tennessee's Partner*, which had at its center a memorably affable performance by future president Ronald Reagan.

Tennessee's Partner (1955)

Like *Escape to Burma* and *Pearl of the South Pacific*, *Tennessee's Partner* was shot in Superscope. However, while Eastman House has a scope print of *Pearl*, it had only a flat print of *Tennessee's Partner* available for screening. Fortunately, the film is now accessible in a DVD with letterboxing.[83]

Tennessee's Partner is the kind of effortless-looking Dwan film that one almost hates to submit to analysis. Although it has both plot and architectural convolutions, it also has a stirring simplicity.

Almost forty years earlier, Dwan had filmed another adaptation of Bret Harte's work, *The Half-Breed* starring Douglas Fairbanks. Dwan told Bogdanovich that *Tennessee's Partner* was the only one of the Bogeaus films that he could recall initiating himself as "this was a good honest story, and I liked Bret Harte. I always looked for things of his, and this seemed to be a natural and it was public domain. I believe the original story was more tragic than ours, but it was very definitely downbeat. And it was a short story, so we had to stretch it out some way or other."

Tennessee's Partner is indeed a terse short story, only several pages long. It tells of two mining partners known by the simple appellations of Tennessee and Tennessee's Partner. Tennessee runs off with his partner's wife. But when some time later, Tennessee returns, without the wife, his partner is the first to greet him and with warmth. Tennessee has evoked some distrust among the citizens of Sandy Bar with his gambling but his exploits as a highwayman really do him in. When he is put on trial, his partner's ill-advised attempt to free him with a bribe only seals his fate. After Tennessee is hanged, his friend comes for the body. After that, the partner's health begins to decline until the day when he once again can see his old friend.

At least one critic has seen in this story not an intimate tale of friendship but a veiled chronicle of betrayal and revenge.[84] Harte himself, however, wrote in his memoir of the California Gold Rush Days, "The Argonauts of '49," "To be a man's 'partner' signified something more than a common pecuniary or business interest; it was to be his friend through good or ill report, in adversity or fortune.... [T]here were partners whom even the grave could not divide — who remained solitary and loyal to a dead man's memory.... The heroic possibilities of a Damon and a Pythias were always present."[85]

Dwan could certainly see the mythic possibilities in the plot, however much he might have to deviate from the basic storyline. And there were basic affinities between Dwan and Harte, particularly in the Bogeaus films. Harte himself had been dubbed by one of his early biographers "Argonaut and Exile." Harte could have grasped the rapidity of the community degeneration into a lynch mob in *Silver Lode*; he once outraged the citizenry with his condemnation of a massacre of Indians and "barely escaped with his life."[86]

Harte also dwelt on a world of outcasts and of the communities of that era that offered "havens of refuge." Harte could suggest the sense of malice and distrust that existed under the facade of respectability.

Tennessee (John Payne), the Duchess (Rhonda Fleming) and Cowpoke (Ronald Reagan) are the three principals in *Tennessee's Partner* (1955).

If Harte's story was both too dark and brief for a feature-length Hollywood movie of the era, Dwan and his collaborators were still able to exploit Harte for further source material. John Payne's Tennessee finds a more likely match in Harte's master gambler John Oakhurst, particularly as described in "The Outcasts of Poker Flat," mustached, and garbed in black clothes. (Oakhurst has also been cited as a likely inspiration for television's 1950s gambling hero Maverick, first name Bret.) Also drawn from the same story are the characters of "the Duchess," more obviously here a lady of ill repute, and that of Tennessee's Partner, "Cowpoke," likely drawn from a personage known as "The Innocent."

Dwan also shared with Harte a fascination with the get-rich atmosphere of the frontier towns. In discussing *Belle Le Grand*, Dwan said he was "crazy" about Virginia City. "I like the romance of it — queer, strange, weird history. They were looking for silver, and throwing all that gray mud away until they found out it was silver." The quintessential American town in his previous major Western before *Tennessee's Partner* was called Silver Lode. Certainly there was a parallel between these budding *nouveau riche* towns of the nineteenth century frontier and the economic boom of 1950s America. Indeed, one of the likely explanations for the enormous popularity of the Western at this time was this parallel in empire-building.

The scenario for *Tennessee's Partner* also appears to have drawn from the situations of *Silver Lode*. Dan Ballard came to Silver Lode with $20,000 he had won gambling and used it to jumpstart his upward mobility which saw him as a solid citizen marrying the daughter of the richest man in town within two years. An incident from his past in which he killed a man after a card game in self-defense (the same one where he won the $20,000) is brought back in a twisted manner. Respectability brought Ballard many friends but most of them fell away as the doubts mounted and circumstances turned against him. Near the end of *Silver Lode*, Ballard bitterly denounces the townspeople who had turned on him. Although he is seen escorting Rose out of the church to a supposed "happy ending," he already seems quite disillusioned with humanity.

Dwan's Western *Tennessee's Partner* could almost be a sequel to *Silver Lode* as Payne's character, known only as Tennessee, and now a total cynic, has founded his own gambling establishment. The first glimpse we get of it is through the point of view of old prospector Grubstake McNiven (Chubby Johnson) staring through a window. This reversal of the visual scheme of *Silver Lode* (character looking into the window rather than out) suggests that Payne–Ballard–Tennessee has now established his own little world where he can play by his own rules.

Tennessee's gambling parlor is only part of the activities in that edifice. The other section is known as the Marriage Market where entertainment and refreshments are provided by elegant and beguiling young women. (The censors were insistent that the women be shown selling drinks so it could be inferred that they had a legitimate occupation and were not prostitutes.[87]) This is Grubstake's first view and what he sees, as Myron Meisel describes it, "is a cornucopia of flowers, mirrors, chandeliers...."[88] Before Grubstake gains access to the window on the other side (he is looking for someone to help finance his "big stake"), there is a scene of the Duchess (Rhonda Fleming) instructing her half-dressed girls on how to make men spend freely and land them as husbands. Duchess also cautions them against having any designs on Tennessee, who is "mine." As she explains the rules of the game, her charges can be seen in a mirror above her, suggesting something of the illusory and self-absorbed world of the Marriage Market. It is a world where "pleasure does not come cheap," that both mirrors and exploits the get-rich-quick ethos of its patrons.

We return to Grubstake making his way to the gambling window where he peers in to see Tennessee deeply engaged in a poker game with three other men. The Marriage Market complements the gambling and at one point during a big card game, there is a cut from the busy gambling hall to the women waiting to sell their wares in the Marriage Market. The juxtaposition is a reminder that while treated as two separate spheres, they are also parallel worlds of commerce.[89]

Except for one sore loser, Tennessee's game partners seem amiable. But after listening to this threatening rival, Judge Parker comments to Tennessee, "For a change, I'd like to see you killed." Later, after Tennessee agrees to help finance Grubstake's claim and speculates that it might pay off, his other fellow gambler, the cigar-chomping Turner (Anthony Caruso), shoots back, "You won't live to see it."

After Tennessee collects his winnings, Dwan camera tracks behind him as he glides up the scarlet-carpeted stairs, as if ascending to his own private fortress. Tennessee has not only learned to accept the hatred of his fellow man (which so embittered Ballard) but to exploit it as a business resource. When Duchess, Tennessee's partner in running the Marriage Market-gambling hall, points out to him that customers "crowd in every night hoping to see you get shot," Tennessee responds, "It's good for business." Duchess yearns for him but Tennessee's suspicions of human nature and of women keep him footloose. Still, they have a relationship of sorts that augments their business arrangement. As they kiss, Dwan dissolves to a shot of a rider entering Sandy Bar; he will have a strong effect on their relationship.

When one of Tennessee's foes takes potshots at him, the wandering cowboy, without knowing what the shooting is about, plunges like Don Quixote into the fray, in the process becoming Tennessee's steadfast friend. That character is played by Ronald Reagan. His simple explanation of why he aided Tennessee is that he doesn't like "folks who hurt you when your back is turned."

Cooped up in jail together while the law tries to unravel what transpired, the two men begin to get acquainted. "I'm a stranger here," Reagan's Cowpoke explains, sounding like a Nicholas Ray character; but the deeper meaning here is that his character is not attuned to the treacherous ways of Sandy Bar. Tennessee and Cowpoke have both known loneliness but Tennessee maintains that he is completely friendless. Cowpoke remains upbeat that one doesn't realize what friends you have until the time comes. His optimism is borne out when Duchess and her ladies, all prepared to testify on Tennessee's behalf, assure the release of the two men.

Cowpoke and Tennessee affirm their friendship by rooming together but their inherent contrariness reveals itself in habits such as Tennessee retiring just before daybreak as Cowpoke is about to begin his day. When Cowpoke suggests to Tennessee

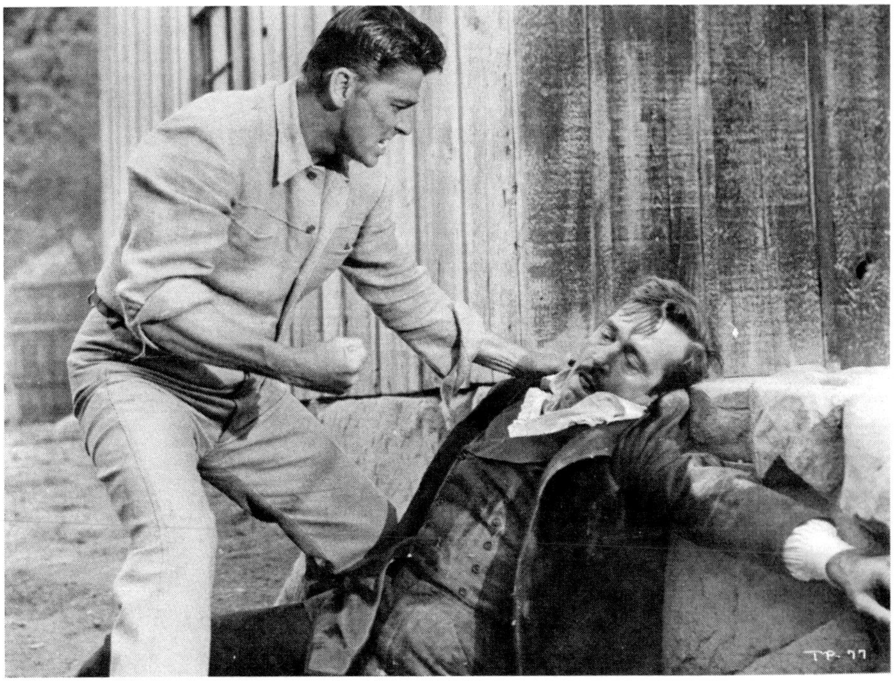

Cowpoke (Reagan) savagely beats an unresisting Tennessee (Payne) but it is Cowpoke who learns the bitter lesson in *Tennessee's Partner* (1955).

that "you ought to get married," the reaction is one of complete distaste. Tennessee's staunch preference for Cowpoke's company registers less an indication of latent homosexuality than of stubborn misogyny despite Duchess' love for him. Cowpoke, on the other hand, speaks blissfully of his upcoming wedding.

Cowpoke is just as much an idealist as Tennessee is a cynic. Reagan was in his mid-forties when he played the role but still handily projects the good-natured boyishness of the character and articulates the innate optimism that would later serve him well as a politician. Unfortunately, Cowpoke is totally ignorant that the woman he is looking forward to marrying is a former lover of Tennessee and a gold digger who's even called Goldie!

It's up to Tennessee to confront Cowpoke with the truth about Goldie in a way that looks like the cruelest kind of betrayal. He does so by running off with Goldie, who was one of his "discards," and then leaving her on a boat departing San Francisco. (She quickly recovers, meeting another attractive prospect.) Cowpoke is crestfallen and humiliated in Sandy Bar. But Tennessee has kept his faith with his friend in his own way.

The friendship between Tennessee and Cowpoke should be seen against the framework of relationships in the film. The Marriage Market works in tandem with the gambling casino; Grubstake's appeal for help requires a bet on the accuracy of his claims for having found gold. Relationships are largely reduced to gambles. But although Cowpoke is known as "Tennessee's Partner," there is really no business relationship between them. Their relationship has a purity that Tennessee and Duchess do not have but might aspire to.

On the other hand, Cowpoke had further complicated his relationship with Goldie by tempting her with a wedding gift of $5,000 in gold.

Tennessee's gamble on Grubstake seems to have paid off: When he returns, the Marriage Market is overflowing with people who want to see the "new millionaires." Tennessee returns from his sojourn with Goldie to find things changed. He now views the Marriage Market through a window, Grubstake's p.o.v. shot at the beginning, suggesting that his sudden acquisition of wealth has led, for the moment at least, to a loss of control. The situation is indicative of the overall instability brought on by the California gold discovery in that period.

Tennessee goes off to Cowpoke's mine and faces him head-on. When an enraged Cowpoke hammers away at Tennessee, beating him brutally, Payne's character puts up no fight until the infuriated Cowpoke realizes that Tennessee's "betrayal" was born out of friendship. He also returns the $5,000 Cowpoke had "gambled" on Goldie. Tennessee justifies his behavior with Cowpoke's line, "I don't like people who hurt you when your back is turned." As Cowpoke reaches out to place his hand on Tennessee's shoulder, Dwan's camera looks down on their reconciliation from a slightly elevated angle, not high enough to be Olympian, but both detached and intimate enough to let their friendship take on the aura of a fable.

Shortly thereafter, when the old prospector is murdered, the sheriff and many of the townspeople (on the basis of circumstantial evidence) are wrongly convinced that Tennessee is the murderer. Tennessee is back to the same situation as Ballard in *Silver Lode* with a lynch mob at his heels, though this time with an honest lawman to restrain them.

As the real culprit is discovered, the ever-protective Cowpoke takes a bullet intended for Tennessee. As Tennessee stands over his friend's body, the camera tilts up to his face as Tennessee, lost in grief, realizes, "I never even knew his name."

Tennessee, the cynic who insisted on having "too many women," finds happiness in marrying his long-suffering sweetheart Duchess. Cowpoke, who had idealized marriage, dies single, betrayed, without even his proper name marked on his grave.

Dwan's sense of irony in his films, while persistent, does not overwhelm the narrative or upset broader concerns. Here irony defers to the mysterious natural order of things. People meet, form bonds and affect each other in unpredictable ways.[90]

Dwan commemorates Cowpoke's death and its effect with a beautifully haunting long shot as Duchess and Tennessee, clad in black, meet and clasp hands against a bleak horizon. Their romantic union is sealed with a recognition of mortality and loss. This scene originally had some dialogue including the judge's eulogy and Tennessee offering his thanks to Cowboy. Dwan makes all the necessary points wordlessly in this single shot.[91] It may also be in keeping with the Griffith tradition of editing that the dark beauty of the shot provides a link to the next scene.

The ensuing sequence shows Tennessee and Duchess celebrating their wedding and departing Sandy Bar. They now have the money to find a more hospitable and comfortable place of refuge.

Slightly Scarlet (1956)

Payne again plays a cynic in *Slightly Scarlet*, now in a modern big city setting and adapted from James Cain's novella *Love's Lovely Counterfeit*. Again, the story has an idealist (of sorts) but this time it is Payne's romantic interest, once more played by Rhonda Fleming, who's working for a reform candidate for mayor. But there is an added wrinkle. Fleming is also caring for her sister, a kleptomaniac out on parole.

Dwan pulled a major casting coup by having probably the two sexiest young redheaded stars of the period, Fleming and Arlene Dahl, play the sisters. Their physical resemblance encompassing two sharply divergent (and complementary) personalities added an extra edge. (The two actresses even shared a common birth date.) Given the closeness of the two stars in appearance and age, it may have been better that Stanwyck, for all her vast talent, dropped out of the project. John Alton's Technicolor cinematography capitalized not only on the red-haired actresses but adapted film noir to a color scheme of garish colors and still menacing shadows.

Arlene Dahl and Rhonda Fleming are the two sisters of different temperaments in *Slightly Scarlet* (1956).

men adds, "Remind me not to send my son to college ... if I ever have a son." The Grace–Caspar rivalry is a perverse footnote to the Dwan lost father–son relationships.) Striking an unusually judgmental tone, Caspar tells "Genius" that he is just a "chiseler ... you're not crooked and you're not straight."

Through Dietz and Caspar, we see Ben as a bookish dreamer, always planning and not even letting physical humiliation unhinge his plans or blow his cool. He is morally ambivalent or amoral as he straddles the ethical fence in trying to get what he wants.

June has taken Dorothy to her not-so-modest home and Dorothy understands how June has used her wiles to get ahead. ("You must be quite a secretary," she wisecracks, surveying the house.)

Dorothy's kleptomania has sprung from emotional wants. We later learn that it was the satisfaction she felt in stealing a charm bracelet that their mother had given to June that ignited her illness. Dorothy acts the free spirit as she manifests kleptomania and nymphomania while June must be more calculated to get ahead. But both sisters suffer from emotional needs and oddly complement each other. In their first scene together, Dorothy wears dark blue while June is in yellow and white. There is a little more here than the usual color coordination of good and evil. For most of the film Dorothy will be seen in the darker colors as if she represents the id and darker impulses of her sister. Dahl's fiery and flamboyant performance as Dorothy is totally in key with this dichotomy.

Dwan introduces the three major characters wordlessly under the credits (each encased in his or her own shot) as we see Dorothy Lyons (Dahl) being released from prison and her sister June (Fleming) in a car waiting for her. Another auto contains Ben Grace (Payne), who is secretly observing and photographing them. While the photo-taking is for a soon-to-be apparent reason, it also introduces a voyeuristic interest in the sisters. In succeeding scenes, we get two views of Ben and his various schemes. To Police Lt. Dave Dietz (Frank Gerstle), Ben is a "dreamer" who will some day be pulled out of the river.

Ben is next seen at the residence of mobster Sol Caspar. When he first enters Caspar's hangout, Ben finds Caspar following the mayoralty campaign, in the first of two scenes, by watching television like the characters under siege in *Silver Lode* watching through the windows. Indeed, Caspar is with his gang watching the publisher Marlowe endorse Frank Jansen (Kent Taylor) for mayor on TV as someone who will unseat the current mayor, who is Caspar's puppet.

We grasp something of Ben's scheming when he tells Caspar that both the candidate and his secretary June Lyons are clean as a whistle and there is nothing to be used on them. When Ben tells Caspar that he is not "smart" to use physical violence against Jansen or his backers, Caspar retorts that Ben will never be a boss. "An operator runs things," he explains. "You've go no jet engine in your belly to operate. You'd rather read a couple of good books. Wait ... let me show you something."

Caspar calls in his men, telling them that he will enact what they will do to Marlowe and proceeds to assault Ben. As a demonstration of Ben's inability to run things, Caspar is exhibiting a bit of guerrilla theater. (Caspar in an aside to his

This duality asserts itself in the first meeting June has with Ben. Dorothy is on the terrace sunbathing while June receives Ben in the living room. Ben has come to offer his services to the Jansen campaign and plays an audiotape incriminating Solly Caspar in the murder of Jansen's backer Marlowe. June hesitates about using it as Ben speculates whether she "has the guts."

Beyond the political tensions of the campaign, an erotic drama is also being played. Dwan intercuts the scene of Ben and June with shots of Dorothy on the patio showing an aroused and increasing interest in the male visitor. As Ben and June sit on a sofa in the foreground, we can still see Dorothy in the background through the picture window, clearly focusing on Ben through her body language.

But if this is voyeurism, it is double-edged, at least. When Ben first enters, he observes Dorothy on the terrace and then turns to June gesturing at the window and says, "Nice-looking girl." June quickly changes the subject since by innuendo he may also be referring to June. At one point, as Ben makes his pitch, we see Dorothy in the background, almost directly behind June's head, focused into gazing at Ben. At this point, Dwan cuts to Dorothy's stare of desire, then cuts back to the two-shot with June ostensibly pondering what Ben is saying. But the juxtaposition of the shots suggests that June shares Dorothy's romantic interest. In long shot, Dorothy can almost be seen directly behind June's head in the picture window, as if she was a bubble in a comic strip more clearly expressing what June is thinking.

Although their initial meeting was edgy, ending with June slapping Ben when he hinted at blackmail because of Dorothy's condition, June eventually accepts Ben's help. After telling Jansen that she can't marry him at the present time, June goes to Ben's apartment as if keeping an assignation to accept his offer.

When Ben first approaches her, he tells June that she is not an idealist like Jansen but "you're a practical girl," alluding to the way she has exploited her position, noting that he doesn't "trust people who aren't a little greedy."

When Jansen wins the mayoral election, Ben and June leave the campaign headquarters to celebrate alone at a restaurant. Summing up her feelings, she observes, "The strangest thing for me tonight ... all those people ... I don't know them. They don't know me. All of a sudden, I realized that you and I and Frank, all of us, were really working like the devil for them ... to help somebody else ... [*chuckles*] I don't think I was ever that altruistic before...."

June's interest in Jansen's politics may have been originally just "practical" but she has clearly caught the bug and has developed genuine political ideals, even if a desire for respectability may be part of it. And perversely, it is Ben who has guided her to this epiphany.

Ben's courting of June is part of his plan to insert his police buddy David Dietz as chief of police where he can return favors to Ben. After he makes his pitch for Dietz, Ben kisses June in the doorway with Dorothy looking on. "Why didn't you invite him in?" Dorothy asks as if echoing June's thoughts while living vicariously through her.

But Dorothy has reached the point where she must make her own desires explicit. That night as they prepare for bed, June innocently asks Dorothy if she wants anything. As June stares into a mirror (almost shrouded in darkness), Dorothy snaps back, "Ben Grace." June tries to dismiss this as an infatuation with the first man she sees available but Dorothy from her bed insists, "Look, I don't expect *you* to understand my feelings.... All head and no heart, planning every move to better yourself. I'm not like you. I've got a heart. And I've got to do what it tells me, no matter what."

Dorothy's outburst is both bluntly honest and misguided. She has followed her heart, but her dependence on emotions with no thought is much of her problem. In talking of her preference for Ben, she contrasts herself with June, who is "all head." But Ben is even more cerebral and more unfeeling than June.

Dorothy is on firmer ground when she finagles Ben into taking her to her analyst and tells Ben, "We're two of a kind — both bad." Yet Ben and Dorothy are more amoral than evil.

Behind the camera on *Slightly Scarlet* (1956) from left to right are cinematographer John Alton (wearing visor), Dwan, Ted De Corsia and Arlene Dahl. Members of the film crew also survey the scene. There was much intrigue in the making of the film.

After Dorothy is arrested for another shoplifting incident, June calls upon Ben to free her, which he does through his connections with Dietz. It is only then that June realizes the web of corruption Ben Grace has spun. Ben lives in the same house as Solly Caspar and operates 30 gambling locations, which Dietz permits to function. June, now the committed reformer, says with disgust, "It's the same old system."

To Ben, gambling establishments (as in *Tennessee's Partner*) are not thievery but responses to human vices that will always exist. He tells June that if he was removed, someone else would just take his place and he wants to get his share of the money.

The roundelay and voyeurism of *Slightly Scarlet* are all of a piece. Characters spy on other characters who have qualities they lack, and each is trying to stay ahead in a game of one-upsmanship. At one point, referring to herself and Dorothy, June asks Ben, "Are you sure you don't want both of us?" Ben really has no interest in Dorothy but he clearly would like June to be more like her sister and less conscientious. Dorothy looks to Ben for the emotional support she feels she is not getting from June. June depends on Ben for his pragmatism while expressing shock at his ethical shortcomings. Ben dismisses Caspar as a "low-grade moron with delusions of grandeur" but he lives in Caspar's house and, while claiming to spurn his methods, wants to take his place.

Matters are brought to a head when word of Dorothy's illegal release (she was on probation) reaches Mayor Jansen. Jansen tells June that Dorothy must give herself up, and Ben must also report to him for what he had done.

Dorothy flees rather than go back to an institution of any kind. In a worthy doppelganger effect, she has left a message in lipstick on the bedroom mirror: "Goodbye Sister."

Caspar returns to his house where he finds a drunk and sultry Dorothy projecting her bare legs over the couch as she waits for Ben. She readily takes Caspar's invitation to join him and he takes her to the beach house where Caspar's money is hidden. Ben, alerted of Caspar's return, is also planning to return there for the money stashed in Caspar's safe.

June intercepts Caspar's call for Ben and goes to the beach house to find her sister. Caspar tries to kill her for her role in exposing him but June outmaneuvers him and shoots him. The gunshots drive Dorothy into hysteria and the apparent breakdown that had long been feared. As she is comforted in the bedroom, Dorothy asks June to take care of her.

For the first time in the film, the dress colors for the two sisters are reversed in seemingly absolute fashion. June is in black and Dorothy wears white. There is in Dorothy's plea a hope for a change and rebirth. June in her shooting of Caspar has become even more drawn into the moral ambiguities of the story.

Ben arrives and quickly packs up Caspar's littered cash on the floor and asks June to come with him but she refuses. But Caspar was not mortally wounded by June and shoots Ben. Weakened by his gunshot wound and knowing he can't get far, Ben calls Dietz and asks for help, knowing that Caspar's gang will soon be with him. Caspar's men arrive a little sooner than expected. When Caspar promises that the two women will be spared if Ben gives up, Ben agrees despite June's protests.

The beach house setting brings to an apogee the expressionistic effects of Alton's lighting. The melodramatic goings-on here are lit in a dark, vertiginous blend of black, yellow and orange. Todd McCarthy noted that "the film features scenes of confrontation and violence that nearly match the tension and power of those Alton helped create in the 1940s."[92]

Pools of darkness and ominous shadows are in evidence from Ben's first visit to Caspar's house. Without in any way detracting from Alton's brilliant effects, it may be also fair to observe that Dwan probably had some input in the visual scheme. In the scene in which Marlowe is surrounded by Caspar's thugs, his plight is dramatized with giant, threatening shadows. Note the same effect in the photo displayed in Chapter 5 from *The Iron Mask* in which the young king is surrounded by his abductors.

By the same token, Van Nest Polglase's sets also play an important role in the visual design. This is particularly true with June's spacious home and is even more in evidence with the beach house, which has a garish color coordination of orange furniture, yellow light shades and blue carpet as well as imposing red doors.

The latter house also has a short staircase, as does June's home. The platform at the top of the staircase in June's house proved a suitable location for Dorothy's spying on activity below. Dorothy also sometimes appeared on the platform like a distorted shadow behind June.

But the platform here is used for more theatrical effect. (We are told that the beach house, in fact, was once a roadhouse.) After his first frustrating look at the TV screen in the movie, Caspar produced his own theatrics of power when he demonstrated to his men how Ben would just *take* a beating. But now Caspar is preparing for an even bigger performance. A large

Ben Grace (John Payne) in a smoke-filled room with gangsters watching a threat to their livelihood on television in *Slightly Scarlet* (1956). Note the large background shadow and compare to the shot from *The Iron Mask* in Chapter 5.

chair is turned around and placed at the foot of the stairs for Caspar, giving him a front row seat. Ben, however, refuses to come down the stairs.

What follows might be called the Sado-Masochistic Theater of the Absurd. Ben remains on the platform and uses it as a stage to taunt Caspar. Realizing that the women are almost certainly still in danger and calculating that the police will soon be there, Ben tries to stretch out the time before the inevitable and directly implicate Caspar. (It is no accident that he is named "Grace.") To do so, he goads Caspar and sardonically refers to him as "Big Man" who "now works on the brain level." One obvious irony is that Ben the "Genius" has also tried to be the "Big Man," whom he is now directly facing, and some of his own self-hatred may be in evidence as he is literally asking for it.

Soon fed up with Ben's soliloquy, Caspar seizes a gun, declaring, "Little by little, I'm going to cut you to pieces." As Caspar shoots him piecemeal, Ben manages to stay standing, ready for the next blow. The police arrive shortly and, after getting in one last shot at Ben, Caspar tosses the gun away. (That'll fool them!) June kneels beside the wounded Ben as he is being loaded onto a stretcher, urging him to hang on. Ben manages to murmur, "Can't say I'm worth it" and June asks that she be the judge of that.

She rises to see Frank Jansen standing beside her and their exchange of looks makes clear that Jansen knows she is in love with Ben. Dorothy then emerges from the bedroom, calling out to June as if awakening from a sleep. Jansen restrains June, and then goes to the top of the stairway to lend Dorothy his support.

In this wordless and eloquent final sequence of *Slightly Scarlet,* there are then shots of each of the three principals, balancing the shots of them under the credits at the beginning. But this time, Ben is supine and Dorothy shares her frame with Jansen, a supportive father figure who has entered the picture. In long shot, we then see Ben being wheeled away at the right of the frame, Dorothy with Frank at the top of the staircase on the left and June standing in the middle. There is then a return to a close-up of June, still clearly caught in the middle, whipping her head back and forth between Dorothy and back in Ben's direction, before settling on Dorothy. Again there is a shot of Dorothy with Frank looking hopefully in June's direction. In a return close-up, June gives her an encouraging nod, and then in long shot all exit off the makeshift stage.

As it shows June poised between the flawed man she loves and the mentally confused sister she wants to love and protect, *Slightly Scarlet* ends by gracefully evoking the dangers and hopes of human relationships. The film's title then zooms out onto the screen, in garish scarlet, perhaps suggesting how we are all tainted.

Though it has been slighted by a number of Dwan enthusiasts and many others, *Slightly Scarlet* is arguably Dwan's finest film and as close to a masterpiece as he has ever gotten. It is undeniably an overheated melodrama that still suffers from loose ends (how does Ben hope to keep his subterfuge from June and the mayor when he moves into Caspar's house?), some naïve characterizations and censorship problems. These elements may keep it from true masterpiece status. Its excesses are both part of its flaws and virtues. The nature of its overblown melodrama permits Dwan to loosen some of his emotional restraints. Dahl's performance may seem a bit over-the-top but it is needed to compensate for the restrictions of censorship and also as a contrast to the more reserved June. In fact, Dahl, Fleming and Payne all acquit themselves well.

As a combination of film noir and woman's film, however, *Slightly Scarlet* has affinities with the notable melodramas then being made at Universal by Douglas Sirk. In fact, the scriptwriter Blees had written two films for Sirk, including *Magnificent Obsession.* Interestingly, where Sirk dwells on reflective surfaces, Dwan more often uses transparent ones to find the truths in his characters.

Far from being a defect, the balance of soap opera and film noir is one of Dwan's more perceptive symmetries. (The first film noir made in color, John Stahl's 1945 *Leave Her to Heaven,* also encompasses these two domains.) The characters pursue a tortured search for happiness while being inevitably drawn to the abyss. Ben's scheming and Dorothy's erratic behavior dominate much of the film but our identification settles in the last shots on the less compromised June, who emerges at the end as the film's moral center.

Slightly Scarlet has also been attacked as a bowdlerization of Cain's 1942 novella. The book, set in the Midwest, is indeed stronger on many realistic details of big city corruption and gives an intricate account of gambling operations and of how ostensibly innocuous pinball games could be modified to serve racketeering interests. But if the book is stronger in details of verisimilitude, the film is more compelling in its handling of the key relationships. Dorothy does not appear in the novella until the final chapters and she instantly provides Ben with a good "clean" relationship that exorcises the exploitative one with June. Dorothy's kleptomaniac problems, for the most part, have been conveniently dispelled. Blees' script is clearly superior to Cain's story. By remaining focused on Ben's relationship with June, the movie acknowledges the complexity and the coexistence of manipulative and genuine feelings while Dorothy presents a complex link between them. In contrast to the complicated and somewhat indeterminate conclusion of the movie, the book has something of a grotesque Hollywood ending. A dying Ben evades questions by marrying Dorothy so that he can't testify against her, thanks to the presence of a Runyonesque gangster with credentials as a self-made minister, permitting him to perform the wedding ceremony. Cain said it was the only novel he wrote with the movies in mind.[93]

The River's Edge (1957)

It is perhaps fitting that for this finale of four major films, Dwan returned to Fox, the studio that had provided him with employment throughout most of the 1930s and early 1940s. It was also the studio that in 1927 permitted him his last fling with location shooting in New York. This time, working with Bogeaus' production company, Dwan shot the first of three films in Mexico and the story is actually set around the Mexican border.

Dave Kehr has described *The River's Edge* as "sort of a Field and Stream noir."[94] Nicolas Saada writing for Cahiers du Cinema saw the film as the crossroads of three genres, the western, film noir and the adventure film.[95]

Dwan was aided by the pairing of major male stars Anthony Quinn and Ray Milland. Milland had owed Fox one more film and liked the script. (Leicester also co-wrote the title song.)

Debra Paget plays Meg Fowler, a city lady with a shady past who has incurred charges of parole violation. Ben Cameron (Quinn) has married her, saving her from prison, and taken her to live with him on his ranch near the Mexican border. But her "salvation" has deteriorated into a strained marriage in crisis, as Meg finds it hard to adapt to the Spartan demands of ranch life. Then Meg is approached by Nardo Denning (Milland), her old gangster boyfriend, who is on the lam with a million dollars in a metal suitcase. As Nardo revives Meg's love, he also enlists Ben's aid to get across the border. Ben agrees because Denning has implicated Meg in a murder but Ben also begins to see remunerative rewards in the trek.

The journey also becomes a competition between the two men for Meg's love.

Whereas *Silver Lode*, *Tennessee's Partner*, and *Slightly Scarlet* all transpired against a backdrop of mob passions and political machinations, *The River's Edge* is an elemental three-person drama with a primal battleground. Other characters appear only briefly and intermittently. As if distilling the essence of all Dwan's narrative variations, here we have the triangle pure and simple. There are no distractions except the cash that Denning carries as the trio embark to a perilous journey against a harsh landscape and submit to a test of survival and sexual dominance. The landscape is given both more character and realism through the use of actual Mexican locations and the breadth of CinemaScope photography.

There are also obvious connections to *Slightly Scarlet* so that *The River's Edge* qualifies as a sequel of sorts. Meg, like Dorothy in the previous film, has a criminal past and is on parole. And Denning seeking to get away with a suitcase full of money starts out as if continuing Ben Grace's aborted flight near the end of *Slightly Scarlet*. John Payne's personae had grown progressively darker through each of the preceding films and if we look upon Denning as his successor, that extension has crossed a moral border. But Grace's character is not simply transferred to Denning. There is also some of Grace in Quinn's Ben Cameron, who with his plans for his ranch is also a "dreamer" like the "Ben" of the earlier film. And like Grace, Cameron also straddles the moral fence. With the gender alterations of each of these four films, Dwan could develop characters and then split their personalities in the next film.

Although Alton did not serve as cinematographer, some of the color scheme of *Slightly Scarlet* carries over into *The River's Edge*. In the first shot of the film, Denning drives into the scene in a garish pink Thunderbird (actually Dwan's own car), visually at odds with the rustic colors of the desert Western setting. His succinct description of Meg to the gas station operator is, "Redhead, about five foot three." And Debra Paget's hair is indeed dyed red to match the hair color of the female leads of *Slightly Scarlet*. As Ms. Paget recalled, this was because she had recently been performing with that hair color in Las Vegas.[96] (Dwan, of course, could have asked her to change the color if he thought it inappropriate.) Throughout the journey that constitutes the second part of the film, Paget's Meg is dressed in an orange shirt to complement the allure of her red hair. The film had a more than slightly-scarlet look to it as Dwan said, "I picked the location because of the red dirt. I liked that since we were working in color."[97] Cameron and Denning are seen respectively in black and white outfits, more purely monochrome than in the dark and light contrasts of the two sisters in the previous film.

Milland's Denning, sporting a white shirt and hat, has the appearance of a dandy. Cameron is the Westerner, a "natural" man who knows the rugged mountain terrain around the border so well that he is often sought as a guide. He may be less sophisticated than Denning but his cunning and powers of observation make him a worthy adversary.

Some reviewers, such as John L. Scott in the *L.A. Times*, noticed that this was a reversal of roles for Quinn and Milland. At the time, the latter was usually the pure white Anglo hero. Although he had won two Best Supporting Oscars, in melodramas Quinn's multi-ethnic characters, often Indians or Hispanics, were usually villains so Dwan's casting coup went against the conventions of the day.[98]

From the very first shots of the ranch, it is made clear that the provocatively dressed city girl Meg seems out of place and her marriage to Ben is tottering. A shot of a scorpion ensconced in Meg's slipper (before she kills it) also nicely signals that there is trouble in paradise.

Meg's dissatisfaction is also reflected in her inattention to Cameron's instructions, resulting in the inadvertent loss of a jar of calf medicine, an exploding stove and a shower faucet that expels muddy water. Ben ignores Meg's pleas to sell his ranch and her protests that there is no fun in their lives. She now wants to leave him.

Cameron reminds her of how they came to be married and of the man who failed to protect her. As she stares into an oval mirror, she seems to be reflecting on her life and what led her to this juncture. (This is one of Dwan's films where mirrors rather than windows predominate.) Now Cameron pleads with her not to go. He also accuses her of still loving the man who betrayed her, even as she professes to hate him.

As Cameron continues to plead that she stay, Denning comes calling at the door, saying that he is looking for a guide and wants to employ Cameron, who is supposed to be the best guide around. Cameron refuses to do so even when Denning offers twice the usual fee. Meg, of course, does not reveal their relationship and acts coolly. But then Cameron asks that Denning take his wife into town so he can stay at home and do other things. Meg at first resists, then takes this to mean that Cameron now wants them to split and admonishes him, "Remember, Ben, that's the way you wanted it."

From the moment Meg sees Denning in the Cameron doorway, the melody for the romantic song "You'll Never Know" is heard on the track and re-appears as a motif throughout the film, sometimes perversely. An Oscar-winning song from a 1943 Fox opus called *Hello, Frisco, Hello* (which starred John Payne!), it is used to conjure memories of Meg and Denning's life together in San Francisco. The appearance of the music is apparently cued by Meg's last response to Cameron about what remains of her feelings towards Denning: "Once you love somebody, you can never be sure. Even when it's changed to hate, you never know whether it's just the other side of love."

After they leave, Cameron rifles through the drawers of Meg's dresser and finds a picture of Denning that Meg had kept so it's clear that Cameron had a good idea, if not certainty, who Denning is. Thus, Cameron's insistence that Meg leave with Denning constitutes a kind of test. Throughout the film, Cameron will continue to lay out tests like scenarios for Meg and/or Denning to follow.

As Preston Sturges demonstrated in his film *Unfaithfully Yours,* where Rex Harrison's symphony conductor indulges in all kinds of vengeful fantasies about his wife and her lover, a suspicious husband has a fertile imagination through which he may be running various scenarios. The ever-practical Ben methodically works like a director to try these scenarios on his wife and her former lover to see where these may lead.

En route to town, Denning tells Meg that he did try to make it to Meg's hearing but was seriously injured by a collision with a truck and was laid up for months. When Meg doubts his credibility, Denning shows her his scars.

Once in town, Denning and Meg check in at separate rooms at the local hotel. Meg is seen briefly enjoying a luxurious bubble bath as "You'll Never Know" again sounds on the track. A riposte to the earlier scene of Meg being soiled in the shower, it conveys in one cheesecake shot how she has become readjusted to life with Denning. At dinner, Denning explains how he has acquired a stash of one million dollars but that the law does not know who has it. Their love rekindled, Denning and Meg plan to run off together.

But driving out of town, the couple is stopped by a border patrolman (Frank Gerstle, the chief of police in *Slightly Scarlet*) who asks to check Denning's trunk. Knowing that he has his suitcase of money there, Denning puts the car in reverse and runs over the patrolman. When Meg rushes out to see if she can help the injured man, Denning appears to be gunning for her with the car and follows her onto the grass. Jumping out of the car, Denning runs to the screaming Meg and says that he was just coming back for her, explaining that he put the car into reverse by accident. This brings another dimension to the unknowability of his acts. Was he indeed capable of wanting to kill her as a witness when the car chased after Meg? And could his feelings suddenly change back to love when he stopped the car and ran out to embrace her?

Back in town, Cameron has sold his ranch in hopes of getting Meg back, and then learns that she and Denning have left their hotel. When Cameron goes to the police station to file a missing person report, he sees the dying patrolman brought in and hears his last words that he was hit by a pink sports car.

Cameron drives back to the ranch where he finds his wife with Denning and tells them, "You really deserve each other." Denning now needs Cameron's help desperately to cross over to Mexico using a mountain route. Meg also needs to escape because the hit-and-run killing endangers her parole. Knowing how critical Denning's plight is, Cameron demands $10,000 to do the job. Denning reluctantly agrees and goes to get the money in another room. The seemingly all-seeing Cameron, spying the oval mirror from the doorway, observes Denning taking the money out of his metal suitcase; he then urges Denning to hold on to the money for the time being.

As the trio makes its way through the hills and mountains, they come across an old prospector played by Chubby Johnson, virtually recreating his role from *Tennessee's Partner*. When during the climb, the suitcase's contents spill onto the ground in view of the old man, Denning shoots him in the back so he can't tell the police.

At nightfall, Cameron leaves Meg and Denning together and the two quarrel over Denning's killing of the old man. Meg is clearly becoming concerned that Denning also plans to murder Cameron and she suggests to Denning that they break away now, falsely claiming that they are only five miles from the border.

But subsequent shots show that Cameron is on a hill looking down at the couple from an angle that shows he has chosen a bird's eye view. Again, he has left them to stew in their own juices as he observes and maintains his own form of control.

Denning and Meg stumble onto a farm where a panicky Denning shoots what turns out to be a cow. Meg, sickened by his murderous impulses, flees and gets tangled in a barbed wire fence. Cameron follows them to the scene and pacifies the angry farmer by having Denning pay him $500 for the cow.

The relationships now begin to shift with the injured Meg becoming closer to Cameron, warning him that Denning wants to kill him. Cameron replies, "We have a lot in common. I want to kill him." The two men have indeed begun to resemble each other.

Sounding almost like the suave Denning, Cameron talks of wanting to buy expensive things for Meg with the suitcase's contents. All three of the characters have been caught up in the corruption.

Dwan uses the widescreen images of the rugged terrain to convey the isolation of the characters. The widescreen also permits Dwan to use his compositions to show the shift in romantic allegiance. This becomes even more evident when the trio seeks shelter in a studio set cave, as Denning walks to the cave wall far from where Meg and Cameron situate themselves.

While Cameron continues to try to manipulate events to his advantage, he also has been forced by circumstances; first in desperation to sell his ranch and then accepting the twisted opportunity to take flight with Meg and Denning. *The River's Edge* may be the only film where a man's wife runs off with her lover and the husband runs off with them as their guide. Cameron is in a way Denning's prisoner but he also dictates terms to him, assumes control of their expedition and hopes to enrich himself. But behind all of this is the struggle between the two men for Meg and Meg's internal struggle over which of them to choose.

The cave becomes a primal arena for the conflicts between the characters, visualizing the primitive circumstances to which they are reduced. Meg's arm wound is seriously infected and Cameron must sterilize his knife to cut out the gangrene. However, there is no way to build a fire with everything they have carried dampened by the rain ... everything except the money in Denning's suitcase.

Cameron demands his fee ($10,000 minus the $500 Denning deducts for the cow) and proceeds to light it to get the fire going. As Cameron ignites the money, Dwan cuts to reaction shots of Denning, who can only recoil from the sight. In the process, Cameron not only shows his love for Meg but gets a leg up on his game of one-upsmanship with Denning, who seems incapable of such an act. But when Cameron needs more money from Denning, Denning risks all by pouncing on his adversary.

Struggling on the ground, the two combatants are frozen by the sudden appearance of a rattlesnake poised to strike. Cameron then calls to Meg to get the hidden rifle. In a highly theatrical moment where the filmmaker tugs at the viewer's credulity, Meg must with one arm debilitated, pick up the rifle and fire accurately on her first shot as Cameron goads her to do it as "I showed you." The same Meg who had showed inattention to Cameron's instructions at the beginning, here comes through. The former femme fatale is now the reformed Eve who slays the serpent under her husband's tutelage.

As night falls, there remains the standoff between Cameron and Denning. For this, the resourceful Cameron must construct still another scenario. While Denning is asleep, Cameron empties the bullets from his handgun but, as if wanting to see the full dramatic effect on Denning, he separates the bullets from the shells with his teeth and then puts the shells back in the revolver. Denning takes the bait and seizes the gun while Cameron is ostensibly asleep.

The next day when Denning learns that they already have passed the border, he pulls out the handgun to do away with Cameron. But his shots have no effect. Cameron, savoring the moment, laughingly shows Denning that he has retained the bullets. But Cameron overplays his hand; as he laughs, Denning throws the gun at him, knocking him down and giving Denning the advantage. In the course of their fight, a huge rock breaks loose and pins Cameron's left leg.

Seeing that Cameron's situation looks hopeless, Denning then tells Meg to join him in making his getaway but she refuses.

Before he leaves, Denning says that he can use some instructions. Cameron then gives him a choice: If he keeps going straight, he will come to a sign that points to the village of Santa Isabel to his left. There, he can give the villagers some money and tell them where to rescue Meg and himself. The alternative is to take the road opposite San Isabel where he can go to make good his escape and charter a plane. Denning says he likes the second choice better and sets off.

But Cameron has actually created another test for Denning. Soon after he leaves, Cameron tells Meg to get a stick and with that leverage, it is not too difficult to remove the rock. With Meg's help, Cameron can now set off after Denning, determined to kill him.

Dwan cuts from the pursuers to Denning arriving at the Santa Isabel signpost and appears to hesitate about which way to turn but there is a cut back to the couple before he makes his choice.

The battle for the gun in *The River's Edge* (1957) between Ben (Anthony Quinn) and Nardo (Ray Milland) is interrupted by the intervention of a snake.

Meg (Debra Paget) and Ben (Quinn) ponder Nardo's sacrifice before his freshly dug grave in *The River's Edge* (1957).

help, and the way to San Isabel leads to Denning's body. Cameron asks, "How do you like that? Probably the first decent thing he's done in years and he gets himself knocked off for it." There is a further twist of destiny to Denning's death since according to his story to Meg at the beginning, it was an accident with a truck that incapacitated and seriously injured Denning when he tried to attend Meg's hearing.

Seeing Denning's body, Meg begins to cry. Cameron does not resent her for doing so. "He deserves a few tears. Go on and cry. The guy loved you and didn't want you to die." The strains of "You'll Never Know" again appear on the track. They were played perversely after Denning committed his murders and now appear again with a different meaning.

Throughout the second half of the film, Cameron had competed with Denning for Meg and seemed to win every round. Cameron may be a simple farmer but he established himself as a man of greater cunning than his city-slicker adversary. (Quinn is impressive in showing that intelligence under his macho swagger.) But in the end, Denning did something Cameron couldn't top: He died for the woman he loved. Meg's feelings for Denning are again aroused at his sacrifice. It is humbling for Cameron. At Denning's freshly dug grave, all doubts about what to do are settled as he tells Meg, "Let's go back and face the music." Denning's intrusion and sacrifice have not only prompted Cameron and Meg to look back at the past but at the darker personalities in themselves.

Rather than succumb to the cynicism of noir, Dwan has tweaked noir as he has the Western to show the strange alchemy of human relationships. A character like Denning can be as much of a catalyst for good as Cowpoke's idealist.

In the original synopsis to the film, this was to be followed by a scene of Cameron and Meg encountering children along the river joyfully gathering up the hundred dollar bills. But this happy change of mood at the end, like the one in the *Around the World* script, was discarded.[99]

After seeing Cameron and Meg bunk down for the night, we again cut back to Denning. He is on a mountain road moving towards his left so if we have been viewing him from a consistent angle, he would appear to be heading towards Santa Isabel. He tries to stop a truck on the narrow road but the sleepy driver fails to notice him in time and accidentally knocks Denning off the cliff. The suitcase opens and we see the money floating over the valley, most of it settling in the river. The imagery evokes the climax of *The Treasure of the Sierra Madre*.

The next morning, Cameron awakens to see the surreal image of a raven dropping a $100 bill from its beak. Cameron quickly surmises that something has happened to Denning. He gathers up some cash he finds on the river and then looks for Denning, quite literally following the money. Meg admonishes him, asking, "Are you after the man or the money?" and Cameron promptly drops the money as he continues. Meg, the fallen woman of classic noir, who had enmeshed the honest Cameron into a web of murder, has now become Cameron's conscience. But there is still another twist.

The money route clearly shows that Denning was going for

10. The Final Act

Piety then needs a counterpoise, something to prevent it from being exercised in an excessively rigid way and this it has, in most intellectual temperaments, in the quality I would call playfulness.— Richard Hofstadter, *Anti-Intellectualism in American Life*

After *The River's Edge*, Dwan made three more films including the aforementioned *Enchanted Island.*

Dwan's second film at Fox after *The River's Edge* was *The Restless Breed*, a Western which was not produced by Bogeaus but by Edward Alperson, another independent producer who had a distribution contract with Fox. Nor did Dwan have the assistance of his other usual collaborators behind the camera to help him cope with this low-budget effort. Some of his former supporting players do turn up such as Jim Davis, Leo Gordon, Myron Healey, and Joe Devlin.

The Restless Breed was scripted by Steve Fisher, who had previously worked with Dwan on *Woman They Almost Lynched.* The film was one of the last made by Anne Bancroft in her 1950s stint in Hollywood before she returned to the stage and finessed a career makeover as the star of *The Miracle Worker* on Broadway. As the leading lady of *The Restless Breed*, she was the last nascent major star to appear in a Dwan movie.

Among the children who appeared in the film was seven-year-old Evelyn Rudie, who had played one of John Wayne's children in John Ford's *The Wings of Eagles*. Ms. Rudie recalls that Dwan was "detailed and friendly" and that he spoke to the child actors with professional respect. Rudie said that Dwan talked like "he really understood the acting process, that it came from a real organic place and that we weren't just sort of puppets, that now we smile and now we cry." She found Dwan "way more friendly" than Ford, who behaved "more like he was moving pieces on a chessboard."[1]

During the period in which Rudie worked on the film, which she estimates to have been anywhere from five days to a week and a half, she remembers Dwan working congenially with the actors and production staff. She recalls seeing producer Alperson on the set only once; after being introduced to the cast and crew, he just stood there watching for about an hour and left.

As Angelita, Anne Bancroft tends to other half-breed children in *The Restless Breed* (1957). Evelyn Rudie is the second child from the right (Ms. Rudie is now co-artistic director of the Santa Monica Playhouse with her husband Chris DeCarlo).

The Restless Breed is a basic revenge story with few narrative links to the four major films previously discussed, but Dwan's style strongly asserts itself. He deals with what must have been a minuscule budget, reportedly only about $200,000,[2] by using his repertory of skills and strategies in coping with a handful of flimsy-looking sets that must be used repeatedly. It is also a case where, given unpromising material, Dwan does not provide just peripheral benefits but rises to the occasion, even if it may be viewed as a triumph of style over content. And various elements of Dwan's style are used to the maximum in this movie. A number of critics have noted the stress on voyeurism and Myron Meisel says the film "exists as little more than an elaborate Chinese box of voyeuristic situations, as each character in turn spies on others." Comparing it to other Dwan films, especially to *Tennessee's Partner,* Meisel adds, "No such adornment lends texture to the voyeurism in *The Restless Breed*; rather the film is a relentless joke on the infinite possibilities for voyeurism in any conventional plot."[3]

And Dwan's curtain call for his players here seems teasingly facetious. As their names appear below them, each of the actors is seen framed in a window. Yet *The Restless Breed* seems too meticulously designed to be a total joke.

When asked by Bogdanovich if he thought his audience recognized the film as a comedy, Dwan replied, "Well, it's hard to say. I sneak into a theatre where it's playing and listen. Somebody will start laughing and somebody else will say, 'Shhh!' Then I know it's all right. One's taking it seriously, the other one's having a good time. If people start to laugh and get shushed, I know we've got it. One of those things — take your choice."[4]

Like any other tale-teller, Dwan's reaction should not always be trusted but *The Restless Breed* is a film of both playfulness and purposefulness. The film moves away from the triangular relationships and the older, more experienced leads of Dwan's RKO pictures. This is more of a "coming of age" story as its young hero, Mitch Baker (Scott Brady), appears traumatized by the murder of his father, a federal agent. He becomes so embittered that he decides to quit law school and to disavow the law itself in order to find his father's killer. This regeneration of the lost father theme appears as intensely here as it did in the Fairbanks film of over forty years earlier, *The Good Bad Man.* The hero's vengeful quest seems to interest Dwan less than the way it alienates him from others. As in the Fairbanks picture, the quest represents something of an identity crisis. As his desire for vengeance drives him from his father's ideals, Mitch refuses to reveal his name to anyone.

The most striking thing about this movie, to even a casual viewer, is that for a revenge story, *The Restless Breed* seems like a very gentle picture. Part of the reason is that the avenging hero Mitch stays at a house with children and a virginal young woman and that she seems to succumb to first love with him. The key villain is absent for most of the film, while a peace-loving minister appears omnipresent. Also, there is a steady stream of songs and background music in the film, composed by the producer's son, Edward Alperson, Jr. These included the three songs listed in the credits plus snatches of two others.[5] (The songs were recorded in Rome to save money.) Among the songs is the recurrent and delicate "Angelita" theme music, sometimes following the driving main theme and ultimately supplanting it.

This thematic tension is set up in the first scene in a Secret Service office where Mitch learns the details of his father's murder. The account is depicted in a flashback without the use of spoken dialogue; just a voice-over of the Secret Service agent (James Flavin) narrating the events like a hybrid evocation of Dwan's beloved silent cinema. In the flashback, the father's features are never clearly seen and are sometimes hidden in shadowy lighting. Mitch's father was gathering information in a Texas border town about a criminal group known as Newton's Raiders, smuggling guns to Mexico. A gang informant spies on him and alerts Newton (Jim Davis), who leaves his secret hideout to enter the town and shoot the undercover agent in the back.

The incident took place in a town called Mission. Mitch resolves to go there. In another nod to stressing the importance of the few sets he had to work with, Dwan's protagonist must then walk through the same streets and stay in the same buildings as we have seen his father enter, literally re-tracing his father's footsteps. Mitch learns that there was only one person who knew his father's identity, an unordained minister, the Reverend Simmons, who operates a mission in the town of Mission. (Yes, this is a playful film.)

Another complication is that Mitch takes his father's gun but refuses to take his badge or to seek his vengeance with any kind of official authority. This was during Hollywood's celebration of youthful rebellion in the early post–James Dean era. The lyrics of the theme song telegraph this message:

> I belong to the restless breed
> Lots of action is what I need.
> No more rules than a toppled weed.
> ... I do what I want to.
> I like what I want to....[6]

Also established at the outset is that both Mitch and the minister (Rhys Williams) are unorthodox in their pursuits, being respectively un-deputized and unordained. Mission, Texas, is no Dwan refuge except for vicious outlaws who want to hide from the law. The real sanctuary is in the script's knowing wordplay of the mission presided over by the Reverend Simmons where Mitch, like his father, will find a haven. The twin missions of Mitch and the reverend (for revenge and nonviolence, respectively) will there assert themselves. Evoking another of Dwan's early Fairbanks films, the Reverend Simmons cares for half-breed children who have been rejected both by the Indians and by their white fathers.

When Mitch arrives in Mission, his coach driver tells him, "People here get killed for looking the wrong way," to which Mitch replies, "I'll keep my eyes closed."

Actually, very few people in Mission are not looking at someone. Voyeurism flourishes here more than in any Dwan film. What is strikingly different are the large amount of close-ups, which Dwan usually avoids. Whereas the voyeurism in previous films was often expressed in framing the looker with his object or taking his point of view, here it is the look itself that is the focus of Dwan's attention.

People look for different reasons and with Mitch, his looking or snooping is usually quite pragmatic and followed shortly by action. He studies the setup in the saloon where Cherokee (Leo Gordon) and his cohorts have killed three previous sheriffs and where the latest victim has been claimed shortly after his arrival. Mitch, taking the law into his hands, enters with his gun pointed and knows just where to anticipate trouble.

Mitch is given free lodgings at the Reverend Simmons' mission where he is able to observe the half-breed foundlings whom Simmons takes care of including Angelita (Bancroft), who is crossing the boundary into womanhood.

One thing that Dwan objected to about the movie was that, "after it was finished, a very funny thing happened. Rhys Williams played a kindly old man who'd taken in this waif—Anne Bancroft — and had been a father to her. Now, long after I left the picture, Alperson, the producer, got a painting of her in this low-cut dancing costume, put it on the wall, and made a scene with Rhys Williams looking at this painting with a lecherous leer, as though he wanted this girl. Well, when I saw that, I flipped. Just horrible bad taste — took all the gentility out of this nice old guy and made him a real dirty old man."[7]

Actually, the reverend does not have a leer when he looks at the picture. (Dwan may have convinced Alperson to drop the shot.) A more compelling objection would be, "Why the minister would have such a picture in his house?" If he is sincere and wants to discourage Angelita from becoming a barroom dancer, why hang such a picture on the wall? And if Simmons is indeed a lecher, why would he want to advertise it by having a suggestive picture of his ward so displayed?

Whoever shot the scenes with the picture on the wall showed the same facility of Dwan to let an image accumulate power and meaning through repetition. The picture first appears when Angelita engages in some of her free-spirited dancing and is intercut with close-ups of the Reverend Simmons looking concerned. Shots of the painting recur, reminding us of the potential volatility of Mitch living in proximity with Angelita. (Mitch sleeps in the barn.) There are two long shots of Simmons looking at the picture, as if contemplating its meaning. It is as if he has the painting there to remind him of some mystery, the temptation to sin and evil or the budding adulthood and sexuality of Angelita. (The picture is lit by a lamp on a table below it, making it resemble an altar painting.) Mitch tells Angelita that he considers her "half-angel, half-woman."

Besides persistent shots of Simmons looking at what is happening before him, there are even more shots of another figure who is snooping. That is James Allan (Scott Marlowe), a juvenile who informed Newton in the flashback about Mitch's father. Strangely, although he has been warned of Allan's presence and his potential for harm, Mitch never seems concerned about looking out for Allan, though he remains tight-lipped about telling anyone anything about himself.

Throughout the film, there are frequent cutaways to Allan observing things or eavesdropping. Some shots just show his eyes looking through a peephole. On one level, the recurrent peephole shots suggest the prurient nature of Allan's behavior. But the repeated image of his eyes also suggests something godlike which knows and sees all.

Allan is often seen alone in the camera frame as if in his own world. For most of the film, he has only a couple of terse lines of dialogue that could easily be missed. One might get the impression that he is mute. At another point, he is shown playing with a noose like a strangely morbid child. He has two opportunities to dispatch Mitch with his revolver but each time, he relents. When he finally learns Mitch's true identity, Allan rushes to tell Cherokee about it and asks to be given a chance to kill Mitch himself. He seems more confident because Mitch is drunk at this point. But Allan's effort as a gunman is totally hapless; as Mitch shoots wildly, Allan panics and drops his gun. In his only other bit of extended dialogue, Allan tries to give his version to the bartender, who quickly surmises the truth. Allan is laughed out of the saloon.

Allan's voyeurism is also his imprisonment. His few actions outside of informing are all ineffectual. His few passages of dialogue reveal the longing to do more that is suggested by his voyeurism.

The balance between the gazes of Allan and Simmons is one of Dwan's delicate symmetries in this film. Aside from peephole shots of Allan's eyes, the close-ups of Simmons are tighter and his countenance more expressive whether deep in thought or showing concern or both. Simmons is especially watchful of Angelita, whom he wants to be a "decent young woman," and there is no questioning of his motives though perhaps of his excessively protective methods. He is also observant of Mitch, both as potential seducer and dangerous gunman. If Allan is in imprisoned longing, Simmons' looks are those that seek judgment.

Interestingly, Simmons is as impotent as Allan is in the movie. He has succeeded in raising his half-breed wards but most of his actions are ineffectual or counterproductive. He is unable to stop the violence in the town or to persuade anyone to testify against the murderers. He can't get Mitch to identify himself or later to give up his lust for revenge. The reverend does manage to nurse the wounded Cherokee but only so that he recovers to contact Newton and assist him in returning to Mission. When Simmons tries to stop Mitch from exhibiting two outlaws on stage, his distraction permits the villains to jump Mitch. On the other hand, when the reverend refuses to participate actively in gambling, just by sitting at the table and holding the cards, as Mitch requests, he wins all the money.

But if the reverend is ineffective in his actions, he is right in his judgment that Mitch "is here for some purpose, some sinful purpose."

Caught between the watchful eyes of Allan's youthful longing and Simmons' aged judgment are the actions of Mitch and Angelita. Mitch first tries to steal a kiss from her when she is mopping the floor, then is thwarted by the Reverend Simmons. Later, after listening to Simmons' admonitions against him, he gives her a kiss through barred windows. Angelita is visibly exhilarated but it is still a game for Mitch.

In the next scene, we see the bright sky of a new morning, one of many of Dwan's "sky" shots in the film with its sense of divine overview. Mitch and then his "observer" Allan are seen in successive medium shots. While both are isolated, in the small church in the background of Mitch's shot, the congregation sings a hymn expressing appreciation of the new day and the fact that as a community they are "never alone."

The children come out of the church, gather around Mitch and ask him if he is an archangel, someone who has come to deliver them. The reference is to how Mitch has brought a stability and quiet to the lawless town. It also links him with that other "half-angel" Angelita, who has been cast off by her parents just as Mitch has lost his father. Despite Mitch's supposed sophistication, the film sings a song of innocence around both of them.

Mitch's carefree attitude toward Angelita dissipates when he sees her reaction to his plans to thwart an ambush. He tells her that things weren't "funny" any more when he "saw a terrible scared look in your eyes." For Mitch and Angelita, each look can carry an impetus to act and change.

Mitch's vulnerability becomes more apparent when he meets his father's old friend, Marshal Steve Evans (Jay C. Flippen), who is pursuing Newton the legal way. This character is reminiscent of another Marshal Evans, Marshal Bob Evans, who in the 1916 *The Good Bad Man* revealed to the protagonist who his real father was, while also serving as a surrogate father. When Mitch refuses to drop his quest for revenge, Evans threatens to have him hanged for murder if he kills Newton, even in self-defense. He then disowns Mitch "in the name of your father." A distraught Mitch heads for the bar to drown his troubles.

Scott Brady as Mitch pursues the guarded Angelita (Bancroft) in *The Restless Breed* (1957).

Though drunk, Mitch returns to Angelita's window, referring to her as the "girl in a cage." But in reverse angle, we also look at Mitch through the same barred window and only to her can he confess his hurt at what the marshal told him. Mitch too is imprisoned in his loneliness but where Angelita suffers from her lack of freedom, Mitch is cut off by his desire to answer to no one.

Mitch's despair helps produce a change in Angelita, whom Mitch now calls "half-angel, all-woman." Angelita asserts her independence by going to Mitch's hotel room and trying to convince him that he must not try to kill Newton. (And this time she initiates the kiss.) Her influence seems to tip the balance. As Newton arrives in town, Mitch remains in his hotel room. In their twin arrival at adulthood, Angelita must learn to break restraints just as Mitch must learn to observe them.

When Evans' attempt to arrest Newton leaves the aged marshal fatally wounded, Mitch runs out and is rewarded for his self-control by Evans' final act of giving him his badge to pursue Newton. Mitch, ever methodical, manages to trap Newton and Cherokee and guns them both down when they resist arrest. Angelita breaks free of Simmons' grip to enter the saloon. As he embraces her, Mitch throws away his gun.

Dwan's film may be viewed as a tragedy that gives birth to a comedy of maturity and restored innocence. It is also a movie replete with playful touches: In the closing curtain call, Mitch breaks out of character to smile at the audience, then extends his head out of the "window" to turn it both ways as if he is still "observing" things. The complexity of Dwan's style not only transcends a trite plot but carries Dwan's obsession with voyeurism to the level of abstraction.

In the previous films, voyeurism, as it exists, can be attributed to the plots and thematic designs of each film. Here it is shrouded in mystery, as if an inherent part of the human condition. Just as we are buoyed by the liberation of Angelita and Mitch, we are haunted by the imprisonment of Allan and Simmons and their twin gazes that extend from youth to late middle age.

Voyeurism can also be taken as an allegory of cinema itself. The young snoop in the film is referred to as James Allan in the flashback but in the end credits his name appears only as "Allan"—not "Allen" as most last names might be spelled but "Allan" as in "Allan Dwan." And if this is one of Dwan's little jokes, we might ask, who is not more of a voyeur than a director who must watch the actors perform every scene every way; watch the "dailies," then look at the films in various stages of post-production until completion? As both insight and in-joke, this suggestion of the director as voyeur precedes Michael Powell's cameo in *Peeping Tom* by three years.

In his curtain call shot, Scott Marlowe's "Allan" does not look into the camera and at the audience but off to the side as if he still cannot break loose from spying on something somewhere...

Dwan's playfulness here, like his mysticism, takes measured appreciation of the folly of human beings.

Evelyn Rudie recalls that Dwan was not actually present when the curtain calls were shot. But she remembers that the actors were given instructions to "Look through the glass and stay in character."[8] Alperson Jr. said that the curtain call cameos were used by his producer-father "several times previously."[9]

With all its merits, *The Restless Breed* may not add up to a major film. But it is Dwan's demonstration that even modest works of art can have illuminative power and complex structure. And as he grasped that he was reaching the end of his career, it was a lesson Dwan relished, exhibiting it with humor and gusto.

Evelyn Rudie recalled that many years later, when she had become co-director of the Santa Monica Playhouse, she met Anne Bancroft once more. She told Bancroft that they had once worked together. When this puzzled the actress, Rudie told her that she was one of the children in *The Restless Breed.* They proceeded to have a "lovely talk" about the experience. The film had stuck in Bancroft's memory and she said she remembered it as a "very poignant moment" in her life.

When asked about *The Restless Breed* being an unusually gentle Western, Rudie responded, "It was gentle. The whole tone of the film was gentle. The tone of the on-set feelings with all the people were gentle." Edward Alperson, Jr., commented, "For my money, *The Restless Breed* was the best picture my father ever made."[10]

An Optimistic Tragedy

After their collaboration on *Enchanted Island*, Bogeaus made his next two films without Dwan, but with director Byron Haskin. The first of those was the 1958 *From the Earth to the Moon* (1958), based on the Jules Verne novel.

It is not clear why Dwan went on hiatus for about two years although he may have been wearied by the experience of shooting *Enchanted Island.* On March 11, 1958, as production wound up on *From the Earth to the Moon*, Bogeaus wrote Dwan a letter in which he seemed nostalgic about their association and remarked that "it seems rather strange that you are not about the set."[11] He concludes by saying, "I certainly hope you are in the best of health and some day in the near future will be ready for 'another one.'"

As with his previous three features, Bogeaus' next film, *Jet Over the Atlantic,* was shot in Mexico. Haskin and the production manager Clarence Eurist worked hard and succeeded in keeping the budget down to $185,000. The film was basically completed and all expenses had been paid. But after all their efforts to rein in the budget, Haskin said that Eurist was shocked to see that claiming script expenses, Bogeaus suddenly wrote an additional $75,000 on the budget sheet. Haskin said that he later heard that by the time the budget was turned in, it was reported as $350,000.

Haskin had agreed to a deferment in payment. He was to get participation money based on profits but said that every time "the income got close to the cost, they'd slap another $75,000 on it. So I had no possible chance ever, of getting any participation money." According to Haskin, the film's star, George Raft, was also not paid.[12] Don Siegel had described Bogeaus as "the worst faker I had ever run into."[13] Haskin considered him "a phony from way back."[14]

Bogeaus reunited with Dwan for his next picture which he would try to launch, again in Mexico, with some new shenanigans. It was the last film for both Bogeaus and Dwan.

Of this movie, entitled *Most Dangerous Man Alive*, Dwan remembered, "In the first place, there was a deception about it. Even I got hooked. Bogeaus said it was to be a pilot for a television series in two episodes and employed everybody on that basis. But when he presented the two parts to the syndicates in Mexico, they said, 'This is a script that's cut in half. It's a continuous story, so it is not a television film but a feature. Therefore, you can't make it on TV terms.... You must take a full crew and do it at full feature rates.' Well, as a matter of fact, that's what it was."[15]

In his interview with Bogdanovich, Dwan claimed that this judgment by the syndicates "tripled" the budget and that he was forced to take special measures including drastically speeding up the schedule. "What should have been shot in five weeks was done in one." Dwan also told Bogdanovich that the film was made in 1958 even though it wasn't released until 1961. Asked why, Dwan replied, "They just didn't let it escape until then."[16]

Dwan's reminiscences in the last paragraph have become a part of movie lore. Numerous reference books have repeated the story of the science fiction film that sat on the shelf for three years. Even this author accepted Dwan's account in an article about the Walter Reade Theater's Dwan retrospective in 2003.[17] But Dwan's recollections here are not just the stuff of legend; they are pure myth.

The contract to make *Most Dangerous Man Alive* for Bogeaus' latest production company, Trans-Global Films Inc., was signed by Dwan and is dated April 23, 1960.[18] It stipulated that Dwan's employment on the film would begin two days later. Actor Gregg Palmer, who appeared in the movie, remembers it as being shot in 1960 and said he was given a bracelet during the making of the picture which has the words "May 9, 1960" inscribed on the back.[19]

Both Palmer and another of the film's actors, Steve Mitchell, also discounted the idea that the film was shot in one week. They estimate that it was shot somewhere between a month and six weeks. Debra Paget believes that it was shot in no less than four weeks. As Palmer put it, "It takes five days just to have lunch."[20]

Why did Dwan make those bogus claims? He may have confused *Most Dangerous Man Alive* with the Howard Hughes presentation *Montana Belle,* which sat on the shelf for almost four years. But if there was confusion, it was at least partly willful. As Dwan told Mizrahi, he did not like the science fiction genre and probably considered it a comedown.[21] So it was one way of venting about the film. Dwan might have also thought that people would be more forgiving of the film's flaws or more impressed if he said it was shot in just a week.

Along with James Leicester and Phillip Rock, one of the credited writers for *Most Dangerous Man Alive* was the Australian actor Michael Pate. But Pate said in an interview that the story had originally been written by actor Leo Gordon. According to Pate, Gordon "came to me with it and I helped him rewrite it. At that time, it was called *The Atomic Man.* Leo eventually came back to me because he needed some quick money, so I bought out his interest in the story idea, and I later turned it over to my [producer] father-in-law Joe Rock and my [writer] brother-in-law Phillip Rock. The three of us optioned the treatment out in various ways, and Benedict Bogeaus took a final option on it."[22]

The star of the film, Ron Randell, was also Australian. Randell played the title character, a gangster framed for murder by his underlings. With the former boss out of the way, his subordinate, played by Dwan veteran Anthony Caruso, takes charge, both of his position and of his former mistress (Paget). Randell manages to escape from the police and stumbles into a freak accident that renders him indestructible.

Also in the cast were Elaine Stewart, Tudor Owen and another Dwan regular, Morris Ankrum. Playing a police lieutenant was thirty-three-year old Gregg Palmer. Palmer recalled the first day of shooting in a lava quarry twelve miles outside of Mexico City. Dwan looked at him and then asked his crew, "Where's his hat?" Dwan felt that a police detective could not be without a hat. When a hat was not forthcoming, Palmer suggested to Dwan, "I'll use yours." Dwan demurred and removed his hat to show sun blotches on his head. But Palmer had a solution for that too. He requested a beach umbrella and then pounded it into the earth. The umbrella now made for a six-foot shade for the director.

Dwan now surrendered his hat to Palmer but said to him with a twinkle in his eyes, "Cowboy, you ruin my hat and you're finished in the business." With that, the two became friends and "Cowboy" became Dwan's sobriquet for Palmer. Palmer said that after the film, he and Anthony Caruso were invited to dinner at Dwan's home in Pacific Palisades.

It's not surprising that Dwan would find a brash problem-solver to be a kindred spirit. Palmer had heard that Dwan was a rough, tough director but he found him to be a "pussycat" with a "good sense of humor." Palmer remembered of Dwan, "When he laughed, he had a warm laugh that lit up the room." The actor and director palled around off the set.

Palmer recalled one evening when they were sitting in the hotel lobby and they saw the fiftyish Bogeaus seated with a young woman. Dwan told Palmer, "Look at that guy with that beautiful young lady. She should be sitting with you, Cowboy." Dwan then arranged for Bogeaus to be paged to respond to a non-existent phone call. Dwan gave his off-set direction to Palmer, "When I say, 'Move,' you move." As Bogeaus went to the phone and waited patiently for his party to come through, Dwan and Palmer walked over to the woman and introduced themselves.

While the hapless Bogeaus continued to wait for his call, Dwan and Palmer learned that the young woman was a resident of the area. Dwan prodded her. "The cowboy here likes to swim. Why don't you invite him for a swim?" Palmer did get an invitation to the lady's home and said he met "a lot of people" there. He also got well acquainted with the lady, who later gave him the aforementioned bracelet.[23]

Bogeaus, however, could still make Dwan nervous when he came to the set. Palmer recalled that once Bogeaus approached Dwan before a scene was shot, concerned over what they would do because Ankrum, playing the police captain, was too sick to work. (He had succumbed to the Mexican water.) Dwan told Bogeaus not to worry; he would simply give all of Ankrum's dialogue to Palmer and they would just use one policeman in the scene and not two. Palmer noted that Dwan "didn't want Ben around the shoot.... Allan was in control of his set. I'll tell you that."[24]

The term "set" here is purely figurative. There were no sets on *Most Dangerous Man Alive.* Given the budget problems, there was not enough money to pay for sets. Everything was shot on location. For interiors, a hotel room or lobby or any spaces that could be borrowed or rented were used. Steve Mitchell credited production manager Clarence Eurist with insuring that a suitable location was always available.[25]

Not only were there no sets but there were no costumes, at least for some performers, and those actors wore their own clothes. This created some concern for a scene where a smoke bomb would be used. Bogeaus assured the actors that there would be no problem. But Palmer said that when the bomb went off, it sprayed a liquid that burned holes in his clothes, Caruso's and other bystanders.

Bogeaus said that he would later send a check to their agents. Caruso, who had worked with Bogeaus several times, told Palmer, "I'm getting my check here. You get yours too." Both Caruso and Palmer were reimbursed in Mexico.[26]

There was a different problem for star Ron Randell. He had an offer to go to Spain to work in the Samuel Bronston big-budget production *King of Kings.* But the start date conflicted with his schedule on *Most Dangerous Man Alive.* According to Mitchell, Bogeaus made Randell take a cut in his salary to get out of his contract.

When he found out about this, Dwan angrily approached Randell: "Why didn't you come to see me? I'm the damned director."[27] Dwan explained that he could have arranged to shoot all of Randell's scenes before he was required to leave.

Bogeaus also had not dropped his bad habit of trying to get away without paying his employees. Mitchell, who played Devola in the film, recalled, "Bogeaus was a nice guy, he was charming. But when it came to money, if there was any way he could screw you out of it, he would screw you out of it."[28]

According to Mitchell, several of the *Most Dangerous Man Alive* actors were not paid for overtime work or for damage done to their clothes. Many months later, by a chance encounter with a Columbia executive at Danny's Hideaway Restaurant in New York, Mitchell said he learned that Columbia had made a deal with Bogeaus to distribute the film. Mitchell called the Screen Actors Guild in Hollywood which he said then protested to Columbia that there was a lien on this film. While Columbia had no obligation to pay the actors, they did have a contract with SAG. Columbia, therefore, had to tell Bogeaus that they could not complete the deal until the actors were paid. So Bogeaus was again forced to pay.

Mitchell recalled that during the time he was trying to sue the producer, he was walking in the polo lounge of the Beverly Hills Hotel and he saw Bogeaus walking with someone. Bogeaus greeted Mitchell with a big smile, then told his associate, "This is the actor's that's suing me." Mitchell responded, "I'm going to get you, Ben." It was done without rancor and Mitchell recalled that after Bogeaus was forced to pay, he told Mitchell that he would have a part for him in his next film.

In contrast, Mitchell found Dwan to be "probably one of the nicest directors" and one who was "totally considerate."[29]

Most Dangerous Man Alive was largely dismissed by critics. In the *New York Times*, Howard Thompson reported, "At the most crucial moments of *Most Dangerous Man Alive* the audience howled."[30] *Variety* did not even consider it acceptable second-feature fodder, believing that "it may be an unwelcome companion with which to burden major theatrical product aimed at enlightened 1961 audiences."[31]

Most Dangerous Man Alive suffers from its low budget and far-out plotting. It has the threadbare look of many of the low-budget science fiction films that proliferated in the 1950s and early 1960s. But even as the plot lays absurdity upon absurdity, the strength of character and narrative involvement and the zest of Dwan's direction makes it well worth watching. It is a work of pinch-penny grandeur telling the story of a comic-book Lear, who after grasping hoodlum supremacy only finds betrayal and Midas-like isolation.

The film begins *in media res* with one member of the gang, Devola (Mitchell), bringing news that Eddie Candell has escaped from custody. This terrifies Eddie's former mistress Linda Morrow (Paget) who is now living with Eddie's usurper, Andy Damon (Caruso). It was Linda's perjured testimony that led to Candell's conviction for murder.

Candell is then seen isolated in a bleak landscape, an image that sums up his situation for most of the film. A flashback reveals the incident that triggered Eddie's downfall: A meeting of Candell's gang associates, known publicly as the International Vending Machine Company, listen to Damon's rant on how Candell is promoting himself. Damon quotes from a magazine that has Candell on the cover with the caption, "From Rackets to Riches." Illustrations from the article are shown that include Eddie's purchase of a mansion for Linda, his financial interest in thoroughbreds, his enjoyment of yachting and his championing of his "protégé" Carla Angelo (Elaine Stewart). Candell might be said to prefigure a future flamboyant gangster, the "Dapper Don," John Gotti. In fact, the article even refers to Candell as the "dapper president" of his company. Damon denounces Candell as a "publicity hound" who is endangering the organization by putting the spotlight on them.

But Candell's quest for celebrityhood may also be seen as something Dwan distrusted in the latter part of his career, a case of someone quite literally trying to raise his head above the Mob. Eddie's sense of hubris, which develops exponentially in the course of the story, is thus revealed as the source of his downfall. When Eddie arrives and interrupts the meeting, one member of the gang tries to assassinate him and Candell shoots him in self-defense. Eddie is then knocked out from behind and the gang conspires to frame him for murder.

We are returned to the image of Eddie lost in a wasteland and suddenly realizing, from hearing a loudspeaker countdown, that he is in a nuclear testing zone. He rushes to a TV camera as he is seen framed in a TV screen pushing against the lens in front of him and gesturing for attention. In a reverse angle shot, we see Dr. Meeker (Tudor Owen) and other scientists in a secluded room watching the image and Meeker trying frantically to phone the control tower. Shots are intercut of Candell and Meeker until we see a stock shot of a nuclear explosion. But after the blast, Candell's hands are seen amazingly rising before the TV camera. Candell comes up from the ground and stands, looking disheveled and dazed but miraculously walking away from the camera.

The staging of Eddie's metamorphosis before a camera that sees it all and records it is an adroit bit of direction by Dwan. It also provides a documentary record to be seen by the police. As in many of the sci-fi films of this era, the scientist explains that a mutation process was triggered by the nuclear explosion. Here the culprit is something called Cobalt Element X. According to Dr. Meeker, Candell's living tissue has become fused with steel and the steel will continue to work its way into his body. He is, as Meeker says, now a "man of steel," a popular reference of the time to the comic-book and TV hero Superman. But while the mutation renders Candell seemingly invincible, the long-range effects may drive him to madness.

Science fiction film aficionados have pointed to similar plots in the 1956 *Indestructible Man* and *Man Made Monster* (1941). But Dwan departs in crucial ways from the science fiction formula. *Most Dangerous Man Alive* fastens onto the Manichean struggle for Eddie's life and soul. The gangster enemies, who want him destroyed and who arouse his need for vengeance, include the satanic-sounding Damon and Devola. The woman who proves to be Eddie's only steadfast companion is Carla Angelo. Her name evokes not only Angelita from *The Restless Breed* but female "angels" from other Dwan movies.

Ron Randell appears to have become invincible in *Most Dangerous Man Alive* (1961).

Candell's "accident" has rendered him both something more than human and something less than human, particularly in his sense that he is no longer capable of human feeling. Dwan's direction frames Eddie's plight with a recurrent emphasis on sensuousness. At the beginning of the film, Linda is seen in bed, awakened by a phone call. When she hears that the caller wants to speak to Damon, she calls to him and carries the phone to her left. In the next shot, we see Damon in bed taking the phone from his right. Dwan avoids the antagonism of the censors, who insisted at the time that a man and woman, even if they are married, must not be shown in the same bed, by keeping Linda and Damon in separate shots. In keeping with the letter of the law, there is no master shot of them in the same bed but the implication is clear that this is the case and that Linda is now in bed with Candell's rival.

In his first encounter with his gang since his metamorphosis, Eddie learns that he is impervious to bullets and manages to take Linda captive. With Linda bound and gagged in a stolen truck full of dynamite, Eddie goes to see Carla, the only person he trusts. She is at first incredulous when he tries to explain what has happened to him but putting her hands on his chest she realizes that it seems to be freezing. Carla puts Eddie to bed and, trying to find a way to comfort him, she cradles him with the warmth of her body.

Carla's intense bond to Candell is interrupted by the police; Eddie must flee to another location with Linda in tow. At the new hideout, it is Linda's turn to appeal to Eddie to recall some emotional vestige of their relationship. Eddie can only repeat "I'm not the same any more." Linda, insisting that she can make him the same, gets Eddie to repeat one of their erotic rituals. As she holds out her leg, Eddie, with great delicacy, slowly pulls off her nylon stocking. Dwan's camera elegantly observes this bit of foreplay in one uninterrupted take but Eddie seems to recoil when it's over. Candell puts Linda's hand over his bare chest and asks, "Can you make that flesh and blood again?" As Linda removes Eddie's shirt and embraces him, it is clear that they will make love. But Candell's hunger to feel human is unsatisfied and Linda will continue to be his prisoner.

Eddie's newfound prowess increases his sense of megalomania while simultaneously arousing his horror at what's become of him. "I feel nothing," he laments. Dwan's mingling of the two genres is wonderfully balanced; the sci-fi metaphor elucidates the plight of a gangster potentate who wants to regain his lost humanity.

The duel between Carla and Linda to restore human feeling to Candell recalls the triangular relationships of the best of the earlier Dwan–Bogeaus films. (In fact, since *The River's Edge* was the last major film of that vein with two men and a woman, *Most Dangerous Man Alive* keeps up the gender alternation.) But there is little doubt that Carla is Eddie's best bet.

Both the police and his gangster rivals are now after Candell, while neither is quite sure how he can be killed. For the most part, Dwan does not apply noir imagery to *Most Dangerous Man Alive*. However, when Carla brings Dr. Meeker to see and possibly help Eddie, Candell stops her from turning on the light in his room and lingers in the shadows. He does not want to be seen and suggests that he has degenerated further: "I only hate," he says ruefully. "Yes, Carla, sometimes I hate even you. If you were to see me now, I would kill you." Throughout the exchange, Dwan keeps Candell in separate shots from Carla and Meeker, magnifying the sense of distance between them, when they are only a few feet away from each other.

Falling deeper into despair, Candell observes, "I'm not flesh any more. I'm steel. I want to be flesh again ... to feel. I want to feel ... I want to die. I don't even know if I can die."

When Carla reasserts that she loves him, Eddie turns on the light, revealing his features and challenges, "Love me now." Carla moves stoically out of her frame and, in the next shot, enters Eddie's frame. Burying her head in his bosom, she tells Eddie, "I've always loved you." Candell then consents to being Meeker's "guinea pig."

Although the makeup on Randell is far short of conveying a horrific change, the emotions in the scene are worthy of a Lon Chaney film. (One wonders how Dwan's career would have developed had he continued working with Chaney.) Elaine Stewart's poignant performance is also a plus. While we know, by the rules of the genre and censorship of the time, that Candell is doomed, this romantic affirmation shines fable-like through the film. Of all the director's autumnal output, *Most Dangerous Man Alive* is the one that best fits Jean Lourcelles' description of Dwan's late films as "optimistic tragedies."[32]

Candell is still caught between the gangsters and the police.

Debra Paget as the bad girl, Randell's former girlfriend, tries to revive his sense of feeling by re-enacting their erotic ritual of removing her stocking in *Most Dangerous Man Alive* (1961).

Both sides keep Eddie under close observation and when one side loses sight of him, the other's spies take over, so he can never stay secluded for long. The police are convinced that Eddie is a monster-killer and have no idea of the struggle taking place within him.

And this is the fundamental irony in all the technological paraphernalia that permit "Big Brother" voyeurism to flourish, the sheer unknowability of what a human being is like to all but his most intimate contacts and probably not completely knowable to them either. In *Silver Lode*, we saw how difficult it was for the townspeople to come to terms with the kind of man Ballard was and how they easily turned from one extreme to another. Candell comes to his end in a quarry outside of town where he is cornered by the police and the army, which will use flame throwers to destroy him. The grandiose use of the military power to bring down Candell recalls not only numerous sci-fi climaxes of the 1950s but the finale to Walsh's *White Heat* where James Cagney's Cody Jarrett seals his doom with a spectacular explosion. Critic Bruce Eder has pointed out that the climax combines the endings of both Walsh's *White Heat* and *High Sierra* and we might add with a little of *King Kong* thrown in as well.[33] Michael Henry Wilson goes even farther and sees Candell coming to "his Golgotha above the town."[34] One can make this point as with the Passion Play scene in *Silver Lode*. But as in the earlier case, Dwan, unlike Ford, is not as whole-hearted or reverential and uses such iconography to add his own riffs.

The first cracks in Candell's composure are depicted in the quarry scene but it is not entirely clear if they are created by Element X. Up until this point, Candell had worked for vindication rather than revenge, only killing in self-defense.

When Linda tries to run to the police to tell them the true story, Damon shoots her in the back. Enraged after seeing Linda murdered, Candell goes after Damon and throws him over the precipice before the horrified onlookers.

Whether it was from the cobalt force working within him or because of his remaining feelings for Linda, bitterness now takes over Candell completely. Taking Carla to another summit, he points out the city below. Sounding more like an Old Testament God than Christ, Candell tells her, "Looks good? It isn't, Carla. It's rotten. I'm going to rip that rotten world apart and throw it to the winds."

But after he launches into a diatribe of megalomania, proclaiming that he will make the police and everyone else crawl, something happens, a miracle of sorts. Carla notices that Eddie's hands feel warm again and his face is back to normal. When rifle shots are fired at Eddie, he bleeds. He has become a human being again, just as the men with flame throwers are closing in to kill him.

Is Eddie now redeemed by his recognition of corruption? Or by his suffering and his love for Carla? Eddie embraces Carla but, noticing that Lt. Fisher has crept nearby, he thrusts her off the ledge, out of harm's way and into Fisher's arms.

Candell now faces the end with pure theatricality. He knows that he's lost his powers but as the flames are poured on him, he continues to shout defiantly that nothing can stop him, that he will rip the world apart. Dwan, now in his mid-seventies, no doubt empathized with Eddie's defiance.

Dwan's unrealistic depiction of Candell's destruction is weirdly allegorical and suggests another miracle. Eddie seems wrapped in a fog and untouched as the flames are sprayed around him. His clothes disappear without him being immolated. After he falls to the ground, his body dissolves into dust.

Four figures (Capt. Davis, Meeker, Fisher and Carla) gather around his remains like the party around Stryker's body at the end of *Sands of Iwo Jima*, with each of the men in close-up making some pithy sum-up. Only Carla says nothing but looks down in sorrow and anguish. It is befitting Dwan's origins in the pre-talkie era that he makes her silence the most eloquent comment of all.

Dwan told Peter Bogdanovich, "I deplored tragedy ... I don't like unhappy endings." But he ended both his last major silent film (*The Iron Mask*) and his final movie with the death of his protagonist. Was that because of Dwan's sense of symmetry or sheer accident? And as disparate as they are, both *The Iron Mask* and *Most Dangerous Man Alive* end with mystical conclusions of cosmic unity. In his interview with Bogdanovich, Dwan derided the deaths of the lovers in the Republic production *Surrender* but aside from the films above, did Dwan also forget *While Paris Sleeps* and *Sands of Iwo Jima,* not to mention the semi-tragic endings of *Tennessee's Partner* and *Frontier Marshal*? It is not even clear if Ben Grace will survive long at the end of *Slightly Scarlet.*

Most Dangerous Man Alive seems like a compendium of many of the director's films. Aside from the references already made, Eddie shares the isolation of Mitch in *The Restless Breed,* the gangster background of the protagonists in *Angel in Exile* and *Slightly Scarlet,* the enmity of the community against the stars of *Young People, Rendezvous with Annie, Belle Le Grand, Silver Lode* and *Tennessee's Partner,* and the sense of terror evoked by the appearance of Doc Halliday in *Frontier Marshal.* The transformation to superman even suggests the Douglas Fairbanks comedies. And Anthony Caruso's Damon was the last of Dwan villains to be thrown off a cliff, as if in homage to Jack Richardson's heavies.

In their abstract imagery set against impoverished budgets, both *The Restless Breed* and *Most Dangerous Man Alive* stand as striking summaries and codas to Dwan's work.

Two decades later, director Wim Wenders paid tribute to *Most Dangerous Man Alive* in his 1982 film *The State of Things,* about a film crew stranded in Portugal when their financing suddenly disappears. The film they are working on looks like a mixture of Roger Corman's *Day the World Ended* and *Most Dangerous Man Alive.*

The producer of the film, played by Allen Goorwitz, has been playing risky games with shady financial backers and is now being hunted. In a clandestine meeting in a trailer he says to the film's director, "Allan Dwan should see us all now. *The Most Dangerous Man Alive.* That's me." Dwan's title character could be an apt symbol for people living at the edge in the film business.

Like Eddie Candell, Dwan had fought hard to the end, making his film against all adversity. But his career now appeared over.

The Accidental Family

One of Robin Wallace's earliest memories of her godfather occurred shortly before her eighth birthday and after she saw his film *The River's Edge.* She was horrified to see his new 1956 Thunderbird auto disabled in the movie.

When Robin next visited Allan Dwan, she was angry at him. She asked him, "Why did you crash the T Bird, Godfather?"

Her godfather laughed. "I didn't crash my T Bird. My T Bird is fine. That was all fake. That was Hollywood."[35]

That was when Robin first learned what young Henry Hathaway heard Dwan trying to explain to his Flying A colleagues early in the century, that movies were an illusion.

Robin loved visiting her godfather at his sumptuous residence, which he shared with her aunt at 355 South Mapleton Drive in the very exclusive Holmby Hills, adjacent to Bel Air. He was kind and generous to Robin and her younger sister. And even in a movie town like Los Angeles, it was unusual to be in close contact with a film director who could tell her so much about the motion picture industry. Robin recalled that in those early days, she would usually see her godfather several times a year, on birthdays, Easter and Christmas.

As she grew older, Robin became increasingly curious about her godfather, who always seemed to be with her Aunt Bonita, and what their relationship was. When she was about ten,

Dwanine (left) and Robin (right) get giant stuffed bunnies from godfather Allan Dwan on the occasion of his sixty-ninth birthday on April 3, 1954 (courtesy Robin Allana Wallace).

Robin asked her mother, "Are they going to get married or something?" Her mother testily and cryptically responded, "Your aunt has been in love with him for years."[36]

The story of how that relationship developed goes back to 1937 when Bonita Simmons left her home in Terrell, Texas, to find a better life in California working as a nurse. She went with the hopes of earning enough money to bring out the rest of the family, whose struggles predated the Depression. After her father drank himself to death, Bonita's mother Tennessee Bertha (named for where her family had its roots) married William Fraley. He fathered a daughter, also named Tennessee and nicknamed Tennie, in late 1915. Presaging Bonita's future journey, Fraley also went to California trying to find opportunities. But he became fatally ill, allegedly because of the lack of heating in the train as it moved through the Donner Pass. His death was ascribed to inflammatory rheumatism, which sounds dubious, leaving Tennessee with two daughters to raise. Fraley's child was only three months old at the time of his death.

After her second husband's death, Tennessee Bertha used different skills to keep her family going, taking in laundry and raising some cotton though it's not clear if the land involved was her own or rented. She also worked as a nurse. Robin Wallace believes that is where Bonita got her initial training for her future vocation.[37]

Bonita not only found employment as a nurse in California but was able to obtain the training to become a physical therapist. In 1938, she brought her mother and sister out to live with her. A brother followed later.

In the early 1940s, Bonita Simmons was called upon for an important assignment: She was to be nurse to the wife of Allan Dwan. Marie Dwan suffered from a number of health problems and in a 1940 newspaper article was referred to as a semi-invalid.[38] She had suffered two publicized mishaps in the last decade. In the spring of 1929, she "narrowly escaped death when her roadster skidded into a water hydrant and then caromed into a high tension power line pole, knocking it down."[39] Mrs. Dwan suffered only slight injuries. No explanation for the accident was given in the brief news item but there may have been a connection with an incident that transpired seven years later. On January 9, 1936, Mrs. Dwan drew a suspended jail sentence of forty-five days and a $150 fine as well as having her license suspended when she pleaded guilty to driving while intoxicated.[40] As noted in Chapter 8, on her death certificate it was cited that she suffered from portal cirrhosis of the liver so Mrs. Dwan may well have had a chronic problem with alcohol. Robin Wallace also believes that she contracted an infection in one of her visits abroad.

Both Tennie and Bonita were attractive-looking women but photos reveal Bonita had the beauty of a movie star. Bonita was captivated by her new employer, whom she found strongly intelligent and witty. Wallace believes that "she really loved him ever since she met him."

Mrs. Dwan was now on an irrevocable path of decline. While the precise timing of her death in 1949 may have been a shock, it was not totally unexpected. The catalogue of maladies on her death certificate confirms what must have been the fragility of her existence during her later years.

After his wife's death, Dwan dismissed most of his servants but Bonita was kept on as his housekeeper. They were certainly in love by this time and giving her this job was one way to maintain their intimacy while squelching gossip. It was the beginning of a union that would last longer than either of Dwan's marriages.

Bonita now shared Dwan's life and when he went on location for a movie, she traveled with him, designated as his assistant. She also joined him on vacations. They always maintained a professional appearance. Robin recalled that her aunt usually addressed him as Mr. Dwan and very rarely heard her refer to him as Allan. Dwan always kept a picture of Marie on his dresser.

After a bad experience with a second husband, who decided after returning from the war that he wanted his freedom, Tennie had married Robert Foster in 1947. Through Bonita, Tennie had known Dwan for years and the couple respected him highly, quickly accepting Dwan as one of their own. When

A young Bonita Simmons (right, holding cat) with her sister Tennie in a snapshot from 1936 (courtesy Robin Allana Wallace).

their first child, a daughter, was born, she was named Robin Allana, her middle name being in honor of the director, whom they designated as her godfather. For their second child, another daughter, born in 1951, the father came up with the name Dwanine.

Dwan and Bonita Simmons were in many respects a couple but Bonita also maintained a separate residence in Van Nuys. The relationship was a bit open-ended. Bonita was not resentful when Dwan would have one of his girlfriends stay over at his house.

Robin recalls that in the late 1950s, Dwan had two redheaded girlfriends. In fact, Bonita told her, "Your godfather really likes redheads and likes to cast them in his films." (Bonita had chestnut brown hair.) Again, one is reminded of Hawks' comment about Dwan falling for a redhead in the 1920s and Dwan's own expression of his obsession in *Slightly Scarlet.*[41]

The two women alternated spending the weekend with Dwan. Robin said that Bonita accepted this. When the weekend sojourns began, both women were in their forties while Dwan was in his early seventies.

Also, as in *Slightly Scarlet,* there were apparent personality differences between the two women. One was in her early forties and had appeared in a bit role in Dwan's *Woman They Almost Lynched.* Robin remembers her resembling Gwen Verdon and said she was very friendly to her and her sister. Apparently at Dwan's suggestion, at some point in Dwanine's childhood, this redhead became her godmother. (Tennie, on the other hand, considered her ditzy and thought she looked like a hooker.)

The other woman was older, in her late forties and was living off the alimony of her wealthy ex-husband. She had the harder personality and was much more aloof. Robin thought she resented members of her family being present. Tennie said she was "like a vampire."

Bonita's tolerance of this situation may have had its limits. As Wallace recollects, around 1965 or 1966, the two women disappeared and Dwan proposed marriage to Bonita. Robin suspected that after all this time, Dwan may have thought he needed to "make an honest woman of her."

However, there was a condition to this proposal. Dwan, who remained a devout Roman Catholic, insisted that Bonita convert to Catholicism. Up to that time, Bonita had been a non-denominational Protestant who admired figures ranging from Aimee Semple McPherson to Oral Roberts. Bonita's own great-uncle had been a fire-and-brimstone Pentecostal preacher.

Dwan had his way but there was an unexpected effect to Bonita's conversion. Once she became a Catholic, Bonita decided that she would remain chaste. She continued to live with Dwan but the relationship had to be platonic. It's likely that guilt for her "living in sin" played a role here but at any rate it was now Dwan's turn to acquiesce. Bonita also accepted Catholicism on her own terms and continued to donate to Oral Roberts.

Robin remembers Dwan as being very kind and indulgent with her and her sister. On Easter, he gave them large stuffed bunnies. Robin also recalls her godfather giving her his baby ring which had a diamond in it. Robin wasn't able to wear it until she was eleven. (Dwan laughed when she told him, "Godfather, you must have been a big baby!") When she was in her teens, Robin lost the diamond and feared that her godfather would be angry with her. But Dwan was unperturbed and told her not to worry, that he would replace the diamond, and he did. Dwan also told her that when she graduated from high school, he would provide the funds to send her to Vassar.[42]

Robin's maternal grandfather had died when her mother was an infant and her paternal grandfather was in distant Indiana. So Dwan became the grandfather figure in Robin's life. She remembers that he always devoted attention to her and her sister and was happy to listen to them.

Dwan also continued to keep up with all that was new, especially in technology. Robin recalls a visit to Dwan's house in the late 1950s when her godfather was eager to show off his new color television set. But he was frustrated because at the time it was difficult to find anything being shown in color. (Dwan was also sure to let Tennie and her children know when any of his films were being broadcast on television.)

Despite his age, Dwan did not live in the past and was receptive to new things. In the 1960s, while youth embraced them, the Beatles were very much reviled by the older generation. But Robin vividly remembers Dwan telling her he had seen the Beatles in their movie *Help!* and recommending it to her as a good film to see.

Robin does remember clashing with her godfather on another emerging issue of the time, the Vietnam War. Robin recalls, "I was a child of the 1960s so we kind of butted heads." Dwan had a profound respect for the military and urged Robin to be "grateful."[43] At the time, Robin fretted about her boyfriend, whom she believed was about to be drafted. Coincidentally, her boyfriend, like Dwan, was Canadian. Dwan assured her that Canadians would not be drafted. However, times had changed and Robin's boyfriend was indeed inducted into the military.

Robin also noted that while Dwan "was conservative in his values, he was liberal in other ways." He was not ideological and not particularly interested in politics. She thought his views were "amazingly kind of balanced."[44]

As she was growing into adulthood, Robin had ambitions of her own: She wanted to become an actress. She recalled Dwan coming to see her in all of her appearances in school plays. However, he discouraged her from getting into show business. Robin said her first thought was that this was his way of telling her he didn't think she was talented. But she also considered that perhaps her godfather wanted to spare her the kind of things she was bound to face in an acting career.

Robin married her beau David Wallace in 1967 and like many young people, and particularly young women of the time, her ambitions were forgotten in the practical demands of marriage.

When Robin had children of her own, Dwan showed the same attentiveness and consideration to them he had to Robin and her sister. Her godfather also became a surrogate grandfather to her children. He had now long been accepted in the family as a kind of patriarch. Robin still remembers him sitting like a little monarch in the big red chair in her parents' living room.[45]

Dwan never had children. There is one source who claims that in 1913, apparently not long after Dwan allegedly impregnated Beatrice Van, he incurred an accident which made him sterile. But nothing has been found to confirm this. Robin believes that Dwan was probably too much of a workaholic during his relatively brief marriage to Pauline Bush, and that Marie Dwan was never in good condition to have children. Bonita was unable to have children because of a medical operation in the 1940s to remove fibroids.

Just as he had started his career as an accidental director, Dwan had now developed his own family by accident. And as with his earlier incarnation, Dwan had thrust himself completely into his new role and achieved stature. Sometimes problem-solving could be a matter of serendipity and seizing the opportunity. Overall, his 1950s films would show far less interest in lost father figures.

But while he was finding satisfaction in his personal life,

Robin Foster and her husband Dave Wallace in 1969 (courtesy Robin Allana Wallace).

Dwan's career as a director had stalled. Robin recalls that in his last decade of filmmaking, Dwan had already shown some frustration that he was not being permitted to do all that he could to raise the quality of his films.

In the early 1960s, Dwan told Robin that he had been offered to direct the 1963 American International film, *X: The Man with the X-Ray Eyes*, starring Ray Milland. But although he had enjoyed working with Milland on *The River's Edge*, Dwan turned down the project. Dwan told his goddaughter that he just didn't think it was going to be a good film. Actually, *X*, directed by Roger Corman, turned out be a better film than most people would have expected. But more importantly, Dwan may have grasped that after *Most Dangerous Man Alive*, he was now being typed as a director of low-budget science fiction films, a status from which he would never recover. Having already directed numerous second features, this was a line he would not cross. At approximately this time, director Jacques Tourneur (the son of Maurice, who had been a member of Associated Producers), had agreed to make films for AIP. His work for them constituted the last two films of his career and in the judgment of his biographer Chris Fujiwara and others, it was his nadir.[46] So another reason why Dwan so disparaged *Most Dangerous Man Alive* may have been that he felt it threatened to banish him to this pariah status.

The indefatigable Bogeaus had founded yet another venture, collaborating with Dwan's friend and the former RKO president, James Grainger. In April 1959, they had formed Inter-Continent Releasing Organization Inc. and Inter-Continent Films. The former, run by Grainger, would be the distribution arm while Bogeaus would head the production company.[47] Among the projects announced were two films that Dwan planned to direct, *The Glass Wall*, based on a novel by Cecil Gilmore and set in an insane asylum, and the long-awaited remake of *The Bridge of San Luis Rey*. But the only film made under this arrangement was the hapless *Jet Over the Atlantic*.

Bogeaus was losing his knack for raising money. His various escapades, including putting Columbia in an awkward situation with SAG, may have also caught up with him. Dwan said that Bogeaus left the film business for a while and "when he tried to come back he found that all of his old friends had gone out of the business or were dead. And he just didn't rate with the big outfits as someone they needed to have on their staff."[48] In 1966, Bogeaus formed yet another company, still promising to make *The Glass House*.[49] In 1967, with Hollywood increasingly drawn to big-budget musicals, Bogeaus talked of making a musical out of the life of the legendary Paul Bunyan.

Dwan observed that Bogeaus "was always looking for a subject he could take to the majors and put over." Bogeaus died of a heart attack on August 23, 1968, at the age of sixty-four. "Even up to his death, he was still groping around, looking for the thing to make."[50]

Bogeaus could be maddening, penny-pinching, conniving and deceitful. But he had permitted Dwan to make ten films with little interference and with someone who, at least occasionally, shared his sensibility. With all his erratic qualities, he provided Dwan with a bulwark as the old studio system crumbled. He had remained, through all of this, Dwan's partner. Dwan remembered, "We liked each other very much."[51]

Another project that almost got Dwan back into the director's chair was called *Marine!* It was based on the book about Lieutenant General "Chesty" Puller, the only Marine to have won five navy crosses and who was responsible for evacuating men out of the Chosin Reservoir area during the Korean War. It would give Dwan an opportunity to revisit the story he had told in *Hold Back the Night* and as he had done before, to refine it or view it from another angle. The script had been co-written by Harry Brown, who had done the original script for *Sands of Iwo Jima*, and by Beirne Lay, Jr., who had co-written another celebrated war film of 1949, *Twelve O'Clock High*. Dwan said that ex–Marines seeking to help Puller had contributed $100,000 to the amateur producer to help get the project going. This encouraged Dwan to come out of his forced retirement to see if he could salvage this project, which had been turned down by nearly every major studio.

The film had been budgeted at five million dollars so Dwan re-wrote the script to pare the budget down to two million. He was able to get the project approved by Jack Warner. But Warner Bros. insisted that the two million dollars would have to be raised before *Marine!* could be put into production. Unfortunately, this was something the producer could not achieve and in the interim in 1966 Jack Warner sold his studio. At this point, Dwan said he left the project and the film was never made.[52] Producer James Ellsworth, a Virginia businessman, did succeed in having the project produced as an hour-long documentary directed by John Ford, titled *Chesty: A Tribute to a Legend*. It was later released in a 28-minute video edition.

But another crisis was engulfing Dwan beyond the apparent loss of his career. The vast wealth he had accumulated over a lifetime was vanishing.

Dwan had bought a canyon that consisted of nothing but forest but it would later become part of Bel-Air. Gregg Palmer remembered Dwan's real estate holdings and that Dwan greeted him at his residence by saying, "Welcome to Dwan's Manor." Dwan's dinner guests were served steak that he said was shipped to him directly from the stockyards in Chicago.

Dwan was reaping a great financial harvest as homes on the canyon were built and sold. But as the fifties progressed and real estate values fluctuated, Dwan's investments seemed to be slipping. His goddaughter recalls that around 1957, Dwan moved out of the South Mapleton residence and into one of the still opulent Sunset Towers apartments.

In 1959, Dwan moved to a house in Pacific Palisades. While imposing, it was not as splendid as the one at South Mapleton Drive. It was while living here that Dwan's finances took a catastrophic dive, hitting bottom around 1963 or 1964.[53] Dwan was not a man to be reckless with his investments, so it is surprising that his holdings would not have been more diversified. But he was certainly not the first Hollywood figure to lose his fortune through bad management. And as the Madoff scandal of the early twenty-first century has demonstrated, some very prominent and savvy investors have made the error of putting

The back view of Dwan's mansion at 355 South Mapleton Drive (courtesy Academy of Motion Picture Arts and Sciences).

all their trust in a supposed master financier whose operation proved to be totally bogus.

Robin got her first inkling of her godfather's plight when her Aunt Bonita confided to her that Dwan would be unable to honor his promise to send her to Vassar. Another valuable piece of jewelry that had been promised to Robin, had to be sold instead. By the mid–1960s, after living for a time in an apartment at North Stanley Avenue in Hollywood, Dwan reached the point where he had to vacate and move in with Bonita.

In 1979, Anita Loos, who was by then living in New York, made a last visit to California. Her niece Mary drove her around so that she could pay a final visit to many of her old friends from the film industry.

Both Anita and Mary had written scripts for Allan Dwan and looked forward to seeing him. Mary remembered, "Anita and I had both known Allan when he lived in a Brentwood estate, but now we headed to the San Fernando Valley, where he was sharing the home of his former housekeeper. That kind and gifted man had lost almost everything because of a wretched business manager, and now he and the housekeeper combined Social Security checks to get by."[54]

The Looses were pleased that Dwan "was his old cheery self, surrounded by current magazines and books."[55]

There was also some reason for Dwan to smile. For while he had lost his career and his money, some measure of his fame was coming back.

The Entertainer

In the mid–1960s, one man spearheaded the effort to reevaluate silent movies and to shake away the popular misconception that they were too primitive to be enjoyed any longer. Following what had become for him a deep passion for silent film, budding film historian Kevin Brownlow left his native England to come to America and seek out the major figures of that period.

In his seminal book on the silent film era, *The Parade's Gone By...*, Brownlow wrote of his experience: "When meeting such distinguished veterans as Dwan, preconceived ideas tend to make the actual encounter somewhat startling. Sparse facts, mixed with rumor and much supposition, had created for me a none-too-easy subject for an interview; I anticipated an elderly, rather fragile man, greatly embittered, impatient and short-tempered. For while the silent days were the peak years of his career, he has since kept himself in the background."[56] Brownlow noted Dwan's popular mantra about the danger of getting one's head above the crowd and being destroyed by the mob.

He then recalled, "The stout man with the breezy grin who opened the door was, I assumed a friend or a business associate; he was too youthful to fit my image. But when he swept me through to a study, decorated with stills from *Robin Hood*, my illusion was dispelled. Any question of age seemed ludicrous; the undiminished enthusiasm, the vitality, and the hilarious sense of humor proved that Dwan as a person hadn't changed much. From this encounter alone I fully understood why people like Douglas Fairbanks and Gloria Swanson selected him as a favorite director."[57]

Dwan demonstrated to Brownlow a facility that would for years astonish interviewers who had come to meet a failing old man. Brownlow observed, "Recalling the past was no effort; the anecdotes flowed in brisk profusion, as though we were talking between takes on a silent picture."[58]

It was as if Dwan had long been waiting in the wings for this moment.

In December 1964, Brownlow was the first interviewer to penetrate Dwan's obscurity and he would continue to interview Dwan over the years. In the late 1970s, Brownlow and David Gill produced the documentary series *Hollywood* about the silent era and Dwan topped their list of people to be interviewed. At the time they contacted him, Dwan was in his nineties and suffering from a cataract. Concerned about the prospect of losing him, they quickly made an appointment for an interview. Despite his eye problem, Brownlow and Gill "found him so riveting that we filmed sixteen ten-minute magazines on him, a record for the series. When we returned to visit him a few months later, we found he had completely recovered, and was in far better shape."[59]

The next man to interview Dwan did not concentrate on the silent era alone. Peter Bogdanovich had already interviewed John Ford and other directors but was now directing questions at "auteurs" who had been celebrated in French cinema journals such as *Cahiers du Cinema*, while neglected in their own country. Former *Times* critic Eugene Archer and burgeoning auteur theorist Andrew Sarris were Bogdanovich's immediate influences. Bogdanovich learned that Dwan lived close to him in the San Fernando Valley. He found in Dwan not only a neglected director but a film pioneer apparently forgotten and virtually unknown to many film buffs. Bogdanovich interviewed Dwan for nine non-consecutive days during the winter of 1968 and the fall of 1969. A book was published of their interview spanning Dwan's entire career, first appearing in the U.K. in 1970 under the title of *Allan Dwan: The Last Pioneer*. A year later it was published in the United States and coincided with a retrospective of Dwan's films at New York's Museum of Modern Art.

Dwan reprised for Bogdanovich his philosophy of the importance of not becoming too famous: "Let the other fellow get the kudos if he wants it. You have the pleasure of doing your job and making it last a long time, until you're ready to stop. That's why I say don't get too big."[60]

But Dwan now had been forced to stop making films. When he was first interviewed by Brownlow, he still had hopes of making *Marine!* but at this juncture Dwan knew that his directorial career was over. And so he now embraced fame, or

Dwan visits the set of *At Long Last Love* (1975). Burt Reynolds is in the center and Peter Bogdanovich at right. Bogdanovich's note to Dwan reads, "Dear Allan — A little memento of your lovely visit — As ever — Peter — 12/74" (Allan Dwan papers. Collection number 3566. American Heritage Center, University of Wyoming).

what bit of it he could find. He impishly tested how far he could embellish stories. His goddaughter Robin recalled that Dwan told her that after being ignored for so long, he felt like a relic that had been suddenly taken out and examined and he decided he was going to have some fun with the process. As some of his gross exaggerations became evident, some dismissed Dwan as a braggart. But one has to tread carefully here. Usually, even his most exaggerated stories contain some kernel of truth. And even some of Dwan's tales that appear to be questionable, have been confirmed by newly found evidence.

Dwan happily gave out copies of Bogdanovich's book to friends and fans. As with Brownlow, Dwan forged a friendship with Bogdanovich that lasted for the rest of his life.

Dwan was eighty-six when *The Last Pioneer* was published in the U.S. and in the last decade of his life, a steady stream of film historians beat a pathway to his door to interview this repository of memories going back nearly to the beginning of the film industry.

Among those interviewers was Joe Adamson, whose extensive 1979 interview with Dwan, centering mostly on Dwan's work at the Astoria studio, is now held by the Museum of the Moving Image in Queens, New York. Adamson had already interviewed numerous veterans of Hollywood's Golden Age but found a striking contrast with Dwan. Adamson recalled that in getting these figures to dredge up their memories of the past, "you get very used to the kind of bitterness that comes from a long association with a business as ungrateful as the movie business.... [W]hat comes up is a general feeling of disappointment or even rage, stemming from long histories of being used, even exploited, without the hoped-for gratitude or repayment ever materializing[.] And Dwan was refreshingly free from that kind of bad feeling."[61]

Although the veteran director was now ninety-four years old, he had lost little, if any, of his zest and energy that he had displayed to Brownlow when he was seventy nine. Adamson remembered, "I was apparently more conscious of his age than he was. After an hour of this non stop monologue, I was sure he must be wiped out for the day; I would take his slightest pause for breath at the conclusion of the story as my cue to leave and would begin composing graceful exit lines. But before I could get them out, I would find him rattling on into the next anecdote. He didn't *want* to quit. Old entertainers never die, they just crawl into corners and play to smaller houses."[62] If Dwan was no longer a director, he was still a storyteller.

Dwan could be free with advice to his former interviewers when they were making films. Dwan corresponded with Brownlow when the latter was making the 1975 *Winstanley*. Brownlow says, "Some of this advice was hilarious. I complained that we were trying to recreate the 17th century under a direct flight path to London airport. 'It's a make-believe world [wrote Dwan] so relax and enjoy it. One of your characters has a phobia. At the most unexpected times he imagines that a fierce demon is about to attack. He falls to his knees and covers his ears until the roar of the demon (the airplane) passes.... Note: the sound of the plane can be augmented by additional shrieks and cries of banshees. At an appropriate time you may have your character fall to his knees but no demon comes — silence. He is cured. (No charge).'"[63]

Dwan visited the set when Bogdanovich directed *Nickelodeon* (1976), a frenetic comedy cum drama, based on stories about Hollywood's early days that Bogdanovich heard from Ford, Walsh, McCarey and especially Dwan. Bogdanovich believed that "the compromises that were made caused the film to fail both artistically and commercially. I was especially sorry it did not live up to Dwan's wonderful stories."[64] Bogdanovich explained that among other things, he had wanted to shoot the film in black and white and have as its stars Jeff Bridges and John Ritter. Ryan O'Neal and Burt Reynolds were the more potent box-office draws cast as the leads.[65]

Nickelodeon was not the only film script inspired by Dwan's film-pioneering adventures, though it's the only one produced to date. Brownlow wrote a screenplay entitled *Shooting Tomorrow on the Western Street*, which he says was submitted to Warner Bros. by producer Sanford Lieberson in 1970. According to Brownlow, "the script had characters based on Dwan and Victor Fleming and Neilan on one side, and von Stroheim on the other." Brownlow later heard that "Robert Redford lay on an agent's sofa and discussed it for half an hour, before turning it down in favor of *The Great Waldo Pepper*. That's as close as it came."[66]

A film historian and occasional screenwriter, Joseph McBride spent much time with Dwan, listening to his stories of the film industry's early days. McBride had also interviewed and corresponded with John Ford and gotten to know many of his associates well. McBride penned a scenario called *California, Here I Come* that was inspired by the experiences of both directors. He was finishing it just as he read the announcement about Bogdanovich's new project. McBride tried to get Bogdanovich to read his script and Bogdanovich was indeed interested. But Bogdanovich had committed himself to *Nickelodeon* since this project seemed likely to go into production.

However, Bogdanovich was not satisfied with the *Nickelodeon* script (then called *Starlight Parade*) and thought it needed rewriting. McBride tried for some time to get permission from the producers to let Bogdanovich see his script but after some delay, they refused. With the looming competition from *Nickelodeon*, it was then too late for McBride to market his script.[67] It was Bogdanovich who injected into the screenplay the stories he had heard from Dwan and others.

Bogdanovich wanted *Nickelodeon* to pay tribute to Dwan in more ways than one. "I told him that if the picture did some business and I made any money, I'd give it to him. But it didn't."[68]

Howard Mandelbaum recalled that Dwan made a face when the subject of *Nickelodeon* was brought up.[69] However, Dwan clearly appreciated Bogdanovich's friendship and, in talking to other interviewers, sounded genuinely proud that a director so commercially successful was continuing to ask him for advice.

Dwan now hoped to get back into the business, as he had in 1935, by selling a screenplay. He may have thought that with the help of a young director like Bogdanovich he could make the right connections. Bogeaus had long fought to do a remake of *The Bridge of San Luis Rey* but after he divorced Dolores Moran in 1962, she gained the rights to the project in the divorce settlement. Bogdanovich made an arrangement with Moran that gave him and Dwan an option to put a film deal together but it never happened.

When Dwan was interviewed by Gary Morris and Howard Mandelbaum in September and October of 1978, he told them he had just put the finishing touches on a script called *A Bullet with Love*.[70] Mandelbaum recalled that Dwan noted the similarities it had to *Slightly Scarlet*.[71] Mandelbaum also remembered that Dwan's tone about the making of another film would change from meeting to meeting. He sometimes sounded enthusiastic but on other occasions would say things like "I know I'm never going to make another movie." Dwan undoubtedly savored the opportunity to be writing scripts again but as time wore on, he may have also realized that he was sharing a fantasy with his respectful interviewers.

Dwan was most likely talking about *A Bullet with Love* when he described a scene from a script he was working on to Joe Adamson. In the screenplay, a woman (suspected of shooting the man she has lived with) is questioned by a detective who Dwan thought could have been played by "someone like Telly Savalas." The woman tells the detective that at 2:30 A.M. she walked from the East River to Park Avenue. The detective scoffs at her story, observing that nobody walks that far that late in New York (again Dwan's favorite city) without being mugged. "I don't get mugged," the woman explains by grabbing the detective by the wrist and flipping him over, landing him on his backside. She then asks him somewhat incongruously, "Are you going to marry me?"[72] We are back with one of Dwan's assertive heroines besting a hapless male in a line stretching back to Calamity Anne.

While Dwan would win marks for fortitude for his script hustling in his nineties, he did not make another comeback. Another prospect was for a documentary made on Dwan's life. In 1975, a San Diego–based producer, George J. Mitchell, planned to make a fifty-minute documentary on Dwan for public television. In a letter Mitchell wrote to one organization seeking sponsorship, he said he had already shot some color footage of Dwan for the project. However, the proposal never got off the ground.[73]

In 1972, Dwan was honored by the Screen Directors Guild. Not everyone was apparently informed about the occasion and Dwan received a letter from Mexico from one party who learned too late. "I didn't know about them honoring you at the Screen Directors Guild or I would have been there. I've got to say Notre Dame had one good man." The letter was from John Wayne.[74] Largely through the efforts of critic Kevin Thomas, Dwan was also honored with a Lifetime Achievement award in 1976 by the Los Angeles Film Critics organization.

There was one major honor that still eluded him. A noted film historian would lead the fight to get Dwan an honorary Oscar.

Joseph McBride was a journalist for *Variety* in the 1970s and had already begun writing acclaimed books of Hollywood film directors that would include such names as John Ford, Orson Welles, Frank Capra and Steven Spielberg. Like other young cinema pilgrims, he also pursued the path to Dwan's door, initially going to see him with another distinguished film historian-to-be, Patrick McGilligan.

McBride followed up on a suggestion he made informally to Walter Mirisch, then president of the Academy of Motion Picture Arts & Sciences, by writing Mirisch a letter dated December 8, 1975. He proposed that Allan Dwan receive an honorary Academy Award.

McBride noted that Dwan's "greatest successes came before the Academy Awards began." McBride cited in particular the example of *Robin Hood* and wrote, "If the Oscar had been given that year, Dwan would certainly have won it. And that was only one of his many critical and financial successes in the silent era."[75]

After citing quotes from Bogdanovich and Brownlow, McBride then noted Dwan's many technical achievements, including the crane shot from *Intolerance* and his claim to having invented the mercury vapor arc lamp.

McBride ended on a personal note from his meetings with Dwan. "My final reason for suggesting Allan Dwan for an Oscar is that he is such a lovely human being."[76]

McBride received a reply dated December 9 that his proposal would be considered by the Academy early the next year. But no Academy Award would be forthcoming for Allan Dwan.

Reunions and Partings

When Jack Warner sold Warner Brothers, he was the last of the founders of the major studios to relinquish control. Warner remained with his company for a time but finally left in 1969. By then, Warners was controlled by Kinney, a parking lot company.

The industry decline that Dwan had seen and exploited during the death throes of RKO had now run its course. The old studio system had collapsed completely and the studios were becoming subsidiaries of larger corporations.

Dwan was not pleased with the changes taking place. Commenting to Adamson on the proliferation of producer credits, Dwan griped that now "everybody is a producer." But more characteristically Dwan accepted and adapted to the change with his indefatigable sense of humor. Noticing the long lines that were then materializing for movie premieres, Dwan suggested to Adamson that a good profit could be made by stationing trucks with portable toilets near the theaters and charging the waiting moviegoers fifty cents a head for relief.[77]

Dwan's former associates also looked for ways to cope with the changed landscape.

After a 1941 film attempt at a comeback, *Father Takes a Wife,* failed to revive her film career, Gloria Swanson turned to business and to acting on stage. From her home in New York, she continued to write to her former lover Marshall Neilan in California. A voluminous collection of their correspondence in the 1940s and 1950s exists in the Gloria Swanson Collection in the Harry Ransom Center at the University of Texas.

According to Neilan's biographer Jack Spears, Neilan's friendship with Zanuck and Raymond Griffith helped get him a job at 20th Century–Fox as a writer in the 1940s though Spears observed he turned in few ideas. Neilan's letters to Swanson suggest that his job was more in the line of story editor. He tried to find for Swanson properties that Fox owned that he thought might be suitable vehicles for another comeback attempt for her.

But in 1949, Swanson was asked by writer-director Billy Wilder about her availability for what she thought would be a bit part. It was actually the lead role in a project produced by Wilder and his writing collaborator Charles Brackett. There was a hitch in that Swanson was asked to audition for the role, at least as a formality. In her autobiography, Swanson wrote that she was hesitant to do so, feeling that she did poorly in screen tests. Her correspondence with Neilan indicates that she had done a screen test in 1947 and perhaps the lack of response from that test accounted for her reluctance.[78]

She sought advice from old friends Dwan, Neilan, director George Cukor and actor Clifton Webb. All urged her to submit to the test. The role she was auditioning for was that of a former silent film star living in a mansion that is a shrine to her departed fame, while she wallows in the illusion that a screenplay she is writing will be her ticket to a stellar comeback. The film was *Sunset Blvd.*, an instant classic steeped in the ambience of Hollywood Gothic, black comedy and film noir.

Mary Pickford, Pola Negri and, seemingly most improbably, Mae West were considered for the star role of Norma Desmond early in the proceedings but by the time the script was finished, Wilder and Brackett were focused on Swanson. Since the filmmakers planned to mix fact with fiction, Swanson presented them with interesting opportunities. Not only was she a genuine star of the silent era, who had long been out of the cinema limelight, but her home studio had been Paramount, which was Wilder and Brackett's production company and distributor. Cecil B. DeMille, playing himself as Norma's former director, was still working at Paramount and his scenes were shot on the set of *Samson and Delilah.* He had actually been involved with Swanson's early career and, as a star director, was recognizable to the public. Erich von Stroheim, who had apparently long ago reconciled with Swanson, was cast as her butler, who was also her former husband and director with the Stroheim-esque moniker of Max von Mayerling. And a clip from *Queen Kelly* would be used in the movie.

But the invisible presence of Allan Dwan also hovered over the film. In the story, Norma Desmond's idea for a comeback script has her starring as Salome and she enlists the screenwriter who has stumbled into her house as a collaborator. This is something of an in-joke since Dwan's *Stage Struck* opens with a sequence in which the daydreaming waitress played by Swanson imagines herself to be the world's greatest actress playing Salome in lurid Technicolor. Like Dwan, Norma disdained the transition to sound films. A reference is made in *Sunset Blvd.* to Norma having Rod La Rocque as one of her house guests and in fact, Swanson had starred with La Rocque and fallen in love with him while acting in Dwan's *A Society Scandal.* H.B. Warner, who appears as one of Norma's "waxworks" card players, had been Swanson's leading man in Dwan's *Zaza.* A second of the three waxworks, Anna Q. Nilsson had appeared in four

Allan Dwan silents and the third, Buster Keaton had made a cameo gag appearance in Dwan's *Tide of Empire*, though it was cut.

Max solemnly tells the screenwriter that one of Norma's admirers was a maharajah who came seeking one of the star's silk stockings and then strangled himself with it. This is an outrageous reminder of Swanson's prank of having her fiancé disguise himself as a maharajah to Dwan. The gaudy use of leopard skin in Norma's limousine also harkened back to the leopard skin pillows and rugs in the Mercedes that picked up Dwan and Rosson in Paris in 1925 as part of that same practical joke. And of course, Swanson's Charlie Chaplin imitation had been earlier enacted in *Manhandled*. (Reportedly, Wilder and Brackett had suggested to Swanson that as Norma Desmond, she would impersonate Douglas Fairbanks. Swanson countered, "Why don't I do the Chaplin thing I did in *Manhandled*?")[79] Even the clip of *Queen Kelly* has a Dwan connection since he was one of the directors whom Swanson asked to advise her on what to do with the footage. And the man who had directed that footage had once been Dwan's assistant director.

More importantly, Dwan had given Swanson experience in kidding her star image in several of their films together, most notably in *Stage Struck*. There is a striking convergence in the waitresses' daydreams and Norma's delusions of returning grandeur. Dwan had become increasingly conscious of the destructive power of fame. Although Dwan saw this destruction coming from the resentment of the "mob," it was not a great distance to the need for fame itself becoming a rampaging id.

Gloria Swanson makes her final descent and prepares for her close-up in *Sunset Blvd* (1950). Her association with Dwan was reflected in the film in interesting references and in-jokes. Could Dwan have been in that final scene?

Ironically, the director-writer was the same Billy Wilder who had been Dwan's bogus tour guide in Germany in 1927.

According to one source, Dwan is actually in the final scene of *Sunset Blvd.* Charles Foster wrote that Swanson once said, "When all the newsmen and photographers are waiting for me to leave the mansion at the end of the film after I have been charged with murder, one of the photographers and you can see him very clearly, is Allan Dwan. I paid the extra hired to do the job to hand over his camera to Allan. He told me it was the only time in his entire career he had been seen on camera."[80]

Dwan is not recognizable in the scene though there are some newsmen and photographers with their backs to the camera or whose features are not discernable. Swanson makes no mention of this in her autobiography nor does Dwan in all the interviews researched for this book. So Dwan's physical presence in the film remains a mystery. Perhaps the story itself is another inside joke.

Joseph McBride has cited an incident late in Dwan's life that is evocative of *Sunset Blvd.* In 1975 when McBride was a reporter and reviewer for *Daily Variety*, he invited Dwan to attend with him a sneak preview of the movie *Nashville* on the Paramount lot. Remembering the scene in *Sunset Blvd.* when Norma Desmond had difficulty getting through the studio gate, McBride decided that he would make sure that Dwan would feel far more welcome. He therefore called Bob Goodfried, the veteran head of Paramount publicity, to ask him to have a studio representative greet Dwan.

But Goodfried responded that they were too busy to do that. McBride recalled, "I tried to explain his [Dwan's] great importance in the history of the studio, but to no avail. I don't know if I quoted to Goodfried Norma Desmond's line from that scene in *Sunset Blvd.*—'Without me, there wouldn't be any Paramount studio'—but I had that on my mind."[81]

In his letters to Swanson, Neilan was a persistent cheerleader for her winning the Oscar for *Sunset Blvd.* But although she received her third Academy Award nomination, Swanson, like Dwan, never took home the big prize.

In November 1944, when Dwan was working for Edward Small, Neilan wrote to him saying that he had a script that Dick Rowland of Fox was anxious for Dwan to direct. Neilan added a postscript: "As soon as I get on my feet I will take care of that indebtedness I owe you. Sorry it has been so long overdue but I was helpless to take care of everything. The God damn government clipped me untill [sic] I at long last got them paid off and am now in the clear."[82]

After years of unrealized projects, Neilan finally got an opportunity but this one had him acting before the cameras. Budd Schulberg, his friend since the days when Schulberg's father B.P. was supervisor at Paramount, helped get Neilan a role in the 1957 film *A Face in the Crowd*, scripted by Schulberg and directed by Elia Kazan. Neilan played the media-challenged politician Senator Fuller, who is given an image makeover by the charismatic Lonesome Rhodes, played by Andy Griffith. Neilan might have continued with an acting career: Schulberg wanted him for his next film, *Wind Across the Everglades*. But, Neilan was stricken with throat cancer. He died on October 27, 1958, at the age of sixty-seven.

Swanson made only three more theatrical films after *Sunset Blvd.*, none of them significant. But she remained active on radio, television and stage. When she was feted on the TV show *This Is Your Life*, Dwan appeared as one of the important people in that life.

As early as 1938, Swanson had written to Dwan asking for his help in writing her autobiography. At that time, Swanson had seemingly given up on her film career and was about to move back to New York. In her letter, she addressed Dwan as "Pop."[83] This effort would not go far. Swanson tried again in the 1970s and frequently consulted Dwan. Her book was published in 1980.

In 1977, for the official fiftieth anniversary of the sound film, Dwan was among the silent veterans interviewed by Guy Flatley of the *New York Times*. At Bonita's Van Nuys bungalow, Dwan told Flatley, "Gloria was an amazing personality, a versatile actress and a very vital person. She's a great-great grandmother and yet she looks like a blushing bride. She kills me. She's my outstanding star of stars. Gloria, Raoul Walsh and I had a reunion not long ago right here in this living room. I said, 'Come on, tell the truth now. What kind of affair did you two have?' They didn't confess a thing but their faces were rosy red."[84] Both Swanson and Walsh were discreet about the affair in their autobiographies. Walsh was only two years younger than Dwan but Swanson did not regard him with the same paternal diffidence.

Dwan had more to say about Walsh, who was now totally blind. "All he has now are his memories. I go to see him when I can. And, as I say, we talk and talk on the phone. I tell him about a new story I'm working on, and we swear that we'll shoot it together, making use of whatever we retain as picturemakers. 'You figure out the gags,' I tell him, 'and I'll shoot it and let you see the rushes.' 'See it,' he says, 'how can I *see* it? 'Don't worry,' I say, 'I have a new device that will make it possible. If there's a barroom brawl, some guy will hit you in the nose and you'll feel it.' Raoul pauses. Then he says, 'Oh! Okay, that sounds fine.'"[85]

For his friend, Dwan could still enact the roles of inventor, problem-solver, entertainer and fantasist.

Walsh died on December 31, 1980. At a meeting of the Simi Valley City Council on February 9, 1981, a resolution was passed honoring the community's late citizen. Accepting the resolution on behalf of Walsh's widow was Allan Dwan. In his address to the City Council, Dwan observed, "Now, this man that you are honoring tonight ... is one of the greatest men I have ever met; he's a personal pal as well as a wonderful example. Raoul Walsh was a student, a hard-working ... sensitive man who made great motion pictures, some of the greatest, and made millions of dollars for the people he worked for, as well as for himself."[86]

Orson Welles, King Vidor and Allan Dwan at the 1978 Los Angeles Film Critics' Awards, where Welles paid tribute to pioneers Vidor and Dwan. Citing Shakespeare's *Julius Caesar*, Welles asked, "When comes there such others? We shall not look upon their like again" (Allan Dwan papers. Collection number 3566. American Heritage Center, University of Wyoming).

Dwan concluded by saying, "So what will we say, life is real, life is earnest, and the grave is not its goal. Dust thou art and to dust returned was not spoken of the soul! So keep your souls clean...."[87]

There was still one more tribute ahead for Dwan. Although he did not receive its Oscar, the Academy of Motion Picture Arts and Sciences sponsored an evening celebrating his career while Mayor Tom Bradley of Los Angeles designated April 25 as Allan Dwan Day. The mayor's proclamation was recited to the audience by Peter Bogdanovich, who appropriately hosted the evening. Film clips from twelve Dwan films were shown, interspersed with comments from Dwan and Bogdanovich. Congratulatory telegrams from Swanson and Fairbanks Jr. were read as well as a cable from President Reagan, who said it "was a treat and honor" to make films with Dwan.[88] The evening concluded with a screening of *Manhandled.*

Dwan now had only a few months to live. His brother Leo had died in 1964, leaving no heirs, and so Dwan had no real family left except for Bonita and her relatives. Pauline Bush died in 1969. Robin does not recall ever hearing her godfather mention her.

Dwan appeared to be in good health even at the age of 96. He had lived long enough to see one of his former actors become the fortieth president of the United States. "Taught him everything he knows," Dwan used to joke after Reagan was inaugurated in January of 1981. (Meeting the future president at a party in the 1970s, Bogdanovich recalled that when he mentioned that he knew Dwan, "Reagan's face transformed completely from pleasantly bored to excited." Reagan then asked, "How *is* Allan? Give him my best, will you? I remember him *very* fondly.")[89]

On November 12, Dwan suffered a stroke and was taken to St. Joseph Medical Center in Burbank. Robin Wallace recalled that in the initial hours after the stroke, Dwan only seemed "a little confused and not very coordinated."[90] Within a few hours, his condition changed dramatically. Wallace remembered that little was done for him medically; perhaps at that time there was nothing that could be done to halt his deterioration. Dwan appeared to have fallen into something close to a vegetative state. One of Dwan's visitors, druggist Max Marks, who had known him for forty years, found him barely able to breathe and only with the help of artificial respiratory aids.

Bonita told one reporter that the only time Dwan smiled after his stroke was when she told him Notre Dame had won a football game.[91] Wallace soon realized that her godfather would never recover but Bonita clung to the hope that Dwan's resilience might yet surface.

Dwan remained unresponsive. On Friday, December 18, he was moved to the Motion Picture & Television County House in Woodland Hills. He died there on December 21.

In his will (recorded on September 10, 1981), Dwan left all his personal possessions to Bonita with the provision that her sister Tennie would get them in the event of Bonita's demise. Bonita was named executrix with Robin and her sister Dwanine assigned as backups. While he had been invigorated and moved by his late friendships, these four women, as the will suggests, had become his family and were probably the most important people to Dwan as he neared the end of his life. But he could leave them little. Dwan had no money in the bank. Bonita later donated some of his photographs and papers to the Margaret Herrick Library.

On December 23, a Requiem Mass was said for Dwan at St. Cyril's of Jerusalem in Encino. The funeral ended with his body's interment at San Fernando Mission Cemetery. Dwan had visited the mission when shooting the 1929 *Tide of Empire* and must have been smitten with its beauty and tranquility. A soloist sang a composition of Dwan's called "From Now Until Eternity."

Robin Wallace was surprised by the crowd that came to the funeral and by the fact that TV cameras were also present. Among the mourners was Peter Bogdanovich, who also served as one of the pallbearers. Also present were the critic Kevin Thomas and the widow of actor Richard Arlen.[92]

One anticipated guest did not appear: Gloria Swanson was apparently struggling with her own health problems. She died slightly over a year later, on April 4, 1983.

Next to Mr. Dwan

Trying to assess how many films Allan Dwan worked on in his lifetime can be something of an ongoing parlor game, and Dwan did not always make the process easier. Kevin Brownlow has commented, "He was so full of colorful anecdotes you could not always be sure which had actually happened. He also exaggerated the number of pictures he'd made."[93]

There has been speculation, fueled by Dwan himself, that he may have been involved with as many 1,000 movies. This largely stems from what were supposed to be Dwan's extensive writing credits before he turned to directing. Given the period involved in his work at Essanay and Flying A, however, it is unlikely that he wrote much more than 100 scenarios before commencing his directorial career. The total amount of films that Dwan was involved in as director, writer, producer, supervisor or in any other capacity was probably somewhere around 500.

Dwan mastered his craft at Flying A and, by the end of his tenure there, was growing more ambitious. At Universal, he made his first notable flings with consciously artistic efforts. At Famous Players, he made the full conversion to making feature films.

At Triangle, he alternated between making more strenuously physical films with Fairbanks and more intimate dramas with female stars. In the early 1920s, working at Mayflower Productions and then with the independent Associated Producers, he again shifted to making more prestigious and serious films.

Unfortunately, nearly all of these films have disappeared. It's possible that Dwan did not prove fully suited for this kind of filmmaking but the results may have been provocative.[94]

After bouncing back to commercial success with *Robin Hood,* he moved to Paramount where he was able to work with the independence and atmosphere he desired on the East Coast. This period was dominated by his work with Swanson, and his artistic efforts were tied to serving and developing the star's screen personality. But here too, he could be adventurous when he could escape the more routine projects imposed upon them.

After the breakup with Swanson, he made a number of different kinds of films though none won him the kind of attention he had with his big star pictures. Again the survival rate of those films is low.

In short, we can chart some of the dynamics of Dwan's silent film career but full critical evaluation is impossible since so little survives aside from his films with Doug and Gloria. Though he embraced self-promotion, he never sought to be the star of his films in the way of DeMille, Vidor and some other notable directors.

The 1930s for Dwan was a struggle for survival followed by a renewed commercial viability late in the decade. He then turned to comedy almost obsessively, examining it like an experimental device and often probing its relation to the more dramatic parts of the story. He seemed to distill in this process what Bogdanovich has called Dwan's ability to see the "ridiculousness in people's behavior"[95] which he applied to both comedies and dramas in his years at Republic. Ironically, it was at this small and disparaged studio that Dwan made his best known film, *Sands of Iwo Jima.* The film dug a niche in the nation's consciousness and was admirable in many respects though it fell short of the greater realism and poetry of World War II films like Ford's *They Were Expendable* and Wellman's *The Story of G.I. Joe.*

Seen in perspective, many of the director's oddball movies at Republic appear part of Dwan's preparations and tests for his more accomplished 1950s films with Bogeaus that attracted the attentions of foreign critics. While still essentially B movies, these films showed a greater measure of refinement in Dwan's exposures of the darker and more perplexing parts of human nature. The aforementioned quartet of Bogeaus films starts with *Silver Lode,* named after the town in the movie. The central core of characters is set in contrast to the ensemble cast of the community, as were the narratives of *Young People, Rendezvous with Annie, Driftwood,* and *Woman They Almost Lynched.*

With the final film of the four, *The River's Edge,* Dwan had moved 180 degrees, away from all sense of community as a trio of characters account for all the important *dramatis personae.* They journey into an increasingly isolated and desolate landscape as if moving to the beginning of time, until the denouement yanks them back to the responsibilities of civilization and the quartet of films comes full circle. Michael Henry Wilson observed, "Dwan nudged his projects towards the fable, apologue or parable even when he portrayed historical figures.... His oeuvre is thus detached from any contemporary reality—seemingly impervious to the zeitgeist."[96]

Perhaps that is why Dwan grew angry with the political pigeonholing question about *Silver Lode* although that indeed provided the context for telling his fable. Wilson refers to Dwan's films as Moral Tales, suggesting a seemingly improbable link between Dwan and Eric Rohmer. But if Dwan's "texts" are far less sophisticated than Rohmer's, Dwan can, by orchestrating his narrative and character twists, in Wilson's words, "make the drama yield a rich morality—what must be called a moral beauty."[97] Perhaps even the four cited Bogeaus films taken collectively don't amount to a great film, but they still constitute one of the most striking moral journeys in cinema history.

Rohmer himself, writing as a critic in the 1950s, contrasted Walsh, Dwan, Minnelli, Kelly and Donen with Bresson, Renoir, Rossellini and Ophuls. Rohmer contended that the latter group held "their art in great esteem, and it pays off." Rohmer believed that the first group "display less consideration for their art. In return, they receive less in absolute value but proportionately more than the others do."[98]

Yet, Dwan's films of this period made without Bogeaus, *Hold Back the Night* and *The Restless Breed,* are peculiarly meditative films with the former suggesting the link between war and all human endeavors of perseverance.

In *Most Dangerous Man Alive,* Dwan expertly applied the 100 percent use of real locations to convey the desolation and rootlessness of the characters even more strongly than in *The River's Edge.* His ubermensch in the film provokes the collective fear and hatred of nearly everyone while being blinded by his own delusions of grandeur, suggesting a cautionary tale on the dangers of fame. Even when rediscovering the frailty of his humanity, the protagonist chooses to thrust himself against all the powerful forces arrayed against him.

Despite Dwan's disavowal of tragedy and the steadfastness of his serene disposition, it is unusual that a number of his films deal with suicides, suicide attempts and suicidal situations including *The Dancing Girl, An Innocent Magdalene, The Forbidden Thing, Stage Struck, Tin Gods, Chances, While Paris Sleeps, The Inside Story, Surrender, Slightly Scarlet* and *Most Dangerous Man Alive.* The censors objected to a scene in the script of *Rendezvous with Annie* showing that "your sympathetic lead Jeffrey is contemplating suicide."[99] Part of the art of Allan Dwan may have come from the tension in repressing his inner turmoil (vide his 1919 nervous breakdown) beneath his sunny exterior just as his businessman persona held his dreamer side in check. In one of the excised parts of the *Last Pioneer* interview, Bogdanovich pointed out the contradiction of Dwan's emphasis on being a businessman and his assertion that he liked making pictures so much that he would do it for nothing.[100]

Bogdanovich found much of Dwan's advice to be helpful in his career as a director. He felt he came to know the truth of

Dwan's words about the dangers of raising one's head above the mob when his own career suffered a downturn after a string of hits. He ruefully acknowledged, "I've got the scars on my neck to prove it."[101]

In 2009, Bogdanovich did have the satisfaction of finally seeing *Nickelodeon* released on DVD in a version much more to his liking, including a conversion to black and white as he intended it to be shot.

Like his 1950s protagonists, Dwan found a place of refuge in his Holmby Hills home with Bonita Simmons and in the other places they inhabited as his fortune dwindled. While his troubles in paradise pursued him as they did his characters, she remained his bedrock of support. Yet to most visitors to his home (actually *her* home), she was simply his housekeeper.

Ms. Wallace believes that Peter Bogdanovich came the closest to understanding the true relationship that existed between Dwan and Bonita Simmons. However, as he states in his book *Who the Devil Made It*, Bogdanovich didn't know Dwan was living in her home until after his death. He poignantly remembered her as "dear Bonita Simmons."[102]

For most interviewers, Dwan could have Bonita serve a myriad of functions. In a 1979 interview for a local newspaper, Dwan says he is living at the home of his sister. Later a drink is served to him by his day-nurse. The "sister" and "day-nurse" are both roles played by Bonita Simmons.

In this article, the drink brought to him is a vodka martini topped with a shaved dill pickle. Dwan chuckles to the interviewer, "Guess that's her idea of an olive."[103] Robin Wallace strongly suspects that the pickle was a signal by Bonita to cut down on the blarney for that interview. Or perhaps she resented the reference to the house being owned by Dwan's non-existent sister.

Bogdanovich was not the only interviewer who did not know whose home he was visiting. Never faltering in his pride, Dwan was resourceful in coming up with subterfuges but his interviewers could grasp he was not telling the full truth. Dwan explained to Howard Mandelbaum, "I'm more comfortable in a smaller place." Mandelbaum remembered the "faded postcard he showed us of his mansion was from the 1920s. My impression was that wealth and comfort were long gone."[104]

Another visitor, Joe Adamson, remembered being told that "Dwan's housekeeper would not or could not stay with him around the clock at his palatial estate, and when his health declined to the point where this kind of attention was necessary, he moved in with her. Thus it was that I found the immortal Hollywood veteran and pioneer Allan Dwan in an unpretentious and totally unremarkable suburban tract home, dressed in pajama tops and slacks, being watched over by the smallish, pleasant woman who called herself his housekeeper."[105]

Bonita was seventy-two years old when Dwan died in 1981. She was still an active person and, needing the money, she took on another job, serving as caretaker to an elderly woman whose family had, in effect, abandoned her.

In early 1995, Bonita suffered a stroke. At the time, Tennie took over caring for her sister, who appeared to be nearing the end of her days. But Bonita proved resilient despite her infirmities. And in a quirk of fate, it was the younger sister Tennie who died the following year.

In late 2000, Bonita suffered another stroke and recovery did not seem possible. She was placed in a hospice. Robin remembers her aunt begging to be permitted to come home for Thanksgiving. But her condition was too fragile and she was having difficulty swallowing.

Bonita Simmons died of pneumonia on January 1, 2001, three months short of her ninety-second birthday. She was cremated according to her wishes. Her ashes and those of her sister were retained in Robin Wallace's home.

When Wallace was contacted for this book in the fall of 2009, she was the only survivor of the four women mentioned in Dwan's will. Her younger sister Dwanine had died in 1998 from diabetic complications. (Her father died in 2004.) Ms. Wallace lives with her husband Dave.

In response to the research queries for this book, Wallace sifted through various family papers. While going through her mother's paperwork, she made a surprising discovery. After her first stroke, her Aunt Bonita had left with her mother instructions for what to do with her remains. But because Tennie died

Probably the last photograph of Dwan and Bonita together. Do her eyes reveal some special concern about "Mr. Dwan"? This photograph was taken at Bonita's Van Nuys home around September 1981 (courtesy Robin Allana Wallace).

first, the paper remained with her personal documents and no one in the family was aware of it at the time Bonita died.

The note left by her Aunt Bonita to her mother was dated February, 12, 1995. It read:

> Tennie,
>
> Honey, when the time comes for me to leave this world, please have me cremated and my ashes placed at the mission next to where Mr. Dwan was buried. Please tell all the children I love them. I can never thank you and Bob enough. God bless you and keep you. I love you all.[106]

Even more than thirteen years after his death, she still referred to him as "Mr. Dwan."

The note also contained rubbings from the stone indicating that Bonita's name had been placed on Dwan's tombstone and only the year of her death needed to be inscribed. Now living in central California, Robin had not seen Dwan's Mission gravesite for decades.

The director with the impish sense of humor may have had the last laugh on his biographer as the very writing of the book had caused an unforeseen event. It suggested that after years of research and contemplation, in the end, the author, like countless others, was only following Dwan's direction and capping things with the kind of mystical final twist the filmmaker favored.

Robin and her family now plan to travel to Los Angeles in 2013 to have her aunt's ashes placed next to Allan Dwan's grave.

Dwan's relationship with Bonita had been his longest with any woman and apparently the happiest of his life. Like many aspects of his career, it did not happen in a conventional manner. The relationship had never been recognized in public and both parties, raised in an era of a different sense of propriety, were content to keep it that way, as long as they could enjoy each other's company.

As meticulously as he had prepared his films, Dwan had planned to have his relationship with Bonita acknowledged in death. Wallace noted, "I don't think that my aunt had her name placed on the stone. The marker was designed by my godfather — it has all his earmarks. He has his initials, in his hand, written on it, and I think that my Aunt Bonita was surprised about the stone's design herself. The grave is for a married couple and the headstone is placed that way." (Bonita had actually already purchased a plot for herself at the same cemetery where her mother was buried.)

Wallace added, "I think this was his last gesture to my aunt about his wishes to join him. I think if she had her name placed on the stone, her first name 'Bonita' would be on it — instead her middle name 'Amanda' is on the stone.... My godfather was always very keen to put his unique personal marks on everything. His initials are on the silver and on the silver ice bucket and pitcher, cufflinks, etc."[107]

Dwan had demonstrated his usual efficiency in his preparations but there had been a snag in its execution that had delayed Bonita's physical return to him for over a decade. But as with the problems he had encountered in life, a solution was found and Dwan would be reunited with Bonita forever.

His last exile was over.

Filmography

This filmography does not include Dwan's early writing credits, most of which are lost. He wrote many of the Flying A films he directed.

The two television programs Dwan directed, that were broadcast in 1955 and 1956 and were not covered in the main text, are briefly discussed here.

The portion of this filmography dealing with Dwan's directorial career at the American Film Manufacturing Company (1911–1913) has been compiled with the generous help of film historian Dana Driskel of Santa Barbara. This is altogether fitting since it was Dana's predecessor as the pre-eminent film historian of the Flying A Company, Timothy F. Lyons, who researched most of the material regarding Dwan's work at American in the filmography for Peter Bogdanovich's groundbreaking book *Allan Dwan: The Last Pioneer*. Additional information obtained by Driskel's continuing research has shown that Lyons was a bit too generous in attributing Flying A films to Dwan's direction. However, even at this date there remain some titles that are possibly but not definitely identified as the work of Dwan. These titles are indicated by an asterisk (*).

1911

Shot at San Juan Capistrano

**A Cowboy's Sacrifice* (May 18); *A Western Dream, Branding a Bad Man* (split reel) (May 22)

Shot at Lakeside

Rattlesnakes and Gunpowder (May 29); *The Sheepman's Daughter* (June 1); *The Sagebrush Phrenologist*; *The Elopements on Double L Ranch* (split reel) (June 5); *$5000 Reward—Dead or Alive* (June 8); *The Witch of the Range* (June 12); *The Cowboy's Ruse*; *Law and Order on the Bar L Ranch* (split reel) (June 15); *The Yiddisher Cowboy*; *The Broncho Buster's Bride* (split reel) (June 19); *The Hermit's Gold* (June 22); *Actress and the Cowboys*; *The Sky Pilot's Intemperance* (split reel) (June 26); *A Western Waif* (June 29); *The Call of the Open Range* (July 3); *The Ranch Chicken*; **The School Ma'am of Snake* (split reel) (July 6); *Cupid in Chaps* (July 10); *The Outlaw's Trail* (July 13); *The Ranchman's Nerve* (July 17); *When East Comes West* (July 20); *The Cowboy's Deliverance* (July 24); *The Cattle Thief's Brand* (July 27); *The Parting Trails* (July 31); *The Cattle Rustler's End* (Aug. 3); *Cattle, Gold and Oil* (Aug. 7); *The Ranch Girl* aka *The Ranch Girl's Rustler* (Aug. 10); *The Poisoned Flume* (Aug. 14); *The Brand of Fear* (Aug. 17); *The Blotted Brand* (Aug. 21); *Aunty and the Cowboys* (shown on a split reel with the documentary *Annie Harris in Chicago Swimming Marathon*, which was shot by another director in Chicago) (Aug. 24); *The Western Doctor's Peril* (Aug. 28); *The Diamond Smugglers* aka *The Smuggler and the Girl* (Aug. 31); *The Cowboy and the Artist* (Sept. 4); *Three Million Dollars* (Sept. 7); *The Stage Robbers of San Juan* (Sept. 11); *The Mother of the Ranch* (Sept. 14); *The Gunman* (Sept. 18); *The Claim Jumpers* (Sept. 21); *The Circular Fence* (Sept. 25); *The Rustler Sheriff* (Sept. 28); *The Love of the West* aka *Western Love* (Oct. 2)

Shot at La Mesa

The Miner's Wife (Oct. 5); *The Land Thieves* (Oct. 9); *The Cowboy and the Outlaw* (Oct. 12); *The Three Daughters of the West*; *The Caves of La Jolla* (split reel) (Oct. 16); *The Lonely Range* (Oct. 19); *The Horse Thief's Bigamy* (Oct. 23); *The Trail of the Eucalyptus* (Oct. 26); *The Stronger Man* (Oct. 30); *The Water War* (Nov. 2); *The Three Shell Game* (Nov. 6); *The Mexican* (Nov. 9); *The Eastern Cowboy* (Nov. 13); *The Way of the West* (Nov. 16); *The Test* (Nov. 20); *The Master of the Vineyard* (Nov. 23); *Jolly Bill of the Rolicking R* aka *Sloppy Bill of the Rolicking R* (shot at Lakeside) (Nov. 27); *The Sheriff's Sisters* (Nov. 30); *The Angel of Paradise Ranch* aka *The Girl of the Ranch* (Dec. 4); *The Smoke of the Forty-Five* (Dec. 7); *The Man Hunt* (Dec. 11); *The Last Notch* (Dec. 18); *The Gold Lust* (Dec. 21); *The Duel of the Candles* (Dec. 25); *Bonita of El Cajon* (Dec. 28)

1912

Bronco Bustin' for Flying "A" Pictures aka *Bucking Horses*; *The Misadventures of a Claim Agent* (split reel) (Jan. 4); *The Winning of La Mesa* (Jan. 8); *The Locket* (Jan. 11); *The Relentless Law* (Jan. 15); *Justice of the Sage* (Jan. 18); *Objections Overrules* (Jan. 22); *The Mormon* (Jan. 25); *Love and Lemons* (Jan. 29); *The Best Policy* (Feb. 1); *The Real Estate Fraud* (Feb. 5); *The Grubstake Mortgage* (Feb. 8); *Where Broadway Meets the Mountains* (Feb. 12); *An Innocent Grafter* (Feb. 15); *Society and Chaps* (Feb. 19); *A Leap Year Comedy* (Feb. 22); *The Land Baron of San Tee* (Feb. 26); *An Assisted Elopement* (Feb. 29); *From the Four Hundred to the Herd* (March 4); *The Broken Ties* (March 7); *After School* (March 11); *A Bad Investment* (March 14); *The Full Value* (March 18); *A Tramp's Gratitude* (March 21); *Fidelity* (March 25); *Winter Sports and Pastimes of Coronado Beach* aka *Coronado'a New Year's Day* (documentary) (March 28); *The Maid and the Man* (April 1); *The Agitator* aka *The Cowboy and the Socialist* (April 4); *The Ranchman's Marathon* (half of split reel) (April 8); *The Coward* (April 11); *The Distant Relative* (April 15); *The Ranch Detective* (April 18); *The Driftwood* (April 22); *Her Mountain Home* aka *The Eastern Girl* (April 25); *The Pensioners* (April 29); *The End of the Feud* (May 2); *The Wedding Dress* aka *Her Wedding Dress* (May 6); *The Myth of Jamasha Pass* (May 9); *The Other Wise Man* (May 13); *The Haters* (May 16); *The Thread of Life* (May 20); *The Wandering Gypsy* (May 23); *The Reward of Valor* (May 27); *The Brand* (May 30); *The Green-Eyed Monster* (June 3); *Cupid Through Padlocks* (June 6); *For the Good of Her Men* (June 10); *The Simple Love* (June 13); *The Weaker Brother*; *A Fifty-Mile Auto Contest* (split reel) (June 17); **The Wordless Message* (June 20); *The Evil Inheritance* (June 24); *The Marauders* (June 27); *The Girl Back Home* (July 1); *Under*

False Pretenses (July 4); *Where There's a Heart* (July 8); *The Vanishing Race* aka *The Vanishing Tribe* (July 11); *The Fatal Mirror*; *Point Loma-Old Town* (documentary) (split reel) (July 15); *The Tell-Tale Shells* (July 18); *Indian Jealousy*; *San Diego* (documentary) (split reel) (July 22); *The Canyon Dweller* (July 25); *It Pays to Wait* (July 29); *A Life for a Kiss* (Aug. 1); *The Meddlers* (Aug. 5); *The Girl and the Gun* (Aug. 8); *The Bad Man and the Ranger* (Aug. 14); *The Outlaw Colony* (Aug. 15); *The Land of Death* (Aug. 19); *The Bandit of Point Loma* (Aug. 22); *The Jealous Rage* (Aug. 26); *The Will of James Waldron* (Aug. 29)

AT SANTA BARBARA

The Greaser and the Weakling (Sept. 2); *The Stranger at Coyote* (Sept. 5); *The Dawn of Passion* (Sept. 9); *The Vengeance That Failed* (Sept. 11); *The Fear* (Sept. 16); *The Foreclosure* (Sept. 19); *White Treachery* (Sept. 23); *Their Hero Son* (Sept. 26); *Calamity Anne's Ward* (re-released on November 23, 1916, as *Calamity Anne Guardian*) (Sept. 30); *Father's Favorite* aka *The Favorite Son* (Oct. 3); *Jack of Diamonds* aka *Queen of Hearts* (Oct. 7); *Reformation of Sierra Smith* aka *The Lost Watch* (Oct. 10); *The Promise* (Oct. 14); *The New Cowpuncher* (Oct. 17); *The Best Man Wins* (Oct. 21); *The Wooers of Mountain Kate* aka *Mountain Kate* (Oct. 24); **One, Two, Three* (Oct. 28); *The Wanderer* (Oct. 31); *Maiden and Men* (Nov. 4); *God's Unfortunate* (Nov. 7); *Man's Calling* (Nov. 11); *The Intrusion at Lompac* (Nov. 14); *The Thief's Wife* (Nov. 18); *The Would-Be Heir* (Nov. 21); **Jack's Word* aka *A Man's Word* (Nov. 25); *Her Own Country* (Nov. 28); *Pals* (Dec. 2); *The Animal Within* (Dec. 5); *The Law of God* (Dec. 9); *Nell of the Pampas* (Dec. 12); *Daughters of Señor Lopaz* (Dec. 16); *The Power of Love* (Dec. 19); *The Recognition* (Dec. 23); *Blackened Hills* (Dec. 26); *Girl of the Manor* (Dec. 28); *Loneliness of Neglect* (Dec. 30)

1913

The Fraud That Failed (Jan. 4); *Another Man's Wife* (Jan. 6); *Calamity Anne's Inheritance* (re-released February 16, 1917) (Jan. 11); *Their Masterpiece* (Jan. 13); *The Awakening* (Jan. 16); *The Silver Plated Gun* (Jan. 23); *Women Left Alone* (Feb. 1); *Calamity Anne's Vanity* (re-released November 30, 1916) (Feb. 8); *The Romance* (Feb. 15); *The Finer Things* (Feb. 17); *Love Is Blind* (Feb. 22); *High and Low* (March 1); *The Greater Love* (March 3); **The Jocular Winds* (March 6); *Calamity Anne—Detective* (re-released February 23, 1917) (March 10); **When a Woman Won't* (March 17); *An Eastern Flower* (March 22); **Cupid Never Ages* (March 24); *Calamity Anne's Beauty* (March 29); *Matches* (April 3); *Woman's Honor* (April 12); *In Another's Nest* (April 17); *Boobs and Bricks* (April 21); *Calamity Anne's Trust* (April 26); *Oil on Troubled Waters* (April 28); *The Road to Ruin* (May 3); **Human Kindness* (May 8); **Angel of the Canyons* (May 12); **The Great Harmony* (May 17); *Calamity Anne Parcel Post* (May 22); *The Ashes of Three* (May 26); *Her Big Story* (May 31); *The Wishing Seat* (June 5); **The Marine Law* (June 21); *Travelers of the Road* (September 20)

PRODUCER

The Wooers of Mountain Kate (1912); *The Ways of Fate* (1913)

From here on, all films are assumed to be directed by Dwan unless otherwise noted. The following abbreviations are also used:

D= Director, P=Producer, S= Screenplay,
C= Cinematographer, E= Editor, M=Music

1913

In Slavery Days (Universal-Rex) D: Otis Turner. S: Otis Turner, Dwan. Cast: Robert Z. Leonard, Margarita Fischer, Jane Ainsley, Edna Maison, Iva Shepard. 2 reels. Released May 22, 1913.

The Spirit of the Flag (Universal–101 Bison) S: Wallace Reid. Cast: Wallace Reid, Pauline Bush, Jessalyn Van Trump, Arthur Rosson, David Kirkland, Marshall Neilan. 2 reels. Released June 7, 1913.

In Love and War aka *The Call to Arms* (Universal-Bison) S: Dwan. Cast: Pauline Bush, Marshall Neilan, Wallace Reid. 2 reels. Released June 17, 1913.

Women and War (Universal-Bison) S: Wallace Reid. Cast: Pauline Bush, Jessalyn Van Trump, Wallace Reid, Marshall Neilan. 2 reels. Released June 21, 1913.

The *Powder Flash of Death* (Universal–101 Bison) S: Dwan. Cast: Wallace Reid, Marshall Neilan, J.D. Kirkland, Pauline Bush, Jessalyn Van Trump. 2 reels. Released July 8, 1913. Re-released as *The Menace*.

The Guerilla Menace (Universal–101 Bison) Cast: Wallace Reid, Marshall Neilan. Released June 24, 1913. No director for this film has been previously acknowledged but one of Reid's biographers, David W. Menefee, said he found in an archive a photo of Neilan and Reid with their credits and that of Dwan on the back. So this film may be classified as a possible but unconfirmed Dwan credit.

The Picket Guard (Universal-Bison) S: Arthur Rosson, from a poem by Ethelin Elliot Beers. Cast: Wallace Reid, Pauline Bush, Marshall Neilan, Jessalyn Van Trump, David Kirkland. 2 reels (1,830 ft.). Released July 15, 1913.

This photograph from *The Guerilla Menace*, showing Marshall Neilan and Wallace Reid, carried a Dwan credit on the back (from the collection of David W. Menefee, author of *Wally: The True Wallace Reid Story*).

Mental Suicide (Universal-Rex) S: Wallace Reid. Cast: Pauline Bush, Jessalyn Van Trump, Wallace Reid, David Kirkland. 1 reel. Released July 27, 1913.

Robinson Crusoe (Universal–101 Bison) D: Otis Turner. S: Dwan, from the novel by Daniel Defoe. Cast: Robert Z. Leonard, Edward Alexander, Charles Travis, Margarita Fischer. 3 reels. Released July 29, 1913.

Man's Duty (Universal-Rex) S: Maurice De La Parelle. Cast: Wallace Reid, Marshall Neilan, Jessalyn Van Trump, Pauline Bush. 1 reel (955 ft.). Released Aug. 10, 1913.

The Animal (Universal-Rex) S: Dwan. Cast: Marshall Neilan, Wallace Reid, Pauline Bush, Jessalyn Van Trump, D. Barlow. 1 reel (995 ft.). Released August 17, 1913.

The Harvest of Flame D: Wallace Reid, Dwan. S: Wallace Reid. P: Dwan. Cast: William Walters, Pauline Bush, Marshall Neilan, Wallace Reid. 1500 ft. Released Aug. 21, 1913.

Uncle Tom's Cabin (Universal-Imp) D: Otis Turner. S: Dwan. Cast: Margarita Fischer, Gertrude Short, Harry A. Pollard, Edward Alexander, Iva Shepard. 3 reels. Released Aug. 25, 1913.

The Wall of Money (Universal-Rex) S: Marshall Neilan. Cast: Wallace Reid, Pauline Bush, Marshall Neilan, Jessalyn Van Trump, James MacQuarrie. 2 reels. Released Sept. 21, 1913.

The Echo of a Song (Universal-Rex) S: Maurice De La Parelle. Cast: Pauline Bush, Murdock MacQuarrie, Jessalyn Van Trump, Gertrude Trump. 1 reel. Released Oct. 12, 1913.

The Criminals (Universal-Rex) S: Maurice De La Parelle. Cast: Jessalyn Van Trump, Pauline Bush, Murdock MacQuarrie, Arthur Rosson, Richard Rosson, William Lloyd, William Walters. 2 reels. Released Oct. 19, 1913.

The Restless Spirit (Universal-Victor) S: Dwan, from Thomas Gray's poem *Elegy Written in a Country Churchyard*. C: Walter Prichard. Cast: J. Warren Kerrigan, Pauline Bush, Jessalyn Van Trump, William Worthington, George Periolat. 3 reels. Released Oct. 27, 1913.

Jewels of Sacrifice (Universal-Rex) S: Maurice De La Parelle. Cast: Pauline Bush. 1 reel. Released Nov. 2, 1913.

The Primeval Test (Universal-Rex) D: Otis Turner. S: Dwan. Cast: Robert Z. Leonard, Margarita Fischer, John Burton, Reese Gardner. 2 reels. Released Nov. 6, 1913.

Back to Life (Universal-Victor) S: Maurice De La Parelle Cast: J. Warren Kerrigan, William Worthington, Pauline Bush, Lon Chaney, Jessalyn Van Trump. 2 reels. Released Nov. 24, 1913.

The Barrier of Bars (Universal-Victor) Cast: J. Warren Kerrigan, Jessalyn Van Trump, George Periolat, William Worthington. 1 reel. Released Dec. 1, 1913.

Red Margaret, Moonshiner (Universal–Gold Seal) S: Jeanie Macpherson. A: Pauline Bush, Lon Chaney, Murdock MacQuarrie, James Neill. 2 reels. R: Dec. 9, 1913. Re-released Dec. 21, 1916, as a one-reeler, re-titled *Moonshine Blood*.

Bloodhounds of the North (Universal–Gold Seal) S: Arthur Rosson. A: William Lloyd, Pauline Bush, James Neill, Murdock MacQuarrie, Lon Chaney. 2 reels. Released Dec. 23, 1913.

The Field Foreman (Universal–Victor) A: J. Warren Kerrigan, Jessalyn Van Trump, William Walters, Edith Boswick, George Periolat, Clara Breyers. 1 reel. Released Dec. 29, 1913.

He Called Her In (Universal) S: Dwan, from a poem by James Whitcomb Riley. A: Pauline Bush, Jessalyn Van Trump, Murdock MacQuarrie. 1 reel. Dubious credit

The Chase Dubious credit

The Battle of Wills (Western Features Film Company) Dwan is said to have made this film for a new company begun by Aubrey Kennedy but no record has been found of its release.

1914

The Lie (Universal–Gold Seal) S: Jeanie Macpherson. Cast: Murdock MacQuarrie, Pauline Bush, Lon Chaney, William Lloyd, Richard Rosson, Arthur Rosson, Fred McKay, James Neill. 2 reels. Released Jan. 6, 1914.

The Honor of the Mounted (Universal–Gold Seal) S: Arthur Rosson. Cast: Pauline Bush, Lon Chaney, Murdock MacQuarrie, James Neill, Gertrude Short. 2 reels. Released Feb. 17, 1914.

Remember Mary Magdalene (Universal-Victor) S: Dwan. Cast: Pauline Bush, Murdock MacQuarrie, Lon Chaney. 1 reel. Released Feb. 23, 1914.

Discord and Harmony (Universal–Gold Seal) S: Arthur Rosson, based on an incident in the life of Beethoven. Cast: Pauline Bush, Murdock MacQuarrie, Lon Chaney, Allan Forrest, James Neill, John Burton. 3 reels. Released March 17, 1914.

The Menace to Carlotta (Universal-Rex) aka *Carlotta the Bead Stringer* S: Lon Chaney. Cast: W.C. Dowlan, Pauline Bush, Murdock MacQuarrie, Lon Chaney, John Burton. 1 reel. Released March 22, 1914.

The Embezzler (Universal–Gold Seal) S: Dwan. Cast: Pauline Bush, Murdock MacQuarrie, Lon Chaney, William C. Dowlan, William Lloyd, Richard Rosson, Gertrude Short. 2 reels. Released March 31, 1914.

The Lamb, the Woman, the Wolf (Universal–101 Bison) S: Dwan. Cast: Pauline Bush, Lon Chaney, Murdock MacQuarrie. 3 reels. Released April 4, 1914.

The End of the Feud (Universal-Rex) S: Richard Rosson. Cast: Murdock MacQuarrie, Pauline Bush, Lon Chaney, William Lloyd, William C. Dowlan. 1 reel. Released April 12, 1914.

The Test (Universal-Nestor) D: Wallace Reid. S: Allan Dwan. Cast: Wallace Reid, Dorothy Davenport, Tom Santschi, Ed Brady. 2 reels. Released April 15, 1914.

The Tragedy of Whispering Creek (Universal–101 Bison) S: Dwan, Lon Chaney (each credited in separate publications). Cast: Murdock MacQuarrie, Pauline Bush, Lon Chaney, William C. Dowlan, George Cooper, Mary Ruby, John Burton, William Lloyd, Doc Crane. 2 reels. Released May 2, 1914.

The Unlawful Trade (Universal) S: George Cooper. Cast: Pauline Bush, William Lloyd, George Cooper, William C. Dowlan, Lon Chaney, Murdock MacQuarrie. 1 reel. Released May 14, 1914.

The Forbidden Room (Universal–101 Bison) S: Bess Meredyth. C: L.O. Bartholomew Cast: Murdock MacQuarrie, Pauline Bush, William C. Dowlan, Lon Chaney, John Burton. 3 reels. Released June 20, 1914.

The Hopes of Blind Alley (Universal–101 Bison) S: Dwan, Murdock MacQuarrie. Continuity: Grace Johnson. C: L.O. Bartholomew Cast: Murdock MacQuarrie, Pauline Bush, George Cooper, William C. Dowlan. 3 reels. Released July 4, 1914.

The Great Universal Mystery (Universal-Nestor) Cast: King Baggot, Pauline Bush, Ford Sterling, William Clifford, Lois Weber, Lee Moran, Ella Hall, Hobart Henley, William Welsh, Betty Schade, Leah Baird, Howard Crampton, Al Christie, Carl Laemmle, Maurice Fleckles, Herman Fichtenberg, Allen Curtis, Florence Lawrence, Francis Ford, Robert Z. Leonard, Cleo Madison, Victoria Forde, Murdock MacQuarrie, Ethel Grandin, Alexander Gadin, Rupert Julian, Edna Maison, Edmund Mortimer, Frank Crane, J.C. Graham, Wilfred Lucas, F.A. Van Husan, J. V. Bryson, Henry MacRae, J. Warren Kerrigan, Grace Cunard, Herbert Rawlinson, Phillips Smalley, Eddie Lyons, William Shay, Irene Wallace, Matt Moore, Marie Walcamp, Frank Smith, William C. Dowlan, Herbert Brenon, Isadore Bernstein, Otis Turner, Bob Thornby, David Horsley, Fred Balshofer. 1 reel. Released July 10, 1914.

Richelieu (Universal–101 Bison) S: Dwan, from the play by E. Bulwer Lytton. Cast: Pauline Bush, Murdock MacQuarrie, William C. Dowlan, Lon Chaney, Robert Chandler, Edna Maison, James Neill, Edythe Chapman, William Lloyd, Richard Rosson, Frank Rice, John Burton. 4 reels. Released Sept. 26, 1914. (According to a review in *Moving Picture World*, a six-reel version had been released and/or previewed in March.)

The Trey of Hearts (Universal–Gold Seal) 15 episode serial. D: Wilfred Lucas. S: Dwan, Bess Meredyth. Story: Louis Joseph Vance. Cast: Cleo Madison, Edward Sloman, George Larkin, Ray Hanford, Thomas Walsh, Charles Brinley, Doris Pawn, George Backus. Released Aug. 4 to November 10, 1914.

The Unwelcome Mrs. Hatch (Famous Players) Dwan's direction of this film is unconfirmed. Adapted from a play by Mrs. Burton Harrison. Cast: Henrietta Crosman, Walter Craven, Harold Lockwood, Lorraine Huling, Gertrude Norman. 4 reels. Released Sept. 10, 1914.

Wildflower (Famous Players) S: Dwan, Eva Unsell. Story: Mary Germaine. Cast: Marguerite Clark, Harold Lockwood, James Cooley, Jack Pickford. 4 reels. Released Oct. 15, 1914.

The County Chairman (Famous Players) S: Dwan, from a play by George Aide. Cast: Maclyn Arbuckle, Wellington Playter, Harold Lockwood, Daisy Robinson, William Lloyd, Helen Aubrye, Wilis P. Sweatnam. 5 reels. Released Oct. 26, 1914.

A Small Town Girl (Universal–101 Bison) S: Beatrice Van. C: L.O. Bartholomew. Cast: William Lloyd, Richard Rosson, Pauline Bush, Rupert Julian, Murdock MacQuarrie, Lon Chaney. 3 reels. Released Nov. 7, 1914.

The Straight Road (Famous Players) Adapted from a play by Clyde Fitch. Cast: Gladys Hanson, William Russell, Arthur Hoops, Iva Shepard, Lorraine Huling. 4 reels. Released Nov. 12, 1914.

Damon and Pythias (Universal-Rex) D: Otis Turner. S: Dwan. xxxxx: Bulwer Lytton. Cast: William Worthington, Herbert Rawlinson, Cleo Madison, Anna Little, Frank Floyd, Helen Wright. 6 reels. Released Nov. 23, 1914.

The Conspiracy (Famous Players) Adapted from a play by Robert B. Baker, John Emerson. Cast: John Emerson, Lois Meredith, Francis Byrne, Harold Lockwood, Iva Shepherd, Hal Clarendon, Dodson Mitchell, Edward Durand. 4 reels. Released Dec. 10, 1914.

1915

The Dancing Girl (Famous Players) Adapted from a play by Henry Arthur Jones. Cast: Florence Reed, William Russell, Fuller Melish, Eugene Ormonde, Malcolm Williams. 5 reels. Released Jan. 11, 1915.

The Country Boy (Lasky Feature Play Company) D: Fred Thompson. P: Dwan. From a play by Edgar Selwyn, Cecil DeMille. Cast: Marshall Neilan, Loyola O'Connor. 5 reels. Released Feb. 18, 1915. Dwan's credit is unconfirmed.

David Harum (Famous Players) Adapted from a novel by Edward Noyes Westcott. C: Hal Rosson. E: William Le Baron. Cast: William H. Crane, Kate Meeks, Harold Lockwood, May Allison, Hal Clarendon, Russell Bassett. 5 reels. Released Feb. 22, 1915.

The Love Route (Famous Players) Adapted from a play by Edward Peple. Cast: Harold Lockwood, Winifred Kingston, Donald Crisp, Jack Pickford. 4 reels. Released Feb. 25, 1915.

The Commanding Officer (Famous Players) Adapted from a play by Theodore Burt Sayre. Cast: Alice Dovey, Donald Crisp, Marshall Neilan, Douglas Gerrard, Jack Pickford. 4 reels. Released March 25, 1915.

May Blossom (Famous Players) Adapted from a play by David Belasco. Cast: Gertrude Robinson, Donald Crisp, Marshall Neilan, Russell Bassett, Gertrude Norman. 4 reels. Released April 15, 1915.

The Pretty Sister of Jose (Famous Players) Adapted from a novel by Frances Hodgson. Cast: Marguerite Clark, Jack Pickford, Rupert Julian, Teddy Sampson, Gertrude Norman, Dick Rosson, William Lloyd, Edythe Chapman. 5 reels. Released May 31, 1915.

A Girl of Yesterday (Famous Players) S: Mary Pickford. Story: Wesley C. MacDermott. Cast: Mary Pickford, Marshall Neilan, Jack Pickford, Frances Marion, Glenn Martin, Donald Crisp, Douglas Gerrard, Kenneth Douglas. 4 reels. Released Oct. 7, 1915.

The Foundling (Famous Players) P: Mary Pickford. S: Frances Marion. Cast: Mary Pickford, Robert Cain, Gertrude Norman. 5 reels. The film was destroyed in a fire before its scheduled release of Dec. 27, 1915. It was then remade with Pickford again in the lead but with some other cast changes. The new version, directed by John O'Brien, was released in 1916.

Jordan Is a Hard Road (Fine Arts–Triangle) S: Dwan. From a novel by Gilbert Parker. P: D.W. Griffith. Cast: Frank Campeau, Dorothy Gish, Owen Moore, Sarah Traux, Ralph Lewis, Mabel Wiles, Fred Burns, Lester Perry, Jim Kid, Walter Long. 5 reels. Released Dec. 19, 1915.

1916

Betty of Graystone (Fine Arts–Triangle) P: D.W. Griffith. S: F.M. Pierson. Cast: Dorothy Gish, Owen Moore, George Fawcett, Kate Bruce, Albert Tavernier, Kid McCoy, John Beck, Warner P. Richmond, Grace Rankin, Macey Harlan, Eugene Ormonde. 5 reels. Released Feb. 20, 1916.

The Habit of Happiness (Fine Arts–Triangle) P: D.W. Griffith. S: Dwan, Shannon Fife. Cast: Douglas Fairbanks, George Fawcett, Dorothy West, George Backus, Grace Rankin, Macey Harlan, William Jefferson. 5 reels. Released April 2, 1916.

The Good Bad Man (Fine Arts–Triangle) P: D.W. Griffith. S: Douglas Fairbanks. C: Victor Fleming. Cast: Douglas Fairbanks, Joseph Singleton, Bessie Love, Sam De Grasse, Mary Alden, George Beranger, Pomeroy "Doc" Cannon, Fred Burns. 5 reels. Released May 7, 1916.

An Innocent Magdalene (Fine Arts–Triangle) P: D.W. Griffith. S: Roy Sumerville. Story: Granville Warwick (a D.W. Griffith pseudonym). Cast: Lillian Gish, Spottiswoode Aitken, Sam De Grasse, Mary Alden, Seymour Hastings, Jennie Lee, William de Vaull. 5 reels. Released June 18, 1916.

The Half-Breed (Fine Arts–Triangle) P: D.W. Griffith. S: Anita Loos. From the novella *In the Carquinez Woods* by Bret Harte. Cast: Douglas Fairbanks, Alma Rubens, Sam De Grasse, Jewel Carmen, Tom Wilson, Frank Brownlee, George Beranger. 5 reels. Released July 30, 1916.

Manhattan Madness (Fine Arts–Triangle) P: D.W. Griffith. S: Charles T. Dazey. Story: E.V. Durling. Cast: Douglas Fairbanks, Jewel Carmen, George Beranger, Ruth Darling, Eugene Ormonde, Macey Harlan, Warner P. Richmond. 5 reels. Released Oct. 1, 1916.

Fifty-Fifty (Fine Arts–Triangle) P: D.W. Griffith. S: Dwan, Robert Shirley. Cast: Norma Talmadge, J.W. Johnston, Marie Chambers, Ruth Darling, H.S. Northrup, Frank Currier, Dodson Mitchell, Warner P. Richmond. 5 reels. Released Oct. 22, 1916.

1917

Panthea (Talmadge–Selznick Pictures) S: Dwan. From a play by Monckton Hoffe. C: Roy Overbaugh, Harold Rosson. Assistant Directors: Erich von Stroheim, Arthur Rosson. Cast: Norma Talmadge,

Earle Fox, Roger Lytton, Murdock MacQuarrie, George Fawcett, Erich von Stroheim, Frank Currier, Norbert Wicki, Herbert Barry, Jack Meredith, Henry Thorpe, William Abbington, Winifred Harris. 5 reels. Released January 1917.

The Man Who Made Good (Triangle) D: Arthur Rosson. Supervisor: Dwan. S: Robert Shirley. C: Roy Overbaugh. Cast: Jack Devereaux, Winifred Allen, Henry P. Dixon, Barney Gilmore. 5 reels. Released May 13, 1917.

American That's All (Triangle) D: Arthur Rosson. Supervisor: Dwan. S: Robert Shirley. C: Roy Overbaugh. Assistant Director: Dick Rosson. Cast: Jack Devereaux, Winifred Allen, Walter Walker, Mrs. Blanche Davenport, Charles Mussett, George Renavent. 5 reels. Released June 3, 1917.

Her Excellency the Governor (Triangle) D: Albert Parker. Supervisor: Dwan. S: Robert Shirley. C: Roy Vaughn. Cast: Hedda Hopper (billed as Elda Millar), Wilfred Lucas, Joseph Kilgour, Regan Hughston, Walter Walker, Edith Speare, Albert Perry. 5 reels. Released July 1, 1917.

A Successful Failure (Triangle) D: Arthur Rosson. Supervisor: Dwan. S: Robert Shirley. C: Roy Overbaugh. Assistant Director: Dick Rosson. Cast: Jack Devereaux, Winifred Allen, George Senaut. 5 reels. Released July 22, 1917.

The Food Gamblers (Triangle) D: Albert Parker. Supervisor: Dwan. S: Robert Shirley. C: Roy Vaughn. Cast: Wilfred Lucas, Hedda Hopper (billed as Elda Millar), Mac Barnes, Russell Simpson, Jack Snyder, Eduardo Ciannelli. 5 reels. Released August 5, 1917.

Grafters (Triangle) D: Arthur Rosson. Supervisor: Dwan. S: James W. Adams. C: Roy Overbaugh. Assistant Director: Dick Rosson. Cast: Jack Devereaux, Frank Currier, Anna Lehr, Irene Leonard, George Siegmann, Robert Crimmins. 5 reels. Released Aug. 26, 1917.

The Haunted House (Triangle) D: Albert Parker. Supervisor: Dwan. S: Robert Shirley. C: Roy Vaughn. Cast: Winifred Allen, Dick Rosson, Albert Parker, Albert Day, Mac Barnes, Mabel Wright, Eddie Kelly. 5 reels. Released Sept. 16, 1917.

Fighting Odds (Goldwyn Picture Corporation) P: Arthur Hopkins. S: Roi Cooper Megrue, Irvin S. Cobb. C: Rene Guissart. Art Director: Hugo Ballin. Cast: Maxine Elliott, Henry Clive, Charles Dalton, George Odell, Regan Hughston, William T. Carleton, Eric Hudson. 5 reels. Released Oct. 7, 1917.

Cassidy (Triangle) D: Arthur Rosson. Supervisor: Dwan. S: Larry Evans. C: Roy Overbaugh. Cast: Dick Rosson, Frank Currier, Pauline Curley, Mac Alexander, Eddie Sturgis, John O'Connor. 5 reels. Released Oct. 21, 1917.

The Man Hater (Triangle) D: Albert Parker. Supervisor: Dwan. S: Mary Brecht Pulver. C: Roy Vaughn. Assistant Director: Thomas F. Tracey. Cast: Winifred Allen, Jack Meredith, Jessie Shirley, Robert Vivian, Harry Neville, Marguerite Gale. 5 reels. Released Oct. 28, 1917.

A Case at Law (Triangle) D: Arthur Rosson. Supervisor: Dwan. S: William Dudley Pelly. C: Roy Overbaugh. Cast: Dick Rosson, Pauline Curley, Ed Sturgis, Jack Dillon. 5 reels. Released Nov. 18, 1917.

For Valor (Triangle) D: Albert Parker. Supervisor: Dwan. S: Robert Shirley. Adapted from the story *Melia-no-Good* by I.A.R. Wylie. C: Roy Vaughn. Assistant Director: Thomas F. Tracey. Cast: Winifred Allen, Richard Barthelmess, Mabel Ballin, Henry Weaver. 5 reels. Released Nov. 25, 1917.

A Modern Musketeer (Artcraft–Famous Players–Lasky) P: Douglas Fairbanks. S: Dwan. From the magazine story *D'Artagnan of Kansas* by F.R. Lyle, Jr. C: Victor Fleming. Cast: Douglas Fairbanks, Marjorie Daw, Frank Campeau, Kathleen Kirkham, Tully Marshall, Eugene Ormonde, ZaSu Pitts. 5 reels. Released Dec. 31, 1917.

1918

From Two to Six (Triangle) D: Albert Parker. Supervisor: Dwan. Adapted from Arthur Stringer's *The Bottom Thief.* C: Roy Vaughn. Cast: Winifred Allen, Earle Fox, Forrest Robinson, Robert Fisher, Margaret Greene. 5 reels. Released Feb. 17, 1918.

Headin' South (Artcraft–Famous Players–Lasky) D: Arthur Rosson. Supervisor: Dwan. P: Douglas Fairbanks. C: Hugh McLung, Harry Thorpe. Cast: Douglas Fairbanks, Frank Campeau, James Mason, Catherine MacDonald, Jack Holt, Marjorie Daw. 5 reels. Released Feb. 25, 1918.

Mr. Fix-It (Artcraft–Famous Players–Lasky) S: Dwan. From a suggestion by Ernest Butterworth. P: Douglas Fairbanks. C: Hugh McClung. Cast: Douglas Fairbanks, Wanda Hawley, Marjorie Daw, Frank Campeau, Catherine MacDonald, Leslie Stuart, Ida Waterman, Alice Smith, Mrs. H.R. Hancock. 5 reels. Released April 15, 1918.

Bound in Morocco (Artcraft–Famous Players–Lasky) S: Dwan. P: Douglas Fairbanks. C: Hugh McLung. Cast: Douglas Fairbanks, Pauline Curley, Tully Marshall, Edythe Chapman, Frank Campeau, Jay Dwiggins, Marjorie Daw. 5 reels. Released Aug. 5, 1918.

He Comes Up Smiling (Artcraft–Famous Players–Lasky) S: Frances Marion. From a novel by Charles Sherman and a play by Byron Ongley and Emil Mytray. P: Douglas Fairbanks. C: Joseph August. Cast: Douglas Fairbanks, Herbert Standing, Bull Montana, Albert MacQuarrie, Marjorie Daw, Frank Campeau, Jay Dwiggins, Kathleen Kirkham. 5 reels. Released Sept. 15, 1918.

Dwan began work on Fairbanks' *Arizona* as either director or supervisor but withdrew during shooting. It is not known if any of Dwan's footage was in the final cut.

1919

Cheating Cheaters (Select Pictures Group) P: Lewis J. Selznick. S: Kathryn Stuart, from a play by Max Marcin. C: Arthur Edeson. Cast: Clara Kimball Young, Anna Q. Nilsson, Jack Holt, Frederick Burton, Frank Campeau, Nicholas Dunsew, Mayme Kelso, Tully Marshall, Edwin Stevens, Jess Singleton, Eleanor Hancock, W.A. Caroll. 5 reels. Released Feb. 1, 1919.

Getting Mary Married (Cosmopolitan-Select) P: Marion Davies. S: John Emerson, Anita Loos. C: H. Lyman Broening. Cast: Marion Davies, Norman Kerry, Matt Moore, Frederick Burton, Amelia Sum merville, Constance Beaumar, Elmer Grandin. 5 reels. Released April 19, 1919.

Sahara aka *Forbidden Fire* (Hodkinson) D: Arthur Rosson. Supervisor: Dwan. P: J. Parker Read, Jr. S: C. Gardner Sullivan. C: Charles Stumar. Cast: Louise Glaum, Matt Moore, Edwin Stevens, Master Pat Moore, Nigel de Brulier. 7 reels. Released June 29, 1919.

The Dark Star (Cosmopolitan–Paramount–Artcraft) S: Frances Marion. From a novel by Robert W. Chambers. C: H. Lyman Broening. Cast: Marion Davies, Norman Kerry, Dorothy Green, Matt Moore, Ward Crane, George Cooper, Arthur Earle, G. Butler Conblough, Emil Hoch, James Laffey. 6 reels. Released July 27, 1919.

Soldiers of Fortune (Mayflower-Realart) P: W.W. Hodkinson. From a novel by Richard Harding Davis. C: H. Lyman Broening, Sol Polito. Associate Director: Arthur Rosson. Assistant Director: James Hogan. Cast: Norman Kerry, Anna Q. Nilsson, Ward Crane, Pauline Starke, Melbourne McDowell, Wallace Beery, Wilfred Lucas, Philo McCullough, Herold Lindsay, Frank Wally, Fred Kohler. 7 reels. Released Nov. 22, 1919.

1920

The Luck of the Irish (Mayflower-Realart) S: Dwan. Story: Harold McGrath. C: H. Lyman Broening, Glen MacWilliams. Cast: James Kirkwood, Anna Q. Nilsson, Ward Crane, Harry Northrup, Ernest Butterworth. 6 reels. Released Jan. 15, 1920.

A Splendid Hazard (Mayflower–First National) D: Arthur Rosson. P: Dwan. S: Harold McGrath. C: Glen MacWilliams. Cast: Henry B. Walthall, Rosemary Theby, Ann Forrest, Hardee Kirkland. 6 reels. Released Sept. 26, 1920.

In the Heart of a Fool (Mayflower–First National) P: Dwan. S: Lillian Ducey, from a novel by William Allen White. C: H. Lyman Broening. Cast: James Kirkwood, Anna Q. Nilsson, Mary Thurman, Philo McCullough, Ward Crane, John Burton, Margaret Campbell, Percy Challenger, Arthur Hoyt. 7 reels. Released Oct. 23, 1920.

The Forbidden Thing (Associated Producers) P: Dwan. S: Dwan. Story: Mary Mears. C: Tony Gaudio. Cast: James Kirkwood, Helen Jerome Eddy, Marcia Manon, King Baggot, Gertrude Claire, Jack Roseleigh, Arthur Thalasso, Newton Hall, Harry Griffith, Katherine Norton. 6 reels. Released Nov. 7, 1920.

1921

A Perfect Crime (Associated Producers) P-S: Dwan. Story: Carl Clausen. C: H. Lyman Broening. Cast: Monte Blue, Jacqueline Logan, Stanton Heck, Hardee Kirkland. 5 reels. Released March 27, 1921.

The Scoffer (Mayflower–First National) P: Dwan. S: Lillian Ducey. Story: Val Cleveland. C: H. Lyman Broening. Cast: Mary Thurman, James Kirkwood, Philo McCullough, Rhea Mitchell, John Burton, Noah Beery, Eugenie Besserer, Georgie Stone, Bernard Durning, Ward Crane. 7 reels. Released March 1921.

A Broken Doll (Associated Producers) P-S: Dwan. Story: *Johnny Cucabod* by Wilbur Hall, adapted by Lillian Ducey. C: H. Lyman Broening, L. William O'Connell. Cast: Monte Blue, Mary Thurman, Mary Jane Irving, Les Bates, Lizette Thorne, Arthur Millette, Jack Riley. 5 reels. Released June 12, 1921.

The Sin of Martha Queed (Mayflower–Associated Exhibitors) S: Dwan. C: Tony Gaudio. Cast: Mary Thurman, Joseph J. Dowling, Eugenie Besserer, Frank Lee, Niles Welch, George Hackathorne, Frank Campeau, Gertrude Claire. 6 reels. Released Oct. 6, 1921.

1922

The Hidden Woman (Nanuet Amusement Corporation–American Releasing Corp.) P: Dwan. Cast: Evelyn Nesbit, Crauford Kent, Murdock MacQuarrie, Ruth Darling, Albert Hart, Russell Thaw, Mary Alden, Jack Evans. 5 reels. Released April 2, 1922.

Robin Hood (Fairbanks Picture Corporation–United Artists) P: Douglas Fairbanks S: Lotta Woods. Story: Elton Thomas (a collective pseudonym), based on tales of Robin Hood. C: Arthur Edeson. Second Cameraman: Charles Richardson. Art Director: Wilfred Buckland. Assistant Art Directors: Irvin J. Martin, Edward M. Langley. Costumes: Mitchell Leisen. E: William Nolan. Assistant Director: Richard Rosson. Literary Consultant: Edward Knoblock. Research Director: Dr. Arthur Woods. Cast: Douglas Fairbanks, Wallace Beery, Enid Bennett, Sam De Grasse, Paul Dickey, William Lowery, Roy Coulson, Billie Bennett, Merrill McCormick, Wilson Benge, Willard Louis, Alan Hale, Maine Geary, Lloyd Talman, Kid McCoy, Bull Montana. 10 reels. Released Oct. 18, 1922.

Superstition (Lee–Bradford Corp.) Cast: Jack Devereaux, Vera Searl, Stafford Windsor. 5 reels (4,480 feet). Released Nov. 22, 1922. Some confusion surrounds this unreleased 1917 Triangle production, which was ultimately sold to Lee Bradford, who distributed it on a states rights basis. It is almost certainly *The Jinx Jumper* which was announced on the Triangle schedule for August 26 release and then yanked for *Grafters*. At least one modern source thought this was just a title change but while Devereaux starred in both films, according to the Triangle release chart of the August 26, 1917, issue of *Motion Picture News*, Devereaux's co-star in *The Jinx Jumper* was Vera (also cited as "Veta") Searl, who was not listed in the cast of *Grafters*. Also, according to Triangle's publicity magazine, this film dealt with superstitions, not thievery. The picture was most likely supervised by Dwan and directed by Arthur Rosson, who helmed all the other Devereaux Triangle features.

1923

The Glimpses of the Moon (Famous Players–Lasky–Paramount) P: Dwan. S: E. Lloyd Sheldon, Edfrid Bingham. From a novel by Edith Wharton. C: Hal Rosson. Cast: Bebe Daniels, Nita Naldi, David Powell, Maurice Costello, Rubye De Remer, Charles Gerard, William Quirk, Pearl Sindelar. 6 reels Released March 25, 1923.

Lawful Larceny (Famous Players–Lasky–Paramount) S: John Lynch. From a play by Samuel Shipman. C: Hal Rosson. Cast: Hope Hampton, Conrad Nagel, Nita Naldi, Lew Cody, Russell Griffin, Yvonne Hughes, Dolores Costello, Gilda Gray, Florence O'Denishawn, Alice Maison. 5,503 feet. Released July 23, 1923.

Zaza (Famous Players–Lasky–Paramount) P: Dwan. S: Albert Shelby Le Vino. From a play by Pierre Berton, Charles Simon. C: Hal Rosson. Cast: Gloria Swanson, H.B. Warner, Ferdinand Gottschalk, Lucille La Verne, Mary Thurman, Yvonne Hughes, Riley Hatch, Roger Lytton, Ivan Linow, Helen Mack. 7,076 feet. Released Sept. 16, 1923.

Big Brother (Famous Players–Lasky–Paramount) P: Dwan. S: Paul Sloane. From a novel by Rex Beach. C: Hal Rosson. Cast: Tom Moore, Edith Roberts, Raymond Hatton, Joe King, Mickey Bennett, Charles Henderson, Paul Panzer, Neill Kelley, William Black, Martin Faust, Milton Herman, Florence Ashbrook, Yvonne Hughes, Charles Hammond. 7 reels (7,080 feet). Released Dec. 23, 1923.

1924

A Society Scandal (Famous Players–Lasky–Paramount) P: Dwan. S: Forrest Halsey. From the play *The Laughing Lady* by Alfred Sutro. C: Hal Rosson. Cast: Gloria Swanson, Rod La Rocque, Ricardo Cortez, Allan Simpson, Ida Waterman, Thelma Converse, Fraser Coalter, Catherine Proctor, Wilfred Donovan, Yvonne Hughes, Catherine Coleburn, Marie Shelton, Dorothy Stokes, Cornelius Keefe. 6 reels. Released March 24, 1924.

Manhandled (Famous Players–Lasky–Paramount) P: Dwan. S: Frank Tuttle. Story: Arthur Stringer. C: Hal Rosson. E: William Le Baron. Cast: Gloria Swanson, Tom Moore, Lilyan Tashman, Ian Keith, Arthur Housman, Paul McAllister, Frank Morgan, M. Collosse, Marie Shelton, Carrie Scott, Frank Allworth, Ann Pennington, Brooke Johns. 6,998 feet. Released Aug. 4, 1924.

Her Love Story (Famous Players–Lasky–Paramount) P: Dwan. S: Frank Tuttle. From the story *Her Majesty, the Queen* by Mary Roberts Rinehart. C: George Webber. C: Gloria Swanson, Ian Keith, George Fawcett, Echling Gayer, Mario Majeroni, Sidney Herbert, Donald Hall, Baroness de Hademann, Paul Panzer, Jane Auburn, Bert Wales, General Lodijensky. 7 reels (6,750 feet). Released Oct. 6, 1924.

The Wages of Virtue (Famous Players–Lasky–Paramount) S: Forrest

Halsey. From a novel by Percival Christopher Wren. C: George Webber. Cast: Gloria Swanson, Ben Lyon, Norman Trevor, Ivan Linow, Armand Cortez, Adrienne D'Ambricourt, Paul Panzer, Joe Moore. 7,093 feet. Released Nov. 10, 1924.

Argentine Love (Famous Players–Lasky–Paramount) P: Dwan. S: Gerald Duffy. Story by Vicente Blasco-Ibanez. Adaptation: John Russell. C: Roy Hunt. Cast: Bebe Daniels, Ricardo Cortez, James Rennie, Mario Majeroni, Russ Whital, Alice Chapin, Julia Hurley, Mark Gonzales, Aurelio Coccia. 6 reels. Released Dec. 29, 1924.

1925

Night Life of New York (Famous Players–Lasky–Paramount) P: Dwan. S: Paul Schofield. Story: Edgar Selwyn. C: George Webber. Cast: Rod LaRocque, Ernest Torrence, Dorothy Gish, Helen Lee Worthing, George Hackathorne, Arthur Housman, Riley Hatch. 6,998 feet. Released July 25, 1924.

The Coast of Folly (Famous Players–Lasky–Paramount) P: Dwan. S: Forrest Halsey. From a novel by Coningsby Dawson. Adaptation: James Creelman. C: George Webber. Cast: Gloria Swanson, Anthony Jowitt, Alec B. Francis, Dorothy Cumming, Jed Prouty, Eugene Besserer, Arthur Housman, Lawrence Gray, Charles Clary, Richard Arlen. 7,001 feet. Released Sept. 12, 1924.

Stage Struck (Famous Players–Lasky–Paramount) P: Dwan. S: Forrest Halsey. Story: Frank R. Adams. Adaptation: Sylvia La Varre. C: George Webber (including two sequences in Technicolor). Assistant Director: Joe Pasternak. Cast: Gloria Swanson, Lawrence Gray, Gertrude Astor, Marguerite Evans, Ford Sterling, Carrie Scott, Emil Hoch, Margery Whittington. 6,691 feet. Released Nov. 16, 1924.

Fifty-Fifty (Encore Pictures–Associated Exhibitors) D: Henri-Diamant Berger. Story: Dwan. C: Henry Cronjager. Cast: Hope Hamption, Lionel Barrymore, Louise Glaum, J. Moy Bennett, Arthur Donaldson, Jean Del Val. A remake of Dwan's 1916 film.

1926

Sea Horses (Famous Players–Lasky–Paramount) P: Dwan. S: James Shelley Hamilton. From a novel by Francis Brett Young. Adaptation: Becky Gardiner. C: James Howe. Cast: Jack Holt, Florence Vidor, William Powell, George Bancroft, Mack Swain, Frank Campeau, Allan Simpson, George Nichols, Mary E. Dow, Dick La Reno, Frank Austin. 6,565 feet. Released Feb. 22, 1926.

Padlocked (Famous Players–Lasky–Paramount) P: Dwan. S: James Shelley Hamilton. From a novel by Rex Beach. Adaptation: Becky Gardiner. C: James Howe. Cast: Lois Moran, Noah Beery, Louise Dresser, Helen Jerome Eddy, Allan Simpson, Florence Turner, Richard Arlen, Charles Lane, Douglas Fairbanks, Jr., Charlot Bird, Josephine Crowell, Andre Lanoy, Irma Kornelia. 6,700 feet. Released Aug. 4, 1926.

Tin Gods (Famous Players–Lasky–Paramount) P: Dwan. S: James Shelley Hamilton. From a play by William Anthony McGuire. Adaptation: Paul Dickey, Howard Emmet Rogers. C: Alvin Wyckoff. Associate Producer: William LeBaron. Cast: Thomas Meighan, Renée Adorée, Aileen Pringle, William Powell, Hale Hamilton, John Harrington, Joe King, Robert E. O'Connor, Delbert Emory Whitten, Jr. 8,568 feet. Released Sept. 6, 1926.

Summer Bachelors (Fox) P: Dwan. S: James Shelley Hamilton. From *Summer Widowers* by Warner Fabian. C: Joseph Ruttenberg. Cast: Madge Bellamy, Allan Forrest, Matt Moore, Hale Hamilton, Leila Hyams, Charles Winninger, Clifford Holland, Olive Tell, Walter Catlett. 6 reels. Released Dec. 18, 1926.

1927

The Music Master (Fox) P: Dwan. S: Philip Klein. From a play by Charles Klein. C: George Webber, William Miller. Assistant Director: Clarence Elmer. Cast: Alec B. Francis, Lois Moran, Neil Hamilton, Norman Trevor, Charles Lane, William T. Tilden, Helen Chandler, Marcia Harris, Kathleen Kerrigan, Howard Cull, Armand Cortez, Leo Feodoroff, Carrie Scott, Dore Davidson, Walter Catlett. 7,754 feet. Released Jan. 23, 1927.

The Military Academy at West Point (Fox Movietone News) 1 reel. Released April 29, 1927.

The *Joy Girl* (Fox) P: Dwan. S: Frances Agnew. Story: May Edginton. C: George Webber, William Miller (with two Technicolor sequences). Cast: Olive Borden, Neil Hamilton, Marie Dressler, Mary Alden, William Norris, Helen Chandler, Jerry Miley, Frank Walsh, Clarence Elmer, Peggy Kelly, Jimmy Grainger, Jr. 5, 877 feet. Released Sept. 24, 1927.

East Side, West Side (Fox) S: Dwan. From a novel by Felix Riesenberg. C: George Webber. Art Director: Sam Corso. Cast: George O'Brien, Virginia Valli, J. Farrell MacDonald, June Collyer, Holmes Herbert, Dora Davidson, Sonia Nodalsky, John Miltern, Frank Dodge, Dan Wolheim, John Dooley, John Kearney, Edward Garvey, Frank Allsworth, William Fredericks. 7 reels (8,154 feet). Released October 22, 1927.

French Dressing (First National) P: Dwan. S: J.L. Campbell. Story: Adelaide Heilbron. Adaptation: Pauline Forney. C: Ernest Haller. E: Terrell Morse. Cast: H.B. Warner, Clive Brook, Lois Wilson, Lilyan Tashman. 6,344 feet. Released Dec. 10, 1927.

1928

The Whip Woman (First National) D: Joseph C. Boyle. P: Dwan. S: Earle Roebuck. Story: Forrest Halsey, Leland Hayward. C: Ernest Haller. Cast: Estelle Taylor, Antonio Moreno, Lowell Sherman, Hedda Hopper, Julanne Johnston, Jack Ackroyd, Loretta Young. 5,087 feet. Released Feb. 11, 1928.

The Mad Hour (First National) D: Joseph C. Boyle. P: Dwan. S: Tom J. Geraghty, from *The Man and the Moment* by Elinor Glyn. C: Ernest Haller. Cast: Sally O'Neill, Alice White, Donald Reed, Larry Kent, Lowell Sherman, Norman Trevor, Eddie Clayton, James Farley, Rose Dione, Tully Marshall, Margaret Livingston, Jack Eagan, Kate Price, Mary Foy, Iona Holmes. 6,625 feet. Released March 4, 1928.

The Big Noise (First National) P: Dwan. S: Tom J. Geraghty. Story: Ben Hecht. Titles: George Marion, Jr. C: Ted Pahle. E: Doris Farrington, Terry Morse Cast: Chester Conklin, Alice White, Bodil Rosing, Sam Hardy, Jack Egan, Ned Sparks, David Torrence. 6 reels (7,412 feet). Released March 25, 1928.

Harold Teen (First National) D: Mervyn LeRoy. P: Robert Kane, Dwan. S: Tom J. Geraghty, from the comic strip by Carl Ed. C: Ernest Haller. E: Leroy Stone. Cast: Arthur Lake, Alice White, Mary Brian, Lucien Littlefield, Jack Duffy, Jack Eagan, Ben Hal, William Bakewell, Lincoln Stedman, Jane Keckley, Hedda Hopper, Virginia Sale. 7,541 feet. Released April 21, 1928.

1929

The Iron Mask (Elton Corporation–United Artists) P: Douglas Fairbanks S: Lotta Woods, based on *The Three Musketeers*, *Twenty Years After* and *The Man in the Iron Mask* by Alexandre Dumas, pere, and the memoirs of D'Artagnan, Richelieu, and Rochefort. Titles and Dialogue: Elton Thomas (collective pseudonym). C: Henry Sharp. Production Designer: Maurice Leloir. Art Director: William Cameron Menzies. Set Directors: Laurence Irving, Burgess Beall, Ben Carré, Miles Borg. Costumes: Leloir, Mary Hallett, Gilbert Clark. E: William Nolan. Assistant Director: H. Bruce Humberstone. Cast: Douglas Fairbanks, Marguerite de la Motte, Leon Barry, Belle Bennett, Dorothy Revier, Rolfe Sedan, William Bakewell, Gordon Thorpe, Vera Lewis, Nigel De Brulier, Ulrich Haupt, Lon Poff, Charlie Stevens, Henry Otto, Stanley J. Standford, Gino Corrado, Robert Parrish, Florence Turner, Fred Cavens, Madame Chalif, Princess Galitzine, Baronne d'Estournelle de Constant. 8,659 feet (silent), 8,855 feet (with talking scenes). Released March 9, 1929.

Tide of Empire (Cosmopolitan-MGM) S: Waldemar Young, from the novel by Peter B. Kyne. Titles: John Colton, Joe Farnham. C: Merritt B. Gerstad. E: Blanche Sewell. Cast: Renée Adorée, George Duryea, William Collier, Jr., George Fawcett, Fred Kohler, James Bradbury, Sr., Harry Gribbon, Paul Hurst. 6,552 feet. Released March 23, 1929.

The Far Call (Fox) S: Seton I. Miller, Walter Woods, from the novel by Edison Marshall. C: Hal Rosson. Cast: Charles Morton, Leila Hyams, Ulrich Haupt, Dan Wolheim, Charles B. Middleton, Arthur Stone, Stanley J. Sandford, Pat Hartigan, Bernard Siegel, Charles Gorman, Willie Fung, Warren Hymer, Frank Chew, Randolph Scott, Ivan Linow, Harry Grip, Sam Baker. Synchronized: 5,313 feet. Silent: 5,282 feet. Released April 28, 1929.

Frozen Justice (Fox) S: Sonya Levien, from a story by Eijnar Mikkelsen. Dialogue: Owen Davis. C: Harold Rosson. Second Unit Location Photography: Charles G. Clarke. E: Harold Schuster. Cast: Lenore Ulric, Robert Frazer, Louis Wolheim, Ulrich Haupt, Laska Winter, Tom Patricola, Alice Lake, Gertrude Astor, Adele Windsor, Warren Hymer, Neyneen Farrell, El Brendel, Lou Morrison, Charles Judels, Joe Rochay, The Meyers Sisters, George MacFarlane, Landers Stevens, Jim Spencer, Arthur Stone, Jack Ackroyd, Gertrude Chorre. 7,170 feet. Released Oct. 13, 1929.

South Sea Rose (Fox) S: Sonya Levien, from the play *La Gringa* by Tom Cushing. Dialogue: Elliot Lester. C: Hal Rosson. E: Harold Schuster. Songs: L. Wolfe Gilbert, Abel Baer. Sets: W.W. Darling. Costumes: Sophie Wachner. Cast: Lenore Ulric, Charles Bickford, Kenneth McKenna, J. Farrell MacDonald, Elizabeth Patterson, Tom Patricola, Ilka Chase, George MacFarlane, Ben Hall, Daphne Pollard, Roscoe Ates, Charlotte Walker, Emile Chautard. Released Dec. 8, 1929.

1930

What a Widow! (Gloria Productions–United Artists) P: Dwan. Executive Producer: Joseph P. Kennedy. S: Josephine Lovett. Dialogue: James Gleason, James Seymour. C: George Barnes. Art Director: Paul Nelson. E: Viola Lawrence. M: Josiah Zuro. Songs: Vincent Youmans. Cast: Gloria Swanson, Owen Moore, Lew Cody, Margaret Livingston, William Holden, Herbert Braggiotti, Gregory Gaye, Adrienne D'Ambricourt, Nella Walker, Daphne Pollard. 90 minutes. Released Sept. 13, 1930.

Man to Man (First National) S: Joseph Jackson, from the *Saturday Evening Post* story *Barber John's Boy* by Ben Ames Williams. C: Ira Morgan. E: George Marks M: Louis Silvers, Erno Rapee. Costumes: Earl Luick. Cast: Grant Mitchell, Phillips Holmes, Lucille Powers, Barbara Weeks, Dwight Frye, Russell Simpson, Paul Nicholson, Robert Emmett O'Connor, George Marion, Otis Harlan, Bill Banker, Charles Sellon, James Hall, Johnny Larkins. 68 minutes. Released Dec. 6, 1930.

1931

Chances (First National) S: Waldemar Young, from a novel by A. Hamilton Gibbs. C: Ernest Haller. Art Director: Esdras Hartley. M: David Mendoza. Costumes: Earl Luick. E: Ray Curtiss. Cast: Douglas Fairbanks, Jr., Rose Hobart, Anthony Bushell, Mary Forbes, Holmes Herbert, Tyrell Davis, Edmund Breon, Harry Allen, Edward Morgan, Florence Britton, Billy Bevan. 71 minutes. Released July 18, 1931.

Wicked (Fox) S: Kenyon Nicholson, Kathryn Scola, from a story by Adela Rogers St. Johns. Associate Producer: John W. Considine, Jr. C: J. Peverell Marley. E: Jack Dennis. Sound: George Leverett. Cast: Elissa Landi, Victor McLaglen, Theodore von Eltz, Una Merkel, Allan Dinehart, Oscar Apfel, Irene Rich, Blanche Payson, Kathleen Kerrigan, Eileen Percy, Mae Busch, Blanche Frederici, Lucille Williams, Alice Lake, Ruth Donnelly, Edmund Breese. 55 minutes. Released Sept. 18, 1931.

1932

While Paris Sleeps (Fox) Story and Screenplay: Basil Woon. Associate Producer: William Sistrom. C: Glen MacWilliams. Art Director: William Darling. E: Paul Weatherwax. Sound: George Leverett. Costumes: Guy S. Duty. Assistant Directors: Earl Rettig, Fred Spencer. Cast: Victor McLaglen, Helen Mack, William Bakewell, Jack La Rue, Rita Roy, Maurice Black, Dot Farley, Lucille LaVerne, Paul Porcasi, Eddie Dillon. 66 minutes. Released May 8, 1932.

Dwan was hired by Columbia to direct FAITH but was fired after three days. He was replaced for one day by Roy William Neill and later by Frank Capra. Dwan's footage was discarded by Capra. By the time of its release, the title was changed to *American Madness*.

Her First Affaire (A St. George–Sterling Production–Associated British) S: Dion Titheradge, Brock Williams, from the play by Frederick Jackson and Merrill Rogers. P: Frank Richardson. C: Geoffrey Faithfull. Art Director: James Elder Wills. E: Dr. Seabourne. Costumes: Gilbert Clark. Cast: Ida Lupino, George Curzon, Diana Napier, Harry Tate, Muriel Aked, Arnold Riches, Kenneth Kove. 72 minutes. Released December 1932 (U.K.), Feb. 17, 1933 (U.S.).

1933

Counsel's Opinion (London Films–Paramount) P: Alexander Korda. S: Dorothy Greenhill, Arthur Wimperis, from the play by Gilbert Wakefield. C: Phil Tannura. Cast: Henry Kendall, Binnie Barnes, Cyril Maude, Lawrence Grossmith, Francis Lister, Harry Tate, Mary Charles, Margaret Baird, Stanley Lathbury. 76 minutes.

I Spy, American title: *The Morning After* (BIP–Wardour Films) S: Dwan, Arthur Woods. P: Walter C. Mycroft. C: James Wilson. Cast: Sally Eilers, Ben Lyon, H.F. Maltby, Harry Tate, Andrews Englemann, Harold Warrender, Dennis Hoey, Henry Victor, Marcelle Rogez. 69 minutes. U.S. release: Aug. 27, 1934.

1934

Hollywood Party (MGM) Uncredited directors included Richard Boleslavsky, Dwan, Russell Mack, Charles Reisner, Roy Rowland,

George Stevens. Animated sequence by Walt Disney. Production Supervisors: Howard Dietz, Harry Rapf. S: Howard Dietz and Arthur Kober. Songs: Richard Rodgers, Lorenz Hart, Walter Donaldson, Gus Kahn, Nacio Herb Brown, Arthur Freed, Howard Dietz, Walter Donaldson. C: James Wong Howe, Hal Rosson. E: George Boemler. Choreography: Seymour Felix, George Hale, Dave Gould. Cast: Jimmy Durante, Charles Butterworth, Polly Moran, Lupe Velez, Jack Pearl, Stan Laurel, Oliver Hardy, Frances Williams, Eddie Quillan, June Clyde, George Givot, Arthur Treacher, Richard Carle, Ben Bard, Tom Kennedy, Robert Young, Ted Healy and the Stooges. 68 minutes. Released May 1934.

1935

Black Sheep (Fox) Executive Producer: Sol M. Wurtzel. S: Allen Rivkin. Story: Dwan. C: Arthur Miller. E: Alexander Troffey. Art Director: Duncan Cramer. Song: "In Other Words I'm In Love": Music by Oscar Levant, lyrics by Sidney Clare. Costumes: Royer. Cast: Edmund Lowe, Claire Trevor, Adrienne Ames, Tom Brown, Herbert Mundin, Eugene Pallette, Jed Prouty, Ford Sterling, Joseph W. Reilly, Billy Bevan, David Torrence, Robert Elliott, Reginald Sheffield, Maude Turner Gordon, Del Henderson. 75 minutes. Released June 14, 1935.

Navy Wife (20th Century–Fox) P: Sol M. Wurtzel. S: Sonya Levien, from the novel *Beauty's Daughter* by Kathleen Norris. Additional Dialogue: Edward T. Lowe. C: John Seitz, Rudolph Maté. E: Alfred De Gaetano. Costumes: Rega. Cast: Claire Trevor, Ralph Bellamy, Jane Darwell, Warren Hymer, Ben Lyon, Kathleen Burke, George Irving, Anne Howard, Jonathan Hale, Ruth Gillette, John Kelly, Susan Fleming, Jed Prouty, Murray Alper. 69 minutes. Released Nov. 29, 1935.

1936

Song and Dance Man (20th Century–Fox) P: Sol M. Wurtzel. S: Maude Fulton, from a play by George M. Cohan. C: Barney McGill. Songs "You're My Favorite One," "On a Holiday in My Playroom," "Join the Party," "Let's Get Going," "Ain't He Good-Looking?" and "Dancing in the Open" by Sidney Clare, Lew Pollack. E: Alfred De Gaetano. Choreography: Fanchon. Assistant Director: Aaron Rosenberg. Cast: Claire Trevor, Paul Kelly, Michael Whalen, Ruth Donnelly, James Burke, Helen Troy, Lester Matthews, Ralf Harolde, Gloria Roy, Margaret Dumont, Billy Bevan, Irene Franklin. 72 minutes. Released March 13, 1936.

Human Cargo (20th Century–Fox) P: Sol M. Wurtzel. S: Jefferson Parker, Doris Malloy, from the novel *I Will Be Faithful* by Kathleen Shepard. C. Daniel B. Clark. E: Louis R. Loeffler. Art Director: Duncan Cramer. Costumes: William Lambert, Gwen Wakeling. Cast. Claire Trevor, Brian Donlevy, Alan Dinehart, Ralph Morgan, Helen Troy, Rita Cansino [Rita Hayworth], Morgan Wallace, Herman Bing, John McGuire, Ralf Harolde, Wade Botelier, Harry Woods, Wilfred Lucas, Tom Ricketts. 66 minutes. Released June 19, 1936.

High Tension (20th Century–Fox) P: Sol M. Wurtzel. S: Louis Breslow, Edward Eliscu, John Patrick. Story: J. Robert Bren, Norman Houston. C: Barney McGill. E: Louis R. Loeffler. Art Director: Duncan Cramer. Costumes: William Lambert. Song "And That Woman Made a Monkey Out of Me" by Sidney Clare. Cast: Brian Donlevy, Glenda Farrell, Norman Foster, Helen Wood, Robert McWade, Theodore von Eltz, Romaine Callender, Joseph Sawyer, Hattie McDaniel, Murray Alper. 63 minutes. Released July 17, 1936.

15 Maiden Lane (20th Century–Fox) P: Sol M. Wurtzel. S: Lou Breslow, David Silverstein, John Patrick. Story: Paul Burger. C: John Seitz. E: Alex Troffey. Art Director: Duncan Cramer. Costumes: Herschel. Assistant Director: Samuel Schneider. Sound: George Leverett, Harry M. Leonard. Cast: Claire Trevor, Cesar Romero, Douglas Fowley, Lloyd Nolan, Lester Matthews, Robert McWade, Ralf Harolde, Russell Hicks, Holmes Herbert, Natalie Moorehead, Patricia Patrick. 64 minutes. Released Oct. 30, 1936.

1937

Woman-Wise (20th Century–Fox) P: Sol M. Wurtzel. S: Ben Markson. Story: Mark Kelly. C: Robert Planck. E: Alfred De Gaetano. Art Director: Lewis Creber. Sound: George Leverett, Harry M. Leonard. Song: "You're A Knockout": Sidney Clare, Harry Akst. Cast: Rochelle Hudson, Michael Whalen, Thomas Beck, Alan Dinehart, Douglas Fowley, George Hassell, Astrid Allwyn, Chick Chandler, Pat Flaherty. 71 minutes. Released Jan. 15, 1937.

That I May Live (20th Century–Fox) P: Sol M. Wurtzel. S: Ben Markson, William Conselman. C: Robert Planck. E: Louis R. Loeffler. Art Director: Lewis Creber. Costumes: Herschel. Cast: Rochelle Hudson, Robert Kent, J. Edward Bromberg, Jack La Rue, Frank Conroy, Frank Kelsey, George Cooper, DeWitt Jennings, Russell Simpson, William Benedict. 70 minutes. Released April 30, 1937.

One Mile from Heaven (20th Century–Fox) P: Sol M. Wurtzel. S: Lou Breslow, John Patrick, from stories by Judge Ben Lindsey, Robin Harris and Alfred Golden. C: Sidney Wagner. E: Fred Allen. Art Director: Bernard Herzbrun. Costumes: Herschel. Assistant Director: Samuel Schneider. Cast: Claire Trevor, Sally Blane, Douglas Fowley, Fredi Washington, Bill Robinson, Joan Carol, Ralf Harolde, John Eldredge, Paul McVey, Ray Walker, Russell Hopton, Chick Chandler, Eddie "Rochester" Anderson, Howard Hickman. 68 minutes. Released Aug. 13, 1937.

Heidi (20th Century–Fox) P: Darryl F. Zanuck. Associate Producer: Raymond Griffith. S: Walter Ferris, Julien Josephson, from the novel by Johanna Spyri. C: Arthur Miller. E: Allen McNeil. Art Director: Hans Peters. Set Director: Thomas Little. Costumes: Gwen Wakeling. Song "In Our Little Wooden Shoes" by Lew Pollack, Sidney Mitchell. Cast: Shirley Temple, Jean Hersholt, Marcia Mae Jones, Sidney Blackmer, Arthur Treacher, Thomas Beck, Pauline Moore, Helen Westley, Mary Nash, Mady Christians, Sig Rumann, Delmar Watson, Egon Brecher, Christian Rub, George Humbert. 88 minutes. Released Oct. 15, 1937.

1938

Rebecca of Sunnybrook Farm (20th Century–Fox) P: Raymond Griffith. S: Kart Tunberg, Don Ettlinger, from the novel by Kate Douglas Wiggin. C: Arthur Miller. E: Allen McNeil. Art Directors: Bernard Herzbrun, Hans Peters. Set Decorator: Thomas Little. Songs: "An Old Straw Hat" by Mack Gordon, Harry Revel; "Alone with You," "Happy Ending," "Crackly Grain Flakes" by Lew Pollack, Sidney D. Mitchell; "Come and Get Your Happiness" by Sam Pokrass, Jack Yetten; "Toy Trumpet" by Lew Pollack, Sidney D. Mitchell and Raymond Scott. Music Director: Arthur Lange. Choreography: Geneva Sawyer, Nick Castle. Cast: Shirley Temple, Gloria Stuart, Randolph Scott, Jack Haley, Phyllis Brooks, Helen Westley, Bill Robinson, Alan Dinehart, Slim Summerville, J. Edward Bromberg, William Demarest, William Wagner, Dixie Dunbar, Carroll Nye, Gary Breckner, Sam Hayes, Paul Hurst, Ruth Gillette, Paul Harvey, Franklin Pangborn, Clarence Hummel Wilson, Eily Maylon, Mary McCarty, Raymond Scott Quintette. 81 minutes. Released March 18, 1938.

Josette (20th Century–Fox) P: Gene Markey. S: James Edward Grant, from a play by Paul Frank and George Fraser, based on the story of Ladislaus Vardnai. C: Harry Mescal. E: Robert Simpson. Art Directors: Bernard Herzbrun, David Hall. Set Decorator: Thomas Little. Costumes: Royer. Songs: "May I Drop a Petal in Your Glass of Wine," "In Any Language," "Where in the World" by Mack Gordon, Harry Revel. Choreography: Nick Castle, Geneva Sawyer. Musical Director: David Buttolph Cast: Simone Simon, Don Ameche, Robert Young, Bert Lahr, Joan Davis, Paul Hurst, William Collier, Sr., Tala Birell, William Demarest, Ruth Gillette, Armand Kaliz, Ferdinand Gottschalk, Lilian Porter, Maurice Cass, Lynn Bari. 73 minutes. Released June 3, 1938.

Suez (20th Century–Fox) P: Darryl F. Zanuck. Associate Producer: Gene Markey. S: Philip Dunne, Julien Josephson. Story: Sam Duncan. C: J. Peverell Marley. E: Barbara MacLean. Art Directors: Bernard Herzbrun, Rudolf Sternad. Set Decorator: Thomas Little. Costumes: Royer. Special Effects: Fred Sersen. Second Unit Director: Otto Brower. Cast: Tyrone Power, Loretta Young, Annabella, J. Edward Bromberg, Joseph Schildkraut, Henry Stephenson, Sidney Blackmer, Maurice Moscovich, Sig Rumann, Nigel Bruce, Miles Mander, George Zucco, Leon Ames, Rafaela Ottiano, Victor Varconi, George Renavent, Frank Reicher, Carlos De Valdez, Jacqueline Lory, Albert Conti, Brandon Hurst, Marcelle Corday. 104 minutes. Released Oct. 15, 1938.

1939

The Three Musketeers (20th Century–Fox) P: Darryl F. Zanuck. Associate Producer: Raymond Griffith. M. Musselman, William A. Drake, Sam Hellman, from the novel by Alexandre Dumas, pere. Additional Dialogue: Sid Kuller, Ray Golden. C: J. Peverell Marley. E: Jack Dennis. Art Directors: Bernard Herzbrun, David Hall. Set Decorator: Thomas Little. Costumes: Royer. Songs "Chicken Soup," "Song of the Musketeers," "Voila" and "My Lady": Samuel Pokrass, Walter Bullock. Music Director: David Buttolph. Cast: Don Ameche, Al Ritz, Jimmy Ritz, Harry Ritz, Binnie Barnes, Lionel Atwill, Gloria Stuart, Pauline Moore, Joseph Schildkraut, John Carradine, Miles Mander, Douglass Dumbrille, John King, Russell Hicks, Gregory Gaye, Lester Matthews, Egon Brecher, Moroni Olsen, George Renavent, Gino Corrado. 73 minutes. Released Feb. 17, 1939.

The Gorilla (20th Century–Fox) P: Darryl F. Zanuck. Associate Producer: Harry Joe Brown. S: Rian James, Sid Silvers, from the play by Ralph Spence. C: Edward Cronjager. E: Allen McNeil. Art Directors: Richard Day, Lewis Creber. Set Decorator: Thomas Little. Costumes: Gwen Wakeling. Cast: Jimmy Ritz, Harry Ritz, Al Ritz, Anita Louise, Patsy Kelly, Lionel Atwill, Bela Lugosi, Joseph Calleia, Edward Norris, Wally Vernon, Paul Harvey, Art Miles. 66 minutes. Released May 26, 1939.

Frontier Marshal (20th Century–Fox) P: Sol M. Wurtzel. S: Sam Hellman, from the book *Wyatt Earp, Frontier Marshal* by Stuart N. Lake. C: Charles G. Clarke. E: Fred Allen. Art Directors: Richard Day, Lewis Creber. Set Decorator: Thomas Little. Costumes: Herschel. Cast: Randolph Scott, Nancy Kelly, Cesar Romero, Binnie Barnes, John Carradine, Ward Bond, Edward Norris, Eddie Foy, Jr., Lon Chaney, Jr., Chris Pin Martin, Joe Sawyer, Del Henderson, Harry Hayden, Ventura Ybarra, Charles Stevens, Tom Tyler. 71 minutes. Released July 28, 1939.

1940

Sailor's Lady (20th Century–Fox) P: Sol M. Wurtzel. S: Frederick Hazlitt Brennan. Story: Lt. Commander Frank "Spig" Wead. Additional Dialogue: Lou Breslow, Owen Francis. C: Ernest Palmer. E: Fred Allen. Cast: Nancy Kelly, Jon Hall, Joan Davis, Dana Andrews, Mary Nash, Larry "Buster" Crabbe, Kay Aldridge, Harry Shannon, Wally Vernon, Bruce Hampton, Charles D. Brown, Selmer Jackson, Edgar Dearing, Edmund MacDonald, William B. Davidson, Kane Richmond. 66 minutes. Released July 5, 1940.

Young People (20th Century–Fox) P: Harry Joe Brown. S: Edwin Blum, Don Ettlinger. C: Edward Cronjager. E: James B. Clark. Art Directors: Richard Day, Rudolph Sternad. Set Decorator: Thomas Little. Costumes: Gwen Wakeling. Songs "5th Avenue," "Tra-La-La," "I Wouldn't Take a Million," "The Mason-Dixon Line," "Young People": Mack Gordon, Harry Warren. Choreography: Nick Castle, Geneva Sawyer. Cast: Shirley Temple, Jack Oakie, Charlotte Greenwood, Arleen Whalen, George Montgomery, Kathleen Howard, Minor Watson, Frank Swann, Frank Sully, Mae Marsh, Sarah Edwards, Irving Bacon, Charles Halton, Arthur Aylesworth, Olin Howlin. 78 minutes. Released Aug. 30, 1940.

Trail of the Vigilantes (Universal) S: Harold Shumate. C: Joseph Valentine, Milton Krasner. E: Edward Curtiss. Art Directors: Jack Otterson, Harold MacArthur. Set Decorator: R.A. Gausman. Costumes: Vera West. Cast: Franchot Tone, Broderick Crawford, Peggy Moran, Andy Devine, Warren William, Mischa Auer, Porter Hall, Samuel S. Hinds, Charles Trowbridge, Paul Fix, Harry Cording, Max Wagner. 75 minutes. Released Dec. 13, 1940.

1941

Look Who's Laughing (RKO Radio) P: Dwan. S: James V. Kern, Don Quinn, Leonard L. Levinson, Zeno Klinker, Dorothy Kingsley. C: Frank Redman. Art Director: Van Nest Polglase. E: Sherman Todd. M: Roy Webb. Special Effects: Vernon L. Walker. Cast: Edgar Bergen, Jim Jordan, Marian Jordan, Lucille Ball, Lee Bonnell, Dorothy Lovett, Harold Peary, Isabel Randolph, Walter Baldwin, Neil Hamilton, Charles Halton, Harlow Wilcox, Spencer Charters, Jed Prouty, George Cleveland. 78 minutes. Released Nov. 21, 1941.

Rise and Shine (20th Century–Fox) P: Mark Hellinger. S: Herman J. Mankiewicz, from *My Life and Hard Times* by James Thurber. C: Edward Cronjager. E: Allen McNeil. Art Directors: Richard Day, George Dudley. Set Decorator: Thomas Little. Costumes: Gwen Wakeling. Songs "I'm Making a Play for You," "Central 2-2-0-0," "I Want to Be the Guy," "Hail to Bolenciewicz," "Get Thee Behind Me, Clayton": Leo Robin, Ralph Rainger. Choreographer: Hermes Pan. Cast: Jack Oakie, Linda Darnell, George Murphy, Walter Brennan, Milton Berle, Sheldon Leonard, Donald Meek, Ruth Donnelly, Raymond Walburn, Donald MacBride, Emma

Dunn, Charles Waldron, Mildred Gover, William Haade, Dick Rich, John Hiestand. 92 minutes. Released Nov. 21, 1941.

1942

Friendly Enemies (Small Productions–United Artists) P: Edward Small. S: Adelaide Heilbrun, from a play by Samuel Shipman, Aaron Hoffman. C: Edward Cronjager. E: William Claxton. Art Director: John DuCasse Schulze. Set Decorator: Edward G. Boyle. M: Lucien Moraweck. Costumes: Royer. Cast: Charles Winninger, Charles Ruggles, James Craig, Nancy Kelly, Otto Kruger, Ilka Gruning, Greta Meyer, Addison Richards, Charles Lane, John Piffle. 95 minutes. Released June 26, 1942.

Here We Go Again (RKO Radio) P: Dwan. S: Paul Gerard Smith, Joe Bigelow. Story: Paul Gerard Smith. Material for Fibber & Molly: Don Quinn. C: Frank Redman. E: Desmond Marquette. M: Roy Webb. Songs "Delicious Delirium," "Until I Live Again": Mort Greene, Harry Revel. Special Effects: Vernon L. Walker. Cast: Edgar Bergen, Jim Jordan, Marian Jordan, Harold Peary, Ginny Simms, Bill Thompson, Gale Gordon, Isabel Randolph, Jerry Maren (as Charlie McCarthy), Ray Noble and His Orchestra. 77 minutes. Released Oct. 9, 1942.

1943

Around the World (RKO Radio) P: Dwan. S: Ralph Spence. Special Material: Carl Herzinger. C: Russell Metty. E: Theron Warth. Art Directors: Albert S. D'Agostino, Al Herman. Set Decorators: Darrell Silvera, Claude Carpenter. M: George Dunning. Songs "Candlelight and Wine," "They Chopped Down the Old Apple Tree," "Don't Believe Everything You Dream," "He's Got a Secret Weapon," "Great News in the Making," "A Moke from Shamokin'," "Roodle-De-Doo": Jimmy McHugh, Harold Adamson. Choreography: Nick Castle. Cast: Kay Kyser, Mischa Auer, Joan Davis, Marcy McGuire, Georgia Carroll, Harry Babbitt, Ish Kabibble, Sully Mason, Julie Conway, Diane Pendleton, Kay Kyser Orchestra, Jack and Mae, Little Fred's Football Dogs, Robert Armstrong, Wally Brown, Alan Carney. 81 minutes. Released November 1943.

1944

Up In Mabel's Room (Small Productions–United Artists) P: Edward Small. S: Tom Reed, from a play by Otto Harbach, Wilson Collison. Additional Dialogue: Isobel Dawn. C: Charles Lawton. E: Richard Heermance, Grant Whytock. Art Director: Joseph Sternad. Set Decorator: Edward G. Boyle. M: Michel Michelet. Special Effects: George Emick. Cast: Marjorie Reynolds, Dennis O'Keefe, Gail Patrick, Mischa Auer, Charlotte Greenwood, Lee Bowman, John Hubbard, Binnie Barnes, Janet Lambert, Fred Kohler, Jr., Harry Hayden. 76 minutes. Released April 7, 1944.

Abroad with Two Yanks (Small Productions–United Artists) P: Edward Small. S: Charles Rogers, Wilkie Mahoney, Ted Sills. Story: Fred Guiol. Adaptation: Edward Seabrook, Tedwell Chapman. C: Charles Lawton, Jr. E: Richard Heermance. Assistant to Producer–Supervising Editor: Grant Whytock. Art Director: Joseph Sternad. Costumes: Odette. Cast: William Bendix, Helen Walker, Dennis O'Keefe, John Loder, George Cleveland, Janet Lambert, James Flavin, Arthur Hunnicutt, Willard Jilson, Herbert Evans, William Forrest, John Abbott. 80 minutes. Released Aug. 4, 1944.

1945

Brewster's Millions (Small Productions–United Artists) P: Edward Small. S: Siegfried Herzig, Charles Rogers, Wilkie Mahoney, from a novel by George Barr McCutcheon and a play by Winchell Smith and Byron Ongley. C: Charles Lawton, Jr. E: Richard Heermance. Art Director: Joseph Sternad. Musical Director: Louis E. Forbes. Cast: Dennis O'Keefe, Helen Walker, Eddie "Rochester" Anderson, June Havoc, Gail Patrick, Mischa Auer, Joe Sawyer, Nana Bryant, John Litel, Herbert Rudley, Thurston Hall, Byron K. Foulger, Barbara Pepper, Joseph Crehan, Neil Hamilton. 79 minutes. Released April 7, 1945.

Getting Gertie's Garter (Small Productions–United Artists) P: Edward Small. S: Dwan, Karen De Wolf, from a play by Wilson Collison, Avery Hopwood. Additional Dialogue: Joel Bigelow. C: Charles Lawton, Jr. E: Walter Hanneman, Truman K. Wood. Art Director: Joseph Sternad. Set Decorator: Henry Zane. Cast: Dennis O'Keefe, Marie McDonald, Barry Sullivan, Binnie Barnes, Sheila Ryan, J. Carrol Naish, Jerome Cowan, Vera Marshe, Don Beddoe, Frank Fenton, Richard LeGrand. 73 minutes. Released Nov. 30, 1945.

1946

Rendezvous with Annie (Republic) Associate Producer: Dwan. S: Mary Loos, Richard Sale. C: Reggie Lanning. E: Arthur Roberts. Art Director: Hilyard Brown. Set Decorators: John McCarthy, Jr., George Milo. M: Joseph Dubin. Musical Director: Cy Feuer. Dance Director: Fanchon. Costumes: Adele Palmer. Special Effects: Howard Lydecker, Theodore Lydecker. Cast: Eddie Albert, Faye Marlowe, Gail Patrick, Philip Reed, C. Aubrey Smith, Raymond Walburn, William Frawley, James Millican, Wallace Ford, Will Wright, Lucien Littlefield, Edwin Rand, Mary Field, Richard Sale, Bob Foy, Mike Frankovich. 89 minutes. Released July 22, 1946.

1947

Calendar Girl (Republic) Associate Producer: Dwan. S: Mary Loos, Richard Sale, Lee Loeb. Story: Lee Loeb. C: Reggie Lanning. E: Fred Allen. Art Director: Hilyard Brown. Set Decorators: John McCarthy, Jr., George Milo. M: Leo Arnaud. Songs "A Lovely Night to Go Dreaming," "I'm Telling You Now," "Calendar Girl," "At the Fireman's Ball," "New York's a Nice Place to Visit," "Let's Have Some Pretzels and Beer," "A Bluebird Is Singing to Me": James McHugh, Harold Adamson. Musical Director: Cy Feuer. Dance Director: Fanchon. Costumes: Adele Palmer. Special Effects: Howard Lydecker, Theodore Lydecker. Cast: Jane Frazee, William Marshall, Gail Patrick, Kenny Baker, Victor McLaglen, Irene Rich, James Ellison, Janet Martin, Franklin Pangborn, Gus Schilling, Charles Arnt, Lou Nova, Emory Parnell. 88 minutes. Released Jan. 31, 1947.

Northwest Outpost (Republic) Associate Producer: Dwan. S: Elizabeth Meehan, Richard Sale. Story: Angela Stuart. Adaptation: Laird Doyle. C: Reggie Lanning. E: Harry Keller. Art Directors: Hilyard Brown, Fred Ritter. Set Decorators: John McCarthy, Jr., James Redd. M: Rudolf Friml. Second Unit Director: Yakima Canutt. Special Effects: Howard Lydecker, Theodore Lydecker. Technical

Consultant: Alexis Davidoff. Cast: Nelson Eddy, Ilona Massey, Joseph Schildkraut, Elsa Lanchester, Hugo Haas, Erno Verebes, Lenore Ulric, Peter Whitney, Tamara Shayne, George Sorel, Rick Vallin, Countess Rosanska, Dina Smirnova, The American G.I. Chorus. 91 minutes. Released June 25, 1947.

Driftwood (Republic) S: Mary Loos, Richard Sale. C: John Alton. E: Arthur Roberts. Art Director: Frank Arrigo. Set Decorators: John McCarthy, Jr., George Milo. Costumes: Adele Palmer. M: Nathan Scott. Special Effects: Howard Lydecker, Theodore Lydecker. Cast: Ruth Warrick, Dean Jagger, Walter Brennan, Charlotte Greenwood, Natalie Wood, Jerome Cowan, H.B. Warner, Margaret Hamilton, Hobart Cavanaugh, Francis Ford, Alan Napier, James Bell, Howard Chamberlin, Teddy Infuhr, James Kirkwood, Ray Teal. 88 minutes. Released Sept. 15, 1947.

1948

The Inside Story (Republic) S: Mary Loos, Richard Sale. Story: Ernest Lehman, Geza Herczeg. C: Reggie Lanning. Art Director: Frank Arrigo. Set Decorators: John McCarthy, Jr., George Milo. E: Arthur Roberts. M: Nathan Scott. Costumes: Adele Palmer. Cast: Marsha Hunt, William Lundigan, Charles Winninger, Gail Patrick, Gene Lockhart, Florence Bates, Hobart Cavanaugh, Allen Jenkins, Roscoe Karns, Robert Shayne, Will Wright, William Haade, Frank Ferguson, Tom Fadden. 87 minutes. Released March 14, 1948.

Angel in Exile (Republic) D: Dwan, Philip Ford. P: Herbert J. Yates. S: Charles Larson. C: Reggie Lanning. Art Director: Frank Arrigo. Set Decorators: John McCarthy, Jr., George Milo. E: Arthur Roberts. Costumes: Adele Palmer. M: Nathan Scott. Cast: John Carroll, Adele Mara, Thomas Gomez, Barton MacLane, Alfonso Bedoya, Grant Withers, Paul Fix, Art Smith, Howland Chamberlin, Tom Powers, Ian Wolfe, Elsa Lorraine Zepeda. 90 minutes. Released Nov. 1, 1948.

1949

Sands of Iwo Jima (Republic) Associate Producer: Edmund Grainger. S: Harry Brown, James Edward Grant. Story: Harry Brown. C: Reggie Lanning. Art Director: James Sullivan. Set Decorators: John McCarthy, Jr., Otto Siegel. E: Richard L. Van Enger. Costumes: Adele Palmer. M: Victor Young. Special Effects: Howard Lydecker, Theodore Lydecker. Cast: John Wayne, John Agar, Adele Mara, Forrest Tucker, Wally Cassell, James Brown, Arthur Franz, Julie Bishop, Richard Webb, James Holden, Peter Coe, Richard Jaeckel, Bill Murphy, George Tyne, Hal Fieberling, John McGuire, Martin Milner, Leonard Gumley, William Self, Colonel D.M. Shoup, USMC, Lt.-Col. H.P. Crowe, USMC, Captain Harold G. Schrier, USMC, Rene A. Gagnon, Ira H. Hayes, John H. Bradley. 108 minutes. Released Dec. 31, 1949.

1950

Surrender (Republic) Associate Producer: Dwan. S: James Edward Grant, Sloan Nibley. Story: James Edward Grant. C: Reggie Lanning. Art Director: James Sullivan. Set Decorators: John McCarthy, Jr., Charles Thompson. E: Richard E. Van Enger. M: Nathan Scott. Song "Surrender": Jack Elliott and John Carroll. Special Effects: Howard Lydecker, Theodore Lydecker. Cast: Vera Hruba Ralston, John Carroll, Walter Brennan, Francis Lederer, William Ching, Maria Palmer, Jane Darwell, Roy Barcroft, Paul Fix, Esther Dale, Edward Norris, Howland Chamberlin, Norman Budd, Nacho Galindo, Jeff York. 90 minutes. Released July 31, 1950.

1951

Belle Le Grand (Republic) S: D.D. Beauchamp. Story: Peter B. Kyne. C: Reggie Lanning. E: Harry Keller. Art Director: James Sullivan. Set Decorators: John McCarthy, Jr., George Milo. Costumes: Adele Palmer. M: Victor Young. Special Effects: Howard Lydecker, Theodore Lydecker. Cast: John Carroll, Vera Hruba Ralston, William Ching, Muriel Lawrence, Hope Emerson, Henry Morgan, John Qualen, Stephen Chase, Charles Cane, Marietta Canty, Glen Vernon, Grant Withers, Thurston Hall. 90 minutes. Released Jan. 27, 1951.

The Wild Blue Yonder (Republic) P: Herbert J. Yates. S: Richard Tregaskis. Story: Andrew Geer, Charles Grayson. C: Reggie Lanning. Art Director: James Sullivan. Set Decorators: John McCarthy, Jr., Charles Thompson. E: Richard Van Enger. Costumes: Adele Palmer. M: Victor Young. Songs: "The U.S. Air Force" by Robert Crawford; "The Heavy Bomber Song" by Victor Young, Ned Washington; "The Man Behind the Armor Plated Desk," special lyrics by Dwan; "The Thing" by Charles R. Green. Special Effects: Ellis F. Thackery, Howard Lydecker, Theodore Lydecker. Cast: Wendell Corey, Vera Hruba Ralston, Forrest Tucker, Phil Harris, Walter Brennan, Ruth Donnelly, Harry Carey, Jr., Penny Edwards, Wally Cassell, James Brown, William Ching, Richard Erdman, Philip Pine, Martin Kilburn, Hal Baylor, Joe Brown, Jr., Jack Kelly, William Witney. 98 minutes. Released November 1951.

1952

I Dream of Jeanie (with the Light Brown Hair) (Republic) S: Alan LeMay, inspired by the life of Stephen Foster. C (Trucolor): Reggie Lanning. Art Director: Frank Hotaling. Set Decorators: John McCarthy, Jr., James Redd. E: Fred Allen. Costumes: Adele Palmer. Choreography: Nick Castle Dance Company. Special Effects: Howard Lydecker, Theodore Lydecker. Cast: Ray Middleton, Bill Shirley, Muriel Lawrence, Eileen Christy, Lynn Bari, Richard Simmons, Robert Neil, Andrew Tombes, James Dobson, Percy Helton, Glenn Turnbull, Louise Beavers, James Kirkwood, Carl "Alfalfa" Switzer, Freddie Moultrie, Rex Allen. 90 minutes. Released June 15, 1952.

Montana Belle (RKO Radio) P: Howard Welsch. Associate Producer: Robert Peters. S: Horace McCoy, Norman S. Hall. Story: M. Coates Webster, Howard Welsch. C (Trucolor): Jack Marta. Art Director: Frank Arrigo. Set Decorators: John McCarthy, Jr., George Milo. E: Arthur Roberts. Costumes: Adele Palmer. M: Nathan Scott. Songs: "The Gilded Lily" by Portia Nelson, Margaret Martinez; "My Sweetheart Is the Man in the Moon" by James Thornton. Special Effects: Howard Lydecker, Theodore Lydecker. Cast: Jane Russell, George Brent, Scott Brady, Forrest Tucker, Andy Devine, Jack Lambert, Ray Teal, Rory Mallinson, Roy Barcroft, Dick Elliott. 82 minutes. Released Nov. 7, 1952.

1953

Woman They Almost Lynched (Republic) S: Steve Fisher. Story: Michael Fessier. C: Reggie Lanning. Art Director: James Sullivan.

Set Decorators: John McCarthy, Jr., George Milo. E: Fred Allen. Costumes: Adele Palmer. M: Stanley Wilson. Songs: "How Strange" by Victor Young, Peggy Lee; "All My Life" by Sidney Mitchell, Sam Stept. Special Effects: Howard Lydecker, Theodore Lydecker. Cast: John Lund, Brian Donlevy, Audrey Totter, Joan Leslie, Ben Cooper, James Brown, Nina Varela, Ellen Corby, Fern Hall, Minerva Urecal, Jim Davis, Reed Hadley, Ann Savage, Virginia Christine, Marilyn Lindsay, Nacho Galindo, Richard Simmons, Gordon Jones, Frank Ferguson, Post Park, Tom McDonough, Richard Crane, James Kirkwood. 90 minutes. Released March 20, 1953.

Sweethearts on Parade (Republic) Associate Producer: Dwan. S: Houston Branch. C (Trucolor): Reggie Lanning. E: Fred Allen. Art Director: James Sullivan. Set Decorators: John McCarthy, Jr., James Redd. Costumes: Adele Palmer. Choreography: Nick Castle Dance Company. Twenty-one Songs with Music by Thomas Haynes Bayly, Johann Strauss, Michael William Balfe, Gaetano Donizetti, Marion Dix Sullivan, William Shakespeare Hays, Friedrich von Flotow, Stephen Collins Foster, James E. Spilman, Franz von Suppe, James Bland, Vincenzo Bellini, Frederick William Nichols Crouch, Anton Rubenstein, Henry Tucker, G. Bicknell. Special Lyrics for "Mating Time," "A Rovin," "Love Is a Pain" and "Wanderin'" by Dwan. Special Lyrics for "Romance" by Robert Armbruster, Lucille Norman. Special Effects: Howard Lydecker, Theodore Lydecker. Cast: Ray Middleton, Lucille Norman, Eileen Christy, Bill Shirley, Estelita, Clinton Sundberg, Harry Carey, Jr., Irvng Bacon, Leon Tyler, Marjorie Wood, Mara Corday, Muriel Lawrence. 90 minutes. Released July 15, 1953.

Flight Nurse (Republic) S: Alan LeMay. C: Reggie Lanning. Art Director: James Sullivan. Set Decorators: John McCarthy, Jr., Charles Thompson. E: Fred Allen. M: Victor Young. Songs: "The Nurse's Prayer" by Edith A. Ayne; "Gimme My Shute" ("Blue Tail Fly"), "Mushi-Mushi," traditional, lyrics by Dwan. Costumes: Adele Palmer. Technical Advisors: Col. Phil B. Cage, Capt. Lillian M. Kinkela. Special Effects: Ellis F. Thackery, Howard Lydecker, Theodore Lydecker. Cast: Joan Leslie, Forrest Tucker, Arthur Franz, Jeff Donnell, Ben Cooper, James Holden, Kristine Miller, Maria Palmer, Richard Simmons, James Brown, Hal Baylor, Morris Ankrum. 90 minutes. Released Nov. 4, 1953.

1954

Silver Lode (RKO Radio–Pinecrest Productions) P: Benedict Bogeaus. Production Supervisor: Leon Chooluck. S: Karen De Wolf. C (Technicolor): John Alton. Art Director: Van Nest Polglase. Set Director: Charles Thompson. E: James Leicester. M: Louis Forbes. Costumes: Gwen Wakeling. Cast: John Payne, Dan Duryea, Lizabeth Scott, Dolores Moran, Emile Meyer, Harry Carey, Jr., Morris Ankrum, John Hudson, Robert Warwick, Stuart Whitman, Alan Hale, Jr., Frank Sully, Hugh Sanders, Florence Auer, Roy Gordon, Edgar Barrier, John Dierkes, Myron Healey, Joe Devlin. 80 minutes. Released June 1954.

Passion (RKO Radio–Filmcrest Productions) P: Benedict Bogeaus. S: Joseph Leytes, Beatrice A. Dresher, Howard Estabrook. Story: Joseph Leytes, Beatrice A. Dresher and Miguel Padilla. C (Technicolor): John Alton. Art Director: Van Nest Polglase. Set Decorator: John Sturtevant. E: Carlo Lodato. M: Louis Forbes. Costumes: Gwen Wakeling. Cast: Cornel Wilde, Yvonne De Carlo, Rodolfo Acosta, Raymond Burr, Lon Chaney, Jr., John Qualen, Anthony Caruso, Frank De Kova, Peter Coe, John Dierkes, Richard Hale, Rozene Kemper, Rosa Turich, Stuart Whitman, James Kirkwood, Robert Warwick. 84 minutes. Released Oct. 6, 1954.

Cattle Queen of Montana (RKO Radio–Filmcrest Productions) P: Benedict Bogeaus. S: Robert Blees, Howard Estabrook. Story: Thomas Blackburn. C (Technicolor): John Alton. Art Director: Van Nest Polglase. Set Decorator: John Sturtevant. E: Carlo Lodato. M: Louis Forbes. Costumes: Gwen Wakeling. Cast: Barbara Stanwyck, Ronald Reagan, Gene Evans, Lance Fuller, Anthony Caruso, Jack Elam, Yvette Dugay, Morris Ankrum, Chubby Johnson, Myron Healey, Rodd Redwing, Hugh Sanders, Byron K. Foulger. 88 minutes. Released Nov. 18, 1954.

1955

It's Always Sunday (Hal Roach Studios; episode for the *Screen Director's Playhouse* television series) S: D.D. Beauchamp. Story: Jesse Goldstein, Frank Fox. C: Ed DuPar. Art Director: William Ferrari. E: Bert Jordan. Cast: Dennis O'Keefe, Sheldon Leonard, Fay Wray, Chick Chandler, Grant Withers, Eilene Janssen, Robert Easton, Terry Rangno, Diane Jergens, Jimmy Hayes. 29 minutes. First broadcast: March 28, 1955.

This was the first of two half-hour programs Dwan did for television. Since the episodes were done for the benefit of the Directors Guild, Dwan said the money the directors earned was turned over to the Guild. Copies of Dwan's contracts indicate that he was paid $825 for each episode.

It's Always Sunday, one of Dwan's lighter fables, deals with a minister (Dennis O'Keefe) who is an "easy mark" for anyone who comes his way. Somehow he is still able to afford a house in the pristine, prototypical suburbia of 1950s sitcoms. His faith in his fellow man is tested when he encounters a hobo who seems to have wandered out of a 1930s Hollywood movie. (There is even a reference to the WPA.) Sheldon Leonard plays the vagrant with his usual Runyonesque demeanor. The reverend's house is often filled with visitors, all of whom become entangled in the minister's ongoing charitable projects. He appears about to be undone by his gullibility when he is rescued by serendipity (Providence?) and his own combination of absent-mindedness and cunning, in the process giving credence to his sermon to "Trust thyself." Fay Wray has a key role as the minister's omniscient wife, who understands and admires his innate dignity while finding his naïveté endearing.

Escape to Burma (RKO Radio–Filmcrest Productions) P: Benedict Bogeaus. S: Talbot Jennings, Hobart Donevan, from the story "Bow Tamely to Me" by Kenneth Perkins. C (Superscope and Technicolor): John Alton. Art Director: Van Nest Polglase. Set Decorator: Fay Babcock. E: James Leiscester. M: Louis Forbes. Costumes: Gwen Wakeling, Lucille Sothern. Special Effects: Lee Zavitz. Cast: Robert Ryan, Barbara Stanwyck, David Farrar, Murvyn Vye, Robert Warwick, Reginald Denny, Lisa Montell, Peter Coe, Anthony Numkena. 87 minutes. Released April 9, 1955.

Pearl of the South Pacific (RKO Radio–Filmcrest Productions) P: Benedict Bogeaus. S: Jesse Lasky, Jr., Talbot Jennings, Richard Landau. Story: Ann Hunger. C (Superscope and Technicolor): John Alton. Art Director: Van Nest Polglase. M: Louis Forbes. E: James Leicester. Costumes: Gwen Wakeling. Cast: Virginia Mayo, Dennis Morgan, David Farrar, Murvyn Vye, Lance Fuller, Basil Ruysdael, Lisa Montell. 85 minutes. Released July 4, 1955.

Tennessee's Partner (RKO Radio–Filmcrest Productions) P: Benedict Bogeaus. S: Milton Krims, D.D. Beauchamp, Graham Baker,

Teddy Sherman. Story: Bret Harte. C (Superscope and Technicolor): John Alton. Art Director: Van Nest Polglase. Set Decorator: Alfred Spencer. E: James Leicester. M: Louis Forbes; Song "Heart of Gold": Lyrics by Dave Franklin. Costumes: Gwen Wakeling. Cast: John Payne, Rhonda Fleming, Ronald Reagan, Coleen Gray, Anthony Caruso, Leo Gordon, Myron Healey, Morris Ankrum, Chubby Johnson, Joe Devlin, John Mansfield, Angie Dickinson. 87 minutes. Released Sept. 21, 1955.

1956

Slightly Scarlet (RKO Radio) P: Benedict Bogeaus. S: Robert Blees, from the novel *Love's Lovely Counterfeit* by James M. Cain. C (Superscope and Technicolor): John Alton. Art Director: Van Nest Polglase. Set Decorator: Alfred Spencer. E: James Leicester. M: Louis Forbes. Cast: John Payne, Rhonda Fleming, Arlene Dahl, Ted De Corsia, Kent Taylor, Lance Fuller, Ellen Corby, Buddy Baer, Frank Gerstle, Roy Gordon, Myron Healey, Thayer Roberts, Gloria Victor, George E. Stone. 99 minutes. Released Feb. 8, 1956.

Hold Back the Night (Allied Artists) P: Hayes Goetz. S: John C. Higgins, Walter Doniger, from a novel by Pat Frank. C: Ellsworth Fredericks. Art Director: Hilyard Brown. Set Decorator: Joseph Kish. M: Hans J. Salter. E: Robert S. Eisen. Cast: John Payne, Mona Freeman, Peter Graves, Chuck Connors, Audrey Dalton, Bob Nichols, John Wilder, Stanley Cha, Nicky Blair, Nelson Leigh, John Craven, Robert Easton. 75 minutes. Released July 29, 1956.

High Air (Hal Roach Studios; episode for the *Screen Director's Playhouse* television series) S: A.I. Bezzerides. Story: Borden Chase. C: Jack MacKenzie. Art Director: William Ferrari. Set Decorator: Rudy Butler. Cast: William Bendix, Dennis Hopper, John Alderson, Leo Gordon, Hal Baylor, William Doty, Don Kennedy, Mike Ragan, John Mitchum, Duane Thorson. 29 minutes. First broadcast: September 12, 1956.

In *High Air*, the always economical Dwan used the time-limited format of the TV anthology episode to provide one of his most intense efforts and one of his strongest evocations of the "lost father" theme, during a decade when that obsession slipped from the forefront of his work. (*The Restless Breed* is the notable exception.)

The story returns Dwan to his beloved New York City but literally under the surface where sandhogs labor in tunnels below the East River. After an opening montage, no daylight or exterior is seen for the rest of the episode. Worker Joe Redman (William Bendix) encounters his son Steve (Dennis Hopper), whom he has not seen in years since Joe is estranged from his wife. Joe is chagrined to learn that his son has quit school and his study of engineering to begin work as a sandhog. Joe is angered by this betrayal of the blue-collar worker's dream (seeing one's son get a good education and find a better station in life than his father). Joe softens as he and Steve talk together for the rest of the program. A bonding takes place as the pair go through Joe's work ritual, moving from the locker room at the opening to the decompression chamber and finally to the tunnel where they perform their work. When a tear in the tunnel wall endangers Steve, Joe throws himself into the puncture to plug the hole.

The felicitous epilogue sounds both inventive and improbable. We learn that Joe has been sucked from the tunnel into the river and rescued on its surface. Through his acceptance of his son and his sacrifice for him, Joe has been given a metaphoric rebirth.

1957

The River's Edge (20th Century–Fox–Elmcrest Productions) P: Benedict Bogeaus. S: Harold Jacob Smith, James Leicester, from the story "The Highest Mountain" by Harold Jacob Smith. C (CinemaScope and De Luxe Color): Harold Lipstein. Art Director: Van Nest Polglase. E: James Leicester. M: Louis Forbes. Special Effects: Lee Zavitz. Cast: Ray Milland, Anthony Quinn, Debra Paget, Harry Carey, Jr., Chubby Johnson, Byron K. Foulger, Tom McKee, Frank Gerstle. 87 minutes. Released April 1957.

The Restless Breed (20th Century–Fox–Alperson Productions) P: Edward Alperson. Executive Producer: Richard Einfield. S: Steve Fisher. C (in Widevision and Eastmancolor): John W. Boyle. Art Director: Ernst Fegte. Set Decorator: Howard Bristol. M: Edward Alperson, Jr. Choreography: Miriam Nelson. E: Merrill G. White. Special Effects: Jack Cosgrove. Cast: Scott Brady, Anne Bancroft, Jay C. Flippen, Jim Davis, Leo Gordon, Rhys Williams, Myron Healey, Scott Marlowe, Eddy C. Waller, Harry Cheshire, Gerald Milton, Dennis King, Jr., James Flavin, Billy Miller, Marilyn Winston, Evelyn Rudie, Clegg Hoyt, Marty Cariosa, Joe Devlin, Fred Graham. 81 minutes. Released May 1957.

1958

Enchanted Island (RKO Radio–Warner Bros.–Waverly Productions) P: Benedict Bogeaus. S: James Leicester, Harold Jacob Smith, from the novel *Typee* by Herman Melville. C (Technicolor): George Stahl. Art Director: Hal Wilson Cox. E: Albert E. Valenzuela. Cast: Dana Andrews, Jane Powell, Don Dubbins, Frederick Ledebur, Ted De Corsia, Arthur Shields, Less Hellman, Carlos Leon, Augustin Fernandez. 93 minutes. Released Nov. 8, 1958.

1961

Most Dangerous Man Alive (Columbia) P: Benedict Bogeaus. S: James Leiscester, Phillip Rock, from "The Steel Monster" by Philip Rock, Michael Pate; Original story: Leo Gordon (uncredited). C: Carl Carvahal. E: Carlo Lodato. M: Louis Forbes. Costumes: Gwen Wakeling. Cast: Ron Randell, Debra Paget, Elaine Stewart, Anthony Caruso, Gregg Palmer, Morris Ankrum, Tudor Owen, Steve Mitchell, Joel Donte, Jay Novello. 82 minutes. Released June 1961.

Unrealized Projects

The Book of Esther (1938)
Will You Marry Me? (1959) Comedy set in Rhode Island
The Glass Wall (first announced in 1959)
The Bridge of San Luis Rey (first announced in 1959)
Marine! (1966)
A Bullet with Love (1970s)

Chapter Notes

Chapter 1

1. The description of Dwan at the 1976 Los Angeles Film Critics Awards comes from critic Kevin Thomas and the physical description of Dwan from writer Joseph McBride. The awards dinner was held on December 21, 1976. The screenwriter recommended to Dwan by Thomas was James Costigan, then best known for his work on his 1975 TV movie *Love Among the Ruins*, directed by George Cukor and starring Katharine Hepburn and Laurence Olivier.

2. Letter from Martin Scorsese to Allan Dwan, November 2, 1976, Allan Dwan Collection, University of Wyoming.

3. Aljean Harmetz, "Hollywood, from A to Zukor," *New York Times*, February 4, 1973.

4. Allan Dwan, "Canada *Has* a Movie Future But Certain Restrictions Must Be Removed," *MacLean's*, February 1, 1920, in Douglas Fetherling, ed., *Documents in Canadian Film* (Peterborough, Canada: Broadview Press, 1988), p. 24.

5. Untitled document, Allan Dwan file, Margaret Herrick Library.

6. *Notre Dame Scholastic*, vol. 40, 1906-07, October 20, 1906, p. 94.

7. Charles Foster, "Allan Dwan," *Stardust and Shadows: Canadians in Early Hollywood* (Toronto: Dandurn Press, 2000), p. 96.

8. *Notre Dame Scholastic*, April 6, 1907, p. 430.

9. Kevin Brownlow, *The Parade's Gone By...* (New York: Ballantine, 1968), p. 111.

10. *The Dome*, Notre Dame yearbook, 1907.

11. Interview with Robin Foster Wallace, October 30, 2009.

12. Uncredited newspaper clipping features photograph of Dwan captioned "Heads College Club." The story, dated October 19, states that at Notre Dame "Dwan was unanimously chosen by the members of the Illinois club as president." The story notes that Dwan is a member of the class of 1907 and will graduate "next June." Allan Dwan file, Margaret Herrick Library.

13. Fetherling, ed., *Documents in Canadian Film*, p. 24.

14. Ibid., p. 25.

15. Ibid.

16. Dwan, "Canada *Has* a Movie Future," in Fetherling, ed., *Documents in Canadian Film*, pp. 25–26.

17. Ibid., p. 27.

18. Ibid.

19. Peter Bogdanovich, *Allan Dwan: The Last Pioneer* (New York: Praeger, 1971), p. 15.

20. Ibid., p. 16.

21. He also told Bogdanovich he had been an assistant to Charles Steinmetz. Ibid., p. 15.

22. The text actually gives the name as "Richetta" but this is an apparent typo. Ricketts had been appointed director in January 1908.

23. Dwan, "Canada *Has* a Movie Future," in Fetherling, ed., *Documents in Canadian Film*, pp. 26–27.

24. Ibid., p. 27.

25. Adela Rogers St. Johns, "Artistic Efficiency—That's Dwan," *Photoplay*, August 1920, p. 57.

26. *Moving Picture World*, August 6, 1920, p. 37, 72.

27. Doris Irving, "How the Director Knows," *Picture Play*, June 1923, p. 92.

28. Allan Dwan, "The Director," in Charles Reed Jones, ed., *Breaking Into Movies* (New York: Unicorn Press, 1927), p. 145.

29. "How Allan Dwan Paid Interest on a $10 Loan," *Washington Post*, March 20, 1921, p. 6.

30. Maude S. Cheatham, "The Dynamic Allan Dwan," *Motion Picture Magazine*, December 1919, p. 82.

31. Ibid.

32. *Santa Barbara Morning Press*, November 6, 1912, p. 3.

33. "The Movie Lots Beg to Report," *Pittsburgh Post-Gazette*, March 4, 1936, p. 10.

34. Ezra Goodman, "Dwan of the Movies," *New York Times*, May 7, 1950.

35. Bogdanovich, *Allan Dwan*, p. 16.

36. Brownlow, *The Parade's Gone By...*, p. 111.

37. Brownlow interview for TV documentary series *Hollywood*, 308, take 1, p. 3.

38. Tay Garnett, *Directing: Learn from the Masters*, Anthony Slide, ed. (Metuchen, NJ: Scarecrow Press, 1996), p. 50.

39. *Photoplay*, August 1920, p. 57.

40. Bogdanovich, *Allan Dwan*, p. 16.

41. "Biography of Allan Dwan," 20th Century–Fox publicity release given to the author by Kevin Brownlow.

42. David Kiehn, *Broncho Billy and the Essanay Film Company* (Berkeley: Farwell Books, 2003), p. 39.

43. Bogdanovich, *Allan Dwan*, p. 16.

44. Timothy Lyons, *The Silent Partner: The History of the American Film Manufacturing Company* (New York: Arno Press, 1974), p. 61.

45. Bogdanovich, *Allan Dwan*, pp. 16–17. Dwan's presence in Tucson was noted in a December 17, 1910, article in the *Tucson Citizen* on page 5. The piece noted that for the picture company, "the mountains will be their stages and they will act a series of 'stories' for the benefit of the moving picture machine. The company includes Charles Kaufmann, D. Edgar Price, Mr. and Mrs. F. Beal, Allen Duvan [sic]...."

46. Fetherling, ed., *Documents in Canadian Film*, p. 28.

47. *Moving Picture World*, May 27, 1911, p. 1186. This story, which refers to Dwan as being now the producer in charge, also notes, "Mr. Hamilton is no longer in charge. Mr. Beal is no longer connected with the American company."

48. Fetherling, ed., *Documents in Canadian Film*, p. 28.

49. *New York Times* obituary for Thomas Ricketts, January 21, 1939. The obituary cites a recent interview in which Ricketts said that after leaving Flying A, he started a new company with Al Christie. This was actually the Nestor Company, founded by David Horsley. Ricketts said that when he made *The Best Man Wins* in California, Dwan was his assistant. *The Best Man Wins* was released in December 1911 and since by that time Dwan had been directing movies for Flying A for over six months, it is unlikely that he would have worked on that film. However, since Ricketts had been making pictures for Nestor since early 1911, it is possible that Dwan did work as an assistant on one or more of those movies.

50. Bogdanovich, *Allan Dwan*, p. 17.

51. Fetherling, ed., *Documents in Canadian Film*, p. 28.

Chapter 2

1. Kevin Brownlow, *The War, the West and the Wilderness* (New York: Alfred A. Knopf, 1979), pp. 224–235.

2. "The American Western Company," *Moving Picture World*, June 24, 1911, p. 1439.

3. "Newsy Items from El Cajon Valley," *Moving Picture News*, May 20, 1911, p. 26.

4. "Allan Dwan on Eastern Trip," *Universal Weekly*, August 2, 1913, p. 2.

5. Bogdanovich, *Allan Dwan*, pp. 17–18.

6. *Moving Picture World*, May 27, 1911, p. 1186.

7. Ibid.

8. If Charles Earle was instead a phantom, where did his name come from? The actual name of the nineteenth-century California bandit known as "Black Bart" was Charles Earle Bolles. Bolles dropped out of sight in 1888 and was never heard from again. It may have been an inside joke at Flying A that he had returned to direct Westerns for American.

9. "The Famous 'Flying A' Cowboy Films—Popular Western Subjects," *Moving Picture News*, June 3, 1911.

10. Bogdanovich, *Allan Dwan*, p. 18.

11. "Stories of the Films," *Moving Picture World*, May 27, 1911.

12. "Comments on the Films," *Moving Picture World*, June 10, 1911.

13. Bogdanovich, *Allan Dwan*, p. 18.

14. Fred J. Balshofer and Arthur C. Miller, with Bebe Bergsten, *One Reel a Week* (Berkeley: University of California Press, 1967), p. 50.

15. Dana Driskel interview with Dwan, September 7, 1978, transcript.

16. Bogdanovich, *Allan Dwan*, p. 19.

17. William Mann, *Behind the Screen: How Gays and Lesbians Shaped Hollywood, 1910–1969* (New York: Viking Penguin, 2002), p. 2.

18. Ibid.

19. "Universal Screen Stars: Pauline Bush: Her Autobiography," *Universal Weekly*, July 4, 1914, p. 13.

20. *Moving Picture World*, June 13, 1911, p. 1249.

21. Bogdanovich, *Allan Dwan*, p. 20.

22. Dwan, "Canada *Has* a Movie Future," in Fetherling, ed., *Documents in Canadian Film*, p. 29.

23. *Moving Picture World*, July 11, 1914, *Photoplay*, April 1915.

24. *Santa Barbara Morning Press*, July 17, 1912, p. 7.

25. Mann, *Behind The Screen*, p. 1.

26. Gary Morris, "Angel in Exile: An Interview with Silent Movie Pioneer Allan Dwan, December 1980," *Bright Lights Film Journal*, Issue 17, September 1996.

27. Bogdanovich, *Allan Dwan*, p. 21.

28. *Moving Picture News*, Sept. 30, 1911, p. 28.

29. Bogdanovich, *Allan Dwan*, p. 21.
30. "Permanent Home, 2 Troupes for American Film Company Here," *Santa Barbara Morning Press*, November 5, 1912, p. 3.
31. Bogdanovich, *Allan Dwan*, p. 21.
32. Ibid., p. 24.
33. Garnett, *Directing: Learn from the Masters*, p. 57.
34. Ibid.
35. Ibid.
36. Rudy Behlmer, *Henry Hathaway* (Metuchen, NJ: Scarecrow Press, 2001), pp. 2–5.
37. Bogdanovich, *Allan Dwan*, p. 22.
38. Jack Spears, "Marshall Neilan," *Hollywood: The Golden Era* (New York: A.S. Barnes, 1971), pp. 281–82.
39. Driskel interview with Dwan, p. 3.
40. *Santa Barbara Morning Press*, November 5, 1912, p. 5.
41. Bogdanovich, *Allan Dwan*, p. 22.
42. *Santa Barbara Morning Press*, November 5, 1912, p. 5.
43. "Santa Barbara," *Moving Picture World*, August 24, 1912.
44. Bogdanovich, *Allan Dwan*, p. 22.
45. "'Flying A' Players Arrive in Santa Barbara," *Santa Barbara Morning Press*, July 7, 1912, p. 2.
46. *Moving Picture World*, August 24, 1912.
47. Bogdanovich, *Allan Dwan*, p. 24.
48. *In the Days of Flying A: The Reminiscences of Mr. and Mrs. Roy Overbaugh*, Santa Barbara Historical Society, p. 7.
49. "Victor Fleming," American Film Company website, March 25, 2008.
50. Lyons, *The Silent Partner*, p. 138.
51. Ibid., p. 140.
52. Ibid.
53. Bogdanovich, *Allan Dwan*, p. 25.
54. The film made use of Santa Barbara's Mission Canyon and the old mission itself.
55. Scott Simmon, *The Invention of the Western: A Cultural History of the Genre's First Half-Century* (Cambridge: Cambridge University Press, 2003), p. 34.
56. "Louise Lester—'Calamity Anne,'" *Moving Picture World*, January 8, 1913.
57. "*Calamity Anne* Is Real," *New York Dramatic Mirror*, August 27, 1913, p. 27.
58. *Motion Picture News*, October 16, 1915, p. 51.
59. *Motography*, April 15, 1916, p. 890.
60. "Head of American Film Co. Visits 'Flying A' Players," *Santa Barbara Morning Press*, November 1, 1912.
61. *Moving Picture World*, February 17, 1912, p. 580.
62. *Santa Barbara Morning Press*, November 21, 1912, p. 3.
63. "Permanent Home, 2 Troupes for American Film Company Here," *Santa Barbara Morning Press*, November 5, 1912, p. 3.
64. "Wallace Reid Named Director of Second Flying A Company," *Santa Barbara Morning Press*, November 21, 1912, p. 3.
65. Ibid.
66. "American Film Company Becomes Fixture in Santa Barbara," *Santa Barbara Morning Press*, November 24, 1912, pp. 1–2.
67. *Santa Barbara Morning Press*, November 21, 1912, p. 3.
68. "American Film Head Kicks, Then Boosts for Santa Barbara," *Santa Barbara Morning Press*, February 9, 1913, p. 3.
69. "Notes from the Flying A Studio," *Santa Barbara Morning Press*, January 21, 1913, p. 5.
70. Ibid.
71. *Santa Barbara Morning Press*, January 14, 1913, p. 6.
72. Bogdanovich, *Allan Dwan*, pp. 27–28.
73. Ibid., p. 28.
74. Ibid.
75. *Santa Barbara Morning Press*, April 13, 1913, p. 3.
76. Ibid.
77. Ibid.
78. *Santa Barbara Morning Press*, March 26, 1913, p. 3; *Motion Picture News*, April 12, 1913, p. 15.
79. Allan Dwan file, Margaret Herrick Library.
80. "Notes from the 'Flying A' Studio," *Santa Barbara Morning Press*, April 15, 1913, p. 3.
81. Bogdanovich, *Allan Dwan*, p. 28.
82. Brownlow interview, 310, take 1, pp. 13–14. Engel must have been Joseph Engel who is cited in the section "The Unwelcome Feature Film."
83. Ibid., p. 15; Bogdanovich, *Allan Dwan*, p. 28.
84. In the Brownlow interview, Dwan has to first meet with Universal's co-founder and president, Carl Laemmle, in New York before settling on $1,000 per week. However, in a 1913 interview, appearing in the next section of this chapter, Dwan acknowledges that he did not meet Laemmle until *after* he started working at Universal.
85. "Personals," *Santa Barbara Morning Press*, April 22, 1913.
86. "Notes from the Flying A Studio," *Santa Barbara Morning Press*, April 15, 1913, p. 3.
87. E.J. Fleming, *Wallace Reid: The Life and Death of a Hollywood Idol* (Jefferson, NC: McFarland, 2007), p. 55.
88. *Moving Picture World*, May 10, 1913, p. 582.
89. Brownlow interview, 310, take 1, pp. 15–16.
90. Driskel interview, September 7, 1978.
91. I.G. Edmonds, *Big U: Universal in the Silent Days* (South Brunswick, NJ: A.S. Barnes, 1977), introduction.
92. "Changes in Universal Staff," *Moving Picture World*, May 10, 1913, p. 582.
93. "Laemmle Controls Universal," *Moving Picture World*, June 21, 1913, p. 1237.
94. *Santa Barbara Morning Press*, Feb. 16, 1913, p. 1.
95. Bogdanovich, *Allan Dwan*, p. 27.
96. *Universal Weekly*, July 5, 1913, p. 25.
97. *Moving Picture News*, July 5, 1913, p. 34.
98. *Moving Picture World*, July 19, 1913, p. 321.
99. *Moving Picture World*, July 26, 1913, p. 430; August 16, 1913, pp. 744–745.
100. Fleming, *Wallace Reid*, p. 57.
101. Spears, *Hollywood: The Golden Era*, p. 283.
102. Ibid. According to Spears, Neilan took over direction of the film when Dwan took ill.
103. *Universal Weekly*, August 2, 1913, p. 2.
104. *New York Dramatic Mirror*, August 27, 1913, p. 31. This item said that Kerrigan began his first picture for Universal, *Shon the Piper*, on August 18. This was either an error or changed by the front office.
105. Bogdanovich, *Allan Dwan*, p. 30.
106. *Universal Weekly*, September 20, 1913, p. 26.
107. *Universal Weekly*, October 11, 1913, p. 12.
108. Ibid.
109. Bogdanovich, *Allan Dwan*, p. 30.
110. *Universal Weekly*, September 20, 1913, p. 26.
111. Bogdanovich, *Allan Dwan*, p. 30.
112. *Universal Weekly*, October 11, 1913, p. 12.
113. *Moving Picture World*, October 25, 1913, p. 382.
114. *Motion Picture News*, October 18, 1913, p. 36.
115. Bogdanovich, *Allan Dwan*, p. 30.
116. Edmonds, *Big U* introduction.
117. *Moving Picture World*, November 8, 1913, p. 619.
118. Bogdanovich, *Allan Dwan*, pp. 30–31.
119. Jon Mirsalis, Lon Chaney website. Also cited in Michael F. Blake, *The Films of Lon Chaney* (Lanham, MD: Madison Books, 2001), pp. 4–5.
120. *Moving Picture World*, May 2, 1914, p. 674. The *Universal Weekly*'s coverage of its film (April 25, 1914, p. 8) refers to *The Tragedy of Whispering Creek* as being written by Dwan but also notes, "Mr. Chaney has used his own ideas in working out the character, as a pervert, in this play and what he has given us is startling to an unusual degree." It's possible that both Dwan and Chaney contributed to the writing.
121. *Universal Weekly*, April 18, 1914, p. 8.
122. *Universal Weekly*, December 6, 1913, p. 5.
123. Excised portion of Bogdanovich interview, tape 3–196, Lilly Library, Indiana University.
124. *Universal Weekly*, July 4, 1914, p. 13.
125. Robert Birchard, e-mail posted to Silent Film Group on May 11, 2001, confirmed in Mr. Birchard's e-mail to author, February 19, 2007. This extended quote is used with the explicit permission of Robert Birchard.
126. *Universal Weekly*, December 6, 1913, p. 5.
127. *Universal Weekly*, January 17, 1914, p. 33.
128. *Moving Picture World*, April 11, 1914, p. 11.
129. "Long Features Doomed!" *Universal Weekly*, June 6, 1914, p. 3.
130. "$50,000 Gift to Universal Exhibitors to Help Boom Fall Business," *Universal Weekly*, August 29, 1914, p. 5.
131. *Moving Picture World*, September 19, 1914, p. 1628.
132. *Motion Picture News*, September 26, 1914, p. 54.
133. *Universal Weekly*, July 25, 1914, p. 25.
134. Bogdanovich, *Allan Dwan*, p. 32.
135. Neal Gabler, *An Empire of Their Own: How the Jews Invented Hollywood* (New York: Crown, 1988), p. 28.
136. Brownlow interview, 310, take 1, p. 16.
137. *New York Dramatic Mirror*, October 28, 1914, p. 30.
138. Curtis Nunn, *Marguerite Clark: America's Darling of Broadway and the Silver Screen* (Fort Worth: Texas Christian University Press, 1981), p. 53.
139. Ibid., p. 54.
140. Bogdanovich, *Allan Dwan*, p. 33.
141. Joe Adamson interview, 1979, Museum of the Moving Image, CD Side #1.
142. Foster, *Stardust and Shadows*, pp. 107–08.
143. Ibid., p. 107.
144. *New York Dramatic Mirror*, May 1, 1914, p. 23.
145. *New York Dramatic Mirror*, July 15, 1914, p. 23.
146. Bogdanovich, *Allan Dwan*, p. 33.
147. *Variety*, August 21, 1914, p. 17.
148. Bogdanovich, *Allan Dwan*, p. 33.
149. *Motion Picture News*, October 24, 1914, p. 41.
150. *New York Dramatic Mirror*, October 14, 1914, p. 38.
151. Nunn, *Marguerite Clark*, p. vi.
152. Ibid., p. 57.
153. Marguerite Clark, "From Comic Opera to Motion Pictures," *American Magazine* 84 (July–December 1917), p. 42 as cited in Nunn, *Marguerite Clark*, p. 54.
154. *Motion Picture News*, December 19, 1914, p. 49.
155. "A Picture Caught in the Making," *Moving Picture World*, September 26, 1914, p. 1760. In his essay "The Cliff and the Flume," Bill Krohn makes the point that many of Dwan's films, and, he argues, his best ones, "grow out of spatial paradigms," usually showing the contrasts or connections between two locales. See *Allan Dwan: The Name Beneath the Title*, Giorgio Gosetti, ed., English edition (Torino: Lindau, 2002), pp. 135–43.
156. Ibid.

157. *Motography*, January 23, 1915, p. 152.
158. Ibid.
159. *Motion Picture News*, January 23, 1915, p. 45.
160. Brownlow interview, 310, take 1, p. 17.
161. *New York Dramatic Mirror*, March 3, 1915.
162. Bogdanovich, *Allan Dwan*, p. 33.
163. Ibid, pp. 33–34.
164. Ibid., p. 34.
165. Brownlow interview, 311, take 1, p. 18.
166. Patrick Robertson, *The Guinness Book of Movie Facts and Feats* (New York: Abbeville Press, 1991), p. 114.
167. *Variety*, February 26, 1915, p. 25.
168. *Moving Picture World*, February 13, 1915, p. 969.
169. *New York Dramatic Mirror*, March 10, 1915, p. 27.
170. *Moving Picture World*, June 12, 1915, p. 1787.
171. *New York Dramatic Mirror*, June 2, 1915, p. 28.
172. Ellen Whitfield, *Pickford: The Woman Who Made Hollywood* (Lexington: University of Kentucky Press, 1997), pp. 137–38.
173. Booton Herndon, *Mary Pickford and Douglas Fairbanks* (New York: W.W. Norton, 1977), p. 94.
174. Ibid., p. 240.
175. Cari Beauchamp, *Without Lying Down: Frances Marion and the Powerful Women of Early Hollywood* (New York: Scribner's, 1997), p. 45.
176. Bogdanovich, *Allan Dwan*, p. 35.
177. *New York Dramatic Mirror*, March 17, 1915, p. 29.
178. *New York Dramatic Mirror*, April 7, 1915, p. 26.
179. *Motography*, May 8, 1915, p. 730.
180. Ibid., March 6, 1915, p. 350.
181. Unidentified and undated magazine clip sent from Kevin Brownlow to author.
182. "A Girl of Yesterday," *Moving Picture World*, October 9, 1915, p. 290.
183. "Mary Pickford to Star In Her Own Story," *Moving Picture World*, May 22, 1915, p. 1280.
184. *Motion Picture News*, May 22, 1915, p. 51.
185. *Variety*, April 23, 1915, p. 19.
186. *Motion Picture News*, May 15, 1915, p. 43.
187. *Moving Picture World*, May 22, 1915, p. 1280.
188. Frances Marion, *Off with Their Heads: A Serio-Comic Tale of Hollywood* (New York: Macmillan, 1972), p. 23.
189. Adolph Zukor with Dale Kramer, *The Public Is Never Wrong: The Autobiography of Adolph Zukor* (New York: Putnam, 1953), pp. 141–144.
190. Bogdanovich, *Allan Dwan*, pp. 34–35.
191. *Los Angeles Times*, May 25, 1915.
192. *A Girl of Yesterday* review, *Moving Picture World*, October 23, 1915, p. 632.
193. *A Girl of Yesterday* review, *Motion Picture News*, October 23, 1915, p. 82.
194. *A Girl of Yesterday* review, *Wid's*, October 14, 1915.
195. *Photoplay*, December 1915, p. 89.
196. *Motion Picture News*, June 12, 1915, p. 52.
197. *Moving Picture World*, June 26, 1915, p. 2082; "Mary Pickford and Company Return, " *Moving Picture World*, July 3, 1915, p. 75.
198. Ibid., July 3, 1915, p. 75; *Motion Picture News*, July 3, 1915, p. 52.
199. *New York Dramatic Mirror*, June 9, 1915, p. 26; "Film Flashes," *Variety*, June 18, 1915, p. 16.
200. "Coast Film Folk Flock to Static Club Dance," *Motion Picture News*, June 12, 1915, p. 68.
201. *Motography*, June 19, 1915, p. 1023.
202. "Claiming Director Dwan," *Variety*, July 2, 1915, p. 17.
203. *Motography*, September 25, 1915, p. 601.
204. "*Zaza* Famous, Found Intact In Vault After Fire," *Motion Picture News*, October 2, 1915, p. 54.
205. See change in "List of Current Film Release Dates" for Paramount Pictures Corporation from *Moving Picture World*, September 4, 1915, p. 1748, to same list from September 11, 1915, p. 1920.
206. "Looking Ahead with the Producers," *Motion Picture News*, August 28, 1915, p. 55; "Manufacturer's Advanced Notes," *Moving Picture World*, August 28, 1915, p. 1498; "Mary Pickford Combines Pathos and Humor in *The Foundling*," *Motography*, August 28, 1915, p. 409.
207. *New York Dramatic Mirror*, January 15, 1916, p. 28.
208. *Variety*, January 14, 1916.
209. Bogdanovich, *Allan Dwan*, p. 35.
210. *New York Dramatic Mirror*, May 26, 1915, p. 26.
211. *Moving Picture World*, May 15, 1915, p. 1058.
212. *Variety*, July 2, 1915, p. 17.
213. *New York Dramatic Mirror*, March 10, 1915, p. 28.
214. D.W. Griffith, and James Hart, *The Man Who Invented Hollywood: The Autobiography of D.W. Griffith* (Louisville, KY: Touchstone, 1972), pp. 92–94; Robert M. Henderson, *D.W. Griffith: His Life and Work* (New York: Oxford University Press, 1972), pp. 150–151.
215. Kalton C. Lahue, *Dreams for Sale: The Rise and Fall of the Triangle Film Corporation* (South Brunswick, NJ: A.S. Barnes, 1971), pp. 26–30.
216. "Two Dollar Admission Price Is Triangle's Aim," *Motion Picture News*, August 14, 1915, p. 43.
217. "Better Films for Masses Not Classes," *Motography*, October 30, 1915, p. 885.
218. "Dwan and Helen Ware Join Big Feature Combine," *Motion Picture News*, July 10, 1915, p. 66.
219. "Dwan Was Not Head Director," *Motion Picture News*, July 17, 1915, p. 84.
220. "In the Picture Studios," *New York Dramatic Mirror*, August 18, 1915, p. 32.
221. "Their Lieutenants: Some Directorial Triangulations," *Photoplay*, March 1916, p. 46.
222. Karl Brown, *Adventures with D.W. Griffith* (New York: Farrar, Strauss and Giroux, 1973), pp. 98–99.
223. *New York Dramatic Mirror*, April 22, 1916.
224. Anthony Slide, *The Kindergarten of the Movies: A History of the Fine Arts Company* (Metuchen, NJ: Scarecrow Press, 1980), p. 8.
225. Bogdanovich, *Allan Dwan*, p. 35.
226. Ibid., p. 36.
227. Brown, *Adventures with D.W. Griffith*, pp. 154–55.
228. Bogdanovich, *Allan Dwan*, p. 36.
229. Lillian Gish with Anne Pinchot, *The Movies, Mr. Griffith and Me* (London: Columbus Books, 1969), p. 175.
230. 9. Ibid., p. 170. In his posthumously published autobiography, Griffith cameraman Billy Bitzer confirms the balloon story but does not say who suggested the tracking shot (*Billy Bitzer: His Story* [New York: Farrar, Straus and Giroux, 1973], p. 135).
231. Joseph Henabery and Anthony Slide, *Before, In and After Hollywood: The Autobiography of Joseph Henabery* (Metuchen, NJ: Scarecrow Press, 1997), p. 331.
232. Kevin Brownlow, e-mail message to author.
233. "Fine Arts Activities," *Moving Picture World*, September 11, 1915, p. 1816.
234. Brownlow, *The War, the West and the Wilderness* (New York: Alfred A. Knopf, 1979), pp. 281–83.
235. Diana Serra Carey, *The Hollywood Posse: The Story of a Gallant Band of Horsemen Who Made History* (Norman: University of Oklahoma Press, 1996), p. 145.
236. Brownlow, *The War, the West and the Wilderness*, p. 283.
237. *Wid's*, December 2, 1915.
238. Brownlow interview, 313, take 1, p. 30 Available plot synopses suggest that Campeau's character was attending a revival, not leading one.
239. Bogdanovich, *Allan Dwan*, p. 40.
240. Ibid.
241. *New York Times*, November 22, 1915, p. 11.
242. *Moving Picture World*, November 20, 1915, p. 1501.
243. *Motography*, November 27, 1915, p. 1143.
244. *Variety*, November 26, 1915.
245. *Wid's*, December 2, 1915.
246. Letter from Tim McCoy to Allan Dwan, December 8, 1965, Dwan file, Margaret Herrick Library.
247. *Variety*, October 29, 1915, p. 20.
248. *New York Dramatic Mirror*, September 18, 1915, p. 24.
249. *Motography*, December 4, 1915, p. 1171.
250. Channing Pollock, "The Discovery of Fort Lee," *Photoplay*, December 1915, pp. 68–69.
251. "Their Lieutenants," *Photoplay*, March 1916, photo caption, p. 43.
252. *Variety*, June 16, 1916, p. 26.
253. *Photoplay*, May 1916, p. 110; *Photoplay*, February 1916, p. 104.
254. *Photoplay*, May 1916, p. 110.
255. *Motion Picture News*, December 20, 1919.
256. *Motion Picture News*, December 20, 1919, p. 980.
257. Andrew Sarris, "Diary of a Schizocritic," *New York Film Bulletin*, May 15, 1962, from Sarris's anthology *Confessions of a Cultist: On the Cinema, 1955–1969* (New York: Simon & Schuster, 1970), p. 45.
258. Phone conversation with Howard Mandelbaum and e-mail to author, February 14, 2010.
259. John Dorr, "The Griffith Tradition," *Film Comment*, March 1974, pp. 48–49.
260. Ibid., p. 51.
261. Ibid., p. 49.
262. Bogdanovich, *Allan Dwan*, p. 26.
263. Myron Meisel, "Allan Dwan," *American Directors, Volume I*, Jean-Pierre Coursodon and Pierre Sauvage (New York: McGraw-Hill, 1983), p. 108.
264. Donald Phelps, "The Runners," *Covering Ground: Essays for Now* (New York: Croton Press, 1969), p. 72.
265. Coursodon and Sauvage, *American Directors, Volume I*, p. 110.
266. *Film Comment*, March 1974, p. 51.
267. *Motography*, November 27, 1915, p. 1143.
268. Stuart Oderman, *Talking to the Piano Player: Silent Film Stars, Writers and Directors Remember* (Boalsburg, PA: BearManor Media, 2005), p. 47.

Chapter 3

1. Percy Hammond, "Shakespeare, the Shrewd Showman Crowds the Lyric," *The Chicago Tribune*, May 1, 1910.
2. Alistair Cooke, *Douglas Fairbanks: The Making of a Screen Character* (New York: Museum of Modern Art, 1940), p. 14.
3. *Moving Picture World*, October 19, 1915, p. 233.
4. John C. Tibbetts and James M. Welsh, *His Majesty, the American: The Cinema of Douglas Fairbanks Sr.* (South Brunswick, NJ: A.S. Barnes, 1977), p. 87.
5. John Ten Eyck, "Catching Douglas Fair-

banks on the Run," *The Green Book Magazine*, October 1914, p. 628.

6. Gaylyn Studlar, *This Mad Masquerade: Stardom and Masculinity in the Jazz Age* (New York: Columbia University Press, 1996), p. 28.

7. Ibid., pp. 46–47.

8. "Brenon Forms Independent Company," *Motography*, July 29, 1916, p. 258.

9. Studlar, *This Mad Masquerade*, pp. 13–14.

10. Tibbetts, *His Majesty, the American*, p. 23.

11. Studlar, *This Mad Masquerade*, p. 52.

12. Robert Frost, "The Figure a Poem Makes," *Selected Poems of Robert Frost* (New York: Holt, Rinehart and Winston, 1967), p. 2. Frost refers to a poem ending "in a clarification of life — not necessarily a great clarification, such as sects and cults are founded on, but in a momentary stay against confusion."

13. Unpublished 1978 Allan Dwan interview with Richard Koszarski, supplied to author by Mr. Koszarski, pp. 7–8.

14. Herndon, *Mary Pickford and Douglas Fairbanks*, p. 142.

15. Ibid.

16. Richard Schickel, *His Picture in the Papers* (New York: Charterhouse, 1973), p. 43.

17. Herndon, *Mary Pickford and Douglas Fairbanks*, p. 140.

18. Bogdanovich, *Allan Dwan*, p. 42.

19. Herndon, *Mary Pickford and Douglas Fairbanks*, p. 241.

20. Ronald L. Davis interview with Douglas Fairbanks, Jr., October 1982, p. 13, Oral History Collection on the Performing Arts, DeGolyer Library, Southern Methodist University, Dallas, Texas, A1980.0154.

21. Ibid.

22. Herndon, *Mary Pickford and Douglas Fairbanks*, p. 143.

23. Adolphe Menjou and M.M. Musselman, *It Took Nine Tailors* (New York: Whittlesey House, 1948). Also cited in Richard Koszarski, *Fort Lee: The Film Town* (Rome: John Libbey, 2004), p. 166. Menjou can be glimpsed in a shot of Clarice's friends at the dinner table.

24. Tibbetts, *His Majesty, the American*, p. 38.

25. Ibid., p. 43.

26. Ibid., p. 45.

27. Douglas Fairbanks, "Styles in Farce," *The Green Book Magazine*, January 1913, p. 98.

28. Cooke, *Douglas Fairbanks: The Making of a Screen Character*, p. 18.

29. *Philadelphia Telegrapher*, May 4, 1916, from Robin Locke Collection, Vol. 461, p. 68.

30. Bogdanovich, *Allan Dwan*, p. 41.

31. *New York Times*, March 13, 1916; *New York Times Film Reviews, Vol. 1*, p. 13.

32. Review of *Hell's Hinges*, *Moving Picture World*, February 2, 1916, p. 1147.

33. *Motion Pictures*, November 1917, from Locke Vol. 460, p. 123.

34. Herndon, *Mary Pickford and Douglas Fairbanks*, p. 143.

35. *Cleveland Plain Dealer*, May 7, 1916.

36. Bessie Love, *From Hollywood with Love* (London: Elm Tree Books, 1981), p. 56.

37. Herndon, *Mary Pickford and Douglas Fairbanks*, pp. 144–45.

38. Love, *From Hollywood with Love*, p. 58.

39. *New York Dramatic Mirror*, April 22, 1916, p. 42.

40. *Motion Picture News*, April 22, 1916, p. 2381.

41. *Moving Picture World*, April 22, 1916, p. 643.

42. *Wid's*, April 13, 1916, 502.

43. Herndon, *Mary Pickford and Douglas Fairbanks*, p. 58.

44. Love, *From Hollywood with Love*, p. 29.

45. Bogdanovich, *Allan Dwan*, p. 39.

46. Excised portion of Dwan interview, tape 4–39, and previous page marked only as "Griffith," Bogdanovich Papers, Lilly Library, Indiana University.

47. *Wid's*, June 18, 1916, p. 638.

48. Charles Affron, *Lillian Gish: Her Legend, Her Life* (New York: Scribner's, 2001), p. 102.

49. *Motion Picture News*, May 20, 1916, p. 3041.

50. Brownlow, *The War, the West and the Wilderness*, pp. 334–335.

51. *Motography*, June 17, 1916, p. 1364.

52. Herndon, *Mary Pickford and Douglas Fairbanks*, p. 144.

53. Ralph Hancock and Letitia Fairbanks, *Douglas Fairbanks: The Fourth Musketeer* (New York: Henry Holt, 1953), p. 13. This same story is recounted in the *Cleveland News*, September 2, 1919, "Douglas Fairbanks — Himself — Fifth in a Series" by Carl Wilmore, Robin Locke Collection Vol.172, p. 29, at the Billy Rose Theatre Division, New York Public Library, which may have been the original source.

54. Herndon, *Mary Pickford and Douglas Fairbanks*, p. 16.

55. Ibid., p. 109.

56. Bogdanovich, *Allan Dwan*, p. 42.

57. Andrew Brodie Smith, *Shooting Cowboys and Indians: Silent Western Films, American Culture and the Birth of Hollywood* (Boulder: University Press of Colorado, 2003), p. 166.

58. *Motion Picture News*, April 8, 1916, p. 2064.

59. George N. Fenin and William K. Everson, *The Western: From Silents to the Seventies* (New York: Penguin, 1977), p. 92.

60. Diane Kaiser Koszarski, *The Complete Films of William S. Hart: A Pictorial Record* (New York: Dover, 1980), p. xix.

61. Smith, *Shooting Cowboys and Indians*, p. 168.

62. Scott Simmon, *The Invention of the Western Film: A Cultural History of the Genre's First Half-Century* (Cambridge: Cambridge University Press, 2003), p. 86.

63. Ibid., p. 129.

64. *New York Times*, July 10, 1916, from *New York Times Book Reviews, Volume 1*, p. 19.

65. Bret Harte, *In the Carquinez Woods*, in *In the Carquinez Woods and Other Tales* (Boston: Houghton Mifflin, 1884), p. 6.

66. Henry Nash Smith, *Virgin Land: The American West as Symbol and Myth* (Cambridge: Harvard University Press, 1950), p. 55.

67. Ibid., p. 89.

68. Simmon, *The Invention of the Western*, p. 130.

69. Douglas Fairbanks, "Why I Was Disappointed in the Grand Canyon," *Ladies Home Journal*, February 1918.

70. "The Shadow Stage," *Photoplay*, October 1916, p. 76.

71. *Motography*, July 22, 1916, p. 214.

72. *New York Times*, July 10, 1916, from *New York Times Book Reviews, Volume 1*, p. 19.

73. *Motion Picture News*, July 22, 1916, p. 452.

74. George Blaisdell, "Douglas Fairbanks in New York," *Moving Picture World*, June 24, 1916, p. 2213.

75. *Motography*, September 16, 1916, p. 675.

76. Smith, *Shooting Cowboys and Indians*, pp. 178–79.

77. *Los Angeles Times*, November 23, 1917, p. 113.

78. Heywood Broun, "Fairbanks at Best on Screen," *New York Tribune*, September 11, 1916, p. 7.

79. Anita Loos, *A Girl Like I* (New York: Viking, 1966), p. 162.

80. Bogdanovich, *Allan Dwan*, p. 42.

81. *Motography*, January 29, 1916, p. 234.

82. Hancock and Fairbanks, *The Fourth Musketeer*, p. 123.

83. Kevin Brownlow, "From Now Until Eternity," in Gosetti, *Allan Dwan: The Name Beneath the Title*, p. 93.

84. Bogdanovich, *Allan Dwan*, p. 42.

85. Undated scrapbook clipping, Billy Rose Theatre Division, New York Public Library, New York *Telegraph*, "Fairbanks Nearly Blinded in Films." Fairbanks refers to it obliquely in an article in *Motography*, September 30, 1916, p. 758.

86. *Motography*, June 24, 1916, p. 1440.

87. *Motion Picture News*, June 24, 1916, p. 3884.

88. Lahue, *Dreams for Sale*, p. 85.

89. *Motography*, November 14, 1916, p. 1041.

90. *Photoplay*, January 1917, pp. 102–103.

91. *Photoplay*, April 1917, p. 76.

92. Dwan interview with Joe Adamson, September 1979, CD, Museum of the Moving Image.

93. *Motion Picture News*, June 17, 1916, p. 3762.

94. *Variety*, July 21, 1916, p. 17.

95. Brownlow, interview with Dwan, p. 41.

96. "Norma Talmadge's Own Co.," *Variety*, September 29, 1916, p. 21.

97. Richard Koszarski interview with Dwan, Tape 7, Reel #1, p. 4.

98. Bogdanovich, *Allan Dwan*, p. 43.

99. *Variety*, January 12, 1917, p. 21.

100. *Variety*, January 12, 1917.

101. *Photoplay*, April 1917, pp. 77–78.

102. Bogdanovich, *Allan Dwan*, pp. 43–44.

103. Kenneth MacGowan, *Behind the Screen: The History and Techniques of the Motion Picture* (New York: Dell, 1965), p. 198.

104. *Wid's*, January 11, 1917, p. 24.

105. Jeanine Basinger, *Silent Stars* (New York: Alfred A. Knopf, 2000), p. 146.

106. Bogdanovich, *Allan Dwan*, p. 43.

107. *Variety*, January, 5, 1917, p. 23.

108. Bogdanovich, *Allan Dwan*, p. 44.

109. Terry Ramsaye, *A Million and One Nights: A History of the Motion Picture Through 1925* (New York: Simon & Schuster, 1926), p. 752.

110. Alvin H. Marill, *Samuel Goldwyn Presents* (South Brunswick, NJ: A.S. Barnes, 1976), p. 19.

111. A. Scott Berg, *Goldwyn: A Biography* (New York: Ballantine, 1989), p. 72.

112. Slide, *The Kindergarten of the Movies*, p. 63.

113. *Motion Picture News*, September 2, 1916, p. 1351.

114. *Motion Picture News*, November 4, 1916, p. 2815.

115. *Variety*, January 12, 1917, p. 1; *Motion Picture News*, January 27, 1917, p. 546.

116. Slide, *The Kindergarten of the Movies*, p. 68.

117. Ramsaye, *A Million and One Nights*, p. 773.

118. Excised portion of Dwan interview, I-191, 1917, Peter Bogdanovich Papers, Lilly Library, Indiana University.

119. *Motion Picture News*, July 7, 1917, p. 110.

120. *Motion Picture News*, March 31, 1917, p. 1987.

121. *Motography*, April 7, 1917, p. 723.

122. *Motography*, April 21, 1917, p. 807.

123. *Motography*, April 7, 1917, p. 724.

124. *Moving Picture World*, April 21, 1917, p. 409.

125. *Motography*, June 2, 1917, pp. 1185–86.

126. *Motography*, April 14, 1917, p. 780; *Motion Picture News*, April 21, 1917, p. 440.

127. *Wid's*, March 22, 1917, p. 182.

128. *Motion Picture News*, May 12, 1917, p. 3016.

129. *Variety*, May 4, 1917.

130. *New York Dramatic Mirror*, May 15, 1917, p. 28.

131. *Wid's*, June 7, 1917, p. 366.

132. Kevin Brownlow, *Behind the Mask of Innocence: Sex, Violence, Prejudice, Crime: Films of Social Conscience in the Silent Era* (London: Jonathan Cape, 1990), p. 237. Referring to *Every Woman's Problem*

the author cited it "as one of the few surviving suffrage films...."

133. *New York Dramatic Mirror*, July 7, 1917, p. 15.

134. *Moving Picture World*, July 14, 1917, p. 255.

135. *Wid's*, July 5, 1917, p. 422.

136. *Moving Picture World*, July 14, p. 255.

137. *Motography*, August 11, 1917, p. 297.

138. *New York Dramatic Mirror*, August 11, 1917, p. 19.

139. Eduardo Ciannelli's name is recognizable to cinephiles for a long career in the sound era as a character actor, most notably as the evil guru in *Gunga Din*.

140. *Variety*, August 10, 1917, p. 23.

141. *Wid's*, August 9, 1917, p. 510.

142. *Photoplay*, November 1917, reviewed by Kitty Kelly, p. 132.

143. *New York Dramatic Mirror*, August 11, 1917, p. 19.

144. *Variety*, August 10, 1917, p. 23.

145. *Wid's*, August 9, 1917, p. 510.

146. "Dwan to Produce Pictures with Vital Topical Themes," *Motion Picture News*, September 1, 1917, p. 1456; "Dwan Favors Timely Topics," *Moving Picture World*, September 1, 1917, p. 1403.

147. *New York Dramatic Mirror*, October 20, 1917, p. 18.

148. *Motography*, October 27, 1917, p. 890.

149. *Motion Picture News*, October 27, 1917, p. 2951.

150. *Photoplay*, January 1918, p. 126.

151. *Triangle Magazine*, October 6, 1917, p. 12.

152. *Motion Picture News*, November 24, 1917, p. 3636.

153. "Give Us Entertaining Plays," *Motion Picture News*, January 12, 1918.

154. *Motography*, November 10, 17, p. 976, December 1, 1917, p. 1142.

155. Joseph Henabery and Anthony Slide, *Before, In and After Hollywood: The Autobiography of Joseph Henabery* (Metuchen, NJ: Scarecrow Press, 1997), p. 153.

156. Herndon, *Mary Pickford and Douglas Fairbanks*, p. 111, 152.

157. Lahue, *Dreams for Sale*, p. 166. The reference to Dwan having "moved East" to accept the job is inaccurate because he was already working in New York when he shot his last film, *Fighting Odds*.

158. Ibid., p. 116.

159. Loos, *A Girl Like I*, p. 97.

160. Anita Loos, *Kiss Hollywood Good-by* (New York: Viking, 1974), p. 10.

161. Henabery and Slide, *Before, In and After Hollywood*, p. 167.

162. Anita Loos, *The Talmadge Girls: A Memoir* (New York: Viking, 1978). In the earlier *A Girl Like I* (p. 178) Loos had written more generously of Fairbanks' reaction to the *Ladies Home Journal* article: "Doug had an honest basis for resentment; that I was the first to write his own personality into a film was true enough, and that he was no actor Doug freely admitted. But he didn't need me; his unusual talents would have come to the fore in either the theater or films without outside help from anyone."

163. Henabery and Slide, *Before, In And After Hollywood*, p. 157.

164. Loos, *The Talmadge Girls*, pp. 33–34.

165. Loos, *A Girl Like I*, p. 178.

166. Samuel Goldwyn, *Behind the Screen* (New York: George H. Doran, 1923), p. 138.

167. Craig W. Campbell, *Reel America and World War I* (Jefferson, NC: McFarland, 1985), p. 62.

168. *Wid's*, October 4, 1917, p. 630.

169. Herndon, *Mary Pickford and Douglas Fairbanks*, p. 168. Dwan also mentions the detour to Kansas in Boganovich, *Allan Dwan*, p. 45.

170. "A Novel Banquet," *Los Angeles Times*, October 27, 1917, p. 113.

171. Bogdanovich, *Allan Dwan*, p. 48.

172. Fetherling, ed., *Documents in Canadian Film*, p. 30.

173. *Motion Picture News*, October 6, 1917, p. 2393.

174. Kevin Brownlow interview for TV series *Hollywood*, p. 64.

175. *Motion Picture News*, January 12, 1918, p. 295.

176. *Variety*, January 4, 1918.

177. *Wid's*, January 3, 1918, p. 840.

178. Hancock and Fairbanks, *The Fourth Musketeer*, p. 175.

179. *Moving Picture World*, February 23, 1918, p. 1095.

180. "Fairbanks Is Active," *Progress-Advance*, January 24, 1918, p. 177.

181. "To Direct 'Doug,'" *Los Angeles Times*, October 7, 1917.

182. "Fairbanks Makes Wild West Wild," *Moving Picture World*, May 26, 1917, p. 1268.

183. *Motion Picture News*, March 9, 1918, p. 1453.

184. *Variety*, March 1, 1918, p. 43.

185. *Progress-Advance*, March 14, 1918.

186. *Progress-Advance*, March 21, 1918, p. 337.

187. *Motion Picture News*, April 20, 1918, p. 2417.

188. *Photoplay*, July 1918, p. 79.

189. *Moving Picture World*, April 27, 1918, p. 519.

190. *Theatre*, September 1918, p. 47.

191. *Motion Picture News*, September 21, 1918, p. 1923.

192. *Wid's*, September 15, 1918, p. 21.

193. *Wid's*, August 25, 1918, p. 2.

194. *Picture Play Magazine*, December 1918, p. 295.

195. "Plays and Players," *Photoplay*, December 1918, p. 79.

196. Memorandum of Agreement Dated September 1918, Allan Dwan file, Margaret Herrick Library.

197. *Motion Picture News*, December 14, 1918, p. 3535.

198. *Motion Picture News*, December 21, 1918, p. 3618; *Motion Picture News*, December 28, 1918, p. 3790.

199. *Photoplay*, March 1919, p. 69.

200. *Arizona* was re-made in 1931 starring Laura LaPlante and John Wayne. Subsequent films with that title such as the 1940 *Arizona* with Jean Arthur have no relation to the original play.

201. "Plays and Players," *Photoplay*, January 1919, p. 82.

202. "Plays and Players," *Photoplay*, February 1919, p. 82.

203. "Rubbernecking in Filmland," *Moving Picture World*, November 23, 1918, p. 821.

204. Richard Schickel, *Harold Lloyd: The Shape of Laughter* (Boston: New York Graphic Society, 1974), p. 9.

205. *Ladies Home Journal*, September 1922, p. 120.

206. *Motion Picture News*, June 12, 1920, p. 4796.

207. *Wid's*, January 18, 1921, p. 1.

208. The contract dated December 20, 1921, consisted of a letter from Dwan listing terms which were approved by Fairbanks. From the files of the Margaret Herrick Library.

209. "Doug Picks Three," *Wid's*, February 4, 1922, p. 1.

210. Allan Dwan, "Notes from a Talk to *Photoplay* Students at Columbia University," Margaret Herrick Library.

211. Hancock and Fairbanks, *The Fourth Musketeer*, p. 193.

212. Brownlow, *The Parade's Gone By...*, p. 285.

213. Bogdanovich, *Allan Dwan*, p. 54.

214. Robert Florey, *Le Film Montreal*, October 1922, as cited in Brownlow, *The Parade's Gone By...*, Booton Herndon, *Douglas Fairbanks and Mary Pickford* and Jeffrey Vance and Tony Maietta, *Douglas Fairbanks* (p. 126).

215. On January 22, 1923, Dwan gave a lecture to Columbia University students on filmmaking. Surviving notes reveal that he mentioned showing Fairbanks the recently completed sets for *Robin Hood* without citing any displeasure on Fairbanks' part. However, with the possibility of Dwan and Fairbanks working together again in the future still a possibility, it is understandable that he might have been discreet on this subject. Dwan, "Notes from a Talk to *Photoplay* Students at Columbia University."

216. "Fairbanks Picture Costly," *Motion Picture News*, May 27, 1922, p. 2959.

217. After three trials, Arbuckle was acquitted of all charges.

218. *Motion Picture News*, May 27, 1922, p. 2959.

219. Bogdanovich, *Allan Dwan*, p. 57.

220. Ibid., p. 62.

221. Ibid., pp. 59–60.

222. *Motion Picture News*, September 9, 1922, p. 1253.

223. A film called *Robin Hood Jr.* was released several weeks after the debut of the Fairbanks epic.

224. "High Praise Given Fairbanks Picture," *Moving Picture World*, November 4, 1922, p. 56.

225. Bogdanovich, *Allan Dwan*, p. 63.

226. At least one report, *Moving Picture World*, November 11, 1922, says the actual starting time of the second showing was 11:15 P.M.

227. "Fairbanks Picture Takes New York by Storm," *Motion Picture News*, November 4, 1922, p. 2405.

228. "Robin Hood Rides Upon the Screen," *Literary Digest*, November 18, 1922, as cited in Vance, *Douglas Fairbanks*, p. 315.

229. *Moving Picture World*, March 24, 1923, p. 454.

230. *Motion Picture Magazine*, February 1923, p. 99.

231. "Pictures and People," *Motion Picture News*, December 9, 1922, p. 2900.

232. Alan Hale actually played Little John a third time in the 1950 *Rogues of Sherwood Forest*.

233. Carey, *Doug & Mary*, p. 131.

234. John Aberth, *A Knight at the Movies: Medieval History on Film* (New York: Routledge, 2003), p. 166.

235. Interviews of H. Bruce Humberstone conducted by Jim Desmarais and David Shepard provided courtesy of Directors Guild of America.

236. Herndon, *Mary Pickford and Douglas Fairbanks*, p. 222.

237. *Photoplay*, February 1923, p. 70.

238. Brownlow interview with Dwan, transcript, p. 66.

239. Ibid.

240. In the article "What Photography Means to Robin Hood" in the December 1922 issue of *American Cinematographer*, Edeson is cited for filming each scene as a master artist paints. As mentioned earlier, Dwan himself acknowledged that Edeson painted with light. The article also notes that in examining the charts and blueprints made of the layout of the sets, "he [Edeson] and Allen [sic] Dwan, his director, poured, much as if they were planning a battle, and figured the angles at which the camera would be placed for the actual filming" (p. 15). In the *Motion Picture News* column "Pictures and People," it was noted that there "are several shots in Douglas Fairbanks in Robin Hood which show that someone endowed with true artistic perception was

on the job. We know that Allan Dwan can compose some mighty effective scenes...." The anonymous columnist opines of the visual artistry, "Undoubtedly Messers. Dwan and [Wilfred] Buckland cooperated to give the picture the full advantage of their combined talent (*Motion Picture News*, November 11, 1922, p. 2400).

Chapter 4

1. Paul Hubert Conlon, "Art and Money: Allan Dwan Is a Director with Big Ideas," *Los Angeles Times*, November 23, 1917, p. 113.
2. Ibid.
3. Ibid.
4. Adela Rogers St. John, "Artistic Efficiency—That's Dwan," *Photoplay*, August 1920.
5. Ibid.
6. Tibbetts, *His Majesty, The American*, p. 39.
7. Rogers St. Johns, "Artistic Efficiency—That's Dwan."
8. Betsy Bruce, "The Camera Shy Director," *Motion Picture Magazine*, September 1920, p. 104.
9. *Theater*, January 1927, p. 38.
10. "Allan Dwan on Eastern Trip," *Universal Weekly*, August 2, 1913, p. 2.
11. Bruce, "The Camera Shy Director," p. 104.
12. *Wid's Daily*, November 14, 1918.
13. *Moving Picture World*, Nov. 23, 1918, p. 821.
14. Giebler, "Rubbernecking in Filmland," *Moving Picture World*, December 14, 1918, p. 1197.
15. Bogdanovich, *Allan Dwan*, p. 49.
16. *Motion Picture News*, January 4, 19, p. 112.
17. *Motion Picture News*, July 12, 1919, p. 599.
18. Julian Johnson, *Photoplay*, July 1919, p. 104.
19. Fred Lawrence Guiles, *Marion Davies* (New York: McGraw-Hill, 1972), p. 81.
20. Ibid., pp. 81–82.
21. Ibid., p. 89.
22. Bogdanovich, *Allan Dwan*, p. 49.
23. *Motion Picture News*, April 19, 1919, p. 2531.
24. *Variety*, April 11, 1919, p. 55.
25. Bogdanovich, *Allan Dwan*, p. 49.
26. *Photoplay*, November 1919, p. 115.
27. *Moving Picture World*, August 16, 1919, pp. 1019–1020.
28. *Wid's Daily*, August 24, 1919, p. 14.
29. *Wid's Daily*, October 15, 1926, p. 5.
30. William Randolph Hearst to Joseph Moore, April 23, 1919, Joseph Moore Papers, Library of Congress.
31. Moore to Hearst, April 24, 1919, Moore Papers, LOC.
32. Ibid.
33. Hearst to Moore, April 24, 1919, Moore Papers, LOC.
34. Ibid.
35. Hearst to Moore, April 26, 1919, Moore Papers, LOC.
36. Ibid.
37. Moore to Hearst, April 26, 1919, Moore Papers, LOC.
38. Hearst to Moore, July 30, 1919, Moore Papers, LOC.
39. Bogdanovich, *Allan Dwan*, p. 49.
40. Ibid.
41. Benjamin Hampton, *History of the American Film Industry: From Its Beginnings to 1931* (New York: Dover, 1970), p. 217.
42. Ibid., p. 218.
43. Ibid., p. 216.
44. Bogdanovich, *Allan Dwan*, p. 50.
45. *Motion Picture News*, August 26, 1919, p. 1441.
46. *Moving Picture World*, August 30, 1919, p. 1266.
47. Bogdanovich, *Allan Dwan*, pp. 49–50.
48. Gianna Maria Babando, "Hollywood in San Diego: The Administration of Local Shooting in Parks," *Journal of San Diego History*, Winter 1992, Volume 38, Number 1.
49. Giebler, "Rubbernecking Filmland," *Moving Picture World*, July 12, 1919, p. 201.
50. Ibid., p. 202.
51. *Motion Picture News*, October 11, 1919, p. 2893.
52. Ibid.
53. *Moving Picture World*, February 22, 1919, pp. 453–454.
54. *Photoplay*, February 1920, p. 74.
55. *Wid's Daily*, November 16, 1919, p. 9.
56. Allene Talmey, *Doug, Mary and Others* (New York: Macy-Masius, 1927), p. 51.
57. Louis Pizzitola, *Hearst Over Hollywood* (New York: Columbia University Press, 2002), pp. 174–75.
58. *Moving Picture World*, November 28, 1924, p. 302.
59. Scott Eyman, *Mary Pickford* (New York: Donald I. Fine, 1990), p. 79.
60. Maurice Kahn, "The Infant Approaches Manhood," *Wid's Daily*, May 24, 1928, p. 21.
61. Hampton, *History of the American Film Industry*, p. 177.
62. Charles Chaplin, *My Autobiography* (London: Bodley Head, 1964), p. 237. Also cited in Tino Balio, *United Artists: The Company Built By the Stars* (Madison: University of Wisconsin Press, 1976), p. 12. According to Chaplin's biographer, David Robinson, both Fairbanks and Chaplin hired private detectives to spy on delegates to the convention. Their reports survive in the Vevey Archive. David Robinson, *Chaplin: His Life and Art* (New York: McGraw-Hill, 1985), pp. 267–68.
63. Ramsaye, *A Million and One Nights*, p. 795.
64. Balio, *United Artists*, pp. 25–26.
65. *Moving Picture World*, February 1, 1919, p. 615.
66. Ibid.
67. Elizabeth Peltret, "Where Do We Go from Here?" *Motion Picture*, May 1919, p. 56.
68. Ibid. The italics are from the original article.
69. Frank Case, *Tales of a Wayward Inn* (New York: Garden City, 1938), p. 88.
70. Herndon, *Mary Pickford and Douglas Fairbanks*, p. 240. "Doug" referred to a game Fairbanks invented that was a variation on badminton.
71. Peltret, "Where Do We Go from Here?," p. 57.
72. Hampton, *History of the American Film Industry*, p. 214.
73. *Motion Picture News*, January 4, 1919, p. 71; *Moving Picture World*, January 4, 1919, p. 53.
74. *Wid's Daily*, August 18, 1918, p. 1.
75. Hampton, *History of the American Film Industry*, pp. 215–216.
76. Ibid., p. 218.
77. "Tucker Specials," *Wid's Daily*, February 19, 1919, p. 1.
78. Ibid.
79. *Wid's Daily*, August 18, 1918, p. 2. In an advertisement that appeared in *Wid's Daily* on October 14, 1921,Gunning acknowledged among other things that he had been an associate of Tucker for four years.
80. *Wid's Daily*, February 20, 1919, p. 1.
81. *Moving Picture World*, December 13, 1919, p. 777.
82. "Plays and Players," *Photoplay*, January 1920, p. 120.
83. Hampton, *History of the American Film Industry*, p. 242.
84. "Plays and Players," *Photoplay*, February 1920, p. 101.
85. *Wid's Daily*, December 9, 1919; *Motion Picture News*, December 13, 1919, pp. 4228–4229.
86. "'Big Six' Prize Is Still Unpicked," *Variety*, April 23, 1920, p. 47.
87. *Moving Picture World*, March 6, 1920, p. 1604.
88. *Wid's Daily*, March 1, 1920, p. 1.
89. Ibid., p. 2.
90. Hampton, *History of the American Film Industry*, p. 244.
91. *Variety*, January 17, 1920, p. 65.
92. *Motion Picture News*, July 31, 1920.
93. Ramsaye, *A Million and One Nights*, p. 813.
94. *Photoplay*, May 1920, p. 65.
95. *Photoplay*, February 1920, p. 74.
96. *Photoplay*, December 1920, p. 123.
97. Carey, *Doug & Mary*, p. 70.
98. Decree, Filed October 23, 1919, Second Judicial Court of the State of Nevada, Margaret Herrick Library.
99. "Allan Dwan Starts The Filming of New and Costly Feature," *Motion Picture News*, December 13, 1919, p. 4308.
100. *Moving Picture World*, September 18, 1920, p. 387.
101. *Motion Picture News*, October 23, 1920, p. 3275.
102. *Moving Picture World*, October 2, 1920, p. 690.
103. *Wid's Daily*, January 15, 1920, p. 8.
104. Ibid.
105. *Photoplay*, February 1919, p. 82.
106. Unpublished Kevin Brownlow interview with Howard Hawks, June 30, 1967.
107. Jack Spears, "Marshall Neilan," in *Hollywood: The Golden Era* (South Brunswick, NJ: A.S. Barnes, 1971), p. 279.
108. Ibid., p. 298.
109. Kenneth Anger, *Hollywood Babylon* (San Francisco: Straight Arrow Books, 1975), p. 76.
110. Spears, *Hollywood: The Golden Era*, p. 279.
111. Dorothy Manners, "The Man Behind the Megaphone," *Picture Play Magazine*, February 1925, p. 69.
112. Ibid., pp. 69–70.
113. Ibid., p. 70, 110.
114. Ibid., p. 110.
115. Spears, *Hollywood: The Golden Era*, p. 288.
116. *Moving Picture World*, December 13, 1919, p. 787.
117. *Photoplay*, February 1921 p. 95 The review of *The Forbidden Thing* was one of several credited not to Burns Mantle, who had written the main reviews in that issue, but to "*Photoplay* Editors."
118. *Motion Picture News*, November 27, 1920, p. 4153.
119. *Variety*, December 3, 1920.
120. *Wid's Daily*, November 21, 1920, p. 7.
121. Thomas H. Ince Papers, Library of Congress.
122. Cut from Bogdanovich interview, tape 2–1, Bogdanovich Papers, Lilly Library, University of Indiana.
123. Todd McCarthy, *Howard Hawks* (New York: Grove Press, 1997), p. 51, 52. As in his interview with Bogdanovich, Dwan does not say specifically which of his Associated Producers Hawks financed, although Hawks appears to say he financed them all.
124. Unpublished Brownlow interview with Hawks, June 30, 1967.
125. Spears, *Hollywood: The Golden Era*, p. 291.
126. Ince Papers, LOC.
127. *Moving Picture World*, September 25, 1920, p. 441.
128. Bogdanovich, *Allan Dwan*, p. 52.
129. Larry Swindell, *Screwball: The Life of Carole Lombard* (New York: William Morrow, 1975), pp. 30–32.

130. *Photoplay*, July 1921, p. 68.
131. *Motion Picture News*, March 5, 1921, p. 1859.
132. *Los Angeles Times*, January 7, 1921.
133. Ibid.
134. Ibid.
135. Cut from Bogdanovich interview, tape 2–1, 2–2, Bogdanovich Papers, Lilly Library, University of Indiana.
136. Special Meeting, Board of Directors, United Artists Corporation, January 8, 1921, Minutes, United Artists Corporate Records, Wisconsin Center for Film and Theater Research.
137. Letter from General Manager of Distribution to Ince, January 14, 1921, Thomas H. Ince Papers, LOC.
138. "Abrams Reported in Deal for Associated," *Variety*, January 28, 1921, p. 47.
139. Letter from F.B. Warren to G. Gardner Sullivan, December 8, 1920, Thomas H. Ince Papers, LOC.
140. "Films' Serious Financial State; Report Banks scary of Trade," *Variety*, December 17, 1920, p. 47.
141. Gene Smiley, *Rethinking the Great Depression* (Chicago: Ivan R. Dee, 2002), pp. 48–49.
142. *Wid's Daily*, May 14, 1921; *Variety*, May 27, 1921, p. 38. In 1924 the New York Supreme Court awarded Warren $39,500 in damages.
143. Joseph McBride, *Hawks on Hawks* (Berkeley: Univ. of California Press, 1982), p. 16.
144. *Oakland Tribune*, December 26, 1922, p. 8.
145. "A.P. to Hold Big Sales Drive," *Motion Picture News*, June 4, 1921, pp. 3437–3438.
146. *Motion Picture News*, June 25, 1921, p. 119.
147. Correspondence from F.B. Warren to members of the Associated Producers included a rundown of members receiving copies. Tucker's name was included in surviving correspondence as late as January 1921. In correspondence beginning in February, beneath the names of the other members was the entry, "None sent to Mr. Tucker, withdrawn." Thomas H. Ince Papers, LOC.
148. *Motion Picture News*, December 3, 1921, p. 2985.
149. *Moving Picture World*, December 10, 1921, p. 710.
150. *Motion Picture News*, December 3, 1921, p. 2985.
151. *Variety*, November 25, 1921.
152. *Wid's Daily*, June 16, 1921, p. 6.
153. Letter from Price to Ince, August 13, 1921, Thomas H. Ince Papers, LOC.
154. *Variety*, August 19, 1921, p. 37.
155. *Wid's Daily*, August 27, 1921, p. 1.
156. *Motion Picture News*, September 17, 1921 p. 1482.
157. *Variety*, September 9, 1921, p. 43.
158. *Wid's Daily*, December 13, 1921, p. 4.
159. *Photoplay*, January 1922, p. 91.
160. Brownlow interview with Dwan, pp. 41–42.
161. Brownlow, *Behind the Mask of Innocence*, p. 150.
162. Brownlow interview, pp. 42–43.
163. Brownlow interview, p. 42.
164. *Harper's Weekly*, April 29, 1916, p. 459; *Kine Weekly*, January 1, 1924.
165. Chris Fujiwara, *Jacques Tourneur: The Cinema of Nightfall* (Jefferson, NC: McFarland, 1998), p. 17.
166. Pizzatola, *Hearst Over Hollywood*, pp. 222–224. The rumors were spurred by the strangely reserved and sometimes contradictory coverage by the Hearst press. In his book, Pizzatola draws on a December 1924 investigation and other sources for another explanation, that Ince had been drinking heavily on board and had succumbed to "bad liquor." The fear of conviction for bootlegging operations would account for Hearst's attempt to contain the scandal and limit information.
167. *Film Daily*, January 18, 1922, p. 4.

Chapter 5

1. Emily W. Leider, *Dark Lover* (New York: Faber and Faber, 2003), p. 231.
2. Ibid., p. 228.
3. *Variety*, February 15, 1923, p. 47.
4. *Photoplay*, February 1922.
5. Bogdanovich, *Allan Dwan*, pp. 65–66.
6. Gloria Swanson, *Swanson on Swanson* (New York: Random House, 1980), p. 192.
7. Dwan interview with Adamson, CD, side #1, Museum of the Moving Image.
8. Ibid
9. Ibid.
10. Dwan interview with Adamson, CD, side #3, Museum of the Moving Image.
11. Dwan interview with Adamson, CD, side #4, Museum of the Moving Image.
12. Robin Wallace mailing to author, March 27, 2011.
13. *Film Daily*, April 10, 1924 "Proof," p. 1.
14. *Moving Picture World*, February 17, 1923, p. 703.
15. Hermione Lee, *Edith Wharton* (New York: Alfred A. Knopf, 2007), p. 594.
16. Bebe Daniels and Ben Lyon, *Life with the Lyons: The Autobiography of Bebe Daniels & Ben Lyon* (London: Odahms Press, 1953), p. 105; "Cuts and Flashes," *Film Daily*, January 30, 1923, p. 4.
17. *New York Times* review, April 3, 1923, p. 23.
18. Ibid.
19. *Photoplay*, June 1923, p. 67.
20. Edward Wagenknecht, *The Movies in the Age of Innocence* (Norman: University of Oklahoma Press, 1962), p. 209.
21. *Oakland Tribune*, December 26, 1922, p. 8.
22. Kevin Thomas interview with author.
23. Anthony Slide, *Silent Players* (Lexington: University Press of Kentucky, 2002), p. 267.
24. Leider, *Dark Lover*, p. 202.
25. Kevin Thomas interview with author.
26. *Moving Picture World*, March 10, 1923, p. 235.
27. Slide, *Silent Players*, p. 163.
28. *Motion Picture News*, August 4, 1923, p. 563.
29. Dwan interview with Adamson, CD, side #3, Museum of the Moving Image.
30. *Moving Picture World*, August 4, 1923, p. 406.
31. *New York Times* review, July 24, 1923, p. 24.
32. Spears, *Hollywood: The Golden Era*, p. 182.
33. Doris Irving, "How the Director Knows," *Picture Play*, June 1923, p. 59.
34. Swanson, *Swanson on Swanson*, p. 24.
35. Ibid., p. 151.
36. Ibid., p. 192.
37. Ibid., pp. 180–181; also Neilan letter.
38. Graham Russell Gao Hodges, *Anna May Wong: From Laundryman's Daughter to Hollywood Legend* (New York: Palgrave Macmillan, 2004), p. 36.
39. Agreement By and Between Gloria Swanson, Herbert Somborn, and Famous Players–Lasky Corporation, March 22, 1923, Gloria Swanson Collection, Harry Ransom Humanities Research Center, University of Texas at Austin.
40. Swanson, *Swanson on Swanson*, p. 181.
41. Ibid., p. 193.
42. Ibid.
43. *Film Daily*, April 17, 1923, p. 1.
44. "In The East," *Film Daily*, June 17, 1923, p. 4.
45. *Film Daily*, February 8, 1923, p. 6.
46. Bogdanovich, *Allan Dwan*, pp. 65–66.
47. Dwan interview with Adamson, CD, side # 3, Museum of the Moving Image.
48. Swanson, *Swanson on Swanson*, p. 194.
49. Ibid., p. 196.
50. Bogdanovich, *Allan Dwan*, p. 66.
51. Dwan interview with Adamson, CD, side #4, Museum of the Moving Image.
52. Dwan interview with Adamson, CD, side #3, Museum of the Moving Image.
53. Dwan interview with Adamson, CD, side #5, Museum of the Moving Image.
54. Swanson, *Swanson on Swanson*, p. 196.
55. *Zaza, A Comedy Drama in Five Acts*, adapted by David Belasco from the French of Pierre Berton and Charles Simon, microfilm copy, Billy Rose Theatre Division, New York Public Library.
56. This account of *Zaza* is based on a viewing of the version provided by the Library of Congress. This print is 6,601 feet long; the release version was 7,076.
57. Dwan interview with Adamson, CD, side #5, Museum of the Moving Image.
58. Swanson, *Swanson on Swanson*, p. 196.
59. *Variety* review, October 8, 1915.
60. Lawrence J. Quirk, *The Films of Gloria Swanson* (Secaucus, NJ: Citadel Press, 1984), p. 152.
61. *Photoplay*, December 1923, p. 72.
62. "Newspaper Opinions," *Film Daily*, September 20, 1923, p. 4.
63. Swanson, *Swanson on Swanson*, p. 196.
64. *Film Daily*, January 10, 1923, p. 1.
65. *Moving Picture World*, September 8, 1923, p. 92.
66. "Dwan May Go West," *Film Daily*, May 8, 1923, p. 3.
67. *Moving Picture World*, September 22, 1923, p. 362.
68. Paramount Publicity Sheet, "Big Brother," "A Real Tie-Up," Billy Rose Theatre Division, New York Public Library.
69. Paramount publicity sheet, "Big Brother," "Jesse Lasky Comments Upon 'Big Brother.'"
70. Paramount publicity sheet, "Big Brother," "Here's A Synopsis of the Story — Along With Cast."
71. Allen Corliss, "That Mean Guy, Hatton," *Photoplay*, November 1916, p. 58.
72. Paramount publicity sheet, "Big Brother," "A Page from the History of New York's Gangland."
73. Brownlow, *Behind the Mask of Innocence*, p. 200.
74. *New York Times* review of "Big Brother," December 24, 1923, p. 12.
75. Paramount publicity sheet, "The Bottom Has Dropped Out of the Price of Food," "Big Brother."
76. Bogdanovich, *Allan Dwan*, p. 68.
77. Brownlow interview, slate 322, take 1, p. 80.
78. Brownlow, *Behind the Mask of Innocence*, p. 203.
79. Dwan interview with Adamson, CD, side #1, Museum of the Moving Image.
80. Paramount publicity sheet, "Big Brother," "No Grease Paint Used in Picture *Big Brother*."
81. *New York Times* review, December 24, 1923, p. 12.
82. *Variety* review, December 27, 1923.
83. *Photoplay*, February 1924, p. 63.
84. Swanson, *Swanson on Swanson*, p. 211.
85. Ibid. The *New York Times* review also mentioned that "Mrs. Thelma Converse, sister of Mrs. Reginald Vanderbilt, plays a minor role in this production" (March 10, 1924, p. 18).
86. *Moving Picture World*, January 19, 1924, p. 193.

87. Swanson, *Swanson on Swanson*, p. 213.
88. Bogdanovich, *Allan Dwan*, p. 68.
89. Ibid., pp. 68–70.
90. *Motion Picture News*, March 22, 1924, p. 1330.
91. *Variety* review, March 12, 1924.
92. *Photoplay*, May 1924, p. 54.
93. *Film Daily*, January 22, 1924, p. 1.
94. *Motion Picture News*, January 26, 1924, p. 361; *Photoplay*, April 1924, p. 74.
95. Swanson, *Swanson on Swanson*, p. 203.
96. Frank Tuttle and John Franceshina, *They Started Talking* (Boalsburg, PA: BearManor Media, 2005), p. 31, See also *Film Daily*, January 29, 1924.
97. Ibid., p. 32.
98. Swanson, *Swanson on Swanson*, p. 203; Tuttle and Franceshina, *They Started Talking*, p. 32.
99. Tuttle and Franceshina, *They Started Talking*, p. 33.
100. Swanson, *Swanson on Swanson*, p. 209.
101. Tuttle and Franceshina, *They Started Talking*, p. 34.
102. Ibid.
103. Bogdanovich, *Allan Dwan*, p. 71.
104. Swanson, *Swanson on Swanson*, p. 210.
105. Tuttle and Franceshina, *They Started Talking*, p. 35.
106. Paramount publicity sheet.
107. Swanson, *Swanson on Swanson*, p. 211.
108. *New York Times* review, July 29, 1924, p. 9.
109. Ibid.
110. *Motion Picture News*, June 21, 1924, p. 2997.
111. Harriette Underhill, "On the Screen," *New York Herald Tribune*, July 29, 1924, p. 6.
112. Swanson, *Swanson on Swanson*, p. 277.
113. *New York Times* review, October 7, 1924, p. 26.
114. *New York Morning Telegraph* quoted in "Newspaper Opinions," *Film Daily*, October 9, 1924.
115. *Moving Picture World*, February 24, 1923, p. 761.
116. *Moving Picture World*, June 23, 1923, p. 637.
117. *Variety*, June 14, 1923, p. 18.
118. Ibid.
119. *New York Times Encyclopedia of Film*, "Pictures Appeal to A Dream Mind," April 18, 1923, "Action, Not Words, Wanted," May 20, 1923.
120. Swanson, *Swanson on Swanson*, p. 214. Also reported in *Photoplay*, September 1924, p. 84.
121. Swanson, *Swanson on Swanson*, pp. 215–16.
122. Ramsaye, *A Million and One Nights*, p. 825. Swanson wrote that before departing for Europe and discussing *Madame Sans-Genes* with Halsey, they decided that the film "should be done in France with a French director on the actual locations..." (*Swanson on Swanson*, p. 215). It's possible that she changed her mind or Paramount overruled her that by the terms of her contract that she would be making all her films with Dwan. But the French still had the final say.
123. Daniels and Lyon, *Life with the Lyons*, p. 133.
124. Ibid.
125. Joe Pasternak, as told to David Chandler, *Easy the Hard Way* (New York: Putnam, 1956), p. 68.
126. Ibid., p. 70.
127. Ibid., pp. 70–71.
128. *New York Post*, November 24, 1924, p. 13.
129. *Moving Picture World* review, November 29, 1924, p. 548.
130. *Motion Picture News* review, November 22, 1924, p. 2645.
131. *Variety* review, November 26, 1924.
132. Mordaunt Hall, *New York Times* review, December 23, 1924, p. 16.
133. Ibid.
134. *Motion Picture News*, November 1, 1924, p. 2210; *Moving Picture World*, November 1, 1924, p. 26.
135. Swanson, *Swanson on Swanson*, p. 232.
136. Ibid., pp. 234–36.
137. Bogdanovich, *Allan Dwan*, pp. 75–76.
138. Dwan interview with Adamson, CD, side #2, Museum of the Moving Image. Dwan said that Swanson and her assistant Jane West used to make crank calls to strangers, suggesting that she was dallying with their husbands.
139. *Film Daily*, January 19, 1925, p. 1.
140. Excised portions from Bogdanovich interview, tape 2–56, tape 2–57, Bogdanovich Papers, Lilly Library, University of Indiana.
141. Swanson, *Swanson on Swanson*, p. 242.
142. *Film Daily*, February 27, 1925, p. 1.
143. *Moving Picture World*, November 8, 1924, p. 166.
144. Bogdanovich, *Allan Dwan*, p. 76.
145. Ibid.
146. Ibid.
147. *Photoplay*, May 1925, pp. 40–41.
148. Bogdanovich, *Allan Dwan*, p. 76.
149. *Photoplay*, June 1925, p. 102.
150. *Moving Picture World* review, July 25, 1925, p. 432.
151. *Photoplay*, September 1925, p. 51.
152. Bogdanovich, *Allan Dwan*, p. 76.
153. Louise Brooks interview with Kevin Brownlow, Rochester, New York, 1965, p. 28.
154. Barry Paris, *Louise Brooks* (New York: Alfred A. Knopf, 1989), p. 97.
155. Brooks interview with Brownlow, pp. 26–27.
156. Ibid., p. 28.
157. Swanson, *Swanson on Swanson*, p. 261.
158. Ibid., pp. 262–63.
159. Ibid., p. 263.
160. Ibid.
161. *Variety*, March 4, 1925, p. 28.
162. Pasternak, *Easy the Hard Way*, p. 82.
163. Swanson, *Swanson on Swanson*, p. 267. It should be pointed out that on page 323 of her autobiography, Swanson also admitted, "I had found in two years of marriage to Henri that I could turn on the Marquise de la Falaise de la Coudraye and be very cold and grand and formal at will, as, for example when I wanted to terminate an interview or get through customs quickly, or put down a phony." So she may have turned on the royal persona whenever she found it useful.
164. Dwan interview with Adamson, CD, side #2. In her 1965 interview with Kevin Brownlow and elsewhere, Louise Brooks said that while shooting at the Astoria Studios, "we were working next door to the Allan Dwan–Gloria Swanson *Coast of Folly*. And ... we'd see Allan over on his set walking around shooting this and and shooting and ... about about 11:30 MISS SWANSON would arrive ... she'd sit down in the director's chair — her little tiny legs crossed. His chair! And ALLAN would smile.... And she'd say, 'Well, I think we ought to do....'" The problem with Brooks' story is that *The Coast of Folly* was not shot in Astoria but in California. Brooks started at Famous Players too late to see most of the Dwan–Swanson films in production. Most of the only remaining Dwan–Swanson picture at Famous Players, *Stage Struck*, was shot in West Virginia. Brooks could have visited the set for the Technicolor sequences shot in Queens but Brooks was making no films at that time. It's possible that Brooks is confusing this incident with the filming of *Fine Manners* when Swanson *was* reported to be sitting in Frank Tuttle's director's chair.
165. Herbert Howe, "Returning to Hollywood," *Photoplay*, May 1925, p. 80.
166. Swanson, *Swanson on Swanson*, p. 267.
167. *New York Times* review, August 31, 1925.
168. *Variety* review, September 2, 1925.
169. Ibid.
170. Bogdanovich, *Allan Dwan*, p. 76.
171. "Example for Assistant Directors by Alan Dwan with Swanson Film," *Variety*, September 16, 1925, p. 31.
172. Swanson, *Swanson on Swanson*, p. 271.
173. Renita Ashley, "Almost Changed the City's Name to Gloria, West Va," *Photoplay*, November 1925, p. 32.
174. Dwan interview with Adamson, CD, side #4, Museum of the Moving Image.
175. Dwan interview with Adamson, CD, side #3, Museum of the Moving Image.
176. Dwan interview with Adamson, CD, side #2, Museum of the Moving Image.
177. Swanson, *Swanson on Swanson*, p. 274.
178. *Photoplay*, November 1925, p. 33.
179. Swanson, *Swanson on Swanson*, p. 274.
180. Pasternak, *Easy the Hard Way*, p. 87.
181. *Photoplay*, November 1925, p. 128.
182. Ibid.
183. Ibid., p. 129.
184. "Gloria Swanson and the Filming of *Stage Struck*," *Wetzel Democrat*, August 27, 1925, West Virginia Archives.
185. Pasternak, *Easy the Hard Way*, p. 87.
186. Ibid., p. 88.
187. Dwan interview with Adamson, CD, side #4, Museum of the Moving Image.
188. Bogdanovich, *Allan Dwan*, pp. 78–79.
189. "Paramount Lineup," *Motion Picture News*, May 16, 1925.
190. Bogdanovich, *Allan Dwan*, p. 78.
191. Swanson, *Swanson on Swanson*, p. 275.
192. Ibid.
193. *Variety*, December 16, 1925, p. 37.
194. Famous Players–Lasky Corporation Inter-Office Communication, September 23, 1925, Gloria Swanson Papers, Harry Ransom Humanities Research Center, University of Texas at Austin.
195. *Photoplay*, November 1925, p. 98.
196. Dwan interview with Adamson, CD, side #3, Museum of the Moving Image.
197. *Variety* review, November 25, 1925.
198. *New York Times* review, November 16, 1925, p. 19.
199. *Movie Magazine*, January 1926.
200. *Moving Picture World* review, November 28, 1925, p. 343.
201. *Photoplay*, February 1926, p. 48.
202. Swanson, *Swanson on Swanson*, p. 276.
203. Dwan interview with Adamson, CD, side #2, Museum of the Moving Image.
204. Swanson, *Swanson on Swanson*, p. 280.
205. Tuttle and Franceshina, *They Started Talking*, p. 35.
206. Swanson, *Swanson on Swanson*, pp. 280–81.
207. "Swanson Directing Final F.P. Picture," *Variety*, May 5, 1926, p. 1.
208. *Motion Picture News*, April 10, 1926, p. 1577.
209. *Photoplay*, July 1926, p. 76.
210. Ibid., p. 102, Richard Rosson photo caption.
211. Gloria Swanson caption, *Photoplay*, September 1926, p. 106.
212. Swanson, *Swanson on Swanson*, p. 276.
213. *Wid's*, March 14, 1926, p. 8.
214. Bogdanovich, *Allan Dwan*, pp. 80–81.
215. *Variety* review, February 24, 1926.
216. Budd Schulberg, *Moving Pictures: Memories of a Hollywood Prince* (Chicago: Ivan R. Dee, 1981), p. 188.
217. Dwan interview with Adamson, CD, side #2, Museum of the Moving Image.

218. Ivor Montagu, *With Eisenstein in Hollywood* (New York: International, 1967), p. 49.
219. Allan Dwan, "Adaptation," *Motion Picture Director*, June 1926, included in Richard Koszarski, *Hollywood Directors, 1914–1940* (New York: Oxford University Press, 1976), pp. 154–59.
220. Richard Buller, *A Beautiful Fairy Tale: The Life of Lois Moran* (Pompton Plains, NJ: Limelight Editions, 2005), pp. 45–46.
221. *Photoplay*, August 1926, p. 54.
222. "Newspaper Opinions," *New York Post*, in *Film Daily*, August 16, 1926.
223. *Moving Picture World*, August 28, 1926, p. 544.
224. Matthew Bernstein, *Walter Wanger, Hollywood Independent* (Berkeley: University of California Press, 1994), p. 58.
225. Ibid., pp. 59–60.
226. Ibid., p. 58.
227. Brownlow, *The Parade's Gone By...*, p. 497.
228. Dwan interview with Adamson, CD, side #2, Museum of the Moving Image.
229. *New York Times* review, September 20, 1926, p. 21.
230. The "lost father" theme does surface in the lost *Her Love Story* when the royal family banished Swanson's commoner husband and had his son raised as the son of the man Swanson was forced to marry. The countess in *The Coast of Folly* was one of the few occasions when Dwan used the device of a "lost mother."
231. *Moving Picture World* review, October 2, 1926, p. 307.
232. *Moving Picture World*, June 12, 1926, p. 537.
233. *Film Daily*, May 27, 1926, p. 1.
234. *Variety*, June 4, 1926, p. 6.
235. Richard Koszarski, *An Evening's Entertainment: The Age of the Silent Feature Picture, 1915–1928* (Berkeley: University of California Press, 1990), pp. 212–13.
236. Madge Bellamy, *A Darling of the Twenties* (Vestal, NY: Vestal Press, 1989), p. 80.
237. *Motion Picture News* review, December 31, 1926, p. 2540.
238. *New York Times* review, December 20, 1926, p. 28.
239. Buller, *A Beautiful Fairy Tale*, p. 200.
240. *Variety* review, January 19, 1927.
241. Matthew Bruccoli, ed., *F. Scott Fitzgerald's The Great Gatsby: A Literary Reference* (New York: Carroll & Grant, 2000), p. 55.
242. Buller, *A Beautiful Fairy Tale*, p. 160, 186.
243. *Film Daily*, September 3, 1926, p. 12.
244. Bogdanovich, *Allan Dwan*, pp. 83–84.
245. Ibid., p. 84.
246. *Film Daily*, April 25, 1927, p. 1.
247. *Motion Picture News*, May 6, 1927, p. 1668.
248. *Variety*, May 4, 1927, p. 27, for appendix 7 minutes long.
249. *Film Daily*, May 1, 1927, p. 1.
250. Donald Crafton, *The Talkies: American Cinema's Transition to Sound, 1926–1931* (New York: Scribner's, 1997), p. 96. *The Jazz Singer*, highly touted for its historical significance, did not premiere until over five months after the West Point newsreel.
251. Bogdanovich, *Allan Dwan*, p. 82.
252. Ibid.
253. Betty Lee, *Marie Dressler: The Unlikeliest Star* (Lexington: University Press of Kentucky, 1997), p. 158.
254. Ibid., p. 159.
255. Ibid.
256. *New York Times* review, September 6, 1927, p. 34.
257. *Variety* review, September 7, 1927.
258. *Film Daily*, June 5, 1927, p. 21.
259. *Film Daily*, June 1, 1927, p. 7.
260. *Film Daily*, June 5, 1927, p. 21.
261. "Fox Picture Outlay $15,000,000," *Motion Picture News*, March 25, 1927, p. 1036.
262. "Sheehan Places Fox Studios on Coast In 'A-1'" Position," *Moving Picture World*, June 25, 1927, p. 589.
263. Leonard Maltin, "FFM Interviews George O'Brien," *Film Fan Monthly*, No. 119, May 1971, pp. 24–25.
264. *Film Daily*, July 27, 1927, p. 2.
265. *Film Daily*, July 29, 1927, p. 1.
266. Ibid., p. 1, 4.
267. Swanson, *Swanson on Swanson*, pp. 293–94.
268. *New York Times*, August 17, 1927, p. 27.
269. *Miami Daily News*, January 16, 1927, p. 10.
270. Charlotte Chandler, *Nobody's Perfect* (New York: Simon & Schuster, 2002), p. 45.
271. Ibid., pp. 45–46.
272. Ibid.
273. Maurice Zolotow, *Billy Wilder in Hollywood* (New York: Putnam, 1977), p. 34.
274. *Moving Picture World*, July 30, 1927, p. 311.
275. *Film Daily* review, December 25, 1927, p. 6.
276. *Variety* review, December 14, 1927.
277. Ibid.
278. "Newspaper Opinions," *Film Daily*, February 21, 1928, p. 4; "New *Photoplays*," *New York Post*, p. 8.
279. *Photoplay*, May 1928, p. 55.
280. *Washington Post* review, April 23, 1928.
281. *Motion Picture News*, May 12, 1928, p. 1588.
282. *Washington Post* review, April 23, 1928.
283. Ibid.
284. *Motion Picture News*, May 12, 1928, p. 1588.
285. Mervyn LeRoy as told to Dick Kleiner, *Mervyn LeRoy: Take One* (New York: Hawthorn Books, 1974), p. 82.
286. *Film Daily*, January 31, 1928, p. 3; *Film Daily*, February 3, 1928, p. 8.
287. Contract between Dwan and Douglas Fairbanks Film Corporation, June 25, 1928, Allan Dwan file, Margaret Herrick Library.
288. Bogdanovich, *Allan Dwan*, p. 82.
289. Hancock and Fairbanks, *The Fourth Musketeer*, p. 221.
290. Ibid.
291. William Bakewell, *Hollywood Be Thy Name: Random Collections of a Movie Veteran from Silents to Talkies to TV* (Metuchen, NJ: Scarecrow Press, 1991), p. 110.
292. Bogdanovich, *Allan Dwan*, p. 83.
293. Bakewell, *Hollywood Be Thy Name*, p. 50.
294. Bogdanovich, *Allan Dwan*, p. 85.
295. Dwan interview with Brownlow, slate 324, take 1, p. 5, p. 98.
296. There was at least one case, however, when another voice was used in place of Fairbanks' for the prologue. That was in the re-issue of *The Iron Mask* in the 1950s which used the narration of Douglas Fairbanks, Jr., in place of intertitles. For the first release of that version Fairbanks Jr.'s voice was post-synchronized to his father's lip movements.
297. Edward Bernds, *Mr. Bernds Goes to Hollywood* (Lanham, MD: Scarecrow Press, 1999), p. 62.
298. Scott Eyman, *The Speed of Sound: Hollywood and the Talkie Revolution* (New York: Simon & Schuster, 1997), p. 321.
299. Bakewell, *Hollywood Be Thy Name*, p. 110.
300. Ibid.
301. Ibid.
302. Interviews of H. Bruce Humberstone conducted by Jim Desmarais and David Shepard provided courtesy of Directors Guild of America, Inc.
303. Ibid.
304. Hancock and Fairbanks, *The Fourth Musketeer*, p. 187.
305. Coursodon and Sauvage, *American Directors, Volume I*, p. 111.
306. Herndon, *Mary Pickford and Douglas Fairbanks*, p. 268.
307. This comes from the last stanza of the prologue poem:

> Friends were friends in those brave days
> Athos, Porthos, Aramis, I
> Graved our hearts with a mystic phrase
> Bound our lives with a mystic tie.
> Come! Stir your souls with our ringing call
> Of ALL FOR ONE AND ONE FOR ALL.
> Come on! Come on! Come on!

308. Other shots worth citing include the queen giving birth, the nuns taking Constance's body, the River Castle in the lightning storm.
309. *Film Daily*, February 25, 1929, p. 1.
310. *Photoplay*, February 1929, p. 53.
311. *Film Daily*, February 25, 1929, p. 2.
312. *Film Daily*, March 3, 1929, p. 1.
313. *Film Daily*, March 19, 1929, full page ad, p. 3.
314. Balio, *United Artists: The Company Built by the Stars*, p. 93.
315. Eyman, *The Speed of Sound*, pp. 379–80.
316. Bogdanovich, *Allan Dwan*, p. 85.
317. Ibid., pp. 105–06.
318. Koszarski, *An Evening's Entertainment*, p. 211.
319. Ibid., p. 211.
320. Bogdanovich, *Allan Dwan*, p. 85.

Chapter 6

1. Peter B. Kyne, *Tide of Empire* (New York: Grosset & Dunlap, 1927), p. 32.
2. Ibid., p. 285, Kyne's attitude towards "half-breeds" is also evident in the citation from Kevin Brownlow in "Fairbanks Without the Smile" in chapter three.
3. "Want Fairbanks Film Changed," *Wid's Daily*, August 2, 1918, p. 1.
4. Bradley King memo, March 21, 1928, MGM Collection, USC.
5. *Tide of Empire*, Daily Production Reports, MGM Collection, USC.
6. Bogdanovich, *Allan Dwan*, pp. 85–86.
7. *Photoplay*, December 1928, p. 55.
8. *Film Daily*, March 20, 1929, p. 4.
9. *Motion Picture News*, May 8, 1926, p. 2250.
10. Tag Gallagher, *John Ford: The Man and His Films* (Berkeley: University of California Press, 1986), p. 544; Joseph McBride, *Searching for John Ford* (London: Faber and Faber, 2003), pp. 158–159.
11. Bogdanovich, *Allan Dwan*, p. 85.
12. *New York Herald Tribune*, October 28, 1929, p. 10.
13. *Variety*, October 30, 1929.
14. *New York Times* review, December 7, 1929, p. 19.
15. *Photoplay*, January 1930, p. 52.
16. Letter from Doris Berman, secretary to Dwan to Pierre Bedard, production manager for Swanson, April 25, 1927, and letter from Bedard to Dwan, May 18, 1927, Gloria Swanson Collection, Harry Ransom Humanities Research Center, University of Texas at Austin.
17. Swanson, *Swanson on Swanson*, p. 295.
18. Ibid.
19. *Variety*, August 17, 1927, p. 5.
20. *Photoplay*, October 1927, p. 42.
21. Swanson, *Swanson on Swanson*, p. 296.
22. Excised portion of Bogdanovich interview, tape 3–249, Bogdanovich Papers, Lilly Library, Indiana University.
23. Ibid., tape 3–250.

24. Cari Beauchamp, *Joseph Kennedy Presents* (New York: Alfred A. Knopf, 2009), p. 119.
25. Swanson, *Swanson on Swanson*, p. 340.
26. Ramsaye, *A Million and One Nights*, caption to photo opposite p. 824.
27. Ibid., p. 329.
28. Ibid.
29. Ibid.
30. Axel Madsen, *Gloria & Joe* (New York: William Morrow, 1988), p. 245.
31. Swanson, *Swanson on Swanson*, p. 373.
32. Richard Koszarski, *The Man You Love to Hate: Erich von Stroheim and Hollywood* (Oxford: Oxford University Press, 1983), p. 230.
33. At one point, Kennedy unsuccessfully tried to arrange a loan-out from MGM of director Sam Wood to finish *Queen Kelly*. The director Swanson once regarded as too prosaic momentarily appeared as a potential savior. Beauchamp, *Joseph P. Kennedy Presents*, p. 291.
34. Joseph P. Kennedy to the Marquis de la Falaise, March 13, 1929, in Amanda Smith, ed., *Hostage to Fortune: The Letters of Joseph P. Kennedy* (New York: Viking, 2001), p. 81; also cited in Beauchamp, *Joseph P. Kennedy Presents*, p. 251.
35. Beauchamp, *Joseph Kennedy Presents*, p. 272.
36. Swanson, *Swanson on Swanson*, p. 397.
37. Ibid.
38. Madsen, *Gloria & Joe*, p. 223.
39. Swanson, *Swanson on Swanson*, p. 373; Madsen, *Gloria & Joe*.
40. *Photoplay*, December 1920, p. 123.
41. Swanson, *Swanson on Swanson*, p. 397.
42. Gloria Swanson Collection, Harry Ransom Humanities Research Center, University of Texas at Austin.
43. Swanson, *Swanson on Swanson*, p. 398.
44. Ibid.
45. Ibid.
46. Bogdanovich, *Allan Dwan*, p. 90.
47. Ibid., p. 89.
48. Swanson, *Swanson on Swanson*, p. 399.
49. Bogdanovich, *Allan Dwan*, pp. 89–90. Dwan also maintained in his version that he suggested to Kennedy that a Cadillac be given to the winner. However, it seems unlikely that he would have been so cavalier with his producer's money.
50. Ibid., p. 90.
51. *Film Daily*, March 13, 1930, p. 8.
52. *Photoplay*, June 1930, p. 134.
53. Bogdanovich, *Allan Dwan*, p. 90.
54. Unpublished 1978 Allan Dwan interview with Richard Koszarski, supplied to author by Mr. Koszarski, p. 26.
55. Swanson, *Swanson on Swanson*, pp. 400–401.
56. Donald Albrecht, *Designing Dreams: Architecture in the Movies* (New York: Harper & Row in collaboration with the Museum of Modern Art, 1986), p. xiv.
57. *Variety*, April 2, 1930, p. 63.
58. Letter from Paul Nelson to Gloria Swanson. The letter is dated only "August 19th" but since in it Nelson asks Swanson how she is satisfied with "the picture," it is almost certainly from 1930. (Nelson also mentions Soviet director Sergei Eisenstein being in Hollywood.) Also letter from Nelson to Swanson, April 20, 1959, in which Nelson states, "Remember you started my career." Gloria Swanson Collection, Harry Ransom Humanities Research Center, University of Texas at Austin.
59. *Variety*, April 16, 1930, p. 31.
60. Albrecht, *Designing Dreams*, pp. xvi–xvii.
61. Madsen, *Gloria & Joe*, pp. 266–267.
62. Swanson, *Swanson on Swanson*, p. 401.
63. Bogdanovich, *Allan Dwan*, p. 90.
64. Balio, *United Artists: The Studio Built By the Stars*, p. 83.
65. *New York Times*, October 4, 1930, p. 15.
66. *Variety*, September 17, 1930.
67. *Motion Picture News*, September 20, 1930, p. 52.
68. Richard Barrios, *A Song in the Dark* (Oxford: Oxford University Press, 1995), p. 320.
69. Beauchamp, *Joseph Kennedy Presents*, p. 213.
70. Ibid., p. 389.
71. Warner Bros. contract, Wisconsin Center for Film and Theater Research, Warner Bros. Collection.
72. Warner Bros. press sheets for *Man to Man*, Wisconsin Center for Film and Theater Research, Warner Bros. Collection.
73. William K. Everson notes, Theodore Huff Society, May 24, 1971, The New School, June 11, 1986.
74. Ibid.
75. Ibid.
76. January 5, 1931, agreement between Allan Dwan and First National Pictures, Wisconsin Center for Film and Television, Warner Bros. Collection.
77. Douglas Fairbanks, Jr., *Salad Days* (New York: Doubleday, 1988), p. 169.
78. Todd McCarthy, *Howard Hawks: The Grey Fox of Hollywood* (New York: Grove Press, 1997), p. 122.
79. Warner Bros. Archives Collection, USC.
80. Bogdanovich, *Allan Dwan*, p. 92.
81. *Film Daily*, March 10, 1931, p. 7.
82. *Chances* script treatments, Retake April 11, 1931, Warner Bros. Archives Collection, USC.
83. William K. Everson notes for *Chances*, Program 8; November 17, 1967.
84. A. Hamilton Gibbs, *Chances* (Boston: Little, Brown, 1930).
85. *New York Times* review, June 12, 1931, p. 27.
86. Coursodon and Sauvage, *American Directors, Volume I*, p. 112.
87. Fairbanks, *Salad Days*, p. 170.
88. Ibid.
89. Bogdanovich, *Allan Dwan*, p. 93.
90. *New York Times* review, September 19, 1931.
91. *Variety* review, September 22, 1931.
92. Bogdanovich, *Allan Dwan*, p. 94.
93. Ibid.
94. *Film Daily*, February 19, 1931, p. 9.
95. *While Paris Sleeps*, MPAA/PCA file, Margaret Herrick Library.
96. Bogdanovich, *Allan Dwan*, p. 94.
97. The New School, notes for *While Paris Sleeps*, Film Series 20: Program #8, November 22, 1974.
98. *While Paris Sleeps* File, Margaret Herrick Library.
99. Fox publicity sheet, "Do You Know," *While Paris Sleeps* file, Margaret Herrick Library.
100. Letter from Jason S. Joy to Al Rockett, January 22, 1932, *While Paris Sleeps* file, Margaret Herrick Library.
101. Letter from Jason S. Joy to Will Hays, January 25, 1932, *While Paris Sleeps* MPAA file, Margaret Herrick Library.
102. *While Paris Sleeps* MPDAA summary, May 9, 1932, *While Paris Sleeps* MPAA file, Margaret Herrick Library.
103. Letter from Joy to Rockett, February 23, 1932, *While Paris Sleeps* MPAA file, Margaret Herrick Library.
104. Memo to Fox included with letter from Paul Claudel, French embassy to Will Hays, July 26, 1932.
105. *Variety* review, June 14, 1932.
106. Ibid.
107. Mark A. Vieira, *Sin in Soft Focus: Pre-Code Hollywood* (New York: Harry N. Abrams, 1999), p. 211.
108. Joy to Hays, February 3, 1932.
109. Basil Woon, *Incredible Land: A Jaunty Baedeker to Hollywood and the Great Southwest* (New York: Liveright, 1933), pp. 84–85.
110. Joseph McBride, *Frank Capra: The Catastrophe of Success* (New York: Simon & Schuster, 1992), p. 249.
111. Ibid., p. 251.
112. Edward Bernds, *Mr. Bernds Goes to Hollywood* (Lanham, MD: Scarecrow Press, 1999), p. 151.
113. Ibid.
114. McBride, *Frank Capra*, p. 200.
115. Author interview with Howard Mandelbaum.
116. Excised portion of Bogdanovich interview, tape 2–203, tape 2–204, Lilly Library, Indiana University.
117. Ibid., tape 2–204, 205.
118. Bogdanovich, *Allan Dwan*, pp. 94–95.
119. "Chatter Page," *Variety*, November 1, 1932.
120. Bogdanovich, *Allan Dwan*, pp. 95–96.
121. William Donati, *Ida Lupino: A Biography* (Lexington: University Press of Kentucky, 1996), pp. 17–21.
122. *New York Times*, September 21, 1941, p. X3.
123. *Variety*, December 27, 1932.
124. Donati, *Ida Lupino*, p. 22.
125. *Kine Weekly*, December 8, 1932, p. 1.
126. *Observer*, May 7, 1933, cited in Karol Kulick, *Alexander Korda: The Man Who Could Work Miracles* (New Rochelle, NY: Arlington, 1975), p. 81.
127. Harry Kendall, *I Remember Romano's: The Autobiography of Henry Kendall* (London: MacDonald, 1960), p. 132.
128. "Long Shots," *Kine Weekly*, March 30, 1933, p. 4.
129. Thomas Schatz, *The Genius of the System* (New York: Pantheon, 1988), pp. 159–160.
130. *Variety*, August 29, 1933.
131. David Quinlan, *British Sound Films: The Studio Years, 1929–1959* (Totowa, NJ: Barnes & Noble Books, 1984), p. 89.
132. *Variety* obituary, June 27, 1933.
133. *Pittsburgh Post-Gazette*, October 30, 1933, p. 10.
134. Strangely enough, there was some basis of truth to the story. In 1933. Paramount had produced a hit film called *King of the Jungle* where Buster Crabbe played a character called Kaspar the Lion Man. Crabbe was then signed by independent producer Sol Lesser to star in a serial called *Tarzan the Fearless*. But after that, Crabbe's rivalry to MGM's Tarzan star Johnny Weissmuller faded.
135. *Hollywood Reporter*, January 19, 1934, p. 1.
136. Bogdanovich, *Allan Dwan*, pp. 98–99.
137. Ibid., p. 99.
138. *Variety*, May 29, 1934.
139. Bogdanovich, *Allan Dwan*, p. 98.
140. Ibid.
141. Balio, *United Artists: The Company Built by the Stars*, p. 84.
142. Excised portions of Dwan interview, tape 2–144, Bogdanovich Papers, Lilly Library, Indiana University.
143. Sarris, *The American Cinema*, p. 235.
144. Bogdanovich Papers, excised portion from book, tape 2–198, 199.
145. Bogdanovich, *Allan Dwan*, p. 100.
146. Excised portions for *The Last Pioneer*, tape 2–194, Bogdanovich Papers, Lilly Library, Indiana University.
147. Ibid., tape 2–195.
148. *Hollywood Reporter*, June 13, 1935, p. 2.
149. Excised portions of *The Last Pioneer*, tape 2–196, Bogdanovich Papers, Indiana University.
150. Brian Taves, "The B Film: Hollywood's

Other Half," in Tino Balio, *Grand Design: Hollywood as a Modern Business Enterprise, 1930–1939* (New York: Scribner's, 1996), p. 318.

151. Release from Harry Brand, publicity director, 20th Century–Fox, December 9, 1935.

152. Bogdanovich, *Allan Dwan*, p. 10.

153. Meisel, "Allan Dwan," in Coursodon & Savage, *American Directors, Volume I*, p. 112.

154. Bogdanovich, *Allan Dwan*, p. 102.

155. Gene Ringgold, *The Films of Rita Hayworth* (Secaucus, NJ: Citadel Press, 1974), p. 66, 68.

156. Bogdanovich, *Allan Dwan*, p. 102.

157. *Hollywood Reporter*, April 18, 1936, p. 3.

158. *New York Times* review, May 16, 1936, p. 11.

159. Bogdanovich, *Allan Dwan*, p. 102.

160. Excised portion of *The Last Pioneer*, tape 2–198, 199, Bogdanovich Papers, Indiana University.

161. *Variety* review, July 15, 1936.

162. John Cocchi, *Second Feature* (Secaucus, NJ: Carol, 1991), p. 122.

163. *Hollywood Reporter*, September 25, 1936, p. 2.

164. Bogdanovich, *Allan Dwan*, p. 103.

165. *New York Times*, May 10, 1937, p. 23.

166. Danny Peary, *Cult Movie Stars* (New York: Simon & Schuster, 1991), p. 564.

167. *Variety*, July 2, 1937.

168. Sol Wurtzel papers, Margaret Herrick Library.

169. Anne Edwards, *Shirley Temple: American Princess* (New York: William Morrow, 1988), p. 75.

170. Andrew Sarris, *The American Cinema: Directors and Directions, 1929–1968* (New York: Da Capo Press, 1996), p. 45.

171. Shirley Temple Black, *Child Star: An Autobiography* (New York: Warner Books, 1988), p. 184.

172. Bogdanovich, *Allan Dwan*, p. 106.

173. Robert Windeler, *The Films of Shirley Temple* (Secaucus, NJ: Citadel Press, 1978), p. 187.

174. In her autobiography, Shirley Temple Black provides a retort to Dwan's contention that Zanuck was unable to make a trade for her, noting that MGM had acquired the rights to L. Frank Baum's *The Wizard of Oz* and wanted her to star in their film. Mrs. Black wrote that Louis B. Mayer was willing to loan out both Jean Harlow and Clark Gable to acquire her for *Oz*. In addition, she would also be loaned out to MGM to make a film with Gable. Mrs. Black says that the deal was capsized by Harlow's premature death. However, according to Aljean Harmetz, author of *The Making of the Wizard of Oz*, Mayer did not even consider purchasing the rights to *Oz* until at least the fall of 1937. Actual purchase was not made until February 1938 though an inter-office memo suggests that casting decisions began in late January 1938. Harlow died on June 1, 1937, and *Heidi* was filmed that June.

In an e-mail to the author, Ms. Harmetz does note that according to a 1965 edition of the pamphlet *Screen Facts* (Issue #12), Mayer had agreed to loan Harlow and Gable to Fox to appear in *In Old Chicago* but for whatever reason this never transpired

175. Black, *Child Star*, p. 193.

176. Ibid., p. 192.

177. Fred Lawrence Guiles, *Tyrone Power: The Last Idol* (San Francisco: Mercury House, 1979), p. 44.

178. Black, *Child Star*, p. 193.

179. Mandelbaum Morris interview, p. 15.

180. Bogdanovich, *Allan Dwan*, p. 108.

181. Black, *Child Star*, p. 192.

182. Windeler, *The Films of Shirley Temple*, p. 187.

183. Edwards, *Shirley Temple*, p. 107.

184. Black, *Child Star*, p. 196.

185. Ibid.

186. Ibid., p. 196.

187. Bogdanovich, *Allan Dwan*, p. 107.

188. *Heidi*, conference with Mr. Zanuck, February 10, 1937, on treatment of January 29, 1937, USC Fox Script Collections

189. HR, April 29, 1937, p. 18.

190. Conference with Mr. Zanuck on temporary script of April 30, 1937, USC Fox Script Collections.

191. The new ending for *Heidi* was apparently written while the film was still in production and the revision is dated August 28, 1937. It still differs somewhat from the ending finally shot in that Heidi pronounces herself so happy that she could sing and proceeds to sing "Happy Ending." For the last eight bars she is accompanied by the "harmonious voices of the invisible girls...." *Heidi* film script, 20th Century–Fox Collection, Courtesy Lilly Library, Indiana University.

192. *New York Times* review, November 6, 1937, p. 14.

193. Ibid.

194. *Variety*, November 10, 1937.

195. HR, October 9, 1937, p. 3.

196. Bogdanovich, *Allan Dwan*, pp. 109–10.

197. Ibid., p. 110.

198. Black, *Child Star*, p. 204.

199. John Gallagher interview with Don Ameche, *Quirks* review, August 1987.

200. Robin Wallace phone conversation with author.

201. *Variety*, March 9, 1938.

202. Ibid.

203. *New York Times*, March 26, 1938, p. 12.

204. Lester and Irene David, *The Shirley Temple Story* (New York: Putnam, 1983), p. 100.

205. HR, December 14, 1937, p. 8.

206. "News of the Screen," *New York Times*, April 5, 1938, p. 19.

207. *Suez*, March 29, 1937, treatment, Zanuck copy, USC Fox Scripts Collections.

208. Zachary Karabell, *Parting the Desert: The Creation of the Suez Canal* (New York: Alfred A. Knopf, 2003), p. 266.

209. Memo to Darryl F. Zanuck, from Jason S. Joy, June 29, 1937, *Suez* file, USC Special Collections.

210. *Suez*, June 25, 1937, treatment, Philip Dunne to Darryl Zanuck, Gene Markey, July 3, 1937, "Report on 'Suez' Treatment by Sam Duncan," p. 1, *Suez* file, USC Special Collections.

211. Ibid., p. 2, 4.

212. Karabell, *Parting the Desert*, p. 124.

213. *Suez* conference with Mr. Zanuck on first draft continuity of February 3, 1938, dated March 1, 1938, p. 1, *Suez* file, USC Special Collections.

214. Conference with Mr. Zanuck, April 18, 1938, on final script of April 8, 1938, pp. 3–4.

215. Ibid., p. 5.

216. Loretta Young as told to Helen Ferguson, *The Things I Had to Learn* (Indianapolis: Bobbs Merrill, 1961), p. 245.

217. Joe Morella and Edward Z. Epstein, *Loretta Young: An Extraordinary Life* (Santa Barbara: Landmark Books, 1987), p. 113.

218. Guiles, *Tyrone Power*, p. 41.

219. Morella and Epstein, *Loretta Young*, pp. 113–14.

220. Guiles, *Tyrone Power*, p. 43.

221. Philip Dunne, *Take Two: A Life in Movies and Politics* (New York: Limelight Editions, 1992), p. 66.

222. Bogdanovich, *Allan Dwan*, p. 111.

223. Ibid., p. 116.

224. Letter from Joseph I. Breen to Jason S. Joy, April 11, 1938, *Suez* PCA file, Margaret Herrick Library.

225. *Suez* conference with Mr. Zanuck, March 1, 1938, on first draft continuity of February 3, 1938, p. 1, USC Fox Scripts Collection.

226. *Suez* conference with Mr. Zanuck, March 28, 1938, on temporary script of March 18, 1938, p. 13, 17, USC.

227. As a film hero, Lesseps is not totally an anomaly in Hollywood films of the period and in *Mr. Smith Goes to Washington*, released a year later, James Stewart's idealistic senator is treated like a wayward child by heroine Jean Arthur.

228. Michael Henry Wilson, "Allan Dwan's Moral Tales at the Edge of Paradise," in Gosetti, ed., *Allan Dwan: The Name Beneath the Title*, p. 125.

229. *New York Times* review, October 15, 1938, p. 21.

230. Guiles, *Tyrone Power*, p. 44.

231. Ibid.

232. Gary Morris, ed., *Action! Interviews with Directors from Classical Hollywood to Contemporary Iran* (London: Anthem Press, 2009), p. 15.

233. Letter to Fox Film Corporation from unnamed representative of Paul de Lesseps, October 21, 1938, Twentieth Century–Fox Legal Records (Collection 95), Performing Arts Special Collections, Charles E. Young Research Library, UCLA.

234. *Suez*, order by judge in chambers, 18 January 1939, copy-translation, Twentieth Century–Fox Legal Records (Collection 95), Performing Arts Special Collections, Charles E. Young Research Library, UCLA.

235. Ed Sullivan, "Looking at Hollywood," *Chicago Daily Tribune*, February 17, 1939, p. 19.

236. Agreement between 20th Century–Fox and Allan Dwan, February 2, 1939, Allan Dwan file, Margaret Herrick Library.

237. "High Salaries Paid in Nation in 1937 as Listed by Treasury," *New York Times*, April 8, 1939, p. 7.

238. Brownlow, *The War, the West and the Wilderness*, p. 280.

239. Michael Blake, *Hollywood and the O.K. Corral* (Jefferson, NC: McFarland, 2007), p. 32.

240. Allen Barra, *Inventing Wyatt Earp: His Life and Many Legends* (New York: Carroll & Graf, 1998), p. 343.

241. Casey Tefertiller, *Wyatt Earp: The Life Behind The Legend* (New York: John Wiley & Sons, 1997), p. 329.

242. *Frontier Marshal*, first draft screenplay by Sam Hellman, "Main Characters" page, USC Fox Script Collection.

243. Solomon, *Twentieth Century–Fox: A Corporate and Financial History*, pp. 25–26.

244. Memo from Hellman to Wurtzel, April 22, 1939, *Frontier Marshal*, revised story outline, April 24, 1939, USC Fox Script Collection.

245. Bogdanovich, *Allan Dwan*, p. 119, 121.

246. Letter from Mrs. Wyatt Earp to Sol Wurtzel, June 17, 1939, *Wyatt Earp*, Twentieth Century–Fox Legal Records (Collection 95), Performing Arts Special Collections, Charles E. Young Research Library, UCLA.

247. Ibid.

248. Ibid.

249. Memo from Wurtzel to Zanuck, June 20, 1939, with Zanuck reply typed on bottom, *Wyatt Earp*, Twentieth Century–Fox Legal Records (Collection 95), Performing Arts Special Collections, Charles E. Young Research Library, UCLA.

250. Letter from George Wasson to Mrs. Wyatt Earp, June 27, 1939, marked as "Letter Not Sent," *Wyatt Earp*, Twentieth Century–Fox Legal Records (Collection 95), Performing Arts Special Collections, Charles E. Young Research Library, UCLA.

251. Bogdanovich, *Allan Dwan*, p. 122.

252. Letter from Mrs. Wyatt Earp to Sol Wurtzel, June 17, 1939, page two, *Wyatt Earp*, Twentieth Century–Fox Legal Records (Collection 95), Performing

Arts Special Collections, Charles E. Young Research Library, UCLA.

253. Barra, *Inventing Wyatt Earp*, p. 304.

254. D.H. Lawrence, *Studies in Classic American Literature* (New York: Penguin, 1923), p. 9.

255. *Frontier Marshal*, conference with Mr. Zanuck on second draft screenplay of May 10, 1939, USC Fox Script Collection.

256. Sam Hellman, *Frontier Marshal* revised story outline, April 24, 1939, USC Fox Script Collection.

257. As if to underline their similarities, the film has attributed to Halliday some of Earp's characteristics. While the historical Doc came from Georgia, it is revealed in the story that he came from Illinois as did Wyatt and the date given for Halliday's birth on the tombstone at the end of the film is not the actual year of his birth but Earp's (1848).

258. Errol Flynn's hero in *Dodge City* was a much more fictionalized version of Earp than *Frontier Marshal*. Another Western of 1939 was MGM's lesser known *Let Freedom Ring* with Nelson Eddy leading a popular revolt against a corrupt railroad tyrant.

259. *Hollywood Reporter*, July 7, 1939, p. 7.

260. *Hollywood Reporter*, July 12, 1939, p. 7.

261. *New York Times*, July 29, 1939.

262. Lindsay Anderson interview with John Ford, in Anderson, *About John Ford* (New York: McGraw-Hill, 1981), p. 222.

Chapter 7

1. At this time, a number of the Fairbanks swashbucklers were being re-made. In 1938 Warner Bros. had released *The Adventures of Robin Hood* starring Errol Flynn, and the same year that Fox's *Three Musketeers* came out, producer Edward Small would be turning out *The Man in The Iron Mask*. The following year the Korda Brothers would produce *The Thief of Bagdad* in color while Fox would release a new version of *The Mark of Zorro* starring Tyrone Power. Perhaps as the film industry turned to increasingly ambitious and costly productions, it recognized the Fairbanks films of the twenties as having set the gold standard.

2. *The Three Musketeers*, conference with Mr. Zanuck on treatment of May 3, 1938, dated May 6, 1938, USC Fox Script Collection.

3. *One For All*, formerly *The Three Musketeers*, temporary script, August 29, 1938, memo from Julian Johnson to Darryl F. Zanuck, August 30, 1938, USC Fox Film Collection.

4. *The Three Musketeers*, conference with Mr. Zanuck on temporary script of August 29, 1938, dated August 31, 1939, USC Fox Script Collection.

5. *One For All* formerly *The Three Musketeers* Script memo, Harry Joe Brown to Darryl F. Zanuck, August 31, 1938, USC Fox Script Collection.

6. HR, February 4, 1939, p. 2.

7. "An Interview With Edward Norris," *Films of the Golden Age*, Issue #25, Summer 2001, p. 48.

8. HR, February, 15, 1939, p. 11; AFI Catalogue 1931–1940, "The Gorilla" [1939].

9. HR, May 18, 1939, p. 2.

10. *Variety*, November 23, 1927.

11. *The Gorilla*, conference with Mr. Zanuck on temporary script of January 9, 1939, recorded January 13, 1939, USC Fox Script Collection.

12. *The Sweetheart of Turret One*, screen treatment by Frank Wead, Margaret Herrick Library.

13. Bogdanovich, *Allan Dwan*, p. 122.

14. Ibid.

15. Notes for The New School, William K. Everson, Film Series 58: Program #9, April 22, 1988.

16. *Trail of the Vigilantes*, assistant director's daily report, Friday, October 11, 1940, USC Universal Script Collection.

17. Memo to Dan Kelley from M.F. Murphy, "Paul Fix — Trail of the Vigilantes," December 6, 1940, USC Universal Script Collection.

18. "Daily Committee Meeting," January 6, 1941, p. 2, USC Universal Collection, Box 789/24987.

19. Blackie Seymour, "Pentagram Profiles: Peggy Moran 1918–2002," *Classic Images*, No. 331, January 2003, p. 74.

20. Notes for The New School, William K. Everson, Film Series 58: Program #9, April 22, 1988.

21. Ibid.

22. Gene Blottner, *Universal Sound Westerns, 1929–1946: The Complete Filmography* (Jefferson, NC: McFarland, 2003), p. 352.

23. Notes for The New School, William K. Everson, Film Series 58: Program #9, April 22, 1988.

24. *Variety* review, December 11, 1940.

25. Seymour, "Peggy Moran," *Classic Images*, January 2003, p. 74.

26. *Young People* (*The Come-Back*), outline dictated by Mr. Zanuck, October 19, 1939, p. 1, USC Fox Scripts Collection.

27. *Young People*, outline dictated by Mr. Zanuck, October 19, 1939, p. 6, USC Fox Scripts Collection.

28. Memorandum from Mr. Zanuck (on temporary script of 2/28/40), March 2, 1940.

29. Black, *Child Star*, p. 310.

30. Memorandum from Zanuck (on temporary script of 2/28/40), March 2, 1940.

31. Black, *Child Star*, pp. 314–316.

32. David, *The Shirley Temple Story*, p. 108.

33. Another film of 1941, *The Wild Man of Borneo*, was based on a play co-authored by Mankiewicz.

34. *New York Times* review, December 6, 1941, p. 14.

35. Jack Oakie, *Jack Oakie's Double Takes* (San Francisco: Strawberry Hill Press, 1980), p. 58.

36. Thomas and Solomon, *The Films of 20th Century–Fox*, p. 118.

37. Excised portions from Bogdanovich book, tape 3–21, Bogdanovich Papers, Lilly Library, University of Indiana.

38. Bogdanovich, *Allan Dwan*, p. 123.

39. RKO Records for *Look Who's Laughing*, UCLA files.

40. Betty Lasky, *RKO: The Biggest Little Major of Them All* (Engelwood Cliffs, NJ: Prentice Hall, 1984), p. 181.

41. Bogdanovich, *Allan Dwan*, p. 124.

42. Ibid.

43. Edward Small Collection, Production files, USC Script Collections.

44. *New York Times* review, July 22, 1942, p. 19.

45. *Variety* review, November 24, 1943.

46. Marcy McGuire interview with author.

47. Ibid.

48. *Around the World*, script treatment, April 13, 1943, by Ralph Spence, UCLA Film Collections.

49. Bogdanovich, *Allan Dwan*, p. 193. A check of government records has not shown that Dwan was in the employment of the United States government but these records are based on payroll information. Thus, if Dwan's work was totally gratis, it would not have been recorded. This period of voluntary service would serve to explain Dwan's very limited production record for 1943, one of only two years in the decade where less than two Dwan movies were released. That was in 1946 but the following year, he had three films in release, the first of which appeared in late January, suggesting that he was busy shooting it in late 1946.

50. Bogdanovich, *Allan Dwan*, p. 132.

51. *New York Times* review, October 26, 1944, p. 19.

52. Bogdanovich, *Allan Dwan*, p. 129.

53. Edward Small as told to Robert E. Kent, *You Don't Have to Be Crazy to Be in Show Business But It Helps! Autobiography of Edward Small* unpublished manuscript, USC Cinema Library, p. 321.

54. Ibid., p. 322.

55. Production cards, Edward Small Collection, USC.

56. Small, *Autobiography of Edward Small*, p. 323.

57. Bogdanovich, *Allan Dwan*, p. 129, 131.

58. Small, *Autobiography of Edward Small*, p. 324.

59. Ibid., pp. 323–324.

60. Ibid., p. 321.

61. Memorandum, January 10, 1942.

62. HR, October 19, 1943, p. 1.

63. Letter from Joseph Breen to Edward Small, August 16, 1943, Edward Small Collection, USC.

64. Edward Small Productions Inc. Statement of Income and Expenses for *Up in Mabel's Room*, March 29, 1947, Edward Small Collection, USC.

65. Letter from Edward Small to Harry Kosiner, January 3, 1945, Edward Small Collection, USC.

66. Letter from Joseph Breen to Small Productions, May 11, 1945, Edward Small Collection, USC.

67. Letter from Will Hays, MPPDA, to Harry Kosiner of Edward Small Productions, June 22, 1945, Edward Small Collection, USC.

68. Both films were also made as silent movies by director E. Mason Hopper.

69. In an essay on Dwan's comedies, Kent Jones maintains that "Mabel is the swifter, more grueling of the two, Gertie the funnier and more purely deranged, and perhaps the more deeply neurotic on the one hand, and more joyous on the other...." Kent Jones, "Love and/or Money," in Gosetti, ed., *Allan Dwan: The Name Beneath the Title*.

70. August 31, 1945, preview of *Getting Gertie's Garter*, Edward Small Collection, USC.

71. Donald Phelps, "The Runners," *Covering Ground: Essays For Now* (New York: Croton Press, 1969), p. 69.

72. Jones, "Love and /or Money," in Gosetti, ed., *Allan Dwan: The Name Beneath the Title*.

73. Bogdanovich, *Allan Dwan*, p. 132.

74. Phelps, *Covering Ground*, p. 69.

75. *Motion Picture Herald*, April 1945.

76. HR Review, August 8, 1946.

77. Jones, "Love and /or Money," in Gosetti, ed., *Allan Dwan: The Name Beneath the Title*.

78. Letter from Joseph I. Breen to Allen Wilson, Republic Prods., August 17, 1945, MPDAA files, Margaret Herrick Library.

79. Memo for the files, October 10,1945, Re: RENDEZVOUS WITH ANNIE [Republic], MPDAA files, Margaret Herrick Library.

Chapter 8

1. Meisel, "Allan Dwan," *American Directors, Volume 1*, Coursodon and Sauvage, p. 114.

2. Dwan's comment is essentially correct, at least for his tenure at Republic. The most expensive film in Republic's history, *The Last Command*, came after *Sands of Iwo Jima* but it was made in 1955 long after Dwan had left the studio. John Ford also made two films at Republic during the early 1950s, *The Quiet Man* and *Rio Grande*, which are cited in Jack Mathis' book *Republic Confidential* as costing more than *Sands of Iwo Jima*. (Mathis had the Republic files in his possession.) See Jack Mathis, *Republic Confidential* (Barrington, IL: Jack Mathis Advertising, 1992). Ford was given more leeway due to his high status as a director, although according to Joseph McBride, Yates fought hard but unsuccessfully to keep Ford's

budgets down. According to McBride's book *Searching for John Ford*, Republic Pictures documents in Ford's files list the negative cost for *The Quiet Man* as $1,446,661; in *Republic Confidential* the figure is $1,698,254. Nearly all of the films budgeted in excess of $1 million in Mathis' book have extensive cost overruns. It's possible that in these figures, Yates used studio overhead to make the budgets appear higher and his profits therefore lower.

3. Bogdanovich, *Allan Dwan*, p. 149.
4. HR, September 21, 1945, p. 1.
5. Ronald L. Davis interview with Mary Loos, July 26, 1990, p. 12, Oral History Collection on the Performing Arts, DeGolyer Library, Southern Methodist University, Dallas, Texas, A1980.0154.
6. Bogdanovich, *Allan Dwan*, pp. 138–39.
7. Mathis, *Republic Confidential*, p. 267.
8. Bogdanovich, *Allan Dwan*, p. 141.
9. Gavin Lambert, *Natalie Wood, A Life* (New York: Alfred A. Knopf, 2004), p. 55.
10. Ibid., p. 54.
11. Bogdanovich, *Allan Dwan*, pp. 141–142.
12. Wilson, "Allan Dwan's Moral Tales At The Edge of Paradise," in Gosetti, ed., *Allan Dwan: The Name Beneath the Title*, p. 119.
13. *New York Times* review, October 20, 2006.
14. For more on this see Larry Suid, *Guts and Glory: Great American War Movies* (Reading, MA: Addison-Wesley, 1978), pp. 96–97 and Randy Roberts and James S. Olson, *John Wayne: American* (New York: Free Press, 1995), p. 319.
15. Bogdanovich, *Allan Dwan*, p. 144.
16. Ezra Goodman, "From the Halls of Montezuma to Hollywood," *New York Times*, August 7, 1949.
17. Larry Suid interview with Grainger, July 30, 1975, p. 6.
18. Larry Suid interview with David Shoup, April 2, 1975.
19. Ibid., p. 3.
20. Ibid., p. 7.
21. *The Making of Sands of Iwo Jima*, documentary.
22. Suid interview with Fribourg, p. 6.
23. *The Making of Sands of Iwo Jima*, documentary.
24. Suid interview with Fribourg, p. 6.
25. William Self interview with author.
26. Andrew McLaglen interview with author.
27. Letter from Wayne to Larry Suid, June 15, 1977.
28. Ibid.
29. Suid interview with Fribourg, p. 7.
30. Letter from Wayne to Larry Suid, June 15, 1977.
31. Mathis, *Republic Confidential*, p. 267.
32. Goodman, "From the Halls of Montezuma to Hollywood," *New York Times*, August 7, 1949.
33. Mathis, *Republic Confidential*, p. 267.
34. *New York Times* review, December 31, 1949, p. 9.
35. In the final shooting script, Dunne's perspective is given a little more power as he relates a recurring dream of seeing the men of his squad, the living and the dead all united as they go into an amtrac. The scene was probably considered too eerie and fatalistic to be used. Script copy provided by courtesy of Leonard Maltin was Fribourg's copy.
36. Jeanine Basinger, *The World War II Combat Film: Anatomy of a Genre* (New York: Columbia University Press, 1986), p. 165.
37. Letters from Joseph Breen to Allen A. Wilson of Republic Pictures, May 12, June 21, June 23, August 5, August 19, 1949, *Sands of Iwo Jima* MPAA file, Margaret Herrick Library. In the June 23 letter, Breen mentions that he suggested to Steve Goodman, the studio code contact, that the woman be portrayed as "a cheap café hostess," with the whole scene taking place in the bar and the child running into the bar to see his mother. Goodman said he would take up the matter with Dwan, who was apparently not won over. The censors also had conferences with Grainger and Grant. On August 5, after inspecting a re-write, Breen noted that there had been a "great change" but that the character still appeared to be a prostitute. This impression still clearly exists in the finished film but perhaps because the woman was shown to be a caring mother and the overall effect of the scene was uplifting, the censors let it pass.
38. Ron Kovic, *Born on the Fourth of July* (New York: Akashic Books, 1976, 2005), p. 65.
39. Philip Caputo, *A Rumor of War* (New York: Holt, Rinehart and Winston, 1977), p. 6.
40. Roberts and Olson, *John Wayne: American*, p. 558.
41. John Wayne letter to Larry Suid, June 15, 1977.
42. James Bradley and Ron Powers, *Flags of Our Fathers* (New York: Bantam Books, 2000), pp. 92–93, 115, 124–25, 224–25, 230–33.
43. "Letters," *American Film*, December 1985, p. 8.
44. "Letter to the Editor," *American Film*, January–February 1986, p. 67.
45. Richard D. McGhee, *John Wayne, Actor, Artist, Hero* (Jefferson, NC: McFarland, 1990), p. 189.
46. McGhee elaborates that "Stryker is transformed into the American flag, into the men who are His witnesses, into the mist which embraces all in the end." McGhee's mystical reading of the scene follows from his assumption that, "as a secular story, it uses religious iconography for patriotic meanings."
47. Death certificate for Marie Shelton Dwan, dated March 25, 1949, Dwan file, Margaret Herrick Library.
48. Louella O. Parsons, "Mrs. Allan Dwan, Wife of Director, Dies in Sleep," March 14, 1949, unspecified publication, Dwan file, Margaret Herrick Library.
49. Roberts and Olson, *John Wayne: American*, p. 274.
50. Joseph Kane interview with Charles Flynn and Todd McCarthy in Flynn and McCarthy, eds., *King of the Bs* (New York: E.P. Dutton, 1975), pp. 321–22.
51. Roberts and Olson, *John Wayne: American*, p. 274.
52. Maurice Zolotow, *Shooting Star: A Biography of John Wayne* (New York: Simon & Schuster, 1974), p. 252.
53. Bogdanovich, *Allan Dwan*, p. 148.
54. Jim Meyer, "Vera Ralston, Skating to Stardom," *Classic Images*, April 2010, p. 77.
55. Bogdanovich, *Allan Dwan*, pp. 148–49.
56. Hedda Hopper, "Looking at Hollywood," *Chicago Daily Tribune*, July 24, 1950, p. A5.
57. Bogdanovich, *Allan Dwan*, pp. 167–68.
58. Ibid., p. 149.
59. Author interview with Richard Erdman, 2007.
60. Ibid.
61. Author interview with Joan Leslie.
62. McCarthy and Flynn, eds., *King of the Bs*, p. 322.
63. Bogdanovich, *Allan Dwan*, p. 149.
64. Phone conversation with Howard Mandelbaum and email from Mandelbaum to author, February 21, 2010.
65. Richard Maurice Hurst, *Republic Studios: Between Poverty Row and the Majors* (Metuchen, NJ: Scarecrow Press, 1979), p. 21.
66. Ken Emerson, *Doo-Dah: Stephen Foster and the Rise of American Popular Culture* (New York: Simon & Schuster, 1994), p. 13.
67. Bogdanovich, *Allan Dwan*, p. 150.
68. Ezra Goodman, "Dwan of the Movies," *New York Times*, Sunday, May 7, 1950.
69. Tennessee Williams described what he experienced after the success of his play *The Glass Menagerie* as "the catastrophe of success" in "On a Streetcar Named Success," *New York Times*, November 30, 1947. Joseph McBride used Williams' phrase for the title of his 1992 biography of Frank Capra.
70. Coursodon and Sauvage, *American Directors, Volume I*, p. 114.
71. Mathis, *Republic Confidential*, p. 360.
72. Except for clip from *I Dream of Jeanie* in the opening montage.
73. *Variety* review, July 29, 1953.
74. Letter from Harry Carey, Jr., to author, October 17, 2006.
75. Author interview with Joan Leslie, January 2005.
76. Author interview with Lillian Kinkela, January 13, 2005.
77. Leslie interview.
78. Ibid.; Kinkela interview. Also confirmed by "Franz Replaces Andrews," HR, June 4, 1953, p. 1. The story states that the New York stage actor Tod Andrews "withdrew from the picture."
79. *Los Angeles Times*, July 10, 2005. The quote cited was given to the *Times* in 1991 by Kinkela's longtime friend, retired Air Force Col. Barney Oldfield.
80. Lawrence H. Suid, "Hollywood, the Marines and the Korean War," *Marine Corps Gazette*, March 2002, p. 43.
81. Excised portion of Bogdanovich interview, tape 3–242, Bogdanovich Papers, Lilly Library, Indiana University.
82. Ibid., unnumbered.
83. Suid, "Hollywood, the Marines and the Korean War," *Marine Corps Gazette*, March 2002, p. 43.
84. Agreement between Dwan and Republic Pictures to direct *Montana Belle*, September 25, 1948, Allan Dwan Collection, University of Wyoming.
85. Thomas F. Brady, "Hollywood Recants," *New York Times*, April 10, 1949, p. X5. According to Brady's article, Republic owned 33 percent of *Montana Belle*, permitting Fidelity to collect roughly $150,000 of the $225,000 profit.
86. Jane Russell, *Jane Russell: An Autobiography, My Path and My Detours* (New York: Franklin Watts, 1985), p. 97.
87. Jeanine Basinger, *A Woman's View: How Hollywood Spoke to Women, 1930–1960* (New York: Alfred A. Knopf, 1993), p. 466.
88. Bogdanovich, *Allan Dwan*, p. 151.
89. Author interview with Joan Leslie.
90. Author interview with Audrey Totter, February 1, 2005.
91. Excised material from Bogdanovich, tape 4–47, Bogdanovich Papers, Lilly Library, Indiana University.
92. Basinger, *A Woman's View*, p. 465.
93. "Dialogue of a Schizocritic," in Sarris, *Confessions of a Cultist*, p. 45.
94. Roger McNiven, "Women Larger Than Life: Program Notes 1: Allan Dwan's *Woman They Almost Lynched* (1953)/*Slightly Scarlet* (1956)," *Bright Lights Film Journal*, May 2009, Issue 64.
95. Ibid.
96. Gosetti, ed., *Allan Dwan: The Name Beneath the Title*, p. 122.

Chapter 9

1. Bogdanovich, *Allan Dwan*, p. 157.
2. Thomas M. Pryor, "Rags to Riches: Or the Hectic Saga of Benedict Bogeaus, Producer and Man of Many Affairs," *New York Times*, November 25, 1945, Section X, p. 3. Having been born in 1904, Bogeaus was actually forty-one years old at the time.

3. Ibid.

4. Jim Marshall, "Nothing to It," *Collier's*, May 18, 1946.

5. Virginia McPherson, "Ben Bogeaus: A Fabulous Man — Really!" *Hollywood Citizen-News*, December 29, 1945.

6. Marshall, "Nothing to It," *Collier's*, May 18, 1946.

7. "Dorothy Lamour Wins," *Spokane Daily Chronicle*, April 20, 1951, p. 9; *Telegraph Herald* [Dubuque, IA], April 20, 1951, p. 11.

8. "Bogeaus Files for Court Relief from Creditors," *Hollywood Citizen-News*, August 11, 1952.

9. *Hollywood Citizen-News*, October 15, 1952; *Variety*, October 16, 1952.

10. "Bogeaus Sues UA for $2,000,000," HR, April 11, 1955.

11. Don Siegel, *Don Siegel: A Siegel Film: An Autobiography* (London: Faber and Faber, 1993), pp. 147–150.

12. Bogdanovich, *Allan Dwan*, p. 154.

13. Ibid., p. 155.

14. Ibid.

15. Gary Morris and Howard Mandelbaum, "Angel in Exile," *Bright Lights Film Journal*, vol. 2, Issue 4, no. 8, 1979, p. 13. This interview is included in Morris, ed., *Action! Interviews with Directors from Classical Hollywood to Contemporary Iran* (London: Anthem Press, 2009).

16. Bogdanovich, *Allan Dwan*, p. 155.

17. Ibid., p. 162.

18. Simon Mizrahi, "Entretien aec Allan Dwan," *Presence du cinema*, no. 22–23 (Fall 1966) pp. 21–22, cited in English translation in Fujiwara, *Jacques Tourneur: The Cinema of Nightfall*, p. 210.

19. Bogdanovich, *Allan Dwan*, p. 156.

20. Ibid., pp. 155–56.

21. Jean Lourcelles, "Allan Dwan," *Presence du Cinema*, Fall 1996, p. 9.

22. V.F. Perkins, "The Cinema of Nicholas Ray," in Ian Cameron, *Movie Reader* (New York: Praeger, 1972), p. 65.

23. *Los Angeles Times*, March 9, 1954, p. A9.

24. "The Runners," in Phelps, *Covering New Ground*, p. 71.

25. Author interview with Robert Blees, 2004.

26. Bogdanovich, *Allan Dwan*, p. 158.

27. Ibid.

28. Al DiOrio, *Barbara Stanwyck* (New York: Coward McCann, 1984), p. 180.

29. Ella Smith, *Starring Barbara Stanwyck* (New York: Crown, 1974, 1985), p. 255.

30. Phil Hardy, ed., *The Aurum Film Encyclopedia: The Western* (London: Aurum Press, 1983), p. 231.

31. *New York Times* review, May 21, 1955, p. 11.

32. Morris and Mandelbaum, "Angel in Exile," *Bright Lights Film Journal*, p. 13.

33. Author interview with Lisa Montell Janti.

34. Smith, *Starring Barbara Stanwyck*, p. 259.

35. Ibid.

36. Bogdanovich, *Allan Dwan*, p. 158.

37. Leonard Maltin, ed., *Leonard Maltin's Movie and Video Guide* (New York: Penguin, 2004).

38. Phelps, *Covering Ground*, p. 70.

39. An earlier draft of the script had George dying and Dan and Rita replacing him as Michael's children. *Pearl of the South Pacific*, RKO Scripts Collections, UCLA.

40. Edwin Schallert, "Harte Classic Augments $25,000,000 Program," *Los Angeles Times*, April 15, 1955, p. A7.

41. Letter from Breen to Maurice Pirar of Universal, September 20, 1945, *Slightly Scarlet* MPAA file, Margaret Herrick Library.

42. Memorandum to files re: *Love's Lovely Counterfeit*, November 19, 1947, MPAA, *Slightly Scarlet* file, Margaret Herrick Library.

43. "Kurt Neumann to Direct Stanwyck in Counterfeit," HR, Thursday, June 9, 1955, p. 2.

44. Blees interview with author.

45. Ibid.

46. Ibid.

47. "Bogeaus, Stanwyck In Conflict Over 'Counterfeit' Deal," HR, July 7, 1955, p. 1.

48. "Rhonda Fleming Succeeds Babs Stanwyck in Film Given 'Scarlet' Retitling," HR, July 13, 1955 p. 9.

49. Axel Madsen, *Stanwyck* (New York: HarperCollins, 1994), p. 312. Madsen said that the injury caused her to miss working in Dwan's *Pearl of the South Pacific* but that had been completed months earlier so Madsen probably meant *Slightly Scarlet*.

50. Arlene Dahl interview with author, April 2005.

51. HR, July 14, 1955, p. 1.

52. Dahl interview with author.

53. Ibid.

54. Ibid.

55. Dahl interview with author.

56. Letter from Geoffrey M. Shurlock to William Feeder, RKO-Radio Pictures, July 20, 1955, MPAA file, Margaret Herrick Library. The MPAA had sent a response to the original script on July 8.

57. Bogdanovich, *Allan Dwan*, p. 163.

58. Ibid., pp. 163–64.

59. Dahl interview with author.

60. Letter from Sherlock to Feeder, July 20, 1955.

61. MPAA/PC Certification, October 14, 1955, Certificate #17646, *Slightly Scarlet* MPAA/PC file, Margaret Herrick Library.

62. Todd McCarthy, Introduction to John Alton, *Painting with Light* (Berkeley: University of California Press, 1995, 1949), p. xxviii.

63. Morris and Mandelbaum, "Angel in Exile," *Bright Lights Film Journal*, p. 13.

64. Vincente Minnelli with Hector Arce, *Vincente Minnelli: I Remember It Well* (London: Angus & Robertson, 1974), p. 241.

65. McCarthy, Introduction to Alton, *Painting with Light*, pp. xxvi–xxviii.

66. Ibid., p. xxviii.

67. *Variety*, February 15, 1956.

68. *New York Times*, March 17, 1956, p. 13.

69. Jean-Luc Godard, *Godard on Godard*, Jean Narboni and Tom Milne, eds. (New York: Viking, 1972), p. 66.

70. Richard B. Jewell with Vernon Harbin, *The RKO Story* (New York: Arlington House, 1982), p. 245.

71. Excised portion of Bogdanovich interview, tape 3–258, Bogdanovich
Papers, Lilly Library, Indiana University.

72. Jane Powell, *The Girl Next Door ... And How She Grew* (New York: William Morrow, 1988), pp. 177–78.

73. Bogdanovich, *Allan Dwan*, p. 166.

74. Powell, *The Girl Next Door*, p. 178.

75. *New York Times*, Andrews' obituary, December 19, 1992.

76. De Wolf was cited as a blacklist victim in Paul Buhle and David Wagner, *Blacklisted: The Film Lover's Guide to the Hollywood Blacklist* (New York: Palgrave Macmillan, 2003), but she was not on the Red Channels list. After *Silver Lode*, she was still able to work on numerous television programs between 1954 and 1959. A search by the Writers Guild has found no surviving relatives who could be contacted for more information. De Wolf died in 1989.

77. Simon Mizrahi, "Entretien Avec Allan Dwan," *Presence du Cinema*, Autumn 1966, p. 23.

78. Phone conversation with Howard Mandelbaum and email from Mandelbaum to author, February 21, 2010.

79. In the original script titled *Desperate Men*, there was still more political symbolism in the dialogue with lines such as Paul Herbert referring to sending Ballard's telegrams saying, "Gosh, I feel like Paul Revere going to send out the message." The little girl's Independence Day speech was also more pointed. She proclaims, "No bloody mailed fist can tear us from our loved ones. No officer of the Crown can deprive us of our liberty, our property, or our reputation without—" before she is interrupted. From Karen De Wolf, script for *Desperate Men*, dated September 14, 1953, RKO Radio Pictures Studio Records (Collection 3), Performing Arts Special Collections, Charles E. Young Research Library, UCLA.

80. Coursodon and Sauvage, *American Directors, Volume 1*, p. 114.

81. Simon Mizrahi, "Entretien Avec Allan Dwan," *Presence du Cinema*, Autumn 1966, p. 23.

82. It should be also pointed out that Daniel Mainwaring worked on the scripts of both *The Phenix City Story* and *Invasion of the Body Snatchers*.

83. In December 1953 Bogeaus announced that *Silver Lode* would be shot in a widescreen process known as Scenicsope, "a new anamorphic widescreen system, which can photograph from the normal dimensions to a 2.90 to 1 aspect ratio." HR, December 10, 1953, p. 1. *Silver Lode*, however, was not released in widescreen in the United States but was converted to Superscope for demonstration purposes and may have been shown in that format abroad. It has also been claimed that Silver Lode was shot in 3-D and while that may have been announced, no evidence has been found to confirm that and according to R.M. Hayes it was shot flat. See R.M. Hayes, *3-D Movies: A History and Filmography of Stereoscopic Cinema* (Jefferson, NC: McFarland, 1989), p. 314. The 3-D element may have been one of Bogeaus' extravagant ideas that Dwan jettisoned.

84. Gary Scharnhorst, Introduction to Bret Harte, *Bret Harte: The Luck of Roaring Camp and Other Writings* (New York: Penguin, 2001), p. xii.

85. Bret Harte, "The Argonauts of '49," in Harte, *Bret Harte: The Luck of Roaring Camp and Other Writings*, pp. 240–41.

86. Ibid.; Introduction by Gary Scharnhorst to Harte, *Bret Harte*, p. ix.

87. Letter from Geoffrey Shurlock to William Feeder, May 8, 1955, MPAA file for *Tennessee's Partner*, Margaret Herrick Library.

88. Coursodon and Sauvage, *American Directors, Volume 1*, p. 115.

89. Viewers of Dwan's 1932 *While Paris Sleeps* may recall that a white slaver tried to disguise his trade by telling Manon his "models" served as a "matrimonial market" to the wealthy in South America.

90. Although this is not spelled out in the credits, *Tennessee's Partner* was a revamping of a 1949 screen treatment by the two of the credited writers, Graham Baker and Teddi Sherman. In that version, Tennessee also runs off with Goldie to protect Cowpoke from her. But in the earlier treatment, Cowpoke is unable to stop a mob from lynching Tennessee for the false accusation of the murder of Grubstake. When the real murderer is revealed, he is also lynched. In this more sanitized scenario, Duchess is a singer at the saloon, who winds up marrying the saloon's owner, a character named Irish. *Tennessee's Partner*, RKO Radio Pictures Studio Records (Collection 3), Performing Arts Special Collections, Charles E. Young Research Library, UCLA.

91. *Tennessee's Partner*, RKO Radio Pictures Studio Records (Collection 3), Performing Arts Special Collections, Charles E. Young Research Library, UCLA.

92. McCarthy, Introduction to Alton, *Painting with Light*, p. xviii.

93. James M. Cain, Preface to *The Butterfly*, in

Cain, *Three By Cain: Serenade, Love's Lovely Counterfeit, The Butterfly* (New York: Vintage, 1989), p. 355.

94. Dave Kehr, DVD review, *New York Times*, July 11, 2006, p. E3.

95. Nicolas Saada, "River's Edge d'Allan Dwan," *Cahiers du Cinema*, No. 536, pp. 10–11.

96. Debra Paget interview with author, May 2010.

97. Excised portion of Bogdanovich interview, tape 3–259, Bogdanovich Papers, Lilly Library, University of Indiana.

98. *Los Angeles Times* review, April 11, 1957.

99. *The River's Edge*, Twentieth Century–Fox Produced Scripts (Collection 10), Performing Arts Special Collections, Charles E. Young Research Library, UCLA.

Chapter 10

1. Evelyn Rudie interview with author.
2. Letter from Edward Alperson, Jr., to author, March 30, 2005.
3. Meisel, "Allan Dwan," in Coursodon and Sauvage, eds., *American Directors, Volume I*, p. 115.
4. Bogdanovich, *Allan Dwan*, p. 166.
5. Those songs were *Caliope* and *Black Sunday*.
6. Permission for use of lyrics of Edward Alperson, Jr., granted by Fred Bock Music Co.
7. Bogdanovich, *Allan Dwan*, p. 166.
8. Rudie interview with author.
9. Letter from Alperson to author, April 19, 2005.
10. Ibid.
11. Letter from Bogeaus to Dwan, March 11, 1958, Allan Dwan file, Margaret Herrick Library.
12. *A DGA Oral History: Byron Haskin*, interviewed by Joe Adamson, Directors' Guild of America and Benevolent Foundation (Metuchen, NJ: Scarecrow Press, 1984), p. 238.
13. Siegel, *Don Siegel*, p. 146.
14. Haskin interview with Adamson, p. 239.
15. Bogdanovich, *Allan Dwan*, p. 167.
16. Ibid.
17. *Classic Images*, June 2003, p. 32.
18. Contract for *Most Dangerous Man Alive*, Allan Dwan file, Margaret Herrick Library.
19. Gregg Palmer interview with author.
20. Author interviews with Gregg Palmer, Steve Mitchell and Debra Paget.
21. Simon Mizrahi, "Entretien Avec Allan Dwan," *Presence du Cinema*, Autumn 1966, p. 23.
22. Tom Weaver, "The Vampire from Down Under," *Fangoria* #113, June 1992, p. 18.
23. Gregg Palmer interview with author.
24. Ibid.
25. Steve Mitchell interview with author.
26. Palmer interview with author.
27. Mitchell interview with author.
28. Ibid.
29. Ibid.
30. *New York Times* review, July 5, 1961.
31. *Variety* review, June 14, 1961.
32. Jean Lourcelles, "The Optimistic Tragedies," in Gosetti, ed., *Allan Dwan: The Name Beneath the Title*.
33. Bruce Eder, review of *Most Dangerous Man Alive*, All Movie Guide, All Media Guide.
34. Michael Henry Wilson, "Allan Dwan's Moral Tales at the Edge of Paradise," in Gosetti, ed., *Allan Dwan: The Name Beneath the Title*.
35. Robin Wallace interviews with author.
36. Ibid.
37. Ibid.
38. *San Antonio Light*, March 2, 1940.
39. *Variety*, June 5, 1929, p. 42.
40. *Modesto Bee and Herald News*, California, January 10, 1936.
41. Robin Wallace interviews with author.
42. Ibid.
43. Ibid.
44. Ibid.
45. Ibid.
46. Fujiwara, *Jacques Tourneur*, pp. 270–75.
47. Philip K. Scheuer, "Grainger, Bogeaus Start New Company," *Los Angeles Times*, April 21, 1959, p. C9.
48. Bogdanovich, *Allan Dwan*, p. 167.
49. Betty Martin, "Movie Call Sheet," *Los Angeles Times*, September 20, 1966, p. C10.
50. Bogdanovich, *Allan Dwan*, p. 167.
51. Ibid., p. 155.
52. Excised portion of Bogdanovich interview, tape 3, 274–75.
53. The full impact of Dwan's financial losses apparently did not hit until 1964. Correspondence with his attorneys at Wadsworth, Fraser & McClung indicate that Dwan was still living at Pacific Palisades on May 5. When their next preserved letter was sent to him on October 8, Dwan was living in an apartment at 1347 North Stanley Avenue. Dwan file, Margaret Herrick Library.
54. Anita Loos, *Anita Loos Rediscovered*, Cari Beauchamp and Mary Loos, ed. and ann. (Berkeley: University of California Press, 2003), pp. 255–56. Dwan would also be able to draw from his DGA pension.
55. Ibid., p. 256.
56. Brownlow, *The Parade's Gone By...*, p. 110.
57. Ibid., pp. 110–111.
58. Ibid., p. 111.
59. Brownlow, "From Now Until Eternity," in Gosetti, ed., *Allan Dwan: The Name Beneath the Title*, p. 96.
60. Bogdanovich, *Allan Dwan*, p. 39.
61. Joe Adamson e-mail to author, February 14, 2010.
62. Adamson, Introduction to Allan Dwan interview.
63. Brownlow, "From Now Until Eternity," in Gosetti, ed., *Allan Dwan: The Name Beneath the Title*, p. 96.
64. Peter Bogdanovich, *Who the Devil Made It* (New York: Alfred A. Knopf, 1997), p. 48.
65. Peter Bogdanovich interview with author, October 10, 2005.
66. Kevin Brownlow e-mail to author, June 21, 2011.
67. Bogdanovich recalled that the script that became *Nickelodeon* was originally called *Starlight Parade* and was written by W.D. Richter. It was then attached to director Arthur Penn. In a re-write of the Richter script, Bogdanovich incorporated stories he had heard from the directors McCarey, Walsh, Ford and especially, Dwan. He never read the McBride script. (Bogdanovich interview with author, April 2010.) McBride recalled that he learned from Dwan that fearing competition, one of *Nickelodeon*'s producers asked Dwan to stop helping McBride with his script. "Dwan was apologetic about this but said he had to follow their wishes." (Joseph McBride e-mails to author, June 8, June 14, and September 21, 2011.)
68. Peter Bogdanovich interview with author, October 10, 2005.
69. Howard Mandelbaum interview and e-mail to author, February 21, 2010.
70. Gary Morris and Howard Mandelbaum, Introduction to "Angel In Exile," *Bright Lights Film Journal*, vol. 2, Issue 4, no. 8, 1979, p. 12.
71. Mandelbaum e-mail to author February 21, 2010.
72. Adamson interview, CD Side #2, Museum of the Moving Image.
73. Letter from George J. Mitchell, president of Centurion Films to Henry G. Gardner, director of fine arts, Balboa Park, Allan Dwan file, Margaret Herrick Library.
74. Letter from John Wayne to Allan Dwan, December 6, 1972, Allan Dwan file, Margaret Herrick Library.
75. Letter from Joseph McBride to Walter Mirisch, December 8, 1975, Wisconsin Center for Film and Theater Research.
76. Ibid.
77. Adamson interview, CD, side #1, Museum of the Moving Image.
78. Letter from Marshall Neilan to Gloria Swanson, February 3, 1947, Gloria Swanson Collection, Harry Ransom Humanities Research Center, University of Texas at Austin.
79. Sam Staggs, *Close-Up on Sunset Boulevard: Billy Wilder, Norma Desmond and the Dark Hollywood Dream* (New York: St. Martin's Griffin, 2003), p. 100.
80. Foster, *Stardust and Shadows*, p. 114.
81. Joseph McBride e-mail to author, November 21, 2011.
82. Letter from Neilan to Dwan, November 16, 1944, Allan Dwan file, Margaret Herrick Library.
83. Letter from Swanson to Dwan, January 5, 1938, Gloria Swanson Collection, Harry Ransom Collection, University of Texas at Austin.
84. Guy Flatley, "The Sound That Shook Hollywood," *New York Times*, September 25, 1977.
85. Ibid.
86. Transcript of Simi Valley City Council meeting of February 9, 1981, dated February 13, 1981, Dwan file, Margaret Herrick Library.
87. Ibid.
88. "Hail Allan Dwan: 96 and Story Rich," *Variety*, May 13, 1981.
89. Bogdanovich, *Who the Devil Made It*, p. 45.
90. Robin Wallace interviews with author.
91. James Bacon, obituary, *Los Angeles Herald Examiner*, December 22, 1981.
92. Robin Wallace interviews with author.
93. Brownlow, "From Now Until Eternity," in Gosetti, *Allan Dwan: The Name Beneath the Title*, p. 96.
94. Aside from The *Sin of Martha Queed*, which is stored at the BFI, Kevin Brownlow has informed the author that he has recently discovered a print of *The Scoffer*.
95. Author interview with Peter Bogdanovich, April 2010.
96. Wilson, "Allan Dwan's Moral Tales at the Edge of Paradise," in Gosetti, ed., *Allan Dwan: The Name Beneath the Title*, p. 118.
97. Ibid., p. 122.
98. Erich Rohmer, *The Taste for Beauty*, Carol Volk, trans. (Cambridge: Cambridge University Press, 1989), p. 152.
99. Letter from Joseph I. Breen to Allen Wilson, January 24, 1946, PCA files, Margaret Herrick Library.
100. Excised portion of Bogdanovich, *Allan Dwan* Papers, page unnumbered before tape 4–17, Lilly Library, University of Indiana.
101. Author's interview with Peter Bogdanovich, April 16, 2010.
102. Bogdanovich, *Who the Devil Made It*, p. 44.
103. Rip Rense, "Allan Dwan: Today He Directs Simpler Scenes," *The Valley News*, Friday, June 22, 1979, p. 21; Rip Rense, "Allan Dwan: Today He Directs Simpler Scenes," *The Valley News*, Friday, June 22, 1979, p. 21.
104. Mandelbaum interview and e-mail to author, February 21, 2010.
105. Adamson introduction to Dwan interview.
106. Copy of document provided to author by Robin Wallace.
107. Mailing from Robin Wallace to author, March 27, 2011.

Selected Bibliography

Aberth, John. *A Knight at the Movies: Medieval History on Film.* New York: Routledge, 2003.
Affron, Charles. *Lillian Gish: Her Legend, Her Life.* New York: Scribner's, 2001.
Albrecht, Donald. *Designing Dreams: Architecture in the Movies.* New York: Harper & Row in collaboration with the Museum of Modern Art, 1986.
Allgood, Jill. *Bebe and Ben.* London: Robert Hale, 1975.
Alton, John. *Painting with Light.* Berkeley: University of California Press, 1949, 1995.
Anderson, Lindsay. *About John Ford.* New York: McGraw-Hill, 1981.
Anger, Kenneth. *Hollywood Babylon.* San Francisco: Straight Arrow Books, 1975.
Bakewell, William. *Hollywood Be Thy Name: Random Collections of a Movie Veteran from Silents to Talkies to TV.* Metuchen, NJ: Scarecrow Press, 1991.
Balio, Tino. *Grand Design: Hollywood as a Modern Business Enterprise, 1930–1939.* New York: Scribner's, 1996.
_____. *United Artists: The Company Built by the Stars.* Madison: University of Wisconsin Press, 1976.
Balshofer, Fred J., and Arthur C. Miller, with the assistance of Bebe Bergsten. *One Reel a Week.* Berkeley: University of California Press, 1967.
Barlett, Donald L., and James B. Steele. *Howard Hughes: His Life and Madness.* New York: W.W. Norton, 1979.
Barra, Allen. *Inventing Wyatt Earp: His Life and Many Legends.* New York: Carroll & Graf, 1998.
Barrios, Richard. *A Song in the Dark.* Oxford: Oxford University Press, 1995.
Basinger, Jeanine. *Silent Stars.* New York: Alfred A. Knopf, 2000.
_____. *A Woman's View: How Hollywood Spoke to Women, 1930–1960.* New York: Alfred A. Knopf, 1993.
_____. *The World War II Combat Film: Anatomy of a Genre.* New York: Columbia University Press, 1986.
Beauchamp, Cari. *Joseph Kennedy Presents.* New York: Alfred A. Knopf, 2009.
_____. *Without Lying Down: Frances Marion and the Powerful Women of Early Hollywood.* New York: Scribner's, 1997.
Behlmer, Rudy. *Henry Hathaway.* Metuchen, NJ: Scarecrow Press, 2001.
Bellamy, Madge. *A Darling of the Twenties.* Vestal, NY: Vestal Press, 1989.
Berg, A. Scott. *Goldwyn: A Biography.* New York: Ballantine, 1989.
Bernds, Edward. *Mr. Bernds Goes to Hollywood.* Lanham, MD: Scarecrow Press, 1999.
Bernstein, Matthew. *Walter Wanger, Hollywood Independent.* Berkeley: University of California Press, 1994.
Bitzer, Billy. *Billy Bitzer: His Story.* New York: Farrar, Straus and Giroux, 1973.
Black, Shirley Temple. *Child Star: An Autobiography.* New York: Warner Books, 1988.
Blake, Michael F. *The Films of Lon Chaney.* Lanham, MD: Madison Books, 2001.
_____. *Hollywood and the O.K. Corral.* Jefferson, NC: McFarland, 2007.
_____. *Lon Chaney: The Man Behind the Thousand Faces.* Vestal, NY: Vestal Press, 1993.
_____. *A Thousand Faces: Lon Chaney's Unique Artistry in Motion Pictures.* Vestal, NY: Vestal Press, 1995.
Blottner, Gene. *Universal Sound Westerns, 1929–1946: The Complete Filmography.* Jefferson, NC: McFarland, 2003.
Bogdanovich, Peter. *Allan Dwan: The Last Pioneer.* New York: Praeger, 1971.
_____. *Who the Devil Made It.* New York: Alfred A. Knopf, 1997.
Bradley, James, and Ron Powers. *Flags of Our Fathers.* New York: Bantam Books, 2000.
Braff, Richard E. *The Universal Silents: A Filmography of the Universal Motion Picture Manufacturing Company, 1912–1929.* Jefferson, NC: McFarland, 1999.
Brown, Karl. *Adventures with D.W. Griffith.* New York: Farrar, Straus and Giroux, 1973.
Brownlow, Kevin. *Behind the Mask of Innocence: Sex, Violence, Prejudice, Crime: Films of Social Conscience in the Silent Era.* London: Jonathan Cape, 1990.
_____. *The Parade's Gone By...* New York: Ballantine, 1968.
_____. *The War, the West and the Wilderness.* New York: Alfred A. Knopf, 1979.
Bruccoli, Matthew, ed. *F. Scott Fitzgerald's The Great Gatsby: A Literary Reference.* New York: Carroll & Grant, 2000.
Buhle, Paul, and David Wagner. *Radical Hollywood: The Untold Story Behind American's Favorite Movies.* New York: New Press, 2002.
Buller, Richard. *A Beautiful Fairy Tale: The Life of Lois Moran.* Pompton Plains, NJ: Limelight Editions, 2005.
Cain, James M. *Three By Cain: Serenade, Love's Lovely Counterfeit, The Butterfly.* New York: Vintage, 1989.
Cameron, Ian, ed. *Movie Reader.* New York: Praeger, 1972.
Campbell, Craig W. *Reel America and World War I.* Jefferson, NC: McFarland, 1985.
Carey, Diana Serra. *The Hollywood Posse: The Story of a Gallant Band of Horsemen Who Made History.* Norman: University of Oklahoma Press, 1996.
Carey, Gary. *Doug & Mary: A Biography of Douglas Fairbanks & Mary Pickford.* New York: E. P. Dutton, 1977.
Case, Frank. *Tales of a Wayward Inn.* Garden City, NJ: Garden City, 1938.
Chandler, Charlotte. *Nobody's Perfect.* New York: Simon & Schuster, 2002.
Chaplin, Charles. *My Autobiography.* London: Bodley Head, 1964.
Cocchi, John. *Second Feature.* New York: Citadel Press, 1991.
Cooke, Alistair. *Douglas Fairbanks: The Making of a Screen Character.* New York: Museum of Modern Art, 1940.
Coursodon, Jean-Pierre, and Pierre Sauvage. *American Directors, Volume I.* New York: McGraw-Hill, 1983.
Crafton, Donald. *The Talkies: American Cinema's Transition to Sound, 1926–1931.* New York: Scribner's, 1997.
Daniels, Bebe, and Ben Lyons. *Life with the Lyons: The Autobiography of Bebe Daniels & Ben Lyon.* London: Odahms Press, 1953.
David, Lester, and Irene. *The Shirley Temple Story.* New York: Putnam, 1983.
DiOrio, Al. *Barbara Stanwyck.* New York: Coward McCann, 1984.
Donati, William. *Ida Lupino: A Biography.* Lexington: University Press of Kentucky, 1996.
Drazen, Charles. *Korda: Britain's Only Movie Mogul.* London: Sidgwick & Jackson, 2002.
Dunne, Philip. *Take Two: A Life in Movies and Politics.* New York: Limelight Editions, 1980, 1992.
Edmonds, I.G. *Big U: Universal in the Silent Days.* South Brunswick, NJ: A.S. Barnes, 1977.
Edwards, Anne. *Shirley Temple: American Princess.* New York: William Morrow, 1988.
Emerson, Ken. *Doo-Dah: Stephen Foster and the Rise of American Popular Culture.* New York: Simon & Schuster, 1994.
Eyman, Scott. *Mary Pickford.* New York: Donald I. Fine, 1990.
_____. *The Speed of Sound: Hollywood and the Talkie Revolution.* New York: Simon & Schuster, 1997.
Fairbanks, Jr., Douglas. *Salad Days.* New York: Doubleday, 1988.
Fetherling, Douglas, ed. *Documents in Canadian Film.* Peterborough, Canada: Broadview Press, 1988.
Fenin, George N., and William K. Everson. *The Western: From Silents to the Seventies.* New York: Penguin, 1977.
Fitzgerald, F. Scott. *The Short Stories of F. Scott Fitzgerald.* Ed. Matthew J. Bruccoli. New York: Scribner's, 1989.
Fleming, E.J. *Wallace Reid: The Life and Death of a Hollywood Idol.* Jefferson, NC: McFarland, 2007.
Flynn, Charles, and Todd McCarthy, eds. *King of the Bs.* New York: E.P. Dutton, 1975.
Foster, Charles. *Stardust and Shadows: Canadians

in Early Hollywood. Toronto: Dandurn Press, 2000.

Frank, Pat. *Hold Back the Night.* Philadelphia: J.P. Lippincott, 1951, 1952.

Frost, Robert. *Selected Poems of Robert Frost.* New York: Holt, Rinehart and Winston, 1967.

Fujiwara, Chris. *Jacques Tourneur: The Cinema of Nightfall.* Jefferson, NC: McFarland, 1998.

Gabler, Neal. *An Empire of Their Own: How the Jews Invented Hollywood.* New York: Crown, 1988.

Gallagher, Tag. *John Ford: The Man and His Films.* Berkeley: University of California Press, 1986.

Garnett, Tay. *Directing: Learn from the Masters.* Ed. Anthony Slide. Metuchen, NJ: Scarecrow Press, 1996.

Gibbs, A. Hamilton. *Chances,* Boston: Little, Brown, 1930.

Gish, Lillian, with Anne Pinchot. *The Movies, Mr. Griffith and Me.* London: Columbus Books, 1969.

Godard, Jean-Luc. *Godard on Godard.* Ed. Jean Narboni and Tom Milne. New York: Viking, 1972.

Goldwyn, Samuel. *Behind the Screen.* New York: George H. Doran, 1923.

Gosetti, Giorgio, ed. *Allan Dwan: The Name Beneath the Title.* Torino: Lindau, 2002.

Griffith, D.W., and James Hart. *The Man Who Invented Hollywood: The Autobiography of D.W. Griffith.* Louisville, KY: Touchstone, 1972.

Guiles, Fred Lawrence. *Marion Davies.* New York: McGraw-Hill, 1972.

_____. *Tyrone Power: The Last Idol.* San Francisco: Mercury House, 1979.

Hagen, Ray, and Laura Wagner. *Killer Tomatoes: Fifteen Tough Film Dames.* Jefferson, NC: McFarland, 2004.

Hampton, Benjamin B. *History of the American Film Industry: From Its Beginnings to 1931.* New York: Dover, 1970.

Hancock, Ralph, and Letitia Fairbanks. *Douglas Fairbanks: The Fourth Musketeer.* New York: Henry Holt, 1953.

Hardee, Jr., Lewis J. *The Lambs Theatre Club.* Jefferson, NC: McFarland, 2006.

Hardy, Phil, ed. *The Aurum Film Encyclopedia: The Western.* London: Aurum Press, 1983.

Harte, Bret. *In the Carquinez Woods and Other Tales.* Boston: Houghton Mifflin, 1884.

_____. *The Luck of Roaring Camp and Other Writings.* New York: Penguin, 2001.

Haskin, Byron. *A DGA Oral History: Byron Haskin.* Interview by Joe Adamson. Directors' Guild of America and Benevolent Foundation. Metuchen, NJ: Scarecrow Press, 1984.

Hayes, R.M. *3-D Movies: A History and Filmography of Stereoscopic Cinema.* Jefferson, NC: McFarland, 1989.

Henabery, Joseph, and Anthony Slide. *Before, In and After Hollywood: The Autobiography of Joseph Henabery.* Metuchen, NJ: Scarecrow Press, 1997.

Henderson, Robert M. *D.W. Griffith: His Life and Work.* New York: Oxford University Press, 1972.

Herndon, Booton. *Mary Pickford and Douglas Fairbanks.* New York: W.W. Norton, 1977.

Hodges, Graham Russell Gao. *Anna May Wong: From Laundryman's Daughter to Hollywood Legend.* New York: Palgrave Macmillan, 2004.

Hoffman, Lt. Col. Jon T. *Chesty: The Story of Lieutenant General Lewis B. Puller, USMC.* New York: Random House, 2001.

Hurst, Richard Maurice. *Republic Studios: Between Poverty Row and the Majors.* Metuchen, NJ: Scarecrow Press, 1979.

Jewell, Richard, with Vernon Harbin. *The RKO Story.* New York: Arlington House, 1982.

Karabell, Zachary. *Parting the Desert: The Creation of the Suez Canal.* New York: Alfred A. Knopf, 2003.

Kendall, Henry. *I Remember Romano's: The Autobiography of Henry Kendall.* London: MacDonald, 1960.

Kennedy, Matthew. *Edmund Goulding's Dark Victory: Hollywood's Genius Bad Boy.* Madison: University of Wisconsin Press, 2004.

Kiehn, David. *Broncho Billy and the Essanay Film Company.* Berkeley: Farwell Books, 2003.

Kimbell, Bobby Ellen, ed., with assistance of William E. Grant. *American Short-Story Writers Before 1880.* Detroit: Gale, 1988.

Koszarski, Diane Kaiser. *The Complete Films of William S. Hart: A Pictorial Record.* New York: Dover, 1980.

Koszarski, Richard. *An Evening's Entertainment: The Age of the Silent Feature Picture, 1915–1928.* Berkeley: University of California Press, 1990.

_____. *Fort Lee: The Film Town.* Rome: John Libbey, 2004.

_____. *Hollywood Directors, 1914–1940.* New York: Oxford University Press, 1976.

_____. *Hollywood on the Hudson.* New Brunswick, NJ: Rutgers University Press, 2008.

_____. *The Man You Love to Hate: Erich von Stroheim and Hollywood.* Oxford: Oxford University Press, 1983.

Kovic, Ron. *Born on the Fourth of July.* New York: Akashic Books, 1976, 2005.

Kulick, Karol. *Alexander Korda: The Man Who Could Work Miracles.* New Rochelle, NY: Arlington House, 1975.

Kyne, Peter B. *Tide of Empire.* New York: Grosset & Dunlap, 1927.

Lahue, Kalton C. *Dreams for Sale: The Rise and Fall of the Triangle Film Corporation.* South Brunswick, NJ: A.S. Barnes, 1971.

Lambert, Gavin. *Natalie Wood, A Life.* New York: Alfred A. Knopf, 2004.

Lasky, Betty. *RKO: The Biggest Little Major of Them All.* Engelwood Cliffs, NJ: Prentice Hall, 1984.

Lawrence, D.H. *Studies in Classic American Literature.* New York: Penguin, 1923.

Lee, Betty. *Marie Dressler: The Unlikeliest Star.* Lexington: University Press of Kentucky, 1997.

Lee, Hermione. *Edith Wharton.* New York: Alfred A. Knopf, 2007.

Leider, Emily W. *Dark Lover.* New York: Faber and Faber, 2003.

Lentz, Robert J. *Korean War Filmography: 91 English Language Features through 2000.* Jefferson, NC: McFarland.

LeRoy, Mervyn, as told to Dick Kleiner. *Mervyn LeRoy: Take One.* New York: Hawthorn Books, 1974.

Lewis, Judy. *Uncommon Knowledge.* New York: Pocket Books, 1994.

Lindsay, Vachel, edited with commentary by Myron Lounsbury. *The Progress and Poetry of Movies: A Second Book of Film Criticism.* Lanham, MD: Scarecrow Press, 1995.

Loos, Anita. *A Girl Like I.* New York: Viking, 1966.

_____. *Kiss Hollywood Good-By.* New York: Viking, 1974.

_____. *The Talmadge Girls: A Memoir.* New York: Viking, 1978.

_____, edited and annotated by Cari Beauchamp and Mary Loos. *Anita Loos Rediscovered.* Berkeley: University of California Press, 2003.

Love, Bessie. *From Hollywood with Love.* London: Elm Tree Books, 1981.

Lyons, Timothy James. *The Silent Partner: The History of the American Film Manufacturing Company.* New York: Arno Press, 1974.

MacGowan, Kenneth. *Behind the Screen: The History and Techniques of the Motion Picture.* New York: Dell, 1965.

Madsen, Axel. *Gloria & Joe.* New York: William Morrow, 1988.

_____. *Stanwyck.* New York: HarperCollins, 1994.

Maltin, Leonard, ed. *Leonard Maltin's Movie and Video Guide.* New York: Penguin, 2004.

Mann, William. *Behind the Screen: How Gays and Lesbians Shaped Hollywood, 1910–1969.* New York: Viking Penguin, 2002.

Marill, Alvin H. *Samuel Goldwyn Presents.* South Brunswick, NJ: A.S. Barnes, 1976.

Marion, Frances. *Off with Their Heads: A Serio-Comic Tale of Hollywood.* New York: Macmillan, 1972.

Mathis, Jack. *Republic Confidential.* Barrington, IL: Jack Mathis Advertising, 1992.

McBride, Joseph. *Frank Capra: The Catastrophe of Success.* New York: Simon & Schuster, 1992.

_____. *Searching for John Ford.* London: Faber and Faber, 2003.

_____, ed. *Hawks on Hawks.* Berkeley: University of California Press, 1982.

McCarthy, Todd. *Howard Hawks.* New York: Grove Press, 1997.

McGhee, Richard D. *John Wayne, Actor, Artist, Hero.* Jefferson, NC: McFarland, 1990.

Menefee, David W. *Wally: The True Wallace Reid Story.* Albany, GA: BearManor Media, 2011.

Menjou, Adolphe, and M.M. Musselman. *It Took Nine Tailors.* New York: Whittlesey House, 1948.

Minnelli, Vicente, with Hector Arce. *Vincente Minnelli: I Remember It Well.* London: Angus & Robertson, 1974.

Montagu, Ivor. *With Eisenstein in Hollywood.* New York: International, 1967.

Morella, Joe, and Edward Z. Epstein. *Loretta Young: An Extraordinary Life.* Santa Barbara: Landmark Books, 1987.

Morris, Gary, ed. *Action! Interviews with Directors from Classical Hollywood to Contemporary Iran.* London: Anthem Press, 2009.

Munden, Kenneth W. *The American Film Institute Catalog of Motion Pictures Produced in the United States.* New York: R.R. Bowker, 1971.

Nunn, Curtis. *Marguerite Clark: America's Darling of Broadway and the Silver Screen.* Fort Worth: Texas Christian University Press, 1981.

Oakie, Jack. *Jack Oakie's Double Takes.* San Francisco: Strawberry Hill Press, 1980.

Oderman, Stuart. *Talking to the Piano Player: Silent Film Stars, Writers and Directors Remember*. Boalsburg, PA: BearManor Media, 2005.
Ohmart, Ben. *Don Ameche: The Kenosha Comeback Kid*. Albany, GA: BearManor Media, 2007.
Paris, Barry. *Louise Brooks*. New York: Alfred A. Knopf, 1989.
Pasternak, Joe. *Easy the Hard Way*. New York: Putnam, 1956.
Peary, Danny. *Cult Movie Stars*. New York: Simon & Schuster, 1991.
Phelps, Donald. *Covering Ground: Essays for Now*. New York: Croton Press, 1969.
Pizzitola, Louis. *Hearst Over Hollywood*. New York: Columbia University Press, 2002.
Powell, Jane. *The Girl Next Door ... And How She Grew*. New York: William Morrow, 1988.
Quinlan, David. *British Sound Films: The Studio Years, 1929–1959*. Totowa, NJ: Barnes & Noble Books, 1984.
Quirk, Lawrence J. *The Films of Gloria Swanson*. Secaucus, NJ: Citadel Press, 1984.
Ramsaye, Terry. *A Million and One Nights: A History of the Motion Picture Through 1925*. New York: Simon & Schuster, 1926.
Ringgold, Gene. *The Films of Rita Hayworth*. Secaucus, NJ: Citadel Press, 1974.
Roberts, Gary L. *Doc Holliday: The Life and Legend*. Hoboken, NJ: John Wiley & Sons, 2006.
Roberts, Randy, and James S. Olson. *John Wayne: American*. New York: Free Press, 1995.
Robertson, Patrick. *The Guinness Book of Movie Facts and Feats*. New York: Abbeville Press, 1991.
Robinson, David. *Chaplin: His Life and Art*. New York: McGraw-Hill, 1985.
Rohmer, Eric. *A Taste For Beauty*. Translated by Carol Volk. Cambridge: Cambridge University Press, 1989.
Russell, Jane. *Jane Russell: An Autobiography, My Path and My Detours*. New York: Franklin Watts, 1985.
Sarris, Andrew. *The American Cinema: Directors and Directions, 1929–1968*. New York: Da Capo Press, 1996.
_____. *Confessions of a Cultist: On the Cinema, 1955–1969*. New York: Simon & Schuster, 1970.
Schatz, Thomas. *The Genius of The System*. New York: Pantheon, 1988.
Schickel, Richard. *D.W. Griffith: An American Life*. New York: Simon & Schuster, 1984.
_____. *Harold Lloyd: The Shape of Laughter*. Boston: New York Graphic Society, 1974.
_____. *His Picture in the Papers*. New York: Charterhouse, 1973.
Schulberg, Budd. *Moving Pictures: Memories of a Hollywood Prince*. Chicago: Ivan R. Dee, 1981.
Siegel, Donald. *Don Siegel: A Siegel Film: An Autobiography*. London: Faber and Faber, 1993.
Simmon, Scott. *The Invention of the Western Film: A Cultural History of the Genre's First Half-Century*. Cambridge: Cambridge University Press, 2003.
Slide, Anthony. *The Kindergarten of the Movies: A History of the Fine Arts Company*. Metuchen, NJ: Scarecrow Press, 1980.
_____. *Silent Players*. Lexington: University Press of Kentucky, 2002.
Smiley, Gene. *Rethinking the Great Depression*. Chicago: Ivan R. Dee, 2002.
Smith, Amanda, ed. *Hostage to Fortune: The Letters of Joseph P. Kennedy*. New York: Viking, 2001.
Smith, Andrew Brodie. *Shooting Cowboys and Indians: Silent Western Films, American Culture and the Birth of Hollywood*. Boulder: University Press of Colorado, 2003.
Smith, Ella. *Starring Barbara Stanwyck*. New York: Crown, 1974, 1985.
Smith, Henry Nash. *Virgin Land: The American West as Symbol and Myth*. Cambridge: Harvard University Press, 1950.
Solomon, Aubrey. *Twentieth Century–Fox: A Corporate and Financial History*. Metuchen, NJ: Scarecrow Press, 1988.
Spears, Jack. *Hollywood: The Golden Era*. New York: A.S. Barnes, 1971.
Sragow, Michael. *Victor Fleming: An American Movie Master*. New York: Pantheon Books, 2008.
Staggs, Sam. *Close-Up on Sunset Boulevard: Billy Wilder, Norma Desmond and the Dark Hollywood Dream*. New York: St. Martin's Griffin, 2003.
Studlar, Gaylyn. *This Mad Masquerade: Stardom and Masculinity in the Jazz Age*. New York: Columbia University Press, 1996.
Suid, Lawrence H. *Guts and Glory: Great American War Movies*. Reading, MA: Addison-Wesley, 1978.
Swanson, Gloria. *Swanson on Swanson*. New York: Random House, 1980.
Swindell, Larry. *Screwball: The Life of Carole Lombard*. New York: William Morrow, 1975.
Talmey, Allene. *Doug, Mary and Others*. New York: Macy-Masius, 1927.
Tefertiller, Casey. *Wyatt Earp: The Life Behind The Legend*. New York: John Wiley & Sons, 1997.
Thomas, Tony, and Aubrey Solomon. *The Films of 20th Century–Fox: A Pictorial History*. Secaucus, NJ: Citadel Press, 1985.
Tibbetts, John C., and James M. Welsh. *His Majesty, the American: The Cinema of Douglas Fairbanks Sr.* South Brunswick, NJ: A.S. Barnes, 1977.
Tuttle, Frank, and John Franceshina. *They Started Talking*. Boalsburg, PA: BearManor Media, 2005.
Vance, Jeffrey, with Tony Maietta. *Douglas Fairbanks*. Berkeley: University of California Press, Academy of Motion Picture Arts and Sciences, 2008.
Vaughn, Stephen. *Ronald Reagan in Hollywood: Movies and Politics*. Cambridge: Cambridge University Press, 1994.
Vieira, Mark A. *Sin in Soft Focus: Pre-Code Hollywood*. New York: Harry N. Abrams, 1999.
Wagenknecht, Edward. *The Movies in the Age of Innocence*. Norman: University of Oklahoma Press, 1962.
Wakemen, John, ed. *World Film Directors, Volume I 1890–1945*. New York: H. W. Wilson, 1987.
Walsh, Raoul. *Each Man in His Time*. New York: Farrar, Straus, Giroux, 1974.
Whitfield, Ellen. *Pickford: The Woman Who Made Hollywood*. Lexington: University of Kentucky Press, 1997.
Windeler, Robert. *The Films of Shirley Temple*. Secaucus, NJ: Citadel Press, 1978.
Woon, Basil. *Incredible Land: A Jaunty Baedeker to Hollywood and the Great Southwest*. New York: Liveright, 1933.
Young, Loretta, as told to Helen Ferguson. *The Things I Had to Learn*. Indianapolis: Bobbs-Merrill, 1961.
Zolotow, Maurice. *Billy Wilder in Hollywood*. New York: Putnam, 1977.
_____. *Shooting Star: A Biography of John Wayne*. New York: Simon & Schuster, 1974.
Zukor, Adolph, with Dale Kramer. *The Public Is Never Wrong: The Autobiography of Adolph Zukor*. New York: Putnam, 1953.

Websites

There are many websites on a variety of film-related subjects. Given the circumstances of the Internet, their existence is often ephemeral. Here are some that I found of particular interest.

http://www.filmandmedia.ucsb.edu/flyinga/ The American Film Company: Run by Dana Driskel, this website is highly informative and offers many interesting details about this pioneering film company. As the process of discoveries goes on, this website is continuously updated.

http://www.lonchaney.org/ The Lon Chaney Home Page. Another longtime website, run by Jon Mirsalis, who, like Dana Driskel, is a very dedicated cinephile who strives for accuracy and keeps his site updated. As with the website above you will find interesting and rare photos.

http://mikegrost.com/dwan.htm Allan Dwan. Run by the enthusiastic Mike Grost, this is one of the few (only?) sites dedicated to Allan Dwan.

http://nitanaldi.com/ Nita Naldi, Silent Vamp. A relatively new website about this cult star. It is run by Donna Hill, whose dedication to the silent film and to Rudolph Valentino in particular is well known on the Internet.

http://www.sandiegohistory.org/journal/index.html Journal of San Diego History. Online issues contain some interesting articles on the early history of filmmaking in that community.

http://www.wvculture.org/history/archivesindex.aspx West Virginia Archives. Interesting information can be found on this site on the making of *Stage Struck* in the 1920s.

Index